Black Cowboys of Texas

NUMBER EIGHTY-SIX

*Centennial Series
of the Association
of Former Students
Texas A&M University*

Black Cowboys of Texas

Edited by Sara R. Massey

INTRODUCTION BY ALWYN BARR

Texas A&M University Press
College Station

Frontispiece: "Coaley" Owens worked as a cowboy
on the J Buckle Ranch. He later worked for thirty-
six years as a cowboy and cook on the Kiowa and
Comanche Indian Nation ranches of S. B. Burnett.
He received a monthly $30 pension after Burnett's
death. At ninety years of age he was living in
Benjamin, Texas, with Burnett's nephew. Courtesy
Panhandle-Plains Historical Museum Research
Center, Canyon, Texas

The paper used in this book meets the minimum
requirements of the American National Standard
for Permanence of Paper for Printed Library
Materials, z39.48-1984. Binding materials have
been chosen for durability.

Library of Congress Cataloging-in-Publication Data

Black cowboys of Texas / edited by Sara R. Massey.
   — 1st ed.
       p.   cm. — (The centennial series of the
Association of Former Students, Texas A&M
University ; no. 86)
   Includes bibliographical references and index.
   ISBN 0-89096-934-5 (alk. paper)
   1. Afro-American cowboys—Texas—History.
2. Afro-American cowboys—Texas—Biography.
3. Ranch life—Texas—History. 4. Cattle trade
—Texas—History. 5. Texas—History—
1846–1950. 6. Texas—Race relations.
I. Massey, Sara R. II. Series.
F391.B58 2000
976.4—dc21   99-055339
                         CIP

Contents

Part 3. Twentieth-Century Cowboys   215

Illustrations

Preface

If no one remembers, do we have a past?

Historians have written little about the African Americans who are a part of the history of Texas. Books on Texas history written by the noted trinity of Texas historians—Walter Prescott Webb, Eugene C. Barker, and T. R. Fehrenbach—have been reprinted over the decades. Many Texans continue to consider these notable men the authorities on Texas history. However, if we rely on Webb, Barker, and Fehrenbach for our knowledge, African Americans had no place of significance in the history of Texas. Within the context of the nineteenth and most of the twentieth century, African Americans were not perceived as important enough to mention beyond slavery. They worked for their masters and made some of them very rich, but they weren't part of the Texas saga. Bill Moyers, in a 1997 speech before the Texas State Historical Association, called the omission, the distortion, the "prettying up" of history, the eternal lie. "Sometimes ignoring the stories of those who have been less visible can lead to some pure and nearly eternal lies—even fatal lies."[1] The lives of African American men and women are entwined in the history of Texas, though the stories of only a few are yet in the history books. The people in this book are real. The events actually occurred. The places exist. This is not a work of fiction.

The cowboy was nurtured in Texas, as a result of the availability of wild mustangs and Longhorn cattle. The cowboy learned his craft from the vaqueros of New Spain and Texas when it was the northern territory of Mexico. We have heard the story of the Anglo cowboys who worked the ranches of Texas, but there is more to be known about the cowboys. There were the nameless African American cowboys who worked beside the vaqueros and Anglo cowboys.

Texas is a unique state with a raucous history. It was a place of confluence, where cultures came together and stayed over time. The mingling of the cultures as each group tried to make a home and gain a livelihood was neither easy nor painless. The land had been home for numerous Native American tribes when claimed by Spain in the sixteenth century. Two centuries later the people of Mexico won their independence from Spain, and the land, with its scattered peoples, became the northern territory of the province of Coahuila. In 1836 the recently arrived "ungrateful" immigrant settlers successfully rebelled against the authority of Mexico and the Republic of Texas was formed. In a few short years the Republic of Texas became a state of the United States—and quickly the new state was entangled in another war, the Mexican War (1845–48). Next came the Civil War, with Texas joining the Confederacy in 1861. At the end of the war, the slaves in Texas were freed, but not until June 19, 1865.

In less than sixty-five turbulent years (1800–65), the area of Texas evolved from a few scattered haciendas granted to Spanish patrons and roaming Indian tribes to a land dominated by European and Euroamerican settlers with their African and African American slaves. Embroiled in three wars and with four governments, the people of Texas simultaneously tried to build new homes, earn livings, and survive attacks from the angry Indians who did not want them there. The people were diverse—Europeans and Euroamericans, Indians of both Mexico and Texas, Africans, and African Americans.

The labor of the African Americans formed the basis of the cotton plantations established in East Texas and later contributed to the cattle industry. For most settlers coming to Texas, raising stock was just part of farming, but over the years, the homesteads of the European immigrants and Euroamericans with slave labor were expanded to include more land. Some ranches grew to massive size. Many haciendas were lost when uninformed or misinformed landholding patrons neglected to file legal claims required by the new laws of the United States. Life was difficult, and some owners sold their slaves to purchase cattle in order to get started in the cattle business.

The cattle and horses brought over two centuries had multiplied and spread throughout the area. Much of the Texas landscape was ideal for cattle and horses, a vast prairie covered with grass. "The natural vegetation was plentiful . . . On the coastal prairies the tall grass used to grow almost as tall as a man on horse back . . . Away from the coast country the mesquite grass of the black prairies, renowned for its abundance and nutritious qualities, would, especially when the fall season was dry, lose its green color and become yellow like hay, but retain its food value, and cattle and horses would eat it with the avidity as when it was green, and thus remain in good living condition until spring came again."[2]

Cattle doubled in number every four years, creating vast herds of wild roaming cattle with long horns extending six feet.

Buffalo or deer could be no wilder (than wild cows). These cattle would not graze on open ground in the daytime, but would seek the densest thickets or lie with their heads on the ground like deer, listening and sniffing, on the lookout for danger of any sort, and ready for a mad rush through the jungles to a place of safety . . . These cattle were wild creatures which could not only flee from a human being like other wild animals, but could fight and would do so as promptly as any grizzly bear I ever saw. . . . The Americans who first undertook to handle these cattle for profit found that they had the task, not only of securing a market for them, but of getting Americans who could do a Mexican vaquero's work. . . . The instructors in the art of cowboy work were Mexicans. Soon there was formed a nucleus of cowboys, added to rapidly as the years rolled by.[3]

Through the centuries, the vaqueros, Indians of Mexico, learned the skills and acquired the equipment from the Spanish to capture, gentle, herd, and tend the cattle and horses. The roundup, branding, the western saddle, roping, and the clothing of cowboys all originated with the vaquero. This Spanish heritage produced the *remuda*, rodeo, ranch, chaps, cinches, and lariat. The vaqueros excelled at the art of horsemanship. They captured mustangs, tamed, and trained them for the work of rounding up the wild cattle. From these beginnings, Euroamerican cowboys and African American cowboys emerged on the ranches of Texas.[4]

The cattle industry grew in Texas between 1850 and 1880, although the Civil War retarded development and expansion for a while. The Euroamerican men of the new state of Texas went off to war, leaving behind the women, the children, the elderly, and the African Americans to maintain their small farms and ranches. They tended the cattle, broke horses, raised the crops, cultivated the gardens, and fought off the surviving Indians tribes, most notably the Apaches and Comanches. With the end of the Civil War, the Euroamerican men came home to resume their lives. Unbranded cattle, numerous and free for the taking, grazed on the abundant open ranges.

During the decade and a half following the Civil War, Longhorn cattle were the economic salvation of Texas. They were gaunt and wiry, independent and perverse. As a product of the wilderness they did well where blooded cattle would have perished of drought, travel, and thirst. They were more easily handled than blooded stock, both in the roundup and upon the trail. Because of breadth of horn they spaced themselves better under herd—

keeping plenty of room—thus traveling with greater ease, less heat, and less loss of flesh. Their hoofs were tougher, their legs longer, and their endurance greater than high-grade "stuff." They ranged a much wider scope of country, went longer without water, suffered more hardships, and took better care of themselves upon the range or in stampedes than any other breed. Old age did not find them toothless as it often finds improved cattle, and in breeding usefulness they lived nearly double the span of their successors.[5]

Cattle in Texas were cheap, but there was money to be realized if cattle could be gotten to the markets in California, New Orleans, or the East Coast. The long cattle drives, fraught with danger, began around 1866, and by the 1870s herds headed north every spring for the new railroad at Abilene, Kansas. The cattle drives, often as long as twelve hundred miles, could take three to four months to complete, depending on the fickleness of the weather, the Indians, stampedes, and other problems encountered along the way.[6] From harsh beginnings filled with hardship and loss, millions of dollars were made by the settlers, now ranchers in the burgeoning cattle business. "The total number of cattle driven from Texas from 1866 to 1885 inclusive is estimated at about 5,720,000"[7] not including cattle driven to closer shipping points, Indian agencies, or northern territories. Cowboys, lots of cowboys, were needed to round up the cattle and to catch and tame the horses necessary to take the herds to market. With the confluence of people in Texas all struggling for a livelihood, the cowhands included young men and a few women of several cultural groups—the Mexican vaquero, the Euroamerican and European cowboy, Indian cowboy, and the African American cowboy.[8]

The life of the cowboy was filled with dangers from Indians, rattlesnakes, windstorms, prairie fires, and desperadoes, but in 1874 Joseph McCoy, who helped create the shipping depots for cattle in Abilene, Kansas, described the camp life of cowboys as one filled with comforts: "There are many comforts enjoyed in camp life, out on the great plains in the summer season, not the least among which is the delightsome breeze which so gently sweeps over the land, bringing health, vigor, and 'the balm of a thousand flowers' upon its wings. The freedom and hilarity which naturally abounds, coupled with the jovial hilarity inevitable to robust health, to which may be added the often recurring sharp appetite for the feasts of game often provided by the skill of some semi-nimrod herder, all conspire to render camp life upon the broad plains a joy forever."[9]

Mr. McCoy surely must not have driven cattle to Abilene himself, and the tall tales of the cowboys when they arrived must have been glowing, because the life of the cowboy was really not that charming. The cowboy has been portrayed as a loner who wandered from ranch to ranch tending the cattle and working the roundups. This stereotype of the cowboy is not completely true. Most vaqueros remained on one ranch all their lives and raised families there. The African American cowboys working cattle on farms and ranches in the Coastal Bend area also stayed on a "home" ranch, as did others such as the Paynes in the Big Bend region and George Adams of Sanderson.

The number of African American cowboys in Texas during the height of the cattle drives from 1866–95 is disputed. In 1925, George W. Saunders, president of the Texas Trail Drivers Association, stated, "35,000 men went up the trail with herds," and of this number, "about one third were negroes and Mexican."[10] The figures used by Saunders came from the cattle owners, ranchers, and trail drivers who were on the drives of 1866–95 and were members of the Texas Trail Drivers Association when he was president in the 1920s.

Kenneth Wiggins Porter confirmed Saunders's information for the same years by examining existing "lists of trail-herd outfits which identify their members racially. These lists also demonstrate the Negroes out-numbered Mexicans by more than two to one . . . slightly more than 63% whites, 25% Negroes, and slightly under 12% Mexicans."[11] Philip Durham and Everett L. Jones in *The Negro Cowboy* used Saunders's figures to state that 5,000 black cowboys were on the cattle drives out of Texas.[12] Thus the major sources of past information on the number of black cowboys in Texas ultimately relied on Saunders's statement or the examination of the lists of Texas trail-herd outfits with the racial identification for the three decades of cattle drives following the Civil War, 1866–95.

Quintard Taylor, Jr., refutes these figures, stating, "Black Texas cowboys, who were more numerous than in any other western state or territory, nonetheless constituted 4% of the total Texas herders in 1880 and 2.6% by 1890."[13] The only source of data cited for Dr. Taylor's 4 percent for 1880 was information from Terry Jordan's *Trail to Texas: Southern Roots of Western Cattle Ranching*, which speaks only about blacks moving from East Texas to West Texas up to 1880. Jordan states, "Blacks accompanied the Anglo rancher migration to West Texas, where sixty-eight of them worked as cowboys by 1880. While these blacks made up only 4 percent of the cowboy work force, a far lower proportion than claimed by some historians, their presence in West Texas is undeniable."[14] Jordan is not talking about African American cowboys in all of Texas, just West Texas. His information does not include the large number of African American cowboys not emigrating who remained in East Texas and the southern triangle of Texas. Jordan's statistics do not address African Americans coming in from Mexico or those entering from the area west of Texas. Taylor cites only Jordan in concluding that African American cowboys were only 4 percent of the total cowboys going up the trails. No census data for 1880 was provided.

To calculate the 2.6 percent for 1890, Dr. Taylor presents the population census of 1890 and 1910. Saunders, Porter, and Durham and Jones were speaking of cowboys working on the Texas cattle trails during the years of 1866–95 while Taylor used census data for 1890 and 1910.

The accuracy of the numbers obtained by the U.S. census in 1890 cited by Taylor for the nonwhite population of Texas must be questioned. The 1890 census was taken twenty-five years after the emancipation of African Americans in Texas. Census takers went house to house, but it was often the West Texas ranch owners, if available, who provided the count for the (cow) hands on the ranches. This often resulted in African Americans being counted as whites. African Americans were undercounted in even less isolated places than West Texas in the 1890s.

It should be noted that any use of the 1890 population data is questionable as the manuscript was destroyed by fire. Only the population totals of the published census are available. The 1890 (and 1910) population census for Texas used by Taylor to calculate his percentages are for the stock raisers, stock herders, drovers (cowboys), and feeders. This does not include the wranglers who cared for the horses or the cooks, who were also cowboys and included many African Americans. It does not include those who were seasonal help or all the extra cowboys who were hired only for big roundups and branding.

The 1890 census figure for the total white stockraisers, stock herders, drovers, and feeders was 17,819, and the total nonwhite, including Chinese, Japanese, Indians, Negroes, and Mexicans, was 473.[15] The census for stockraisers, stock herders, drovers, and feeders must be considered invalid in terms of the total African American cowboys in Texas.

Taylor's use of census data for 1910 is not relevant, as the time of the great cattle drives in Texas was past and not addressed by George Saunders or any of the previously stated authors.

The boom years of the trail drives (1866–85) were over by the time of the 1890 census used by Taylor, and many cowboys were looking for work.[16] By 1890, the glory days of grazing Longhorn cattle on the open range and catching mustangs were past. The years of finding unbranded cattle were gone. Herding vast numbers of cattle up the trail had ended for most ranchers. Fencing was underway using the new barbed wire, and by 1885, the XIT had 162 miles of fencing completed, with only 35,000 acres yet to fence by the end of

1886.[17] The railroads had come to Texas; African American cowboys were no longer hiring on for seasonal work, and some, including Mathew Hooks, went to work for the railroad or as freight haulers, as did Jim Perry. Many cowboys of the trail crews were settling down as cowhands on ranches where they could find work, doing the daily chores of tending cattle in fenced pastures with windmills being installed for water. Others were "in transit," searching for work and trying to figure out what to do now that their skills were no longer needed. After 1885, the great cattle drives had ended, though a few trail drives taking young stock to high feeding grounds in Wyoming, Montana, and Dakota continued. Ike T. Pryor of San Antonio, who embarked in the cattle business in the region south of San Antonio in 1871, states it differently:

> The estimated number of cattle that passed up the cattle trail from 1870–90—twenty years—is some where around ten million head. It is safe to estimate one-half million a year, because many years there were almost a million head driven up the trail. . . . Think of the vast army it took to handle these drives during the years mentioned. Each year an average of five hundred thousand cattle were moved in two hundred herds. It took twenty-four hundred men to drive these herds and fourteen thousand four hundred saddle horses. . . . The ten million cattle that were moved in twenty years from Texas to the northwest were driven in four thousand herds of twenty-five hundred each. It took forty-eight thousand men to drive all these cattle, unless a man repeated his trip from year to year. It took a total of two hundred and eighty-eight thousand saddle horses and quite all these horses remained in the northwest . . .
>
> I mention these facts to show the magnitude the trail business reached before the driving of herds ceased in 1890. This was about the last year of much trail activity, because in 1884 the price began to drop on Texas cattle, both in Texas and in the northwestern states.[18]

Census figures are traditionally the final authority for most scholars, but other evidence must be considered. African Americans were typically undercounted in the population census. The estimates of Saunders, who lived his life in Texas at the time surrounded by the cowboys and ranchers, including Ike Pryor, remain valid. Porter's re-examination of the written lists of trail herd outfits makes it much more plausible that the total number of African American cowboys herding cattle up the trail 1866–95 was 8,700, or twenty-five percent as originally claimed by Saunders in 1925. "He knew that there were eight cattle herds ahead of them, and, from the top of a small promontory, he saw seven herds behind them, and the dust of thirteen more on the other side of the river. 'All the cattle in world seemed to be coming up from Texas.'"[19]

An additional complicating factor remains. Counting cowboys on the cattle drives in 1866–95 is not counting all the cowboys. Not all cowboys went up the trail. During the cattle drive years many cowboys had to remain at the ranch or base camp. There were still massive herds of cattle to tend. This fact alone gives strength to the argument that during the second half of the nineteenth century there were certainly more cowboys, including African American cowboys, than our records to date would indicate.

Being a cowboy was not glamorous. "Cowboys were poorly fed, underpaid, overworked, deprived of sleep, and prone to boredom and loneliness."[20] They choked in the dust, were cold at night, and suffered broken bones in falls and spills from horses spooked by snakes or prairie dog holes. The cowboy work centered on the fall and spring roundups, when scattered cattle were collected and driven to a place for branding, sorting for market, castrating, and in later years, dipping in vats to prevent tick fever.

Being African American cowboys though also meant surviving discrimination, bigotry, and prejudice, as well as escaping death. The lives of the African American cowboys tell the story of skill and grit, as they did what was necessary to gain the trust and respect of those who controlled their destiny. For these men and women it meant being the best—at roping, at bronc busting, at taming mustangs, at calling the brands, controlling the remuda, or topping off horses. They knew that if there were an outlaw horse to be broken, it was their job. If someone had to ride an extra night watch, it was their job to do. That's just the way it was. They were made the butt of jokes, went to the back room to eat, and tried not to fight back. They made fun of themselves or did "the shamble," because they had to. Some say skill and the scarcity of labor counted more in the West, which may be true, but African American men and women earned respect the hard way—by becoming the very best at their work.

From scattered courthouse records, writings, and interviews, a few of the African American cowhands who were a part of the history of Texas are now remembered. Peter Martin, who was freed after the 1836 Texas Revolution, hauled freight to assist the insurgents in their rebellion against the Mexican government while building a herd of cattle that allowed him to own, through a proxy, rental houses in town. Ben Kinchlow, a free black, was raised in Matamoros during the Republic period to ensure his freedom. He served as an unofficial guide with McNelly's Rangers and later herded cattle "up the trails." Bose Ikard, a friend of Charles Goodnight, went on Goodnight's first cattle drive opening the Goodnight-Loving Trail but today is only remembered by locals as a handyman! Johanna July, a Black Seminole woman who wasn't very good at cooking and sewing, had her own method of taming horses in the Rio Grande for the soldiers at Fort Duncan. Cowhand Jim Kelly was good with his gun and worked the ranches of the Print Olive clan, enforcing their version of law in the wild West. Louis Power, the mulatto grandson of empresario James Power, became a ranch foreman on the O'Connor Ranch. Daniel Webster Wallace saved his money and became a West Texas rancher. These cowboys along with others across the state became the mentors for those who came after them such as T. J. Williams, A. J. Walker, and the Reverend Mack Williams. African American cowboys were a valuable part of the cattle industry of Texas.

This book about the lives of African American cowboys of Texas is the product of many fine researchers. They traveled to interview that one person who remembered or to the courthouse to find the death certificates or deeds. They tramped deserted homesteads and read scores of county histories with little substantive information about anyone of African American heritage. It was important to research these African American cowboys now. Another decade will see the passing of the grandchildren and community members. With their passing will go the valuable memories.

The lives of these men and women who worked cattle and horses are told in the individual styles of the authors. The authors, as diverse as their subjects, include a folklorist, academics, a lawyer, a priest, a film producer, historians, artists, a soldier, an oral historian, a teacher, a museum director, and a musician. They all believe in the importance of history. The books that are written and published are about more than what is preserved in documents and archives. They are also about the choices authors make in deciding what they write. This book was written by twenty-seven people who chose to stop their lives and said, "Yes, this work must be done now."

As writers, we have used historical materials and documents in which we encountered the language and attitudes of the nineteenth and twentieth century that we find offensive today. We apologize to those readers we might offend, but in order to present a clear historical record, we used the words, phrases, and attitudes as found at the time they were written. We cited our sources in detail because there is so little available on this topic. We decided to include rather than exclude any relevant citations. We hope this work encourages others in their hometowns to bring to life the stories of the many people of color whose lives enriched our history.

We dedicate this book to the African American cowboys who were alone in life and never married because there were no African American women living nearby, to the angry African American cowgirls who fought to do what they knew how to do regardless of the views of others, and to the African American cowboys who labored from dawn to dusk. They are Texas cowboys.

NOTES

1. Bill Moyers, "The Big Story: A Journalist Looks at Texas History," *Southwestern Historical Quarterly* 101:1 (July, 1997): 4.

2. Daniel Evander McArthur, "The Cattle Industry of Texas, 1865–1918," (M.A. thesis, University of Texas at Austin, 1918), pp. 86–87.

3. James M. Cook, *Fifty Years on the Old Frontier* (Hartford: Yale University Press, 1923) as quoted in Louis J. Wortham, *A History of Texas: From Wilderness to Commonwealth*, vol. 5 (Fort Worth: Wortham-Molyneaux Company, 1924), pp. 142–43.

4. For a detailed discussion of the cultural origins of cattle ranching in Texas, see Terry G. Jordan, *North American Cattle-Ranching Frontiers* (Albuquerque: University of New Mexico Press, 1993), pp. 208–40. The Texas system of cattle ranching incorporated cultural contributions from both Mexico and the South.

5. J. Evetts Haley, *The XIT Ranch of Texas and the Early Days of the Llano Estacado* (1929; reprint, Norman: University of Oklahoma Press, 1967), pp. 182–83.

6. The buffalo herds, essential to the Indian way of life, were decimated during these years. Between the mid-1860s and 1883, the buffalo population in North American was reduced from an estimated 13 million to a few hundred. *Texas Parks and Wildlife* (June, 1997), p. 6.

7. McArthur, "The Cattle Industry," 1918, p. 164.

8. Numerous origins for the word cowboy have been found. African American folklorists say that just as there were "house boys," there were "cow boys." The "cow boys" were African Americans who herded cows, pushing them along with sticks, as their parents had in Africa.

9. Joseph G. McCoy, *Historic Sketches of the Cattle Trade of the West and Southwest* (Kansas City, Mo.: Ramsey, Millett and Hudson Printers, 1874; reprint, Columbus, Ohio: Long's College Book Co., 1951), p. 268.

10. J. Marvin Hunter, comp. *The Trail Drivers of Texas*, vol. 1 (1925; reprint, Austin: University of Texas Press, 1985), p. 453.

11. Kenneth W. Porter, *The Negro on the American Frontier* (New York: Arno Press and The New York Times, 1971), p. 495.

12. Philip Durham and Everett L. Jones, *The Negro Cowboy* (New York: Dodd, Mead and Company, 1965), pp. 44–45.

13. Quintard Taylor, *In Search of the Racial Frontier: African Americans in the American West, 1528–1990* (New York: W. W. Norton and Company), pp. 157–58.

14. Terry G. Jordan, *Trails to Texas: Southern Roots of Western Cattle Ranching* (Lincoln: University of Nebraska Press, 1981), pp. 143, 146.

15. U.S., Bureau of the Census, *Population of the United States, 1890*, Part II (Washington, D.C.: GPO, 1897), pp. 532–626. "At least three definitions of the term 'Negro' existed in the United States: the legal, the social, and the census. The U.S. Bureau of Census does not recognize the term Negro as such, choosing instead—for purposes of enumeration . . . to divide racial data into 'white' and 'nonwhite.' Nonwhite includes Negroes, American Indians, Chinese, Japanese, Filipinos . . . anyone with even the slightest trace of Negro ancestry is automatically classified as nonwhite by the Census Bureau. . . . Most nonwhites are Negroes. . . For practical purposes, in any one listing, nine out of 10 nonwhites can be regarded as Negroes," in Harry A. Ploski and Roscoe C. Brown, Jr., comps. and eds. "Population Growth and Distribution," *The Negro Almanac* (New York: Bellwether Publishing, Inc., 1967), p. 217.

16. See Jack Weston, *The Real American Cowboy* (New York: New Amsterdam, 1985), pp. 155–56.

17. J. Evetts Haley, *The XIT Ranch of Texas and the Early Days of the Llano Estacado* (1929; reprint, Norman: University of Oklahoma Press, 1967), p. 86.

18. Wortham, *A History of Texas*, vol. 5, pp. 165–67.

19. E. C. "Teddy Blue" Abbott and Helena Huntington Smith, in *We Pointed Them North: Recollections of a Cowpuncher,* Ron Tyler, ed. (1939; reprint, Chicago: R. R. Donnelley and Sons, Company, 1991), p. xxvi.

20. Joe A. Stout, "Cowboy," in *The Reader's Encyclopedia of the American West*, Howard R. Lamar, ed. (New York: Thomas Y. Crowell Company, 1977), p. 268.

Black
Cowboys
of Texas

Introduction

ALWYN BARR

Black cowboys in Texas played diverse roles in ranching as it evolved over the period from the early 1700s to the 1990s. Those African American vaqueros and drovers also lived in societies where racial attitudes, political and legal systems, and social relations underwent significant transitions during the same three hundred years. To place the biographical chapters of this volume in perspective, this introduction offers a brief account of the major economic patterns that molded Texas ranching and the important political and social developments that shaped African American life in those three centuries.

The first persons of African ancestry who herded cattle in Texas worked on ranches near the major settlements at San Antonio de Béxar, La Bahía (Goliad), and Nacogdoches during the eighteenth century when Spain governed the region. In 1792 the Texas population of 2,992 included 34 people listed as Negro, meaning of African ancestry. The same Spanish records also registered 414 persons as mulattoes, usually of mixed Spanish and African ancestry, although some might also have had Indian forebears. Thus these people with African ancestry represented 15 percent of Texas society.

Africans had come to New Spain (colonial Mexico) usually as slaves, primarily from 1580 to 1650, yet owners brought few slaves to frontier Texas. Spanish law forbade slave meetings and acquisition of weapons, but enforcement in Texas remained limited since the region counted only thirty-six slaves in 1783. Slavery began to decline in New Spain after 1650 and increasing intermarriage occurred. The diverse society that emerged in colonial Mexico included an ethnic hierarchy that placed Spaniards born in Spain at the peak, with Spanish Creoles born in America next. Below them came mestizos, of Spanish and Indian ancestry, Indians, mulattoes, lobos of black-Indian ancestry, and blacks. Yet economic success could improve a person's official status. Furthermore, few Spaniards of unmixed ancestry moved to the frontier, so most settlers reflected some version of mixed ancestry. Thus a degree of flexibility and opportunity existed for persons of black or partially African family background. For example, in 1810 Pedro Ramírez herded cattle on a ranch along the San Antonio River, while Narciso la Baume owned a ranch near Nacogdoches in the same year.[1]

On this same Texas frontier cattle raising developed between 1689 and the 1730s when early Spanish expeditions to establish official control of the region brought with them from the Mexican highlands large herds as a basis for settlements. While earlier entradas had driven hundreds of cattle into the region, the Marqués de Aguayo who came in 1721 to build new presidios and confirm Spanish sovereignty added 4,800 cattle to the province. Mission Indians under the direction of friars raised the largest herds during the early eighteenth century. From the 1750s to the 1770s the missions at La Bahía and San Antonio together claimed at least twenty-one thousand cattle as well as numerous horses and sheep, while Nacogdoches focused more on horse raising. During the late 1740s Jose de Escandón led the founding, along the Rio Grande in what was then Tamalipas, of new settlements that included even greater herds of cattle brought from the Gulf coastal area of Mexico, although estimates of the numbers vary widely. In the 1760s soldiers at Béxar and La Bahía entered ranching by gathering wild cattle that had strayed from mission herds, although priests also charged them with rustling. The ranchers and missions raised cattle to consume most of the meat locally, while they sold tallow and hides to markets in other parts of Spanish territory, especially in Coahuila and Nuevo León. Smugglers also took cattle and products into French Louisiana. After Spain acquired Louisiana from France, legal cattle drives moved at least eighteen thousand head into the colony along the Mississippi River. Following secularization of the missions in the 1790s ranchers dominated cattle raising, although joined by some mission Indians who acquired small herds. One observer in 1806 estimated there were a hundred thousand cattle in Texas above the Nueces River, with even more between the Nueces and the Rio Grande.[2]

When Mexico won its independence from Spain through a revolution from 1810 into the early 1820s, Texas society and economic activity met serious disruptions from fighting and its population declined considerably. To stimulate recovery in the region the Mexican government promoted new settlements from within Mexico and by immigration from the United States and Europe. Those patterns also caused the growth of the African American population and the further development of ranching.

Cattle raising in Texas expanded in the area between the Guadalupe River and the Rio Grande with the appearance in the 1820s of new ranchers from the Mexican coastal area led by Martin de León. People of mixed ancestry who included some mulattoes and blacks usually owned and herded the range stock in that region. Through agreements beginning with Stephen F. Austin, people primarily from the southern United States began to immigrate into East Texas during the same period. There on the coastal prairies near the Gulf of Mexico they developed herds of cattle, including some brought from the southern states and some gathered from the wild cattle or Mexican herds already there. The ranchers in that region included a few free blacks from the United States, like Robert Thompson in what became Montgomery County, who entered Texas seeking greater economic opportunity. The Ashworths, who raised thousands of cattle on extensive lands near the Louisiana border, were also involved in interracial marriages. Along with other couples involved in mixed marriages they sought a more relaxed social setting with less racial prejudice. They found Mexican society open to their participation in some public social occasions, had legal status and access to the courts, and joined in local politics. Because most free blacks lived among the Anglo settlers, however, they generally aided the Texas Revolution in 1835–36 to protect their interests from both the Mexican army and their neighbors who would resent any other attitude.[3]

The African American slave population of Texas in the 1820s and early 1830s increased far more rapidly than the free black population as new Anglo settlers from the United States brought with them their bondsmen. Since Mexican laws of the period reflected a trend toward abolition of slavery, leaders in Texas won a temporary agreement that those laws would not apply to the province as a means of stimulating immigration. Many Anglos legally listed their slaves as indentured servants to avoid emancipation pressures. Slaves arrived overland through Louisiana, a long march often made difficult by summer heat or winter cold as well as by the ropes or chains used to control them. Other bondsmen came with owners or slave traders by ship, including some smuggled in from the West Indies. The number of slaves increased rapidly, reaching about five thousand by 1836.[4]

Most of the newly arrived slaves labored as agricultural workers on farms and plantations, following patterns developed in the American South. Smaller numbers of bondsmen worked as house servants or as laborers in towns. Yet another smaller number like Willis, a slave for future governor Francis R. Lubbock, herded cattle in the coastal prairie region, often on foot in the southern style but increasingly by horseback in the Mexican pattern. For some slaves the Texas Revolution offered an opportunity to seek freedom as dozens escaped to the Mexican army in areas that it occupied. Many went with the

Mexican soldiers holding Goliad and San Antonio, who withdrew to the Rio Grande after the defeat of Santa Anna at San Jacinto.[5]

The successful war for Texas independence set the stage for a Republic of Texas led by Anglos who shaped its laws regarding slavery and race. The constitution of the republic recognized slavery and opened the way for increased immigration by slaveholders with their bondsmen from the southern United States. The first U.S. census after the annexation of Texas counted more than 58,000 slaves in 1850. Ten years later their numbers had grown to more than 182,000—about 30 percent of the population in the state on the eve of the Civil War. Thus the plantation and farming areas had expanded to include East Texas and parts of North and Central Texas.[6]

Cattle raising with some use of slaves also increased in the coastal plains along the Gulf and spread into the inland prairies of North, Central, and South Texas. A few cattle drives occurred in the 1850s to Louisiana, Missouri, and the gold fields of California. Packing plants emerged in Gulf ports to prepare hides and tallow as well as some salted meat for shipment by water to points along the Gulf and Atlantic coasts of the United States. Slaveholders, as a precaution against opportunities for escape to Mexico, limited their use of slaves as drovers to areas above the Nueces River.[7]

Slaves, whether they worked in plantation fields or on ranch lands, usually lived in one room cabins. Their food consisted of meat, bread and molasses, corn and sweet potatoes, although some could add vegetables from small gardens they maintained. Work clothes on farms and ranches included two sets of pants and shirts, or dresses for women, some sewn by slaves.

After working for six days from dawn to dusk, slaves could have some time for rest and social life on Saturday night and Sunday. Owners allowed or encouraged church attendance in separate seats or segregated meetings. Bondsmen usually attended Baptist or Methodist services, where they often heard sermons on obedience from white ministers or black preachers under white supervision.

Many slaves went through wedding ceremonies and formed families, although the law provided them no official marriage status or protection from sale and separation. Some slaveholders forced their attentions on slave women, who could be punished for resisting the directions of an owner.[8]

To limit escapes and resistance most whites opposed literacy for bondsmen, which left more than 90 percent of slaves unable to read and write. Laws restricted slave travel, meetings, and access to weapons. On plantations, farms, and ranches some owners tried paternalistic approaches in directing slaves, but resistance, or what owners saw as failures to follow orders and complete tasks as they wished, often led to whippings or other physical punishment. Yet perhaps the most important long-term limitation on the economic status of slaves came in the form of laws that designated them property, thus making them unable to own other property including land, which provided the primary source of opportunity in the nineteenth century.

Slaves responded to the controls, limitations, and punishments of slavery in diverse ways. To avoid whippings and to gain better treatment many bondsmen sought to play the roles expected of them by owners, including labor and outward acceptance of their status. Slaves folklore such as the "Old John" tales reflected inner feelings of resentment and hopes of outwitting slaveholders. To emphasize brotherhood and hope, slaves also held secret religious meetings.

Often bondsmen engaged in subtle retaliation for unjust punishments, by theft from slaveholders and by breaking tools or destroying some part of an owner's property. Slave foremen, usually called drivers, who supervised other bondsmen, could lighten punishment and set a steady work pace that did not cause collapse.

Numerous slaves, despite the odds against success and the threat of punishment, sought freedom through escape to Mexico, to Kansas, or to Indians on the frontier. Some like a group from Bastrop in 1844 might have been cowboys, for they escaped on horseback. By 1855, perhaps as many as four thousand men and women had run away to Mexico. Individual bondsmen who at times resisted punishment or killed owners usually faced execution if caught. Fears of slave revolt arose on several occasions among white Texans from the Texas Revolution through the Civil War. Two moments of crisis came with the discovery of possible plots in Colorado County and nearby areas during the fall of 1856 and with a series of fires blamed on slaves in North and Central Texas during the summer of 1860. In each instance several slaves faced hanging or whipping for possible participation in the plots. Because slaves who labored on plantations or herded cattle in Texas contributed important but unpaid labor, they lived with social restrictions on their daily lives and limits on their legal and economic status.[9]

A few slaveholders freed individual slaves or allowed them to earn their freedom. Yet Texas laws excluded immigration by free blacks into the republic or the state for fear they provided an example that undermined slavery. Thus the population of free African Americans increased little after the Texas Revolution and according to the censuses declined from 397 to 355 in the 1850s, although the actual numbers probably were slightly larger. This small group lived scattered on farms and in towns across East and Central Texas. Laws also excluded free blacks from voting, testifying against Anglos in court, and marrying whites. Legal efforts to eliminate property ownership by free African Americans ultimately did not include those who lived in Texas before its independence. In 1850, four of the thirty-eight owners who herded at least five hundred cattle from the Sabine River to the Trinity River came from mixed ancestry. Yet free people of color, such as the Ashworth ranchers of Jefferson County, had to defend themselves against court cases and threats of violence or enslavement. Some lost land and cattle in those struggles. Clearly, free black status had become more circumscribed in the transition from Mexican to Anglo-American leadership in government.[10]

African American status underwent another major change when the Confederate states including Texas lost the Civil War. The U.S. government ended slavery completely with the Thirteenth Amendment to the Constitution in 1865. Yet the new status of former slaves in the southern states remained unclear. Former slaveholders sought continued dominance over African American life and labor through Black Codes adopted by the Texas government in 1866. Those laws rejected black voting and testimony in court against whites and allowed Anglo landowners major controls over laborers. African Americans in Texas and the South celebrated emancipation and sought land for farming or raising animals, or at least wage earning jobs. Further concerns of the freed people included reuniting families separated by slave sales, seeking education, forming their own churches, and gaining some voice in state government.

Congress continued the Freedmen's Bureau, adopted the Civil Rights Act of 1866, and passed the Fourteenth Amendment to the Constitution to provide some protection against violence by the first Ku Klux Klan and unfair law enforcement including labor contracts. The bureau also opened the first schools available to African Americans in most parts of the South and Texas. In 1867 Congress responded to continuing problems in the former Confederate states by adding the Reconstruction Acts that granted voting rights to African American males. An election in 1868 for delegates to a Texas constitutional convention produced success for the new Republican Party that included most black voters. Republicans won a majority of seats, with nine African Americans among the delegates. Led by G. T. Ruby, the black delegates urged equal rights in the new state constitution, which eliminated some of the previously discriminatory laws. Republicans elected a legislative majority and Gov. E. J. Davis, who received the support of most African American voters in 1869. The governor and the legislature then organized an integrated state police force to oppose violence, as well as public schools that included African Americans for the first time, although on a segregated basis. The state government granted greater legal equality while African Americans sought with less success to gain desegregated public accommodations.[11]

As a large migration of white southerners came to Texas, the Democratic Party representing primarily former Confederates won back control of the state government in the early 1870s. The number of black legislators declined, although some served in the 1880s and the 1890s. N. W. Cuney and other African Americans did continue as leaders of the Republican Party into the 1890s. With white law enforcement officers exercising less restraint on violence toward blacks, Texas ranked third among the states in lynchings during the late nineteenth and early twentieth centuries. Segregation also emerged in public accommodations such as hotels, restaurants, and theaters during the same period. Separate public schools for African Americans began to receive less funds than white schools in the last decades of the nineteenth century.

Despite new forms of discrimination that limited their opportunities, African Americans found areas where they continued to achieve some advances. The growing group of black teachers formed an association in 1884 and their efforts increased African American literacy from about 25 percent in 1880 to more than 60 percent in 1900. Although founded with limited funding, several church-supported colleges such as Wiley College in Marshall began to offer further educational possibilities for black students in this period, while the state created Prairie View A&M College near Hempstead. As a result of new opportunities in education, some black writers, attorneys, and doctors joined ministers, teachers, and merchants in a developing African American middle class. Those groups in turn formed fraternal organizations such as Masons and Knights of Pythias. Black congregations organized Baptist conventions and conferences of the various Methodist denominations to promote cooperative programs within the denominations. Richard Henry Boyd, a former cowboy, became a minister and in the 1890s rose to secretary for the home mission board in the National Baptist Convention that represented most black Baptists.

In the late nineteenth century with its mixture of freedom from slavery balanced against new forms of discrimination, most African Americans sought economic opportunity in rural areas. The vast majority had received no wages under slavery and had no savings when emancipated. Since they could not buy land without funds, most chose to farm as sharecroppers or tenants, thus renting and working small plots as families with a degree of autonomy. Their earnings remained low, but a limited number saved enough to acquire a few acres. A small but growing group moved into towns that offered more safety and greater diversity of occupations, including a few skilled positions such as carpenters and blacksmiths. More of the urban workers labored as less skilled teamsters or at unskilled work loading ships or wagons. Many employers reserved both skilled jobs and foremen's positions for Anglos.[12]

A limited number of black Texans, like Ike Word who used his roping skills in Goliad County, herded cattle on ranches primarily on the coastal prairie or in South and Central Texas. Another small group found places on the new spreads in West Texas as the tide of settlement advanced. Many of these black cowboys worked on the rapidly growing trail drives out of Texas. While recent studies have argued for a smaller percentage of black cowboys than earlier accounts had estimated, the new studies show the largest numbers of African Americans herding cattle worked in Texas—one-third of all black cowboys in 1890 and two-thirds in 1910. Their jobs ranged from breaking wild horses to serving as cooks. Life on ranches and drives seemed to involve less discrimination than in more settled areas. Yet blacks seldom became foremen, although a few rose to be trail bosses like Al Jones. Few could save enough money to buy land and cattle or find Anglos willing to sell to them. Furthermore whites often identified individuals with terms such as "Nigger Add."[13]

Despite these limitations, black cowboys found places in cattle ranching as the industry expanded into new areas during the postwar period. Wild cattle that had drifted away from ranches in South Texas existed in growing numbers, with estimates of up to five million. Thus new cattlemen emerged by gathering these unbranded "Mavericks." A demand for meat and cattle to create new herds in the North stimulated prices of up to $30 a head—ten times the price in Texas. Trail drives to railroads in Missouri and Kansas soon moved up the Sedalia and Chisholm Trails through Central and North Texas, then across the Indian Territory that became Oklahoma. By one estimate almost one-and-a-half-million head of Longhorns had been taken north between 1867 and 1871. As the railroads spread westward and new ranches appeared in Colorado, Wyoming, and the northern plains, new routes developed across West Texas and New Mexico to become the Western and Goodnight-Loving Trails. A later estimate placed the number of cattle driven north at more than five million by the mid-1880s. While the sale of so many cattle created several wealthy ranchers, the drovers encountered problems that ranged from storms and extreme heat and cold, to flooded rivers and stampedes. Indians who opposed the shift from buffalo to cattle on the plains cut out some steers or harassed drives.[14]

The great postwar trail drives lasted only about twenty years, however, for major changes began in the 1880s. High profits from cattle led to the purchase of land and herds by northeastern and British businessmen who began to fence their holdings. Farmers also joined the move into West Texas seeking to purchase public land used but not owned by ranchers. The improvement of barbed wire in the 1870s by J. F. Glidden provided a means of controlling land in the 1880s. Ranchers used the wire to keep farmers away from water and roads they needed to sustain new crops. Farmers used wire to keep cattle off their fields. People on both sides reacted by cutting fences and demanding action by the Texas legislature as Texas Rangers and county lawmen struggled to control the problem. New laws punished fence cutting, as well as fencing public land or denying proper access to landowners. Compliance emerged slowly in the late 1880s. Yet ranchers survived the end of the trail drives because new railroads were built into West and South Texas in that decade, while the use of windmills made it possible to tap underground water.

Texas ranchers faced further transitions because the vast numbers of cattle by the 1880s left them more susceptible to changing climate conditions in the form of droughts in the summers and freezing storms in the winters, especially during the period 1885 to 1887. Thousands of cattle died. Concerns in the Midwest about disease carried by Texas cattle led to quarantine laws that forced the sale of herds at much reduced prices.[15]

The diverse changes resulted in the emergence of huge ranches that could better survive the new situations. Older areas such as the coastal region and South Texas saw the rise of the Kennedy Ranch and the even larger King Ranch that encompassed more than a million acres. When the U.S. Army forced the Comanches and other Plains Indians onto reservations in the 1870s, the way opened for the expansion of ranching into the new South Plains, Panhandle, and Trans Pecos areas of West Texas. The JA Ranch of Charles Goodnight and the XIT Ranch, with its three million acres granted to Illinois businessmen for construction of the new Texas capitol, then emerged in this region.

With the transformation to fenced ranches came efforts to improve the quality of livestock. Hereford cattle became the most widespread new breed, although many ranchers raised Angus or Durham breeds that also came from Europe or the Midwest. Especially in the Hill Country west of Austin and San Antonio some ranchers raised both cattle and sheep or goats, contrary to popular stereotypes of conflict between owners of different animal herds. As early as the 1870s ranchers formed the Cattle Raisers Association of Texas to oppose rustling. Later the organization lobbied the state and federal governments on other issues such as railroad regulation. In the early twentieth century the wealthiest ranchers began to diversify their investments to include banking, various merchant enterprises, and oil. Others like George Littlefield made part of their land available for sale to farmers. A boom in cattle prices during World War I ended in the 1920s with a decline, followed by a need for federal credit assistance during the depression of the 1930s. These changes probably hit smaller ranchers hardest forcing some out of business. When owners of large ranches bought the lands of those forced to sell, the average size of the remaining ranches increased. In the 1950s nineteen ranches each held at least a hundred fifty thousand acres. Texas continued to rank first in the nation in cattle production, counting over fifteen million head being raised for beef consumption in the 1970s. In another change during the second half of the twentieth century, trailer trucks transported more cattle to market than the railroads. A growing number of cattle were also fattened in feedlots, rather than in ranch pastures. Thus new trends further reduced the roles of cowboys.[16]

The changes in the cattle industry came during a period when Texas society also underwent significant changes. Together those developments forced African Americans to face a variety of transitions beginning in the 1890s and continuing into the twentieth century. In the first half of the century black Texans met growing restrictions on political participation and increasing segregation in public places.

During the first decade of the twentieth century the state government imposed a poll tax requirement for voting, the Democratic Party excluded African Americans with a white primary, and white Republicans reduced the roles of blacks even within the party of Lincoln. These limitations resulted in a major decline in African American participation in the political process. In response, blacks such as Lawrence Nixon, a doctor in El Paso, fought back through court cases against the white primary, but achieved only limited success.

As African Americans lost their political voice, they found it even more difficult to oppose lynching, which continued in significant numbers into the 1930s. One mob burned down the courthouse in Sherman to kill its victim. A second Ku Klux Klan arose in the 1920s to intimidate African Americans and other racial and religious minorities in Texas and across the nation. Race riots with whites attacking blacks broke out in Texas and in other states during both world wars, most often over job competition. Middle class African Americans in Texas organized chapters of the National Association for the Advancement of Colored People, beginning in the second decade of the century, to seek legal protection from the violence and discrimination.

As Texas cities grew in the twentieth century, with an accompanying growth of a black urban population, segregation of public accommodations became more rigid as streetcars and residential areas joined schools, libraries, hotels, restaurants, and theaters as places of required separation. In response African Americans boycotted the newly segregated streetcars in several cities at the turn of the century. Blacks also continued to organize their own social and fraternal groups as well as businesses to meet the needs of the black community.

Among these limitations on black status, restrictions on African American economic opportunity ranked with the most important. Most black Texans continued as farmers in the early twentieth century with 30 percent owning usually small plots of land while 70 percent remained sharecroppers or tenants. A smaller but growing number became urban workers. Yet the depression of the 1930s created high black unemployment in towns because some employers gave white workers preference, especially for skilled positions. In other cases blacks, as the most recently hired workers with the least skills and experience, became the first to lose jobs. An even greater impact of the depression resulted as sharecroppers lost their land when owners took it out of production because of low prices. New programs of the Franklin Roosevelt administration also aimed at reviving prices by reducing the size of crops. Those trends forced thousands of sharecroppers out of agriculture.[17]

World War II in the early 1940s revived the economy with new jobs in war industries and on farms producing food for the military. The growing African American middle class in Texas also won a court judgment outlawing the white primary in 1944. That opened the way to more voting by African Americans, who turned to the Democratic Party largely because the depression-era jobs programs of the Roosevelt administration had included blacks. African American teachers lobbied with some success for equal salaries in the 1940s. Heman Sweatt then broke down the first barrier to integrated higher education when he won access to the University of Texas law school in a 1950 court case. Civil rights organizations used boycotts and protests to desegregate public accommodations in Texas and southern cities during the 1960s, while court cases reduced segregation in public schools. The Civil Rights Act passed by Congress in 1964 further restricted discrimination in jobs. That resulted in an increase of the African American median income in Texas from 37 percent of the median white income in 1940 to 60 percent by the 1970s. Black businesses also increased in number but still remained below the percentage of the black population.[18]

Black cowboys found their lives and status reflecting some of the new social and economic trends of the twentieth century, while varying from others. When the trail drives ended the demand for drovers also declined, thus many of those who had herded cattle north began to seek new employment. Mathew "Bones" Hooks, for example, found work with the Santa Fe Railroad as a porter. Just as the number of farmers including black farmers declined by the late twentieth century, the number of cowboys including black cowboys declined in the same period.

Yet the fenced ranches, large and small, still needed some cowboys. Especially in the older areas along the coast and in South Texas ranchers employed a variety of hands—Anglo, Hispanic and African American. The limited number of black cowboys who had acquired land and cattle of their own, such as D. W. "80 John" Wallace in Mitchell County of West Texas, worked hard to make the necessary transitions and retain their place in the changing patterns of ranching. Wallace began to raise Durham and Hereford cattle, and joined the Cattle Raisers Association of Texas. Away from the ranches African American cowboys and ranchers faced segregation in the early 1900s. But a new generation in the late twentieth century could enjoy the greater flexibility of a society moving toward desegregation.[19]

The growing towns and cities of the twentieth century also had an increasing number of people who had lost their ties to the land but wished for some contact with the lifestyle of an earlier era. The emergence of rodeos reflected the development of cowboy skills into a form of entertainment. No one represented the potential of rodeos better than Bill Pickett who grew up in Central Texas as a black cowboy but later joined the 101 Ranch Wild West Show based in Oklahoma. He then became a premier rodeo cowboy as he developed daring new bulldogging methods, such as throwing a steer by seizing its upper lip in his teeth. He made appearances across the nation including New York City as well as in Europe and Latin America during an eventful career that included working with the cowboy comedian Will Rogers.[20]

In addition to rodeos, urban audiences found that movies about the West offered another form of entertainment with increasingly romantic ideas about cowboys. White motion picture producers and directors created an all-white West or restricted African Americans to minor or comic roles on the silver screen during the first half of the twentieth century. In response, black movie producers worked with smaller budgets to offer westerns with African American actors for black movie theaters. Bill Pickett appeared in two early movies including one titled *The Bulldogger* in 1923. Actor Clarence Brooks from San Antonio served as the villain in several other black westerns. The increasing desegregation of Hollywood pictures and roles in the second half of the twentieth century provided at least occasional inclusion of African Americans with positive roles in western films with ranch settings.[21]

From the Spanish frontier to the motion pictures of the twentieth century, black cowboys in Texas joined other Texans in herding cattle over the span of three centuries and in several different regions of the state. They labored on open range ranches, trail drives, and fenced ranches. They worked in changing political climates from Spanish colony to Mexican province to one of the United States. They lived in evolving social situations where discrimination existed to different degrees in different periods. At times, especially in early twentieth-century literature and movies, their very existence received no mention. Yet throughout the changes black cowboys have claimed a variety of roles in the history of Texas and American ranching, as the following chapters so clearly reveal.

NOTES

I wish to thank Paul Carlson for his helpful comments on an earlier draft of this introduction.

1. Donald E. Chipman, *Spanish Texas, 1519–1821* (Austin: University of Texas Press, 1992), pp. 188–89, 206–207; Alicia V. Tjarks, "Comparative Demographic Analysis of Texas, 1777–1793," *Southwestern Historical Quarterly* 77 (January, 1974): 291–338; Jack Jackson, *Los Mesteños: Spanish Ranching in Texas, 1721–1821* (College Station: Texas A&M University Press, 1986), p. 475; Carlos E. Castaneda, *Our Catholic Heritage in Texas, 1518–1936*, vol. 5 (Austin: Von Boeckmann-Jones Company, 1936–58), p. 418; Alwyn Barr, *Black Texans: A History of African Americans in Texas, 1528–1995* (1973; Norman: University of Oklahoma Press, 1996), p. 3.

2. Jackson, *Los Mesteños;* Terry G. Jordan, *North American Cattle-Ranching Frontiers: Origins, Diffusion, and Differentiation* (Albuquerque: University of New Mexico Press, 1993), pp. 86–158.

3. Jordan, *North American Cattle-Ranching Frontiers,* pp. 150, 156–58, 170–89; Jackson, *Los Mesteños,* pp. 585–617; Barr, *Black Texans,* pp. 3–6, 10.

4. Randolph B. Campbell, *An Empire for Slavery: The Peculiar Institution in Texas, 1821–1865* (Baton Rouge: Louisiana State University Press, 1989), pp. 10–34; Barr, *Black Texans,* pp. 13–17.

5. Campbell, *An Empire for Slavery,* pp. 35–49; Paul D. Lack, *The Texas Revolutionary Experience* (College Station: Texas A&M University Press, 1992), pp. 238–52.

6. Campbell, *An Empire for Slavery,* pp. 50–66.

7. Ernest Staples Osgood, *The Day of the Cattleman* (Minneapolis: University of Minnesota Press, 1929), pp. 1–23; Campbell, *An Empire for Slavery,* pp. 62–64.

8. Campbell, *An Empire for Slavery,* pp. 115–76, 201–203; Barr, *Black Texans,* pp. 20–23. See also Ron Tyler and Lawrence Murphy, eds., *The Slave Narratives of Texas* (1974; reprint, Austin: State House Press, 1997).

9. Campbell, *An Empire for Slavery,* pp. 96–114, 177–89; Barr, *Black Texans,* pp. 23–34. See also T. Lindsay Baker, *Till Freedom Cried Out: Memories of Texas Slave Life* (College Station: Texas A&M University Press, 1997).

10. Campbell, *An Empire for Slavery*, pp. 110–14; Barr, *Black Texans*, pp. 7–12. See also George R. Woolfolk, *The Free Negro in Texas, 1800–1860: A Study in Cultural Compromise* (Ann Arbor: University Microfilms, 1976).

11. James Smallwood, *Time of Hope, Time of Despair: Black Texans during Reconstruction* (Port Washington: Kennikat, 1981); Barr, *Black Texans*, pp. 39–69. See also Barry A. Crouch, *The Freedmen's Bureau and Black Texans* (Austin: University of Texas Press, 1992); and Merline Pitre, *Through Many Dangers, Toils and Snares: The Black Leadership of Texas, 1868–1900* (Austin: Eakin Press, 1985).

12. Lawrence D. Rice, *The Negro in Texas, 1874–1900* (Baton Rouge: Louisiana State University Press, 1971); Barr, *Black Texans*, pp. 70–111.

13. Barr, *Black Texans*, pp. 58, 91. For discussion of the number of black cowboys see Philip C. Durham and Everett L. Jones, *The Negro Cowboys* (New York: Dodd, Mead, 1965), pp. 44–45, and Kenneth W. Porter, *The Negro on the American Frontier* (New York: Arno Press, 1971), pp. 494–521, who believe there were at least five thousand black cowboys in the West; while Jordan, *North American Cattle-Ranching Frontiers*, pp. 214–15, 220–21, and Quintard Taylor, *In Search of the Racial Frontier: African Americans in the American West, 1528–1990* (New York: W. W. Norton & Company, 1998), pp. 156–63, believe there were less than half that number.

14. Jordan, *North American Cattle-Ranching Frontiers*, pp. 208–36; Osgood, *Day of the Cattleman*, pp. 24–113.

15. Jordan, *North American Cattle-Ranching Frontiers*, pp. 236–40, 267–75; Osgood, *Day of the Cattleman*, pp. 114–258.

16. J. W. Williams, *The Big Ranch Country* (1954; Lubbock: Texas Tech University Press, 1999); Harwood P. Hinton, "Introduction," *History of the Cattlemen of Texas* (1914; reprint, Austin: Texas State Historical Association, 1991); Jimmy M. Skaggs, *Prime Cut: Livestock Raising and Meatpacking in the United States, 1607–1983* (College Station: Texas A&M University Press, 1986), pp. 61–68, 166–218; Rupert N. Richardson, Ernest Wallace, and Adrian Anderson, *Texas: The Lone Star State* (Englewood Cliffs: Prentice-Hall, 1981), p. 309.

17. Barr, *Black Texans*, pp. 112–72. See also Darlene Clark Hine, *Black Victory: The Rise and Fall of the White Primary in Texas* (Millwood: KTO Press, 1979).

18. Barr, *Black Texans*, pp. 173–247. See also Chandler Davidson, *Race and Class in Texas Politics* (Princeton: Princeton University Press, 1990).

19. Ron Tyler and Douglas E. Barnett, eds., *The New Handbook of Texas* (Austin: Texas State Historical Association, 1996), 3:688, 6:804–805.

20. Bailey C. Hanes, *Bill Pickett, Bulldogger: The Biography of a Black Cowboy* (Norman: University of Oklahoma Press, 1977).

21. Thomas Cripps, *Slow fade to Black: The Negro in American Film, 1900–1942* (New York: Oxford University Press, 1977), pp. 273–74; Henry T. Sampson, *Blacks in Black and White: A Source Book on Black Films* (2d ed.; Metuchen: Scarecrow Press, 1995), pp. 288–89, 294–95, 360–61, 387, 433.

Part 1

The Early Cowboys

During the early 1800s Texas was a part of Mexico. Tribes of Comanches, Apaches, and Kiowas roamed the vast unsettled land. Until the 1860s settlement was primarily in East Texas, along the Gulf coast, and inland along the rivers. East Texas was considered the black belt, with most of the African American population along the Brazos, Trinity, Nueces, Sabine, Colorado, and Red River bottoms. Other pockets of settlement developed along the Rio Grande and in South Texas.

Many settlers came to the region to escape debt in the United States. They were willing to take a chance starting a new life on the frontier. It was hard work to scrape a living from the land, but the settlers were young, and their children matured early. By fifteen or sixteen years of age, if they could do the work, they were considered adults. This was certainly true for the African Americans.

Life was complicated by the dangers of living surrounded by the migratory Indian tribes. In 1840, a Mr. Clopton sent "his negro girl out to drive up the cows . . . The girl found the cattle and began hallooing at them to drive them home. This drew the attention of the Indians to her, who were concealed near by in the bottom, and several of them crept up to her under cover of the tall sedge grass, and shot the poor creature a number of times with arrows until she fell dead. They then scalped her and concealed themselves again in the bottom."[1]

Even though slavery was illegal in Spanish and Mexican Texas, owners circumvented the laws. The majority of African Americans in the region were slaves. There were isolated examples of free African Americans such as cowboy Ben Kinchlow and horse breaker Johanna July. Cowboys worked on small farms, or ranches, as they were called in Texas. For the new ranchers, building a herd took time, even though cattle were free for the taking. These were years of learning by experience. Few who came to Texas knew the ways of wild cattle, how much land was needed to feed them, where to sell them, how to break horses, and still clear the land and grow food for the family. As the settlers learned, so did the African Americans. The African Americans learned to herd cattle and break horses right alongside their owners. Tending the cows and horses on a small ranch was just one of the many chores done by the African American cowboys. Trailing herds to a market was still in the distant future.

Life on the frontier was a fragile life. For African Americans, life was primarily confined to the homestead. Leaving the homestead was dangerous for a slave and required a pass. Bounty hunters from the South came to the area hunting for runaways, and stories of runaways were numerous. But the work of the cowhand was essential to the newly arrived settlers building a life on the Texas frontier, and caring for cows and horses was usually the responsibility of the African Americans who were the early African American cowhands of Texas.

NOTES

1. J. W. Wilbarger, *Indian Depredations in Texas* (Austin: Hutchings Printing House, 1889; reprint, Austin: Pemberton Press, 1967), pp. 269–70.

Figure 1. Group of Black Cowboys on Horses. Stock hands of Thomas W. Jones, 1880s. Jones is standing in the foreground. Third cowboy from left holds TJ brand of Thomas Jones (1840–95), son of George Ranch founder Henry Jones. Courtesy George Ranch Historical Park, Richmond, Texas

Chapter 1

Remembrances

Black Cowboy Life in Texas

T. LINDSAY BAKER

"I was jes' a small boy workin' on de ranch when I heard talk 'bout conscriptin' de men for de war what was agoin' to set de slaves free," remembered Jack Bess from his days as a slave boy in Gonzales County, Texas. Even though he thought the prospect of freedom was *"too good to be true,"* he kept on working *"wid my hosses and my cattle . . . jes' like dere wasn't no war, 'cause dat was all I ever knowed how to do.*[1]

Living in the 1930s in the home of his daughter in San Angelo, Jack Bess was one of several thousand elderly African Americans interviewed by field workers from the Federal Writers' Project of the Works Progress Administration during the depths of the Great Depression. Bess was one of a number of interviewees who worked as black cowboys in Texas. Because these interviews were with African Americans who had been working cowboys during the heyday of Texas ranching in the nineteenth and early twentieth centuries, their remembrances give us particularly personal views into past life on the range.[2]

A field worker interviewed Sam Jones Washington in Fort Worth, where he had worked in meat-packing plants in later life. Sam had grown up in Wharton County, where as a slave he had begun his working life caring for his master's cattle. His remembrances began with the question,

• • •

"How old I is?

"I's 16 year old when surrender come. I know dat, 'cause of massa's statement. . . . I seed plenty slave days.

"Massa [Sam] Young run de small farm 'long de Colorado River and him don't own many slaves. . . . I fust run errands and den massa larn me to ride, soon's I could sit de hoss. Den I stays out with the cattle mos' de time and I's tickled. I sho' likes to ride and rope dem cattle and massa allus fix me up with good clothes and good hoss and good saddle. I stays dere till long after surrender.

"Us have stampedes from de cattle. Dat am cust'mary with dem critters. Dat mean ride de hoss to turn de cattle. Us ride to side de leader and crowd him and force him to turn, and keep forcin' him, and by and by dem critters am runnin' in de circle. Dat keep dem from scatterment. Dat sho' dangerous ridin'. If de hoss throw you off dem cattle stamp you to death. . . .

"I sho' 'joys dat business, 'cause we'uns have de good times. Us go to town and have fun. One time I comes near gittin' in trouble, but it ain't my fault. I's in town and massa, too, and a white man come to me and him show de drink. 'Who you 'long to, nigger?' he say. 'I's Massa Young's nigger,' I says, polite-like. 'You looks like de smart nigger and I's de notion smack you one,' he say. 'You better not smack me any,' I says. You understand, dat de way massa raise me. I don't understand some cruel white mens gits de arg'ment, jus' for de chance to shoot de nigger. Massa am standin' near by and him come up and say, 'If you touches dat nigger, I'll put de bullet through you.' Dat man see massa have no foolishment in he words and gets gwine. But if massa am not dere, Gabriel blow he horn for dis nigger's Jubilee, right den, yes, sar. . . .

"De war? White man, we'uns didn't know dere am de war. We seed some sojers at the start, but dat all. One day massa say to me, 'After dis, you gits $15.00 de month wages.' I works for him three more years and den he sold out. Den I goes farmin' till 1905. I works in de packin' plants here in Fort Worth den, till I's wore out."[3]

When a Works Progress Administration field worker interviewed former slave Tom Holland in Madisonville, Texas, the elderly man related memories of his boyhood in Walker County. As a teenager, Holland prided himself in his ability to break horses for riding:

"I chopped cotton and plowed and split rails, then I was a horse rider. In them days I could ride the wildest horse what ever made tracks in Texas, but

I's never valued very high 'cause I had a glass eye . . . I'd make a dollar or fifty cents to ride wild horses in slavery time and massa let me keep it. I buyed tobacco and candy and if massa cotch me with tobacco I'd git a whippin', but I allus slipped and bought chewin' tobacco."[4]

Daniel Phillips, Sr., who a field worker interviewed as an old man in San Marcos, had grown up in the vicinity and also had worked with his master's horse herd as a young man.

"I was a slave to Dr. Dailey and his son, Dr. Thomas Dailey . . . I was born in Stringtown just after they arrived in 1854 . . . Dey has a plantation at Stringtown and a ranch on de Blanco River . . .
"Marse Dailey raised cotton and co'n on de plantation. On de ranch dey ketches wild horses and I herds dem. When I'm on de ranch I had to drive de wild horses into de pen. De men cotches de wild horses and I has to drive 'em so's dey won't git wild again.
"Lots of dem wild horses got colts and I has to brand dem . . .
"When de war's over I didn't know about it. Marse Tommy comes to de ranch when I'm herdin' de wild horses. He says, 'Dan, you'se free now.' I say, 'Wha' dat mean, Marse Tommy?' He say, 'Dat mean you can live with you mammy and you pappy, and what you makes you kin keep.'"[5]

John Price, who came to Southeast Texas as a slave about 1861, observed how Texas cattlemen supported the Confederate cause during the Civil War by driving cattle overland across Louisiana to markets at New Orleans. He described the drives to his interviewer in Liberty:

"Dey drive beefs and have two rivers to cross to git dere, de Sabine and de Neches. Dey 'liver 'em by so many head and iffen dey ain't have 'nough, other mens on the prairie help 'em fill out de number what dey needs. I's rid many a wild hoss in my day and dat's where I make my first money for myself."[6]

R. C. Smith, interviewed in Alderson, Oklahoma, as part of the WPA slave narrative interview effort in Oklahoma, found himself on a West Texas ranch as a direct consequence of the Civil War. His master, Presley R. Smith, sent him from Arkansas to a ranch on the Texas frontier for "safekeeping." This was a location where he would be less likely freed by invading Union troops. Smith recounted the events this way:

• • •

"My master refugeed me to Texas at the outbreak of the War. We went down in the winter and it was awful cold. We crossed the Indian Territory . . . We went out in west Texas on a ranch. The Kiowa and Comanche Indians give them a lot of trouble. They was always slipping into the country and stealing horses and cattle.

"The owner of the ranch had a boy named Charley. He and I would ride, rope calves, and play around. We had good times together. His father would let us go with the boys sometimes when they went on round-ups.

"One day the men started out to round-up and brand the young stock and we wanted to go. Charley's father, for some reason, did not want us to go and he told us to stay at home. After they left he saddled his horse and started after them. He said that his father would let him stay with the outfit if he just caught up with them. I wouldn't go with him so he went without me. I can still see him as he turned and waved to me just before he rode out of sight. I couldn't help wishing that I could go with him but I dassent disobey the Master.

"Nobody ever saw Charley again. They tracked his horse for several miles. That was easy as his horse had shoes on it. His horse was running and there was other tracks along with his that we supposed belong to a band of Kiowas or Cheyennes. They were hidden and the cowboys passed them, but when Charley come by they surprised him and finally captured him. I'm sure they killed him for he would a come back if he could have. I always wished I'd gone with him for they wouldn't bother a nigger, but they sure had it in for white folks. I missed my friend, so I could hardly stay on at the ranch. I never had no good times any more."[7]

Monroe Brackens, who also came to Texas as a boy, shared memories of cowboy life both as a slave and as a freedman following emancipation. He spent most of his life in the Frio Valley near Hondo, Texas, where a WPA field worker interviewed him over sixty years ago.

"I was bo'n in Mississippi, in Monroe County. I'm 84 years old. My master, George Reedes, brought me, my father and mother and my two sisters to Texas when I was two years old.

"My master settled here at a place called Malone, on the Hondo River . . . He went into the stock business. Our house there was a little, old picket house with a grass roof over it out of the sage grass. The bed was made with a tick of shucks and the children slept on the floor. The boss had just a little lumber house. Later on he taken us about 20 miles fu'ther down on the Hondo, the Old Adams Ranch, and he had a rock house. I was about six years old then. I had some shoes, to keep the thorns outa my feet, and I had rawhide leggin's. We just had such clothes as we could get, old patched-up clothes. They just had that jeans cloth, homemade clothes.

"I was with George Reedes 10 or 12 years. It was my first trainin' learnin' the stock business and horse breakin'. He was tol'able good to us, to be slaves as we was. His brother had a hired man that whipped me once, with a quirt. I've heard my father and mother tell how they whipped 'em . . .

"I was on the Adams Ranch on the Hondo when my master came out and told us we were as free as he was. He said we could stay on and work or could go if we wanted to. He gave my mother and father 50 cents a piece and 25 cents for the children. We stayed awhile and then went west to the Frio.

"I used to be along with old man Big-foot Wallace in my early days. He was a mighty fine man. I worked for the people that was gathering stock together there . . . I used to go up to his camp down on the San Miguel. He lived in one part and his chickens in the rest of his house . . . He used to run stock horses and had a figger 7 on the left shoulder for his brand and the tip of each ear split was his earmark.

"The last man I broke horses for was Wilson Bailey. I was there about 12 years. He raised just cavi-yard—we called it a cavi-yard of horses, just the same thing as a remuda. We called 'em that later, but we got that from the Spanish. We would get up in a tree with our loop till the horse came and drop it down on him. When they were so spoilt, we got 'em in a sort of cavi-yard and drove 'em under trees and caught 'em in a snare. We had lots of wild horses, just this side of Pearsall. 'Bout the only way I'd get throwed was to get careless. We'd ketch 'im up, hackamore 'im up, saddle 'im up and get on 'im and let 'im go. Sometimes he'd be too wild to pitch, he'd break and run and you had to let 'im run himself down. I used to rather ketch up a wild horse and break 'im than to eat breakfast."[8]

Although the goal of the field workers in the WPA slave narratives project was to record remembrances of slavery days, many of the interview transcripts contain recorded memories of individuals' later lives. Consequently the slave narratives occasionally provide lengthy accounts of Texas black cowboy life in the years that followed emancipation in 1865. Because some of these narratives provide accounts of the trail-driving days of the 1860s and 1870s, they represent especially valuable sources about the black cowboy experience during this significant phase in the cattle industry for which relatively few African American sources are available. John Sneed, for example, drove cattle on the Chisholm Trail a number of times for noted Austin-area cattlemen, on one occasion tangling with a puma:

"I followed the cattle till I's 'bout 26. I's went up de Chisholm Trail eight or nine time and druv for Massa Blocker and Jedge Brackenridge and others. On one stampede I rode 24 hours straight and after we rounds up all de cattle, I goes to sleep under a tree. Dat day I has on a buckskin coat I in gen'ral wore and I feels somethin' grab dat coat and bite my side. I rouses up and sees de big panther draggin' me off to de thicket. I has de six-gun but I couldn't git to it. Every once in a while dat panther lay me down and sniff at my nose. I jes' hold de breath, 'cause if dat panther cotch me breathin' dat been de end of me. He drug me to some bushes and den goes off a li'l way and give de yell. Dat yell make me turn cold, 'cause it sound jes' like a man screamin'. Den dat cat dug a shallow hole. I eases out my old gun, takes careful aim and den says, 'Thank you, old man,' and he turns to look at me and I shoots him right 'tween he eyes. After 'while, dat cat's mate and cub come runnin', 'cause he yell for dem, and I kilt dem, too."[9]

Tom Mills, who came to Texas from Alabama as a slave in 1862, spent half a century working cattle in the South Texas area for the stock that were driven up the cattle trails and later shipped by rail to markets in the North. Like John Sneed, Mills had his own encounter with a puma, as well as meeting many of the other dangers and excitements in his long working life as a cowboy:

"When I got to workin' for myself (after freedom), it was cow work. I done horseback work for fifty years. Many a year passed that I never missed a day bein' in the saddle. I stayed thirteen years on one ranch. The first place was right below Hondo City. His name was Talley Burnett and I was gettin' $7.50 a month. Went to work for that and stayed about three or four months and he raised my wages to what the others was gettin' and that was $12.50. He said I was as good as they were. Then I went to Frio City. I done the same kind of work, but I went with the people that nearly raised me, the Rutledges . . .

"I married when I was with them and I worked for them after that. That was when we would work away down on the Rio Grande, when Demp Fenley and Lee Langford and Tom Roland and the two Lease boys and one or two more was deliverin' cattle to the Gold Franks' ranch. He wanted 8,000 two-year-old heifers. He had 150,000 acres of land and wanted cattle to stock it. Some taken a contract to deliver so many so these men I was with went down below Laredo and down in there. We wound that up in '85. In '86, I went to Kerr County ranch out there on the head of the Guadalupe River. I stayed there two years and a half, till they sold out. This man I was workin' for was from Boston and he leased the ranch and turned it over to me and I done all the hirin' and payin' off and buyin' and ever'thing. When he sold out, I left and went on the Horton ranch about thirteen months.

"My first wife died in 1892 . . . I married again in Bandera and quit ranchin' and went to stock farmin' for Albert Miller, then leased a place from Charley Montague for two years, then went over into Hondo Canyon and leased a place there in '98. We stayed there till 1906, then came to Uvalde. I leased a place out here, about two hundred acres, four miles from town, and had odd jobs around here too. Then, about 1907, we went to Zavala County and stayed till 1919. I leased a place here, then, and finally settled at this place I'm on now (at Uvalde) and have been here ever since . . .

"I know when we used to camp out in the winter time we would have these old-time freezes, when ever'thing was covered in ice. We would have a big, fat cow hangin' up and we could slice that meat off and have the best meals. And when we was on the cow hunts we would start out with meal, salt and coffee and carry the beddin' for six or eight men on two horses and carry our rations on another horse. I guess it would scare people to hear 'em comin' with all them pots and pans and makin' all that racket.

"When we camped and killed a yearlin' the leaf fat and liver was one of the first things we would cook. When they would start in to gather cattle to send to Kansas, they would ride out in the herd and pick out a fat calf, and they would get the "fleece" and liver and broil the ribs. The meat that was cut off the ribs was called the fleece. It was a terr'ble waste, for many a time, the hams wasn't even cut out of the hide, jes' left there . . .

"I remember when I was a little fellow at John Kanady's . . . . One day, he came there and put me on his horse. He had loosened up his girt, and I got out there a little ways and one of the cows turned back. The horse was a regular old cow pony and when that cow turned back, the old horse turned just as quick and the saddle slipped and I stayed there.

"Oh, pshaw! they turn so quick you have to be on the lookout. You have to watch the horse as well as the cow. Some of them horses get pretty smart. One time they were cuttin' cattle and a fellow brought a cow to the edge of the herd and the cow turned back and when she did, the horse cut back too and left him there. When he went from under him, that fellow's spur left a mark clear across the saddle as he went over. It was my saddle he was ridin' and that mark never did leave it . . .

"No, I never did go up on the trail. I've helped prepare the herd to take. Usually, there would be one owner takin' his cattle up on the trail. They had no place to hold the cattle, only under herd. Usually, they would start with a thousand or fifteen hundred head, but they didn't put 'em all together till they got away out on the divide. They would have 'em shaped up as they gathered 'em and jes' hold what they wanted to send. It didn't take so many men, either, because they all understood their business.

"I was jes' thinkin' about when Mr. Demp Fenley and Rutledge was here. They had about nine hundred head of cattle. We brought 'em right in below Pearsall, right about the Shiner ranch, and delivered 'em there. But before we got there at a little creek they called Pato, they was hardly any place to bed the cattle because they was so much (prickly) pear. Mr. Rutledge and I always bedded the cattle down, and then I would go on the last relief, usually about the time to get up, anyway. He used me all the time when they would get ready to go to camp in the evenin', and we'd spread 'em out and let 'em graze before beddin' 'em down. Sometimes he would give me a motion to come over there, and I knew that meant an animal to throw. He always got me to do the ropin' if one broke out. Well, we was comin' on with those cattle and they was a steer that gave us trouble all the time. As soon as you got away, he would walk out of the herd. Well, we got the cattle all bedded down and they were quiet, but that steer walked out. I was ridin' Mr. Fenley's dun horse, and Mr. Rutledge says to me, 'I tell you what we'll do. We'll ketch that steer out here and give 'im a good whippin'.' I says, 'We'll get into trouble, too.' Well, he was to hold 'im away from the herd and I was to rope 'im, but the steer run in front of him and out-run 'im. If he would have run in behind him, I would 'a caught 'im, but that steer beat 'im to the herd and run right into the middle of 'em. And did he stampede 'em! Those cattle run right into the camp, and the boys all scramblin' into the wagon and gettin' on their horses without the boots on. One steer fell and rolled right under the chuck wagon. You know, we run those cattle all night, tryin' to hold 'em. It was a pear flat there, and next mornin' that pear was all beat down flat on the ground. They sure did run, and all because of that foolishness. Mr. Rutledge got me and told me not to tell it, and I don't reckin to this day anybody knows what done that.

"I never told you about the panther about to get on to me, did I? Well, we was out on the Rio Grande, about thirty-one or thirty-two miles beyond Carrizo. It was at the Las Islas (The Islands) crossin'. I was about three days behind the outfit when they went out there. That was in July, and they was a law passed that we had to quit wearin' our guns the first day of July and hang 'em on the ho'n of our saddle. When I got to the outfit, the boys was gettin' pretty tired herdin'. They had to bring 'em out about six miles to grass and to this little creek. We would put 'em in the pen at night and feed 'em hay. They were waitin' there for them to deliver some cattle out of Mexico. The Mexkin [*sic*] told me they was somethin' out there where they were herdin' sheep that was scarin' the sheep out of the pen at night. I had seen some bobcats, but I laid down under one of these huisache trees and went to sleep. I had my pistol on and was layin' there and about two o'clock, I woke up. I turned over and rested myself on my elbow and looked off there about 12 feet from me and there stood a big old female panther. She was kind of squattin' and lookin' right at me. I reached right easy and got my Winchester that was layin' beside me and I shot her right between the eyes. Well, I had one of her claws here for a long time. She had some young ones somewhere. I imagined, though, she was goin' to jump right on me. It wasn't no good feelin', I know. She was an awful large one.

"Oh, my goodness! I have seen lobos, eight or ten in a bunch. They're sure mean. I've seen 'em have cattle rounded up like a bunch of cow hands. If you hear a cow or yearlin' beller at night, you could go next mornin' and sure find where they had killed her. They would go right into the cow or calf and eat its kidney fat first thing. I tell you, one sure did scare me one time. I was out ridin', usually ropin' and brandin' calves, and I came across a den in the ground. I heard somethin' whinin' down there in that hole. It was a curiosity to me and I wanted to get one of those little wolf pups. That was what I thought it was. I got down there and reached in there and got one of those little fellows. They was lovos (lobos). They are usually gray, but he was still black. They are black at first, then they turn gray. He was a little bit of a fellow. Well, I got him out and the old lovo wolf run right at me, snappin' her teeth, and my horse jerked back and came near gettin' away. But I hung (on) to my wolf and got to my horse and got on and left there. I didn't have nothin' to kill her with. I was jes' a boy, then. I took that pup and give it to Mrs. Jim Reedes, down on the Hondo, and she kep' it till it began eatin' chickens.

"I had a bear scare, too. That was in '87, about fifty years ago. Well, Ira Wheat was sheriff in Leakey in Edwards County, then. I went down there, and I was ridin' a horse I broke for a sheriff in Kerr County. I came to Leakey to see Wheat—you see they was burnin' cattle (running the brands) all over that country then. As I was ridin' along, I seen some buzzards and I rode out there. Somethin' had killed a hog and eat on it. I knowed it was a bear afterwards, but then I went on down to Leakey and started back, I got up on the divide, at the head of a little canyon and I seen those buzzards again. I seen two black things and I jes' thought to myself them hogs was comin' back and eatin' on that dead hog. I rode up and seen that it was two bears and I made a lunge at 'em and the old bear run off and the little cub ran up a tree. I thought,

'I'll ketch you, you little rascal.' So I tied my horse and I went up the tree after the cub and when I was near 'im, he squealed jes' like a child. I tell you, when it squealed that way, here came that old bear and begin snuffin' around the tree. My horse was jes' rearin' and tryin' to break loose out there. I tell you, when I did get down there and got to him, I had to lead him about two hundred yards before I could ever get on him. He was sure scared. Like it was when I was a boy down on the Hondo one time and I could hear horses comin' and thought it was Indians and after awhile, I couldn't hear nothin' but my heart beatin'."[10]

Not all the remembrances in the slave narratives of Texas cowboy life come from men. Julia Blanks, a San Antonio native, as a freedwoman in the 1870s married a cowboy who worked on the Adams Ranch in the Frio Valley. Her remembrance of being a ranch wife and sometimes cook for the ranch personnel sheds valuable light on the lives of working black cowboys and their families, especially her observations on foodways and daily activities.

"After I married the second time, we lived on the Adams ranch on the Frio and stayed on that ranch fifteen years. We raised all our chillen right on that ranch. I am taken for a Mexkin [sic] very often. I jes' talk Mexkin back to 'em. I learned to talk it on the ranch . . . All my neighbors here is Mexkins. They used to laugh at me when I tried to talk to the hands on the ranch, but I learned to talk like 'em.

"We used to have big round-ups out on the Adams ranch. They had no fences then. The neighbors would all come over and get out and gather the cattle and bring 'em in. He would notify his neighbors they were goin' to gather cattle on a certain day. The chuck wagon was right there at the ranch that is, I was the chuck wagon. But if they were goin' to take the cattle off, they would have a chuck wagon. They would round-up a pasture at a time and come in to the ranch for their meals. Now on the Wallace ranch, they would always take a chuck wagon. When they were gettin' ready to start brandin' at the ranch, my husband always kep' his brandin' irons all in the house, hangin' up where he could get his hands on 'em. Whenever they would go off to other ranches to gather cattle, you would see ever' man with his beddin' tied up behind him on his horse. He'd have jes' a small roll. They would always have a slicker if nothin' else. That slicker answered for ever'thing sometimes. My husband slep' many a night with his saddle under his head.

"He used to carry mail from San Antonio to Dog Town, horseback. That was the town they used to call Lodi (Lodo), but I don't know how to spell it, and don't know what it means.[11] It was a pretty tough town. The jailhouse was made out of 'dobe and pickets. They had a big picket fence all around it. They had a ferry that went right across the San Antonio River from Floresville to Dog Town. I know he told me he come to a place and they had a big sign that said, 'Nigga, don't let the sun go down on you here.' They was awful bad down in there. He would leave Dog Town in the evenin' and he would get to a certain place up toward San Antonio and camp, and once he stopped before he got to the place he always camped at. He said he didn't know what made 'im stop there that time, but he stopped and took the saddle off his horse and let 'im graze while he lay down. After a while, he saw two cigarette fires in the dark right up the road a little piece, and he heard a Mexkin say, 'I don't see why he's so late tonight. He always gets here before night and camps right there.' He knew they was waylayin' 'im, so he picked his saddle up right easy and carried it fu'ther back down the road in the brush and then come got his horse and took him out there and saddled 'im up and went away 'round them Mexkins. He went on in to San Antonio and didn't go back any more. A white man took the mail to carry then and the first trip he made, he never come back. He went down with the mail and they found the mail scattered somewhere on the road, but they never found the man, or the horse, either.

"On the Adams ranch, in the early days, we used to have to pack water up the bank. You might not believe it, but one of these sixty-pound lard cans full of water, I've a-carried it on my head many a time. We had steps cut into the bank, and it was a good ways down to the water, and I'd pack that can up to the first level and go back and get a couple of buckets of water, and carry a bucket in each hand and the can on my head up the next little slantin' hill before I got to level ground. I carried water that way till my chillen got big enough to carry water, then they took it up. When I was carryin' water in them big cans my head would sound like new leather—you know how it squeaks, and that was the way it sounded in my head. But, it never did hurt me. You see, the Mexkins carry loads on their heads, but they fix a rag around their heads some way to help balance it. But I never did. I jes' set it up on my head and carried it that way. Oh, we used to carry water! My goodness! My mother said it was the Indian in me—the way I could carry water.

"When we were first married and moved to the Adams ranch, we used to come here to Uvalde to dances. They had square dances then. They hadn't commenced all these frolicky dances they have now. They would have a supper, but they had it to sell. Every fellow would have to treat his girl he danced with . . .

"Another thing, we used to have big round-ups, and I have cooked great pans of steak and mountain orshters. Generally, at the brandin' and markin', I cooked up many a big pan of mountain orshters. I wish I had a nickel for ever' one I've cooked, and ate too! People from up North have come down there, and when they were brandin' and cuttin' calves there, they sure did eat and enjoy that dinner.

"The men used to go up to the lake, fishin', and catch big trout, or bass, they call 'em now; and we'd take big buckets of butter—we didn't take a saucer of butter or a pound; we taken butter up there in buckets, for we sure had plenty of it—and we'd take lard, too, and cook our fish up there, and had corn bread or hoe cakes and plenty of butter for ever'thing, and it sure was good. I tell you— like my husband used to say—we was livin' ten days in the week, then.

"When we killed hogs, the meat from last winter was hung outside and then new meat, salted down and then smoked, we put in there, and we would cook the old bacon for the dogs. We always kep' some good dogs there, and anybody'll tell you they was always fat. We had lots of wild turkeys and I raised turkeys, too, till I got sick of cookin' turkeys. Don't talk about deer! You know, it wasn't then like it is now. You could go kill venison any time you wanted to. But I don't blame 'em for passin' that law for people used to go kill 'em and jes' take out the hams and tenderloin and leave the other layin' there. I have saved many a sack of dried meat to keep it from spoilin'.

"We would raise watermelons, too. We had a big field three mile from the house and a ninety-acre field right by the house. We used to go get loads of melons for the hogs and they got to where they didn't eat anything but the heart.

"I used to leave my babies at the house with the older girl and go out horse-back with my husband. My oldest girl used to take the place of a cowboy, and put her hair up in her hat. And ride! My goodness, she loved to ride! They thought she was a boy. She wore pants and leggin's. And maybe you think she couldn't ride!

"After we left the ranch, we took up some state land . . . After my husband got sick, we had to let it go back . . . My husband has been dead about nine-teen years."[12]

James Cape, born a slave in Southeast Texas, became a working ranch hand while still in bondage. After emancipation he discovered that inadvertently he had become associated with a band of rustlers. Fearing for his life, should the thieves be apprehended by law officers while he was with them, he escaped, only to join company with members of a gang of armed robbers.

· · ·

"I's bo'n in yonder southeast Texas and I don' know what month of de year for sho', but 'twas more dan 100 years ago . . .

"When I's old 'nough to set on de hoss, dey learned me to ride, tendin' hosses. 'Cause I's good hoss rider, dey uses me all de time gwine after hosses. I goes with dem to Mexico. We crosses de river lots of times. I 'members once when we was a drivin' 'bout 200 hosses north'ards. Dey was a bad hail storm comes into de face of de herd and dat herd turns and starts de other way. Dere was five of us riders and we had to keep dem hosses from scatterment. I was de leader and do you know what happens to dis nigger if my hoss stumbles? Right dere's whar I'd still be! Marster give me a new saddle for savin' de hosses. . . .

"I's free after de war and goes back to Texas, to Gonzales County, and gits a job doin' cowboy work for Marster Ross herdin' cattle. And right dere's whar I's lucky for not gettin' in jail or hanged. It was dis way: I's in town and dat man, Ross, say to me, 'I understan' you's a good cowhand,' and he hires me and takes me way out. No house for miles 'fore we comes to de ranch with cattle and I goes to work. After I's workin' a while, I wonders how come dey brings in sich fine steers so often and I says to myself, 'Marster Ross mus' have heaps of money for to buy all dem steers.' Dey pays no 'tention to de raisin' of cattle, jus' brings 'em in and drives dem 'way.

"One time Marster Ross and six mens was gone a week and when dey comes back, one of 'em was missin'. Dey had no steers dat time and dey talks 'bout gittin' frusterated and how one man gits shot. I says to myself, 'What for was dey chased and shot at?' Den I 'members Marster Bob Houston don tol' me 'bout rustlers and how dey's hanged when dey's caught, and I knows den dat's how come all dem fine steers is driv in and out all de time. But how to git 'way, dere's de puzzlement. I not know which way to go and dere's no houses anywhere near. I keeps gettin' scarter, and ever' time somebody comes, I thinks its de law. But Marster Ross drives de cattle north and I says to him, 'I's good hand at de drive. Kin I go with you nex' time you goes north?' And not long after dat we starts and we gits to Kansas City. After Marster Ross gets shut o' de critters, he says, 'We'll res' for couple days, den starts back.' I says to me, 'Not dis nigger.'

"I sneaks 'way and was settin' on a bench when 'long comes a white man and he's tall, had dark hair and was fine lookin'. He says to me, 'Is you a cowhand?' So I tells him I is, and he says he wants a hand on his farm in Missouri and he says, 'Come with me.' He tells me his name was James and takes me to his farm whar I tends cattle and hosses for three years and he pays me well. He gives me more'n I earns. After three years I leaves, but not 'cause

I larned he was outlaw, 'cause I larned that long time afterwa'ds. I's lonesome for Texas and dat's how I comes to Fort Worth and here's whar I's stayed ever' since."[13]

Reflecting on changes that he had seen during his life, Joe Oliver summarized the lives of the cowboys he had known during his life of slavery and freedom in Hill County. Oliver noted:

"... de farmer soon begun to put all dis land in cultivation so bye an' bye the cowboy had to go further west; some of dem didn't go away, dey jes stayed an' hung up his spurs an' went to plowin' de land an' turnin' his pasture into a cotton an' corn field, but while dey was here dey made hit worth dey time for dey wuz one of the best folks dat ever lived in dese parts."[14]

NOTES

1. U.S., Works Progress Administration, Federal Writers' Project, Slave Narratives, Texas, Part 1, Box A930, Manuscript Division, Library of Congress, Washington, D.C., pp. 72–73, cited hereafter as Texas Slave Narratives, Part 1. The quotations in this chapter present the actual words in dialect as spelled inconsistently by the WPA Slave Narrative Project personnel in the 1930s.

2. The Slave Narrative Project of the Federal Writers' Project was undertaken between 1937 and 1939 in seventeen states with sufficient black population to record the remembrances of elderly African Americans who had been born into slavery. Texas was one of the seventeen states in which the interview project was undertaken, although Texan memories of slavery are also recorded in interviews made across the Red River in Oklahoma. The narratives in effect are texts prepared from field notes written down by field workers, who asked interviewees a set list of questions. From the notes the field workers prepared rough drafts of the interview notes, which project editors then placed in a more standard form before they forwarded them to project headquarters in Washington. There the "official" set of slave narratives went to the Manuscript Division of the Library of Congress, where 2,300 of the interviews are preserved and available today. Not all the narratives, however, ended up being sent to Washington. In Texas additional typescripts of WPA slave narratives are preserved in such repositories as the Center for American History at the University of Texas at Austin, in the Houston Metropolitan Research Center in Houston, and at the Special Collections at the University of Texas at Arlington. In Oklahoma additional narratives not sent to Washington, including the remembrances of some Texans, are preserved in the Archives and Manuscripts Division of the Oklahoma Historical Society.

The slave narratives, as is true of any other primary sources, must be viewed critically. Often, for example, the memories of slavery come from individuals who experienced bondage as children, so they viewed the institution of slavery through juvenile eyes. As the elderly informants related their memories, their remarks were influenced by the racial etiquette of the day; many interviewees dared not offend white people who they perceived as agents of the government on which they depended for pensions. Further, some interviewees had sharp memories and others had difficulty remembering their early years. Users of the narratives necessarily must approach them with the same caution with which they would approach any other historical sources.

For background on the WPA Slave Narrative Project, see Norman Yetman's fine overview, "The Background of the Slave Narrative Collection," *American Quarterly* 19 (fall, 1967): 534–54. For articles dealing with the use of the slave narratives as primary evidence, see John W. Blassingame, "Using the Testimony of Ex-Slaves: Approaches and Problems," *Journal of Southern History* 41 (Nov., 1975): 473–92; Paul D. Escott, "The Art and Science of Reading WPA Slave Narratives," in *The Slave's Narrative*, Charles T. Davis and Henry Louis Gates, Jr., eds. (New York: Oxford University Press, 1985), pp. 40–48; C. Vann Woodward, "History from Slave Sources," *American Historical Review* 79 (Apr., 1974): 470–81.

The slave narrative interviews undertaken in Texas are available in published form in George P. Rawick, ed., *The American Slave: A Composite Autobiography*, Series 1, vols. 4–5 (Westport, Conn.: Greenwood Press, 1972); Supplement, Series 2, vols. 2–10 (Westport, Conn.: Greenwood Press, 1979). Selections from these interviews are also available in Ronnie C. Tyler and Lawrence R. Murphy, eds., *The Slave Narratives of Texas* (Austin: Encino Press, 1974). For interviews with Texas ex-slaves interviewed as part of the Oklahoma Slave Narrative Project, see T. Lindsay Baker and Julie P. Baker, eds., *Till Freedom Cried Out: Memories of Texas Slave Life* (College Station: Texas A&M University Press, 1997).

3. U.S., Works Progress Administration, Federal Writers Project, Slave Narratives, Texas, Part 4, Box A392, Manuscript Division, Library of Congress, pp. 138–40, cited hereafter as Texas Slave Narratives, Part 4.

4. U.S., Works Progress Administration, Federal Writers' Project, Slave Narratives, Texas, Part 2, Box A931, Manuscript Division, Library of Congress, p. 144, cited hereafter as Texas Slave Narratives, Part 2.

5. U.S., Works Progress Administration, Federal Writers' Project, Slave Narratives, Texas, Part 3, Box A931, Manuscript Division, Library of Congress, pp. 183–84, cited hereafter as Texas Slave Narratives, Part 3.

6. Texas Slave Narratives, Part 3, p. 199.

7. Rawick, ed., *The American Slave*, Supplement, Series 1, vol. 12 (Westport, Conn.: Greenwood Press, 1979), pp. 284–85; also available in T. Lindsay Baker and Julie P. Baker, eds., *The WPA Oklahoma Slave Narratives* (Norman: University of Oklahoma Press, 1996), p. 400.

8. Texas Slave Narratives, Part 1, pp. 124–25, 128–29.

9. Texas Slave Narratives, Part 4, pp. 50–51.

10. Texas Slave Narratives, Part 3, pp. 99–106.

11. Mrs. Blanks here probably was referring to Lodi, about six miles northwest of Floresville in Wilson County, Texas, which became the seat of Wilson County on its organization in 1867.

12. Texas Slave Narratives, Part 1, pp. 100–102, 103–105.

13. Texas Slave Narratives, Part 1, pp. 193–96.

14. U.S., Works Progress Administration, Federal Writers' Project, Slave Narratives, Texas, "Reference[:] Interview with Joe Oliver, R. F. D. Mart-Waco Road," typescript, 1937, p. 8, WPA Records: Slave Narratives, Box 4H361, Center for American History, University of Texas at Austin.

Chapter 2

Peter Martin

A Stockraiser of the Republic Period

MICHAEL RUGELEY MOORE

The earliest references to African American cowboys in Texas are clouded in the anonymity of slavery. Prior to the general emancipation in 1865, few Afro-Texans appear in records depicting the cattle industry. Yet the importance of these men in the launching of Texas' nineteenth century livestock industry is significant. Peter Martin, born a slave in the first decade of the nineteenth century, is among the many Texas slaves who worked cattle for white owners. Yet he is virtually unique in Texas history as one of a handful of African Texans who received manumission during the Texas Republic, and who managed his own cattle herds in the era before the Civil War eliminated slavery from the state.

Peter, the slave of Wyly Martin, was born in Georgia during the period 1800–10, probably in Sumter County. Peter had served Wyly "from his boyhood," presumably including the decade that Wyly Martin served in the United States Army on the northwestern frontier up to 1822. After leaving the military, Wyly immigrated to Texas, and with Peter's assistance, brought over a hundred head of cattle from Louisiana to Austin's Colony in 1824. The settlement of Austin's Colony along the lower Brazos and Colorado Rivers in the 1820s began the first legal movement of sizable numbers of Anglo and African families to Mexican-owned Texas. Mexico's National Colonization Law of 1823 granted each settler a labor of land (177 acres) for farming, and a *sitio* or league of land (4,428 acres) if the colonist planned to raise livestock.[1]

Wyly Martin received a league of land in present Brazoria County in 1824, and by 1830 petitioned Austin for an additional league of prairie land in present Fort Bend County to establish a stock farm—as ranches were known at the time. Martin's Fort Bend neighbor, Henry Jones, received his stockraising league in 1824, and had already established a successful stock farm on lands adjoining the Brazos when Martin received the second league. Cattle raising in Austin's Colony commenced on a small, subsistence level as soon as the colonists arrived. As time progressed, and more cattle were imported and captured from the prairies, the herds increased to commercial-sized operations in the early 1830s.[2]

The branding of cattle was an important indicator of ownership. Austin required his settlers to record the brands to be used on their cattle with the alcalde's office in San Felipe. One visitor to the colony commented that "the rules observed in respect to them are very strict." Henry Jones and neighbor Wyly Martin recorded their marks or brands in 1825. While many African Americans tended their owners' cattle before emancipation, few owned cattle themselves. In 1831, however, Jim, "a man of color belonging to the Est[ate] of A. Jackson" recorded his brand in San Felipe, the first African American to do so.[3]

The efforts of slave laborers and the expanding markets for cotton and cattle helped Henry Jones and fellow colonists expand subsistence-level farms into extensive plantations and ranches. By 1840, Jones owned sixteen slaves and eight hundred head of cattle, making him one of the ten largest stockraisers in the Republic of Texas. Despite Wyly Martin's 1830 assertion to Stephen F. Austin that he intended "to devote a considerable portion of my means to the raising of Stock," Martin's success at ranching was more limited than Henry Jones's. Martin's one hundred head of cattle imported in the 1820s had dwindled to seventy-five head by 1840.[4]

Henry Jones and Wyly Martin established close connections in the years before Martin's 1842 death. Martin served as godfather to Jones's daughter, Polly, born in 1826. Jones at times rented one of Martin's three slaves, and during the colonial period, "after the custom of the times Peter was allowed to marry one of Henry Jones' slaves." Peter's marriage to Judith would remain a stable union until his death in 1863. Peter was a trusted worker who managed Martin's plantation and cattle herds, and may have also assisted the stockraising efforts of Henry Jones.[5]

Although there were wild cattle on the prairies of Texas—a legacy of the Spanish mission efforts in East Texas, these cattle were difficult to capture and domesticate. The colonists preferred to import cattle from Louisiana to begin their stock farms. As a result of Spanish occupation and trading in Louisiana, a Spanish-derived breed of cattle and partially Hispanicized livestock traditions flourished on the prairies in the southwestern portion of the state.[6]

African Americans are closely associated with the movement of these cattle from Louisiana to Texas during the early years of settlement. Colonists, aided by their slaves, often drove Spanish horses and mules to Louisiana to trade for cattle. In at least one case, an unfortunate young male slave was taken to Louisiana and traded for sixty head of cattle to be brought back to Texas.[7]

Yet the value of other African Americans to the beginning of these stock farms exceeded that of chattel to be traded for cattle. Many slaves developed cattle-working skills in this early period. Peter Martin managed Wyly Martin's property and stockraising operations during the period before the Texas Revolution. Wyly Martin focused his efforts on the political arena of Austin's Colony, serving in a variety of offices including that of alcalde. Wyly's direct involvement tending stock can be doubted due both to his other political obligations and his reputation as a person who avoided physical labor. Wyly trusted Peter's management of the property, and Peter "endeared himself to his master, by fidelity and good conduct." In addition to managing Wyly's plantation, Peter also launched a freight-hauling business, and "transacted business by his own account by Consent of his master" prior to the Revolution.[8]

During the Texas Revolution, Peter served both as an aide to his master and independently hauled supplies for the Texian army. On the eve of revolution in 1835, Wyly Martin acted as interim administrator of the colony at San Felipe. Peter managed Martin's camp and hunted to keep his table supplied with game. Peter also used his own resources to support the revolt. He "rendered material aid to the government by Hauling . . . military stores and provisions for the use of the Army." Peter used his wagon and team to haul supplies from San Felipe to the Texian army at San Antonio in the fall of 1835, being paid $180 for the services.[9]

Wyly Martin desired to give Peter his freedom in recognition of his faithful service and to ensure that Peter would not be treated poorly by a future owner. Wyly Martin's will, dated September 3, 1833, first promised Peter his manumission, to take effect upon Wyly's death. After the revolution, however, Wyly began to take steps to free his slave.[10]

Wyly could manumit Peter at his own discretion, but the Constitution of the Republic of Texas did not permit a "free person of African descent . . . to reside permanently in the republic, without the consent of Congress." Wyly desired that Peter be able to continue to live in Fort Bend County, so he took steps to ensure that the new government would respect Peter's freedom. Wyly petitioned Congress in 1839 to authorize Peter's residence, to which they agreed after a heated debate concerning the precedent it would be setting. This act of Congress made Peter the first emancipated slave legally permitted to remain in Texas.[11]

Peter's emancipation became formalized in 1842 following the death of his owner. Peter had taken the last name of Martin at least as early as 1835, yet only after his emancipation did his full name begin to appear in legal documents. Congressional debates indicated that Peter had accumulated wealth of as much as $16,000. Although this value was exaggerated, Peter's business activities enabled him to purchase property and to hire his wife from her owner, so the family could be together. As a freedman in antebellum Texas, Peter had to have a white man serve as his guardian. Mills M. Battle and later William Ryon, Henry Jones's son-in-law, served as guardians and held the title to Martin's homestead and property in trust for Peter.[12]

In addition to his home in the town of Richmond, Peter also possessed cattle and horses during the Republic period. He may have received his start in the stock business from a portion of the increase of Wyly Martin's cattle, possibly explaining the lack of growth in Wyly's herd. In 1842, the year of his emancipation, Peter is first listed on the county tax rolls with 100 head of cattle, which increased to 125 head in 1844, and 225 head two years later. To work these cattle he owned two horses in 1842, and five by 1845; throughout the remaining antebellum years, Peter owned between five and seven horses for use in tending cattle and pulling his wagon. In 1845, his herd of 200 head of cattle ranked him twenty-third among the 146 stockraisers in Fort Bend County.[13]

Settlers who arrived during the colonial years had the largest cattle herds in 1845. Henry Jones, owner of Peter's wife, Judith, possessed 1,325 head, and Jones's neighbor, Joseph Kuykendall, led the county with 1,400 head. Yet the average herd for the county that year was only 127 head, making Peter owner of fifty-seven percent more cattle than the average of white farmers in the area. Fort Bend County also ranked high among all Texas counties in cattle ownership in this time. In 1840, Jones and Kuykendall's cattle herds ranked them as the seventh and sixth largest ranchers, respectively, in Texas. Ten years later, Fort Bend County remained a principal stockraising center of the state, with the fifth highest number of cattle of any Texas county.[14]

Although Peter owned no ranching lands, his marriage to Jones's slave Judith and other connections to the Jones family ensured Peter access to the Jones prairie lands as range for his cattle. In 1842, for example, Henry Jones owned or controlled almost fifteen thousand acres in Fort Bend and Brazoria Counties. Peter had livestock dealings with the Jones and Ryon families throughout the antebellum period, as indicated by the fact that his cattle had the brand of Henry Jones's daughter, Polly Ryon, and were counterbranded with his own brand at the time of his 1863 death. Although it was mentioned that Peter had his own brand, it unfortunately was not recorded in the Fort Bend County brand books.[15]

In the late 1840s or early 1850s Martin sold most of his cattle herd, possibly to purchase additional property in Richmond. In 1853, Martin bought four Richmond town lots and erected a dwelling for his family, rental houses, a smokehouse, and other improvements. Told that a freedman risked holding property in his own name, he had William Ryon hold title to the property in trust for him and his family. In later years Peter had various occupations: peddler, cook, and boarding house manager.[16]

Peter's death in April, 1863, caused more than emotional grief for his family. His wife, Judith, was sold to a new owner later that year, and his Richmond home and property were sold for Confederate money—which quickly became worthless. Judith resented the sale of what she felt was her property and after the end of the Civil War, and her emancipation, she filed suit to reclaim it. Polly Ryon helped finance Mrs. Martin's successful suit, which, after appeal to the Texas Supreme Court in 1873, upheld her rights to the property and the proceeds of its sale. The sale of Peter's estate, the court ruled, created a trust in favor of his wife, Judith Martin, and his children, and though the trust was inoperative so long as they remained slaves, after their emancipation, it was valid and enforceable in their favor. Having recovered her house and property, Judith continued to live on this Richmond property until her death in 1890.[17]

The general emancipation in 1865, celebrated thereafter as "Juneteenth," not only enabled Judith to inherit Peter's property; it also brought the emancipation of her children. Fourteen children were born to the couple during their twenty-plus years of marriage, although only one daughter was living at the time of the 1872 court case. After freedom, descendants of Peter and Judith Martin continued to work on the ranch lands originally granted to Henry Jones, now managed by his daughter, Polly Ryon. George Martin, Peter's grandson, worked as a "stock hand" for J. B. Wheat and J. H. P. Davis throughout the late nineteenth century. Both Wheat and Davis were sons-in-law of Polly Ryon. In 1906, George Martin made at least two trips to St. Louis accompanying trainloads of ranch cattle to market.[18]

African American cowboys, many born into slavery on the Jones-Ryon plantations, provided the labor to expand the ranching operations in the postbellum years. Polly Ryon managed the Jones ranching operations in the late nineteenth century, expanding it to an estate worth $200,000 that included more than twenty-five thousand acres and eight thousand head of cattle at the time of her death in 1896.[19]

While difficult and often dangerous work, the life of a cowboy at the time was often better—economically and socially—than the hardscrabble life of a sharecropping farmer. The Bob Jones family is one example of the economic opportunities available in ranch work for newly freed slaves. When freedom came, Bob was about thirty years old and had been born as a slave of Henry Jones. Within three years of his emancipation, he owned five horses and forty head of cattle—making him the owner of the second highest number of cattle among African Americans in Fort Bend County that year. Over the next few years, Bob Jones expanded into farming, cotton ginning, and other businesses. His son, Y. Union Jones, worked for the Ryon Farm and Pasture Company as a cowboy beginning in the 1880s, and then rented a large farm from the Ryons by the age of thirty. Y. U. Jones later went into business with his father in the partnership of Robert H. Jones and Son. Y. U. Jones continued to prosper and became "one of Texas' most progressive farmers, ranchers and business men, regardless of race or color."[20]

The rates of pay for black cowboys on this ranch in the late nineteenth century varied according to their skills and permanence in the job. Wes Mack, making $20 per month, was the highest paid and presumably was serving as a foreman or top hand on the Ryon Ranch. Rufus Powell, known as a first-rate cowboy, worked for $15 per month in the early 1890s. Henry Armstrong worked for the Wheat Ranch division of the Ryon Farm and Pasture Company at a rate of $10 per month in 1893 and received an increase to $12 per month after March, 1894. Neal Cook was only paid $8 per month in 1896 at the same ranch. Other hands worked by the day rather than the month; daily hands on the Wheat Ranch made $0.65 per day during the spring roundup of 1896. The "cow wagon" cook—the term used locally rather than chuck wagon—Richard Jackson made only $15 per month in 1899.[21]

The slaves brought by Austin's colonists, such as Henry Jones and Wyly Martin, began an important tradition of ranch work by African Americans in Southeast Texas. Descendants of these families formed a stable rural community into the twentieth century. Labor contracts and farming on shares replaced slavery, and the expanding cattle markets of postbellum America provided good wages to younger generations of African Texans that worked as cowboys. Continued political, social, and economic dominance by the descendants of the former slaveholders, however, greatly affected the lives of the African American families who remained on the land. In the early twentieth century, Mamie George inherited the Jones-Ryon Ranch headquarters, and emigrant Czech, Polish, and German families supplanted African Americans as tenant farmers on the George Ranch. Descendants of these European farmers turned to ranch work, and, combined with the hiring of Hispanic ranch workers from South Texas after mid-century, led to the end of more than century of black cowboys as the principal ranch workers on this land.

Although little is known of the actual cattle-working activities of Peter Martin, his management of Wyly Martin's stock farm in the 1820s and 1830s certainly establishes him as one of the region's first African American cowboys. Unlike the majority of slave cowboys who labored in obscurity, Peter's story is known because of his two encounters with the legal system—the congressional debates surrounding his manumission and the legal efforts of his widow to inherit his property after the Civil War. Peter's own successful stockraising during the Republic of Texas period demonstrated his ability to use the ranching skills learned in slavery to provide for his family. Despite later pursuing other occupations, he owned cattle throughout the remainder of his life. Although never called a "cowboy," Peter Martin represents the experiences of many slaves who tended cattle in early Texas. Yet he also emerged, through his own talents and the rapport developed with his owner, to become one of the first African American ranch foremen and independent cattlemen in Texas.[22]

NOTES

1. Bureau of the Census, Seventh Census of the United States, 1850, Schedule 1 (Free Inhabitants), Fort Bend County, MSS, Washington, D.C.: National Archives, p. 236; Bureau of the Census, Eighth Census of the United States, 1860, Schedule 1 (Free Inhabitants), Fort Bend County (Washington, D.C.: National Archives), p. 372; "Capt. Wiley Martin," in J. H. Kuykendall, "Sketches of Early Texians," MSS, Center for American History, University of Texas, Austin, pp. 21–22; Petition of Wyly Martin, November 5, 1839, MSS, Texas State Archives, Austin; Thomas H. S. Hamersly, *Complete Regular Army Register of the United States from 1779 to 1879* (Washington, D.C.: T. H. S. Hamersly, 1880), p. 606; Wyly Martin to Stephen F. Austin, July 31, 1824, in Eugene C. Barker, ed., *The Austin Papers*, vol. 1 (Washington, D.C.: GPO, 1924), pp. 862–63; Wyly Martin to Stephen F. Austin, Dec. 14, 1830, Stephen F. Austin Papers, MSS, Center for American History, University of Texas, Austin, Texas; David B. Gracy, ed., *Establishing Austin's Colony* (Austin: The Pemberton Press, 1970), p. 36.
2. Martin to Austin, December 14, 1830, MSS, S. F. Austin Papers; "The Estate of William Stiles, Decd. to Henry Jones," William Stiles Succession Records, File #1, Fort Bend County Clerk's Office, Richmond, Texas; David Dary, *Cowboy Culture: A Saga of Five Centuries* (Lawrence: University of Kansas Press, 1981), p. 69.
3. Anonymous, *A Visit to Texas in 1831* (Houston: Cordovan Press, 1975), p. 37; Austin Colony Brand Book, MSS, Austin County Courthouse, Bellville, Texas, p. 16.
4. Gifford White, ed., *The 1840 Census of the Republic of Texas* (Austin: The Pemberton

Press, 1966), p. 45; Martin to Austin, December 14, 1830, MSS, S. F. Austin Papers; Fort Bend County Tax Roll, 1840, MSS, George Memorial Library, Richmond, Texas, p. 7.

5. Martin to Austin, *Austin Papers*, vol. 1, pp. 862–63; Martin to Austin, Dec. 14, 1830, MSS, S. F. Austin Papers; "The Estate of William Stiles, Decd. to Henry Jones," William Stiles Succession Records, File #1, MSS, Fort Bend County Clerk's Office, Richmond, Texas; Becht v. Martin 37 TEX 719–720 (1872–1873); Clarence Wharton, *History of Fort Bend County* (San Antonio: The Naylor Company, 1939), p. 25.

6. Two interpretations of Hispanic influences in Colonial Louisiana are found in Jack Jackson, *Los Mesteños: Spanish Ranching in Texas, 1721–1821* (College Station: Texas A&M University Press, 1986), pp. 173–221, 586–88, and Terry G. Jordan, *North American Cattle-Ranching Frontiers* (Albuquerque: University of New Mexico Press, 1993), pp. 120–22, 156–58, 184–89.

7. "Biographies of Leading Texans," Part II, MSS, Texas State Archives, Austin, Texas, p. 397–403; J. Marvin Hunter, comp., *The Trail Drivers of Texas* (1925; reprint, Austin: University of Texas Press, 1985), p. 733.

8. Becht v. Martin 37 TEX 727–728 (1872–1873) Texas State Archives, Austin, Texas; "Capt. Wiley Martin," in J. H. Kuykendall, "Sketches of Early Texians," p. 24.

9. Wharton, *History of Fort Bend County*, pp. 70–71; Harriet Smither, ed., *Journals of the Fourth Congress of the Republic of Texas, 1839–1840*, vol. 1, Senate Journal (Austin: Von Boeckmann–Jones, Co., 1929), p. 64; R. R. Royall to the General Council of Texas, Dec. 18, 1835, Adjutant General Papers, Folder 19, MSS, Texas State Archives, Austin.

10. Will of Wyly Martin, Sept. 3, 1833, Succession of Wyly Martin, Fort Bend County Probate, vol. A, MSS, George Memorial Library, Richmond, Texas, p. 293.

11. *Laws of the Republic of Texas*, vol. 1 (Houston: Office of the Telegraph, 1837), p. 19; Randolph B. Campbell, *An Empire for Slavery: The Peculiar Institution in Texas, 1821–1865* (Baton Rouge: Louisiana State University Press, 1989), p. 111; Becht v. Martin, 37 TEX 719 (1872–1873); P. E. Peareson, "Brief and Argument for Appellees," Julius Becht vs. Judith Martin, et al., No. 1353, Supreme Court of Texas, 1873, MSS, Texas State Archives, Austin, p. 2; Harold Schoen, "The Free Negro in the Republic of Texas," *Southwestern Historical Quarterly* 40 (Oct., 1936): 103; "Capt. Wiley Martin," in Kuykendall, "Sketches," p. 23.

12. Succession of Wyly Martin, June 27, 1842, Fort Bend County Probate, vol. A, pp. 292–95; Royall, Dec. 18, 1835, Adjutant General Papers, Texas State Archives; Smither, *Journals of the Fourth Congress*, p. 64; P. E. Peareson, "Brief and Argument for Appellees," Julius Becht vs. Judith Martin, et al., No. 1353, Supreme Court of Texas, 1873, p. 2; Guardianship of Peter Martin, Fort Bend County Probate Minutes, bk. B, MSS, George Memorial Library, Richmond, Texas, p. 289; Becht v. Martin 37 TEX 723 (1872–1873).

13. Fort Bend County Tax Rolls, 1842, p. 77; 1844, p. 108; 1845, pp. 125–27.

14. Fort Bend County Tax Rolls, 1845, pp. 125–27; White, *The 1840 Census of the Republic*

of Texas, p. 45; J. D. B. DeBow, *Statistical View of the United States, 1850* (Washington: United States Government, 1854), pp. 308–19.

15. Fort Bend County Tax Roll for 1842, p. 75; Peareson, "Brief and Argument for Appellees," Julius Becht vs. Judith Martin, p. 2; "Capt. Wiley Martin," in Kuykendall, "Sketches," p. 23; Becht v. Martin 37 TEX 728–729 (1872–1873).

16. Wharton, *History of Fort Bend County*, p. 156; Seventh Census of the United States, 1850, Fort Bend County, Texas, p. 236; Becht v. Martin 37 TEX 728 (1872–1873); Peareson, "Brief and Argument for Appellees," Julius Becht vs. Judith Martin, et al., No. 1353, Supreme Court of Texas, 1873, p. 2; Petition of Judith Martin, et al., filed Oct. 23, 1871, Fort Bend County District Court, p. 2, Texas State Archives, Austin, Texas.

17. P. E. Peareson, "Brief and Argument for Appellees," Julius Becht vs. Judith Martin, et al., No. 1353, Supreme Court of Texas, 1873, p. 2; W. S. Jones and wife to James Barnett, Nov. 18, 1863, Fort Bend County Deeds, Book G, MSS, George Memorial Library, Richmond, Texas, p. 576; Becht v. Martin 37 TEX 719–720 (1872–1873); Oliver Brown to J. H. P. Davis, Feb. 24, 1892, J. H. P. Davis Papers, Box 2, Folder 3, MSS, George Ranch Historical Park Archives, Richmond, Texas.

18. J. H. P. Davis Ledger, "1899–1914 Accounts of People," J. H. P. Davis Papers, MSS, George Ranch Historical Park Archives, Richmond, Texas, pp. 12–13, 15, 82.

19. "Inventory Property of Ryon Farm & Pasture Company, February 29, 1896," ledger, vol. C, "1897–1898 Ryon Farm and Pasture Co.," MSS, George Ranch Historical Park Archives, Richmond, Texas, p. 2.

20. Fort Bend County Tax Rolls, 1868, p. 615; A. W. Jackson, "A Sure Foundation," MSS, George Memorial Library, Richmond, Texas, pp. 536–37; Y. U. Jones Probate, no. 2277, Fort Bend County Probate Minutes, vol. Y, MSS, George Memorial Library, Richmond, Texas, p. 555.

21. Ryon Farm and Pasture Company, ledger C, p. 6; Ryon Farm and Pasture Company, ledger B, p. 130; Pay Roll Wheat Ranch, Ryon Farm and Pasture Company, Apr., 1896; ledger, "1899–1914 Accounts of People," MSS, George Ranch Historical Ranch Archives, Richmond, Texas.

22. The portion of Polly Ryon's estate inherited by granddaughter Mamie George has been preserved as a 23,000-acre ranching historic site in Fort Bend County. The George Ranch Historical Park preserves the ranching landscapes of the Jones and Martin leagues, artifacts and archives of Southeast Texas ranching, and the stories of the African and Anglo families who created this ranching culture. The 1830s stock farm of Henry Jones has been reconstructed, and interprets lives of the Jones family as well as that of Peter and Judith Martin. The 1890s ranch of Polly Ryon and 1930s ranch of Mamie George is also presented to the public at this living history museum of Texas ranching.

Figure 2. Robert Lemmons. Courtesy George Willems, Carrizo Springs, Texas

Chapter 3

Robert Lemmons

A Black Texan Mustanger

ALLAN O. KOWNSLAR

I worked alone and acted like I was a mustang. I made the mustangs think I was one of them. Maybe I was in them days. After I stayed with a bunch long enough they'd foller me instid of me having to foller them. Show them you're the boss. That's my secret.

So spoke Robert Lemmons in 1931 to folklorist J. Frank Dobie as he recalled his days during the late 1800s when he worked alone, stalking wild horses that roamed Dimmit, Zavala, and Frio Counties in South Texas.[1]

Lemmons was a black Texan cowboy and one of the few black Texan mustangers or *mesteñeros* that also included Bill Nunn, Will Crittendon, and Joe McCloud. Among them, Lemmons demonstrated the most unique way to catch wild horses, usually bringing them into captivity looking and feeling as fit as they did on the day he first encountered them.

Mustangs hunted by Lemmons were horses that began to roam the American West as early as the late 1500s. They acquired their name from the Spanish adjective *mesteño* from *mesta*, meaning an unbranded animal "belonging to the grazers." The horses the Spanish brought to Mexico from Spain were of a mixed breed. As noted by one scholar, they included: "the Andalusian horse of Southern Spain[, which] was the product of a mixing of native stock with others from North Africa and Arabia. Out of the generally light, hardy, and swift Oriental stock of the Near East came the Arabian horse. . . . In North Africa another excellent breed also developed from the Oriental stock—the Barb, so named because it was found in the Berber or Barbary States."[2]

As the mustangs spread throughout the North American continent, domesticated horses joined the wild herds and their descendants acquired some of the bloodlines of the Spanish horses. As a result, "certain recognizable types had appeared. One of these was the claybank, coyote dun, or buckskin, a golden colored animal with black mane and tail. It usually had horizontal 'zebra' stripes on its legs and a dark line along its spine and down its shoulders. Another type of dun was the grulla, which was the color of the sand-hill crane, or, as some said, mouse-colored. Grullas were also line-backed and striped on their legs. Both of these types were noted for their exceptional endurance and made excellent cow ponies. Cowboys were eager to own them."[3]

Within a mustang herd, a stallion led a *manada* or group of mares. The group varied in number but usually included between twenty to thirty-five horses that grazed over a twenty-five- to fifty-square-mile area.

People who saw the herds during their rapid decline by the end of the nineteenth century told the same basic stories. One person was John Young, who tried unsuccessfully to catch a mustang stallion and his mares. Although Young failed in the attempt, he continued to marvel at the existence of such horses. As he recalled:

Watching the habits of the mustangs was with me a frequent source of interest. Their breeding season was the early spring months, and then the stallions were in continual combat. Every old stallion would be busy fighting the young stallions, including the yearlings, out of his *manada,* and the young stallions would be maneuvering to steal a mare or so each; in addition to fighting off these young upstarts the old stallions had to guard against each other. The strongest and best stallions kept the most mares. Thus, under conditions undisturbed by man, the breed would have a tendency to improve, selective breeding rather than inbreeding being the natural tendency . . .

Day and night the stallion was on guard to keep his bunch together and to protect them. If he wanted to run, he gave a signal snort and fell in behind them, biting chunks of hide and flesh out of any laggard or recalcitrant mare. If the mares were well trained, all the stallion had to do was to snort and take the lead; after he got his *manada* well going, he took the lead anyhow and kept it. Sometimes he had to fight from the front in order to turn the running mares back or to swerve them.

The bunches of young stallions that took up with each other were not so compact. They were constantly scattering. In nearly every bunch of mustangs were a few saddle horses with an occasional mule. The saddle horses were not afraid of man, but they were harder to catch than the mustangs, for they would run and dodge with more intelligence. Sometimes we might get a cross-run on a bunch of mustangs and cut or rope the saddle horses out, but we never caught a mule. A mule that had taken up with mustangs was always alert, ready to "whistle" when he saw a man. One could never slip up on a bunch of mustangs that contained a mule, and the mule never tired on a run.[4]

Stallions leading *manadas* were almost impossible to catch, but catching mustangs became a necessity. Texans who took cattle on the long drives to railheads in Kansas required sometimes as many as a hundred good horses. More often than not, that many domesticated horses were not immediately accessible. Thus, wild mustangs had to be caught and tamed. During the 1870s and 1880s, the years of the big cattle drives, those horses, once assembled, were more vital than their equivalent numbers in cattle.[5]

There were five basic techniques for capturing mustangs. One was roping. It could mean waiting in a tree beside a water hole and then roping the mustang when it walked nearby. Another method involved a man on horseback running with a mustang and looping a rawhide lariat over its head. This method often injured the animal as it was thrown violently to the ground. Corralling was another method. It, too, sometimes made use of a water hole. "The usual method was to find some water hole that was visited by wild horses. A large circular corral of poles, boards, or wire then was built around it. A light-weight gate, opening inward, was placed on the side from which the animals usually approached. Perhaps a smaller corral was attached to a side. For some time the mustangs would be permitted to water there, until the fear of human scent had gone. In the summer when most of the water holes were dry and the horses desperate for water, they returned. When it came time to use the trap one man secreted himself on the 'off-wind' side, holding a rope with which to spring the trap closing the doors."[6]

When corralling, mustangers built pens with V-shaped wings sometimes a half-mile from the main gates. Then, cowboys would run the mustangs into the pens and keep them circling until they became exhausted. If the head stallion continued to be a major problem, he was often shot. If a herd were too large, the pen would become overcrowded with the result that many if not most of the horses would trample one another to death in their attempts to escape. This method could also cause danger to cowboys attempting to capture the mustangs. "[For] every ten horses captured and broken, two or three saddle horses were either killed, wind-broken, or crippled. Cowboys have been seen to sit down beside their horse thus used up and cry like babies at their loss, although in their eagerness to catch the wild ones and their excitement in the chase they had spurred the horse until there was a raw place on either side as big as a dollar. [An observer] once saw a man whose horse had collapsed under him, pull out his Winchester, shoot into the escaping band of mustangs, then throw his arms about his pony's neck and sob in remorse for what he had done."[7]

Nicking or creasing was also a risky way to capture mustangs. "To nick a mustang the hunter aimed a rifle to send a ball—in later days a bullet—just through the top of the animal's neck, at the root of the mane, a little in front of the shoulder. Here a nerve center—connected with the spinal cord and the brain—may be so shocked as to stun or temporarily paralyze the horse, causing it to drop to the ground senseless for a minute or two, in which brief time it could be securely roped and tied down. The chief disadvantage of this method was that if the aim at the moment of the shot was not accurate the whole attempt was an instantaneous failure, for if the shot did not strike the exact spot for which it was intended the animal either fled because the bullet missed its mark, or dropped dead with a broken neck."[8]

Another author recalls, "One old mustanger says to 'talk of going out to catch horses this way is pure bunk. I have tried it many times and have broken their necks scores of times and never caught a horse that way and never knew anyone else who did.'"[9] Indeed professional mustangers shied away from such a practice because it usually resulted in either the death or escape of forty-nine of the fifty horses sought.

Equally dangerous for mustangs was catching them in a trap. It involved the use of a snare that "would be secreted on a trail familiar to a herd, and the horses either were driven down the mountain path or else the trapper waited until they came to water. When trapped by the foot or the neck the horse made new arrangement of the mountain scenery. If the end of the rope were tied to a log the animal took the whole trap for a long ride . . . [Wise horses] would use cattle as leaders. Consequently, if a trap caught anything, it often was a steer. . . . The mortality among animals snared was high, a great majority being choked to death."[10]

Probably the most humane effort consisted of what came to be known as a "walk down." Usually two men on horseback using fresh mounts or alternating with other riders would continue to follow in a circular movement a mustang herd using a single ranging area. The mustangers hoped to tire out the horses or for them to become so used to the mustangers that the horses could be easily caught. The "walk down" was not always successful, as the lead stallion could have his *manada* outlast the mustangers.

When successful, the walk down involved using a full moon so that one could keep the herd moving at night. These animals could be driven for three or four days and nights, at a slow speed, until they were finally exhausted and crazy for water. One old horse catcher does not believe that exhaustion is the sole explanation of why the horses, after being "walked down" no longer feared man. He believes that because of the former association of the mustang or his ancestors with man, he felt secure in man's presence again. Regardless of the reason, the exhausted horse could be roped or driven into a corral. Feeling ashamed of his conduct, one cowpuncher who helped "walk down" a herd of eighty in four days wrote: "Some would lie down; then the stringing rawhide end of a lariat would be snapped at them and strike unerringly where the vaquero intended it to. Up they would get, and reel ahead. It was night when the men got them to camp, and they kept those that were not literally fagged out on the move nearly all night—moving backward and forward."[11]

The "walk down" was Robert Lemmons's favorite method for catching wild mustangs and made him foremost among the most successful of the mustangers. However, unlike others, he not only worked alone, but he used the most humane techniques to catch the horses.

This unusual man was born a slave without a formal name in Lockport, Caldwell County, Texas. The exact date of his birth is unknown, but Robert Lemmons claimed it was November 20, 1848, the same date as listed on his death certificate.[12]

He was the son of Cecelia, also known as Celia, Sealy, or Gus. While still a young slave girl, Cecelia was a gift from Aaron Burleson to his daughter, Matilda, and his son-in-law, Levi English, when they married during 1838. About ten years later she gave birth to Robert. His father's name is unknown.[13] While still in his early years, Robert was given to John, called "Bud," the son of Levi and Matilda English. Although Robert was still a slave, he and John English apparently became good friends.

For several years, the English family, primarily due to problems with Indians, moved to Bexar, DeWitt, Atascosa, and Frio Counties, finally settling in the Carrizo Springs area in early 1863. Robert, his mother, and his siblings went as well, with Robert driving a four-yoke team of oxen. Once there, he helped the English family build a herd of Longhorn cattle.[14]

The Carrizo Springs area is only a short day's walk to Mexico, and Robert easily could have gained his freedom at any time. Instead, perhaps because of his youth, his fear of facing the world alone, or his not wishing to cross country where he could encounter Comanches, he elected to remain with the English family. In doing so, he became an early survivor among the few blacks to live in the area. Many of the others made their way either to Eagle Pass or Mexico.[15]

Lemmons was freed from slavery due to an unusual circumstance. On July 4, 1865, John English and two others died of wounds after joining others, including Robert, pursuing Comanches who had attacked one of the nearby settlers earlier that day. As Lemmons told an interviewer in 1933, Levi English "was so grieved over the loss of his son that he told Bob he could have his freedom."[16] Although it was then customary for freed slaves to adopt the surname of their former masters, Lemmons did not, perhaps because the English family opposed it.[17]

It was not long, however, until Lemmons acquired a formal name. Soon after he left the English family he worked for a nearby rancher named Duncan Lammons or Lemmons, with whom Robert developed a lasting relationship. As Lemmons recalled: "When I was set free, I was about 17 years old. The slaves didn't have names, only those of their masters, so I had to stand around and hunt me a name. Old man Duncan Lemons [Lammons] come along and I told 'im my trouble so he took me to Eagle Pass and bogused my name. So that's how I got the name, Lemons. I stayed with old man Duncan till he died, and he taught me everything I knowed about stock. I guess I caught about 103 mustangs for 'im."[18]

Spellings of his surname later appeared either as Lammons, Lemmons, Lemon, and Lemons. Robert's death certificate carries the name Lemons; his will, Lemmons (and in parentheses "sometimes spelled Lammons"); his marriage license, Lemmons; his registration of a cattle brand, Lemons; and the General Index to Deeds for Dimmit County, Lemmon. His tombstone has the name Robert Lemmons, the same way he spelled his name when writing it.

Lemmons's quick sense of humor was obvious in an episode involving himself, Duncan, and some others "when they had to form a circle to fight off a small band of Indians. [Duncan] Lammons told Bob to stand behind him and protect him from the back. Hearing Bob laughing, Lammons turned to see Bob watching the Indians, not protecting him. Bob had become so fascinated with the improvised spurs of sharp, Y-shaped branches the Indians had tied to their feet, that he had forgotten to fight."[19]

After the death of Duncan Lammons, Lemmons worked as a cowboy. While still a young man, he hired out to a woman taking cattle to market. He could not remember her name but did say she was quite skilled with horses. Her husband was away on business at the time, so Lemmons and about twenty men made a cattle drive, with Lemmons also serving as the woman's personal servant. Every lunchtime he prepared a pallet for the woman where she had her meal. One day a Mexican cowboy sat down on the pallet beside her. She told him to leave. He did not, so she shot and killed him. With that, as Lemmons recalled, the woman was "outside the law." She quickly left her foreman in charge of the herd, and, to Lemmons's amazement, took him with her as she sought and finally located her husband. What happened to the woman after that is unclear today, but Lemmons remembered being extremely anxious during the whole affair and greatly relieved to get back to Carrizo Springs.[20]

For a time, Lemmons worked as a freight hauler, a skill he had learned with the English family. He first hauled cotton from Lockhart to the Brownsville area and returned with a load of salt gathered from El Sal del Rey, a lake outside Edinburg. Later he made trips from Dimmit County to El Sal del Rey, hauling molasses and returning with salt. Janie Helen Bowe Blitch related one episode during the latter trips that remained quite vivid in Lemmons's memory:

Mr. Jodie Tumlinson [of Dimmit County] was herding some cattle through in the general area. Bob considered Mr. Jodie to be short-tempered, but the cattleman loved fine horses. When his prize horse needed to be rested and taken back to Dimmit County, Mr. Jodie, without Bob's knowledge, tied his good mount to the rear of [Bob's] freight wagon. Bob first learned of the horse when a bullet flipped his hat off and grazed his scalp. Stumbling earlier, the horse had apparently fallen and continued to be pulled by the fastened rope. It had choked and been dragged to death. Riding up about this time, Mr. Jodie saw his dead horse, became infuriated, and shot at Bob. Afterward, he told Bob that he didn't mean to kill him but only to scare him. [One woman who heard the story commented] "Bob wasn't sure— at least it was too close for Bob to believe that anything but the Lord had spared him." In retrospect, however, Bob did recall that the oxen had seemed to be pulling "awful hard." To verify the shooting, Bob later showed [a neighboring ranch] family the remaining scar on his head and said he also kept the hat with its bullet hole.[21]

While still in his early twenties, Lemmons began to teach himself to read and began acquiring a sizable estate.[22] Through buying and leasing land he had assets of $1,140 by the end of 1870, and ten years later, he had an estate that included over a thousand acres stocked with cattle, sheep, horses, and goats.[23] His cattle brand as registered in Dimmit County was "4R+."[24]

Although financially secure, Lemmons continued to hire out his talents in ranching and even loaned money to white ranchers during the Great Depression of the 1930s. It is possible that some of those ranchers never repaid him.[25]

Lemmons married once, outliving his wife. On September 3, 1881, he married Barbarita Rosales. The couple had eight children: Edward, Manuel, Joseph, Ina, Lucinda, Marcela, Robert, Jr., and Fernando. Only Robert, Jr., Ina, and Lucinda lived to adulthood and only Robert, Jr., who died in 1958, outlived his father by nine years.[26]

As Lemmons acquired property and livestock, a transformation occurred in the way whites addressed him. During his early years in Dimmit County, he was known as "the English Nigger" or "the Lemmons Nigger." As he became a successful mustanger and rancher, people called him "Bob Lemmons." During his later years he was known as "Uncle Bob" to many of the local white residents.

This name progression was evident in an account about Lemmons's religious beliefs as noted by the Reverend Bruce Roberts, formerly the pastor of the First Baptist Church of Carrizo Springs. During the first years of his pastorate in Carrizo Springs, Roberts assumed that Lemmons did not attend the Baptist church services because he thought Lemmons was a Roman Catholic, as was Barbarita Rosales, Lemmons's wife. One day Roberts happened to ask Lemmons about his religious views and was astonished to learn that Lemmons was a charter member of the very church where Roberts had his pastorate. As Lemmons told Roberts, "Well, Sir, I guess you know that in January 1879, Brother L. S. Cox, a Baptist preacher, came here and held a meeting. He baptized a good many people—baptized them in the Carrizo Creek. Well, I, too, was baptized, and I have never changed my faith."

For a time, Lemmons faithfully attended religious services, but he stopped going when one family seemed to object to being in church with a black man. Even though he had not been in the Baptist church for forty years, Lemmons added:

> "But I love God, and I have never changed my faith."
> Bruce Roberts responded, "Uncle Bob, I want you to come to our services."
> His humble reply was, "Well, Sir, if you think it will be all right, I'll be happy to come."
> I placed a chair [sort of a special Amen Chair] in the church near the front in the right-handed aisle, and that was known as Uncle Bob's chair as long as I was pastor of that Church. One day I met him in town and he said,

"Brother Roberts, you will never know what it has meant to me to get to come to your Church. Sometimes I wish we could be off to ourselves and we could pray together."

I told him that my study was in the little room adjoining the garage, and that I would love to have him come any time. He came, and we never had a prayer there but that I had a feeling that I was praying with one who knew God, and knew the way to the Throne.[27]

Other examples of a growing local regard for Lemmons included a story about the death of Ina, his daughter. The *Carrizo Springs Javelin* on August 23, 1913, noted not only her death but added that "Bob Lammons [Lemmons] is one of the few negro residents of the county, and has by industry and economy acquired a competence and the respect and liking of his white neighbors." In 1984 one of the foremost historians of Dimmit County concluded that Lemmons had become a "legend in his own time. From slave to prosperous rancher, with nationally-recognized talents in horsemanship, he became much sought-after to tell his life story. He was humble and self-conscious, though, and rarely gave detailed information about his past, except to describe his mustanging. He was a colorful storyteller, though, and many residents today remember the hours spent listening to him tell about the old days."[28]

Storytelling aside, it was Lemmons's special talent with horses that separated him from others. When stalking wild mustangs or doing other outdoor work Lemmons had a "habit of putting mesquite leaves in the top of his hat to help protect his head from the sun. This was probably a device learned during his long days of riding in the South Texas heat. He also believed that [drinking] ice water would kill a person if swallowed while he was warm [or overheated]. Though he was a fantastic horseman, Bob would not go near a horse with light colored eyes, such as glassy blue; he warned that these animals were possessed with a devil and should be avoided."[29]

An old-timer recalled when Lemmons helped manage someone else's ranch:

> The cowpunchers were selecting their horses. These horses had been fed corn all winter, and were slick and fat and full of ginger. They had not been ridden all winter, and some of them were sure to make the boys pull leather. There was a big hog-backed, dun-colored horse that had glass eyes, and a stripe down his back. He was an outlaw. Many of the boys picked this horse, but after Lemmons told them what he was they selected something else. A cowpuncher said, "Bob, I'll ride that horse."

Lemmons said, "If you do, you do it at your own risk."

The boy said, "I can ride him."

The horse was rode, and say! He fought like a tiger. They had to hogtie and blindfold him in order to put the saddle on. They let him up, and, fellows, he sure could make the stirrups crack together over his back. He just squealed and bucked. Lemmons held the horse and the cowpuncher tried to mount him, but he whirled around, never still. Finally the boy got his left foot in the stirrup and his hand on the horn of the saddle. He pulled the bronc's head around, and as he whirled, he swung into the saddle, and Bob Lemmons pulled the blind away. That bronc went up in the air like he was shot out of a cannon and when he hit the ground you could not see daylight under him. He pitched and then went to bawling and bucking . . . The puncher lost his right stirrup and hooked his right spur in the cinch, and was sure riding.

We were sitting up on the corral fence and the bronc came straight for it. We fell off, like turtles off a log. Just then the bronc whirled and bucked down along the corral, the boy staying with him. The bronc quit pitching and started to run towards the creek, and it looked as if he were going over a high bluff, the cowpuncher all the time quirting hell out of him. He ran for a mile or so and the cowpuncher rode him back to the corral, a subdued horse for the time being, but not yet broken. The blood was running out of the rider's mouth. The horse had bucked so hard that some small blood vessel in the boy's head had broken. He got all right, and he broke the big dun outlaw.[30]

Lemmons's early adult physical appearance was mostly black with maybe a trace of Indian blood. He exhibited "a medium complexion, high cheek bones, and straight hair."[31] Another description of Lemmons stressed that his "soft long hair" was viewed as a positive symbol. Wearing it shoulder length, Bob said, "It gives me strength," which suggests a biblical Samson. His assertions certainly show a combination of individuality and pragmatism.[32]

It was that "combination of individuality and pragmatism" that made famous his "walk down" of wild mustangs. J. Frank Dobie described the Lemmons technique as one in which he never tried to starve or physically exhaust the horses. If Lemmons lost sight of the herd, he simply followed its tracks. One time he did not see the horses for five days. Once he had convinced them to accept his presence, he would work to become their leader. This involved moving them to stranger ground where they "would surrender more readily than at home." As he acted out his role as a mustang, he "let them see him smelling for danger. Sometimes to show his power, he would not allow them to drink. When he was ready, he would ride into the water with them." At night he slept near the herd, and when "awakened by a restless nicker, he would saddle, round up the *manada* in the manner of a stallion, and leave with it." If another human being came in sight of the herd, Lemmons would watch that individual with apparent alarm and then lead the horses in flight. If he had to temporarily leave the herd, he "would upon returning come with the wind so that they would smell him and not be alarmed. Thus day and night, for week following week, across prairies and through thickets, huddled in rain, spread out on the ground in sunshine, listening in starlight to the encircling coyote concerts, lingering for the grazers as unhurried as the shadow of a circling buzzard, this lone man in primeval silence and space lived with the mustangs and, except in not eating grass and in having the long, long thoughts that only a human being can have, lived as one of them."[33]

Seven years before the mustanger's death, Lemmons recalled to Florence Fenley:

I've ketched a good many mustangs, and I've seen as many as two hundred runnin' when bunches got throwed together. Of course, when night come, they'd split up, and each stallion would get his own band together.

You didn't want to get one of them big bunches in a pen, because they'd kill one another too bad. They'd just run right over anything that got in their way. You had to keep 'em circlin' after you got 'em in the pen. If you didn't know how to circle 'em with blankets and such, you'd get 'em killed. But of course you want to know how I started out after 'em. . . .

I wouldn't want nothing much to hinder me when I went out after a band of horses. I learned to keep the same outfit all the way through too. After I got 'em to where they'd let me stay with 'em, I couldn't change horses, or saddle or hat. Not even a canteen, because they'd know it as soon as I come to 'em and they got the wind of me. When they begun to get used to me, I never let 'em get too clost to my horse, and when I'd leave 'em for a little while and come back to 'em, I let 'em keep the wind on me so they'd know it was me.

When I'd spot the bunch I wanted, I went toward 'em in a walk. They'd watch me a little while and come toward me to try to figure me out. Then when they made sure it was a man on a horse, they'd break and run. They'd run clean out of sight, but I never put my horse out of a walk and I knew they'd circle back to their range no matter how far they run. I'd keep that up for days and they'd run from me every time they saw me, but they wouldn't run so far. Pretty soon I could ride up in a short distance of 'em. It wasn't long before they wouldn't run from me, and then I got 'em to where they trusted me, because ever' time they'd scare, I'd scare and run as hard as they did. Sometimes, I'd scare first and away we'd go, with me in the lead and them follerin' me. I'd soon have a whole bunch runnin' with me everywhere I went.

We had spies out from the ranch to watch which way I had 'em headed, and they'd put grub out for me at certain places. If I'm goin' north, they'd keep grub for me ahead, and if I'm goin' south, they'd do the same. . . . We always had it understood where they was to leave grub next day, and when the mustangs got to follerin' me, they'd go with me to the place because, by then, I was working 'em around toward the pens we were goin' to put 'em in.

A horse has a heap o' sense. When I'd first get after 'em, they'd sure watch me, even after they got used to me. I'd follow 'em to water when I seen they need water bad, and let 'em keep the wind on me. I'd ride right into the water with 'em and as soon as they'd see it was me, they'd run out, but they'd come right back.

On the day we got ready to pen 'em, I'd work 'em around in the neighborhood of the corrals the boys had ready. There'd be wings built out from the gate a-ways, but when everything was ready and I had 'em just right, I'd scare, and away I'd go with them after me. On that day, I'd run right into the pen and I had to keep ridin' after I got in there too till they'd open a gate for me to let me out. Once a [Mexican worker] had the gate in charge and when he seen me comin', he got excited and went to slip the bars out of the gate but pushed 'em in, instead, and nearly got me killed. I told Mr. Lemons I didn't want to work with that fellow again.

We'd circle the horses after we got 'em in the pen, till they finally stopped. Some of 'em was awful mean and hard to handle, but they're a heap easier to tame than you'd think, after all. A lot of times when you'd spot a bunch of horses, you'd think they were mustangs, but you'd find out you had horses that had just gone wild.

It wasn't uncommon for horses to get taken off by Indians and then go wild if they got clean away. I followed a bunch clean down to Oakville in Live Oak County once and they carried me right to the owner. I worked 'em about a week and I wanted 'em to go north, but no, they wanted to go south, so I went on with 'em. We got to the place where they come from and they went right to the very ranch house. The owner was sure glad to see 'em and paid me for the return of 'em. There were nine head of young horses and five head of old mares. They sure were wild. Somebody had stole 'em, and carried 'em off and they got loose. We ketched a good deal of horses like that. The most I ever ketched was twelve head. That is, I saved twelve head out of the bunch and killed five.

Shucks, I could ride as good now as I ever could, if I could see. That bunch of cattle you hear comin' in now belongs to me. Erskine Rhodes is bringin' 'em in. He takes care of my stuff for me and moved me down here on his place where he could look after me better. My place joins him on the west. I ride sometimes yet, but Erskine says I'm getting too old and might get hurt since I can't see. I've spent most of my life on a horse and wouldn't know what to do if I couldn't get on one any more.[34]

As Lemmons began to lose his eyesight during his later years, he lived in a home provided for him on the Erskine Rhodes Ranch just outside Carrizo Springs. On the ranch Janie Helen Bowe Blitch, granddaughter of Erskine Rhodes, helped to care for him until his death on December 23, 1947.

In his last will and testament, dated February 20, 1937, Lemmons expressed his gratitude to Erskine Rhodes. He stated how Rhodes "has over a period of many years assisted me in the working and management of my cattle business and has practically managed it and done it all for me, and in addition he has constantly looked after my personal welfare, day and night, in sickness and in health, and he has done all that without compensation, and the reason I make the bequests, herein made to him, is because I want to show to him my love and appreciation for his help and kindness."[35]

Lemmons not only made Erskine Rhodes his independent executor but left him half of his cattle, up to 724 acres of land, and half of his cash. Robert Lemmons, Jr., also was to receive half of his cash. Another of Lemmons's friends, Louisa Guerra, was to get 13.5 acres of land, presumably the land on which she lived. The remaining 545.5 acres, as Lemmons stated in the will, was to go "to my legal heirs in the respective proportions that they would inherit under the law of descent and distribution of Texas." If for some reason his heirs did not receive his bequests, Rhodes was to receive all that remained except for Louisa Guerra's getting half of the remaining land designated for Lemmons's heirs.[36]

The funeral for Lemmons was held at the First Baptist Church of Carrizo Springs. The Reverend Bruce Roberts, then pastor in Uvalde, Texas, conducted the service before a full house. The church choir provided the music, and the town's leading citizens served as pallbearers. Robert Lemmons was then laid to rest in the old Tejano cemetery located within the city limits. He is probably the only black buried there. On his tombstone are the words *En Paz Descante Su Alma* (May His Soul Rest in Peace).

Yet, long before Lemmons's death, J. Frank Dobie paid him perhaps one of his greatest tributes. In praising Lemmons, Dobie wrote that there "are men whom bees will not sting. There are men whom a fierce yard dog will not bark at, much less bite. What is it inside some individuals that makes horses untamable by others, submit to them gently? I am not talking about fake horse-whisperers, though I think there have been some who were not fakes. Back in the days of open range and long trails, when *remuda* men for months at a stretch guarded, grazed, watered and moved over an unpeopled world with the saddle horses of isolated cow outfits, one now and then led instead of driving his *remuda*. The horses would follow him like mules magnetized by a bell mare. . . . Bob Lemmons . . . actually became the leader of a band of wild horses that followed him into a pen as fresh as they had been when he first sighted them."[37]

NOTES

1. Robert Lemmons as quoted in J. Frank Dobie, *The Mustangs* (Boston: Little, Brown and Company, 1952), pp. 235–36.

2. Don Worcester, *The Spanish Mustang: From the Plains of Andalusia to the Prairies of Texas* (El Paso: University of Texas at El Paso Press, 1986), pp. 1–2.

3. Ibid., p. 42.

4. John Young, "The Reminiscences of John Young," in J. Frank Dobie, *A Vaquero of the Brush Country* (Boston: Little, Brown and Company, 1943), pp. 227–28.

5. Philip Durham and Everett L. Jones, *The Negro Cowboys* (Lincoln: University of Nebraska Press, 1965), p. 162.

6. Walker D. Wyman, *The Wild Horses of the West* (Caldwell, Idaho: Caxton Printers, Ltd., 1945), p. 239.

7. Will C. Barnes, "Wild Horses," *McClure's Magazine,* Apr., 1909, pp. 285–94, passim; Will James, "Piñon and the Wild Ones," *Saturday Evening Post,* May 19, 1923; Wyman, *Wild Horses,* pp. 239, 242.

8. O. W. Nolen, "Nicking the Mustang," in J. Frank Dobie, Mody C. Boatright, and Harry Ransom, eds., *Mustangs and Cow Horses* (Dallas: Southern Methodist University Press, 1940), p. 44.

9. Wyman, *Wild Horses,* p. 225; Dobie, et al., eds., *Mustangs and Horses,* p. 75.

10. Wyman, *Wild Horses,* p. 226.

11. Ibid., p. 234.

12. Death Certificate of Robert Lemmons, Dimmit County, File No. 43, Texas Department of Health, Bureau of Vital Statistics, State of Texas, Dec. 30, 1947. Lemmons's tombstone lists 1846 as his birthdate, but there is neither collaborating

evidence to support that nor is his birthdate listed among the slave records of Caldwell County.

13. Bruce Roberts, *Springs from the Parched Ground* (Uvalde, Tex.: Hornby Press, 1950), p. 103.

14. "Sketch of Ed B. English of Carrizo Springs," in J. Marvin Hunter, ed., *The Trail Drivers of Texas* (1925; reprint, Austin: University of Texas Press, 1985), p. 495.

15. "Wildest Days Were Prior to 1880," *Carrizo Springs* (Texas) *Javelin,* Oct. 20, 1955; Verner Lee Bell, "Uncle Bob Lemmons," *Carrizo Springs* (Texas) *Javelin,* Aug. 10, 1933.

16. Robert Lemmons, quoted in Verner Lee Bell, "Uncle Bob Lemmons," *Carrizo Springs Javelin,* Aug. 10, 1933.

17. Janie Helen Bowe Blitch, "Old Bob and the Pit and Allusive Revelations," (M.A. thesis, University of Texas at Austin, 1970), p. 4; and Crystal S. Williams, History of Dimmit County, MSS, Dimmit County Clerk's Office, 1960. Janie Blitch noted that "most of the incidents not otherwise identified [in her thesis about Lemmons] were supplied by Mrs. Genevieve Rhodes, who heard Bob Lemmons' stories when he lived on her family's ranch."

18. Robert Lemmons, interview by Florence Fenley in "Turns 'Mustang' to Catch Mustangs," *Uvalde Leader News,* Sept. 13, 1940; *The Cattleman,* Sept., 1940.

19. Crystal S. Williams, A History of Dimmit County; Blitch, "Old Bob," p. 4.

20. Blitch, "Old Bob," p. 5.

21. Ibid., pp. 7–9, passim.

22. Ironically, Duncan Lammons remained illiterate throughout his lifetime.

23. General Index to Deeds, Book 4, 1887, Dimmit County Clerk's Office, Dimmit County, Tex.

24. Records of Marks and Brands: May 29, 1882, vols. 1, 2, Dimmit County Clerk's Office, Carrizo Springs, Tex.

25. Bell, "Uncle Bob Lemons," *Carrizo Springs Javelin,* Aug. 10, 1933; Blitch, "Old Bob," p. 11.

26. Records of Marriages, 1881, Dimmit County Clerk's Office, Carrizo Springs, Tex.; Probate Document, vol. 2, no. 685, Dimmit County Clerk's Office, Carrizo Springs, Tex., p. 101.

27. Roberts, *Springs from the Parched Ground,* pp. 104–105.

28. Tidwell, *Dimmit County Mesquite Roots,* p. 233.

29. Blitch, "Old Bob," p. 10.

30. Evan G. Barnard, *A Rider of the Cherokee Strip* (New York: n.p., 1936), pp. 71–72; Dobie, et al., eds., *Mustangs and Cow Horses,* pp. 302–303.

31. Laura Knowlton Tidwell, *Dimmit County Mesquite Roots,* vol. 1 (Carrizo Springs, Tex.: Wind River Press, 1984), p. 233.

32. Blitch, "Old Bob," p. 10.

33. J. Frank Dobie, *The Mustangs,* pp. 236–38, passim.

34. Robert Lemmons, interview by Florence Fenley in "Turns 'Mustang' to Catch Mustangs," *Uvalde Leader News,* Sept. 13, 1940; *The Cattleman,* Sept., 1940.

35. Estate of Robert Lemmons, Feb. 20, 1937, Document 490, Dimmit County Clerk's Office, Carrizo Springs, Tex.

36. Ibid.

37. Dobie, *The Mustangs,* p. 240.

Figure 3. Henrietta Williams Foster, "Aunt Rittie." Sketch by Mark Kohler,
Courtesy of Louise S. O'Connor, Victoria, Texas

Chapter 4

Henrietta Williams Foster, "Aunt Rittie"

A Cowgirl of the Texas Coastal Bend

LOUISE S. O'CONNOR

Since 1970, I have been photographing and interviewing residents in a four-county area of the Texas Coastal Bend encompassing Victoria, Goliad, Refugio, and Aransas Counties. I grew up in this culture as a fifth-generation member of an Irish pioneer ranching family. We arrived in Texas with the Power-Hewetson Colony in 1834.

Many of the ranches in this area were carved out of the Power-Hewetson land grant acquired in 1828 from the Mexican government. Mexico was seeking Catholic settlers for the northern reaches of their empire in New Spain. Mexico, after the Mexican Revolution, hoping to stem the flow of Americans encroaching on them from the north, offered enormous land grants to anyone who would bring in Catholic settlers.

Because of the English penal codes being enforced against the Irish at the time, and because they were of the Catholic faith, they were prime candidates to settle the area that was to become Texas. Little did Mexican officials know that within two years, because of the rape of the Mexican Constitution of 1824 under which they had agreed to settle, the Irish pioneers would take part in the revolt and help take the Texas area away from Mexico. The young Irish settlers who helped win the war seemingly had had quite enough of oppression from governmental entities. Though rag-tag and unorganized, their anger, their zeal, their determination, and energy enabled them to help defeat a much larger and more organized army from the south.

When they returned from war, they went about the business of building a republic as well as their ranches and farms. It is from these early land holdings and acquisitions that the great ranches of the Texas Coastal Bend were born. On these ranches were the people who formed a unique culture of Europeans, Irish, Africans, and Mexicans. It is with the descendants of these pioneers that I have worked for seventeen years, interviewing and photographing them to preserve the last vestiges of a dying culture.

Henrietta W. Foster was one of these pioneers. She was a rare person in her time, a woman who worked cattle with men, as their equal. She was African American by birth, which made her most uncommon in the pastures and cowpens of the Texas Coastal Bend. Females, except in the rarest of instances, did not work cattle, and black women were normally confined to the fields or homes of the large landowners. "Aunt Rittie" was a person of honor and great strength. It was not easy to step out of the restrictions imposed on African Americans of the era, but she did and became a legend in the Texas Coastal Bend.

I discovered Henrietta Foster for the first time when I began interviewing the Coastal Bend cowboys in 1982. She was always referred to as "Aunt Rittie." I had heard my father, Tom O'Connor, Jr., mention the name many times but only within the context of his father, Thomas O'Connor (II), calling his daughter "Rittie." As I became more and more interested in the few women who actually worked cattle in the early days, I began to realize that her name came up anytime I mentioned cow women. Mentioning Aunt Rittie would set off a firestorm of stories and incredulous commentary. She was an ex-slave and could tell many stories about her life in slavery. She is unique among the many characters that inhabited the region and was as tough as any man.

Aunt Rittie was a sight. She was born in Mississippi and had six sisters. They came from there on a boat to McKamey when she was eighteen. Some people here bought her as a slave. She was separated from her sisters and nieces. There was six of them, all girls. They split them up and sold them as slaves. She was the healthiest one of the bunch.

Old man Mitchell, Buddy Shelton's grandfather (Isaac Newton Mitchell), bought her and she was a slave to him (on a ranch west of Victoria). She said they would pick cotton, clean up and cook and then they would go down on the river and have church. They sang the old hymns in secret. You know, they didn't allow the slaves to have church or school. They couldn't read or write. If you were caught at either, they would give them a good lashin'.

She did laundry for Mrs. Mitchell and Mrs. Shelton. They made a slide to pack water from Miss Ellie Moss' house to Aunt Rittie's house to do laundry. She did all those great big skirts they used to wear. She ironed with those big pot irons they heated on the fire. She said life was tough. She felt bad about the way she was treated. They didn't hardly have any food or clothing. She didn't like being separated from her sisters. She never knew where they went.

She didn't like goin' to the back door. She told me she and "Doc" Mitchell got in a ruckus one time over her cattle because she didn't like the way he was handlin' them. She kept them on his place and she took all twelve to her place and raised them right there, all twelve of them.

Aunt Rittie married Charles Foster and had a place up there on San Diego Street in Refugio. She paid twenty-five dollars for it and she paid it out a quarter a week. She didn't get paid but a dollar and a half a week.

Her place was off from Uncle John Thornton's. She got in a fight with him over her land. She went out there and told him he was stealin' her land. She accused him of puttin' his crops on her property. She gave him a good cussin' when he went out there to see her about that land problem. She went and got a hammer and knocked a hole in his head and beat him until it was a wonder the law didn't come right away. She thought he was dead and ran to tell the law that she had killed John Thornton. Then she said she wanted him put in jail for stealin' her land if he wasn't dead. She had knocked a big hole in his head, but she hadn't killed him, so they let her go. She wasn't afraid of anyone.

She worked cattle bareback with the men and she would go out in the cow camps with the different cow crowds. She liked to ride horses and it was said she was the only woman that worked with the men. Aunt Rittie would move around and go with the cow crowd from the different ranches. Wherever men were workin' cattle, she was workin' with them. She rode sidesaddle and bareback on her white horse. She could ride like an Indian because she was half-Indian.

Aunt Rittie had no education, but she always said she hoped us children didn't have to live like her. She wanted us to get an education. She saved her little money and sent my mother to college. She didn't want her to have to do the work she had to do.

She midwifed and taught my mother how to be one. She knew how to fix a woman so she couldn't have children. Aunt Rittie didn't want no children because she had seen women have such hard times, so she once told my mother she was real lucky to be here. My mother studied this in college, too. Aunt Rittie had to quit midwiffn' because her sight started failin' her.

Great-grandma was a character. She was mean and gave people so much trouble, nobody wanted to take care of her when she got old. She would sit and drink all the time. She became an alcoholic. She couldn't see, but she could find that bottle and she could raise hell. She wasn't scared of no one and she didn't take no foolishness off nobody. Aunt Rittie could cuss and lay people out and she could "hoodoo" people away from the house if she didn't like them. She once was so mad at some woman in town, she said she would rather pick with the chickens than work for her. She said she didn't pay her right.

Aunt Lizzie took care of her first and when she passed in 1926, my mother took her on. Rittie died in 1928. She was over one hundred years old when she died.[1]

I was the oldest, born in 1901. Aunt Rittie was my great, great-grandma. I was around her a lot. She told me lots about slavery. She was twelve when she got sold to the Mitchells. She was in Indianola in the big storm.

Aunt Rittie was a midwife, a cow rider, and a slave. She was lots of things. She was real dark and she wasn't educated, but she knew lots of things that educated people didn't know.

There once was an old Mexican guy got stabbed at Cinco de Mayo. His intestines were all hangin' out and someone took him to Aunt Rittie. She sewed him up with black thread. She knew how to doctor cattle, too.

Rittie knew how to keep a woman from having kids. She was married to a Williams and a Foster, but Aunt Lizzie Dunman was the only child she ever had. She did it with herbs, but I don't know what it was. I didn't know ABC about things like this. Rittie knew a lot about herb medicines.

Mrs. Izzie Shelton said Rittie killed a man once for tryin' to rape and molest her. They kidnapped her, but she always carried a knife and she got away. She could cuss right smart when she was mad, too. There was always lots of strange "hoodoo" goin' on around here. Aunt Rittie knew how to stop it.

Some of her sayin's were: "The bird flies high, but it's gotta come down," and "Go and pick with the chickens." She also said, "We never know where we gotta waller."

She didn't die until she was way up in her hundreds. She died in 1926 or so, somewhere around that big freeze in the twenties.[2]

She was rough. Aunt Rittie would tear you up. She was a little woman, but she was somethin' else. She would whoop a man as quick as that. We never did get to be around her much because we lived out on the ranch, but I know she was something else.[3]

Rittie could ride a horse better than a man could. They say she followed the O'Connor cow crowd around and worked right out there with the men. She was a little woman and she was a *bad* (tough) woman. She slept on the ground and rode them horses. It wasn't like it is now. When you went out in those days, you stayed out sometimes as long as a month.

The old hands who knew her say you felt about her just like a man and that's the way you better act, or that woman would kill you. She had a butcher knife with her all the time and she'd cut your throat. So they felt just like they did with any other bad man out there. They didn't bother her. She was ready for any trouble and the men were afraid of her. She would put a club on you if you didn't act right.

She wore those old long dresses and she rode straddle over the horse. She could throw calves and do anything else a man could and maybe better. She said she was brought up like that and worked all around this area.[4]

She could get me to do anything she wanted. She'd say, "Where you goin', boy." I would say, "No where." She'd say, "I want you to do so and so." I would always say, "Yes, Ma'am."[5]

She made the best light bread. The only time I ever had to stay around her all day, I cried.[6]

◇ ◇ ◇

She was an ex-slave. She was so old she had seen the stars fall. She worked for Mama O'Connor and Grandpa Dennis. I can remember Papa taking me to see her one time. He wanted to see her before she died. She may have been his nursemaid when he was a child.[7]

Henrietta Williams Foster appears to have been the Coastal Bend combination of Gloria Steinem, the Tasmanian Devil, and Rosa Parks. She is buried in Refugio, Texas, and remains in the folklore of the county as the legendary Aunt Rittie.

NOTES

1. Josephine Spriggs Green, interview by Louise S. O'Connor, Refugio, Tex., May 11, 1990.
2. Desaline Spriggs Barefield, interview by Louise S. O'Connor, Seadrift, Tex., Oct. 15, 1990.
3. Lela Edwards Williams, interview by Louise S. O'Connor, Refugio, Tex., May 11, 1990.
4. Simmie Rydolph and Monroe "Bailey" Shaw, interview by Louise S. O'Connor, Refugio, Tex., Mar. 1, 1983.
5. Ibid., Monroe "Bailey" Shaw.
6. Ibid., Simmie Rydolph.
7. Tom O'Connor, Jr. (III), interview by Louise S. O'Connor, Victoria, Tex., Nov. 18, 1986.

Chapter 5

Johanna July

A Horse-Breaking Woman

JIM COFFEY

Tradition rests as heavily on the Mexican border as the heat in summer. Tradition is seen everywhere and is testimony to the way the people interact with each other and their surroundings over time. It is not unusual to see a truck pulling a two-horse trailer with saddled horses and its driver with jeans tucked into boots adorned with gal-legged spurs. The cowboys seen on the border use roping techniques that were born in another century but find themselves at home today in this desert country. The traditions of the border cowboy are deep and exist in the backgrounds of two cultures, Mexican and Anglo. In Val Verde and Kinney Counties of Southwest Texas, a third cultural force swings into the saddle; that force is the Black Seminole cowboy who created a unique brand of cowboy tradition.

The Black Seminoles created their own cowboy traditions beginning with their cattle work in Florida. It was a tradition based on their history and heritage. By examining the experiences of these people, another face of the Texas cowboy emerges.

The traditions of the Black Seminoles have been passed on by their storytellers and elders. During the depression of the 1930s, federal writers came to hear the stories of how the Seminoles came to be in Texas. They told their stories in Gullah, in Spanish, and in English to those who listened. One of these storygatherers was Mrs. Florence Angermiller, who found in the Black Seminole community at Brackettville a woman who typified the spirit of the people whose search for freedom took them from Florida to a home in Mexico via Indian Territory (Oklahoma) and finally into Texas. The story was a long one.

From British colonization to the early 1800s, slaves and free blacks fleeing the cancer of slavery found refuge with the Seminoles in their South Florida homeland. The ex-slaves were accepted and became bilingual in the Seminole language. Some lived with the Seminoles, while others set up separate communities. In the Seminole communities, blacks kept arms, farmed their own crops, and were considered near-members of the larger Seminole family rather than slaves.[1] Through the years the Seminoles and African Americans intermarried and fought against the United States Army. The close ties between the two groups developed in Florida would be continued as wars and misfortune forced them to new lands.

When the Seminoles were forced to move from Florida, their black allies went with them west to Indian Territory. There, the blacks and Seminoles established separate towns but were reduced to poverty and dependence. Over time, conflicts and hostilities with both the Anglos and the slave-holding Creek Indians aroused some of the blacks and the Seminoles to leave. So began the second part of their odyssey.

In 1849, about two hundred Seminoles and blacks left the reserve without the permission of Indian Agents or government officials. They headed for Mexico after leaving word that they would kill anyone who tried to stop them. Nine months later, they crossed the Rio Grande at Eagle Pass and, with their silver necklaces, colorful turbans, and weapons shining in the sun, rode into exile seeking a new homeland. Other groups leaving later were not so lucky—they met hostile Texans and Plains Indians.[2]

The Mexican government settled the new immigrants in two small military colonies at Musquiz and Nacimiento de Los Negros. The Mexican government negotiated with the Black Seminoles to stop raiding Comanches, bandits, and other unsavory types from coming into the region and to farm while not being involved with more bellicose duties.[3] At its peak population in 1850, this colony provided a home for more than seven hundred Black Seminole men, women, and children.[4] The presence of this free colony across the border bothered many Texans, who regarded the residents as runaway slaves. It was here that the People, as they called themselves, began once again the keeping and herding of cattle as learned in Florida, adapting now to the parched lands of Northern Mexico. It would be the skills of the cowboy—searching, hunting, herding—that would serve them and their children in the decades ahead.

In 1870, the United States Army, desperate for translators and scouts familiar with the border country and its collection of dialects, made a deal with John Horse (Juan Caballo as he was known in Mexico) and John Kibbetts, both Black Seminole leaders, to supply scouts and trackers to the army. The understanding between the two groups, the Army and Seminoles, was never made very clear to the recruits. The Black Seminoles understood that they would be provided with pay, provisions for their families, and grants of land for their service.[5] The group under John Kibbetts agreed and moved into Texas on July 4, 1870. They settled at Fort Duncan near Eagle Pass and Fort Clark at Brackettville. During the summer and fall of 1871, more scouts, their families, and others came from Mexico, bringing the total Black Seminole community in Texas to about 150.[6]

It was during the second migration from Mexico, that John Horse brought his people from Mexico and with them was one of the most unusual of the early Black Seminole cowboys, unusual because this "cowboy" was a woman.

Johanna July was born in Mexico in 1857 or 1858. The community she was born into was typical of the many small villages in the area. It was a gathering of adobe *jacals* in which extended families lived together, cooking outdoors. In most Seminole communities at the time, the girls learned to cook, sew, and take care of the family, while the boys learned to catch horses and hunt. For Johanna, things were turned around. She learned to fish the deep pools for catfish and scanned the countryside to find the lairs of the coyote. Johanna learned from her father, Elijah July, about the animals and the terrain. She began to learn the ways of horses and how to herd the stock, usually goats and some cattle. She grew to love this life and began to spend more time with the stock than she did learning the domestic skills performed by the women of the period.[7]

Adam Wilson, one of the later scouts, taught her to ride sidesaddle. Whether this was a nod to what was considered "womanly" at the time or not is conjecture. Two groups of women riders would have been seen in Mexico at this time: Indian women usually rode astride, and Mexican women rode sidesaddle.[8] Besides riding sidesaddle, Johanna often rode bareback, with only a braided rope looped around the horse's neck and then half-hitched over its nose. Later she rode with a pad or saddle blanket in place of a saddle. As a horsewoman she entered the world of the vaquera.

"I couldn't ride a hoss like dey do dese days . . . I couldn't straddle 'em. I didn't use no bridle either just a rope around deir necks and looped over de nose. We called it a 'nosin,'—same as a half-hitch . . . Right today I don't like a saddle an' I don't like shoes. I can sure get over de ground barefooted."[9]

The needs of the family dictated the jobs the children did. For Johanna, that job was simple—to work with horses. Years later, perhaps brightened by the sunset of a long life, she remembered that mostly she rode. She herded horses for her extended family and daily moved the goats and cattle from the *jacals* to the pastures for feed. While working the stock, she probably herded using a long pole to goad the stock in the same manner that vaqueros of old had used *medias*.

The skills she developed stood her in good stead when the family moved into Texas in 1871. Settling at Eagle Pass, she kept up the routine she had developed in Mexico, herding the livestock. As the family resettled, Johanna found herself living what later generations would call a "tomboy" life, as that was what she knew. With the death of her father, her life became dictated by her abilities with the stock and the taming of wild horses. Her sisters and mother cooked and took care of the domestic chores. She took care of horses.

In later years, she recalled that her brother, Joseph, left the family, although his burial in the Seminole Cemetery in Brackettville suggests that he drifted back into the family at some time. Her mother remained head of the family and directed life for Johanna and her sisters.

Religion was important in the life of the Black Seminoles, and it became a mixture of their experiences from the places they had been. The Baptist religion of Johanna's grandmothers became mixed with that of Roman Catholicism they had encountered in Mexico. Johanna maintained Lent, Good Friday, Easter, and Christmas celebrations, combined with the fasting, chanting, and celebrations of the Seminole culture. When she was baptized, she secured a place in the community.[10]

In the Black Seminole community the interpretation of dreams played an important role and provided a guide for young women. Both male and female deacons heard and interpreted dreams, and this service was provided the young Johanna.[11] Although her father was dead, the near reverence in which older members of the community was held extended the family for Johanna in the tight-knit community. She learned much from the U.S. Army scouts, such as Adam Wilson, who had taught her to ride. She learned the basics of tracking and observation that made the scouts so successful and would aid her in several future escapades.

From the scouts and some of the vaqueros she met she learned the folklore of horses. She learned the colors of horses such as *grullo* for the dark grays, *prieto* for the blacks, *cabos negros* for those with black mane and tail, and *estrello* for those with a star on their forehead. The superstitions of horses became something by which she lived. Many people believed white horses were special, but on the border, the white horse was one you would see at night, and that was not always something a person wanted. She knew that the *bayo cabos negros,* a dun with black stockings, black mane, and tail, could take the rough handling that would be the lot of the cowboy or scout's horse, and that the *bayo anarnajado,* or foundation of the palomino, would be "dead before he is tired." She knew that if a horse turned over when he wallowed, he was a good horse, and she knew that strong, agile, short-coupled ponies were more likely to endure.[12]

Johanna expanded her knowledge of caring for horses by working with them and watching the people around her. By observation she learned when and where she could water a horse. She saw horses with colic and watched as they rolled on the ground, trying to ease the stomach pains. She would struggle to walk them to keep them off the ground, but mostly she rode.

As she grew into her teens, her riding skills improved, as well as her skills in training horses. Breaking horses in South Texas followed a time-worn routine. The *domador,* or horse breaker, roped a horse and tied it to a tree. After a day or more, the horse would be saddled, a blindfold or *tapojo,* tied over its eyes, and, perhaps, the right hind leg tied up if the horse was inclined to kick. When the horse became accustomed to the weight of the saddle, it would be led in a circle and finally ridden. Generally, it was the *jinite,* or a younger horse trainer, who did the riding. It was he who learned the truth of the phrase, *"Nunca hay caballo ensillado que a alguno no se le ofrece viaje"* or "There is never a saddled horse that doesn't offer a journey to someone."[13] Perhaps because Johanna spent so much of her time alone and would not have had the advantage of the needed help, or because of her sidesaddle riding, Johanna developed her own method of gentling horses.

"I would pull off my clothes and get into de clothes I intended to bathe in and I would lead 'em (the horses) right into de Rio Grande and keep 'em in dere till dey got pretty well worried . . . I would swim up and get 'im by de mane an' ease up on 'im. He couldn't pitch and when I did let 'im out of dat deep water he didn't *want* to pitch."[14]

Generally, the horse would be tired from its swimming and would be less likely to have the strength to buck. The number of times she would have to expose the horse to this water treatment depended on the nature of the horse. There were times when the horse found its footing in shallow water and began to run with the young girl, but the running and danger of being thrown were a part of the life she accepted. The horse, thus gentled, became part of the herd that she moved and watched during the day.

"Sometimes dey wasn't so w're out an' would take a runnin' spree wid me when dey got out in shallow water where dey could get deir feet on de ground, and dey would run clear up into de corral. But I was young and I was havin' a good time."[15]

The border country of the 1870s was still subject to incursions by both Indian and border outlaws. A herd of horses was always a prime target for roving bandits. Johanna found this to be true early in her career. Early one morning she had moved her horses away from the village at Fort Duncan. She searched out one of the *vegas,* or meadows, to graze the horses and to cut hay.

After she had worked for awhile, she became tired and looked around for a place to take a nap. "Suppose I lay down here an' take myself a nap an' den finish cuttin' my hay, but I thought, 'No, I better go on and cut my hay,' an' about den, I seen de hosses gettin' nervous.'"[16]

Later, she attributed her escape to divine intervention. As she checked the horses, she found them milling, snorting, and pointing their ears, signs that usually indicated strangers in the area. She glanced in the direction the horses were looking and saw two Indians slowly circling the herd. She undoubtedly remembered stories of the treatment of captive Black Seminoles, who had fallen into the hands of Plains Indians during the trek from the Indian Territory or recalled how two of the children had been scraped with knives to see how deep the color of their skin was.[17] She also knew she had to take care of the horses, so she called to "Bill," the big bay horse, she had gentled. When he moved, the herd moved with him. She placed the hacamore, a braided bridle, on a little gray named "Charley" and grabbed a handful of mane as she swung onto his back. She kicked him into a lope and started a run for the fort. As she glanced back over her shoulder, she could see the Indians in pursuit. She leaned lower over Charley's neck, whipped him into a run, and, followed by the horse herd, began the horse race of her life. The herd strung out behind her and crossed the meadows near the fort. Her pursuers, seeing that they would not catch the herd, broke off the chase, and the frightened girl and her horses swept into the fort.

She told her story to the guard, who sent out scouts. They apprehended the Indians as they crossed into Mexico.[18] While this was not the only incident in which Johanna escaped on horseback from a life-threatening situation, it was one that remained with her for the rest of her life. As terrifying as the desperate race must have been, it did not keep her away from her horses. "Dat didn't break me. I was always out wid dem hosses."[19]

Johanna had become a young woman and been noticed by many of the men around Fort Duncan. One was a young man named Lesley who had seen the tall, barefoot girl in the bright homespun dresses, with hair in thick braids, long gold earrings, and necklaces strung around her throat.[20] The young couple married and moved west to Fort Clark to join the Black Seminole community there.

At Fort Clark, the Seminoles lived near Las Moras Creek at the center of the fort. The community, numbering about 150 people, lived in small houses with thatched roofs that surrounded the community church. Johanna and her husband set up housekeeping there, but it was far from a happy union.

Johanna's expertise was that of a vaquera, not a housewife. The skills she had developed over her short life had been aimed in one direction: that of caring for stock and living outdoors. Her new life required that she carry out the activities that her mother and sisters had done for her. All the confidence she had felt, the successes she had known, were not enough to sustain her in a life where she was expected to cook, sew, and take care of the house. She burned beans and cut her sewing fabric wrong. Her new husband responded to her shortcomings with violence. Instead of enjoying the roaming life she had known, she found herself tied to one place. Instead of to her horses, she was bound to a small rock and adobe house. Instead of her free life, she found the life of a prisoner. Her husband's reaction to her inability to live up to his expectations moved from harsh words to using his fists.

The settlement at Las Moras Creek might as well have been Devil's Island, because Johanna began to dream of escape. She had to escape from this life, or there would be no life. It was not a dream that came to her lightly. She made her decision after a particularly vicious encounter with her husband. She would return to Fort Duncan and her family. She could no longer live with her violent husband.

Late in the afternoon, Johanna left the house and crossed Las Moras Creek. The creek was viewed by many of the Seminoles to have a spiritual importance in their lives. When Johanna crossed the creek, she hoped for a return to her old life. She took a knife and stripped the fiber from a Spanish dagger plant. Her mind focused on plaiting the fiber into a hacamore that she used as a bridle on a horse she found in a field near the fort. As the cannon fired to end the day for the soldiers at the fort, Johanna was ending her day as a married woman in an abusive marriage.

"I couldn't get dat old pony out of a trot, and I rode dat forty-five miles dat night. As I got to Fort Duncan I heard de sentry call out, 'Four o' clock an' all is well!' I know I said to myself, 'All may be well, but I don't feel so well after dis ride!'"[21]

She met two groups on the trip home. One group she thought might have been Texas Rangers.

"Whar you headed for? and I tole 'em, Fort Duncan, an' dey let me pass an' didn't offer to hurt me. I guess dey was rangers. De next bunch I met was about a mile from de fort. Dey didn't speak an' I didn't either."[22]

Lesley was not one to let a wife go easily. His grief and anger escalated with each trip he made to Fort Duncan. Each rejection of his pleas for her to return seemed to irritate the situation even more. After four trips, asking her to return, the physical abuse she had dealt with at Las Moras went a step further.

"He come down dere three or fur times to get me but I wouldn't go. He shot at me two different times, but he missed me, den he tried to rope me, but de Lawd fixed it so my head was too low and de rope wet over. I got to the brush an' he never could find me. He would have killed me, an' I knowed it!"[23]

Life changed little for Johanna as she got older. After her husband died, she married two more times, both to men with whom she worked at the job she knew well, that of horses and herding. She married Ned Wilkes and continued to break horses as well as trap and hunt, but even with her name changes she was still known in the community as Johanna Lesley.

"After he died I married twice mo'. I helped my last husband break hosses and mules. I 'member one bad mule. He was the meanest one I ever had any dealin's wid. He was 'hip-shotten.' I had to tie his good front leg to his good back leg an', don't you know, he'd catch me by de clothes and toss me and shake me if he could get hold of me. I never did break 'im, I got 'fraid of 'im. I've had some awful scrapes. . . . down here on de Fadillas ranch I've had mules run away wid me an' sometimes tear de wagon to pieces."[24]

After 1910, Johanna moved back to Brackettville and with her husband lived there for the rest of her life. The small house she had on a hill near the cemetery on the northeast side of town was the one in which she raised her children and at least one granddaughter, Ora Mae. Sundays were a time for visiting, and "Aunt Chona," as she became known, always found time for the children.[25]

She continued to maintain her fierce independence. In the 1930s, a train ran from San Antonio to Del Rio, crossing part of the old fort. Johanna frequently took the train from Brackettville to visit family in Eagle Pass. The fact that the train didn't stop where she wanted didn't deter her. She would stand on the track, and the engineer would blow the whistle and yell, "Get out of the way, old woman." She would stand her ground, saying, "I'm going to stand on this track 'cause I am going to catch you today."[26] In 1933, others noted she was still lively and able to cut a cord and a half of wood.[27]

"My last husband has been dead eight years now. My first husband was so mean to me I suppose dat was why de Lawd fixed it so I didn't divo'ce him an' he didn't divo'ce me, an' now what little bread I'm gettin', I'm gettin' it right off of him."[28]

The woman who came out of obscurity ended her life the same way. The date of her death is not remembered. People remember dates by what was happening at the time, and her nephew, William Warrior, believes she died after World War II. She was buried in the Seminole Cemetery west of Brackettville, but her grave is lost among the Medal of Honor winners of the scouts and the latter-day cowboys. Few in the community remember her to-day. Warrior remembers her as "that old lady who rode sidesaddle," and her great-granddaughter, Izola Resberry, remembers the wonderful tortillas she used to make as she went barefoot around the house, refusing to wear shoes except outdoors.[29]

The only known picture of Johanna was taken in 1934 with her sisters and other family members. She is a tall woman, standing slightly apart from the group. The separateness, caught accidentally, might well describe her life. In a land rich in tradition, Johanna created her own. Johanna July was always a little separate from the rest.[30]

NOTES

1. Scott Thyboyn, "Against all odds, Black Seminole who won their freedom," *Smithsonian* 22:5 (Aug., 1991): 90–101.

2. Kenneth W. Porter, "The Seminole-Negro Scouts, 1870–1881," *Southwestern Historical Quarterly* 55:3 (Jan., 1952): 358–77.

3. Ibid., p. 205.

4. William Kerrigan, "Race, Expansion, and Slavery in Eagle Pass, Texas, 1852," *Southwestern Historical Quarterly* 101:3 (Jan., 1998): 283.

5. Ibid.

6. Ibid., p. 206.

7. Johanna July's life falls into two parts, the years Johanna remembered and recalled for Florence Angermiller, and the life remembered by those still living in Brackettville and Del Rio. It probably is not unusual that the two are slightly different. Those people unfamiliar with the Angermiller interview expressed surprise that she had led the life she had in an earlier generation. In an interview with Ethel Warrior, I was told that Johanna's life was not that unusual for a woman of the period and that there were at least two other women who worked stock and broke horses. William Warrior and his wife Ethel provided invaluable information and memories of Johanna.

8. Glenn R. Vernam, *Man on Horseback* (Lincoln: University of Nebraska Press, 1972), pp. 222–23, 387–88.

9. U. S., Works Progress Administration, Federal Writers Project, American Life Histories: Johanna July. Interview by Florence Angermiller. American Memories Collection, Library of Congress, 1936–1940. Online, Aug., 1996. (http://www.lcweb.loc.gov/)

10. Conger H. Jones, "Old Seminole Scouts Still Thrive on Border," *Frontier Times* 11:8 (May, 1934): 329.

11. Ibid., p. 330.
12. J. Frank Dobie, et al. *Mustangs and Cow Horses* (Austin, Texas Folklore Society, 1940), p. 24.
13. Ibid., p. 276.
14. July, interview by Angermiller, Online.
15. Ibid.
16. Ibid.
17. Thyboyn, "Against all odds . . ." p. 96.
18. July, interview by Angermiller, Online.
19. Ibid.
20. The young man she married, "Lesley" is not mentioned on any lists of the scouts. He may have been associated in some fashion with the organization as a horse breaker, or he may have just migrated with one of the groups of Seminoles who moved up from Mexico.
21. July, interview by Angermiller, Online.
22. Ibid.
23. Ibid.
24. Ibid.
25. Ethel Warrior, interview by Jim Coffey, Del Rio, Tex., July 3, 1998.
26. William Warrior, interview by Jim Coffey, Del Rio Tex., May 12, 1998.
27. July, interview by Angermiller, Online.
28. Ibid.
29. Izola Resberry, telephone conversation with Sara R. Massey, Aug. 15, 1998.
30. This photograph is the personal property of Izola Resberry and not available for publication.

Figure 4. Edward "Sancho" Mozique. Courtesy Fort Concho National Historic Landmark, San Angelo, Texas

Chapter 6

Edward "Sancho" Mozique

A Buffalo Soldier Turns Cowboy

KEN POLLARD AND VICKI J. HAGEN

Westward moving pioneers, following a vast Concho River tributary system of West Texas, settled in the Concho Valley. As the pioneers traveled the Concho and its tributaries, they found it bordered by the high plains to the north, wind-blown desert to the west, and the dreaded Pecos River with its Horsehead Crossing to the southwest. Comanche raiding parties roamed unchecked, and Apaches hid in its narrow valleys. At this confluence of the Concho Rivers was Fort Concho and the town of San Angelo.[1] This was to become the home of the Buffalo Soldier and West Texas cowboy Edward "Sancho" Mozique.

Edward "Sancho" Mozique[2] was born a slave June 10, 1849, in Columbia, South Carolina. He and his family were owned by "the widow Green." Just prior to the Civil War, "the widow Green" gave Sancho, his mother, and his six brothers and sisters to her nephew, Dr. Edward Fleming, as a wedding present. Sancho Mozique and his family lived with the Flemings in Spartanburg, South Carolina, until the war ended and then Sancho returned to Columbia. He was just sixteen when the emancipation proclamation was read.[3] In an interview with J. Evetts Haley in 1946, Sancho said that his name came from his father, who was a "French creole out of New Orleans."[4]

In July, 1866, following the Civil War, Congress passed legislation establishing two cavalry and four infantry units to be made up of African Americans. The Ninth Cavalry was formed in New Orleans under the command of Colonel Edward Hatch and saw service at Forts Stockton, Davis, McKavett, and other Texas frontier posts. They carried out their duties under the most trying of conditions. The units were charged with protecting stage and mail routes, building and maintaining forts, and establishing law and order in an area full of outlaws and raiding Comanches, Cheyennes, Kiowas, and Apaches. In 1875, after eight long years on the Texas frontier, the Ninth Cavalry and their headquarters were transferred to the District of New Mexico.[5]

The Tenth Cavalry was formed at Fort Leavenworth, Kansas, under the command of Civil War hero Benjamin H. Grierson. Between 1866 and 1875 the units were moved from Fort Leavenworth to Fort Riley, Kansas, and later to other forts in Kansas and Indian Territory (Oklahoma). In April, 1875, the Tenth Cavalry was moved to Fort Concho in West Texas.[6] The regiment's mission in Texas was to protect the mail and travel routes, control Indian movements, provide protection for settlers from outlaws, and gain a knowledge of the area's terrain.

Mozique told the *Standard Times* on his hundredth birthday that he had been taught to fear the blue-coated Union soldiers and would hide from them. Eventually, he and three friends overcame their fear and enlisted.[7] In 1875, Sancho Mozique, at twenty-six years of age, was assigned to Company E of the Tenth Cavalry. He listed his trade as a carpenter and was sent to Jefferson Barracks near St. Louis, Missouri, to receive training before being transferred west to Fort Concho. Sancho arrived at Fort Concho in July, 1875, after a long, 230-mile march from Austin.[8] In 1936, Sancho told a Works Progress Administration interviewer, "I was a soldier for five years, enrolling in 1875 on the 23rd day of February. I was discharged in 1880."[9]

When Sancho Mozique's company arrived in Texas in 1875, the garrison of the Buffalo Soldiers in Texas was changing, with the Ninth Cavalry moving to New Mexico and the Tenth Cavalry being reassigned. When Colonel Grierson and the Tenth Cavalry arrived at Fort Concho and saw the neighboring village of San Angelo, their spirits fell. The post was in a sad state of disrepair. During an inspection in 1875, the post surgeon described living conditions as "primitive." "Sweaty horse blankets and saddles were routinely kept inside the poorly ventilated barracks. The porches were full of holes into which dirty rags had been stuck, and everywhere there were broken windows. The outhouses were so filthy that soldiers were reluctant to use them, which in turn, caused medical problems."[10] This was the location of Sancho's new assignment.

The village of Saint Angela (San Angelo) consisted of about two dozen "hovels," each one a whiskey shop or "something worse." The sheriff was a saloonkeeper and a gambler. "Robbery and murder were frequent, and the only jail was the crumbling guardhouse at the post." Within a few days of his arrival however, Grierson had stone quarrying details set to work, and repairs were soon underway. The parade ground was overgrown with weeds, some up to three feet high. This provided work for the occupants of the guardhouse.[11]

The work week at the post was seven days, with rations consisting of beans, potatoes, beef, or pork and the occasional vegetable from a post garden. The Tenth Cavalry in Texas scouted 34,420 miles of uncharted terrain, opened more than 300 miles of new roads, laid over 200 miles of telegraph lines, and produced excellent maps, detailing water holes, mountain passes, and grazing areas that would allow settlement of the area by ranchers.[12]

Sancho Mozique was assigned to the carpenter's shop of the quartermaster's section. He worked under the direction of Dennis Keating, the fort's wheelwright. As Sancho was an expert carpenter, he was not sent out for any field duty. Because of his carpentry skills, he received $10.60 a month above the $13.00 to $16.00 an ordinary private earned. He was also an active member in the Tenth Cavalry band, under the direction of bandmaster Lieutenant Robert Smither.[13]

Mozique seemed to be on good terms with the post commander, Colonel Grierson. Sometimes, he would go hunting and give Mrs. Grierson whatever he killed that day.[14] He recalled Grierson's young daughter, "Edie," singing, "Oh, happy day when Jesus washed my sins away." Edith Grierson, daughter of the colonel, died September 9, 1878, of typhoid fever. Sancho helped Dennis Keating make the coffin for her burial.[15] The Griersons buried Edie in the civilian cemetery near the post and built a small rock wall around her grave.

In a 1946 interview with J. Evetts Haley, Sancho described San Angelo when he first came. "There wasn't anything else there when I came except there [were] a few dugouts with Mexicans living in them, very few homes. Lots of dance halls later." He also described the various saloons in town. A Mr. McDonald had a saloon in a picket building with a dirt floor. George B. Jackson, an African American businessman, owned the Blue Ribbon Saloon. Sarge Nasworthy owned "Sarge's Place," a combination dance hall and saloon. Sancho went on to describe both the appearance of the town and the characters who inhabited it.[16]

Sancho was honorably discharged from the army on February 24, 1880, at Fort Concho. He remained in the area and worked as one of the first carpenters in San Angelo, helping erect many of the town's early buildings, including the Tankersley's Concho Hotel. Because lumber was scarce and expensive, there wasn't much demand for a carpenter; and the jobs soon ran out.[17]

Sancho periodically moved from San Angelo to look for carpentry work. His quests took him to New Mexico, El Paso, Dallas, San Antonio, and Houston, but he always returned to San Angelo and remained there until his death.[18] Edward Mozique married Alice Johnson, who was born July 4, 1875, in San

Angelo. She was the daughter of Belva Johnson, born in Kentucky, and Angeline Taylor, born in Louisiana.[19]

Mozique turned to ranch work and to cooking. The Texas Longhorn had the stamina, adaptability, and the capacity to sustain long marches and the hostile West Texas conditions. Successful ranching in the Concho Valley included diversification with special breeds of livestock.[20] Sheep were also brought into the Concho Valley and often fared better in those locations where grass and terrain were not suited for cattle. Sancho worked for a number of ranchers in the area, including M. L. Mertz, George Richardson, and J. D. Sugg. At times, his wife worked on the ranches as well.[21]

Sancho worked at the old corral at Kickapoo Springs Ranch as a cook. According to an interview with the *San Angelo Standard Times* in 1934, Sancho started cooking after his discharge from the army and worked in several early-day hotels and restaurants in San Angelo. A good cook was always valuable on the ranch and especially during the roundup.[22]

In 1885, I started working for Mr. Mertz (M. L. Mertz) at the old corral at Kickapoo Springs, about 37 miles from the present site of San Angelo, Texas. This place was known as the first stage stand. A huge corral encircled the large livestock stable which was surrounded by large pecan trees. This building was made of rock, having a roof of lumber. There was a room at the east side of this stable where my brother-in-law and I slept. On the west side, the livestock were kept. During the day, these animals were not molested in any way, but at night, they made such a noise and became so frightened that they had to be removed, sometimes in the middle of the night. Some say this stable was 'hainted, I don't know whether it was or not, but I do know that it was impossible to keep animals in that stable at night. There was something in there that frightened them to death! I tried to keep my horse in this 'hainted stable, but one night I was awakened by a terrible noise and commotion. My horse was charging about and I had to get up and see what was causing the trouble. I found my horse in a nervous condition, practically scared to death! He was sweating and panting and this was wintertime, not summer. It was cold too, this fact was verified by my sleeping inside. I had to remove my horse finally. A new stable was built and the old one was abandoned.

The general talk was among colored folk that it was the custom of the witches to tie the horse's manes together, in order to make a stirrup. One colored man was asked what did the witches do without two stirrups. The old man replied, "We leaves that up to the spirits." I have never seen a horse whose manes have been tied, other than by man, but I have known people who have seen horses with manes tied and knotted, said to have been done so by supernatural causes.[23]

Mozique told the *San Angelo Standard Times* that the Indians were not half as bad as the cowboys who caused "more shooting and trouble than we ever had with the Indians." Careless cowboys were frequently the cause of prairie fires.[24]

Even though he was not a fighting soldier, Sancho was good with firearms. While stationed at Fort Concho, he often hunted buffalo when a small herd roamed near the fort. Buffalo hides brought $1.00 to $1.50. An army private could always use additional money, but Sancho was more interested in the meat—especially the buffalo tongue, which was considered a delicacy.[25]

Sancho loved to hunt and trained bird dogs for a number of years. He was considered an excellent bird hunter and claimed he had never shot a bird on the ground. In his later years Sancho spent his days fishing alone on the Concho River.[26]

"I sold game to the market and to the few residents who were living where the town of San Angelo now stands. I did this type work for four years. I sold quail, two for 25 cents, wild turkey, $1.50 each, hens, $1.25 each, plovers, $1.00 per dozen. I sold fish by the string."[27]

Sancho retired from being a cook at the Sugg Ranch in 1931 to take care of his wife, who was in very poor health. Alice Mozique died on October 8 or 15, 1948, from influenza and toxemia. She was buried in Fairmont Cemetery in San Angelo.[28]

"In 1946, on his 97th birthday, Mazique had pledged (after the doctor ordered it) to cut down on his chewing (tobacco). His 'chaw' had been a Mazique trademark over the years while cooking for the cowboy outfits" in the Concho Valley.[29]

Sancho was interviewed February 15, 1936, as a person who knew more about San Angelo, its first location, and its strange, lawless origin than possibly any of the present residents. When old "Zique" was asked if he knew another story, he repeated the following:

I know one funny incident that occurred on a fishing party. Grimes, a colored friend of mine, Collins, better known as Crow because of his dark hue, and I went to the river one night to fish. Grimes was a ventriloquist and he decided to have some fun with Crow. He told him there was a turtle tied by the boat and to go and fetch it. Crow proceeded to do what he was told, regardless of the impending darkness. On his way back, the fun started. The turtle had been sticking his head out and trying to bite Crow's leg. Finally he craned his neck and said to Crow, "Mr. Crow, what are you going to do with me?" Crow just took time enough to state, "I'se gwine to drap you right heah!"[30]

In 1951, Sancho fell and fractured his arm. His son, Edward, was living with him and taking care of him. While he was in the hospital, he contracted pneumonia, and, on April 20, 1951, Sancho Mozique died, two months short of his 102nd birthday. His recipe for a long life was that he "always made it a practice of going to bed early, getting up early and using plain common sense in the matter of life."[31] The Reverend L. C. Young of St. Paul's AME Church conducted the funeral services for Sancho.[32]

Through drought, floods, blizzards, and gunplay, Sancho Mozique watched San Angelo grow. He never quite overcame his amazement that this was the place he was sent as a soldier to protect against Indians.[33] Sancho Mozique came to Texas as a Buffalo Soldier, a carpenter, and worked on area ranches as a cowboy and cook. He lived to see the transformation of San Angelo from a rough town into a respectable city of over 60,000 people at the time of his death.

NOTES

1. Gus Clemens, *The Concho Country* (San Angelo, Tex.: Newsfoto Yearbooks, 1981), pp. 90–95. San Angelo was known by several different names during the period 1875–83: San Angela, Saint Angela, and Sainta Angela. Eventually, the U.S. Postal Department changed the name to San Angelo. Due to its unsavory reputation, soldiers at Fort Concho referred to the town as "Over the River." The officers and their wives preferred the community of Ben Ficklin, which was near the fort. This community was washed away in the 1882 flood.

2. Sometimes spelled Mazique.

3. *San Angelo Standard Times,* Apr. 3, 1934.

4. Sancho Mozique, interview by J. Evetts Haley, Oct. 20, 1946, J. Evetts Haley Collection, Nita Stewart Haley Memorial Library, Midland, Tex. Sancho Mozique did not elaborate on the fact that his father was from New Orleans and he was from South Carolina. Given the time of Mozique's birth, his father could have been sold to someone from New Orleans.

5. William H. Leckie, *The Buffalo Soldiers: A Narrative of the Negro Cavalry in the West* (Norman: University of Oklahoma Press, 1976), pp. 6–8, 81–84, 112.

6. Ibid., pp. 112, 6–8, 16, 141.

7. *San Angelo Standard Times,* June 10, 1949.

8. Ibid., Apr. 3, 1934, June 10, 1949.

9. Edward "Sancho" Mozique, interview, Feb. 15, 1936, in *Heritage Quest: The Genealogy Magazine* 73 (Jan./Feb., 1998): 28. Given the date of this interview it was probably conducted under the auspices of the Works Progress Administration.

10. William H. Leckie and Shirley A. Leckie, *Unlikely Warriors: General Benjamin H. Grierson and His Family* (Norman: University of Oklahoma, 1984), p. 225.

11. Ibid.

12. Ibid.

13. *San Angelo Standard Times,* Apr. 3, 1934.

14. *San Angelo Standard Times,* Apr. 10, 1949.

15. Bill Green, *The Dancing Was Lively, Fort Concho, Texas: A Social History, 1867–1882* (San Angelo: Fort Concho Sketches Publishing Company, 1974), p. 91.

16. Sancho Mozique, interview by Haley, Oct. 20, 1946.

17. *San Angelo Standard Times,* Apr. 10, 1949.

18. Ibid.

19. Death Certificate of Alice Johnson, Tom Green County Records, vol. 16, San Angelo, Tex., p. 313; *San Angelo Standard Times,* Apr. 21, 1951.

20. Clemens, *The Concho Country,* p. 108.

21. Ibid., p. 110.

22. *San Angelo Standard Times,* June 10, 1949.

23. Edward "Sancho" Mozique interview, *Heritage Quest,* p. 28.

24. *San Angelo Standard Times,* June 10, 1949.

25. Ibid.

26. *San Angelo Standard Times,* Apr. 3, 1934.

27. Edward "Sancho" Mozique interview, *Heritage Quest,* p. 28.

28. *San Angelo Standard Times,* June 10, 1949.

29. Ibid.

30. Edward "Sancho" Mozique interview, *Heritage Quest,* p. 28.

31. *San Angelo Standard Times,* Apr. 21, 1951.

32. Record of Funeral, Tom Green County Library, San Angelo Library, San Angelo, Tex.; Death certificate, Tom Green County Courthouse, San Angelo, Tex.

33. *San Angelo Standard Times,* June 10, 1949.

Part 2

Cowboys of the Cattle Drives

The Civil War in Texas had the unexpected effect of creating the African American cowboy. Within sixteen years of annexation to the United States, Texas joined the Confederacy. Successful ranchers formed regiments and went off to war, leaving behind their wives, children, and African American slaves to maintain and preserve the welfare of their ranches. Most of the "outdoor" work became the responsibility of the African Americans. Some African Americans took this opportunity to escape to the western frontier of Texas. Others used the opportunity to acquire the skills of cowhands. But maintaining the cattle herds and claiming ownership of the cattle on the open range was difficult at best, and during the war it was almost impossible. There were just too few "hands" to do the work. Barbed wire had yet to be invented, so the cattle continued to roam the grasslands and returned to the wild. Fear of the Indians was still a major concern, but giving firearms to African Americans was unthinkable. When the owners returned from war there were few resources, and money was scarce. Most of their small herds had returned to the wild and multiplied by the thousands.

Finding their herds decimated, the primary concern of the owners was once again acquiring horses, rounding up the wild cattle, and putting on their marks to build herds. Some owners sold their slaves for cattle to get the cash to start again. Others fell back on selling the cattle for the "hide and tallow" business to get cash. But with the 1865 emancipation proclamation in Texas, the ranchers lost a primary source of labor. African Americans were free, and reconstruction was under way.

Free African Americans who had held together the ranches of their owners during the war had learned the skills it took to work with cattle and horses. They could top off a horse, throw a cow, pull calves from mud bogs, and pop those 'horns out of the brush. Their skills were now in demand as ranchers worked to build their herds. The ranchers needed help, lots of it, to reclaim the cattle from the wilds. So these cowboys went to work, and the law required a wage be paid. But the major issue was finding a market to sell the cattle. A three- to five-dollar beef in Texas could bring ten times that much back east in the big population centers. In East Texas a few ranchers herded cattle to Gulf coast ports and shipped them to New Orleans or drove cattle south into old Mexico. A few herds were driven to California. Fortunes could be made if cattle could just be gotten to a major market.

Abilene[, Kansas,] in 1867 was a very small, dead place, consisting of about one dozen log huts, low, small, rude affairs, four-fifths of which were covered with dirt for roofing . . . Abilene was selected (for the rail depot) because the country was entirely unsettled, well watered, excellent grass, and nearly the entire area of country was adapted to holding cattle. It was the farthest point east at which a good depot for cattle business could have been made . . . The shipment of '67 reached almost 1,000 cars, all of which, except seventeen, went over the Hannibal & St. Joe Railroad to Chicago, were there packed, largely on the owners' account. The seventeen cars spoken of went to St. Louis, over the Missouri Pacific.[1]

In the thirty years following the Civil War the cattle drives taking cattle to the railroad shipping points in Kansas, Missouri, and Colorado began. The Chisholm, the Western, the Shawnee, and the Goodnight-Loving Trails, with numerous "spurs" or branches, were pounded in the prairie grasses of Texas. There were no signposts or markers, just deep, dusty ruts going north. Millions of Texas cattle were moved in vast herds to the northern shipping points and sold. In 1887, "Colonel Fant had a contract with the government to furnish beef for the Indians in the Indian Territory, so he employed about a hundred Negroes and Mexicans to drive his herds up the trail every year or work the cattle he sold and shipped by train to Ardmore, Oklahoma."[2]

Each ranch had to do spring and fall roundups to form a herd. Each drive required many cowboys. Men who were skilled in the ways of cattle and horses, who could withstand the rugged life fraught with dangers, and who were loyal and trustworthy were needed. Help was scarce. Skilled cowboys were in peak demand, and the African American cowboys were there.

NOTES

1. Joseph G. McCoy, *Historic Sketches of the Cattle Trade of the West and Southwest* (Kansas City, Mo.: Ramsey, Millett and Hudson Printers, 1874; reprint, Columbus, Ohio: Long's College Book Co., 1951), pp. 44, 50, 51.
2. William Loren Katz, *The Black West* (Garden City, N.Y.: Doubleday and Company, Inc., 1971), p. 144.

Figure 5. Ben Kinchlow. Courtesy Sabinal Canyon Chapter, Daughters of the American Revolution

Chapter 7

Ben Kinchlow

A Trail Driver on the Chisholm Trail

JOHN H. FULLER

Ben Kinchlow was an African American cowboy, neither famous as an outlaw nor legendary in the history books, but he was a part of the trail-driving legacy of Texas. His life began as a free black in Texas' post–Republic period, when most African Americans were slaves, and ended in the late 1930s. His life spanned an era that saw the growth of Texas from a few plantations along the Gulf coast to a state that served the nation by supplying beef and cotton to eastern markets. Ben's life is a look back into Texas history, with the glamour of cowboy legends, the hardships of slavery, and the cultural diversity of Texas.

From the establishment of the mission settlements in the northern provinces of New Spain to the Texas Revolution, many African Americans and Native Americans were slaves. Slavery, though not official policy, existed and was continued to provide for the economic welfare of the new settlers arriving in the area. After the Texas Revolution, the newly formed republic legalized slavery, and free African Americans were at risk of being sold back into slavery. With the annexation of Texas in 1845 the laws of the United States became official, but there was little noticeable change in slaves' conditions.

While African Americans in Texas existed under the laws of slavery until after the Civil War, there was always the urge to be free. Stealing away to freedom, as told in most narratives, meant escaping to Canada, where the British government had abolished slavery in 1834. In Texas, with the northern border at such a distance, escape north was unimaginable. There did exist a second option, Mexico. Mexico was closer, but the perils of crossing desolate areas, the possibility of encounters with unfriendly Indian tribes, and the uncertainty of survival presented a dissuasive alternative for escape. Still, in spite of the risky conditions, many slaves took the opportunity to escape into Mexico.

As early as 1845 slaves were making their escape to Mexico. The *Houston Telegraph* and *Texas Register* reported on the escape of twenty-five Negroes from the city of Bastrop: "They were mounted on some of the best horses that could be found and several of them were well armed. It is supposed that some Mexican has enticed them to flee to the Mexican settlement west of the Rio Grande."[1]

Some runaways were not so successful in their attempts to reach freedom in Mexico. An article posted Thursday, April 29, 1853, in the *Texas Ranger* and *Lone Star* paper told of their failure:

Two Negroes Shot
We learn from a gentleman just in from the West, that a couple of negroes belonging to Mr. Lott on the San Antonio river, stole two of the best horses he had on his plantation some ten or twelve days ago, and made off for Mexico. They succeeded in making their way to the neighborhood of Brownsville, when they were overtaken by a party of U.S. soldiers, who ordered them to surrender. They refused to do so, and manifesting a disposition to resist any attempt that might be made by the soldiers to retake them, were immediately shot down.

The killing of the negroes has been a serious loss to Mr. Lott, as they were two of the most valuable hands he had upon his place.[2]

Slaves who were successful in escaping to Mexico were allowed by the Mexican government to live there and become citizens, in spite of efforts by the United States to establish extradition agreements. To escape from slavery with the possibility of being recaptured and punished took persons of extraordinary courage and determination. One such person was Lizaar Moore, a half-white slave woman owned by Sandy Moore, whose plantation was located along the Brazos River bottom in Wharton County. In 1847, Lizaar Moore had obtained her freedom and, with her two sons traveling in an "ambulance" (fancy wagon), crossed into Mexico. One-year-old Ben Kinchlow was one of the sons. Arriving in Mexico, Lizaar Moore and her sons settled in the border area of Matamoros. At the time of Ben's journey to Mexico, Texas had been annexed as a state, but the strict slave laws of the republic were still enforced. It could be argued that the laws no longer existed, but a letter by Governor E. M. Pease, January, 1856, to the state legislature in reference to the status of two free Negroes stated: "It has been the policy of Texas, since the commencement of her revolution to prevent free Negroes and mulattos from coming here to reside. . . . I think the policy heretofore pursued by the State, of excluding free Negroes and mulattos, is a wise one and should be adhered to . . ."[3]

Ben's mother would have been concerned about the status of her sons having been born to her as a free black. Would they have the same rights as a free person or no rights as a slave? As Ben told of his early life to a Works Progress Administration field worker in 1938, his mother was a free person at the time of her travel to Mexico and that they had means to live on until his mother obtained a job washing clothes. She was charging $2.50 a dozen for men's clothing and $5.00 for women's. Ben stated that it "earned her a lot of money at that time."[4]

Young Ben grew up during the 1850s and 1860s in the Matamoros border region, across the Rio Grande from Brownsville—the gateway to Mexico. Ben told that when he was growing up it was necessary for neighbors to work together for survival, with the necessities of life being communally shared.

The way we lived in those days—the country was full of wild game, deer, wild hogs, turkey, duck, rabbits, 'possum, lions, quails, and so forth. You see, in them days they was all thinly settled and they was all neighbors. Most settlements was all Meskins mostly; of course there was a few white people. In them days the country was all open and a man could go in there and settle down wherever he wanted and wouldn't be molested a-tall.

Sometime when we wanted fresh meat we went out and killed. We also could kill a calf or goat whenever we cared to because they were plenty and no fence to stop you. We also had plenty milk and butter and homemade cheese.

We didn't have any sugar, and a very rare thing to have flour. The deer was here by the hundreds. There was blue quail—my goodness. You could get a bunch of these blue top-knot quail rounded up in a bunch of pear and, if they was any rocks, you could kill every one of 'em. If you could hit one and get 'im to flutterin', the others would bunch around him and you could kill every one of 'em with rocks.

We lived very neighborly. When any of the neighbors killed fresh meat we always divided with one another. We all had a corn patch, about three or four acres. We did not have plows; we planted with a hoe. We were lucky in raisin' corn every year. Most all the neighbors had a little bunch of goats, cows, mares, and hogs. Our nearest market was forty miles, at old Brownsville.

When I was a boy I wo'e what was called shirt-tail. It was a long loose shirt with no pants. I did not wear pants until I was about ten or twelve. The way we got our supplies, all the neighbors would go in together and send into town in a dump cart drawn by a mule. The main station was at Brownsville. It was thirty-five miles from where they'd change horses. They carried this mail to Edinburg, and it took four days. Sometimes they'd ride a horse or mule. We'd get our mail once a week. We got our mail at Brownsville.

Our house was a log cabin with a log chimney da'bbed with mud. The cabin was covered with grass for a roof. The fireplace was the kind of stove we had. Mother cooked in Dutch ovens. Our main meal was corn bread and milk and grits with milk. That was a little bit coarser than meal. The way we used to cook it and the best flavored is to cook it out-of-doors in a Dutch oven. We called 'em corn dodgers. Now ash cakes, you have your dough pretty stiff and smooth off a place in the ashes and lay it right on the ashes and cover it up with ashes and when it got done, you could wipe every bit of the ashes off, and get you some butter and put on it. M-m-m' I tell you, its fine.[5]

Just as Ben and his family had escaped to Mexico, riding in an "ambulance," other slaves continued to escape from Texas to seek freedom in Mexico. Brownsville was located on a frequently used route for escaping slaves. The Lower Valley farmers came to the area to ship their cotton to the eastern markets. Transportation of cotton to Brownsville was by wagon and mule, usually driven by slaves. Mexican inhabitants offered encouragement and help to runaway slaves. The escape of a slave, worth between $500 to $1,200, was a sizable loss to any plantation owner. Runaway slaves became such a problem that the U.S. government passed the Fugitive Slave Act in 1850, making it illegal for any citizen to assist an escaped slave. Ben recalled the shipping of cotton to Brownsville and the opportunistic escape of slaves.

"While I was yet on the border, the plantation owners had to send their cotton to the border to be shipped to other parts, so it was transferred by Negro slaves as drivers. Lots of times, when these Negroes got there and took the cotton from their wagon, they would then be persuaded to go across the border by Meskins. That is how lots of Negroes got to be free. The way they used to transfer the cotton—these big cotton plantations east of here—they'd take it to Brownsville and put it on the wharf and ship it from there. I can remember seeing, during the cotton season, fifteen or twenty teams hauling cotton, sometimes five or six, maybe eight bales on a wagon. You see, them steamboats used to run all up and down that river. I think this cotton went out to market at New Orleans and went right out into the Gulf."[6]

In Mexico, young Ben learned to ride and break horses. "I can get my hoss saddled in the mornin' and when I throw my leg over his back, I never move my leg, but ride all day like that, sittin' straight."[7] Ben and others learned to ride horses and tend cattle while exiled in Mexico. Although the lives of slaves in Texas were primarily relegated to the raising of crops and the tending of a few cows and hogs for slaughter, survival in Mexico was more dependent on the ability to work cattle. The majority of Texas slaves had little experience working with horses and cattle prior to the outbreak of the Civil War. Slaves were so valued for their field service that most plantation owners would rather hire white horse trainers to break and train their horses. The cowboy skills acquired by black runaways in Mexico through working with the Mexican vaqueros resulted in the African American cowboy being a valuable asset to Texas ranchers in the post–Civil War cattle roundups and drives to market.

Ben stated that he stayed in Mexico about twelve years before moving across the border from Matamoros to Brownsville, where he lived until emancipation. From 1846–61 various U.S. troops were garrisoned at Fort Brown as protection to settlers against the Indians.[8] How Ben was able to escape being returned to slavery while living in Brownsville is unknown. A return to Texas for most African Americans during the 1850s would have resulted in severe punishment and their return to slavery, as illustrated by the arrest and return to slavery of John Horse (Caballo), leader of the Black Seminoles and a Mexican citizen. John Horse was arrested in Eagle Pass, Texas, also on the border, by Texas Rangers in 1851 and returned to slavery. His freedom was purchased for $500, equivalent to buying him as a slave, by his trusted friend Wild Cat, leader of the Seminoles residing in Mexico. John Horse had previously acquired his freedom in the United States, but this was of no consideration in his return to slavery.[9]

While the Civil War raged in the northern and mid-west states, Texas saw few major battles, which left the state in a position to continue its agricultural interest unobstructed. Ranch work during the Civil War was relegated out of necessity to the old men, small boys, women, and the slaves. An important result of the Civil War was the increase in the number of cattle in the state. Cattle during the Civil War were left to graze and multiply on the open ranges. By 1866 it was estimated there were over three million wild Longhorns in Texas, and many hungry appetites to the north.[10]

East Texas in 1865 was heavily populated, with the western part of the state, above the headwaters of the Brazos and Colorado Rivers, relatively devoid of settlements. A major deterrent to the establishment of settlements in the western part of the state was the presence of the Comanches, lawless Texans, and Mexican bandits. In 1874 the legislature created two Ranger forces to cope with the situation. Major John B. Jones led the frontier battalion, consisting of six companies and an organization called the Special Force with thirty men under the leadership of Captain Leander McNelly. The creation of the Rangers displaced the existing state police, which was composed of about forty percent black men.[11]

I commenced workin' for Cap'n McNelly and his rangers in '72 as a guide, an' I worked with 'em about 18 months. I was about 19 when I joined 'em, so of course I couldn't draw state pay. But I didn't let that bother me, 'cause I knowed I could more than make my wages after I got in the company, by gambling. Sometimes, I would have $100 or $125 I had won off the soldiers dealing monte or seven-up. There wasn't no craps in them days. We played luck too. Never had no shenanigans—stealin' a man's money. . . .[12]

They was all dependin' on me guidin' 'em. We was after cow rustlers and bandits comin' over from Mexico and there was no way for 'em to get to the cow ranches after they crossed the Ryo [sic] Grande except to come across that road. That's where it was easy for me to pick up a trail. I would follow that road for a certain distance and come back and report. If I found a trail, he'd ask me how many they was and which way they was goin' and I would tell 'im. He would give 'em two or three days to make their roundup and then we'd always meet 'em or catch 'em when they went to cross back over the Ryo Grande with the cattle.

The worst combat we had was on the Palo Alto Prairie, one of Santa Ana's battlegrounds. About twelve or fifteen miles east of old Brownsville, they was 16 of the bandits and 15 of 'em killed, all Mexkins except one white man. One Mexkin escaped. The Cap'n just piled 'em all in a pile and sent word to the authorities at Brownsville what shape they was in and where to find 'em.

I guess they was over 200 head of cattle with them bandits that time. It was open country and they'd get anybody's cattle. They just got 'em off the range. They mostly would cross that road at night, and by me gettin' out early next mornin' and findin' that trail, I could tell pretty much how old it was. I reckon that place wasn't over thirteen miles from Brownsville and our camp was thirty-five miles. I guess it must have been twenty-five miles from our camp to where we had that battle. We sure went there to get 'em. I trailed them horses and I knowed from the direction they was takin' that they was goin' to those big lakes called Santa Lalla. They was between Point Isabel and Brownsville and that made us about a forty-five mile ride to get to that crossin', to a place called Bagdad, right on the waters of the Ryo Grande.

We got our lunch at Brownsville and started out to go to this crossin'. I knowed right about where this crossin' was and I says to the cap'n, "Don't you reckon I better go and see if they was any sign?" We stayed there about three hours and didn't hear a thing. And then the cap'n said, "Boys, we better eat our lunch." While we was eatin', we heard somebody holler, and he said, "Boys, there they are!" And he said to me, "Ben you want to stay with the horses or be in the fun?" And I said, "I don't care." So he said, "You better stay with the horses; you ain't paid to kill Meskins." I went out to where the horses were. The rangers were afoot in the brush. It was about an hour from the time we heard the fellow holler before the cattle got there. When the rangers placed themselves on the side of the road, the Meskins didn't know what they was goin' to get into.

The Meskins was all singin' at the top of their voices and they was comin' on in. The cap'n waited till they went to crossin' the herd, he waited till these rustlers all got into the river behind the cattle, and then the cap'n opened fire on the bandits. They was in the water, and he just floated 'em down the river.[13]

So began the Texas Ranger life of the earliest known African American to be associated with the Special Force or what became McNelly's Rangers. Ben was working for John Cunningham on the Bare Stone Ranch about thirty-five miles above Brownsville when he became acquainted with Captain McNelly. With his knowledge of the territory Ben initially drew maps of roads for the Rangers. After becoming acquainted with them, he asked McNelly for a job working with the Rangers. McNelly responded to Ben, "I'd like to have you all right, but you couldn't come here on state pay, and under no responsibility."[14] Ben agreed to be a guide for the Rangers at no pay and served with the Rangers until the death of McNelly.

Ben's having acquired cattle- and horse-handling skills in Mexico, along with good tracking skills, and his knowledge of the border territory around Brownsville, made him invaluable to the Rangers. Ben spent about eighteen months with the Rangers, but he did not receive pay for his services. Ben is described as the earliest recorded Negro in service to the Rangers, but because he did not receive pay or sign an affidavit of service, no official record exists of Ben's service.

The Texas Rangers were disbanded and became scouts for the Confederate army in 1865. They were not officially reorganized until 1874. The official existence of a state-sanctioned Ranger force in 1872 is questionable. It is possible that Ben's recollection of his service dates is incorrect. The Battle of Palo Alto Prairie did take place, and the account as given by Ben is authenticated by the comments of several members of McNelly's Rangers.[15]

With the death of Captain McNelly, Ben's guiding service with the Rangers ended, and he headed east toward Matagorda County doing the work he enjoyed, working cattle and breaking horses. Traveling home to Matagorda County, where his mother had returned earlier after leaving Brownsville, Ben worked on several ranches en route. He worked on the Banqueta Ranch on the Agua Dulce Creek for two months, and then he continued east, where he signed on with the King Ranch. He did ranch work there for four months, with horse breaking his main responsibility. Ben told of his experience breaking horses:

> They was one thing I was put in this world for was to judge a hoss. I can tell when I look at 'im whether he is any account or not. We left a ranch in Victoria County an' I bet you they would be two-hundred-and-fifty Mexkin hosses to cull out, an' I bet they was three differ'nt herds when we was classin' out them hosses. We rode there for about a month. They was an openin' out in front of the pens an' we'd pen them hosses in that corral, an' I don't care what hoss you roped, you had 'im to ride. You'd saddle 'im in the corral an' get on 'im an' they would open tha gate for you' an' there would be several line riders away out from the pens in that openin' to catch the hosses that got away with the saddles on. I was sho' lucky. I never had one of them hosses to throw me. I don't say it because it's myself, but there never was a hoss that ever throwed me out of my saddle. I don't mind 'em pitchin' no more'n nothin'. A hoss could outwind me now but if it wasn't for that, no hoss could throw me. I used to have wind enough to stay with the meanest an' toughest, but of co'se I cain't do it now.[16]

After arriving in Matagorda County and staying with his mother for a short time, Ben worked as a cowhand on the Tres Palacios, tending cattle and doing pasture work. Ben stated that he worked for Mr. Moore for twelve years in Matagorda and then another eight years when he lived in the Stockdale area.

> . . . when I was about twenty-one, I began punchin' cattle. For my first ridin', I broke a mule an' rode 'im bareback. I didn't care nothin' about a saddle. About the year of '75 was the time when I was into my work good. I done all kinds of cow an' hoss work, but of co'se, after I gat to doin' real

cattle punchin', I had to have a saddle. My first job was breakin' hosses an' when I got hard down to breakin' em', I broke sixty-two head on one ranch for Jim Merryman. He give the "21" brand . . .

I used to get four-bits a head for every Maverick I roped out an' branded. You know people couldn't get out to brand up all their stock and after the calves were a year old, they were considered Mavericks. They had quit their mother, then. Yes, instead of brandin' em' up for myself, I got four-bits a head to make the other man rich. Well, I didn't want nothin' them days but a pair of boots, a six-shooter an' a big hat. As for saddles, they was rigged with the pure old rawhide. Nearly ever'thing them days was made of rawhide. Our riatas were made of rawhide an' we had another rope we used for ropin' that was called "cabresto." It was made out of hoss tails an' manes. The first outfit I ever had they furnished it to me. You see, we made most of it ourselves, all 'cept the old saddle tree an' we rigged it up with rawhide. We would jes' kill a big yearlin', an cut it half in two an' make our leggin's. In rainy weather, we would have to commence takin' up our rawhide stirrups an' in dry weather, we'd have to begin lettin' 'em out. That's because when rawhide gets wet it stretches so bad. Anyhow, we had a pretty good outfit. We could rope any big bull or cow that come along. I wore these reg'lar old Mexkin spurs with a sort of short shank but a big rowel. I carried a .45 six-shooter. We had to wear our guns all the time and we tucked 'em down in our belts under our leggin's. We carried guns mostly for the Indians, but lots of times they was dirt done that the Indians didn't do.[17]

In most photographs of cowboys, they are packing holstered six shooters, wearing chaps and ten-gallon hats. In reality, though, most cowboys stuck their six shooters in their belts as did Ben.[18] African American cowboys working on most ranches in Texas were prohibited from carrying guns. On the cattle drives it was a different story. Cowboys stored their rifles in the chuck wagon and carried their guns for protection from Indians and cattle thieves. They arrived at the end of the trail carrying their pistols. Packing a pistol and shooting up the town of Abilene landed one African American cowboy in the town's newly built stone jail, earning him the distinction of being the first prisoner of the jail and the first to break out when the trail crew busted him out of jail.[19]

The prominence of the cowboy was created by the trail drives with large cattle herds from the coastal plains and brush country of Texas to the rail-heads in the north after the Civil War. The word cowboy became synonymous with a Texas trail drover. From 1867–85 the cowboys on the long trail drives were herding cattle through thunderstorms, blizzards, and chasing Comanches as the herds crossed the Red River into Indian Territory to reach the Kansas and Nebraska railheads.

Major cattle drives to the north started in 1867, with the building of the railroad to Abilene, Kansas, and the subsequent beginning of the Chisholm Trail. The Chisholm Trail started on the Rio Grande at Brownsville, led to Austin, Waco, Fort Worth, crossing the Red River at Red River Station, through Indian Territory (Oklahoma) to Wichita, Kansas, and ended at the final destination of Abilene, Kansas. At the height of the cattle drives north from 1870–75, cattle sold for $20 to $35 a head, a sizable profit when compared to the $5 to $10 selling price in Texas. Ben Kinchlow was in his prime as a working cowboy at this time, being around the age of twenty-five—the average age of cowboys herding cattle to the north.

I went up the trail five or six times. Charley Word, Ab Blocker, George West, W. G. B. Grimes, Able and John Pierce was all big trail drivers then. Goin' up the trail you never was out of sight of a herd. The Trail was so worn, that the dust would be knee-deep to the cattle. You could ride right up to the rear of the cattle an' you couldn't see the cattle for the dust. It sho' was slow goin', but whenever we struck good range where there was grass an' water, we always grazed 'em. If the cattle was strung out good on the trail, the lead cattle would be at least four miles ahead of the rear cattle an' sometimes fu'ther.

Out on the Sol West ranch, there was a ranch hand there, a colored man or yellow nigger, by the name of Armstead Bankhead. We was gettin' our hosses out of the pen ant he roped a hoss for me to ride. Mr. West said, "Armstead, since you roped that hoss, you better ride 'im"; an' so Armstead got on 'irm ant hoss made two or three jumps an' off Armstead went. He tried it again an' off he went. Fin'ly, Mr. West asked 'im if he wanted to try it again, but Armstead said, "No, I cain't ride that hoss!" I'd been standin' aroun' watchin' it, so I said, "Take your saddle off ant let me show you how to ride that hoss, Armstead!" An' he did. Did that hoss pitch? My goodness! But I rode 'im down. We was headed for Nebraska that trip, I believe, an' we turned the outfit over to another bunch up on the South Platte River.[20]

Ben referred to working for Sol West on his ranch and going north herding cattle. Sol West made his first cattle drive up the Chisholm Trail in 1871. In 1874, Mr. West was put in charge of a cattle drive to Ellsworth, Kansas, earning him the distinction of being the youngest man who ever "bossed" a herd up the trail.[21] No official record of the trail crew exists, but Ben could easily have been a member of Sol West's first cattle drive, and undoubtedly joined Sol West on some of his twelve successive trips herding cattle from Texas to Colorado, Kansas, and Nebraska.

Leo Tucker, a cowboy with John May and Joel Bennett on an 1874 trail drive, told the story about one of the hardest and most eventful trips he had made. A blizzard hit the trail near Hell Roaring Creek. "That night was the coldest I ever experienced. Snow, sleet, and ice were one and a half feet deep, and our stock suffered. Our loss was not as heavy as some of our neighbors, under Sol West, whose horses froze under their riders. West, Boyce McCrab and Al Fields lost many of their horses."[22] Sol West reported "the horses ridden by the boys had actually frozen to death with their riders on them during our progress of about five miles. My horse was the last to go down."[23]

Ben also told of his experience with bad weather going up the trail with Sol West.

Goin' up the trail ain't all fun, you betcha. Sometimes they'd come a freeze in late spring an' ketch us an' I tell you we had fun then. We went up the trail generally in the spring, you see, an' I remember one spring we was goin' up with the West cattle an' had a good open spring an' about the middle of April was when we received our herd an' we moved off the ranch to Victoria Prairie.

We was goin' to brand out our cattle at the pens an' then the bad weather commenced. We had about one hundred head of hosses in our remuda an' it commenced rainin' an' freezin'. We had to herd them cattle an' you'd go out to see where your old hoss was an' saddle 'im up, an' it would be so dark you couldn't see 'im but you could hear 'im snort. The wind would be blowin' and you'd have to drag that old stiff saddle an' blanket up the old hoss an' the rain would be freezin' almost when it hit. We'd put a bunch of cattle in the pens an' put the road brand on 'em an' it would be burnin' an' hurtin' 'em when we turned 'em out, so they'd take to the river an' swim across an' we had to get across the best way we could to bring 'em back. Well, we'd get that bunch back about the time they turned another bunch out an' the same thing would take place.

Our cook on that trip was Pancho Silgaro, an' I tell you he was a cook too. I reck'n he thought we wasn't havin' trouble enough so he an' Mr. King went to town after supplies one day. When they got all loaded up, the mules stampeded right in town an' run off with the wagon an' scattered provisions all over Victoria. They had flour, molasses, beans, bacon an' all kinds of stuff mixed up an' scattered for a mile. They fin'ly got most of it gathered up an' come on out to camp.

On that trail drivin', we'd start with about twenty-four hands an' they wouldn't have but expert hands, either. They didn't want no sleepy-heads a-tall. By the time we got to Austin or Gonzales, ever' hand would be tried out, an' if you wasn't pretty good, they'd turn you loose an' hunt some others. We always left the ranch with a couple set of hands an' when we got to Austin or Gonzales, twelve of the men would turn back to the ranch an' the other twelve would go on with the herd. They' be six on one relief an' six on the other relief at nights, but if the cattle got along all right, it would soon be to where two men could handle 'em at night an' let the others rest.[24]

The hardships that the cowboys had to endure were numerous. Driving a herd of two thousand cattle on a thousand-mile journey that lasted from three to six months with encounters of Indians, rustlers, and Kansas farmers was a major achievement. The cowboys always had to be on guard for sign of trouble. Regardless of the weather the cowboys pointed the cattle northward and fended off the harsh conditions as best they could. A cowboy had to stay in his saddle all day and bear it, whether it was freezing rain, misty rain, heavy rain, or rain with hailstones. Ben faced it all on his trips up the trail.

I've stood up of many a bad night, dozin'. It would be two weeks sometimes, before we got to lay down on our beds. I have stood up between the wagon wheel and the bed (of the wagon) and dozed many a night. Maybe one or two men would come in and doze an hour or two, but if the cattle were restless and ready to run, we had to be ready to run, we had to be ready right now. Sho!

Those stormy nights, thunderin' and lightnin'! You could just see the lightnin' all over the steers' horns and your horse's ears and mane too. It would dangle all up and down his mane. It never interfered with you a-tall. And you could see it around the steer's horns in the herd, the lightnin' would dangle all over 'em. If the hands (cowboys) or the relief could get to 'em before they got started a runnin', they could handle 'em, but if they got started first, they would be pretty hard to handle. . . .[25]

The worst thing you got to watch in a stampede is to keep out of the middle of the herd when you get 'em to millin'. When you get a herd turned an' millin' you can handle 'em but you cain't hardly stay out of the middle of the herd to save your life. One night after a stampede, Mr. Pulliam rode up on me in the middle of the herd an' he said, "Who's that?" I said, "It's Ben!" An' he got in the middle of 'em.

Another peculiar thing about herdin' at night in case of stampedes is that you want to always build your bed down with your head away from the cattle. Always sleep with your feet toward the herd. If you don't, an' they stampede, you will get up an' run away from 'em instead of toward 'em ever' time. The thing is to get to your hoss an' get on 'im. Your hoss is always at camp right at the wagon, saddled an' ready to go. The herd was always bedded down about fifty or seventy-five yards away from the wagon. No, you don't never want to run from the herd, but toward 'em when a stampede starts. Pshaw! I never did see a stampede run over a man. I don't know how they ever got that started. Maybe if you got right square in front of 'em before they saw you an' they couldn't turn, they would knock you down and run over you, but I never did see it, an' I reck'n I've seen as many stampedes an any man ever saw.[26]

Poisonous snakes were another consistent problem with which the cowboy had to contend. From the start of the trail drive in South Texas to the end of trail, snakes were a constant menace. There were rattlesnakes in South Texas, water moccasins along the Colorado and Brazos Rivers, and more rattlesnakes in North Texas and Oklahoma. On every trail drive there was always a cowboy who could tell about a bad experience with a snake, and without medical attention an encounter with a poisonous snake could be disastrous for a cowboy or his horse.

Many a thing could happen out on the trail, or out on the ranch gatherin' cattle. I've had worlds of rattlesnake experiences. One time down here on the Irvin ranch, I seen the biggest snake layin' right by the trail, an' befo' I could turn my hoss, he struck. He missed my hoss, but he (the snake) was so sho' he got 'im, he flopped over on his back befo' he knowed he missed. Whenever they strike anything an' hang their fangs in it, they always flop on their backs to tear their fangs loose. This sho' was a big one.

I had a hoss bit later on at the Anderson ranch. The snake hung his fang in my hoss' leg an' he couldn't get loose. His fangs hung an' my hoss reared an' plunged till he stepped on the snake with his hind foot an' pulled the snake loose. I took him home an' took my pocket-knife an' scarified the place an' then packed salt petre in the cut an' bound it up. Then I put kerosene on the place an' it never did swell.[27]

The cowboy became unique in our history. He would take a dangerous situation, make it an ordinary occurrence, and treat it in a light-hearted manner. Ben told about one of these situations on the trail.

* * *

I'll tell you something funny happened on that trip where we left the herd on the South Platte River. We was waitin' for the other outfit an' had to graze our herd on the river. That South Platte was a hundred miles long. Mr. Tom Pulliam was first boss an' Mr. Bob Rice was second boss, an' one day Mr. Pulliam says to Bob Rice, "Bob, I believe I'll go out an' hunt some range for the cattle. They've been here long enough," an' Mr. Rice says, "All right." Along in the evenin' Mr. Pulliam hadn't got in yet an' Mr. Bob says, "Ben, don't you feel like eatin' some good range meat?" Of co'se I said yes an' he says, "Well, we'll ride out an' get one this evenin'!" So we saddled up an' rode out an' pretty soon we found a nice fat range heifer an' he took his rifle an' shot 'er. He told me to get down an' bleed 'er an' I did, but when I straightened up an' looked, I saw a rider comin' across the hill an' I sure got restless for I thought it was a range rider. I said to Mr. Rice, "Look yonder, that sure is a range rider an' he's comin' right here!" Mr. Rice says, "Well, we'll jus' have to put him, hoss an' all in the river. Will you help me?" I was afraid to say no because he was a kind of desperado himself an' if it was a range rider rode up there, I knowed Bob Rice would kill 'im an' put him, hoss an' all in that river. But it turned out to be Mr. Pulliam. He'd come back to camp an' knowed about where we were. He jus' rode on out to where we was gettin' the meat. I sho' was scared for awhile.

Once we took a herd up to Dakota an' that trip was the first "chip races" I ever saw. Them girls up there would run races to see who could pick up the most buffalo chips. They wasn't no wood up there to burn, so they used buffalo chips instead of wood. I've cooked with many a chip. Them big old girls could sure gather 'em on them races. They'd have lots of fun, too.

They called them people up there "grangers." We call 'em "nesters" down here. They didn't have no fences aroun' their farms an' one day we throwed our herd off to graze. It was on Sunday an' the old granger that owned a certain little place there was gone to church an' the place was all left alone. The old man had his harness hangin' in a shed an' our cattle was grazin' all aroun' his place, so one old steer got in the shed an' got one of the bridles of the harness hung on his head an' grazed off with it on. About that time, the old granger an' his family come home an' he ordered us off his place. We had a big, black Nigger with the herd an' after 'while, the granger come up to him an' wanted to know who was the boss of the outfit an' the Nigger pointed to me an' told him I was the boss. He come to me an' wanted to know if I was the boss an' I told him no an' pointed to another man close to me an' he went to him. That man told him no, he wasn't the boss an' pointed back to the big, black Nigger an' told 'im that Nigger was the boss. The granger went back to the Nigger and said, "Are you the boss here?" An' the Nigger said, "No." The granger was gettin' pretty mad an' says, "Well, where in the hell is the boss." Then he looked over at the steer an' said, "Now, younder's a steer with one of my bridles on his head an' I want it taken off an' you go do it!" About then, he went to the house an' come out with a great long gun an' that Nigger—he was Paul Boggins—he had to rope that steer to get the bridle an' when he got it off an' brought it back, the granger said, "Now, I'll give you ten minutes to get these cattle off this land. This land is mine an' I want 'em off, so you better get 'em off in ten minutes!" We sho' got 'em off too. We never thought that was half as funny as the old steer walkin' aroun' with his bridle on.[28]

Ben's account of his days on the trails paralleled those told by others. It took a special individual to survive months of driving cattle through unimaginable conditions, but the African American cowboys such as Ben Kinchlow did survive and returned year after year for another adventure. "Goin' up the trail ain't all fun, I can tell you, but it is the prettiest sight on earth when you have a big herd of cattle on the trail and get 'em to grazin' if a person knows how to shape 'em up. You can ride along and watch 'em and it looks like every steer is takin' the same step and a mouthful of grass at the same time. You couldn't know how pretty that sight is unless you saw it. If it was so I could, I'd go back to a cattle ranch now where I could see the work go on. Of co'se they ain't no more trail drivin', but I like to be aroun' stock."[29]

Between cattle drives and roundups, Ben worked on a number of ranches in Texas. He later settled down in the Uvalde area with his second wife, Eliza Dawson. In 1939 Ben was ninety-one years old and had been married to Eliza for forty years when he was interviewed by a field worker with the WPA Federal Writers Project. Ben did not have children by Eliza, but he had had six children by his first wife, Christiana Temple, whom he wed in 1879 in Matagorda County.[30]

Ben lived a full and complete life as a free black in the days when that was hard to do. After fleeing to Mexico with his mother he grew up in the Brownsville area where he learned the skills of handling cattle and horses. He returned to the Matagorda area of his birth with the skills of a cowboy. He arrived just in time for the boom years of the trail drives north. His life as a black cowboy is representative of the many black cowboys working the ranches of Texas.

NOTES

1. Philip Durham and Everett L. Jones, *The Negro Cowboy* (1965; reprint, Lincoln: University of Nebraska Press, 1983), p. 16.

2. *The Texas Ranger and Lone Star Newspaper,* Apr. 20, 1853, Texas Historical Archives, Austin, pp. 2–3, 9. This Mr. Lott is the same man for whom George McDow, profiled in another chapter, often worked.

3. Governor E. M. Pease, letter to State Legislature, Jan., 1856, Governor's Papers, Texas Historical Archives, Austin.

4. Florence Fenley, *Oldtimers: Their Own Stories* (Austin: State House Press, 1991), p. 134.

5. U.S., Works Progress Administration, Federal Writers' Project, Slave Narratives of Texas, Box A931, Part 2, Interview by Florence Angermiller, Manuscript Division, Library of Congress, Washington, D.C., pp. 261–65.

6. Ibid., p. 265.

7. U.S., Works Progress Administration, Federal Writers Project. American Life Histories: Ben Kinchlow: Range Lore and Negro Cowboy Reminiscences Before and After 1875. Uvalde County, District 15. Interview by Florence Angermiller. American Memories Collection, Library of Congress, 1936–1940, p. 1, Online, July, 1998. (http://www.lcweb.loc.gov/)

8. Walter Prescott Webb, ed., *Handbook of Texas,* vol. 1 (Austin: Texas State Historical Association, 1952), p. 61.

9. Juan Manuel Maldonado, Colonia Militas de Rio Grande, Milican en Piedra Negras, letter to Office of the Chief Justice of the Military Colony of the Rio Grande, Sept. 22, 1851, Texas Ranger Archive Papers, Texas Historical Archives, Austin.

10. Patrick Dearen, *A Cowboy of the Pecos* (Plano, Tex.: Republic of Texas Press, 1997), p. 29.

11. Alwyn Barr, *Black Texas: A History of African Americans in Texas, 1528–1995* (1973; reprint, Norman: University of Oklahoma Press, 1996), p. 48.

12. WPA, "Ben Kinchlow," Online, p. 1.

13. U.S., Works Progress Administration, *Ben Kinchlow,* pp. 20–24.

14. Ibid., p. 20.

15. George Durham, *Taming the Nueces Strip: The Story of McNelly's Rangers* (Austin: University of Texas Press, 1962), p. 8. Mr. Durham stated that he joined the Rangers in 1875 and was involved in the Palo Alto fight. His service with the Rangers would be after the date given by Ben for the Palo Alto fight. This suggests Ben's recollection of his service dates with the rangers was incorrect when he was interviewed by Works Progress Administration (WPA) workers.

16. WPA, "Ben Kinchlow," Online, p. 6.

17. Ibid., p. 2.

18. Photographs of Deadwood Dick, Isom Dart, Ben Hodges, and other Negro cowboys show them with six-shooters in their belts.
19. Durham, *Negro Cowboy*, pp. 55–56.
20. WPA, "Ben Kinchlow," Online, p. 7.
21. J. Marvin Hunter, ed., *The Trail Drivers of Texas* (1925; reprint, Austin: University of Texas Press, 1986), pp. 128, 136.
22. Ibid., p. 704.
23. Ibid.
24. WPA, "Ben Kinchlow," Online, p. 14.
25. U.S., Works Progress Administration, *Slaves Narratives*, Part 2, p. 12.
26. WPA, "Ben Kinchlow" Online, pp. 11–12.
27. Ibid., p. 19.
28. Ibid., p. 8.
29. Ibid., p. 10.
30. Ben's great-grandson, also named Ben Kinchlow, is co-host of the Christian Broadcasting Network's "700 Club" and has written an autobiography entitled *Plain Bread* (Shippensburg, Penn.: Treasure House, Destiny Image, 1997).

Figure 6. Neptune Holmes with Shanghai Pierce (right) and A. P. Borden (left). Courtesy of Wharton County Historical Museum, Wharton, Texas

Chapter 8

Neptune Holmes

A Lifetime of Loyalty

KITTY HENDERSON AND CHARLIE WOODSON

Few Texans are unfamiliar with the names of Richard King, Charles Goodnight, or Shanghai Pierce. These men and their deeds are never forgotten when the history of the Texas cattle industry is told, but there are those whose stories have not been told. The deeds of the African American cowboys of Texas are equally important for a more complete story of the cattle industry of Texas. These men rode side-by-side with the cattlemen, helped drive the herds to market, mended the fences, and frequently carried the gold used to buy cattle. They appear sometimes in faded photographs, mounted quietly, but proudly, on their horses, often beside their employers. The many African American cowboys were there when ranching controlled the Texas economy and for- tunes were made by the cattlemen. Their hard work, their loyalty, and their skills remain as faded as the old photographs, but they were no less important to the success of the vast ranches of history.

Undiscovered stories of the African American cowboy are nestled in the legends of famous ranches and ranchers. One such story is that of Neptune Holmes—the right-hand man of Abel "Shanghai" Pierce, one of Texas' most picturesque cattle barons.

Abel Head Pierce was a tall man with a brusque manner and a booming voice that could be heard for miles. He was a native of Rhode Island with a few years of schooling. His restless nature led him to Texas, stowed away on a schooner bound for Indianola.[1] He acquired the nickname from a pair of spurs with un- usually long shanks with long rowels that he bought from a South Texas black- smith. The Rhode Islander turned cowboy remarked, "Why, they make me look like a Shanghai rooster."[2] At nineteen he went to work for E. A. Deming in Matagorda County splitting rails, but he soon moved on to work for coastal rancher W. B. Grimes as a cowboy.[3] From all accounts, Grimes was a harsh task master with a deceiving nature. Nevertheless, Pierce learned his trade well and was known for his ability to quickly tame a wild horse and understand the ways of skittish cattle. In 1855, at twenty-one, he became a boss driver for Grimes, who had several African American slaves working as cowboys.[4]

Life on the Grimes Ranch was not easy for Pierce. It's said that Pierce asked for his first year's pay of two hundred dollars in cows and calves. When the time came, Grimes paid Pierce at the rate of fourteen dollars each for pregnant cows. Unfortunately, however, the cattle were old stock, unfit to be sold, and the majority of them died soon after calving.[5] In the eyes of Grimes, he was "teaching a Yankee the cow business."[6] The relationship between the two men ended when Pierce returned to the ranch after serving with the First Texas Cavalry for the Confederacy during the Civil War. Knowing he would need money after the war, Pierce had asked Grimes to keep his back pay of five hundred dollars until he returned. Pierce went to his old boss to claim his pay—Grimes gave it to him in worthless Confederate dollars.[7]

This event triggered the beginning of the vast Pierce empire. Pierce and his brother, Jonathan, who arrived in Texas before the Civil War, established El Rancho Grande at Tres Palacios in Matagorda County. By 1871, they had more than 100,000 head of cattle spread over miles of grassy range with fifty cowboys working the roundup, but after the death of his wife, Shanghai converted his cattle to gold and went to Kansas City for eighteen months.[8] Upon his return to Texas, Shanghai, Jonathan, and Daniel Sullivan began to buy land in Wharton and Matagorda Counties. Before long, the company owned 500,000 acres—including the land where W. B. Grimes grazed his cattle. They were sending thousands of cattle up the trails and shipping more by rail. Shanghai Pierce was the undisputed king of coastal ranchers.

Along with his brother Jonathan and other business partners who helped Pierce build his vast empire there was Neptune Holmes. Holmes, an African American man, traveled alongside Pierce for over thirty years, just as committed to cattle as the legend himself.

Neptune spent most of his life as an employee of Shanghai Pierce. Just when and how he came to work for Pierce is unknown. The 1880 Jackson County census indicated Neptune was born in 1852 and listed his parents from South Carolina,[9] but his death certificate listed his parents, Isaac Holmes and Sarah Wilson from Texas.[10] In all probability, his parents came to Texas as slaves during the Republic period. Matagorda and Wharton Counties were in the heart of cotton plantations and nearly all the first settlers brought their slaves with them as "indentured servants" and were allowed eighty acres for each slave.[11] Neptune's grandson, Bill Holmes, recalls that Sarah worked for either Shanghai or his brother Jonathan at the original Pierce brothers ranch, El Rancho Grande.[12] Neptune had three brothers, Arthur Green, Horace "Dick" Holmes, and Allen Holmes and a sister who lived in Bay City, Texas, but her name is not remembered.

Family history recounts that Neptune began working for Shanghai when he was a child. El Rancho Grande was started in 1866, when Neptune was about fourteen years old. Chris Emmett, in *Shanghai Pierce, A Fair Likeness,* states that Neptune rode with "Mr. Shang," Neptune's name for Shanghai, for thirty-five years.[13] Accordingly, that would suggest Neptune worked for him until 1901. Shanghai Pierce died in 1900, but it can be concluded that Neptune was at least in his early teens when he started with Shanghai. It is likely that Sarah and Isaac, along with their four children, were workers on the ranch and associated with the Pierce family. The early years of Shanghai and Neptune's association were during reconstruction in the heart of the "Black Belt" of Texas. Slaves were freed, and many stayed on the plantations and ranches as employees.

Nep's grandson, Bill, now in his nineties, recalls that Neptune did all kinds of cowboy work on Pierce's BJ Ranch: breaking horses, punching cows, branding, dehorning, fencing, dipping, and driving stock.[14] During 1871 and '72 Pierce was shipping five hundred cattle a week to Cuba to provide beef for the soldiers in their war against Spain. Cowboys, many of them African American,[15] were there as part of the gathering crew and the loading crew, night-herding to keep the cattle quiet. Pierce became one of the largest trail drivers of Texas, and his steers became known as "Sea Lions."[16] When Pierce reached Kansas he would say, "Well boys, here are my sea lions; they came right up out of the Gulf of Mexico."[17] The origin of Neptune's name remains unknown, but with Pierce's cattle known as "sea lions," there is an obvious connection to Neptune, the Greek mythological king of the seas, as Neptune Holmes was the guardian of Pierce's "sea of cattle on a vast ocean of grass."[18]

Nep is remembered for his deadly aim with a six-shooter and his loyalty to Shanghai. In 1883, Neptune was working the cattle on the trail near Ogallala. Seth Mabry bought Shanghai's herd and horses as well, and Neptune, along with William Chin and others, had their wages raised and were hired on to take the herd toward Denver. Shanghai later wrote his bookkeeper, "take Neptune one side and tell him I will fix up with him the balance when I Come home but for him to tell the other boys he only got $25 per Mo."[19] There was clearly some "understanding" between the two men. Over the years wherever you found Shanghai Pierce, you also found Neptune Holmes. Whether it was on the open range, on the trail to Kansas City, paying the crews at the various trail camps, or buying cattle, Neptune was there protecting the gold and "Mr. Shang."

Neptune is described by Chris Emmett as an almost illiterate servant who slept with the money and followed Pierce wherever he went, whenever he was called. He was always "Old Nep" even though he was not so old.[20] Family stories and family attitudes present a different view of the relationship between the two men. No one truly knows whether Neptune could read or write or knew arithmetic, but there is no doubt that his relationship with Shanghai Pierce was a unique one. Pierce was a man with a strong and powerful personality, and he was not one to suffer fools lightly. He made big deals for big money, and that money was entrusted to Neptune. Neptune, at forty-four years of age, was there when Shanghai in 1896 went from town to town buying gold to pay off bank notes. This continued for sixteen days, with Neptune holding the horses and the two of them hauling the gold.[21] Shanghai had learned his lesson when Mr. Grimes had paid him in worthless Confederate notes. He used gold in his many transactions, and it was Neptune's job to keep it safe.

Another time, Shanghai got interested in leasing lands in Indian Territory and was invited to Washington. Neptune said, "Mr. Shang, hadn't we better stay out of that p'litical bizness you don't know nothing about, and stay with our cows we do know somethin' about?" Shanghai did not go to Washington.[22] Author Emmett seems to have presented Neptune as the African American stereotype of the 1950s, rather than raise the possibility that Pierce, as an astute and tough rancher, relied on a person he knew he could trust and who got the job done.

Neptune was married to Priscilla Chin, whose father, William Chin, also worked as a cowboy on the Pierce Ranch. They had nine children, five sons and four daughters.[23] Census data for Jackson County in 1880 lists Priscilla's occupation as keeping house and Neptune's as a stock driver.[24] In his later years, Neptune was a pensioner on the Pierce estate. He continued to ride his horse with his six-shooter at his side and advise and check on crews well into his eighties.[25] He was paid well for the times and for his years of allegiance to Shanghai. Bill Holmes recalls that Shanghai offered Neptune as much land as he wanted, but Nep declined, fearing he would fall victim to unkind souls after Pierce's death and lose the land.[26] Neptune did accept about seventy acres for his immediate family and the comfortable house where he and Priscilla lived at Pierce Station, a community Pierce envisioned becoming the county seat. Neptune took his pay to the bank because he wanted to provide for his children's education. Schools for African American children were established in Wharton County during reconstruction, and all nine of Neptune's children received high school diplomas.

Neptune Homes remained at Pierce Station until his death at eighty-two from pneumonia on February 4, 1934. He was buried at the Mount Olive Baptist Church in Mackay, Texas. Blacks, whites, and Hispanics attended the services, crying unabashedly at the passing of one of the true cowboys.[27]

A few years before Shanghai Pierce died, he had commissioned a statue of himself made out of gray marble by Frank Teich of San Antonio. The statue, which was to be "higher than any statue of any Confederate general, a fair likeness of myself, big enough to be buried under, so people can look at it and say, 'There stands old Pierce,'" is in the Hawley Cemetery near Blessing, Texas.[28] But Shanghai Pierce didn't pay the tombstone maker until the statue passed inspection. "'It looks just like you, Mr. Shang,' Neptune reported—and then Mr. Shang wrote the check."[29]

NOTES

1. Wayne Gard, *Rawhide Texas* (Norman: University of Oklahoma Press, 1965), p. 80; Chris Emmett, *Shanghai Pierce, A Fair Likeness* (Norman: University of Oklahoma Press, 1953), p. 4.
2. O. W. Nolen, "Shanghai Pierce," *Cattleman* 31:7 (Dec., 1944): 31. Both C. L. Douglas, *Cattle Kings of Texas* (Fort Worth: Branch-Smith, Inc., 1968), p. 34, and Gard, *Rawhide Texas*, pp. 80–81, claim his nickname originated from an unknown person commenting on his too tight and too short pants, whereas Nolen stated it came from a comment of Pierce himself who as a Rhode Islander had a knowledge of chickens.
3. Nolen, "Shanghai Pierce," p. 31.
4. Douglas, *Cattle Kings*, pp. 35–36.
5. Ibid., pp. 31–32; Gard, *Rawhide Texas*, p. 80.
6. Annie Lee Williams, *A History of Wharton County, 1846–1961* (Austin: Von Boeckmann–Jones Company, 1964), p. 154.
7. Douglas, *Cattle Kings*, p. 37; Gard, *Rawhide Texas*, p. 80.
8. Douglas, *Cattle Kings*, p. 43; Gard, *Rawhide Texas*, p. 81.
9. U.S. Bureau of Census, Jackson County, 1880, Clayton Genealogical Library, Houston, Tex.
10. Death Certificate, Office of Vital Statistics, Wharton County Courthouse, Wharton, Tex.
11. Williams, *History of Wharton County*, p. 105.

12. Bill Holmes, interview by Charlie Woodson, Granado, Tex., Sept. 19, 1998.

13. Emmett, *Shanghai Pierce*, p. 47.

14. Holmes interview.

15. Emmett, *Shanghai Pierce*, p. 123, mentions Negro cowmen Robert and John Norman, Charlie Ellis, Ed Roberts, Jasper Singleton, Gabriel Sims, and Podo, the tall Kaffir from Zululand as working for Pierce.

16. Matagorda Historical Commission, *Historic Matagorda County*, vol. 1 (Houston: D. Armstrong Co., Inc., 1986), p. 178.

17. Williams, *History of Wharton County*, p. 156.

18. Emmett, *Shanghai Pierce*, p. 47, states that Neptune Holmes—the Old Nep of-the-sea-of-waving-grass—who rode in the wake of his boisterous master, just happened along to help still the anxiety of many a Texas cattleman from that day on.

19. Emmett, *Shanghai Pierce*, pp. 133–34.

20. Ibid., p. 47.

21. Ibid., pp. 266–67; Maria Sandoz, *The Cattlemen* (Lincoln: University of Nebraska Press, 1978), p. 110; Philip Durham and Everett L. Jones, *The Negro Cowboys* (Lincoln: University of Nebraska Press, 1965), p. 26.

22. Emmett, *Shanghai Pierce*, p. 176.

23. Holmes interview.

24. Census, Jackson County, 1880.

25. Holmes interview.

26. Ibid.

27. Ibid.

28. Emmett, *Shanghai Pierce*, p. 47; Douglas, *Cattle Kings*, p. 58.

29. Emmett, *Shanghai Pierce*, p. 46; Douglas, in *Cattle Kings*, p. 58, recounts this story but states it was Jesse Duncan who told Mr. Shang that the statue resembled him.

Figure 7. George McDow. Courtesy Della Mae McDow Bennett, Corpus Christi, Texas

Chapter 9

George McDow

A Black Cowboy

IRA V. LOTT

Pettus would rather have George McDow by his side
in a fight than any other man.[1]

George McDow (1855/60–1942) was born in Goliad County, Texas. He lived in St. Paul, one of the small rural settlements formed by ex-slaves, some of whom worked as cowboys after the Civil War. Goliad was the center for the cattle industry at that time. "Roaming the plains of Texas were great herds of semi-wild cattle that had been abandoned by the Mexican owners. During the WAR these animals were used to help feed the soldiers, but after the disbandment of the army many discharged soldiers gathered for themselves herds of varying sizes. These wild animals were gradually tamed and corralled. The first pens which were constructed for the purpose of corralling these cattle were in Goliad."[2]

McDow left no personal memories of his life as an early cowboy of Texas; however, James Edward Pettus, trail boss, and Pettus family members left records regarding the trail driving days and their crews.[3] Accurate information about McDow's early years is limited. George McDow was born into slavery in Texas. His mother, Harriet, and stepfather, John Shelton, were born in Mississippi. The Sheltons and George, along with the Perrymans, Duncans, Taylors, and other families, lived for many years in a settlement located where Dry Creek and Manahuilla Creek converge in Goliad County. In 1858, Manahuilla Creek was a stream of good size surrounded with post-oak and mesquite trees.[4]

According to Joe Duncan, who was born in the St. Paul settlement, the settlers farmed their own land and were responsible for all community affairs. South of the cluster of homes was a one-room frame church that was also used as a school. A community cemetery was in the same area. Duncan remembered gardens with sweet potatoes, peanuts, watermelons, and other vegetables. There were cotton patches where the women chopped, thinned, and picked cotton. The people also worked on neighboring farms and ranches, sometimes earning $1.00 a day. Duncan's father and six uncles worked as cowboys for the Pettus, Lott, and O'Connor families. Lee Duncan, his uncle, went on several trail drives.[5]

The family Bible indicates: "George McDow's father, Ben Mack was owned by Dr. Lipston (Lipscomb), and sold by Dr. Lipson (Lipscomb) to someone in Mississippi."[6] It is likely that George's last name was at one time Mack, as Mrs. Jesse Pettus-Wallace wrote: "These are the years J. E. Pettus went up the trail—'77, '78, '79, '80 and '82. In '80, Ed Lott went with him. In '82 two white men: Johnson and Diebrel (Diebel). Negros mostly. George Mac(k) (McDow) and George Flood they went in the years of the '80s."[7]

McDow reached manhood in the St. Paul settlement and was married to his first wife, Alice, until her death prior to 1900. The 1900 U.S. census indicates George McDow was a widower, and there were four sons in the home.[8] Alice's death and the place of her burial are unknown, but the most likely place is the cemetery where the St. Paul community was located. The entire area is now farm land that has been chained and root plowed.[9]

In 1906, McDow married Lucy Perryman, a neighbor, and to this union was born a son and daughter, Amos and Della Mae. Lucy worked for the James E. Pettus family as a housekeeper and cook off and on for many years. The family lived then in the town of Goliad, where McDow spent the remainder of his life. An active member of Calvary Baptist Church, he had become a deacon, fulfilling pastoral responsibilities as called for by members of the congregation, all the while providing for his family as a farmer. He enjoyed reading the Bible, newspapers, and the *Farmers Almanac* while sitting beneath a pecan tree located near his home. At the time of his death in 1942, he was known as a man who had a special interest in his family, the Masonic Lodge, and various community groups.[10]

In her memoirs, Mrs. Wallace wrote about George McDow and George Flood, the cook, who were part of the trail crews. The backgrounds and upbringings of George McDow and George Flood were similar. Both men were born slaves to slave parents who had been brought to Texas. Emancipation and the cattle industry provided opportunities to recreate themselves as free men. Both lived their lives in Goliad County and worked as cowboys at approximately the same time for either Pettus or Lott. Mrs. Wallace wrote: "George Flood (a negro) went up the trail to Kansas with J. E. Pettus in the cattle drives in the 70's and 80's. He also went with Col. Suggs in 1884. George was born in Goliad in the house where Mrs. Ragland now lives. Classie Small was George's mother. Linas Flood was George's father. Linas was born in Kentucky and owned by a man named Beverly. . . . George Flood, before he married, worked for Reeds, then for Mr. Tom Campbell, Weiss Ranch. In 1890, he began working for J. E. Pettus for 15 years. . . . Bill Johnson (a negro) also went up the trail with J. E. Pettus. . . . Alex Pettus and Frank Pettus (both negroes) also went up the trail with Ed Lott."[11]

Late in his life, James Edward Pettus recalled his trail life in a newspaper article:

J. E. (Jim) Pettus, 50-year Resident of Goliad, Tells About Times When Cattle Meant Hard Work And Money

He talks of moving herds of cattle over a great distance of land in dangerous times, the day to day struggles, the fears, and the exhilaration of accomplishment and finally heading back home to Texas. . . . "I rode the range, when it was new, with my father's cattle and horses and many a pleasant memory is mine as I hark back to cow camps, long before barbed wire fence days. The songs that we sang to the cattle; of sleeping, dead to the world, with water running round our bedding and trickling down our backs as the rain pelted on our hat brims pulled over our faces for protection. Of stampedes and everything else in God's world to make us miserable, but strange to say none of 'em did, we slept, ate, rounded-up, branded, marked and drove cattle as free hearted and happy as if we had been on a lark of some kind."[12]

He confessed fear of Indian attack, trouble with the "nesters" (farmers) who hated cattlemen, and the beauty of the country they were crossing. His preference to "have George McDow by his side in a fight" is convincing evidence that this McDow must have been an exceptional cowboy.[13]

Pettus described his first drive in 1877 to the Red River where his cattle were sold for "good money." Accompanying him was W. J. Lott, with whom Pettus had formed a partnership after borrowing money from his older brother, William Albert, to pay for his share of the stock. The cattle drive apparently was a success, for the experience "set him going." The following year, 1878, Pettus and Lott started up the trail with 3,800 Longhorns heading for Dodge

City, Kansas. "Three more herds of cattle leave this week for the Kansas Market—one by J. E. Pettus of 1,800 head, one by W. J. Lott of 1,900 head, and the other by D. R. Fant of 2,000 head, besides a large herd of horses of 1,200 head also by D. R. Fant. If a few more thousand of these inferior Mustang ponies were taken off the range it would be a great benefit to the balance of the stock left. Horse stock are selling at six to eight dollars per head when the whole remuda is taken."[14]

Pettus took cattle up the trail each succeeding year until 1882. The trail drives that Pettus made with his men were vivid in his mind even though fifty years had passed:

Speaking of trail drives in general, there is very little difference in them when you've learned all there is to know about 'em. Of course, trouble and worry varied, as it does in every kind of business. But, for the most part, trail drives were of a "whatness." There were banks full, streams to swim and cross over, chuck wagons to fix with poles and ropes, cowboy style, stampedes of longhorns, as wild as the country that bred them. Bucking broncs, and long, hard, drives in scorching, sizzling, heat that rose like waves from a red, hot furnace. And not a drop of water for men or animals. Sand storms that filled mouth, eyes and ear. Choking, binding, cutting and stinging the skin with minute particles that pricked you like a thousand needles. And for contrast, there were blizzards that whipped out of the North, at a moment's notice, carrying sleet and snow that nipped the hides of horses and cattle, lashing them like rawhide whips into a dead run, with every cowboy doing his darnedest to head the leaders or get them into a mill and no time to think of faces frozen in an icy mask, hands so numb they couldn't guide with the bridle reins, feet frozen to the stirrups and all sense of direction muddled up, until nothing was clear, by the force of wind and swirling snow.

Did we ever complain? Sure we did, to ourselves, nobody else. For no matter how rocky it came, we had sense enough to know that nobody was responsible for us running our heads into the same noose year after year. So, we took the medicine the doctor ordered, the bitter with the sweet, cussed a string as long as the best calf rope in the outfit, and said nothing.

Then the other side of the picture was altogether different and as desirable as one could ask, when the sun hung like a big ball of gold reflected in clear water along with the blue sky and piles of white clouds the prairies, as far as eye could see, spread out like green velvet spotted over with every color of wild flower imaginable and thousands of cattle grazing or lying there chewing their cuds. Then, in late evening, when it began to get dark and millions of stars popped out one by one, or the full moon rose bright as day, and the outfit sat cross legged round the campfire swapping yarns, cutting the pigeon wing on the familiar tunes of the day. Times like that a fellow was fascinated with the work he wouldn't quit for anything and when suffering and privation rolled around he was fixed, so he couldn't be so there was no use arguing about it and most of us stayed on and enjoyed whatever was handed out to us.[15]

The last trail drive of Pettus with his crew was to Ogallala, Nebraska, with seven thousand Longhorns—a doubleheader: "It took a long time to drive through, so we decided to double-up and see how it worked. And I'm telling you, we got ourselves plenty of experience before we got that 7,000 head sold. Not a one of us cared about repeating the dose. And it cured my trail fever, sound and well, never did run a temperature after that. But it took five years and a double herd to do it."[16]

It is likely that George McDow was a part of these last cattle drives with Pettus and enjoyed the return trip to Texas. "We almost always sold our saddle horses with the cattle, and we did it this time. Sometimes one of the boys wanted to keep out his ponies and ride back to Texas horseback and of courses that was his privilege but for the most part riding the cushions looked too good to pass up by boys who had all they wanted for a while of sand in their craws and sun in their eyes. The best way to get back to Goliad was by way of Galveston, Indianola and Victoria, and that was the way we took."[17]

There is no evidence of either Pettus or McDow having made another drive up the trail. The entertaining Pettus family oral history is clear that whenever the "nesters" (farmers) made trouble along the trail, George McDow was always the first man willing and ready to volunteer for a fight with them.[18]

NOTES

1. Anne Bode and Patsy Light, "San Antonio River Valley (West of Goliad) Rural Historic District," National Register of Historic Places, Section 8, The Daughters of the Republic of Texas Research Library, San Antonio, p. 212.
2. James Lee Martin, *History of Goliad from 1836–1880* (M.A. thesis, University of Texas at Austin, 1937), p. 57.
3. Pettus-Wallace Papers: 1836–1977. Unpublished. The Daughters of the Republic of Texas Library, San Antonio. The memoirs of Pettus descendants, Mrs. Jesse Pettus-Wallace and her father, James Edward Pettus record the course of McDow's early life and his life on the trail.

4. John C. Reid, *Reid's Tramp or A Journal of the Incidents* (1858; reprint; Austin: Steck Company, 1935), p. 44.
5. Bode and Light, National Register of Historic Places, p. 196.
6. Della Mae McDow Bennett, McDow Family Bible, Corpus Christi, Tex. The two spellings of Lipston and Lipson are as noted in the Bible.
7. "Mrs. Jesse Pettus-Wallace Memoirs," Pettus-Wallace Papers: 1836–1977, The Daughters of the Republic of Texas Research Library, San Antonio.
8. "Population Schedules of the Twelfth Census of the United States, 1900," no. T623, roll 1638, Goliad, Tex. (n.p., National Archives Microfilm Publications).
9. Bode and Light, National Register of Historic Places, p. 199.
10. Della Mae McDow Bennett (daughter of George McDow), interview by Ira Lott, Corpus Christi, Tex., Mar. 8, 1998.
11. "Mrs. Jesse Pettus-Wallace Memoirs," Pettus-Wallace Papers: 1836–1977.
12. Cora Melton Cross, "Stories of the Old Trail Drivers of Long Ago," *Semi-Weekly Farm News of Dallas, Texas,* Aug. 26, 1930, p. 2.
13. Bode and Light, National Register of Historic Places, p. 212.
14. Beth White, *Goliad Remembered, 1836–1940* (Austin: Nortex Press, 1987), p. 46–47.
15. Cross, "Stories of the Old," p. 2.
16. Ibid.
17. White, *Goliad Remembered,* p. 48–49.
18. Anne Bode (granddaughter of James Edward Pettus), interview by Ira Lott, Goliad, Tex., Apr. 13, 1998.

Figure 8. Bose Ikard. Courtesy Mary Kemp, Weatherford, Texas

Chapter 10

Bose Ikard

Splendid Behavior

BRUCE M. SHACKELFORD

The short era of the great cattle drives, from the end of the Civil War in 1865 until the early 1880s, was a time when men could rise above their upbringing and education and, through difficult and dangerous work, gain not only financial fortunes, but the respect of their peers. Hard work and danger overlooked most differences among men except ability, bravery, and a man's dedication to his outfit. Like the brief florescence of the trail drives, after their great adventures on the trail, many of these men faded into obscurity. Bose Ikard was one of these men. Historians have kept for us some stories that include Bose Ikard. Other stories, probably equally as rich, never shall be known.

What is positively known is that Bose was born into slavery in Summerville, Noxubee County, Mississippi.[1] The exact birth date of Bose Ikard is unclear, as three dates appear in various records. The most likely date of his birth is June of 1847.[2] Bose Ikard's mother, named "King," was a slave owned by Dr. Milton Ikard. Legal documents identify his father as "Ikard."[3] "Ikard" was most likely Dr. Milton Ikard, the owner of both Bose and his mother. Portraits of Bose Ikard and his owner Dr. Ikard reveal such a striking resemblance that even descendants of Dr. Ikard believe that Bose's father was the doctor. Charles Goodnight, a friend of the Ikards, was of the same belief.[4]

In July of 1847, in Mississippi, a "legitimate" son was born to Dr. Milton Ikard, William Susan Ikard. With less than a month's difference in their ages, W. S. Ikard and Bose Ikard grew up together; one a legitimate son of the doctor, the other a slave. The two boys left Mississippi with the Ikard family and three other slaves, arriving in Texas in 1852. The slaves brought to Texas with Bose were one man and two mulatto women.[5] The family first settled near Honey Grove, and then the family settled on Grindstone Creek, in Parker

County, approximately nine miles southwest of present-day Weatherford, Texas.[6]

In 1852, Parker County was the edge of Euroamerican settlement in North Texas. Comanche and Kiowa Indian raiders found Parker County and the surrounding counties fertile grounds for their horse-stealing efforts. Confrontations between the hostile neighbors occurred with some regularity.[7] When the Ikard clan arrived in Parker County the family took up the primary enterprise of the area, cattle raising. The Ikards and several of their neighbors would later be known throughout the western cattle industry. One of the neighbors, Charles Goodnight, led Bose Ikard out of slavery and into the history books.

Growing up through the 1850s and 1860s Bose sharpened his skills of herding cattle and riding horses for Dr. Ikard. During the Civil War, W. S. Ikard served with Mason's Company, Texas Cavalry, Texas State Troops, Confederate States of America. Battles took place hundreds of miles from the Ikards' Parker County home, leaving the soldiers of Billy Mason's Company more concerned with Indian raids and marauding white renegades around North Texas than fighting Yankees.[8] After the war the Ikard slaves were free to leave. How many slaves Dr. Ikard held at the end of the war is unclear. After the Ikard family's arrival in Parker County, one of the mulatto women belonging to Dr. Ikard had already been sold for a thousand dollars worth of cattle to a neighboring stockman, Oliver Loving.[9] The transaction started the Ikards in the business of raising cattle. There is no record of whether the woman sold was Bose's mother or someone else. At the close of the war Ikard bestowed the remaining slaves with the surname of "Ikard" as a "gift."[10]

All of the Ikards' slaves remained with the family for some time after the end of the Civil War.[11] Bose worked cattle for the Ikard family with all its frontier dangers. An interview with W. S. Ikard by Texas historian J. Evetts Haley detailed an incident that occurred while Bose was gathering cattle in late 1865 or early 1866:

> After the War Sam Newberry, Bose, and some other white men were out in Parker County working cattle. They had already gathered some cattle and Milton, my brother, was holding them. The other hands were out hunting more cattle and ran onto an Indian trail. It was raining and they took their trail, but on account of the rain they'd lose the trail every little while, but would keep on straight for half a mile or so and would strike it again. They followed it about fifteen miles and came upon the Indians near Rock Creek Bluff. "Milt," my brother, Bose, and Sam Newberry, Delbert Doss, and another fellow or two were the only ones who could keep up with the

Indians. Bose saw they had one of his own horses and yelled, "Oh yes, damn you, you've got my hoss!" They went on chasing them and Delbert Doss was killed. "Milt" held the body across the horse for fifteen miles back.[12]

Dangerous encounters of this sort had been the life of cowboys in Parker County since its settlement and doubtless Bose Ikard participated in other incidents. Bose Ikard's working status with his former master changed in the summer of 1866. On the sixth day of June, 1866, legendary cattleman Charles Goodnight, a neighbor of the Ikards, pointed a herd of cattle west to establish what became known as the Goodnight-Loving Trail. Traveling with Goodnight was Bose Ikard. Bose had been given a letter of recommendation by W. S. Ikard[13] and arrived at the Goodnight trail wagon in the company of Oliver Loving.[14] Goodnight's first journey west was the beginning of Bose Ikard's entry into the history of the cattle industry.

Unlike previous trails established before the Civil War that led north, Goodnight chose to head west, with Colorado as his eventual goal. If the cattle market was down on his arrival he reasoned, he would graze the cattle on good pasture until the market improved. By heading due west to Fort Phantom Hill, then southwest through Buffalo Gap, he avoided trouble in the Indian lands in Oklahoma Territory.[15] Besides Bose Ikard, the notorious "One-armed" Bill Wilson accompanied Goodnight and the fifty-four-year-old Oliver Loving. The joining of the Goodnight and Loving herds made a total of two thousand Longhorn cattle to be driven west.[16]

From the hardships of the first cattle drive Bose Ikard forged a friendship with Charles Goodnight that would last through his lifetime and into death. The rugged trail through the Texas desert made for extreme working conditions for the cattle and the crew. At one point, near Castle Gap, east of the Pecos River, the herd went three days without water.[17] The stretch of the trail near Horsehead Crossing on the Pecos River gained a reputation among trail drivers and cowboys as the worst stretch of trail in Texas. Except for cattle, rattlesnakes were about the only living thing the riders observed along the rugged stretch of the trail.

On the first drive, with all of its difficulties, Goodnight never made it to Colorado. When the cattle and crew reached Fort Sumner, New Mexico, the U.S. Army was paying a good price for steers to feed the Navajo and Mescalero Apache Indians interred at Bosque Redondo. A deal was made for the Goodnight-Loving steers, and Goodnight left, in all likelihood with Bose at his side, to return the seven hundred miles home to Texas. Loving continued on to Colorado with his stock cattle, which he sold in the vicinity of Denver.[18]

The trip up the trail in 1867 was fraught with more difficulties than the first 1866 journey, and it was about this trip that Goodnight later made his first mention of Bose Ikard. After an encounter with Indians that resulted in an arrow in the neck of one of the cowboys, a terrific storm blew up on the Texas plains above the Clear Fork of the Brazos River.[19] Some of the herd stampeded, running around the slowly moving main herd. Strong winds blew, and by one o'clock in the morning all that could be seen through the blackness was electricity glowing on the horses' ears.[20] Bose Ikard, considered one of the best nightriders that ever worked for Goodnight, drifted with the herd through the stormy night. Toward morning, the herd began to settle, and Goodnight headed to camp to wake the cook. At first light the herd again stampeded, heading straight for the camp. Goodnight told the following story to J. Evetts Haley: "By this time it was light enough to see. I kept going up the side of the cattle as fast as possible, wondering why Bose had not turned the front. When I had almost caught up with him, he looked back and saw me, and immediately his horse shot out like lightening [sic] and he threw the leaders around. After we got them circled, I asked him why he had not turned them sooner. 'I tell you, sah,' answered the cautious Bose. 'I wuzn't sartin who had dis herd 'til I saw you. I t'ought maybe de Indians had 'um.'"[21]

Other encounters with trouble continued to plague the trip up the trail. In late July, Oliver Loving left the herd for Santa Fe against Goodnight's wishes, with "One-armed" Bill Wilson along for the ride. Loving's plan was to be on time in Santa Fe for the letting of cattle contracts in early August. Three days from the herd, Loving and Wilson were attacked by Comanches on the Pecos River; Loving received two wounds. The episode, which is now legendary, ended in Loving's death from infection at Fort Sumner a short time later on September 25, 1867. In February of 1868, Loving's body was exhumed from a Fort Sumner grave and hauled the seven hundred miles back to Weatherford, Texas, for final burial. Records are unclear, but Bose Ikard is believed to have been among the cowboys that accompanied Loving's body home.[22]

1869 was the final year on the Goodnight-Loving Trail for Bose Ikard. On the trail he excelled as a bronc rider, a night herder, and, when needed, he cooked meals for the crew. Goodnight returned to the ranch in Colorado, advising Bose to stay in Weatherford and farm. Bose wanted to return with Goodnight to Colorado, but race finally intervened in their relationship. The sparse black population in the Rocky Mountain area led Goodnight to advise Bose against taking up residence in Colorado.[23] Bose Ikard followed Goodnight's advice and took up farming in Parker County. In later years Goodnight would remember his ally on the trail:

. . .

There was a dignity, a cleanliness, and a reliability about him that was wonderful. . . . His behavior was very good in a fight, and he was probably the most devoted man to me that I ever had. I have trusted him farther than any living man. He was my detective, banker, and everything else in Colorado, New Mexico, and the other wild country I was in.

We went through some terrible trials during those four years on the trail. While I had a good constitution and endurance, after being in the saddle for several days and nights at a time, on various occasions, and finding I could stand it no longer, I would ask Bose if he would take my place, and he never failed to answer me in the most cheerful and willing manner, and was the most skilled and trustworthy man I had.[24]

After this time, except for census reports, little factual information is known about Bose Ikard until his death. Eleven years after his adventures on the trail with Goodnight, Bose is listed as a "farmer" in the 1880 U.S. census. In the late 1860s, between trips up the trail, Bose married Angeline. Angeline was born into slavery in Texas on August 19, 1853. They had six children, five of whom survived childhood.[25] Angeline Ikard died May 29, 1902.

The white Ikard child with whom Bose was raised, William Susan Ikard, moved from Parker County to a ranch south of Wichita Falls, Texas, where he became a major influence in the Texas cattle industry. W. S. Ikard was mentioned in cattle industry books and was well known by the most important ranchers in the region. It is argued that W. S. Ikard brought the first purebred Hereford cattle to Texas, and, in fact, he probably did import the first "Royal" stock from England. In later life, W. S. Ikard served as vice president of the North Texas Cattle Raisers Association and vice president of the Henrietta, Texas, National Bank. W. S. Ikard died in 1934 in Henrietta.[26]

Bose lived out his life in obscurity in Weatherford, Texas. His neighbors remembered him in later years as a handyman who did yard work and ran errands.[27] Goodnight sent Bose money from time to time and maintained some contact.[28] Bose Ikard died from influenza at the Seton Infirmary in Austin, Texas, on January 4, 1929.[29] Like his old neighbor Oliver Loving, his body was carried back to Weatherford for final burial. Ikard was buried in the old Greenwood Cemetery in Weatherford.[30] His published obituary tells nothing of his adventurous life as a cowboy on the Goodnight-Loving trail or his role as Charles Goodnight's most trusted friend:

. . .

Bose Ikard, Colored, One of Old-Time Negroes Of City
Buried Here Monday

Bose Ikard, colored, one of the old-time negroes of Weatherford and Parker County, died at Austin, Friday, January 4. The body was shipped to Weatherford, arriving here Sunday, and funeral services and burial took place Monday afternoon. Bose Ikard was well known to nearly all of the older residents of Weatherford where he lived for perhaps fifty years. He was very old, being variously guessed from 85 to 90, by those who knew him. He had been living in Austin but a short time.[31]

Upon learning of Bose's death, Goodnight began plans for erecting a monument with a fitting tribute to his friend. Goodnight contacted T. W. Stanley, superintendent of the Weatherford public schools, to design the granite monument. Rawlins marble yard completed the stone and engraved the epitaph. Goodnight's attention caused a local stir in Weatherford, and on June 8, 1929, the Weatherford newspaper published a proper obituary for Bose Ikard under the headline, "CHAS. GOODNIGHT ERECTS MONUMENT TO NEGRO FRIEND BURIED HERE."[32] The epitaph from the marker was published in the newspaper as follows:

Served with me four years on the Goodnight-Loving Trail, never shirked duty or disobeyed an order, rode with me in many stampedes, participated in three engagements with Comanches, splendid behavior.
—C. Goodnight

NOTES

1. W. S. Ikard, "Bose Ikard," interview by J. Evetts Haley, Jan. 26, 1932, J. Evetts Haley Collection, Nita Stewart Haley Memorial Library, Midland, Tex.
2. W. S. Ikard interview; U.S. Census, Parker County, 1880, nos. 387, 396 (Washington, D.C.: GPO). The year of Bose Ikard's birth is in some dispute although the month of June is fairly consistent. By subtracting Bose's age (thirty-seven) given in an 1880 Census of Parker County, 1843 is calculated as his year of birth, although this year is not given in the census. His Texas death certificate lists Ikard's birthday as June 5, 1854. A number of sources cite the Ikard family as arriving in Texas in 1852, making the 1854 birth year incorrect. The most-often cited birth date, and the one cited in this chapter, comes from an interview with W. S. Ikard conducted by J. Evetts Haley on January 26, 1932, in which W. S. Ikard states, "Bose Ikard, the

nigger slave, was born in June 1847. I remember the date as I was born on July 7th of the same year."

3. Standard Certificate of Death, Rep. No. 5569, 7231, Texas State Department of Health, Bureau of Vital Statistics, Austin, Texas.

4. Kent Biffle, "Ikard Reunion Marked By an Odd Twist," *The Dallas Morning News,* Sun., Oct. 21, 1990.

5. Mrs. Lynn Boyd, "Sketch Of Lineage and History of Dr. Milton Ikard and His Sons," Ikard Surname File, Genealogy Department, Weatherford Public Library, Weatherford, Tex.; Doctor Milton Ikard, a "hydropathec doctor," was born in 1812 in Franklin County, Tennessee. He also taught school when he arrived in Honey Grove, Texas.

6. Ibid.; J. Evetts Haley, *Charles Goodnight: Cowman and Plainsman* (Norman: University of Oklahoma Press, 1949), p. 242.

7. Doyle Marshall, *A Cry Unheard: The Story of Indian Attacks In and Around Parker County, Texas 1858–1872* (n.p.: Annetta Valley Farm Press, 1990), p. 75.

8. Confederate Pension, File No. 50238, Clay County, Tex., Texas State Archives, Austin.

9. W. S. Ikard interview; W. S. Ikard interview in "The Ikards In Texas," Ikard Surname File, Genealogy Department, Weatherford Public Library, Weatherford, Tex.

10. Karen Ikard Ferguson, letter, Sept. 21, 1994, Ikard Surname File, Genealogy Department, Weatherford Public Library, Weatherford, Tex.

11. W. S. Ikard interview.

12. Ibid.

13. Ikard Smith, "The Real Lonesome Dove or Truth Can Be Stranger Than Fiction" (Fort Worth: The Cattle Raisers Museum, n.d., photocopy), p. 5.

14. Haley, *Charles Goodnight,* p. 242.

15. Ibid., p. 127.

16. Ibid., pp. 127–28.

17. Ibid., pp. 130–31.

18. Ibid., pp. 139–40.

19. The area discussed is northeast of present-day Abilene, Texas.

20. Haley, *Charles Goodnight,* pp. 166–67.

21. Ibid.

22. Ibid., pp. 170–80.

23. Ibid., p. 242.

24. Ibid.; "Chas. Goodnight Erects Monument to Negro Friend Buried Here," *The* (Weatherford) *Daily Herald,* June 8, 1929.

25. Mary Kemp, "Bose Ikard (1843–1929)," application for Texas Historical Marker, Bose Ikard File, J. Evetts Haley Collection, Nita Stewart Haley Memorial Library, Midland, Tex.

26. Ikard Smith, "The Real Lonesome Dove," p. 5; "W. S. Ikard," in *Historical and Biographical Record of the Cattle Industry and the Cattlemen of Texas and Adjacent Territory*, (1895; reprint, New York: Antiquarian Press, Ltd., 1959).

27. Mary Kemp, interview by Bruce Shackelford, Weatherford, Tex., May 4, 1998.

28. Ikard Smith, "The Real Lonesome Dove," p. 15.

29. Certificate of Death, Rep. No. 5569, 7231, Texas State Department of Health, Bureau of Vital Statistics, Austin.

30. Mary Kemp, "Bose Ikard (1843–1929)," application for Texas Historical Marker.

31. "Bose Ikard, Colored, One of Old-Time Negroes of City Buried Here Monday," *The* (Weatherford) *Daily Herald*, Jan. 7, 1929.

32. "Chas. Goodnight Erects Monument to Negro Friend Buried Here," *The* (Weatherford) *Daily Herald*, June 8, 1929.

Figure 9. James Kelly. Courtesy Paul W. Stewart, Denver, Colorado

Chapter 11

James Kelly

The Ebony Gun

JAMES SMALLWOOD

Although they are not usually mentioned in American history textbooks, African Americans made up about twenty-five percent of the cowboys who rode the western ranges of the "cattle kingdom" that blossomed in the latter nineteenth century. The following is the story of one of those "invisible" cowboys who worked for the infamous Print Olive clan of Texas, who became one of the family's trail bosses, and who served as one of their gunmen. He also functioned as one of their regulators whenever the Olives believed that certain enemies deserved extralegal justice.[1]

Born in Williamson County, Texas, circa 1839, James "Jim" Kelly was the son of free blacks—former slaves who had been manumitted upon the death of their master. "Uncle Amos" and "Aunt Phoebe" Kelly both had worked with the Olive family.[2] Little is known about Jim Kelly's early life except that he grew up on James Olive's Williamson County ranch and was, in fact, named after Olive. After he reached his teenage years, young Kelly worked on the ranch, trailing cattle and breaking horses; he was called peerless in his ability to train horses. In the late 1850s he went to West Texas to escape the secessionist crisis and the growing white hostility toward black people, free or slave. After riding the range for a rancher there, when the Civil War ended, he returned to the Olive's cattle empire, where he again became a wrangler, horse breaker, and trainer. Again it was said, around the county, that the Olives had the best horses in the area because James's skills were so sharp. In addition to working with horses and cattle, he rekindled his friendship with young Isom Prentice "Print" Olive, who would soon take over his father's ranch.[3]

As a grown man, James Kelly was quite an imposing figure. Slim and ruggedly handsome, he stood six feet six inches tall. Besides his skills as a cowboy,

143

he had learned to be most proficient with weapons, whether they be hand-guns, rifles, or shotguns. So, "gunslinger" could be added to James's list of vocations, and he used his gun on various occasions to help members of the Olive clan. Observers noted that Kelly was not an "Uncle Tom" or a "Sambo." Rather, he took pride in being who he was, and he looked at all men, black or white, as equals.[4]

By the time James returned to the Olive Ranch in Williamson County, rustling had become common and was a serious problem for the Olives. Every steer that disappeared was lost money for the family. Print Olive, his brothers, Kelly, and other cowboys sometimes traded shots with thieves whenever they were seen. On one occasion Print and an alleged rustler, Dave Fream, fought a duel on horseback, one in which Print killed the thief but was in turn se-verely wounded.[5] Problems finally became so severe that the Olive bunch be-came a "gun outfit," according to E. C. "Teddy Blue" Abbott who worked for the family for a time. Kelly's gunslinging skills made him the top enforcer or regulator for the Olives. Under his supervision, all the ranch hands began wearing arms and were told to use them first and ask questions later if they came upon strangers near Olive cattle. Men who did not have experience with weapons turned to Kelly for their training. The Olive clan became a "tough outfit," according to Abbott, who added that the Olive brothers "were violent and overbearing men." They had "black eyes just like a rattlesnake's and a temper to match." Abbott met Kelly and other Olive cowhands and summed them up thus, "[I]t takes a hard man to work for them, and believe me, they had several of those all the time."[6]

In one 1876 incident, authorities in Lee County, adjacent to Williamson, found two dead men, known only as Turner and Crow, wrapped in cow hides, this being a clear signal that rustlers in the area would not be tolerated. The "death of the skins" was an old Spanish method of torture. Turner and Crow were staked out and wrapped in green cowhides carrying the Olive brand. The hides contracted before the rays of the sun, and both men died only after suffering excruciating pain. Most likely, Kelly helped Print Olive and his broth-ers dispatch the two thieves.[7]

By the time of the cowhide killings, the long drives were underway. Texas cattlemen would round up their cattle and make the trek north to the nearest railhead. The first long drives went over the Sedalia Trail to Sedalia, Missouri, in 1865. Then as the railroads pushed farther west, new trails were cut, and eventually the herds could be driven—through open country all the way—to railheads in Kansas and other points westward.[8]

In 1866, Print Olive, along with wrangler Kelly, and Print's brothers—

Thomas, Ira, and Bob—managed a roundup for the entire Williamson area and drove several thousand head northeastward to Sedalia. Jim Kelly served as one of several trail bosses on the drive. By wisely investing his money and continuing to make the long drives for yet more profits, Print soon had one of the largest spreads in Texas. Notably, the spring, 1869, drive took him, Kelly, and two thousand head (eight hundred were Print's own) to Fort Kearny, Nebraska. After delivering at the fort, Olive and Kelly drove a herd of young steers from Dobytown to a range in Central Nebraska, north of the Platte River. Olive and Kelly were impressed with the lush range where blue stem grasses grew as tall as the withers on their saddle horses. One day Print and Jim would return. Meanwhile, the two men headed south, back to Williamson County, their saddlebags stuffed with gold coins and paper currency.[9] A later drive in 1871, to Abilene, Kansas, was also noteworthy. After selling Olive cattle, Print and Jim returned home with $50,000.[10]

The 1872 drive to Ellsworth, Kansas, was memorable for both Print Olive and Jim Kelly. On May 28, Print turned out a big steer herd from his pens and marched them up the Chisholm Trail. Jim went along, serving as a trail boss and as a wrangler. Trouble developed almost immediately. There were stampedes every night for a week.[11] Then, a gunfight almost developed at camp one night when "Bushy" McGuire, a new man who rode right swing, made one too many racist remarks to Jim, after Kelly had criticized him for allowing some of the saddle stock in the *remuda* to stray. After listening to quite enough talk, Kelly pulled his .44, cocked the hammer, and stuck it right under Bushy's nose. Jim softly said, "[I]f Mr. Print does not say take it down, I'm going to blow your head off your shoulders." Print said "take it down" just in the nick of time.[12] Bushy would live another day—but not much longer—because yet more travail developed.

After Olive's herd crossed Deer Creek and entered Kansas from the Cherokee Outlet in Indian Territory, the men made a stop at C. H. Stone's log cabin supply store. Nearby, a dozen sod homes were clustered in an area that would eventually become Caldwell, Kansas. First, Print and Jim were forced to deal with one of their young riders, a boy who had "discovered" the Gold Nugget, a bawdy house, and a seventeen-year-old beauty inside. Even with Kelly's help, Print still had trouble dragging the boy away from his new love and back to camp. Then, Olive and Kelly had to deal with Bushy McGuire again.[13] The hotheaded McGuire, most likely drunk, forced a gunfight on another Print man, Gene Lyons, who calmly pulled a revolver and killed the young hotspur. Riding up to the spot of the killing, Jim—on his favorite horse, Chowder, a bald-faced black sorrel—was heard to mutter, "he (Bushy) sure picked the wrong man (to fight with) this time."[14] Jim and others could only bury the body and hope Lyons would be spared by the law, for he had killed Bushy in self-defense.

Subsequently, the McGuire episode was resolved by a Caldwell judge, who did indeed rule self-defense and set Lyons free. Print, Jim, Lyons, and the other men drove the herd onward without further incident. The herd crossed the three forks of the Nenescah River, Antelope Creek, Indian Run, Rattlesnake Creek, and the big Arkansas River; thence, the cowboys headed the herd straight north and soon reached Ellsworth, Kansas, where new troubles awaited. On July 3, 1872, after selling his herd of three thousand head and making a $45,000 profit, Print headed for a saloon where he joined a poker game.[15]

To ensure the peace, the barkeep made all men turn in their weapons, including all guns and knives, to be stored on a back-bar. Excitement developed when James Kennedy, a card cheating gambler, accused Print Olive of doing exactly what he (Kennedy) was doing—namely dealing seconds and dealing from the bottom of the deck. Olive's vocal hostility drove Kennedy, who was making verbal threats, out of the saloon. The next night, Print was at the crowded tables again. Unnoticed, Kennedy entered, slipped through the throng, went to the back-bar, grabbed a revolver, and started firing at the leader of the Olive clan. The first shot hit Print in the hand, the second in his groin, and the third in one of his thighs. Kennedy was preparing to fire a fourth round point-blank to kill his quarry when, as providence had it, Jim Kelly came to Print's rescue.[16]

Before Kennedy's attack, Jim and a vaquero friend walked by the front door of the saloon. Seeing Print playing cards, the two men decided to stop, take chairs, and watch the townspeople in their comings and goings. Then, Kelly heard Kennedy's rapid firing. Still sitting down, Jim swiveled his head, saw what was happening, quickly drew his own gun, and fired through the open window, his shot hitting Kennedy in the thigh. While other men took custody of the gambler and disarmed him, Jim ran to his friend, who was grievously wounded but destined to survive. Kelly had saved Print's life and stayed with him in Ellsworth to help nurse him back to health while the other Olive men headed home. When Print was well enough to move around, the two men boarded a train and headed south, going back to the Olive family ranch.[17]

As Print recovered, both he and Kelly noted that, by the 1870s, Texas was changing—and not for the better according to the cowmen. The free range was now passing from the scene, and rustlers were ever present. The Olive clan believed in swift justice; they sometimes took the law into their own hands. Consequently, legal troubles continued to dog the family.[18] After a series of outrageous events, several bizarre killings, and uproarious court cases, Print decided to move the clan northward and establish a new ranch. Print chose Colorado as a site for a new spread, but area cattlemen knew about the Olive men's run-ins with the law and would not accept them.[19]

Print then set his sights on the Loup River country in Central Nebraska, an area he had seen on an earlier long drive.[20] Later, in February of 1877, the area was organized and became Custer County. Located on the South Loup River, Custer City became the new county seat; it was about twenty-eight miles north of Plum Creek, which sat astride the Union Pacific Railroad. The area that Print had selected had ample water and lush grasses for stock, in addition to being close to a railhead. Further, Custer became a thriving town as a supply depot for the cattle "barons." Soon, the Olive men helped make stockraising the leading industry of the area, and Print personally became the richest man in the new county and one of the wealthiest in the entire state.[21]

To establish a new "empire," in 1876, Kelly and others helped Print drive fifteen thousand head of cattle to the Loup River and Corral Canyon area, where Print was prepared to claim range. Kelly then began exploring the new range while other men began building shelters and pens. Print's brother Bob, who in an effort to elude Texas lawmen had changed his last name to Stevens, arrived in the Corral Canyon area later, and Kelly met him at the Union Pacific's station in Plum City. Print left word for Bob to join Kelly scouting the area. After provisioning themselves at Ogallala, Bob and Kelly, each leading a pack horse, began their explorations. Six days out of Ogallala, the pair came across an unclaimed range in the sand hills area of Central Nebraska. They also encountered a band of Sioux, whose women and children followed the warriors. Both cowboys placed their hands near their Winchesters as the Sioux party rode on without incident.[22]

Their scouting completed, Bob "Stevens" and Jim stopped at Plum Creek, a small village. Bob went to sign into the town's hotel and sent Kelly to the saloon to buy whiskey. (Bob could cope with his "stomach problems," but only if he had his nightly drinks). Kelly walked into the saloon, stopping at the end of the bar. He asked proprietor Bill Green, "a big ruddy-faced Irishman," for a bottle of bourbon. Green continued to serve his other customers but ignored Kelly, all the while making racial epithets about "colored cowpunchers." After hearing a bit more of such talk, Jim got Green's attention. He put his hand on his revolver, and averred, "I come here to buy a bottle of whiskey, not to be made the fool by a bartender . . . pass me a quart of that bourbon and I'll be peacefully on my way." In the dead silence that followed, Green decided that he had better, indeed, hand a bottle to the black gunslinger. Watching Kelly leave, another Texas cowboy told Green, "That's Nigger Jim, Print Olive's bad nigger. Pay you to treat him right or leave him alone."[23]

After Print arrived in Custer County, the Olive spread, eventually to number thirty-one thousand beeves and several thousand horses feasting on lush grasses, quickly became the largest in the region.[24] To help police the range against rustlers, area ranchers formed the Custer County Livestock Association, electing Print as its first president. Jim became, naturally, the association's chief enforcer.[25] Speaking of Kelly, E. C. "Teddy Blue" Abbott, who rode with the Olives into Nebraska, said that Jim was quite a character. He added that people "called him Olive's bad nigger, because he was a gunman and fighter." Continuing, Abbott also noted that the Olives often sent Jim ahead to "talk turkey" to settlers who established homesteads not with intentions of working them but with plans to charge the trail herds that crossed their land big fees for water. Abbott added, "that big black boy with his gun would sure tell them punkin rollers (farmers) where to head in at. He'd roll up his eyes like a duck in a thunderstorm and grit his teeth . . . (and) most of the settlers were poor northern folks that had never seen many niggers and was scared of them." Abbott concluded, saying, "when they saw Kelly they would come down quick enough from twenty dollars to five dollars as the price for watering the herd."[26]

Unfortunately, the Olive bunch, Kelly included, did not just terrorize "shady" homesteaders who only wanted to control the water rights. As more and more farmers moved into the area, they all became "fair game" as a confused situation developed. Many new farmers, who claimed 160 acres under the 1862 Homestead Act, had no fencing materials, so they plowed a furrow around their holdings. Legally, the furrow was the same as a barbed-wire fence. Cattle barons knew that, but their cattle did not. The stock would wander at will over boundary furrows; to protect their holdings, some farmers shot and killed such wanderers. The minute they were able to obtain barbed wire, real fences would go up.[27]

Whenever Olive cattle were killed or when they were bloodied by barbed wire, the clan—led by Kelly—would strike back. They purposely drove cattle across boundary furrows and dared farmers to fight. They cut any fences that were erected. They burned farmers' crops. In general, they terrorized the "sodbusters." In Custer and Plum City, verbal confrontations between area farmers and Kelly (and his boss Print) became frequent. There would be no compromise by Print Olive. Either the cattlemen or the farmers would dominate the region, and Print intended the issue to be settled in favor of the cowmen.[28]

The struggle between cattle barons and "sodbusters" was compounded by a general lack of real law enforcement in the West that became the haunt of all manner of malefactors. Robbers, murderers, gamblers, and renegade Indians all created a situation where, as one writer noted, there was "no law west of Kansas City [and] no God west of Fort Scott."[29]

Given the tensions between the Olives and area farmers, trouble was not long in finding Print and his right "arm," James Kelly. In 1878, problems developed between the Olives and two local homesteaders, Ami W. Ketchum and Luther Mitchell, whom the Olives charged with killing some of their cattle that had strayed over a furrow boundary. Print and Bob ("Stevens") Olive also charged that the two sodbusters were stealing Olive cattle. Ketchum and Mitchell countered by saying that the Texans were trying to force farmers and smaller ranchers from the range in Custer County. The aforementioned "Teddy Blue" Abbott, while working for the Olives, charged that Ketchum and Mitchell were stealing and butchering Olive cattle and selling the sides as elk meat. In addition, county authorities had recently arrested a man named Manley for cattle rustling, and in his confession he implicated Ketchum. Further, a man named McIndeffer, who acted as a spy for area ranchers, also swore that Ketchum was a thief. Regardless of any facts, regardless of whether Manley and McIndeffer could be believed, Ketchum was finally branded as a rustler by Buffalo County Sheriff Dave Anderson, who deputized Bob "Stevens" to bring Ketchum and Mitchell in to stand trial. To ensure swift justice, Print placed a $700 reward for bringing in the pair just in case his brother's posse could not find them. Once at the Ketchum place, Bob and his posse of three became involved in a gunfight, during which Mitchell shot Bob, who, as a result, died a short time later.[30]

The surviving posse members arrested Ketchum and Mitchell at the Ketchum place, put them in irons, threw them into a wagon, and began the trip back to Plum Creek. The wagon was intercepted by another posse led by Print Olive, his "right hand" James Kelly, and Green, the barkeep of the town's saloon. In all, there were seven men in the party. After talking to the two prisoners and getting nothing but ill-mannered remarks, Print shot Ketchum in the side, knocked him out of the wagon, and said, "Swing 'em." Both men were hanged from a lone elm tree not too far from Plum Creek. Later, after both prisoners were dead, two Plum Creek men accidentally set the bodies on fire, the act later blamed, erroneously, on Print, who had already left the scene before the bodies were burned.[31] Later, when a local newspaper ran a story accusing the Olive men of "heinous" murder, Print, with Kelly at his side, went from saloon to saloon in Plum Creek, saying that "there weren't enough men in the whole goddam state of Nebraska to take him."[32]

Although Print, Kelly, and others were later arrested, eventually taken to Hastings, and tried for manslaughter, charges were dismissed against Jim and several other men. They were freed perhaps because the jury was intimidated by area ranchers and their retainers or because Kelly and some others did not participate directly in the lynchings. However, in February of 1879, Print and Frederick Fisher were convicted of murder, sentenced to life, and taken to the Nebraska State Penitentiary.[33] There, Kelly and several of the Olive clan frequently visited Print whenever they could free themselves from their cattle and horse herds.

In 1879, Jim returned to the Olive family ranch in Texas and reported to Ira Olive, who was planning a new drive. With Ira as the head trail boss and Kelly as one of the other bosses, the cowboys rounded up a big herd of cattle and a horse herd seven thousand strong. Along the way, trouble developed between Kelly and Ira. One day, Ira began haranguing Kelly about some problem. While "cussing" the black cowboy, Ira pulled his rifle from the scabbard on his horse and hit Jim across the mouth with it. Kelly lost two front teeth, but, out of respect for other members of the Olive family, Jim did not retaliate. He was passive in the face of Ira's hostility. Cowhand "Teddy Blue" Abbott, still a teenager, intervened, telling Ira, "if you hit that boy again, I [will] shoot [your] damn eyes out."[34] Abbott said that Ira knew he was wrong for hitting the faithful Jim, and that Ira put the gun back in the scabbard, spurred his horse, and rode away, intending to check on another part of the herd. The drive to Loup River country then continued without further violence. Jim could have sought revenge later and most likely could have killed Ira, but the black cowboy's feelings for Print and the memory of his namesake James Olive were too strong to harm any member of his family.[35]

Meanwhile, Print and Fisher languished in prison, but finally, within a year, the two men faced an appeals court wherein the presiding judge ordered a new trial, because they should have been, but were not, tried in Custer County where the murders were committed. When the new trial convened, surprisingly no witnesses came forward to testify against Olive and Fisher; therefore, the charges against them were dismissed.[36] Freed, Print went back to his ranch and worked the next area roundup along side his friend, Jim Kelly, who was not too many years away from retirement.[37]

When Kelly decided to retire from the range is not known. He may have retired shortly after the Olives' roundup of 1880; alternately, he may have lasted until the hard winters of the mid-1880s and the decline of the cattle market. Either way, information about the last years of Jim's life are lost in the past, for no sources exist that provide detailed information. It is known that he spent his last years in Ansley, Nebraska. In February of 1912, he died at the age of seventy-three and was buried in the town's cemetery.[38]

NOTES

1. For a survey of black cowboys see Philip Durham and Everett L. Jones, *The Negro Cowboys* (New York: Dodd, Mead and Company, 1965); Philip Durham and Everett L. Jones, *The Adventures of the New Cowboys* (New York: Bantam Books, 1969); William Katz, *The Black West: A Documentary and Pictorial History*, rev. ed. (Garden City, N.Y.: Doubleday Anchor, 1973); and Paul W. Stewart and Wallace Yvonne Ponce, *Black Cowboys* (Broomfield, Colo.: Phillips, 1986). For a survey of the black experience in Texas, see Alwyn Barr, *The Negroes in Texas* (2nd ed.; Boston: American Press, 1996). A useful bibliography of blacks in the West can be found in Bruce A. Galsrud, comp., and Sharon Smith-Savage, ed., *African Americans in the West: A Bibliography of Secondary Sources* (Alpine, Tex.: University Center for Big Bend Studies, Sul Ross State University, 1998).

    A selection of articles that go into some depth on the general story of black cowboys include Kenneth W. Porter, "Negro Labor in the Western Cattle Industry, 1866–1900," *Labor History* 10 (summer, 1969): 346–74; W. Sherman Savage, "The Negro Cowboys on the Texas Plains," *Negro History Bulletin* 24 (Apr., 1961): 157–58, 163; W. Sherman Savage, "Negroes on the Cattlemen's Frontier," *Midwest Journal* 6 (1954–55): 35–48; Harold Preece, "American Negro Cowboys," *Real West* 9 (Jan., 1966): 26–30; Barbara J. Richardson, "Black Cowboys Also Rode," *Password* 31 (spring, 1986): 29–34, 41; La Vere Anderson, "The Cowboys," in *Saddles and Sabers: Black Men in the Old West* (Champaign, Ill.: Garrard, 1975); Gale Gill, "Texas Trail Ride: Negro Cowboys," *Ebony* 18 (May, 1963): 115–22, 124; Jack Lowry, "The Forgotten Cowboys," *Texas Highways* 38 (Aug., 1991): 4–11.

2. Stewart and Ponce, *Black Cowboys*, p. 4; Harry E. Chrisman, *The Ladder of Rivers: The Story of I. P. (Print) Olive* (Denver: Sage Books, 1962), pp. 34–35, 313; Dan L. Thrapp, *Encyclopedia of Frontier Biography*, vol. 2 of 2 (Glendale, Calif.: Arthur Clark Company, 1988), p. 768. Although primary and secondary sources that mention Kelly are sparse, it is possible to find bits of information here and there.

3. Stewart and Ponce, *Black Cowboys*, p. 4; Chrisman, *Ladder of Rivers*, pp. 35, 77. The noted J. Marvin Hunter, *The Trail Drivers of Texas* (1925, reprint; Austin: University of Texas Press, 1985), contains only one reference to the Olive family and none to Jim Kelly.

4. Steward and Ponce, *Black Cowboys*, p. 4; Chrisman, *Ladder of Rivers*, p. 77.

5. Thrapp, *Frontier Biography*, vol. 2, p. 1080.

6. Edward Charles "Teddy Blue" Abbott and Helena Huntington Smith, *We Pointed Them North: Recollections of a Cowpuncher* (1939; reprint, Norman: University of

Oklahoma Press, 1955), p. 32; and see Thrapp, *Frontier Biography,* vol. 2, pp. 768, 1080.

7. Robin Dutton, "Isom Print Olive (1840–1886)," in Ron Tyler, ed., *New Handbook of Texas History,* vol. 4 (Austin: University of Texas Press for the Texas State Historical Association, 1996) p. 1145; Richard W. Slatta, *The Cowboy Encyclopedia* (New York: W. W. Norton & Company, 1994), p. 266.

8. For comments about both the Sedalia Trail and the Chisholm Trail, see W. P. Anderson to Luther A. Lawhon, n.d., in Hunter, *Trail Drivers of Texas,* pp. 13–15. For the Chisholm Trail, see C. H. Rust to Lawhon, n.d., ibid., pp. 37–41, and George W. Saunders to Lawhon, n.d., ibid., pp. 959–71.

9. Dutton, "Print Olive," in *Handbook of Texas,* pp. 1145–46; Chrisman, *Ladder of Rivers,* p. 93.

10. Thrapp, *Frontier Biography,* vol. 2, p. 1080.

11. Chrisman, *Ladder of Rivers,* pp. 102–104.

12. Ibid., p. 104. Author Chrisman and others have created a dialect and used it in quotes. I have rejected that practice and have tried to use proper English.

13. Ibid., pp. 102–104, 113.

14. Ibid., pp. 114.

15. Ibid., pp. 117–22; Stewart and Ponce, *Black Cowboys,* p. 4.

16. Thrapp, *Frontier Biography,* vol. 2, p. 768; Chrisman, *Ladder of Rivers,* p. 122; Stewart and Ponce, *Black Cowboys,* p. 4.

17. Chrisman, *Ladder of Rivers,* pp. 122–24; Stewart and Ponce, *Black Cowboys,* p. 4.

18. See *Austin Statesman,* Mar. 30, 1876, for a contemporary report about area rustlers, shoot-outs, and killings; Chrisman, *Ladder of Rivers,* pp. 124–46; Dutton, "Print Olive," *Handbook of Texas,* vol. 4, pp. 1145–46.

19. Dutton, "Print Olive," *Handbook of Texas,* pp. 1144–46; Chrisman, *Ladder of Rivers,* pp. 129–43.

20. Dutton, "Print Olive," *Handbook of Texas,* pp. 1145–46; Chrisman, *Ladder of Rivers,* pp. 146–96; James C. Olson, *History of Nebraska* (Lincoln: University of Nebraska Press, 1955), p. 199.

21. Harrison Johnson, *Johnson's History of Nebraska* (Omaha: H. Gibson, 1880), pp. 273–74.

22. Chrisman, *Ladder of Rivers,* pp. 190–93; Stewart and Ponce, *Black Cowboys,* p. 4.

23. Chrisman, *Ladder of Rivers,* p. 196.

24. S. D. Butcher, *Pioneer History of Custer County [Nebraska]* (Broken Bow, Nebr.: Privately printed, 1901), pp. 42–44; A. O. Jenkins, *Olive's Last Round-Up* (Loup City, Nebr.: Privately printed, 1930), passim; David Dary, *Cowboy Culture: A Saga of Five Centuries* (New York: Alfred A. Knopf, 1981), pp. 320.

25. Dutton, "Print Olive," in *Handbook of Texas,* vol. 4, pp. 1145–46; Thrapp, *Frontier Encyclopedia,* p. 1080.

26. Abbott and Smith, *We Pointed Them North,* p. 34.

27. Dary, *Cowboy Culture,* pp. 319–20.

28. Ibid., p. 320.

29. A short, convenient summary of lawlessness in some areas of the "Cattle Kingdom" and the conflicts between ranchers and homesteaders can be found in Alan Swallow, ed., *The Wild Bunch* (Denver: Sage Books, 1966), p. 13–28.

30. Abbott and Smith, *We Pointed Them North*, p. 34; Butcher, *Custer County*, pp. 42–44; Dutton, "Print Olive," *Handbook of Texas*, vol. 4, pp. 1145–46; Thrapp, *Frontier Encyclopedia*, p. 1080; Chrisman, *Ladder of Rivers*, pp. 234–39; Dary, *Cowboy Culture*, p. 320; Everett Dick, *The Sod-House Frontier, 1854–1890: A Social History of The Northern Plains from the Creation of Kansas & Nebraska to the Admission of the Dakotas* (New York: D. Appleton–Century Company, 1943), p. 152.

31. (Lincoln) *Nebraska State Journal*, Jan. 30, 1879; Chrisman, *Ladder of Rivers*, pp. 224, 248–54; Dutton, "Print Olive," *New Handbook of Texas*, vol. 4, pp. 1145–46; Abbott and Smith, *We Pointed Them North*, pp. 34–35; Dary, *Cowboy Culture*, p. 320. The bodies may have been set afire on purpose, see Butcher, *Custer County*, p. 51.

32. Mari Sandoz, *The Cattlemen: From the Rio Grande across the Far Marias* (1958, reprint; Lincoln: University of Nebraska Press, 1978), p. 228; and see Durham and Jones, *Negro Cowboys*, pp. 82–83.

33. Dick, *Sod-House Frontier*, p. 152.

34. Abbott and Smith, *We Pointed Them North*, p. 33.

35. Ibid.

36. Butcher, *Custer County*, pp. 61–62; Dary, *Cowboy Culture*, p. 320; Chrisman, *Ladder of Rivers*, pp. 86, 408; Dutton, "Print Olive," *New Handbook of Texas*, vol. 4, pp. 1145–46; Dick, *Sod-House Frontier*, p. 152.

37. Chrisman, *Ladder of Rivers*, p. 309; Thrapp, *Frontier Biography*, vol. 2, p. 768; Butcher, *Custer County*, pp. 61–62. Stewart and Ponce, *Black Cowboys*, p. 5. Print Olive moved his operations to Dodge City, Kansas, in the early 1880s and again in 1885, this time to start a spread near Trail City, Colorado. Diversifying, he built stables, started a wagon yard, and opened a saloon in the new cow town of Trail City. In 1886, while arguing about a $10 debt over a livery bill, Joseph J. Sparrow— Print's one-time trail boss—shot and killed Olive. For Print's death, see Jenkins, *Olive's Last Round-Up*; Abbott and Smith, *We Pointed Them North*, p. 35; and Slatta, *Cowboy Encyclopedia*, p. 266.

38. Chrisman, *Ladder of Rivers*, p. 217; Thrapp, *Frontier Biography*, vol. 2, p. 768; Stewart and Ponce, *Black Cowboys*, p. 5.

Chapter 12

Bill "Tige" Avery

"Rare Back There, Boy, Rare Back"

LAWRENCE CLAYTON

One of the most competent and colorful cowboys of the Texas ranges was Bill "Tige" Avery, who worked most of his life for J. A. Matthews and later Joe B. Matthews of Shackelford County. The Matthews family was among the first whites to enter that area in the 1850s, and they soon controlled huge stretches of rolling ranch land around what is today Albany. J. A. Matthews established a partnership using the MO Brand and later divided the property. He took control of what became known as the Lambshead Ranch, a viable working ranch run by his youngest son, Watkins Reynolds Matthews, until 1997, when Watt died at ninety-eight years of age. Family members still operate the ranch. Most of Avery's life was spent in the ranch country north of Albany, or in other associations with the Matthews family, from sometime in the 1880s until his death in 1935.

How the name "Tige," probably short for "Tiger," came to be Avery's nickname is unknown, and where he came from is unclear. It is known that this ex-slave was a thoroughly competent cowboy who held his own in what was largely, in this region at least, a white man's world. Watt Matthews, who as a child knew Avery, recalled that Avery was about five feet eight inches in height and was of medium build.[1] Avery said he was the same age as J. A. Matthews, Watt's father, who was born in 1853. No one, including Tige, knew for sure.

Tige had extensive experience working with cattle and made several trips up the trail with the herds. Although the drives to Kansas ended in the 1880s with the expansion of the railroad system into Texas, ranchers continued to drive their cattle to the northern ranges to establish herds of breeding stock and to fatten steers on the rich northern grasses. Driving the herds was cheaper than shipping the animals by rail.

How many trips Avery made is not recorded, but undoubtedly one of the most memorable experiences occurred in 1881 when he made a drive to the Indian agencies of Montana. John Hendrix recounted that on this trip a late blizzard caught the herd along the Platte River in Nebraska. When the temperature hit zero, the boss of the herd ordered the men to let the herd drift and for the men to go to the wagon. The men crawled into their bedrolls in an effort to avoid freezing, but Tige spread his roll over the boss, a young but unidentified member of the Reynolds family. Tige stated his intention of finding shelter in the wagon. The young boss, instead, insisted that Tige get in the roll with him, and they survived. Unfortunately, the horses all died. Another trail crew that had pitched camp in a sheltered draw shared their horses, many of which survived because of the shelter. After the crews gathered the cattle that had drifted south before the storm, the drive continued.[2]

Another challenging drive with more freezing weather occurred in 1892. Tige accompanied Phin Reynolds and a group of cowboys driving over four thousand head of cattle to the Reynolds Cattle Company Ranch in the Dakota Territory. The cattle had been wintered on ranges belonging to Charles Goodnight near the town named for the old-time cattleman. They crossed the Canadian River about fifteen miles above Adobe Walls, a famous Panhandle landmark. They went on to cross the Arkansas River at Lamar and then drove past Chevington on the Union Pacific Railroad line. By the end of May these two herds, one under the direction of Tot Richards of Throckmorton and the other with Tom Matthews of Albany, were driving through southern Colorado. In close proximity were four additional herds of cattle belonging to the famous XIT Ranch of the Texas Panhandle. Just after dark on June 1, about twenty-five miles north of Hugo, Colorado, a devastating snowstorm hit the herds and scattered the cattle, mixing the six herds into one enormous herd of almost fifteen thousand wild and frightened animals. The cattle drifted more than twenty-five miles in front of the strong north winds. Only the drift fences on the Union Pacific Railroad right-of-way stopped them. Even more devastating was the dangerously cold weather and wind for the men, who gathered at the wagons and bedded down together under tarpaulins with all their clothing and other belongings to survive the storm. Because they did stay under cover, snuggled in their "soogans" throughout the storm, all the men survived. Included were Will Poer of Marfa, Will Matthews of Albany, and Avery. Avery laid his bed beside Phin Reynolds's roll, and Reynolds, without thinking, said as he crawled under the tarpaulin, "My God, what is that I smell?" Tige retorted, "It's just me, Mr. Reynolds!"[3]

The horses, however, had no such protection. All of the saddle horses brought from the Texas ranges perished in the storm. They had been cut from the herd at the Reynolds's Long X Ranch in West Texas and were in poor condition. Only twenty-seven horses and a mule brought from Dakota managed to survive the onslaught of wind and snow. It took the cowboys from the Reynolds and the XIT herds six days to round up and separate the cattle, thanks to the road brands on the animals. Phin Reynolds, who was in charge of the herds, wired to Albany and had fresh horses sent to him by rail. Curiously, though the XIT cattle losses ran into several hundred head, their horse losses were none. The Reynolds herds suffered far fewer losses in cattle than the XIT. The drive was successfully completed, and the men returned to the Clear Fork country of Texas. Phin Reynolds recalls that when Avery saw a mule frozen to death on its feet, the black cowboy swore a willingness to "have gotten in bed with Jay Gould himself" to keep warm.[4]

Avery was known for his quick repartee in speech and his sense of humor. Once Ethel Matthews Casey said something to Avery in German, and he quickly responded that he was not up on his German at that time.[5] He described a storm as "dark and terlugious and interrogating trouble." The actual meaning of this expression is unknown, but it was Avery's standard expression for an impending storm. After his Colorado experience, he had every reason to be concerned. Another time on a cold day on the Lambshead Ranch the cowboys were out working, and Avery volunteered that if the men were cold, he would lope on up ahead and build a fire, so they could warm up when they got there. He spurred his horse with his "chicken bones" (spurs) and rode on.[6]

On another occasion he wanted to communicate with kinfolks in a location no longer discernible and had a local man of some considerable education write his letter. Watt Matthews remembered that the man wrote in a fine Spenserian hand, and Tige simply dictated to him what was to be written. As the letter was nearing conclusion, the scribe asked Avery if he had anything else he wanted to add. In characteristic humor, Tige asked that the man add, "Please excuse poor writing and spelling," perhaps assuming that his poor language skills would show up in the letter. The scribe, taking the incident in stride, reportedly included that wording in the letter.[7]

A bachelor in his later years, Avery may have been married early in life, though nothing is known about his wife. It is known that he had at least one stepdaughter, because Matthews remembered that she wrote Avery seeking money for several causes and that he wrote back a clever response, declining to send money. "I'd like some of the same ingredients," he said to her.[8]

As a cowboy Tige was unparalleled. Jack Pate recalled that Avery always rode with his stirrups hobbled, or tied together under his horse's stomach, a technique riders use to stay on bucking horses.[9] He was an outstanding roper, but had one hand severely injured by a rope burn. He knew cattle and ways to handle them. He was what Judge Matthews said a good cowboy should be. He could see a cow this spring and remember what brand she wore and where he had seen her the year before. He could also remember the quality of the calf and know whether to cull her or not. He moved cattle without disturbing them and was efficient and careful in his work.[10] Although he had little or no formal education and was unable to read or write, he mastered every brand in the region. He recognized them quickly and knew the home range and the owner's name.

Avery enjoyed attending the Texas Cowboy Reunion at Stamford, and Pate recalled that he would often sit in the grandstands during the bucking horse events and holler out to the contestants, "Rare back there, boy, rare back." If the rider happened to be thrown by the furiously bucking horse, Tige would shout to the dust cloud, "I told you to rare back!"[11] Avery also had good control of a pack of greyhounds kept on the ranch. He could make them race each other and return to him on command. This always worked unless they were chasing a coyote, and then he had little control over the dogs. They often slept in his quarters, and he referred to them as his "chilluns."

Just as he was good with dogs, he was also good with children. He often captured baby killdeer birds and carried them home in the front of his shirt so that the children could play with them. Watt Matthews remembered that Tige took him under supervision anytime he was working on the ranges of the ranch, and that Tige and Francis Gober trained Watt to be the excellent cowman that he became. The children respected Tige, and he was always kind and gracious but firm with them, especially when they were working cattle. Tige treated others respectfully. Pate recalled that when Tige was introduced to someone, he would take off his hat, put it under his arm, and shake hands with the person to whom he was being introduced.[12]

A humorous but potentially deadly game Avery played was with an old ram kept at the Lambshead headquarters. Avery would get down on his hands and knees and entice the ram to charge. At the right moment, he would duck his head to the ground, and the ram would go over the top of his hunched body. Once, however, as he ducked his head to the ground, Tige hit his eye on a broom weed stub and, startled, raised his head just as the ram arrived. It butted Avery on the top of his skull and knocked him unconscious for a time. He recovered. However, none recall if he played this game with the ram again.[13]

Each fall the Matthews family left the ranch and moved to town so that the children could attend school. They took with them Charlie Standifer to cook and help with the other chores in town. Many a winter Tige spent on Lambshead with Francis Gober and one or two other men, looking after the stock and doing the winter chores. During these periods Avery served as cook for the crew until the Matthews family moved back to the ranch in the spring for the summer's work ahead. He was quick to hand the dishtowel to Standifer and resume his preferred role as cowboy.

His relationship with the white cowboys was excellent. He worked all his life among white cowboys and felt little affinity for other blacks who moved into the area later. He seems much like Isaac Jefford in Elmer Kelton's novel *Wagontongue,* in which the black was a primary helper for the rancher.[14] One notes the significant parallel between Avery and Judge Matthews and Jefford and Major Estel Lytton, the rancher in Kelton's novel. Avery was unable to get along with other blacks after he retired from his cowboying days and moved to Albany.[15]

One of his close associates was Francis Gober, longtime foreman of the Lambshead Ranch. The long hours they spent together welded a strong bond. When Gober died, Watt Matthews took Tige to the funeral in Throckmorton. Tige sat at the back of the church. At the end of the service, the funeral director rose and said there was among those in the audience one who was especially close to Gober and that this man should come first to view the open casket. When his name was called, Tige, with his hand held over his heart and his head bowed, was the first to file by Gober's coffin.[16]

During his later years, Avery also helped other ranchers. Josephine Williams, an Albany native, recalls as a child seeing Avery at the house of her Aunt Clara or John Smith, another relative in Albany. She recounts that he helped with a herd of unruly bulls. Several of the wild animals broke away from the herd and ran into the house of Richard King, Josephine's father. She laughingly recalls that the family, much startled by the activity, darted into the other rooms for safety but eventually had to go back and open one of the doors of the house to let the animals out.[17]

Age took its toll on Avery, as did strong drink. Ethel Matthews Casey, daughter of J. A. Matthews, said that Avery "injured himself" with strong drink.[18] Matthews, a judge in Shackelford County, fired Avery at least a half a dozen times, but always hired him back. Avery stayed with the Matthews family, except when he was drunk, and then he retreated to the house of John Smith, or that of Josephine Williams's Aunt Clara. During his later years he worked for the Wells Fargo Company in Abilene. He quit because he did not like the work. Pate recalled that Tige said, "I'd rather be Mr. Joe Matthews' poodle dog than the express man in Abilene."[19] He then worked for several years as a janitor at the First National Bank of Albany where the Matthews and Reynolds families have long played prominent roles.

Tige retired completely by the early 1930s, but Judge Matthews continued to pick him up every morning and take him to the ranch. Watt Matthews remembered that the judge would pick up Avery and ask him if he had had breakfast. Avery often responded that he'd only had a cup of coffee. The judge insisted that Avery get into the car, and they drove to the ranch, where Avery no doubt caught up on his missed meals.[20] At other times, Ethel Matthews Casey recalled, he would "sit on the curb" of the main street of Albany and, if he saw a member of the Matthews family driving down the street, he would run "to the middle of the street" to indicate an available parking place.[21] At games of the local football team, Avery, an avid fan, would stand in the Albany end zone, and if the team scored, he would go onto the field and dance a jig, roll over, and shout in the air. Morris Ledbetter identifed Avery as one of the best fans the Albany Lions team had.[22]

By 1935, Tige was no longer able to follow this routine. The time came for the Texas Cowboy Reunion, an important annual event at nearby Stamford. Avery had been a frequent attendee, but he became ill at the event and was hospitalized in Stamford. He had beside his bed a new pair of boots given to him by his friends. He died not long after in the Stamford hospital. At the funeral Watt Matthews arrived at the cemetery and saw the small crowd but found that no minister was there to conduct the services. Matthews calmly stepped in and conducted the service himself by reminiscing about Avery's life and experiences, particularly his life on the trail, and reciting the Twenty-third Psalm. Then he saw his old friend and teacher laid to rest.[23]

July, in ranch country, is still as busy as it was then, so Tige lay at rest in Stamford for many years. Later, Watt decided to have the body exhumed and returned to the ranch. After some confusion, resulting from a poorly marked grave, Tige's remains were located and the bones exhumed. These were bare of flesh, and the coffin had rotted away. To be sure that the bones being moved were those of Tige, Watt himself examined the skull, readily recognized the forehead of Tige, and concluded that these were indeed the right bones. He had them placed in a simple wooden box to serve as a casket and buried in the Matthews-Reynolds Cemetery at Reynolds Bend on the Lambshead Ranch. In a fitting tribute to Avery, Watt had the stone marker inscribed, "Bill 'Tige' Avery, fine black cowboy." Tige's remains rest today on the range he rode and loved.[24]

Later, Jimbo Reynolds, a descendent of the original Reynolds brothers and a noted cowman on the Wyoming ranges, broke a black gelding that became a fine cutting horse. Watt Matthews, who began riding this horse when it was three years old, rode him in a cutting event in Stamford and later in Graham. The name of the horse was "Tige" Avery. The legacy of this fine black cowboy lives on at Lambshead Ranch, where he is remembered today as a kind and gentle man who was a thoroughly effective cowboy.

NOTES

A version of this chapter appeared in *Cowboys Who Rode Proudly,* produced by the Haley Library.

1. Watt Matthews, interview by Lawrence Clayton, Lambshead Ranch, Aug. 19, 1991.
2. John M. Hendrix, *If I Can Do It Horseback: A Cow-Country Sketchbook* (Austin: University of Texas Press, 1964), p. 163.
3. Matthews interview.
4. J. R. Webb, "Chapters from the Frontier Life of Phin W. Reynolds," *West Texas Historical Association Year Book* 20 (Oct., 1945): 140.
5. Ethel Matthews Casey, *Reminiscences* (El Paso: Carl Hertzog, 1979), p. 12.
6. Matthews interview.
7. Ibid.
8. Ibid.
9. Jack Pate, telephone interview by Lawrence Clayton, Aug. 21 and 23, 1991.
10. Matthews interview.
11. Pate interview.
12. Ibid.
13. Matthews interview.
14. Elmer Kelton, *Wagontongue* (New York: Ballantine, 1972).
15. Matthews interview.
16. Ibid.
17. Josephine Williams, interview by Lawrence Clayton, Albany, Tex., Sept. 1, 1991.
18. Casey, *Reminiscences,* p. 12.
19. Pate interview.
20. Matthews interview.
21. Casey, *Reminiscences,* p. 12.
22. Morris Ledbetter, interview by Lawrence Clayton, Albany, Tex., Aug. 15, 1991.
23. Matthews interview.
24. Ibid.

Figure 10. George Adams. Courtesy James W. Davis, San Antonio, Texas

Chapter 13

George Adams

A Cowboy All His Life

KENNETH W. HOWELL

On September 29, 1939, George Adams quietly died in the small town of Sanderson, Texas. He had succumbed to pneumonia. Shortly afterward, the ninety-five-year-old black cowboy was buried near the grave of C. F. Cox, Sr., his former boss, in the Cedar Grove Cemetery at Sanderson. Two years prior on his death bed, Cox had requested that his good friend be laid to rest beside him. The only deviation from his dying wish was that Adams was placed at the foot of his grave instead of at his side. In 1939, the burial of an African American in a white cemetery no doubt brought up racial questions and caused tension among members of the Cox family and the citizens of Sanderson, as segregation was a part of mainstream America—even in death. Thus, Adams's grave became a testament to his life. Cox's last request was fulfilled only because Adams was "well respected and well liked," both by the Cox family and the community.[1] How Adams achieved such distinction is his life's story.

George Adams, also known as "7D George" and "Nigger George," came to Southwest Texas sometime around the 1870s. Unfortunately, little is known about his life before this time. Relatives of C. F. Cox speculated that Adams was born a slave and escaped from bondage sometime around the start of the Civil War. Considering that many runaway slaves took refuge in the West before and during the war, these presumptions have some merit. However, whether or not Adams was actually a slave is unknown.[2]

Another questionable aspect of Adams's life is where he lived before his arrival in Southwest Texas. If he ran away at the start of the Civil War, as claimed, approximately twenty years are unaccounted for preceding his arrival in Pecos County in the 1870s. It is likely that he was working as a cowboy somewhere in the brush country of Texas—probably in the areas south and

163

west of San Antonio. This inference is based on the fact that he frequently told his friends and co-workers stories about the "brush" country. The regions mentioned above are covered in thick brush. It was also noted that he wore a heavy coat nearly year-round. Because working cattle in heavy brush would have necessitated such apparel, it is easy to see how Adams would have grown accustomed to wearing regularly an article of clothing used by other cowboys only during inclement weather.[3]

When he reached the Trans-Pecos area in the late 1800s, Adams found work on the famed 7D Ranch whose brand was the figure 7 and a lowercase *d* on a common vertical line.[4] The ranch was located on Comanche Creek, four miles east of Fort Stockton, Texas. It is likely that Adams worked for this outfit until the Western Union Beef Company was sold to John T. McElroy in 1899.[5]

While working for the 7D, Adams acquired a reputation for being a "top hand," or excellent cowboy. His ability to ride and rope soon became legendary throughout the region. One story Adams used to tell illustrates his expertise in handling horses. According to his account, he and another cowboy came upon a wild "strawberry roan" horse. The two cowboys managed to rope and saddle the stallion. Then, Adams mounted the excited beast, which caused it to pitch violently. Suddenly, the horse reared up and fell completely over on its back. Adams jumped clear, and he was able to get back in the saddle before the horse could get to its feet again. After this happened repeatedly, the two cowboys decided to take the stallion up to the top of a high bluff overlooking the Pecos River. Once they reached the bluff, the other cowboy took a turn at the outlaw horse. Once again, the horse reared and flipped over backward. Only this time, there was no ground to break the horse's fall. It went over the cliff and landed in the Pecos. The horse swam to the bank of the river where it was caught before it could escape with Adams's saddle. Still, the horse repeated its act when a rider tried to mount him. The two men eventually gave up for the day and led the horse back to the ranch, putting it in a 7-foot-high corral. When the cowboys returned the next morning they were amazed to find the holding pen empty. During the night, the stallion had cleared the top rail and returned to the wild.[6] Adams and his friend were unsuccessful in taming this animal, but the encounter with the wild horse illustrates their expert horsemanship. If they had not been skillful riders, a serious injury could easily have occurred.

"7D George" was also known for his proficiency with a lariat. In fact, Adams gained such notoriety with a lasso that he became part of the region's folklore. One popular story tells of an old outlaw steer that used to drink from the

Pecos River near a 7D horse camp. The old steer would always send another steer to check to see if anyone were around the watering hole before going down to drink. The scouting steer often "reported" that 7D men were there, and the old steer would say, "Let's go git a drink." One day, however, the scouting steer reported that George was there. To this, the old steer said rather quickly, "Let's git. It's that big nigger from the 7D's." The point of the story was simple. Any steer not wanting to find itself at the end of Adams's rope had better not cross his path, because he rarely ever missed.[7]

Early in his career at the 7D, Adams pushed cattle up the Goodnight-Loving and Chisholm Trails. One trip remained permanently etched in his mind. The 7D Ranch had sent some cattle north to Wyoming. Once the cattle were sold and the hands paid their wages, some of the cowboys, including Adams, went to one of the gambling houses in town. Adams reported, "I kinda forgot and gets so interested in one table that when I looks around agin, the room is just filled with men with guns and afore I know what is going on, all them fellers have their guns out all ready to shoot." It did not take Adams long to consider his options. He continued, "It shore did scare me so I just fall down on my hands and knees and starts to crawl out from there. I even crawls between some of the legs to get to that door." As he was crawling, one of the men in the casino saw him and shouted, "Look at that little negro!" Apparently, the others found Adams's actions humorous. At this point, tensions relaxed, and the men holstered their guns. Adams, however, continued to crawl out the door. He later stated, "I [was] ... sure glad to get outside again. It seem to me clumps of mesquite and cactus would always look good to me after that!"[8]

During the late 1800s, Pecos County was a popular outlaw retreat. Naturally, anyone riding the range looking for cattle was eventually going to run into a group of miscreants. An interviewer once asked Adams if he had ever seen the Ketchums, a notorious outlaw band from the Trans-Pecos area. He replied, "Sho! I has seen 'em plenty o' time. Why I'se been right in their camp. They's jest folk like anybody else. They was jest like everybody else in dis country at de time."[9] Not only was this a comment on the wild and rugged life of Southwest Texas during this era, but it also revealed Adams's attitude toward others. He viewed everybody in the region as equals. This explains in part why Adams had few enemies during his lifetime.

After he left the 7D Ranch, Adams worked briefly for the T5 outfit. The T5, more properly known as the Independence Cattle Company, was located on Independence Creek at Independence Spring and was the first big ranch established in the area now known as Terrell County. Despite the large number of cattle owned by the operation, the early owners consistently had problems rendering the payroll. Thus, it was hard for the ranch manager of the operation to keep good cowboys. Nevertheless, when the roundups began, a group of T5 cowboys always went down the Pecos River to gather and herd the company's cattle back toward the ranch.[10]

Adams ended his stint with the T5 in 1902. From then until his death, he worked as a cowboy for the C. F. Cox Ranch, located in Brewster and Terrell Counties. Most of the ranch was situated in Brewster County, but the town closest to the ranch's headquarters was Sanderson, Texas. The small Terrell County town, approximately forty miles from Cox's home, boasted a thriving population of 112 in 1900. Though meager in size, the town did serve as one of the few connections to the "outside world."[11]

George Adams was a steadfast worker and loyal friend to the Cox family, especially C. F. Cox, owner and operator of the ranch. Coleman Foster Cox was born on November 16, 1855, near Evansville, Arkansas. He came to Fannin County, Texas, in the early 1870s, where he lived and worked for his uncle, Burwell Cox. It was during this time that C. F. Cox became familiar with the sheep business. It is also probable that he became interested in politics at this time, as, reportedly, he was a staunch Republican. After approximately a year on his uncle's range, Cox set out on his own, leaving with a small herd of sheep, a horse and saddle, a dog, and a gun. Cox made his way to Throckmorton County, where he bought two ranches near Throckmorton, Texas.[12]

While ranching in Throckmorton, Cox was introduced to Claudia Vannerson, who became his wife. They were married in Greenville, Texas, on November 25, 1896. Cox and his new wife lived in Throckmorton until 1900, at which time he purchased eighty thousand acres in Brewster and Terrell Counties. The Cox family moved to the area shortly afterward and lived on the new ranch until C. F. Cox died in 1937. Cox's sheep were herded to Brewster County from Throckmorton by Harry des Landes and two other men. They moved the six thousand sheep to the location through San Angelo in the spring of 1900.[13]

George Adams and C. F. Cox developed a close relationship in the thirty-five years that they knew each other. Cox grew to respect Adams and eventually considered him part of the family. Their friendship was solidified during Adams's early days on the ranch when he homesteaded eight sections of land for Cox. Once Adams obtained title to the land, he sold it to his boss. In this way, the Cox ranch increased in size, and the two men became more or less partners. Clearer evidence of this partnership is illustrated by another event in the lives of these two men. During the 1930s, C. F. Cox, like many Americans, suffered economic hardship from the Great Depression. At one point, Cox was unable to make his mortgage payments at the Sanderson bank. Just as the bank was about to foreclose, Adams put his cattle up as collateral, and Cox's loan was renewed. Thus, because of this act of Adams, future generations of the Cox family were able to maintain ownership of the ranch.[14]

When Adams arrived at the Cox Ranch, there was already a man named George working for the outfit. Thus, the other hands began to call him "7D George" in order to distinguish him from the other cowboy. Later, Adams was known simply as "Nigger George."[15]

For thirty-eight years, Adams basically did the same work. He checked cattle, rode fences, pulled cattle out of the mud in stock ponds when dried because of drought, joined in roundups of sheep and cattle, doctored livestock, and trained horses.[16] For these services, George was often paid in cattle. He had little need for cash money, so when it came time to settle his wages, Cox would tell George, "brand you a cow, you have earned it." This happened so frequently that Adams soon stopped branding the cattle, especially when his boss went back into the sheep business. At that point, Cox considered all the cows to be the property of his African American "partner."[17]

Adams maintained a simple existence working on the Cox Ranch. He never learned to read or write, but he spoke both English and Spanish fluently. Though not a religious man, he did subscribe to a philosophical way of life. Using cowboy logic, he rationalized his views about the world and God. As with many cowboys, the wide-open prairie was his church, the saddle his pew, Mother Nature his pastor, and he never missed a sermon.

Adams's entertainments were also simple. Once a year, he would go to Sanderson for the annual ranch rodeo. He led the rodeo parade every year, and at the rodeo grounds, he would buy beer for all his friends. He also supplied the cattle for the roping events. At home, "7D George" enjoyed playing cards and checkers with Bill Davis, one of C. F. Cox's grandsons, and others.[18] Another pastime the old cowboy enjoyed was smoking or chewing tobacco. According to Jim Davis, Bill's younger brother, Adams ordered an annual supply of tobacco leaves through the mail. The leaves were sent to him in a large tin container. "George would crumple these big tobacco leaves up and chew them. When he got all the juice out of them, he would put the plug on top of a fence post to let it dry out. Once the chewed leaves dried, he would smoke them in his pipe." The thought of smoking chewed tobacco leaves may not be a pleasant one, but it is indicative of Adams's resourcefulness.[19]

Adams's living conditions and diet were sufficient but rudimentary. He first lived in an old bunkhouse at the ranch headquarters, but later moved to another site after Cox's death. His later home was an old storeroom that was previously used for storing horse tack. Adams's diet seemed to be more tolerable than his housing. Though his diet was simple and consisted primarily of meat, beans, and bread, it was cooked well. "7D George" was an excellent cook, and frequently he prepared two of his favorite dishes—biscuits and "por jo," a kind of tomato dumplings.[20]

Aside from casual acquaintances with other cowboys and his relationship with the Cox family, Adams had only one close friend, Ross Anderson. Anderson was another African American cowboy who worked for the Cox Ranch during the 1930s. Adams's younger friend was best remembered for his abilities as a hunter. He was said to have owned the best "panther dogs" in the area. The dogs were used in hunting cougars (more commonly referred to as panthers by people living in the Southwest Texas region), wolves, and coyotes. These wild animals represented a serious threat to the ranchers' livestock, and anyone who could eliminate the "killers" effectively was held in high regard. Anderson was also a noted horse trainer, a skill he acquired while working for the Second United States Cavalry stationed at Brackettville, Texas.[21]

In his younger days, Adams attended some of the "panther" hunts with C. F. Cox and Anderson but only when coerced. One reason for his lack of interest was that he did not own a gun. No one can remember ever seeing Adams carry a pistol or rifle with him on the range. Perhaps his dislike for such weapons was a result of his unpleasant experience at the gambling house in the Wyoming cattle town years before.[22]

Though it is evident that he enjoyed a great deal of freedom in Southwest Texas, George Adams was aware of certain racial barriers present within the area. He never joined white cowboys at social functions, dinners, or in their conversations, unless they invited him. Yet, as further testament to his standing with the Cox family and other ranch hands, his presence was always requested.[23]

Like other African Americans in the West, Adams faced the harsh realities of racial prejudices. Though cowboys were judged on their abilities to rope and ride, race was still an issue. Black cowboys continuously had to perform their duties with better-than-average skills to gain recognition from their white counterparts.[24] This one fact alone made African Americans some of the best cowhands ever to have worked on the open range. George Adams certainly gained recognition from the men who worked with him. In their conversations, his abilities were discussed at greater length than was the color of his skin.

African American cowhands, especially old, experienced ones, taught young, inexperienced cowboys the ways of ranch life. Often the old-timers' students were the ranch owners' sons or relatives.[25] This was certainly the case with Jim and Bill Davis. Adams took both boys under his wing and instructed them in how to be cowboys. In many cases, black cowboys were often hired because they could handle wild horses.[26] Considering that C. F. Cox started out as a sheep rancher, "7D George" was probably hired to train Cox's horses. Only after working for Cox did he learn the sheep business.

George Adams's life was the epitome of the African American cowboy in the West. Black cowboys for the most part were ex-slaves from Texas seeking a fresh start on life, or they were moving west to escape restrictions placed on them by Southern governments.[27] Adams was assumed to be a runaway slave. Adams's life was similar to the lives of many African American Texans during the late nineteenth and early twentieth centuries, but it was also the exception in some ways. Unlike many African American cowboys, Adams became in many respects his own boss and for all practical purposes a partner with a white rancher.[28] He was able to remain a cowboy all of his life and continued working until the week before his death.[29] Many black cowboys were forced into other occupations when the cattle drives from Texas ended in the late 1800s.

Adams earned and retained the respect of men in Brewster and Terrell Counties during his lifetime. Perhaps this was in part due to C. F. Cox's reputation throughout the region, or maybe the area was still wild enough in the early 1900s that people had more on their minds than the color of a man's skin. Although present in Terrell County, racial prejudices toward blacks did not appear to be as strong as they were in East Texas. Men were judged on their abilities to work.

George lived his life alone in the midst of the Cox family and never married. His life illustrates the African American cowboy experience in Southwest Texas. His is a story of hard work and competence—a life lived with dignity.

NOTES

1. Alice E. Downie, ed., *Terrell County History: Its Past and Its People* (San Angelo: Anchor Publishing Company, 1978), p. 241; *The Sanderson Times*, Sept. 29, 1939; Jim Davis (grandson of C. F. Cox), interview by Ken Howell, San Antonio, Tex., Apr. 11, 1998; Bill Davis (grandson of C. F. Cox), interview by Ken Howell, San Antonio, Tex., Apr. 10, 1998. There seems to be some question as to how Adams actually died. According to Jim Davis, he died of pneumonia. Apparently, a family traveling from California stopped at the Cox Ranch shortly before Adams died. They professed to be relatives of the aged black cowboy, but Adams repudiated their

claims. Nevertheless, they stayed a few days and proceeded to take care of the elderly, but healthy, Adams. The newly arrived "relatives" set out at once to clean up George's cabin. They also felt compelled to clean up George as well. Thus, they removed his long-handle underclothes, which he wore year-round, and put him in "short underwear." After several nights, Adams caught a fever from the cold September air. He was brought to the Davis's home, where he slept in Jim Davis's bed until he died. However, Bill Davis remembered him dying of prostate cancer. Official cause of death could not be determined as the county clerk's office in Terrell County reported the death certificate lost.

2. Jim Davis interview; Bill Davis interview; Downie, *Terrell County History*, p. 242. Adams claimed to be about seventeen when he ran away. However, he never gave a reason why he ran away, nor did he ever actually admit to being a slave to either Jim or Bill. Because Adams supposedly had no living relatives and no wife or children, no known family stories exist about his early life.

3. Jim Davis interview.

4. There is some question as to the location of the 7D Ranch. Jim and Bill Davis claim that the ranch was located in "La Pryor County," though present-day La Pryor is located in Zavala County. Julia Smith, "Seven-D Ranch," in Ron Tyler, ed., *The New Handbook of Texas*, vol. 5 (Austin: Texas State Historical Society, 1996), p. 979; T. R. Haven, "Sheep-Cattlemen Antagonism on the Texas Frontier," *West Texas Historical Association Yearbook* 18 (Oct., 1942): 15, places the ranch's location close to Fort Stockton, Pecos County, Texas. It is possible Adams could have worked at both locations. The *Terrell County History* states the 7D Ranch, when it was owned by the Western Union Beef Company in the 1880s and 1890s, was headquartered at San Antonio, with supply bases established at Fort Stockton, Uvalde, Toyah, Sheffield, Ozona, and Del Rio. Adams was probably working at the supply base at Fort Stockton when the company began liquidating its stocks in 1897. This would put him in the proximity of the Cox Ranch, where he went to work in 1902.

5. Smith, "Seven-D Ranch," *New Handbook of Texas*, vol. 5, p. 979.

6. Roy D. Holt, "Allergic to Riders," *Sheep and Goat Raisers* (Oct., 1950): 33–34. A "strawberry roan" is a reddish brown colored horse.

7. Downie, *Terrell County History*, p. 242.

8. Ibid.

9. Ibid.

10. Ibid., p. 49.

11. Walter G. Downie, "Terrell County," in Ron Tyler, ed., *The New Handbook of Texas*, vol. 6 (Austin: Texas State Historical Society, 1996), p. 262; Jim Davis interview; Jim Davis, interview by Sara R. Massey, San Antonio, Tex., Apr. 7, 1998; Downie, *Terrell County History*, p. 326.

12. Downie, *Terrell County History*, p. 325; Margaret Vannerson, ed., *The Family History* (Redwood City, Calif.: Nona Lael [Vannerson] Trimble, 1961), p. 45; Bonnie Cox Sellers, *Our Family Heritage* (Riverside, Calif.: A to Z Company, 1980), pp. 42–43.

13. Ibid., Claudia was C. F. Cox's second wife. He was previously married to Eunice Edsall while living at Throckmorton. Their marriage produced no children. C. F. and Claudia had three children: Mary, Neta, and C. F. Cox, Jr.

14. Jim Davis, interview by Howell. It was not uncommon for ranch workers to homestead land and sell it to their boss. Both parties benefited. The owners obtained more property, and the ranch hand gained a quick monetary reward. However, using Adams's cattle as collateral for the Cox bank note was an unusual case.

15. Jim Davis, interview by Howell; Jim Davis, interview by Massey. Jim told the story that when he was a young boy in school his teacher taught him that African Americans should be addressed as "Negroes" rather than "niggers." In order to impress the man whom he admired, he ran up to George after school and called him, "Negro George." Reportedly, Adams quickly angered and said something to the effect, "Why you little smart-mouth, you better never call me that again. I was born 'Nigger George' and I'll die 'Nigger George.'"

16. Jim Davis, interview by Massey. The Cox Ranch during various times in the early 1900s ran sheep, cattle, and horses. In the 1920s the ranch had a horse herd of approximately seven hundred head. In the 1930s, the ranch ran about eight hundred to nine hundred cattle.

17. Jim Davis, interview by Howell.

18. Bill Davis interview; Jim Davis, interview by Howell.

19. Jim Davis, interview by Howell.

20. Bill Davis interview; Jim Davis, interview by Howell.

21. Jim Davis, interview by Howell.

22. Ibid.; Jim Davis, interview by Massey.

23. Jim Davis, interview by Howell.

24. Kenneth Wiggins Porter, "Negroes on the Frontier," Howard R. Lamar, ed., *The Reader's Encyclopedia of the American West* (New York: Thomas Y. Crowell, 1977), p. 820.

25. Kenneth W. Porter, "Negro Labor in the Western Cattle Industry, 1866–1900," *Labor History* 10 (summer, 1969): 350.

26. Ibid.

27. Joe A. Stout, "Cowboy," in Lamar, ed., *The Reader's Encyclopedia of the American West*, p. 268.

28. Jim Davis, interview by Howell.

29. Ibid., Adams accumulated a nice herd of cattle while working on the Cox Ranch. After his death, Adams's herd was sold by the Cox family.

Figure 11. Charley Willis and wife Laura. Courtesy Franklin Willis, Los Angeles, California

Chapter 14

Charley Willis

A Singing Cowboy

JIM CHILCOTE

A number of years ago I was asked to sing for a convention of physicians at an evening "Wild West Show." Present were a number of rodeo cowboys, ropers, bulldoggers, bronc riders, and several bull riders. While we waited behind the chutes, the cowboys stretched out, unkinked ropes, resined rigs, checked cinching, and talked rodeo. Despite the fact that several of them had just met, they became a tight-knit group within minutes, for what bound them had little to do with where they were from, where they had attended school or from what social strata they had originated. They were all cowboys, talking stock, spurs, horses, rigs, and bruises.

Just before the end of the rodeo, after the calves had been roped, the broncs busted, and the songs sung, the arena lights went out—a blown breaker no doubt. With the bulls yet to be ridden, I wondered how the master of ceremonies would deal with the disappointed crowd. Within moments, however, the bull riders bounded into the middle of the dark arena for a quick meeting. They had come to ride bulls and were not about to get cheated out of the fun. Immediately, cowhands sprang to their trucks, arranged them at one end of the arena and turned on their headlights in an attempt to illuminate the scene. That evening, to the deafening cheers of the dazzled audience, by the dim, striated, and woefully inadequate light, three cowboys made the most daring bull rides I've ever seen. All three bull riders were African American cowboys.

What those cowboys had done that night spoke volumes about pride, spirit, guts, and the cultural history of being a cowboy. Later, I happened to make the acquaintance of Will Arthur (Artie) Morris, an accomplished country singer, who told me of his great-grandfather, Charley Willis, a black cowboy who went "up the trail" in 1871. Remembering those bull riders, I decided to learn his story.

Charley Willis was born in 1850 in Milam County, Texas. After the Civil War, Charley was freed, and he went to work for E. J. Morris on the Morris Ranch near Bartlett, Texas, in Bell County. He continued to work off and on at the ranch for over twenty years, breaking horses and doing all the other jobs of cowboys.[1] It is believed that his wife, Laura, was part Seminole and probably migrated to Texas from Mexico with other Black Seminoles during the Civil War.[2]

The 1880 census lists Charles Willis in Milam County with wife Laura, age twenty-six, and four children: Andrew, age ten; Magdalene, age eight; Joshua, age six; and Clemmer, age two. The birth dates given are: Laura, 1854; Andrew, 1870; Magdalene, 1872; Joshua, 1874; and Clemmer, 1878. A census error listed Clemmer, or "Bud" as he was later called, as a daughter rather than a son.[3]

In 1871, Charley Willis at twenty-one took to the trail with one of ten herds driven north to Wyoming by the Snyder brothers, well-known cattle drovers from Georgetown, Texas.[4] This drive, terminating in Cheyenne, was roughly two thousand miles round-trip on horseback and would have taken several months to complete with all the dangers inherent in herding cattle a long distance. The year that Charley went up the trail marked the all-time peak of trail activity for the era. Cattle drive figures for the years 1868 through 1885 show that 1871 was the bumper year, with over six hundred thousand head of cattle being driven on the trails.[5] That Charley was an accomplished cowboy seems beyond question, given the length of his employment with E. J. Morris, as well as his hiring on with the Snyder brothers for the trail drive. It was a common practice at that time for cowboys to hire on with other ranchers for the long trail drives. His job of breaking horses was not for the soft or faint-hearted. Breaking horses was reserved for the best and toughest cowhands, and given the investment involved in a large-scale trail drive, cattle ranchers wanted to procure the most experienced cowboys obtainable. His photograph suggests that he was rather small and wiry, a favorable combination for working green saddle stock.

During his trek with the Snyder herds up to Wyoming, Charley was exposed to all aspects of trail driving along with the sweat and dangers. One element of cowboy life Willis certainly experienced was "singing to the herds." As cattle drovers were quick to discover, Longhorns were prone to stampede at the slightest provocation unless within earshot of the human voice, hence the phenomenon of "the singing cowboy." In fact, "some cattle drovers, realizing the value of music to a trail herd actually hired singers to take part in the drives."[6]

· · ·

Some trail bosses didn't like to hire a fellow who couldn't sing. We boys would consider it a dull day's drive if we didn't add at least one verse. On bad, dark nights the cowboy who could keep up the most racket was the pet of the bunch. We called him the bellwether, and he always brought up his side of the herd. . . . When the trail hand gargled his throat . . . he usually had a practical purpose. In threatening weather, when the cattle began to drift and showing signs of stampeding, a hymn or a ballad might quiet them . . . Songs were the best antidote to rumbling in the sky or the howl of a lobo wolf on a distant hill. . . . the cowboy puncher who could sing better than the average had an advantage. In his long days in the saddle, songs helped to speed the hours and to keep him from growing lonesome. In the evening around the campfire, they gave a bit of diversion before the tired men hit their bedrolls. The hands on night guard used songs not only to keep the cattle quiet but to keep themselves awake.[7]

"What you would hear as you passed your partner on guard would be a kind of low hum or whistle, and you wouldn't know what it was. Just some old hymn tune, likely as not—something to kill time and not bad enough to make the herd want to get up and run. . . . The cowboy hardly ever knew what tune he was singing his song to, just some old, old tune that he had heard and known as a boy."[8] While the repertoire of the cowboys was anything but high-brow, it was likely to include "hymns, bawdy ditties, familiar ballads, cowboy songs of communal authorship, popular songs of the day, and poems that had been put to music with either original or borrowed tunes."[9] "Methodist hymns were popular . . . although good old-fashioned Negro minstrel songs have been found equally effective in soothing the breast of the wild Texas steer . . . after the men had sung a few lullabies to the steers, they (the steers) all lay down and started snoring."[10]

Charley must have had an ear and an aptitude for music, because he returned to Texas singing some of the trail tunes endemic of the cowboy. "Horses, which play an essential and intimate part in the daily life of the trail hand, were the heroes of many of his (the cowboy's) songs."[11] On one trip Charley returned singing the oldest traceable version of the song "Goodbye Old Paint." Family tradition suggests that he authored the song, which is possible. No one knows if Charley had a horse named "Ol' Paint," as most cowboys did not own horses,[12] but the song continued into history.

Sometime around 1885 when Charley was breaking horses for E. J. Morris, he taught the song "Ol' Paint" to E. J.'s son Jesse, replete with a Jew's harp accompaniment.[13] Jesse Morris, later to become an accomplished cowboy himself, received his first lessons on the fiddle from another black cowboy on the Morris Ranch, Jerry Neely, and continued playing Charley Willis's version of "Ol' Paint" throughout his life.[14] In 1947, at the request of folk musicologist John Lomax, Jesse Morris recorded "Goodbye Old Paint" for the Library of Congress.[15] The preservation of the song was commented on by the director of the repository at the time: "Morris . . . has the oldest known version: he traces it to the point of first origin, Charley (Willis)."[16] Jim Bob Tinsley says, "Credit for saving it from obscurity must be given to three Texans: a black cowboy (Willis) who sang it on the trail drives, a cowboy who remembered it (Morris), and a college professor who put it down on paper (Lomax)."[17] "Goodbye Old Paint," as sung by Charley Willis:

Goodbye Old Paint

My foot's in the stirrup, my pony won't stand,
Goodbye Old Paint, I'm off to Montan'.

Repeating chorus:
Old Paint, Old Paint, I'm a-leavin' Cheyenne,
Goodbye Old Paint, I'm a-leavin' Cheyenne.

Old Paint's a good pony, he paces when he can,
Goodbye little doney, I'm off to Montan'.

Go hitch up your horses and feed 'em some hay,
An' set yourself by me as long as you'll stay.

We spread down the blanket on the green grassy ground,
While the horses and cattle were a-grazin' around.

My horses ain't hungry, they won't eat your hay,
My wagon is loaded and rollin' away.

My foot's in the stirrup, my bridle's in hand,
Goodbye little Annie, my horses won't stand.

The last time I saw her was late in the fall,
She was ridin' Old Paint and a-leadin' Old Ball.[18]

Cowboys rarely had good singing voices. "If he had one to start with, he always lost it bawling at cattle, or sleeping out in the open, or tellin' the judge he didn't steal that horse. . . . Cowboy songs were always song by one person, never by a group."[19] Charley, like most cowboys, probably didn't have a trained voice, but the song he conceived someplace on the trail drive is now an enduring cowboy ballad.

Sometime after his return from Wyoming, Charley and Laura took up residence in DaVilla, Texas, some fifteen miles southwest of Cameron in Milam County. The family homestead, approximately six acres, is situated adjacent to the DaVilla Cemetery, near the school and Baptist church. The family home no longer exists, but a walk on the site with Artie Morris turned up pottery shards, broken glass, and rusty remnants of pots and pans from the old homestead.

It is unclear when Charley died. Vyree Willis Moore, great-granddaughter of Charley and Laura, has no recollection of Charley, whereas she remembers Laura quite well.[20] It is likely that Charley died about 1930. A walk through the DaVilla Cemetery with Vyree failed to confirm the location of Charley's grave, as a draw had widened over the years, eroding the earth and washing away many of the markers that Vyree remembered from her childhood.[21]

The legacy of Charley Willis and his wife Laura is substantial. In addition to the four children listed in the 1880 census, two more were born later, Victoria and Ruth. Two descendants carry on the Willis family tradition. "Goodbye Old Paint" continues to be sung by the Willis family and Artie Morris. Artie, a great-grandson of Charley, lives in Fischer, Texas, and is a singer of country and western music. He is a national performer who counts among his honors being invited backstage at the Grand Ole Opry in Nashville. Clarence Gonzales, another great-grandson of Willis, led a lengthy life as a rodeo cowboy from the late 1940s through the early 1970s. Living now in Richmond, Texas, Clarence used to compete in all events, but his forte was bull riding. He won honors in rodeos at such places as Madison Square Garden and the Boston Garden.

Today, hundreds of descendants participate in the Willis Connection, an organization founded by Willis descendant Franklin Willis of Los Angeles, California. Willis Connection members, as a means of celebrating their family heritage, continue to attend annual family reunions, correspond regularly, and support a newsletter.[22] The legacy of Charley Willis, an African American cowboy who drove cattle up the trail in the 1870s continues not only in his descendants, but also in our country and western music today as we sing "Goodbye Old Paint."

NOTES

1. Jim Bob Tinsley, *He Was Singin' This Song* (Orlando: Florida University Press, 1982), p. 124.
2. James Brown, telephone interview by Jim Chilcote, May 7, 1998.
3. U.S. Government, *1880 Census* (Washington, D.C.: Department of Commerce, Division of Census).
4. Tinsley, *He Was Singin' This Song*, p. 124.
5. William Forbis, *The Cowboys* (New York: Time-Life Books, 1973), p. 162.
6. Tinsley, *He Was Singin' This Song*, p. 7.
7. Wayne Gard, *The Chisholm Trail* (Norman: University of Oklahoma Press, 1954), p. 243.
8. N. Howard "Jack" Thorp, *Songs of the Cowboys* (1908; reprint, New York: Clarkson N. Potter, Inc. 1966), pp. 16, 18–19.
9. Tinsley, *He Was Singin' This Song*, p. 7.
10. Gard, *Chisholm Trail*, p. 243.
11. Ibid., p. 244.
12. Joe A. Stout, "Cowboy," in Howard R. Lamar, ed., *The Reader's Encyclopedia of the American West* (New York: Thomas Y. Crowell Company, 1977), p. 269.
13. Tinsley, *He Was Singin' This Song*, p. 7.
14. Ibid., p. 125.
15. Duncan Emrich, *Cowboy Songs, Ballads, and Cattle Calls from Texas*, LP Record No. AAFS L28 ca. 1948 (Washington, D.C.: Archive of American Folk Song, Library of Congress, 1949).
16. Duncan Emrich, *Folklore on the American Land* (Boston: Little, Brown, and Company, 1972), pp. 489–92.
17. Tinsley, *He Was Singin' This Song*, p. 123.
18. Ibid., p. 122.
19. Thorp, *Songs of the Cowboys*, p. 16.
20. Vyree Willis Moore (great-granddaughter), interview by Jim Chilcote, Temple, Tex., Mar. 31, 1998.
21. James Brown, great-grandson of Charley Willis, supports the view that Charley was interred at the DaVilla Cemetery, as he reports having seen the marker sometime in the late 1970s during a pilgrimage to the Willis homestead.
22. For more information, contact: Franklin Willis, *Willis Connection*, 5914 South Cimarron, Los Angeles, Calif. 90047.

Figure 12. Daniel Webster "80 John" Wallace. Courtesy D. W. Wallace Estate and the Institute of Texan Cultures, San Antonio

Chapter 15

Daniel Webster Wallace

A West Texas Cattleman

JOYCE GIBSON ROACH

The herd starts in the morning . . .

The boy, called Webster, went to the barn at the end of a cotton-patch day, did his chores, carved his name on the wall and left to be a cowboy. Scores of early-day Texas stories of the last third of the 1800s begin in similar ways— leaving home for various reasons to take up life on the cattle ranges of the West. Daniel Webster Wallace had no reason to succeed beyond merely a cowboy's life. Yet, he did, and never once is it recorded that the man complained of the sorrows, trials, or tribulations of getting by or making do in a white man's world, in spite of the brand he carried for a nickname—80 John.

The most reliable narrative of Wallace's life was written by his daughter, Hettye Wallace Branch, *The Story of 80 John: A Biography of One of the Most Respected Negro Ranchmen in the Old West*.[1] Her biography is the source of nearly all published stories and accounts of Wallace after 1960.

The story of Daniel Webster Wallace's life opens with the familiar details of a slave child's beginnings. Before he was twelve years old, he was sent to the fields to chop weeds or plow for thirty cents or so a day. He was not enthusiastic about it, was accused of daydreaming, and had the reputation for being listless and even stupid, at least while he was in the rows and furrows.

He was unenthusiastic—it was true. He did, indeed, daydream, and he listened. What he heard were the cowboys yelling in the distance or talking about drives up the long trail.

On one particular day—who can say why—Webster decided that he would not stay any longer in the dirt or afoot. "The herd starts in the morning . . ." He knew the hour, the place, and direction that Mr. O'Daniel, the master, would take the herd—northwest.

At the close of that day, the boy embedded his name into the timbers of the barn like a signature to a covenant made with himself, and then went to bed. But he couldn't sleep. Arising at 3:30, Webster put on his clothes and hat, stuffed his coat under his arm, and, shaking for fear he'd wake his mother, silently and under cover of darkness, began his life as a cowboy.

Webster's leave-taking and his life-changing decision would not necessarily have been unusual for a white adolescent in the 1860s, but it is easy to presume that it was unthinkable for a black child. One notices that the circumstances of Wallace's life were different both in his childhood and young adulthood in the wide-open spaces of the Texas frontier where matters were likely to take unlikely turns, where need took precedence over any other consideration, even color, where a man's business was obscured and hidden by vast expanses. Under any other conditions of time and place and without some luck his story might not have been possible.

Daniel Webster Wallace was born in Texas, Victoria County, on September 15, 1860. His mother, Mary Wallace, originally from Virginia, was sold in Missouri to Mary O'Daniel for one thousand dollars and may have been separated from her husband and three other children. Mention is made of two younger brothers for whom Webster later became responsible. Information about any other family members except for his mother is obscure.[2]

From his birth, Webster enjoyed a status better than most. His mother, because of her looks—"the way she held her head in walking" and "the neatness and the coil of long black hair at the nape of her neck"—became a house servant as opposed to working outside as a field servant. Mrs. O'Daniel was pleased with Mary's work and allowed her to bring the baby to the house to attend to his needs. Mary served as wet nurse to Mrs. O'Daniel's son, Dial, who was a few months younger than Webster. Later evidence reveals that when Mary was given her freedom she preferred to stay with Mrs. O'Daniel on the three acres provided for her. As the baby, Webster, became a child, he was left to his own devices in his mother's house, which was substantial for a slave. Consisting of two large rooms with a hall between and a lean-to in the back for a kitchen, the little boy played with stick horses crafted for him by his mother.

There was a little schooling, presumably in a segregated setting, but Webster never liked what went on, especially when the dunce cap was placed on his head. He was accused of being a dreamer. His later life revealed that he was anything but stupid, in spite of the fact that he was negative about learning at that stage in his life. He was tall for his age, and it may have been easy to assume that he was slow when, in fact, he was merely too young to do what was expected of him.

Yet, Webster apparently watched and listened to the cowboy life going on around him and acted on his dreams. When he showed up early on that spring morning of the drive about which he'd heard, he pleaded, "Please, sir, let me go with you." The boss took pity on him. He was warned that he had to stay aboard a horse but was given a gentle one. When the herd moved out, Webster was riding point with the boss while others took middle and drag positions. There is no reason to believe that Webster was taken along for any other reason except to give him an adventure and to allow him to participate as a tagalong with a front-row seat.

For the drive to Coleman County, Webster was paid fifteen silver dollars, indicating that he did work on the drive, but he didn't go home to spend his days telling tales about his adventure. He, instead, considered it a chance, a leg up, a beginning. He hunted immediately for another job and ended up working the summer for Sam Gholson, who had a reputation as a buffalo hunter and Indian fighter.[3] It was from this man that Webster was introduced to the basics of cowboying, working on the open range searching out strays that wandered as far as a hundred miles off the home grounds, learning brands and earmarks, and wrangling horses, which included snapping out broncs.

When Gholson pulled out and went elsewhere, Webster went to work for the Nunn outfit. Whatever skills were begun under Gholson's tutelage were expanded, honed, and perfected with Nunn. The narrative of that time reveals that he came into his own as a cowhand. His life on the range reads as well as Andy Adams's *Log of a Cowboy* and ranks with Charlie Siringo's autobiography of his trail-driving days, *Riata and Spurs*.[4]

There were lone expeditions after straying horses and cattle. Nunn's herd contained eight thousand head, with no fences to contain them. A wild ride, fleeing before the Comanches, brought death for one of Webster's comrades who tried to outride them rather than dropping to the ground as the others knew to do. The boy was wrapped in his bedroll and buried in a shallow grave with no marker.

Webster learned what a man's handshake meant. While sharing the work of roundup and branding with a neighboring herd, he came across a bully who bragged about what he had done to Negroes. When the man got personal, Webster called him to task. As was the custom, someone drew the line and the fight began. After Webster knocked his detractor down, the man got up and offered to shake hands. They became friends, shared heading and heeling as partners, and enjoyed each other's company until the friend, never named, went to New Mexico with his boss's herd.

Interspersed with work on the open range were recollections of activities undertaken against boredom and loneliness. Webster was challenged to rope a buffalo from horseback because he had gained the reputation as a fine roper, but also because he was an excellent horseman. He did, not once but several times. Drinking, playing poker and shooting craps, horse races, mock trials and punishments, pranks such as putting dead snakes in bedrolls helped to pass the time.

It was during Webster's interlude with Nunn that he buried yet another friend. Apparently, a young man, again unnamed, got sick and was in terrible pain. Appendicitis may have been the cause. When the crew got ready to move cattle to market, the boy begged not to be left alone. The cook noticed that the boy was too sick to ride and put him in the chuck wagon. He died in agony speaking of his mother and of the lonesomeness of the prairie. When he was buried, rolled in his bedding, in another prairie grave, Webster stayed long enough to place a stone for a marker before riding on.

Occasionally, someone was sent from the ranch to get mail and tobacco. The nearest point to get both was forty miles away. On one such trip, Webster received a letter that changed the direction of his life once again. It was a letter from Mrs. O'Daniel saying that his mother was dying. It had taken the letter at least a month to arrive, and it took a month for Webster to ride to Fayette County where the O'Daniel family now lived. His mother was already dead by the time he arrived. Mrs. O'Daniel had taken in Webster's two small brothers. He took them both and rode four hundred miles to Buffalo Gap in Runnels and Taylor Counties near Abilene to work for Clay Mann. The year was 1877. Webster was all of seventeen years old.

If Nunn taught Webster to be a cowboy and to "ride for the brand" as the saying goes, it was with Mann he learned to be his own man, a cowman and rancher. He added firearms along with ropes to his equipment and became the right arm of a man who would later back him in his own enterprise.

Clay Mann's business was far-flung. He had land and cattle in Mitchell, Kent, and Coleman Counties in Texas, and other holdings in New Mexico and Chihuahua, Mexico. Such an empire had to be defended against Indians all identified as Comanches. Hettye Wallace Branch alludes to her father's Indian blood although a tribal designation is absent, "He considered himself brave as most any man; he too had Indian blood in his veins."[5]

Desperadoes and outlaws gave equal concern, but the biographer is quick to express her father's opinion that the renegades "hid behind the Indians and used them for an excuse of terrorism."[6] Horse thieves and cattle rustlers added to the trouble. Range wars were fierce, with one outfit challenging another often with guns blazing or at least with rifles at the ready. Ambush was common, by killers hired and otherwise. Wallace went well armed, as did other men of the range, honest and dishonest alike, in order to protect Mann's interests and his own life, especially when business took him on scouting forays hundreds of miles from headquarters. If color was ever a hindrance in the pursuit of business conducted amidst lower types of range life or in vengeful company, no mention is made of it. The reason may lie not in Wallace's reluctance to speak of it, but in the conditions of the vast expanses of space where the prejudices of the old order did not have the same power. It seems safe to say that everybody was from cautious to suspicious to downright afraid of everybody else, and yet generous, helpful, and trusting to a fault when need arose. As Branch noted, "The struggles for existence made men sympathetic."[7] If Wallace did encounter prejudice, he apparently did not allow himself to become overwhelmed or hampered by it.

Wallace's recounting of life on the range with Mann's outfit expands to complete a portrait of life and times before barbed wire or law enforcement. Trail driving was complete with stampede: "The clouds came closer and so low they seemed to have been touching the ground, then would suddenly rise and fall yards away. The boys' only light was a flash of lightning, or the balls of fire on the cows' horns; even the saliva of the cows appeared to have been made of fire."[8]

With streaks of lightning and claps of thunder, the stampede is on. Wallace is in the lead, trusting his life to his horse until he realizes he can stand no more. Turning his horse away to safety, he escapes with his life. Other rememberers—in the best tradition of storytellers—might have found it easy to end the story in a different way by claiming to have turned the herd and stopped the stampede. Not Wallace.

Swimming the herd across was almost as dramatic as stampedes, but Wallace had learned to swim as a child in the Navidad and Guadalupe Rivers and so felt safe if his horse should fail. Gambling, dance halls, drinking, shooting, and fighting offered diversity from the monotony of stampedes and river crossings. Where the drive ended is vague, possibly Kansas, but Wallace and the crew sold the extra horses, shipped their saddles, and returned to Texas.

In 1877, the same year that Wallace signed on with Mann, the rancher drove a herd to Colorado City, where he planned to center his Texas activities. The cattle carried the 80 brand, burned from "backbone to belly." It was from this same brand that Wallace got the name that identified him for the rest of his life—80 John. There is no doubt that he was Clay Mann's top man, offering his employer fealty and his best efforts without question and putting the boss's interests first, but, as much was said of other reputable men of the range. Was

80 John a label that branded him like a slave or was it merely an identification tying him to the ranch's interests? Would such an identification have been used with a white man? Because neither Wallace nor other sources make anything of it, the matter must remain speculative.

It is clear that Wallace had little time to ponder anything. He was instead too busy responding to mavericks, coping with deep snow and the terrible drought of 1883, working the roundups without pens or corrals, fighting prairie fires, and riding horses—his own favorite was called Peck because "he was no bigger than a half of bushel."[9] The cowboy was trusted to carry and exchange large sums of money to buy and sell cattle far from home. At other times he remained at home to protect both the boss's family as well as the ranch. He constantly tallied cattle and attended to the details of being an expert horseman.

In the same year of the drought and maybe because of it, Mann decided to develop his Bovita Ranch in Mexico. He sent his brother, John, a cousin, John Bailey, and three others—a Mr. Rainey as wagon boss, Joe Clardy, and 80 John—and a few other cowboys, unnamed. Early after their arrival in Mexico, Wallace took the lead as first rider through a mountain pass, but for some reason decided to drop back with the other riders, allowing John Mann and Joe Clardy to lead. Indians ambushed the group and both John Mann and Joe Clardy were killed. What was left of the crew returned to Texas shortly after, and Mann sold the ranch in 1886 to Randolph Hearst.[10]

By 1884, the 80 brand was established back in the Colorado City area, and Wallace and Mann had come to an agreement whereby John drew only ten dollars a month from his thirty dollar a month pay and saved the rest. In two years he was able to buy some steers, which he branded "Wallace" extending from hip to shoulder in an act reminiscent of young Webster's carving his name into the barn timbers. The steers were run on the Mann range along with the 80 brand, driven to market and sold. Wallace's future was secured. He was by then twenty-four years old.

It was during this period that Wallace witnessed the coming of the Texas and Pacific Railroad and the fencing of the ranges. He saw Colorado City become the center of West Texas commerce and trade, the development of the freighting industry using oxen and whackers proficient with the black snake whip, the great blizzards and drifts of 1884 and '85, and horse racing—in which the quarter horse named 80 Gray, raised by Mrs. Mann, won races from Texas to New York City.[11]

By the time Wallace was twenty-five years old he had bought two sections of land near Loraine in Mitchell County, homesteaded it, and had decided to go back to school. He observed that not all the "cattle barons," as they are identified by Branch, could write their names. Some merely signed with an X. Finding out about a segregated school in Navarro County, Wallace enrolled there for a few months in the second grade each year for two years. Whatever embarrassment and daydreaming he suffered as a child apparently had left him. After improving to his own satisfaction, he left but not before he had met, courted, and won Laura Dee Owen, who was finishing high school with the intention of becoming a teacher.

Wallace brought Laura Dee home, after their marriage in 1888, to two rooms and a dugout on one of the Mann ranches. Mann died in 1889. Wallace, after working for the Mann brand for fourteen years, decided to go it on his own in 1891. For a short time he partnered with Dave Roberson, another black rancher, but the arrangement didn't last long.

In order to get established, Wallace had to continue working for wages in such jobs as loading cattle from stock pens in Colorado City, but he now had a hand, Laura. Together they built the herd and a *remuda* of horses, changed the brand to a D-triangle on the hides of the Durham cattle he bought, endured the worst of weather conditions, and entertained friends such as some of the O'Daniels from Flatonia, fed hungry Indians and travelers, faced up to drought, moved the herds to Oklahoma only to sell for enough to pay his debts. And he went broke.

Wallace let no wind gather round his failure. On the way back from Oklahoma, he stopped by Fort Worth to see Winfield Scott, a former rancher and friend in Mitchell County.[12] Scott gave Wallace a letter of credit for ten thousand dollars with which he bought Hereford cattle to try on the range, made improvements, and invested in one of the first windmills used in the area.[13] Wallace changed his brand one last time to a D on the hip and the running W on the right side.

Then it was back to business at Loraine near Colorado City for the next twenty years or so. They were years complete with witching for water, coping with fever ticks, screw worms, prairie dogs, and dust storms. Wallace shipped cattle to market instead of driving them, and he secured corrected titles to his properties, which eventually amounted to 8,820 acres covering eleven square miles with no mortgages due. Oil was discovered on some of his land. Another drought necessitated his moving the herd to New Mexico, where he stayed for ten months to save ninety percent of his cattle. He fenced and cross-fenced his land, built barns, sheds, and a modern home.

Such activities kept Webster and Laura and their family of four—three daughters, Mary, Hettye, and Eula, and a son, Carson—busy right up to 1929. The Great Depression, however, did not ruin the Wallace enterprises as it did many ranchers' and farmers' businesses. Wallace never applied for government aid and did not sign waivers on cotton crops. He lost only seventy-five of his cattle to the government slaughter programs in 1934. Wallace's life was filled with acts of good will and charitable deeds during the same time he carved out his empire. He loaned money to friends to buy homes, fed the hungry and needy, and provided for old friends in need. He educated his own children, made it possible for others to attend school, and supported his church, helping to pay for the Baptist church in Loraine. A school was named after him in Colorado City because of his generous gifts.

For his personal enlightenment and pleasure, he joined the Texas and Southwest Cattle Raisers Association, actively engaging in its programs and attending meetings. He enjoyed Mitchell County reunions and often spoke of early times. John M. Hendrix of Abilene, Texas, writing for *The Cattleman* magazine in 1936, reported: "in a manner deferential and in language wholly lacking in Uncle Remus dialect, he tells them of their country as he first saw it more than half a century ago, unsullied by barbed wire and train smoke, a cowman's paradise of running water, grass covered hills, and wide fertile valleys where antelope played, and the South Texas cows of Mister Clay Mann grazed among the still fresh carcasses of the slaughtered buffalo."[14]

In his seventies, Wallace continued to ride horses, and by the accounts of others he was always an excellent horseman. His favorite was his cowpony, Blondie. It was after a ride in the autumn of 1939 that the rancher foretold his own death. Laura was out in the yard working when she heard someone call. Supposing it was Wallace, she went inside and asked what he wanted. "Nothing," was the reply. A second call brought her back, and when Wallace said again that he did not call her, she went to look around to see if anyone else might be there. Laura went back to say that she had found no one around. Her husband looked at her and said, "Three months from now you will know who called."[15]

In the winter, Wallace became seriously ill and never rallied. One night he asked Laura, "How long has it been since you heard the call?"[16] When she responded that it had been about three months, the husband, father, and rancher without peer said that he was dying.

He couched death in terms of going on a long trip. Did he recall the long drives through snow and rain with St. Elmo's fire illuminating the horns of the cattle and streaks of lightning revealing their stampede? Did he remember the thirsting animals he brought to better pasture through Indian Territory and treacherous terrain? Whatever his recollections, the man with strength failing asked that "On Jordan's Stormy Banks I Stand," be sung at his funeral.

On Jordan's stormy banks I stand and cast a wishful eye,
to Canaan's fair and happy land where my possessions lie.
Oh, I'm bound for the Promised Land . . .

The image of death as "pale horse, pale rider" comes to mind as Wallace waited to be carried away perhaps on the back of his own mount. Mr. M. H. O'Daniel came, but Wallace was too weak to talk. Yet the man's visit stirred memories of his early days with the O'Daniels.

When Wallace was able, he talked to the family about future plans, reminding them to treat each other and everybody else right, to carry on the business in a responsible way. Part of getting ready to cross over was remembering his past life. At one point he said to his wife, "I have reviewed my life from six years until now. I have harmed no man. I am ready to go; what do you think of me?" Laura responded with a kiss and these words, "You have always been my ideal, don't you know?" He took stock of his possessions: "I care nothing about my land and my cattle—I love my family. . ."[17]

The dying think their own thoughts and are enfolded in places of the mind where none can know or enter. Early Tuesday morning, March 28, 1939, Daniel Webster Wallace saw a woman come into his room. He recognized her, knew that she was calling, lifted his hand to her, and smiled. And then he passed. Was it his mother? Did she wait to help him swim the cattle across one more swollen stream?

O'er all those wide extended plains shines one eternal day . . .
Sweet fields arrayed in living green and rivers of delight . . .
I'm bound for the Promised Land . . .

From carving his initials on a barn wall, to carrying the nickname of someone else's cattle brand, to gouging out a place for himself in cattle history of his own making, the life of Daniel Webster Wallace is imprinted in the hard-packed dirt of Texas' cattle country. He is enshrined wherever men speak or sing of the old days among the herd.

The herd starts in the morning . . .

NOTES

1. This chapter is based on materials from Hettye Wallace Branch, *The Story of 80 John: A Biography of One of the Most Respected Negro Ranchmen in the Old West* (New York: Greenwich Books Publisher, 1960) unless otherwise noted. An endnote in W. Sherman Savage's *Blacks in the West: Contributions in Afro-American and African Studies,* no. 23 (Westport, Conn.: Greenwood Press, 1976) indicates that another daughter identified as "Mrs. Wallace Fowler" began work on the biography but that the unfinished manuscript was completed by Hettye. Without the first name it can not be determined whether it was Mary or Eula, because both sisters married Fowler brothers. Additional information is available in Bertha Auburn Webb, "D. W. '80 John' Wallace: Black Cattleman, 1875–1939," M.A. thesis, Prairie View Agricultural and Mechanical College, 1957.

2. R. C. Crane, "D. W. ('80 John') Wallace, A Negro Cattleman on the Texas Frontier," *West Texas Historical Association Yearbook* 28 (Oct., 1952): 113–18. This article is written from an interview with Wallace in 1934. He mentions his father and mother both coming to the farm of Mary Carr. Is Mary Carr the Mary O'Daniel referred to in Hettye Wallace Branch's biography? Branch does not mention the name of Carr but the other details match. Obituary notices at the time of Wallace's death in 1939 mention two brothers, Richard Irving of Oklahoma and Charlie Gilroy of Loraine.

3. Gholson's reputation as an Indian fighter rests on one recorded incident in 1871 when the Texas Rangers and eighteen cowboys, one of them Gholson, overtook a small Comanche band with stolen horses. A. C. Greene who notes the incident in *900 Miles on the Butterfield Trail* (Denton: University of North Texas Press, 1995), p. 51, cites Elkins and McCarty's 1929 printing of *Indian Fighting on the Texas Frontier.* See also J. Evetts Haley, *Charles Goodnight: Cowman and Plainsman* (Norman: University of Oklahoma Press, 1949), p. 218.

4. Andy Adams, *Log of a Cowboy* (Boston: Houghton Mifflin, 1903) and Charles Siringo, *Riata and Spurs* (Boston: Houghton Mifflin, 1927).

5. Branch, *The Story of 80 John,* p. 22.

6. Ibid., p. 23.

7. Ibid., p. 39.

8. Ibid., pp. 24–25.

9. Ibid., p. 28.

10. Ibid., p. 30.

11. Ibid., p. 34. That 80 Gray was a Quarter Horse of Steel Dust lineage, see "Betting Was Strictly Private Affair in West Texas Races," *Fort Worth Star Telegram,* n.d.

12. Ibid., p. 4. Winfield Scott, a self-made man who had ranching enterprises around Colorado City, came to Fort Worth in 1889. In addition to ranches, he owned sizable business property in Fort Worth, built such buildings as the Texas Hotel,

and eventually bought Thistle Hill, owned by W. T. Waggoner. See Judy Alter, *Thistle Hill* (Fort Worth: Texas Christian University Press, 1988).

13. Information found among Wallace files dated October 25, 1973, "Re: Windmill Type Well: 80 John Wallace" with the word or name, Sance, at the end indicates that Travis Branch, son-in-law of Wallace who took over the ranching operation after Wallace's death, testified that "in reference to the truth that 80 John drilled the first windmill type well in West Texas, his personal knowledge is limited." He indicated that a "Miss Billie Wolfe, collector of items at Texas Tech in Lubbock claims that the records of the Eclipse Windmill Co. reveal that 80 John was one of the first ranchers to buy parts to build such a well."

14. John M. Hendrix, "Tribute Paid to Negro Cowmen: Nearly All Larger Cow Outfits Had one or more Negro Cow Punchers, *Cattleman* 22 (Feb., 1936): 26.

15. Branch, *The Story of 80 John*, p. 50.

16. Ibid., p. 51.

17. Ibid.

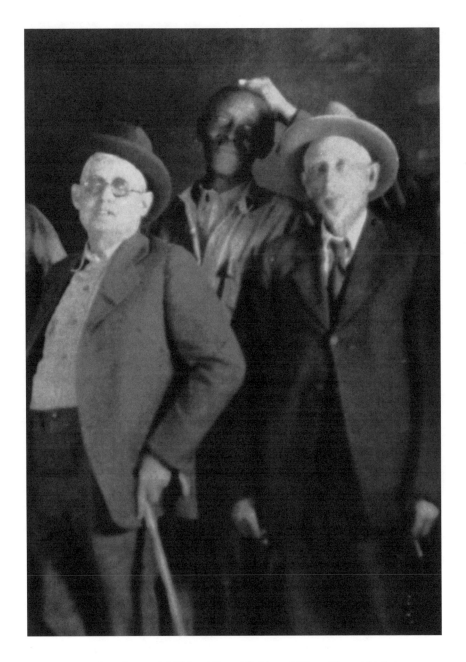

Figure 13. Addison Jones with Edgar Harral (left) *and Victor Harral* (right).
Courtesy Southwest Collection, Special Collections Library, Texas Tech University,
Lubbock

Chapter 16

Addison Jones

*"The Most Noted Negro Cowboy
That Ever 'Topped Off' A Horse"*

MICHAEL N. SEARLES

Addison Jones gained fame and prominence during his lifetime. In a time when most cowboys were known little farther than their place of employment, Addison Jones, or "Nigger Add" as he was called, was recognized and respected by cattlemen, working cowboys, town folk, and cowboy poet-song writers in parts of Texas and the Southwest. His acclaim emanated from two distinct sources: his extraordinary abilities as a cowboy bronc rider and the good fortune of having his talent put into poetry and song.[1]

Addison Jones's birth and early life are clouded in uncertainty; however, several cowboys who knew him and scholars of the western range believed that he was born a slave in either Gonzales or Hays County.[2] His death certificate, completed by his wife, stated that he was born in Gonzales County in 1845. While no records have been found to describe Add's childhood and adolescent years, it is probable that he grew up working cattle and riding horses. If Gonzales County was the place of his nativity, his parents could not have selected a better birthplace. *The Handbook of Texas* notes that some of the first cattle drives began in Gonzales County. Author J. Evetts Haley, who wrote about many of Add's exploits, mentions Gonzales County as a place where it is said that men were born to leather and raised on horses. Jones was closely associated with George Washington Littlefield: legendary cattleman, banker, and philanthropist. Littlefield was born in Panola County, Mississippi, and in 1850, when he was eight, moved with his parents to Gonzales County, Texas. The relationship established between the Littlefield family and Add apparently continued to his death in 1926.[3] While his name first appeared in numerous accounts of the Littlefield (LFD) ranch, a cattle business in eastern New

Mexico and West Texas, not until recently did the name of Addison Jones appear in print.[4] Most references are made to Old Ad(d), Old Negro Add, or "Nigger Add." The use of the appellation "Nigger" was common throughout the old West to describe black cowboys at the time. Cecil Bonney, a contemporary cowboy acquaintance of Add, stated that the term "nigger" was used with respect and affection; however, we cannot really know how Add or other black cowboys felt about it.

Black cowboys associated daily with white Southerners and working class men who carried many contemporary prejudices and resented black cowboys as an economic and social threat to their status. Of greater concern to black cowboys than hostile feelings and the use of an epithet was the violence, ill treatment, and blatant discrimination they sometimes faced. John M. Hendrix of Abilene, Texas, a cowman for many years, explained what was expected of black cowboys around the turn of the century. "They (black cowboys) did as much as possible to place themselves in the good graces of the (white) hands. This most often took the form of 'topping,' or taking the first pitch out of the rough horses of the outfit as they stood saddled, with back humped, in the chill of the morning, while the (white) boys ate their breakfast. It was not unusual for one young negro to 'top' a half dozen hard-pitching horses before breakfast . . . It was the negro hand who usually tried out the swimming water when a trailing herd came to a swollen stream, or if a fighting bull or steer was to be handled, he knew without being told it was his job."[5]

We may never know whether Addison Jones chose the cowboy life or if the cowboy life chose him, but we do know that many young black men tended cattle in antebellum South Carolina, Georgia, Alabama, Mississippi, Louisiana, and Texas.[6] The practice of using black cowboys, sometimes to the exclusion of whites and Mexicans, occurred on some ranches in the Coastal Bend of Texas. Even in West Texas and Eastern New Mexico where blacks were few, John Chisum and George Littlefield employed black cowboys to the chagrin of more than one white cowboy. The use of black cowboys by Littlefield and his nephew J. Phelps White prompted J. Evetts Haley to explain: "With no loss of the sense of benevolent mastery or social hierarchy Littlefield loved his Negroes. They were a part of his early life, a part of his embattled retinue in his unremitting economic struggle, a part of his southern tradition."[7]

The planter, according to T. R. Fehrenbach, author of *Lone Star: A History of Texas and the Texans,* "could value a good Negro to a poor white man." Jones's "privileged status," however, was more than paternalism. Add, recognized as an outstanding cowboy and bronc buster, perfected myriad skills of singular value to a ranching operation like Littlefield's.

His skills with horses made him especially valuable to the LFD. It was often Add who trained young cowboys to handle and prepare the horses that were to be ridden the next day. Hiley T. Boyd, Jr., remembered stories his father told about his cowboy days and a roundup he made with Old Add. H. T. Boyd, Sr., wrote that Add would handle a horse wagon with "two or three hundred saddle horses and two or three hundred broncs."[8] Haley further acknowledged that Add was a welcome sight at roundups, because "when the wagons started and the horses were fresh, he sapped out the salty ones for the boys who dreaded to ride them. It was nothing unusual for him to top off several horses of a morning in order to get the pitching out of their systems before the outfit started on the drive. . ."[9]

The life of a cowboy was filled with long hours, foul weather, and lonely, monotonous work. Anyone who wanted to try his hand was given the opportunity. During the years of the cattle drives, Irish, German, Canadian, English, Jewish, Native American, African American, and Mexican cowboys moved cattle along the Texas trails. Although anyone could try his hand at cowboying, many found the work not to their liking.

Skill and grit were the two ingredients that distinguished those who adopted the cowboy life and those who left it behind. Each cowboy was expected to know or quickly learn his work and to do it without complaint. The life was best suited to young men, and by the time a cowboy reached his mid-thirties, he was getting "old." Talent and skill were distributed among cowboys the way they randomly appeared in other lines of work; however, some were better than others. Some cowboys were good bronc riders while others were good ropers, but rarely was a cowboy exceptional in the array of skills needed in the cattle business.

Addison Jones was the exception who distinguished himself in all areas of cow work. Add gained his reputation among men who were skilled, devoted to the cowboy life, and hesitant to give praise. Yet all of the conditions notwithstanding, Add became a legend in West Texas and Eastern New Mexico, and earned the accolade "the most noted Negro cowboy that ever 'topped off' a horse." The man who issued this high praise was historian and biographer J. Evetts Haley. Yet Haley was not alone in his tribute; numerous cowboys who knew Add described him as an outstanding cowboy.

Add did not leave any memoirs and may have had a limited ability to read and write. What is known about Add comes from two sources: the papers of the men who worked with him and public documents that recorded his marriage, a property deed, and his death.[10] In many cases, references to Add appeared as essential footnotes in the history of the Littlefield ranch. Cecil Bonney in his

Looking Over My Shoulder: Seventy-five Years in Pecos Valley made the point this way: "One cannot tell about the LFD without telling about 'Nigger Add.'"

V. H. Whitlock, who wrote under the pen name Ol' Waddy, a nickname for an old cowhand, recorded stories Add had told him about "Black Jack" Ketchum, a Texas cowboy-outlaw who, with his brother Sam, wreaked havoc in Texas and New Mexico.[11] In *Cowboy Life on the Llano Estacado,* Whitlock referred to Add as "an expert horseman, a good rider and roper," and paid special homage with the phrase "the most famous Negro cowpuncher in the Old West." These statements were particularly significant given the number of cowhands with whom Bonney and Whitlock had worked during their long careers as cowboys.

According to Whitlock, Add, who was not averse to fun, said that he could "look a horse square in the eye and almost tell what it was thinking." Those who saw Add ride often agreed. He was known to stick to the saddle and ride almost any horse he mounted. Some cowboys had never seen a horse that Add could not ride; however, one horse, Whistling Bullet, did temporarily get the best of Old Add. Whistling Bullet was one of those horses that gained notoriety as an outlaw horse. Horses often acquired this status through indiscriminate breeding and ill treatment and were thought to be only suitable for bucking contests. In true cowboy fashion, Add had another chance to test his mettle against this outlaw, and this time, according to District Judge Pat Boone of Littlefield, Texas, Add became the "only bronc-buster that ever rode old Whistling Bullet."[12]

Every rancher knew a cowboy who was a good bronc buster, but the work was dangerous, and even those who were considered successful usually lasted only a few years. The rigors on the body included falls, broken arms and legs, and having lungs torn loose by the violent jolting of the horse. After working for just a few months, many "busters" found themselves spitting up blood. Bronc busters were often a solitary and daring breed of men. Many became busters hoping to make fast money. They often worked exclusively as bronc busters and traveled from ranch to ranch or town to town, picking up work when they had a mind to.

Addison Jones did not fit this profile. He worked for the Littlefield family practically all of his life and continued to "take the sap" out of horses into his sixties or seventies. While Add was not a freelancer, he liked the daring associated with breaking horses. The danger involved in breaking horses was so great that common sense dictated that a cowboy not make the job more risky than it was. Yet, lurking inside many cowboys was a bravado that called for achieving some feat that had never been done, and "Old Black Add" may have garnered the self-esteem associated with "swapping ends with a wild bronc" that otherwise was denied him.

Addison Jones discovered a unique technique for bringing down a horse. Just how he developed this skill and how long it took to perfect it is unknown, but those who witnessed it first-hand were amazed at what they saw. The fool-hardy nature of the feat also made it an ideal cowboy activity. Numerous cow-boys made references in memoirs to Add's remarkable athleticism, and J. Evetts Haley provided the following description: "He (Add) would tie a rope hard and fast around his hips, hem a horse up in the corner of a corral or in the open pasture, rope him around the neck as he went past at full speed, and where another man would have been dragged to death, Add would, by sheer skill and power on the end of the rope, invariably flatten the horse out on the ground."[13]

Add was often described as a short man with broad shoulders, bowlegs, and a powerful, heavy-set build. Add was very strong, but strength alone would have been insufficient to accomplish this consummately daring act consis-tently. Timing and confidence were crucial in bringing down a mustang weigh-ing as much as eight hundred pounds. Although Add exhibited remarkable consistency, he was not always successful. V. Whitlock and Add worked to-gether at the Bar F horse camp when all their horses got loose and left them afoot. Add tied two ropes together, securing the end of one rope hard and fast to his hips. He slipped up on the horses while they were drinking and lassoed one. He then attempted to flatten the horse as he so often did; however, this time it was Add that was snatched down and dragged for about a half-mile before he got the upper hand.

Add's roping skills were renowned far beyond catching a horse at full speed. He had the knack of catching any horse at which he tossed a rope. He often used a sixty-foot rope, which would allow him to throw to the far side of a *remuda* and catch a bronc with deadly accuracy. According to cowboy Mat E. Jones, Addison's status as a roper was recognized by the wagon bosses, who "would even let Ad rope horses out of the corral."[14] Add's confidence and the casual manner with which he roped were often a point of conversation with the cowboys that knew him. Eugene Price relayed the following story: "Add would wrap the end of his rope around his hips, and holding the end of the rope and the coils of it in his left hand, he'd slip around the remuda until he got a chance at the horse he wanted, then he'd smear that big loop all over the front end of the frightened little bronc. Maybe the loop would take up properly around the pony's neck, or maybe he'd jump a foreleg through, but it was all the same to Add."[15]

Add's confidence, braggadocio, and secure status with the LFD most likely made him feel like a "privileged character," as some of the cowboys suggested. Add was willing to breach much of the protocol that existed between black and white cowboys. While most black cowboys, especially former slaves, did not try to anger or embarrass white cowboys, Add would at times cross the line. Mat E. Jones related another story that became legend on the LFD that demonstrated the temperament of Addison Jones. A white cowboy, Cliff Robertson, came to the LFD from a neighboring ranch as a "rep" or representative. Ranches often sent seasoned cowboys to roundups to make sure that their stock was identified, properly branded, and returned to the home ranch. Add rode up to change his horse as Cliff was about to select a favorite mount to begin his "rep" work. As Add was changing his horse, he asked, "What horse you want, lint?" The term lint was a derisive one that referred to a young, inexperienced cowboy out of East Texas with "cotton lint still his hair."

Cliff stated that he would catch his own horse, but he missed with his throw. Add then roped the horse (some say by the hind leg) and began to pull it out. Cliff, both embarrassed and insulted, came after Add either with his rope doubled or a knife to cut the rope. At this point, Bud Wilkerson, the LFD range boss rode between them and said to Add, "Drag the horse out, and I will tend to the lint." Cliff Robertson was so angered by the experience that he saddled his horse and went back to his home ranch.

Add frequently traveled to other ranches where he could not depend on the protection and goodwill of the LFD bosses. On one occasion, Add was a "rep" at the neighboring Hat Ranch. While waiting for the horses to be brought in, Add went to the water bucket to get a drink. Finding the bucket empty, he followed a standard cowboy procedure to fill the bucket. The Hat Ranch used a large, fifty-gallon tank with a hose from which water had to be siphoned. To get the water started, a cowboy had to "suck the gut." When Add began to start the water, a white cowboy, Tom Ogles, picked up a neck yoke and hit him on the back of the neck, knocking him out. This incident begs the question of racism in the West.

Addison Jones, while attending a "colored" dance in Eddy, New Mexico, laid out with one punch a town black who insulted him. Mat Jones, who related the story, said that Add held out his arm and patted it saying, "When I straighten a fellow, I gets fruit." This same Addison Jones, after being struck by Tom Ogles, said nothing. After he regained consciousness, he waited for the *remuda* as if nothing had happened, caught his horse, and rode back to the LFD. This incident provided reasonable credence to the position that a black cowboy had limitations that were not placed on his white counterpart. Apparently, Add's "sucking the gut" violated an unwritten taboo on the Hat Ranch, and he was more willing to accept the embarrassment of the assault by Tom Ogles than to "straighten him out."

A popularly held conviction by many that had some acquaintance with the West was that no racial discrimination existed. Cecil Bonney makes that exact statement in *Looking Over My Shoulder* when he said that Add's appellation "Nigger Add" was given not out of derisiveness but in respect, even affection, because "there was no discrimination on the range in those days." Others also pointed to the closeness that black and white cowboys on the range sometimes exhibited. As a way of confirming an unbiased atmosphere, Bonney mentioned that "Tom White (a wagon boss) and Nigger Add would sleep in the same bedroll as protection against the elements." Some of Add's experiences though would indicate Bonney was in error.

An amusing story developed out of Tom and Add's sleeping arrangements, which Elvis Fleming related in his article on Addison Jones: "Ralph Whitlock described Add's bed as the best one he ever saw on the range. It took two men to load the all-blanket bedroll. Judge Boone states that his father '. . . said that Tom White, straw boss of the LFD, was too stingy to buy his own bedroll and always shared Add's when visiting his chuck wagon.' Ralph Whitlock adds to that story by saying that Add once told Phelps White, 'Mist' Phelps, I wish you would buy Mist' Tom a bed; he keeps me lousy all the time!' Tom was Phelps's younger brother."[16]

Add's humor must be understood within the reality that he was never to receive the status as a cowboy that would have been his if he were white. Despite Cecil Bonney's statement that Add "was considered the tophand of all the Negro cowboys who came to the large cow outfits on the Pecos" and Jack Thorp's reference to Add as the "LFD outfit's range boss," V. Whitlock clarified Add's status: "He was a good cowhand, but because of the custom in those days, he never became what was known as a 'top' hand."

When Thorp, an early cowboy songwriter-collector, rode into Add's camp in March, 1889, on his first song hunt he found Add and his men "pitched at the tail of their chuck wagon" during a roundup. The job of "calling brands" was given to Add, who had perfected the art of reading and calling the cattle brands.[17] Thorp made several favorable comments about Add's abilities, the wide recognition and reputation he enjoyed, and the fact that Add worked South Texas colored hands almost entirely.[18] The reference to Add working "colored hands almost entirely" also indicated a standard practice of not allowing black cowboys to supervise white ones. Even in cases like Add's, where a black cowboy had many years of experience, he was still not "qualified" to tell white men what to do, so he worked all-black cowboy crews.

Add remained a cowboy and stayed in West Texas and Eastern New Mexico all of his life. Many of the black cowboys who worked with him, however, are lost to history. In various accounts, they often were referred to as young, transient, and itinerant. There was no indication whether these cowboys left because of racist treatment or for greener pastures. For those few black cowboys for whom some record exists, the issue of loneliness and the absence of permanent female companionship seemed to have been an issue.

For most of his life, Addison Jones was single. His life was such that he may have decided that it was not the kind of life that a married man should live. However, if he were the marrying kind, he would have to face a very serious question: Whom could he marry? In many parts of the West, the scarcity of black women destined black cowboys to bachelorhood. In New Mexico Territory in 1900, one year after Add married, the black population was 1,610, with only 587 females. In 1910, in Chaves County, which included Roswell, the total black female population was 108. The number of nubile black women in both Chaves County and the surrounding area could have easily been less than 20.[19]

George McJunkin or "Nigger George," a contemporary black cowboy in West Texas and Eastern New Mexico, was faced with the same dilemma. His biographer's words were poignant, "He wished he had a family, but how could he marry? There were no black women in the valley. George liked some of the young Mexican women, and they liked him, but Mexican men strongly opposed marriages of their womenfolk to non-Mexicans. On the other hand, if he and a white woman wanted to become man and wife, the white men of the valley would not stand for that. They respected George as a skilled cowboy, but not one of them would like it if he married a white woman. They all had been taught—and still believed—that such a thing was wrong."[20]

In 1883, at the age of twenty, Rosa Haskins came from Texas to the Pecos Valley. Rosa or Rosie was well known in Roswell and cooked at Nellie C. Pearce's rooming house for tuberculars and for a number of prominent families. Add was more fortunate than George McJunkin, who never married. Add found, courted, and married Rosa Haskins in Roswell on December 7, 1899. Add was fifty-four and Rosa was thirty-six. The record is not clear whether Add enjoyed eternal marital bliss; however, there was a clear record of how the notification of his marriage was received by others. Thorp, who mistakenly cited Christmas for the marriage, related the response from ranchers and friends of Add upon hearing of his wedding. "Late in life Add got himself engaged to a colored girl and told a few friends he would be married on Christmas Day. The news spread. Every cowman or outfit wanted to send a present, but ranches were far apart and nobody knew what the other fellow was sending. So on his wedding day Add and his bride went to the Roswell freight depot to claim his gifts which they had been told were there and found NINETEEN COOKSTOVES!"[21]

Addison Jones remained an active part of the LFD long after he could do the daring feats of his youth. V. Whitlock told of being assigned to break horses with a young cowboy nicknamed "Wrang." Charlie Walker, LFD wagon boss, told Whitlock that "Old Negro Add" would go and help him handle the horses. Add was too old and crippled to take an active part in riding the young, unbroken horses; he was to guide the horses away from the fences and catch them when they threw off the two would-be bronc busters.[22]

Whitlock had a great deal of respect for Add and remembered when he could not only ride them but knew every one of the 120 horses in the Bar F *remuda* by name. It was also Whitlock who recalled an event that cowboys remembered whenever Add's name was mentioned. Whitlock and a cowboy friend were about to leave Roswell by "order of the judge" when they saw Add in front of the Grand Central Hotel. Add was sitting on Sunflower, the LFD's most powerful roping horse, waiting to get a letter for the roundup boss. While the cowboys were waiting, they saw a milk wagon coming down the street toward them at full speed without a driver.

"Add reached down and pulled the latigo strap on his cinch one hole tighter. He jerked down his rope, double-half-hitched one end to the saddle horn and built a big loop in the other end. As the team passed by, he jumped Sunflower alongside it and dropped a big 'blocker' around both of the horses' necks. He threw the slack in his rope over the wagon, dropped his weight over his left stirrup and turned off as if he was 'fairgrounding' a big steer. Sunflower stacked the whole shebang in the middle of the street. Both horses went down, the wagon toppled on its side with the tongue broken, and milk and broken bottles scattered over a wide area."[23] Whitlock ends the story with the comment that when the driver came and removed Add's rope, Add was reported to have said, "Them horses sure would've tore things up if I hadn't caught them."

Add's tongue-in-cheek humor was standard cowboy fare and indicative of Add's approach to life. He helped establish the cattle industry in the West, lived a full life, and rode until he could no longer mount a horse. He never lost his love for cowboying and was seen riding in the old-timer parades in Roswell during his declining years. Addison Jones outlived many of his contemporaries and, according to former Texas and New Mexico sheriff Bob Beverly, "died knowing full well that his efforts had been recognized and appreciated by the really great cowmen of Texas and New Mexico."[24] In making his mark in the

Pecos Valley, Jones followed a path similar to other black cowboys whose skill and reliability prompted those who employed them to lament their passing and salute their lives.

NOTES

The chapter subtitle comes from J. Evetts Haley, *George W. Littlefield: Texan* (Norman: University of Oklahoma Press, 1943), p. 181.

1. N. Howard (Jack) Thorp, a cowboy, song writer/collector, was the first person to make a systematic effort to collect cowboy and songs of the range. He wrote a poem entitled "Whose Old Cow?" that he put to music. It memorialized "Nigger Add" as an expert on cattle earmarks and brands in a song about a roundup. The song was listed by N. Howard Thorp, *Songs of the Cowboy* (1908; reprint, New York: C. N. Potter, 1966) pp. 248–49, and John Lomax, *Cowboy Songs and Other Frontier Ballads* (New York: Macmillan Co., 1920), pp. 362–63. The words to the song as written in Lomax are as follows:

Whose Old Cow?
   'Twas the end of round-up, the last day of June
      Or maybe July I don't remember
   Or it might have been August 'twas some time ago
      Or perhaps 'twas the first of September.
   Anyhow, 'twas the round-up we had at Mayou
      On the lightning rod's range, near Cayo
   There were some twenty wagons, "more of less" camped about
      On the temporal in the Cañon.
   First night we'd no cattle so we only stood guard
      On the horses, somewhere 'bout two hundred head
   So we side-lined and hoppled, we belled and we staked
      Loose'd our hot-rolls and fell into bed.
   Next morning 'bout day break we started our work
      Our horses like possums felt fine
   Each "one 'tending' knitten!" none trying to shirk
      So the round-up got on in good time.
   Well we worked for a week 'till the country was clear
      And the bosses said "now, boys, we'll stay here
   We'll carve and we'll trim 'em an' start out a herd
      Up the east trail from old Abilene.
   Next morning' all on herd an' but two with the cut
      An' the boss on Piute, carving fine
   'Till he rode down his horse and had to pull out
      An' the new man went in to clean up.

Well after each outfit had worked on the band
There was only three head of them left
When Nig Add from LFD outfit rode in
A dictionary on earmarks an' brands.
He cut the two head out told where they belonged
But when the last cow stood there alone
Add's eyes bulged so he didn't 'no just what to say
'Ceptin' boss, der's something here monstrous wrong.
White folks smarter'n Add, an' maybe I'se wrong
But here's six months wages dat I'll give
If anyone'll tell when I reads dis mark
To who dis long horned cow belongs.
Overslope in the right ear an' de underbill
Left ear swallerfork an de undercrop
Hole punched in center, an' de jinglebob
Under half crop, an' de slash an split.
She's got O Block an' lightnin' rod
Nine forty-six an' A bar eleven
T terrapin an' ninety-seven
Rafter cross an' de Double prod.
Half circle A an' diamond D
Four cross L an' three P Z
B W I bar, X V V
Bar N cross an' A L C
So, if no' o' you punchers claims dis cow
Mr. Stock 'Sociation needn't git alarmed
For one more brand more or less wont do no harm
So old Nigger Add'l just brand her now.

2. Bob Beverly, interview by J. Evetts Haley, recorded by hand, June 27, 1946, J. Evetts Haley Collection, Nita Stewart Haley Memorial Library, Midland, Tex. Bob Beverly was a well-established, turn-of-the-century cowboy who later became a sheriff and tax collector for Midland County, Texas; a cattle inspector for the Texas and Southwestern Cattle Raising Association; brand inspector and sheriff of Lea County, New Mexico. In the conversation between Haley and Beverly, they discussed "Nigger Add" and a black cowboy identified as "Old Nigger Bob." Beverly who was uncertain as to whether they were from Hayes [Hays] or Gonzales County told a story of these two boyhood friends Add and Bob who met near Amarillo as the herds they were driving met. That evening with the two crews camped near each other, Add and Bob swapped stories of their growing up together. Addison Jones's death certificate, which gives Gonzales, Texas, as his birth place, was completed by his wife Mrs. Addison Jones.

3. Haley, *George W. Littlefield, Texan.* J. Phelps White and Tom White, George Littlefield's nephews and partners as well as wagon boss, Bud Wilkerson also

maintained a close working relationship with Add. On several occasions, white cowboys made comments that Add was a "privileged character" at the LFD. See Mat E. Jones, *Fiddlefooted* (Denver: Sage Books, 1966), p. 115, and Cecil Bonney, *Looking Over My Shoulder: Seventy-Five Years in the Pecos Valley* (Roswell, N.Mex.: Hall-Poorbaugh Press, Inc., 1971), pp. 140–41, for other cited instances when Tom White and Add shared a bedroll to protect them from the severe weather.

4. Connie Brooks, *The Last Cowboys: Closing the Open Range in Southeastern New Mexico, 1890s–1920s* (Albuquerque: University of New Mexico Press, 1993), p. 72; Kenneth Wiggins Porter, a leading authority on blacks in the West, writes a bibliographic essay on Addison Jones but only refers to Add as "Nigger Add" [Old Add, Old Negro Ad] and gives his birth and death as fl. 1889–c. 1906 in Rayford W. Logan and Michael R. Winston, eds., *Dictionary of American Negro Biography* (New York: W. W. Norton & Company, 1982), pp. 5–6; J. Evetts Haley did know Add's last name was Jones, as was clearly indicated in several interviews he conducted. However, Haley apparently did not consider it important, because he never printed it in the histories or biographies he wrote. Ed Harral, interview by J. Evetts Haley and Hervey Chesley, recorded by hand, Roswell, N.Mex., June 13, 1939, J. Evetts Haley Historical Collection, Nita Stewart Haley Memorial Library, Midland, Texas. See C. W. Walker, W. W. Walker, W. D. Walker, interview by J. Evetts Haley, recorded by hand, Dunlap, N.Mex., Aug. 5, 1937, J. Evetts Haley Collection, Nita Stewart Haley Memorial Library, Midland, Texas. Cecil Bonney states that Add's wife Rose was a cook and housekeeper for some of Roswell's oldest families, among them J. P. Church and John W. Rhea.

5. John M. Hendrix, "Tribute Paid to Negro Cowmen," *Cattlemen* 22 (Feb., 1936): 24.

6. Peter H. Wood, *Black Majority: Negroes in Colonial South Carolina from 1670 through the Stone Rebellion* (New York: Alfred A. Knopf, 1974), pp. 30–34. Wood puts forth an argument that suggests one source of the term cowboy may have come from the slave experience. Terry G. Jordan, *North American Cattle-Ranching Frontiers: Origins, Diffusion, and Differentiation* (Albuquerque: University of New Mexico Press, 1993), pp. 112–13, 117, 121, 177, 180, 188–89, 213, 215, 220–21.

7. Haley, *George W. Littlefield, Texan*, p. 181.

8. Hiley T. Boyd, Jr., interview by David Gracy, tape recording, May 19, 1969, Southwest Collection, Texas Tech University, Lubbock.

9. Haley, *George W. Littlefield, Texan*, pp. 181–82.

10. Marriage certificate, Deed—1885, Chaves County Clerk, Roswell, New Mexico, has records of Add's marriage to a Miss Rosa Haskins and a deed indicating his purchase of land in New Mexico Territory in 1885. Death certificate: Addison Jones, Bureau of Vital Records & Health Statistics, Santa Fe, N.Mex.

11. This is the same Ketchum known by George Adams, another black cowboy who lived in Brewster County.

12. Elvis E. Fleming, "Addison Jones, Famous Black Cowboy of the Old West,"

    Treasures of History III (Roswell, N.Mex.: The Historical Society for Southeast New Mexico, 1995), p. 36.

13. Haley, *George W. Littlefield, Texan*, p. 184.

14. Jones, *Fiddlefooted*, p. 115. Mat E. Jones is one of the cowboys who knew and worked with Add. Mat seemed not to be especially fond of Add and expressed a kind of glee when Add got what Mat thought he deserved.

15. Eugene H. Price, *Open Range Ranching on the South Plains in the 1890's* (Clarendon, Tex.: Clarendon Press, 1967), p. 52.

16. Fleming, "Addison Jones," *Treasures of History III*, p. 38.

17. Thorp, *Songs of the Cowboy*, p. 248.

18. N. Howard (Jack) Thorp, *Partner of the Wind: Story of the Southwestern Cowboy* (Caldwell, Idaho: Claxton Printers, Ltd., 1945), p. 22.

19. U. S. Bureau of the Census, *Negro Population, 1790–1915* (Washington, D.C.: GPO, 1918), pp. 150, 821.

20. Franklin Folsom, *Black Cowboy: The Life and Legend of George McJunkin* (Niwot, Colo.: Roberts Rinehart Publishers, 1992), p. 85.

21. Thorp, *Partner of the Wind*, Appendix I.

22. V. H. Whitlock, *Cowboy Life on the Llano Estacado* (Norman: University of Oklahoma Press, 1970), p. 173.

23. Ibid., p. 225.

24. Bonney, *Looking Over My Shoulder*, p. 141.

Figure 14. Jim Perry. Courtesy Southwest Collection, Special Collections Library, Texas Tech University, Lubbock

Chapter 17

Jim Perry

XIT Hand

RON W. WILHELM

Among the many legendary figures associated with the three-million-acre XIT Ranch in the Panhandle of Texas was James (Jim) Perry. In various accounts of XIT history, Jim Perry was hailed as the best rider, roper, and cook in Texas. The few details of Jim's life on the XIT were told not by Jim, himself, but by his white co-workers and their wives. Their recollections created an image of Jim Perry as an accomplished cowboy, respected for his considerable talents with a rope and skillet as well as for his generous nature.

Although Jim was born in Texas on February 2, 1858, his birthplace and early years are unknown. The 1900 Oldham County census data indicate both Perry's mother and father were natives of Alabama.[1] Yet the 1910 Hartley County census information indicates that they were both born in Texas.[2] Such confusion may have resulted from different people giving the information. It is unclear whether Jim or his parents were born free or were enslaved.

Prior to working for the XIT, Perry punched cattle in the 1870s for the Horse Shoe T Cross Ranch near Double Mountains in Stonewall County. The ranch was owned by Sauls and Armstrong of Austin and managed by Neil Moneil at the time.[3] Perry's association with Colonel A. G. Boyce, later general range manager of the XIT, apparently began when both men were working on the Horse Shoe T Cross.[4]

Inconsistencies exist regarding Perry's beginnings at the XIT. Nordyke related that Perry had participated in the last, big, general roundup in 1886 before the XIT was fenced.[5] Hunter attributed Jim's arrival to Colonel A. G. Boyce, who supposedly brought Jim from Boyce's family home in Williamson County when he became general range manager in 1887.[6] Regardless of the starting date, Perry's association with the ranch lasted off and on for another twenty years.

The XIT Ranch resulted from a land-exchange deal to build a state capitol in Austin. In 1879, the Texas state legislature set aside 3,050,000 acres of land in the Panhandle of Texas to be sold so that a new capitol could be constructed. The Taylor, Babcock and Company of Chicago, Illinois, consisting of Abner Taylor, A. C. Babcock, John V. Farwell, and Charles B. Farwell, was awarded the contract. They accepted the deal having never seen the land in question. After Babcock toured the high plains in 1882, the company's initial plan to open the land to settlers for farming was altered to establish a ranch. From its beginnings in 1885 until 1912, the XIT Ranch was arguably the largest ranch in the state and probably the largest fenced range in the world.[7]

As was the case with most of the cowboys on the XIT, Perry's duties were varied and changed with the seasons.[8] His considerable talents as a bronc buster and roper soon gained him acclaim among the other cowboys on the ranch. Former XIT cowhand W. T. Brown remembered, "Not only was Jim the best cook, but the best Negro that ever lived, as well as the strongest and the best rider. . . . If they (the broncos) throwed me he would ride them for me."[9]

Jim was often designated to handle particularly tough roping assignments. Yet, despite his prowess, he did not always come out on top. One such costly incident occurred during the general roundup in 1886.

Comedy and sorrow mingled with the hustle and bustle that morning. Jim Perry, a Negro and one of the best riders and ropers ever to hit the West, was celebrating that year with a new Apple Horn saddle, so named because the horn looked remotely like an apple. Since a puncher had to buy his own saddle, the latter was a considerable index of his worth. A man might have to ride a ten-dollar nag, but he wanted a forty-dollar saddle, anyhow. So Jim had saved his money and bought the Apple Horn. It had cost a little more than forty, and he was anxious to try it out. In his remuda was a horse named Bald Hornet, which had the bad habit of stampeding out of the rope corral. That morning the wagon boss had decided to teach the outlaw a lesson. "Jim," he said to the Negro cowboy, "when Bald Hornet breaks out this morning, I want you to get your string on him an' break his damn' neck, if you can. I'll try to handle the horses so he'll break out close to you."

Jim took his stand. As Bald Hornet plunged through the remuda and over the rope that enclosed the corral, Jim's lariat followed him and settled firmly into place. Quickly Jim gave it a wrap around the horn of the new saddle. The lasso grew taut against the pull of the Hornet, now charging forward at full speed, and in a moment Jim's torn saddle horn whistled through the air. Jim's eyes rolled wetly, as he gazed forlornly at the ruined saddle.[10]

This failed roping effort cost Jim some money and pride, but another incident could have cost him his job.

One day, Jim and "Scandalous" John McCanless, an XIT cowboy known for his outlandish practical jokes, encountered an antelope near ranch headquarters in Channing. Hunter reported, "Riding up to the big barn, they found an antelope inside and decided to rope it. McCanless drove the antelope toward the door, where Jim waited with lasso ready. He missed on the first try and almost ran his horse down in an attempt to catch the swift animal, with no success."[11] Both men risked being fired over this escapade because they had broken XIT Ranch rule number ten, written by ranch general manager Abner Taylor in 1888, which read, "Employees are not allowed to run mustangs, antelope or any kind of game on the company's horses."[12] Perry's job, at least, was probably saved because he clearly had Col. Boyce's support and respect. According to XIT folklore, "Col. Boyce had a standing offer to bet any amount of money that Jim could rope and tie a steer faster than any man in the state."[13]

Jim Perry's talents did not end when he put his lariat aside after branding season. In his later years, he also worked as cook on the XIT and was arguably one of the cowhands' favorites. Perry drove the chuck wagon out of the ranch headquarters in Channing during the summer and drove freight wagons from there to Amarillo during the winter.[14] After a particularly severe winter in 1888, Colonel Boyce decided that the ranch could not be managed as a single range and created seven divisions, each division with its own foreman, range and wagon bosses, fencers, windmill crews, freight outfits, including chuck wagons, and cowboys.[15] Long after the ranch was sold in 1912, reunions of the old-timers, cowhands, and their wives were held in Dalhart each August beginning in the 1930s. Often the talk revolved around which division had the best cook.

Former XIT cowboy J. W. Standifer remembered that Jim Perry was "a Negro cook from Austin, Texas and what a cook! He could make the best son-of-a-gun (calf testicle stew) I ever ate, and I never had a truer friend."[16] Even though many cowboys seemed to grumble about the chuck fare as part of their job description, the chuck for the XIT was reputed to be better than average. Typically, Perry and the other cooks would prepare sourdough biscuits, potatoes, beans, coffee, beef, dried fruits, and a small amount of various canned vegetables.[17]

J. Evetts Haley presented one of the more detailed accounts of the importance of the chuck wagon and cook to the ten to twenty-five cowboys of each division on the XIT, "An ill-tempered cook would often ruin the morale of a cow camp. A good-humored one who did his work well always improved it."[18] By all published accounts, Jim Perry represented the latter category.

During the winters as a freighter, Perry was responsible for daily hauling ten to eleven thousand pounds of ranch supplies twenty to twenty-five miles.[19] In this manner, Jim and other freighters supplied the ranch divisions with materials needed by the more than 150 cowboys to maintain the six thousand miles of fence, numerous windmills, and their riding stock of 1,000 horses in addition to the more than 150,000 head of cattle. Evidently Perry brought the same ability to his freight-hauling work that he had to his roping and cooking duties and clearly won the lasting respect and friendship of more than one cowhand. Mrs. Allen Willbanks, wife of a former XIT cowboy, recalled one of Jim's visits to their line camp during a particularly fierce norther:

> They had a colored man on the ranch that they called Jim. He was a good Negro man. Everybody thought lots of old Jim. He would come to our camp and spend the night when he had to bring out a load of casing or rods for the windmills. One time when he came out he made out his hot roll, or bed, in a tepee we had for the men to sleep in, and away in the night one of the coldest snowstorms came up. Mr. Willbanks called Jim and told him to bring his bed into the shack we were living in or he would freeze to death. He did come in and made his bed down on the floor.
>
> The next morning Jim built the fire, and he said, "I tell you, Mr. Willbanks, you would have had a dead shine in camp if you had not called me into the house last night." After that Jim would slip off to our camp and bring us eggs, chickens, or anything else he could get to bring us to eat. He thought so much of us that Mr. Willbanks would tease me and say that I would give him, Jim, the best chair in the front room to smoke his Meerschaum pipe to make me mad.[20]

Jim Perry earned the respect of his white contemporaries through his hard work and distinguished abilities. Clearly he was a man who appreciated quality, whether in his work, equipment, or clothing. Reminiscing about Jim Perry, J. W. Standifer recalled: "He loved to dress up and go to town and show off before the other Negroes. He one time had a twenty-dollar hat. He wore it to Fort Worth and got mixed up with some city slicks. This other Negro told him he didn't want to be recognized in that part of town, and for them to exchange hats, but when the town Negro got his hand on Jim's twenty-dollar hat he skipped out, and that was the last of Jim's hat as far as he was concerned."[21] Apparently, Jim was generous to a fault.

Although he could not read or write, according to the 1910 Hartley County census data, Jim parlayed his prowess and knowledge as a cowpuncher into respect and friendship from his white counterparts, many of whom, including his boss, Colonel A. G. Boyce, had served in the Confederate army. Even though ability with a horse and rope counted for more on the High Plains of Texas than the color of a man's skin, the cowboy society established on the XIT merely reproduced the dominant social mores extant at the time throughout the post–Civil War South. For example, Jim Perry, as other black cowboys of the day, did not escape being called the derogatory name "Nigger." Indeed, long after Jim died, residents in the Channing-Tascosa area commonly referred to an old line camp as "Nigger Jim's."[22]

In conversations with his close white friends, Jim confided that he was aware that his abilities as a cowman far exceeded the status relegated to him by a prejudiced society. In spite of Colonel Boyce's standing bet to test Jim's abilities with a rope, one account suggested, "Jim was acknowledged to be one of the best riders and ropers in Texas, although he was not permitted to compete in round-ups against white cowboys, perhaps for fear that he might show them up."[23]

Jim, always savvy as to how to survive in a white-dominated society, was careful never to charge racism. However, in the XIT literature that mentions Jim Perry, one can find a quote often attributed to him, "If it weren't for my damned old black face I'd have been boss of one of these divisions long ago."[24] His use of self-deprecating humor in this instance and his previous reference to himself as a "shine," may be interpreted appropriately as a survival strategy. On the one hand he communicated that he was prevented from achieving a professional and social status equal to his abilities, but then he softened his criticism of a prejudiced society by placing the blame on himself and his skin color as an indication to his white contemporaries that he knew "his place" in their world.

Interestingly, Jim Perry, as an employee of the XIT Ranch, had the right to vote at a time when other blacks and women were denied it. The owners and management of the XIT intended to control local politics and to influence state politics to protect and enhance their interests against other ranchers and a growing number of farmers. One of the owners, Charles B. Farwell of Chicago, an aspiring presidential candidate of the Republican Party, served as a U.S. senator from Illinois. Another owner, Abner Taylor, charged with the construction of the Texas state capitol in exchange for the XIT land, was elected a congressman from Chicago.[25] These men understood how to use their political connections to manipulate Panhandle politics and to do it, they needed the votes of all of their employees, including Jim Perry. His wife, Emma, once confided to her friend, Mrs. Bobbie (Robert E. Lee Edwards) Morris, "Before the elections he is Mr. Perry, but after the voting, he is just 'Nigger Jim' again."[26]

Three known photographs of Jim exist. Apparently all three were taken at Jim's camp on what became the Bivens's place. In one photograph, Jim is playing a fiddle. In another, Jim is holding a rifle, and, in the third photograph, Jim is being accosted in a mock hold-up at gunpoint by I. J. Lamar, a bookkeeper and stenographer who began work at the XIT in 1907.[27]

Jim married late in life at the age of fifty. The marriage records of Hartley County show he married Emma Beaseley on September 29, 1908.[28] She was twenty-seven at the time. The 1910 Hartley County census data indicate that Emma and both of her parents were born in Texas, that Emma was literate, and that the couple had no children.[29] No other information regarding later children was found. In the 1910 Hartley County census data, Jim's occupation was listed as "manager, general farming" and apparently he was renting his homestead when the census was taken.[30] He and Emma lived in the Channing-Tascosa area, and they enjoyed visits with Al and Bobbie Morris, who owned an apple orchard on the old Casimiro Romero place near Tascosa.[31]

Perry did not survive an operation for a brain tumor at the Trans-Canadian Clinic in Dalhart in 1918.[32] He was buried in the center of the old section of the Channing Cemetery in plot number twenty-seven.[33] His gravestone read "James Perry, February 2, 1858–August 2, 1918, 60 years and 6 months." Ben Carlton Meade, a Panhandle resident, wrote of Perry, "The only negro cowhand in the Tascosa-Channing area known to current residents and the only negro buried in this cemetery; known as 'Nigger Jim' to his contemporaries, but so well liked by all that there was no dissent in burying him in a white cemetery as one might expect in that time."[34] Yet, as recently as May, 1998, not twenty yards away from Perry's grave, a Confederate battle flag decorated the grave site of another cemetery resident as a silent reminder of the social restrictions under which Jim Perry lived even as one of the most respected cowboys on the XIT Ranch.

NOTES

1. U.S. Bureau of the Census, Census of 1900, Oldham County Texas (Washington, D.C.: GPO).

2. U.S. Bureau of the Census, Census of 1910, Hartley County, Texas (Washington, D.C.: GPO).

3. William Carey Newton, interview by Adele Howell, transcript, c. 1939, Panhandle-Plains Museum, Canyon, Tex.

4. *The XIT Brand,* Aug., 1939, p. 40.

5. Lewis Nordyke, *Cattle Empire: The Fabulous Story of the 3,000,000 Acre XIT* (New York: William Morrow and Company, 1949), pp. 138–39.

6. Lillie Mae Hunter, *The Book of Years* (Hereford, Tex.: Pioneer Book Publishers, Inc., 1969), p. 112.

7. For a detailed description of the founding of the ranch, see J. Evetts Haley, *The XIT Ranch of Texas and the Early Days of the Llano Estacado* (Norman: University of Oklahoma Press, 1967).

8. For a detailed description of cowboys' duties on the XIT see J. Evetts Haley, Ibid., and Cordia Duke and Joe B. Frantz, *6,000 Miles of Fence: Life on the XIT Ranch of Texas* (Austin: University of Texas Press, 1969).

9. Duke and Frantz, *6,000 Miles of Fence,* p. 172.

10. Nordyke, *Cattle Empire,* pp. 138–39.

11. Hunter, *The Book of Years,* p. 113.

12. Nordyke, *Cattle Empire,* p. 271.

13. Hunter, *The Book of Year,* p. 113.

14. *The XIT Brand,* Aug., 1939, p. 40.

15. For a description of the division of the ranch in Boyce's plan, see Nordyke, *Cattle Empire,* or Haley, *The XIT Ranch of Texas.*

16. Duke and Frantz, *6,000 Miles of Fence,* p. 172.

17. Nordyke, *Cattle Empire,* p. 142.

18. Haley, *The XIT Ranch of Texas,* p. 153.

19. Ibid., p. 98.

20. Duke and Frantz, *6,000 Miles of Fence,* p. 164.

21. Ibid., p. 172.

22. Vera Morris, telephone interview by Ron Wilhelm, Channing, Tex., May 29, 1998. Perry's residence at the camp, east of Channing that became the Bivens family's Seven X Ranch, was not verified.

23. Hunter, *The Book of Year,* p. 112.

24. Duke and Frantz, *6,000 Miles of Fence,* p. 172.

25. For background on the ranch owners, see Nordyke, *Cattle Empire,* or Haley, *The XIT Ranch of Texas.*

26. Morris interview.

27. These photographs are in the collection of the XIT Museum in Dalhart, Tex.
28. Frances Ingmire, *Hartley County, Texas Marriage Records, 1891–1924,* book 1 (St. Louis, n.d.).
29. Census of 1910, Hartley County.
30. Ibid.
31. Morris interview.
32. *The XIT Brand,* Aug., 1939, p. 40.
33. Morris interview.
34. Ben Carlton Meade, Jim Perry File, XIT Museum, Dalhart, Tex., n.d.

Part 3

Twentieth-Century Cowboys

The twentieth century saw major changes occurring for many African American cowboys. The days of the cattle drives had ended as railroads moved into Texas. Getting cattle to market was now easier. It took fewer men and horses to drive the smaller herds to market at the nearby shipping points. Free cattle, once taken from the open range, were no longer available. Efforts to breed the best stock now became important to ranch owners. Few groups of wild horses remained, and some owners took up horse breeding. The new barbed wire changed the West, as ranges were fenced and owners fought for water. Cowboys began building and tending windmills to insure a good supply of water for the herds. The Indians were now confined to the government reservations. The introduction of official law and order was making the West safe for women and children of European descent. Gone were the opportunities for ranchers to amass great fortunes quickly.

For cowboys, including African American cowboys, it was a time of transition, as fewer cowboys were needed on the ranches. Most work became seasonal, with cowboys needed for the spring and fall roundups and branding. Cattle were brought to a central point, branded, and returned to the pastures. Ranch owners kept a few cowboys who had proven their worth and diversity in the years of the big cattle drives, but most cowboys were out of work. Some went to work on the railroad, as Mathew Hooks did. Some took this opportunity to settle down and get married like Addison Jones. Some, like Daniel Wallace, used their savings to start their own ranches. Often the owners gave cattle in exchange for wages. Some cowboys, including George Adams, stayed on the ranch and built their own herds. And still others tried their luck at rodeos. But it was not easy for African Americans as they entered the twentieth century.

> If an Albany or Jacksboro resident had been asked during the 1880s
> whether class distinctions existed in the community, the answer would
> have been an emphatic, "No, we're all alike out here." Yet the newspapers,
> mirroring much of the life of the area reveal that definite layers of social
> stratification did exist in the towns . . . The most obvious stratification, of
> course, was the system of caste which restricted the social, political, and
> economic opportunities of the small Negro population of the towns. The
> Negroes' residences were grouped together, generally in the least desirable
> sections of the towns . . . they attended their own churches and schools
> . . . celebrated events in their own areas . . . performed menial household
> tasks for white residents . . . but the larger economic opportunities in the
> towns were definitely closed to them.[1]

Few Texas communities wanted African Americans in *their* towns, so buying land and houses was very difficult. Starting a business was virtually impossible. Education for their children was segregated. Some jobs were available as servants in the homes of the wealthy, in laundries, as cooks. Lynchings were frequent. It was not particularly safe for African Americans, regardless of how skilled or loyal they had been as cowboys. The African American cowboys of Texas got by as best they could, raising their families, and telling fondly the tales of the "old" days when they were as good as any cowboy throwing his saddle on a horse at dawn and riding out to bring in the herd.

NOTES

1. Warren Kendall Agee, "A Study of Small-Town Life in the Texas Cattle Country, 1880–1890, as Reflected in the Press of the Area and Period" (Ph.D. dissertation, University of Minnesota, June, 1955), pp. 354–55.

Figure 15. Mathew "Bones" Hooks. Courtesy Southwest Collection, Special Collections Library, Texas Tech University, Lubbock

Chapter 18

Mathew "Bones" Hooks

A Pioneer of Honor

ANA CAROLINA CASTILLO CRIMM

Dear Sir:

I wish to pay tribute to you on the occasion of the banquet given to you by the members of your Church, for it is men of your kind and spirit who make this world a better place in which to live. I wish tonight to present you with a lone white flower, a guerdon of honor, that I have been sending for the past fifty-two years in honor of the pioneer men and women who have helped to make this Panhandle County of ours one of the "white" spots of the nation, for it is one of the traditions of the Panhandle to give honor to whom honor is due. With heartfelt greetings to you and yours, and God bless you.

—Mathew Bones Hooks

Mathew Hooks, one of the first black horse wranglers and bronc busters in the Texas Panhandle, is probably best known for honoring the early pioneers with a white flower, a symbol that he later extended to others of equal courage and merit. Hooks grew up with the Panhandle, watching it change over a period of seventy-five years, as he developed from wrangler and cook, to bronc buster and horse trainer, to hotel and railroad porter, and finally to town builder and civic leader for the black community of Amarillo. He had a true sense of history and a love of the early settlers that he shared, through his prodigious memory, with journalists, writers, and scholars, as well as school children, college students, and anyone who was interested in listening. His homespun philosophies entertained and engaged his audiences as he told the tales of the old days, of the early pioneers of the Panhandle. He actively preserved the history of the area and joined half a dozen old-timers organizations. With other pioneers, he helped found the Panhandle Plains Museum where his scrapbooks and papers are preserved.

Mathew Hooks refused to be cowed by a society grown increasingly racist in the years after the Civil War. The black communities that he founded, first in Clarendon and later at North Heights in Amarillo, became a haven where blacks could live in comfort and safety with their own businesses and their own homes. He recognized the contributions of his white friends, but Mathew Hooks had to fight his own battles for his rights and the rights of his people. In the end, his dedication, his drive, and his ambition personified the courage and grit of the Panhandle people whom he honored with his white flowers.[1]

Mathew Hooks was born November 3, 1867, in the small community of Orangeville in Robertson County, Texas,[2] to Alex and Annie Hooks. The couple had received their freedom two years earlier, from Warren (or perhaps Cullen) Hooks,[3] a plantation owner in Bowie County, Northeast Texas. The plantation, which employed as many as sixty-six slaves, was located near the present community of Hooks, on Highway 82, twenty-five miles west of Texarkana. Alex Hooks, while still a slave, was gifted with a native ability and a will to improve. He learned to read and write from "Old Man" Hooks who broke the law to teach the bright young slave. Instead of hiring a white clerk, Warren Hooks put Alex in control of the plantation bookkeeping.[4]

With the end of the Civil War in 1865, the South was struggling to fit free blacks into its structure. Alex and Annie, who needed to find jobs and make decisions that had long been made for them, moved to Orangeville, where Alex became a community leader, something that may have later inspired his son. Alex, by putting his gifts of reading and writing to work, led the way in education, in Christian concepts, and in furthering the growth and development of his people. He willingly shared his talents as a teacher and preacher with the rapidly growing black communities.[5]

Their son, Mathew, was the first of their eight children. As Mathew said, he was the first thing they had ever owned. If the first five years of a child are the formative years, Mathew Hooks was blessed with a head start. From his family, he learned courage, determination, and strong Christian concepts. His home life, as he said later, made him what he was. "I can see young men," he said, "and see right away the effect their home has had on them. . . . Men are just grown up boys and they act just the same when they grow up as when they were boys."[6] He benefited from his parents' biblical teachings and their strict moral code. He never smoked or drank and avoided conflict whenever he could. Mathew's father taught his young son to read and write, and Mathew, supported by his own cheerful personality and inveterate good humor, learned quickly to work hard and to follow through with whatever he started. "When I get an impulse to do something," he said, "I stick to it 'til I get it done . . . If I have to wait two hours to see a man I want to see, I wait. When the time is ripe to do a thing, it's right, and that's the time to do it."[7] He also developed a sense of responsibility at an early age. As the eldest of eight children, it was often Mathew's duty to care for his four younger brothers and three sisters. "They made me rock the cradle for my brothers, and I've been rockin' somebody's cradle ever since."[8]

As a youngster, Mathew was thin and wiry, which earned him the nickname "Bones." He was also energetic, and by the time he was seven, he could do a man's job. He worked to help his parents by driving the butcher's wagon around town and learned to harness and handle oxen and mules. Two years later, in 1874, D. Steve Donald, a cattleman from Denton County along the Red River north of Dallas, traveled to Robertson County on a cattle-buying trip. He needed someone to drive the camp wagon back to Denton, and Warren Hooks, Alex's old boss, assured Donald that young Mathew could handle the job. Mathew, on his first trip away from home, drove the camp wagon hitched to two oxen, Buck and Jerry, back to Denton with Donald and the herd of cattle. Donald, who paid for Mathew's return home, was impressed with the young boy's willingness and skill. The following summer, on another cattle-buying trip, Donald once again hired Mathew, only this time he provided him with his own mule, named Dinamite, on which Mathew made the return trip. For the next four years, Mathew continued to work for Donald and finally remained in Denton, because he was "old enough to make a hand."[9]

It was while Mathew worked for Steve Donald that he learned to ride and break horses. The cowboys on the DSD Ranch, as Hooks said, "made me the best bronc rider in the country. But they weren't trying to make me a rider, they were trying to get me throwed."[10] The teasing cowboys would put young Mathew on any horse that looked like it would buck him off. According to J. Frank Dobie, bucking was not usually a vicious act, but a natural instinctive response by horses to get rid of any clawed and fanged animal on their backs. Dobie, in his book on mustangs, described a story told to him by a cowboy: "That dun struck out pitching right through the middle of the herd. He pitched for half a mile right and left, backwards and forwards. There was no getting his motion. He pitched till we were both broke down and I was bleeding at nose, mouth, and ears . . ."[11]

Such bucking was not uncommon, and riders such as Mathew Hooks had to put up with broncs who might buck, jump, or rear. The worst were the broncs with the "belly full of bedsprings."[12] A horse like that tried everything to get rid of a cowboy on its back, "pawing for the moon, breaking in two half way up, sunfishing on the way down, and then hitting the earth hard enough to crack open his rider's liver."[13] Some horses never did quit fighting and remained unbroken outlaws. Others might become killers, throwing themselves over backward on a rider or rolling on a rider to crush him. Horses and their pitching ability were frequently judged by their color. According to Hooks, "a sorrel steel dust is a hard pitcher; a bay hondo hasn't much pitch in him."[14] Most horses, however, found out quickly that the rider, especially when it was Mathew, could not be removed by any gyrations, regardless of their force, and the horse might as well give in and accept the burden.

After an uncounted numbers of falls, Mathew learned to hang onto the horse by whatever means was necessary. There were no predetermined rules such as those that bind modern rodeo cowboys to keep their spurs above the shoulders of the horse or not grab the horn (pulling leather). Mathew's light weight, his long legs, and his wiry frame were perfectly suited to bronc riding. He was sometimes put on the horses bareback or without a bridle. "One day the boys got me on a big gray horse, and turned him out of the corral, him pitching and running, and me without a bridle or any way to hold or guide him."[15] Through grit and determination, Mathew stayed on for twelve miles until the cowboys finally herded Mathew and his mount into camp. Mathew also learned that there were only four directions a horse could jump, and it did not take him long to judge the horses and outguess their movements. "We used to say that if you could ride a horse as far as three jumps, you could usually ride him, but you were usually thrown by the second jump."[16] Within a few years, Mathew, like a persistent tick, could hang onto a horse until it gave up pitching and accepted him in the saddle.

By the time he had become a teenager, he was confident that he could stay on any horse alive. An outlaw horse belonging to the DSD Ranch called "Old Bill" had been written off as unridable and was in use as a wagon horse. One Sunday, Mathew determined he would ride "Old Bill" while the family was at church. He saddled the horse in the barn so if the horse did buck him off it would not take off with the boss's saddle. When he climbed on, the horse exploded, broke through the barn door, "knocked over the stile block at the gate and took out up the road with me in the saddle."[17] Several miles later, Mathew met the family, coming back from church in the buckboard, and managed to pull Old Bill to a stop. The astounded family asked him what made him think he could ride the outlaw. Mathew replied that the horse was made like all other horses, and if the cowboys could ride them, "I figured Old Bill could be rode, too."[18]

Mathew learned to love horses and willingly rode whatever was available. The demand for horses was great. Cowboys needed horses to work the cattle, and money was good in the cattle industry, which was booming during the late 1870s and early 1880s. Both cowboys and horses were needed to supply cattle to the ever-growing market—Mathew's skills were in demand. By the time he turned fourteen, he broke and trained horses as well as working as a horse wrangler. When a new horse was brought in, Mathew rode him daily, earning the horse's trust, until the horse was bridlewise. He was paid between $3 and $5 per horse or $25 per month with board. This money was as good as cowboys got, although it was not an easy job. While riding the horses, Mathew developed a friendship with each of the animals. As friends, he named the horses after anything and everything. "I gave them every name I could think of . . . after the people I knew, what they looked like, any peculiarity they had like Fox Trot or Run Away . . . after the bosses, the hands, . . . after owls, hawks and coyotes. I even named one Miss Sally Chisum after Mr. Chisum's daughter."[19]

After Mathew had broken the horses to ride, the cowboys would take one or two of the newly broken horses to add to their string. Each cowboy had between seven and ten horses, most of them smaller Spanish mustangs, weighing around nine hundred pounds. Each cowboy might have a pet pony, but he also had "a cutting horse, a bridle horse, a night horse, a roping horse, a saddle horse and a packing horse."[20] The night horses had to be the safest and most dependable, because, in an emergency such as a cattle stampede, a cowboy would have to jump on the horse without saddle or bridle, and the horse would carry him out of danger with nothing but his headstall and rope. These horses were often smart enough to bring a man back to camp if he were lost.[21] The saddle horses were used for the daily duty of the roundup and were worked hard all morning for four to five hours in search of the elusive cattle. At lunch, the cowboys rode in and changed their exhausted, sweating mount for a second horse out of their string and rode out for a long, hot afternoon of gathering more cattle. Once the cattle were herded together, cowboys switched to their roping or cutting horses for separating the cattle to be branded. Some horses, like one Mathew called Chubby, were natural cow ponies and would follow a steer without being guided. "If you did not catch the steer that he was after, he got mad and shook his head from side to side and backed his ears."[22] Once, a cowboy who was riding Chubby failed to rope a cow. The horse began to shake his head angrily, and Mathew commented, to the embarrassment of the cowboy and the glee of his companions, "That's the first time that Chubby has been disappointed that bad in a long time!"[23]

As a horse wrangler, it was Mathew's duty to feed, doctor, and care for all of the horses. If there were 20 to 25 men on a roundup and each one had 7 to 10 horses, the *remuda,* or horse herd, might number from 140 to 250 horses. In the morning, the men would saddle their horses and, while they were at breakfast, Mathew rode the kinks out of each horse until it had quit bucking. Sometimes, on a cold morning, the spirited horses would give the young boy a considerable workout. Mathew accepted the job, because, as he noted, "The only thing I have found that a white man was afraid of was a rattlesnake and a pitching horse. I do not know why, but they were."[24] After the cowboys had left to begin scouring the gullies and draws for hidden cattle, Mathew took the herd of horses to graze on nearby grass pastures.

When Mr. Donald began driving cattle into Oklahoma Indian Territory just across the Red River, Mathew worried about Indian raids. The cowboys had assured him that Indians could steal a horse right out from under a man, even with the horse tied to him, and he'd never know it. One afternoon while grazing the horses, Mathew lay down to take a nap and tied his mule, Dinamite, to his arm. The cowboys, finding him asleep, untied the mule, and began to whoop like all the Indians in the world. Mathew recounted, "I awoke to see my mule gone and thought the Indians had me sho'. I left there fast and the boys had to head me off on their horses."[25]

By the time Mathew turned sixteen in 1884, Steve Donald had moved his operations west to Henrietta, near Wichita Falls. One afternoon, Mathew, on Dinamite, noticed a group of cowboys with a *remuda* and wagon coming across the prairies. It was J. R. Norris and his men returning to the JRE Ranch on the Pecos River in West Texas. Young Mathew rode Dinamite out to investigate the group, and, when asked if he were a cowboy, the tall, gangly black boy answered that he was. The cowboys began teasing him about his mule, telling him that no cowboy rode a mule. At the insult, Mathew challenged them to a race against Dinamite. They let him choose the horse he would run against, and, much to the chagrin of the cowboys, Mathew and Dinamite beat their horse and rider. Mr. Norris, evidently impressed with the courage of the young boy, invited him to come out west and become a real cowboy. Norris offered Mathew a new pair of boots and five horses for Dinamite if Mathew would go with them. Mathew answered, "Right here's where you get traded off, old mule." He turned Dinamite loose on the range and joined the JRE outfit for his first trip to West Texas. From then on, he rode horses.[26]

Few people, in 1850, would have guessed that the Panhandle of Texas would ever amount to much. Captain R. B. Marcy of the U.S. Cavalry, who was searching for Indians at the time across the dry grasslands and rolling hills, stated, "This country is, and must remain, uninhabited forever."[27] Joseph McCoy, who opened Abilene, Kansas, and began the shipment of cattle to the East Coast, had examined the Panhandle and declared the seven million acres were absolute desert. For those who finally took the chance on settling the Panhandle, the greatest problems would not be the desert-like conditions, the dried grass, or the lack of water, but the over-abundance of buffalo and Indians. During the 1870s and 1880s, those problems were being solved by American military troops who were removing the latter, while buffalo hunters massacred the former. By 1876, reconstruction ended, and the cattle boom began. Charles Goodnight, familiar with the Panhandle, which he had traversed on his way to Colorado, and certain he could rid the area of the few remaining buffalo, brought sixteen thousand head of cattle from Colorado into the protected Palo Duro Canyon. With capital from John G. Adair, the English lord, Goodnight and Adair formed the JA Ranch and began the development of the Panhandle.[28]

The two earliest towns in the area were Mobeetie and Tascosa, both of unsavory character, and towns that Mathew did not enjoy visiting on the annual trail drives. Mobeetie, some eighty miles northeast of present-day Amarillo, had developed in 1874 as a supply store for buffalo skinners on Sweetwater Creek. It later became the southern terminus of the Jones-Plummer Trail, and as such, was inundated periodically with cowboys either coming or going from the railheads in Kansas. Mobeetie also served Fort Elliott, established in 1874 to remove the Plains Indians. Several troops of black soldiers, also known as Buffalo Soldiers, were stationed at the fort and their families made up the small community of blacks in Mobeetie. The town consisted of a supply store, owned by Charles Rath and Bob Wright, and numerous saloons. A scattering of homes made of buffalo skins gave the town its first name, Hidetown, which the city fathers changed in 1879 to the Indian word Mobeetie, which may have meant sweet water.[29]

Tascosa, the second major settlement in the Panhandle, lay approximately forty miles northwest of present-day Amarillo, on the Canadian River. Tascosa, from the Spanish word *atascosa* meaning boggy or swampy, was at the beginning of the Dodge City Trail, and like Mobeetie, was periodically overrun with rowdy cowboys looking for a drink, a poker game, and a fight, usually in that order. Founded in 1876 by Spanish sheepherders, Tascosa was soon taken over by Charles Goodnight and his cowboys. Saloons flourished, along with general stores, which freighted in as much as fifty thousand pounds of merchandise monthly from Dodge City for the local cattlemen, including the XIT Syndicate, Goodnight's JA Ranch, and numerous smaller ranchers. Tascosa, like Mobeetie, was considered a den of iniquity and, therefore, not a place where Mathew Hooks liked to go.[30]

Mathew Hooks, brought up in a Christian tradition, preferred the town of Clarendon, established in 1878 just fifty miles southeast of Amarillo. Founded as a "Christian community" by the Reverend Lewis Henry Carhart, a Methodist minister, and his brother-in-law, Alfred Sully of New York, it was once again the backing of English investors that made the town possible. The town leaders carefully controlled the few saloons and prohibited any rowdy behavior from the cowboys who wandered through. One saloon owner refused to serve liquor to any young boys, and the town's citizens were so honest that bags of money could be safely left behind the saloon counter while a ranch owner transacted business in town. Their jail, although they built one, soon fell down from disuse. The boisterous, thrill-seeking cowboys wanted little to do with a town that they dubbed "Saints' Roost." Mathew, as a religious man who neither smoked nor drank, liked the God-fearing town. "Clarendon," he said, "was the white spot of civilization. Prohibition started there; colleges started there; everything good got its start in Clarendon."[31]

Claiming to be a Christian town, however, did not necessarily mean that the town accepted black citizens. Mathew was told that Negroes were not allowed in town. "But," he said, "I did not believe that, and that is the very reason why I am here today; I still don't believe it."[32] He was determined to be part of the Christian town, and by quiet perseverance, he made friends with the citizens, many of whom were small ranchers who used his services to break or train horses. It took several years and several persistent attempts, but he was eventually accepted by the residents and allowed to buy a small plot of land and build a home. "Friendship," he told a class of students in 1933, "can be more useful to you than anything else."[33]

Settlers, still wary of Indian raids in the 1870s, did not rush to the area, and only the hardiest of souls remained. Mathew Hooks was amazed by the ability of the early settlers to survive. Water was their greatest need, and they learned to find water holes by following birds to water in the mornings and to backtrack by following the birds' path from the water in the evening. They also learned to avoid areas where there were neither trails nor animals, which meant an absence of water. Mathew described the trail drive from Portales, New

Mexico, to Texico, a stretch of some sixty miles where there was no water. "When you knew you couldn't get water, it was awful. You would just moan and grunt. The cook sometimes saved dish water from one meal to another. We also had a barrel of clean water that we kept for the coffee. One night I felt that I just had to have some water, so I got a little rubber hose and after everybody had gone to bed, I slipped up and stuck my hose in the first water I came to. It was the dishwater. I just fell back and groaned."[34]

Life was hard for those scratching out a living in the Panhandle. Settlers on the caprock—the flat plains that seem to stretch forever from the Canadian River in the north to the Pecos River in the south—built homes of sun-dried adobe bricks or stacked sod, which made cool, comfortable homes, although they might not be the most civilized looking buildings. Mathew recalled that he could always tell where a settler lived from the kind of fuel they used. For those who lived on top of the caprock, today known as the Edward's Plateau west of Post, fuel was dried cow dung, or cow chips. Those below the caprock, in the rolling, hump-backed hills west of Abilene, used scrub wood. Mathew also noted that settlers found their directions on the unmarked plains by knowing that the wind usually blew from the southwest. In one instance he was riding from Mobeetie back to Clarendon and ran into two of the ranchers, Mr. Tom Turner and Judge Wilson, but the wind was blowing so badly that they could hardly see. "They asked me where Mobeetie was and I told them it was in the direction of the wind, if it was not covered up."[35]

Mathew Hooks particularly admired the tenacity of the women. "Credit for the advancement on the Plains belongs to the pioneer mothers. . . . When the men brought their wives to the Plains the women demanded milk cows, chickens, schools, churches and all the other attributes of civilization and culture."[36] The men, he recalled, were satisfied with camping in tents and accepted the saloons and gambling in Tascosa and Mobeetie. It was the women who demanded civilization, worked for churches, and finally achieved the stability that encouraged other settlers to come. Women such as Mrs. Goodnight, Mrs. Bugbee (wife of Thomas S. Bugbee, the second man to establish a ranch in the Panhandle), and Mrs. Patrick, were, as viewed by Mathew, "the very strongest of characters . . . who have seen all the modern things come."[37] When the women determined to vote Clarendon dry, Mathew said, "I thought it would be just as easy to bring the Canadian River in and vote it dry. But those women got to working, and after a while Clarendon was dry."[38] Often alone, the women suffered the births and deaths of their children, sacrificing for the success of their husband's ranches. They also defended the lonely young black cowboy from the teasing or harassing that he often endured. One woman stopped a group of cowboys who were firing blanks at Mathew's feet. Another pioneer housewife, when a cowboy objected to eating with Mathew at the same table, replied, "Everyone is treated alike at my table."[39] Mathew responded in kind, caring for their children, as he had his own brothers and sisters. Mothers trusted him with their young sons, knowing that Mathew would teach them the horse skills that he knew so well. The mothers also treated him as a son. One mother was concerned over her young son picking up Mathew's only curse word, "'y God," short for "By God." The mother offered to buy Mathew a Sunday suit if he would stop the habit, which Mathew immediately did.[40] Mathew knew that for the mothers, as it was for him, the hardships were the worst and the need for courage the greatest.

The people of the Panhandle were, from Mathew's point of view, different from settlers elsewhere. "The climate and conditions here make them differ-ent. . . . I have seen one kind of man come here and stay awhile, and he just can't stand it, he just breaks down."[41] But another kind, much like Mathew himself, did not let the country phase him, and that was the kind who re-mained. "One was a pioneer," he said, "and the other was just pioneering."[42] It took the pioneers to settle the Panhandle, and Mathew always admired them for their strength, for he, too, knew what it took to survive in the Panhandle.

By the time Mathew Hooks arrived in West Texas, there were already a number of successful ranches. The cattle boom had been going strong for almost ten years, and with the removal of both the Indians and the buffalo from the Panhandle plains, the land was perfect for cattle, despite the earlier concerns of people such as Captain Marcy. Among the early ranches were the Frying Pan, north of Amarillo, the T-Anchor near what would become Ama-rillo, the Two Buckle and Matador at the bottom of the Panhandle, the Bar CC, the 777, the Turkey Track and the Bar T along the Red River in the north; along the New Mexico border were the XIT, the LX and the 6666, the Quar-ter Circle T, and the Laurel Leaf; and along the Oklahoma line were the Dia-mond Tail and the Rocking Chair.[43]

Mathew's skill at horse breaking and training was in demand by all of the ranchers. He worked for almost all of them, including the XIT, the largest of the ranches, which would not outlast the century. In 1882, Texas lawmakers traded three million acres of Panhandle land to Matthias Schnell and A. R. Birck for the construction of the Texas state capitol. A Chicago firm, Taylor, Babcock and Co., bought out the Schnell-Birck contract, and chose the land for the XIT in the ten counties along the New Mexico border, north and west of present-day Amarillo. The ranch was run by a syndicate made up of En-glish investors who intended to subdivide the land for farming and sell it off.

Until the population in the area increased, however, the investors ordered the huge acreage fenced using the newly invented barbed wire. By 1886, over 781 miles of land had been fenced and the ranch had imported over 150,000 head of high-grade, purebred cattle, worth over a million dollars.

Mathew continued to work part time for the JRE Ranch during his first years in the area, as well as hiring out to other outfits when they needed a horse trainer or a wrangler. He made friends with owners of the smaller as well as the larger ranches and soon became a popular and well-liked worker. His friendships sometimes got him into trouble. Once, Mathew hired out as a wrangler to two cowboys who were illegally gathering cattle. When the ranch owner and his cowboys surrounded the group, justice was swift and merciless. The two cowboys were hung and the rope had dropped over Mathew's neck. "Skillety" Bill, an acquaintance from the Frying Pan Ranch (hence his name), and a member of the vigilante group, intervened. While the group waited, he questioned Mathew and, convinced that Hooks had been unaware of the intentions of the two cattle thieves, Skillety Bill let him go and told him to clear out of the country quick.[44]

After his narrow escape, Hooks left the Panhandle and returned to Henrietta in North Texas. He worked horses in Oklahoma until the threat of the hanging had passed, and then he returned to the Panhandle. During the summers he worked for most of the local ranchers. At different times he worked for Mr. George Brookshire of the Hashknife outfit, Billie Johnson of the "W" Ranch, Mr. Nash of the 7D range, Mr. Perry Autman of the PX outfit, the Cowan Ranch, which was located around the Davis and Guadalupe Mountains, the LX ranch, whose headquarters were near Dalhart, and the Chicago "C" outfit, which tried and failed to raise Polled Angus cattle. Not all land was owned outright. The large ranches controlled the ranges wherever their cattle grazed, usually to a natural boundary such as a river or mountain range. "One fellow would be northeast of the mountains and that would be his range, then some other fellow would be located to the southeast of the mountains and that would be his range."[45] Between five hundred and one thousand cattle might graze on any given range, some belonging to the big ranch, and others to the smaller ranches. "When a man bought a brand and the cattle, that gave him the right to the range. When he bought the brand and cattle of another range, the boys would gather up all the cattle they could find and turn them over to the buyer. When he bought the remnant, he got the range which included a section or two of land."[46]

Hooks remembered the ranches and their owners. The Hashknife was bought by Bill Ross, who moved the ranch to Arizona. T. J. McElroy, whose range extended from south of the Pecos to El Paso, bought the last remnants of the 7D, which had existed around Fort Stockton. Other outfits, such as the LX, had never established a headquarters but only maintained a chuck wagon with thirty or forty men.[47]

Not all of the ranches were large outfits. "When the big outfits began to dwindle down as the country became more settled, sometimes the cowboys would branch off and start a little outfit of their own," Hooks explained. "Then they would grow into big ranches."[48] The smaller outfits were allowed to run their cattle on the same ranges as the big ranchers as long as the roundups were done jointly. According to Hooks, the ranchers, both large and small, were good neighbors and got along well.

When roundup time came, all the cattle owners would combine their forces to collect the cattle. Calves were branded with the same brand as their mothers thus ensuring that the owner of the cow could claim the calf. When calves were missed, they were called mavericks and could be claimed by whoever caught and branded them. In one instance, Mathew was riding with Joe White when they spotted a big two-and-a-half-year-old maverick. Mathew explained, "Mr. White wanted to get that big one first; it's sort of natural with white men to want the biggest and best thing first. If it had been a little one, he would have let me rope that one first."[49] Normally, a calf would not be branded unless a representative from each of the ranches was part of the group to prevent accusations of cattle theft, but in this case, because it was an older maverick, the men went ahead with the branding. Mathew stopped to build a fire to brand the calf and began heating the short branding iron that they always carried for just such emergencies. Mr. White, meanwhile, chased the maverick over the top of the hill. Mathew suddenly heard Mr. White yelling for him. When Mathew topped the hill, he found that Mr. White had roped the hind legs of the calf, but the calf had escaped the rope, and Mr. White was holding onto the calf by its tail.

"I jumped down, but when I got a hold of him, Mr. White turned loose and started to run. Mr. Joe lit out, and me right after him, and the yearling right after me. . . . when I passed Mr. Joe, I said, 'There he is again!' I heard a jingling, and it was his spurs as his feet went up in the air. A cow can't hook anyone on the ground because its horns are so long. That is one thing a fellow learns if he is willing to lie there and learn his lesson. I ran a while and rested a little bit, and went to catch my horse. I said, 'Do you want me to rope him?' He said, 'What do you think I want?' 'Well, I don't know; if you don't want him, I don't,' I said. He told me that the next time I started running not to start after him."[50]

Cattle were rounded up in the spring and fall, just after calving season, so the young calves could be branded. There were no fences during the early days of cattle ranching in the Panhandle. All the cattle from the different ranches roamed together on the ranges and had to be rounded up and divided with everyone sharing in the effort. For a roundup, the largest ranch would furnish the chuck wagon, and the other ranches would send their cowboys. In this way, no one rancher had to pay for a larger work force than he absolutely needed, but there were sufficient men to find the cattle on a range that might extend hundreds of miles. All the cattle in a fifteen-mile area were collected in one day, and the herd was moved along to the next fifteen-mile section for the next day's roundup. Mathew recalled that cattle liked hiding in the canyons and draws, and ranchers built a drift line near present-day Lubbock to keep the cattle out of the canyons. When the cowboys had amassed a sizable herd, the calves were cut out and branded. Once the entire range was cleared of cattle, which might take as much as four months, the cattle that were to be sold were separated and bunched together for the drive north.[51]

Trail drives, which usually began in May from either Tascosa or Mobeetie, would reach Kiowa, Kansas, in September, and the cowboys would be back home by Christmas. Hooks made many trail drives from the Pecos country with such outfits as the TJ and the Hashknife. The smaller ranchers would put their sale herds in with the large herds going to market and trust the large rancher to pay them for the cattle upon their return. For the most part, Hooks recalls, as long as the ranchers knew each other, "the little fellows got along fine with the big fellows."[52] The huge and sometimes arrogant syndicate ranchers, however, were considered fair game by some of the small ranchers.

Some time later, while Mathew was working for the XIT Syndicate, a young local rancher asked for his help to get one of the prized purebred bull calves from the syndicate's immense, but carefully fenced, pastures. As an employee, Mathew Hooks could come and go through the gates easily, and it took no time to find and separate a good calf and herd him across the country. Part way across the pastures, however, Hooks found a better calf and let the first one go. He herded the second little bull to his waiting friend who tied the calf up to keep it from returning to its mother and weaned the calf in four days. Many years later, after having earned a reputation for honesty and integrity, Hooks was called into court to testify before a grand jury investigating cattle thefts. He found that the judge was none other than the young rancher whom he had helped. The judge asked Hooks, "Do you know of anyone stealing cattle . . ." then paused, and pointedly added, ". . . now?" Hooks was able to answer truthfully, "No, boss, not now."[53]

Much of the law and order of the country, during the early years, was controlled by vigilantes. These men were usually cowmen determined to stop the cattle and horse theft that had become rampant by the 1880s. According to the cattlemen's associations, as much as forty percent of the cattle that arrived in Dodge City were listed as stolen. In spite of Mathew's early run-in with the vigilantes, his honesty earned him a place as one of their group. They bound themselves together by a password, a casual word that could be passed along in a general conversation unnoticed by others. Though Mathew Hooks refused to divulge this password during his lifetime, he said he would leave it somewhere in his files at the Panhandle-Plains Museum. When word went out among the vigilantes that there was to be a "gathering" or a "trial," the group would come together at a predesignated place, usually with a handy tree. Mathew Hooks held the horses while the committee members conducted their trial under the tree. When the trial was concluded, the accused was usually hung. One young man, after receiving his sentence, asked two favors. The first was to take his boots off, because he had promised his mother that he would not die with his boots on, and the second was to be hung by a man who had never rustled cattle or horses himself. The rope passed from hand to hand around the circle of vigilantes, who soon withdrew for a council. The decision was to let the young man go "if he made a solemn promise he would leave the country right quick and never come back." He left.[54] According to Hooks, there were only twelve to fifteen hangings during the time he was in the Panhandle.[55]

Although many of the ranchers did not realize it at the time, the terrible winter of 1885 and the subsequent drought in 1886, combined with the dreaded tick fever, ruined the free-range cattle industry not only in the Panhandle, but throughout Texas. The freeze in January and February of 1886 was so severe that it killed cattle all the way to South Texas. Hooks, who was in Henrietta for the winter, saw so many dead cattle that "you could have put the dead cows three feet apart and had enough to reach to Colorado."[56] Dozens of ranchers went out of business that year, losing all their cattle to either the freeze or the drought that followed. The only operations that would survive into the twentieth century turned to fenced pastures, cattle dipping, and upgraded programs of cattle breeding.[57]

During 1886, Mathew Hooks found there was little need for his services in the Panhandle. Hooks, who had gathered a small herd of horses and cattle as his pay for working roundups, sold his B brand and his herd and moved back to Northeast Texas to be with his family. Briefly, he invested his money in a grocery store in the town of Wamba in Bowie County, near Texarkana. After about eighteen months, he arrived one day to find a sign on his door that read, "We give you thirty-six hours to get out," signed by the "White Caps of Sand Gall Gizzard."[58] He closed up the store and "gave 'em thirty-three hours of that back."[59]

Like the other pioneers who had learned to love the arid plains of the Panhandle, Mathew chose to return to Clarendon and the Pecos. After visits to family and friends in Denton, Dallas, and Henrietta, he was back in the Pecos country breaking broncs for T. J. McElroy, Autman, and others by the end of 1887.[60] The cattle business had declined somewhat, as absentee investors and English speculators were weeded out by the freeze and drought of '86, but the completion of the Fort Worth and Denver City Railway just south of Clarendon by 1887 provided new impetus for the remaining ranchers.[61] Mathew's skills were again in demand as horses were needed to trail the cattle from the Pecos River, starting in early March, to reach the railheads along the Fort Worth and Denver Railway in the northern part of the Panhandle in time for the summer shipping.

Although the Fort Worth and Denver shipped cattle year-round, the majority of cattle were shipped after the spring roundup and again after the fall roundup. Because shipping by rail was still in its infancy, most railroads did not supply enough cattle cars to carry the larger number of cattle during the spring and fall. Fourteen cattle cars were provided in each out-bound train, so only a few cattle could be taken from each man's herd. The rest of the herd had to be fed at the owner's expense while waiting in the lots along the railroad line, something that might take as long as a month or more. Mathew was responsible for feeding the horses of the *remuda* until he and the cowboys could take them back to the ranches on the Pecos. Often, he and some of the cowboys were detailed to take the horses back early, leaving only a few to work the cattle in the pens until they were all sold. Many of the ranchers, still used to the trail drives and not interested in paying the high cost of feed at the railhead, would often trail the cattle on to Dodge even with the railroad already in the area. The last of the trail drives to Dodge that Mathew rode with as a wrangler came over the trail in 1896. By then, the railroads had sufficient cattle cars to handle the volume of cattle coming out of the Panhandle, but the cattlemen and cowboys were never fond of the men who checked the cars and decided which cattle to ship. The cowboys called them "bald faced,"[62] not necessarily a derogatory term, but one that came from the white collars the men wore that made them look like the newly introduced "bald-face" or white-faced Hereford cattle.[63]

During his years in the Panhandle, Mathew Hooks became friends with

Tom Clayton when the two men worked for Charles Goodnight on the JA Ranch. "Tommy was one of those boys who liked the open country and horses and cattle."[64] Clayton and Hooks pooled their resources and became partners in the horse business. Each had something the other lacked. "Tom tried hard to be a great rider but he didn't have the physical make-up. On the other hand, I didn't have any business sense and Tom had a pretty good head."[65] The Clayton family was from the Pecos region, so, sometime in the late 1880s or early 1890s, the two men left the JA Ranch at Palo Duro Canyon and returned to the Pecos country in the south. Working from Tom Clayton's small ranch, the two men—Hooks now in his early twenties—began breaking and training horses and selling them throughout the Panhandle. "We made a fine team and I was closer to him than I ever was to any other white man."[66]

During 1894, the two men, with some of the ranch cowboys, were working horses near the Davis Mountains in the Pecos country. Tommy's horse fell, crushing him. Several of the cowboys laid Tommy in a wagon and took him to town, leaving Mathew with the *remuda*. Deeply concerned for his friend, Mathew "went out and picked a bouquet of the white flowers that Tommy liked so well and I asked the boy to take them to my friend to cheer him up and remind him of the happy days we rode together."[67] The cowboy asked what he should do with the flowers if Tommy were dead. "Just put them on his grave," Mathew answered. When the flowers arrived, Tommy had died, but, as Mathew had requested, his mother laid the small bouquet of white flowers on Tommy's coffin. From this beginning, in honor of his departed friend, and out of respect for the courage and stamina of the early settlers of the Panhandle, Mathew Hooks sent white flowers to the funerals of all the early pioneers. He also began to send flowers to others who showed the same kind of courage and compassion. "I like to give them to distinguished people because of the meaning the flower has for me and because of my respect for the white people," he said.[68]

By the 1890s, times were changing. After the death of Tommy Clayton, Mathew Hooks reassessed his situation. Although Hooks continued to break and train horses, the country was settling up as farmers and merchants came on the railroads. The early ranchers who had made it through the freeze of '86 profited from the limited number of competitors for the cattle market. With their newly acquired wealth, they had built elegant new homes for which they needed servants. Prior to 1880, many towns in the Panhandle had forbidden Negroes to live or even stop over in their towns. The 1880 census indicates, there were a total of fifty-one Negroes in the Panhandle, including a handful of black cowboys and the small community of thirty-one black families at

Mobeetie.[69] Among the black cowboys, Mathew counted Dan Sowell of the Figure 4 Ranch, Henry Mangum of the TJM, Bill Freeman at the Quarter Circle Heart, Charles Fowler and Edward Jones at the LFDS, and Brook Lee of the Diamond Tail.[70] The blacks were often harassed, and although there might be from eight to ten who lived and worked in the area for a short time, they were often run off by the townspeople. "Sometimes there would be only one or two left, and sometimes there would not be any."[71] Eventually, blacks from other parts of Texas and the South arrived to work as domestic help in the fine homes of the newly rich ranchers. The community of Clarendon evidently accepted the new arrivals, perhaps based in part on their friendship with Mathew Hooks. In 1894, the town fathers agreed to let Mathew Hooks have land for a Negro church. With a very limited number of blacks in the area, Mathew brought both a preacher from Fort Worth as well as the beginnings of a small congregation, most of whom were able to find employment in the homes of Clarendon's citizens. It was Mathew's first success at building a black community but not his last.[72]

In the waning years of the nineteenth century, the Panhandle was no longer the frontier Mathew had known when he arrived ten years earlier. Newspapers were becoming more readily available, and Mathew, like the ranch owners, kept up with the national news, in particular the struggles of the Populist movement. In 1896, the farmers and ranchers were determined to put the Great Populist, William Jennings Bryan, in the White House. Mathew was working on the Cowan spread at the time, and he and the rest of the hands rode into town to vote. "There were only eight other people besides myself who were going to vote from that section of the country. They said they would throw me in the creek, if I did not vote for Bryan."[73] Mathew, ever his own man, voted for McKinley. Hooks bet Mr. Ross, the Cowan foreman, his horse against fifty dollars that McKinley would win. When they finally saw a copy of the *El Paso Herald*, "it was giving three to one on McKinley's being elected."[74] When McKinley won, much to the dismay of the nation's Populists, Mathew collected. An occasional friendly wager was not against Mathew Hooks's principles.

As civilization, with its roads and towns, spread across the plains, the demand for horse breakers declined. He married Anna Crenshaw, and the couple settled down at his home in Clarendon. "My wife," Mathew said, "was a good woman, a good cook and a wonderful housekeeper,"[75] but, as he said, it was hard for her to adjust to his brand of humor. "It took some time," he said, "but she got better at telling jokes."[76] Mathew found out that she also had a powerful sense of intuition. "I found out when she said not to do a thing, I'd better listen." Anna suggested a move to Amarillo so that Mathew, now thirty-three years old, could leave the dangerous job of breaking horses.[77]

By 1900, Amarillo was well established, having been founded in 1887 by a group of Colorado City merchants along the right-of-way of the Fort Worth and Denver City rail line. The newly opened Elmhurst Hotel, in need of workers, hired Anna and Mathew Hooks, who moved from Clarendon to Amarillo, although Mathew continued to claim Clarendon as his home. Anna was employed washing and ironing the hotel linens, and Mathew went to work as a porter for the hotel. For nine years, the couple worked hard, made a decent living, and Mathew continued his friendships with the early ranchers and settlers who had remained in the area.

Although there was still considerable prejudice against the black families, Mathew became a staunch supporter of the new civic organizations that were being formed. Mathew served on jury duty, the first black in Potter County to do so. He was also vitally interested in any organizations that related to the old days. He joined the Old XITs, men who had worked, at one time or another, for the XIT Ranch, which had gone into receivership by the early 1900s. He was also a charter member of the Western Cowpunchers Association of Amarillo and the Western Cowboys Association in Montana. Without fail, he attended the annual meetings of the Old Settlers Reunion at Pampa and the Old Settlers Reunion at the Tri-State Fair.[78] According to Judge James D. Hamlin, "During the last twenty-five years there has not been an important meeting of any kind, conventions, or old settler get-together meetings that Bones is not present, bringing a carnation wrapped in tissue paper which he asks the presiding officer to present with his compliments to the most important guest in attendance."[79]

It was at one of the reunions of the Amarillo Cowboys that his old friends called on Mathew to produce some of his well-known range chili. When he at last pronounced the huge pot of chili done, everyone anxiously lined up for a serving, but Hooks would not allow anyone to eat until he had said grace. He got on his knees and bowed his head, while his old friends, most of them "too stove up to get on their knees," also bowed their heads.[80] His chili prayer was captured for posterity by one of the members in attendance: "Lord God, You know us ole cowhands is forgetful. . . . We just know daylight and dark, summer, fall, winter and spring. But I sure hope we don't never forget to thank You before we is about to eat a mess of good Chilli. We don't know why in Your wisdom, You been so doggone good to us. The Heathen Chinee don't have no Chilli ever, the Frenchmen is left out. The Rooshins don't know no more about Chilli than a hog does about a side saddle. Even the Meskins don't get a good wiff of it unless they stay around here. Chilli eaters is some of your chosen people. We don't know why You is so doggone good to us. But Lord God, don't never think we ain't grateful for this Chilli we is about to eat. Amen."[81]

In 1909, Mathew Hooks was offered a job as a porter on the Santa Fe Railroad, and he joined what many perceived as a prestigious group. The black porters, who had serviced the elegant Pullman Company sleeping cars for the railroad lines since 1867, were considered the elite of the black labor force. Although they were still underpaid and dependent on tips to make a living wage, they not only had steady jobs but also the opportunity to travel around the country. One wonders whether the cheerful and garrulous Hooks talked as freely and openly with his passengers as he had with his fellow cowboys. Hooks toured the United States, visiting cities as far away as Chicago and San Francisco. He also learned of the efforts by A. Philip Randolph to form a union among the porters. Because blacks made up the vast majority of the workforce on the railroads, Randolph formed the Brotherhood of Sleeping Car Porters in 1925. Mathew Hooks, as an independent cowboy and the only black among the white ranchers of the Panhandle preferred to place his faith in the paternalism of the white supervisors of the Pullman Company. "One thing about the white folks," he said, "if you do something worthwhile, they will give you credit for it."[82] During the formation of the union in 1925, the company ferreted out the labor leaders and fired any union organizers. In retaliation, Randolph planned a strike in 1928, but without extensive support from the membership, the effort failed, leaving the union members angry and defensive and Mathew Hooks thankful that he had not joined the union. The brotherhood slowly declined and was not revived until 1933 with the support of Franklin Delano Roosevelt and the New Deal. By that time, Mathew Hooks was in his sixties and had retired from the railroad on a disability pension.[83]

Mathew Hooks had never given up his love of horses and the excitement of bronc riding. During 1910, only a year after he had gone to work for the Santa Fe Railroad, he overheard a group of ranchers discussing horses on their train ride back to the Panhandle. "Because I don't like to miss any horse talk," he "sort of hung around dusting the seats."[84] The men were discussing a horse belonging to Mart Davidson of Pampa whom no one had been able to ride. Hooks, even at forty-three, was certain he could ride the horse, and finally, when he could stand it no longer, he broke into the conversation. "I can ride that horse," he stated, quietly confident. The men smiled and assured him that no one could. Ever the gambler, Mathew bet the men $25, an enormous amount of his salary, that he could. The group accepted his bet and determined to have

Davidson bring the horse to the train station at Pampa when the train passed through on its return run. Two days later, when the train pulled into Pampa, Mathew got out, removed his coat and porter's cap, and climbed aboard the horse. The horse had been justly described as "a thousand pounds of dynamite," and sitting astride the pitching animal was certainly worse than being on a "hurricane deck," but Mathew rode the horse to a standstill. As the train's passengers cheered, enjoying the one-man rodeo, Mathew climbed off, calmly collected his money, donned his porter's uniform, and reboarded the train.[85] It was a feat that made Mathew Hooks famous up and down the railroad line for the remainder of his twenty years with the Pullman Company.

In 1930, Hooks, then sixty-three years old, had worked on the railroad for over twenty years. His wife, Anna, had died ten years earlier, in 1920, and he had buried her at the Llano Cemetery in Amarillo. He had married again, briefly, but the marriage ended in divorce, and he did not remarry. He had seen the Panhandle change and grow, and although he had not supported A. Philip Randolph, he had been influenced by the growing feeling of black pride that was being espoused by not only Randolph, but Marcus Garvey, W. E. B. DuBois and other black leaders. He knew that there was a need for more black communities such as the one he had started thirty-five years earlier at Clarendon. "When I was a boy," he said, "everywhere I went, folks would say, 'We're not goin' to let any Negroes live here.'" I said to myself, "When I get grown I'm goin' to build a town right beside yours, and not let any white folks live there."[86]

When he retired from the railroad, he used his savings and his pension to build a town for his people that would be a credit to the black community. "I wanted our people to have an exclusive town and show the white man we could live as decent and law-abiding citizens so that when one black man committed a crime, the white man couldn't say all darkies were like that."[87]

Mathew Hooks joined sixty other members of the black community in Amarillo to make their dream come true. A parcel of land northwest of Amarillo had been platted for the construction of West Texas State University, but when the Amarillo city fathers failed to encourage its establishment, the board of regents moved the location of the university to Canyon. Hooks and the black leaders asked to purchase the land as a community exclusively for blacks. In September, 1930, the Amarillo City Commission approved the sale of a twenty-eight-square-block parcel, "bounded on the south by Miller Heights, on the north by Thompson Park, on the east by North Madison Street and on the west by North Hayden Street."[88] North Heights grew rapidly into a successful residential and business community for the blacks of Amarillo. One hundred and thirty-five families built comfortable and attractive homes, in addition to a community center, an auditorium, Methodist, Baptist and Holiness churches, and the Fred Douglas Elementary School and Patten High School in which the principal's wife ran the cafeteria.[89] There were also garages, gas stations, and a drug store/general store, owned by Mathew Hooks, at First and Harrison with a second floor where Mathew lived most of the remainder of his life.

In 1932, Hooks and the sixty charter members of the community dedicated a park with lights and a water fountain between Northeast Twenty-first and Twenty-second Streets and between Davidson and Washington. They planted trees, each one named after a child of the community, so that the children could watch their trees grow as they grew. The black community appreciated the efforts of the aging cowboy, and, within the year, the town fathers decided to rename the park in honor of Mathew Hooks. A statue was later erected for him in the park and to this day, on June nineteenth, emancipation day, celebrations are still held in Mathew Hooks Memorial Park, with baseball games, barbecues, and speeches.[90]

In 1932, Mathew Hooks, concerned over the underprivileged boys in the community, formed the Dogie Club. Hooks called himself the Head Wrangler and spent his time teaching and educating any of the black boys of the community who were poor or fatherless. The club, which met frequently, helped the young boys learn pride and good citizenship. The boys benefited from the lessons, and many went on to become successful members of the community. At the beginning of World War II, Hooks helped in a recruiting drive for the Selective Service among the young black men of the area. A number of his "Dogies" joined the military and fought with valor in World War II, returning with pride to their West Texas community. Hooks received a certificate of acclamation from the U.S. government for his assistance that he saved in his growing number of scrapbooks.[91]

Mathew Hooks was also active in founding historical groups. In 1933, he founded the Colored Panhandle Pioneer Club. The only requirement was that members had to have lived in the Panhandle for more than twenty-five years. At the first meeting on June ninth at the North Heights Community Center, there were over sixty black pioneers. As Hooks said, "Folks, it was some roundup. Those mavericks told their experiences in this country when there weren't nothing much but rattlesnakes and dust storms."[92] He was also interested in preserving the history of the area that he saw rapidly slipping away at every funeral he attended. He joined other like-minded old-timers in setting up the Panhandle Plains Museum and Library and eventually left his extensive scrapbook collection to the museum. His scrapbooks showed his eclectic range of interests with clippings on world affairs, juvenile problems, crime prevention, politics, and welfare. In 1936, Hooks's scrapbooks were chosen because of their broad coverage and extensive details to represent the history of Negroes in the Panhandle at the Texas Centennial in Dallas. Three years later, in 1939, Mathew Hooks was invited, as the Texas representative, to display the scrapbooks again at a national exhibit in Detroit for the "Seventy-Five Years of Negro Progress."[93]

By the 1940s, Hooks had become "the most famous cowhand still living."[94] Part of his fame came from his white flowers that appeared, for over fifty years, at the funeral of every pioneer from the early Panhandle days. His "Guerdons of Honor" also spread to anyone who had benefited mankind. The Amarillo floral company kept a list of his gifts and with each one went the same note explaining his desire to honor the pioneer men and women who had built the Panhandle, in particular his friend Tom Clayton. Among those to whom he gave flowers, the Old Soldiers organization received the largest number, eighty-two, while the next largest number, sixty white flowers, went to the Confederate Reunion Plainsmen, also know as the Sky Busters. During World War II, Hooks sent fifty-seven flowers to a WAVES unit known as the Blue Bonnets, and forty-seven to the Rangerettes, a Women's Army Air Corps unit. Five flowers went to the Scouts of England, and President and Mrs. Franklin Roosevelt each received a flower. The notes of acknowledgment from the presidential couple, as well as from the many other recipients, are carefully preserved in his scrapbooks. When the United Nations Conference met in San Francisco, Hooks sent forty-eight flowers, one to each of the national representatives, some of whom he had met when he was a porter on the trains. During the years from 1930 to 1951, whenever a new building was opened or a church was dedicated in Amarillo, one of Mathew Hooks's white flowers appeared. By the end of his life, Hooks had sent over five hundred white flowers to people from all walks of life and had become famous for his thoughtfulness.[95]

By 1949, at eighty-one years of age, Mathew Hooks had begun to suffer a debilitating illness. Without children or a wife to care for him, he was admitted to Wyatt Memorial Hospital in Amarillo. Unfortunately, the income from his store as well as his life savings had been spent on his young Dogies and to help anyone who had asked for money. His stay in the hospital used up what little was left of his resources. When he was finally released, he was neither able to care for himself nor did he have any money left to hire help. Hearing of his problems, the *Amarillo Globe* ran a story detailing his plight. Friends and funds appeared from everywhere. With the money that was collected, his friends hired a housekeeper, Mrs. Leecie Silas, who left her work at the Amarillo Hotel to devote her attention to caring for Hooks.[96]

Mathew Hooks passed away on February 2, 1951, in Amarillo at eighty-three years of age. One brother, Clem Hooks of Hubbard City, Texas, and a sister, Mrs. Eva Lipscomb, of San Diego, survived him.[97] The funeral, held at the Mt. Zion Baptist Church, was attended by dozens of Amarillo citizens. One old white pioneer friend, John Trolinger, had made a vow with Mathew—"whoever was living when the other died, should offer a white flower as a symbol of friendship between the races."[98] Trolinger carried out the promise and placed a lone white flower on his coffin.[99] Mathew Hooks was buried beside his wife, Anna, in Llano Cemetery.

Mathew Hooks had come to the Panhandle with the earliest settlers. As he said, "Folks talk about Judge Bean and the Law West of the Pecos, but there wasn't no law out here then."[100] He watched the improvements and comforts of life slowly develop in the area, and he played an active part in the many changes that had taken place. Mathew Hooks helped improve the lot of the early black settlers, first at Clarendon and later at Amarillo. "I've lived through two ages, the horse age and the automobile age. I liked horses and about the time I got to where I liked autos, they started flying."[101] Although he did go flying when his wife had insisted on it, he decided he would not be able to go with the airplanes as he had with the horse and the auto. He had lived a good life and considered himself fortunate. "One time I owned some oil land and could see myself a millionaire. Then I went broke. I got hurt on the railroad and was retired on a pension and I couldn't live like I had before. So I reached up and pulled down my desires to fit my income and now I am a millionaire."[102] He shared his philosophy of life with a class of college students in 1933. "One of the finest things in the world is the friendships you establish when you are young. . . . You can keep friendship always. You may lose everything, but you can't lose that."[103] He believed that if a man loved his country and had faith in that country, it would bring him comfort, life, and friends. For Mathew Hooks, the Panhandle country brought him everything he had hoped for, and his beloved country was enriched by his presence.

NOTES

1. The extensive collection of the Hooks scrapbooks, interviews, and memorabilia are gathered at the Panhandle-Plains Museum and Library at West Texas A&M

University in Canyon. Further sources are in the McCarty Papers at Amarillo Public Library.

2. Hooks in a July 15, 1939, interview, states that he was born in Orangeville, Robertson County, Texas. Ron Tyler, ed., *The New Handbook of Texas*, vol. 4 (Austin: Texas State Historical Society, 1996), p. 1164, cites the only town listed with such a name as located in Fannin County, near the Red River, not in Robertson. Likewise, a history of Robertson County reveals no Orangeville, at any time, in that county.

3. The 1860 Fannin County Census Records list a Cullen or Collin Hooks who owned sixty-five slaves. The name Warren Hooks appears in an undated newspaper clipping from the *Amarillo Globe* in the Hooks Scrapbooks.

4. "Bones Hooks," *Amarillo Globe*, n.d., Mathew Hooks file, Amarillo Public Library, Amarillo, Tex.

5. "Bones' Bits," Farm and Ranch, *The Amarillo Press*, n.d., Mathew Hooks file, Amarillo Public Library.

6. "Old Bones," interview with History 413, Apr. 16, 1933, typescript, Panhandle-Plains Museum Library, West Texas A&M University, Canyon.

7. Barbara C. Spray, "Mathew Bones Hooks," in Amarillo Genealogical Society, *Texas Panhandle Forefathers*, vol. 1 (Dallas: National ShareGraphics, 1983), p. 77.

8. Ibid.

9. "Recollections of Early Day Texas: Mathew (Bones) Hooks," interview by A. B. Hays, Amarillo, Tex., July 15, 1939, manuscript interview file, Panhandle-Plains Museum Library, West Texas A&M University, Canyon.

10. Guy Saunders, "The Empty Saddle," Clara T. Hammond, comp., *Amarillo* (Amarillo: George Autry, Printer, 1971), p. 139.

11. J. Frank Dobie, *The Mustangs* (Boston: Little, Brown and Company, 1934), p. 304.

12. Ibid.

13. Ibid.

14. Jean Ehly, "'Bones' Hooks of the Panhandle," *Frontier Times* 37:4 (June–July, 1963): 21; "Old Bones," interview with History 413 transcript, p. 5.

15. "Recollections: Bones," interview with Hays manuscript, July 15, 1939.

16. Interview with History 413 transcript, Apr. 16, 1933.

17. "Empty Saddle," *Amarillo*, p. 140.

18. Ibid.

19. Interview with History 413 transcript, Apr. 16, 1933.

20. Ibid.

21. Ibid.

22. Ibid.

23. Ibid.

24. Ibid.

25. "Recollections: Bones," interview with Hays manuscript, July 15, 1939.

26. Ibid.; interview with History 413 transcript, Apr. 16, 1933; Genealogical Society, *Texas Panhandle Forefathers*, vol. 1, p. 76.

27. "The Empty Saddle," *Amarillo,* p. 231.
28. Ibid., p. 232.
29. Frederick W. Rathjen, *The Texas Panhandle Frontier* (Austin: University of Texas Press, 1973), pp. 230–31; "Mobeetie," Tyler, ed., *New Handbook of Texas,* s.v., pp. 784–85.
30. Rathjen, *Texas Panhandle Frontier,* pp. 230–31; "Tascosa," Tyler, ed., *New Handbook of Texas,* s.v., pp. 209–10.
31. "Clarendon," Tyler, ed., *The New Handbook of Texas,* s.v., pp. 129–30; George Turner, "Black Cowboy 'Bones' Hooks Left his Mark on Frontier West's Lore," *Amarillo Globe Times,* Nov. 14, 1973; Ehly, "Bones Hooks," *Frontier Times;* Amarillo Genealogical Society, *Texas Panhandle Forefathers,* vol. 1, p. 76.
32. Interview with History 413 transcript, Apr. 16, 1933.
33. Ibid.
34. "Recollections: Bones," interview with Hays manuscript, July 15, 1939.
35. Interview with History 413 transcript, Apr. 16, 1933.
36. "The Empty Saddle," *Amarillo,* p. 139.
37. Interview with History 413 transcript, Apr. 16, 1933.
38. Ibid.
39. U. S., Works Progress Administration, Federal Writers Project. American Life Histories: Bones Hooks. American Memories Collection, Library of Congress, 1936–40. Online, July, 1998. (http://www.lcweb.loc.gov/)
40. Ibid.
41. Ibid.
42. Ibid.
43. "Empty Saddle," *Amarillo,* pp. 232–33.
44. Ibid.
45. Interview with History 413 transcript, Apr. 16, 1933.
46. Ibid.
47. Ibid. The 7D ranch is the same ranch that black cowboys George Adams, Daniel Webster Wallace, and members of the Payne family worked.
48. Ibid.
49. Ibid.
50. Ibid.
51. Ibid.
52. Ibid.
53. Ibid.; "How the Vigilantes Worked," folder 166, McCarty Papers, Amarillo Public Library.
54. To date the password has not been found in museum records. "Vigilantes Worked," folder 166, McCarty Papers.
55. Ibid.
56. Interview with History 413 transcript, Apr. 16, 1933.
57. "The Empty Saddle," *Amarillo,* pp. 233–34; Ehly, "Bones Hooks," *Frontier Times,*

p. 20; Alwyn Barr, *Black Texans: A History of Negroes in Texas, 1528–1971* (Austin: Jenkins Publishing Co., 1973), p. 91.

58. "Recollections: Bones," interview with Hays manuscript, July 15, 1939.

59. Ibid.

60. "Death Takes Bones Hooks," *Amarillo Daily News*, Feb. 3, 1951.

61. Rathjen, *Texas Panhandle Frontier*, pp. 245–46.

62. Interview with History 413 transcript, Apr. 16, 1933.

63. Ibid.

64. "Recollections: Bones," interview with Hays manuscript, July 15, 1939, p. 5.

65. Ehly, "Bones Hooks," *Frontier Times*, p. 21.

66. Ibid.

67. "Recollections: Bones," interview with Hays manuscript, July 15, 1939, p. 5; "The Empty Saddle," *Amarillo*, p. 139.

68. "Recollections: Bones," interview with Hays manuscript, July 15, 1939, pp. 5–6.

69. Rathjen, *Texas Panhandle Frontier*, p. 237.

70. W. Sherman Savage, *Blacks in the West* (Westport, Conn.: Greenwood Press, 1976), p. 92.

71. Interview with History 413 transcript, Apr. 16, 1933.

72. *Texas Panhandle Forefathers*, vol. 1, p. 76; Ehly, "Bones Hooks," *Frontier Times*.

73. Interview with History 413 transcript, Apr. 16, 1933.

74. Ibid.

75. Amarillo Genealogical Society, *Texas Panhandle Forefathers*, p. 76.

76. Ibid.

77. Ibid.

78. "Mathew Hooks," *The Afro-American Texans* (San Antonio: Institute of Texan Cultures, 1987), p. 17; *Amarillo Press*, July 4, 1996.

79. J. Evetts Haley and William Curry Holden, *The Flamboyant Judge: James D. Hamlin* (Canyon: Palo Duro Press, 1972), p. 103.

80. "Matthew [*sic*] 'Bones' Hooks Chilli Prayer," African Americans: Matthew [*sic*] "Bones" Hooks Vertical File, Institute of Texan Cultures, San Antonio.

81. Ibid.

82. "Empty Saddle," *Amarillo*, p. 140.

83. Paula Pfeffer, *A. Philip Randolph: A Pioneer*, p. 24; "Mathew Hooks," *The Afro-American Texans*, p. 17; "Empty Saddle," *Amarillo*, p. 140.

84. Ehly, "'Bones' Hooks," *Frontier Times*, p. 22; Savage, *Blacks in the West*, p. 92.

85. Savage, *Blacks in the West*, p. 92.

86. "Bones Bits," Farm and Ranch, *Amarillo Press*, n.d.

87. "Empty Saddle," *Amarillo*, p. 139.

88. Amarillo Genealogical Society, *Texas Panhandle Forefathers*, p. 76.

89. Ibid.

90. Amarillo Genealogical Society, *Texas Panhandle Forefathers*, p. 76; "Empty Saddle," *Amarillo*, p. 139; Turner, "Black Cowboy," *Amarillo Globe Times*, Nov. 14, 1973.

91. Amarillo Genealogical Society, *Texas Panhandle Forefathers*, p. 77.
92. Ibid.
93. Turner, "Black Cowboy," *Amarillo Globe Times*, Nov. 14, 1973; Amarillo Genealogical Society, *Texas Panhandle Forefathers*, p. 77.
94. Jean M. Burroughs, *On the Trail: Life and Tales of 'Lead Steer' Potter* (Santa Fe: Museum of New Mexico Press, 1980), p. 136.
95. Ehly, "'Bones' Hooks," *Frontier Times*, p. 23.
96. "Empty Saddle," *Amarillo*, p. 141.
97. Savage, *Blacks in the West*, p. 92.
98. Ehly, "'Bones' Hooks," *Frontier Times*, p. 54.
99. Ibid.
100. *Amarillo Press*, newspaper clipping, July 4, 1996.
101. Ibid.
102. "Empty Saddle," *Amarillo*, p. 140.
103. Interview with History 413 transcript, Apr. 16, 1933.

Figure 16. Louis Power. Courtesy Louise S. O'Connor and the Texas Coastal Bend Collection, University of Texas, Austin

Chapter 19

Louis Power

A Hero's Hero

LOUISE S. O'CONNOR

The name of Louis Power always elicits outbursts of praise and wonderment from those who knew him. Even those who did not have the privilege of his company have heard the stories, and the stories are legion. He was and is a household word in the Coastal Bend of Texas. He is legendary in the world of cowmen and cowhands, a hero, a teacher, and, by unanimous vote, the best cowman that ever lived. Anytime people are gathered and talking about cattle, Louis Power's name still comes up, just as it did almost a hundred years ago. An article in the Goliad paper, during the dipping years of 1918–22, claimed that he dipped more cattle in one day than anybody in the county.

Louis Power was the mulatto grandson of the Irish empresario James Power. In 1809, James Power learned from Stephen F. Austin about the empresarioships being granted by the Mexican government to bring in colonists. James Power and James Hewetson received a contract as empresarios from the governor of Coahuila and Texas in 1828. Power married in 1832, and his son, James, Jr., was born a year later.

The son, James Power, Jr., married Frances Bower, and they had three children. Following his wife's death in the 1870s, James Power, Jr., lived with a black woman at the Power Ranch on Melon Creek. It was from this relationship that Louis was born.[1] Louis apparently knew his father and a half-brother James. When his brother was dying he sent for him, but Louis, knowing he was an embarrassment to the white side of his heritage, declined to go see his brother, preferring to stay away to spare the family the discomfort of his presence.

Louis Power was born on the O'Connor Melon Ranch in 1875 and was raised in the Shelly Field area of the ranch. He spent most of his childhood on that ranch and, as a fairly young man, began carrying out jobs on all the O'Connor ranches as a boss.

I live on the O'Connor Duke Ranch now, down on the San'tone River, but I was born in Refugio County on the Melon Creek back in 1875. I've spent all my life on O'Connor land, and I never really knowed anyone but O'Connors to live on this land, back to the original Mr. Tom . . .

I never really have knowed how big that ranch is. I started out bossin' the country east of Melon creek and west of Copano Creek from 1904 until they divided the land in 1907. After that, I went to the Duke Ranch for Mr. Joe O'Connor except for a couple years . . . when I farmed for Mr. Tom O'Connor (II).[2]

Louis was illiterate but created a language of his own that he used to count, keep ranch records, and his own personal business. Very few people ever saw the language he created. His niece, Rosie Terrell Jones, used to help him with his bookkeeping when his records had to be translated into English for use by others. She once described it as a form of hieroglyphics. He would use symbols and pictures to keep his records.

He was considered a totally honest man, skilled in the ways of cattle and handling men. If he counted cattle in a sale, his count was accepted without question. His word was his bond, and it was never questioned by his employers, his employees, his friends, or the people with whom he did business. He could count cattle faster and more accurately than anyone. He would put a knot in a piece of string for every one hundred head of cattle he counted, and he never missed the count to anyone's knowledge. The old cowhands that worked with him and for him commented that he could count faster than you could run cattle by him. This was always said with total admiration and incredulity.

At the age of twenty-five, Power was in charge of the 1907 division of the O'Connor Ranches after the death of Dennis M. O'Connor (I) in 1900. He went on to become foreman of the Duke Division of the O'Connor Brothers Ranches in an era when blacks did not become bosses. He was a genius at understanding a "cow brute" and at handling cattle. His ability to think like a cow made his work easier, his men's work easier, and life easier for the cattle. He was just as adept at handling men and the everyday tasks of the ranch as any modern-day, high-level corporate manager.

The men who worked for him would tell how he made them want to be like him. They called him an honest man, true in everything he did and said.

They still live by his teachings fifty years after his death. Those who knew him well loved him without qualification. Those who did business with him respected him to the point of awe. After years of interviewing in the community in which he was born, grew up, lived as an adult, and died, I began to suspect the group assembled would have genuflected if they had dared, when I mentioned his name, so honored was he by all.

My father tells the story of his toughness. A wild nerve (tic deloreaux) afflicted Louis in the face. It was so painful that it would "have felled" an ordinary person. He would simply ignore it until it became unbearable, and then he would submit to having the nerve shot with alcohol to subdue it for awhile. It was reported that he refused any form of anesthesia and never made a sound when the treatment was taking place.

Being a mulatto was painful for him. He fit in no world, black, white, or Mexican. He would eat by himself and lived by himself because he never felt fully comfortable in the other worlds. Others who were half-black were treated as full-blooded blacks in black society. Louis was not treated as an equal in black society. He was considered a cut above. In his time, there was also no place for him in white society. He had to keep a proper distance from his employees, so he did not feel entirely welcome in any place in his world at the time. He once told Tom O'Connor, Jr., that there was "a special place in hell for a white man who put his blood in black veins."[3]

> Let me tell you what happened to me one time. I was in Mr. Huson's (Hobart) office as secretary and Louis walked in one day. He was paler than me and very polite. I always tried to be nice and get in conversations with people who come in the office.
>
> He wrote his name down in the register, Louis Power, and I said, "Power? Are you kin to the Power family here?" He smiled and said, "I just don't know about that, Ma'am." All I could think of to say was, "Uh, oh, and it's about time we talked about something else. You have to remember that I came from another part of the world." That was the end of that conversation, but he was such an elegant gentleman about the whole thing.[4]

It is said that my grandfather, Thomas O'Connor [II] once whipped old man Hugh Roy Cullen and threw him off the ranch because Cullen made some comment about having to eat with Louis.

"He was a big man with copper-colored skin and reddish hair. He was very Irish looking, slow-talking, slow-moving, and very bowlegged. He was an authority figure wherever he was. The fact that he had a position of prestige, yet was one of them in color, gave him a place of special respect among his men and his community.

"I had heard of him all my life, but never had any personal experience with him until I took over the Duke Ranch in 1941 when my brother was drafted in World War II. Louis had been running the Duke Ranch since 1907. He once said he had been around the Duke Ranch since the 1890s.

"Louis was in his early seventies when I took over the Duke. He was still riding horseback and was active at that time. He knew what an old cow would be thinking tomorrow. He was absolutely without peer when it came to knowing a cow, her ways, how to handle her and what she needed to be healthy and make you money. He knew every cow on that ranch, her mother, where she was born and if she would or wouldn't survive the winter. His knowledge of cattle was incredible. His mind was uncluttered with anything but that herd of cattle, taking care of his cowhands, and the Duke Ranch. That was his world."[5]

"When I first ran away from home, I wandered around until I got back to the O'Connor Duke Ranch, where Mr. Louis was. He was a good man and a good boss and he knew cattle. He couldn't write his name, but he could look at a bunch of cattle and tell you how many there was. When he counted, he didn't count one, two, he counted bunches at a time.

"He could look across a pasture and tell if a calf following its mother was a bull or a heifer. He knew a bull walks behind and a heifer walks up side her, just like a foal. He could tell the way an animal moved as far as he could see if he had screw worms in its body. He learned all that just watching cattle. He was on a ranch from the time he was a boy.

"He was an honest man with true sympathy and compassion for others. He had a lot of experience and knowed all the signs of mighty near everything. He would look at a man's horse and tell if he had been to the windmill he was told to go to. He could tell how the horse was sweated. He knowed things by nature. He had great experience in life. He also had lots of secret parts about him I didn't know.

"When we were working and especially if we were driving cattle, he could tell every crooked move you made. He never hollered at you, he was easy to work for. He was a man never laughed much; he hardly ever had a conversation. He would just shake his shoulders if he was real tickled.

"We always knew when it was cow working time coming up. Uncle Louis would drag two or three hard twist ropes behind his horse for two or three weeks."[6]

"Louis Power was foreman of the O'Connor Duke Ranch. He was a fine fella. One time a friend of mine had a bunch of cattle stampede and Louis Power was nearby. He ran ahead of the herd and stopped the stampede. He could talk to the cattle and make them stop stampeding. He could take them out of a stampede.

"Whenever he counted cattle, nobody would question his count. He would tie a knot in his bridle rein for every one hundred head he counted. He could really use a whip. He could pop that whip right between a cow's eyes.

"He could drink a good bit of whiskey. He would just put his finger in that hole and roll the jug over. He used to like horse races, but he would never bet for himself. He would always give his money to a white man to bet for him. I guess he thought it was out of place for him to bet."[7]

"Uncle Louis could measure the distance between his fence posts by a horse's step. He could step off property that way also. He didn't have anything surveyed. Everyone took his word. He wasn't pretty near right, he was right."[8]

"We don't know the year when he moved the family out to the farm of Mr. Tom O'Connor [II] out on the Melon Ranch. We do not know how long we were there before Mr. Joe O'Connor ask him to leave his plows and tractor and come over and start riding and fixing on the windmill.

"All that was pleasure for us. We never did have to pick cotton but very little. Papa didn't want us in the field. He hired men, but he work hard himself. We didn't have no income, so we thank God for a father like that and a loving mother.

"We do not know how long he was at this place, but you know, Mr. Joe O'Connor was very nice to Papa and the family and he moved him up higher at the Duke Ranch, knowing that Papa was not getting any younger. Papa would come to Refugio to see us often. We did not live at the Duke Ranch all the time.

"Papa never went to school a day in his life. We children say that it was God gave him his wisdom, knowledge, and understanding. We loved him, but God loved him most."[9]

• • •

"He taught me how to work cattle and do everything. In 1917, at the Duke, he used to tell Mr. Sitterle to let me go help with the cow crowd. He put me to cuttin' cattle in 1917. I cut cattle until I quit working in 1947.

"He was born near the creek by the big house at the Melon Ranch. He knew everything about the Copano Pasture and he knew everything about cattle.

"One time, Mr. Jim Welder bought some steers from Louis and asked Louis how many days it would take for him to gather them. Louis said, 'Three or four days.' Mr. Welder said, 'If you can gather them in that few days, I will buy you a pair of boots in Victoria.' Louis did it and he got the boots. He delivered those steers to Vidauri in three days.[10]

Louis Power died in 1946 of prostate cancer. He rode horseback and worked almost to the end. Tom O'Connor, Jr., took care of him in his final illness and loved and respected him until the day he died. It was that way with everyone who knew him. The men he mentored and worked with are some of the finest men that ever lived, and he was their hero.

NOTES

1. Tom Shelton, interview by Sara R. Massey, San Antonio, June 29, 1998.
2. Louis Power, interview by Verlin Vandenburge, ca. 1941, in Louise S. O'Connor, *Cryin' for Daylight: A Ranching Culture in the Texas Coastal Bend* (Victoria: Wexford Publishing, 1989), p. 139–40.
3. Tom O'Connor, Jr. (III), interview by Louise S. O'Connor, Gaffney Ranch, Victoria, Tex., Nov. 18, 1990.
4. Joyce Anderson Winsor, interview by Louise S. O'Connor, Refugio, Tex., Mar. 24, 1995.
5. Tom O'Connor interview.
6. Milam Thompson, interview by Louise S. O'Connor, Gaffney Ranch, Victoria County, Tex., 1987.
7. Herbert "Blue" Albrecht and Ralph Bego, interview by Louise S. O'Connor, Goliad, Tex., June 21, 1990.
8. Willie Brown, Jesse Jones, L. V. Terrell, interview by Louise S. O'Connor, Gaffney Ranch, Victoria County, Tex., 1987.
9. Verlee Power Crittenden, Rachel Power Hayes, Adele Power Osborne, Delores Power, and Elneta Power Roland (all daughters of Louis Power), interview by Louise S. O'Connor, Victoria, Tex., 1983.
10. Rafael de la Garza, interview by Louise S. O'Connor, Victoria County, Tex., 1983.

Figure 17. Monroe Payne. Courtesy Nora Payne Geron and the Archives of the Big Bend, Sul Ross State University, Alpine, Texas

Chapter 20

The Paynes of Texas

Black Seminole Cowboys of the Big Bend

MARILYN DELL BRADY

The Big Bend region of Texas, where the Rio Grande dips south around the Chisos Mountains, was one of the last areas of the state to be settled. As the ranch country of Central Texas and the Panhandle filled, new land was opening in the Big Bend. Anglo ranchers began to enter the area by the 1850s. After the arrival of the railroad in 1881, they came in greater numbers, taking control of the rare water holes and vast stretches of land. While some ranchers fenced their land and controlled the breeding of their cattle, roundups and cattle drives to the railroad towns of Marfa, Alpine, or Marathon continued until the mid-twentieth century. Some men who worked as cowboys in the Big Bend were Mexican, native to the region or to the villages on either side of the Mexican border. Anglo men, often from previously ranched sections of Texas, joined them as ranchers and as cowboys. Also from the East came African Americans, some of them descended from slaves.[1]

In addition, there was the Payne family, whose racial and cultural legacy was complex, and whose stories have been preserved by their own oral histories and essays.[2] All claim as their ancestors Natividad Mariscal, one of the elite Seminole Negro Indian scouts who had fought throughout the Big Bend region and beyond in the Indian wars of the 1870s and 1880s, and his wife, Antonia Payne, a member of the Black Seminole community. Their sons, Monroe and John, were born near Fort Clark and were American citizens, but the family returned to Nacimiento, Coahuila, after Mariscal finished his enlistments. In the early 1900s, first Monroe and then John Payne crossed back into Texas and settled in the Big Bend region, where they and their sons became known as exceptionally fine cowboys. Monroe's sons, Thomas, Rocky, and Marcello, and John's son, Blas, followed in their fathers' footsteps. John's daughter, Ruth, married Morgan Gordon, the son of an ex-slave and an out-standing cowboy himself. Some of the next generation also worked on ranches. The varied lives and work of these black cowboys earned them accolades, especially for breaking horses, and helped some of them advance to positions of ranch foremen. Praise and respect could not, however, totally erase racial discrimination on the West Texas frontier.

The descendants of Natividad Mariscal Payne are justly proud of his service as a Seminole scout. These were the men who tracked Apaches and Comanches for the United States Army in West Texas and played a unique role in the opening of the land for railroads, ranching, and mining. The Black Seminoles, as they were called, were generally descended from the African Americans who had fled slavery to join the Seminole Indians in Florida in the 1700s and early 1800s. Accepted into the tribe as "vassals and allies," they intermarried with the Seminoles and with them resisted the invasion of the U.S. Army into their lands. In the 1840s, many of both groups were removed to Indian Territory, present-day Oklahoma. There blacks found themselves threatened with enslavement by members of the "civilized tribes" who practiced plantation slavery like Southern whites. Along with some Seminoles, blacks escaped to Mexico and were granted land at Nacimiento, Coahuila, in exchange for protecting inhabitants from raiding Indians. When the Civil War ended slavery in the United States, many Black Seminoles enlisted as scouts in the U.S. Army, where they served with distinction in the Indian wars of West Texas. From their days in Florida, Indian Territory, and Mexico, the Black Seminoles worked with cattle and horses. As Kenneth Porter notes, the early dynasties of the Seminoles were named "cowkeepers." The Black Seminoles knew animals, they knew the land, and they perfected the skills that they passed from generation to generation.[3]

Although he served as a Seminole Negro Indian scout for eight years, there is no evidence that Natividad Mariscal was either a Seminole or a Negro. Racial lines among the Black Seminoles were fluid, and tribal and family identity seems to have been based more on function than heredity. Mischa Benson Adams, an anthropologist, claims that kinship at Nacimiento was "more like a basket, than a family tree." Nato, as he was called, seems to have been a Mexican who arrived in the Black Seminole community at Nacimiento with Fidel Soria, variously called his brother, cousin, or close friend, seeking refuge after his own Indian captivity. He may have started a family there. In 1876, he went to Fort Clark at Brackettville, Texas, where the Seminole scouts and their families had a second community along Las Moras Creek. He served among the scouts until 1884, in the Big Bend region, in Mexico, and throughout Trans-

Pecos Texas, tracking hostile Indians, building roads, and providing essential escort duty to investors and engineers seeking to develop mines and railroads.[4]

Little is known about Antonia Payne, the woman he married in Brackettville. Her name establishes that she was a Payne, one of the largest and most influential families among the Black Seminoles and was almost certainly of African descent.[5] After living for a time at Las Moras, Antonia, Natividad, and their children returned to Nacimiento. Monroe and John grew up there and, according to local narratives, Monroe was a wild youth. In 1894, he married Jesusita Vasquez at Nacimiento, and his brother, John, married her sister, Refugia Vasquez. Both were the daughters of Santiago and Juanita Mireles Vasquez. At both Nacimiento and Las Moras, interracial marriages were common, and the women, like their husbands, were probably of mixed racial descent.[6]

Monroe Payne left Mexico and came to the Big Bend of Texas in 1904 with his wife, Jesusita, and their three oldest children, Maria, Thomas, and Batana, all of whom had been born in Nacimiento. They probably followed the old route from Santa Rosa along the west side of the Sierra del Carmen to Boquillos, Mexico, where they crossed the Rio Grande. Initially, Monroe worked for Max Ernst, perhaps hauling goods for his trading post. He also hired out to do short-term jobs for several ranchers in southeast Brewster County.[7]

Shortly after his arrival, Monroe Payne became ranch foreman for Lou Buttrill, who had a large ranch in the Rosillos Mountains. Payne and his family lived in a three-room rock house near the Buttrill family's dwelling. The Payne house was about twenty feet square, with glass windows, a fireplace, stove, and an outhouse. Not required to work for the Buttrills, Jesusita Payne took care of her home and children and grew a large vegetable garden. More children were born to the family. The ranch was quite isolated, and the children never attended school. The Payne family saw few other people except Buttrill's cowboys and purchasers of Buttrill's cattle and horses. The trip to Marathon took several days, and they rarely went, as Mrs. Buttrill occasionally shopped for them there. The Paynes shopped in the village of San Vicente on the Rio Grande, described as having "lots of farmers and houses." Monroe kept dogs, used to hunt panthers, and always carried a pistol, which his son, Rocky, never saw him use. Son Tom raised Spanish goats. Lou Buttrill involved Tom and Rocky in ranch work while they were still quite young. Tom, who was six years old when the Paynes arrived, got fifty cents for his first job as a cowboy, and Rocky, who was born while the family lived at the ranch, remembers being a "little, bitty cowboy" for Buttrill.[8]

While working for Buttrill, Monroe Payne started his own enterprises, buying land and animals of his own. Some of the land was probably to extend

Buttrill's holdings, a common practice in the region. He also bought and sold lots in Marathon and began his own freighting business. He had mules, horses, and three big wagons that he used to carry hay and oats for the horses of the soldiers at Glenn Springs and to haul ore from the mining company in Boquillos to the railroad in Marathon. When the mining stopped, and the soldiers left, Payne found other articles to haul and continued in the business until his death. In 1916, he bought his first truck, a Ford, from Casner's newly opened dealership in Alpine. In addition, he leased land on the Rio Grande where some of his family farmed. His son, Rocky, described it as a "big farm—about half a section." On it the family raised corn, wheat, and all kinds of vegetables for nearby ranchers. The farm also had some hot springs.[9]

By 1914, the Payne family had moved from the Buttrill headquarters across Nine-Point Draw to Bone Springs on the main road to Marathon. They were living there when Monroe Payne was caught in events surrounding the raid at Glenn Springs and the kidnapping of Jesse Deemer from his store. In 1924, Payne drew up a legal deposition about the kidnapping in an attempt to gain compensation from the Mexican government. Payne's statement differs significantly from most accounts of the kidnapping, which have depicted him as a passive victim seized and rescued alongside Deemer. Payne describes how he had gone to Mexico to check on the cattle he owned there. He encountered the raiders, who forced him to take them to Boquillos, where Deemer and the contents of his store were taken. Payne makes clear that he passed over opportunities to escape in order to insure Deemer's safety before the U.S. Cavalry rescued them. A newspaper man covering the raid remarked that the large, powerful, black Payne was "a person such as I have never seen before—but everybody in the Big Bend is like nobody I ever saw before."[10]

Shortly after the raid, the Buttrills decided to sell out and move off the Rosillos Mountain ranch. About the same time, the Payne family moved into a spacious adobe house in the Mexican part of Marathon. From there, Monroe Payne continued to run a variety of enterprises. He rented houses in town, sold water from his windmill, and sold water to his Mexican neighbors at ten cents for a fifty-five-gallon barrel. Although he quit most of his cowboying, he continued to work roundups for the Stillwells, Bensons, and other ranchers.[11]

His grandchildren recall Monroe as a "jack of all trades" who created his own work, rather than depending on employment by others. His children and grandchildren learned from him the value of hard work and the need to go after what they needed. "If you have a body, you can go out and earn it," Monroe advised.[12] By 1920, he had become relatively well off and was listed in the U.S. manuscript census for 1920 as being a farmer who owned his own home and land. In addition, he was listed as now being white. Although the census taker may have made a common mistake, Monroe Payne could have been following the more fluid definitions of race traditional in New Spain and Mexico. Color mattered, but wealth and upward mobility could move a person to a "lighter" racial category.[13]

Not all of Monroe Payne's enterprises were legal or successful. The *Alpine Avalanche* stated that he was arrested for bootlegging *sotol* from Mexico in 1921.[14] Undocumented "tales" of the Big Bend area depict him as a legendary outlaw, willing to be a "hired gun" and a cattle thief on his visits to Mexico. One story tells how Payne refused to show deference when getting water at Bone Springs. Instead of letting a white cowboy fill his water barrels first, Payne gave him a pistol-whipping. The white cowboy rushed back to his ranch headquarters and returned with a friend who was an excellent marksman, but no shots were fired. Although legends claim that Payne was killed in a gunfight, he died at home in 1952.[15]

Meanwhile, Monroe Payne's sons had begun to work as ranch hands. Tom, the eldest, was closest to the image of the cowboy as a loner and wanderer. Except for a brief marriage that his wife "quit," he remained single and worked for different ranchers at various jobs. After his father's involvement in the Boquillos kidnapping, he claimed he had "bad luck." "My dad ruined me," and for some unspecified reason caused Tom to be jailed in Marathon. Sometimes Tom herded cattle or goats, but he preferred herding sheep and did that most often. His work consisted of "Up at four or five. Get horse. Get truck loaded. Feed sheep." Herding sheep allowed him to "just stay out on the ranch and look around." Sometimes he worked with five or six other cowboys, "wet Mexicans" whose illegal presence meant extra carefulness. He described going out on the ranch for three or four months and earning $20 or $30. Then he would return to Marathon to buy clothes, "a little candy" and give his money to his mother.

Tom Payne had a strong pride in how long and how hard he had worked. In addition to herding, he once went by bus across the Mississippi River to Wisconsin to pick pumpkins. He claimed his hardest job was doing pick-and-shovel work in the cold as boss of three or four other men. Always, however, he returned to his mother in Marathon and to ranch work in the Big Bend. When he got too old to earn a full wage, he said, he just kept on working and accepted half pay.[16]

Like his father, Rocky Payne achieved a permanent position as ranch foreman, but he remained more focused on ranching. After leaving Buttrill's ranch, Rocky worked on the family farm on the Rio Grande for a short time, and then was employed by several different ranchers. He reported spending about half the time on the ranch and half out with the cattle, also returning with money for his mother. At one point, Rocky worked roundups at the Gage Ranch, one of the largest ranches in the area. He remembered getting up at five and working till dark. The cook would "fix bacon and meat for breakfast," and then the cowboys would "go gather up cattle." Crews of twenty men would drive the herd thirty or forty miles a day and then camp for the night. Sometimes there would be a singer or a guitar player, but more often "they sat a right good while, talking." Rocky believed that it had been "a good wagon to be with." Not having attended school, he credited the older cowboys with having taught him all he knew.[17]

Rocky Payne became widely known in the Big Bend region for his ability to break horses. Travis Roberts broke horses at the Gage Ranch with Rocky and claimed he was "as good a rider as I ever saw."[18] Ted Gray, a local rancher, included Rocky in his memoirs, naming him among "the four good Negro cowboys in the Alpine area." All four were "good *jinetes*" or bronc riders, leading Gray to comment, "A horse seems to have some kind of recognition for a colored cowboy—they have a different way with horses. They were all comics, and you could joke with them and have a little fun." After breaking horses with Rocky Payne, Ted Gray observed his particular technique. He "always quirted the horse on the neck instead of the flank" presumably to keep the horse from "ring-tailing."[19] When Gray was wagon boss for the Kokernot Ranch, Rocky was part of his outfit. Once, after the major part of the cattle had been rounded up and shipped, they went after wild cattle north of Alpine. Gray encountered a three-year-old bull dragging a rope. When he asked whose rope it was, Rocky responded, "It's his'n. I gave it to him just a little while ago over there in that brush thicket. He can have it now."[20] Rocky also assured Ted that it was important to hold off castrating the horses until the right "sign," referring to the zodiac. Otherwise, "them horses will all have a weak back, or they'll stumble, or something." Although Gray did not agree about "signs," he called Rocky "quite an old Negro cowboy."[21]

In 1935, when Rocky Payne was thirty-one years old, he became foreman for Zeb Decie, who had recently married and acquired Que Decie Ranch, south of Alpine. Rocky remained in that position for twenty years. At first, he made $30 a month, the going rate, but by 1955 he was making $175. As foreman, he had great responsibility. His children commented on how well he knew animals and could do all the various other skills necessary on a ranch. Decie placed great trust in both his ability and his honesty.

Shortly after coming to Alpine, Rocky married Cruz Bustamante. As his own parents had done at the Buttrills, the couple lived near the Decies on the ranch. Rocky had not attended school and could neither read nor write when he first married. After counting the horses and cows, he would tell the numbers to his wife who would write them down. "Then he'd bring the paper to Mr. Decie." The couple's three oldest children, Nora, Rocky, Jr., and Manuel grew up on the ranch. When Nora was born, Zeb Decie gave Rocky Payne his first cow. In subsequent years, Rocky raised his own cattle along with those belonging to the ranch. Cruz Payne was not employed by the Decies and devoted her primary attention to her family and the large vegetable garden. The children did chores, helped with the garden, milked the family cows, and played around the ranch. Nora Payne Geron described going on a roundup and cattle drive with her father and the Decie outfit when she was about six. As the oldest child, she claimed her father sometimes treated her like a son until her brothers were old enough to become involved in the ranch. As the older children started school, they boarded during the week with their mother's mother in Alpine, gladly returning to the ranch on weekends. When Manuel, the third child, started school, Rocky Payne built a house in town for his wife and children where they lived during the week when school was in session. The family still spent weekends together, often at the ranch, and even went out weekday evenings because the children missed helping with the chores.

Rocky described Que Decie as a "small operation" where he and one other man worked regularly and other men helped out as needed. He also claimed that he only worked about half a day, showing up at noon or going into Alpine. Nora challenged her father on both accounts, remembering the ranch stretching for miles and her father leaving the house at five in the morning and returning after dark, when his wife and children had finished in the garden. The depression and World War II passed by Rocky Payne. After retiring from the ranch in 1955, he did a variety of jobs on nearby ranches as well as picking cotton and working in the oil fields near Kermit, Texas.[22]

Marcello Payne, the younger brother of Thomas and Rocky, shared their love and commitment to ranching. For a time he worked with Rocky at the Gage Ranch, where they cut horses together. He went on to spend the rest of his life on ranches around Marathon, where Rocky's son, Manuel, joined him during the summers when he was growing up. Following in the family tradition, Manuel broke horses when he was in high school in the 1950s. After school was over, he would go out and break two or three horses, earning $75 a horse for spending money. Although he went on to have a steady job with the highway department, Manuel continued to work for ranchers on the weekends.[23]

While Monroe Payne and his family were settling into life in the Big Bend region, his brother, Juan or John, remained in Mexico and, after 1910 became involved in the Mexican Revolution. His son, Blas, claimed that John fought four years while soldiers took the crops his wife, Refugia, and the children needed to survive. Blas forcefully asserted that his father had fought "for Revolution," rather than for any particular side.[24] John's grandson, Morgan Gordon, Jr., tells a different version. He says that John Payne was an officer for the Federales, fighting to defend the Diaz government. Then he deserted and followed his brother into the United States where they both held citizenship because of their birth at Fort Clark. Gordon remembers hearing that John Payne originally came alone and was followed by his wife and their five children. Monroe Payne met the family at the river crossing near Boquillos. The Rio Grande was flooding, and the mules pulling the family wagon balked at entering it. Only after Monroe tricked them by taking the bell mule across first were they willing to cross.[25] Arriving in Brewster County, the family stopped at Bone Springs, where Monroe and his family were living. John Payne began doing hired work for several ranchers, and then he took a job at the Combs Ranch south of Marathon. He became ranch foreman and stayed with the Combs until his death. Like the other Payne men, he was known for his ranching expertise.

Blas Payne, John's oldest son, worked at the Combs Ranch all of his life as well, starting when he was still in his teens. When his father died, Blas took his place as foreman. Eventually he became too old to continue as a cowboy and became caretaker of the remnants of Camp Peña Colorado, a former military post on the Combs Ranch. He and his mother lived in an abandoned building there, and he is buried on the hill overlooking "the Post," as the local people call it.[26]

Blas Payne claimed that his grandfather, Nato Mariscal, while serving with the Seminole scouts, had discovered the spring at Peña Colorado and built the structures there.[27] In his later years Blas lived in the old officers' quarters that he claimed his grandfather had built, where individuals interested in the Seminole scouts frequently visited him. Over the years, Blas told excellent stories that became increasingly elaborate.[28] Other family members, official army records, and the research of Kenneth Porter, the first scholar to focus on the Seminole scouts, offer strong evidence contrary to some of his most known tales. For example, they establish that Natividad Mariscal was not really Isaac Payne, the trumpeter for John Bullis, the white commanding officer for the scouts, and, therefore, he was not one of the four scouts who earned Congressional Medals of Honor. In fact, muster rolls and other records indicate that Nato Mariscal and Isaac Payne were two different individuals who actually served among the Seminole Indian Negro scouts at the same time.[29]

Blas Payne is often acclaimed as "the best cowboy ever seen," an undocumented title Kenneth Mulroy assigned Blas's photograph in his book on Black Seminoles.[30] Joe Graham, a scholar of ranch history, confirms the validity of Blas's title. Graham grew up near Marathon, and, during the summers of his high school years, he worked on the ranch with Blas Payne. Graham still credits him as being "the best cowboy I ever saw." Graham also remembers that Blas went to the kitchen of the local ice cream parlor while the other cowboys enjoyed themselves in the front.[31] Like other African American cowboys, Blas Payne found that admiration for his skills on the ranch did not always translate into acceptance as an equal when in town.[32]

Although Monroe's children took Mexican partners when they married, John's oldest daughter married an African American. Rita, as she was called in Mexico, or Ruth as she became in Texas, married Morgan Gordon, an ex-slave with his own fine reputation as a black cowboy. Morgan Gordon's mother had been a slave, with few good choices after emancipation. When Morgan was about twelve, a man she was with in Goliad beat him with double-barbed wire. Leaving home, Gordon grew up on his own as he moved through Arkansas and Oklahoma. When he got in trouble a sheriff in Arizona sent him back to Texas. Once there he drove cattle to railroad heads in Kansas for the 7D ranch in present-day Terrell County.[33] When Mexican raiders took the other horses but not Gordon's, the trail boss got angry at him, and he quit to deal cards at a gambling place in Alpine. In 1910, the census taker found him in Marathon, working in the *guayule* factory and giving his age as forty-four.[34] Then he began working as a cowboy and later foreman for Jim P. Wilson, Sr., on his large ranch in Green Valley, south of Alpine. He stayed there for forty-four years, retiring on full pay when he could not continue his full-time duties and then worked as he could. Morgan Gordon also continued to do roundups and wrangle horses. He was still so good that George Benson would try to arrange the schedule so that both Morgan Gordon and Monroe Payne would be available to work his roundups in south Brewster County.[35] His son, Morgan, Jr., called him a "hell of a cowboy," and recalled that he also used to take his "paint" mules and wagon and go down to the Rio Grande to get *sotol* to sell.[36]

Morgan Gordon was about Monroe Payne's age, but his wife, Rita (Ruth), was the daughter of Monroe's brother, John, and much younger than he was. She did not live on the Wilson Ranch, and their children were born in Alpine.

While Gordon, Sr., was on the ranch, she and the children spoke Spanish with each other and with their Mexican neighbors. Gordon spoke perfect "Mexican," but did not want his children to grow up speaking it. Upon returning home, he would yell, "You no damn Mexican. Speak English." He and his wife cared deeply about educating their children, not an easy task for black parents. The school in Alpine that the black community created was located on his land and named the Morgan School.[37]

Morgan Gordon, Jr., or Sonny as he is still called, was also drawn to ranching while a young boy. Leaving the schooling his parents tried to provide, he began working with horses when he was eleven. Stanford, a black cowboy known for his skill at breaking horses, tutored him. Sonny described him as "a savvy old man" who never directly criticized his errors but would later calmly point out how someone else had handled the same situation. While still teenagers, various people asked Sonny and his brother, Martin, known as Caboose, to come break their horses.[38] Stanford, also, got Sonny started working on the Gage Ranch, where he first hired on as a horse wrangler for a roundup. Still in his teens, Sonny was responsible for moving about a hundred horses from the place where the outfit had slept to the site the chuck wagon cook picked for their noon stop and for having fresh horses ready for the cowboys. He was good enough at the job that he became a "full-fledged cowboy" for the Gage Ranch. Eventually Sonny left Gage and went to ranch east of Fort Stockton, where he was left alone with beans, potatoes, some colts he had broken, and some sheep to herd. One evening he startled the colt he was riding, and it started to run. When the colt tore between a rare fence post and one of the few trees on the place, Sonny fell to the ground. Neighbors eventually found him, alone and badly wounded. After he healed, he joined the U.S. Army and served for twenty years. As he put it, when he got wounded in Korea, someone was there to take care of him.[39]

Despite the praise, trust, and advancement that the Payne men received for their skills, they still faced discrimination for being of African descent and for looking "colored." To varying degrees, they articulated their resentment. Monroe and John Payne were children of mixed parentage that included some degree of African ancestry. They both married women who also seemed to be of mixed heritage. When they came to Texas, even a tiny amount of African "blood" defined a person as "colored," a word contemporaries used frequently to describe them and their children. As "colored," they all faced discrimination and responded to it in different ways.

Other than his legendary pride, little can be known about how Monroe Payne felt about his racial identity or how whites viewed him. Alberto Garcia, one of his Mexican neighbors, grew up running errands for Payne and spoke about his place in the community. When asked how the Mexicans regarded Monroe Payne, he stated that some "shied away from him." Garcia, himself, took a different view, reporting, "Well, Monroe Payne was a colored fellow, but to me he wasn't a colored fellow. To me, he was one of us because I went to him there, so he would help after I helped him all of the time. Anything that they had, they would give me."[40]

After his marriage, Rocky's family went by the name of Mariscal and moved largely in the Mexican community when not on the ranch. Rocky's Roman Catholic baptismal and marriage certificates gave his name as Rocque Mariscal. Deciding to go by the name of Payne when Nora started the second grade, the family later had problems over their legal identity. Rocky Payne did not, however, tell his children that they had any possibility of African descent until the oldest were grown. When she was in college in Alpine, a local Anglo historian told Nora Payne that her grandfather was a Seminole scout. Only then did she begin to ask questions about her ancestry. Acceptance of the children as Mexicans made it easier for Rocky's children to attend public schools in Alpine and eventually Sul Ross State University.[41] It also indicates a deep acceptance of the family within the Mexican community.

Both Rocky and Marcello Payne married Mexican women, and, to some degree, blended into the Mexican community. This had been a common and accepted practice in New Spain, and some of the Buffalo Soldiers continued it when they came to the Big Bend region. Texas, however, had had strong laws against interracial marriage since its founding as a republic. While no evidence has been found that the laws were enforced in Brewster County, families in El Paso were arrested for unknowingly having broken them. African Americans there protested that their children were being made illegitimate and collected money to help with the defense of those affected. They noted that they had been soldiers in the area and that they had married and had children "without any thought of violating the law."[42]

Travis Roberts was more outspoken than the Paynes themselves about the discrimination from the other cowboys that Rocky and Marcello faced. After claiming "those Seminoles always liked me," Roberts went on to protest, "Those other boys, they'd used to throw off on them because they were colored people, and I didn't believe in that." He told how, when the men were holding a herd and taking turns going to lunch, the Paynes did not get their fair share of time to eat. "I knowed they never got enough to eat. It wasn't five minutes and they'd be on their way back." According to Roberts, who was white himself, the Paynes could be depended on for help, unlike the other white cowboys. "I didn't give a damn about those gringos. Those old kids would hide behind a bush over on a ridge, and you think they'd come help you. . . . I just detested most of them." At calf roping, Travis and his partner formed one team and the Paynes another. "Do you think those other boys ever offered to relieve us? We flanked all the calves. Them Niggers, they did their part and we did ours."[43]

Unlike Monroe's children, John Payne's daughter, Ruth, married an ex-slave whose African descent was clearly visible. Although they also lived with Mexicans, the Gordon children faced greater discrimination than the young Paynes. Because of Jim Crow laws, they could not attend either the Anglo schools or the school provided for Mexican children. Although segregated from Anglos, Mexicans were legally defined as white. Occasionally, when black parents could gather over a dozen children from the surrounding area, they could bring in a young teacher from Prairie View A&M. Sonny remembers going to school with some cousins and a few other children in the living room of his grandmother's home in Marathon. Other years they held school in Marfa or Alpine. The problems Sonny and his brothers had going to school led his father and others to found the Morgan School.

Being black also contributed to Sonny Gordon's decision to become a cow-boy. Sonny felt there were only three acceptable things that a black man could do: wash dishes till he learned to cook, work in a filling station, or shine shoes. If he could become a cowboy, however, he could "buy $20 boots and strut around town."[44] Racial definitions, which were fluid for Rocky Payne's chil-dren, did not yield for the Gordons.

Yet, discrimination did not diminish the high regard that the Payne and Gordon cowboys earned. Their ancestors, African, Native American, and Mexican, had handled cattle and horses for generations in a variety of settings and cultures. The Paynes of the Big Bend were part of this complex, intermin-gling tradition. Like many other black cowboys, individual Paynes were par-ticularly known for their skill and daring in breaking horses. Unlike earlier African American cowboys on the classic cattle drives to Kansas, however, some of the Paynes held top positions on the ranches where they worked.[45] Because they excelled as cowboys, ranchers in the Big Bend gave them enor-mous responsibility. Despite discrimination both on and off the ranches, the Paynes and the Gordons are widely remembered and respected today for their special qualities as cowboys.

Natividad Arisolo Mariscal (Nato) "Seminole Negro Indian Scout"
    Married Antonia Oriola Payne
Children:
    Monroe   b. 1872, Brackettville, d. 1952, Marathon
    John   b. 1878, Brackettville, d. 1941, Marathon
    Differing accounts of their siblings

Monroe Payne 1872–1952
                Married Jesusita Vasquez, 1880?–1965
                Parents: Santiago and Juanita Mireles Vasquez
                Came to Brewster County 1904
Children:
    Mary   b. ?, Mexico, married Lewis Roach
    Thomas   b. 1898, Mexico, d. 1989, Alpine
    Batana   b. 1904, Mexico, d. 1925, Marathon
    Rocky   b. 1906, Marathon, d. 1986, Alpine
                Married Cruz Bustamante, 1936
                Children: Nora Payne Geron, Rocky Payne, Jr., Manuel Payne,
                    Larry Payne, Susie Payne Acosta
    Marcello   b. 1909, d. 1975
    (Chello)
                Married Francisca Garcia
                Children: Elida Eilguerez, Monroe Payne
    Santiago
    Ramona

John Payne 1878–1941
                Married Refugia Mariscal Vasquez, 1859?–1964
                Parents: Santiago and Juanita Mireles Vasquez
                Came to Big Bend c. 1914
Children:
    Otilia   Married Lewis Bly
    Blas   Married Genoveva Garcia, remarried Catrina Baeza
    Rita/Ruth Married Morgan Gordon
                Children: Morgan, Jr., Martin, Lewis, Monroe
    John
    Cuca   Married Arthur Simmons

NOTES

1. Robert Utley, "The Range Cattle Industry in the Big Bend of Texas," *Southwestern Historical Quarterly* 69 (1966): 421–41; U.S., Censuses for Brewster, Presidio, and Jeff Davis Counties, 1870 and 1880, MSS, Archives of the Big Bend, Sul Ross State University, Alpine, Tex.

2. Thomas Payne, interview by Jim Cullen, Alpine, Tex., June 10, 1983; Thomas Payne, interview by Virginia Wulfkuhle, Alpine, Tex., Aug. 19, 1984 (notes in the possession of the author); Rocky Payne, interview by Jim Cullen, Alpine, Tex., June 12, 1983; Blas Payne, interview by Theresa Whittington, Camp Peña Colorado, Tex., May 3, 1976; Nora Payne Geron and Manuel Payne, interview by Marilyn Dell Brady, Alpine, Tex., Feb. 26, 1998; Marcello Payne, "The Monroe Payne Family," in AnneJo Perry Wedin, *The Marvelous Marathon Basin: A History of Marathon, Texas, Its People and Events* (Austin: Nortex Press, 1989), pp. 449–50; Payne File, Wedin Collection. With the exception of the interview by Wulfkuhle, all citations are transcribed in the Archives of the Big Bend, Sul Ross State University, Alpine, Tex.

   Additional interviews by Marilyn Dell Brady with Nora Payne Geron, Pecos, Tex., June 21, 1998; and Morgan Gordon, Jr., Pecos, Tex., July 1, 1998, are not transcribed.

3. Kevin Mulroy, *Freedom on the Border: The Seminole Maroons in Florida, the Indian Territory, Coahuila, and Texas* (Lubbock: Texas Tech University Press, 1993); Kenneth W. Porter, *The Black Seminoles: History of a Freedom-Seeking People* (Gainesville: University of Florida, 1996), rev. & ed. by Alcione M. Amos and Thomas Senter.

   Terry Jordan, *Trails to Texas: Southern Roots of Western Cattle Ranching* (Lincoln: University of Nebraska Press, 1981) discusses the ways in which African, Anglo, and Native American methods of herding blended in early Florida, Georgia, and the Carolinas. Kenneth Porter, "The Cowkeeper Dynasty of the Seminole Nation," *Florida Historical Quarterly* 30 (1952): 341–49.

4. Accounts of when and by whom Mariscal was captured vary widely. Donald Swanson, ed., "Enlistment Records of Indian Scouts Who Served in One of the Scout Detachments at Fort Clark, Texas," *Seminole Negro-Indian Detachment, August 1872–September 1914* vol. 1 (Bronte, Tex.: Ames American Printing Co., 1985); Col. Isaac Payne, IV, "A History of the Payne-Huddleston Families, 1795–1998," MSS, author's possession, Albuquerque, N.Mex., 1998.

   For information on the Seminole scouts in West Texas, see Thomas Britten, "The Seminole-Negro Indian Scouts in Big Bend," *Journal of Big Bend Studies* 5 (1993): 69–80; Thomas Britten, "The Dismissal of the Seminole Scouts," *Fort Concho and the South Plains Journal* 24 (1992): 54–77; and Edward Wallace, "General John Lapham Bullis, The Thunderbolt of the Texas Frontier," *Southwestern Historical Quarterly* 54 (1951): 452–61; and 55 (1951): 77–85.

5. "Notes on the Payne Family of the Seminole Nation in Florida, the Indian Territory, Mexico, Texas, and Oklahoma," Kenneth W. Porter Collection, Schomburg Center for Research on Black Culture, New York City Public Library.

For a more detailed account of the stories relating to the ancestry of the Paynes, see Marilyn Dell Brady, "Monroe Payne: Descendent of a Black Seminole and Successful Entrepreneur in Brewster County, Texas," forthcoming.

6. Thomas and Rocky Payne interviews, 1983; Marcello Payne, "The Monroe Payne Family," in Wedin, *The Marvelous Marathon Basin*, pp. 449–50. Refugia Vasquez Mariscal Payne, Jesusita's sister who married John Payne, claimed that she had been born a slave, see Charles Hunter, *El Paso Herald Post*, Jan. 20, 1962. Her family could have been among those who escaped slavery in Texas by going to Nacimiento in the 1850s. Jesusita makes no such claim. Both women are listed as being white and born in Mexico, in the U.S. Manuscript Census for Brewster County, 1910 and 1920. Some Kickapoos shared the land at Nacimiento with the Black Seminoles, and Vasquez or his wife might have been related to them. Information on Seminoles at Nacimiento is based on notes from the Kenneth Porter Collection, Schomburg Center for Research on Black Culture, New York Public Library, New York.

7. Thomas and Rocky Payne interviews, 1983; Totsy Nelle Hitchcock, "Representative Individuals and Families of the Lower Big Bend, 1895–1925" (M.A. thesis, Sul Ross State University, 1960), pp. 29–34.

8. Thomas and Rocky Payne interviews, 1983; Virginia Wulfkuhle, *Buttrill Ranch Complex: Brewster County, Texas* (Austin: Texas Historical Commission, 1989).

9. Brewster County Tax Assessment Records, 1908, 1909, 1911, 1912; Monroe Payne file, Casey Collection; Thomas and Rocky Payne interviews, 1983; Blas Payne interview, 1976.

10. Thomas and Rocky Payne interviews, 1983; Blas Payne interview, 1976. Deemer died before the deposition was filed, and there is no evidence that any money was paid.

Several other historians are somewhat closer to Payne's account. Elton Miles, *Stray Tales from the Big Bend* (College Station: Texas A&M University Press, 1993), pp. 101–13; Wedin, *The Marvelous Marathon Basin*, pp. 449–50. W. D. Smithers, "Bandit Raids in the Big Bend Country," *West Texas Historical and Scientific Society* 19 (1963): 74–105, notes that Payne saved Deemer's life, a point made by Monroe's sons in their interviews. Jesse Deemer agreed that "his friend Munroe Payne" saved his life, Cas Edwards, newspaper clipping, Payne folder, Casey Collection, Archives of Big Bend.

The quotation is from Miles, *Stray Tales*, pp. 104–105.

11. Alberto Ureta Garcia, interview by John Klingman, Marathon, Tex., Feb. 21, 1998, Center for Big Bend Studies, Sul Ross State University, Alpine, Tex.; Mischa Benson Adams (granddaughter of George Benson), personal communication, 1998.

12. Nora Payne Geron and Manuel Payne interview, 1988.

13. Rocky Payne interview, 1983; U.S. Manuscript Census for Brewster County, 1920, in which Monroe Payne and his family are listed in Marathon, and Munroe Payne and

his family are also listed in south Brewster County, where he is said to rent his home and work as a ranch hand. The point about Hispanic definition of race is made repeatedly in scholarship on late colonial and early national Mexico.

14. *Alpine Avalanche,* Apr. 28, 1921. Nora Payne Geron confirmed that her grandfather often bootlegged *sotol,* a fermented drink made from *sotol* plants found abundantly in the Chihuahuan Desert.

15. Miles, *Stray Tales,* pp. 101–04, 123; Notes on Brewster County Death Records, Payne file, Casey Collection, Archives of Big Bend.

16. Thomas Payne interview, 1983.

17. Rocky Payne interview, 1983.

18. Travis Roberts, interview by Jim Cullen, July 26, 1986, Archives of Big Bend, Sul Ross State University. Travis was the son of Jim Roberts, boss of the Gage Ranch.

19. Barney Nelson, *The Last Campfire: The Life Story of Ted Gray, A West Texas Rancher* (College Station: Texas A&M University Press, 1984), p. 32. The others that Gray named were Staffrod Bligh, who taught Rocky's nephew, Morgan Gordon, Jr., to break horses, Pat Bligh, and Morgan Gordon, Sr., the ex-slave who married John Payne's daughter.

20. Nelson, *The Last Campfire,* pp. 74–75. Morgan Gordon, Jr., Rocky's nephew, tells the same story about him.

21. Ibid., p. 150.

22. Rocky Payne interview, 1983; Geron and Manuel Payne interview, 1998.

23. Geron interview, 1998.

24. Blas Payne interview, 1976.

25. Gordon interview, 1998.

26. Blas Payne interview; Gordon interview.

27. Mariscal's involvement at Camp Peña Colorado is possible. In the early 1880s, Seminole scouts had helped to build the camp and the road from Fort Clark to Fort Davis that it guarded. No evidence was found, however, about Mariscal or that he discovered the springs. Britten, "The Seminole-Negro Indian Scouts in Big Bend," pp. 69–80; Britten, "The Dismissal of the Seminole Scouts, pp. 54–77; and Eddie Guffee, "Camp Peña Colorado, Texas, 1879–1893," (M.A. thesis, West Texas State University, 1976).

28. Comparison of Blas Payne interview in 1976 with the one reported in the *Houston Chronicle,* Aug. 15, 1982.

29. Swanson, "Enlistment Records,"pp. 30, 34. When Kenneth Porter interviewed in Nacimiento in the 1940s, he talked to Julia Payne, wife of Isaac Payne. It was clear that she was never married to Natividad Mariscal, Kenneth Porter, "Notes on the Payne Family," Porter Collection, Schomburg Center. Other family members make this claim, as did whites such as Travis Roberts, 1986.

30. Mulroy, *Freedom on the Border,* p. 100.

31. Joe Graham, comment on a paper at the Center for Big Bend Conference, Nov. 15, 1997.

32. The same point is made about black cowboys on trail drives to Kansas by Kenneth Porter, "Negro Labor in the Western Cattle Industry, 1860–1900," *The Negro on the American Frontier* (New York: Arno Press, 1971), pp. 494–523.

33. Black cowboys George Adams and Daniel Webster Wallace also worked on the 7D Ranch.

34. U.S. Manuscript Census for 1910: Brewster City, Marathon, Tex. *Guayule* plants, which grew wild in the Big Bend, could be processed to produce rubber. A factory was built in Marathon, but the process proved impractical. Wedin, *The Marvelous Marathon Basin,* pp. 114–27.

35. Gordon interview, 1998; Mischa Benson Adams (granddaughter of George Benson), personal communication, 1998.

36. Gordon interview, 1998.

37. Gordon interview, 1998; Abelardo Baeza, "La Escondida: History of the Morgan School in Alpine, Texas, 1929–1954," *Journal for Big Bend Studies* 6 (1994): 85–98.

38. Caboose was supposed to be Ruth and Morgan's last child. Instead Martin and Louis followed. Gordon interview, 1998.

39. Ibid.

40. Garcia interview, 1998.

41. Geron and Manuel Payne interview, 1998.

42. *El Paso Evening Tribune,* Oct. 9, 1983, clipping file, El Paso Public Library.

43. Travis Roberts interview, 1986.

44. Gordon interview, 1998.

45. Other research on black cowboys, focusing on trail drives before 1900, claims that such advancement was almost impossible. Porter, "Negro Labor," pp. 507–09; Alwyn Barr, *Black Texans: A History of African-Americans in Texas, 1528–1995* (Norman: University of Oklahoma Press, 1996) 2nd ed., pp. 91, 149.

Figure 18. Richard "Bubba" Walker (right) *with Ike Barnes. Courtesy John W. Walker, Wilson County, Texas*

Chapter 21

Richard "Bubba" Walker

Best Cowhand Wilson County Ever Had

LEE N. COFFEE, JR.

Just inside the Wilson County line, approximately twenty-one miles north-east of Pleasanton, Texas, is a rural communal area known as Dewees, an aging ranch community that once ". . . was to sprawl over three counties. The 90,000 acre ranch included portions of Wilson, Karnes, and Atascosa counties."[1] In this ranching community lived Richard "Bubba" Walker. He was known as the best cowboy who ever rode a horse in Wilson County, Texas. As a third-generation cowhand, Bubba Walker's skills were valued by community ranchers, cattle magnates, and friends.

While visiting the Wilson County community during the "Christmas Along The Corridor Celebration of 1997," I asked a resident if he knew any black cowboys in the area. He, quickly, told me of a cowboy known by many community ranchers as "Bubba," a hard-working cowhand who had worked many years on the Dewees Ranch. Twenty-four years after his death, his life still influences people in the area.

Richard, or "Bubba" to his family and friends, was the youngest of ten children born to Jim and Eliza (Edwards) Walker. Though Bubba was not born in the saddle, he was certainly born for the saddle. "At an early age, he followed in the footsteps of his father, a rancher, and found his life's work."[2] Bubba was born in Floresville, Texas, on July 24, 1899. The son of a cowboy father living in the heart of the cattle industry, he quickly adapted to the lifestyle that his grandfather had learned during the previous generation. It was a lifestyle that would capture and hold the interest of his father, his brothers, and his children, along with other African Americans over the years.

James (Jim) Walker was taught to break horses by his enslaved father, who was reportedly brought to Texas from Alabama, and was taught to break horses by his owner in the late 1840s. Family history recalls that "... Jim Walker said, they were taught to break horses during slavery. They were taught by having to sit on the fence of the pen of wild horses, and made to jump off onto the backs of wild horses."[3] Apparently, this procedure for breaking horses was common among black cowboys in the South Texas region during the nineteenth century.

In September of 1872, Frank Collinson, a seventeen-year-old Englishman, arrived in San Antonio, Texas. He spent more than fifty years in the southwestern United States. Mr. Collinson watched former enslaved blacks break horses on the Noonan Ranch near Castroville: "I made friends with the Negro cowhands and asked them every step of the procedure in breaking a bronco and did my best to carry out their advice. . . . They were top hands, and there was nothing about bronco-busting that they did not know."[4]

He was particularly observant watching Link, a fearless bronc buster and former slave. He was "a master at breaking horses. He would often climb to the top rail of the big corral gate, and when the horses dashed through, would drop astride onto the back of the biggest, wildest mare he could see. The mare would pitch furiously, but Link would cling on like a big panther and jump or fall off when he got ready. I never saw him hurt, or never saw him thrown."[5]

When James Walker married Eliza Edwards, on December 30, 1880, she was living with the Edwards family on George Monkhouse's land.[6] With a vision of the future, and a growing family, Jim Walker began to take steps to secure additional property for himself and his family in the Wilson County area. On March 17, 1888, Jim Walker paid E. W. Herrington $31 and gave him a promissory note for the purchase of his first acre of land in Wilson County.[7] Prior to November 8, 1892, Jim Walker teamed with his father-in-law, Andrew Edwards, on two separate occasions to purchase land that totaled over seventeen acres.[8]

Growing up after the turn of the century, Bubba was surrounded by his brothers who were experienced cowhands and horse handlers. Obie Walker, Bubba's older brother, was the second oldest son of Jim and Eliza Walker. He "was considered to be one of the best ranch hands in Southwest Texas, and owners of ranches would refer him to other ranches, and to other parts of the state."[9] This was done because ". . . he was this good cowboy, and other ranchers would hire him when they had problems on their ranches."[10] John Walker, Obie's nephew, credited him as a ". . . helluva cowboy . . . there never was a horse that could throw him."[11]

While Bubba was a teenager, Obie broke broncos and did ranch work on many ranches in Wilson, Atascosa, La Salle, and other surrounding counties. Obie may have taught his younger brother horsemanship skills when he came back home. Obie was frequently being referred to other ranchers in South Texas and as far west as Marfa and Presidio Counties.[12] Sources indicate that Obie was drafted into the United States Army from Presidio County during World War I. Presidio County is located five hundred miles west of his birthplace.[13] World War I ended before Bubba became eligible to register for the Selective Service Act, but by this time, Bubba was already working as a cowboy.[14] Initially, he worked for the ranchers in Wilson County, like the Dewees family, but he soon began to hire out with ranchers in the neighboring counties.

The Dewees Ranch was established by two brothers, John O. and Thomas Dewees, after the Civil War. John, the elder of the two brothers, fought with the Thirty-second Texas Cavalry during the Civil War. After the war ended, he reportedly "stole a white mule from a Yankee and rode home to Texas with 25 cents in his pocket. . . . Eleven years after returning from the Civil War, John O. Dewees in partnership with his brother, Thomas Dewees, and J. F. Ellison, began driving cattle to northern markets."[15]

During the height of the Dewees and J. F. Ellison partnership, they probably marketed more Longhorns than any other South Texas cattlemen.[16] Records to prove that any of the Walkers worked for the Dewees Ranch prior to the turn of the century don't exist; however, in 1874, it is known that the Dewees brothers employed black cowboys to work their cattle on many occasions. White ranchers had great respect for the skills of the black cowhand because, "To be a good cowboy, one needed first of all to be a good man, for a wild Longhorn had no more respect for a Texan than for a Negro."[17] They hired black cowboys based on the availability of jobs. "When there are more jobs than men to fill them, there is less discrimination."[18]

Before the turn of the century, some of the more prominent ranchers in the region were related by marriage, and at least two of them had descendants who would hire Richard "Bubba" Walker. The Irvin children, Anna and Alice, married John O. Dewees, and Thomas M. Peeler, respectively, and their brother, William Irvin, married Medina Dewees.[19] These two cattlemen, coupled with the family ties of the Irvin children, had very profitable marriages.[20] They were in positions to employ Jim Walker (Bubba's father), and other black cowboys to help manage ranches covering more than two hundred thousand acres and all the Longhorn cattle that the four South Texas counties could handle.

There are several accounts of these extended families working together to move cattle "up the trail" during the 1870s. L. B. Anderson, a drover from Seguin, said, "The outfits of Dudley, Tom and myself were gathering cattle on the Dewees' ranch, when one morning a Negro and myself were rounding up a bunch of cattle . . ."[21] In another account he continues with ". . . Tom Lay was having some fun with a Negro . . . and the cattle became frightened at the noise the boys made."[22] These black cowboys were working for the Dewees or neighboring ranches when cowboys were still driving cattle to market.

Several years after the great trail drives went north during the waning years of the nineteenth century, some of the ninety thousand acres of Dewees property was divided and sold. In the twentieth century, John O. Dewees was still recognized as "one of the leading stockraisers and financiers in the section of the State in which he resides."[23]

As a third-generation cowboy, Bubba could break a horse, ride a herd, toss a rope, and cut a steer from the herd for branding. He was competent to perform the important maintenance functions of burning prickly pear to feed Longhorns, vaccinating cows, or castrating young steers with the precision expected of a man born in the saddle.[24] These were the essential skills that all ranch owners expected their hands to possess, and it was no different for Rosa Dewees, the wife of John E. Dewees. After the death of her husband in 1918, Rosa continued to manage the property until her death in 1966.[25]

Jamie Harris, great-niece of Bubba, remembers that Mrs. Dewees hired "Uncle Bubba and a lot of African Americans from the counties around there for different kinds of positions."[26] They helped with all the tasks inherent in the operation of a large ranch. By the 1930s, the Dewees Ranch had become a self-supporting homestead. "At the peak of its production, the ranch sustained a commissary, a school and homes for its employees. (It) was known as the Dewees Community."[27] Bubba spent many years in the saddle on the Dewees Ranch. As on any ranch, the work could last from sunup till sundown, with no consideration for overtime. When John Walker, Bubba's son, worked with his father, he earned $5 a day, but he admits of his father that "I reckon back in his day, he was getting less."[28]

John Walker, a native of Floresville, and now a fourth-generation cowboy from the Walker family used "to help guys down in Floresville, if they had little ranches. The biggest ranch I worked on was over in Charlotte for Frank Thompson."[29] Just like his father, John worked as a cowboy, off and on, twenty-five to thirty-five years. Although he had the same ability to stay in the saddle as his Uncle Obie, he did admit to being thrown. "You wouldn't be a cowboy if you hadn't got thrown."[30] When asked how long his father worked as a cowboy, John quickly responded, "All his life . . . he did it till he died." With the twinkle of remembrance in his eyes, a trait he seems to have inherited, he commented, "I'd been following my daddy around since . . . before I could get on a horse, he used to help me up on a horse. I went off to college, and when I came back, I'd be right back there with him."[31]

John also worked on the Dewees Ranch with his father, ". . . if he had something for me to do, then we'd go do cattle work. . . . That Dewees ranch at the time was so big, and different people had bought into the ranch that I don't know just how big it was."[32]

Many cities in the South Texas region are credited as being a starting point for the "Texas Trail Drives," but only Pleasanton, Texas, is known as "The Birthplace of the Cowboy."[33] This fact is partly in recognition of the two patriarchs from the Dewees and Peeler families. They laid a foundation in the Southwest Texas cattle industry that remains today. There are several other significant ranches in the region, but few have the rich history of the Peeler Ranch.

In 1882, Mr. and Mrs. Thomas M. Peeler "moved to Atascosa County and established the Basin Hill Ranch near Cambellton, later named the 7LP Ranch for the 'seven little Peelers,' five boys, and two girls born to Tom and Alice."[34] Graves Peeler was one of the "seven little Peelers," and, in 1932, he also entered the cattle business. The Walker brothers frequently worked as ranch hands for Graves Peeler. Graves is credited with helping to preserve the Texas Longhorns. "After near extinction, the Longhorn breed is being revived throughout the U.S. today. It was the Peeler stock that provided the origin for many such herds."[35]

In the early 1950s, Graves recruited Bubba and his brothers Walter and Buster, along with other black cowboys, Ike Barnes and Beanie Roberts, and Alonzo Peeler to participate in a spectacular roundup and picnic that occurred on the Peeler Ranch in McMullen County. The ranch was owned by the Peeler family and managed by Alonzo and his brother, Graves, of McMullen County, Texas. The Tom Peeler family remembered the event. They "were rounding up and branding Longhorn cattle . . . and we had pictures taken at this Bar-B-Q that was at Uncle Graves Ranch. The photographers were there taking the photographs for *Life* Magazine, and I remember handing my daughter up to the black cowboy; he was on horseback, and I handed my daughter up to him so she could ride in the saddle with him. This man from *Life* Magazine developed the pictures of the roundup, and sold them all over the country, but they were originally in *Life* Magazine."[36]

John recalls his father telling him about the event. He proudly displays two pictures[37] from the barbecue in his home. The largest is the same picture that hangs proudly on the wall in the Peelers home. The inscription reads: "The Last of the Texas Longhorns." Mounted on horseback, Bubba sits beside his two brothers, Walter and Buster, amidst fourteen other cowhands. He was identified by his great-niece by "this hat that he has on. I saw him in a photograph and he was way in the distance, but I could identify him because of this hat, and the way he rolled the brim."[38] Alonzo and Graves Peeler are mounted in the foreground, with a hundred head of Longhorn cattle between them and the cowhands in the back. The scene is complete with chuck wagon, *remuda*, and the vast expanse of Texan frontier. The picture illustrates the ethnic flavor of the Texas ranching heritage and its cattlemen, refuting the myth that blacks were always relegated to the job of a "belly cheater" or cook.[39]

Bubba also participated in the cattle roundup for a movie. "It was made on the Peeler Ranch in Pleasanton, or somewhere out that way."[40] Tom E. Peeler, grandson of the family patriarch also recalls his Uncle Graves doing the roundup for the movie, "He had the largest herd of Longhorn cattle in the U.S. . . . John Wayne made a movie, and he purchased steers for that movie from my Uncle Graves."[41] These were the animals used in the filming of the John Wayne movie, *The Alamo.*

During the 1940s, Bubba had a full-time job at Kelly Air Force Base in San Antonio, Texas, supporting his wife, Helen, and their two children, Richard, Jr., and John W. Walker. However, he continued working as a ranch hand on the various ranches in Wilson and surrounding counties. As a result of his hard work, he was able to send both John and Richard, Jr., to Prairie View A&M University prior to their enlisting in the U.S. Army during World War II.[42]

Richard "Bubba" Walker made many friends as he worked in South Texas. Throughout his life, he was known for sharing his skills with other cowboys. One of his protégés was Ike Barnes, another black cowboy, who worked as a cowhand on ranches in the region. Mrs. Harris recalled his mentoring Ike on several occasions. "My Uncle Bubba was like a father to Ike."[43] In 1979, Ike Barnes was selected for the prestigious "Working Cowboy Award" given at a gala rodeo in Pleasanton. He is one of two African Americans to receive this award since its inception in 1966.[44]

Bubba is remembered today. His family recalls his twinkling eyes and contagious laugh that was so filled with mirth that it often made you want to laugh along with him.[45] He stood six foot one inch, and, when mounted, he sat very tall in the saddle. Bubba kept his hat tilted on the top of his head, and the brim was rolled in its characteristic way. He was able to toss a rope whether mounted or afoot and had "cowboy" flowing though his body as much as any Texan that worked a cattle ranch.

"A Tribute to a Friend"

The late Richard "Bubba" Walker, yes he was Black, but he had a heart of gold, we rode side by side day after day, and I learned a lot from him, for I know he was the best cow-hand that Wilson County ever had. I hope that I have the same impact on someone's life, as some of these people I have written about had on me. God rest their souls.

—Earl D. Gilley[46]

For over a century, the men from the Walker family contributed to the ranching industry of South Texas and participated in the making of Texas history. As a result, many friends, cattle magnates, and community residents considered Richard "Bubba" Walker to be the best "cowhand that Wilson County ever had" or cowboy that ever rode a horse.

NOTES

1. Diane Jimenez and George Southern, *Wilson County History* (Dallas: Taylor Publishing Company, 1990), p. 60.
2. Richard "Bubba" Walker, Funeral Notice, Nov. 20, 1974.
3. Mrs. Jamie (Walker) Harris, great-niece of Richard "Bubba" Walker, interview by Lee Coffee, Jr., San Antonio, Tex., Feb. 9, 1998.
4. Frank Collinson, *Life in the Saddle* (Norman: University of Oklahoma Press, 1963), p. 15.
5. Ibid., p. 16.
6. Marriage Records: 1878–1891, vol. B, certificate #756, Wilson Country Courthouse, Floresville, Tex., p. 91; Harris interview.
7. Index to Deeds Reverse: 1860–1889, vol. 1, bk. S, Wilson County Courthouse, Floresville, Tex., p. 205.
8. Index to Deeds Reverse: 1890–1902, vol. 2, Wilson County Courthouse, Floresville, Tex., pp. 593, 595; Deed Records, vol. 2, Wilson County Courthouse, Floresville, Tex., pp. 88, 93.
9. Harris interview.
10. Ibid.
11. John W. Walker, son of Richard "Bubba" Walker, interview by Lee Coffee, Jr., San Antonio, Tex., Mar. 23, 1998.
12. Harris interview.
13. Ibid. Draft registration in possession of Mrs. Jamie (Walker) Harris.
14. Maurice Matloff, ed., *American Military History* (Washington D.C.: GPO, 1969), pp. 373–74.
15. Jimenez, *Wilson County History*, pp. 59–60.
16. Ibid., p. 60.
17. Philip Durham and Everett L. Jones, *The Negro Cowboys* (1965; reprint, Lincoln: University of Nebraska Press, 1983), p. 44.

18. Ibid.

19. Jimenez, *Wilson County History,* p. 60.

20. J. Marvin Hunter, ed., *The Trail Drivers of Texas,* 2nd ed. (1925, reprint, Austin: University of Texas Press, 1996), p. 204.

21. Ibid., p. 205.

22. Ibid.

23. John Henry Brown, *Indian Wars of Texas* (Austin: L. E. Daniel Publishers, 1988), p. 665.

24. Harris interview.

25. Jimenez, *Wilson County History,* pp. 59–60.

26. Ibid.

27. Ibid., p. 60.

28. John W. Walker interview.

29. Ibid.

30. Ibid.

31. Ibid.

32. Ibid.

33. HOW "BIRTHPLACE OF THE COWBOY" GOT ITS NAME, pamphlet, 32nd Annual Pleasanton Cowboy Homecoming Rodeo, p. 59. "Pleasanton was within the area described by history as being the cradle of the cowboy," and as W. K. Daetwyler, former publisher of *The Pleasanton Express,* stated: ". . . any other town within the area could have made the same valid claim, but Pleasanton was the first to stake that claim, and historic justice is being served when the slogan, *THE BIRTHPLACE OF THE COWBOY,* is applied to Pleasanton."

34. *Atascosa County Centennial* (Atascosa County, Tex.: Atascosa County Centennial Association, 1956), n.p.

35. *Atascosa County History* (Dallas: Taylor Publishing Company, 1984), p. 270.

36. Tom E. Peeler (grandson of Tom M. Peeler), interview by Lee Coffee, Jr., Pleasanton, Tex., May 5, 1998.

37. Harvey Patterson & Son, *Photograph #90–360* (San Antonio: Institute of Texan Cultures, 1954).

38. Harris interview.

39. George T. Martin and Jim and Judy Lanning, eds., *Texas Cowboys: Memories of the Early Days* (College Station: Texas A&M University Press, 1984), p. 133.

40. John W. Walker interview.

41. Tom E. Peeler, telephone interview by Lee Coffee, Jr., May 4, 1998.

42. Harris interview.

43. Harris, telephone interview by Lee Coffee, Jr., Mar. 26, 1998.

44. 32nd Annual Pleasanton Cowboy Homecoming Rodeo, August 15–16 1997.

45. Harris interview, Feb. 9, 1998.

46. Martha Baird, telephone interview by Lee Coffee, Jr., May 8, 1998.

Figure 19. Troy John Williams. Courtesy C. A. "Tony" Sherman, Missouri City, Texas

Chapter 22

Troy John Williams

The Tennis Shoe Cowboy

C. A. "TONY" SHERMAN

Making 50 cents a day was a lot of money for a 12-year-old boy in those days. I would work from sun up to sun down to help my parents make ends meet. Back in them days, if you were big enough, you had to go to work. I was kinda small for my age, but I was strong. I thought I could keep up with those older guys working around Bay City and Live Oak.[1]

Troy John Williams was born December 6, 1922, one of four children of Levi and Alfreda Williams. Alfreda was the daughter of cowboy John Norman, the son of Nathaniel and Biddy Norman. On his father's side of the family, his grandfather was Troy Taylor, whose father was a white landowner. Troy started his own ranching business some fifteen years after slavery ended. After accumulating over four hundred acres around Matagorda County, Taylor passed his holdings to his son Levi, who knew the value of hard work and sacrifice.

When T. J. turned twelve, he rode to work at the Hawkins and Sanders Ranch on the back of his father Levi's horse.

That old horse was big and stout. My dad had good control of that horse which really impressed me. Most of the time, I am sure that horse knew what to do before my dad was ready for him to do it. I mean it was like they had their minds synchronized. My dad was tough with people, but real gentle with his horse. Fact of the matter is I think that horse was his first and real love.

When I was 13, I was hired by the Hawkins Ranch to keep the cows out of the rice fields. There were no fences back then and I had to run after them. I worked the cows for two years till I was 15, making that 50 cents a day. My daddy gave me a wagon and team of mules. I worked with those mules every day, and I got good at controlling 'em. I went to the 5X Ranch boss and asked for a job hauling rice. My mother did not want me to work for Mr. Broughton, because he was real mean to his workers. It was well known that he freely kicked his workers, but I was determined! One of the other workers convinced my mother to let me stay. Mr. Broughton said I was too little to work but he liked my wagon and team. He let me continue hauling that rice.

Because T. J. was not big enough, he did not know how to lead his wagon. As a result, it turned over many times after traveling only about a block. "Mr. Broughton saw that I was really trying," said T. J., "so he told me to haul as much as I could." After a while, T. J. was given a job hauling water to the field hands.

When T. J. was finally paid, he had a total of $18 in his pocket. When he took the money home to his mother, she kept all but 25 cents. Each week thereafter, he had to save 25 cents until he accumulated $10. He left the money in his pants pocket and forgot to remove it when it was time to wash them. When his mother found the money, T. J. was left penniless. He started the routine over again until he saved another $10. This time he gave it to his oldest sister to keep for him. She went off and got married and took his money with her. After that, T. J. started doing business with the local bank.

In 1937, at the age of seventeen, Troy John Williams began breaking horses. By that time, he had learned the values of hard work and sacrifice that his father and grandfather had taught him. He had saved his money for the past several years, but it was now time to develop his talents in working with horses. The first year, he charged $5 every time he broke one. Later, he raised his price to $7.50 a horse. "There were some who questioned who broke who," said T. J., but he managed to save enough money to buy a cow for $35. Then he saw a horse he wanted to buy that cost $300. Although he had lots of money in the bank, his mother said, "No," but he went to the bank, borrowed the money he needed, and bought the horse.

After buying the horse and training it for some time, T. J. sold it for $1,000. With that money, he was able to pay off his loan and purchase twelve acres of land. T. J. believed in land ownership. He had a sharp eye for business and would always be seen in places where deals were being made. In his mid-twenties and owning twelve acres, a small herd of cows, and a couple of horses, T. J. was well on his way to making an impact in the county. He began to increase his training of horses in the areas where no one else was doing it. He believed that he could make a living at training horses to "cut cattle" from the rest of the herd. To him, cutting horses had more value than ones for roping, but training horses that belonged to residents of his county meant a limited income. "You have to train a whole lot of horses to make a living at $12 to $15 dollars a horse. I've had almost every bone in my body broken more than once. I figured out early that I needed to train people right along with the horse. And I'll tell you what, the horse always had more common sense than the person I was training. You just can't get up on the horse acting like you are scared, and shy. You have to let that horse know that you are in charge and he is going to have to take orders from you."

Troy John's early years were spent working the ranch and training people and horses. His business was successful enough for him to purchase an additional twenty acres of land. Cattle ranching was the order of business. "You could get a good price for a herd, if you bred with good bull stock," said T. J. During and after World War II, T. J. worked all over South Texas. In addition to training, he actively engaged in ranch work, which included roping, branding, breaking horses, and giving riding lessons. In the early 1950s, the cowboys of Texas began to compete with each other on what has developed into the rodeo circuit.

In the early 1960s, T. J. spent quite a bit of time training a quarter horse named "Ick" to become a cutting horse. The horse belonged to a man named Otis Sweeney of Bay City, Texas. Mr. Sweeney refused to allow any other cowboy to ride his horse. As T. J. recalls, Alvin, Texas, had a really big competition, probably the biggest of the year. "Mr. Otis came to me and told me he wanted me to ride Ick in that show for him. Now I ain't no dummy, you see. I knew those white folks over there were not going to let me ride that horse in that rodeo. But, old man Sweeney insisted. He said I was going to be the one to ride him and nobody else. So I said, 'Mr. Sweeney, you know that they don't let Negroes in that place, let alone ride in competition.' Well, he wasn't going to hear it! You just get him over there and be ready to ride."

That was the beginning of many breakthroughs for T. J. He had trained many of the horses in the competition as well as many of the riders, but allowing him to go head-to-head against them was another matter. Nevertheless— due to Mr. Sweeney's prestige in and around Bay City—those strong negative voices soon quieted down, at least enough to allow T. J. to sign up.

• • •

I never like to brag, but I kicked their butts with that horse. I had him humming, you know what I mean? Them white folks could see it too. They were hollering and yelling all kinds of stuff at me, but they knew that horse won. At the end of the competition, I waited for the score, as did 7,000 other folks. When they posted the score, we won. I couldn't believe it! That was a really big deal for me. But, you know what? They refused to give me my money. I was mad as I could be, but I couldn't show it. I took my hat off, bowed my head and waved my hat in the air. I was bigger than them. That money meant a lot to me, but it meant more to me to know that I won. I had to keep a smile on my face.

Ick and T. J. left the arena and returned to Live Oak empty handed. Several days later, Otis Sweeney came to visit T. J. with a check from the rodeo. After some discussion, T. J. advised Mr. Sweeney that he did not want the money, and that he was satisfied to boast that he had won. In the world of cowboys, a man's reputation was paramount. No matter what happened at Alvin, T. J. was the top trainer and rider of cutting horses in Texas. That was a fact.

On occasion, other African American rodeo cowboys had the opportunity to visit with T. J. at Live Oak. There, with his wife Doris, T. J. developed the premiere training center for rodeo cowboys and casual riders as well. Myrtus Dightman, Norman Williams, and nephew John Reeves were among those who benefited from just being around T. J. Many performers for the Houston Livestock Show and Rodeo were trained by T. J. in the fields of cutting horse competition, roping, and barrel racing. T. J.'s greatest contribution to the advancement of the African American cowboy in rodeo competition was his ability to cross the line of color and compete with all cowboys. "A man is a man, no matter what color he happens to be. That horse don't care what color you are. Are you man enough to ride him?"

There were times on the rodeo tours that cowboys had periods of down time—no competition. During such times, many of them slept or drank or sat around telling tall tales. On one occasion, T. J. observed a spirited cowboy practicing roping. He observed him dismount his horse, plant the heel of his boot in the muddy turf, and prepare to run along his rope to tie down the calf at the other end. As the cowboy dismounted, his right foot got caught in the mud, and a loud snap was heard by many. The cowboy broke his ankle in multiple places. "That was the nastiest break I had ever seen. Man that guy was in so much pain, he was yelling and hollering like a stuck pig. It was something awful to see. I made a pledge to myself, that I would never wear boots in competition again."

To the day he died, T. J. only wore tennis shoes when he worked his horses. "You've done it again, T. J.," I said. "You have created a first in cowboy attire wearing those tennis shoes while you work." He replied, "It doesn't matter what you got on your body that counts, it's what you got in your head. There is no way anybody with common sense will blame me for doing something that makes sense."

T. J. Williams has been a role model for any and everybody. From the small-town rodeo cowboys to the city and county officials, they all looked up to this gentle cowboy giant. Perhaps due to his extensive involvement with the RV Ranch and the Jackson brothers or as president of the Southwestern Cowboy Association, T. J. Williams was considered a cowboy's cowboy. He was recently recognized by the Centennial Commission of Bay City as a Matagorda County history maker.

Well into his fifties, T. J. was still competing. In a cutting-horse competition in Houston in the late 1980s, T. J. was seen by the All-Pro football cornerback Mel Blount, who invited him to come to his ranch in Vidalia, Georgia, to teach wayward teens how to ride. As Mel put it, "You won't regret it." T. J. accepted the invitation and headed for the other side of the country, to work with some top cutting horses—and train kids in horsemanship. His plans were to develop some of the steeds into competitions for cash.[2]

Back home, his son Tracy was tending his herd of 250 cattle, and times were getting tough. A Texas drought was taking its toll on the herd, so after four months T. J. headed back to Texas to salvage his herd and make some deals. T. J. had seven children, five sons and two daughters. His son Tracy carries on T. J.'s cowboy tradition. He has been a finalist in the Professional Rodeo Cowboys Association's calf-roping contests. T. J. continued to train cutting horses until his death at seventy-three in 1995. Willie Rollins, a stepson, memorialized T. J. in a song he wrote and recorded:

The Black Texas Cowboy

Down in Live Oak Texas, a little town on the coast
Lived a Black Texas Cowboy, and I don't mean to boast
But he's the finest fellow you'd ever want to meet.
If you talked with him for a minute, you'll know he's hard to beat.
He's a quiet strong man, always courteous and polite.
The folks down home, they all know I'm right
When I say this man is a king, a gentleman, a priest
A husband, a father, and last but not least . . . he's a cowboy.

He enters rodeo competition all through the years
All other ranchers and cowboys respect him and fear
The ability of this man to train a horse.
Although sometimes the judging is a real farce
But this man was strong in body and mind
And he can take the pressures of being one of a kind.
In the heart of his wife he has untold fame
And the cowboys everywhere knew his name.
Every thing on his right hand had at one time been broken
But to this sturdy built man, it was just one of life's little tokens.
When he looked back on his own life there were no regrets
For the life of the cowboy is the best life yet.
His deeds have now become legendary and through my life
I hope to carry his courage and strength
'cause I'm a fan of T. J. Williams . . . my mama's old MAN.[3]

NOTES

1. Except as noted all material for this chapter is from T. J. Williams, interview by Tony Sherman, Live Oak, Tex., Aug., 1989.
2. Doris Williams, interview by Tony Sherman, Live Oak, Tex., July, 1998.
3. This song was written and privately recorded by Troy's stepson Willie Rollins.

Figure 20. A. J. Walker. Courtesy Alan Govenar, Dallas, Texas

Chapter 23

A. J. Walker

Cowboy and Rodeo Organizer

ALAN GOVENAR

The social and economic organization of white-owned ranches in Texas prior to World War II inhibited the advancement of black cowboys to managerial positions. Historians Philip Durham and Everett Jones state, "the Negro cowboy was welcomed as a hand or even as a top hand, though rarely as a foreman."[1] The mid-twentieth century life of black cowboy A. J. Walker indicates things hadn't changed much.

Institutionalized racism imposed obstacles not only for ranch cowboys, but it was also prevalent among rodeo competitors as well. Even the most famous professional black cowboy from Texas, Bill Pickett, encountered difficulties. Despite international acclaim as a bulldogger, his biographer, Colonel Bailey Hanes, wrote that Pickett's promoter "was wise enough not to identify Pickett as a Negro. During Pickett's life, at most contests, Negroes were automatically barred from competition because most whites felt that it was below their dignity to compete with a black man, even if he carried more than one-half Indian and white blood in his veins."[2]

Racist attitudes toward black cowboys persisted into the 1960s, when the passage of civil rights laws began to affect ranching and rodeo professions. A. J. Walker, in Raywood, Texas, recalls the difficulties he had trying to compete in the Professional Rodeo Cowboys Association rodeos. "White cowboys didn't really like having the black cowboys around. They look at you crazy. They do anything they could to you. We stayed out of their way. We had a bunch of black cowboys, but we didn't have any trouble."[3]

Avoiding trouble, however, was not always possible. Vincent Jacobs, who met Walker at a rodeo in Crosby, Texas, in the 1950s, says, "Usually, we had a hard time. We had to stay back and sometimes, we'd be bumped against and spit on, but we stayed in there and fought back for as long as we could."[4]

Generally, black cowboys were respected because of their horsemanship and skill, but they had limited opportunities for social or economic mobility. Born March 7, 1930, the year his family moved to Southeast Texas from Opelousas, Louisiana, Walker began to ride horses at age four and saw his first rodeos on nearby ranches.

> There were just little ranch rodeos back in them times. The range was loose then. We didn't have any fences. They would turn all their horses and cows loose on the highway and in the pastures. They eat out there and a bunch of them would get out there and round them up in the open prairie. Some of them would hold the horses and bulls and cattle and others would get off and ride them, rope and everything, just like in the rodeo. I was just old enough to remember them doing it on Saturday evenings about round-up time. Just before it get cold, they round-up them cattle. They have a ranch rodeo and then they take them off to auction, or whatever you wanted to do. They'd do steer dogging and roping. They rope the head and the heel. They didn't do bull riding like they do now. Mostly, they use them big year-lings. I never did compete in them, I was too young.[5]

A. J.'s father, Tom Walker, worked as a sharecropper on land owned by a white farmer and rancher named Hubert Smith in Raywood. "My dad was a ¾ farmer," A. J. says, "meaning the boss man got ¼ and we got ¾, but I imagine at first he was a ½ farmer because when he first got over here he had to buy some horses and mules. Then after a while, he became a ⅔ farmer and then ¾. He paid the boss man less."[6]

Tom Walker raised corn, peas, okra, and cucumbers to sell but had to supplement his income by doing seasonal work cutting and chopping rice for white landowners in the fall of the year. In time, A. J. says, his father was able to buy a few head of cattle, and over the years the herd grew to about thirty and forty head. "My daddy used to say he'd cowboy until the cowboys come. He didn't go out to be no cowboy, but he'd ride till the real cowboys got there."[7]

A. J. began working mules when he was seven years old. "We raised mules, working mules. I'd ride the mule while my daddy was working them. I'd go to sleep sitting up on those mules, and he'd hit one of them and wake me up, you know. As far as I can remember, I was near about big enough to go to school. We had our general mules and stuff and I just start riding them. Then I started riding calves. Not long after that I started rodeoing and riding them heifers and a few of them bull calves and roping them calves. And that's something we like to do; me and all my brothers, we done the same thing."[8]

By the time he was twelve, A. J. was breaking horses, and soon he got to the point where he felt he was good enough to compete on the rodeo circuit. Initially, his father disapproved, but A. J. would "just take off and dad didn't know. I just put my bull rope and rigging in a satchel and go off down the road. He didn't know where I was going." A. J. rode his first bull in 1946 at the county fair in Anahuac, Texas. "That was a real rodeo, bull riding and bareback riding. I rode my horse bareback, but I got bucked off the bull. I had never been on a bull before. Around the house I had been riding yearlings, little half grown bulls."[9]

A. J. recalls that the only cowboys he ever saw when he was growing up were black cowboys. "The only white was the boss man, the man who owned the ranch. We worked for him, and the only white boys we saw were his sons or members of his family. Them white boys would get on the horses after you got them broke. The boss man or the boss man's son would take them. But the black cowboys did all the work. The black cowboys broke the horses, took care of the cattle, and did whatever needed to be done."[10]

It wasn't until A. J. left home in Southeast Texas that he began to meet white working cowboys, who were not only ranch hands but also competed in rodeo. As a child A. J. never made a distinction between rodeo and ranch cowboys. "There was never much money to be made at the little ranch rodeos and the only cowboys, who competed, worked on the ranch."

At age twenty-two, A. J. started working for Everett Colbert in Dublin, Texas, a white rancher and rodeo producer. A. J. had heard about the job from Ed Hamm, a black cowboy in Houston, who also was going to work for Colbert. Colbert had negotiated a major contract to supply the livestock for a rodeo to be held in Madison Square Garden in New York City and needed cowhands to take care of the stock.

Before we left we had to haul the hay and then help load the stock on the train. We went in the boxcars. The bulls were on each end and we sat in the middle of the car. We left Dublin and went to Fort Madison, Iowa first. We stayed in Fort Madison for about a month. We had to feed the stock and work them, get them in shape for the rodeo. Then we left Fort Madison and went to New York. I forget how long that took, but it took us a week to come back to Texas. I went on the train and came back on a truck. We had three trucks, loaded with steers.

When we got to New York, we had to go to Long Island, to the stock-yards to unload all the stock there. We had to get them company-owned, union trucks to take the bulls. But we (the black cowboys) had to lead the horses. Each man had nine horses to lead from Long Island to Madison Square Garden. We had to go right downtown, all the horses. We led them horses on the street, and we had people watching from the time we left to the time we got there. We had 500 head of bucking horses and 500 head of saddle horses.[11]

A. J. and the other black cowboys stayed for a month in New York City, living with the bulls in the basement of Madison Square Garden. He did get the opportunity to compete in the rodeo, although the black cowboys were segregated from the white cowboys. "They didn't like the blacks and the whites to be together. We'd have to get on the bulls behind the chutes. They wanted us to stay in the back until after the white rodeo was over. We couldn't go in the same places the white guys go in. We'd ride after the show. It would be for the same prize money, but you couldn't ride at the same time as them white cowboys. We ride after all the folks (in the audience) had left, and all the white cowboys were gone. You'd be competing for the same money as the white cowboys. They just wanted your entry fees."[12]

At Madison Square Garden, A. J. did place first as part of the team wild horse race. The prize was a saddle, and A. J. and the two other cowboys (one black and one white) who competed as a team had to flip a coin to see who was going to get it. As it turned out, A. J. says the white cowboy out of Stephenville won the saddle.

When A. J. returned to Texas, he joined the Texas Rodeo Cowboys Association and competed in the circuit of small, black rodeos in Texas, Oklahoma, Kansas, and Louisiana. "We'd work during the week, and rodeo on the weekend. We were all black cowboys, who came from all over to compete with one another. There wasn't a lot of money in it, but it was lots of fun."[13]

In 1964, A. J. joined the Professional Rodeo Cowboys Association but only won one event—a bareback buckle in Houston at the Diamond L Ranch. The competition in PRCA was tough, and the expenses of trying to travel the circuit were high. A. J. preferred to stay in Texas, where he worked a construction job and continued to maintain his part of the forty-acre homestead that his father had bought in 1941. "The land was good; most of it was up on the hill, away from the marshland. I had to quit school early because we was buying this land out here, and I had to help pay for it. I finished the ninth grade, and then had to go to work. We had to pay 40 dollars an acre for that land.

That was a lot of money back then. We raised cotton and corn and food for the children to eat. We all lived in the same house, until I built my own after I married. After my father died, the land was divided up between me and my brothers and sisters."[14]

Given the restrictions imposed by segregation and discrimination, relatively few opportunities existed for African American cowboys to acquire land. However, in Southeast Texas, in the Raywood area between Beaumont and Houston, some African Americans were able to build their own ranches as a result of their hard-earned efforts and as a consequence of unforeseen circumstances.[15]

A white rancher, E. R. Taylor, built the Taylor-Stevenson Ranch, located just south of the Astrodome in Houston, in 1869. Family records indicate he married his slave, Ann, and their children inherited and developed the ranch. According to Mollie Stevenson, Taylor's great-granddaughter, "Ann was able to cure E. R. Taylor, who was suffering from tuberculosis, through the use of teas and potions."[16] During Taylor's lifetime, the ranch raised cattle, sheep, cotton, and vegetables, but after his death, oil was discovered, and livestock and farming became less important.

Another African American ranch is the Jackson Ranch, which encompasses more than 10,000 acres in Chambers County. The ranch dates from the 1880s and was probably an offshoot of the Jackson Ranch in South Texas. Nathaniel Jackson came to South Texas in 1857 from Alabama in five covered wagons with his family and eleven freed slaves. In Texas, Jackson purchased approximately 5,535 acres of land from E. D. Smith of Hidalgo County, a lawyer-merchant, who was an heir of Narciso Carvazos. Carvazos had received the original Spanish land grant in 1767.[17]

The details of Jackson's life are sketchy, although it is known that shortly after his arrival Jackson built his ranch home, probably of adobe and thatch, beside the Old Military Road that ran from Brownsville to Hidalgo. Reportedly, he was a devout man, who constructed an adobe and palm thatch chapel, which was a forerunner to the wooden structure, built around 1883, which still stands today.

During his lifetime, Jackson grew sugar cane, beans, yams, corn, and other vegetables in the rich alluvial soil along the Rio Grande, and pastured cattle and sheep on the drier lands north of the river. Over the years, Jackson became quite prosperous and was widely known for his generosity. When the Civil War broke out, Jackson was an ardent abolitionist who openly supported the federal cause and opposed Texas' secession from the Union. According to legend, Jackson offered refuge to runaway slaves along the border. Today, the

Jacksons in Anahuac and elsewhere in Southeast Texas claim to have mixed racial ancestry. Quentin Jackson, who was a local judge, recalled that the white and black Jacksons got together for family reunions when he was growing up.[18]

Many of the African Americans who live in Southeast Texas, however, migrated to the state from Louisiana, looking for land and work. Elton Laday, born in 1920, was originally from Ville Platte, Louisiana, but came with his family to Cheeks, Texas, near Beaumont, when he was two years old. Although his father, Odine Laday, owned a fifty-acre ranch, Elton grew up baling hay and working as a cowhand on cattle drives for some of the white ranchers in the area. Each year, Elton remembers, about fifteen cowboys drove approximately three hundred to four hundred cattle from Cottonwood. The cattle were fed on the native grass during the spring and summer months and then moved across the inter-coastal canal to Port Bolivar, where they were able to feed on salt grass from October to March or April, when they were brought back.[19]

Laday, like A. J. Walker, continues to operate his own ranch. In recent years, he has built his own rodeo arena with his son, following the model established by his friends and neighbors. A. J. decided to build his own rodeo arena in the early 1960s: "There were so few opportunities for black cowboys at that time. I wanted to give them a chance that they might not have otherwise. They might win a little money and have a lot of fun. And maybe, get a start on something that would carry them on through life. Maybe even, help them get into professional rodeo. All of them boys want to ride, try to ride."[20]

Concurrent with his work to build his own rodeo arena in the 1960s, A. J. and his friends, who were also cowboys and owned their own small ranches, started to meet on a regular basis to organize their efforts. Together, they formed the Anahuac Saltgrass Cowboys Association. Comprised at first of a loosely knit group of men and women with shared interests, the ASGCA was designed to help promote African American rodeos in Southeast Texas. The ASGCA usually meets three times a year (in December, April, and October) to coordinate rodeo schedules at the different ranches that host rodeos. Today, there are nearly six hundred members; of these, about fifty are white. Membership in the ASGCA is required in order to compete in the rodeos. Initially, membership was $10 but has now risen to $30. Membership fees are used to help defer some of the promotional costs associated with the individual rodeos.

In 1967, A. J. opened his Circle 6 Ranch rodeo to the public. At first, all the cowboys who competed were black, but in time, the rodeo began to attract white cowboys from the surrounding area. "Over the years the rodeo has grown. Today, we have more than 100 cowboys who compete on a regular basis (about

55 calf ropers, 22 bull riders and 25 steer wrestlers) with approximately 400–500 people in attendance. Admission to the rodeo started at $3 for adults and $1 for children, but today costs $5 for adults and $1 for children. It costs us a lot more to put on rodeos than it did when we started. We have to pay the announcer $125, and we put $300 into the pot for prize money. The entry fee for the cowboys is $25 and a $7 stock fee for each animal they ride. We think it's fair and we try to show everyone a good time."[21]

In addition to organizing rodeos, A. J. also has built a small dance hall adjacent to the rodeo arena. "It's only open during the time we have the rodeo going. People can get a beer or soft drink, something to eat, take a break, and then after the rodeo is over, we have a dance. We used to hire Zydeco bands from Louisiana, but they've gotten too expensive. Now, we have a DJ and he plays whatever the people want to hear."[22]

Today, there are seven rodeo arenas sanctioned by the ASGCA, located in Southeast Texas at Raywood, Cheeks, Double Bayou, Hankamer, and Beaumont. Each ranch schedules its own rodeos during the season from April to October. A. J. says that he usually hosts three or four rodeos every year. "It depends on the weather, how many cowboys are around, and how we did at the last rodeo."[23]

Although the Circle 6 Ranch does provide some revenue, A. J. has had to supplement his income with farm, construction, and truck-driving jobs. For A. J. rodeo is more than a job, it is a way of life. "I've been doing this a long time. It's been tough, but I've liked every bit of it."[24]

NOTES

1. Philip Durham and Everett Jones, *The Negro Cowboys* (1965; reprint, Lincoln: University of Nebraska Press, 1983).
2. Colonel Bailey C. Hanes, *Bill Picket, Bulldogger* (Norman: University of Oklahoma Press, 1977), p. 40.
3. A. J. Walker, interview by Alan Govenar, Raywood, Tex., Apr. 1, 1998. See *The Hard Ride: Black Cowboys at the Circle 6 Ranch*, prod. Documentary Arts and dir. Alan Govenar, 26:38 min., 1996, videocassette; *Alfred Snuff Johnson: Black Cowboy Blues and Church Songs* (Dallas: Documentary Arts, 1994), audiocassette.
4. Vincent Jacobs, interview by Alan Govenar, Raywood, Tex., Mar. 4, 1993.
5. Walker interview.
6. A. J. Walker, interview, Mar. 4, 1993.
7. Walker interview.
8. Ibid.

9. Ibid.

10. Walker interview, Feb. 23, 1998.

11. Walker interview, Feb. 22, 1998.

12. Walker interview, Mar. 30, 1994.

13. Walker interview, Feb. 23, 1998.

14. Ibid.

15. For more information, see Alan Govenar, "African-American Ranching in Texas," in Joe S. Graham, *Ranching in South Texas: A Symposium,* Kingsville, Tex., 1994, pp. 80–85; Alan Govenar, "Musical Traditions of Twentieth Century African American Cowboys," in Francis E. Abernethy, Patrick B. Mullen, and Alan Govenar, eds., *Juneteenth Texas: Essays in African American Folklore,* Texas Folklore Society (Denton: University of North Texas Press, 1996), pp. 195–208.

16. Molly Stevenson, interview by Alan Govenar, Houston, Tex., Dec. 3, 1993.

17. Frances W. Isbell, Hidalgo County Historical Commission, Hidalgo, Tex., letter to Alan Govenar, Nov. 4, 1993; Mary Alice Ramirez, "Nathaniel Jackson—1858," MSS, Hidalgo County Historical Commission, Hidalgo, Tex.; Deed Records of Hidalgo County, Deed Book C, p. 119; Deed Book A, Hidalgo County Historical Commission, Hidalgo, Tex., p. 315; Hidalgo County Census—1860, Hidalgo County Historical Commission, Hidalgo, Tex.

18. Quentin Jackson, telephone interview by Alan Govenar, July 12, 1994.

19. Elton Laday, interview by Alan Govenar, Raywood, Tex., Mar. 4, 1994.

20. Walker interview, Mar. 31, 1998.

21. Walker interview, May 4, 1998.

22. Walker interview, Apr. 1, 1995.

23. Walker interview, Apr. 27, 1994.

24. Walker interview, Mar. 4, 1993.

Figure 21. Mack Williams, Sr. Courtesy the Reverend Mack Williams, Sr., and the Institute of Texan Cultures, San Antonio

Chapter 24

Mack Williams, Sr.

Nobody's Fool

ANTHONY P. GRIFFIN

Her hair laid immaculately; its whiteness paid tribute to her years. She waited patiently, recognizing that she, too, would not be allowed to enter the church to pay her last tribute to the Reverend Mack Williams.[1] Her clothes were well tailored. She spoke to no one as she waited; her eyes did likewise. A graceful willow tree framed her purposeful stance; the willow swayed as the Gulf water played a quiet refrain—from ashes to ashes, dust to dust. The clouds slowed their pace, held their tears, but seemingly expressed their sorrow and respect none the same. The sky was gray, heavy, moist. I knew we all came for the same purpose, some with Jesus hanging from their necks, others with symbols of their employment. There were those whose appearance reflected the various stages of Reverend Mack's life and contributions: rangers, ranchers, preachers, priests, laborers, the children of laborers, and yes, old cowboys.

I didn't know whether she had come because of Reverend Mack's cowboy past, his former presidency of the Tivoli Lions Club, or his membership with the American Red Cross, the American Cancer Society, or because of his previous induction in the Cowboy Hall of Fame. Somehow, though, I knew that she too had laughed at his stories. I tried not to stare; I knew I wasn't doing a good job.

I guess we all knew that because of the sheer number of those who came to pay tribute that there would be little chance of entering the church. Our procession of patience was unavoidable; no house of faith was large enough in this South Texas town to accommodate our visit. I am sure that those who were of the Catholic faith didn't object to this Baptist preacher/cowboy/park ranger lying in state in their chapel. Time's dance slowed ever so slightly.

301

The front door of the church opened. She differed; her hair was exceedingly black. She, too, wore black. She was at least two generations younger; they stood no more than three feet apart. Of different races, ages, but they were part of the collective assembled on this April morning. As she exchanged hugs with those who were part of my observation room, the wind's gentle grace removed her hat and placed it on the sidewalk. I adjusted my weight from one foot to the other. The sun peaked and then escaped quickly behind its saddened brethren. The sea birds could be heard in the distance playing their song. We continued our pilgrimage.

A quiet refrain, a tear, a hand of reassurance. "Father, I stretch my hand to thee." We of different faiths and histories continued to wait. Time's slow dance allowed me to revisit why I was in Tivoli, Texas.

When I was asked to write a chapter on a black cowboy, living or otherwise, I said yes before I actually realized that I too was part of the unwritten history of the black cowboy. When I accepted, I knew that I was not a historian, but I appreciated history. Saying yes didn't mean I was professing to be a writer by trade, but the allure of the interplay of words, and how words allowed us to taste, smell, and see that which was not present had always astonished me.

Listening to the caller tell me how exciting the project would be caused my fears to manifest themselves on the hairs that covered my arms. I rubbed my arms slowly as if the rubbing would persuade the hairs to lay flat and slay my fears. It was when I cradled the phone I realized that I didn't know any black cowboys—mythological or otherwise. Sure, I knew folks who owned horses and participated in urban trail rides, but I knew that wasn't what I was being asked to study and then write about.

Apprehension, worry, and distress all created an intense fear as I catalogued my limited and rather humorous range of knowledge of the real or mythological West. Durango Kid—no. Roy Rogers—no. Hop-Along-Cassidy—no. John Wayne—of course not. The oft-conflicting but defining worlds of historians, cultural commentators, entertainers, and television all conspired to increase my anxieties. As I cursed my own shortcomings, I knew my ignorance of the historically invisible didn't mean that the black cowboy didn't exist. With my fear came my confession—even though I knew the written and unwritten history of urban workers of my father's generation, I had not made the same conscious connection with respect to those who toiled in rural America. For every roadway, Woolworth, or "concrete monuments attesting the supposed greatness of others" built from the sweat of urban workers of color, I had ignored that the cattle industry, of Reverend Mack's grandfather's, father's, and his generation, required laborers, cheap labor, and lots of it.[2] I had not thought of any of this until the request to write, but even though the request brought fear and anxiety, it also brought a sense of historical relief and sense of purpose.[3] The request was also coupled with a plea of urgency. History sung its song.

"Reverend Mack is ill. You should visit with him as soon as possible."[4]

Spring gently blew a reminder of its impending visit. The sun's dance increased its pace as if it were competing for our attention. Ironically, the rebirth brought by the season's change, and the ever present energy of the sun, did not erase my thoughts of impending death. Entering the hospital, I noticed that Sunday's grace had robbed the hospital of its visitors; the chairs longed for company; the floor's surface announced both our presence and path. I longed for a bridge between my anxiety and the anticipated interview.

"Do you know where I can find the Reverend Mack Williams?"

I read once that "ignoring the stories of those who have been less visible can lead to pure and nearly eternal lies—even fatal lies." The words were those of Bill Moyers, a modern-day historian. My text was actually a speech that Moyers had given. I knew what Moyers spoke of when he spoke of pure and eternal lies of written and oral history.[5] I remember in school questioning the voices of history that were fed to us and wondered whose voices we were actually hearing. I felt that some of what I was told was true, but the faces, hands, and bodies of my great-grandparents, grandparents, and parents were not seen, heard or felt; I knew that some of what was being told was simply not true. As the slide-tap, slide-tap, slide-tap dance of our feet played against the floor, I knew that history's call for a consistent truth was the reason I had said "yes" so readily.

Walking, I assume, causes the physiological expulsion of energy; I didn't anticipate it would cause my internal anxiety to continue its assault. My partner in this dance of anticipation was Sara Massey with the Institute of Texan Cultures. Sara had agreed to travel to Victoria from San Antonio to introduce me to "my cowboy." I had traveled from Galveston. Sara's interest was clear— sometime ago, Sara had recorded Mack Williams's oral history for the Institute.[6] Prior to our trip, I had read the transcript. I had studied the pictures of Buzzard Williams, Thornton Williams, Roy Williams, and Mack Williams. I had studied the videos, but despite visiting with "my cowboy" in these other mediums, I still needed to hear his voice. Also for some reason I needed to touch his hand. When the elevator's doors opened, I sincerely hoped that death would slow its march.

Sara's raspy voice punctuated the solitude of the hospital room. "Reverend Mack, I want you to meet someone."

The smell of death permeated the room; I remembered the smell from childhood when I spent summers at my grandparents' Central Texas farm. The farm was also where I was able to observe my surroundings more closely. I learned that humans are no different from animals when death is impending. One summer, death visited my Muh Chest's extra bedroom quite often.

"Why, Muh Chest?"

"Baby, they have come for prayer and comfort."

I always remembered that—they didn't die in the hospital; they didn't tie themselves to machines; they died in the room over from where my grandparents slept.

"My cowboy" moved slowly as the nurse raised his body—the taming of the wild was now just a fond remembrance. Although his voice and supple skin belied his age, his physical condition, his cancer did not. His spirit, his laugh, and his words conveyed a richness for life. He understood that I had come to interview him, to write about him, and to learn more of his unwritten history as a black cowboy. I'm sure others had intruded into his space to do likewise. I had seen him tell about the life of a cowboy on video. I had watched him disarm his audiences with humor. I had seen him weave his tale in order to tell us about a life we didn't know, didn't fully appreciate, or in some sense may have found objectionable. In one particular story, he told of relationships, marriage, and of men and women. With his straw hat tilted ever so slightly, he moved comfortably about the room. "We got married. And about two months passed, I hadn't been to town. We didn't own much. We had a tackle box, a two burner oil stove and a five gallon lard can. We put our groceries in that. I made us a toolbox also."

As I listened, the realness of his story was quite evident. Part of me understood that the description of poverty was not provided to seek our pity—to the contrary.

One night I came in, I said, "Don't cook no supper tonight." I said, "I just eat at the place."

She said, "I'll cook anyway. I'll eat with you."

It was just the two of us, way out there. I told her that, "I'm goin' to town with (the) boys."

She said, "What time you comin' back?"

I said, "About ten o'clock."

It was almost seven miles to town, walking, you know, down the dirt road. We didn't have no car of no kind, not even a Model T. So we went on down the road. We sung all the way there. Sung all the way back. I told her that I would be back about ten. So we got there.

I watched the audience watch Reverend Mack. I saw the wood-burning stove that was used to heat my grandparents' small farmhouse.[7] I smelled the biscuits cook in the oven. I became a participant in his story.

> My father told me, "Now when you marry, you put your foot down. You's the boss of your house."
> I said, "Yes, sur."
> He said, "Don't give her an inch cause, cause she take a mile."
> "Yes, sur."
> "You be the boss!"
> I told him, "Yes, sur."
> He told me all this. "You don't knows thems women. You marry one of them and then they want to go bossin' and you have to bring all the money to them."
> I told him alright.

As he would say the refrain in reference to his father, Reverend Mack would whisper.

> We went to town, thirteen or fourteen of us. Cattle on the side looking at us. So finally, we got to town. We got all sprewed up with that Sweet Lucy. We came back and walked to the house. I looked at the door and backed up a little bit. Finally, I made it to the door. I knocked.
> She said, "Who is that?"
> I heard my father's voice. "Put your foot down."

The audience moved forward as Reverend Mack whispered his father's misguided wisdom. The audience roared when it realized that his father's encouragement caused his words to become emboldened.

> I said, "Me!"
> She came and turned that little latch. She had that Mother Hubbard Lamp. A Mother Hubbard Lamp hangs on the wall, with a nail, that has a reflector in the back of it.
> I said, "It's me!"

She opened the door, she said, "Where you been?"
He whispered, I heard that voice, "Put your foot down."
"Where you been?"

Again he raised his voice and explained,

I said, "Bout my business."
She came up with that hand, pow! Slapped me.
He whispered again, "Put your foot down."

He stared at the audience, smiled, and then increased his pace.

We got together. Man, we mixed it up.
She said, "You wait!"
She take that little old lamp and put it on the dresser. And, boy, we got back at it. Tearing up the house wrestlin'. So finally, I got her down on her hands and knees. She was beggin' me. I mean she actually begged me. She weighed 250 and I weighed 140 pounds, but she begged me.

He stopped, smiled again, and provided the most invariable punch line.

You know what she was saying, "You come out from under that bed, you coward or what!"

He laughed; they laughed. I wondered to myself whether his humor and appreciation of life was forged from the years of solitude on the range. He continued.

We had one of those iron beds with that old timey springs in it. I crawled up under that bed. After the while she in the bed, griping, groaning and the bed went down like this. Sprang all down. About four o'clock, I crawled from under there and reached and grabbed there and got the latch and keys and went to work.
The boys said, "Where you been?"
I said, "I went to the house."
That's what happened.[8]

The nurse lowered his body; he asked whether she could wait, "Párese, párese."[9] His body told another story at this time—his high cheek bones evoked images of his grandmother, Fannie Williams, a Cherokee; his dark and supple skin, his height told of Izeah Weathers, his "momma's father," "an African," "a Watusi." I saw in his exceedingly thin frame his grandfather, Thornton, and his father, Buzzard. Although the voices of technology outside the hospital door forced us to remain in the present tense, his voice, his illness, his stories allowed us to straddle both worlds. He still gestured with his hands; he still told his stories, but not with as much force. We listened, Sara and I. Mrs. Williams stood guard in the corner of the room. I'm sure she knew all of the stories, after sixty-two years of marriage, but she didn't let on.

He sang a song of both high and low. He sang his song. "They were moved from one place to the other. First, the Butlers. They were sold to the Butlers. Then after they moved there, the Butlers sold them to the Thorntons. So my grandfather kept the name Thornton. And his brother kept the name Butler. He killed a man everywhere he went. He didn't want to work."

Reverend Mack chuckled when he mentioned his great uncle's being a belligerent slave. The audience joined in his laughter. "And the last name we got was Williams. Then the O'Connors, they didn't name us. They just got us. We kept that name Williams. And they didn't name us O'Connor. I wish they haddah, maybe I could claim part of the land."

I realized when listening to Reverend Mack that his words told an all-encompassing story. He allowed his audience to participate in his story; he used the language of his heritage and culture; he told the story from his perspective as the grandchild of a slave. He chuckled after wishing out loud about laying claim to the land.

History's song sometimes sings a different verse. The difference became most profound when I revisited the words of the heirs to the land:

> The relationship between the ranchers and their cowhands is also the result of the patron system, which has links with feudalism, Latin American peonage, and Southern slavery. It was a system in which a large landowner would maintain a permanent labor force on his land. These workers were paid subsistence wages, but their needs—and those of their families—were taken care of from the crib to the grave. The owner provided for their housing, food, medical care, transportation, place of worship, and their children's education. Thus, the ranches became self-contained communities, with generation after generation living and working together in the same place. I tried for six years, almost on a daily basis, to get someone who had experienced the *patron* system to criticize it. I was never successful, even though the interviewees were free to say whatever they chose.[10]

I understood the extreme pride of the land's heirs. History's lore told them of Thomas O'Connor's arrival from Ireland to Texas in 1834, of his having fought in the Battle of San Jacinto—the youngest Texan to do so. "When O'Connor died in 1887, he left the ranch to his children, who left it to their children, and so on down the line."[11]

The late author James Baldwin explained the chasm best in a speech given in 1980. He probably understood what Reverend Mack was telling us. He told the same story, but in a different manner:

> Actually, we all know something very important that has brought me here. Let me try to spell it out for you, again. And let me suggest that the argument concerning Black English is one of the most dishonest arguments in the history of a spectacularly dishonest nation. I kid you not. I grew up in Harlem. I was a shoe-shine boy. I scrubbed toilets. And I can still cook. I was dealing with cops before I was seven years old and sleeping in basements before I was ten, watching my mother and my father, my brothers and my sisters, in the land of the free and the home of the brave, living as though everyday was going to be our last. Now how exactly do you expect me to explain that, to describe that to Greer Garson when she comes to teach English. There is an irreducible gap between my teacher and my experience, between my teacher and my education. . . . I tell you something else, a very important matter. The language forged by Black people in this country, on this continent, as the choir just told you, got us from one place to another. We described the auction block. We described what it meant to be there. We survived what it meant to be torn from your mother, your father, your brother, your sister. We described it. We survived being described as mules. . . .[12]

As best I could figure, he was a cowboy from birth. Reverend Mack described it as being born in the middle of a pasture, "so I was born a cowboy."[13] His daddy's daddy was a cowboy. His daddy was a cowboy. He was a cowboy. He spoke of his Aunt Dovie, his Aunt Lenoa, Little Fanny, and Uncle Sam.[14] He laughed when he spoke of his Uncle Jimmy, "He wore women's shoes. Real high heels. He was a character."[15] He said his grandfather died in 1914, the same year that he was born.[16] Four generations of Butlers, Thorntons, Williams,[17] were products of slavery, of the Southern caste system, and an understanding of that which was necessary for survival. His slow and deliberate movements continued; he explained that he worked in those pastures of love until 1945.[18] When he tried to tell me some of the stories I had read, his slender hands would grab the rail, he would heave his chest, he would attempt to hide the pain—somehow he would always laugh. Somehow I felt that he wanted me to see the Woolworth building. Roy Rogers—yeah, Roy Rogers.[19] As he talked, the light in the room seemed dimmer. Time slowed its dance. Reverend Mack continued to grip the bed's rail lightly. "Párese." "Párese."

He told me that "we made seventy five cents a day, but it increased to two fifty during the war." I knew he watched for my reaction. He laughed again, and then expressed that a cowboy is a happy man; I understood what he meant and why he laughed, but I didn't tell him I understood. I asked him about his favorite horse. I asked him how many horses he worked at one time; he told the story of a black cowboy's life as if he wanted us to avoid the eternal lie.

I remembered when I was a child, we spoke in terms of "he told me," "she told me." I found that in my conversation with Reverend Mack his words allowed me to relate in that sense—"my," "mine," "yours," "mamma," "daddy." Images of Louis Wright, my mother's father, joined our conversation—"my," "mine," "yours," "Muh Chest," "Daddy Louis." Dad Louis also expressed that his greatest pleasure was the smell, taste, and touch of nature. When Reverend Mack laughed, I saw Louis Wright's red-sand skin, instead of Reverend Mack's rich, chocolate tones. They shared a mutual laugh; I truly believe the laugh spoke of their mutual mistress—Mother Nature. So when Reverend Mack told me of the buzzards attacking newborn calves, the Texas sky opened up, the rush of the summer heat filled my nostrils, the gentle rock of the horse's back was felt as he led me to the buzzards' site. Sand cuts, sticker burrs, and unbearable heat, little appreciated then but appreciated now—warm plums, ripe watermelons, the smell of livestock. Mother Nature captivated us with her dance, with her song, with her touch.

"Thank you, Reverend Mack."

"Thank you."

The clouds at this time released some of their sorrow. She turned and looked skyward. Her eyes remained focused; her hair retained its immaculate appearance. The wind played its quiet refrain; its presence was felt. I knew that Reverend Mack was still smiling. He could no longer tell the nurse to wait. He could no longer watch over his herd; he could no longer brag about being the "El Coyote Prieto." Coyotes could now rest assured that the black cowboy was no longer scheming their demise. Párese no more.

The church's doors opened again. An usher, flush with heat, immediately lowered her body to the steps. Her white dress fanned out; fans of comfort were not far behind. One of the funeral attendants quickly moved a chair through the crowd, placed it on the grass and helped her to a higher position. At this time, she moved from her position and turned to walk away. The usher wiped her brow; she wiped her tears. I knew at this time that "my cowboy's" story was told by the presence of those of different hues, tongues and attire. We were poor, wealthy, pampered, unfortunate, frightened, disenfranchised, and worthy. We were cowboys, vaqueros, cowmen, and ranchers. She with immaculate hair and she with exceedingly black hair were part of his heritage. He wanted us to dispel the eternal lie:

> They sent me to a deal about four years ago to Cody, Wyoming, because they say, "There are not any black cowboys." I stepped in just when somebody said that, "There are not any black cowboys."
> I hit the floor and said, "What? What's that about not any black cowboys?"
> They said, "Come on up here, you supposed to been up here, you were on this panel. I wanted to know whether there were any black cowboys."
> I said, "There were black cowboys ever since my grandfather got off the boat." And I want you to think about it, about black cowboys. You think that the slave owners would have a bunch of blacks there and not put them to work on the horses?[20]

He wanted history to recognize the hours and hours of work and the generation and generations of those who survived. Somehow, I knew that when the Lone Ranger reared his horse Silver in the air and sung his most familiar chant, Reverend Mack patted Blue Heaven[21] on her flank and chuckled at history's song.

> *Precious Lord, take my hand,*
> *Lead me on, let me stand,*
> *I am tired, I am weak, I am worn.*
> *Through the storm, through the night*
> *Lead me on to the light,*
> *Take my hand, precious Lord,*
> *Lead me home.[22]*

NOTES

The name of this chapter derives in part from Louise S. O'Connor, *Cryin' for Daylight: A Ranching Culture in The Texas Coastal Bend* (Austin: Wexford Publishing, 1989), wherein O'Connor, when speaking of cowhands/cowboys, entitled a chapter, "Fools on Good Horses: The Cowhands." It seems to this author that they should be more appropriately referenced as "Nobody's Fool."

This chapter has some built-in limitations—that is, it provides only a snapshot of the subject's life and deals with his life as a cowboy from birth (1914) until 1945. The chapter does not address in any significant manner the subject's life as a minister or his work as a park ranger.

1. Mack Williams, Sr., was born on November 16, 1914, and died on April 9, 1998. He was born on the O'Connor/Williams Ranch in Tivoli, Texas. He was buried on the same ranch. Mack Williams married Alice Mae Barefield Williams on December 25, 1936; two children were born of this union. Both sons preceded him in death— Roy Allen died in a truck accident at the age of twenty-six, and Mack Williams, Jr., died at the age of fifty from cancer. Mrs. Williams was also a product of the ranch culture, as she was born on the Fagan Ranch, an adjoining ranch.

    The significance of race, history, and politics cannot be ignored. Louise O'Connor describes the building of the O'Connor land mass this way: "The building of the O'Connor ranches started in 1836, the year Texas declared its independence from Mexico. Every soldier who fought with Sam Houston for the Texas cause was awarded a land grant of 650 acres." *Cryin' for Daylight,* p. 15; Edward Everett Dale, in *The Range Cattle Industry: Ranching on the Great Plains from 1865 to 1925* (Norman: University of Oklahoma Press, 1960), p. 113, n. 53, mentions the O'Connor Ranch in the context of the accumulation of land from land grants made by Mexico or the Republic of Texas: "Belonging to the first type were men like Col. Richard King, who acquired the Santa Gertrudes Ranch in 1853, and laid the foundations of the famous 'King Ranch' of Texas. Others of the same type were Captain Kenedy of the Kenedy Ranch of Nueces County, O'Connor of the O'Connor Ranch and numerous others."

2. Ernest Staples Osgood, *The Day of the Cattleman* (Minneapolis: University of Minnesota Press, 1929), pp. 28–29, has an early description of the cattle industry in 1880 (after the Civil War). The colonization of Texas was also based on the ranching industry. "If a married man declared himself a farmer, he received 177 acres [negroes excepted]—one 'labor'—of agricultural land. If he was also engaged in stock raising, a grazing tract sufficient to complete a square league, or 4,440 acres, was added. If unmarried, he received one-fourth of the above amount. And the government could increase these allotments in proportion to the size of the family, with a limit of eleven square leagues for any one family. For the colonist, the over-all cost of a square league was only $180. . . . From 3,500 Anglo-Texans in 1821, it zoomed to

54,000 in 1841 and to 400,000 in 1860. Correspondingly, cattle increased from a few score of thousands in the 1820s to an estimated four million in 1860—making a ten-to-one majority for *Bos taurus* over *Homo sapiens*;" C. H. Towne and E. N. Wentworth, *Cattle & Men* (Norman: University of Oklahoma Press, 1955), p. 153.

3. "The Texas cities—San Antonio, Houston, Dallas, and Fort Worth—constitute an anomaly in the discussion of the black urban West. In 1910 because no Texas city exceeded 100,000 inhabitants they were not among the region's largest urban centers. Yet the Texas cities' combined African American populations totaled 65,949, and Houston's 23,929 residents exceeded the combined black population of the five largest cities in the West. Nineteenth-century black urban Texas emerged in the shadow of slavery." Quintard Taylor, *In Search of The Racial Frontier: African Americans in the American West, 1528–1990* (New York: W. W. Norton & Company, Inc., 1998), pp. 208–209; Howard Beeth and Cary D. Wintz, ed., *Black Dixie: Afro-Texas History and Culture in Houston* (College Station: Texas A&M University Press, 1992).

4. My caller was Sara R. Massey with the Institute of Texan Cultures. She had initially persuaded me to participate in this project. She told me that there was little written about Mack Williams, that the Institute possessed oral history materials and that the same would be provided to me; I promised to see him as soon as possible.

5. Bill Moyers, "The Big Story: A Journalist Looks at Texas History," *Southwestern Historical Quarterly* 101:1 (July, 1997): 4–6. Bill Moyers explains it best when he writes,

> Sometimes ignoring the stories of those who have been less visible can lead to some pure and nearly eternal lies—even fatal lies. . . . It's not only that the depiction of slavery was just prettied up, it was flat out deceitful. Any youngster reading *Texas History Movies* could have reasonably concluded that black people enjoyed being owned body and soul by a master. Of course it was some of the masters—or some of their children and grandchildren—who were telling those tales. Not until many years later did it occur to me to wonder how these stories would have sounded had they been written by children and grandchildren of the slaves. . . . As schoolchildren we read—and this is a direct quote— that "Any man who inherited slaves was bound to free one-tenth of the number." That was a lie; slaves were legally designated chattel, not flesh-and-blood, and any man who inherited slaves was no more bound to free a single one of them than he was obligated to liberate a portion of his cotton fields, his pigs, or his grandmother's silver. . . . "Slaves could change masters at will," we read. Another lie. And we read, "The law provided for the education of Negroes even while they were slaves,"— this we read under the picture of a little barefoot black child in a shabby schoolroom spelling "K-A-T." In truth, the law provided for the severe

punishment of any slaves caught educating themselves, but many black children and adults who, in their hunger for knowledge, accepted the terrible risk, learned to spell a heck of a lot better than that.

Moyers refers to *Texas History Movies* (Austin: Texas State Historical Association, 1986).

6. The Other Cowboy Forum: Mack Williams, prod. Institute of Texan Cultures, 1 1/2 hrs., Sept., 1997, 2 videocassettes; *Workin' from Can't to Can't: African American Cowboys in Texas,* prod. Institute of Texan Cultures, 27 min., 1995, videocassette; Rev. Mack Williams, Sr., interview by Anthony Griffin, Victoria, Tex., Mar. 1, 1998; Rev. Mack Williams, Sr., interview with Sara R. Massey, Austwell, Tex., Sept. 27, 1996, transcript, vertical files, Institute of Texan Cultures, San Antonio.

7. Unfortunately, the legacy of the black farms may become a historical relic. See Roger Thurow, "Soiled Legacy: Black Farmers Hit The Road to Confront a 'Cycle of Racism,'" *Wall Street Journal,* May 1, 1998, p. 1.

> In 1920, African-Americans owned 14% of the nation's farms; by 1992, the proportion was down to 1%. In the next agriculture census, it will likely be a mere fraction of a percent, and black farmers will be deemed statistically irrelevant. They have been done in by the same economic hardships and urban migrations that have imperiled all small family farms, plus one other thing: racism. The USDA admits as much, in various reports over the past two decades and in recent individual rulings. When Mr. Shaffer applied for an equipment loan, a USDA county official told him: "All you need is a mule and a plow." USDA investigators looking into the denial of Mr. Halls' application for crop-disaster relief found a county loan officer referring to a black community as a "baby factory." In a complaint that is part of the suit, Abraham Carpenter, an Arkansas farmer, says a county official deemed his disaster-relief request "too much money for a nigger to receive."

8. The Other Cowboys Forum: Mack Williams, videocassette 2.

9. Mack Williams's primary language was Spanish. He joked about not being able to speak a lick of English at one time; he constantly apologized for his limited use of words at other times. The apologies, although sincere, helped to form the endearing nature of storytelling and the oral history that he was so capable of presenting.

10. See Louise O'Connor, *Cryin' for Daylight,* p. 46. An interpretation of the historical context of beliefs, tradition, and one's view of the world is important in the context of Coastal plain cultures that had the influence of Mexicans, Africans, and Europeans; Arnoldo De León, in *They Called Them Greasers: Anglo Attitudes toward Mexicans in Texas, 1821–1900* (Austin: University of Texas Press, 1983), pp. ix, x, expresses the same in this context: "It also points to the fact that those who have traditionally dominated Texas history have published works that reveal, in fact and

interpretation, serious flaws, deficiencies of research, and detectable bias, especially concerning the relationships between whites and Mexicans. Strongly influenced by Eugene C. Baker, Walter Prescott Webb, and Rupert N. Richardson, other historians have uncritically followed their mentors' paths, overlooking a long racist and ethnocentric tradition toward blacks and Indians that was transposed upon native Texas *castas* as a matter of course."

11. Erin Davies, "The Biggest Ranches," *Texas Monthly,* Aug., 1998.

12. James Baldwin, "Black English: A Dishonest Argument," in Geneva Smiterman, ed., *Black English and The Education of Black Children and Youth* (Detroit: Harlo Press, 1981).

13. Tim Delaney, "Cowboy Folklorist Mack Williams' Rites Set in Tivoli," *Victoria Advocate,* Apr. 11, 1998, p. 14A.

14. Williams, interview by Massey, transcript, p. 7.

15. Ibid., p. 34.

16. Ibid., p. 8.

17. The Other Cowboys Forum: Williams, videocassette 1.

18. Williams, interview by Massey, transcript, p. 24.

19. Quintard Taylor describes mine and others of my generation ignorance of history; surely our ignorance is not bliss. Taylor writes, "Philip Durham and Everett Jones offered a succinct reason for the twentieth-century invisibility of nineteenth-century black drovers: 'When the West became a myth . . . the Negro became the invisible man. . . There was no place for him in these community theatricals. He had been a real cowboy, but he could not easily pretend to be one.'" Taylor, *In Search of the Racial Frontier,* p. 162.

20. The Other Cowboys Forum: Williams, videocassette 2.

21. Williams, interview by Griffin, Mar. 1, 1998; "Blue Heaven was gray, not blue, a mingling gray" was how Reverend Mack described his favorite horse.

22. Thomas E. Dorsey, "Take My Hand, Precious Lord," in H. L. Gates and N. Y. McKay, eds., *The Norton Anthology of African American Literature* (New York: W. W. Norton & Company, 1997), p. 20.

Conclusion

History lasts a long time. As adults, we carry with us the history we learned in school, the pictures and words from the books we read. It is important that history be told truthfully and inclusively with no persistent omissions. Historians of each generation re-examine history within the context of the issues of their own time. The civil rights era of the twentieth century necessitated such a re-examination. The history of the United States is being reconsidered from diverse perspectives to arrive at a more inclusive and accurate understanding of the past. A society that denies a group of people its history participates in another insidious example of racism. The history of Texas and the West is not exempted.

Books and movies about cowboys are numerous, but only in meeting the Reverend Mack Williams and hearing the stories of his days as a cowboy did it become clear that something was missing from the traditional history. The history of African Americans is about much more than slavery. The stories of the lives of the African American cowboys provide another picture of life on the Texas frontier, and there are many more stories that can never be told.

The accounts of ordinary African American working cowboys—doing their jobs day after day—are difficult to trace, but they exist. Their names, culled from books and articles about the Texas cattle industry, include Bill Freeman of the Quarter Circle Heart; Charles Fowler of the L.F.D.S.; Sam Hext of San Saba County; Brook Lee of the Diamond Trail; Boot Stevenson of the George Dewe Ranch; Negro Sam, Jack Harvey, and Buck Moore with the U.L.A. outfit of Foard County; Henry Mangum of the T.J.M. Ranch; Dan Sowell of the Figure 4 Ranch; Mose Burton with the LH7 Ranch; Jack Brinkley, foreman on the Reverend William States Jacobs Ranch of Harris County; Old Pleas with the J.J. Ranch of Archer County; and Cal West with Jim Scott. Others include Jeff Charleson of the Guadalupe community; Gus Jones, foreman on the Joe D. Hughes Ranch of Chocolate Bayou in Harris County; Emanuel Organ of Bushy Creek; Dave Gill of Hudspeth County; George Glen with R. B. Johnson; Mose Herron of the Pleasant Creek community; Sherman Russaw of the Widow Ryan's Ranch near Dead Creek; Bill Coleman with the Spade Ranch of Wharton County; "Nat" Robinson of the Victoria area; "Toad" Green; Sandy Wimbish; Steve Ray of Sandy Point; Bill Junius with L. L. Shield; Old Frank with the Chisum family; Tom Ball with J. F. Welder, Jr., of Victoria County; Will Gordon of the Pearson Ranch; Ellis Miller, associated with Dr. Ledbetter of Winchester; George Grant of the De Costa community; Rob Remer with the Blocker boys; Heck Bazy with Tom L. Burnett of Iowa Park; and "Coaley" Owens of the J Buckle Ranch. There are more: "Big Mouth" Henry, "Nigger" Ed, "Goat," and Britton Johnson, whose wife and children were kidnapped by Comanches in 1864. "Under the generous treatment of his master he became the owner of a large number of horses and cattle, and when peace, like an angel of mercy, with healing on her wings, blessed the country and gave him his freedom, he tried every pathway to recover his lost ones."[1] Britton Johnson found and joined the tribe holding his family in captivity. In 1865 with his family he escaped from the Comanches and returned home. Six years later as he returned from gathering his cattle he and two other men were attacked and killed by the Indians who had not forgotten him. The African American cowboys of this anthology are not a few isolated examples; they are representative of the many African American cowboys in the cattle industry of Texas.

In Texas, a brand had to be recorded by the county clerk to prove ownership as well as identify the cattle. The primary purpose of roundups has always been to brand the cattle to prove ownership. African Americans registered their brands for the same purpose. "Button" Evans was born in 1822 in Vicksburg, Mississippi, and was once owned by a Mr. Stroud, who lived near Groesbeck, Texas. "Button" recorded his Pitcher brand in Texas on September 3, 1877. Austin Williams of West Columbia, a cowboy for Jordie Farmer, registered his brand, the Dash Seven Connected brand. He was "as good a cow hand as I've ever known. He was black as tar and big as a mule, and he used a long rope."[2] Old Frank, another African American cowboy, worked with the Chisum family. He refused to take his freedom and remained with the Chisums all his life. However, when Jesse Chisum died, Frank refused to keep his VF herd with the family's cattle. "I want to see that VF brand and know that the animal belongs to me alone, not to a company."[3]

These were working African American cowboys of Texas history. They may be recorded at the courthouse as white or with another name or with different spellings, as Robert Lemmons (Lammons, Lamons, Lemons, Lemon), or their death certificates may be lost, as was that of Charley Willis. Clearly there were African American cowboys who worked in every phase of the Texas cattle industry.

Many of these cowboys began working at twelve or thirteen years of age. They acquired their skills by experience, herding the cattle with sticks, as did Johanna July, riding a mule, as did Bones Hooks, or, like Bose Ikard, driving a wagon. In old age, many recalled their cowboy years fondly, dismissing the hardships and terrors like Tige Avery's near-death experience, snuggled with another cowboy to survive the freeze. As the Texas frontier expanded westward, so went the African American cowboys, 80 John Wallace, George Adams, and Monroe Payne.

The cowboys were remembered as Addison Jones, "the most noted Negro cowboy that ever 'topped off' a horse" and Bubba Walker, "the best cowhand Wilson County ever had." The stories were filled with hyperbole. It seems unlikely that all of these cowboys could be so conspicuously good, but it is necessary to remember that the African Americans of the time were invisible doing their jobs, not important enough to mention. For stories of African American cowboys to be remembered over time they had to be absolutely outstanding, whether as mustangers, bronc busters, or as riders of outlaw horses—as did Bones Hooks beside the tracks of the Santa Fe Railroad. African American cowboys went against the odds when they joined crews or herding outfits. They had to be the very best just to keep working.

Also recalled were "humorous" incidents, things perceived as funny enough to be remembered by the ranchers, such as George Adams's crawling under the tables of the bar as guns were drawn, Tige Avery bucking heads with the ram, or the exploits told of Addison Jones. He had developed behaviors that made others laugh. It was how he endured the attitudes of the other folks. He knew the rules! George Adams had feared for his life and was surely shamed in the retelling of his escape. And there was the smell of Tige Avery as he crawled into his bedroll—we laughed. These "humorous" tales remind us of the culture and attitudes these cowboys endured in their lifetime to live in Texas, not to be shot, not to be lynched, and to have daily work as cowboys.[4]

". . . in the 1870s and 1880s, blacks were a common sight on the trails. Nonetheless, they did encounter prejudice. There were many men in Texas who hated a black as much as they did a Yankee. Poll Allen, the leading cowboy with John Husley's outfit, was such a man. When, in 1878, Husley picked up an unidentified black who wanted to work and brought him to the Twenty-two Ranch, Allen objected. During a drive to Kansas, he would not allow the black to eat or sleep anywhere near the rest of the outfit. Finally, Allen ran him off by shooting at him. In accordance with the custom of the region, no questions were asked."[5]

Several of these cowboys were remembered because they were the respected "companions" of important, successful white ranchers. Bose Ikard carried money for Charles Goodnight when they returned after selling cattle. Neptune Holmes carried bags of gold for his boss, Shanghai Pierce. This was a good business strategy at the time, as no one would think a black man had any money. These cowboys had proven to their bosses (masters) that they were loyal and trustworthy.

Often they helped raise and train the young sons and grandsons of the owners to ride horses and drive cattle, as George Adams trained Bill and Jim Davis on the C. F. Cox Ranch and Bones Hooks taught youths in Clarendon. They were doing what their parents and grandparents had done for decades, caring for the children of the whites. As cowboys, these men were relatively safe and secure in a region and time filled with violence, especially for African Americans.

Numerous sources quote Jim Perry, a cowboy on the XIT Ranch. "If it weren't for my damned old black face I'd have been boss of one of these divisions long ago."[6] That was true for him and other African American cowboys. It was rare for any owner to allow African Americans to issue orders to white cowboys, but there were exceptions. Louis Power was made foreman of the Duke Division on the O'Connor Ranch; cowboys of the Payne family worked as foremen in Brewster County. It is, also, possible that Addison Jones was boss of an all-black crew that Jack Thorp met one night when he began his song-collecting rides.[7]

A cook was the second-most important person of any group of cowhands. Beyond doing the duties as cook, he was the doctor, barber, caretaker of all belongings, and "peacekeeper." Jim Perry did become a cook and was known as one of the best, as was "Coaley" Owens, pictured in this volume's frontispiece.

It was mentioned that many of these cowboys could neither read nor write. This was also true for many of the other twenty-five thousand Texas cowboys at the time. The descendants of Louis Power tell how he drew pictures and gave them to a family member to change into written words. It is more surprising that *any* of the African American cowboys were literate, such as Bones Hooks, given the laws prohibiting the education of African Americans. It is not mentioned that many owners of the small and large ranches of the period, also, could not read or write. As Hooks told us, it was the frontier woman who brought civilization, churches, and schools to the West. The struggle to become literate for African Americans continued well into the twentieth century, which was the situation the Paynes of Brewster County faced as they tried to educate their children. And the struggle continues today. "The cow country was no utopia for Negroes, but it did demonstrate that under some circumstances and for at least a brief period white and black in significant numbers could live and work together on more nearly equal terms than had been possible in the United States for two hundred years or would be possible again for nearly another century."[8]

W. E. B. DuBois said in 1903, ". . . the problem of the Twentieth Century is the problem of the color line."[9] At the end of the twentieth century it can be said, "Yes, it was." With the fulfillment of DuBois's prophecy, we enter the twenty-first century having a more complete history of the past and knowledge of the African American cowboys who worked in the cattle industry along with the thousands of other cowboys on the Texas frontier and those who continue the work today. After 1865, all these African American cowboys were free men and women. They received wages for their work or got cattle instead. Most lived out their lives near the ranches where they had worked. Most married, though it was usually later in life, when their years as cowboys were over.

The African American cowboys of the past shared a great moment in the history of Texas that continues in the lives of African American cowboys today. They were working hard as cowboys when Texas was young. They were very good. They were *Texans*.

NOTES

1. J. W. Wilbarger, *Indian Depredations in Texas* (Austin: Hutchings Printing House, 1889; reprint, Austin: Pemberton Press, 1967), pp. 579–82.

2. Leonard Stiles Branding Iron Collection, No. 217, No. 757. MSS, Fort Worth: Texas and Southwest Cattle Raisers Foundation and Museum.

3. Jean M. Burroughs, ed., "Black Cowboys on the Open Range," *Greater Llano Estacado Southwest Heritage* 7 (summer, 1977): 13–14.

4. Humor was often a subtle means of rebellion. James Smallwood, in *The Struggle for Equality: Blacks in Texas* (Boston: American Press, 1983), p. 9, states that "the Sambo façade . . . often hid from whites a spirited and shrewd bondsperson." The African-American cowboys of the 1880s in Texas certainly had experiences necessitating them to assume façades.

5. W. J. Elliot, "The Spurs," in W. Sherman Savage, *Blacks in the West* (Westport, Conn.: Greenwood Press, 1976), p. 88.

6. Cordia Duke and Joe B. Frantz, *6,000 Miles of Fence: Life on the XIT Ranch of Texas* (Austin: University of Texas, 1969), p. 172.

7. N. Howard "Jack" Thorp, *Songs of the Cowboys* (1908; reprint, New York: Clarkson N. Potter, Inc., 1966), p. 16.

8. Kenneth W. Porter, "Negro Labor in the Western Cattle Industry, 1860–1900," *The Negro on the American Frontier* (New York: Arno Press and *The New York Times*, 1971), p. 522.

9. W. E. B. DuBois, *The Souls of Black Folk* (1903; reprint, New York: Fawcett Publications, 1970), p. iv.

Contributors

T. Lindsay Baker, a native of Cleburne, Texas, has written multiple books on Texas and the American West, among them *The WPA Oklahoma Slave Narratives* and *Till Freedom Cried Out: Memories of Texas Slave Life*. He is a fellow of the Texas State Historical Association and is director of the Texas Heritage Museum at Hill College.

Alwyn Barr is professor and former chair of the history department at Texas Tech University. He teachers American history courses on African American history, the Civil War, the South, and Texas history. He has written and edited seven books, including *Black Texans: A History of African Americans in Texas, 1528–1995*, and *Black Leaders: Texans for Their Times*. He has served as president of the Texas State Historical Association and served as an advisory editor on nineteenth century and African American history for the *New Handbook of Texas*.

Marilyn Dell Brady is an independent scholar who researched the Paynes as a research associate at the Center for Big Bend Studies at Sul Ross State University in Alpine, Texas. Her Ph.D. is from the University of Kansas, and previously she was an associate professor at Virginia Wesleyan College.

Jim Chilcote, a fifth-generation San Antonioan and cousin of cattle drover John R. Blocker, is a writer, singer, and the founder of the Arbuckle Boys cowboy western band. He has written and performed the stage play "Trail Drive—1871."

Lawrence Clayton is the dean of liberal arts at Hardin-Simmons University in Abilene, Texas. He is the author of *Historic Ranches of Texas* and numerous other books.

Lee N. Coffee, Jr., is a first sergeant with Company A, Brooke Army Medical Center of the U.S. Army. He is well known for his living history portrayals of Buffalo Soldier and Medal of Honor awardee Sergeant Emanuel Stance.

Jim Coffey is an education specialist in gifted and talented education and amateur historian with the Region XV Education Service Center in San Angelo, Texas.

Ana Carolina Castillo Crimm, a Mexican by birth, has a Ph.D. from the University of Texas at Austin and is currently an assistant professor of Latin American history at Sam Houston State University. Her work focuses on the cultural survival of the Mexican Americans of Victoria, Texas.

John H. Fuller is a professor of electrical engineering at Prairie View A&M University. He has written numerous articles in scientific and professional journals in the field of engineering and is a member of the Prairie View Trailriders and the Western Heritage Multicultural Trailriders. He is also actively involved with the Seminole Negro Indian Scouts Cemetery Association in Brackettville, Texas.

Alan Govenar is a writer, photographer, folklorist, and documentary filmmaker. He has a Ph.D. in the arts and humanities from the University of Texas at Dallas and is the author of numerous books, including *Meeting the Blues* and *Portraits of Community: African American Photography in Texas*.

Anthony P. Griffin is a practicing attorney in Galveston, Texas. His publications include "The First Amendment and the Art of Storytelling," in *Speaking of Race, Speaking of Sex* by Henry Louis Gates, Jr., Anthony P. Griffin, Donald E. Lively, William B. Rubenstein, and Nadine Strossen, with a preface by Ira Glasser, and *Is the Diminution of Civil Rights the Road to a Color-Blind Society? The Law of Mea Culpa Notwithstanding*, published in the Thurgood Marshall Law Review.

Vicki J. Hagen is a ten-year veteran research historian with the Texas Parks and Wildlife Department, Texas Buffalo Soldiers, and Exploring Texas Roots educational programs.

Kitty Henderson is the education coordinator for the Community Heritage Development Division of the Texas Historical Commission and an adjunct professor at Austin Community College.

Kenneth W. Howell has been a social studies teacher with the Athens (Texas) Independent School District and has written *An Antebellum History of*

Henderson County, Texas, 1846–1861. He is currently a doctorate student at Texas A&M University in College Station.

Allan O. Kownslar is a professor of history at Trinity University and writer of social studies school textbooks including *People and Our World, Discovering American History,* and *The Texans: Their Land and History.* He is a past president of the Texas Association for the Advancement of History.

Ira V. Lott is a Roman Catholic priest with the Missionary Oblates of Mary Immaculate of Texas, a religious order ministering to the poor. He has an interest in genealogy and has spent the past year researching his family heritage in the Goliad area.

Sara R. Massey is an education specialist with the Institute of Texan Cultures developing instructional materials and web sites for teachers of Texas history. She has a doctorate in curriculum and instruction and degrees in American history, counseling, home economics, and secondary education. She has been an associate professor at Incarnate Word College, University of Southern Maine, and the University of Hartford. She has spent the past ten years in education on the Hopi Indian Reservation in Arizona.

Michael Rugeley Moore is director of the Fort Bend Museum Association and George Ranch Historical Park, in Richmond, Texas. He has received the Leadership in Education Prize from the Texas State Historical Association as well as the Nancy Hanks Memorial Award for Professional Excellence given by the American Association of Museums.

Louise S. O'Connor, a fifth-generation descendant of an early settler of Texas, has been collecting oral histories of the "old timers." She has spent the past seventeen years interviewing people of Coastal Bend Texas and has compiled their stories into the books *Cryin' for Daylight* and *Tales From The San'tone River Bottom,* volumes 1 through 4.

Ken Pollard, a seventeen-year veteran with the Texas Parks and Wildlife Department, began the Texas Buffalo Soldier educational program and continues to work with the program.

Joyce Gibson Roach is an author, columnist, and folklorist. She is a three-time Spur Award winner from the Western Writers of America for her book

The Cowgirls; short nonfiction, "A High Toned Woman," from *Hoein' the Short Rows;* and short fiction, "Just As I Am," from *Women of the West.* She has served as president of the Texas Folklore Society and is a fellow of the Texas State Historical Association.

Michael N. Searles is an assistant professor of history at Augusta State University in Augusta, Georgia. His area of specialization is blacks in the American West, and he does presentations throughout the year on the African American cowboy.

Bruce M. Shackelford is a fifth-generation Texan and a descendant of rancher Tolbert Burford. He is an independent consultant in the historical content of American Indians and the American West.

C. A. "Tony" Sherman is a descendant of Joshua Houston, servant to General Sam Houston, a county commissioner, and owner of Tony Sherman's School of Art and Gallery in Missouri City, Texas. He is a writer and artist known for his portrait sculptures and paintings and serves as a member of the Texas Arts Commission.

James Smallwood is a native of East Texas and is a professor of history at Oklahoma State University. He is the author and/or editor of more than twenty books. His *Time of Hope, Time of Despair: Black Texans During Reconstruction* won the Texas State Historical Society's Coral H. Tullis Award in 1982 for the best book of the year on Texas history.

Ron W. Wilhelm is an associate professor of education at the University of North Texas with degrees in curriculum and instruction, special education, and social science. He has many publications in the field of education and has written extensively in Spanish.

Charlie "Rock" Woodson is an admissions counselor at the University of Houston and a historiography specialist with the Fort Bend County Historical Commission.

Bibliography

PUBLISHED BOOKS AND ARTICLES

Abbott, Edward Charles "Teddy Blue," and Helena Huntington Smith. *We Pointed Them North: Recollections of a Cowpuncher.* Introduction by Ron Tyler. 1939. Reprint, Chicago: R. R. Donnelley and Sons Company, 1991.

Adams, Andy. *Log of a Cowboy.* Boston: Houghton Mifflin, 1903.

Adams, Effie Kaye. *Tall Black Texans: Men of Courage.* Dubuque, Iowa: Kendall Hunt Publishing Co., 1972.

Anderson, La Vere. "The Cowboys." In *Saddles and Sabers: Black Men in the Old West.* Champaign, Ill.: Garrard, 1975.

Atascosa County Centennial. Atascosa County, Tex.: Atascosa County Centennial Association, 1956.

Atascosa County History. Dallas: Taylor Publishing Company, 1984.

Baeza, Abelardo. "La Escondida: History of the Morgan School in Alpine, Texas, 1929–1954." *Journal for Big Bend Studies* 6 (1994): 85–98.

Baker, T. Lindsay, and Julie P. Baker, eds. *The WPA Oklahoma Slave Narratives.* Norman: University of Oklahoma Press, 1996.

———, eds. *Till Freedom Cried Out: Memories of Texas Slave Life.* College Station: Texas A&M University Press, 1997.

Baldwin, James. "Black English: A Dishonest Argument." In Smiterman, Geneva. *Black English and The Education of Black Children and Youth.* Detroit: Harlo Press, 1981.

Barker, Eugene C. "The African Slave Trade in Texas." *Southwestern Historical Quarterly* 6:2 (June, 1902).

———. *The Life of Stephen F. Austin, Founder of Texas, 1793–1836.* Nashville: Cokesbury Press, c. 1925.

———, ed. "The Austin Papers." In *Annual Report of the American Historical Association for the Year 1919.* Vol. 2, Part 1. Washington: GPO, 1924.

Barnard, Evan G. *A Rider of the Cherokee Strip.* New York, Houghton Mifflin Company, 1936.

Barnes, Will C. "Wild Horses." *McClure's Magazine,* April, 1909.

Barr, Alwyn. *Black Texans: A History of African Americans in Texas, 1528–1995.* 1973. Reprint, Norman: University of Oklahoma Press, 1996.

———. *The Negroes in Texas.* 2nd ed. Austin: University of Texas Press, 1996.

Barr, Alwyn, and Robert A. Calvert. *Black Leaders: Texans for Their Times.* Austin: Texas State Historical Association, 1981.

Beeth, Howard, and Cary D. Wintz, eds. *Black Dixie: Afro-Texan History and Culture in Houston.* College Station: Texas A&M University Press, 1992.

Bell, Verner Lee. *Memories of Peter Tumlinson Bell.* Saint Jo, Tex.: S. J. T. Printing Company, 1980.

"The Black Cowboy." *Texas: Houston Chronicle Magazine,* May 25, 1986, p. 14.

Blassingame, John W. "Using the Testimony of Ex-Slaves: Approaches and Problems." *Journal of Southern History* 41 (November, 1975): 473–92.

Bonney, Cecil. *Looking Over My Shoulder: Seventy-Five Years in the Pecos Valley.* Roswell, N.Mex.: Hall-Poorbaugh Press Inc., 1971.

Branch, Hettye Wallace. *The Story of 80 John: A Biography of One of the Most Respected Negro Ranchmen in the Old West.* New York: Greenwich Books Publisher, 1960.

Britten, Thomas. "The Dismissal of the Seminole Scouts." *Fort Concho and the South Plains Journal* 24 (1992): 54–77.

———. "The Seminole-Negro Indian Scouts in Big Bend." *Journal of Big Bend Studies* 5 (1993): 69–80

Brooks, Connie. *The Last Cowboys: Closing the Open Range in Southeastern New Mexico, 1890s–1920s.* Albuquerque: University of New Mexico Press, 1993.

Brown, John Henry. *Indian Wars of Texas.* Austin: L. E. Daniel Publishers, 1988.

Burroughs, Jean M., ed. "Black Cowboys on the Open Range." *The Greater Llano Estacado Southwest Heritage* 7 (summer, 1977): 13–14.

———. *On the Trail: Life and Tales of "Lead Steer" Potter.* Santa Fe: Museum of New Mexico Press, 1980.

Butcher, S. D. *Pioneer History of Custer County* (Nebraska). Broken Bow, Nebr.: Privately printed, 1901.

Campbell, Randolph B. *An Empire for Slavery: The Peculiar Institution in Texas, 1821–1865.* Baton Rouge: Louisiana State University Press, 1989.

Casey, Ethel Matthews. *Reminiscences.* El Paso: Carl Hertzog, 1979.

Castaneda, Carlos E. *Our Catholic Heritage in Texas, 1518–1936.* Austin: Von Boeckmann-Jones Company, 1936–58.

Chipman, Donald E. *Spanish Texas, 1519–1821.* Austin: University of Texas Press, 1992.

Chrisman, Harry E. *The Ladder of Rivers: The Story of I. P. (Print) Olive.* Denver: Sage Books, 1962.

Clayton, Lawrence. *Watkins Reynolds Matthews: A Biography.* Abilene: Hardin-Simmons University Press, 1990.

Clements, Gus. *The Concho Country, Newsfoto Yearbooks.* San Angelo, Tex., January, 1971.

Collinson, Frank. *Life in the Saddle.* Norman: University of Oklahoma Press, 1963.

Cook, James H. *Fifty Years on the Old Frontier as Cowboy, Hunter, Guide, Scout, and Ranchman.* Fort Worth: Wortham-Molyneaux Company, 1923. As quoted in Louis J. Wortham, *A History of Texas: From Wilderness to Commonwealth.* Vol. 5. Norman: University of Oklahoma, 1924.

Crane, R. C. "D. W. Wallace ('80 John'), A Negro Cattleman on the Texas Frontier." *West Texas Historical Association Yearbook* 28 (October, 1952): 113–18.

Cripps, Thomas. *Slow fade to Black: The Negro in American Film, 1900–1942.* New York: Oxford University Press, 1977.

Crouch, Barry A. *The Freedmen's Bureau and Black Texans*. Austin: University of Texas Press, 1992.

Dale, Edward Everett. *The Range Cattle Industry: Ranching on the Great Plains from 1865 to 1925*. Norman: University of Oklahoma Press, 1960.

Dary, David. *Cowboy Culture: A Saga of Five Centuries*. Lawrence: University of Kansas Press, 1981.

Davidson, Chandler. *Race and Class in Texas Politics*. Princeton: Princeton University Press, 1990.

Davies, Erin. "The Biggest Ranches." *Texas Monthly,* August, 1998, pp. 119, 120.

Davis, Alvin G. "Black Cowboys and Ranchers in Texas. *Heritage* (winter, 1994): 1–12.

Dearen, Patrick. *A Cowboy of the Pecos*. Plano, Tex.: Republic of Texas Press, Wordware Publishing, Inc., 1997.

DeBow, J. D. B. *Statistical View of the United States*. Washington: U.S. Government, 1854.

De León, Arnoldo. *They Called Them Greasers: Anglo Attitudes Toward Mexicans in Texas, 1821–1900*. Austin: University of Texas Press, 1983.

Dick, Everett. *The Sod-House Frontier, 1854–1890: A Social History of the Northern Plains from the Creation of Kansas & Nebraska to the Admission of the Dakotas*. New York: D. Appleton-Century Company, 1943.

Dobie, J. Frank, Mody C. Boatright, and Harry R. Ransom, eds. *Mustangs and Cow Horses*. Dallas: Southern Methodist University Press, 1940.

———. *On the Open Range*. Dallas: Southwest Press, 1931.

———. *The Longhorns*. New York: Bramhall House, 1951.

———. *The Mustangs*. Boston: Little, Brown and Company, 1952.

Dorsey, Thomas A. "Take My Hand, Precious Lord." In *The Norton Anthology of African American Literature,* edited by H. L. Gates and N. Y. McKay. New York: W. W. Norton and Company, 1997.

Douglas, C. L. *Cattle Kings of Texas*. Dallas: Cecil Baugh, 1939; Fort Worth: Branch-Smith, Inc., 1968; Austin: State House Press, 1989.

Downie, Alice E., ed. *Terrell County History: Its Past and Its People*. San Angelo, Tex.: Anchor Publishing Company, 1978.

Downie, Walter G. "Terrell County." In *The New Handbook of Texas,* edited by Ron Tyler and others. Vol. 6. Austin: Texas State Historical Association, 1996.

DuBois, W. E. B. *The Souls of Black Folk*. 1903. Reprint, New York: Fawcett Publications, 1970.

Duke, Cordia, and Joe B. Frantz. *6,000 Miles of Fence: Life on the XIT Ranch of Texas*. 1961. Reprint, Austin: University of Texas Press, 1969.

Durham, George. *Taming the Nueces Strip: The Story of McNelly's Rangers*. Austin: University of Texas Press, 1962.

Durham, Philip, and Everett L. Jones. *The Negro Cowboys*. New York: Dodd, Mead, 1965. Lincoln: University of Nebraska Press, 1983.

Dutton, Richard C. "Isom Prentice Olive (1840–1886)." In *The New Handbook of Texas History,* edited by Ron Tyler and others. Vol. 5. Austin: University of Texas Press, 1996.

Ehly, Jean. "'Bones' Hooks of the Panhandle." *Frontier Times* 37:4 (June–July, 1963): 20–23.

Emmett, Chris. *Shanghai Pierce.* Norman: University of Oklahoma Press, 1953.

Emrich, Duncan. *Folklore on the American Land.* Boston: Little, Brown, and Company, 1972.

Escott, Paul D. "The Art and Science of Reading WPA Slave Narratives." In *The Slave's Narrative,* edited by Charles T. Davis and Henry Louis Gates, Jr. New York: Oxford University Press, 1985.

Everett, Diana. *The Texas Cherokees: A People Between Two Fires, 1819–1840.* Norman: University of Oklahoma Press, 1990.

Fehrenbach, T. R. *Lone Star: A History of Texas and the Texans.* Toronto: Macmillan Company, 1968.

Fenley, Florence. *Oldtimers: Frontier Days in Uvalde Section of South West Texas.* 1939. Reprint, Austin: State House Press, 1991.

Fife, Austin E. and Alta S. *Cowboy and Western Songs.* Ojai, Calif.: Creative Concepts Publications, 1969.

Fleming, Elvis E. "Addison Jones, Famous Black Cowboy of the Old West," *Treasures of History III.* Roswell, N.Mex.: The Historical Society for Southeast New Mexico, 1995.

Folsom, Franklin. *Black Cowboy: The Life and Legend of George McJunkin.* 2nd ed. Niwot, Colo.: R. Rinehart Publishers, 1992.

Forbis, William. *The Cowboys.* New York: Time-Life Books, 1973.

Gard, Wayne. *Rawhide Texas.* Norman: University of Oklahoma Press, 1965.

———. *The Chisholm Trail.* Norman: University of Oklahoma Press, 1954.

Gill, Gale. "Texas Trail Ride, Negro Cowboys." *Ebony* 18 (May, 1963): 115–22, 124.

Gillespie, A. S. "More About Negro Cowmen." *Cattleman* 23 (June, 1936): 32.

Glasrud, Bruce, comp. *African Americans in the West: A Bibliography of Secondary Sources.* Edited by Sharon Smith Savage. Alpine: Center for Big Bend Studies, Sul Ross State University, 1998.

Goodnight, Charles. "Managing a Trail Herd." In *Texas History for High Schools and Colleges,* edited by Eugene C. Barker. Dallas: Southwest Press, 1929.

Govenar, Alan. "Musical Traditions of Twentieth Century African American Cowboys." In *Juneteenth Texas: Essays in African American Folklore,* edited by Francis Abernethy and others. Publication of the Texas Folklore Society. Denton: University of North Texas Press, 1996.

Gracy, David B., ed. *Establishing Austin's Colony.* Austin: The Pemberton Press, 1970.

Grant, Bruce. *The Cowboy Encyclopedia.* New York: Rand McNally, 1951.

Gray, Frank S. *Pioneer Adventures.* Cherokee, Tex.: n.p., 1948.

Green, Ben K. *A Thousand Miles of Mustangin'.* Flagstaff, Ariz.: Northland Press, 1972.

———. *Wild Cow Tales.* New York: Alfred A. Knopf, 1969.

Green, Bill. *The Dancing Was Lively, Fort Concho, Texas: A Social History, 1867–1882.* San Angelo: Fort Concho Sketches Publishing Co., 1974.

Greene, A. C. *900 Miles on the Butterfield Trail.* Denton: University of North Texas Press, 1994.

Grimes, Roy. *300 Years in Victoria County.* Victoria, Tex.: Victoria Advocate Publishing Co., 1968.

Hale, Will. *Twenty-Four Years A Cowboy and Ranchman.* Norman: University of Oklahoma Press, 1975.

Haley, J. Evetts. *Charles Goodnight: Cowman and Plainsman.* 1936. Reprint, Norman: University of Oklahoma Press, 1949.

———. *George W. Littlefield, Texan.* Norman: University of Oklahoma Press, 1943.

———. *The XIT Ranch of Texas and the Early Days of the Llano Estacado.* Chicago: Lakeside Press, 1929. Reprint, Norman: University of Oklahoma Press, 1967.

Haley, J. Evetts, and William Curry Holden. *The Flamboyant Judge: James D. Hamlin.* Canyon, Tex.: Palo Duro Press, 1972.

Hamersly, Thomas H. S. *Complete Regular Army Register of the United States from 1779 to 1879.* Washington, D.C.: T. H. S. Hamersly, 1880.

Hammond, Clara T., comp. *Amarillo.* Amarillo: George Autry Printer, 1971.

Hanes, Col. Bailey C. *Bill Picket, Bulldogger: The Biography of a Black Cowboy.* Norman: University of Oklahoma Press, 1977.

Hardman, Peggy. "Bob Lemmons." In *The New Handbook of Texas,* edited by Ron Tyler and others. Vol. 4. Austin: Texas State Historical Association, 1996.

Harmon, John H. "Black Cowboys are Real." *The Crisis: Periodical of the NAACP* 47 (September, 1940): 280–81, 301–302.

Hendrix, John M. *If I Can Do It Horseback: A Cow-Country Sketchbook.* Austin: University of Texas Press, 1964.

———. "Tribute Paid to Negro Cowmen." *Cattleman* 22 (February, 1936): 24, 26.

Hine, Darlene Clark. *Black Victory: The Rise and Fall of the White Primary in Texas.* Millwood: KTO Press, 1979.

Hinton, Harwood P. "Introduction." *History of the Cattlemen of Texas.* 1914. Reprint, Austin: Texas State Historical Association, 1991.

Holt, Roy D. "Allergic to Riders." *Sheep and Goat Raisers,* October, 1950, pp. 33–34.

Hunter, J. Marvin, comp. *The Trail Drivers of Texas.* 1925. Reprint, Austin: University of Texas Press, 1985.

Hunter, Lillie Mae. *The Book of Years.* Hereford, Tex.: Pioneer Book Publishers, Inc., 1969.

Jackson, Jack. *Los Mesteños: Spanish Ranching in Texas 1721–1821.* College Station: Texas A&M University Press, 1986.

James, Will. "Piñon and the Wild Ones." *Saturday Evening Post,* May 19, 1923.

Jay, William, and James Freeman Clark. *The Free People of Color.* 1838. 1839. Reprint, New York: Arno Press and The *New York Times,* 1969.

Jenkins, A. O. *Olive's Last Round-Up.* Loup City, Nebr.: *Sherman County Times,* 1930.

Jimenez, Diane, and George Southern. *Wilson County History.* Dallas: Taylor Publishing Company, 1990.

Johnson, Harrison. *Johnson's History of Nebraska.* Omaha: J. Gibson, 1880; New York: Arno Press, 1975.

Jones, Conger H. "Old Seminole Scouts Still Thrive on Border." *Frontier Times* 11:8 (May, 1934): 329.

Jones, Mat E. *Fiddlefooted.* Denver: Sage Books, 1966.

Jordan, Terry G. *North American Cattle-Ranching Frontiers: Origins, Diffusion, and Differentiation.* Albuquerque: University of New Mexico Press, 1993.

———. *Trails to Texas: Southern Roots of Western Cattle Ranching.* Lincoln: University of Nebraska Press, 1981.

Katz, William Loren. *The Black West: A Documentary and Pictorial History.* Garden City, N.Y.: Doubleday Anchor, 1973.

Kelton, Elmer. *Wagontongue.* New York: Ballantine, 1972.

Kerrigan, William T. "Race, Expansion, and Slavery in Eagle Pass, Texas, 1852." *Southwestern Historical Quarterly* 101:3 (January, 1998): 275–301.

Lack, Paul D. *The Texas Revolutionary Experience.* College Station: Texas A&M University Press, 1992.

Lanning, Jim and Judy, eds. *Texas Cowboys: Memories of the Early Days.* College Station: Texas A&M University Press, 1984.

Laws of the Republic of Texas, Passed at the Session of the Fourth Congress. Houston: Telegraph Power Press, 1840.

Laws of the Republic of Texas, Passed at the Session of the Fifth Congress. Vol. 2. Houston: Printed by Order of the Secretary of State, 1841.

Leckie, William H. *The Buffalo Soldiers, A Narrative of the Negro Cavalry in the West.* Norman: University of Oklahoma Press, 1967.

———. *Unlikely Warriors: General Benjamin Grierson and His Family.* Norman: University of Oklahoma Press, 1984.

Lowry, Jack. "The Forgotten Cowboys." *Texas Highways* 38 (August, 1991): 4–11.

MacGregor, Karen, and Tammy Wiloth. "Black Pioneers of Shackelford County." *Old Timer Magazine* 7 (1980): 10–13.

Marshall, Doyle. *A Cry Unheard: The Story of Indian Attacks In and Around Parker County, Texas.* [Texas]: Annetta Valley Farm Press, 1990.

Matagorda Historical Commission. *Historic Matagorda County.* Vol. 1. Houston: D. Armstrong Co., Inc., 1968.

"Mathew Hooks." *The Afro-American Texans.* San Antonio: Institute of Texan Cultures, 1987.

Matloff, Maurice, ed. *American Military History.* Washington, D.C.: GPO, 1969.

Matthews, Sallie Reynolds. *Interwoven: A Pioneer Chronicle.* 3rd ed. Austin: University of Texas Press, 1977.

McComb, David G. *Texas: A Modern History.* Austin: University of Texas Press, 1989.

McCoy, Joseph G. *Historic Sketches of the Cattle Trade of the West and Southwest.* Kansas City, Mo.: Ramsey, Millett & Hudson Printers, 1874. Reprint, Columbus, Ohio: Long's College Book Co., 1951.

Miles, Elton. *Stray Tales from the Big Bend.* College Station: Texas A&M University Press, 1993.

Moyers, Bill. "The Big Story: A Journalist Looks at Texas History." *Southwestern Historical Quarterly* 101:1 (July, 1997).

Mozique, Edward "Sancho." Interview, February 15, 1936. In *Heritage Quest: The Genealogy Magazine* 73 (January/February, 1998): 28.

Mulroy, Kevin. *Freedom on the Border: The Seminole Maroons in Florida, the Indian Territory, Coahuila, and Texas.* Lubbock: Texas Tech University Press, 1993.

"Negroes on the Cattlemen's Frontier." *Midwest Journal* 6 (1954–55): 35–48.

Nelson, Barney. *The Last Campfire: The Life Story of Ted Gray, A West Texas Rancher.* College Station: Texas A&M University Press, 1989.

Nolen, O. W. "Nicking the Mustang." In *Mustangs and Cow Horses,* edited by J. Frank

Dobie, Mody C. Boatright, and Harry Ransom. Dallas: Southern Methodist University Press, 1940.

———. "Shanghai Pierce." *Cattleman* 31:7 (December, 1944): 31.

Nordyke, Leslie. *Cattle Empire: The Fabulous Story of the 3,000,000 Acre XIT.* New York: William Morrow and Company, 1949.

O'Connor, Louise S. *Cryin' for Daylight: A Ranching Culture in the Texas Coastal Bend.* Austin: Wexford Publishing, 1989.

Olson, James C. *History of Nebraska.* Lincoln: University of Nebraska Press, 1955.

Osgood, Ernest Staples. *The Day of the Cattleman.* Minneapolis: University of Minnesota Press, 1929.

Payne, Marcello. "The Monroe Payne Family." In AnneJo Perry Wedin, *The Marvelous Marathon Basin: A History of Marathon, Texas, Its People and Events.* Austin: Nortex Press, 1989.

Perrigo, Lynn I. *The American Southwest: Its Peoples and Cultures.* New York: Holt, Rinehart and Winston, 1971.

Pfeffer, Paula F. *A. Philip Randolph: A Pioneer of the Civil Rights Movement.* Baton Rouge: Louisiana State University, 1990.

Pitre, Merline. *Through Many Dangers, Toils and Snares: The Black Leadership of Texas, 1868–1900.* Austin: Eakin Press, 1985.

Porter, Kenneth W. "Negroes and Indians on the Texas Frontier, 1983–1876." *The Journal of Negro History* 41:3 (July, 1956): 185–214; 41:4 (October, 1956): 285–310.

———. "Negro Labor in the Western Cattle Industry, 1866–1900." *Labor History* 10 (summer, 1969): 346–74.

———. "Negro Labor in the Western Cattle Industry, 1866–1900," *The Negro on the American Frontier.* New York: Arno Press and The *New York Times*, 1971.

———. "Negroes on the Frontier." *The Reader's Encyclopedia of the American West,* edited by Howard R. Lamar. New York: Thomas Y. Crowell, 1977.

———. *The Black Seminoles: History of a Freedom-Seeking People.* Revised and edited by Amos Alcione and Thomas Senter. Gainesville: University of Florida, 1996.

———. "The Cowkeeper Dynasty of the Seminole Nation." *Florida Historical Quarterly* 30 (1952): 341–49.

———. "The Seminole-Negro Scouts, 1870–1881." *Southwestern Historical Quarterly* 55:3 (January, 1952): 358–77.

Preece, Harold. "American Negro Cowboys." *Real West* 9 (January, 1966): 26–30.

Price, Eugene H. *Open Range Ranching On the South Plains in the 1890's.* Clarendon, Calif.: Clarendon Press, 1967.

Rathjen, Frederick W. *The Texas Panhandle Frontier.* Austin: University of Texas Press, 1973.

Rawick, George P., ed. *The American Slave: A Composite Autobiography.* Series 1, vols. 4–5. Westport, Conn.: Greenwood Press, 1972; Supplement, Series 2, vols. 2–10. Westport, Conn.: Greenwood Press, 1979.

Reid, John C. *Reid's Tramp or A Journal of the Incidents.* 1858. Reprint, Austin: Steck Company, 1935.

Rice, Lawrence D. *The Negro in Texas, 1874–1900.* Baton Rouge: Louisiana State University Press, 1971.

Richardson, Barbara J. "Black Cowboys Also Rode." *Password* 31 (spring, 1986): 29–34, 41.

Richardson, Rupert N., Ernest Wallace, and Adrian Anderson. *Texas: The Lone Star State.* Englewood Cliffs: Prentice-Hall, 1981.

Robert, Wilma Pinkston. "'80 John' Wallace: The Black Rancher Who Died Wealthy." *Oeste, The Magazine for West Texas* 1:1 (December, 1975): 54–56.

Roberts, Bruce. *Springs from the Parched Ground.* Uvalde, Tex.: Hornby Press, 1950.

Sampson, Henry T. *Blacks in Black and White: A Source Book on Black Films.* 2d ed.; Metuchen: Scarecrow Press, 1995.

Sandoz, Mari. *The Cattlemen: From the Rio Grande Across the Far Marias.* New York: Hastings House, 1958. Reprint, Lincoln: University of Nebraska Press, 1978.

Saunders, Guy. "The Empty Saddle." In *Amarillo,* compiled by Clara T. Hammond. Amarillo: George Autry Printer, 1971.

Savage, W. Sherman. *Blacks in the West: Contributions in Afro-American and African Studies,* No. 23. Westport, Conn.: Greenwood Press, 1976.

———. "The Negro Cowboys on the Texas Plains." *Negro History Bulletin* 24 (April, 1961): 157–58, 163.

Schoen, Harold. "The Free Negro in the Republic of Texas." *Southwestern Historical Quarterly* 39 (April, 1936): 292–308; 40 (July, 1936): 26–34; 40 (October, 1936): 85–113; 40 (January, 1937): 169–99; 40 (April, 1937): 267–89.

Sellers, Bonnie Cox. *Our Family Heritage.* Riverside, Calif.: A to Z Company, 1980.

Siringo, Charles. *Riata and Spurs.* Boston: Houghton Mifflin, 1927.

Skaggs, Jimmy M. *Prime Cut: Livestock Raising and Meatpacking in the United States, 1607–1983.* College Station: Texas A&M University Press, 1986.

Slatta, Richard W. *The Cowboy Encyclopedia.* New York: W. W. Norton & Company, 1996.

Smallwood, James. *The Struggle for Equality: Blacks in Texas.* Boston: American Press, 1983.

———. *Time of Hope, Time of Despair: Black Texans during Reconstruction.* Port Washington: Kennikat, 1981.

Smith, Julia. "Seven-D Ranch." In *The New Handbook of Texas,* edited by Ron Tyler and others. Vol. 5. Austin: Texas State Historical Association, 1996.

Smither, Harriet, ed. *Journals of the Fourth Congress of the Republic of Texas 1839–1840.* Vol. 1. Senate Journal. Austin: Von Boeckmann–Jones Co., 1929.

Smithers, W. D. "Bandit Raids in the Big Bend Country." *West Texas Historical and Scientific Society* 19 (1963): 74–105.

Speir, Thomas Earl. "Mustangs." In *The New Handbook of Texas,* edited by Ron Tyler and others. Vol. 4. Austin: Texas State Historical Association, 1996.

Spray, Barbara C. "Mathew Bones Hooks." *Texas Panhandle Forefathers,* edited by the Amarillo Genealogical Society. Vol. 1. Dallas: National ShareGraphics, 1983.

Stewart, Paul W., and Wallace Yvonne Ponce. *Black Cowboys.* Broomfield, Colo.: Phillips Publishing, 1986.

Stout, Joe A. "Cowboy." In *The Reader's Encyclopedia of the American West,* edited by Howard R. Lamar. New York: Thomas Y. Crowell, 1977.

Swallow, Alan, ed. *The Wild Bunch.* Denver: Sage Books, 1966.

Swanson, Donald, ed. "Enlistment Records of Indian Scouts Who Served in One of the Scout Detachments at Fort Clark, Texas." *Seminole Negro-Indian Detachment, August 1872–September 1914.* Vol. 1. Bronte, Tex.: Ames American Printing Co., 1985.

Taylor, Quintard. *In Search of the Racial Frontier: African Americans in the American West, 1528–1990.* New York: W. W. Norton, 1998.

The Texas Almanac for 1857 with Statistics, Historical and Biographical Sketches, etc." Galveston: Richardson and Co., 1856; Reproduction, Irving, Tex.: Glen's Sporting Goods, 1986.

Thorp, N. Howard (Jack). *Partner of the Wind: Story of the Southwestern Cowboy.* Caldwell, Idaho: Caxton Printers, Ltd., 1945.

———. *Songs of the Cowboy.* 1908. Reprint, New York: Clarkson N. Potter, Inc., 1966.

Thrapp, Dan L. *Encyclopedia of Frontier Biography.* 3 vols. Glendale, Calif.: The Arthur H. Clark Company, 1988.

Thurow, Roger. "Soiled Legacy: Black Farmers Hit the Road to Confront a 'Cycle of Racism.'" *Wall Street Journal,* May 1, 1998, p. 1.

Thyboyn, Scott. "Against all odds, Black Seminole who won their freedom." *Smithsonian* 22:5 (August, 1991): 90–101.

Tidwell, Laura Knowlton. *Dimmit County Mesquite Roots.* Vol. 1. Carrizo Springs, Tex.: Wind River Press, 1984.

Tinsley, Jim Bob. *He Was Singin' This Song.* Orlando: Florida University Press, 1982.

Tjarks, Alicia V. "Comparative Demographic Analysis of Texas, 1777–1793." *Southwestern Historical Quarterly* 77 (January, 1974): 291–338.

Towne, Charles Wayland, and Edward N. Wentworth. *Cattle & Men.* Norman: University of Oklahoma Press, 1955.

Tyler Ron, and Douglas E. Barnett, eds. *The New Handbook of Texas.* Austin: Texas State Historical Association, 1996.

Tyler, Ronnie C., and Lawrence R. Murphy, eds. *The Slave Narratives of Texas.* Austin: Encino Press, 1974.

U.S. Bureau of the Census. *Census of 1870. 1880. 1910. 1920. Brewster County, Presidio County, Jeff Davis County.* n.p. National Archives Microfilm Publication.

———. *Population of the United States, 1890.* Washington, D.C.: GPO, 1897.

———. *Eighth Census of the United States, 1860.* Washington, D.C.: GPO, 1864.

———. *Population Schedules of the Twelfth Census, 1900. Goliad, Texas.* No. T623, Roll 1638. n.p., National Archives Microfilm Publications.

———. *Census of 1880: Parker County.* No. 387, 396. Washington, D.C.: GPO.

———. *Census of 1900: Oldham County, Texas.* Washington, D.C.: GPO.

———. *Census of 1910: Hartley County, Texas.* Washington, D.C.: GPO.

———. *Negro Population, 1790–1915.* Washington, D.C.: GPO, 1918.

Utley, Robert. "The Range Cattle Industry in the Big Bend of Texas." *Southwestern Historical Quarterly* 69 (1966): 421–41.

Vannerson, Margaret, ed. *The Family History.* Redwood City, Calif.: Nona Lael (Vannerson) Trimble, 1961.

Vernam, Glenn R. *Man on Horseback.* 1964. Reprint, Lincoln: University of Nebraska Press, 1972.

A Visit to Texas in 1831. Houston: Cordovan Press, 1975.

Wallace, Edward. "General John Lapham Bullis, The Thunderbolt of the Texas Frontier." *Southwestern Historical Quarterly* 54 (1951): 452–61; 55 (1951): 77–85.

Webb, J. R. "Chapters from the Frontier Life of Phin W. Reynolds." *West Texas Historical Association Year Book* 20 (October, 1945): 140.

Webb, Walter Prescott. *The Handbook of Texas.* Vol. 1. Austin: Texas State Historical Association, 1952.

Weston, Jack. *The Real American Cowboy.* New York: New Amsterdam, 1985.

Wharton, Clarence. *History of Fort Bend County.* San Antonio: The Naylor Company, 1939.

White, Beth. *Goliad Remembered, 1836–1940.* Austin: Nortex Press, 1987.

White, Gifford M., ed. *The 1840 Census of the Republic of Texas.* Austin: The Pemberton Press, 1966.

Whitlock, V. H. *Cowboy Life on the Llano Estacado.* Norman: University of Oklahoma Press, 1970.

Wilbarger, J. W. *Indian Depredations in Texas.* Austin: Hutchings Printing House, 1889. Reprint, Austin: Pemberton Press, 1967.

Williams, Annie Lee. *A History of Wharton County, 1846–1961.* Austin: Von Boeckmann–Jones Company, 1964.

Williams, J. W. *The Big Ranch Country.* 1954. Reprint, Lubbock: Texas Tech University Press, 1999.

Wood, Peter H. *Black Majority: Negroes in Colonial South Carolina from 1670 through the Stone Rebellion.* New York: Alfred A. Knopf, 1974.

Woodward, C. Vann. "History from Slave Sources." *American Historical Review* 79 (April, 1974): 470–81.

Woolfolk, George R. *The Free Negro in Texas, 1800–1860: A Study in Cultural Compromise.* Ann Arbor: University Microfilms, 1976.

———. "Turner's Safety-Valve and Free Negro Westward Migration." *The Journal of Negro History* 50:3 (July, 1965).

Worcester, Don. *The Spanish Mustang: From the Plains of Andalusia to the Prairies of Texas.* El Paso: University of Texas at El Paso Press, 1986.

"W. S. Ikard." *Historical and Biographical Record of the Cattle Industry and the Cattlemen of Texas and Adjacent Territory.* Reprint, New York: Antiquarian Press, Ltd., 1959.

Wulfkuhle, Virginia. *Buttrill Ranch Complex: Brewster County, Texas.* Austin: Texas Historical Commission, 1989.

Wyman, Walker D. *The Wild Horse of the West.* Caldwell, Idaho: Caxton Printers, Ltd., 1945.

The XIT Brand, August, 1939, p. 40.

Yetman, Norman. "The Background of the Slave Narrative Collection." *American Quarterly* 19 (fall, 1967): 534–54.

Yoakum, H. *History of Texas from its first settlement in 1685 to its annexation to the United States in 1946,* 1855. Reprint, Austin: Steck-Vaughn Company, n.d.

Young, John. "The Reminiscences of John Young." In J. Frank Dobie, *A Vaquero of the Brush Country.* Boston: Little, Brown and Company, 1943.

NEWSPAPERS

Alpine Avalanche, April 28, 1921.

Amarillo Globe Times, November 14, 1973.

Amarillo Press, July 4, 1996.

Austin American Statesman, March 30, 1876.

Bell, Verner Lee. "Uncle Bob Lemmons." *Carrizo Springs Javelin,* August 10, 1933.

"Betting Was Strictly Private Affair in West Texas Races." *Fort Worth Star Telegram,* n.d.

Biffle, Kent. "Ikard Reunion Marked By an Odd Twist." *The Dallas Morning News,*
    Sunday, October 21, 1990.

"Bones' Bits," Farm and Ranch, *The Amarillo Press,* n.d., Mathew Hooks file, Amarillo
    Public Library.

"Bones Hooks." *Amarillo Globe,* n.d., Mathew Hooks file, Amarillo Public Library.

"Bose Ikard, Colored, One of Old-Time Negroes of City Buried Here Monday." *The*
    (Weatherford) *Daily Herald,* January 7, 1929.

"Chas. Goodnight Erects Monument to Negro Friend Buried Here." *The* (Weatherford)
    Daily Herald, June 8, 1929.

Cross, Cora Melton. "Stories of the Old Trail Drivers of Long Ago." *Semi-Weekly Farm
    News of Dallas, Texas,* August 26, 1930.

"Death Takes Bones Hooks." *Amarillo Daily News,* February 3, 1951.

Delaney, Tim. "Cowboy Folklorist Mack Williams' Rites Set in Tivoli." *Victoria
    Advocate,* April 11, 1998, p. 14A.

El Paso Evening Tribune, October 9, 1983.

Fenley, Florence. "Turns 'Mustang' to Catch Mustangs." *Uvalde Leader News,* September 3,
    1940.

Houston Chronicle, August 15, 1982.

Hunter, Charles. *El Paso Herald Post,* January 20, 1962.

Nebraska State Journal (Lincoln), January 30, 1879.

San Angelo Standard Times, April 3, 1934; April 10, 1949; June 10, 1949; April 21, 1951.

The Sanderson Times, September 29, 1939.

The Texas Ranger and Lone Star Newspaper, April 20, 1853. Texas State Archives.

Turner, George. "Black Cowboy 'Bones' Hooks Left his Mark on Frontier West's Lore."
    Amarillo Globe Times, November 14, 1973.

"Wildest Days Were Prior to 1880." *Carrizo Springs Javelin,* October 20, 1955.

Willems, George, and John Willems. "Dimmit County: The First Hundred Years, 1880–
    1980. *Carrizo Springs Javelin,* October 28, 1980.

UNPUBLISHED MATERIALS

Accounts of People, 1899–1914. Ledger. George Ranch Historical Park Archive,
    Richmond, Tex.

Adjutant General Papers. Texas State Archives, Austin, Tex.

African Americans: Robert Lemmons. Vertical Files. Institute of Texan Cultures, San
    Antonio.

Agee, Warren K. "A Study of Small-Town Life in the Texas Cattle County, 1880–1890, as Reflected in the Press of the Area and Period." Ph.D. dissertation, University of Minnesota, 1955.

Austin Colony Brand Book. Austin County Courthouse, Bellville, Tex.

Austin Papers. Center for American History, University of Texas, Austin.

Becht v. Martin Case Papers, No. 1353. Texas State Archives, Austin.

Bennett, Della Mae McDow. McDow Family Bible. Corpus Christi, Tex.

"Biographies of Leading Texans." Texas State Archives, Austin.

Blitch, Janie Helen Bowe. "Old Bob and the Pit and Allusive Revelations." M.A. thesis. University of Texas at Austin, 1970.

Bode, Anne, and Patsy Light. San Antonio River Valley (West of Goliad) Rural Historic District, National Register of Historic Places, Section 8. The Daughters of the Republic of Texas Library, San Antonio.

Boyd, Mrs. Lynn. "Sketch Of Lineage and History of Dr. Milton Ikard and His Sons." Ikard Surname File. Genealogy Department, Weatherford Public Library.

Brady, Marilyn Dell. "Monroe Payne: Descendent of a Black Seminole and Successful Entrepreneur in Brewster County, Texas." Forthcoming.

Brewster County Death Records, Payne File, Casey Collection, Archives of Big Bend, Sul Ross State University, Alpine, Tex.

Col. Isaac Payne, IV. "A History of the Payne-Huddleston Families, 1795–1998." Manuscript, in possession of author, Albuquerque, N.Mex., 1998.

Confederate Pension. Clay County, Texas. File No. 50238. Texas State Archives, Austin.

Curlee, Abigail. "A Study of Texas Slave Plantations, 1822–1865." Ph.D. dissertation, University of Texas, Austin, 1932.

Death Certificate of Addison Jones. Bureau of Vital Records & Health Statistics, Santa Fe, N.Mex.

Death Certificate of Alice Johnson. Tom Green County Records. Vol. 16. County Courthouse, San Angelo, Tex.

Death Certificate of Bose Ikard. Rep. No. 5569, 7231. Texas State Department of Health, Bureau of Vital Statistics, Austin.

Death Certificate of Edward Mozique. Tom Green County Records. Vol. 16. County Courthouse, San Angelo, Tex.

Death Certificate of Neptune Holmes. Office of Vital Statistics, Wharton County Courthouse, Wharton, Tex.

Death Certificate of Robert Lemmons. File No. 43. December 30, 1947. Department of Health, Bureau of Vital Statistics, State of Texas, Dimmit County Clerk, Carrizo Springs, Tex.

Deed Records of Chaves County. 1885. Addison Jones. Chaves County, Roswell, N.Mex.

Deed Records of Fort Bend County. Peter Martin. Book G. George Memorial Library, Richmond, Tex.

Deed Records of Hidalgo County. Nathaniel Jackson. Books A and C. Hidalgo County Historical Commission, Hidalgo, Tex.

Deed Records of Wilson County. Richard Walker. Book 2. Wilson County Courthouse, Floresville, Tex.

District Court Minutes. Peter Martin. Vol. F. George Memorial Library, Richmond, Tex.

Edwards, Cas. Payne Folder, Casey Collection, Archives of Big Bend, Sul Ross State University.

Estate of Robert Lemmons. Document 490. February 20, 1937. Dimmit County Clerk, Carrizo Springs, Tex.

Ferguson, Karen Ikard, letter. September 21, 1994. Ikard Surname File. Genealogy Department, Weatherford Public Library.

Fort Bend County Probate. Peter Martin. Vols. A, B, and Y. George Memorial Library, Richmond, Tex.

General Index to Deeds. 1887. Robert Lemmons. Book 4. Dimmit County Clerk, Carrizo Springs, Tex.

Graham, Joe S., and others. Ranching in South Texas: A Symposium. Kingsville, Tex., 1994.

Guffee, Eddie. "Camp Peña Colorado, Texas, 1879–1893." M.A. thesis, West Texas State University, 1976.

Haley, J. Evetts. "A Survey of Texas Cattle Drives to the North, 1866–1895." M.A. thesis, University of Texas, 1926.

Haynes, Rose Mary F. "Some Features of Negro Participation in Texas History Through 1879." M.A. thesis, Texas College of Arts and Industries, 1948.

Hidalgo County Census, 1860. Nathaniel Jackson. Hidalgo County Historical Commission, Hidalgo, Tex.

Historical Marker: D. W. "80 John" Wallace, 1860–1939." Mitchell County. Wallace Vertical Files. Institute of Texan Cultures, San Antonio.

Hitchcock, Totsy Nelle. "Representative Individuals and Families of the Lower Big Bend, 1895–1925." M.A. thesis, Sul Ross State University, 1960.

"How the Vigilantes Worked." Folder 166. McCarty Papers, Amarillo Public Library.

Index to Deeds Reverse: 1860–1889. Richard Walker. Vol. 1, Book S. Vol. 2. Wilson County Courthouse, Floresville, Tex.

Isbell, Frances W., letter to Alan Govenar. November 4, 1993. Nathaniel Jackson. Hidalgo County Historical Commission, Hidalgo, Tex.

Jackson, A. W. A Sure Foundation. MSS. George Memorial Library, Richmond, Tex.

J. H. P. Davis Papers. George Ranch Historical Park Archives, Richmond, Tex.

Kemp, Mary. "Bose Ikard (1843–1929)." Application for Texas Historical Marker, Bose Ikard File. J. Evetts Haley Collection, Nita Stewart Haley Memorial Library, Midland.

Kuykendall, J. H. "Capt. Wiley Martin." In "Sketches of Early Texians." Center for American History, University of Texas at Austin.

Maldonado, Juan Manuel, Colonia Militas de Rio Grande, Milican en Piedras Negras, letter to Office of the Chief Justice of the Military of the Rio Grande. September 22, 1851. Texas Ranger Archives, Waco, Tex.

Marriage Certificate: Addison Jones. Chaves County, Roswell, N.Mex.

Marriage Records: 1878–1891. Richard Walker. Vol. B, Certificate #756, Wilson County Courthouse, Floresville, Tex.

Marriage Records: 1891–1924, Texas. Jim Perry. Book 1. Hartley County. St. Louis, Mo.

Martin, James Lee. History of Goliad from 1836–1880. M.A. thesis, University of Texas at Austin, 1937.

"Matthew [sic] 'Bones' Hooks Chilli Prayer." African Americans: Matthew [sic] "Bones" Hooks Vertical File, Institute of Texan Cultures, San Antonio.

McArthur, Daniel Evander. "The Cattle Industry of Texas, 1685–1918." M.A. thesis, University of Texas at Austin, 1918.

McDonald, David. "Vaqueros: Role Models for Anglo-American Cowboys, the Origins of Cattle Ranching in Texas." Manuscript, Texas Parks and Wildlife, 1996.

Meade, Ben Carlton. Jim Perry File. XIT Museum, Dalhart, Tex.

"Mrs. Jesse Pettus-Wallace Memoirs." Pettus-Wallace Papers: 1836–1977. The Daughters of the Republic of Texas Library, San Antonio.

"Notes on the Payne Family of the Seminole Nation in Florida, the Indian Territory, Mexico, Texas, and Oklahoma." Kenneth Porter Collection. Schomburg Center for Research on Black Culture, New York Public Library.

Payne File. AnneJo Perry Wedin Collection. Archives of the Big Bend, Sul Ross State University.

Payne, Monroe. Casey Collection, Archives of Big Bend, Sul Ross State University.

Peareson, P. E. "Brief and Argument for Appellees." *Julius Becht vs. Judith Martin*, et al., Number 1353. Supreme Court of Texas, 1873. Texas State Archives, Austin.

Pease, E. M., letter to State Legislature. January, 1856. Governor's Papers. Texas State Archives, Austin.

Petition of Judith Martin, et al. Filed October 23, 1871. Texas State Archives, Austin.

Petition of Wyly Martin, November 5, 1839. Texas State Archives, Austin.

Pettus-Wallace Papers: 1836–1977. The Daughters of the Republic of Texas Library, San Antonio.

Probate Document. Robert Lemmons. Vol. 2, No. 685. Dimmit County Courthouse, Carrizo Springs, Tex.

Ramirez, Mary Alice. "Nathaniel Jackson—1858." Manuscript, Hidalgo County Historical Commission, Hidalgo, Tex.

Robert Lemmons. Vertical Files. Dimmit County Public Library, Carrizo Springs, Tex.

Records of Marks and Brands. May 29, 1882. Vols. 1, 2. Dimmit County Clerk, Carrizo Springs, Tex.

Records of Marriages, 1881. Robert Lemmons, Dimmit County Clerk, Carrizo Springs, Tex.

Ryon Farm and Pasture Co. 1897–1898. Ledger. Vols. B and C. George Ranch Historical Park Archives, Richmond, Tex.

Smith, Ikard. "The Real Lonesome Dove or Truth Can Be Stranger Than Fiction." The Cattle Raisers Museum, Fort Worth, Texas, n.d. Mimeographed.

Tax Assessment Records. 1908, 1909, 1911, 1912. Brewster Country, Archives of the Big Bend, Sul Ross State University.

Tax Rolls. Fort Bend County. George Memorial Library, Richmond, Tex.

Webb, Bertha Auburn. "D. W. '80 John' Wallace: Black Cattleman, 1875–1939." M.A. thesis, Prairie View Agricultural and Mechanical College, 1957.

William Stiles Succession Records. File #1. Fort Bend County Courthouse, Richmond, Tex.

Williams, Crystal S. A History of Dimmit County. Manuscript. Dimmit County Clerk, Carrizo Springs, Tex. 1960.

Will of Wyly Martin, September 3, 1833. Succession of Wyly Martin. Fort Bend County Probate, Vol. A, MSS, George Memorial Library, Richmond, Tex.

Wortham, Sue Clark. "The Role of the Negro on the Texas Frontier, 1821–1836." M.A. thesis, Southwest Texas State University, 1970.

U.S., Eighth Census of the United States, 1860. Fort Bend County. Schedule 1. National
Archives, Washington, D.C.

U.S., Census of 1880. Jackson County, Clayton Genealogical Library, Houston.

U.S., Seventh Census of the United States, 1850. Fort Bend County. Schedule 1. Fort
Bend County. National Archives, Washington, D.C.

U.S., Works Progress Administration (WPA), Federal Writers Project. Slave Narratives,
Texas. Part 1, Box A930. Part 2, Box A931. Part 3, Box A931. Part 4, Box A392.
Manuscript Division, Library of Congress, Washington, D.C.

U.S., Works Progress Administration (WPA), Federal Writers' Project. Slave Narratives,
Texas. "Reference[:] Interview with Joe Oliver, R. F. D. Mart-Waco Road." Tran-
script, 1937. WPA. Records: Slave Narratives. Box 4H361. Center for American
History, University of Texas at Austin.

INTERVIEWS

Adams, Mischa Benson (granddaughter of George Benson). Personal communication,
1998.

Albrecht, Herbert "Blue," and Ralph Bego. Interview by Louise S. O'Connor. Goliad,
Tex., June 21, 1990.

Baird, Martha. Telephone interview by Lee N. Coffee, Jr. May 8, 1998.

Barefield, Desaline Spriggs (great-granddaughter of Henrietta Williams Foster).
Interview by Louise S. O'Connor. Seadrift, Tex., October 15, 1990.

Bennett, Della Mae McDow (daughter of George McDow). Interview by Ira Lott.
Corpus Christi, Tex., March 8, 1998.

Beverly, Bob. Interview by J. Evetts Haley. June 27, 1946. Handwritten. J. Evetts Haley
Collection, Nita Stewart Haley Memorial Library.

Bode, Anne (granddaughter of James Edward Pettus). Interviews by Ira Lott. Goliad,
Tex., April 13 and May 27, 1998.

Boyd, Hiley T., Jr. Interview by David Gracy. May 19, 1969. Audiocassette. Southwest
Collection, Texas Tech University.

Brown, James (great-grandson of Charley Willis). Telephone interview by Jim Chilcote.
May 7, 1998.

Brown, Willie, Jesse Jones, and L. V. Terrell. Interview by Louise S. O'Connor. Gaffney
Ranch, Victoria County, Tex., 1987.

Crittenden, Verlee Power, Rachel Power Hayes, Adele Power Osborne, Delores Power,
and Elneta Power Roland (all daughters of Louis Power). Interview by Louise S.
O'Connor. Victoria, Tex., 1983.

Davis, Bill (grandson of C. F. Cox). Interview by Ken Howell. San Antonio, April 10,
1998, audiocassette. Research Library, Institute of Texan Cultures, San Antonio.

Davis, Jim (grandson of C. F. Cox). Interview by Ken Howell. San Antonio, April 11,
1998, audiocassette. Research Library, Institute of Texan Cultures, San Antonio.

———. Interview by Sara R. Massey. San Antonio, April 7, 1998, audiocassette.
Research Library, Institute of Texan Cultures, San Antonio.

de la Garza, Rafael. Interview by Louise S. O'Connor. Victoria County, Tex., 1983.

Garcia, Alberto Ureta. Interview by John Klingman. Marathon, Tex., February 21, 1998, Transcript. Center for Big Bend Studies, Sul Ross State University.

Geron, Nora Payne (granddaughter of Monroe Payne) and Manuel Payne (grandson of Monroe Payne). Interview by Marilyn Dell Brady. Alpine, Tex., February 26, 1998. Transcript. Archives of the Big Bend, Sul Ross State University.

Geron, Nora Payne. Interview by Marilyn Dell Brady. Pecos, Tex., June 21, 1998. Archives of the Big Bend, Sul Ross State University.

Gordon, Morgan, Jr. (grandson of John Payne). Interview by Marilyn Dell Brady. Pecos, Tex., July 1, 1998. Archives of the Big Bend, Sul Ross State University.

Green, Josephine Spriggs (great-granddaughter of Henrietta Williams Foster). Interview by Louise S. O'Connor. Refugio, Tex., May 11, 1990.

Harral, Ed. Interview by J. Evetts Haley and Hervey Chesley. Roswell, N.Mex., June 13, 1939. Handwritten. J. Evetts Haley Historical Collection, Nita Stewart Haley Memorial Library.

Harris, Jamie Walker (grandniece of Richard Walker). Interview by Lee N. Coffee, Jr. San Antonio, February 9, 1998.

———. Telephone interview by Lee N. Coffee, Jr. March 26, 1998.

Holmes, Bill (grandson of Neptune Holmes). Interview by Charlie Woodson. Granado, Tex., September 19, 1998.

Ikard, Bose. Interview by J. Evetts Haley. January 26, 1932. J. Evetts Haley Collection, Nita Stewart Haley Memorial Library.

Ikard, W. S. Interview in "The Ikards In Texas," Ikard Surname File, Genealogy Department, Weatherford Public Library.

Jackson, Quentin. Telephone interview by Alan Govenar. July 12, 1994.

Jacobs, Vincent. Interview by Alan Govenar. Raywood, Tex., March 4, 1993.

Kemp, Mary. Interview by Bruce Shackelford. Weatherford, Tex., May 4, 1998.

Laday, Elton. Interview by Alan Govenar. Raywood, Tex., March 4, 1994.

Ledbetter, Morris. Interview by Lawrence Clayton. Albany, Tex., August 15, 1991.

Matthews, Walt. Interview by Lawrence Clayton. Lambshead Ranch, August 19, 1991.

Moore, Vyree Willis (great-granddaughter of Charley Willis). Interview by Jim Chilcote. Temple, Tex., March 31, 1998.

Morris, Vera. Telephone interview by Ron Wilhelm. May 29, 1998.

Mozique, Edward "Sancho." Interview by J. Evetts Haley. October 20, 1946. Transcript. J. Evetts Haley Collection, Nita Stewart Haley Memorial Library.

Newton, William Carey. Interview by Adele Howell. Transcript, c. 1939, Panhandle-Plains Museum, Canyon, Tex.

O'Connor, Tom, Jr. (III). Interview by Louise S. O'Connor. Gaffney Ranch, Victoria, Tex., November 18, 1986, November 18, 1990.

"Old Bones." Interview with History Class 413. April 16, 1933, Transcript, Panhandle-Plains Museum Library, West Texas A&M University, Canyon.

Pate, Jack. Telephone interview by Lawrence Clayton. August 21, 23, 1991.

Payne, Blas (son of John Payne). Interview by Theresa Whittington. Camp Peña Colorado, Tex., May 3, 1976. Transcript. Archives of the Big Bend, Sul Ross State University.

Payne, Rocky (son of Monroe Payne). Interview by Jim Cullen, Alpine, Tex., June 12, 1983. Transcript. Archives of the Big Bend, Sul Ross State University.

Payne, Thomas (son of Monroe Payne). Interview by Jim Cullen. Alpine, Tex., June 10, 1983. Transcript. Archives of the Big Bend, Sul Ross State University.

———. Interview by Virginia Wulfkuhle. Alpine, Tex., August 19, 1984. Handwritten with Marilyn Dell Brady.

Peeler, Tom E. (grandson of Thomas M. Peeler). Interviews by Lee N. Coffee, Jr. Pleasanton, Tex., May 4 and 5, 1998.

Power, Louis. Interview by Verlin Vandenburge, ca. 1941. In Louise S. O'Connor, *Cryin' for Daylight: A Ranching Culture in the Texas Coastal Bend.* Victoria: Wexford Publishing, 1989.

"Recollections of Early Day Texas: Mathew (Bones) Hooks." Interview by A. B. Hays. Amarillo, Tex., July 15, 1939, Manuscript interview file, Panhandle-Plains Museum Library, West Texas A&M University, Canyon, Tex.

Resberry, Izola. Telephone interview by Sara R. Massey. August 15, 1998.

Roberts, Travis (son of Jim Roberts). Interview by Jim Cullen. July 26, 1986, Transcript. Archives of Big Bend, Sul Ross State University.

Rydolph, Simmie, and Monroe "Bailey" Shaw. Interview by Louise S. O'Connor. Refugio, Tex., March 1, 1983.

Shelton, Tom. Interview by Sara R. Massey. San Antonio, June 29, 1998.

Stevenson, Molly. Interview by Alan Govenar. Houston, December 3, 1993.

Thompson, Milam. Interview by Louise S. O'Connor. Gaffney Ranch, Victoria County, Tex., 1987.

Walker, A. J. Interview by Alan Govenar. Raywood, Tex., March 4, 1993; April 27, 1994; April 1, 1995; February 22–23, 1998; March 31, 1998; April 1, 1998; May 4, 1998.

Walker, C. W., W. W. Walker, and W. D. Walker. Interview by J. Evetts Haley. Dunlap, N.Mex., August 5, 1937. Handwritten. J. Evetts Haley Collection, Nita Stewart Haley Memorial Library.

Walker, John W. Interview with Lee Coffee, Jr. San Antonio, March 23, 1998.

Warrior, Ethel. Interview by Jim Coffey. Del Rio, Tex., July 3, 1998.

Warrior, William. Interview by Jim Coffey. Del Rio, Tex., December 22, 1997; March 18, 1998; May 12, 1998.

Williams, Doris (wife of T. J. Williams). Interview by Tony Sherman. Live Oak, Tex., July, 1998.

Williams, Josephine. Interview by Lawrence Clayton. Albany, Tex., September 1, 1991.

Williams, Lela Edwards. Interview by Louise S. O'Connor. Refugio, Tex., May 11, 1990.

Williams, Mack, Sr. Interview by Anthony P. Griffin. Victoria, Tex., March 1, 1998.

———. Interview by Sara R. Massey. Austwell, Tex., September 27, 1996. Transcript. Research Library, Institute of Texan Cultures, San Antonio.

Williams, T. J. Interview by Tony Sherman. Live Oak, Tex., August, 1989.

Winsor, Joyce Anderson. Interview by Louise S. O'Connor. Refugio, Tex., March 24, 1995.

Works Progress Administration, U.S., Federal Writers Project. American Life Histories: Edward "Sancho" Mozique. Interview. February 15, 1936. American Memories Collection, Library of Congress.

AUDIOTAPES, VIDEOTAPES, AND RECORDS

Alfred Snuff Johnson: Black Cowboy Blues and Church Songs. Dallas: Documentary Arts, 1994. Audiocassette.

Emrich, Duncan. *Cowboy Songs, Ballads, and Cattle Calls from Texas.* LP Record No. AAFS L28 ca. 1948. Washington, D.C.: Archive of American Folk Song, Library of Congress, 1949.

The Hard Ride: Black Cowboys at the Circle 6 Ranch. Produced and directed by Alan Govenar. 26.38 min. Documentary Arts, 1996. Videocassette.

The Other Cowboys Forum: Mack Williams. San Antonio: Institute of Texan Cultures, 1997. Videocassettes.

Workin' from Can't to Can't: African American Cowboys in Texas. Produced and directed by Leslie Burns. 27 min. San Antonio: Institute of Texan Cultures, 1995. Videocassette.

ONLINE

U.S., Works Progress Administration, Federal Writers Project. American Life Histories: Ben Kinchlow: Range Lore and Negro Cowboy Reminiscences Before and After 1875. Uvalde County, District 15. Interview by Florence Angermiller. American Memories Collection, Library of Congress, 1936–1940. Online, July, 1998. (http://www.lcweb.loc.gov/)

U.S., Works Progress Administration, Federal Writers Project. American Life Histories: Bones Hook. American Memories Collection, Library of Congress, 1936–1940. Online, July, 1998. (http://www.lcweb.loc.gov/)

U.S., Works Progress Administration, Federal Writers Project. American Life Histories: Johanna July. Interview by Florence Angermiller. American Memories Collection, Library of Congress, 1936–1940. Online, August, 1998. (http://www.lcweb.loc.gov/)

Index

Brewster County, 166, 169, 257, 262, 318

Brinckley, Jack, 315

bronc busting, 173, 193, 196, 208, 219, 222, 237–38, 274. *See also* horses, breaking

Brookshire, George, 229

Brotherhood of Sleeping Car Porters, 237

Broughton, Mr. 284

Brown, W. T. 208

Brownsville, Tex., 55, 100–105, 113, 295; Chisholm Trail, 108; common escape route for slaves, 102

Bryan, William Jennings, 235

buffalo, 89, 225; chips as fuel, 112; chip races, 112; slaughter of, 188

Buffalo Gap, Tex., 135, 184

Buffalo Soldiers, 85, 225

Bugbee, Mrs. Thomas S., 227

bulldogger, 173, 291

Bullis, John, 262

bull riders, 173, 177, 293

Burleson, Aaron (slaveowner), 53

Burleson, Cecelia, 53

Burleson, Matilda (slaveowner), 53

Burnett, Talley, 28

Burton, Mose, 315

Bushy Creek, 315

Bustamonte, Cruz, 260–61

Butler family (slaveowners), 307

Buttrill, Lou, 257–58

buzzard, 31

C. F. Cox Ranch, 166, 318

calf roping, 30, 266, 287

Calvary Baptist Church of Goliad, 126

Cameron, Tex., 177

Campbell, Tom, 127

Camp Peña Colorado, 262

Canadian River, 155, 225, 227

Cape, James: cattle rustling, 34

Carhart, Reverend Lewis Henry, 226

Carrizo, Tex., 30

Carrizo Springs, 53, 55, 61

Carrizo Springs Javelin, 57

Carvalos, Narciso, 295

Casey, Ethel Matthews, 156, 159

Casimiro Romero place, 212

Castle Gap, 135

Catholic settlers, 67

cattle, x–xii, 4, 10, 40, 119, 248, 249; breeding, 11, 232, 255; cutting, 29, 252; dipping, 232, 247; Durham, 187; in exchange for wages, 167, 216; Hereford, 137, 187; horns of fire, 185, 188; industry, xi, 301–302; Longhorn, xi, xiii, 88, 103, 127, 129, 135, 174, 275, 277; markets, 135; Polled Angus, 229; price of, 108, 128, 145; roping, 30, 266; roundups, 32, 145; rustling, 34–35, 104, 184, 231, 232, 259; shipping by railroad, 96, 233, 255; stampedes, 24, 30, 109, 111, 136, 145, 174, 185, 251; wild, 10, 29, 40, 125, 216, 232

cattle drives, 10–11, 25, 29–30, 40, 43, 96, 103, 129, 135, 145, 154, 174, 216, 255; described, 108, 128, 136; entertainment on, 183; financial opportunity, 126, 133

Cattleman, The, magazine, 188

Cattle Raisers Association of Texas, 11

cattle trails. *See* Chisholm Trail; Goodnight-Loving Trail; Shawnee Trail; Western Trail

Cedar Grove Cemetery, 108

census, xiii–xv, 6, 120, 207, 211, 234, 258, 263

Chambers County, 295

Channing, Tex., 209

Channing Cemetery, 212

Channing-Tascosa, 211

Charleson, Jeff, 315

Charlotte, Tex., 276

Cheeks, Tex., 296

Cheyenne Indians, 26

Chicago "C" Ranch, 229

Chin, Priscilla, 120

Chin, William, 119, 120

chip races. *See* buffalo: chip races

Chisholm Trail, 96, 108–109, 145, 165

Chisos Mountains, 255

Chisum, John, 194

Chisum, Sally, 223

Chisum family, 316

Grant, George, 316
Gray, Ted, 260
Great Depression, 12–13, 56, 73, 166–67, 187
Green, Arthur, 119
Green, Bill, 147, 149
Green, "Toad," 316
Green, Widow, 85
Greenville, Tex., 166
Greenwood Cemetery, 137
greyhounds, 157
Grierson, Benjamin H., 86
Grierson, Edith, 87
Grimes, W. G. B., 108, 118
Grimes Ranch, 118
Grimes (ventriloquist), 89
Grindstone Creek, 133
Groesbeck, Tex., 316
Guadalupe County, 315
Guadalupe River, 185
Guerndons of Honor, 240
Guerra, Louisa, 61
guns, 28, 120, 146, 165, 184, 257; blacks can't carry, 107; six-shooter, 119; Winchester, 31, 147
gunslinger, xvii, 144, 146, 148, 259

Haley, J. Evetts, 85, 87, 134, 136, 193–95, 197, 210
Hamlin, Judge James D., 236
Hamm, Ed, 293
Handbook of Texas, 193
Hanes, Colonel Bailey, 291
hangings, cattle thieves, 232
Hannibal & St. Joe Railroad, 96
Harris, Jamie, 276
Harris, Mrs., 278
Harris County, 315
Hartley County, 207, 210
Harvey, Jack, 315
Hashknife Ranch, 229, 231
Haskins, Rosa, 200
Hastings, Nebr., 150
Hatch, Colonel Edward, 85
Hat Ranch, 198

Hawkins and Sanders Ranch, 283
Hawkins Ranch, 284
Hawley Cemetery, 121
Hays County, 193
Hearst, Randolph, 186
Hell Roaring Creek, 109
Hendrix, John, 155, 188, 194
Henrietta, Tex., 137, 224, 229, 232
Henry, "Big Mouth," 316
Hereford cattle, 11, 137, 187
Herrington, E. W., 274
Herron, Mose, 315
Hewetson, James, 247
Hext, Sam, 315
Hidalgo County, 295
hide and tallow business, 4, 6, 95
Hidetown, Tex., 225. *See also* Mobeetie, Tex.
Holmes, Allen, 119
Holmes, Bill, 119
Holmes, Horace "Dick," 119
Holmes, Isaac, 118
Holmes, Neptune, 117–21, 318
Homestead Act of 1862, 148
Hondo, Tex., 26, 28, 31
Hondo Canyon, 29
Hondo River, 26
Honey Grove, Tex., 133
Hooks, Anna, 236, 238
Hooks, Clem, 241
Hooks, Mathew "Bones," 218–45, 317; breaking horses, 221; Clarendon, 226; horse wrangler, 219; humor, 224; on pioneers, 228; porter, Elmhurst Hotel, 236; porter, railroad, xv, 13, 216, 237; union, refuses to join, 237; white flowers, 234
Hooks, Tex., 220
Hooks, Warren "Cullen" (slaveowner), 220, 221
Horse, John Caballo: Black Seminole translator, 74; returned to slavery, 103
Horsehead Crossing, 85, 135
horses, x, xv, 110, 175, 185, 188, 208; drives, 35, 41; frozen in blizzard, 109, 155–56;

Mertz, M. L., 88
Mexican Constitution of 1824, 67
Mexican Revolution, 262
Milam County, 174, 177
Miller, Albert, 29
Miller, Ellis, 316
Mills, Tom, 28
Missouri Pacific Railroad, 96
Mitchell, Isaac Newton (slaveowner), 68
Mitchell, Luther, 149
Mitchell County, Tex., 184, 186–88
Mobeetie, Tex.: black community 225, 231, 235
Moneil, Neil, 207
Monkhouse, George, 274
Montague, Charley, 29
Moore, Buck, 315
Moore, Lizaar, 100–101
Moore, Mr., 106
Moore, Sandy (slaveowner), 100
Moore, Vyree Willis, 177
Morgan School, 264
Morris, Al, 212
Morris, Bobbie, 212
Morris, E. J., 174–75
Morris, Jesse, 175
Morris, Ruth, 177
Morris, Victoria, 177
Morris, Will Arthur "Artie," 173, 177
Morris Ranch, 174
Moss, Ellie, 68
Mount Olive Baptist Church, 121
Mount Zion Baptist Church, 241
Moyers, Bill, 303, 312n, 313
Mozique, Alice, 89
Mozique, Edward "Sancho," 84–91;
    Buffalo Soldier, 85; wages, 87, 89
Mozique, Edward, Jr., 90
mulatto, 247, 250, 283; social outcast, 249
mules, 221, 224, 292; frozen, 156; in wild
    horse herds, 50–51
Mulroy, Kenneth, 263
Musquiz, Mexico, 74
mustanger, 49
mustangs. *See* horses: wild, mustangs

NAACP, 12
Nacimiento Los Negros, Mexico, 74
Nacogdoches, Tex., 3
Nash, Mr., 229
Nasworthy, Sarge, 87
National Colonization Law of 1823,
    Mexico, 39
Navarro County, 187
Navidad River, 185
Nebraska State Penitentiary, Print Olive
    incarcerated at, 150
Neely, Jerry, 176
Negro Sam, 315
Nenescah River, 146
nestors, 112, 127, 129
Newberry, Sam, 134
"nigger," use of word, 194
"Nigger" Ed, 316
Ninth Cavalry, 85–86
Nordyke, 207
Norman, Biddy, 283
Norman, John, 283
Norman, Nathaniel, 283
Norris, J. R., 224
North Heights, 238–39; black community,
    220
North Texas Cattle Raisers Association,
    137
Nueces River, 19
Nunn, Bill, 49
Nunn, Clay, 183

O'Connor (slaveowners), 307
O'Connor, Dennis M., 248
O'Connor, Joe, 248, 251
O'Connor, Mama, 71
O'Connor, Thomas II, 68, 248–49, 251,
    308
O'Connor, Tom, 248, 308
O'Connor, Tom, Jr., 68, 249, 252
O'Connor Duke Ranch, 248
O'Connor family, 126
O'Connor Melon Ranch, 247
O'Connor Ranch, Duke Division, 318
O'Daniel, Dial, 182

slaves (*cont.*)

Bose, 133; Jim, 40; Jones, Addison, 193; Jones, Bob, 43–44; Kinchlow, Ben, xvi, 100; Lemmons, Robert, 53; Mack, Ben 126; Martin, Peter, 39; McDow, George, 125, 126; Moore, Lizaar, 100; Mozique, Edward "Sancho," 85; Phillips, Daniel, Sr., 25; Shelton, Harriet, 125; Shelton, John, 125; Small, Classie, 127; Smith, R. C., 25; Walker, Jim, 273; Wallace, Daniel Webster "80 John," 182; Wallace, Mary, 182; Williams, Butler, 307; Williams, Thornton, 307; Willis, Charley, 174

Slaveholders: Burleson, Aaron, 53; Burleson, Matilda, 53; Butler, Mr., 307; Creek Indians, 74; Dailey, Dr. (father), 25; Dailey, Dr. Thomas (son), 25; English, Levi, 53; Fleming, Dr. Edward, 85; Green, Widow, 85; Hooks, Warren (Cullen), 220; Ikard, Dr. Milton, 133; Jones, Henry, 40; Lipston (Lipscomb), Dr., 126; Lott, Mr., 100; Loving, Oliver, 134; Martin, Wyly, 40; Mitchell, Isaac Newton, 68; Moore, Sandy, 100; O'Connor, Mr., 307; O'Daniel, Mr., 181; Reedes, George, 26–27; Smith, Presley, R., 25; Stroud, Mr., 316; Thornton, Mr., 307

Small, Classie, 127

Smith, Charley: killed by Indians, 26

Smith, E. D., 295

Smith, Hubert, 292

Smith, John, 158

Smith, Presley R.(slaveowner), 25

Smither, Lieutenant Robert, 87

snakes: rattlesnakes, 111, 135; water moccasins, 111

Sneed, John, 27

Snyder brothers, 174

social mores, 211

social stratification, 216

sodbusters, 148. *See* nestors

Sol West Ranch, 108

songs, 174–75, 177, 193, 287; *Black Texas Cowboy, The* 287–88; *Goodbye Old Paint,* 176; *Whose Old Cow,* 202–203

songwriters, 193, 199, 287

Soria, Fidel, 256

South Loup River, 147

South Platte River, 108, 112

Southwestern Cowboy Association, 287

Sowell, Dan, 235, 315

Spade Ranch, 316

Spanish land grant of 1767, 295

spurs, 117, 173; "chicken bones," 156; *Riata and Spurs,* 183

Stamford, Tex., 159

stampedes, 24, 30, 109, 111, 136, 145, 174, 185, 251

Standifer, Charles, 157–58

Standifer, J. W., 209

Stanford, 264

Stanley, T. W., 138

St. Elmo's fire: illuminates cow horns, 185, 188

Stevens (Olive), Bob, 147

Stevenson, Boot, 215

Stevenson, Mollie, 295

Stillwell family, 258

Stockdale, Tex., 106

Stonewall County, 207

Story of 80 John: A Biography of One of the Most Respected Negro Ranchmen in the Old West, 181

St. Paul, Tex.: founded by ex-slaves, 125–26

St. Paul's AME Church, 90

Stringtown, Tex., 25

Stroud, Mr. (slaveowner), 316

Sugg, J. D., 88

Sugg Ranch, 89

Suggs, Colonel, 127

Sullivan, Daniel, 118

Sully, Alfred, 226

Sul Ross University, 265

Sumiter County, 39

superstition, 88–89

Sweeney, Otis, 285

Sweetwater Creek, 225

swimming the herd, 185, 194

Williams, Doris (wife of TJ), 286
Williams, Fannie, 306
Williams, Josephine, 158
Williams, Levi, 283
Williams, Mack, xvii, 300–315; ancestors, 306–308; Baptist preacher, 301
Williams, Mr. (husband of Henrietta Foster), 70
Williams, Norman, 286
Williams, Roy, 303
Williams, Thornton, 303, 307
Williams, Tracy, 287
Williams, Troy John, xvii, 282–89; ancestors, 283; breaking horses, 284–85; breaks color barrier, 285
Williamson County, 143–44, 207
Willis, Andrew 174
Willis, Clemmer "Bud," 174
Willis, Charley, 172–79; singing, 174–75
Willis, Franklin, 177
Willis, Joshua, 174
Willis, Magdalene, 174
Willis Connection, 177
Wilson, Adam, 76; Black Seminole scout, 75
Wilson, Jim P., Sr., 263
Wilson, Judge, 227

Wilson, One-armed Bill, 135
Wilson, Sarah, 118
Wilson County, 273–75, 317
Wilson Ranch, 263
Wimbish, Sandy, 316
Winchester, Tex., 316
windmills, 11, 187, 216
wolves, 168
women: civilized the West, 227
Word, Charley, 108
Word, Ike, 10
Working Cowboy Award, 278
Works Progress Administration: duties of, 224, 264; interviews, 24–27, 73, 86, 101, 113; purpose of, 36n 2; wrangler, 145
"W" Ranch, 229
Wright, Bob, 225

XIT Ranch, 155, 208–209, 226, 228, 231, 318; last roundup before fencing, 207; state capitol land deal, 207

Young, John, 50
Young, Reverend L. C., 90
Young, Sam (slaveowner), 24

Zavala County, 29, 49

Covent Garden

The Untold Story

Music advisor to Northeastern University Press
GUNTHER SCHULLER

Covent Garden
The Untold Story

Dispatches from the English Culture War, 1945–2000

NORMAN LEBRECHT

Northeastern University Press
BOSTON

First published in 2000 in England by Simon & Schuster UK Ltd, London.
Published in 2001 in the United States of America by
Northeastern University Press, by arrangement
with Simon & Schuster UK Ltd.

All pictures used by kind permission of the Lebrecht Collection.

Library of Congress Cataloging-in-Publication Data

Lebrecht, Norman, 1948–
Covent Garden : the untold story : dispatches from
the English culture war, 1945–2000 / Norman Lebrecht.
p. cm.
Includes bibliographical references and indexes.
ISBN 1-55553-488-0 (cloth : alk. paper)
1. Royal Opera House (London, England). 2. Great Britain – Intellectual life –
20th century. 3. Opera – England – 20th century. 1. Title

ML1731.8.L72 C63 2001
782.1′09431′3209045 – dc21   2001031720

MANUFACTURED IN GREAT BRITAIN
05 04 03 02 01   5 4 3 2 1

For

Elbie, Naama, Abigail and Gabriella

Acknowledgements

I have received tremendous assistance in researching this book from dozens of people in all walks of life, some of whom do not wish to be named. I am particularly grateful to the 12th Earl of Drogheda for letting me look after and quote from his father's papers; to Ken Davison (Lord Brochaine) for his friendship and memories; to the Board of the Royal Opera House for allowing me partial access to their archives; to the ROH archivists Francesca Franchi and Jane Jackson; to the many artists, staff and directors who gave liberally of their time and memorabilia; to my assistants, Joanna Collins and Catherine Best; and to my nearest and dearest who put up with two years of mental absenteeism.

I have been helped in various ways, above and beyond the demands of friendship and collegiality, and sometimes more than they knew, by:

Mary Allen, Peter Alward, Helen Anderson, Peter Andry, Tim Ashley, Dave Ashton, Ewen Balfour, Lady Barbirolli, Richard Bebb, Eduardo Benarroche, Catherine Best, Sir Harrison Birtwistle, Gillian Brierley, Ismene Brown, Teresa Cahill, Patrick Carnegy, Alexander Chancellor, Joanna Collins, Keith Cooper, Jilly Cooper, Sarah Crompton, John Denison, Peter Diamand, Geoffrey Douch, Sir Anthony Dowell, Sir Edward Downes, David Drew, Paul and Francoise Findlay, Eva Foley-Comer, Massimo Freccia, Betty Freeman, Daniele Gatti, Peter Gellhorn, Paul Gent, Valery Gergiev, Lord Gibson, Lord Gilmour, Berthold Goldschmidt, Lord Gowrie, Judy Grahame, Rita Grudzien, Michael Haas, Dame Heather Harper, Seppo Heikinheimo, Gavin Henderson, Lillian and Victor Hochhauser, Manuela Hoelterhoff, Sir Jeremy Isaacs, Alan

Contents

I sometimes think that more has changed since 1945 than in all the years of history there have ever been. I don't know what to make of the end of so many things.

Lou Levov, in Philip Roth's *American Pastoral*

CHAPTER 1

Come into the Garden, Awed

IN THE MIDDLE of most great cities there stands an opera house: part monument, part amenity. In teeming, congested New York, the Metropolitan Opera proclaims its importance with an extravagance of space and wealth. In Paris, the gilded, primping Opéra Garnier has been joined by the towering Opéra Bastille on a site soaked in revolutionary sentiment. In Berlin and Vienna, the opera houses represent the presumptions of an imperial past. In Helsinki, the opera house is dappled, like the country, by a forest lake. The symbolism of an opera house is often so powerful that one can easily forget the place is supposed to be dedicated to pleasure.

London's main opera house has occupied the same site at Covent Garden since 1732. The building burned down twice, in 1808 and 1856, and until the Second World War it was privately owned and operated, presenting seasons of international opera and ballet to coincide with 'the Season' when landed families came to town and presented their marriageable daughters at Court.

The Royal Opera House was a reflection of the country it served. The rich and noble entered by the front doors, were greeted by flunkeys and enjoyed light refreshments at the Crush Bar. The rest of the world entered by side-doors, scrambled up badly-lit stairs and enjoyed the show from on high with few interval luxuries. In a country which had five different classes of rail travel, the stratification was almost democratic.

It became problematic after 1945, when the Royal Opera House was reborn as a public company, in receipt of state subsidy. From this point on, the voting public felt it had a vested interest in the opera house, a right to share in triumphs and apportion blame for failure. The ROH, for its part, purported to conduct a national mission while attaching itself to a social élite. In these tensions and contradictions lay potential for high drama, which exploded at the end of the century when the opera house awoke to discover that it had lost the country upon which it had been moored.

There have been several histories of Covent Garden, some written by former executives, others by dewy-eyed supporters. This writer is neither. As a professional attender over twenty years, I have been unstirred by the majesty of the ROH and unconvinced of the singular importance attached to it by editors and politicians. My fault, no doubt.

Whether watching a rehearsal, being hectored at a press conference or wooed at lunch, embraced by artists or abused by officials, it took no great effort to maintain a position of amused neutrality towards a self-centred enterprise that demanded a diet of undiluted praise. It was made clear in oh-so-many ways that the press were given free tickets to Covent Garden in the interests of public accountability but that this institution was so celestially superior, so unutterably Royal, that criticism was not just superfluous – it would be almost disloyal. Critics and journalists were tolerated so long as we sang from an approved score. One press officer of the Royal Opera House would sit purposefully behind the row of press seats to make sure we all behaved like gentlemen, stayed awake and stayed to the end.

My earliest transgression set in motion a whizzing *pas de deux* that, I later discovered, was danced only in the most exalted circles. In May 1983 I reported that Covent Garden had cancelled an important Verdi production, supposedly for lack of funds but in reality (I learned) because regular telephone contact could not be established with its eccentric German producer. A Puccini production had already been replaced that season because its equally uncontactable Italian designer had built a set that was too large for the ROH stage. They could get it up, but they could not get it down in time for the next production. The Italian conductor, threatening to quit over an ill-prepared diva, was taken aside and firmly told that if he walked out, with the Queen Mother due to attend, he would never work again in Britain.

When a toned down version of this story appeared in early editions of the *Sunday Times*, an irate Covent Garden chairman, Sir Claus Moser, rang the editor, Frank Giles, late on Saturday night demanding that the item be removed. Was it inaccurate? asked Giles. No, said Moser, but it was damaging to the opera house. When Giles refused to withdraw the piece, Moser hinted that the paper might be stripped of its free tickets.

Saturday night head-to-heads between editors and public figures were as common, and mostly as bloodless, as punch-ups outside East End pubs. The only noteworthy aspect of this particular spat was that the ROH was employing a weapon normally reserved for Downing Street, the Bank of England and Buckingham Palace. It was no more than coincidence, surely, that the Secretary to the Board of the ROH at this time was also Secretary to the Cabinet. No other place of entertainment was so conversant with power. No other theatre, museum, sports club or orchestra acted as if its selfish interests were, in fact, the national interest.

Preposterous as this might sound to millions who never set foot in the ROH and switched channels if ever it appeared on television, there was some validity in the confluence of interests. For Covent Garden was always more than a pleasure house. If the Church of England was the Conservative Party at prayer and the Savoy Grill displayed half the Cabinet at trough, Covent Garden epitomized certain aspects and aspirations of the national condition that were all the more interesting for being unrecognized. During half a century of social change, Covent Garden was solid and immovable in its narrow sense of purpose: to produce opera and ballet at the highest standard. Unlike the House of Commons, the BBC, the National Health Service, the Labour Party and other manifestations of the *vox populi*, the ROH stood so far above transient whims of public taste and demands for 'modernization' that it encapsulated a set of freeze-dried English values in a disinterested archival form – like the (supposedly) apocryphal shelf at Oxford University Press where unsold books were taken off and dusted once a century. And come the millennium, when England anguished over its eroding identity, Covent Garden stood out briefly as a template of fading Englishness.

Its human influx was a social cross-section, always more catholic than was caricatured. It ran, in ascending flights of stairs, from the lobby carousel of peers, tycoons, media stars and the odiously rich, up to the closed circle of predatory queens and nightingale fanciers, and beyond to the top gallery of donkey-jackets and student couples with full scores in their laps and coffee flasks in their backpack. Mingled at all levels were little girls all agasp at their first *Swan*

Lake, truck-drivers who would go 'anywhere' to hear Gwyneth Jones, old-age pensioners who 'never missed a *Figaro*', pop singers who freaked out at real voices and couples of every conceivable gender pairing who were there for a birthday, an anniversary, a corporate night out or because their eleven-year-old nephew was playing an urchin in *Peter Grimes*.

The mix varied from night to night. A première or gala audience differed markedly from a Saturday-afternoon ballet house. Verdi pulled a different public from Wagner. In every row there were divergent levels of commitment and privilege. Seats 10 and 11 might belong to Friends who attended pre-curtain talks and Sunday teas, and gave ten pounds to incessant appeals. Their neighbour on either side might be a first-time corporate guest and a fanatical music-buff who had queued all day for returns. That these patrons co-existed without rancour was itself a comment on the English compromise in the three centuries since the last civil war. A comparable conjunction would not have sat peacefully in the Vienna State Opera or the Palais Garnier, especially when the corporates started snoring and the queuers unlaced their pungent footwear.

Over half a century, the social code was rewritten. In 1946, the stalls wore black-tie and the gallery dress uniforms. In 1996, jeans were not uncommon and an ex-POW would greet Japanese moguls at the door. In 1946, the Lord Chamberlain exercised powers of censorship that eliminated acts of nudity, treason or blasphemy. By 1996, the Royal Ballet star Sylvie Guillem danced habitually topless and François Le Roux had his privates on parade in *Gawain*. A new production of the *Ring* ridiculed Wagner to a point where Bernard Haitink could hardly bring himself to conduct it, and homo-erotic images were pasted on street posters to attract a sexually-active audience.

In manners and morals, habits and hobbies, attitudes and ambitions, England changed fundamentally in the second half of the twentieth century. The upheavals were most visible in demographics and wealth distribution. In 1946, any non-white face at Covent Garden would certainly have belonged to a North American soldier or a Latin American diplomat. By 1996, opera appealed to Londoners of Asian and Caribbean descent. When Covent Garden reopened after the war, England was a manufacturing nation with a northern industrial base. When it closed in 1997, England was a post-industrial society that relied on 'invisible earnings' and

London-based service industries. Millennial England with its cluttered domes and multi-cultural correctnesses bore scant resemblance to the late-imperial world of 1946. The past, wrote L. P. Hartley, is a foreign country[1] – and many who chose to live in the past felt like foreigners in their own land. Covent Garden was one of the few points of constancy.

I became aware of its frozenness in time when, in May 1995, I took my eldest sister to watch *La Bohème* with Roberto Alagna and Cynthia Haymon. Beatrice, living on a windswept hilltop in Galilee, had not entered the ROH for forty-five years. While I toddled my first steps she, in her first job as a school secretary, used to visit the opera two or three times a month. It cost her two-and-sixpence (twelve and a half pence in decimal conversion; around two pounds in millennial values) and she developed a teenaged crush on the Irish tenor, James Johnston, before leaving to build a new country.

As we ate ices between acts of *Bohème* and surveyed the human promenade, Beatrice suddenly remarked how familiar it felt, how little had changed. London no longer belonged to her, but Covent Garden was a rock upon which her memories and values could safely be measured. This was the England she had left behind. Her observation sparked a train of thought in my mind. Could it be that an archaic institution like the Royal Opera House represented something more than the sum of its vanities? Was it, perhaps, a repository of unretouched reality, a laboratory specimen of an England we had lost in a wave of Europeanism and heteroethnicity?

Personally, I welcomed the new cosmopolitanism that turned greasy-spoon caffs into spic trattorias and Brylcreemed hair into beaded dreadlocks. I shuttled happily through the Channel Tunnel and rejoiced at the death of little-Englishness and mediocre English art. Every historian, however, feels a responsibility to conserve. In the remote, myopic and often comic self-absorption of Covent Garden there existed, I suspected, a classic model for examining what had happened to my country in my lifetime.

For an opera house to flourish, it must secure and sustain popular approval, fingering the pulse of the majority who never attend opera or ballet yet pay for them through taxes in Europe and tax-breaks in the United States. This is rather like asking a butcher to canvass the views of passing vegetarians, but it has become a prerequisite of modern opera management. Failure to attune to changing rhythms of public mood is a recipe for disaster. Covent Garden, in the second half of its public existence, recklessly courted disaster.

By aspiring to world class, it forsook the common touch. In chasing stars, it alienated earthlings. The higher it rose, the odder it seemed to that kind of Englishman who likes a dash of amateurism in his sport and prefers an honest English trier to a world-slaying foreign genius. Covent Garden, once it joined the Met, La Scala and Vienna as a cornerstone of world opera, lost its local footholds.

A ghetto mentality prevailed. In the minds of directors, staff and performers, the ROH represented an irresistible force of destiny. 'To work at Covent Garden with its wealth of history – let us be bold and say Tradition – would make anyone humble that he or she occupies the room where Melba or Caruso dressed for performances, or where Augustus Harris planned his seasons; it can make the same people proud that, a generation after his death, they are sharing in an attempt to give reality to Richter's dream of a national opera company for England, based on Covent Garden,'[2] marvelled the Queen's cousin, a senior Royal Opera House executive. His sentiments were meaningful, but only to a minority within a cultured minority who adored opera. To the man on the Clapham omnibus, the names of Melba and Caruso might ring a bell, but Harris and Hans Richter struck no chords. What was their dream, and who cared? Opera, the most inverted of arts, was forever invoking ancient gods, whose names usefully separated the true devotee from the cultural tourist. To the buff, going to the opera entailed a day's advance preparation: reading the libretto, studying the score or sampling a recording and, if time permitted, trawling a periphery of composer letters and philosophical essays. In a country where fanaticism is dismissed as bad manners, a schism opened between the committed and the occasional.

Every place where opera and ballet is performed is riddled with cliques and intrigues. Covent Graden was unusual in its unifying sense of purpose. 'People worked here for next to nothing,' said the house manager, Trevor Jones. 'We tried to give the public a sense of coming into something special. Our rewards, and theirs, were those nights when everything came off.'[3] 'The pay was atrocious,' said a 1960s secretary, 'fifteen pounds a week was half what I could have got outside. But you got swept up in the life of the house, the magic.

Everyone hung out in the canteen, stars and plebs and stagehands. It was wonderful.'[4]

Many of those who worked in the offices made opera and ballet as amateurs in their own spare time. They sang in choruses, directed village-hall productions, researched impossibly detailed programme notes and hung out in bars with fellow-devotees. They spent holidays in the crush of Bayreuth, Verona or an English summer school where the art would be mounted by night and studied by day. 'At Covent Garden, everybody loves the opera, from the porter to (the general director) Jeremy Isaacs,' said the international soprano, Angela Gheorghiu. 'I know all the people, the usherettes, the stage hands. If they like a performer, they collect money to buy her flowers. Only at Covent Garden does this happen, nowhere else in the world.'[5]

Only at Covent Garden would you find dancers rehearsing on stage at four in the morning, no other slot being available. Nowhere else did wage clerks stay on past midnight to proofread a report from another department that had to reach the Arts Council by morning. Here alone did stagehands knowingly risk and, on tragic occasion, sacrifice their lives on machinery that was defunct before the First World War and still in use decades later. Only at Covent Garden would the doorman look after the dogs of two dancers who were going on holiday, while the nonagenarian ballet founder, Dame Ninette de Valois, stood in a queue for a cup of canteen tea, shunning special treatment. In no other opera house would a music director, a knight of the realm, take a broom and sweep the pit floor before rehearsal, taking care not to knock down the table on which Puccini had stood during rehearsals for the first *Bohème*.

Such attitudes amounted to a vanishing ethos, preserved by the collective will of an ever-changing group of people who, in some ways, represented the English character at its finest – robust, optimistic, reserved, dry-witted, industrious and uncomplaining. People who, in former times, would have been called 'the salt of the earth'. People who lived for an ideal, but made no big deal of it. People who said 'you don't want to hear about *me*,' as they scuttled off to complete a twenty-hour day. People – artists, stagehands, make-up men, secretaries, programme editors, wig-makers, second violinists – who were the life's blood of the place, and would blush or snarl if you told them so. Singly, they were men and women of little consequence; collectively, they gave devoted service to something larger than themselves, their phlegmaticism calling to mind romanticized accounts of the yeomen of old England and the spirit of the Blitz.

The underside of such dedication was a tunnel vision that led company members to mistrust outsiders and feel threatened by change. True insiders were known as 'Gardeners'. They formed a secretive society, pledged to protect one another and preserve the sacred opera house from external encroachments. The corollary of their English staunchness was a poisonously English parochialism of the kind excoriated by Benjamin Britten in *Peter Grimes* and parodied in *Albert Herring*. As managers came and went, ancillary staff dug themselves into defensive positions, marrying self-interest with the survival of a company that was fast becoming unmanageable. Private papers were ransacked and computers hacked. News of a senior dismissal was leaked to the press before the victim could be told. Factions within the Floral Street offices were at war with one another, and the chairman spoke out at board meetings of 'a nest of vipers'. In the face of danger, the opera house turned inwards like a scorpion and stung itself almost to death in a series of misadventures that enthralled the nation. The full truth of those mortal passions can be revealed in this book for the first time.

There have been several books on Englishness, written either by wrily admiring foreigners or by acidly self-lacerating Brits. This author is neither. Born and raised in post-war London, I lived and worked in other lands and picked up several languages before returning home, convinced that this was still the best place to live and write. Mine was, I realized, an unfashionable choice. England was in decline, its populace unhappy, its world role abandoned. There was more money to be had in America, more fun in Europe and more excitement in the Middle East. The decisive lure of England was its Englishness, that amalgam of the qualities that enables fifty-five million people to live at peace and in comfort on a crowded island. It is a temperate cocktail composed of mild tolerance, good manners, bad food, fair play, mixed weather, anti-intellectualism and a refusal to take life and death too seriously.

That was the top of the coin. The obverse revealed a puzzling attachment to mediocrity and an exclusion of alien ideas. The composer Michael Finnissy viewed the adjective 'English' as 'a tactful euphemism for second-rate or, worse, a limited and limiting culture'.[6] The artist Ron Kitaj re-emigrated to America in 1997, blaming anti-Semitic reviews for the death of his wife. A Lancashire-born Jewish scholar said tellingly, 'Englishness is not available to me.'[7] 'Damn you, England!' said the playwright John Osborne in a famous rejection of Queen and country.

All of these perceptions viewed Englishness as a tangible unity, which it decidedly is not. Even after the devolution of Scotland, Wales and Northern Ireland, this remains a peaceably fissipated island: city knows nothing of country, town never meets gown, them are not us, and 'U' is the opposite of 'non-U'. There are many Englands and varied forms of Englishness. When the New Labour Government backed a measure to abolish fox-hunting, it thought it was attacking the landed gentry. Peaceful mass demonstrations brought threadbare crofters marching on to the streets beside estate-owners' wives in jodhpurs and pearls. They represented the English countryside, united against the spread of urban values. When the rights of hereditary peers were abolished in the House of Lords, it was the life peers who were seen to weep, mourning the passing of eight centuries of tradition.

'The Prime Minister has asked us to help create a new Britain, a new country,' declared one Labour MP,[8] but there will always be an England, and there will always be what the writer Michael Bracewell called 'a need within the psyche of Englishness to look back to an idealized past'.[9] The Royal Opera House catered primarily to that need, which may help explain the passions it aroused. But the ideals were never defined, and the murkier they grew the shakier was the ground on which the ROH stood. This history attempts to trace the parabola, from gleaming post-war ideals to complacent millennial posterity.

The sources of modern history are oral and documentary. At Covent Garden, the paper trail is tantalizingly thin. There is an official archive, which has been officially shut for two years. It has also been stripped of anything remotely contentious. There is no file of correspondence, for example, between the ballet director and the general administrator. There is a file for Lord Goodman, the Arts Council chairman and later a member of the ROH board, but it turned out to be completely empty.

Before I could enter the archives, the board demanded that I obtain the approval of all past chairmen, one of whom refused access to files pertaining to his period. I would later discover that he had little to hide. His response was typically that of an ROH grandee who saw no reason for the public to know what had been going on while he was in charge of a public-funded institution.

Other papers had to be treated with care. Maynard Keynes, by the time of his involvement with Covent Garden, was aware of his frailty and wrote with an eye to posterity. David Webster, the first administrator, never committed himself to paper if he could avoid it, and what he wrote often differed from what he meant.

In the most glaring of lacunae, Ninette de Valois, founder of English ballet, sent her papers for safe-keeping to her mother in Ireland. When she came to visit, she found they had been thrown on the fire. 'I didn't realize you wanted that stuff kept,' said Mum.

Happily, I stumbled across the papers of the 11th Earl of Drogheda, secretary to the ROH Board for six years and chairman for sixteen, conserved in a cardboard suitcase beneath an old gentleman's bed in Chelsea. With the permission of the 12th earl, his son, I have been able to unravel some of the more stubborn mysteries of the formative period. The widows of two music directors, Karl Rankl and Georg Solti, allowed me to examine items from their archives. During the upheavals of the late 1990s, several executives kept diaries and conversation notes, sometimes at the demand of their lawyers. Several of these eye-opening documents passed beneath my incredulous eyes.

Almost every artist and executive whom I approached for information responded positively and generously. There was a collective desire, it seemed, almost an urgency, to discover the past, dispel the clouds and start again on fresh foundations to bring art to an undemanding nation. Impartial as I remain, they have earned my gratitude, admiration and every good wish.

Norman Lebrecht
St John's Wood
July 2000

CHAPTER 2

Drinks at the Bar, 6.45
(1945 European time)

THE WAR ENDED in Europe on 7 May 1945, news of the German surrender being relayed over the BBC as England sat down to lunch. There was no public eruption, but the next morning, VE-Day, thousands converged on Whitehall where Winston Churchill, having addressed Parliament and offered thanks to God at St Margaret's, Westminster, went onto the balcony of the Ministry of Health to tell the milling crowds, 'My dear friends, this is *your* victory . . .'

That night, London was floodlit for the first time in five and a half years, its gutted and gapped glories exposed like a grand dowager's mouth in the dentist's chair. St Paul's stood miraculously intact on a mound of devastation; the National Gallery gleamed once more in Georgian splendour, though its west side was wrecked. On Trafalgar Square, Nelson on his leonine column surveyed a tide of deferred and fairly decorous revelry. The police had been ordered to treat excessive jubilation 'in a fatherly manner',[1] but there was not much to exercise the arm of the law apart from one bright spark who led community singing from on top of the gates of Buckingham Palace and another who set a tree ablaze in Green Park. Pubs began to run dry by eight in the evening and restricted beer-drinkers to half-pints. Two young women hopped into the Trafalgar Square fountains to pose in clinging-wet sweaters with a pair of pop-eyed sailors. But there was no repeat of the unbridled relief and pavement copulations that, in the same streets, greeted the end of the First World War.

Men and women of all ranks and nations donned paper hats, embraced one another and danced into the night but most drew back from acts they might regret in grey daylight. Something in the national mood suggested that this was not the moment for letting go. The war with Japan was still to be won, the full horrors of Hitler's crimes had yet to be absorbed and the immediate future portended as much of a life-and-death struggle as the recent past. Although British losses in battle were barely half the 750,000 toll of the 1914–1918 War, the home front this time was torn to shreds. More than 780,000 buildings had been destroyed or heavily damaged by German bombing. Some 147,000 civilians had been killed or severely injured and many more were in urgent need of rehousing. One-third of the City of London had been laid waste. The merchant fleet was reduced to two-thirds of its pre-war size, eliminating any early resumption of overseas trading.

To pay for the war, the United Kingdom had sold £1,118 million of assets and incurred foreign debts of three billion pounds. The world's richest nation had become its biggest debtor. All it had earned in return was a stubborn independence and a swelling of self-pride. 'When shall the reputation and faith of this generation of English men and women fail?' exulted Churchill on VE-Day. 'I say that in the long years to come, not only the people of this island, but from all over the world, wherever the bird of freedom chirps in human hearts, they will look back to what we have done and they will say, "Don't despair, don't yield to violence and tyranny. March straight forward and die, if need be, unconquered."' Churchill, however, was about to be swept away in an electoral landslide, and the bill for victory was due for payment.

No sooner had the results been declared than the incoming Labour Government faced a stark warning from the Treasury adviser, Lord Keynes, that Britain had 'not a hope of escaping what might be described, without exaggeration, and without implying that we might not eventually recover from it, a financial Dunkirk'. Industry had been turned over to military production and could not quickly be domesticated; export markets had been lost, perhaps for ever; and the United States was about to end its expensive line of credit known as Lend-Lease. Resorting to darkest-hour Churchillian rhetoric, Keynes, the foremost living economist, said the situation could only be saved 'by a combination of the greatest enterprise, ruthlessness and tact'.[2]

Britain was, in a word, broke. Its cities lay in ruins, its citizens were shabbily dressed and its daily food and fuel would be strictly rationed for the next ten years. It had won the war and lost the peace, before the peace had even begun. The country was entering an era of austerity so bleak that unborn historians of a future generation could grasp it only by experiencing conditions in shard republics of the dismantled Soviet empire. Fear of national bankruptcy, added to exceptionally harsh winters, industrial unrest and the threat of nuclear confrontation with the Russians, would give rise to a siege mentality more pervasive and morale-sapping than the fearsome Blitz – an atmosphere captured with only slight exaggeration in George Orwell's apocalyptic novel, *1984*.

The early summer of 1945 was a critical moment that did not permit English people the luxury of relief and rejoicing. It was a time to tighten belts and think of bare necessities. There were neither the resources nor the urge for frivolity. Yet – and this decision would appear all the more striking in light of political attitudes in a later, wealthier age – within weeks of the end of war and with creditors baying at the door, an almost indigent nation resolved without controversy to set up three cost-intensive new cultural institutions: the Arts Council, the BBC's third programme of music, drama and serious talks, and the Royal Opera House, Covent Garden.

In a society that had always left the organization of art in the hands of enthusiastic amateurs and refused to allocate tax revenue to support mere 'entertainments', this triple conception amounted to nothing less than a Damascene conversion, a blinding act of faith. The endowment of three publicly-funded promoters of culture amounted to a penitent admission by the authorities of their moral responsibility for the state of the arts. Setting aside the BBC's initiative, which was the kind of public-spirited gesture the BBC tends to make when its Charter is up for renewal, the founding of the Arts Council and the Royal Opera House at a time when there was not enough gold in Threadneedle Street to pay the nation's energy bills marked a substantial shift in the core values and priorities of the island's inhabitants, the unarticulated quintessentials of Englishness.

'The English will never develop into a nation of philosophers,' wrote Orwell around this time. 'They will always prefer instinct to logic and character to intelligence. But they must get rid of their downright contempt for "cleverness". They cannot afford it any longer. They must grow less tolerant of ugliness and mentally more adventurous. And they must stop despising foreigners.'[3] To survive in a post-war landscape, Orwell believed the English had to shed their chauvinism and philistinism and show more respect for intelligence and ideas, wherever they originated. 'The intellectual atmosphere of England is already very much livelier than it was,' he noted. 'The War scotched if it did not kill certain kinds of folly. But there is still a need for a conscious effort at national re-education.'[4]

Orwell's words were, as so often, reflective and prophetic of the national mood. No serious objection was raised to the introduction of state funding for the arts. A revolution achieved almost by stealth, but with tacit public support, was regarded as one of a series of necessary measures that would modernize the country without altering its character. 'They remained a peaceful and civilized people, tolerant, patient and generous,' was A. J. P. Taylor's assessment of the English at the end of war. 'Traditional values lost much of their force. Other values took their place. Imperial greatness was on the way out; the welfare state was on the way in. The British empire declined; the condition of the people improved.'[5] Times changed, England endured. Amid the irritating privations, most people shared the view that they were building a better country, a New Britain (to borrow a future slogan), and the arts had a vital role to play in improving the national condition.

Ever since the tide of war began to turn, the British had been led, by a sheaf of multi-party Government reports, to look forward to a better, fairer way of life. They were promised free education, the eradication of poverty and, by Labour, a welfare state that would care for everyone from cradle to grave. When the war ended, Britain awoke to Blakeian visions of a New Jerusalem. When Labour was elected, that utopia seemed at hand.

Welfare, however, is a cumbersome behemoth, slow to rise and costly to run. It was 1946 before the National Insurance Act offered decent benefits to the sick and unemployed and November 1948 before the National Health Service provided free health care, dentures and spectacles. These tangible blessings and shibboleths of a caring society took years to organize, against bitter resistance from the medical profession and others. When the war ended, there was need for an immediate sign that *laissez-faire* had been abolished and the caring state had been born. Nothing expensive could be undertaken before a general election, but all parties were united in wanting to give the country a taste of times to come. That appetizer was placed before the House of Commons on 12 June 1945 by the Chancellor of the Exchequer, Sir John Anderson, who announced the introduction of public subsidy for culture by setting up an Arts Council of Great Britain to foster a 'knowledge, understanding and practice of the fine arts'.[6]

If the Welfare State had a defining moment, it was not in the delivery of the first benefit cheque or the cutting of a free tonsillectomy but in this momentous, consensual decree that the arts – the creative voice of the nation – were from now on to be a paternal concern of central government. The new Arts Council was granted £235,000, worth around six million pounds by end-of-century values. Its remit was as modest as its resources – a friendly tweak here, a helping hand there. In the outlay of the first four years, there was nothing for orchestras in London, a hundred pounds for opera in Wales and three thousand for converting a barracks cinema in Salisbury into a fully-fledged arts theatre. By far the largest Arts Council grant, £25,000 and double the next year, was set aside for the Royal Opera House, a symbolic act of favouritism that would join the two bodies in a macabre alliance for the next half-century and almost destroy them both. This shady union was not the fault of any individual or either organization. It was by the expressed will of Government and Parliament that the Arts Council and the Royal Opera House were created inseparably in a single act and with a parallel mission – to revive the nation.

To endow two new agencies at a moment of extreme fiscal stringency and on the eve of a general election required political courage and cross-party consensus. To formulate the legislation alone demanded time that had to be stolen from more pressing matters, yet there is little sign of dissent in the surviving documentation. Covent Garden and the Arts Council were created with as much unity, or sufferance, as the nation had shown in waging war against Hitler. More remarkable still, this double extravagance was impelled and inaugurated not by some impractical dreamer but by the rigorist prophet and architect of national austerity, the high-domed and walrus-eyed Treasury adviser, John Maynard Keynes.

On the day of his Chancellor's statement in the House of Commons, the free-spirited Baron Keynes called a press conference at an address in Bloomsbury, the central London district that had lent its name to a libertarian artists' group in which the eminent economist was a pivotal and beloved figure. Keynes, who planned to become chairman of both the Arts Council and the Royal Opera House, cheerily gave the press his own gloss to the Chancellor's speech. The Arts Council, he said, had many objectives but reopening Covent Garden was absolutely its top priority – 'thereby restoring to this country something it should never have lost'.[7]

Four weeks later, in a prime-time radio address Keynes added: 'We look forward to a time when the theatre and the concert hall and the gallery will be a living element in everyone's upbringing, and regular attendance at the theatre and at concerts a part of organized education.'[8] Culture and creativity were the key to national revival. If England was to rise again, it would rise enlightened from its economic Dunkirk.

'I do not believe it is yet realized what an important thing has happened,' Keynes continued. 'State patronage of the arts has crept in. It has happened in a very *English*, informal, unostentatious way – half-baked, if you like. A semi-independent body is provided with modest funds to stimulate, comfort and support any societies and bodies . . . which are striving with serious purpose and a reasonable prospect of success to present for public enjoyment the arts of drama, music and painting.' He went on to extol the artist 'who walks where the breath of the spirit blows him. He cannot be told his direction; he does not know it himself. But he leads the rest of us into fresh pastures and teaches us to love and enjoy what we often begin by rejecting, enlarging our sensibility and purifying our instincts.'

This was no mere blueprint for a new bureacracy. The dialectics of Keynes's speech left no room for doubt that he was talking about a resurrection of a national spirit in which his infant Arts Council and Royal Opera House would nurture the necessary growth. He talked of preserving not just an English way of art, but Englishness in all its regional and social variants. In the one passage of his talk that sparked controversy Keynes declared: 'Let every part of Merrie England make merry in its own way. Death to Hollywood!'

This rallying cry drew a yelp of protest from the dream factories. Mr J. Pole, publicity director of United Artists, wrote to *The Times* complaining of Keynes's ingratitude for Hollywood's part in winning the war. Keynes, visiting America with a begging bowl ('there is no source from which we can raise sufficient funds except the United States,'[9] he told the Government) hurriedly ate his words. 'What I ought to have said,' he recanted, 'was Hollywood for Hollywood.' His meaning, though, was unmitigated by half-apology. Unless England preserved its Englishness through the arts and the Royal Opera House, the country would be reduced to dependence not just on American material aid but on the crassness of its commercial culture. The British economy might some day recover,

Keynes told his Government, but no country could ever restore a culture that had been allowed to become extinct.

The notion that culture could define nationhood was not a novel proposition. Nationalism had raged through the arts in the nineteenth century as embryonic nation-states applied great art to inflame revolution and justify independence. Verdi was, in no small measure, the catalyst of unified Italy as Beethoven and Wagner were of Bismarck's Germany. Such confluences had no place in English culture, grounded as it was in fine painting and dramatic poetry. Britain had conquered half the world without recourse to its arts and when Victorian romantics painted or poetized a 'spirit of Empire' their effusions were richly embarrassing.

Music, the most inflammatory of arts, played little part in English culture until the ascent of Edward Elgar, whose success was founded more on continental than on national strands. Elgar developed a synthesis of Franco-German orchestral textures, bowing to Berlioz, Gounod and Saint-Saëns in one bar, Brahms and Wagner in the next, albeit in a robustly English manner. Composers who set out to trace native sonorities found themselves half a century behind European researches; Ralph Vaughan Williams and Gustav von Holst, the first to be perceived as nationally 'English', were identifiably so only insofar as their music conscientiously refused to score points and make propaganda for a national agenda. English culture as a whole was individualist, self-contained, phlegmatic, witty and overwhelmingly static, fixed to the page, the canvas and the dramatic stage.

The performing arts, while well-attended, were imported wholesale. No city apart from New York paid higher fees to foreign singers, actors and musicians than imperial London. No metropolis had less by way of year-round entertainment. Opera and ballet were confined to 'the Season' when the landed gentry decamped on the capital to go shopping and display their marriageable daughters. No symphony orchestra existed in London until 1904. A national theatre, first mooted in 1848, did not come into being until 1962. The German rhetorician who defamed England as 'the land without music'[10] was not altogether wide of the mark. It took one world war to persuade English theatres and concert halls to accept indigenous artists and a second to convince the public of their merits.

The catalyst was a woman called Lilian Baylis who, inheriting her Aunt Emma's temperance hall on the wrong side of Waterloo

Bridge, made it her mission at the Old Vic to provide drama and opera at prices that were affordable to all classes. Baylis set her sights high, announcing an annual Shakespeare season in 1914 when no classics were to be seen in the West End. Sybil Thorndike played most of the female leads and the first cycle reached completion with *Troilus and Cressida* in the tercentenary year of 1923, a stark alternative to the prevailing Twenties frivolity.

Lilian Baylis's contribution to English arts and culture cannot be overstated. Over quarter of a century and on cruelly pinched means, she laid the foundations of three great ensembles: the Royal National Theatre, English National Opera and the Royal Ballet. Stout, bespectacled, thick-lipped and almost execrably ugly, her mouth twisted in midlife by a stroke, Baylis spoke in a Cockney accent that provoked middle-class derision and disparagement even from firm supporters. 'Poor dear, she has no imagination of what any opera might be, if only it was put on properly,'[11] exclaimed the music scholar Edward J. Dent, a member of her board. Whatever she lacked in artistic discernment, she made up for with an uncanny knack for recognizing good artists and persuading them to work for pennies – 'doing our bit for the Vic,' they called it. Actors who asked Baylis for a ten-shilling raise were told, 'Sorry, dear, God says No.' She was often to be found by the side of her rolltop desk, 'down on her knees, praying for a tenor'.

The operas Baylis espoused were sung resolutely in English for the greater public edification. 'My people must have The Best,' she declared. 'God tells me The Best in music is grand opera. Therefore my people must have grand opera.'[12] Stagings were unspectacular and the sets were constantly recycled. Opera played three times a week at the Vic, but the appetite for plays grew faster, especially once John Gielgud, Peggy Ashcroft and Ralph Richardson emerged at the head of a thrilling new generation. So 'the Lady', as Baylis was ironically known, decided to keep the Old Vic for drama and to find a new home for opera.

In 1928 she bought and started rebuilding the derelict Sadler's Wells theatre in seedy, run-down Islington. It was a daring move, an act of faith. To fill the bill, she knew, would require more than grand opera. Just as she was surveying her options, the God of her prayers sent along Ninette de Valois, a 'slightly fanatical young woman'[13] in her late twenties who had danced as a *soliste* for Serge Diaghilev and was now determined to create a distinctively British ballet company.

Irish-born and baptized Edris Stannis, de Valois had retired from the stage with arthritis and founded a ballet school. She needed more outlets for her talented pupils. Baylis engaged her to choreograph dance scenes for Shakespeare plays and furnish a *corps de ballet* for the opera. De Valois seized the opening and formed a full-time ballet company. The missionary zeal of 'the Lady' was met by the visionary force of a natural leader who became known to her subordinates as 'Madam'.

Baylis, who died in 1937, clung to the belief that working people could be lured from dreary pubs into the higher temples of art with a promise of entertainment and self-betterment. Some deemed her approach archaic, arguing that more modern works would attract a loyal and enthusiastic following among teachers, young secretaries, shipping clerks and the rest of the educated underclass. But the Lady was set in her ways and unsusceptible to intellectual argument. Others could raise the tone if they liked, and they did. While Gay Young Things bopped and bed-hopped the night away, England was experiencing a high-cultural revolution. Its performing landscape suddenly burst into flower. The number of symphony orchestras doubled as Birmingham, the BBC and Sir Thomas Beecham tapped a surgent demand for good music. Repertory theatres sprang up in several towns. An opera festival was started at Glyndebourne, in the Sussex Downs, by a bullish landowner, John Christie, who had married an English soprano, Audrey Mildmay.

The combined impact of these uncoordinated and often mutually hostile initiatives on English artists was electrifying. Composers and librettists found a market for their works. Home-trained English singers and ballerinas made débuts before a supportive public. A country that had neither opera nor ballet before the war was finding its voice and feet and advancing on the world stage. The legacy of Lilian Baylis and her contemporaries amounted to nothing less than a spontaneous expression of a national will to excel in the unEnglish realm of the lyric arts. The ultimate goal was to present outstanding English performers in immortal English works before a discerning English public.

Covent Garden, meanwhile, continued to serve the nobility with international seasons of opera and ballet, a parade of celebrated singers and dancers under Sir Thomas Beecham's stylish if capricious leadership. An inveterate intriguer and omnivorous wit, Beecham had been the centrifugal force in British opera since the early years of the century, spending most of his father's money and some of his mistress's on seasons and schemes that foundered as much on the shimmer of his brilliant inconstancy as on the rock of English indifference. He fluttered from the dazzle of Diaghilev, whose troupe he imported in 1913 and 1914, to the dreariness of an all-British Opera Company; from the shock value of Strauss, conducting the premières of *Elektra* and a censored *Salome*, to the soporific worthiness of Frederick Delius. A butterfly personality that illuminated all it touched, Beecham lacked the patience to dig foundations and the application to fulfil bureaucratic and legal requirements. Puffed up with vanity and frustrated by mundane obstacles, he directed a withering hail of barbed aphorisms at any would-be national revivers who did not follow his wavery beat.

'The English may not like music,' he opined, 'but they absolutely love the noise it makes.'[14] British music, he snorted, 'is in a state of perpetual promise. It might almost be said to be one long promissory note.' Modern art, he drawled, 'is a gigantic racket, run by unscrupulous men for unhealthy women.'[15] Spying the growing audience at Sadler's Wells he sent Lady Cunard, his moneybags and mistress, on a bid to take financial control of the Vic-Wells Company and send it on provincial tours. Baylis, however, was not prepared to be bought out and bridled in ripe Cockney language at her ladyship's deprecations of the company's musical standards.

Between Beecham's all-stars and the jolly-good-triers there was an unbridgeable gulf in quality, both artistic and social. No English-sung Carmen could match Conchita Supervia's. No one who was anyone in the Covent Garden audience would be seen dead watching opera in English. Nevertheless, despite the disparities, or perhaps because of them, Covent Garden was losing ground. Facing top-note competition from Glyndebourne's Continentals and rising standards at Sadler's Wells, the Royal Opera House was becoming an oddity rather than the apex of artistic life. Beside the constructive, year-round work of home-based companies, its ephemeral seasons seemed extravagant, antediluvian, even ridiculous.

What does England do when war breaks out? runs the joke. It calls up the army and shuts the theatres.[16] While *ganz* Berlin and *tout* Paris flocked to opera and music-halls, London was masked in darkness from September 1939 until Neville Chamberlain's nervous government realized that lack of entertainment was sapping morale and putting artists on the dole. Night-life resumed by official decree in November 1939. Soon after, on 14 December, a meeting took place that would transform the casual status of English arts for all time to come.

It was convened in a private room at the University of London and brought together two Cabinet ministers with little personally in common. Herbrand Sackville, ninth Earl De La Warr, was President of the Board of Education, a lover of bright lights and loose women.* Lord Macmillan, an austere Scottish jurist of great intellect and discretion, was the inept Minister of Information. Both had served in the 1924 Labour administration before drifting into National Governments with the Conservatives; both would soon be sacked.

What tore these two public figures from their duties on a working Thursday in the middle of a war was the guile of a Welsh charmer called Thomas Jones. A former Deputy Secretary to the Cabinet, Jones had been unable to accept retirement when he reached the statutory age in 1930. Having served four Prime Ministers through war, peace, Irish troubles, a General Strike and a financial crash, he had come to consider his counsel indispensable to the nation. For the next decade until Churchill shut him out, this white-haired ex-preacher and sometime economics professor was in and out of Downing Street hustling for many causes, chiefly for easing poverty in Wales and making friends with Germany. Jones had been received by Hitler in his Munich apartment and was over-friendly with his crass ambassador in London, Joachim von Ribbentrop. Using unique access to men in power, he took the former Prime Minister David Lloyd George to see the Führer and almost persuaded the incumbent Stanley Baldwin to follow suit. Known in Whitehall as 'T.J.', Jones wheedled tirelessly for an alliance between Germany and Britain. He voiced some sympathy for Hitler's Jewish victims, but was committed at all costs to achieving an understanding with the master-race.

In or out of office, Tom Jones assiduously blurred the lines between public service and personal favours, between duty and booty. Friends considered him 'incorruptible', but as Lloyd George's closest confidant from 1916 onwards, 'he had not merely touched pitch; he had been up to his neck in it, and not been

* his sister, Lady Idina, was at the centre of a colonial scandal when her husband, Lord Erroll, was murdered in Kenya in 1941, conceivably by her lover

defiled.'[17] Through his friendship with Baldwin, Jones became Secretary of the Pilgrim Trust, endorsed by the New York financier and philanthropist, Edward S. Harkness' Pilgrim Trust, to improve the quality of British life.

T.J. was in clover, sitting on a fortune to spend as he alone saw fit. Baldwin, the trust chairman, trusted him unreservedly and Macmillan, who succeeded as chairman in 1934, was equally friendly if more frugal. Jones sailed to America to survey its many charities. On his return he lavished large amounts on the repair of Lincoln Cathedral, Durham Castle and St David's Cathedral in Wales. Next came gifts to an experimental nursery school in the deprived London borough of Deptford and to Lilian Baylis's ever-needy Old Vic. There were grants to preserve the natural beauty of the Malvern Hills and the grandeur of Parliament Square. Sir Isaac Newton's birthplace was bought for the nation and Jones even passed a proposal, remarkably given his Nazi friendships, to offer relief to Jewish refugees.

But what most concerned the busy Secretary was the blight of mass unemployment. He began looking for 'pivotal people',[18] Gauleiters perhaps, who could lead communities out of the vale of despair by running clubs and recreation centres at which the workless might learn crafts and arts. The idea caught on in depressed Wales where, by 1933, there were one hundred and fifty such centres attended by thirty thousand men. Paying a penny a week, many labourers acquired new skills that enabled them to find or create work; others applied their idle time to reinforcing the principality's enviable choral traditions. T. J. became a hero in his homeland. In the rest of the kingdom, he sought to stem graduate emigration by giving Pilgrim Trust bursaries to impecunious students.

All of his schemes and wheezes came to a halt, however, with the outbreak of a war he had worked so shadily to prevent. The Pilgrim Trust suspended its grants for the duration of hostilities and T.J., now 69, was left casting around for a role. Back home in Wales, he wondered whether his grass-roots arts and crafts movement might not raise spirits across the nation during the Phoney War, perhaps with Government aid. Just then, he took a phone call from 'Buck' De La Warr at the Board of Education, who was thinking along similar lines. Jones proposed a chat with the Pilgrims' chairman, Lord Macmillan.

The oleaginous Jones has left a much-quoted minute of this

historic meeting, a document compromised only by its author's manipulative disingenuousness. 'Lord De La Warr,' wrote Jones, 'was enthusiastic. He had Venetian visions of a post-war Lord Mayor's Show in which the Board of Education led the Arts in triumph from Whitehall to Greenwich in magnificent barges and gorgeous gondolas; orchestras, madrigal singers, Shakespeare from the Old Vic, ballet from Sadler's Wells, shining canvases from the Royal Academy, folk dancers from village greens – in fact, Merrie England. Lord Macmillan's grave judicial calm collapsed suddenly and completely. At the moment he was responsible for the national morale, and in the President's dream he saw employment for actors, singers and painters, and refreshment for the multitude of war workers for the duration. Supply and Demand kissed. Would £25,000 be any use?'[19]

'It is characteristic of our national way of doing things,' wrote Macmillan in his memoirs, 'that the beginnings of what was to become the first State-subsidized organization for the provision and promotion of music, drama and painting for the people were entirely informal and unofficial . . . The Pilgrim Trust made a first grant of £25,000 and Lord De La Warr persuaded the Treasury to contribute pound for pound with us, up to £50,000.'[20]

Four days later, with uncommon haste for Whitehall even in wartime, Macmillan and Jones called on De La Warr at his office. With them were Sir Kenneth Clark, director of the National Gallery, and two of Jones's Welsh cronies, the composer and popular broadcaster Sir Walford Davies and the adult education propagator William Emrys Williams. Having made sure that any decision was stacked in his favour, Jones proposed the formation of a Committee for the Encouragement of Music and the Arts, known as CEMA, to be funded jointly by the Pilgrim Trust and the state.

There was just one hitch. Jones's plan for milking the Treasury was designed, in part, to procure himself a last niche in public life. Unhappily for the little wizard, politics intervened. A fortnight before CEMA's inaugural meeting on 19 January 1940, Lord Macmillan was dismissed by Neville Chamberlain. With time on his hands and a noble desire to serve, Macmillan volunteered to become chairman of CEMA, depriving Jones of one post he wanted. Whitehall then claimed the job of CEMA Secretary for one of its own, a former schools inspector and French linguist called Mary Glasgow. That left T.J. out in the cold, with only a deputy chairmanship for comfort and a seat on the board for his two Welsh chums.

So long as CEMA ran on Pilgrim benefice, Jones continued to be its driving force. But Macmillan, late in 1941, ruled that the Trust might be exceeding its legal remit and would have to withdraw, leaving sole responsibility for funding the arts with the Treasury. Thus, the unintended outcome of Jones's plot, before he trickled off into oblivion, was to make the arts an affair of state – administered at 'arm's length' from political interference but accepted by all parties as a natural concern of central Government.

This was, by any measure, an historic achievement. It was also, in terms of war aims, a victory on the home front as Pilgrim and Treasury money revived the spirits in every corner of the land. CEMA sent six 'Music Travellers' up and down the country; in six months they organized 254 concerts and founded 37 orchestras and 244 choirs. William Emrys Williams circulated 'Art for the People' exhibitions, complete with easy-to-understand lecturers and guides. Sir Walford Davies organized symphony concerts in factory canteens.

When the Blitz began, CEMA put on 'emergency' concerts in air-raid shelters. The demand for distraction swelled. Men in desert fatigues faced Panzer tanks in North Africa with Penguin tracts and Mozart scores in their pockets. The Old Vic gave *The Merchant of Venice* in mining towns and moved office to Burnley. Divisions between serious and popular art narrowed. Every show, high or low, sold out and newspapers remarked on the growth of a mass audience for culture. Covent Garden, meanwhile, served as a Mecca ballroom.

Sadler's Wells Ballet and the London Philharmonic Orchestra – forsaken by its founder, Beecham, who fled the country on the outbreak of war – were sustained by an independent charity, the Carnegie Trust. Other professional ensembles stayed alive by entertaining troops, for which they were paid by ENSA out of army budgets. CEMA saw itself more as 'an extension of the social service',[21] designed to ease unemployment and foster self-help. The priority, for Jones, was to serve the public, not the arts.

CEMA was, nonetheless, the centrifugal force in a cultural upsurge that contributed materially to a myth of mass resistance – 'we can take it' – during the worst of the Blitz. 'The Treasury thought that CEMA would end with the war,' noted Kenneth Clark, who was privy to Whitehall thinking and despised Jones's lowly aims.

The Director of the National Gallery believed in great art, loved grand opera and loathed provincialism. An arrogant young man of inherited wealth who became the nation's chief curator in 1934 at the age of thirty, Clark packed off his canvases to caves in North Wales and engaged the redoubtable Myra Hess to give daily piano recitals in the bare-walled National Gallery. No event of CEMA's so captured the spirit of the times as Dame Myra playing to a thousand men and women in an evacuated, dome-shattered gallery. 'This was what we had been waiting for,' extolled Clark, 'an assertion of eternal values.'[22]

Jones, for his part, sent musicians to 'dreary Dagenhams' and kept them out of the capital, 'where amenities are abundant'.[23] Clark's dissatisfaction increased when Jones's blinkered cronies refused the brilliant actor-manager Donald Wolfit funding for a national tour in May 1940, on the grounds that Wolfit was a 'commercial' London-based enterprise. That Wolfit's lunchtime Shakespeare performances were addressing the same urgent need as Myra Hess's recitals somehow failed to register with the Joneses, locked as they were in their petty rules and pathetic resentments. This fatal misjudgement earned CEMA an unnecessary enemy.

Wolfit had lately performed a sold-out season at the Arts Theatre in Cambridge, enthralling its founder, the economist Maynard Keynes. Puzzled by the denial of subsidy, Keynes consulted Kenneth Clark, who told him that CEMA was frittering away public money on mediocrity. In July 1940, *The Times* ran a leading article attacking CEMA for spending too much on amateur art and too little on professional companies. Keynes, a Treasury advisor, duly summoned the CEMA Secretary, Mary Glasgow and, in her words, 'made mincemeat of me when I tried (as I had to) to justify my masters on the Council. I reeled out into the night, bloody but I hope unbowed, feeling I had been in the presence of a very great man.'[24]

She was not alone in that impression. Clark found Keynes 'every bit as clever and charming as he is reported to have been'.[25] Bertrand Russell, the Cambridge philosopher, wrote: 'Keynes's intellect was the sharpest and clearest that I have ever known. When I argued with him, I felt that I took my life in my hands.'[26] Keynes's brain, said the novelist H. G. Wells, was 'the best in the country'.[27] Even Tom Jones recognized his 'prismatic genius'.[28] Keynes was both an intellectual giant and a bully who used his superior mind like a bulging muscle to daunt would-be rivals and opponents. 'I did not enjoy his company,' said Russell, 'he made me feel a fool.'[29]

To put Wolfit on the road, Keynes personally underwrote a quarter of his losses and advised CEMA to guarantee the rest. The incident brought CEMA into his sights. When offered its chairmanship by 'Rab' Butler, President of the Board of Education and 'the best Prime Minister Britain never had', Keynes hesitated at first, protesting that he suffered from heart disease, was overworked at the Treasury and had no sympathy for CEMA's aims. But Butler was a persuasive man and his father-in-law, the philanthropist Samuel Courtauld, was a friend of Keynes. Butler knew the great economist was 'not impervious to flattery';[30] a peerage clinched it and Keynes became chairman. Upon the tittle of titles does English history turn.

In April 1942 Keynes took charge of CEMA, moved it to Bloomsbury and transferred departmental responsibility from Education to the Treasury, shifting brick walls of authority like so many breeze-blocks. Over the next three years, amid frail health and fiscal crisis, he overcame all obstacles to establish an Arts Council and Royal Opera House. Without Keynes, neither would exist. His appointment might seem fortuitous, a clever improvisation by a rising politician, but the foregoing events indicate that it was part of an organic process – the kind of evolutionary adjustment for which the English system is widely envied and profoundly misunderstood. Whitehall was working in mysterious ways, its wonders to perform.

Officialdom had acted unofficially, creating precedents that foreshadowed all future relations between Government and the arts. CEMA, conceived at an informal meeting of two ministers and run by Whitehall nominees, was funded by the Treasury without formal legislation and, when its directors proved inadequate, they were replaced without a ripple appearing on the public record. This was a manner of administration that had functioned since the reign of Henry the Eighth. Self-selecting from a narrow social and educational base, the senior levels of the civil service clung to unreformed privileges by being acutely sensitive to failure. Their rules were designed to deter hotheads, avert corruption and put the right man in the right job most of the time. They did not always succeed at first, but setting Keynes at the head of arts funding was a mark of the system at its best. Here was a man with all the necessary qualities and a passionate commitment who could also be trusted by the Establishment not to traduce its authority.

Keynes was at once an insider – Eton, Cambridge, Whitehall – and a lion of bohemia; a public official and a self-made millionaire; a servant of the Crown with an independent mind. The arts, he once said, 'owe no vow of obedience'.[31] Without Keynes as arts commissar, England would probably have reverted to its usual state of artlessness and the Royal Opera House would never have risen from the disgrace of a dance-hall floor.

Few men of ideas have exerted such influence on their century as John Maynard Keynes, designer of the modern economy. From the early 1930s when he formulated the *General Theory of Employment, Interest and Money* to the 1970s when it was held responsible for renewed economic crisis, Keynes held sway in the study of economics to the point where anyone questioning his formula was dismissed as stupid or heartless. While never quite a household name, Keynes was widely held to be the 'saviour'* of capitalism as Karl Marx was of communism and Jesus Christ of sinful humanity – an immaculate conceptualizer. His teachings possessed poetic simplicity and empirical apparatus, glorious turns of phrase and just enough historical evidence to convince the doubters.

Before Keynes, economics was taught in England as a minor branch of moral philosophy. After Keynes, economics became a political formula of immense practical value. Until Keynes published his *General Theory* in February 1936, governments were led to believe that economies were intractable and could not be manipulated. Ministers who asked awkward questions were fed a pre-industrial aphorism from eighteenth-century France. Known as Say's Law, this theorem held that 'supply creates its own demand'. Production resulted in income which, in turn, got spent on other products. Unemployment and stagflation were temporary aberrations, adjusting themselves like the weather after a record heatwave. That was the way of the world, said the classical economists, and had been ever since fiscal trade replaced the bartering of goods. *Quod erat demonstrandum.*

What Keynes proposed, in the depths of world Depression, was that Government could, and should, make a difference. By lowering and raising interest rates it could stimulate spending or saving, as

---

* the title of the second volume of Skidelsky's important biography

desired. By borrowing money and spending it on industrial pur-
chases and investments, it could increase levels of employment. The
state, Keynes argued, needed to spend more than it earned in order
to secure jobs for most working men and boost their spending power.
If the public overspent, the swelling of inflation could be curbed by
higher interest rates. It was within the hands of politicians, not God,
to manage supply and demand.

People wanted the moon, said Keynes, and governments were
telling them 'that green cheese is practically the same thing'.[32] One
remedy for reducing unemployment, he joked, was for the Treasury
'to fill old bottles with bank notes, bury them at suitable depths in
disused coal-mines and . . . leave to private enterprise on the well-
tried principles of *laissez-faire* to dig the notes up again.'[33] He was
out to demolish conventional economics including, he assured
George Bernard Shaw, the foundations of Marxism.[34]

Keynes was not acting alone. Cambridge colleagues helped tweak
the General Theory and his favourite pupil, Richard Kahn, is
sometimes credited with co-authorship for having invented in 1931
a multiplier device by which the method could be accurately
applied. It took Keynes five years to put his hypothesis into print, in
which time proof of its validity was building up. Its publication in
three hundred and eighty-four pages, four equations and two curves
marked a watershed in the way economics were practised and the
world was run. 'Never did a book fall more quickly and more
completely into the hands of summarizers, simplifiers, boilers-
down, pedagogues and propagandists,'[35] wrote a Cambridge
disciple.

The *General Theory* had the great merits of readability, rationality
and of being exactly what every humane politican wanted to be true.
Franklin D. Roosevelt's New Deal in the United States was starting
to show – with some help from Keynes who advised the White
House on occasion – that governments could relieve misery and
spend their way out of recession. Hitler's programme of public
works and rearmament was ending Germany's slump. Britain had to
respond. In February 1937, Neville Chamberlain announced
borrowings of four hundred million pounds over five years for arms
manufacture to counter the German threat. Labour, committed to
pacifism and suspicious of Keynes on personal and political
grounds, was inclined to object. But Hugh Dalton, its economic
expert, had read his *General Theory* and talked his party around.

From that point on, Keynes was the guiding light to governments of every complexion. Roy Jenkins, a Labour Chancellor of the Exchequer, called the *General Theory* 'the most important book of the past hundred years'.[36] Even when Keynes seemed discredited in the 1970s oil-fuelled crisis, wise men like John Kenneth Galbraith maintained that Keynes was still right in principle. What had gone wrong was the perversion of his ideas by insipid leaders and greedy trade unionists who claimed a 'right to work' and full employment, while giving little in return.

At the start of the next century, it was too soon to pronounce Keynes dead – for even if his Theory was disputed, the institutions he invented continue to dominate our fiscal and cultural skylines. In 1944 Keynes laid the foundations of the International Monetary Fund and the International Bank for Reconstruction and Development, two aids for helping impoverished nations spend their way out of trouble. The next year, he instituted the Arts Council of Great Britain and the Royal Opera House. All four bodies were fashioned conspicuously in his image.

In Keynes, as in all men of imagination, personal proclivities and prejudices dictated the course of his ideas and the colour of his legacy, intellectual and institutional. One editor of *The Times* and chairman of the Arts Council[37] has argued that Keynes's sexual orientation was responsible for his rejection of the gold standard. Bertrand Russell saw him as a Cambridge cleric, out to redeem the world for academic purity. Some regard Keynes as an Establishment insider, others as a subversive intruder. The extent to which his character formed his economic thought continues to arouse heated debate. Little consideration, however, has been given to Keynes's private, even selfish, grounds for reforming the arts and founding a Royal Opera House. To understand his contributions to the arts one needs to trace the complicated and contradictory desires and talents of this 'practical visionary', the subject of more books than any Englishman of his time[38] except Churchill.

In many of his public deeds, and especially in the arts, Keynes was alert to his own self-interest, yet egotism drove him to ever-greater acts of public benefice. He was tugged in two directions, and over-compensated in both. He was, said his biographer, Robert Skidelsky, 'a buoyant and generous spirit who refused to despair of his country and its traditions, and offered the world a new partnership between government and people to bring the good life within reach of all.'[39]

*

That Keynes was extraordinarily clever was never in question. The eldest of three bright children,* born in June 1883 to a lecturer in moral science and his wife, a future mayor of Cambridge, Maynard (his mother called him John) outshone all other dons' sons and mentally outstripped his bodily development. He grew up weak, lanky and, in a six-year-old self-appreciation that never altered, 'remarkably ugly'.[40] Aged eight, he was taken with his brother to be surgically circumcised, apparently to stop them masturbating. He kept a home in Cambridge all his life and dearly loved his parents, visiting or writing to them weekly and consulting his mother on all matters of well-being, accepting her choice of cardiologist when his health began to fail. It was as much for her vanity as his own that he accepted the barony that came with the CEMA chairmanship.

Winning scholarships to Eton and King's, Keynes discovered a gift for making profound and lasting friendships. In Cambridge, he was elected to a secret intellectual society, The Apostles, which took in one or two of the sharpest undergraduates each year. Here, he met the future writers Lytton Strachey and Leonard Woolf. Together, they formed the nucleus of what became known as the Bloomsbury Group, a gathering of free spirits that embraced Strachey's lover, the artist Duncan Grant, Grant's mistress Vanessa Bell, her art-critic husband Clive Bell and her celebrated sister Virginia, who married Woolf.

Other affiliates included the novelist E. M. Forster, Strachey's brother, James, and Virginia's brother, Adrian Stephen (whom Grant seduced), the painter Roger Fry (who loved Vanessa Bell and Strachey's sister, Phillippa), the novelist David Garnett (who married Vanessa's daughter) and the painter Dora Carrington, who was suicidally infatuated with Strachey.

Bloomsbury was both a physical habitat and a pervasive state of mind. Much has been made by literary gawkers of its inextricable sexual entanglements, but any loosening of Victorian corsets must be viewed in the context of the group's general ethos, which was hedonist, separatist and supremacist. As admirers of the Cambridge philosopher, G. E. Moore, Bloomsberries were dedicated to the pursuit of a 'good life', sampling whatever took their fancy but

* his brother, Geoffrey, became an eminent surgeon; his sister, Margaret, married Professor A. V. Hill, secretary of the Royal Society

refraining from defining 'goodness' or applying rules. Life was a grand experiment in which friends had to be allowed to make mistakes, even when lives were ruined or put at risk. The pleasures of human intercourse and the enjoyment of beautiful objects, were the highest reward, the ultimate good.

For all their high mindedness, Bloomsbury talked low and dirty. When Strachey saw a stain on Virginia's skirt, he asked her loudly if it was semen. 'One can talk of fucking & sodomy & sucking & bushes all without turning a hair,'[41] wrote Vanessa Bell, appreciatively, to Keynes. They saw themselves as being above convention, rejecting religious morality and striving for the betterment of the species. 'In or about December 1910, human character changed,' wrote Virginia Woolf.[42] What united Bloomsbury was a sense of its collective superiority and a contempt for people of lower brows and staider ways.

Sexuality was a glue that bonded the group and sealed its intimacy. Most of the men were primarily homosexual, an affinity that placed them at odds with propriety and the law. Bloomsbury made of their sexual predilection an élitist distinction, espousing a 'Higher Sodomy' that, on physical and ethical grounds, affirmed an elevated set of tastes and values – 'buns, buggery and higher thinking', in the definition of one scion.[43]

Hampered by a lack of physical allure (or sense of self-loathing), Keynes formed a passionate attachment unrequitedly to a Cambridge freshman, Arthur Hobhouse, before bedding the artist Duncan Grant, both objects of Lytton Strachey's desire. When unhappy in love, or out of it, Keynes indulged in casual pick-ups. Homosexuality for Keynes was a code of conduct and a cocking of snoots at the society he served. A physical and spiritual ambivalence ran through the course of his public life.

On 1 August 1914, three days before Britain declared war on Germany, Keynes was approached by a Treasury acquaintance, Basil Blackett, with a request 'to pick your brains for the country's benefit'.[44] Five months on, he joined the most rigorous, secret and powerful Government department and rose so smoothly through its brainy ranks that in March 1919, aged thirty-five, he was sent as the Treasury's chief representative to the Paris peace conference. During the War, Keynes financed the military effort by day and talked pacifism with Bloomsbury at night. His friends were conscientious objectors and he supported them with advice and money, some of it in public commissions. Russell gave up his Cambridge rostrum and went to jail for his beliefs; Keynes kept quiet and made a great career. Nimble-minded and none too fastidious, he papered over the schisms and kept soul and reputation intact. At the Paris peace conference he opposed punitive German repayments; on losing the argument he left the Treasury and published a searing indictment of the peace treaty,[45] recovering self-respect.

While struggling to reconcile conscience with career, Keynes lost sight of the niceties that separate public and private business. When he became rich after the war, it was whispered that Keynes had used Treasury inside knowledge to make his fortune on the Stock Exchange. Keynes's accounts show that he negotiated a thousand-pound overdraft at Barclays days before war broke out and invested half of it in shares. He borrowed another thousand from Roger Fry as speculative capital. During five years in Whitehall, his assets increased eightfold to £16,431,[46] a tidy sum for a civil servant, worth quarter of a million in end-of-century values. There is little doubt that Keynes speculated during the war, albeit prudently, in modest amounts and without necessarily misusing privileged information. It was not, at the time, illegal for a Treasury official to play the markets, although it might have been regarded as improper for a man whose ministerial advice could affect the value of currencies and stocks. Keynes, it seems, refused to recognize the distinction between personal and public interest.

Slightly more compromising was the role he played in helping to acquire for the nation part of the estate of Edgar Degas, who was both an important Impressionist and an astute art collector. A catalogue of the Paris sale of Degas' estate in March 1918 had fallen into the hands of Duncan Grant, who 'suggested to Maynard that he should get the money from the Treasury to buy some of these pictures for the National Gallery.'[47] Anxious to recover Bloomsbury esteem, Keynes wired back: 'Money secured for pictures.' He had persuaded the Chancellor of the Exchequer, Andrew Bonar Law, to release 550,000 francs, equivalent to twenty thousand pounds, on the twin grounds of enriching British art and helping the French balance of payments. Heading for Paris on Treasury business, Keynes took along Sir Charles Holmes, director of the National Gallery, who shaved off his moustache and wore glasses to avoid recognition by art dealers. On the morning of 26 March, with the sound of German guns grimly audible and Debussy's death the night before casting a deeper pall,

Keynes and Holmes pulled off one of the great auction-room coups. Outbidding the Louvre for a Delacroix, they also picked up Manet's *Execution of Maximilian* and works by Corot, David and Ingres. Holmes, according to Keynes, turned down a Cézanne and two El Grecos and came home with quarter of his allowance unspent. The canny Keynes picked up for himself Cézanne's *Apples* for £327, as well as two pictures by Delacroix and a female nude by Ingres.

'As Holmes had a prejudice against Cézanne, no conflict of interest had arisen,' concludes Keynes's biographer,[48] but the position was not quite so pure. Holmes may have shunned Cézanne, but no curator would fail to spend an open cheque unless the Treasury man at his side was murmuring caution. Nothing can be pinned on Keynes, but he would never have owned the Delacroix he coveted had the Director of the National Gallery sensed a competitive ardour. Keynes had gone to Paris on public business and came back with the basis of an opulent private collection (which, by the time he was finished, included four Cézannes, two Braques, a Matisse, two Picassos and Georges Seurat's 1884 study for *La Grande Jatte*). He may not have traduced his position, but he left office much richer than he entered, and with no sense of having bent the rules. He managed, like many of fewer scruples, to convince himself that what was good for Maynard Keynes was good for the nation – a perception that would guide his intense involvement with the performing arts.

Apart from a love of fine art and books Keynes, along with most of Bloomsbury, had little time for the lively arts. Theatre they made mostly for themselves in post-supper *tableaux vivants* and charades. Music was not part of their insular Englishness. No composer of note visited Gordon Square. Virginia Woolf was bored witless at Bayreuth. Keynes in 1907 showed complete lack of enthusiasm when Grant secured tickets for Wagner's *Ring* cycle.[49] War, however, can alter the most settled of habits.

In the autumn of 1918, the exiled Serge Diaghilev introduced his latest troupe to a London public whose liking for dance he had cultivated in four vogue-making visits before the War. Keynes joined the rush for tickets. 'There is no genius in it this year,' he reported to Grant. 'The leading lady, Lopokova, is poor. But the new Nijinski, Mr Idzikovsky . . . has a charm or two.'[50]

Backstage, Keynes and Grant were introduced to the monocled

impresario. At a party given by the scandal-seeking Sitwells, Keynes met Lydia Lopokova, who let him pinch her legs to feel how strong they were. On Armistice Night he met her again and revised his first impression. She was a bubbly dancer with a prodigious technique, twenty-six years old and unhappily married to Diaghilev's Italian business manager, Randolfo Barocchi, from whom she was plotting escape. Her disappearance in July 1919 was the talk of the town, noticed even by Virginia Woolf. Lopokova fled to America for eighteen months, rejoining Diaghilev in Paris and returning with him to London at the end of 1921 in Tchaikovsky's *Sleeping Beauty*, re-scored by Igor Stravinsky and retitled *The Sleeping Princess* because, said Diaghilev, 'Lopokova is no beauty.'

The show was no hit either, but Keynes, who had not seen Lopokova or anyone half as good for three years, was smitten. He watched her night after night in the near-solitude of half-empty stalls, until the run was cut short in February 1922 as Diaghilev ran out of funds. *Sleeping Princess* left such an impression on Keynes that he demanded it for the reopening of Covent Garden in 1946 and invoked its Good Fairy in the last speech of his life to an audience of astonished financiers. Lopokova was now at the centre of his turbo-charged thoughts. Erotically, he was still sharing with Lytton Strachey and E. M. Forster the affections of a Cambridge under-graduate they called 'Sebastian' (his given names were Walter John Herbert Sprott), but the lure of Lydia proved irresistible. He was becoming hopelessly 'entangled', he told Vanessa Bell. She flashed back: 'Don't marry her . . . she'd be a very expensive wife and would give up dancing and is altogether to be preferred as a mistress.'[51] Lytton Strachey called Lopokova a 'half-witted canary' and Grant declared the couple 'utterly unsuited'.[52] Virginia Woolf predicted that Keynes would be reduced to talking in words of one syllable.

Keynes married Lydia the following year, once she had finalized her divorce from Barocchi, and they lived blissfully ever after. Some Bloomsberries believed that theirs was a sexless *marriage blanc* but their correspondence contains much kissing and 'gobbling' and marks of mutual physical infatuation. There was even talk of procreation, and hints of a miscarriage.

'Bloomsbury often missed the point,' wrote the ballet historian Richard Buckle,[53] and never more so than in Lydia's case. The evidence of their eyes should have shown Bloomsbury that she brought Keynes not only domestic happiness, but elements of lightness and laughter that he missed in his cerebral existence. She called him 'Lank' and thought him beautiful; he called her 'pupsik' and 'darling talky'.

'What are you thinking about?' he once asked her.

'Nothing,' said Lydia.

'I wish I could,' remarked Keynes sadly.[54]

And that was her gift to him. She introduced Keynes to a life out of mind and an art that was pure escapism, appealing to all the physical senses and none of the braincells. 'I . . . fluctuate with my hand on any soft skin that belongs to you,' she cooed, 'when you are not intelectual (*sic*) i.e. in the evening.'[55] He in return gave her adoration if not total fidelity. He continued to lust after young men, groping the lissom Frederick Ashton and a fellow-dancer when they came to dinner in Gordon Square while Lydia was 'twiddling her thumbs inside'.[56] His devotion to her, though, transcended such aberrations. For quarter of a century, the desire to please her and promote her art was uppermost in his mind. From the day they married, Keynes became the driving force behind the advancement of English ballet.

'There will be no more dancing, that is all over now,'[57] Keynes's prim sister told the press on their wedding day, but Lydia was not ready to become a housewife. She danced five roles for Diaghilev that autumn and starred in *Pulcinella*, the new Stravinsky-Massine ballet, the following year. At thirty-five she turned out for Diaghilev before the King of Spain, then in 1929 she danced in an early British sound film, *Dark Red Roses*, with George Balanchine and Anton Dolin. Keynes bought an estate at Tilton, on the edge of the Sussex Downs, where Lydia shocked passing ramblers by sunbathing nude in full view of a public footpath. He longed for her to shine before the whole world and encouraged her to take elocution lessons so that she might recite Shakespeare, opposite Michael Redgrave in a staging of the dramatic ballad, *A Lover's Complaint*. Cressida was to have been her next role but then Diaghilev died, in Venice in August 1929, and the crisis in ballet overrode personal ambitions.

Someone had to fill the vacuum, especially in England where the Russian adventurer had cultivated a taste for dance but erected no framework on which it might grow. A committee was formed by two ballet critics, Arnold Haskell and Philip Richardson (founder of *Dancing Times*), together with the music critic Edwin Evans, the ever-enterprising Ninette de Valois and the hyperactive conductor and composer, Constant Lambert. They called themselves the Camargo Society, after an eighteenth-century Belgian dancer, and put on three or four ballets a year in West End theatres on empty Sunday nights and Monday afternoons. Lydia was co-opted as choreographic adviser and assumed 'real impresarial power'[58] by bringing on board as Treasurer the foremost economic thinker in the western world.

Lydia danced and acted in the opening production, *Beauty, Truth and Rarity*, to her husband's delight, although her quirky Shakespeare and Milton recitations drew mixed reviews. She went on to dance William Walton's *Façade* opposite Frederick Ashton – whom she advised to hang up his pumps and become a choreographer – and in Lambert's colourful *Rio Grande*, 'divinely',[59] as Queen of the Whores. 'On all occasions Lydia Keynes was our most outspoken member,' wrote de Valois,[60] whose arch-rival, Marie Rambert, was in the process of founding a Ballet Club at the tiny Mercury Theatre in Ladbroke Grove with the help of her playwright husband, Ashley Dukes, and a who's-who subscriber list topped with serene impartiality by Keynes and Lopokova, Lady Diana Cooper and the sculptor Jacob Epstein. Rambert, known as 'Mim', was a polyglot Polish-Jewish teacher of poor technical skills but possessing an uncanny eye for talent. She spotted and nurtured the gifts of Frederick Ashton and Agnes de Mille, to the envy of de Valois who shamelessly lured Rambert's stars to the Camargo and Vic-Wells. There were, sensed the visiting balletmaster Lincoln Kirstein, 'many factions at odds here',[61] with Keynes and Lydia ranged with de Valois against Rambert, and sometimes vice-versa. Alicia Markova and Anton (Pat) Dolin broke away to form a company of their own.

There was no shortage of ideas or opportunities. Everyone had the feeling they were inventing an English art that might, in time, challenge the half-exiled Russian ballet for world supremacy. All they lacked was money, and Keynes took care of that. He took a begging-bowl to his friend, Samuel Courtauld, and dipped from time to time into his own pocket. He was, said de Valois, 'quite masterly and, when necessary, equally ruthless'.[62] In 1935 Keynes booked two Camargo performances at the Royal Opera House for delegates of an international economic conference, Markova starring in *Swan Lake* and Lydia in *Coppélia*. 'A large sum of money was raised and the Camargo Society closed down after its five years of work – with all its debts fully discharged,'[63] reported de Valois. The Society had served its purpose, sounding the dawn chorus of English ballet and furnishing it with precious experience and repertoire. Two beacons for the future were Ashton's arrival as an exotic choreographer in Lambert's *Rio Grande*; and *Job* with music by the premier English composer, Vaughan Williams, choreographed by de Valois and conducted by Lambert, with Dolin as Satan and a synopsis by Keynes's surgeon brother, Geoffrey.

With the Camargo's liquidation and Lydia in her forties, Keynes cast around for another frame in which to exhibit his trophy-wife. In Cambridge, where he had restored the King's College finances, there was a plot of land left over from a student hostel he had built. The town had ten cinemas and no theatre. Keynes proposed to redress the omission by erecting an Arts Theatre, largely at his own expense, on the vacant plot. He involved himself in the tiniest detail, inspecting everything from pageboys' uniforms to the dressing-room floors. The house opened on 3 February 1936, a day before the *General Theory* was published, with a gala performance by the Vic-Wells Ballet, followed in the third week by Lydia playing Nora in Ibsen's *A Doll's House* and Hilda in *The Master Builder* – to the wry approval of Virginia Woolf ('Lydia very good') and the acute embarrassment of the philosopher Isaiah Berlin, who earned 'a rather severe look'[64] from Keynes.

Lydia made further appearances in Cambridge and London in Molière's *The Misanthrope*, and her farewell in *On the Frontier*, by W. H. Auden and Christopher Isherwood. There was nothing more Keynes could do for her, nor was he any longer in a position to promote her cause as vigorously as before. In May 1937 he collapsed with a severe cardiac infarction. Consultants failed for a whole month to detect a swarming colony of mouth bacteria that were eroding his heart valves and closing up arteries. The infection, exacerbated by heavy smoking, condemned Keynes to a life of invalidity. Lydia nursed him like a hawk, rushing in to press ice-packs to his chest in the middle of lunch and driving away visitors who were likely to tire him. Keynes submitted happily to a kind of second childhood. At fifty-four, he did not need to work again. His investments were worth £506,450 – around sixteen million pounds in modern values – and his *magnum opus* was endorsed by all political parties. Yet, feebly as his heart beat, Keynes's brain was busier than ever.

When war was declared in 1939, Keynes convened in Gordon

Square a group of veterans of the First World War administration who 'denounced the Chamberlain government's lack of coherent policy, criticized the dispersal of Whitehall departments to the provinces and devised alternative strategies for prosecution of the war.'[65] No sooner did Churchill become Prime Minister than he hauled the 'old warhorses' back to the corridors of power. Keynes, having written a pamphlet on *How to Pay for the War*, was given exactly the same job as before – the external financing of the war. He was made officially an Adviser to the Chancellor of the Exchequer, but his brief ranged over any issues he cared to address, from Indian sterling balances to domestic coal supply. He was he liked to say, 'just Keynes', a man anyone could turn to with their problems. He became a Director of the Bank of England, a Trustee of the National Gallery and ultimately the man in charge of the nation's arts. When the United States entered the war, he emerged as Britain's chief negotiator of credits and co-operation, spending extended periods in Washington and at the Bretton Woods conference designing the post-war world. Lydia accompanied him everywhere, lightening his load with kisses and chatter and seldom straying from his sight. Amid the pressures of saving his country from ruin and foreign domination, Keynes reserved a corner of his mind for erecting an eternal edifice to his Lydia and her art.

As chairman of CEMA, Keynes did not disguise what Mary Glasgow tactfully described as his 'strong predilection in favour of the ballet'.[66] Under prim Tom Jones, CEMA had not funded opera and ballet; if the moneyed classes wanted such extravagances, they could find the resources to pay for them. Under the theatre-owning Keynes, the climate changed. First Keynes brought the Vic-Wells under CEMA's umbrella and sent the Ballet Rambert off on regional tours. Then he moved heaven and earth to repatriate the war-stranded dancers of Kurt Jooss from South America and release their master from internment as an enemy alien. Amid tense negotiations at Bretton Woods, he slipped a note to the Soviet delegation asking them to send the Bolshoi and Kirov Ballets for a London season, a request he then got the Foreign Secretary, Anthony Eden, to repeat in Moscow. In New York, Keynes went to the Metropolitan Opera and met, through Lydia, a clutch of Diaghilev survivors who urged him to assert in England the primacy of ballet over opera. He did not, in truth, need much persuasion. Backstage at the Met he renewed contact with Sir Thomas Beecham, who was conducting operas on two rehearsals, divorcing his first wife and staying half a step ahead of his creditors, slipping out through kitchens and back doors to avoid process servers. Beecham reminded Keynes of the arrogant supremacy that musicians arrogated to their art above all others. In the theatre, Keynes was, according to his CEMA drama officer, 'never more than an amateur, with all the tendency of the amateur to dogmatize, much to the irritation of the professional.'[67] In ballet, however, he was, in Ninette de Valois' words, 'a dedicated follower . . . an awesome chairman, a man of sudden dramatic decision, yet possessed of an unblushingly warm heart.'[68]

In the mental compartment reserved for his passion, Keynes had cause for concern that the huge strides made by English ballet in the previous decade were about to be lost in the privations of war. When the theatres shut down, Markova, Dolin and the choreographer Antony Tudor took up offers in America and de Valois was distracted by domesticity. Her husband, a country doctor, was short-handed in his practice. 'Ninette – *wonderful* Ninette – said that a woman's place is in the home and she went away and disappeared,' sniped the sharp-tongued Ashton.[69] Having regrouped the Vic-Wells under his own leadership, Ashton was unwillingly conscripted into the Royal Air Force. With most of its male dancers in uniform, English ballet now fell under the charismatic spell of Robert Helpmann, a witty and outrageous Australian with talents as a Shakespearean actor and a propensity for importuning attractive young men: not, perhaps, the ideal builder of a national art. Even with 'Madam' back from her surgery, the future of English ballet was parlous during the War and Keynes seldom allowed it to slip from his mind.

Opera, all the while, was making a nuisance of itself through the auspices of a National Council of Music, formed by the Glyndebourne owner, John Christie. In six halcyon summers of fading peace, Christie had set new benchmarks for operatic production in England through the rigour of three Hitler refugees: director Carl Ebert, conductor Fritz Busch and administrator Rudolf Bing. Having shut his festival for the duration and dispatched his wife and children to safety in America, the bluff, eccentric Christie had little better to do with his time than bombard the authorities with ideas for a post-war musical utopia. 'I want to crystallize the National Conscience by giving it a constitution and a home (Glyndebourne),' he wrote to the Minister for Aircraft Production, Stafford Cripps, having been brushed off by other politicians. 'The Slums and Poverty of the past would not have been tolerated if the National Conscience had been made aware of these problems,' he ranted. 'We want a better World and we offer service.'[70] Cripps, a future Labour Chancellor, said he was 'extremely interested' and advised Christie to discuss his ideas with Keynes, which was the last thing either man wanted.

Keynes had loathed Christie ever since they were boys at Eton, 'an ancient, implacable hatred'.[71] As near-neighbours in Sussex they avoided each other's eye on the platform of Lewes station and 'pointedly entered different compartments'[72] on the London train. Keynes occupied a realm of ideas and ballet, Christie a vista of farmland and opera. The supreme provider for arts made short shrift of the landowner's submissions. Through the gruesome medium of CEMA's music officer, Steuart Wilson, an English tenor who had once sung for Christie but was not considered good enough to be cast in Ebert's productions, Keynes flatly refused the Glyndebourne Festival access to public subsidy – a fiat that has been upheld by Arts Councils ever since. Personal animus motivated this decision, but with Keynes the personal was indistinguishable from the public: *l'état c'est moi*. He was, come what may, never going to allow the alien and self-interested opera world to leapfrog over his beloved ballet just as the grail of a permanent home came within his grasp.

It is not entirely clear from a wealth of self-congratulatory documentation who first cottoned on to the possibility that Covent Garden might become a state-funded public opera and ballet theatre. Kenneth Clark, who deputized as CEMA chairman in Keynes's absences, claimed credit for this and most other CEMA successes. Keynes seems to have been slightly slow off the mark, pardonably enough given his murderous workload. Once apprised of the opportunity, however, he seized it with terrier-like tenacity and restless ambition. 'The climax of his work for the future came with the opening of the Royal Opera House, Covent Garden,' summarized Mary Glasgow. 'It was a kind of symbol of what he stood for, and an earnest of what he hoped would be realized.'[73]

The Royal Opera House, owned by a property company, had been leased as a *Palais de Danse* to Mecca Cafés in December 1939 for a period of five years, with an option for renewal that Mecca, for its part, was keen to secure. The chairman of Covent Garden Properties

Ltd, Philip Hill, was caught in two minds. To a landlord, Mecca were reliable and responsible tenants who paid a commercial rent. Hill, however, was a sentimental opera lover who had sat on Beecham's opera board in the 1930s and longed to see the house restored to its traditional function. He confided his dilemma to Harold Holt, Beecham's concert agent, who was unable to help but directed him to Leslie Boosey and Ralph Hawkes who ran a music publishing company.

Boosey & Hawkes had urgent need for an opera house. During the war they had come into possession of a clutch of enemy properties and copyrights, including the complete operas of Richard Strauss. On a second front, they had acquired the Paris-exiled Belayev Editions and were negotiating for Serge Koussevitsky's Editions Russes de Musique, commandeering the major copyrights of Russian opera from Mussorgsky's *Boris Godunov* (in Rimsky-Korsakov's orchestration) through to Prokofiev's *Love for Three Oranges* and Stravinsky's *Oedipus Rex*. All they needed was a stage on which to perform them.

Boosey & Hawkes had, in the phrase of the times, 'had a good war'. Aside from publishing music, they had an instrument-making factory at Edgware, on the north-western edge of London, which had been converted for the duration to the exigent manufacture of armaments. Making guns was much better business than making music, and the partners were faced at the end of the war with an unseemly level of profits. Leslie Boosey, it is related, said to Ralph Hawkes: 'some of this money belongs to the nation – we must put it towards the public good.'[74] When Hill came by with the Covent Garden lease in April 1944, they bought it without much thought for cost or practicalities. Their simon-pure intent was 'to secure for Covent Garden an independent position as an international opera house with sufficient funds at its disposal ... giving London throughout the year the best in English opera and ballet, together with the best from all over the world.'

Mecca were outraged at the loss of a nice little dance-hall. On reading Boosey's statement, the directors rushed to law, arguing that the publishers, having no experience as opera and ballet producers, had obtained the lease under false pretences and were liable for Mecca's losses. Boosey and Hawkes went rushing to CEMA, where Kenneth Clark received them with open arms and offered to take over the house. 'I immediately wired to Maynard Keynes at his

arboreal conference and received his enthusiastic assent,' Clark
wrote. 'I then referred the project to the Treasury. I told them frankly
that I had no idea what it would cost, but that state operas on the
continent were known to be very expensive. My enthusiasm must
have melted their hearts, and they agreed.'[75] Thus, on a whim and a
prayer, did Covent Garden become a state concern.

Clark's motives were not entirely impersonal. Immensely rich and
barely forty, he had decided to leave the National Gallery and was
casting around for a bigger role, perhaps as successor to Keynes in
one of his many public capacities. He had put Keynes on the board
of his Gallery, and expected reciprocity. Mad keen on opera and
ballet, Clark coveted the running of Covent Garden for himself – but
Keynes's desire was stronger.

Although absent in the United States between June and August
1944, and again between September and December, Keynes decided
to chair the Covent Garden Committee himself. He brought on
board his friend Samuel Courtauld and his CEMA official Steuart
Wilson, as well as Clark, Boosey and Hawkes. For musical know-
how he recruited the Cambridge scholar Edward J. Dent, who also
advised Sadler's Wells; the dull Royal Academy principal Sir
Stanley Marchant; and the composer William Walton who was
having an affair with Clark's wife, Jane, with the full consent and
encouragement of the National Gallery director who was himself
philandering with, among others, Frederick Ashton's newly-wed
sister, Edith. A cosier set-up for running a public company could
scarcely be envisaged: yet there was nothing furtive or corrupt about
these arrangements. They merely reflected the English way of
making things work, through committees of the great, the good, the
rich and the sycophantically well-connected, looped around old-tie
networks of public school, Pall Mall clubs and private sports and
pastimes.

Objections to the scheme came not from public watchdogs but
from two losers who had been pointedly excluded. Christie attacked
the Covent Garden Committee in letters to the press, the Chancellor,
and anyone who would give him the time of day. 'Keynes refuses to
see me,' he wailed.[76] He applied to buy the building from Hill and
caused enough trouble for Hawkes to urge Keynes to co-opt Christie
on to their committee, if only to shut him up. Keynes, however, was
in no mood for conciliation and allowed his lackey Wilson to goad
the wounded Christie. Beecham, meanwhile, waited in America for

a call from Covent Garden – if not to run the house he knew so well then at least to be chief conductor. He waited in vain. 'They never came near me,' he told his biographers, uncomprehending and bleeding from the worst blow ever inflicted to his splendid pride.[79]

Cast out from Covent Garden, Christie and Beecham formed an anti-Keynes alliance, but soon fell out. Beecham huffed off to form yet another London orchestra, the Royal Philharmonic, and Christie reopened Glyndebourne without him. Neither gave up their smouldering claim to Covent Garden, but both recognized that the battle had been lost. 'Today,' intoned Beecham in September 1946, 'after seven years of operatic deprivation, we are in a pitiable plight. The newer public in this country, mysteriously and miraculously expanded to unprecedented dimensions, has little knowledge of the works of the great Masters, and none at all of a high standard or even correct method of performance. We have touched rock bottom.'[77]

Keynes had got his way again. Before leaving for America to shape the world's financial future, he took steps to secure the operating mechanism of the Royal Opera House. A general administrator was sought by traditional who-do-we-know? methods. David Webster was a Liverpool department-store manager who had kept the local orchestra alive through the war. Clark spotted him first and Holt vouched for his ability, but it was Hawkes who approached Webster, on the recommendation of his man-about-town cousin, Anthony Gishford. Publisher and shop-manager saw eye to eye over lunch at the Ritz Grill and Keynes warmed quickly to the practical, unflustered Webster, endorsing his appointment in July 1944. Gishford, by way of reciprocity, was appointed Public Relations Officer to the Royal Opera House.

All that remained was to organize a season. The Allies had landed in France, the war could end at any moment and it was imperative that Covent Garden should open before the Treasury relented. An opera and ballet company had to be built, borrowed or stolen. Acting under time pressure, Keynes took the felonious option. With Lydia at his side, he urged Ninette de Valois to transfer her troupe lock, stock and tutus, from Sadler's Wells to the Royal Opera House. 'I should expect that Ninette would like to come to Covent Garden,' he told Webster,[79] but de Valois was unwilling to risk fifteen years' effort and a loyal audience in a rash move to an unconstituted new venue. Although tempted by the glamour and centrality of the Royal Opera House, she feared its vast, unmapped emptiness. It was, she said, like being 'given Buckingham Palace, a few dusters and told to get on with the cleaning'.[80]

While de Valois dithered, Hawkes sounded out her choreographer, Frederick Ashton. 'If you won't,' Ashton told de Valois, 'I will.'[81] When Madam finally assented, the Sadler's Wells Governors screamed blue murder. Tyrone Guthrie, the company administrator, threatened to book the Drury Lane Theatre and perform in competition on the ROH doorstep. Guthrie preyed on Madam's well-founded fears, telling her that Covent Garden was 'an artistic graveyard' with a knack of 'swallowing up all but the most powerful and penetrating performers and performances'.[82] Dent, sitting on both boards, plotted merrily with and against Guthrie for maximum personal advantage.

It required a Keynsian device to settle the matter. Hanging around with fellow-peers in the House of Lords lobby while waiting for the King to open Parliament, he sidled up to the half-deaf Sadler's Wells chairman, Lord Lytton, and made him a whispered offer which he followed up with 'a brilliant memorandum'.[83] Lytton, a man of his word who was embarrassed to be thought hard of hearing, stood by whatever Keynes said they had agreed. In November 1945, *The Times* announced the transfer of the Sadler's Wells Ballet to Covent Garden under the headline, 'A Marriage Has Been Arranged'.

The deal that Keynes struck made creative use of his unchecked powers as chairman of both CEMA and the ROH. In exchange for sending its ballet company to Covent Garden, CEMA would pay Sadler's Wells a transfer fee of £15,000, plus a £5,000 top-up to de Valois' ballet school – a bribe by any other name.

On 20 February 1946, the Royal Opera House reopened in the presence of the King and Queen and an audience, 'most of whom were of Keynes' own choice',[84] in a programme that the chairman had picked on personal, sentimental grounds. '*The Sleeping Princess* should make an excellent start,'[85] Keynes instructed Webster. And so it did, with choreography by Ashton, splendiferous sets by the fashionable Oliver Messel and the effulgent Margot Fonteyn in the stellar role. Queen Elizabeth complained that there was nothing to eat in the Royal Box. 'Rationing, your Majesty,' they apologized.

'In my grandmother's Edwardian days,' noted Randolph Churchill, Winston's son, 'the Opera House admittedly presented as brilliant a spectacle as could be found in Europe – two tiers of boxes running all round it, replete with beauty and fashion. The women wore tiaras; the men kid gloves . . . Now the new management has restored the beautiful auditorium almost to its old splendour – not quite, for though the gold and crimson may have returned, the boxes have shrunk to a mere dozen or so on one tier only; and though the audience, headed by the King and Queen and the Prime Minister, contained figures of every known form of distinction, they were not on the whole much to look at; for nowadays nobody has any clothes worthy of the name. It was an "austerity" opening.'[86]

Keynes, while waiting to greet the Royals, suffered a mild heart attack and was hustled away to his box, leaving Lydia and Webster to do the bowing and scraping. 'He soon recovered and was able to watch the ballet,' recalled Ashton, 'while Lydia and I smoked cigarettes on the floor of the box undisturbed, until the house fireman arrived and told us to stop.'[87]

'He heard Tchaikovsky's splendid trumpets which he knew so well, and the march proceeded. He was still feeling tired, and he closed his eyes,' noted Keynes's economist friend, Roy Harrod. 'He thought of Diaghilev's production. There had been a princess, so light and quick, so charming and piquant, so gay and unexpected. His whole being had been filled with joy and exhilaration . . . That other performance had cast its spell upon him and determined his future course of action. It was a pleasant thing to be able to look back on one's life and find in it symmetry and purpose fulfilled.'[88]

Kenneth Clark, who shared his box some nights later, saw Keynes jump when a man in a black cloak passed through the door with a finger to his lips.

'Who is that?' demanded Keynes anxiously.

'That was Death,' said Clark.

Weeks later (and not the next day, as Clark fancied), Keynes was dead. He had just got back from America for the sixth time in as many years, having agreed a ruinous deal for the repayment of Britain's war debts, when the fatal heart attack struck as he rested at Tilton on Easter Sunday. Keynes was six weeks short of his sixty-third birthday; both of his parents attended the funeral.

Foreshortened as it was and widely mourned, few modern English lives have been more richly fulfilled in love, wealth and lasting achievement. No economist ever achieved such mesmeric influence over politics, art and society. Few scholars became so rich. And rare is the public figure in any sphere who enjoys a love as profound as the marriage between Maynard and Lydia Keynes. After his death,

Lydia wore his pyjamas for years – then threw them away. 'When Maynard died I thought I could never live without him, and I suffered a lot,' she said in 1951. 'But now I never think of him.'[89] She did not read his books and after his death seldom attended Covent Garden. Yet it was in tribute to her, above all other motivations, that he had restored the Royal Opera House as a centre of classical ballet.

Had Keynes cared about opera, he would either have struck a deal with Glyndebourne, or incorporated one of the established opera companies, Carl Rosa and Sadler's Wells. By shunning Christie, being 'rude to Rudi'[90] Bing and banning Beecham, he autocratically excluded every available English source of opera. Christie reopened his festival; Bing founded the Edinburgh Festival before heading off to run the Metropolitan Opera; Beecham immersed himself in orchestral politics; and Covent Garden entered the age of state opera innocent as a choirboy.

'It has never been clear to me,' wrote a future chairman of the Royal Opera House, 'whether the question of the Sadler's Wells Opera Company also being transferred to Covent Garden was raised or, if it was, why it was not pursued . . . Much time could have been saved and many subsequent difficulties avoided.'[91]

Unpublished documents show that the question was raised, in fact, only to be fudged, prevaricated and finally quashed. Guthrie, as late as February 1945, was expecting Covent Garden to take both ballet and opera companies from Sadler's Wells.[92] Discussions along those lines continued for several weeks more, but it appears that Keynes was merely stringing Sadler's Wells Opera along as a cover for his main agenda: to open Covent Garden with ballet on top. 'So far as opera is concerned,' he had told Webster four months earlier, 'I expect it is wise to keep Sadler's Wells away from Covent Garden until they are much stronger . . . About the ballet, on the other hand, I feel differently.'[93] His pro-ballet prejudice was no secret at Covent Garden. In a solemn eulogy to Keynes, his co-directors referred to it with a hint of irony as 'the art he loved *perhaps* beyond others'.[94]

As for opera, that was a necessary adjunct that could wait its turn and trust to fate. 'I think it was a mistake,' reflected Guthrie, 'that public money was used to found at Covent Garden another opera company, thus dividing in two the available funds, talent and support, which were barely sufficient for one. I do not know who was responsible. Neither I nor Miss Cross were consulted; we were presented with a quietly accomplished fact. At the time I was too much exhausted either to object or to grasp its implications for the future of opera in Britain.'[95]

Arrogant, intolerant and remorselessly self-serving behind a façade of charm and wit, Keynes founded the Royal Opera House with utter disdain for cultural and constitutional proprieties. By reversing the subordinate relation of ballet to opera, he implanted eternal enmity between the two arts, uglier than in any other opera house. By appointing a committee of cronies, he exposed Covent Garden to accusations of élitism. And by acting as chairman of both CEMA and the ROH, giver and receiver, he locked Government and Covent Garden into an oppressive intimacy that verged on perpetual corruption.

Keynes was the only man in England who could have created an opera house in the tense hiatus between two wars, hot and cold, conventional and nuclear. His monument endures, but the victory he claimed for his beloved ballet was pyrrhic. In the roars of first-night applause the recipe for lasting conflict was writ large.

CHAPTER 3

Enter the Leader
(1946-47)

AMONG PHYSICAL MEMORIES, the one that lingers is the smell. Not the sight of the ravaged city, nor the sound of its damaged engines, nor the touch of rough textures, nor the taste of food processed and spammified almost beyond salivation. It is the smell that most survivors recall – of bodies and clothes unwashed or rinsed in foamless soap; of decomposing foodstuffs sold as fresh; of fetid air, fed by the foul breath of poor diets and damaged digestions. Far from the heavenly dawn depicted by Labour nostalgists, London stank and festered in the birthpang years of the welfare state.

Few districts reeked higher than Covent Garden, where the capital's fruit and vegetable market thundered around the clock and there was neither the available manpower nor the municipal will to clean up and hose down. The market was a world unto itself, a square half-mile where whole harvests were sold on a handshake and stalls passed from father to son for five generations. Under the eye of Bow Street police station and magistrates court, where the most notorious villains were brought for arraignment, the market laid down its own laws and set the tone for the district, its porters and costermongers whistling lascivious comments at petite sopranos and ballerinas scuttling along to rehearsal. To have instituted amid such noxious, leering mayhem a royal opera house, replete with powdered flunkeys and velvet seats, was an act of dottiness or negligence that only the English could have committed in the grave extremity of their post-war circumstances.

In June 1946, rationing was extended for the first time to bread, at nine ounces a week for adults. The country embraced ever deeper privations, as the bill for Keynes's final American deal fell due. 'Our present needs are the direst consequences of the fact that we fought earliest, that we fought longest and that we fought hardest' commented the *Economist*. 'In moral terms we are creditors; and for that we shall pay $140 million a year for the rest of the twentieth century. It may be unavoidable; but it is not right.'[1]

The national mood was turning grumpy, yet there was no objection to the expensive reopening of the Royal Opera House – an acquiescence that can be largely attributed, in part, to a compensatory sense of moral superiority that swept the country. England might have lost its wealth and might, but it could still put on a show for all the world to envy. When, with personal taxes at record heights, the Government authorized local councils to raise sixpence on the rates for arts subsidy, there was again hardly a murmur of demurral.

On 29 September 1946, the BBC inaugurated its high-brow Third Programme with a concert of all-English music, the oldest by Purcell, the newest a world première from Benjamin Britten. Ruined as it was, the country fell back on culture for comfort and joy. Novels sold out within hours of publication. Galleries were packed. Public performance flourished in every form. To meet surgent demand, new orchestras – the Philharmonia and Royal Philharmonic – and a welter of private opera and ballet troupes were formed to augment and challenge state-supported ensembles. Jay Pomeroy, a Russian-born Jewish entrepreneur with a soprano mistress, put on 607 nights of Italian opera at the Cambridge Theatre and made no secret of his aim to take over Covent Garden, going so far as to usurp its aims of building 'a permanent Opera Centre' and training British artists to international standard. The one commodity in London that was not rationed was music, and for many Londoners it was the one relief that kept them going. 'You could always get in, even on first nights,' recalled an avid night-outer. 'It was never hard to get tickets, there was so much going on.'[2] Half-a-crown bought a place in the Covent Garden gallery, 13/6d a seat in the front stalls. Escape from the stench of reality was cheap and easy.

Those with connections scorned the transcendence of art and sought more privileged sanctuaries. Cecil Beaton, the society photographer and designer, talked his way into houses where they drank pre-war Château Yquem and served *marrons glacés* with fresh pineapple. Cyril Connolly, the *bon-vivant* literary editor, spent his summer in France, sponging off the Rothschilds and Lady Diana Cooper, wife of the British ambassador. Arthur Koestler, polemical journalist, lunched in Paris with Albert Camus and André Malraux. George Orwell, England's literary conscience, betook himself to the windswept Isle of Jura, where he composed *1984*.

But for homecoming heroes, escape began with a night at the theatre. Swapping rumpled uniforms for a three-piece demob suit and porkpie hat, they rushed to the box-office and remembered the rewards for the rest of their lives. Denis Healey, a future Cabinet minister, took his fiancée, Edna, to see Laurence Olivier in 'a stupendous double bill'[3] at the Old Vic, followed by a Myra Hess Beethoven recital in the National Gallery. Denis Forman, future head of Granada Television, sneaked into trade previews of every new film. Alan Jefferson, a future opera critic back from peace-keeping duties in Palestine, went straight to Covent Garden to see *Sleeping Beauty*. He went three times more to catch every change of cast but one – Fonteyn, Pamela May, Moira Shearer and Violetta Elvin, then known as Prokhorova; Beryl Grey he found unappealing and gave her a miss. The cost of Oliver Messel's £12,814 production – more than quarter of a million pounds in millennial values – was fully justified by economic utility. The sets were seen in 222 performances over six seasons, leaving an indelible imprint on the minds of a newly-civilianized conscript generation. *Beauty* defined the rebirth of British ballet, a benchmark for future attainments.

A chance to compare it with the world's best soon arrived when Covent Garden invited the Ballet Theater of New York to fill out the last two months of its inaugural season. The Americans danced *Les Sylphides*, followed by Jerome Robbins' choreography of *Fancy Free*, at which the Fourth of July gala première was conducted – at the insistence of his publisher, Ralph Hawkes – by the young composer in person. Leonard Bernstein never raised a baton again at Covent Garden as long as he lived. He came to hate London that cold, wet July of 1946. Foreigners were unable to obtain clothes coupons and he could neither buy himself a sweater nor warm himself on manly flesh picked up off the meat-rack around the emblematic statue of Eros. 'I've worn out Piccadilly in invitation and rejection,' Bernstein told Aaron Copland,[4] flying home the morning after his sole appearance.

Four of the American ballets were choreographed by Antony Tudor, who returned to something less than a hero's welcome. Snubbed in the Crush Bar as a war escapee, he was cold-shouldered by de Valois and Ashton who feared the depth of his intellect.

'Neither Fred nor Ninette spoke to (him),' said one witness.

One night in the crush bar Alan Jefferson, who went to see just about everything at Covent Garden that year, was approached by a portly man of obvious authority. 'I have seen you here before,' said David Webster. 'Will you also go to the opera?'

'Not if it's sung in English,' replied the young buff. 'I can't bear all those syllables left hanging over the end of lines.'

Webster turned on his heel and walked away. He was irked by the comment not because it was unfair but because it touched upon his own crisis of conscience. He had accepted a mission from Keynes to assemble an opera company from native resources, singing in the vernacular. But Webster was a nightingale fancier, smitten by superb voices. Among the greatest nights of his life he numbered a Covent Garden *Otello* on 6 June 1937 when the inimitable Giovanni Martinelli, months short of his sixtieth birthday, sang the title role opposite the Norwegian soprano Eidé Norena and the American baritone Lawrence Tibbett. How could he find or raise such voices in these sceptred isles? More agonizing still, he knew that the new crop of singers in Italy, Germany and Austria were available for little more than the price of a pack of cigarettes, while he was con- scripting inferior English singers to chew a clumsy text. Webster had entered into a Faustian pact. In order to fulfil his dream of managing an opera house, he had mortgaged his soul to the cause of English singing. How to pay lip-service to mediocrity while aiming for excellence would take all of his ingenuity and the rest of his life.

He faced an immediate challenge from the Cambridge Theatre, where the piratical Pomeroy was presenting Mariano Stabile, Giuseppe Taddei and his own mistress Daria Bayan, affectionately known as 'Dascha'. Never one to miss a trick, Pomeroy employed Diaghilev's designer, Natalia Goncharova. For 1946, this was a starry line-up and one that threatened to out-sing the Royal Opera House on its very doorstep.

As a makeshift counterweight, Webster imported the San Carlo company from Naples to give the first post-war operas at Covent Garden. The San Carlo had been popular with British forces who overran the port-city in September 1943 and contained two stunning young tenors in Mario del Monaco and Luigi Infantino. Alone, they were not enough to outgun Stabile and Taddei, but Webster played his trump with a sensational late announcement that the immortal Beniamino Gigli would join the company for four performances –

two *Bohème*s and two double-bills of *Cavalleria rusticana* and *I Pagliacci*. Gigli had been a huge star in England before the war. Hurriedly cleared of fascist collaboration, he came to introduce his lovely daughter, Rina, to his loyal London public. All-night queues formed on Floral Street and there were scuffles for the last tickets. Few in the audience seemed to mind that the performances were barely rehearsed and feebly conducted, or that Rina Gigli was never going to make the big time, except in her father's fond imagination. Gigli was back, and that was all that mattered to long-deprived English opera buffs. His recruitment was a master-stroke by David Webster, the first sign that this roly-poly northern shopkeeper had the makings of a world-class impresario.

Approaching strange men in public places was something David Lumsden Webster did every day of his professional life. As manager of the Bon Marché department store in Liverpool, he was regularly to be found patrolling the main floor, eyeing up customers and chatting them up, eager to anticipate the public's tastes and fancies. As he walked through the store, adjusting display units and praising his staff, his hand would snake out as he passed the confectionery counter and pop a pair of chocolates into his mouth. Webster was not a man to deny himself instant oral gratification.

The love of good things told quickly on his physique. Webster was plump, jowly and bald, with a spatter of dandruff on his shoulder; he was lucky not to live in an age when appearance counted above achievement. Nor did he attempt much by way of diet or sartorial camouflage. David Webster won the confidence of the middle-aged Masons and Rotarians who rule life in provincial cities by looking exactly like one of them, down to the last rumple. His store, on the other hand, was the last word in elegance, much smarter than the neighbouring branch of the John Lewis chain into which it was ultimately amalgamated. Bon Marché, recalled a young shopper, 'was the local fashion house; Lewis's was cheapjack by comparison.'[5] Webster, who rose to General Manager at the age of twenty-eight on a splendid salary of £7,000 a year, had created the most exciting emporium in the English northwest. He was a brilliant organizer with a ruthless streak. 'It's all right to stamp on other people,' he once said, 'til you get to the top. Then you can stop.'[6]

Running a provincial store was never going to satisfy so agile an operator or slake so hungry an ambition, but the opportunity he craved was slow to arrive. A commercial traveller's son, born in Dundee in July 1903, David Webster was raised in a Presbyterian tradition that left him thirsting for glamour and a sniff of grave sin. As a boy, he saw Pavlova dance. As a youth, he hung around stage doors for a glimpse of the great. He read economics as a scholarship boy at Liverpool University and joined an amateur dramatics society before forming his own. He was a decent actor and a dull director who derived most fun from giggling away over 'naughty' revues that he wrote with a friend in his lunch break. Getting to meet John Gielgud and Frederick Ashton were the triumphs of his young manhood; some said he was never really young.[7]

As general manager of Bon Marché, and later of the more important Lewis's, Webster was a figure of local substance. He was elected treasurer of the chamber music guild and on to the board of the Liverpool Philharmonic Society. In committee, he was industrious, quick-witted and hyper-sensitive. A request from the chairman to see his audited accounts was all it took for Webster to threaten resignation. People walked around him on egg-shells; he was too useful to lose.

In June 1939 the Philharmonic Society reopened its concert hall, which had been destroyed by fire, with a gala concert conducted by Sir Thomas Beecham. The hall was an art deco marvel, a shining white landmark in a begrimed port city. It was cleverly designed to accommodate concerts and cinema shows, something for highbrows and low. Three months after the hall opened, war was declared and the Society voted to disband the orchestra and shut the hall. Webster demurred, arguing that music and movies would be needed more than ever in times of stress. Elected chairman, he put the orchestra on a formal contract and reinforced it with London players, among them Anthony Pini as principal cello, Reginald Kell on first clarinet, the oboist Leon Goossens and most of the BBC's evacuated Salon Orchestra. Henry Holst, once Wilhelm Furtwängler's concertmaster in Berlin, became leader. 'Before Webster,' said a freelance musician, 'the Liverpool orchestra was a fiction – they were just boys bussed in from Manchester for the night.'[8] Webster put on thirty-two concerts in the first wartime season. He declared evening dress non-compulsory and threw open the doors to factory workers and servicemen, leading a minor revolution in English social mores.

At the front line of the economic war, its docks pulverized by air raids and its shipping decimated by submarines, Liverpool cried out for musical consolation. Webster, resisting easy populism, insisted on challenging audiences with works that pointed ahead to post-war renewal. Béla Bartók's Concerto for Orchestra received its first UK performance in Liverpool and Michael Tippett's first symphony its world première. The Liverpool orchestra, historically overshadowed by Manchester's Hallé, began to attract national attention. It made records for EMI, including Benjamin Britten's *Young Person's Guide to the Orchestra*, and made its début in London at the BBC Proms. Webster, in musical circles, was regarded as a rising force.

When his store was bombed, he did not have to look far for gainful employment or suffer, like Ashton, the dread hand of the draft board. Requisitioned by a friend in the Ministry of Supply, he was sent around the country to report on production targets. He began meeting serious businessmen, one of whom, Sir Robert Barlow of the Metal Box company, nominated Webster as his successor. He had just signed a contract with Metal Box at £10,000 a year, when Ralph Hawkes took him to the Ritz and hooked him on the Covent Garden line. Webster hesitated, tempted by the glamour but worried about the salary drop. The more he fretted, the more Hawkes pressed. Webster was perfect for the position: a successful executive with a passion for music and a knowledge of stagecraft who had cleverly rescued an important musical organization. That he had no direct experience of opera and ballet was immaterial, even a positive advantage.

For David Webster possessed a superior quality in the eyes of Hawkes and his colleagues. He was, in the most English sense of the word, an *amateur* – an attribute that could qualify him to captain the national cricket team, and hold the highest office in English arts. David Webster had reached the top: he could now stop stamping on people. 'He came to see me just before he took the job,' recalled Delia Barnaby, deputy music critic on the Liverpool *Daily Post*.* 'I said, "Will this mean big cigars?" He said, "might be". He had a nice sense of humour.'

All his adult life, Webster had been drawn to London like a kid to a sweetshop window. Living with his mother in Sunnyside, a blameless middle-class suburb, he hungered for glitter and guilt. Often he would rush from work to catch the 4.10 to London, change

* she wrote under the pseudonym of Norman Cameron, because Liverpool in those days did not trust a woman's musical judgement

clothes in the train toilet, arrive in time for curtain-up, dine afterwards at the Café Royal or the Savoy Grill, and ride the overnight sleeper back home, sauntering into the Bon Marché for breakfast. He once made the round trip five nights running to hear Arturo Toscanini conduct the BBC orchestra at Queen's Hall.

Webster's companion on these jaunts was a young man he had met at a Berkeley Square party in 1931 and promptly recruited on to the Bon Marché payroll. James Cleveland Belle became David Webster's lover and lifelong companion. The intrusive severities of an English law which punished homosexual acts with months of imprisonment forced them to dissimulate – a habit so powerful that Jimmy, even in the liberal 1970s, deleted the specifics of their conjugality from the manuscript of Webster's posthumous biography.* In London, and on summer holidays in Salzburg and New York, the two men enjoyed the freedom of anonymity and the thrill of a chance encounter in a public place, for neither held much with sexual fidelity. In Liverpool, however, they felt inhibited and afraid. Webster, a self-made man, had enemies in high places who wanted to bring him down. 'I had a great friend, Dick Bishop, who was prosecuting solicitor for Liverpool Police and was gunning for David Webster, trying to catch him out,' recalled Delia Barnaby. 'One day at lunch Dick said to me: "David Webster is shaking in his shoes in an absolute panic. He thinks we are going to close in on him, and we are."' Although reluctant to leave his mother, Webster knew he had to escape. The options before him were jail, Metal Box or Covent Garden. He chose Covent Garden.

In August 1944, Webster was given a desk and a telephone in Boosey & Hawkes's offices at 295 Upper Regent Street and told to organize a National Home for opera and ballet. Over the next eighteen months he assembled the entire enterprise from scratch. Stagehands, carpenters and wig-makers had to be hunted and hired, an orchestra, soloists and chorus auditioned, a management structure invented and a purpose defined that would unite 500 men and women in a new-born cause. The legal status of the company and its charter had to be formulated, and the views of eight independent-minded directors taken into consideration. Six different trade unions

---

* Montague Haltrecht, the author, was allowed to retain half-a-dozen veiled references to homosexuality. Jimmy, he discovered, was worried what his nephews might think of his past

had to be consulted and appeased over pay and conditions. Workshop and storage buildings had to be inspected and purchased. A financial plan was required. The Arts Council demanded to be kept informed; the BBC needed to be bullied into making a commitment. All of these issues and more were dealt with by Webster shrewdly, calmly and for much of the time single-handedly. His work did not go unnoticed.

The first task of a successful executive is to earn the trust of his board. Webster showered his directors with a disarming mix of magisterial memos and warmly personal notes. Keynes, often cruel to underlings, was impressed by Webster's eye for detail and ear for scandal. Their correspondence, always formal in address – 'Dear Lord Keynes', 'Dear Webster' – grew cheerful and chatty. Under the heading 'Gossip',[9] Webster kept his absent chairman amused with theatrical tittle-tattle. Keynes, in turn, trusted Webster to look after his aged mother on her first visit to the Royal Opera House; when the retired Mayor of Cambridge mislaid her spectacles in the chairman's box, Webster made sure they were found and returned.[10] Despite a twenty-year age difference and unbridgeable barriers of class and brain, the two men found mutual affinities that enabled them to collaborate on level terms. 'Both,' suggests Webster's biographer, Montague Haltrecht, 'were physically unattractive homosexuals. Keynes would have seen in Webster a fellow-sufferer, a man struggling with secrets and disabilities. Webster, for his part, was undaunted by Keynes's fame, knowing that the great man was vulnerable to the same pressures as himself.'[11]

It was on the rock of Keynes's support that Webster established his authority at Covent Garden, a dominance that would hold sway for quarter of a century. The General Administrator held a menial title and a deferential attitude to famous persons, but Webster made sure that no other person held anything resembling executive power in his house. He was the source of all decisions, the address for all complaints. He let it be known among staff that he could be found on a Friday lunchtimes at the bar of a pub some distance away, behind the Piccadilly Theatre, where anyone with a problem could stand him a drink. He instilled a spirit of shared enterprise, *esprit de corps* and paternalist care. The attentive habits of a good shopkeeper never fully quit his soul.

Alert and obsequious, sharp-eyed and convivial, Webster could not escape his original calling. He longed to shine in his own right, to rub shoulders with twinkling stars and, by rubbing, to promote his own worth rather than his merchandise. He loved taking curtain-calls to make 'an important announcement' to beaming audiences. But the only limelight that came his way was the afterglow of great artists and famous men. The more he craved recognition, the more he needed to cultivate his superiors and mimic them, indulging to the full his shop-floor instinct for snobbery. His first home in London was a suite at the Savoy. He went on to rent and then buy, with Jimmy, a flat in stately Weymouth Street, where they gave formal dinners for those he sought to impress, with his celebrity friends John Gielgud and the playwright, Terence Rattigan, in regular attendance. Webster name-dropped furiously to impress his staff.

When he took possession of Covent Garden from its Mecca tenants on 22 October 1945, Webster's first priority was to pick an office. He chose the biggest pair of interconnecting rooms in the building, and planted his desk at the far end of the inner chamber. The outer room was occupied by a horn-rimmed Scottish secretary, Miss Muriel Kerr, who guarded his door with a baleful glare. Stars were ushered in and gushed over, but most mortals who needed David Webster were made to approach him as foreign ambassadors once approached Mussolini, taking a long, lonely walk down an acre of carpet before reaching the great man at his desk. With lowly envoys, Webster would not even look up from his paperwork. 'What is it?' he would snap, leaving the visitor feeling like a gnat on the Duce's epidermis.

Barely had he been appointed than the board began pressing Webster to appoint an artistic director for the unformed opera company. The ballet had a surfeit of artistic directors – de Valois in charge of policy, Ashton of choreography and Lambert of anything to do with music – and the General Administrator was allowed no say in its programming. All de Valois would let him do was co-ordinate dates and accept her *faits accomplis*. Webster was determined that the opera company should stay under his control, reflecting his own ideas and imagination. So he played for time, refusing to let a conductor into the house until he had established a chain of command in the opera company with himself at the helm.

The kind of man he needed was a knowledgeable mechanic who would look after the nuts and bolts of the orchestral engine, a man rendered so insecure by temperament or situation that he would be eternally grateful for the job, and for Webster's protection. Assembling an ensemble from scratch was beyond the capabilities of a shopkeeper who could barely tell a *spinto* from a spinet. But Webster had learned enough in Liverpool to know that if a high-profile maestro was engaged, his own role would be reduced to the shadows and shallows of general administration. What he required was a musical cipher. He would then have to persuade knowledge-able connoisseurs like Keynes, Hawkes and Clark, as well as the expert musicians Walton and Dent, that such a cipher was not only the best option locally available but also in the company's best interests. The appointment of Covent Garden's first Musical Director was a process that reveals Webster at his most machiavellian.

After a delay, during which he scaled down the job title from Artistic Director, Webster in April 1945 produced a brilliant report which combined the appearance of impartial observation with a slash of character assassination to discredit the candidates he deemed undesirable. Headed 'Conductors for Covent Garden', and never previously published, the three-page memo listed eight candidates in capital letters and no particular order of preference, with Webster's personal favourite carefully camouflaged in the middle.

BEECHAM, Webster began, 'is the obvious name that comes first. There is no doubt that he is the greatest conductor we have produced, and the only first-class conductor of Opera. His drawbacks are, first, that he is not content to conduct, he must also produce . . . then he would like to conduct the whole enterprise, and as an administrator he is unsuccessful.'

This was neatly put. Beecham's claims were irrefutable and Keynes's committee were united in wanting to keep him out. Webster gave them grounds for rejection by implying that Beecham, now sixty-six years old, would seize control of the house and ruin it. Webster had talked to Beecham 'and intimated to him that as we are anxious to build up (a public) institution, he might find that limitation dull.' Beecham was 'not being offered very much work in America' and that 'notwithstanding his artistic success' Edward Johnson, the Metropolitan Opera manager, had found him 'unsatisfactory, and it is rumoured that he is not being engaged again'.

This was, at best, half-true. Beecham had a new agent in America and no shortage of concerts. He had fallen out with the Met, which prized singers above conductors, and was hankering to come home. To suggest that he was on the skids, as Webster did, was a malicious falsehood – but it was exactly what Keynes and Co. wanted to hear. 'The greatest conductor we have produced' was, on the basis of Webster's biased assessment, shut out of Covent Garden with a collective sigh of relief and without so much as the courtesy of an interview. This was unwise. A better judge of conductors would have known that Beecham would not lie low or fade away. Within months, he was back in London, forming a new orchestra and making mischief for Covent Garden – a course he pursued with unremitting malice to his last breath, sixteen years hence. Webster had made a mortal enemy, a man with mysterious connections that reached into the heart of the British establishment and up to the very Throne. He might easily have persuaded Beecham to accept an honorary title at the Royal Opera House with an occasional opera to conduct, but Webster did not want the old magician to cross his threshold. By excluding Beecham, he exposed Covent Garden and himself to attacks on their most vulnerable parts.

Webster's second target for demolition was John Barbirolli, back from seven lean years with the New York Philharmonic Orchestra and now revamping the Hallé. BARBIROLLI, Webster noted, 'is liked by musicians and by singers of this country' and 'is probably the best orchestra trainer resident in this country'. His credentials were outstanding. Webster might also have added that Barbirolli was ambitious, energetic, co-operative, good-looking, experienced in opera, untouched by scandal and just forty-five years old. He was a compelling candidate, almost without fault.

So Webster proceeded to disable him in a single, innuendo-laden sentence. Barbirolli, he wrote, 'has an odd flair for personal popularity, which is inclined to have difficult repercussions for the organizations for which he works.' This was meant, and understood, to imply that Barbirolli was an ego-driven narcissist of alien extraction ('flair' being English code for foreign) who would ensure that any credit for restoring Covent Garden would come his way, outshining the committee and General Administrator. He was neither servile nor malleable. 'His taste in interpretation is often doubtful,' added Webster, implying that this avid interpreter of Elgar and Vaughan Williams was a bit too dusky to pass muster at Covent Garden. The smears did their work, for Barbirolli was never offered the job. (Soon after, he turned down six thousand pounds a year to conduct the LSO.)

Malcolm SARGENT was easily dismissed. 'His reputation in London,' noted Webster, 'is perhaps not so high as it was before the war, probably because he conducts mainly in the provinces (Liverpool Philharmonic Orchestra) . . . and has been conducting too much.' This was wickedly disingenuous. It was Webster himself who had engaged and over-worked Sargent in Liverpool, at the cost of his London reputation. He owed the conductor a fair hearing at Covent Garden, but Webster was not a man to remember his debts.

Albert COATES, who had directed pre-war seasons in St Petersburg, Berlin, Vienna and New York was written off by Webster as too old and in 'doubtful' health. Aged sixty-three, Coates migrated soon after to South Africa, where he conducted the Johannesburg Symphony Orchestra for seven formative years.

The next candidate required diplomatic handling. Constant Lambert, music director of Sadler's Wells ballet, was esteemed by Keynes as 'potentially the most brilliant person I have ever met'.[12] De Valois saw him as 'our only hope of an English Diaghilev'[13] and William Walton, a committee member, was one of his oldest friends. The first Englishman to compose symphonic jazz, Lambert was also an influential essayist and wit, author of the much-read *Music Ho!*, successful in almost everything he touched.

At the ballet, he had educated Ashton in music and nurtured Margot Fonteyn, both culturally and as her first lover. As the central figure in a bohemian circle novelized by Anthony Powell in *A Dance to the Music of Time*, Lambert introduced body-conscious ballet folk to a Fitzrovian warren of ideas, where his painter and poet friends were reciprocally drawn into an awareness of dance. An enemy of romanticism and all things German, mildly anti-Semitic and anti-modern, Lambert adored French forms, foods and finesse. Lame from boyhood operations and often in pain, he sought oblivion in the lap of teenage girls and hard liquor. The sculptor Elizabeth Frink once left Lambert slumped senseless across a bar as she went to a concert at which he was supposed to recite Walton's *Façade*. To her amazement, Lambert walked on stage a few minutes late and gave an immaculate performance. His friends viewed his addictions with amusement. Webster, who disliked and distrusted Lambert, could not risk affronting his supporters.

He delivered a verdict that was curt, factual and damningly

neutral. LAMBERT, began Webster, 'is a very considerable musician'. He had, however, conducted very few operas. 'The internal politics of Sadler's Wells,' insinuated Webster, 'resulted in the fact that although they have had no conductor for years of Lambert's quality, he has never been offered an operatic performance.' He added that Frank Howes, reactionary music critic of *The Times*, 'had the highest opinion of Lambert's possibilities,' and left it at that. Lambert's friends on the committee may have appreciated Webster's discretion in overlooking his riotous personal life; and were probably right in rejecting him for the post. 'Lambert was an excellent ballet conductor when sober,' recalled a Sadler's Wells horn-player, 'but nowhere near as good in opera.'[14] To put it bluntly, said another orchestral musician, 'he was incapable of following a singer or instrumentalist in a *rubato*'.[15]

There were three names left in Webster's hat. Karl RANKL, he suggested, 'is the most likely foreigner resident in England for a high place at Covent Garden. I have had personal experience of his way of handling English musicians and he is very good at the job.' Although the name and track record of this Austrian exile, forty-six years old, were virtually unknown, Webster did not elaborate.

Casting his gaze abroad, he proposed Bruno Walter as the only alien star worth considering. Now in his seventieth year and living in the United States, Walter had been sacked by the Vienna State Opera when the Nazis took over in 1938. He had previously directed the great opera houses of Munich and Berlin, and was a compelling symphonic conductor. WALTER, said Webster, 'is greatly loved in this country and he in his turn loves working here . . . He is good to work with and his presence at Covent Garden would give the whole scheme some cachet.' He could not, however, at such an age be expected to form a company. Walter should be invited only as an honoured guest, Webster felt. Walter felt otherwise, demanding to know who would be training the chorus and orchestra before accepting an engagement. He never conducted again at Covent Garden, though he did make one decisive intervention in its future destiny.

Walter's nomination as the sole overseas candidate exposed the depths of Webster's ignorance or guile, for there were half a dozen other exiles he should certainly have mentioned. Chief among them was Otto Klemperer, 60, architect of Berlin's ground-breaking Kroll Oper and now penniless in New York – as was Jascha Horenstein,

47, formerly of Düsseldorf. George Szell, 48, once of Berlin and Prague, and Fritz Reiner, 57, of Budapest and Dresden, held positions with US orchestras but were open to overtures. Erich Kleiber, 55, former head of the Berlin State Opera, was mouldering in Buenos Aires. Any of these masters was capable of raising an opera house from the foundations up, yet none was considered for Covent Garden – either because Webster had not heard of them, or because he feared their competence and charisma.

The last name on his list was an Englishman working abroad, a quiet fellow who had conducted many operas for Beecham before taking on orchestras in Rochester and Cincinnati. Born into a musical family of Belgian descent, Eugene Goossens was fifty-two years old and looking for a career move after making the awful misjudgement of refusing to pay commission to his all-powerful US manager, Arthur Judson.[16] He was finished in America and dying to come home, where his parents still lived and his oboist brother and harpist sister were active in the London orchestras.

GOOSSENS was thus both qualified and available – a bit too available for Webster's liking. 'He has been conductor of the Cincinnati Orchestra for some 15 years. The fact that he has stayed there so long makes it clear that he has been very satisfactory to Cincinnati, but it might be criticized on the grounds that if he were really first-class he should have gone to a better orchestra,' was his assessment. Given the restricted choice and the urgent need, however, Keynes and his colleagues ordered Webster to engage him without delay. Ralph Hawkes had sounded him out some weeks beforehand, and Goossens had informed his parents that he expected to accept the offer. 'I'll be returning,' he wrote, 'in the most dignified and important role I could possibly return to: something which I think would make you very proud of me – at last!'[17] There was a servile flaw in Goossens character, a damaging weakness that was not publicly evident but which might have been picked up by Webster's man-watching sensors.

Whatever his instructions, the General Administrator was in no rush to issue a contract. In June 1945, three months after hearing from Hawkes, the conductor complained of lack of progress. When summer passed without further word, he agreed to conduct in Australia. In March 1946 after eleven months of inaction from Webster, Hawkes cabled a warning from New York: 'We shall lose Goossens unless we can come to brass tacks immediately. After consultation with Keynes who has spoken to Goossens on telephone I am offering him definite engagement for two years from July at five thousand pounds per annum. He cannot cancel Australian engagement thus arrival London earlier than July impossible. Most important reach provisional conclusions about operatic repertoire before he leaves for Australia.'[18]

A week or so earlier, Webster had sent formal proposals to Goossens couched in terms that were, perhaps, intentionally unappealing. 'Anything that we do by way of opera has more or less to be from scratch,' he wrote. 'Not that England is entirely devoid of good singers, but there are naturally few of them and those few, for obvious reasons, are not well schooled in Opera.' Nevertheless, the company would have to 'give every encouragement to the British artist and consider him first . . . We also intend giving every encouragement to British composers.' It read like a recipe for vocal mediocrity.

All operas would have to be sung in English because 'opera has never really prospered anywhere unless given in the language of the audience attending the performance.' Some of the conducting might be given to Lambert, Sargent, Barbirolli and 'a newcomer here, a Czech named (Walter) Sus(s)kind'.

Webster went on to outline administrative procedure. 'The general direction of the company would be in the hands of yourself and the principal producer, with myself in the Chair.'[19] In other words, every artistic decision would have to be approved by Webster before it went to the board for modification and authorization. No opera director in the world operated under such restraints, and Goossens promptly rejected the proposal on almost every count.

He pointed out that the Met gave opera successfully in the original language; that Covent Garden had only ever flourished with big singers, albeit foreigners; and that you cannot make bricks without straw. Above all, he objected to Webster's triumvirate. 'With regard to the directorial set-up, I am a little inclined to view with misgiving any divided authority. Blame for the shortcomings of a production as well as credit for its good points should fall on the shoulders of a single individual – the artistic director . . . Webster's letter has finally made me realize that I cannot safely undertake the responsibility for a project the artistic outcome of which I cannot foresee.'[20]

Goossens had left the door open but Keynes, incensed by what he saw as ingratitude, told Webster to appoint a more pliant conductor

– adding that if the new man failed 'in the first six months, we shall get rid of him and let Goossens take his job.'[21] Webster was 'delighted'[22] and engaged his privately preferred choice, Rankl.

However, while pleased by Goossens' withdrawal, Webster could not forgive the snub. Goossens sailed for Australia where he served as director of the New South Wales Conservatory and conductor of the Sydney Symphony Orchestra. Whenever he spotted a promising singer, he sent the youngster straight to Webster as a personal favour, when he could have directed them just as easily and perhaps more profitably to an American or European opera company. The kindness was not reciprocated. Whenever Goossens or his agent asked if he might guest-conduct an opera at Covent Garden, Webster's reply was always in the courteous negative.

By 1953, Goossens was almost begging: 'Dear friend Webster . . . This is just to let you know that I would welcome an invitation from the Covent Garden authorities to take charge of some opera performances at the old Theatre in which I formerly appeared so frequently . . . A lifetime's experience of opera is still in me, as befits one who has directed at different times close on sixty operas . . . I venture to think that the press and public would display some interest in my reappearance.'[23] Webster replied that conducting arrangements for the next season were 'almost complete', and offered him free tickets instead. The following year, he proposed Goossens as chief conductor of the ballet, an insult to a musician of his stature.

Goossens was thrown out of Australia in January 1956 after being caught – or, more probably, set up – with a thousand items of pornography in his luggage. The Governors of the BBC reviewed his case and gravely resolved to allow him to conduct their orchestras 'after a suitable interval'. At Covent Garden, however, any engagement was out of the question. Goossens, naïve to the last, could not believe that Webster had ordered his exclusion and continued to address him pathetically as 'Friend'. His final letter, thanking for some tickets, sighs that 'visits to Covent Garden arouse in me an almost unbearable nostalgia'.[24]

Wise as always after the event, Kenneth Clark lamented the dreadful error in his memoirs: 'David Webster didn't really know the field [of conducting] and would not turn to anyone who could advise him in case he would be overshadowed. He chose as Musical Director a minor figure named Karl Rankl and for some years we put on performances which varied between mediocre and bad.'[25] Rankl's appointment was announced on 16 June 1946, together with details of the company's curtain-raiser, Purcell's opera, *The Fairy Queen*, conducted by Lambert. Gushing news like a punctured hosepipe, as if to divert pressure from a faulty headpiece, Webster also let it be known that the choreographer Frederick Ashton was to be 'production consultant' to the opera company, though Ashton's knowledge of opera was limited and his experience non-existent. Ashton had lately created *Symphonic Variations*, the deepest and most enduring of his ballets.

'Who on earth is Rankl?' demanded the press. *The Times*, in a well-briefed leading article, bemoaned the exclusion of Beecham and 'certain other musicians working in America', but hoped that 'Mr Rankl's experience in the direction of half a dozen (*sic*) continental opera houses (would) qualify him for the great task.'[26] Rankl's credentials were taken as read. Little more was known about him in England where he had conducted barely a dozen concerts, but in America some émigré musicians were 'highly amused' when they heard of his sudden eminence.[27]

The fourteenth child of a subsistence farmer from Gaaden, near Vienna, Rankl had served in the trenches during the First World War before being invalided out to study with Arnold Schoenberg, himself newly demobbed. Among the destitute of a defeated nation, Schoenberg's pupils were the poorest of the poor. He taught them without charging a fee and they repaid him by performing all manner of musical drudgery, from selling tickets at his 'private' concerts to making piano reductions of his unplayed scores. When a wealthy patron offered a donation, Schoenberg thanked the 'dear, kind lady' and said he was sending her gift to two young disciples, Hanns Eisler and Rankl, 'both as poor as they are gifted, as ardent as they are sensitive, and as intelligent as they are imaginative'.[28]

After a spell as repetiteur and chorusmaster at Vienna's Volksoper under the crusty Felix Weingartner, Rankl served a traditional musical apprenticeship as conductor in the provincial towns of Reichenberg and Königsberg. He rounded off his training with three years as Otto Klemperer's assistant at the Kroll Oper in Berlin, birthplace of operatic modernism. In 1932, he was named music director in Wiesbaden, one of Klemperer's former posts; but when the Nazis seized power he refused to live in Germany. Graz in his home country gave him the running of its opera house for the next four years. In 1937 he succeeded Szell at the German-language opera house in Prague, a small company in a great musical city. Months later, the German army marched in. Linked to left-wing causes and married to a half-Jewish wife, Adele Jahoda, Rankl fled to England.

The outbreak of war left him stranded and penniless, living on two pounds a week from a Czech charity. In the five years until he obtained a work permit, he was put up in a spare cottage by the Oxford classicist Gilbert Murray, while his wife knitted small items for sale. When officialdom finally relented, he stood in at short notice for two London concerts and was engaged by the Liverpool Philharmonic, where he impressed Webster. After the war, he was invited to audition for the two Australian jobs that were being offered at the same time to Goossens and Lambert. Unable to get travel papers for Adele, Rankl refused to travel alone; when the plane he was booked on crashed en route, Rankl saw it as a mark of providence. Two weeks later, Webster offered him Covent Garden.

In technical respects, he was well qualified. Rankl knew the workings of an opera house inside out and was a good judge of singers and musicians. His ear was acute and his repertoire broad. He knew how to schedule rehearsals and plan a balanced season. He had a well-stocked mind, and was open to new ideas. He 'had a very high opinion'[29] he told an interviewer, of Walton, Britten, Bliss and Vaughan Williams. A high-domed little man in rimless glasses and bow-tie, Rankl looked the part of a central European intellectual as depicted by Christopher Isherwood in *Prater Violet*: ferociously intelligent, professionally stringent yet privately gentle and vulnerable. 'He frightened a lot of people,' said one of his singers, 'but I got to know he liked animals, and I thought if he liked animals there must be a kind side to him.'[30]

Rankl's drawbacks became apparent only when he began to conduct under pressure. He was the kind of conductor who, when unsure of himself, could not leave well alone. He felt the need to indicate every semi-demi-quaver and would work himself into a lather in the quietest passages. He disturbed the audience without greatly elevating the orchestra. When things went wrong in rehearsal, he did not thunder – he nagged. His friendly beam turned fractious and he lacked the native wit to jolly musicians back into good spirits. He spoke a clipped English, rendered directly from the

German. 'Oh, those swine!' he would shout, not realizing how much uglier the word sounded to English ears. 'Rankl was a sweet old thing but a bit of a martinet,' said his assistant conductor, Peter Gellhorn. 'I don't think he wanted to be. He felt always up against it.'[31]

Instead of easing with achievement, his anxiety escalated. 'It was not until he had been stretched beyond his capacity and endurance that he became the frightening hysteric we were later to see,'[32] reflected one musician. At the end of the first season, several players left the orchestra, unable to bear the atmosphere. Rankl tried to mend fences, inviting musicians to a Christmas party at his home in Acacia Road, St John's Wood, where they met his stately wife, Adele, and her 'adopted daughter', a newly-arrived Austrian girl called Christine. This set-up was too continental for simple English folk to fathom, and after a while it got too much for Mrs Rankl, who left to live with her sister in the West Country. Some years later, Karl married young Christine.*

There were social barriers, as well as linguistic and cultural ones, that Rankl could never overcome. Raised in a country where seriousness was a virtue and flippancy a sin, he had no small talk and could not make conversation with Covent Garden grandees. The convivial Clarks threw a thank-you party for him at the end of his first year. 'I am sorry you couldn't come to the Rankl party,' wrote Clark to Webster. 'I hope he enjoyed it – I couldn't tell.'[33] Rankl was the very antithesis of Lambert, who fizzed with bottled bonhomie. The two chief conductors detested one another on sight.

Nevertheless, Rankl's single-minded, strait-laced dedication was precisely what Covent Garden needed. He had six months to form an opera company, and he went at his task with a determination that more famous maestros might not have matched. Between May and early August he held auditions in the crimson-and-chandeliered Crush Bar at Covent Garden and in large halls around the country, extending the search in a quick summer trip to America. Around two thousand singers were heard, among them postal clerks, milkmen, housewives and farmhands. Few had ever sung for money, or could read a score. From these raw voices, Rankl signed up chorus singers for eight pounds a week, and soloists for forty, which seemed like a

---

* Adele Rankl refused to grant him a divorce, and he remarried only after her death in 1963 (Information from Mrs C. Rankl)

fortune. 'I thought I was a millionairess,'[34] said Constance Shacklock, a farmer's daughter from Sherwood Forest, who was taken on for secondary mezzo roles.

Webster played a full part in the search, relishing his opportunity as a talent-spotter. The untrained bass singer Ian Wallace found himself facing the former shopkeeper and a lady he introduced as 'Madame Gerhardt'. Wallace had never heard of the celebrated lieder singer and bluffed his way well enough through two arias to be called back for a further audition with Rankl. Second time round, his enthusiasm did not compensate for a sound that was deemed 'too small' for Covent Garden.

During an audition in Leeds, a Harrogate organist with handlebar moustaches, Douglas Robinson by name, was appointed Chorus Master, a post he held until 1974. At the same session Rankl met an ex-Berliner, Peter Gellhorn, whom Webster had seen working with the Carl Rosa Company. Rankl appointed Gellhorn Head of Music Staff. Norman Feasey, a pre-war Covent Gardenite known as 'the Reverend' returned as Chief Repetiteur, and Reginald Goodall, a bespectacled conductor in his mid-forties, was poached from Sadler's Wells for thirty-five pounds a week.

There was a rush of qualified refugees for the job vacancies but the order was out to buy British. Webster noted that 'apart from Mr Rankl, Peter Gellhorn would be the only foreigner on the musical side'.[35] The fact that both men were naturalized UK citizens was immaterial. It was a matter of island pride that Covent Garden should be crewed with native stock. Rankl, the day their papers arrived, told his wife, 'Liebchen, we are British!' She was promptly dubbed 'the British Liebchen'.

At the opening rehearsals, hardly anyone had ever seen or heard the operas they were meant to be performing, so limited had been the English exposure to opera before the war. Rankl could take nothing for granted; he had to teach the art from scales up.

An orchestra of sorts had been put together by Lambert putting the word around the public bar of The George and other watering holes that there were jobs going at eighteen quid a week in a new band under his cheery baton. Only twelve members of the orchestra had ever played opera before, and the leader, Joseph Shadwick, was so unsuited to the task that he departed after only one season.

There had been no provision for such an orchestra in the original Covent Garden scheme. 'Our plan,' Webster reminded Keynes, 'was to use one of the existing (London) orchestras for the Covent Garden work, but this has not proved practicable. In any case, demobilization has changed the personnel picture and we find that we can form our own orchestra. Constant is convinced that its quality will be high.'[36]

The cost of the orchestra was enormous, over £70,000 a year, but Webster hoped to earn back some money from commercial engagements. Lambert assured the BBC 'that he was trying to make Covent Garden orchestra into a thoroughly efficient and coherent entity, and with that in view he hoped to get them concert and recording work in due course apart from their work in the pit at Covent Garden.'[37] But this was either drunken talk or dangerous self-delusion, for there was no chance of Covent Garden attracting the calibre of musician that played in the London Symphony Orchestra, London Philharmonic or BBC Symphony Orchestra, let alone the golden-handshake Royal Philharmonic and Philharmonia orchestras that Beecham and EMI's Walter Legge were forming from the best demobbed bandsmen. If a musician wanted excitement, he went to work with Beecham, Toscanini, de Sabata and Celibidache at one of the self-employed bands. If he wanted security, he signed up with Boult for a BBC pension and paid holidays. At Covent Garden, all that was on offer was a ten-month contract under conductors of choleric instability. Man for man, Covent Garden was the weakest of London orchestras and remained so. To make up numbers, Shadwick went looking for women players, incurring a reprimand from his union.

Lambert had first crack at the orchestra. After leading it in the curtain-raising *Sleeping Princess*, he set to work on a dazzling venture that would open the new era of opera at Covent Garden. The two hundred and fiftieth anniversary of the death of Henry Purcell had fallen in 1945, and Lambert came up with the idea of reviving his famous but unfamiliar masque, *The Fairy Queen*, as a full-blown three-act opera. Purcell, declared Lambert, 'is by general consent the greatest of English composers and is considered even by those Continentals who still imagine England to be *le pays sans musique* as one of the great classical masters.'[38]

By cutting screeds of Shakespearian dialogue, the masque was kept to an endurable three hours. Professor Edward J. Dent helped modernize the instrumentation. The designer was Lambert's flat-mate, the artist Michael Ayrton; the choreographer was Ashton and the producer was Malcolm Baker-Smith, an associate of the French cinema director, René Clair. *The Fairy Queen* was not an opera but it was about as English as could be, representing a combination of all English arts, a Restoration-era *Gesamtkunstwerk*. To make up for a lack of celebrated singers, or much strong stuff for them to sing, a full galaxy of dancers was trotted out, headed by Fonteyn and Helpmann and augmented by Beryl Grey, Michael Somes, Alexander Grant and the ominously popular Moira Shearer. 'The Sadler's Wells Ballet (Director: Ninette de Valois)' took top billing, above 'Soloists and Chorus of Covent Garden Opera.'

Lambert had invested six months of his short life in *The Fairy Queen*, only to find that Webster was scheming to replace him with Rankl. Webster was not prepared take risks with his opening night, and could not be sure that Lambert would turn up sober. He was forced to back down when Ashton, Ayrton, Helpmann and Baker-Smith wrote an emphatic appeal on Lambert's behalf, backed by a veiled threat of mass resignation:

> The fact that *The Fairy Queen* is more ballet than opera and that the vast majority of the action is choreographic and devolves upon the ballet company, who have worked under Mr Lambert's music direction for many years, indicates that they would be likely to perform with greater confidence under a conductor so experienced in this medium as Mr Lambert.[39]

The opening, on 12 December 1946, was dutifully received. The production was revived once, in 1951, and never again.

Downcast and disillusioned, Lambert slumped into decline. Although newly in love with Isabel Delmer, estranged wife of a war correspondent and former mistress to Miro, Epstein and Giacometti, he went from booze to bust. Between acts of *The Fairy Queen*, he would nip out for a large gin, no tonic. In one pub, he was seen to spend half his weekly pay packet. After a holiday with Ayrton in Italy, he returned to conduct *Turandot* and had a terminal ruction with Webster. The morning after his last scheduled performance, 2 July 1947, Webster gave him the choice of resigning, or getting fired. Isabel, who married him in October, concurred that 'his physical and mental state at this time was such that he could not be relied upon to give *consistently* good performances.'[40]

In his resignation letter, Lambert said he intended to spend more time composing and 'will obviously be unable to give the hundred per cent support to the ballet which I have been able to give in the past.' Webster's reply was gushingly and ungrammatically insincere: 'The Sadler's Wells Ballet owes you an enormous amount of credit for the work they (*sic*) have done. Certainly, no ballet company since Diaghilev has had such an outstanding list of musical works in their repertoire, and as far as English composers are concerned I am quite sure that they have never had such an innings with any other musical institution. It does you enormous credit... I personally am extremely happy that it is likely you are going to do more composing and I am sure the whole musical world will be glad also.'[41] Webster could afford to be generous, having got rid of an enemy at no personal cost.

Lambert never conducted opera again at Covent Garden. De Valois continued to book him for her ballets, and named him artistic director of her second company, at Sadler's Wells, at a paltry five hundred pounds a year. He would merit a footnote in England's cultural renaissance, but no memorial in its central edifice. On 15 August 1951, after conducting *Rio Grande* at the Proms, he collapsed in the street and had to be helped home. Some nights later he woke up delirious, raging against Webster and his interference in *The Fairy Queen*. 'Don't let them take me away,' he pleaded. Rushed to hospital, he died the next morning, two days short of forty-six years old.

The cause of death was broncho-pneumonia and diabetes mellitus. Had the latter condition been diagnosed sooner, it would have been treated with insulin injections and noted as the main cause of his alcoholic thirst. The composer Dennis ApIvor, who observed Lambert with the eye of a qualified physician, believed he drank to stave off boredom. This being England, nobody told him he was killing himself or needed to see a doctor, because what a man drank was his own business – and, anyway, Constant was such fun when drinking. Even Dr ApIvor admitted that 'the volatile and uproarious side of his company, of which I have never seen the like, was probably at least fifty per cent of himself.'[42] Isabel went on to marry Lambert's best friend, the composer Alan Rawsthorne. Both would contribute to Ashton ballets, but neither was engaged by Webster for the Opera. Nor was any tribute to Lambert permitted at Covent Garden. Lambert, said the novelist Anthony Powell, had 'a touch of genius' – a quality too dangerous for David Webster. Constant

Lambert was the first but would not be the last conductor at Covent Garden to collapse in a gutter and die in disgrace.

The winter of 1946-47 was the worst for half a century, vicious winds whistling through the blitzed-out city and a frost piercing its shattered defences. The Thames froze at Westminster Bridge and fuel shortages, causing frequent power cuts, meant there was no relief from the cold either at home or at work. In the warren of Covent Garden's rehearsal rooms and offices, the lights came on for only two hours a day. The cats in the neighbouring market turned feral with hunger. A chorister who stopped to stroke a passing puss was warned she could get her hand bitten off.

The gloom was as pervasive as the cold. Winston Churchill talked of an Iron Curtain dividing Europe. Many awaited the imminent outbreak of a nuclear Third World War. In the literature, the art and the music of that winter, it is hard to find a single note of hope. Vaughan Williams, who so often caught the national mood, was at work on a sixth symphony which would end in hushed despair.

The only happy faces belonged to the 'spivs' and black-marketeers who ran a racket in scarce commodities, turning an overwhelmingly law-respecting country into a society that con-doned law-breaking when it eased officially-imposed deprivation. Like America under Prohibition, England during post-war rationing underwent profound changes in its character and conduct.

On these dark, cold and fearful mornings, Karl Rankl set to work creating an opera company at Covent Garden. The forces at his disposal did not inspire confidence. 'A good many of the men were just out of the forces,' recalled a chorister. 'One was lame, one scarred by burns and all of us were poorly dressed. I was wearing a coat my mother had made me out of an army blanket. We didn't look very well fed either.'[43]

The first production for this pallid and bedraggled assembly was a sun-kissed *Carmen*, the most popular and passionate of operas and the one least suited to the conductor's temperament. Pedantic and bloodless, a counter of crotchets and stickler for formalities, Rankl beat his way metronomically through Bizet's blazing love-tangle. An English pre-war mezzo, Edith Coates, sang the heroine and an Australian ex-policeman, Kenneth Neate, was Don José.

The Queen and several Cabinet ministers turned out for opening night, 14 January 1947. They cheered the ballerina, Beryl Grey, and

little else. Apart from the establishmentarian *Times*, which proclaimed a success, the reviews were as grim as the weather. A sour
pack of critics found little to praise apart from Edward Burra's set
and costumes, and the capable stage direction of Henry Cass. Before
the war, Covent Garden had not bothered with production. No
director was listed on playbills and any shifting around was left to
the stage manager, who chalked crosses on the floor where singers
were supposed to stand. The noticeable difference at the new Covent
Garden was that designers and directors had been recruited from the
thriving theatrical world to enhance the operatic experience.
Otherwise, comparisons with pre-war performances were overwhelmingly unfavourable.

Carmen was followed by Massenet's *Manon*, a relative novelty to
English audiences, conducted by Goodall, adroitly directed by
Ashton and beautifully designed by James Bailey. The singing was
the let-down once again, with the main roles taken by an American,
Virginia MacWatters, who was pretty but slight, and a venerable
English tenor, Heddle Nash, who was born in 1894 and sounded
woodenly Victorian.

And so the season wore on, with few magic moments apart from
the return of Eva Turner as Turandot, a role she had made her own at
La Scala and was now required to relearn in English. 'I pray it goes
well,' she told a friend.[44] The rest of the programme was a line-up of
inspired amateurs and tired professionals. 'I am shocked that
singing of that order can survive the first week of rehearsal in a
respectable opera house,' griped the *New Statesman*'s Desmond
Shawe-Taylor of some roles in *Der Rosenkavalier*. 'Who has the
power of veto at Covent Garden and why wasn't it used?'

On 1 April 1947, Rankl mounted the conductor's box to rehearse
the third act Pantomime in *Der Rosenkavalier*, beating two to the
bar. David Franklin, singing Baron Ochs, recalled the ensuing
embarrassment:

He raised his hands, looked around expectantly and plunged into
his downbeat. With completely deadpan faces, the orchestra
played the prelude to *Carmen*. Rankl . . . snatched the music from
Joe Shadwick's stand – Joe led the orchestra. 'But this is
Rosenkavalier that you have,' said Rankl, 'why you play *Carmen*
– why?' Joe explained to him that on All Fool's Day we play jokes
on our friends. If only Rankl had had the wit – or the humanity –

to realize it, the important word was 'friends' . . . But Rankl told Shadwick not to be silly. 'Rehearse properly,' he said angrily. . . Fifteen minutes later, when he stopped them to clear up some problem in the score, he turned to Shadwick and said anxiously, 'When I come into the pit tonight to conduct *Magic Flute*, what will you play?' 'For God's sake,' said Joe, 'we shall play the *Flute*, of course. This was just a joke.' 'A *joke*?' said Rankl – he couldn't believe it.[45]

In the coffee break, Constance Shacklock overheard him asking a fellow-immigrant, 'what is April Fools, Gellhorn?' On another occasion, as Rankl began his rehearsal, the band struck up 'Happy Birthday!' 'What are you doing? This is not our music? What is this?' he cried. Someone explained patiently that it was a tune rendered affectionately on birthdays. It was 1 October and the band wanted to salute their conductor but Rankl, apoplectic, could not accept it.[46] To him the opera house was a place of service, solemnity and decorum, a temple of the arts. When a large Welsh chorister, arriving late, walked into rehearsal in his outdoor clothes, Rankl rushed up and ripped the hat from his head. For a glowering moment, the two men almost came to blows; neither could understand why the other was so angry.

The bitter, irascible Rankl scarcely resembled the leader of men whom Webster had described to his committee: 'I have had personal experience of his way of handling English musicians and he is very good at the job.' Rankl smoked a pipe and went to cricket matches at Lord's in the hope of penetrating the mysteries of Englishness, but he never learned to relax and form working relationships. He believed fervently in the viability of English-sung opera and the trainability of English singers, but he lacked any powers of public persuasion and was too shy to expose himself to press interviews. Beecham branded Rankl's appointment 'the mystery of mysteries' and his toadies wafted a stink of venom around the press.

'We felt the press had their knives into us from the beginning,' said Gellhorn. 'Nothing we could do was right, and both Rankl and I worked so hard, conducting three or four nights a week. Sunday mornings, I would lie in bed until lunchtime, exhausted.'[47] Rankl kept saying that their efforts would take years to be recognized, but the opening season was a write-off and the public was drifting elsewhere. Covent Garden Opera drew a sixty per cent attendance, an average of twelve hundred spectators a night.

Yet the Arts Council kept faith, more than doubling its grant to £55,000, and some critics knowingly suppressed the deficiencies in service of what they saw as a greater public interest. 'I thought that some of my colleagues . . . should take a longer view,' said Frank Howes of *The Times*, 'even if in detail there was truth in what they were saying. And I think now that the start was right.'[48]

Even in a false dawn, Covent Garden was not without friends. The trustees were astonishingly well-connected and they pounded their address books tirelessly. Clark, in particular, preached the cause around his circle of political, commercial, artistic and sexual conquests. He was forever badgering Webster for free tickets to give to contacts who might be 'valuable allies from many points of view, as well as being charming people' – the targets in this instance being Sir John Anderson, the Independent MP, and his charming wife, Ava. Sir John was not so much a household name as a backyard fixture, his 'Anderson Huts' having sheltered many British families during the terrors of the Blitz. He had served as Home Secretary and Chancellor of the Exchequer under Churchill, and was retained as a nuclear weapons adviser to the Labour Government, with a private secretariat in the Cabinet Office. 'If you could let me have two tickets,' suggested Clark, 'I think it would repay us.'[49]

There had to be a quid pro quo. In return for free seats, the Royal Opera House amassed a list of powerful people who could be called upon in time of need to press its case with Government. Covent Garden became a professional player of the English game of grease-and-favour, always getting more than it gave.

Adversity, as Churchill discovered, brings out the bulldog in the British. The more Covent Garden got bombed with bad notices, the greater was its collective tenacity. 'Everyone, from the top to the bottom, was fired with a deep sense of enthusiasm which it was impossible to ignore,' said the bass-baritone, Michael Langdon. 'I was immediately caught up by it, and it quickly changed from being just a fill-in job to being something I was desperate to do. Above all there was a tremendous amount of fun in what we were doing.'[50]

'We were building a British opera company,' declared Constance Shacklock. 'We were working as a team to build something of value, something the country could be proud of.'[51]

'It was a very special time,' recalled Iris Kells, a chorus girl who was promoted to soloist. 'So many had been in the War. Some of us who were very young were helped along by pre-war singers. Everybody pulled together.'[52]

'The chorus rehearsed in the girls' dressing room at the top of the building, up four noisy flights of concrete stairs,' reminisced Irene Thomas, who went on to amaze the nation with her erudition as a radio panellist on *Round Britain Quiz*. 'There was no proper chorus rehearsal room. We sat in a clutter of make-up boxes, crinoline frames, wigs, mirrors, shoes and dress-rails with Robbie (Douglas Robinson) and the pianist wedged in the corner. But we didn't mind the discomfort . . . we began to forge a company spirit.'[53]

There were rough pubs in the vicinity that opened for market porters at six in the morning and held Last Drinks for singers until after the final curtain. The Nag's Head, opposite the stage door, was a ready haven for the desperate. Its landlord, Wally Pack, was a retired boxer and his wife a mother-surrogate to the homesick, and around the bar there would usually be an old-timer or two from the Beecham era, eager to trade gossip for the price of a scotch. For more substantive nourishment, there was a greasy spoon café in Floral Street that did not look too closely at ration coupons. Deprivation meant that few could afford to be over-fastidious. One prop-boy used to collect fag-ends after the Smoking Chorus in *Carmen* and re-roll them for resale to the cast. Some men from the market doubled as extras in crowd-scenes, others earned a bit on the side helping out as scene-shifters. Michael Manuel, whose father owned a fruit-and-veg stall, was taken on to the staff and became stage manager for the ballet.

A community of allsorts began to emerge, studded with the kind of characters that make every theatre and circus seem larger than life. There was 'Bogey' Ballard, the veteran chief machinist, who knew all the secret passageways in the building and had a horrible knack of turning up on an overhead gantry, shouting 'I heard you!', just as people were disparaging him. There was a stage electrician called Norman who used to pull on rubber gloves and hold together two live wires to produce the lightning-flash in *Don Giovanni*. Sergeant Martin, the moustachioed chief commissionaire in his long red coat with gold buttons, was a sentimental soul who held tickets for the best shows for his wartime commanding officer in the Scots Guards. The repetiteur Eric Mitchell, a former Royal Marine, came to work each morning in black coat and striped trousers. Michael Wood, the beanpole press officer, would walk to the office with a tiny fox-terrier called Henry – unless it rained, in which case he sent the dog ahead by taxi. Wood had his shoes polished to a high gloss three times a week by his former Army batman.

The combination of grey deprivation and lurid eccentricity, external assaults and internal solidarity, created a remarkable sense of unity and purpose. And once the company began touring the country, sharing bedrooms in shabby digs and jokes about their landladies, the cohesion bonded into something far stronger than a place of employment and entertainment. 'We were like a family,' said the stately Shacklock, who stood out for her glamorous, home-made hats. 'I knew every member of the chorus by name, and the ballet too,' she said; fifty years later, she still saw some of them for lunch.

'The great thing about the Garden was the touring,' added Iris Kells, 'it built the company and brought us together.' 'We played cards with the orchestra,' remembered Irene Thomas, 'pontoon, with a suitcase-top as a table.'[54] Some returned from tour newly in love. Irene fell for a Welsh chorister, Eddie Thomas; Kells wed a repetiteur, Leonard Hancock. Shacklock fell for Eric Mitchell when he coached her as Brangäne in *Tristan and Isolde*. They married at the end of the first season in a registry office. Mitchell, whose first marriage had broken up in the war, could not be entered in holy matrimony by the Church of England in the Kensington church where he served each Sunday as organist. Such were the rules that earned England its reputation for bifocality, but few contested the *status quo* at this time, and the Mitchell couple were content to receive a private blessing from their parish priest.

Greater and more lasting than the roll of romantic couplings at Covent Garden was the emergent collective ethos. It pervaded the company from top to pit and must be regarded as David Webster's supreme achievement, arising from his concern for staff welfare, a quality that was rare in class-ridden British industry, outside the Quaker factories and the paternalistic Jewish stores of Tesco and Marks & Spencer. Most chief executives held themselves aloof, descending once a year to join the workers for Christmas lunch and hand out the annual bonus. Bosses were addressed as 'Sir' and subordinates by surname.

Webster, by contrast, was a caring and visible administrator. He was not readily approachable inside the opera house, but would strike up a conversation with any employee who encountered him on the street or in a pub. He usually remembered their names and, if he forgot, called them 'my dear chap'. He was not a daunting figure either in height, dress or demeanour, and seemed to court affection rather than respect. 'In the main, he earned the loyalty of his staff for he brought great dedication to his job and he had a generous nature,' wrote a future chairman, 'although he found it almost impossible to go backstage after a performance to say, "Well done". Why this was, I never discovered.'[55] Some put his reticence down to a natural shyness, which turned to an 'obsessive secretiveness'[56] as his company came under pressure.

Like many gay men, he may have longed for a family of his own and at Covent Garden he created a surrogate of sorts. 'Do you know,' he once reproached the Welsh baritone, Geraint Evans, 'you've never invited me to your home.'[57] To members of the company, this fat, bald, florid little man was a fatherly rock of solidarity.

'Webster was always there for the singers,' said Iris Kells. 'We had very few problems. I don't remember being angry at anything.'

After Keynes, Kenneth Clark thought he deserved to become chairman of the Arts Council, or Covent Garden, or both. He had deputized during Keynes's long absences and knew all the right doors to knock and all the right men to lunch along Whitehall, which perversely worked against him. What Whitehall wanted was to put the genie back in its box. Keynes, with his fluid mind and stealthy charm, had set up a state-funded Arts Council and national opera house that operated at arm's length from the proper authorities. It was time for the Civil Service to claw back control, offering Clement Attlee's hard-pressed Cabinet the means to renege on promises and curb the costs of Keynes's folly. The twin crowns of the arts kingdom were now in the gift of the Prime Minister, acting on the advice of officials who drew their recommendations from a list of the Great and the Good who could be relied upon to show 'worthiness, soundness and discretion' – any quality, that is, except bold imagination. These were the curbs that Whitehall sought to impose upon the arts, and they concurred more or less with the needs of Attlee's Cabinet.

Contrary to popular myth, the architects of the welfare state were no keener on supporting the arts than the most reactionary of Tories. The Labour Government was composed of social reformers, trades union organizers and political strategists, few of whom felt much concern for culture. Their objective was equalization of opportunity in a post-imperial state, an aim that was annoyingly delayed by war debt, a mutinous workforce and the ever-spiralling cost of nuclear defence in the face of a perceived Soviet threat. They had neither the resources nor the inclination to foster the arts as a source of hope and revival. Some ministers regarded the arts as a niggling distraction, others as a necessary palliative: socialist bread and circuses. Either way, the arts needed to be yoked to the machinery of government.

To head the Arts Council, Whitehall and the Labour Government selected a retired officer of the City of London Corporation's Drapers' Company, a man who had sat for years half-noticed as vice-chairman of the Old Vic and Sadler's Wells. Sir Ernest Pooley was six months short of seventy years old and, in Clark's words, 'having no interest in the arts, he could be relied upon not to press their claims too strongly.'[58] Mary Glasgow, the Council's secretary-general, refused to mask her contempt for Keynes's successor and paid for it with her career; Pooley replaced her in 1950 with W. E. Williams, one of Tom Jones's antedeluvian Taffia. In her memoirs, Glasgow reported that she was once told by a drunken civil servant that Pooley was a 'safe little shit' who would not demand money or make trouble because 'we've got something on him'.[59] Whether or not there is substance to this rancorous aspersion, implying sexual (specifically, homosexual) scandal, the grey-faced Pooley chaired the Arts Council for seven lean years; at the end of which, he was created a baronet and got married for the first time, to an old chum's widow.

Under his aegis, the Council's grant rose from an initial £235,000 to £575,000 in 1948, at which point Pooley decided that state benefice had reached its natural limits. 'We don't need any more,' he said, 'an increase will only get us into trouble.'[60] By the time of his departure in 1953, the grant was just £675,000, which included a Coronation year bonus. It is hard to avoid the conclusion that Pooley had been picked to curb the resurgence of British arts, and he did his level best. Subsidy for the arts, he once wrote by way of self-epitaph, 'is frequently both unnecessary and undesirable'.

With the Arts Council emasculated and ruled by a Sadler's Wells man, Covent Garden found itself dangerously isolated. The Trust, alarmed, set out to find a champion whose name would conjure up a

Keynesian measure of awe, not so much from the general public as among the handful of senior mandarins and politicians who had to approve the appointment. Clark might have made a fine figurehead, but in the corridors of power he was dismissed as 'lacking bottom'. What was needed was a man of irresistible intellect and outstanding public service whose word was law in Whitehall. The ideal candidate was found, selflessly or unwittingly, by Clark himself when, in March 1946, he procured a pair of complimentary ballet tickets for the 'valuable' Sir John Anderson, 'who was, in the opinion of Whitehall, the greatest administrator of his day'.[61]

Anderson's public life had been so rich and eventful that he had never spared a flicker of interest for art. 'Administration he was born to and the art of government came not unnaturally as a corollary . . . the arts had never been specifically within his field of operations,' wrote his admiring biographer.[62] 'His knowledge of ballet and opera was minimal, and he did not pretend otherwise,' said a Covent Garden subordinate.[63] A stationer's son from Edinburgh, Anderson excelled in mathematics and philosophy and spent a post-graduate year in Leipzig presciently studying the radioactive properties of uranium. He came top in the Civil Service exams in 1905 with the second highest score in history and was put to work in the Colonial Office, reforming West African currencies. By thirty, he was developing a visionary health insurance system. At thirty-seven he became chairman of the Board of Inland Revenue and, at forty, permanent under-secretary at the Home Office, where he planned the emergency supply and transport mechanism that broke the 1926 General Strike. In between, he had acquitted himself with courage in Dublin during the settlement of the Irish crisis.

He was sent out to settle Moslem-Hindu riots in Bengal in 1932 and escaped an attempt on his life. Six years later, he declined an appeal from Chamberlain to become High Commissioner in strife-torn Palestine, settling instead for a sinecure as an independent MP, representing Scottish Universities. Within eight months he was brought into Chamberlain's Cabinet to organize London's defences. Churchill admired his analytical mind and capacity for hard work, promoting him to Home Secretary and then to Chancellor. He left Anderson in charge of the country when he went abroad, informing the King: 'It is the Prime Minister's duty to advise Your Majesty to send for Sir John Anderson in the event of the Prime Minister and the Foreign Secretary being killed.'[64]

Civil servants called him 'Old Jehovah' and deemed him infallible, albeit self-righteous and woodenly humourless. Anderson had 'without question the most acute brain in Parliament,' said one official. He was 'the only member of the Government able to talk with eminent scientists on equal terms. Scientific papers, consisting mostly of formulae, passed through our office, intelligible only to the Chancellor.'[65] Under Attlee, his command of nuclear technicalities remained indispensable.

In 1946, Anderson took on the chairmanship of the Port of London Authority, an economically sensitive hotbed of industrial unrest, and put his high mind to augmenting his index-linked pension with some rewarding City directorships. In any national crisis, whether flooding in East Anglia or a row with the Russians, someone would send out a call for Anderson and the Solomonian Scot in his high-winged collar would arrive to give solemn and impartial judgement. The initials 'J.A.' on an official memo were enough to put any issue beyond debate. 'Looking back,' wrote a senior colleague, 'I cannot think that he ever made, or caused to be made, a wrong decision.'[66]

In private life he was punctilious and dour. Mourning his beloved first wife, who died during a cancer operation in 1920, he betrayed no emotion at her funeral and required their two tiny orphans to shake hands politely with all present. Falling in love with a Foreign Office widow during the London blackout, he addressed the object of his affections as 'Mrs Wigram' until their marriage. It was mostly to give the French-educated, piano-playing and slightly frivolous Ava a chance to play the grande dame that he was tempted by the Covent Garden chairmanship, though he recalled that it was his assent as Chancellor of the Exchequer which had allowed Keynes to conceive the Royal Opera House project in the first place.

Before accepting the chairmanship, he wanted to be sure he was in possession of all relevant facts. He pressed Webster for details of cash flow and trade conditions. Webster replied that funds were running low, and that Swedish Opera received some ninety-two thousand pounds a year,[67] almost four times as much in state grants as Covent Garden did. Armed with these figures, Anderson wrote to his successor as Chancellor, Hugh Dalton, in a tone so peremptory it sounded more like a military ultimatum than a civil request.

'My dear Dalton,' he began, 'When I mentioned to you a week or two ago that I had been invited to become Chairman of the Covent

Garden Trust in succession to Keynes, I said that I would not feel justified in accepting the suggestion unless I could be assured that the project had been placed on a sound financial basis.'

He was not, he stressed, asking for more money than the Budget had allocated. That would be presumptuous and unprocedural. What he wanted was a copper-bottomed statement of commitment to Covent Garden. 'I want to be assured on two points,' he wrote. 'First that in expressing your offer in terms of so much a year "for the quinquennium" you do not in any way rule out the possibility of a larger payment in certain contingencies before the end of that period and, secondly, that you recognize in the arrangements now contemplated that the State will be assuming a definite obligation to see to it that, subject to others playing their part, Opera will not be let down.'

He went on to berate Dalton for refusing to grant tax relief on gifts to the arts, a veto which (according to Webster) had cost Covent Garden a twenty-five thousand pounds annual donor whose income was subject to 97.5 per cent tax. 'I ask you, therefore,' concluded Anderson combatively, 'to review your attitude in the light of these observations . . .'[68]

No ordinary citizen writing to the Chancellor in such forthright tones would expect to receive more than a dusty reply. But Anderson was no ordinary citizen. He was a supreme civil servant and former Chancellor of the Exchequer who knew that the response to his letter would be drafted not by the man who signed it but by senior Treasury officials whom he had personally raised and trained in the epistolary and administrative arts. The reply was, in effect, pre-ordained by the precise formulation of Anderson's demands, and he did not have long to wait to receive it.

Five mornings later, he sliced open an envelope and read with dry satisfaction a crested document greeting him as 'My dear Anderson'. Dalton began by reiterating the procedure that Anderson had himself put into practice: 'The assistance which the Covent Garden Trust receives from the Treasury will, of course, come to it through the Arts Council,' wrote Dalton. 'You will understand that in general I should wish the Council to feel themselves responsible for the allocation of the funds which Parliament puts at their disposal, and to plan their work ahead in the expectation of an assured but limited grant.'

The commitment Anderson sought was carefully worded in the

language of mandarins, so carefully that the key words have to be emboldened for non-officials to grasp their import.

'I recognize, however,' continued Dalton, 'that the magnitude of the Covent Garden undertaking and the difficulty in present circumstances of estimating its future needs places it in **a special position**, and that the State will be assuming **a definite obligation** to see to it that, subject to others playing their part, **Opera is not let down.** I do not therefore rule out the possibility that **the fulfilment of this obligation might in certain circumstances make it necessary to increase the Treasury grant** to the Arts Council still further than I undertook in my letter [to Pooley] of July 15th. It would, I think, be agreed that these circumstances would not be held to have arisen unless in any year the Trust could show a need for a grant from the Arts Council of an amount exceeding £60,000.

'I am sending a copy of this letter to Pooley.

Yours ever,

Hugh Dalton.'

Anderson was not a man to whoop for joy, but he instructed Webster to inform the Trustees that he regarded 'the terms of the reply as satisfactory' and was now prepared to accept their invitation to become chairman. He was so pleased with the letter that 'he used always to carry (it) about with him in his pocket, taking it out and brandishing it when the need arose.'[69] In his mind it amounted to a constitutional guarantee of Covent Garden's centrality and an irrevocable pledge of financial support. For while he acknowledged that, in theory, 'no Chancellor could commit his successor, the whole history of practical politics was based on the fact that he did.'[70] Anderson held Dalton's letter to be 'morally binding on all future Chancellors';[71] it meant that 'you can close Covent Garden, but you must not starve it'.[72]

This may sound impossibly naïve to post-modern ears which have grown accustomed to senior civil servants being 'economical with the truth', but that is more a measure of how much England has changed in the second half of the twentieth century than a mark of Anderson's gullibility. He belonged to a school which held that government is conducted on a basis of trust and continuity, where an Englishman's word is the bond that ties the hands of future generations and prevents them from disrupting the smooth running of the country. Anderson would himself have cause to be disappointed with the way the rule was applied to Covent Garden, but both he and his immediate disciples upheld the need for a British government to stand by its word, whatever the cost. The retreat from that red line took place only when the country went bust a second time, after the Suez disaster and the loss of empire.

In Anderson's eleven years as chairman of the Royal Opera House, the Treasury developed a resistance to Jehovah's thunderbolts and yielded less than he demanded. Nevertheless, Anderson's letter of intent was a landmark in the company's self-perception. It gave an immediate boost to internal confidence, followed by a lasting glow of self-importance. 'Under the shelter of John Anderson's unshakeable stature the venture of British opera grew lusty and acquired stability,' wrote his biographer. Anderson proved, as expected, a redoubtable chairman. His mastery of any problem from both sides of the argument was an intellectual tour-de-force. He listened closely to unwelcome opinions and delivered judgements that sounded irrefutable. His readiness to delegate had been a feature of his career, and he made no exception in this non-executive role. Ava loved foreign travel and Anderson was content to leave Covent Garden in Webster's hands for long periods, with Clark occupying the Royal Box as deputy chairman.

Webster was not the sort of man Anderson would have chosen to run a Treasury department but, once convinced of his competence, he let him carry on with very little interference. Webster never achieved the cordiality with his second chairman that he had enjoyed with Keynes, and his attempts to charm Ava were lost on a lady who fawned on minor royalty and restricted her contacts with his office to ticket requests. Her husband quickly put a stop to the random leakage of free seats. 'I think there might be something to be said for giving tickets out occasionally to members of the Labour Party,' he suggested, 'but their distribution would have to be in accordance with some plan.'[73] In the mind of a born bureaucrat, there had to be a plan for everything.

Anderson attended opera and ballet dutifully, without displaying any sign of pleasure. When his wife complained about a bad performance, he would reproach her mildly: 'Now, now, Ava, you must remember they are doing their best.'[74]

He was scrupulous in separating his role as a Government adviser from his activities at the Royal Opera House, and every few months his clerk at the Cabinet Office would invoice Webster's secretary, Muriel Kerr, for the sum of one pound to cover Anderson's use of Government postage and stationery for Covent Garden matters.

He ordered formal minutes to be kept of all board meetings and, since the company was publicly funded, felt they should be taken by a qualified civil servant. The Treasury, anxious to keep tabs on its money, supplied a senior official called Denis Rickett, formerly Anderson's confidential assistant on nuclear weapons and soon to become principal private secretary to the Prime Minister, Clement Attlee. Rickett was far too elevated to take physical notes of board proceedings; he left that to his assistant, Miss Bevan, who scribbled away in shorthand and submitted a draft that the senior mandarin then edited into official language. 'There would be vigorous arguments at these meetings and voices were raised in anger,' said an Arts Council observer, 'but if the Board failed to agree on a proposal all that would ever appear in the minutes is the Cabinet phrase: "The Board took note . . ."'[75]

Rickett, who went on to become vice-president of the World Bank, was the first in a distinguished line of Whitehall grandees who took an afternoon off each month to serve as Secretary to Board of the Royal Opera House. No payment was involved, but the officials could attend opera and ballet whenever they liked and more often than some were able to afford on a Whitehall salary. In exchange, Covent Garden gained an invisible friend at the heart of Government and, sometimes, at the Prime Minister's right ear. Its relationship with the Treasury was formally defined, black on white, as *a special position* with *a definite obligation*.

The document that declared these terms grew frayed in Anderson's breast pocket, and a spare copy was kept in the Covent Garden archive, albeit under lock and key. The Royal Opera House did not want the world to know of its unique access. Twenty years after the Dalton letter had been made public in Sir John Wheeler-Bennett's biography of Anderson, the copy that was kept at Covent Garden was still withheld from researchers. 'If to be used publicly,' said a note on the file, 'John Tooley [general director] should agree.' It was only in January 1982 that the letter was finally released to BBC Television for a *Panorama* programme on opera funding.

This discretion was not casual or excessively cautious. It amounted to a tacit recognition by Covent Garden directors that their links with Government were too incestuous to warrant critical scrutiny. The cosiness established by Keynes and Anderson persisted and thickened until the tensions inevitable in an illicit relationship finally erupted in an explosion that almost wrecked the Royal Opera House and set England's performing arts back fifty years, all the way back to the bleak beginnings.

CHAPTER 4

Overture and Beginners
(1947–51)

AMID THE PRIVATIONS of the period, it was not easy to notice that something new was being born, a new nation, a new place in the sun. To returning soldiers and militant workers, the war seemed a wasted effort, the Labour Government a let-down. Class consciousness still segmented the country into unwalled ghettos. A man's station in life was determined by the twang of his accent and the cut of his suit. England had not changed in any of its timeworn ways, except for the worse. Women, who had seized the work-bench during the war, were sent back to hearth and home. Universities made a show of opening their portals to returning heroes, but most students were middle- and upper-class products of prohibitively expensive 'public' schools or rigorously selective grammar schools. The route to a worthwhile occupation was restricted by class and upbringing.

Where one lived was policed by price and prejudice. A frock-coated estate agent in Belgravia would never show properties to a cash-flush street-trader; a Birmingham landlord did not rent rooms to blacks, foreigners and unwed couples. Wages were fixed by an owners' cartel, or a union rate; profits, on the other hand, were untrammelled. Income tax was deducted at source from the working man's weekly envelope; businessmen paid no tax on their off-shore accounts and investments. Industrial inaction, the revenge of the underclass, hit the poor before rich. Rationing, the white flag of economic defeat, was bypassed by the luxuried classes.

Most British homes had no telephone or refrigerator; many had no bathroom and only an outdoor toilet, often shared with neighbours. Fewer than one person in twenty owned a car. Promises of a better tomorrow sounded hollower by the day. A cloud of disillusionment settled across the country as its pivotal decade drew to a close.

'Left governments,' wrote George Orwell in March 1948, 'almost invariably disappoint their supporters because, even when the prosperity they have promised is achievable, there is always need of an uncomfortable transition period about which little has been said beforehand.'[1] These hidden costs of Socialism, added to the debts of war, had ruled out the bestowal of any peace dividend.

Yet events were taking place, within and beyond the island that, between the watery summers of 1947 and 1948, would alter England for ever, both materially and in its battered self-perception. The Empire, which for two hundred years had stoked the nation with mineral wealth, fresh markets and false pride, was about to be dismantled. On 15 August 1947, the union flag was lowered in New Delhi and the subjugated sub-continent partitioned into two states, India and Pakistan. A rage of bloodshed ensued between Hindus and Moslems, a holocaust unleashed by the cavalier incompetence of the viceroy, Lord Mountbatten, and the precipitate haste of the British people to be shot of their past.

In January 1948, Mahatma Gandhi, man of peace, was shot dead while at prayer. That same month, Britain withdrew from Burma. In March, civil war erupted in Malaya. In April, British forces pulled out of Palestine, leaving Jews and Arabs to fight out an unending war. East of Suez, England was speedily ending its dominion.

In Europe, Stalin solidified his eastern bloc with a putsch that in March 1948 ended democracy in Czechoslovakia and precipitated the shocking murder of Jan Masaryk, thrown from a high window of his Foreign Ministry in Prague. The Americans, alarmed at the spreading Soviet hegemony, began pumping Marshall Aid into western dependancies before the month was out. Luxury goods long absent from London appeared in Hamburg shop-windows, to the amazement of British squaddies. The status of their nation was slipping before their unbelieving eyes. Heroism and imperial power had given way to retreat and recession. Despondency set in, akin to defeat. Something had to be done to restore national self-esteem. It was not enough to build quarter of a million homes and announce educational reforms, as the Labour Government was doing. England needed an ideal, a New Jerusalem, something to love and believe in.

On 5 July 1948, that shining icon was unveiled by Aneurin Bevan, minister for health and housing, by the symbolic act of handing the keys to Park Hospital in Trafford, Manchester, to a delegation of doctors, nurses and public administrators. The National Health Service, harbinger of hope, had been born.

Bevan, a self-educated Welsh miner who went down the pit at fourteen, was the only member of Attlee's Cabinet of Old Etonians and union barons who could have prevailed against the combined resistance of the medical establishment, the pensions and insurance industry, the Treasury, the Tories and some of his fellow-ministers. It was a blazing achievement, the greatest by any politician since Lloyd George's social reforms of 1908, and made all the greater by the marginality of its inceptor.

Bevan relished opposition more than he enjoyed government. During the war he had refused to join Churchill's coalition, defending the right to criticize even in a national emergency. A blazing demagogue with a scathing tongue, married to the turbulent and beautiful Scottish MP, Jennie Lee, Bevan lambasted the Conservatives as 'lower than vermin'. To the landed gentry and the Tory press, he was the mouth-frothing hate-figure of a socialist regime that was reducing Great Britain to dull conformity. In every important decision of state, he put principle above practicality.

Bevan envisaged the National Health Service not as a poultice for the poor but as a provider of 'the most up-to-date' medical care for every citizen, 'irrespective of means, age, sex or occupation'. The Service was to be 'comprehensive and free of charge'. Its scope exceeded any system attempted in the most caring and paternalistic of societies, more catholic even than the cradle-to-grave nanny-states of Scandinavia and the Netherlands. Bevan freed hospitals from local control and smashed the resistance of family doctors by bribing senior consultants with honours and bonuses. No one was obliged to join the NHS, but ninety-five per cent of the populace registered within two months, along with nine out of ten GPs.

The dawning of the NHS changed the habits of the nation. Women who formerly had babies at home because they could not afford a hospital bed, now gave birth in state-sheeted safety. No one was now too poor to see a dentist or have an eye-test. No one had to ignore an ache until they could pay to have it examined. A goitred mendicant could be attended by the King's personal oncologist. At dinner one night, Bevan declared, 'tomorrow, thirty thousand people will hear who cannot hear today'.[2] He had spent all week assessing every available hearing-aid, before choosing the most expensive.

Nothing was too good for the national health. Even the rich, who

saw private specialists, rushed to an NHS hospital if they had anything seriously wrong. The charitable nature of lower-order health
care was consigned to the past. The National Health Service, said a
Labour MP half a century later, 'marked the introduction of
Christian values to English public life'.[3]

It was Labour's supreme accomplishment, immunized by public
affection against future restraint. Bevan dreamed that costs would
fall when the nation became healthy, its ailments cured. He later
said, 'we shall never have all we need,' but he was building Utopia,
not a budgetary formula. As British medicine ventured into heart
transplants, test-tube babies and hip-replacements for the over-
eighties, the bills ran into billions and the NHS became Europe's
biggest employer, an over-centralized, cash-guzzling monster. But
such was its iconic status that it became politically untouchable.
Even the free-marketeering Margaret Thatcher was made to
proclaim, 'the National Health Service is safe in our hands'. The
NHS was the first emblem of post-war England, the crucible of a
'caring' society whose soothing unguents replaced the pomp and
circumstance of imperial grandeur.

Thus it was that between the summers of 1947 and 1948, England
retracted its horizons and became another country – a nicer country,
some said, though one still far from self-knowledge and inner peace.
Bevan's hall mat was filled each morning with hate-mail; he was
jostled in the streets by hoodlums roused to outrage by the Tory
press and elderly colonels wrote to *The Times* that the country was
going to the dogs. But in the seminal summer of 1948, England's
cricketers were thrashed by Don Bradman's Australians by four
Tests to nil, and even diehards had to admit that the imperial lion was
looking toothless and in need of a new coat.

Germany had begun its economic miracle and Europe was talking
of unity. England, for its part, set off on a solitary voyage of self-
discovery, a search for creative purpose that would supplant the
'civilizing' goals of building and ruling an Empire. The NHS
represented social justice and scientific progress as putative goals,
but the national aim remained uncertain. What would become of
England when the last patch of red was gone from the atlas and the
powers denied her a seat at the table? Did the Old Country have
anything left to offer the world? Had the war been fought in vain?

One answer, for those who kept a finger on the national pulse, came where it was least expected – in an art where no Englishman had excelled for two centuries and a half, an art dismissed by the greatest of English dictionarists as 'an exotick and irrational entertainment'. On 7 June 1945, a month to the day after peace returned to Europe, Sadler's Wells reopened with a new opera, *Peter Grimes* by Benjamin Britten. The composer was very young, just thirty-one, but not wholly unknown. Before the war he had produced a piano concerto at the Proms and a suite of string variations at the Salzburg Festival. Moving to America with his companion, the tenor Peter Pears, he wrote a mid-Western Singspiel, *Paul Bunyan*, with a text by the expatriate poet W. H. Auden. He received more commissions and was widely performed, but Britten was beset by feelings of guilt and longing. Pears, browsing in a second-hand bookshop in Los Angeles, bought him an 1851 edition of the poems of the anti-romanticist George Crabbe (1754–1832). Some days later Britten read a magazine article by the novelist E. M. Forster, beginning with the words: 'To think of Crabbe is to think of England.'[4] 'I suddenly realized where I belonged and what I lacked,' he said.[5]

Peter Grimes relates the torments of a strong-willed fisherman, hounded by his village after the death of an apprentice boy at sea. It had nothing to do with war, victory, democracy, reconstruction, or any other burning issue, except in the most ethereal and generalized sense. Where others wrote for the here and now, Britten dared to compose in a time and place all his own. He wrote swiftly and surely, the opus number, thirty-three, being greater than his age.

At Sadler's Wells, disgruntled singers declared the work 'a piece of cacophony' and sent an Equity trade union deputation to the governors to complain about Britten's 'excessive' publicity. The rebels demanded a democratic say in the company's repertoire. Joan Cross, chosen by Britten to sing the sympathetic schoolmistress Ellen Orford, resigned as company director. The baritone playing Captain Balstrode jumped ship with six weeks to go, declaring the music 'outlandish'. The hostility arose, it seemed, less from the music than from an awareness that the composer, tenor, conductor, Reginald Goodall, and producer, Eric Crozier, were all conscientious objectors who had sat out the war, and that two of them were blatant homosexuals. A demonstration was threatened for opening night. 'Whatever happens,' said Tyrone Guthrie to Joan Cross in her dressing-room, 'we were absolutely right to do this piece.'[6]

When the curtain fell, the opera was greeted with total silence – a full thirty seconds, according to one report. Then the house erupted, and the curtain-calls were too numerous to count. The audience, wrote Crozier, 'did not know what had happened nor how they could have been so deeply affected'.[7] Over the following days, reviewers pronounced *Grimes* 'a work of genius',[8] 'an astonishing work'.[9] For the next three weeks, the doyen Ernest Newman wrote in the *Sunday Times* of nothing but *Grimes*. An American in London, the distinguished literary figure Edmund Wilson, wrote in his travel diary:

> By the time you are done with the opera – or by the time it is done with you – you have decided that *Peter Grimes* is the whole of bombing, machine-gunning, mining, torpedoing, ambushing humanity which talks about a guaranteed standard of living yet does nothing but wreck its own works, degrade or pervert its own moral life and reduce itself to starvation . . . you feel that you are in the same boat as Grimes.[10]

Every critic seemed determined to find metaphors in an opera that was emotionally as cathartic as it was tonally conservative. The much-touted modernism of *Peter Grimes* lay not in the music – 'it's full of howlers,' the composer sighed in later years – but in an ice-breaking presumption that art could psychoanalyse the English condition, and that England might be redeemed through its arts. 'It looks as if the old spell on British opera may be broken at last!' rejoiced Britten.[11]

Acclaim, however, did not quell the storms. Although *Peter Grimes* would be sung over the next four years on twenty-five foreign stages from Budapest to Los Angeles[12] and became the most performed of post-war operas, petty resentments persisted. The safety curtain was brought down early one night, cutting short the ovations. A BBC broadcast could not be recorded for posterity because the Sadler's Wells orchestra demanded extra money. A studio recording, paid for by the British Council, was cancelled when the company voted to tour Germany instead. After nine packed performances, Britten withdrew the work from Sadler's Wells. Guthrie resigned the day the season ended. Cross, Pears and Crozier followed soon after, forming an English Opera Company to produce Britten's forthcoming works in a joint venture with John Christie of Glyndebourne.

For Covent Garden, the sight of England's ascendant composer linking arms with the arch-enemy at Glyndebourne was life-threatening. If English opera was experiencing a rebirth, parturition could not be allowed to occur in a Sussex country barn. The Royal Opera House had been created, at public expense, to be the acme of national activity in the lyric arts. If the most thrilling new operas were appearing elsewhere and at no cost to the tax-payer, its existence would be foreshortened.

The ROH could, of course, call on other composers, from the genial Vaughan Williams to the languid William Walton who sat upon its Trust. But Britten had, with *Peter Grimes*, vaulted over all English composers, past or present. He was the man of the moment, a musician who transcended the musical ghetto and spoke to the heart of the nation. Unless it could accommodate Britten, Covent Garden could not expect to sustain its centrality, or indeed its survival.

Coming to terms with Benjamin Britten was never going to be easy. A hyper-sensitive soul who viewed the adult race with suspicion verging on contempt, he reserved a special loathing for large cities, long lunches and anything resembling the established order. Politically, he sympathized with the Moscow line on most issues. Professionally, he formed warm and fruitful relationships with writers, directors and many musicians, only to drop them without a word if he felt slighted, or found their usefulness had expired. Colleagues treated him like unwrapped nitro-glycerine. The only man who felt comfortable with Britten was his lifelong lover Pears, a slightly reedy tenor capable of astonishing on-stage intensity and groundless off-stage hatreds.

The Royal Opera House, whose very name resonated with rotten metropolitan privilege, was anathema to Britten. His publisher, Hawkes, was careful not to press its cause on the tetchy composer and Webster, who had commissioned *A Young Person's Guide to the Orchestra* for Liverpool, had no choice but to smile at Britten and say nothing about Christie.

On 12 July 1946 Britten's chamber opera, *The Rape of Lucretia*, began a two-week run at Glyndebourne before going on tour. It contained some of the most beautiful music he ever wrote and featured the operatic début of Kathleen Ferrier, a Blackburn telephonist whose rich contralto voice had enthralled factory audiences during the war. Out of costume she was plain 'Kath', beloved by all. She shared the role with Nancy Evans, wife of the record producer Walter Legge. Both needed a 'great deal of rehearsal before we could achieve [Lucretia's farewell] without bursting into tears'.[13]

Orchestral players found themselves dabbing their eyes and critics fumbled for superlatives. Howes in *The Times* predicted that Britten might 'lift opera out of the dead end in which it has been stuck since the death of Puccini'. There were some dissenters, however. Beverley Baxter, a Tory MP writing for the Beaverbrook press, 'longed for the orchestra to go out and have a drink so that we could hear the words'.[14] William Glock, a future BBC boss, called for 'a re-writing of the whole opera'.[15] Desmond Shawe-Taylor deemed the *Rape* 'less successful'[16] than *Grimes* and, with a year's hindsight, summarized a consensual view that it was flawed by Ronald Duncan's pretentious poesy and by a moralizing Christian ending that sounded both anachronistic and insincere. On tour in Edinburgh, Glasgow, Manchester, Liverpool and Oxford, the *Rape* played to half-empty houses. Christie complained there was 'no music in it'[17] and claimed he had lost eleven thousand pounds; the Arts Council gave him three thousand in compensation.

Britten made no effort to reassure his patron. In October, he declared independence from Glyndebourne, agreeing to return the following summer as a 'guest company' with a revival of the *Rape* and the première of *Albert Herring*, a laconic variation on English rural life. Directed by Frederick Ashton, who disliked Pears and loathed his voice, *Herring* was a tense affair. 'Ben wouldn't speak to Christie or allow him inside his own theatre,' said Ashton. Christie 'hated Ben's music and said so out loud,' reported the opera's designer, John Piper.[18] 'This isn't our kind of thing, you know,' Christie told his guests on opening night,[19] heaving a huge sigh of relief when the composer huffed off to found his own festival at Crabbe's fishing village of Aldeburgh. In 1948 his were still the only new operas seen in England since the war.[20]

Britten now flung down a gauntlet in the direction of Covent Garden, in the manifesto of his English Opera Group. 'We believe the best way to achieve the beginnings of a repertory of English opera,' said Britten, 'is through the creation of a form of opera requiring small resources of singers and players' – the antithesis of Webster's 500-strong payroll. Webster, timing his approach to perfection, took Britten to lunch with Karl Rankl a week later.

Dispensing with courtesies he got straight down to business, asking Britten to write a large opera for Covent Garden, offering a revival of *Peter Grimes* and assuring him that his friends Pears and Cross would be welcomed in the main roles.

'So far as the possibility of your Company finding a home at Covent Garden is concerned,' Webster summarized, 'neither of us can see anything against this, indeed we would be delighted to welcome you here, and to pursue enquiries to make that possible if you, on reflection, say so.

'We would like to assure you that no one connected with us would feel anything but the strongest desire to help and to co-operate with you in any plans you have for your Company . . . Both Karl and myself, however, would very much appreciate being taken into your councils and your discussions, completely unofficially, and we will willingly arrange as I have said as far as is possible for you having the use of any of our artists, or anyone you want . . .

'You need, I am sure, no assurance that both Karl and I feel most warmly to you personally and to your very great talents, and if there is anything that we can do at all to help you to realize your own ambitions for your Company, you have only to ask us.'[21]

The line had been baited and the fish was tempted. In November 1947 Covent Garden put on a new production of *Peter Grimes*, rejecting offers from a desperate Sadler's Wells to buy its original sets at half-cost (£1,050) and borrow half its chorus.[22] Rankl conducted the opening performance, but thereafter gave way to the expert Goodall. With Pears and Cross in the roles they created and stage direction by the steadfast Tyrone Guthrie, the opera was cast for safety. It lacked the shock of novelty yet, on a larger stage, seemed all the more momentous and, on opening night, was augmented in its sea-fog atmospherics by a fortuitous London pea-souper that penetrated every corner of the house.

If Britten could be induced to write a successor, there was every chance of Covent Garden achieving world renown. Yet, despite the accolades, doubts persisted about general standards of performance. Britten, dropping in on a second-cast night, dashed off a furious letter to Webster: 'I went to Covent Garden to see a performance of 'Grimes' recently and I must frankly say I was shocked by it, and I feel that to take the work abroad in this condition would be to its detriment and incidentally to the detriment of English Opera itself. The reasons, I think, are three: 1. Under-rehearsal; 2. A disregard of

dynamics and expression marks that has grown up; 3. Miscasting
. . . I hate to say this, but I feel that unless you can do something
about the performance I shall feel strongly inclined to put pressure
on my publishers to make the tour impossible . . .'[23]

Webster was unperturbed. With Glyndebourne out of the way,
there was nowhere else for Britten to take his operas unless he
wanted to save them for his Aldeburgh outpost. Britten was
important to Covent Garden but no longer essential. Covent Garden,
on the other hand, was now the only place where an English
composer could find a fitting home.

Webster did not bother to acknowledge Britten's asperities. Five
weeks later, he sent him a warm note reporting that 'Peter Grimes
and the Company have had a great success both in Brussels and in
Paris. The Queen of the Belgians was at the first performance.'[24]

In the widening search for a world role, the English fell back on
language. England had given the world the most flexible and utilized
of modern tongues. English was the *lingua franca* of aerodynamics
and air traffic control. It had replaced German as the vernacular of
physics, psychoanalysis and biblical exegesis, and was taking an
unassailable lead in the uncharted infinities of computer science and
space research. It was the resolvent language of the United Nations,
the basis of international law. French and Italian might determine
couture and cuisine, and Russian was the rhetoric of occupied
Europe and dialectical materialism, but English held sway in
finance, technology and the horizons of unfolding knowledge.

It would be ridiculous to pretend that the ascent of English was
due to anything other than the military and economic might of the
United States. Nevertheless, the island that invented the language
maintained an arm-lock on its usage and development, both as
keeper of Shakespeare's chalice and as a prolific source of popular
literature. The world's top-selling children's author, Enid Blyton,
wrote the King's English, as did the most widely-read crime writer,
Agatha Christie. George Bernard Shaw was the most performed
living playwright. Winston Churchill, idle in opposition, was writing
a *History of the English-Speaking Peoples*. T. S. Eliot, who received
the Nobel Prize for Literature in 1948, had chosen (on the advice of
a fellow-American, Ezra Pound) to spend his creative life in
England. P. G. Wodehouse and Noël Coward were the living arbiters
of English wit. Hollywood actors and Ivy League preppies adopted

Oxford accents and wore Savile Row suits. The BBC was the world's most trusted provider of news and information.

With a grip on the American imagination and the currency of mass communications, it was just possible to envisage that England might regain by language the influence it was losing with empire. Those who turned politically rightward favoured a North Atlantic union of English-speaking forces in which England supplied the lexicon of leadership. Leftist thinkers preferred an English-speaking Commonwealth of nations that would unite the scattered shards of Empire and follow the stately procedures of the mother of Parliaments. Either way, the English language appeared to be England's best hope of resurgence, its premier asset.

The supremacy of the King's English was so taken for granted that it was scarcely debated as a cultural issue. Any institution that represented national aims needed to conduct its business in English – the more so if its art-forms had originated in another tongue and place. Italian and German, the parlance of opera, had been reviled for six years as enemy dialects. The Royal Opera House could not be their beachhead in Britain. 'The operas will be given in English,' affirmed Webster in a mission statement to the Arts Council.[25]

The question of opera in English had always been a shibboleth of privilege. The nobility and *nouveau riche* in the nineteenth and early twentieth centuries went to Covent Garden to hear foreign stars sing in foreign tongues. The lower classes made do with cut-price opera in English from Carl Rosa's touring troupe and the Sadler's Wells missionary ensemble. Miss Lilian Baylis wanted her visitors to understand what they heard on the opera stage. She found an ally in a crusty Cambridge professor, Edward J. Dent, who became her most fluent translator.

Dent was a recognizable English type: a bachelor misogynist, born into Yorkshire gentry but living on reduced means, an amateur at everything, fixed in his scholarly prejudices. 'One must look at things from an historical point of view,' was his stock phrase.

As a young Fellow of King's, Dent had planted in E. M. Forster's mind the plot for *A Room with a View*; he is immortalized in Forster's first novel, *Where Angels Fear to Tread,* as the pallid hero, Philip Herriton, who discovered the sap of life on a trip to Italy. Dent was tempted by foreign pleasures, but returned to spend his life in Cambridge, producing learned studies of Scarlatti and Mozart and English librettos for Miss Baylis's operas. Some of his translations were flecked with naïvety, or mischief. His finest line, from Tchaikovsky's *Eugene Onegin*, was, 'Balls in the country are quite a sensation . . . ,' which the chorus used to sing with unusual gusto. Still, beside the general run of opera translations – which, for example, had Colline, needing a shave in *Bohème*, sing: 'The first chance I get, I will scrape acquaintance/ With a beard eraser' – Dent's texts were fluent, musical and even witty.

His outlook was also redeemingly uncloistered. Although he loved Mozart above all composers and played a vital role in his English revival, Dent was an aficionado of modern music, a friend and biographer of Ferruccio Busoni and founder-president of the International Society for Contemporary Music. He was a born committee man. Although infirm and going deaf, he agreed to join the Covent Garden Trust with a view to sabotaging it on behalf of Sadler's Wells. 'I said to Webster,' he reported after a first meeting, 'I wished he could scrap the whole thing and make an entirely new interior out of it, without boxes, on modern democratic lines.'[26] As Sadler's Wells began to crumble Dent, mindful of his translator's royalties, set out to cultivate Webster and define new roles for both houses – both of them singing off his copyrighted sheets. It was Dent who proposed that Covent Garden should be reserved for 'grand opera' and Sadler's Wells for 'opéra comique', a distinction that endured in principle for the next half-century. With unerring self-interest, he also proposed they should jointly publish opera librettos in English.[27]

With Webster, Dent soon found common ground. 'He is rather fat and prosperous looking, not unlike John Christie,' he informed Clive Carey, the Sadler's Wells manager, 'but whereas Christie has the "powdery" pink and white surface of a Raeburn, and looks so Victorian that you almost think he's got mutton-chop whiskers, Webster is pink with a high polish, and ought to be Lord Mayor of some big provincial town.'[28]

Webster encouraged Dent to believe he was a man after his own heart, committed to the performance of opera in English and the creation of an indigenous repertory. Webster was also anxious 'to secure the adoption of standard English versions by schools, teachers and opera companies throughout the English-speaking world'[29] – in accordance with the national agenda.

Amid the debris of an ill-attended opening season, however, Webster was plotting a retreat. 'One of our biggest drawbacks appears to be that we are performing in English,' he reflected at the opening of the 1947-48 season, '. . . it seems incredible that certain sections of the public view opera in English as inferior to opera in foreign languages.'[30]

Early that year, the Austrian legation in London had proposed that the BBC's Third Programme should bring over the Vienna State Opera for a series of live broadcasts. The BBC asked Webster if he might stage the operas and Walter Legge at EMI if he wanted to record them. 'Of course we'll put them on,' cried Webster.[31] Unheard for eight years, the Viennese possessed the world's finest ensemble, albeit one which had embraced Nazism with unexampled enthusiasm. In June, Webster flew to Vienna with contracts for seventeen performances of *Fidelio, Don Giovanni, The Marriage of Figaro* and *Salome*. In September, the Vienna State Opera arrived at Covent Garden to be met by angry demonstrators – not, as feared, concentration-camp survivors, but members of the Musicians' Union, protesting at the engagement of the Vienna Philharmonic Orchestra in place of their Covent Garden pit band.

It did not take more than a minute of Overture to underline the qualitative difference. 'It was a standard of performance people hadn't heard here for years,'[32] exclaimed a BBC official. The celestial voices of Maria Cebotari, Elisabeth Schwarzkopf, Irmgard Seefried, Hilde Gueden and Sena Jurinac, followed by the rippling eroticism of Ljuba Welitsch as Salome, were the talk of the town. Hans Hotter was the Count in *Figaro*, Julius Patzak the Florestan in *Fidelio*, Anton Dermota the Ottavio in *Don Giovanni*, each unequalled in his role. The exiled Richard Tauber was reunited with his former colleagues, singing Ottavio in the last opera of his life before entering hospital with a fatal illness.

Rankl was to have conducted *Figaro* but proved incompatible with the Viennese. Josef Krips took the baton in Mozart, Clemens Krauss in Strauss and Beethoven. Webster scuttled around back-stage signing up young singers. He bypassed Cebotari, Hitler's favourite, and for unaccountable reasons the lustrous Jurinac, who went to Glyndebourne. But in scooping up the cream of Vienna, Webster altered the character and purpose of his company. Gone was the determination to promote 'the British artist'. Covent Garden would become a multinational company, still singing in English to be sure, but not for long.

Hotter returned to sing Hans Sachs in English in *The Mastersingers*, the first Wagner opera since the war (the chorus line 'Honour your German masters' was tactfully amended to 'your noble masters'), followed by Wotan in *The Valkyrie*. His diction was so mangled that Webster and Rankl, without reference to the Trustees, reverted other operas to their original language.

In February 1948, German rang out, harsh and guttural, from the stage of the Royal Opera House, Covent Garden. The opera was *Tristan und Isolde* and all eyes were on Kirsten Flagstad, the magnificent. Flagstad, who had first appeared in 1934 and spent the war in her native Norway, was desperate to sing in London again. Her husband, Henry Johansen, had been arrested as a Nazi collaborator and died in jail awaiting trial. Her American engagements were cancelled; 'we really needed those concerts and the money,' she sighed.[33] More than the income, she physically needed to sing. A heavy-boned, placid woman, apparently without nerves, she would sit knitting and sipping stout in her dressing-room until the stage-call came to go out and die. 'Apart from my work, I am just an average woman,'[34] she said, and meant it.

Her return was a revelation. 'She walked into rehearsal at ten in the morning, folded her arms across her chest and sang full out. I had never heard any sound like it,' recalled Iris Kells. Out in the market, porters stopped in their tracks when Flagstad let rip with 'Tristan, Geliebte!' Her first Tristan, August Seider, was overwhelmed. He was replaced by the resonant though diminutive Swede, Set Svanholm, who reached Flagstad's midriff.

Riding a taxi to work, she often gave a lift to walking choristers and showered many kindnesses on junior colleagues. 'What I loved about Flagstad was that she never made me feel a little secondary artist,' said the fast-maturing Constance Shacklock, who became her constant companion. 'In three months, I didn't know my own voice or my own self. I just wanted to be like her.'

Her attitude was not shared by other imports. Hotter was polite but superior. Schwarzkopf could learn a role in perfect English at twenty-four hours' notice but 'was not particularly friendly'.[35] She had left Vienna and moved in with Legge, joining Covent Garden on sixty pounds a week, which was fifteen pounds cheaper than native principals. Her Aryan beauty and silvery voice won public and critical acclaim.

In addition to Germans, Webster also bagged a brace of Italians –

Paolo Silveri of the San Carlo company and Elda Ribetti, who had married an Englishman. Neither did much for morale and their first appearance in *Rigoletto*, was deemed 'a stupid misuse of public money'.[36] English amateurism could be tolerated, but adequacy and arrogance were unacceptable in foreigners.

As the English lines of his company blurred, Webster was hustled into an unnaturally bold move. A reflective man, known to his board as the Arch Procrastinator, Webster liked to put off major decisions until the problem had gone away or the outcome became inevitable. He was on the way to assembling a professional opera company, but he had yet to imprint his own aesthetic preferences on the enterprise. What Webster loved above all was glamour. He needed to reinforce Rankl's tetchy and tunnel-visioned artistic leadership with a real innovator, preferably an Englishman.

In the autumn of 1947, Webster removed Frederick Ashton's name as Production Consultant from opera playbills, having received a visit from a young job-seeker. Peter Brook had directed a quick and witty *Love's Labours Lost* at Stratford-upon-Avon, followed by a hotly disputed *Romeo and Juliet*. He was being spoken of in some quarters as the white hope of English theatre, and was all of twenty-two years old. Webster, impressed, offered him a job, recanted, kept in touch and finally told the Trustees that he wanted a Director of Productions, a title Brook had invented on the spur of the moment. Webster told them that Brook had 'a first-class musical mind' and was Britain's brightest theatrical spark. His encomium was approximately half-true.

The son of Latvian-Jewish radicals who came to England and invented a popular laxative, Brooklax, Brook grew up in suburban Chiswick with a burning fascination for footlights. At Oxford, he started a University Film Society and directed his first movie. At twenty, he was putting on shows in Birmingham and the West End. He despised the 'niceness' that emasculated contemporary English drama, dominated by Rattigan and Coward, and was drawn more to the caustic absurdities of Cocteau and Anouilh. His directorial style turned dangerously improvisational. Before going to Stratford to direct *Love Labour's Lost*, he recalled,

> I worked it all out beforehand, every move, with little arrows on pieces of paper. Then the first rehearsal began and I gave out the

instructions. Everyone obeyed, but I looked and suddenly realized, 'This is dreadful. Stop, start again.' My plans were no good because they were plans. From that day onwards, I never prepared anything in detail.'[37]

Brook breezed into the Royal Opera House with a brief to shake up its opera productions, which he found 'unbelievably bad'. He had taken piano lessons as a boy from a former teacher at the Moscow Conservatoire, but had limited knowledge of grand opera and no love of its mannered ways. 'I entered the opera with one simple aim,' he wrote, 'to give this sleepy, old-fashioned institution a series of shocks that would jolt it into the present-day world.'[38]

He ran up against the rock of reality in the shape of 'Bogey' Ballard, the wing-collared, octogenarian backstage boss who ruled the bowels of the house. Brook ordered a change of scenery for *La Bohème*; Ballard insisted on doing things the way Mr Puccini had instructed him. Brook went to Webster, suggesting that Ballard should be considered for gentle retirement. Old Bogey, however, was the only man who knew where anything was kept backstage. Decrepit as he was, Ballard outlasted the upstart Peter Brook.

The first production by the new director was Mussorgsky's *Boris Godunov*, an epic work that appealed to Brook's Baltic blood and his love of filmic crowd scenes. Unable to find an English designer who felt the same way, he borrowed a Russian, Georges Wahkevitch, from Roland Petit's Parisian ballet company. *Boris* was a striking success, diminished only by Silveri's tameness in the title role. A year later, when the Bulgarian Boris Christoff made his début, the opera glowered with menace. Christoff and Brook were at each other's throats until the very moment the curtain rose.

Like any young lion let loose in a flamingo pool, Brook wreaked havoc among the singers. No respecter of vanities, he yelled at German sopranos like a Gauleiter, commanding their unquestioning obedience. Some he rejected as too fat or ugly, not normally an impediment to operatic success. He encouraged the sexy Ljuba Welitsch to vamp up Musetta in *Bohème* and steal the show from Schwarzkopf's Mimi. He let off fireworks in the finale of *Figaro*. Some believed he mistook it for another opera, perhaps Strauss's *Ariadne auf Naxos*. 'Peter Brook was different,' commented one singer. 'Whatever else could be said of him, he was different.'[39]

His shortcomings were nakedly apparent and loudly bemoaned.

His musical knowledge was limited and his improvisational style was readily mistaken for indecision. A last-minute change of mind could upset fifteen soloists, two hundred men and women in the *Boris* chorus and a ninety-strong orchestra. Unable or unwilling to act out roles, Brook used verbal imagery that went above the singers' heads. 'Finding out what he wanted was very hard work,'[40] said David Franklin, who sang Colline in the cat-fight *Bohème*. 'I don't believe he had listened to the piece before he produced it,' was Gellhorn's impression.

'I never had the four principal men together in rehearsal at the same time,' Brook complained of that production. 'If three of them were there, the fourth was inevitably away – not resting, as was always claimed to be so important for the voice, but flying to Paris for a quick morning recording, or to a provincial German city to snap up an extra fee for a recital. Instead, a stage manager would stand in for the missing character, holding a large score and enthusiastically singing out-of-tune Lancashire Italian.'[41]

Brook did not disguise his contempt for antideluvian backstage crews and pompous prima donnas. He sought to empower lesser artists by giving choristers and understudies an evening off and two free tickets in exchange for a written report of their impressions. Ninette de Valois and Frederick Ashton were not amused when chorus singers found fault with their ballets, and the initiative was discontinued.

Brook was determined, as Mahler had been in Vienna, to eliminate sloppy traditions. When he cut out the sordid bit of stage business in *Figaro* where the Count rests his hand on Susanna's bosom, Rankl objected, saying he could not conduct to any different action. Brook stood his ground, and Rankl became his sworn enemy. By the time they collaborated in *The Olympians* by Arthur Bliss, Covent Garden's first commissioned opera, the director of productions and the musical director were no longer on speaking terms.

Senior critics, too, resented change. Ernest Newman, aged eighty, grumbled that *Boris Godunov* 'touched for the most part the lowest depths to which Covent Garden has yet fallen'.[42] Newman, on the other hand, adored *The Olympians*, proclaiming Bliss to be England's Verdi and J. B. Priestley his Boito. The opera, a vain attempt to reflect England's hosting of the 1948 Olympic Games, had ten half-sold performances and four on tour before vanishing forever.

Brook provoked a clash of antipodal cultures, New English Theatre versus Old Fogy Opera. The climax came with *Salome*, for which Brook ordered designs from Salvador Dali, the Spanish surrealist. The shimmering 'Palestinian night' of Richard Strauss's score was to be represented by the spread tail of a giant peacock – across which Dali, until Brook dissuaded him, proposed to parade a flying hippopotamus. The costumes were grotesquely uncomfortable even after adaptation by London seamstresses. The pouting Welitsch refused to wear hers and Shacklock, as Herodias, appeared to be entombed in a yellow tent. 'I did not set out to shock,' said Brook. Dali stayed away.

On 11 November 1949, a Friday night, Welitsch earned tumultuous acclaim as the sexiest Salome in memory. 'Salome Lost 7 Veils But She Won 14 Curtains' ran the *Daily Herald*'s headline.[43] Rankl did not come out for a curtain call and Brook faced scattered boos. 'Rankl on the first night refused even to talk to Brook,' recalled Peter Gellhorn.[44]

The heavyweight press, sensing dissension, fomented a full-scale theatrical scandal. Newman, in the sombre columns of a Remembrance Sunday newspaper, denounced 'the most miserable *Salome* I have ever heard,' and demanded to know 'how much longer the London opera public will be expected to tolerate performances and productions at Covent Garden that are for the most part an affront to its intelligence. How long, O Lord, how long, we ask.'[45]

Brook was sacked the next morning – 'I was out on my ear'[46] – and the Director of Productions post was abolished. Salome was taken off after six performances and the sets were jubilantly smashed up by stagehands, acting on Bogey Ballard's orders. On the verdict of two octogenarians who knew little of the world beyond music and opera, England's most brilliant theatrical animator was thrown overboard. *Salome* may have been a mistake and he had made other errors of inexperience, but Brook brimmed with ideas. There is no telling what he might have achieved had he been granted another two years at Covent Garden.

Over the next half-century, Peter Brook became the guiding light and inspiration to every significant British director, from Peter Hall to Deborah Warner. His nine-hour production of the Hindu *Mahabharata* was one of the wonders of the modern world. His Stratford *King Lear* with Paul Scofield in 1962 was a milestone in Shakespearean interpretation and his account that year of *The*

Persecution and Assassination of Marat, as performed by the Inmates of the Asylum of Charenton under the direction of the Marquis de Sade amounted almost to a theatrical rebirth. He took eleven actors on a ten thousand-mile village trek across Africa. He visited Cuba and mounted fiery denunciations of the Vietnam War. In 1967, Brook moved to Paris, establishing an International Centre for Theatre Research and an ever-evolving, borderless culture at the Bouffes du Nord theatre. He never returned to Covent Garden.

In a choice between talent and tradition, the ROH settled for ritual. The company, young as it was, was already too arthritic to experiment in any form that challenged the restrictive, predictable disciplines of singing and dancing. In any artistic revolution, Covent Garden occupied the rearguard. Its stage directors, after Brook, would not frighten the horses, the singers or the Lord Chamberlain, who vetted all productions for nudity and profanity. Rising costs, antiquated working methods and unworkable ideals had led Covent Garden to plump for safety, stasis and compromise. Noël Coward, watching a *Bohème* with Victoria de los Angeles, found the production 'disgraceful' and the tragedy 'hilarious',[47] so flaccid were the company's theatrical values.

Gone was the blazing commitment to Englishness, the English language and an English *Gesamtkunstwerk*. Covent Garden was on the way to becoming just another opera house, a prospect which opera and ballet lovers viewed as a healthy sign of normality and other arts regarded with distaste and detachment. Covent Garden was the agent of its own isolation. It remained to be seen whether the country would support the self-regarding citadel of a pair of costly minority arts.

The first alarm sounded just before the start of the second season when Webster diffidently warned his chairman of impending embarrassments. 'I am especially sorry that we may have to go to the Treasury again this year,' he wrote, 'I was so hoping we could put off the second visit until next year. I thought we would have at least £30,000 against contingencies, but the slump has deprived us of most of this. I am sufficiently optimistic to believe that we shall do better in the Autumn, but that is mere belief.'[48]

If he anticipated a sharp intake of breath, he need not have feared. Sir John Anderson was too seasoned an administrator to be upset by budgetary vacillations. His life had been dedicated to oiling the

wheels of government and shielding officialdom from the consequences of its dutiful errors. He was the problem-solver *par
excellence*. A man who had held the nation's purse-strings in a war
of survival was not going to be daunted by the petty difficulties of a
place of entertainment. Nor was he concerned by the niceties of any
'arm's length' principle. He demanded a complete breakdown of
costs and Webster, ever the perfect shopkeeper, reeled it off in a
dictated memo, probably without having to look at the ledgers.

It cost, he reported, precisely ten pounds less than six thousand a
week to keep the lights on at Covent Garden. The electricity bill
came to £75. Stage hands and stage management earned £445. The
ballet management cost £275, the musical conductors, repetiteurs
and pianists £340, wardrobe and dressers £170. The chorus were
paid £615, the ballet dancers £810 and all the opera soloists together
eleven hundred pounds. By far the largest expense was the
orchestra, assembled by Webster and bleeding his company at the
rate of fifteen hundred and sixty pounds a week, or more than a
quarter of its total outgoings.[49]

This was obviously the key area for making economies. The
musicians were on ten-month contracts and could be dismissed
without penalty at the season's end. The orchestra was, by common
consent, unimpressive. Yet neither Webster nor Anderson apparently
thought of reducing or replacing the orchestra, a move which would
have staunched the company's deficit at a stroke. For Webster,
cutting the orchestra would have meant an admission of error and a
sticky negotiation with the irascible Rankl. For Anderson, it would
have gone against the grain to disestablish part of an organization
and undermine the status quo. The orchestra was thus left
untouched, storing up problems for the future.

Anderson's response to the crisis was twin-track. For ready cash,
he negotiated an ROH overdraft with Sir Jasper Ridley, chairman of
Coutts, the exclusive little bank where the Royal Family kept their
chequeing accounts. For longer-term stability, he went to see the
Chancellor of the Exchequer. The arts-friendly Hugh Dalton had
been forced to resign in November 1947 over an inadvertent leak of
Budget details and his successor, Stafford Cripps, was austerity
personified. Anderson, however, prepared his ground assiduously
with Treasury officials and came away with gold. In January 1948,
Mary Glasgow at the Arts Council heard from a Treasury colleague
that 'when the Chancellor saw your Chairman and Sir John

Anderson, he said that he proposed to ask Parliament to vote £550,000 as a grant for the Arts Council, of which £120,000 would be earmarked for grant to the Covent Garden Trust and would not be available for other purposes.'[50]

Problem solved, or so it must have seemed. In exchange for no extra undertaking on its part, Covent Garden had received a quintupling of its original allowance – along with a direct line to the privy purse that bypassed Arts Council providers. The Anderson deal was not merely high-handed but improper, violating the terms of a Royal Charter. Christie, who knew Cripps, resumed his epistolary attacks on the ROH. He demanded a triple merger of Covent Garden, Sadler's Wells and Glyndebourne. When that was ruled out, he called for panel of professionals – Walton, Legge, Rankl – to take charge of the ROH's weak casting and repertoire, pointedly excluding Webster.

Cripps, mildly concerned, summoned Anderson who assured him that the future health of the ROH was 'more important than any temporary fluctuations in the standard of performance'. This annoyed the crusty Chancellor, who demanded a written report, with specific recommendations for artistic improvements. Anderson set up a sub-committee, which conceded the inadequacy of some productions and the need for appointing an artistic adjutant to the General Administrator. This clipping of Webster's wings seemed to reassure Cripps, who then authorized an even greater gift.

The five-year lease on the building held by Boosey & Hawkes was due to expire at the end of 1949 and the impresario Jay Pomeroy, whose West End opera season was going well, put in a bid for a new forty-two year lease. Leslie Boosey rushed in alarm to the Arts Council. The Government was alerted and in August 1948 a compulsory purchase order was issued, acquiring the Royal Opera House on behalf of the Ministry of Works. This brash intervention in the open market drew bitter criticism in the Tory press, which condemned the purchase as an act of state theft. Boosey, withdrawing quietly, was landed with a £180,000 Ministry of Works bill for 'dilapidation'.

The stage was set for the grand master of malice, the easily-goaded goatee, to deliver his show-stopper. In January 1949, Sir Thomas Beecham addressed the annual conference of the Incorporated Society of Musicians, a grass-roots organization volubly dismayed at the rising numbers of foreign singers at Covent

Garden. Deeming the moment propitious for a full-blown barrage at his enemies, Beecham took his standard precaution of inviting the national press to Brighton to savour his coruscating wit. He began, quietly enough, by asserting that no member of the Covent Garden Trust 'knew anything about opera or had any practical experience of it'. He accused Leslie Boosey and Ralph Hawkes of profiteering from the enterprise, and then turned his fire on the artistic leadership:

> The appointment of an alien, and especially one bearing a German name, to the post of musical director of the British national opera is so incredible that I have from time to time to remind myself that it has actually happened and is not some fantastic dream. It must be, I think, because the hapless set of ignoramuses and nitwits who conspired to bring this about – this disaster – were under the impressions that the functions of a music director in an opera house were of such exotic, intricate and profound a nature that only a person of the sublime intelligence of a Teuton could grasp and manipulate them.

This was classic Beecham – irony wrapped in ridicule and a dubious cloak of patriotism, brilliantly extemporized to produce a roar of laughter and a spatter of morning headlines. He avoided mentioning Webster by name, but castigated his casting and repertoire with the authority, and despair, of a man who had achieved greater things:

> In the bad old days (said Beecham) it used to be our practice to put the horse before the cart and to discover what vocal resources we had at our disposal, and to make our choice of works accordingly. The modern practice it would seem is to select the work and afterwards discover that we have not the singers to take part. That is but one of the symptoms of comparative insanity which prevails in that unfortunate institution and among its backers.

Beecham demanded a public inquiry into this 'strange and un-English way of doing things; let them see the evidence of how the vast sum of £100,000 has been spent in one year with so little to show for it.'[51] Boosey, incensed, reached for his lawyers. Rankl told *The Times* that he 'never replied to any public criticism'. Anderson reached for his pen and composed the dustiest of public-servant replies:

> I have read the remarks attributed to Sir Thomas Beecham with surprise and regret. Sir Thomas's eminent services to music are well known but unfortunately his great gifts are associated with other characteristics including as he has demonstrated again and again an unbridled tongue . . .
>
> As regards Dr Rankl, the musical director, it was necessary in the unanimous judgement of the Trust to have in their possession someone with extensive practical experience of the day-to-day working of an opera house . . . The Trustees have the highest admiration for the manner in which he has addressed himself to his task.
>
> The fact that since the beginning of the present opera season audiences at Covent Garden have maintained an average of nearly ninety per cent of capacity justifies the inference that the public are far from sharing Sir Thomas's dissatisfaction.[52]

Back in Brighton, rebuttal came from an unexpected quarter. Steuart Wilson, ex-singer and Keynes's CEMA sidekick, now Director of Music at the BBC and a member of the Covent Garden Trust, delivered an apparently spontaneous counter-blast. He dismissed Beecham as 'irresponsible and foolish' and claimed, untruly, that the great man had never shown faith in English singers. As for allegations of waste, Covent Garden had a payroll of 599, two hundred fewer than the Paris Opéra, which received five times as much state subsidy.[53]

Beecham returned to the subject some days later in the *Daily Telegraph*, but sounded subdued and especially keen to exempt Webster from blame:

> For the Administrator of this pathetic fiasco I have some compassion. Not so long ago he publicly stated that owing to his inability to find English singers who could fill competently many of the roles in the operas being given at Covent Garden, he had been forced to import a necessary contingent of foreigners. Since then the influx of the alien element has increased, to the manifest chagrin of scores of native vocalists who consider, rightly or wrongly that there is no justification for this invasion. Anyway, it

can be disputed by no one that if we cannot have opera in Covent Garden represented fittingly without the regular appearance of non-British artists in the principal roles, the case for National Opera in this theatre is blown sky-high.[54]

All Beecham wanted was an opportunity to vindicate past glories. Over the following months he cultivated John Denison, the Arts Council's music officer, with a proposal to put on a summer season of operas – two at Covent Garden and one at Sadler's Wells. Denison showed Beecham's letter to Webster – 'I'm treading very carefully, because there will be a delicious rumpus if these negotiations come to grief!'[55] – and the General Administrator sent back a signal that Beecham would be welcome to conduct at Covent Garden, whenever and whatever he liked. Beecham demanded *Meistersinger* with twice the normal chorus, regardless of cost. Webster coolly acquiesced. An influential antagonist had been judiciously neutralized, for the time being at least.

Pomeroy, too, withdrew from the fray, ruined by a devastating bill for three hundred thousand pounds from the Inland Revenue, one of Anderson's former fiefdoms. His retirement meant that no rival opera would play against Covent Garden in the West End. In a bitter parting shot, Pomeroy declared: 'Opera becomes its superlative self only when its ingredients – music, singing and acting – speak with one voice. At Covent Garden, these more often than not are not even on speaking terms.'[56]

Christie also retreated, preoccupied with reopening Glyndebourne in July 1950 and shuttling its productions back and forth to the newly founded Edinburgh Festival. He lost Rudolf Bing to the Metropolitan Opera and, in successive summers, Fritz Busch and Audrey Christie to fatal illness. Vittorio Gui conducted, Sena Jurinac sang and Glyndebourne regained its summer role, separate unto itself.

Covent Garden had survived its winter of political and cultural discontent. Attendances were rising and there was evidence of a committed audience forming around the house as it had done two decades earlier at Sadler's Wells. A monthly *Ballet* magazine, edited by a perceptive aesthete Richard Buckle, had expanded into *Ballet and Opera*, the latter half edited by the King's nephew, the Earl of Harewood, who had mastered the history of opera while in German wartime custody. The journal was sparky enough to receive libel writs from Beecham. By the end of 1949 its two halves were serving separate readerships and split apart. Harewood, who had just married Marion Stein, daughter of Britten's editor, appointed an opera-mad North London schoolmaster, Harold Rosenthal, to edit *Opera* magazine, which became a cheerleader for ROH plans and aspirations.

As a further bolstering of public support, Anderson and his Board (the Trust had been disbanded and reconstituted with the change of property ownership) renewed Webster's contract and fulfilled their pledge to Cripps to repair artistic inefficiencies by appointing a Deputy General Administrator. He was none other than Steuart Wilson, newly knighted and signing himself on all occasions 'Sir Steuart'. Wilson had spent two and a half years at the BBC, making no mark on the Third Programme but vengefully procuring the removal from the BBC Symphony Orchestra of its founder-conductor, Sir Adrian Boult, whose sin, it seemed, had been to take in the wife and four children that Wilson, an avid womanizer, had abandoned in 1932. Wilson promised to replace Boult with John Barbirolli; he failed, and the BBC were landed with Malcolm Sargent. Waspish, snobbish and untrustworthy, Wilson's enforced retirement at the statutory BBC age of sixty was a cause for musical glee – until it was learned that, by calling on old friendships with Professor Dent and other trustees, he had wangled himself a job at Covent Garden. 'I can't understand how Webster ever let him across the threshold,' said his Arts Council successor.[57]

In October 1950, Wilson had his favourite settee, wooden arm-chair and easy chair delivered to Covent Garden by BBC van. He was to be paid £2,500 a year for unspecified duties, and would be allowed to continue teaching, writing and broadcasting, 'subject to the agreement of the General Administrator'. He was recruited mostly for show, to reassure the Chancellor and deflect press criticism. 'His name from the public relations angle is extremely useful to us,' Webster assured Rankl, 'and his direct standing in the musical world is considerably greater than mine.'[58]

Wilson, however, had few friends in Whitehall or Fleet Street and was remembered by the musical public, if at all, as a reedy tenor well short of world class. He did little to raise confidence, outside the house or within. He was a stranger to loyalty and prone to deception. Webster, agreeing to his appointment, must have forgotten the afternoon in 1947 when he returned to the office one day to find

Wilson going through his drawers. Caught red-handed, the interloper had a ready excuse:

Dear David,
   I am afraid that I inadvertently left you somewhat in the dark. At the Trustees meeting, when you were ill, it was agreed between Sir John and myself, that a summary of accounts should be presented to the Arts Council at the Council Meeting on September 25th and that I should get a break down of certain production figures but not circulate them until Sir John had approved. It was in the middle of this that you found me with Lund [the finance officer] and I completely forgot that you had not been at the meeting and had no idea what I was after.[59]

Intrigue entered the premises with Wilson; no one quite knew whom to believe. He would summon singers to his home for private coaching; those who refused had reason to fear that they could lose roles. His rejections were poisonously hurtful. 'You tackled a big hurdle the other day to convince us that you could go beyond what we all thought were limitations in your casting, and I am afraid you didn't convince us, though we would have liked to be convinced,' he told a chorus singer auditioning for solo parts.[60] 'I don't suppose that you have for some time thought that your position at Covent Garden was entirely satisfactory to you or that you were making good enough progress yourself,' he told a bass singer. 'As far as our company is concerned I think I must tell you candidly that I don't see a future for you . . . So I advise you to give up the idea of a career in singing as your livelihood and to return to what you were doing before the War, which I gather was an accountant . . .'[61] Sitting in judgement over England's new artists was an embittered ex-singer who had himself demonstrably failed to break into opera.
   Wilson's appointment and Beecham's appeasement did not resolve the company's problems. They merely postponed the day of reckoning, which was Webster's way of coping with crisis. Beecham made a triumphal return in 1951, conducting *Meistersinger* to roars of acclaim from the old press codgers, who mostly chose to overlook his waning powers of concentration. In the middle of the second act Beecham went off into a reverie and, with the singers improvising for all they were worth, loudly expostulated, 'Good God, where are they?'[62] Blom, in the *Observer*, tactfully remarked: 'There were two

good performances – one on stage, the other in the orchestra – which would not quite go together.'

On their way home from the 1950 Edinburgh Festival, the La Scala company stopped at Covent Garden and, under the baton of Victor de Sabata, showed up more of the local shortcomings. Renata Tebaldi and Tito Gobbi made their mark as ascendant stars and the orchestra was resplendent. Artistically, Covent Garden was a long way from its objectives, and financially its troubles were increasing by the month. A five-fold increase in state funding had been followed by a five-year freeze. Its roof leaked and its backstage was a danger to life and limb. Into the Treasury came a new generation of officials who knew not 'Old Jehovah', and Sir John Anderson's approaches fell on deaf ears.

Other arts were clamouring for money and Sadler's Wells Opera was clambering back to form under a trained pianist and former Treasury clerk, Norman Tucker, who had worked in Anderson's office during the war and knew his way around Whitehall. Tucker refreshed the Wells with English-sung British premières of unfamiliar Verdi – *Simon Boccanegra*, referred to by its conductor as 'Buck-nigger' – and the completely unknown Janáček, in the form of a heart-rending *Katya Kabanova*, sung by Amy Shuard and conducted by a Prague-taught Australian, Charles Mackerras. The Sadler's Wells Theatre Ballet, reconstituted by Ninette de Valois under her assistant Peggy van Praagh, took on a life of its own. A young South African choreographer, John Cranko, produced a startling *Beauty and the Beast* and in April 1950 the elegant Svetlana Beriosova joined the company from the Metropolitan Ballet, New York. To the dismay of de Valois, critics like the *Observer*'s Richard Buckle favoured the underdog company with its fresh crop of legs to the respected pillars at Covent Garden. Another South African, Nadia Nerina, technically the best dancer in town, was poached by Covent Garden, as was the fast-rising Kenneth MacMillan. Sadler's Wells formed reciprocal ties with Lincoln Kirstein at New York City Ballet and was fulfilling a vital function as the nursery of British dance.

Covent Garden could no longer justify its claim for one-fifth of Arts Council funds, especially when the Council chairman, Pooley, had sentimental ties to Sadler's Wells. The Royal Opera House was being bled white by its inconsistent and painfully vulnerable opera company. The one factor which kept Covent Garden in credit was its ballet company, which not only produced a small nightly surplus but was starting to earn decent sums abroad. Webster, escorting its first American tour, sent a jubilant message to Anderson, to be 'passed on to the Chancellor'. In seventy-four performances over nine weeks, he reported, the Covent Garden Ballet had been seen by 225,000 people and received by the President of the United States and the Governor-General of Canada. It had also achieved 'the means of bringing back seventy-five thousand dollars into this country',[63] no mean amount when the Bank of England's hard-currency reserves were critically depleted. With the best ballet in the world, Covent Garden might somehow keep the wolves from its door until the country was prosperous enough to afford greater subsidy.

'It was always the ballet that bailed out the opera,' said Ninette de Valois, late in her centenarian life. 'They'd send the ballet away on a huge tour of the States and we'd come back with a lot of money to run the opera company. You can tour ballet easier than opera. They can't stand the change of climate, the rough and tumble. The voice doesn't stand up to it like legs and feet.'[64]

Madam had succeeded beyond mortal expectations. Under her iron rule English ballet had advanced, in twenty years, from nullity to world conquest. Its début at the Metropolitan Opera House on 9 October 1949, was a landmark in dance history, 'one of the most brilliant ballet openings New York has witnessed in this genera-tion'.[65] New York did not lack for good ballet. In George Balanchine, it had a Diaghilev choreographer who, backed by the monetary and organizational muscle of Lincoln Kirstein, founded New York City Ballet and other troupes. In Martha Graham and Merce Cunningham, Manhattan saw a pair of modern dance-masters, working in a notably American idiom with such forward-looking composers as Aaron Copland and John Cage. The balletic future belonged, it appeared, to the nuclear superpowers who had carved up the dance map between American adventurism on the one hand and hardline Russian traditionalism on the other.

Beside these behemoths there seemed little space for a third force, yet the newcomers of English ballet aimed to show something more than virtuosic novelty. Their repertoire was rich and self-wrought. Their style was discreetly distinctive. Their determination was immense. 'We feel that all the eyes of London and New York are upon us,' said Madam.[66]

When the curtain fell on *Sleeping Beauty*, the first uncut version of the ballet New York had ever seen, the Met exploded. Robert Helpmann heard the applause erupt 'like the sound of a gun'.[67] 'Everyone was hysterical,' recalled Margot Fonteyn. 'Crowds tried to reach the dressing-rooms; the doormen panicked . . . I felt like a person reprieved from the gallows.'[68] De Valois wrote: 'perhaps we shall never experience such a triumph again'.[69] The volleys of acclaim grew from one town to the next. Years later, the *New York Times* critic, John Martin, decided that the inaugural English tour represented 'the greatest opening of the popular audience the ballet had ever known in this country'[70] – a turning-point in American culture.

'That a dancing troupe from Paris would prove to be exhilarating and sexy was somewhat to be expected,' wrote *Variety* in a front-page splash. 'But that a ballet company from stolid Britain, the land of mutton and ale, of tweeds and Scotch whisky, would prove to be exotic and glamorous, was a complete surprise.'[71] Everywhere the dancers went, they were treated as heavenly guests. Some had not seen so much food, drink and leisured abundance since childhood.

Not everything they danced was instantly enjoyed. *Symphonic Variations*, the most thoughtful of Ashton's ballets, was written off as 'watered Balanchine' and De Valois' English *Job* drew a total blank. But America was bowled over by a troupe which tore the heart-strings in *Swan Lake* and could also tickle the ribs in *Façade* and *A Wedding Bouquet*, drily narrated by its conductor, Constant Lambert. This was an ensemble of all-rounders, a family of talents, and a source of boundless invention. America urgently demanded its return the next winter. Over the next three decades and more English ballet became a biennial fixture on the American entertainment scene. Against all odds, England had been granted a seat among the balletic superpowers.

Webster was entitled to a share of the laurels. He had purposefully lured the New York promoter Sol Hurok to Covent Garden's opening night in 1946 and then refused several invitations until Hurok procured the Met and accepted each and every one of Madam's demands. 'What made the whole business difficult,' said Hurok to Webster and De Valois, 'was that you were talking with two heads but one voice.'[72] A flamboyant Russian-born Jew who billed his own name bigger than his artists, Hurok had proposed the usual cuts in *Beauty* and sought to downplay the unknown Fonteyn in favour of the lovely Moira Shearer whose Powell-and-Pressburger film *The Red Shoes* had played fifty-seven weeks in New York. He even talked of replacing Fonteyn altogether with a US-based Russian ballerina. But Webster backed his ballet director and Hurok finally doffed his wide-brimmed fedora to the adamant woman he addressed, in a Russo-Brooklyn accent, as 'Madame de Vulva'.

Her obstinacy would be vindicated by the finest performances anyone had yet seen from Fonteyn, and by a public reaction that stopped two shrieks short of hysteria. 'I think we made it,' Fonteyn cabled her mother coolly. Weeks later, she was on the cover of *Time* magazine, a world star. At first, said Madam, 'it was only Margot . . . They didn't really see beyond her or the *Sleeping Beauty*. Then later they started to accept the choreography of the country.'[73]

Margot, for Madam, had always been the means to her end. English ballet needed a home-grown star, and she had sensed at first sight that Margot was just the star it needed. A fifteen-year-old girl called Peggy Hookham, part-Irish like herself but also English and Brazilian by descent and complexion, had applied to join her ballet school in 1934. Stage-named Margot and taking her mother's maiden name of Fontes, later Fonteyn, she appeared late in 1935 as the bride in Ashton's first Stravinsky ballet, *La baiser de la fée*, and as Odile in an almost-new *Swan Lake*. Alicia Markova was pirouetting out of the company on a high pointe, refusing to play ensemble parts, and Fonteyn slipped sweetly into her roles. One night she played a child whore in *Rio Grande*, the next a twinkling fairy. Having promoted her in an emergency, De Valois protected her from rivals and self-doubt. 'And some have greatness thrust upon them,' was her cabled exhortation to Margot on an early opening night.

Ashton defined her style and Lambert, her secret lover, drew out a piquant eroticism, but Fonteyn was always Madam's creation and fondest hope. 'Margot was her favourite,' said Moira Shearer, the Scots redhead whose cinematic appeal outstripped Fonteyn's stage-bound fame. 'I wasn't one of her girls. She called us all by our surnames, except Margot. After my first *Giselle* in 1948, Miss de Valois came round to my dressing room, screaming at me, purple in the face. She said, who taught you those things? I said, Madame Karsavina. At which point she went white in the face. The next I heard, Margot was taking lessons from Madame Karsavina.'[74]

'Margot had every first night, of every season, every production,' lamented Nadia Nerina with pardonable hyperbole. 'It was very frustrating for other ballerinas.'[75]

Nevertheless, after a decade at Sadler's Wells, Fonteyn's fame was confined to the ballet. She was skin-tight gorgeous, extensively photographed and elegant to a fault, but not quite a public figure. Three post-war factors transformed her status. The larger stage at Covent Garden endowed her with a degree of grandeur that made her seem larger than life and attracted an upper-class fan club. Fonteyn was the first member of the company to acquire snob appeal. 'I am afraid that as Margot is not dancing that evening, it is very difficult to make people buy expensive seats,' explained Kenneth Clark's wife, Jane, to Webster in May 1948. 'The first question everybody asks when we talk about this is what Margot is dancing. If I had known at the meeting, when the date was decided, that she would be in Paris, I should have protested very strongly against having the Gala evening without her.'[76]

What she was doing that springtime in Paris was enjoying her second lover, the dancer-choreographer Roland Petit, who taught her how to dress at Maison Dior and teased out a vein of seductiveness in her gestures. She had her nose surgically reshaped and luxuriated in new-found physical confidence. 'In Margot's life, I was just the person who, at the right time, opened the door,' said Petit.[77] It was American critics who first commented on her lack of English 'thinness and meagreness of temperament'.[78] Transatlantic triumph completed her five-year ascent from English all-rounder to world champion. Margot Fonteyn, as Madam had foreseen, was a human blank page on which history could be written.

She repaid the company's faith with due servility. Her weekly wage in 1950 was £100, thirty per cent higher than any opera singer but well below her escalating market value. La Scala offered her £150 a week to appear in Milan. Hurok dangled six hundred dollars a week for a US tour, more than twice her Covent Garden pay. But Fonteyn was a company girl, body and soul. When she needed to be with her lover, she politely requested leave of absence. When injured, she accepted half-pay. She lived with her mother and had few friends or interests beyond the ballet.

In 1953, fearing she might be lured away, Webster increased her US touring fee to twelve hundred dollars a week, four times her home salary. It was only after her marriage to the Panamanian diplomat Tito de Arias in February 1955, that Fonteyn evinced a need for pecuniary recognition. By 1962, she was making £400 a night at Covent Garden and $24,600 for thirty-six US appearances – all payments being made to a tax-sheltered Panamanian company, Diana, S. A., as befitted her elevated social status and her exceptional position at Covent Garden.

No other dancer had remotely the same allure. Shearer, a shy girl who disliked the bawdy side of ballet life, was dismayed at seeing life-sized effigies of herself outside cinemas where *The Red Shoes* was still showing. She had outplayed Helpmann in the film and was never forgiven for it by the Sadler's Wells old guard; when she stepped out in the title role on the first night of *Cinderella*, not one member of the company wished her luck. In America, she was content to let Fonteyn hog the limelight and shared her sleeping quarters on the company train without complaint. Newly married to the writer Ludovic Kennedy, she soon fell pregnant and retired from the stage, naming Fonteyn as godmother to her eldest daughter. The company's other principals, Beryl Grey, Pamela May and Violetta Elvin, did not presume to contest Margot's supremacy, knowing that Madam would tolerate no challenge.

The male dancers were of lesser calibre. Helpmann, Fonteyn's regular partner, failed to cover up low leaps and weak technique with comic winks and thespian skills. 'He was a pretty poor dancer, but a marvellous mime,' was the collegial verdict.[79] His place was taken by Michael Somes, a large-boned Devonian whose marriage to a fellow-dancer, Deidre Dixon, almost broke Frederick Ashton's heart. Ashton had been smitten with Somes since 1934, but the sexually ambivalent, emotionally repressed Englishman had a mind of his own and a temper to match. On stage, he caught and supported Fonteyn.

If Margot was the magnet for English ballet, Ashton was its creative mind. Most people were drawn to ballet to see beauty, whether of half-naked young bodies with exaggerated cod-pieces and visible bottoms, or of the chaste co-ordination of music and movement. Ashton added an unsought bonus: the prospect of cerebral stimulus. Ashton ballets tended to deal with adult issues rather than nursery stories. *Symphonic Variations* (1948), an abstract for six dancers to music by César Franck, contemplated the state of religious faith, sexual love and English pastoralism after the savagery of war. Liberated by Covent Garden's great spaces from the constraints of the Sadler's Wells stage, Ashton daringly stopped his dancers dead-still, arousing trains of thought about the individual's place in a fast-moving world. It was the first unqualified masterpiece of English ballet, wearing its seriousness without solemnity, its beauty without preening.

His next work was a failure, depicting Richard Strauss' *Don Juan* (1948) as an anti-hero, his virility weakened by austerity, the flaccid Helpmann almost scissored apart by a flying Fonteyn. In Prokofiev's *Cinderella* (1948), the prime roles were given to the Ugly Sisters, danced by Helpmann and Ashton himself with seditious disdain for fairytale endings. Ravel's *Daphnis et Chloe* (1951) he redeemed from romantic excess and presented as a conflict between corporeal and spiritual love. *Tiresias* (1951) touched on the insoluble conundrum of whether men or women get more out of sex. *Sylvia* (1952), with music by Delibes, was a soppy anachronism, written to please Fonteyn's American fans; but most Ashton ballets flung barbed questions at an increasingly receptive audience.

The choreographer had somehow reinvented himself as chronicler of modern England. He made the ballet intellectually respectable, and far more innovative than hidebound opera. Going to the ballet became as much an essential of civilized metropolitan life as reading the latest Graham Greene novel, seeing the new Terence Rattigan play or hearing a Britten première. Ashton was the engine for a ballet of ideas, making a sensual art socially relevant.

This amounted to a sensational leap, for the man as much as for the art. Ashton had grown up half-wild in a South American outpost and achieved little by way of formal education. He was physically lazy and did not seem always to know his own mind, but behind the slack exterior there ticked a busy intellect, allied to a comic streak that could send stiff-lipped royalty into fits of mirth. A voracious reader of classical and modern literature, Ashton infused his ballets with cultural allusions and confused dancers with ideas well above their heads. He could reduce them to tears with his turns and twists, but mostly cajoled them into position. He was exacting rather than tyrannical, and much loved.

Ninette de Valois was a more daunting proposition. 'She was awful to rehearse with,' said Shearer, 'she tore us apart down to the last toenail. But when it came to the performance it was clear that she had seen everything clearly in her mind – unlike Fred, who often seemed to improvise.' As a choreographer, Madam was approaching her nemesis. In 1950 she fashioned a *Don Quixote* to music by the modernist Catalan exile Roberto Gerhard. It was her first ballet in seven years and, as it proved, her last. Although respectfully received at Covent Garden, and despite brave performances by Helpmann and Fonteyn, the ballet bombed in New York. 'After the third of its five scenes, two or three dozen patrons rose from their orchestra seats and, with no apparent attempt to be covert about it, walked from the auditorium. From then until the end, departing figures provided an unbroken counterpoint to the movement on the stage,' reported *Musical America*, its critic, Cecil Smith, adding that 'the débâcle was of Miss de Valois's making . . . neither madness nor fantasy was evoked by the choreography.'[80]

But her appetite for achievement was unspent and, if her creative contribution was at an end, her energies could be applied all the more vigorously to imperial administration. She was in charge of two national companies and the ballet school that fed them with fresh recruits, a position of unparallelled authority. 'She was a very powerful woman,' said Shearer, 'almost a Hitler in her way of running things – though that may have been a good thing at the time. Ninette de Valois was, to me, the antithesis of Diaghilev in running a company. He was entirely generous, and she was closed.'

Others saw her in a gentler light, recalling that she was often racked by arthritic pain. 'She overcame personal feelings,' said Diana Gould who danced for de Valois before marrying the violinist, Yehudi Menuhin. 'To me she was helpful and kind and understanding.'[81]

There was something incorporeal about Madam, as if she did not fully belong to a race of flesh and blood. In an art that glorifies the human form, she dressed in shapeless jackets and skirts, swinging a bulging handbag. Even in her dancing days, she was not one to undress before others or expose bare skin on stage. Where many dancers hopped in and out of each other's beds like overfed rabbits, Ninette de Valois was impervious to lust and untouched by scandal. So detached did she seem from her own physicality that dancers stood before her as if before a heavenly throne. One dancer was fascinated by the contrast between Madam and her brother, the ballet photographer Gordon Anthony. 'Like many ballet fans and hangers-on, he was a tremendous pooftah. Gordon was completely effeminate, while she must have come out with all the male genes in the family.'[82]

'You were either petrified, or you adored her,' said Antoinette Sibley, a pupil at her school. 'She really liked naughty people, and I adored her. I answered her back. Someone like Anthony Dowell, who was reserved and trying too hard, had it much tougher.'[83] Madam had expanded the school in 1947 into a full-scale curricular establishment, taking children from nine years old to university entrance. The first intake were all girls, paying fifty-five guineas a term. A dozen boys were added the following year, most of them on scholarships. 'Madam only took (whom) she wanted and she had an incredible eye,' said one of the teachers.[84] She valued an all-round education and would not accept pupils into her companies until they had passed their School Certificate (GCSE) in at least five subjects. Sitting at a long table, flanked by satraps, she delivered snap verdicts on her charges – this girl bound for glory, that one for university.

She brooked interference from no one. Having loaned Beryl Grey to dance in *Carmen*, she withdrew her one night without notice, over the conductor's objections. 'There was no talking to her,' he sighed.[85] When Webster asked Moira Shearer and her husband to suggest a ballet synopsis to Covent Garden, their plot was dismissed unread by the ballet sub-committee because, said its chairman, Kenneth Clark, 'Ninette naturally feels that any new ideas for a ballet should at an early stage have been submitted to her.'[86] Webster, said his secretary Muriel Kerr, was 'terrified' of Madam and jumped out of his skin when her presence was announced in his vestibule.[87] She attacked him for being 'pro-opera' and fought by all means, fair and foul, to uphold the primacy of ballet at Covent Garden. But she knew that ballet needed to batten on to a thriving opera company to sustain its profile and employment and she was prepared to concede, when pressed, that Webster had his uses as 'a good businessman'.[88]

As the decade ended, the mood curdled. The Labour Government, having weathered economic woe and achieved most of its objectives, trod on a national corn when, in September 1949, Stafford Cripps devalued the pound from four dollars and three cents, to a paltry two dollars eighty. The measure was meant to revive British exports and it succeeded in due course. But the public recoiled in outrage at the humbling of their currency. England evinced an irrational pride in the solidity of sterling. The first Labour premier, Ramsay MacDonald, had sacrificed his last claim to be the people's choice by suspending the gold standard in 1931, causing the pound to lose twenty-five per cent of its value in a week. Now Cripps shrunk sterling by one-third overnight and the backlash was felt by every MP. Never having lost a by-election since the war, the Government saw its support plummet in constituency soundings. In February 1950 Attlee decided to cut and run ahead of a tough Budget, calling a snap election.

He almost lost. A politically oriented advertising campaign by 'Mr Cube', emblem of the sugar monopolists, Tate & Lyle, swayed voters against further nationalizations. Churchill talked of 'setting the people free' under the Conservatives and Labour lacked a counter-punch. Attlee was visibly weary, Cripps was dying of intestinal cancer and the rest of the party were gearing up for a succession struggle between power-clinging pragmatism, represented by Hugh Gaitskell, and the impractical idealism of Aneurin Bevan. Labour scraped home by a wafer-thin majority of eight seats and the post-war agenda was pulled to a stuttering halt.

Unheeded by politicians, the reversal had been foretold in art. George Orwell, in his *1984* valediction, portrayed a futuristic totalitarian state in drab colours that belonged, all too familarly, to 1940s Britain. Any extension of socialism was, inferentially, a threat to liberty. The menace was underlined by massive Communist advances in Europe and China. Intelligent support for any form of Marxist praxis was discredited by Arthur Koestler's influential polemic, *The God that Failed*. Socialism in England had gone as far as it would go.

A nation that boasted of equanimity was mired in misery. Francis Bacon, the finest painter to arise since the war, depicted only suffering and despair. Dylan Thomas, the popular poet, wrote of death and mourning. Graham Greene, the mainstream novelist, wrote of the death of love.

Hopes of creative renewal were scorned by the elysian T. S. Eliot who, in the year of his Nobel Laureateship, gave vent to a bitter diatribe that proclaimed the death of civilization:

We can assert with some confidence that our own period is one of decline; that the standards of culture are lower than they were fifty years ago; and that the evidences of this decline are visible in every department of human activity. I see no reason why the decay of culture should not proceed much further, and why we may not even anticipate a period, of some duration, of which it is possible to say that it will have *no* culture.[89]

Cyril Connolly, whose literary magazine, *Horizon*, had thrived on wartime intellectual ferment, accused the Government of doing 'practically nothing' to help advance the culture. In 1949, he closed the magazine, citing public apathy and a dearth of talent. British cinema turned insular and escapist in a succession of stiff-lipped comedies and war films. English theatre was numbingly polite. The belief that art could rebuild society was fading, and the artistic ventures founded upon this faith were shaken in their very purpose.

At Covent Garden, the worm turned during election month. The commitment to Englishness was weakened yet again and Webster was ordered to summon as many foreign conductors as were needed to bring the opera company up to standard, its existence to be justified by excellence alone. This meant telling Karl Rankl that his job would be abolished. Erich Kleiber had been booked to help out around the sensitive Christmas period. Rankl, who had been assured by Webster that things were improving, was stunned – both by the notice of dismissal and by a crippling anxiety of what might transpire if a celebrated conductor like Kleiber occupied his place in the pit. He loathed Kleiber with a venom that was both personal and political. Kleiber had clung to his post in Berlin for two full years of Hitler's Reich, while Rankl quit Germany the day the Nazis came to power. 'He was a wicked man,' said Rankl of Kleiber.[90]

'I was surprised at your views on Kleiber,' replied Webster with calculated disingenuousness. 'He seems to be one of the few people who share our views – he is all for encouraging local singers and he has done a great deal of this kind of work in South America. He believes in opera in English with the kind of exceptions we have already made . . . (and) he speaks well of you.'[91]

Rankl replied, within hours, in an agitated handwritten note:

'Dear David,

I have read your letter very carefully. The only question I should like to ask is: Are you presenting me with a *fait accompli*, or are your proposals still open to a discussion between ourselves?'[92]

Webster's response was unyielding:

'My dear Karl, The principles in my letter are beyond discussion. . . The office of Musical Director will cease after the 1950-51 season. This is also beyond discussion.'[93]

A more confident, less naïve musician than Karl Rankl would have resigned there and then. His contract stated unequivocally that no musician or singer could be engaged or dismissed without his written consent. By hiring Kleiber behind his back, Webster had committed a flagrant breach of contract and Rankl would have been within his rights to sue for exemplary damages through his eminent firm of lawyers, Rubinstein Nash. He was inhibited by two concerns: a refugee's insecurity, and a deep-seated commitment to the singers and musicians whose talents he had discovered and nurtured. Unable to afford legal action, and impelled by forlorn ideals, Rankl took up his baton for the transformatory season of 1950-51.

He opened with the stomach-churning obligation of a *Flying Dutchman* produced by 'Mephisto' Heinz Tietjen, artistic director at Bayreuth during the Hitler era, upon a set by Emil Preetorius, Goebbels' favourite stage designer. Clemens Krauss, music director in Hitler's Munich, was due later in the season, and one of the new singers, Frederick Dalberg, was a Newcastle-born bass who had changed his name from Dalrymple and plied his trade in Germany during the war. In place of purified Englishness, Covent Garden was leading the way in the appeasement of Nazi sympathizers.

'I see Tietjen's been here,' was Kleiber's comment on entering the auditorium.

'How did you know?' said Rankl, astonished.

'Speakers and microphones everywhere,' said Kleiber. 'Tietjen was always spying on his staff.'[94]

'I felt terribly sorry for Rankl,' said a stage manager. 'He was on his way out and, as well as Kleiber, all these Nazis were coming to Covent Garden. That must have been a bitter taste.'[95]

Rankl's revival of *Salome*, on sets rebuilt from the jettisoned *Olympians*, got the new season into its stride. *Tosca* directed by Christopher West, a former Brook assistant who stayed on as house producer, augured well, despite the unscheduled posthumous reappearance of the heroine, Hilde Zadek, who bounced back into view after landing from her suicide leap on to an oversprung mattress. Rankl and the orchestra seemed to be growing together in confidence, until Kleiber arrived and put the art of performance on an altogether different plane.

Erich Kleiber had earned his spurs not as a provincial conductor in Graz but as head of the State Opera in Berlin for twelve years, resigning in protest against the Nazis' ban on his projected première of Alban Berg's *Lulu*. Married to an American, he had spent a sedate war at the Teatro Colon in Buenos Aires and, on a return trip to Europe was approached by Webster with a princely offer of two hundred pounds a night to conduct at Covent Garden.

The ovation that erupted as he entered the pit to conduct *Der Rosenkavalier* on 6 December 1950, was 'like the cheers of a beleaguered garrison at the sight of the rescuing force.'[96] A schoolboy in the audience felt a 'perceptible difference'.[97]

'Kleiber made me blossom,' declared Constance Shacklock, who sang Octavian. 'He had a way of bringing out the best in everyone. Rhydderich Davies, the Welsh boy, very beautiful voice but not particularly musical, was playing the Attorney and there is one point where he is talking to Baron Ochs and says 'May it please – (pause) – your Lordship . . .'

Kleiber shouted up to him in rehearsal: 'My boy, why do you think Strauss wrote those rests?'

So Rhydderich said: 'I haven't a clue, Sir.'

He said: 'Well, Strauss was an asthmatical – gasp – old boy. Try it again.'

Well poor old Rhydd nearly choked himself.

'Sorry, sir, can't do it,' he cried.

Kleiber said: 'My boy, you can do it. You're an artist.'

There was dead silence. We were awestruck.'

A back-desk cellist was overheard saying, 'I wouldn't have believed I could enjoy a Saturday morning rehearsal so much. And he finished half an hour early.'[98]

Der Rosenkavalier was followed by Tchaikovsky's *Queen of Spades*, *Rigoletto* and *Carmen*, the conductor's appeal spreading like fire both within the company and beyond. Though his American wife, Ruth, liked to kick up a fuss over imagined slights and Kleiber himself would threaten at times to catch the next plane to Buenos Aires, for performers he could do no wrong. 'He was always on our side,' said an orchestral player.[99]

'He was a dear man,' smiled Shacklock. 'He always came to see you before you went on stage, to say: just watch that little note there. As if of all the thousands of notes in the opera, this was the one that mattered. He used to knock and walk in, didn't wait for an answer.

Well one night I was late getting ready. I was decent, but not fully dressed. When he came in I protested, "Herr Kleiber!"

"It's all right my dear," he said. "Firstly, I'm short-sighted. Secondly I'm married. And thirdly, I like what I see . . .'"

'We must do everything in our power to keep him here,' Kenneth Clark told Webster. 'He has made an immeasurable difference. But when all is said and done he couldn't have used the instrument unless Rankl had created it.'[100]

The humourless, unflirtatious Musical Director had, rather nobly, introduced Kleiber to the orchestra before scurrying away to nurse hurt feelings. 'Kleiber got six rehearsals for *Carmen*, which had been in repertoire for three years, while Karl was doing a new *Götterdämmerung* and praying for every rehearsal he could get,' said Christine Rankl.[101] When he came on one night to conduct *Fidelio* and was greeted by shouts from the audience of 'We want Kleiber!', his pride was wounded beyond repair. The news that Kleiber had been booked for *Wozzeck* the following season, an opera that Rankl coveted for himself, was the final straw.

During parallel rehearsals – one at Covent Garden, the other at Kingsway Hall, Holborn – a dispute broke out as to which conductor had first call on the orchestra's two regular trumpeters. Had Webster been around, matters might have been smoothed over, but the General Administrator was in America with the ballet and the problem fell into the domain of his officious deputy, Sir Steuart Wilson. The double-booking had been Rankl's fault, arising from his refusal to help scheduling Kleiber's rehearsals, but Wilson's pompous handling turned a slight scratch into gangrenous wound. 'I again told him that if he would not accept responsibility for Kleiber's rehearsal somebody must, and that it was now important that I should do so,' reported Wilson to Webster in America. 'I therefore regard Rankl's refusal to co-operate in any way, even under protest, in this matter of the rehearsal as being a definite challenge to define the authority of the Musical Director, and I equally definitely take up the challenge and say that he voluntarily abdicated his rights by refusing to co-operate.'[102]

Wilson sent Rankl an ultimatum: 'Will you accept as a compromise that you end your rehearsal at 12.30 p.m. and let all the orchestra go including the two trumpeters who will be here at 12.40?'[103] Rankl acquiesced, but came home and told his young girlfriend that he could not take much more. 'Throw the job in their faces,' she said, 'I'd rather have you alive than dead.'[104] On Webster's return, Rankl formally resigned 'from all my positions with the Covent Garden Opera Company'[105] from the end of July. Since his contract expired on that date and was not to be renewed, his gesture was as toothless as his humiliation by Wilson had been pointless.

A resignation statement was issued, at Rankl's request, because (as Webster told his chairman) 'he has to find work for himself and finds the matter a little delicate without some announcement having been made.'[106] No reason was given but Rankl was thanked by the Directors for his 'immense pioneer work in the formation and training of principals, chorus and orchestra'.

The remainder of his tenure was not so much regretful as pathetic. He conducted *Parsifal* and the *Ring* with considerable panache, to the point that one loyal staffer felt that 'there hasn't been anything better'[107] since his *Götterdämmerung*, with Flagstad as Brünnhilde. On the last night of June, Flagstad and the conductor bade farewell to Covent Garden with *Tristan und Isolde*. Flagstad took twenty-one curtain calls, but there was no tribute to Rankl. Three and a half weeks later in Liverpool, Flagstad made her final operatic appearance and David Webster walked out in front of the curtain in his home town to salute her career. He went on to raise a round of applause for Shacklock who had that night sung her fiftieth Brangäne. But not a word passed his lips about Rankl, who had just given his last performance with the company he had created. 'I wanted to call out, "what about Rankl?",' recalled the bass singer Michael Langdon, 'but I lacked courage. I was young and had my future to think of; I kept my mouth shut.'[108] Rankl was given a lift back to his hotel by a new member of the music staff, Emanuel Young. In the car, he burst into tears.

He was rapidly erased from Covent Garden memory. Hard-up and out of work, Rankl wrote to Webster in September wondering when he could expect the 'handsome cheque' he had been promised if he went quietly. A settlement of one thousand pounds was eventually paid into his account, small recompense for five formative years. He invited Webster to his opening concert as chief conductor of the Scottish National Orchestra the following winter; Muriel Kerr sent personal 'congratulations on your appointment in my home country'[109] but no one from Covent Garden attended. The following year, his name was left out of a Covent Garden history, provoking a protest from Clark and a libel threat from Rankl. 'I am naturally sorry that you should be upset by the omission,' Webster wrote. 'There was no wish either to hurt you nor to omit your name from any place where it should appear. The brochure was intended primarily to be a piece of publicity for the Coronation Season.'[110]

The more the Royal Opera House improved, the more eager Webster was to eradicate traces of Rankl, who now seemed too insignificant to have been associated with so exalted an institution. He remained fond of 'dear Karl' and fretted about his unemployment after his Scottish position folded, volunteering to 'write to a few people to see if they can do anything about him . . . freelance conductors at a reasonable price are not as common as all that.'[111] But he never asked Rankl back to conduct at Covent Garden. As far as Webster was concerned, said Peter Gellhorn, who left the company for a better job at Glyndebourne, 'when it was finished, it was over – he didn't want to know you.'

Rankl might have been the wrong man for the job, but he did more than anyone could have expected from a smalltown *kapellmeister*. The visiting conductors Clemens Krauss and Rudolf Kempe praised his chorus as the best in the world, and some of the singers he discovered and trained were soon taking wing, Shacklock to Moscow, Geraint Evans to La Scala and the Met. 'That first five years of discipline with Rankl is something I'll always be grateful for,' said Shacklock. But Covent Garden, along with the rest of Britain, was keen to cover up those dedicated, stumbling beginnings and stride ahead to a less principled, amnesiac future.

CHAPTER 5

First Act, Forbidden Acts

(1951–59)

THE REBIRTH OF the nation was marked ceremonially on 3 May 1951, a wet Thursday of scurrying morbidity. On a patch of reclaimed marshland on the south bank of the River Thames, diagonally opposite the Mother of Parliaments, the Festival of Britain was opened by the Archbishop of Canterbury, Dr Geoffrey Fisher, who proclaimed a 'belief in the British way of life' and a hope that 'we may continue to be a nation at unity with itself and of service to the world'. National self-reconsecration was the refrain of the Festival Exhibition, which 'unfolded the tale of the continuous impact that this particular land has made on this particular people, and of the achievements that this people has continued to derive from its relationship with the land.'[1]

The particularity was significant. As patriotism was the last refuge of a scoundrel,[2] so insular nationalism had become the rallying cry of returning heroes. 'The belief that Britain will continue to have contributions to make in the future is founded on two factors,' quavered the Exhibition guidebook (price 2/6d), 'the People of Britain and the Land of Britain.'[3] An echo of Goebbelsian rhetoric, *Ein Volk, Ein Land*, pervaded the undertones. 'The "People of Britain" Pavilion shows how the British stock was blended,'[4] explained the guidebook, adding a thoughtful disquisition on 'the problem of space' – or *Lebensraum*. The nation was turning in upon itself with a celebration of Merrie England that was both surreal and anachronistic. A pylon stretched pointlessly into the sky, symbolizing the Vertical Future. A Milk Bar proferred the delights of arable farming. Foreign foodstuffs were banned from the site. English wit and self-mockery were conspicuous by their absence.

The Festival had begun as an open letter written to Stafford Cripps

by Gerald Barry, editor of the *News Chronicle*, in the roseate dawn
of September 1945. Barry drew attention to the approaching
centenary of the Great Exhibition of 1851 in which Britain at the
pomp of empire had displayed its wares and vitality to the world.
The anniversary, he suggested, offered an opportunity for the nation
to affirm to the world and to itself that it had weathered the war and
was poised to invent a better future. Cripps was unimpressed, but his
Cabinet colleague Herbert Morrison, Lord President of the Council,
leaped upon the concept and made it flesh.

Morrison, a muscular London politician who mysteriously
destroyed most of his personal papers, longed to leave a national
monument. The Festival became his pet project. Using his clout at
Party headquarters, he extracted from the Treasury a huge budget of
twelve million pounds, reduced to eleven million in the 1949
devaluation crisis. He made Barry director general and surrounded
him with a council of cultural eminences: Kenneth Clark, T. S. Eliot,
Malcolm Sargent, John Gielgud. Under Tory attack for extravagance, he appointed as chairman Churchill's wartime chief of staff
and close friend, General Lord Ismay.

At the centre of the site was its only permanent edifice, the Royal
Festival Hall, commissioned by the London County Council to
replace Queen's Hall, which had been bombed to rubble on 10 May
1941. Acclaimed as a marvel of modern architecture but acoustic-
ally dull, the brave new concert hall was ringed by temporary
pavilions and a Dome of Discovery, displaying varied aspects of
British life and endeavour. Surfaces were painted in gaudy hues of
red, white and blue and futuristic designs offered a respite from a
decade of utility products. The catering was reassuringly awful.
Anyone who ordered wine was poured British sherry by a
'slatternly'[5] waitress.

Elsewhere, the Festival sprouted a funfair in Battersea Park, a
pageant in Cardiff, an exhibition of Industrial Power in Glasgow, an
opera in Liverpool and a festival ship that stopped at major ports. 'I
want everyone in Britain to see it, to take part in it, to enjoy it,' said
Morrison. 'I want to see the people happy. I want to hear the people
sing.'[6] By the time the pavilions were taken down in October, eight
and a half million people had visited the site, equivalent to one-sixth
of the country's population. 'You came away feeling you could
dance like (Gene) Kelly,' said the budding playwright Arnold
Wesker, 'and, for a few moments, along the road, with one's friends,

you actually did step more lightly and leap a little.'[7]

The press played up the general jollity and Morrison, who skipped an important ministerial meeting of the Council of Europe to show the King and Queen around his creation, was popularly rechristened 'Lord Festival', an appellation that impressed his power-conscious grandson, Peter Mandelson. 'The Festival has been a good thing for all of us,' intoned Archbishop Fisher at the closing ceremony, 'it has been a real family party.'

This airy platitude was vaguely incontestable, but the family party was a dubious choice of phrase. For the Britain that the Festival purported to represent was no longer a family affair. The war had destroyed its cultural homogeneity and the peace its racial purity. Some sixty thousand Hitler refugees, mostly Jews, had arrived before 1939 and an equivalent number followed after 1945. Their cultural impact was explosive. The art publishers Bela Horovitz and Walter Neurath revolutionized dowdy British book design. The music publishers Ernst Roth, Erwin Stein and Alfred Kalmus nurtured young British composers to world fame. Bauhaus-trained architects mocked mock-Tudor semis and altered the urban landscape. Nikolaus Pevsner chronicled *The Buildings of England* and redefined *The Englishness of English Art*. Karl Popper and Ludwig Wittgenstein, Isaiah Berlin and A. J. Ayer, revitalized Oxbridge philosophy. Alexander Korda breathed life into British cinema. Elias Canetti contemplated a cerebral novel that would win him a Nobel prize. Lucien Freud was emerging as the country's most original portraitist. None of these trends or individuals were reflected in the Festival of Britain, which celebrated as restrictive and mythical a vision of national conformity as any Nuremburg Rally.

Nor were Jews and European *émigrés* the only outcasts. An employment boom brought about by the National Health Service and the nationalization of transport had created a sudden need for more nurses, midwives, hospital ancillaries and bus drivers than were locally available. The NHS and London Transport placed job adverts in West Indian newspapers. Young men and women, raised to admire the Mother Country, rushed to apply for positions, many of which offered vocational training. The first 492 immigrants disembarked at Tilbury in June 1948. Wearing thin suits and jaunty hats, they expected to be welcomed, or at least tolerated, by the country they had come to help.

Instead, they faced a brick wall of medieval primitivism and prejudice. Eleven Labour MPs signed a letter of protest to the Prime Minister and a Cabinet committee was formed to examine 'ways which might be adopted to check the immigration into this country of coloured people from British colonial territories'. Landlords put up signs saying 'No Coloureds'. The newcomers were appalled by damp and filthy accommodation. Many houses had no bath or shower. Some used the bathtub for storing coal.

At work, immigrants were shunned or abused. The first black copper in the Metropolitan Police was so ill-treated by colleagues at Bow Street station, opposite Covent Garden, that he recalled crying himself to sleep at night for a whole year. In hospital, patients would shout 'get your black hands off me' at nurses and porters who were trying to look after them. The Festival of Britain turned a blind eye to the fast-changing demographic map of Britain. The Land and the People were a tight little item that excluded aliens from arcadian bliss. Seen with half a century's hindsight, the Festival was aimed at the nation's narrowest instincts, and was thus successful beyond measure.

Morrison was promoted in March 1951 to Foreign Secretary, in place of the dying Ernest Bevin, but Labour was too far gone to be resuscitated. A month before the Festival opened, the party was split down the middle by a blazing Cabinet row between Aneurin Bevan and the pragmatist Chancellor, Hugh Gaitskell, successor to the dying Cripps. Bevan loathed Gaitskell with a passion that was as much physical as political. He called the Chancellor 'a dessicated calculating machine' and his supporters reviled 'the prim set of his mouth (that) seemed to symbolize the primness of his political views'.[8] Gaitskell despised Bevan as a dangerous windbag, and goaded him into action by imposing charges for NHS spectacles and dental care in his first Budget, supposedly to help pay the costs of the Korean War.

It was not the money, thirteen million pounds, that mattered to either man, but the principle and the personal. Bevan objected to any charge for NHS services as a breach of faith, and to British participation in the Korean War as an act of American toadyism. Gaitskell wanted to reinforce the Atlantic alliance with an extra £690 million of rearmament spending, and to bring the NHS back under Treasury control.

When he refused to back down on the charges, Bevan resigned

from the Government, taking with him Harold Wilson, President of the Board of Trade, and John Freeman, a junior minister. When Attlee called a snap election in September, Labour lost by seventeen seats. It hardly mattered that they mustered 176,000 more votes than the Tories and a forty-nine per cent share, higher than in 1945. The vagaries of the first-past-the-post system had produced a result that reflected public sentiment and put paid to a clapped-out administration.

Apart from promptly bulldozing the Festival of Britain site and leaving it derelict for a decade, the Tories neither turned the clock back nor moved it forward. 'Steady as she goes' was the motto, with R. A. Butler as a conciliatory Chancellor and an apolitical Minister of Labour, Walter Monckton, who did his best to befriend the trade unions. 'Little had actually changed,' wrote a Labour historian, 'Attlee's patriotic socialists gave way to Churchill's social patriots.'[9] The ruling dogma became known as 'Butskellism', a centre-ground consensus that bogged the 1950s down in a mire of political stagnancy. Mounting social and industrial disasters were swept, along with any pretence at idealism, beneath the Plimsoll line of both main parties. Wages were allowed to rise at three times the rate of production. Quick-fix housing began to uglify cities and destroy communities. Future leaders would deride the period for its 'retreat from reality'.[10]

The Royal Opera House had a small part to play in the Festival of Britain, and played it shabbily. In 1948, Webster had endorsed an Arts Council scheme to commission new operas for the Festival and stage them at Covent Garden. Dozens of anonymous submissions were read by a selection panel comprised of Constant Lambert and Edward Dent, representing the ROH, Steuart Wilson and Lawrance Collingwood of the BBC, and Eric Walter White of the Arts Council. White was the only member who knew the composers' identities, and he acted with 'great discretion'.[11] There was consternation when the victors were named, not least from Lambert, who found he had chosen *Deirdre of the Sorrows* by his arch-enemy, Karl Rankl. 'By God, I hate that bastard's guts,' he exploded, 'but it's still a good score and my word stands.'[12] The other winners were *Beatrice Cenci*, by Berthold Goldschmidt; *Wat Tyler*, by Alan Bush; and Arthur Benjamin's *Tale of Two Cities*. The composers received an award of three hundred pounds in exchange for granting the Arts

Council the right, for the next two years, 'to nominate the first production'.[13] The Council would 'do its best to bring about' a production, and the composers were led to understand that it would take place at Covent Garden.[14]

Then the back-tracking started. Someone noticed that the operas picked to celebrate the Festival of Britain had been written by three foreigners and a Communist. The Royal Opera House smartly withdrew and the Arts Council blushed deeply and did nothing. Bush, the moment his two-year clause expired, sent his insurrectionist epic to the German Democratic Republic where it appeared in Leipzig in 1955 and remained for decades in the repertory. Benjamin, an Australian, had his Dickens melodrama broadcast by the BBC in 1953. Goldschmidt, a German refugee, was allowed to conduct selections from *Beatrice Cenci* on the Third Programme for his fiftieth birthday that year. Dismayed by Covent Garden's disregard for its commitments – an Englishman's word was, after all, supposed to be sacrosanct – Goldschmidt wrote a letter of protest to *The Times*. The result was that he was shunned by the English operatic establishment and had to wait until 1994 to see *Beatrice Cenci* triumphantly vindicated in Berlin and successfully recorded by Sony. Rankl's *Deirdre* never got that far. His appeals to Webster went unanswered, despite testimony from singers that the opera was performable. After his death in 1968, Rankl's widow placed the score for safe-keeping with an archive in Graz, where it languishes unsung to this day.

In place of the victorious alien operas, Webster put on the tepid première of Ralph Vaughan Williams' *Pilgrim's Progress*, more sacred oratorio than grand opera, and no fewer than nineteen performances of *The Bohemian Girl* by Michael Balfe, a Victorian pot-boiler that had faded from all living memory except for Sir Thomas Beecham's. Opening in Liverpool, where it was billed as the Festival high-point, the opera earned Beecham £150 a night conducting fee, plus 3.5 per cent of box-office takings as a royalty on a performing edition in which he questionably claimed copyright. This torpid anachronism then vanished once again into a mist of its mediocrity. Webster, unable to attack Beecham, avenged himself on the innocent producer, Dennis Arundell, who was blacklisted at Covent Garden.

To an introspective ROH, the Festival of Britain had been an unwanted distraction. Covent Garden was preoccupied with an internal struggle. The Board demanded a new music director. Webster was determined to delay any appointment for as long as possible in order to extend his own authority. Having attended many auditions, he considered himself a connoisseur of singers and a master of casting and looked forward to a period of grace unhampered by a resident conductor. He decided to buy time by seeking a partial replacement and wrote to Sir John Barbirolli in Manchester, asking him to lunch. Barbirolli, whom Webster had spurned in 1945 as too vain, replied warmly: 'As you know I am not much of a luncher, but if you would like to give me a sandwich and a whisky and soda it will be very nice.'[15]

News of their meeting leaked to the press, and Barbirolli was besieged – 'they even got into his hotel bedroom'.[16] Two days later, it was announced that Barbirolli had 'accepted an invitation to be Guest Conductor with the Covent Garden Opera during the 1951/52 Season. The acceptance of this invitation will not involve curtailing his services with the Halle Orchestra.' Both men got what they wanted out of this arrangement and emerged the best of friends, signing their future letters 'love and best wishes'. Webster increased his power and Barbirolli strengthened his hand in contract nego- tiations with the Halle, while securing top whack at Covent Garden – two hundred and fifty guineas for each first night, and one hundred and fifty for subsequent performances.

He opened with *Turandot* and *Aida*, and was not seen again that season. Next year, Barbirolli repeated the same operas, followed by *Bohème*, *Tristan* and two nights of Gluck's *Orfeo ed Euridice* built around the family-favourite contralto, Kathleen Ferrier, who was making her ROH début at the age of forty. Ferrier had breathed new life into the baroque opera at Glyndebourne and her rendering of 'What is Life to me Without you' was reputed to melt granite. But she had undergone a serious operation and Frederick Ashton, who directed and choreographed the production, took care to spare her unnecessary effort. Webster was among the handful of people who knew the gravity of her condition and his decision to authorize the production was a calculated and compassionate risk.

The Sunday before opening night, when his faithful designer Sophie Fedorovitch failed to turn up for the pre-dress rehearsal, Ashton sent an assistant round to her studio. Sniffing gas, he let himself in with a spare key and found the designer prone beside her bed. She had been dead for two days, poisoned by an accidental leak.

During the week, Buckingham Palace announced that the King was gravely ill, and the nation prepared to mourn.

Ferrier, before going on stage, gave Barbirolli a set of blue-enamelled cuff-links and a loving note thanking him 'for making an Orpheus dream come true – and for many other blessings spread over the last three years'.[17] On the second night, 6 February 1953, she made an awkward move and broke her hip in several places, the bone weakened by cancer. She sang out the second act leaning on a stage prop and took her curtain calls on the conductor's arm. 'I shall never forget,' said Barbirolli in a memorial tribute, 'the impish glee with which she literally purred over one of the critics' comments that her movements were an object lesson even to the Sadler's Wells Ballet.'[18] Seven months later, Ferrier was dead.

Barbirolli conducted three listless productions the following season, and nothing more. When Webster half-heartedly raised the vacant music directorship, Barbirolli changed the subject.

Kleiber was the next candidate, but he was both costly and capricious. On his return to Covent Garden, Kleiber restricted himself to eighteen performances of four operas. His involvement climaxed with *Wozzeck*, the atonal opera he had brought into the world more than quarter of a century before, and which was being staged for the first time in Britain. Its tale of a war-weary soldier, brutalized by his officers and comrades and idly betrayed by his mistress Marie, was more topical and radical than any play in the West End, but Kleiber knew the immensity of effort it required. He sent for Reggie Goodall, who had been sacked from Covent Garden after poor reviews and got him to coach the cast for four months and start training the orchestra. Kleiber himself called nineteen sectional rehearsals. 'Just think you are playing a Haydn symphony,' he told the orchestra.[19]

The six performances of *Wozzeck* were poorly attended and deeply perplexing to reactionary critics like Frank Howes who told *Times* readers how 'nasty and depressive it all is'. But the collective achievement surpassed belief. The cast of mostly staff singers hit the toughest passages with stunning accuracy. The antediluvian mechanisms and antiquated backstage bosses coped with fourteen scene changes in under ninety seconds. And the orchestra played for the first time like a frontline ensemble, equal to any task a composer could throw at it. The half-empty house was dotted with enthusiasts who came night after night to experience a work, which as Philip

Hope-Wallace wrote in the *Manchester Guardian*, 'seizes the imagination by the short hairs of the scalp'. *Wozzeck* was the moment Covent Garden came of age and Hope-Wallace credited the transformation to 'Dr Kleiber, a great artist'.[20]

Kleiber, however, was fed up with foggy London winters and fretting for continental activity in Berlin, Vienna and recording studios. He found fault with Webster and became unpredictably perverse, perhaps a symptom of impending illness. After a gripping *Elektra*, directed by Rudolf Hartmann of Munich, Kleiber left London on the eve of the Queen's Coronation, and never returned. Two and a half years later, on Mozart's bicentennial birthday, he was found dead of a heart attack in the bath of a Zurich hotel suite.

Apart from Barbirolli and Kleiber, there was no conductor with strong claims to be the next music director. The names that came Webster's way were ridiculously inapposite. Steuart Wilson volunteered two Englishmen: Anthony Bernard, a sixty-year-old former Shakespeare Theatre conductor, and John Pritchard, aged thirty, who made a messy début in charge of Professor Dent's new translation of Verdi's *Masked Ball*. William Walton, from the boardroom, nominated Harry Blech, a violinist who had formed his own chamber orchestra, the London Mozart Players. The half-deaf Dent, despairing of conductors, told Webster that what he needed was an artistic director and the best man for the job was Aladar Toth of Budapest Opera. Toth, said Dent, spoke 'practically no English' but was 'keenly interested in Purcell' and had put on a *Peter Grimes* 'which was far better in every way than either of the London productions'.[21]

The more far-fetched the suggestion, the more it suited the General Administrator, allowing him time and licence to play fantasy opera and book the conductors and singers of his dreams. Not all of them responded. Early in 1953, he made strenuous efforts to attract Wilhelm Furtwängler for *Meistersinger*, but the Berlin conductor, never the most decisive of men, was unmoved by the proffered honour and died before much progress was made. Each such demise or refusal enabled Webster to convince his board of the lamentable lack of conductors and music directors, and thereby to strengthen his grip on artistic planning.

An intriguing solution was forming in his mind. In the autumn of 1951, Benjamin Britten completed his first Covent Garden opera, *Billy Budd*. He nominated the Austrian conductor Josef Krips to conduct the première on the strength of a fine *Rape of Lucretia* at Salzburg but Krips, receiving his copy of the score six weeks before opening night, declared the photostats unreadable.

Mistrusting other maestros and bypassing the fractious Goodall, Britten asked Peter Gellhorn to commence rehearsals and finally decided, 'however reluctantly'[22] to conduct the run himself. 'He certainly knew his job,' said one orchestral player. 'He also had the ability, unusual in a composer, to explain to us clearly in words what he required from us in music.'[23] Webster, rather meanly, paid him just five hundred pounds for four performances and much preparation.

Britten grumbled about 'the size of the house, state of company, lack of co-operation'.[24] The disorderliness of a grand opera house offended his prim nature. Two months before opening night there was still no singer designated for the title-role until Webster, on an American trip, saw a blond, broad-chested California baritone, Theodor Uppman, and signed him to play Herman Melville's innocent ship-boy, hung at the yard-arm after a murder at sea. 'The fact that an opera is in English does not make it easy to cast,' he told the Ministry of Labour, after protests from the actors' union, Equity. 'I would say categorically that there is no Englishman who is suited to the role of Billy Budd.'[25] Pears played the hapless Captain Vere and Frederick Dalberg the evil Claggart.

Expectations ran impossibly high, for not only was *Budd* a reprise of powerful *Grimes* themes of death and guilt on the high seas but it introduced, as co-librettist with Eric Crozier, the novelist E. M. Forster, who had never written for the stage and had produced no large work since *A Passage to India* back in 1924. 'I feel confident that *Billy* will make all Ben's operas until now look like experiments leading to the first of his great mature works,' wrote Crozier to his future wife, Nancy Evans. 'It will be a tragedy if Morgan does not live long enough to write other works for him.'[26] Forster, happily, enjoyed an Indian summer after *Budd*, but did not work again with Britten. As for the opera, it split opinion from the start and stirred more disquiet as it matured.

The morning papers recorded a 'torrent of applause', but Ernest Newman in the *Sunday Times* derided the libretto and discerned no musical progress on Britten's part; woundingly, he likened the finale to *H.M.S Pinafore* by Gilbert and Sullivan. Younger critics like Desmond Shawe-Taylor and Philip Hope-Wallace damned *Budd* with faint praise. In the *Manchester Guardian*, Hope-Wallace argued that the opera had been dramatically undermined by Britten's decision to give 'the moralizing tenor part' to a non-protagonist, Captain Vere. 'This gives the opera a core of almost German earnestness . . . (and) has the effect of weakening the natural hero Budd and the villain Claggart in spite of their monologues and self-revelations, into little more than abstractions of good and bad,' he observed.[27] Twenty-seven years later, the same critic was 'over-whelmed' by a Covent Garden revival of *Billy Budd* and wondered whether his first response had not been swayed by over-zealous interpreters. In the 1980s, critical wisdom graded *Budd* as second-rate *Grimes*, most tellingly in a television survey of Britten's work.[28] The tide then turned, but commentators could not agree about the meaning of it all. Reviewing a Welsh production in 1998, Michael Kennedy saw the opera as 'the conflict between public duty and private sentiment at a time of national danger'.[29] Peter Conrad, con-versely, noticed 'sweaty bonding rituals of mateship' and applauded the opera for showing 'how homosocial behaviour on board ship approaches but tactfully avoids homosexual declaration'.[30] It was as if two seasoned critics had been watching separate shows, so richly contorted were the possibilities embedded in *Budd*. On the opening night, it was the astute Kenneth Clark who observed that this was 'one of those masterpieces that change human behaviour'.[31] Noël Coward, on the other hand, left the theatre unmoved.[32]

The verdict that mattered was delivered by the opera circuit. Unlike *Grimes*, which circled the world, *Budd* with its single-sex cast was shunned. In Germany, a cut version was staged at Wiesbaden and fast forgotten. Apart from a television airing on NBC in 1952, *Budd* was not seen in America until 1970, by which time Britten had reluctantly halved its four acts, reducing three intervals to one. The original *Budd* was not revived until 1997.

The flaws revealed or perceived in *Budd* gnawed away at Britten's ever-fragile confidence and increased the stomach-churning anxiety that gripped him when he was required to conduct on big occasions. He thanked Webster for his support and looked forward politely to further collaboration,[33] but his first loyalties lay with Aldeburgh and the English Opera Group. Beyond his gaze, meanwhile, powerful forces were conspiring to raise him to high office. Harewood, smitten by *Budd*, arranged with his father-in-law Erwin Stein, who was Britten's editor at Boosey & Hawkes, to nominate Britten as the next music director at Covent Garden. Webster leapt at the idea, not least because Britten would be a non-executive music director who conducted only his own works and maybe a Mozart or two, leaving the General Administrator to select other conductors and casts. But he anticipated boardroom opposition, knowing that Leslie Boosey would not want Britten to be distracted from composing and that William Walton was seething at the praise and favours being showered on his rival.

Walton had entered the war as England's rising composer and ended it an also-ran. Kept in comfort by his mistress, Lady Wimborne, until her death in 1948, he married a young Argentine beauty soon after and was struggling to make an opera out of Chaucer's version of *Troilus and Cressida* while setting up home in exile on the Italian island of Ischia. Although constitutionally lazy and not given to malice, he had blocked a British Council recording of *Grimes* and liked to moan about Britten and his 'coterie'.[34]

Webster, faced with opposition, took his usual course of doing nothing until, nagged by Harewood, he neutrally raised the proposal with the board. Boosey, predictably, declared that Britten was a professional composer who should be absolved from practical duties. Walton, at his last board meeting prior to emigration, wondered whether Britten would be prepared to conduct *Troilus*; Harewood said he would. And there the matter rested. Britten himself was lukewarm to the idea. He would only take the post, he told Webster in November 1952, if he could bring along his English Opera Group. They would be regarded as a clique, warned Webster. A clique, said Britten, was the only way anything got done in music; he hated having to deal with strangers at the best of times.[35]

He was, by now, deep into his next Covent Garden commission, an opera proposed by Harewood and dedicated 'by gracious permission to Her Majesty Queen Elizabeth II, in honour of whose Coronation it was composed'. Harewood, about to be employed by Webster 'in a general kind of capacity',[36] wanted something 'appropriate' for his maternal first cousin's ascent to the Throne, securing the consent of his paternal second cousin, Sir Alan Lascelles, who happened to be the Queen's Private Secretary. Small world, the English aristocracy.

On a skiing week in Austria, Harewood discussed with Britten and Pears England's deplorable lack of a national opera, in the way that Italy had *Nabucco* and Germany *Die Meistersinger*. Britten rose to the bait and conversation turned to the glories of the first Elizabethan era. Harewood proposed Lytton Strachey's history of *Elizabeth and Essex* as a plot, recounting how the Queen's love for a courtier led to his execution. Britten imagined a synthesis of Tudor polyphony with the post-tonal chords of a New Elizabethan era. He chose as librettist the South African-born Bloomsbury poet William Plomer, a circumspect friend of E. M. Forster's. Webster told them to write as large as they liked, confident that any deficit would be covered by an extra Treasury grant for the Coronation.

The first objections were raised by the Sadler's Wells Ballet, which kicked up a fuss at being denied the chance to strut its stuff before the new Queen. Ninette de Valois demanded *jus primae noctis* – either a new ballet performed before *Gloriana*, or a full evening of dance. In the Covent Garden boardroom, ballet backers battled opera buffs. 'O David – dear David – Can nothing be done to stop K. Clark's silly mouth?' wailed Britten to Webster. 'I have, five minutes ago, received yet *another* message from my lord of Upper Terrace about the Ballet v Gloriana situation (it was thru 'the usual channels', of course). I am now informed that there is going to be a short ballet on June 8th *before* poor old Glory Anna. Just like that. Now if anything fresh was settled at your last Board meeting – please can *you* tell me direct and not have just any old trustee sending messages. Anyhow, you know that only over my dead body, dead opera too, will there be a ballet before *Gloriana* that night . . . Excuse scribble, please, but I'm still shaking with temper! love – Ben.'[37]

The composer eventually agreed to write ballet scenes that would be choreographed by the 25-year-old John Cranko, for whom he felt a budding affection. John Piper, his favourite artist, was engaged to design the sets; the director was the EOG's Basil Coleman who had served him well on *Budd*; Joan Cross agreed to play Elizabeth and Pears was to be Essex. Surrounded by friends, Britten composed at high speed, as many as twenty-eight pages of full score in a day. His only discomfort was the conductor John Pritchard, selected by Webster after Britten declined the baton. Pritchard was often late for rehearsals and did not appear to have mastered the score. His lover and agent, Basil Horsefield, had been known to stand in for Pritchard when the conductor was delayed, earning them both a sharp rebuke from Webster.[38]

As *Gloriana* reached completion, clouds gathered. A circle of young critics and acolytes had published during the winter an adulatory survey of Britten's life and works[39] which inflamed envy in musical rivals and pursed many lips for reprisal. In the Coronation Honours List, Britten was created a Companion of Honour, an unusually exalted tribute for a man under forty. English mediocrity awaited its day of reckoning. A coalition of rebuffed composers and sceptical critics murmured together in pubs. Walton whispered to Rawsthorne, who moaned to 'Twelve Tone Lizzie' Lutyens, who drank daily at the BBC. Lutyens dismissed Britten's music as 'brilliant journalism'. To appease the chief moaner, Webster asked Walton to write a Gala reorchestration of the National Anthem, thus annoying Britten.[40]

Adding to his own woes, Britten swelled the enemy ranks by shedding friends and allies without a word of explanation. Tenors who sang higher or better than Pears were made to feel unwanted. Conductors who were over-applauded were not reinvited to Aldeburgh. The tense atmosphere at Britten's festival recalled the fickleness of the Elizabethan Court, where yesterday's golden knight was tomorrow's grim beheaded.

On 2 June 1953, Queen Elizabeth the Second was crowned with pomp imperial in Westminster Abbey. The Conservative Government spent a million pounds on the festivities, aiming to fortify national unity and display England at its most arcadian. Coronation mugs sprouted in every market and food rationing was eased by an extra pound of sugar and four ounces of margarine. The Queen entered the Abbey to the chords of Walton's *Orb and Sceptre* before taking the oath and hearing the surge of Handel's great chorus 'Zadok the Priest' as she was anointed. The first Coronation on live television was watched by twenty million people, more than half the adult population, many of whom purchased a set for that purpose. Almost twelve million tuned in to the radio. Hundreds of thousands lined the processional route. It was the first occasion since the war and the last for forty-four years in which the nation acted in unison. On the morning of the Coronation, *The Times* reported that Sir Edmund Hillary and his sherpa guide, Tenzing, had reached the summit of Mount Everest, supposedly the world's highest peak. England ascendant was the motif of Coronation week. Even at cricket, the national game, there were signs that England was about to regain the Ashes, ending twenty years of Australian dominance.

Six days after the Coronation, *Gloriana* received its première at

Covent Garden before the new Queen and an audience comprised of the highest in the land. The Court and *corps diplomatiques* turned out in force. Evening dress and full decorations were *de rigueur*, the top seats cost six guineas and the interior of the theatre was redecorated for the occasion by Oliver Messel, the Royal Box lined with a cloth of gold. All eyes were on the new Queen and the Establishment felt obliged to attend, either out of a sense of duty or nagged to distraction by the socially-mobile wife of the Covent Garden chairman, Sir John Anderson, himself lately ennobled as the first Viscount Waverley. 'That tiresome, pushing little Lady Waverley was still wriggling her way up the ladder,' noted Cecil Beaton, who was taking photographs at the Palace; 'with her innate vulgarity of yellow, frizzy musical comedy curls and sycophantic flattery, she stuck out a mile.'[41]

The failure of *Gloriana* was rendered almost inevitable by the status of its audience. If the invitation list was inappropriate, the offering was doubly so. Harewood's presumption that the avowedly unmusical new Queen, fresh from her Abbey ordeal, would want nothing better than to spend two and a half hours watching a modern opera was wishful, to say the least. Britten, too, was not without blame. His opera creaked with Plomer's archaisms, assumed a detailed foreknowledge of Tudor history and portrayed the Queen as cruel and capricious, not what was expected in Coronation week. It was a warm night, and Covent Garden was airless. Starched collars wilted with perspiration and yawning broke out in the stalls. Prince Philip was seen reading a green-and-white Penguin crime thriller hidden inside his programme.[42]

'Oliver Messel's decor was superb,' recorded John Colville, the Prime Minister's principal private secretary, 'and the audience – well dressed at Covent Garden for a change – matched it. But the music was above our heads and the episode depicted by the opera, Elizabeth's squalid romance with Essex, totally unsuited to the occasion.'[43]

The response was apathetic. Even those who were moved to applaud did so in a patter since many hands were white-gloved for the occasion. 'An audience of stuck pigs,' Britten called them.[44] 'One of the great disasters of operatic history,'[45] said Harewood. 'A fiasco,' said the Secretary to the Covent Garden Board.[46] The critics performed on cue. Newman in the *Sunday Times* proclaimed that 'the bulk of the music is hardly more than pastiche'. Richard Capell in the *Daily Telegraph* called it 'pageant rather than drama', and Philip Hope-Wallace in the *Manchester Guardian* found himself, at the end of the first act, 'wondering if the opera will ever get off the ground'. The reviews were by no means wholly uncomprehending, but nothing less than hallelujahs would have satisfied the Brittenites and Harewood felt so affronted that he turned witheringly on *Opera* magazine for failing to appreciate 'what the Gala stood for, how it summed up the efforts made for English opera since 1945; how, through it, the arts generally and opera particularly were recognized as they had never been before in England.'[47] The popular press renamed the opera 'Boriana'. Despite healthy attendances drawn by the controversy, the show was a write-off. 'Sic transit Gloriana,' quipped one musical journal. La Scala cancelled its intended production and the American première was done in deepest Cincinnati. The opera redeemed itself at Sadler's Wells in 1966, despite last-ditch efforts by Webster to withhold the rights from a rival company. It contains, notably in the dance sequences, some of the liveliest and happiest music in any Britten opera, but a first-night flop is hard to reverse and four decades passed before the work was considered worthy of a recording.

Gloriana set the seal on Britten's involvement with Covent Garden. He would write and conduct a ballet, *The Prince of Pagodas*, for his friend John Cranko, but no new opera of his would ever come into being at the Royal Opera House. *Turn of the Screw* went to Venice, *A Midsummer Night's Dream* to Aldeburgh, *Owen Wingrave* to BBC television and *Death in Venice* to New York. Although he had warm feelings for Webster, after *Gloriana* Britten did not trust Covent Garden to appreciate his work and protect it from the wolves. His goal was to bring art to the people at every level, from the rudiments of *Let's Make an Opera* to the moral complexities of *Peter Grimes*. Covent Garden's aim was, increasingly, to present exquisite singing for connoisseurs and the moneyed classes. The dichotomy had become irresoluble.

In reputational terms, the failure of *Gloriana* was not Britten's but Covent Garden's. It demonstrated that a company created to foster national opera was unable to accommodate the country's greatest composer. *Gloriana* had been the right opera for the wrong time and place. A prompt revival might have revived Britten's faith in Covent Garden, but the board were cowed by the Royal disgrace and Webster was constrained by their shame from making amends.

He never gave up hope, however, of securing Britten's commitment in a different capacity. Five years after *Gloriana*, Webster wrote a memo to his board about the endless search for a chief conductor. He argued 'that there is no one available or in the offing to whom we should offer the job of Musical Director of opera at Covent Garden,' but declared himself 'in favour of an approach being made to Britten under the Musical Director heading – not because I thought he would take the job but because I thought (that) out of the discussion would come some notion of how Britten could help Covent Garden.'

This was an imaginative leap on Webster's part. Attaching a great composer to an opera company, not as a conductor or for the music he might write but purely for his creative mind and refined taste, was positive thinking of a high order. Webster hastened to reassure his directors, somewhat wishfully, that 'we need not worry about the coterie aspect of Britten ... It is my strong belief that he has outgrown the coterie phase.' He added: 'To me he would be of immense value. His salary would be a matter of opinion but I would have thought about £2,000.'[48]

There is no evidence that Webster ever put this idea to Britten, and his memo received short shrift from a Board whose priorities had shifted ever further away from English opera. Relations between Covent Garden and the composer were doomed to remain sporadic, wary, and mutually unrewarding. An attempt was made to lure Britten to take part in a 1973 Gala celebrating Britain's accession to the European Common Market, but the composer withdrew on grounds of ill health, and was not greatly missed at the Royal Opera House.

The *Gloriana* debacle of the Coronation summer was quickly overshadowed by events of greater moment. Before the month was out, England was agog at news that Princess Margaret, the Queen's younger sister, was keen to marry Group Captain Peter Townsend, a freshly-divorced royal equerry. Divorcees could not remarry in the Church of England, of which the Queen was titular head, and Townsend was packed off to Brussels, leaving the Princess disconsolate and the press in clover.

More sombrely, a fortnight after *Gloriana*, Winston Churchill gave dinner at 10 Downing Street for the visiting Italian premier, made a dazzling speech about the Romans in Britain, sat down heavily and suffered a stroke. Over the next few days he lost the use of his left arm and leg and his doctor, Lord Moran, did not think he would live. Anthony Eden, his deputy, was in America recovering from a gall-bladder operation. The country was being run by senior civil servants, in consultation with the top Tories Lord Salisbury and Rab Butler and the Queen's private secretary, Sir Alan Lascelles. Remarkably, despite the presence at dinner of so garrulous a guest as Kenneth Clark, no word leaked out of Churchill's incapacity. He made a partial return to health and remained in office for two years more, persuading the country that it did not need much by way of leadership beyond a wave of the hat and a cigar-clenched grin. The absence of strategic purpose was demonstrable across politics and industry however, as Britain indulged consumer desires with half a million car sales in 1955, and self-disciplined Germany built the strongest economy in Europe. Inflationary self-delusion was the order of the British decade. The burning issues were questions of class: whether one spoke 'U' (respectable) or 'non-U' (common). The ship of state had an esteemed skipper, but there was no one plotting a course.

The absence of a driving-seat music director made no obvious difference at Covent Garden. The singing and playing continued to improve, and when the Bavarian State Opera brought three Strauss operas in September 1953, there was no rush on the box-office and no blush on English cheeks. The home company could do just as well – and went on to prove it with a run of five Strauss operas under Rudolf Kempe, a tall, reserved Saxon who became a seasonal fixture. After a wooden *Ring* fell flat under the baton of Fritz Stiedry, Kempe took over the production and demonstrated the difference a good conductor could make. The *Daily Telegraph*, under the headline 'Wagner Revealed', declared in an editorial that 'Kempe has restored the *Ring* to us. He has made the orchestra sing and removed the necessity for the singers to bellow, bark, scream or hoot.'

The weakness of the *Ring* was its lack of local content. Apart from the Czech-born Otakar Kraus as Alberich, none of the central parts was entrusted to a British singer. Webster, unhampered by Rankl, splurged his budget on foreign glamour – the magnificent Hotter, Margaret Harshaw from the Met, the Swede Svanholm, Leonie Rysanek and Hilde Konetzni. The director was Rudolf Hartmann, the Bavarian intendant. Amid roars of relief for a redemptive *Ring*, no one seemed to notice that Covent Garden Opera was drifting away from its founding objectives. Vision, rigour and principle were cast overboard. Expedience ruled an eclectic display.

It was in this period of unbridled improvisation that the legend of Webster's omniscience was born. He began to court the limelight of press interviews, assuming a paternalist *gravitas* that verged on pomposity. Publicity articles that flowed from his pen were almost unreadably stuffy. 'It may be that when it is demonstrated that there exists the possibility of operatic careers in this country this somewhat vicious circle may be broken,' is a typical sample of unpunctuated Websterian prose.[49] The frivolous side of his nature, his Pickwickian relish of gossip, was carefully concealed. To the opera public and to most of his staff and directors, Webster was a dusty figure with an uncanny command of company activity. The real Webster was revealed only to an inner circle of trusted allies who met weekly behind closed doors.

'We were an awfully close-knit bunch,' said Elizabeth Latham, who arrived from Stratford as stage manager in 1950. 'We met in Webster's office: Morris Smith and Douglas Robinson, the orchestra and chorus directors, Patrick Terry, the opera company general manager, Webster, Miss Kerr and myself – and Lord Harewood after he joined the staff. We all knew what was going on, there were no secrets. We had this thing called The Bible, which was the scheme for the whole year, and would adjust it as necessary. It seemed amazing to me then, and still does now, that the house could have been run so simply and with such little fuss. I never had a contract. We shook hands, and that was that.'[50]

Their intimacy verged on the conspiratorial. Sir Steuart Wilson, Webster's deputy, was invited to the meetings 'as seldom as we could manage'. Latham, along with the director Christopher West, the production manager John Sullivan and the rest of the weekly group were also made welcome at Webster's Weymouth Street flat, where Jimmy Cleveland Belle was a 'charming, delightful host' and Webster was seen at his most relaxed. With Morris Smith in particular, he would, it was said, 'uninhibitedly, and safely, unburden himself'.[51] Smith, a Coldstream Guards trombonist who lost his playing nerve after being attacked in the park with a parasol by a pacifist lady, let it be known that he belonged to the same masonic lodge as Webster. A below-decks tyrant, Smith gained an 'unenviable reputation'[52] among orchestral musicians whose careers were shadowed by his blatant favouritisms. Successive conductors, and even the chairman himself, were unable to overcome Smith's reactionary prejudice against women players.[53] As much lackey as bully, he would preface his more preposterous decisions with the words, 'Webster says . . .'

The existence of an inner clique, though, barely intruded on the daily life of the company. Latham, who balanced her career with marriage to a Harley Street surgeon, was on formal terms with the General Administrator. 'We were always Mr Webster and Miss Latham,' she recalled. 'He had this extraordinary passive face. One day he came on stage and said, I think you really deserve a rise now, Miss Latham. You will notice it in your bank account next month.' She was getting fifteen pounds for a six-day week – in at eight-thirty a.m. to check the scenery before rehearsal; afternoons taken up by paperwork; at six she raced home to bathe and change for the performance; at midnight she locked up. Her credentials were established not by any closeness to Webster but by her willingness to 'take a coat off and run a flat as well as any stagehand'[54] – and by a remark tossed her way after a week at work by the assistant chief machinist, Ted Lilley. 'Miss,' said Ted, 'Mr Ballard says you know your onions.' Authority in the backstage had not altered appreciably since Puccini's day.

Among the Victorian pulleys and rat-runs, Webster had neither command nor control. He tried in 1947 to assert his management by appointing a fellow-Liverpudlian, Cliff Clifford, as stage manager, but Clifford was cowed by the Ballard gang and Webster knew better than to tangle with a bunch of swarthy lads linked by theatrical heritage and family bloodlines. When snow failed to fall in *Bohème*, or descended with a thump like a feather mattress, Clifford shrugged his shoulders and blamed it on the untamed stage crew. When half the chorus collapsed coughing and the cause was traced to dusty floors, Clifford complained of the lack of a staff cleaner. He was a kindly man, who let stage-struck youngsters take over his prompt corner – 'keep an eye on this for me,'[55] he would say in mid-opera, while he nipped across the road for a drink – but he was too weak to last. 'I had never seen a stage so badly run,' said Latham, who resigned after ten weeks at Covent Garden and went to work at Glyndebourne. Her letter to Webster, outlining Clifford's short-comings, has been removed from the files, but Clifford's contract was not renewed at the end of the 1950-51 season. 'I am particularly sorry that I have not been able to give you this news in person,'[56] wrote Webster, avoiding an unpleasant interview with an old provincial friend.

Latham, resuming her post in September 1951, discovered unplumbed depths of inefficiency, and worse. Wages were being paid to men who never showed up, and probably did not exist. She spotted the fraud when the company went on tour and Latham noticed that the names of her stagehands differed from those on the pay packets. 'We were working with dead men,' she exclaimed. 'We'd write ahead and ask for six hands, but when I checked the wage list none of them were the Bills or Freds we'd been given.' There was also some tinkering with expenses, with pounds fiddled up to guineas. Latham took the discrepancies not to Webster but to the company secretary, Douglas Lund. 'He was excellent,' she noted, 'like a weasel down a rat-hole.' The corruption was silently purged. No trace survives in the archives and Webster does not appear to have informed his Board, let alone called the police. Latham came down soon after with consumption, brought on by stress and overwork, and Webster assured her that he would pay her full salary for six months of recovery. 'My God,' she thought, 'just how much money have I saved them?'

Petty theft and Mickey-Mouse practices were creeping in to British industry and would become endemic in Fleet Street, but in the early 50s they were still unusual in the London theatre and unheard of at Stratford. Webster needed to hush the scandal, not because he feared for his position but because it would have dented his myth of immaculate management.

His awareness of image was ahead of its time, and his use of industrial psychology was equally advanced. 'He knew us all, weaknesses and strengths,' said Latham. His technique was to say little and do nothing, letting others assume that he read their minds, approved their actions and deserved credit for their success. It was only in the very jaws of disaster that he ever acted decisively, and such instances were so uncommon that their rarity greatly magnified the impact of his intervention.

Once, during a rehearsal of Offenbach's *Tales of Hoffmann*, he began to suspect that the conductor, Désiré Emile Inghelbrecht, retired chief of the Paris Opéra, did not know the score. A hurried check revealed that the elegant septuagenarian had never conducted *Tales* in his life. Webster, in full view of the company, sacked the

Frenchman and summoned a new member of the music staff, Edward Downes, to take over. Downes, until lately a horn player at Sadler's Wells, seized his opportunity with both hands and saved the show. Webster was credited with *Hoffmann*'s rescue, even though the problem had arisen from his own cavalier assumption that any maître from the Paris Opéra would know his Offenbach like a Stratford man knew his Shakespeare. Webster's ignorance of conducting lore was absolute, but his bold decision obscured the original error and reinforced his aura as a far-sighted, all-seeing leader of an ever-improving enterprise.

Not that conductors ranked high in Webster's list of priorities. Singers were paramount, and it was to their welfare and development that he devoted most attention. With Rankl gone and Wilson often away on well-paid lecture tours, Webster increased his involvement in the selection process. Rankl's four-cornered trawl of the kingdom had more or less exhausted native resources but a tide of hopefuls began to turn up from the dominions. Sylvia Fisher, who had sung *Aida* on Australian radio, convinced Rankl on her fifth audition to cast her as Leonore in *Fidelio*. Her success smoothed the path for many of her compatriots. Fisher's voice was extolled by *Opera* magazine as 'one of the joys of the present day'[57] and her cheerful, no-worries attitude made her the perfect company singer; she also married the company's Italian coach, Ubaldo Gardini.

Less immediately appealing, at least to the managerial and critical teams, was the New Zealander Joan Hammond, whose mannish demeanour attracted a vociferous clique. Webster was not convinced. He was looking for team players, not prima donnas. The antipodeans he hired were not the kind who answered back. Elsie Morison was poached from Sadler's Wells in 1953 and Marie Collier from Glyndebourne two years later. The tenor John Lanigan was retrieved from Jay Pomeroy's wreckage. 'I had a letter one morning from Webster, asking if I would think of joining to do *Fidelio* and *Bohème* – for me, it was heaven on earth,' said Morison, who was married at the time to a Covent Garden bass, Kenneth Stevenson.[58]

None of these recruitments, however, possessed the elusive gleam that separates the timeless artist from the merely timely. What was needed was a heavenly star, incontestable and irresistible, who would give a rocket-boost to ROH prestige and raise other singers with her to a higher plane of fame. Webster, at auditions, prayed for a Nellie Melba or a Florence Austral to ascend from the antipodes – and prayed doubly hard that she did not apply first to Vienna or New York.

The miracle he was seeking arrived in the mail one morning in the autumn of 1951, in the shape of a testimonial from Eugene Goossens who was still trying to work his way into Webster's favour. 'The bearer of this letter,' wrote Goossens,

> has a magnificent soprano voice and has done excellent work here in concert and operatic performances. Her voice is in the true Austral tradition and she made quite a sensation here recently in her creation of Judith in my opera of that name. Her departure for Europe will be a great loss to Australia for such grand natural voices as hers are all too rare nowadays.

An audition was arranged at the Wigmore Hall at 2.45 p.m. on 16 October, before Sir Steuart Wilson who gave a typically dusty report: 'Starts with a good ring in the voice. Very little stage experience *or gifts by nature*.'[59] The gangling, square-jawed Australian, three weeks short of her twenty-fifth birthday, was advised to return to her studies with Clive Carey and reapply six months later. Second time round, in June 1952, Peter Gellhorn detected an 'unusual solidity' in her voice and suggested that she might, in time, become a dramatic soprano. A third audition was held on 10 July at Covent Garden with Webster himself in the stalls. The tall girl sang 'Non mi dir' from *Don Giovanni* followed by 'Ritorna vincitor' from *Aida* and, while most felt she would at best become a decent understudy for Sylvia Fisher, Webster in his report noted: 'with work, might do better than that'.

Before the week was out, members of the music staff heard her sing Giorgetta in a Royal College production of Puccini's *Il Tabarro*, and the matter was settled. 'I got a telephone call the next day from the Garden,' recalled Joan Sutherland, 'and they said, "My dear, we have decided that you should join the Company, starting in September."'[60] She was to be paid ten pounds a week and was told to learn the First Lady in *The Magic Flute*. Sutherland made her début on 28 October and a week later sang the High Priestess in *Aida*. Four days after that, her recital début at the Wigmore Hall drew a ripple of reviews from critics alerted to her promise by Webster, who was convinced from the outset of her potential. 'This,' he said, 'is the first singer we've had here since the War who is capable of becoming a star.'[61]

But the rise of Joan Sutherland was to be slow and spasmodic. Seven years would pass before she exploded on to the world's consciousness in the Mad Scene of Donizetti's *Lucia di Lammermoor*. Time enough for various members of the Board and the music staff to question her stiff gestures and lack of conventional good looks. After *Lucia*, any fool could have spotted her star quality, but it took courage to keep faith in Sutherland for seven lean years. Webster, however, harboured no doubts. He assured Mrs Sutherland that her daughter was destined for greatness and when Joan slipped out to marry her Svengali-like pianist friend, Richard Bonynge, the General Administrator sent a huge bouquet of red carnations to the church in Ladbroke Grove and gave the young couple a reception at his Weymouth Street flat. No other young singer was so favoured. When Sutherland sent her agent, Joan Ingpen, to beg for Mondays off to have her teeth fixed, Webster's only quibble was, 'are you sure she is seeing the best person?'[62]

Her ascent was delayed by several impediments, not least the onset of pregnancy and the insistent presence of Bonynge, who whipped her off to a throat specialist at the first sniff of a cold and lobbied tirelessly for her advancement. Socially, she held herself slightly apart and shunned the coarse humour of singers. On one occasion, when Geraint Evans's hand touched her bare midriff in a *Figaro* rehearsal, she swung round and belted him across the jaw. She made another baritone swear never to relate that she had let off a thunderous fart as he clasped her to his bosom. Even as an ingenue, she assumed the *hauteur* of stardom.

The immediate obstacle to vertical progress was an historic force far greater than herself. On 8 November 1952, the day after Sutherland's début recital, Maria Callas made her first appearance at Covent Garden, with the Australian trailing her in the minor role of Clothilde, her nurse. Callas, just twenty-eight years old, was a Manhattan-born Greek who had been provoking near-riots in Italian opera houses. Outside of Italy, she was known only in Greece and South America. She possessed a twin-edged reputation, for ferociously intense performances allied to a temperament that brooked no contradiction. Frumpish yet sultry, she was married to a Verona businessman, Giovanni Battista Menenghini, whose role in life was to obstruct anyone who approached Maria, making her own recalcitrance appear moderate by comparison. Before Covent Garden came into her reckoning, she had fallen out badly with her mentor, the conductor Tullio Serafin, and turned down a début at the Met in New York.

The first Englishman to be smitten was the Earl of Harewood, who in August 1947 caught the second or third night of her Italian début in Ponchielli's *La Gioconda*, with Serafin conducting, in the Arena di Verona. Harewood was struck by the tigerishness of her delivery and undismayed by a quavery harshness that marred some high notes. Four years later, he heard her in Verdi's *Sicilian Vespers* in Florence, under Erich Kleiber, and marvelled at her enlarged authority and waistline. Webster turned up soon after with a proposal that she should embrace the role at Covent Garden in English – which was, in a sense, her native tongue. Callas laughed, and countered with an offer to sing *Norma*, in Italian. Webster murmured a noncommital approval which endeared him to Callas, who was accustomed to more emphatic, usually hostile, responses.

Bellini's little diva-pleaser of an opera had last been staged at Covent Garden in May 1930 to suit Rosa Ponselle. Dating from 1831, it was the high watermark of bel canto opera, an early-romantic school that demanded tonal beauty and exaggerated dramatics. If it took a démodé work to catch a Callas, Webster deemed it worth the risk. Meanwhile, EMI's Walter Legge had wormed his way past Menenghini to get Callas's signature on a record contract. London was about to become her stepping-stone to world fame.

Typically for Callas, between consent and consummation, lay months of vacillation. Her London agent, Sandor Gorlinsky, implored her to confirm the ROH dates. Callas demanded a six-month postponement, having accepted a better offer from Mexico City. Webster cabled her new *Norma* dates, assuring her that 'we count on and look forward to your participation'.[63] This time, Callas confirmed – for a fee of two hundred and fifty pounds a night, £100 higher than any other ROH artist, plus ten pounds a day living allowance (equivalent to Sutherland's weekly wage) and return fares for herself, husband and secretary. Webster booked her a suite at the Savoy and filled it with flowers. At her general rehearsal, the orchestra broke into applause.

On opening night, Callas's first big duet with the mezzo-soprano Ebe Stignani earned an ovation and was, against house rules, encored. When she delivered 'Casta diva', the house erupted. If ever a star was born, this was the moment. A great artist had come of age on a great stage, each enhanced by the other. All tickets for the remaining four performances were gone by morning. The first reviews were reserved, Ernest Newman grouching that she is 'slightly sub-Normal' and 'no Ponselle'. Philip Hope-Wallace in the *Manchester Guardian* struck a more admonitory note:

> Her phrasing was often memorable, arresting and even perhaps exaggerated; though she is a most musicianly singer. Yet the flawless vocal emission which is the cardinal quality called for in this exposed and perilous role was not vouchsafed. The voice is uneven. Some things, such as the gliding runs in the first scene and the attacked high notes in the second, were dazzling and amazed the audience. There were some beautiful soft phrases. But the voice did not ride the big final ensemble as it should . . . I myself cannot feel that she is more than a plausible *Norma*. The classical dimension was wanting.[64]

Even at this stage there were *cognoscenti* who voiced concern at her intensity and warned that if she carried on so recklessly she would burn out in her prime. They were stating the obvious. What made Callas so compelling was her reckless passion in performance, risks that she took half-knowing that they could destroy her voice and herself. To her overnight fans, Callas was a revelation. *Opera* magazine raved over her 'fabulous *fioriture*' and 'stupendous' top notes; she appeared twice on its cover in three months. Joan Sutherland, as Clothilde, sidled up to Callas in the wings and whispered shyly that she would like one day to sing Norma. 'Why not?' said the diva. 'It means a lot of work; but why not?'[65]

Callas went from London to open La Scala's season in Verdi's *Macbeth* and then to Florence for *Lucia di Lammermoor*, where the veteran tenor Giacomo Lauri-Volpi, who sang Edgardo to her Lucia, told the press that 'this young artist, with her ability to rouse the multitudes, may yet lead the lyric theatre to a new golden age of singing'.[66] But she was always larger than operatic life. Her visual impact was as stunning as her aural appeal and her instinct was uncanny. The conductor Antonino Votto referred to 'a unity of music, drama and movement . . . an aesthetic phenomenon'. On and off stage, she became the most famous Greek woman since Helen of Troy, a modern immortal. Quarter of a century after her death, she sold more records each year than any living soprano.

Webster, asked to sum her up in one sentence for *Vogue* magazine, reflected that she liberated opera from its inbred artificiality and raised it to an altogether higher plane. She possessed

> a radiant personality steeped in music, a rare feeling for words, their meaning and colour, an acute sense of timing, an innate appreciation of line in music and movement, an ability to make an audience part of her own experience, a capacity to fuse music and drama so that an aria is not a set piece but part of a complete musical and dramatic development within which she can raise a *Tosca* to the level of classical tragedy.[67]

What Callas did for Covent Garden was to raise the English company to world rank. Although she returned only five times, in six roles, the Royal Opera House was pivotal in her life. Falling out with every other major house, she maintained tranquil relations with Webster and his staff. Legge, one of her closest collaborators, called her 'vengeful, vindictive, malicious . . . ungrateful',[68] and she did not seem to care who got caught in the eye of her storms – managers, fellow-artists, police officers, tax inspectors, politicians. Callas possessed an ego the size of Olympus and an insecurity that was never long subdued.

But most testimonies suggest she turned difficult only 'when those around her failed to show the same dedication – when people arrived unprepared or unserious, that's when she'd hit the roof'.[69] Edward Downes, who occupied the prompt box at her début and rehearsed her in other roles, remembered her as 'an exceedingly professional lady. She sang with prodigious intensity all the time. And all the stories about her tantrums, they were never involved with her professional colleagues who were doing their job. She was always there to rehearse, she always worked, there was never any shirking.'[70] A future ROH chairman who took her to lunch with his wife noted: 'what struck us most was her intensely practical and analytical approach to her work.'[71]

At Covent Garden, she threatened once to walk out of *Trovatore* after a clash with James Johnston, a Belfast tenor with his own butcher's business and a slightly whimsical attitude to work. She also blew out the conductor, Alberto Erede, for refusing to accept her tempi in the final aria. But these were rare dissonances amid general harmony. 'She and (Giulietta) Simionato were always going off into peals of laughter,' reported the bass singer Michael Langdon, who overheard them, in mid-performance, discussing the price of knickers at Marks & Spencer. In rehearsal, Callas noticed Langdon's habit of beating time with both hands, clasped behind his back. Sneaking up, she grabbed his wrists just as Erede gave his cue, giggling into his ear, 'now you won't be able to sing, will you?'[72] *Trovatore* was the third of three operas she sang in Coronation month. Her fee was now £400 a night, net of tax.

She was not seen again at Covent Garden for three and a half years, by which time she had slimmed herself down from fourteen stone to ten, telling her hairdresser she aimed to resemble Audrey Hepburn in the film *Roman Holiday*. At one stage she dyed her hair blonde. In Luchino Visconti's May 1955 La Scala production of *Traviata*, conducted by Carlo-Maria Giulini, there were gasps in the stalls at her sudden luminosity. A gorgeous Violetta had emerged from caterpillar fat, investing the role with a sulphurous passion and sickly decline that split Italian critics into warring camps. Many had never seen a more gripping account of the role; others cavilled at her gestures and complained that the voice weakened towards the end, impaired by weight-loss. Callas maintained that she made her voice sound weak to accentuate the consumptive heroine's tragedy.

The Callas that London saw in two *Norma*s in January 1957 was a fully-fledged world star. She had conquered New York and been launched, by her new friend Elsa Maxwell, into high society. The Savoy gave her 'the Callas suite' and Covent Garden paid her hotel bills, plus £500 a night.* The hotel thronged with pressmen and the performances ended with Callas and Stignani in tears, overwhelmed by the blaze of their reception.

She returned in June 1958 for a Gala marking the centenary of Covent Garden's Victorian reconstruction, followed by six *Traviata*s. She was now so expensive that Webster had to raise top ticket prices from four guineas to five, notifying his chairman of the stupendous cost of Callas:

---

* on applying for a work permit, Webster declared to the Ministry of Labour that he was paying Callas £300; he clearly did not want the Government to know how much tax money was flowing to one foreign singer

6 performances @ £500	£3,000.00.00
2 return fares to Milan	£154.10.00
Hotel for 3 people for 23 days	£923.6.10
Tax paid by us	£1,575.6.00
Total	£5,653.22.10
Cost per performance	£942.3.10

Such was the financial pressure that when the BBC's *Monitor* programme sought an interview with the diva, Webster demanded a fifty-guinea 'management fee' on the grounds that Covent Garden were paying all her expenses 'and it did not seem to me very fair to Covent Garden that the BBC should have this artist working for them at what in fact amounts to our expenses.'[73] He took steps to protect her lustre by denying her chief La Scala rival, Renata Tebaldi, the showcase of a new production. Tebaldi sang seldom in London and, though she acquired devoted fans, Webster and Harewood were wedded to Callas.

Webster bragged to his Board of his 'special relationship'[74] with Callas. She was the rock on which the case for an all-English company shattered, the pivot around which Webster was able to turn Covent Garden towards internationalism. Callas, however, was not built to last. By 1958 her voice was plainly fraying. 'Some of us remained only fifty per cent enraptured,' wrote Hope-Wallace. 'Personally, I suffered much.' Not that most fans minded the sudden shrieks. Callas could have recited the A to D telephone directory in E-flat and the house would have hung on to every Brown and Cook in the book. 'Like everyone else,' confessed a budding critic, 'I was converted to opera by Callas.'[75] Every time she sang was an act of defiance, a glove flung in the face of fate and purism. 'Opera is a battlefield,' said the living Callas. 'My weapons are my voice and my technique.'[76] Viewed in retrospect, 'filmed excerpts from Callas's performances attest to the desperate intensity with which she sought to justify opera, regardless of her own vocal or mental survival.'[77]

The fatal acts were about to unfold. On her next trip to London, in 1959, she fell for Aristotle Onassis, the Greek shipowner who coveted her glory and abused her love. Her stage appearances became infrequent as she sat by the phone waiting for Ari to call. Webster called her often, but to no avail. The dramatic finale was destined for London, but not quite yet.

Sweeping into the theatre on the eve of the 1958 Gala, Callas overheard Joan Sutherland rehearsing the aria 'I dreamt that I dwelt in marble halls' from Balfe's *Bohemian Girl*. She stopped to listen and, when told the soprano's name, remembered the ungainly Australian who had sung Clothilde in her own début, less than six years before. She praised the singing to Harewood, and then said: 'She has learnt very well how to copy me.'[78]

Sutherland, apprised of this remark, was delighted. Still awaiting her apotheosis, she took the compliment in the spirit in which it had been intended. Callas was the queen of the operatic walk, and an ambitious singer could do no better than watch, wait and try to outshine her. Sutherland and others at Covent Garden absorbed something of the Callas ardour and her bel canto repertoire, while taking care to avoid her tonal impurity. Legge warned that Callas's example could destroy the next generation of singers; in fact, all she destroyed was herself. Some months after the Gala, the critic Noël Goodwin wrote, with uncanny prescience:

> I predict that if Maria Callas, now thirty-four, goes on performing at the present rate, she will have left no professional singing voice by the time she is forty. Joan Sutherland ... will, within five years, be acclaimed as famous an international star as Maria Callas is now, but she will no longer be a member of the Covent Garden Company.[79]

*

The cost of internationalism was unbudgeted. Engaging foreign stars had been a calculated risk – vocal credibility in exchange for financial exposure – and the first part of the equation was richly fulfilled. Covent Garden was becoming known as 'a singer's house' – more than just a famous stage, it was now a place where artists came to learn their craft. By the mid-1950s, one executive observed, 'singers from all over the world would make special journeys to London to study with the staff',[80] so expert were the repetiteurs and coaches at teaching roles and getting the best out of untapped vocal potential.

Such considerations can moderate a singer's fee demands but the cumulative cost would plunge Covent Garden into an unending cycle of cash crises. When matters grew desperate Webster said nothing to his board, and tried to catch the eye of John Denison, director of music at the Arts Council. 'I got on very well with David,' said Denison, 'and from time to time he'd say to me, "perhaps you could drop round for a chat on Thursday evening?" So I would go to his flat at Weymouth Street, after supper, and we'd take a walk around the block. Then David would say, "we're running out of money, I don't think I can pay the wages next week." In the morning I'd see the Treasurer at the Arts Council and ask for a thousand-pound advance on Covent Garden's next grant. That's how it was done, no forms to fill, no fuss.'[81]

No opera house can live hand to mouth and expect to sustain high standards. In 1952, the overdraft reached £100,000 and closure became a distinct possibility unless an uninterested Tory Government agreed to increase its grant. Papers were produced showing that the French Government gave the Paris Opéra eight times the amount of Covent Garden's stipend and even the Colón in Buenos Aires received twice as much. But the Treasury argued that ROH grants had risen sixfold since 1945, well above inflation.

In February 1952, the Arts Council chairman Ernest Pooley delivered morbid news to the Covent Garden chairman, not without a wry smirk. 'Dear John,' he wrote disingenuously,

You will be disappointed but not, I suppose, surprised, to hear that the best we can do for the Royal Opera House Covent Garden in 1952-53 is a grant of £150,000. In submitting our estimates to the Chancellor of the Exchequer we included a much higher figure for Covent Garden, and I can truly say that we represented your needs very strongly to the Treasury. However, the Chancellor has been unable to give us any increase on our previous year's grant of £575,000 for the whole of our operations and we in turn cannot improve on the sum we voted Covent Garden last year.[82]

Lord Waverley replied, in his dustiest Scottish tones:

My dear Ernest,
    I read your letter of 14th February to my Board yesterday. It is clear that we are confronted by a major financial crisis which will call for grave decisions in the very near future. In view of the care with which the details of our expenditure have already been examined I cannot help feeling very doubtful whether further discussions will prove profitable . . .[83]

Waverley decided not to waste his time on the Arts Council. He went into action on higher ground at the Treasury, his old department, and put in a bid for an exceptional one-off grant, half of it to pay off the overdraft and the other half for 'bricks and mortar' repairs. By summer, he had won the case and got the Chancellor to approve a £90,000 'rescue operation'. This concession was then consolidated the following year into the regular ROH grant, which rose by around sixty per cent. Even this boost, however, failed to stem the losses or guarantee financial stability. Through the 1950s, Covent Garden found itself unable to get by on £240,000 to £270,000 state subsidy, ten times its original allowance (retail prices, from 1946 to 1956, rose by just fifty per cent).

The more Covent Garden was given, the more it spent on foreign singers. The nights might glitter but by day Webster and his team wrestled with the spectre of foreclosure. In Whitehall minds, said Denison, both Covent Garden and the Arts Council were impermanent bodies that could be disestablished without fuss. The insecurity was acute. At Sadler's Wells, with no world stars, the situation was just as grim. The costs of running opera and ballet had risen 'out of all proportion to the income'. The day was gone, lamented its director Norman Tucker, 'when artists could be expected to take a kind of charitable or missionary view of their work at Sadler's Wells'.[84] Yet, as leaders of both houses would rue in later, tougher times, there was still enough cash in hand to enable them to act on impulse and recover from mistakes.

Waverley now decided to go politicking. 'When does Pooley's term end?' he asked Webster in a curt memo, before making sure that the next chairman of the Arts Council would be a trusted friend. At a meeting of the board his eye fell on Kenneth Clark, a founding father who had failed to find a role after his National Gallery era. Clark liked to say that he had only two loyalties in life – to his family and to the Royal Opera House. 'I have not only enjoyed performances there,' he wrote, 'but have developed an affection for the whole place – the auditorium, the foyer and the members of the staff, which is like a family feeling.'[85]

He was the perfect candidate for Arts Council chairman, a Covent Garden stooge, and his appointment was rushed through the 'usual channels' that Waverley was so expert at navigating. Clark's ascent at the prime of life – he was still on the right side of fifty – promised a rekindling of the Keynesian ideal of art for everyman, accessible and comprehensible. But Clark, for all his passion and erudition, turned out to be a terrible disappointment. 'I cannot say that the Arts

Council prospered under my chairmanship, or that I enjoyed my spell of office,'[86] he admitted. There was not enough money to make much difference, he complained, and the Taffia-epoch secretary-general, W. E. Williams, denied him a secretary or an office. 'K. Clark wasn't allowed to know anything,' chuckled John Denison, the music director, 'we just got on with it.'

Clark, truth be told, was easily distracted. He craved fame, and soon took on a livelier post as chairman of the Independent Television Authority. In time, he found his *métier* as presenter of the most illuminating art series ever seen on the small screen. It was as 'Lord Clark of *Civilization*' that Clark entered posterity – though without reaping the contentment that usually accompanies success. Clark was a restless man, beset by a concupiscent urge that verged on the obsessive. 'He was forever looking over your shoulder at any passing woman,' said a Covent Garden associate.[87] His conquests were numerous and he rented a flat in Dover Street for casual assignations. Jane Clark, for her part, took to the bottle.

Soon after taking office, Clark stumbled across a highly irregular arrangement. The Council and the opera house were, he discovered, employing the same accountant and company secretary. Douglas Peter Lund worked mornings for the provider of grants and after-noons for the receiver. Insiders joked that he would write a strong letter to himself demanding financial information, and then carry it from St James's Square to Floral Street on his lunchtime walk to save postage, before replying to himself in equally robust terms.

Lund had been a tax inspector in Newcastle before serving as chief accountant to the Royal Air Force in Italy, where he fell prey to the opera bug. Unwilling to return to provincial monotony, he wangled an introduction through his commanding officer to Leslie Boosey, who found him part-time work at Covent Garden, augmented in 1950 by an extra half-job at the Arts Council. Lund, known as 'Peter' at work and 'Douglas' to friends, was a cautious man who would never have taken the liberty of writing an official letter to himself. Exchanges between Covent Garden and the Arts Council were always conducted and signed by the secretary-general and general administrator. Lund, said his colleagues, merely drafted the letters, in both directions.[88]

Honest as Lund was, Clark saw impropriety in his dual loyalty. 'I mentioned to you the other day the anxiety I feel about our joint employment of Mr Lund,' he told Waverley. 'The fact that Covent

Garden and the Arts Council go halves in their Finance Officer is a matter which could be interpreted very injuriously by such a body as the Public Accounts Committee . . . We on the inside know that Mr Lund's dual role works to our joint advantage – but that could be made to look otherwise from the other side of the fence.'[89]

Waverley dismissed Clark's fears as petty niceties. As far as he was concerned, the Royal Opera House was, like the Royal Family, above reproach and answerable to no mortal authority. He had talked to Lund, he told Clark, and his 'personal feelings are that under practically no circumstances is he prepared to give up Covent Garden.'[90] So Lund was allowed to continue working for both organizations, staying with the Arts Council until 1965 and with Covent Garden until his statutory retirement in 1972. So collusory was the arrangement that when Covent Garden raised his £2,250 salary by ten per cent in January 1955, 'Mr Denison undertook to ascertain whether the Arts Council would be willing to contribute one half of the proposed increase.'[91] On two salaries, Lund earned more than either of his bosses, Webster and Williams.

In addition to his double-role, Lund also did a little freelancing on the side. When Webster engaged foreign stars, he would offer Lund's services to get them the best deal on UK taxes; as a former inspector, Lund knew all the loopholes and could make their ROH sojourn that bit more profitable. 'Perhaps you'll allow Mr Lund to present his bill for looking after Tito's tax?' Webster would remind Gobbi's agent, making sure his chief financial officer got properly recompensed. After he retired, Lund was allowed to keep an office in the Royal Opera House so that he could keep 'in touch with events and with those singers whose tax he looks after'.[92]

Everybody trusted Lund, who died in 1974 and never put so much as sixpence in the wrong column. However, where public money is being handled, it is as important for the bookkeeper to avoid any hint of suspicion as it is for the books to balance. Lund blurred the lines of state funding, casting a shadow of doubt over both giver and receiver and introducing a procedural sloppiness that would, in time, bring both institutions into disrepute. If the Ministry of Defence and Rolls-Royce had been sharing the same accountant, the implications could hardly have been graver.

So close were Covent Garden and the Arts Council, they even shared the same bank. If Coutts got fretful about Covent Garden's credit worthiness, they had only to consult the Arts Council, which bankrolled the ROH. The risk to Coutts in letting the ROH run up large debts was therefore non-existent.

To the pure, it is said, all is pure. It would never have crossed the high mind of a man like Waverley to imagine that ROH dealings with the Arts Council were intended for any purpose other than the greatest public benefit. Nevertheless, he would have been the first to acknowledge that any drift from accepted norms of public conduct can induce a laziness of mind that fosters, if not corruption, then at the very least an inferior form of governance. That Waverley, the Civil Service paragon, should have given Covent Garden the licence to break rules is a paradox almost beyond comprehension. In later years, wags would say that when public men joined the Board of the Royal Opera House, they left their brains at the door.

While Waverley played politics, Webster fixed the press. To justify hugely increased public funding, he needed to show results – and results in the lively arts are measured in high attendances and rave reviews. The press in the 1950s was overcoming its wartime complaisance and, as pages increased, starting to report closely and critically on national enterprises. Tougher verbiage came into play. A new *Tannhäuser* was put down as 'a disgrace';[93] a John Cranko ballet, with Beryl Grey and David Blair, was 'a great disappointment . . . beyond the point of no return'.[94] The grumblings of old Ernest Newman could be ascribed to geriatric dyspepsia, but the new wave of opera and ballet critics were less predictable and they were beginning to question the purpose and viability of the Royal Opera House.

Attendances started to drop, especially for routine revivals sung in English by non-star casts. A run of *Bohème* played to 54 per cent capacity on poor reviews and *Rigoletto* to 46 per cent. Webster cultivated the critics, knowing the glow a good lunch could bring to the next batch of reviews. But he needed to boost confidence in his company and was prepared to use his powers of appointment to sway leading journalists.

The placement of newspaper coverage and dining of editors was generally left to the ROH press officer Michael Wood and his Australian deputy, Bill Beresford, recruited from the *Daily Express*. When Wood went off in 1958 to manage the ballet company, he was succeeded by Beresford. He took as his deputy a girl who had come to Webster's office two years earlier, asking for a job.

'What can you do?' said Webster.

'Well, I can't sing,' said Sheila Porter, 'but I have an Oxford degree in Greats.'

The fact was not lost on Webster that Sheila was the twin sister of Andrew, associate editor of *Opera* magazine and music critic of the *Financial Times*, whose managing director, Viscount Moore, had succeeded Denis Rickett as Secretary to the Covent Garden Board. Sheila Porter was duly recruited as deputy press officer. Beresford, it so happened, lived next door to Andrew Porter on Pembroke Walk. The circle was stiflingly small.

It says much for Andrew Porter's strength of mind that he shut out all intimate connections and wrote some of the most intelligent and combative coverage of Covent Garden over the next two decades. It says just as much for Webster's delicacy that he did not, by word or wink, seek to influence Andrew Porter through his sister. 'It was never a hazard,' she maintained.[95]

The temptations resisted by Andrew Porter were, on the other hand, meat and drink to *Opera*'s editor. Harold Rosenthal had taken charge of the monthly when its founder, Lord Harewood, went to work for Webster in 1953. Rosenthal was also on the ROH payroll, earning three pounds a week as company archivist.[96] He loved being on the inside of an opera house, mingling with stars in the staff canteen. A suburban ex-schoolmaster, he was an exceptionally ugly man with a puppylike desire to please. The director Christopher West, whom Rosenthal considered his friend, quipped that he had 'a face like an arsehole turned inside out'. Others called him 'a slippery little man, so ugly you had to be nice to him'.[97]

Opera, with a circulation of barely five thousand, was acquiring a cachet as the buffs' Bible, authoritative in tone and exhaustive in detail. Many of its reviews criticized Covent Garden productions and some of Rosenthal's editorials challenged aspects of policy. But his belief in the need for a Royal Opera House was absolute and his pages were at its service. A puffy little feature introduced 'new singers at the Royal Opera House'; Sadler's Wells, Glyndebourne and the emergent Welsh National Opera were never given equal weight.

Rosenthal's presence in the Covent Garden corridors was widely resented. Beecham, in 1951, demanded his dismissal. Sir Steuart Wilson complained about 'the general position that *Opera* holds inside the House and I wish that we could make something a little more satisfactory than having their waspish attacks directed at us from the inside.'[98] But Webster was unbothered; when Rosenthal resigned in 1956 to write a glorifying centennial history of Covent Garden, he was still given the run of the house and a modest budget to purchase items for the archives.

Webster believed he had Rosenthal in his pocket. A peep of impartiality from *Opera*, an editorial in praise of Norman Tucker's reforms at Sadler's Wells, drew an enraged response. 'Thank you for your letter of October 27th enclosing the drivel which you propose to publish,' wrote Webster. '. . . As you know I have never objected and never will object to criticism either of this organization or of myself, but to propose to publish such plausible nonsense at this juncture in our careers is really going too far.'[99] Webster threatened to found a rival publication and run *Opera* out of business. Rosenthal, terrified, crawled back into line and so successfully appeased Webster that he felt confident enough, the following year, to put himself forward to succeed Harewood, who was leaving to become Director of the Edinburgh Festival. 'My dear David,' wrote Rosenthal, 'I don't know whom you have in mind as your next Controller of Opera Planning, but I would very much like you to consider me seriously as a possible successor to George. I feel that I could do the job and that my knowledge of the world of opera and its personalities is as good as anyone's.'[100]

Webster ignored the application, which was repeatedly resubmitted. He did, however, accede to the next suggestion from the insistent editor. Rosenthal was forever impecunious and on the look-out for little jobs. He offered to supply Webster with a quarterly listing of the world's leading singers and conductors, where and what they were performing and with whom. The information flowed into *Opera* from its worldwide correspondents and could be made available for a modest financial consideration. Webster, who could have read most of the information in the magazine itself, or obtained it from his fellow-intendants, decided to find value in Rosenthal's idea and agreed to pay him £250 a year in quarterly instalments.[101]

This was no small sum, enough to pay for a family holiday in a luxury resort. Rosenthal drew payments from Covent Garden for a good few years (the termination is not noted on file), at times requesting an advance for 'urgent family expenses'. His income was hidden from the contributors who supplied his data, and from the critics who might have been concerned by his conflict of interests.

Webster made no apparent use of the information he acquired from Rosenthal. He was buying the man, not the material, and seemed content with the bargain. In the struggle to sustain Covent Garden he could safely rely on the unqualified support of *Opera* and its heavily compromised editor.

An air of aimlessness set in, obscured by growing ease. Churchill finally resigned in April 1954, at the age of 79, but his heir was a man of short temper, broken health and no experience in domestic affairs. 'I don't believe Anthony can do it,' said Churchill on his return from the Palace, and Eden soon proved him right. Austerity was ending, but there was no grand design for creating prosperity. The age of anxiety had given way to an epoch of uncertainty. England was planning to muddle through.

The absence of visionary leadership can erode great institutions no matter how efficiently they are administered, and Covent Garden was not alone among the ships of state that were drifting to no obvious purpose. The BBC, the Church, the Royal Navy and the England soccer team which lost its unbeaten home record in a 3-6 defeat to Hungary were all struggling with questions of identity and strategy.

By September 1954, the doubts about Covent Garden's artistic aims were growing intense. The season opened with bad news from abroad. Benjamin Britten's new opera, *The Turn of the Screw*, was premièred in Venice on 14 September and broadcast back home over the BBC Third Programme. Despite carping from Howes in *The Times* and some indiscretions in the French press about the composer's homosexual obsessions, the public response and critical consensus were that Britten had, as the *Manchester Guardian* put it, 'created another masterpiece'.

The opera came to London three weeks later – but to Sadler's Wells, not to Covent Garden. While awaiting its turn at the *Screw*, the Wells put on (at Britten's instigation) the world première of another English opera, *Nelson* by Lennox Berkeley. It was tepidly received and soon discarded, but the spirit of enterprise seemed livelier in Islington than at the slumbrous Royal Opera House. Early Verdi was being promoted by Tucker and young conductors, like Charles Mackerras and Alexander Gibson, were given their head; Gibson would go on to found Scottish Opera. The Welsh National Opera were preparing to make their London début – at Sadler's

Wells, needless to say. The Wells had been drenched in emotion the previous spring when, for the centenary of Janáček's birth, *Katya Kabanova* was sung by a cockney sparrow, Amy Shuard, and conducted by the imposing Czech exile, Rafael Kubelik, who was about to return for a second run. The strengths of this production had led Shawe-Taylor to underline 'the paramount importance of the operatic conductor'. Webster was under pressure to act fast, or miss out.

He had been trying for years to meet Kubelik, who had flown to London in February 1948 on the day the Communists seized power in Prague. The willowy son of a legendary violinist, Kubelik had spent the first half of the war conducting opera in Brno, and the second half as head of the Czech Philharmonic. Stateless in his mid-thirties but well known in the West, he was besieged by attractive offers, accepting a guest conductorship at the Concertgebouw in Amsterdam and in 1950 the music director's baton at the Chicago Symphony Orchestra. His shiny-eyed integrity and an appetite for dissonant new music did not go down well with older subscribers and earned him torrents of vituperation from the *Tribune* critic, Claudia Cassidy. Kubelik, hyper-sensitive to personal slights, quit after three seasons and returned to London with his violinist wife, Ludmilla, who had been left partly disabled and in constant pain after being physically assaulted in Prague.

Webster was smitten by *Katya*. On 6 October 1954, he informed the Ministry of Labour and National Service that he wanted to appoint Rafael Kubelik as music director of the Covent Garden opera company for a period of seven and a half months a year. An official announcement was made the following day.

Kubelik, conducting abroad, issued a statement declaring his faith in Covent Garden's founding covenants. In Brno, operas had been sung in Czech; in London they should be sung in English by local singers of the highest quality. He was thrilled with Shuard, who quickly signed for Covent Garden, and confident he could find more like her. His second run of *Katya* was, if anything, more shattering than the first. He made his Covent Garden début weeks later, in May 1955, with a more familiar Czech masterpiece, *The Bartered Bride*, with Morison, Lanigan, Otakar Kraus and Noreen Berry in the leading roles. Smetana's opera was a perennial favourite at Sadler's Wells and Norman Tucker was left impotently fuming as Webster impudently stole his best conductor, soprano and box-office comedy.

Webster next attempted to steal Sadler's Wells new clothes with two world premières in eight weeks. First, in December 1954, came William Walton's long-awaited *Troilus and Cressida*, seven years in the making, a bid by the former ROH board member to reclaim the rank of top composer. Walton, with a librettist chosen by Lady Wimborne, wisely eschewed the Shakespearean play which depicts Cressida as a heartless tart and opted for the Chaucerian tale which shows her torn between two lovers, Greek and Trojan. However, on reading Christopher Hassall's draft libretto, Walton was beset by doubts and sent the script for a second opinion to Ernest Newman. Later in the process, he asked W. H. Auden and Laurence Olivier to tinker with it.

He was desperate for the opera to succeed and called in favours from famous friends. Olivier, for whom Walton had composed a *Henry V* film score, was named in *The Times*[102] as the opera's producer and Henry Moore, the foremost English sculptor, as its designer. The Cressida role was written for Elisabeth Schwarzkopf and Troilus for Nicolai Gedda; the conductor was to be Malcolm Sargent, who had given the storming first performance of *Belshazzar's Feast*. Of this glamorous line-up, only Sargent signed up – and his contribution was to bring the work to the edge of destruction.

Sargent had not conducted an opera in eighteen years and barely looked at the score before starting rehearsals. He refused to beat time for singers unless the orchestra was playing, ignoring a plea from Peter Pears, who sang the avuncular role of Pandarus. He tinkered with the instrumentation – 'it's my fucking opera and I'm going to write more for the second harp,'[103] exploded Walton, reversing the textual changes – and in the homebound car one afternoon the conductor tried to grope the composer's young wife.

Walton, fearing Sargent might botch the opera deliberately if he took him to task, shared his despair with the visiting Jascha Heifetz, for whom he had written a magnificent concerto. That night after dinner, Heifetz took the conductor aside.

'I gather, Sir Malcolm, that you are coming soon to visit the United States,' he remarked.

Sargent, swelling with pride that his tour should have been noticed by the greatest living violinist, murmured something about his desire to bring great music to the American public.

'Well listen here,' said Heifetz, in an Edward G. Robinson snarl.

'Unless you sit down right now and learn every note of William's opera, I shall make sure every orchestra in America knows that you are a fake who can hardly read music. Got that?'[104]

Sargent knuckled down to his task, but the opera was beyond redemption. A glittering crowd including Olivier and Vivien Leigh, Somerset Maugham, Henry Moore and Yehudi Menuhin thronged the Royal Opera House on opening night to hear Pears overcome a bout of flu, the Hungarian soprano Magda Laszlo make a goulash of Cressida's English and only Richard Lewis as Troilus fulfilling the composer's hopes and expectations. The press did their best to find rousing adjectives, and Howes in *The Times* called it 'a great tragic opera', but the public response was tepid and by the end of a broken run of twelve performances the house was half-empty.

Walton made cuts and adjustments for sundry revivals but the work never caught fire. It lacked big moments and a build-up of dramatic tension. Tuneful and antediluvian, it was old before its time. When a restoration was staged at Covent Garden in 1976, the next critical generation dismissed *Troilus and Cressida* as 'a hopeless old dodo'.[105]

These reservations were alive within Covent Garden even at the time of the première. Many staffers shared the view of Lord Harewood that Troilus was the equivalent of a 'well-made play'. They placed their faith in *The Midsummer Marriage* by Michael Tippett, which some construed as an English reworking of *The Magic Flute*.

Walton and Tippett were human antipodes, one raised in northern poverty, the other in southern comfort. Walton was blunt-spoken and uncluttered. Tippett pursued vague and esoteric ideologies. Walton had gone to war with rousing film scores; Tippett went to jail as a conscientious objector. Walton was well turned out and something of a ladies' man; Tippett was homosexual, slept in a hovel and was likely to turn up in open-toed sandals. Musically, Walton knew the value of every note and never wasted one. Tippett sprawled all over the staves and looked bewildered when told that what he had written was unplayable on strings. He devised his own librettos, which were riddled with abstruse Jungian and Hinduist symbolisms.

The opera was introduced to Covent Garden by Edward Sackville-West. Webster proposed Cranko or Ashton as director and Graham Sutherland as designer; the jobs finally fell to the house director Christopher West and the sculptress Barbara Hepworth –

not that they were able to shed much light on the composer's intentions. John Pritchard was given another chance to make a name for himself, but Tippett found that Pritchard was sight-reading, and 'Webster warned him that unless he learned the score fully he would never conduct at Covent Garden again.'[106]

While Tippett's supporters rallied behind the project, internal opposition crystallized around Sir Steuart Wilson who had warned from the outset that the opera was overlong, its story 'unattractive' and its visual aspects unclear. 'The nature of the music,' he noted, 'is difficult to describe. I have heard one act only on the piano and it appears to me on the whole to be very diffuse and exceedingly restless: every bar seems filled to the uttermost with notes. The experience I have had with Tippett's music is not encouraging from a practical point of view . . .' Tippett's orchestration said Wilson, 'is highly impractical, and requires a vast amount of rehearsal to extricate the composer's meaning . . . A great deal of time will have to be spent in straightening out the badly expressed intentions of the composer. This opinion will, I know, be corroborated by those few conductors who have coped with Tippett's major works.'[107]

Many of the cast came to share his view. 'If you are coming to ask me what it's about, don't bother,' said Otakar Kraus, who sang the King Fisher. 'I don't know who I am, and that's the truth,' said Edith Coates, described as An Ancient. 'I can only say that I know my part,' was John Lanigan's terse comment to an eve-of-première journalist.[108] When Joan Sutherland, as Jenifer, asked Tippett about the meaning of her part, he said: 'Don't worry, darling. Just sing everything beautifully and the rest will take care of itself.'[109] To the press, he responded: 'I have gathered that the singers don't see what I'm getting at, but the whole thing seems perfectly simple to me. This is a story of two sets of lovers, and their different approach towards marriage. It is a piece of depth and imagination, and it is like a crystal ball which you can turn endless ways.'[110] Some of the cast, he later said, were in tears before the première, denying the remarks attributed to them.

Sutherland and Richard Lewis as her lover, Mark, sang as beautifully as the composer could have wished – 'even if their acting was stiff'.[111] Tippett's boldness was widely praised, as was Covent Garden's in staging so perplexing an opera. The theme, said Howes in *The Times,* 'is magnificent.' But the text was called a 'hotch-potch' by Martin Cooper in the *Daily Telegraph,* 'rubbish' by Shawe-

Taylor in the *Sunday Times* and 'nonsense' by Cecil Smith in the *Daily Express*, adding: 'I consider this libretto . . . one of the worst in the 350-year history of opera.'[112] The audience split almost along generational lines, older viewers showing less tolerance for Tippett's ramblings than younger ones who sensed a raw energy in the piece. The composer himself appeared serenely untouched by criticism, and remained so three years later when his second symphony broke down in chaos a few minutes into its broadcast première. 'Sorry,' said the conductor, Sir Adrian Boult, into the live microphone, 'my fault entirely.' The BBC overrode his apology and wrote a letter to *The Times* blaming the composer.

In the course of time, *The Midsummer Marriage* acquired a cultish following and Tippett a coterie of accomplished interpreters. Three of his five operas were premièred at Covent Garden, where he was elevated, *pace* Britten, to the status of Great British Composer. Yet, despite unwavering support from the ROH and the leading German publisher, Schott, none of Tippett's operas caught on abroad or sold out at home. The German première of *The Midsummer Marriage*, in 1998, was laughed off in Munich as an English eccentricity.

Webster's intentions had been of the best, but the double première demonstrated only that the ROH was no place for new music, conventional or adventurous. The second half of the twentieth century would not yield many operatic masterpieces, but none of its few successes originated at Covent Garden, and British composers discovered that they were better off working with almost any other national company, or best of all with Glyndebourne. The creative aspect of Covent Garden's Keynesian mission died an early death in that dull mid-50s winter.

One spring afternoon, at the end of a Board meeting, Waverley cleared his throat and said, 'Webster, would you be good enough to retire for a few moments? I wish to discuss a certain matter with my colleagues.'

When the door shut, the chairman continued. 'David Webster is overburdened,' he said. 'We should find a suitable young man to assist him. I wonder if any of you has a person to nominate.'[113]

Most of those around the table were aware that Sir Steuart Wilson as Deputy General Administrator was fomenting trouble, and that he and Webster were barely on speaking terms. Wilson had formally complained to Waverley of Webster's shortcomings and now sought to address the board, threatening to go public unless his grievances were noted. Waverley stalled, knowing that Wilson was due to retire in August 1955, his sixty-sixth birthday. He was anxious for Wilson to leave without fuss and for his successor to be an aid to Webster rather than a threat. Even Lord Harewood, resourceful as he was, left Webster and Waverley with an uneasy feeling as to his larger, long-term ambitions.

'Mr Chairman,' piped up Edric Cundell, head of the Guildhall School of Music and one of the newer members, 'I am fortunate to have at my school a very able administrator, John Tooley, and would very much regret to lose him . . .'

'Cundell,' rasped Waverley, 'I am much obliged to you. Will you ask Mr Tooley to attend upon me at the Port of London, tomorrow at nine o'clock. I think we can ask Webster to rejoin us.'

Tooley thus slipped into Covent Garden like gin into vermouth. A product of Repton and Magdalen College, Cambridge, he had spent the war in the Home Counties after falling off a motorbike and being rendered unfit for action. The son of an Admiralty civil servant (Waverley, at their interview, never asked about his background), he shocked his family with talk of becoming an oboist, then a singer, before settling for musical management. Personable and quiet, married and thirty-three years old, he had no further urge to see his name up in lights, but would have appreciated a higher wage than the £1,400 he was offered. 'Webster kept salaries depressed by holding his own down,' said Tooley. 'I had a struggle to make ends meet. A lot of younger people on the staff who had children had a tough time. But Webster insisted everybody had to fall in line.'[114]

Tooley busied himself getting to know the House 'and everyone in it, Niebelheim to Valhalla'.[115] Webster was suspicious at first and refused him the title of Deputy, designating him Assistant. He kept Tooley away from his precious opera stars and used him as his go-between in an increasingly fractious relationship with Ninette de Valois. 'Tooley was Ballet,' said singers, 'we were never much aware of him.'[116]

His appointment was, however, the straw that snapped Sir Steuart Wilson's tolerance. Returning from a lecture tour to find his plea to the Board deferred and his job turned over to a stripling, Wilson resigned on 17 April 1955, refusing to work out the last months of his contract. A statement in *The Times* noted that 'when the present season ends the post of deputy general administrator . . . will be discontinued.'[117] The *Daily Mail* added that Wilson was 'withdrawing immediately on leave'. He told the paper: 'The words "withdrawing immediately" were chosen by myself. You must draw your own inferences from them.' This was unusually strong language for a public official, but Wilson would not be drawn on specifics. He said nothing further for three whole months. Then, furious at the world's indifference to his dismissal, he exploded into print in an interview with the most scurrilous of Sunday newspapers.

MUSIC CHIEF LEADS BIG CAMPAIGN AGAINST VICE

ran the *People*'s headline, and the story that followed was as explicit as the times and libel laws permitted:

A campaign against homosexuality in British music is to be launched by Sir Steuart Wilson, until last month (*sic*) Deputy General Administrator of the Royal Opera House, Covent Garden. Sir Steuart, 66, told the *People* last night:

'The influence of perverts in the world of music has grown beyond all measure. If it is not curbed soon, Covent Garden and other precious musical heritages could suffer irreparable harm.

'Many people in the profession are worried. There is a kind of agreement among homosexuals which results in their keeping jobs for the boys.[118]

In classic Sunday-shocker style, the *People* cast around for men of substance to authenticate its scoop. The best they could find was Mr Walford Haydn, 'the famous composer and conductor', who said:

'Homosexuals are damaging music and all the other arts. I am sorry for those born that way, but many acquire it – and for them I have nothing but contempt. Singers who are perverted often get work simply because of this. And new works by composers are given preference by some people if the writer is perverted.'

The newspaper then solicited and reported a rebuttal from Mr David Webster, General Administrator of the Royal Opera House:

'Music is flourishing,' he said. 'It is nonsense to say that there are jobs for the boys as Sir Steuart alleges.'

Wilson's target was unmistakable, and the report must have struck terror into Webster, coming as it did in the midst of a police crackdown against homosexual men and the places where they met. A war on 'vice' had been declared in 1953 by the Tory Home Secretary, Sir David Maxwell Fyfe, in a grotesque reaction to the Muscovite defection of Guy Burgess and Donald Maclean, whose spy ring was predominantly gay. The Metropolitan Police, for their part, were keen to improve arrest rates in order to mask a rise in organized crime and its seeping corruption of the constabulary.

The vice squad were notoriously compromised and eager to cover up with some big 'collars'. They were no respecters of reputation. Lord Montagu of Beaulieu, peer of the realm, was arrested, charged and jailed for a year for having sex in his own beach house with various men at different times. Sir John Gielgud, the greatest living actor, was grabbed in a public lavatory in Chelsea on the evening of 21 October 1953 and convicted the next morning 'for persistently importuning'. He told the court: 'I was tired and had had a few drinks. I was not responsible for my action.' He was fined ten pounds and told by the magistrate 'to see your doctor the moment you leave here'.[119] (The choreographer John Cranko was arrested in the same area, made the same excuse and received the same fine six years later, a traumatic experience that led him to consider emigration.) Britten and Cecil Beaton were interviewed by Scotland Yard.[120] Alan Turing, the computer genius who cracked Germany's wartime codes, committed suicide with a strychnine-laced apple to escape secret-service scrutiny of his homosexual life.

English hypocrisy was enjoying its high noon. At least one member of the Cabinet, the Colonial Secretary Alan Lennox-Boyd, was a practising homosexual. The flamboyant Labour MP and sometime *Express* gossip columnist, Tom Driberg, was a notorious sex-pest who preyed on young working-class males. When he was arrested in a public lavatory and convicted in open court, not a word appeared in any newspaper, thanks to a code of silence imposed by his friend, the press magnate Lord Beaverbrook. Yet it was Beaverbrook's *Sunday Express* that led the pack against less protected miscreants, demanding in Gielgud's case that the nation should 'mark its abhorrence of this type of depravity by stripping from men involved in such cases any honours that have been bestowed on them'.[121] A prominent MP could importune with impunity but the arrest of a little-known choreographer was front-page news in the *Daily Express*, which described Cranko as 'the latest on the list of famous stage names who have been found guilty of this squalid behaviour'. The paper added: 'It has become a sour commonplace in the West End theatre that unless you are a member of an unpleasant free-masonry your chances of success are often lessened.'[122]

Webster, at this time, was acutely vulnerable. Although his private life seemed a model of middle-aged respectability, Jimmy got frisky at parties[123] and Webster himself predated on fanciable youths, who were sometimes repelled by his noxious halitosis. One queenly young man, invited to dinner with Gielgud at Weymouth Street, found himself overcome by tiredness (had the wine been doctored? he wondered) and awoke on a sofa, Webster beside him and Jimmy gazing at them from an overhead gallery.[124] In London's gay underworld Webster was the butt of many in-jokes:

> David Webster, in a public lavatory, whispers to the man in the next stall, 'what do you like?' There is a long pause. Then the man whispers back, 'Callas in *Traviata*.'

Webster sent Fred Ashton into a terrible tizz by threatening to seduce his boyfriend, Dick Beard.[125] On a 1953 tour of Rhodesia, he was reportedly seen in a sauna with other white men and black boys, 'red all over and looking like a boiled lobster'. According to rumour, he so injured an African boy in the act of love that the victim was rushed to hospital and Webster had to be hustled out on the next flight. No trace of any such incident exists in ROH or Government archives. John Denison, who knew Webster well, is convinced that talk of a homosexual scandal was 'all mischief that emanated from Wilson'. Nevertheless, the poison could paralyse a man's career and Webster, at the height of his power, was pursued by the same fears that had forced him once before to leave Liverpool and start afresh.

Alarmed at his exposure, ROH friends brought influence to bear. The Clarks, who knew everyone, invited the head of Scotland Yard to the opera and introduced him to Webster, believing the contact might come in useful.[126] Others moved silently behind the scenes.

Newspapers, like fish, feed off each other; a good story in one is invariably snapped up by the rest. Remarkably, however, not one word of the *People*'s charges of Covent Garden 'vice' appeared in any other corner of the British press – or ever again in the *People* itself. Such omissions are not coincidental, and while the Express group were leading what David Astor, the *Observer* editor, called a 'rabble-rousing . . . witch-hunt' of homosexuals, it would have taken more than gentle persuasion to deflect the hacks. Who called the shots and with what weapons? The finger points unerringly at Garrett Moore, Secretary to the ROH Board and, by day, managing director of the *Financial Times*.

As Waverley ailed, Moore increasingly took the chair at Covent Garden. He knew the press barons as social equals and sat on their Newspaper Proprietors Committee, which adopted a tacit code of practice to the effect that one press baron did not attack another. Beaverbrook had procured press silence on Driberg by convincing his rivals to honour the code. The FT chief, by similar means, quashed the Wilson smears as an assault on his domain. Moore was not a man to boast of conquests, but a wink of satisfaction can be seen in his memoirs when he notes that 'subsequent evidence of the (*People*'s) campaign was strangely lacking'.[127] Strangely, indeed.

It had been a close call. Any tabloid reporter in search of 'jobs for the boys' at Covent Garden need have looked no further than the inner office where most of Webster's team were lifelong bachelors. Christopher West was professedly gay; Morris Smith and John Sullivan were avowedly religious and hostile to women. 'Nobody asked if they were gay,' said Elizabeth Latham, 'one was very careful what one said and did in those days.'[128] In the so-called 'straight' theatre, Covent Garden was known as a gay house, with many of its designers and directors drawn from the unuttered community. Webster, in whose gift these appointments lay, especially favoured Oliver Messel, Michael Benthall (Helpmann's life-partner) and Peter Potter.

The theatre, by tradition, was a haven for minorities and outcasts, a place where intolerance was suspended along with disbelief. Outside, however, the atmosphere was oppressive. Although the gutter press revelled in mock-horror, homosexuality was swept under the carpet in polite society. Playwrights and film-makers skirted the subject, knowing it would not be passed fit for public viewing. The plays of Noël Coward, Ivor Novello and Terence Rattigan, and the novels of Somerset Maugham and Angus Wilson substituted man-woman euphemisms for 'the love that dared not speak its name', a love whose status had not changed since the day of Oscar Wilde's conviction. England's leading painter (Bacon), poet (Auden), composer (Britten), actor (Gielgud), novelist (Forster), and choreographer (Ashton) were all homosexual, an attribute that was unmentionable in studies of their lives and works. Forster was unable to publish his homosexual novel, *Maurice*.

Gay men developed common dialects and mannerisms. Britten, writing to Webster about a mutual friend, spoke in camp tones that he would never have used with Harewood: 'Are all things right now with Johnnie Cranko? I do hope you've had your talk with him, because the poor boy's *really* worried.'[129] Under stress, homosexuals chose colleagues they could trust. Webster favoured Britten and Tippett above all composers and John Pritchard above all local conductors. He identified Maria Callas as a gay icon, more potent than Judy Garland. It would not have taken deep investigation for the gutter press to expose Webster in their terms as an 'evil man' and Covent Garden as a 'den of vice', prompting calls for its closure. Wilson's assault had been designed to bring down Webster and the house around him. He had to be repelled, not so much for Webster's sake as for the survival of the company.

A month after his attack, the departed deputy wrote to Waverley apologizing for his comments in the *People*, 'which he said he had not authorized'.[130] The insincerity of his retraction became apparent within a year when he popped up in the *Daily Telegraph*, demanding a public inquiry into 'the powers at present wielded by the Administrator of the Royal Opera House, Mr David Webster, uncontrolled by the Board of Directors ...'[131] The *Telegraph*, in a leading article, said the Board could 'hardly ignore the criticisms made by their former Deputy General Administrator'. But ignore them they did, in self-imposed silence, and Wilson was left to sputter off into well-deserved obscurity. Years later, in 1970, his widow approached Webster and Tooley for information for a posthumous biography. Webster said: 'He wanted my job – and Mary (his previous wife) egged him on.'[132] Tooley offered to 'help in any way I can' but when he asked to see the files, the archivist replied: 'I have had a good look through the papers which we have sorted so far and I cannot find anything of use related to Steuart Wilson's time here.'[133]

The operatic ups and downs were starting to depress the ballet. Acclaimed in America, the ballet company was losing ground at home. 'The midsummer nights in the Royal Opera House Covent Garden have been ringing to resounding cheers,' editorialized *Dance and Dancers* in August 1955. 'Well-dressed crowds have been milling around in their efforts to get tickets . . . All this excitement has not been for ballet but for the great international stars who have been appearing as guests with Covent Garden Opera.' Ninette de Valois had warned that her public was fickle and could be lured away by an Italian diva with a top B-flat, and her presentiments were being fulfilled. 'You must be *mad* going to the ballet,' was a sneer aimed at balletomanes,[134] who had little to contend in their defence.

The big ballet draw of 1955 was Richard Buckle's memorial exhibition for Serge Diaghilev, seen by 165,000 visitors in Edinburgh and London. De Valois, back in 1931, had claimed a stake in Diaghilev's legacy with *Job*, the first all-English production. Its Covent Garden revival in the summer of 1955 brought the farewell appearance of Anton Dolin as Satan, setting a symbolic seal on the formative era of English ballet. The founders were fading and their heirs lacked the same edge of vitality.

Far too much hinged on the physical endurance of Margot Fonteyn, thirty-six years old, newly married and in sight of middle age. Fonteyn stood at the summit of a stultifying pyramid. Beneath her, five dancers – Beryl Grey, Svetlana Beriosova, Violetta Elvin, Nadia Nerina and Elaine Fifield – cultivated a personal following without attaining universal stardom. Nerina, a South African, had, in Buckle's view, 'three times Fonteyn's strength and technique, but . . . never imposed herself to the same degree as Fonteyn as a personality.'[135] Fifield, an Australian who had been hailed as 'a new Pavlova' at Sadler's Wells, felt stifled by the Covent Garden pyramid and, divorcing the conductor John Lanchbery, opted in 1957 for repatriation. Moira Shearer had retired to have babies, Grey was about to go it alone, and Elvin was on the point of hanging up her shoes.

Beneath the glass ceiling of five ballerinas ranged a motley of has-beens and hangers-on who blocked the path of young hopefuls. The male leads, Michael Somes, Alexander Grant and David Blair, lacked magnetism. The company as a whole lost impetus. Peggy Van Praagh, who ran the second corps at Sadler's Wells, resigned to go freelance and eventually to Australia. Louis Yudkin, the popular stage manager, had been killed in a plane crash in Africa.

The one fruitful resource was the company's flourish of choreographers: Cranko, the young Scot Kenneth MacMillan, and the eternally surprising Fred Ashton who, however, was having a hit and miss season. Frustratingly, his best shot of 1955, *Madame Crysanthème*, with Fifield as heroine (music by Rawsthorne, costumes by Isabel Lambert), opened during a newspaper strike and sank without notices.

The fortunes, present and future, of English ballet rested heavily on the shoulders of Margot Fonteyn, who was willing as ever but weakening. She had missed five months through illness in Coronation Year and Webster reported a gloomy prognosis to the Board. 'I have been concerned about that matter myself,' said Waverley, in a rare interjection on artistic personnel. When Fonteyn returned in *Apparitions* more than fifty bouquets were thrown, house staff shouted 'Margot!' and Webster openly wept. When asked why, he replied: 'If you don't know, you don't deserve to be told.'[136]

Brilliant as she was, Margot could not last forever and there was no alternative in store. Dancers quoted a comment by the novelist Angus Wilson about 'a certain stagnation in English contemporary life', applying it to their own parlous situation.[137]

Ninette de Valois did not take criticism lightly. She went flaring onto the attack, blaming Covent Garden, the press and the public for lack of support. 'The Royal Opera House Covent Garden receives a handsome grant from the Arts Council to which much publicity is given,' she thundered. 'The grant is in respect of opera and ballet. One of its principal services to the public is that it enables the prices of seats to be kept at levels which have increased comparatively little since before the war when compared to increases in the prices of other commodities. Ballet seat prices have increased by something like 25 per cent compared with pre-war, but opera seats are at a much *lower* average price.'[138]

Madam begrudged the dollar profits that her troupe pumped into the ROH and complained that her dancers were unable to get enough stage rehearsals. Her relations with Webster soured, and Tooley shuttled curt messages between them. Yet, at no time then or ever after did she consider secession. 'I don't think opera and ballet should ever be divided,' she declared. 'They haven't been over three hundred years. Why should they now?'[139] Deep down, Dame Ninette knew that her company could not survive unattached to the opera house. Proof, if proof were needed, was supplied in October 1955 by the Ballet Rambert which was going broke on a six thousand pound Arts Council grant and launched an emergency appeal in *The Times*.

The subsidies to Madam's enterprises were not separately published, but her first troupe received a handsome share of Covent Garden's quarter-million pounds, her second ensemble got part of the hundred thousand awarded to Sadler's Wells and her ballet school was getting fifteen thousand a year 'for capital expenditure' under the dubious 1946 deal. Madam's compact with Keynes had been richly rewarded.

On 5 May 1956 she marked her company's quarter-centenary with a three-ballet evening: her own *Rake's Progress*, Ashton's *Façade* (both danced by the ageless Helpmann) and a new Ashton *pièce d'occasion*, *Birthday Offering*, that was so exquisite it outlived the occasion and entered the staple repertoire. 'There was a full house, a hum of excitement and speeches at the end,' reported *The Times* dutifully. Alexander Bland in the *Observer* warned that state patronage of ballet could give rise to 'rigidity, bureaucracy, ossification', which de Valois had managed, thus far, to hold off. But enthusiasm was scarce and it seemed that ballet was losing its iron grip on the public attention.

Three nights later, English theatre rose from its drawing-room doldrums with the eruption at the Royal Court of *Look Back in Anger*, a kitchen-sink rant against class, complacency, the men who fought the war and all the good works that followed, starting with the Festival of Britain. Noël Coward found the play 'electrifying' and Kenneth Tynan, the *Observer* critic, called it 'a minor miracle'. Its anti-hero, Jimmy Porter, spoke for a rising caste of demobbed males who had no cause to respect age and rank. 'I suppose people of our generation aren't able to die for good causes any longer,' said Porter. '. . . If the big bang does come and we all get killed off, it won't be in aid of the old-fashioned grand design. It'll just be for the Brave New-nothing-very-much thank you. About as pointless and inglorious as stepping in front of a bus.'

Laurence Olivier, watching the play, was unmoved at first, but when he returned with his filming partner Marilyn Monroe, her husband, Arthur Miller, proclaimed it 'great stuff'. Olivier went to see the playwright, John Osborne, and asked him to write him a role. In *The Entertainer*, England's most bankable actor embraced the new realism with a fervour that revitalized spoken theatre and made it again the hot ticket in town. The Royal Court, on seven thousand pounds of Arts Council subsidy, was stealing the headlines from the Royal Opera House, on quarter of a million. Angry Young Men now held the stage, and all else appeared outmoded. Osborne's success was soon matched by Harold Pinter and Arnold Wesker. Samuel Beckett was all the rage and a new wave of directors rose with the tide of modern dramatists, chief among them Tony Richardson at the Royal Court and Peter Hall at Stratford-upon-Avon. The centre of energy was shifting towards straight theatre.

If this was bad for ballet, there was worse to come. The new Soviet leader, Nikita Khrushchev, had visited London in April 1956 and, although he failed to impress either Eden or the Labour Party, the resumption of person-to-person politics permitted a semi-thaw in cultural relations. Webster, who had visited Moscow the previous winter, was suddenly rewarded with a visit by the Bolshoi Ballet, the first by any Russian dance troupe since the Revolution. As word got round, there was a rush on the box-office. 'It is doubtful,' reflected *Dance and Dancers*, 'whether in the past history of ballet in England there has been queueing for three nights to book tickets.'[140]

On the opening night, 3 October 1956, the house was crammed with the pride of British ballet: Fonteyn, Ashton, de Valois, Somes, May, Grey, Beriosova, Nerina, Fifield, Cranko, MacMillan, Dolin, Markova, Rambert, Shearer, Helpmann and several who danced elsewhere that night but rushed in to catch the closing moments. The glittering Galina Ulanova, now forty-seven years of age, and her regular partner Yury Zhdanov danced Leonid Lavrovsky's *Romeo and Juliet*. By the end, Fonteyn was in tears. She told reporters, 'I am so dazzled, so dazed. Ulanova is just indescribable. I had no idea, no conception of her. I cannot describe it. I did not watch her technique. One cannot watch technique when watching Ulanova.'[141]

Webster went on stage to interrupt the ovations, which lasted fully an hour and a half. He made a masterly speech, talking of 'the miracle that is Ulanova' and of Britain's 'affection and admiration' for the genius of Russia. The Prime Minister, sitting centre stalls, nodded approvingly. The next morning, every newspaper except the *Financial Times*, splashed the Bolshoi across their news pages. 'They're Just the Best in the World,' proclaimed the *Daily Herald* on its front page.

'What a lot we have to learn!' sighed the ballet historian Mary Clarke. 'Each night I went to the Bolshoi, I felt more ignorant and more lacking in theatre experience.'[142] Altogether the Bolshoi danced twenty-four times that month at Covent Garden and three nights in Croydon, adding *Giselle*, *Swan Lake* and *The Fountains of*

Bakhchisarai to their playbill. The ovations continued to mount and the arguments to rage, with Dolin and others rushing into print to insist that English dancers were every bit as good as the Russians. The contrary evidence was collected at the box-office, which turned in a forty thousand pound net profit from the Bolshoi month, reduced only by subsequent political complications.

After their final appearance in Croydon, the Russians were whisked to the airport to board a waiting fleet of Aeroflots. Moments after the last plane had left British airspace, radios crackled with news of a Soviet armoured invasion of Hungary, suppressing an anti-Communist uprising. Prospects of future cultural contacts receded and the Sadler's Wells Ballet, which had shipped its sets to Leningrad in anticipation of a reciprocal visit, lost eighteen thousand pounds in getting them back. British attention, meanwhile, shifted south and east to Suez, where Eden had ordered an invasion to reverse Gamal Abdel Nasser's seizure of the Suez Canal, which had been held by Britain under a dubious imperial treaty. As the nation split painfully over an unjust and unnecessary war, British ballet heaved a sigh of relief to have escaped further comparisons with the Soviet grandmasters.

The gulf between English effort and Russian expertise had been cruelly exposed, and Ninette de Valois needed to act promptly. She ordered a complete overhaul of the training of male dancers at her school and called in palace contacts to procure, in January 1957, a Royal Charter for her companies and a Damehood of the British Empire for Margot Fonteyn. The Sadler's Wells Ballet thus became the Royal Ballet, outranking the Covent Garden Opera Company. Dame Margot stood on a pedestal above all other dancers.

As for the art, there was not much more Madam could do except play to the national strengths. If the Russians had a flaw, it was the dullness of their sets and the archaic predictability of their choreography. Madam hired good designers (John Piper, Osbert Lancaster, Isabel Lambert) and gave Cranko and MacMillan a license to innovate, the latter drawing his dancers ever deeper into dark realms of suicide, rape and lunacy. Britten's *Prince of the Pagodas* on New Year's Day 1957 was followed the next season by *Ondine*, a brilliant score by a German outcast, Hans Werner Henze, who had met Ashton at William Walton's home on the island of Ischia. Together, they gave Fonteyn her most shimmering role, the pose in which she is cast in stone in a statue in her home town,

Reigate. 'The crown of our creation, the radiant centre of the whole ballet, was Margot, the *assoluta*, the frail instrument, the master's Stradivarius,'[143] wrote Henze, whose cosmopolitan charm was much in demand among the Angry Young Men of bohemian Chelsea.

British composers – Malcolm Arnold, Richard Arnell, Dennis ApIvor, Alexander Goehr and Matyas Seiber were also favoured by Madam's quest for novelty but many of their submissions were rejected by her chief conductor, who complained that 'the composers have only an imperfect idea of what a ballet score should be'.[144] The standard of ballet conducting, post Lambert, was variable. What was unchanged was the voltage of Madam's ambition. If the Royal Ballet could not outdance the blazing Russians, Ninette de Valois was determined that it should outsmart them. 'We belong to the West,' she declared in May 1957. 'To change our style would be to kill our particular individuality, and to confuse the issue of our future place in the history of dancing . . . Today it can be said that the English school has by now absorbed classicism in the main; it is moving forward to a second stage . . .'[145]

The Kubelik era at Covent Garden Opera, brief as it was, was characterized by a gleaming idealism. Kubelik was a believer in human values and human rights. His faith in mankind was pricked only by an endearing lack of self-confidence. Before *Bohème*, an opera he had never conducted before, Kubelik was seen 'simply quivering'.[146] Verismo and bel canto were not his cups of tea, but in Verdi and Wagner, Mozart and the moderns, he was deft and compelling. Polite and patient in rehearsal, his performances glowed with the incandescence of sudden inspiration. Some in the orchestra grumbled that he varied his tempi from one night to the next, but this was ever the mark of a fine conductor: to follow a fleeting fantasy and let each performance be a grand improvisation.

As a conductor Kubelik ranked, in his early forties, among the world's top names. He made records for EMI and Deutsche Grammophon and drew an ROH emolument of £6,500, necessitating an immediate increase in Webster's measly £3,500 salary. He rented a flat in Hampstead and sent his son, Martin, to a local prep school; his much-loved wife, Ludmilla, was physically incapacitated and undergoing repeated bouts of surgery.

Kubelik began in October 1955 as he intended to proceed, with a Verdi *Otello* that was meticulously well prepared and cast, for the most part, from internal resources, with the exception of the Chilean Ramon Vinay as the tragic hero and the Dutch soprano Gré Brouwenstijn as Desdemona. There was to have been a bigger star, but when Tito Gobbi failed to turn up by the end of the first week of rehearsal, Kubelik cancelled his contract. Gobbi, in his memoirs, maintained that his flight had been delayed by fog and it was all a wretched misunderstanding. Edward Downes, who was involved in the rehearsals, had a different recollection:

> Gobbi's agent, Sandor Gorlinsky, rang up to say he was going to miss the first three rehearsals because he had engagements on the Continent and had sung the part of Iago more than a hundred times. Kubelik said: Absolutely unacceptable. He asked me if I knew anyone who could learn Iago in a weekend. So I went round to Otakar Kraus's flat in Notting Hill, and taught him the part.[147]

Gobbi turned up at the theatre with his agent and lawyers. Webster summoned learned counsel. On the opening night Peter Potter, Christopher West's one-legged assistant, anticipated a scandal when he saw Gobbi and his entourage occupying a row of centre-stalls. He and Webster hopped about the gangway behind the grand tier throughout the performance. At the final curtain, Gobbi rose to his feet and cheered Kraus to the echo. *Otello* was hugely acclaimed and, in Harewood's words, 'caused virtually a change of mind in public and critics about the possibilities of the young company'.[148]

Kubelik had called a press conference some weeks before to declare his commitment to performing opera in English with native singers, dispensing as far as possible with international stars who 'come and go and have no idea of real artistic co-operation'. This statement set him irretrievably at odds with the Callas-gaping opera lobby and with star-struck members of the ROH board, but Webster lent his support and the company swelled with the confidence he instilled. 'We learned so much from Kubelik,' said Elizabeth Latham. 'He was one of the few gentlemen that ever entered the theatre, and he imagined everyone else was ticking over just as he was. I don't think he was right for Covent Garden – he was too nice.'[149]

Elsie Morison, who would give up her career nine years later to become his second wife, was captivated by the way 'he understood singers, he breathed with you'. A *Magic Flute*, staged in January

1956 for the bicentenary of Mozart's birth, exemplified Kubelik's aims. The bill was topped by Morison, Jess Walters, Richard Lewis and Adele Leigh – all home-grown, with Shuard, Iris Kells, Josephine Veasey and Joan Carlyle in the supporting roles. Kubelik had refined the concept over seven months with the producer, Christopher West, and the designer, John Piper, and even got to grips with crusty old Professor Dent, inducing him to modify the English translation. The result was a trifle over-serious, but beautifully performed and improving measurably when Sutherland and Pears replaced Morison and Lewis in the revival. Webster found the production over-rehearsed and Rosenthal complained that Kubelik's productions were hogging all the stage time, at the expense of other conductors and guest stars. 'Kubelik's almost fanatical insistence that, when he was preparing a new work, virtually everything else had to go by the board, resulted in the dullest mid-season (1956-57) in memory,' he wrote.[150]

There was also disaffection within. Shacklock, a company founder, resigned at the end of Kubelik's first season to pursue a freelance life that took her to the Bolshoi and the West End, where she wound up trilling the hills alive in *The Sound of Music*. 'I didn't find Kubelik warm,' she said. 'I can't say I didn't get on with him but we weren't on the same wavelength. And then he married Elsie Morison. We were very happy for Elsie.'[151] Fisher also quit, and others turned murmurous. Geraint Evans lost his Papageno role to Jess Walters and Adele Leigh was demoted from Pamina to Papagena. Evans took Leigh to see Webster, saying, 'it's rather disgraceful the way Adele has been treated.' Webster replied: 'I cannot interfere.'[152] (He did, however, implore Kubelik to find something for the Welshman, who 'has had no new part of any worth for some time'.)[153]

Joan Sutherland, Webster's white hope, went into a huff after falling out with Kubelik over her recitatives as the peasant girl in a *Carmen* rehearsal. She made no further headway in Kubelik's time. 'He was not much use to her,' reflected Downes, 'because he didn't understand Italian repertoire and was scared of much of it.'

On the other hand, he was quick to spot a Canadian truck-driver who, dismissed by the senior repetiteur Norman Feasey, was retrieved by Downes and coached for the king's role in an explosive *Ballo* in Maschera in Kubelik's second season. Jon Vickers was proof positive of the case for producing opera in English.

The second season also saw a thrilling but ill-attended *Jenůfa*, a mixed *Meistersinger* in which Sutherland (as Eva) refused to sing out because she felt Kubelik was letting the orchestra overwhelm her, and the first complete staging of Berlioz's *The Trojans* which sold out every seat for eight performances and sent ripples round the world as a miracle of English stagecraft, an object lesson to the French who persisted in demeaning their greatest composer.

In the huge *Trojans* cast there was only one foreigner, the American Blanche Thebom. Vickers was the male lead and, despite refusing to take much direction from the director, John Gielgud, bestrode the stage like a titan. The chorus numbered 120. 'You had to do a lot of coaxing, and try to remember their names and take trouble not to treat them like a lot of cattle,' the great actor reminisced. He also 'quickly came to realize that when the conductor comes on to the scene, he really is the boss'.[154] Kubelik insisted that *The Trojans* should be staged exactly as Berlioz intended, without cuts, gimmicks, updatings, or artificial sweeteners. The opera had never before succeeded at full length.

The only dissension arose in the boardroom, where Isaiah Berlin had been urging that 'a revival of an opera by Vivaldi would rivet international attention in a way in which *The Trojans* will not'[155] and the opera sub-committee chairman, Viscount Moore, offered to resign after Webster, without prior approval, engaged a Rumanian designer, Mariano Andreu, who was suspected to be Gielgud's lover. 'What folly on the part of anyone in Webster's vulnerable position to pick on a man whose chief qualification seems to be close personal association with John Gielgud!' exclaimed Waverley.[156]

The outcome, however, dispelled all clouds. Crabby old Dent, who supplied the translation, told Webster: 'It was a stroke of genius, I felt, to engage John Gielgud as producer. I went to several dress rehearsals and realized all along what difficulties he had to contend with, but he surmounted them marvellously, and I saw how he gradually developed the personalities of Amy Shuard, Jess Walters and A-canius, whose name I don't know but I think she is one of our own people.'[157] A voice from the past, Eugene Goossens, added his blessing: 'I have just come from *The Trojans* and I feel I must tell you – as I just told Rafael – how completely moved and overwhelmed I am by the splendour and sheer precision of the whole production.'[158] In the press, Peter Heyworth reported 'a triumph for the whole company' and Andrew Porter extolled 'a sumptuous and splendid and glorious experience'. 'It was the greatest thing we did,' said Iris Kells.

There was more to come from Kubelik, but not much more. Eager to introduce modern drama, he got Webster to nag his Soviet contacts for the rights to stage Prokofiev's *Fiery Angel* and Shostakovich's *Lady Macbeth of Mtsenk*, both suppressed by Stalin. He proposed to conduct the world première of *The Greek Passion*, by his Czech fellow-exile Bohuslav Martinů, but Sir Arthur Bliss, composer of the ephemeral *Olympians*, persuaded the Board that the score should first be 'seen by one or two competent musicians'. The authorities selected for this task were Edric Cundell of the Guildhall School of Music; John Denison of the Arts Council; and Anthony Lewis, a provincial conductor. Their reports were denigratory and the opera was dropped.[159] Kubelik also talked of staging Rankl's *Deirdre* as an act of contrition, with Morison in the title role, only to be vetoed again by the Board. The discouragements were increasing.

In his third and final season, Kubelik conducted *The Carmelites* by Francis Poulenc, twelve months after its La Scala première, and a new *Tristan und Isolde* (in German) with Vinay and Fisher, alternating with the magnificently ascendant Swede, Birgit Nilsson. The only other new show of a cash-strapped season that coincided with the centenary of the ROH building was a Verdi *Don Carlos*, produced by Luchino Visconti and conducted by Carlo Maria Giulini – an all-foreign, all-star effort with Gobbi, Boris Christoff, Brouwenstijn, Fedora Barbieri and, wonder of wonders, in the title role, Jon Vickers, made in England and the major find of the Kubelik era. The production, said Peter Heyworth in the *Observer*, would be talked of 'for years to come' – and so it was. Giulini and Visconti atttended all of each other's rehearsals, setting a moral example of artistic collaboration. Kubelik's reforms were bearing rich fruit but the Board was in no rush to support him.

Kubelik had warned that he planned his international diary a year in advance, and needed a quick decision on contract renewal.[160] No answer was forthcoming. His own resolve had been weakened by a persistent stream of xenophobic innuendos emanating from a familiar source. In June 1956, assessing an ROH ten-year report, the *Daily Telegraph* critic Martin Cooper cast doubt on the company's aims and wondered whether English voices would ever grow large enough to fill its vast stage. Kubelik, stung, wrote to *The Times* urging critics to 'ignore the snobs and instead fight for communion between the British public and British composers and singers.' Cooper retorted that 'these singers must be worth communing with', and on the very same day, as if by mystic co-ordination, the arch-meddler, Sir Thomas Beecham, reached for his poisoned pen in support of his satrap hacks. Beecham's letter to *The Times* opened with a swipe at the departed Rankl before pouring scorn on Kubelik:

> Now we have another foreigner in charge. But does he possess any of the qualifications for the creation of a truly national organization? It is not a question only of conducting; the modern world positively teems with conductors of every nationality and nearly all of them are highly praised by the press.
>
> What we have got to realize is that Covent Garden has neither accomplished the purpose for which it was established, nor is it ever likely to do so while it remains in the hands of those who are now in charge of it . . . The dignity of our nation is today at stake and we are presenting a sorry spectacle to the outside world.[161]

Kubelik, reading this, promptly offered his resignation, contending 'that my status as a foreigner might be regarded as a handicap to creating British national opera'. His letter, together with a draft blast to *The Times*, landed on the desk of Viscount Moore, who went to the conductor and asked him to stay his hand for twenty-four hours until Lord Waverley had time to act.

The aged chairman summoned a board meeting the following afternoon, at the end of which he dictated a magisterial missive to *The Times*, declaring that the ROH music director had resigned upon reading Beecham's letter. 'The board have informed Mr Kubelik that they are unwilling to accept his resignation,' intoned Waverley. 'They have assured him that he has their entire confidence and that he can rely on their unstinted support in pursuit of the policy he has outlined during his tenure of his present office.'

Kubelik was called to the boardroom to be read this letter. 'He flung his arms wide apart, said dramatically "It is finished," and then embraced the chairman.'[162] There was no more talk of walking out, but the 'unstinted support', he found, was not wholehearted and the critical sniping persisted. Kubelik also felt vicariously the anguish of his dying friend Martinů, whose faith in his final opera had been damaged by Covent Garden's rejection. In the end, Kubelik just slipped away, saying he would be happy to return as a guest conductor. He told Webster he wanted freedom to follow his artistic instincts, and fewer constraints from punitive UK taxes.[163] 'I don't remember why I left,' he told me years later. 'Perhaps I made a mistake. Fate is strange.'[164]

In 1961, after Ludmilla's death, he found fulfilment in Munich as chief conductor of the Bavarian radio orchestra, with which he recorded (among many indispensables) the outstanding *Meistersinger* of all time – only for a contract dispute to prevent its release. Kubelik was never a lucky conductor. In 1973 he became music director of the Metropolitan Opera in New York, but resigned before taking office when Goran Gentele, his co-director, died in a car crash. Kubelik would not fulfil his operatic ideals, but his home life was made happy by Elsie and his final years were uplifted by the velvet revolution that liberated his beloved homeland.

For a brief moment in the 1970s it seemed that Kubelik might return to London as music director of Sadler's Wells, whose manager, Stephen Arlen, was now married to Iris Kells, Elsie's best friend. Kubelik weighed the offer before deciding, wisely, not to risk further exposure to the *Opera* gang who, he felt, had hounded him for reducing Covent Garden's dependence on unruly stars. He never told Elsie his reasons for leaving London. 'He was not a person to dwell on things,' she said. 'He never held a grudge and liked to look ahead, not backwards.'[165] His ROH file has been purged of any mention of his departure.

Brief as it was, the Kubelik era at Covent Garden left a lasting lesson in leadership, both practical and moral. 'Kubelik brought real humanity to his music making,' noted John Tooley. 'He wasn't obsessed with absolute precision of playing but what he wanted was the spirit, the heart of the music, and he knew how to get there.'[166] Harewood felt uplifted by his unusual blend of sincerity and professionalism, reporting in his memoirs that Kubelik's three years at Covent Garden were 'the best of my life'.[167]

What Kubelik brought to the company is best illustrated by Edward Downes. Conducting *Jenůfa* one night in 1959, Downes suffered a haemorhage behind both eyes and was blinded. He groped through to the end of the opera and was rushed to hospital. Next day, a specialist told him there was no hope, his sight was destroyed.

'Kubelik wouldn't accept that,' said Downes. 'He sent me to three surgeons in Switzerland, one of whom operated and restored some of my vision. I was earning twelve pounds ten shillings a week and couldn't afford that kind of treatment. Kubelik paid it all out of his own pocket. He was a good man, in the true sense of the word. If he had stayed at Covent Garden, there is no telling what kind of family company we might have become.'[168]

One morning in 1956, Elizabeth Latham walked on stage as usual at eight in the morning and saw a strange man peering down at her from the gantry.

'Who's that?' she asked a stagehand.

'A spy from the union,' he whispered.

Bogey Ballard having finally retired, his powers had passed to shop stewards and union convenors who had no sympathy for the intensity of effort expected in the non-commercial theatre. Under Ballard, the stage carpenter had been boss backstage. Now, there were norms and national rules to be obeyed and a closed shop to be protected. Three rival unions – NATKE, ETU and T&GWU – fought for dominance backstage. In early 1956 the Musicians Union stopped BBC relays from Covent Garden; months later, the actors and ballet union Equity blocked the televising of *Petrushka*. 'I knew the game was up,' said Latham. 'I could see that this was not going to be the theatre I believed in, so at the end of the season I resigned.'

On one of her last nights, Equity succeeded in having an Italian, Melchiorre Luise, banned from singing the minor part of Sacristan in *Tosca*. Latham had to explain to Luise that he was being replaced on union orders with a British bass, Howell Glynne. Luise watched the opera from the wings and, after the final curtain, went on stage to congratulate his replacement. 'That night finished it for me,' said Latham, who packed her bags and went to Vienna to live with her friend, Hilde Zadek.

Similar scenes were being played out all over the land. As the industries that Labour had nationalized responded to central directives, so their employees banded for strength and protection into the embrace of increasingly powerful unions. More than fifty per cent of all male employees were union members; among working-class men, the figure was closer to eighty per cent. More and more time at work was taken up with union meetings and the number of strikes rose exponentially. Between the end of the war and 1954, two million days were lost to industrial inaction. In the next decade, the loss rose to 3,889,000. Union leaders became key players on the national stage, invited to Downing Street by Harold

Macmillan who saw himself as a 'One Nation' Tory and fostered a spending spree in the interests of social peace and electoral gain.

Macmillan, a wealthy publisher's son married to the Duke of Devonshire's daughter, was the epitome of bourgeois complacency. 'Let's be frank about it,' he told the country in 1957. 'Most of our people have never had it so good.' Two years later he was re-elected in a mini-landslide, but when the concessions he made and the debts he amassed fell due for payment he would be swept from office in an unprecedented ferment of scandal and decay.

Lord Waverley, who had devoted his life to the philosophy and practice of good governance, lived to see his esteemed Whitehall reduced to 'the management of decline' and his country embracing inflationary chaos. He underwent surgery in September 1957 and returned from hospital to deal with a threatened chorus strike. He addressed his pain and his duty stoically to the last. A fortnight before he died, Waverley summoned Ninette de Valois to his bedside, in the 'shabby gloom' of St Thomas's Hospital, south London, a former poor ward that had not been much improved upon under the NHS. He had announced his retirement and was, she recalled,

> relaxed, yet curiously excited and hopeful about Covent Garden's future. 'Lord Moore will be the new Chairman. He's the right man, is he not? I have every faith in young Moore . . .'

Even at the end, said de Valois, he saw things 'with extraordinary clarity'.[169] News of his decline was conveyed to the Queen, who brought forward the Order of Merit that he was due to receive in the 1958 New Year's Honours List. Lord Waverley, dying, was dutifully touched. 'The Civil Service,' he said, 'will be pleased about this.'[170]

CHAPTER 6

Short Interval: Champagne,
Canapés and Nature Calls
(1959–60)

THE NEW CHAIRMAN was – after Keynes, Webster and de Valois – the fourth cornerstone of Covent Garden, the last of its formative figures. Garrett Moore, who had become 11th Earl of Drogheda on the death of his father in November 1957, would chair the board for sixteen years, having served it as secretary for seven. Half his working life was taken up by Covent Garden, both chronologically and in the amount of time and unpaid attention he lavished on it.

Drogheda did not take his responsibilities lightly. 'He was a restless man,' wrote the long-serving *Financial Times* editor, Gordon Newton. 'One never saw him sitting quietly at his desk, thinking. He had two secretaries, one for the *Financial Times* and the other for the Royal Opera House – he became chairman of both – and he always seemed to be dictating something to one of them. He was one of the greatest memo writers of all time. He always carried a pencil and small paper pad in his pocket. As he strode about the place, he would stop and make a note, which would result in someone, somewhere receiving yet another memo later in the day.'[1]

These notes, known as Droghedagrams, landed several times daily on the desks of Newton, David Webster and others who came within his purview. They were tartly phrased, neither critical nor peremptory but politely interrogative: had you noticed that ...? what are your plans for ...? He expected immediate action. Failure to respond resulted, late the same day, in the ultimate Droghedagram: 'When do you think I will be receiving a reply to my previous notes?'

Andrew Porter, the *Financial Times* critic, would finish work around two in the morning, having written his review and checked the galleys for the last edition. Seven hours later, his doorbell would ring. 'The Droghedagrams arrived at nine,' he recalled, 'brought by a boy on a bike.'[2]

At the opera, Drogheda sat 'with a tiny torch to hand, making notes of anything that goes wrong'.[3] Whether he ever indulged his genuine love of music and dance is uncertain for he assumed a dangerously hybrid role of chairman and chief critic. Droghedagrams flowed from the Royal Box down to the prompt corner and on to the side-stage often in the middle of performances, reminding managers of their lapses and artists of his scrutiny. At a dress rehearsal he sent a note to the producer Christopher West saying: 'From now on I want all the action on the prompt side of the stage, because I can't see the other side from the Royal Box.'[4]

'He did not bide time by being either shrewd, over-discreet or patient,'[5] noted Ninette de Valois, who bore his asperities with uncommon restraint, appreciating the sincerity of his concern and attributing his agitation to their common Scots-Irish heritage.

Drogheda cherished his ancestry to the point of insufferable snobbery. In a company which held a Royal Charter and employed the Queen's cousin as its administrator's assistant, he liked to remind people that his forebear was knighted by the *first* Queen Elizabeth and his Earldom dated from an era when the present Buckingham Palace dynasty were mere Electors in some swampish German province. His bloodline was as blue as his eyes, which were piercing though warm, and he looked down an aquiline nose at most of mankind. He recognized, however, the nobility of genius and admitted the likes of Ashton, Fonteyn and Callas to his own superior caste. In art and at work, he was more meritocrat than aristocrat.

Drogheda changed the character of Covent Garden from populist to élitist – decadently, by means of social elevation; progressively, by preaching, pestering and pummelling everyone to raise their sights and achieve the highest standards. His motto might well have been, 'the best for the best'.

His philosopher friend, Isaiah Berlin, summed up Drogheda as 'a curious mixture of painstaking conscientiousness and aristocratic self-indulgence and impatience'.[6] His patrician arrogance could be charming at times, infuriating at others. He was, said a colleague, 'not an easy man with whom to communicate a view which was not wholly palatable to him'.[7] Lord Gibson, his FT chairman, called him 'a great life-enhancer – a man unlike anyone else who ever lived'.[8]

Charles Garrett Ponsonby Moore was born on St George's Day 1910 to ill-matched parents who separated when he was eleven. His father believed in public service and rose to become director general of the Ministry of Economic Warfare. His mother was devoted to pleasure and playboys; she particularly liked racing drivers and was chummy with the flier Amy Johnson. After their divorce, the tenth earl married the ex-Gaiety actress, Olive May. Garrett's upbringing was thus colourfully contrasted, mingling duty with fun, fidelity with fickleness, tradition with fashion, and high seriousness with theatrical sensation.

After Eton and Cambridge, he went to work in the City and dallied with débutantes. Keen on music, he founded a Quartet Society with a friend, Jack Donaldson, at the home of Beecham's patron, Lady Cunard. He got to know Sargent, Walton and other leading lights but seemed languidly unfulfilled. Two fortuitous meetings reshaped his life. In 1932, he was introduced to Brendan Bracken, a red-haired newspaper manager whose resemblance to Winston Churchill was so striking that he fostered rumours of his own bastardy. Bracken had built a small empire consisting of the *Financial News*, *Investor's Chronicle* and *The Economist* which, in due course, he merged with the *Financial Times*. He liked the young Lord and offered him a job selling advertising. Garrett, thrilled by the smell of print and the access it gave to world events, found his métier in newspapers.

Soon after, he found true love. Weekending at Bracken's country house, he met a pianist of arresting looks and was smitten for life. Joan Carr had fled a nightmare marriage to a palm-court violinist and was resuming her career with the help of a wealthy Jewish couple, Violet and Sydney Schiff, who had sponsored her career since childhood. Humbly born, Joan was a couple of years older than her suitor and amorously less ardent. A *roman-à-clef* about her early life suggests that she feared sexual contact after harrowing experiences of marital rape. Alarmed by Garrett's impetuousness, she 'did not know how to deal with what she had reason to call his grim whimsy'.[9] He pursued her to New York, where his persistence paid off and they married at City Hall in May 1935. Their son was born two years later. When the Blitz began Garrett, following a widespread practice among the rich and privileged, sent his wife and son for safety to the United States. He, meantime, served in an anti-aircraft regiment before being seconded by Bracken (now Churchill's Minister of Information) to assist Oliver Lyttelton, a War Cabinet member with responsibilities first for the North African front and then for the Ministry of Production.

By the time he saw Joan again, on a mission to Washington in 1942, she was romantically involved with a Frenchman who stabbed himself melodramatically in the chest when she returned to her husband. The Drogheda marriage was never a conventional relationship. He pursued beauties throughout his life, fancying his chances with the newly-wed Marilyn Monroe, who rented his house while filming *The Prince and the Showgirl*. Joan was equally sought after – 'the most seductive woman since Cleopatra' said an admirer.[10] She cultivated a circle of male friends, mostly intellectual and homosexual, such as John Pope-Hennessy, director of the Victoria and Albert Museum. 'Her quick mind, wide reading and professional talent as a pianist, allied to ethereal beauty and elegance, greatly appealed,' observed the social gadfly James Lees-Milne. 'Moreover . . . her background had been fraught with penury and want, a fact which to her credit she never forgot or glossed over after marriage to Garrett had brought security and comparative affluence.'[11] 'She made you feel as if you were the only person that mattered in the world,' said a senior FT figure. 'I was totally smitten – but for her I don't think things went much further than that.'[12]

Together, Joan and Garrett made a compelling pair. Her musicianship and mental powers gave depth to his shotgun opinions and her charm unruffled many feathers that he had disordered. 'She had an amazingly well-stocked mind,' said a senior Arts Council official. 'Of course, you could talk to her about music, but she was immensely knowledgeable about art and widely read in many other fields.'[13] She sometimes griped that Garrett never read a book from start to finish, simply filleting the salient bits. Her approach was always the more substantive.

It was Drogheda's war record in Whitehall that commended him to Waverley, who grew increasingly fond of him and promoted him in 1954 from Secretary to full board member and chairman of the opera sub-committee. When Drogheda offered to resign after the *Trojans* tiff with Webster, the undemonstrative Waverley wrote him a letter of almost paternal warmth:

My dear Garrett,

I agree that such conduct as you describe is quite intolerable.

But please do nothing rash. You cannot think what a comfort it has been to me to have you as a colleague & in what is, or ought to be, a key position.

I will deal with Webster at the first opportunity.

Yours ever, Waverley[14]

Drogheda had his own ideas on how to deal with Webster, but he needed first to secure the support of his board, which he did by stacking it with friends. Out went Sir Arthur Bliss and Edric Cundell, Philip Nicholls and the Hon. James Smith, all Arts Council nominees. In came Jack Donaldson, his oldest friend who, as his wife admitted, 'was known at that time neither to the other members of the board nor to anyone else in the musical world'.[15] The publisher Mark Bonham-Carter became ballet chairman, less for his dance knowledge than for being a friend of Princess Margaret's. Thomas Armstrong, quiet principal of the Royal Academy of Music, came in to represent musical interests, and William Coldstream, head of the Slade School of Art, added visual expertise.

Not content with these changes, Drogheda added three business-men to the board – Sir Colin Anderson, who donated new lighting for the ROH; Sir Leon Bagrit, a self-made Russian Jew who had bought Kenneth Clark's house in Hampstead and filled it with fine art; and Burnet Pavitt, UK boss of the Hoffmann-La Roche pharmaceutical giant and Lady Drogheda's four-handed piano partner. The chairman intended to raise cash for Covent Garden and reduce its state dependancy. Where his predecessors were public servants and philosophers, Drogheda was an advertising salesman who harried FT guests over lunch until they coughed up, leaving his editor 'squirming with embarrassment'.[16] Even at the Newspaper Publishers Association, of which he was chairman, he would pester fellow-moguls to buy space in his paper, announcing their latest financial transactions. 'It was a bit unnecessary,' said his sometime deputy.[17]

At Covent Garden, he proceeded to soak the rich, compensating them with an exclusive annual gala and regular invitations to share his Royal Box. 'You know quite well why I want to avoid Fridays and Saturdays for first performances,' Drogheda told Webster. 'It so happens that a lot of people, including yourself, take themselves out of London at weekends, and many of them *are the sort of people that we want to be present at first nights.*[18]

Following an American model, he decided to form Friends of Covent Garden and hired a former flying ace, the Hon. Kensington Davison, DSO, DFC, to run it. Davison recruited ten thousand Friends, many of them young and impecunious. He was a tireless populist and a tenacious organizer whose influence was felt in all parts of the house. But the forming of Friends was another step in the retreat from universality. It introduced an effective class system to Covent Garden – outer circle (general populace), inner circle (Friends), Drogheda circle (exceptionally wealthy or well-connected). From this point on, rows of best seats were withdrawn from public sale and reserved for persons of privilege, or for companies who leased up to 140 seats annually under the so-called Premium Stalls Scheme.[19]

These divisions marked a turning point in the social evolution of the Royal Opera House, an abandonment of Keynes's vision of art for all and a reversion to pre-war practices. Change was inevitable, given the inadequacy of public funds to meet the company's soaring ambitions; but the barriers were offensive to poorer attenders and many began to feel excluded – the more so as ticket prices rose steadily to match the pockets of a wealthier clientele. Gallery seats trebled in Drogheda's first three years, from four shillings to twelve. Stalls seats for premium operas were priced at ten guineas and the grand tier at twenty-five guineas, equivalent to more than three hundred pounds in end-of-century values.

None of these inequities troubled Drogheda, who was a short-termist and no kind of strategic thinker. He was, however, alert to his own shortcomings and harvested the fruits of greater minds. Having brought Berlin and the LSE economist Lionel Robbins on board in Waverley's day, he later added the Oxford historian Noel Annan and the art expert Pope-Hennessy. His board meetings took on the sherry-and-rigour haze of an Oxbridge tutorial. 'It was a privilege to sit in,' said a junior staffer. 'You could not have wished for a better education.'[20]

Drogheda positively encouraged confrontation. 'We had great rows at the FT,' said Lord Gibson. 'They would usually end in him saying, "well, I couldn't possibly disagree with you on that" – which meant he had won.' At Covent Garden he bombarded Webster with impossible demands, outrageous ideas and thousands of minute observations, many of them useful and essential. Relations between chairman and chief executive were stormy. 'At times they were on non-speaks,' said one board member. 'I remember going to the Savoy Grill, where everybody who was anyone had lunch in those days, and exclaiming in surprise at seeing David and Garrett closeted at the same table. "They are making peace again," someone said.'[21]

To keep Webster on his toes, Drogheda asked Donaldson to bring on board the obstreperous record producer Walter Legge who, in addition to undermining the management, would procure the return to Covent Garden of his much-missed wife, Elisabeth Schwarzkopf. With his board in place, Drogheda proceeded to review policy. He had been warned by Isaiah Berlin that the company was running off the rails. It needed to abolish English mediocrities and revert to two periods of international opera and two slightly longer seasons of Royal Ballet. The house should shut from July to October or be rented out for the summer, 'vulgarity no object'. Berlin further urged that operas by British composers were 'to be discouraged'; they might be undertaken 'only if financially failure-proof', having been tried out at Sadler's Wells or in the provinces.[22]

This was radical and reactionary, but Drogheda was no reductionist. He intended to continue developing English singers for domestic and export markets, so long as they did not have to sing in English. His reasons, he explained, were artistic and pragmatic. 'I wanted to hear the works given as the composer originally intended,' he argued. 'Then, from the point of view of British singers, the opportunity of learning basic repertory works in the original language added greatly to their ability to obtain engagements overseas.'[23] His decision was soon vindicated as, over the next decade, a flock of Covent Garden singers made the grade at Milan, Munich, Paris and the Met. The world was shrinking and British business could no longer expect that foreigners would follow the Queen's English if it was loudly and slowly enunciated.

The retreat from the vernacular, never formally promulgated or announced, provoked some grumbling among the opera-in-English lobby but no opposition from the Arts Council which was entering one of its transitional phases. Kenneth Clark was about to yield the chair to the Tory peer Lord Cottesloe, and Taffia-Bill Williams was within sight of his pension. The House of Commons, in its first-ever debate on the arts, passed a resolution welcoming the increased popular interest in the arts and endorsing the rule 'that artistic policy should be free from Government control or direction'.[24] But there was precious little control or direction coming from the Council, which was in the process of bungling a merger of the enfeebled Carl Rosa company with Sadler's Wells, almost sinking both companies at a stroke and provoking Harold Rosenthal to devote fifteen pages of his magazine to 'The Opera Crisis'.[25]

Sensing the Council's frailty and the tide of public concern, Drogheda swooped. He ordered Webster to up the ante, telling the press that Covent Garden might not survive another year unless its subsidy was markedly increased. The deficit had reached £183,248 by mid-1959 and Coutts were getting edgy. The Chancellor of the Exchequer, Derick Heathcoat-Amory, was informally approached. He aimed to retire within two years and was thus free to indulge personal fancies. He has been described (by Roy Jenkins) as 'the most obscure Chancellor of the century', but he left two large footprints on the cultural landscape, which is two more than any of his successors.

A theatre-loving squire of slightly louche tastes, Heathcoat-Amory benignly gave the go-ahead to a long-mulled scheme to build a National Theatre on the South Bank of the Thames, down-river from the Royal Festival Hall. This was as bold a boost for the dramatic arts as the inception of Covent Garden had been for lyric theatre. The thespian sector was exultant, the more so since the NT was a pet project of the new Arts Council chairman, Lord Cottesloe, a former governor of Sadler's Wells and the Old Vic who gave it a million pounds and, when the Treasury balked, went to the Party fixer Rab Butler to get more. By the time the last coat of cement and concrete had been slapped on its grimly modern exterior, the NT had cost seven million pounds and was ready to compete with Covent Garden for cultural supremacy.

Worse, from Covent Garden's point of view, the South Bank scheme involved the creation of a second theatre to house the remnants of the Old Vic, the ascendant Royal Shakespeare Company and the impossibly cramped Sadler's Wells. 'Covent Garden said little in public,' recalled Norman Tucker, the Sadler's Wells director, 'but it was clear that the whole South Bank scheme was anathema to David Webster, his chairman Lord Drogheda and other members of the Covent Garden Board. While the Arts Council were pecking cautiously at the scheme with a marked lack of enthusiasm, the

Garden, behind the scenes at least, were definitely antagonistic, fearing, quite without foundation, a tiresome rival in the new house.'[26] Drogheda found himself on opposite sides from Oliver Lyttelton (now Lord Chandos), his wartime boss, who chaired the National Theatre and set about quietly tweaking the Government's ear.

Appreciating that Covent Garden was being downstaged, Heathcoat-Amory ordered the Treasury to come up with a better formula for funding opera. What it proposed was a new deal that granted 43 per cent of the ROH budget, with the rest to be earned at the box office. The uplift was instantaneous and unstoppable. The ROH grant shot up from £362,000 in 1958/9 to £463,000 the next year, and then to half a million. In 1962, with elections approaching, an even more generous formula gave Covent Garden a grant equivalent to 87.5 per cent of its previous year's earnings, 'without limit as to the amount payable'.[27]

This was like giving a small boy a blank cheque in a sweetshop. All Webster had to do was increase his outlay, and Whitehall would foot seven-eighths of the bill. In 1964, the subsidy reached a million pounds, more than forty times the foundation grant of eighteen years before. Amid much back-slapping, two dubious precedents had entered the relationship between Government and the arts. Covent Garden was encouraged to believe that when it ran out of cash, the Treasury would make good. And Whitehall, by treating the ROH as a special case, bypassed the Arts Council and undermined the operating ethic of Keynes's arm's-length principle. The seeds of future disaster had been liberally sown, and with the best of intentions.

The onus of justifying extra public investment fell heavily on the opera company, which gobbled up the new money and kept coming back for more. Webster entered the 1958/59 season knowing it could be his last. Mistrusted by his new chairman and maimed by the loss of Kubelik, he began thinking of changing career for the final decade of his working life. A well-connected London solicitor, Arnold Goodman, secured him a seat on the board of Southern Television. But first he had a crucial season to put on.

There were four new productions on the stocks, including the return of Callas as Cherubini's *Medée* and Kempe conducting *Parsifal*. The opening attraction, if such it could be called, was a salute to the bicentenary of Handel's death with ten nights of

Samson, an oratorio recast for the first time as opera, mutton dressed as lamb. The show, intended as an act of homage to the English choral tradition, was cast internally and promised few excitements. What transpired was that Jon Vickers, fresh from his *Trojans* triumph, took the title role by the scruff and gave an evocation of the blinded Nazarene that would have moved stone walls to tears. Twenty-seven years later, his voice gravelled with age, I saw him recreate *Samson* at Covent Garden on the tercentenary of Handel's birth – and still felt the force of his furious identification with the shackled strongman. Vickers sang four more roles that season, finishing as Parsifal and then flying off to Bayreuth to claim his rightful place on the world stage.

To Webster's relief, the Covent Garden incubator had once again come good, but even he could not have predicted the revelation that was to follow. In *Samson*, Joan Sutherland had sung an Israelite Woman whose only aria is heard near the end. She sang well and was warmly applauded. Webster would have liked her to tackle the big German and Italian diva roles, but her run as Eva in *Meistersinger* had been unhappy and her ubiquitous husband, Richard Bonynge, was steering her into the bel canto range which had reaped such dividends for Callas.

Bonynge proposed Donizetti's *Lucia di Lammermoor*. The uxoricidal opera was last laughed off the stage at Covent Garden after a Toti dal Monte performance in June 1925. The ROH music staff and opera sub-committee saw no reason to revive it, despite (or perhaps because of) Callas's evocation of the role. Walter Legge's opposition was notably vociferous. 'I remember David pushing for it really hard against several members of the board,' said Sutherland's agent, Joan Ingpen.[28] In the end, the board agreed to let Sutherland sing *Lucia,* provided it was conducted by Tullio Serafin, Callas's mentor. The director and designer was to be Franco Zeffirelli, a Luchino Visconti acolyte who had yet to make a name for himself abroad. He arrived at Bow Street to find that the man at the door, Sergeant Martin, had been one of his Scots Guards liberators in wartime Italy.

Sutherland was sent for ten days to Venice to study with the octogenarian Serafin. Back in London, she was manhandled by the director who made Geraint Evans, playing her brother Enrico, throw her repeatedly to the ground. 'Her movements on stage weren't very fluid,'[29] said Evans. Michael Langdon, singing Raimondo, felt that

Zeffirelli had spotted something 'no one realized she possessed'.[30] Serafin, in the pit, bridled at the director's veristic insistence on decking Lucia in a blood-drenched nightgown. 'Permit me to say, sir,' said Sergeant Martin to the director, 'that it's very good.'[31]

In the week of the première, the Brazilian Joao Gibin pulled out as the lover Edgardo and was replaced by the homespun Australian, Kenneth Neate. 'Is Joan going to be very good, Langdon?' fretted Webster. 'Absolutely,' cooed the baritone. 'Good,' sighed the General Administrator, 'I think so, too; I think so too.'[32] He had come close to staking his survival on her success.

Getting ready for the dress rehearsal, Sutherland was told that Callas and Schwarzkopf had come to hear her. With visible trepidation she consented to a joint photocall, pictures of which appeared next day in all the morning papers, Callas in a mink wrap, Sutherland in a flannel dressing gown. 'There were twenty-two photographers crowding into dressing-room five,' remembered Beresford.[33] According to Schwarzkopf, Callas was impressed. 'She will have a great success tomorrow,' said the diva, 'and make a big career if she can keep it up. But only we know how much greater I am.'[34]

On the night of 17 February 1959, a star was born on the stage of the Royal Opera House, an event rare and precious in the annals of art. As soon as Sutherland finished her opening scene, sitting on a rock with harp accompaniment, there were calls for encores. Between acts, Walter Legge came by to offer a recording contract, promising to telephone in the morning. Lord Harewood apologized for leaving early; he was dining at Buckingham Palace. Callas, too, reportedly left before the climax.

In the penultimate Mad Scene, having slain her new husband, running hither and thither to the mocking trills of a flute, Sutherland sang like a woman possessed, her grip on sanity flickering and fading with each swoop of the voice until, on a high E-flat, arms outflung, she fell backwards, the curtain dropped and the house exploded. 'Stay there, darling,' hissed Langdon, as Sutherland tried to rise:

Each time (the curtain) came down she would move as if to get up, and each time I prevented her physically. 'How much longer, Mike?' she kept asking, one eye open to see if the curtain was going back again. It did – seven times, if I recall correctly. When she eventually went out to take her solo call in front of the curtain, the house went wild and it was at least twenty minutes before we could start the final scene.[35]

The morning's reviews paled beside the night's excitements, the critics struggling to preserve critical detachment. Philip Hope-Wallace reported 'a personal triumph for the Australian soprano Joan Sutherland – a future Melba, some people would be ready to declare on the strength of her almost flawless singing of the great scene of the third act.' Andrew Porter ranked Sutherland as 'one of the world's leading prima donnas', raising the roof as no one but Callas could.[36]

Legge typically failed to phone, but an Australian heiress, Louise Hanson Dyer, booked Sutherland to sing on her L'Oiseau Lyre label, employing Decca engineers, who signed Sutherland exclusively for their firm. The BBC relayed *Lucia* live to the nation and Sutherland was courted by opera bosses from Venice, La Scala, Genoa and all the way down to Sicily. Amid the hype and glory, some wondered why it had taken so long for Covent Garden to realize her potential. Her husband suggested that she owed the company few favours. Her agent gave credit equally to Webster for persisting with such a gawky girl and to Zeffirelli: 'she was *choreographed* by him'.[37]

Overnight fame made little obvious impact on the girl they would call 'La Stupenda'. Her first decision was to take three months off, checking into the London Clinic to have her sinuses cleared, an operation which, she was assured, would give her thirty years of trouble-free singing. She returned to a world clamouring for her autograph. She sang two Handel operas – *Alcina* for Cologne Radio and *Rodelinda* at Sadler's Wells, and ended the season with four sold-out *Lucias* at Covent Garden.

Then her contract expired. 'I feel we are to blame for not having sufficient check on her activities,' lamented Drogheda.[38] Serafin suggested that she should follow one Italian-Scot heroine with another, Verdi's Lady Macbeth. Bonynge, however, insisted on Amina in Bellini's *La Sonnambula*, another bel canto role ('he has set my work back by a hundred years,' said Callas) – and that was that. 'They both knew where they were going,' wrote her biographer. 'They were going wherever Richard, and only he, said they should go.'[39]

'Everybody found Ricky difficult,' said Joan Ingpen, 'and poor Joan often didn't know whom to obey.' The following spring,

Bonynge was locked out at Glyndebourne and left banging on the auditorium door after making a pest of himself demanding that she stand centre-stage throughout Bellini's *I Puritani*. Ingpen persuaded him that in Edinburgh, where the opera was transferring, the stage was too small to accommodate his otherwise admirable idea. Bonynge was becalmed, but trouble soon flared again. Ingpen took Sutherland aside and explained that her husband's interference was damaging her career. The big Australian looked back at her with tear-filled eyes. 'If I don't do what he wants,' she said, 'he'll leave me. And I love him.'[40]

A solution was proposed by Sutherland's American agent, Anne Colbert, who said, 'if there's nothing else to do with him, let him conduct her.' 'For Joan, who did not like scenes,' noted her Decca producer, John Culshaw, 'it would mean the end of differences of opinion with strange conductors; for Richard it would mean that he would lose anonymity; and for the agent it meant a lot less trouble (they could be engaged together in what the Americans call a 'package deal') and still more money.'[41]

The only question was whether Bonynge could hack it with the baton. He made a nervous début in January 1962 with the Rome radio orchestra. Well-meaning colleagues and anxious Decca bosses urged him to take lessons with Goossens or Pierre Monteux, but Bonynge resisted options for self-improvement, apart from a few tips that he took from Henry Lewis, a former orchestral player who was married to, and conducting, the mezzo-soprano Marilyn Horne. 'I think (Bonynge) was simply unaware of his own deficiencies as a conductor,' said Culshaw, 'and strangely impervious to the shafts of irony which orchestral players would hurl at him from time to time ... (He) prevented the opera audiences from hearing Joan Sutherland with the great conductors of the age, for it soon became the rule (and there were very, very few exceptions) that to engage Sutherland you had to engage Bonynge as well.'[42]

Sutherland would not hear a word said against Bonynge. When he was booed, she stood wringing her hands in the wings saying, 'it's my fault – I went wrong in the cavatina'. They became the twentieth century's most famous operatic pairing, inseparable as Cav and Pag, forming a Melba-type touring ensemble and ending up in command of Australia's first opera house. Their huge entourage included female attendants for Sutherland and a male valet-cum-chauffeur for Bonynge, in keeping with the style of a Victorian nightingale.

Bonynge steered her into some Verdis and late romantics, but her reputation centred on bel canto. 'I think Ricky limited her,' said Ingpen, echoing a widespread sensation. Others argued that, without Bonynge, Sutherland would have languished undiscovered. 'Joan was a darling, so simple and uncomplicated,' said Adele Leigh who sang beside her throughout the 1950s. 'If it weren't for Richard, she would never have become Dame Joan.'[43]

Whatever the objective truth, Sutherland's involvement with Covent Garden ended with her apotheosis. She would return frequently as a guest artist and liked to declare that 'I have always called Covent Garden my home,'[44] but she showed little sense of obligation. 'You understand that since my very sudden "rise to fame" things have become very complex for me,' she told Webster in December 1959, turning down several roles.[45] Webster, she said, with unintended irony, 'was great at giving people confidence, certainly to me.'[46]

Her departure was a bitter blow, not just for Webster personally but for the collective ideal. Before 1959, singers who rose to fame on his stage, albeit less explosively than Vickers and Sutherland, maintained an attachment to the Covent Garden 'family'. Shacklock, Shuard, Geraint Evans and Adele Leigh enjoyed coming home as 'house stars'. Sutherland took off like a rocket and never looked back. Air travel was becoming easier, the world was getting smaller and the temptations were far too great for a singer to place sentiment above self-interest. Though she would sing a nostalgic Mad Scene at Webster's farewell and end her own career in December 1990 on the ROH stage, Sutherland would spend more of her career in the air than she did in any opera house. 'She belongs as much to Covent Garden and La Scala as she does to the Met,' noted the American singing expert John Ardoin in 1964 – by which time, she belonged nowhere. The rules of engagement were being rewritten and, as Ardoin sadly acknowledged: 'the great names of opera do not reflect the quality of an opera house'.[47] They had become the topping on the cake, the sugary sprinkling that sold the product while rotting a company's finances and fibre.

The flight of star voices from staff contracts destroyed another of Covent Garden's founding assumptions. The dream had been that a national opera company would supply its own stars from English and Empire stock. This chimera was dispelled by ease of travel and an explosion in world fees, which Covent Garden was forced to match and sometimes to exceed. The 60s were about to go consumer mad. 'There will be more food in the shops this Christmas than there has been since 1938,' trumpeted the popular press.[48] Singers were swept up by greed and by a publicity-driven need for status symbols – no longer one sports car but three. Sutherland bought a château in Switzerland, where Melba made do with an Australian ranch.

Rampant materialism ravaged the budgets of major opera houses, but the spiritual damage was greater still. The idea of opera as a collaborative act turned absurd when one soprano was paid more than the entire chorus. To the emergent Me Generation, individuality was the ultimate and community a net for losers. Against this backdrop, Covent Garden's original aspiration to artistic self-sufficiency came to seem as utopian as Nye Bevan's claim that the NHS would cost less each year as the national health improved. Opera was marching out of step with the times, and no one at Covent Garden was able to acknowledge the dysfunction, or redefine the company's purpose. This was a dangerous arrhythmia, and one that would become more pronounced as the century advanced.

At the Royal Ballet, the despondency deepened. Margot Fonteyn had murmured the dreaded r-word, and her murmurings of retirement grew louder and more insistent as a critical birthday approached. 'Margot told me quite plainly,' said John Tooley: '"Physically, I can't keep up the pace. It won't be long."'[49]

Her husband Tito Arias had returned to Panama where, politically sidelined, he plotted a *coup d'état* – his sixth.[50] Fonteyn flew out to lend support, but the *coup* was comic-opera. Arias's flotilla of armoured shrimp boats was routed by the Guardia Nacional and Fonteyn was arrested in Panama City on 20 April 1959, interrogated for two days and deported. Back in London, she changed her status at the Royal Ballet to guest artist and upped her fee. 'Guns don't come cheap,' she told her friend Colette Clark, Kenneth's daughter.[51] Even more quietly, she marked her fortieth birthday on 18 May, a date she had long set down for retirement.

She had been dancing for years on a damaged left foot and relied on sheer willpower some nights to stop her perma-fix smile contorting in anguish. The skin on her high cheekbones was stretched taut as a drum and her trim form seemed more fragile than agile. She ruled out any more *Swan Lakes*, unable to manage thirty-two *fouetté* turns on her painful left foot. Forty was old for a ballerina and Fonteyn was ready to reclaim her life; whether she would spend the rest of it with that philandering wastrel Tito was another matter, a question she needed time and freedom to contemplate.

Her ruminations plunged Madam into action and Webster into despair. Margot Fonteyn was the Royal Ballet's only star. Others in her constellation were approaching their zenith without having earned the authority and allure of a prima ballerina. If Margot quit, it would spell domestic disaster and the end of dollar revenue. All season long, the company trembled. Ashton, her creative source, alert to the shifting of sands, devised his chirpy new ballet, *La fille mal gardée*, for Nadia Nerina and David Blair. It proved his greatest success for half a decade, his signal of comic renewal.

Fonteyn, however, after the Panama fiasco stopped murmuring. Low on funds, she resolved to dance on. Not for the money, she insisted, but because there were certain things she could do which no one else could match, and because the public needed her. 'She was always loved not so much for what she did as for what she was,' noted a shrewd colleague, 'for that emanation across the footlights of a gentle, heartwarming personality which was convincing because the personality seemed so genuine.'[52]

What the year of Margot's wobbles yielded was an accelerated urgency in Madam's mind to spot a successor. In August 1959, a 20-year-old *Swan Lake* extra was summoned to the Director's office and told she was to dance the central roles of Odette-Odile on tour in six weeks' time at the Hippodrome Theatre, Golders Green, a commuter junction on the Northern Line of the London Underground. Antoinette Sibley was a graduate of Madam's ballet school, a Home Counties girl with a mind of her own. 'I felt at ease with her,' said Sibley. 'She called me Sibyl.'[53]

Her partner in *Swan Lake* was to be Michael Somes, Fonteyn's regular and the company's most rigorous trainer. Sibley was rehearsed round the clock and got through her début without incident, followed by a second performance at suburban Streatham. She then went back unremarked to the corps.

Four weeks later, she got a Saturday morning call from Somes. 'You're on tonight,' he said. Nerina was sick and she was to dance Odette-Odile at Covent Garden. 'There's no way,' said Sibley. 'I can't. No, no.'[54] Refusal, however, was inadmissible. Fonteyn, ever the team player, gave up her rehearsal time and guided her through the *fouettés*. A press conference was called to announce that Miss Sibley would be the youngest person ever to dance the role at the ROH. Even if she had fallen twice on her bottom and waltzed off with the wrong swan, she would have rated a mention in the Sunday papers. Sibley, though, was stunning, and glamorous: softer and shapelier than Fonteyn. A full hand of ballet critics phoned in raves, and several of their reviews made the front page. Next morning, Sibley could hardly get out of her house for the throng of photographers.

'Madam wasn't very pleased about it,' said her flatmate, 'because in those days the policy was that it was the company and not the individual that mattered. I think they felt that (Antoinette) had courted that publicity, which she hadn't at all, bless her heart; she'd just gone there and done what she had to do.'[55]

Like it or not, Ninette de Valois had a star in the making. Her response was to put Sibley back in the corps for six weeks before letting her dance another lead role. Then she sent her to South Africa, sharing and studying roles on tour with the experienced Beriosova, Nerina and Beryl Grey. On their return to Covent Garden, in February 1960, Sibley danced in quick succession the Betrayed Girl in Madam's version of *The Rake's Progress*, Aurora in *Sleeping Beauty*, six *Swan Lakes* and *Les Sylphides*. Beriosova said she liked her Aurora better than anyone's except Margot's, and Fonteyn herself taught her *Giselle*. Somes, whose first wife had recently died, moved in with his protégée and later married her, often reducing her to floods of tears in exhaustive training sessions. He was more than twenty years her senior but still a striking figure, the best male dancer England had ever produced, albeit now on his last legs. They made an eye-catching couple, and the romance did Sibley no lasting harm.

Nor was she the lone contender. That season, Covent Garden saw a *Swan Lake* danced by her classmate Lynn Seymour, billed as the first Canadian to dance a leading role with the Royal Ballet. Separated in age by just ten days, Seymour and Sibley shared the same teacher, Winifred Edwards, but specialized in different styles. Sibley was a classical dancer, a perfectly tuned instrument for established repertoire. The darker, more turbulent Seymour was a dramatic interpreter of new work, careering into a symbiotic though non-sexual relationship with the choreographer Kenneth MacMillan. Both dancers bristled with promise and beside them stood a third, Merle Park, two years older and Rhodesian by birth, who sought to embrace both classical and dramatic roles.

These were joyous auguries for the Royal Ballet, its first flush of renewal since entering the House. But no one knew better than Madam how long it took to make a world star, fifteen years in Fonteyn's case, and how many new blooms fell by the wayside. She glowered at the hyperbolic reviews and emphasized the need for relentless hard work. Beyond the patter of silk-shod feet, all she could hear was the ticking of Margot's chronological clock.

Webster played no part in the ballet's progress. His relations with Madam were cool and barely correct. Not one written word between them survives in the ROH archives, but a stray letter in a private collection illustrates graphically the degree to which Webster was excluded from ballet decisions but blamed for any mishaps. On tour in New York, Madam was dissatisfied with arrangements for *La fille mal gardée*. 'My dear David,' she snarled,

> I very much want an interview with you and Sol (Hurok) and will come either to your hotel or his office as soon as I hear that you can arrange it. What happened at the dress rehearsal of *La fille mal gardée* really cannot occur again – there is no Director alive that would accept that.

After a page of complaints about last-minute rehearsal changes, she launched into a series of scarcely-veiled personal threats:

> I am busy collecting a very clear picture of all the demands that are being made on my staff. If I find that anything as steep as some of the things that have already happened are likely to occur again, I promise you that I shall demand a proper hearing in their defence before I leave them. . .
>
> I tried to show you all last summer the way that you are working the Company as a whole. Before I left London, the surgeon in charge of our Company complained of overstrain. Over 200 treatments had to be given to 50 dancers during the rehearsal period. I told him that I knew I was over-taxing everyone and that I welcomed his comments.
>
> I realize that the above is irrelevant to the rest of this letter, but I mention it to show you that the *Fille* rehearsal was the straw that nearly broke the camel's back. The camel, though, was not the writer, but the spirit of the Royal Ballet as a whole.
>
> (signed) Ninette de Valois.[56]

Madam never let Webster venture so much as a suggestion about the Royal Ballet, and he feared her rare visits to his office as a secondhand car dealer fears the taxman. He remained friendly with Ashton, however, and held the purse-strings of both her troupes, after the Sadler's Wells Theatre Ballet was taken over by Covent Garden as its secondary touring company. This anomalous position exposed Webster to uncomfortable situations. At the end of a gruelling, financially successful US tour in 1964, Sibley, Seymour and Park approached him for a pay rise. 'Margot had danced the first nights,' said Sibley, 'but Lynn, Merle and I had carried the tour – we were the backbone of the company. We were very nervous about going to Webster, but I honestly believe he hadn't a clue who we were. This was the only time I ever spoke to him. Introducing us on television some time later, he couldn't even pronounce our names properly.'[57]

If the General Administrator's control of the ballet company was chimerical, his command of the opera company was now under challenge from his new chairman. Drogheda declared that Covent Garden would not be allowed to drift without a music director and that the Board, not Webster, would select and interview the conductors.

The premier candidates were Giulini and Kempe, both of whom were ruled out for knowing little beyond Italian or German opera. The next rank consisted of the Italian Nello Santi (who messed up a Sutherland *Traviata*), the Czech Jaroslav Krombholc, and the Hungarian refugee Georg Solti, who was coming to the end of a nine-year term at Frankfurt-am-Main. Solti was making a name for himself with a recording-in-progress of Wagner's *Ring* that was a marvel of early-stereo, with ear-tweaking stage effects and energized tempi. Harewood was sent to Germany to see him conduct Verdi's *Il forza del destino*. He reported favourably to Webster, who flew out and booked Solti for a December 1959 *Rosenkavalier*.

Solti's arrival at Covent Garden was hardly noticed by a press and public distracted by the return of Elisabeth Schwarzkopf, who had been absent for almost a decade. To first-nighters, her account of the Marschallin, a role she had recorded successfully and sung in sixteen productions, was a huge let-down. Andrew Porter in the *Financial Times* complained of 'artificiality', William Mann in *The Times* accused her of 'archness' and Peter Heyworth in the *Observer* ridiculed her 'toothpaste smile'. Her husband, Walter Legge, stormed into the next board meeting, demanding a motion of censure against British critics; he earned a note in the minutes stating that 'the present state of English music criticism is a national misfortune'.[58] Schwarzkopf never sang again at Covent Garden, and Legge left the Board soon after. Solti blamed Legge for wrecking his wife's performance by shouting instructions at her during every rehearsal.

His conducting was widely admired. Orchestral players told Thomas Armstrong, a member of the Board, that Solti made their fingers tingle. Drogheda was deeply moved and dismissed a counter-proposal to appoint John Pritchard as music director. He turned instead to his wife's piano teacher, a Hungarian called Ilona Kabos whom Solti had known from student days in Budapest. Kabos invited Solti to cocktails with Drogheda at her handsome home in St John's Wood. 'I was instantly attracted,' said Drogheda.[59] Solti, who spoke little English, never forgot the directness of Drogheda's greeting. 'I came into the room,' he recalled years later, 'and Garrett said: "We want you as our next music director, but we cannot pay you – we haven't any money. Oh, and you cannot say No."'

Solti, charmed and flattered, declined the offer, explaining that he did not want another opera post and was on his way to Los Angeles. 'Think it over,' said Drogheda. 'How long?' said Solti. 'Take as long as you like,' said the chairman, 'we haven't got anyone else.' The morning after his last *Rosenkavalier*, Solti flew to Los Angeles to meet his new orchestra and pay respects to the octogenarian Bruno Walter, who had been briefly considered for Covent Garden fifteen years before. Walter, to his surprise, now urged him in the strongest possible terms to take the London post. 'You have to do it,' said Walter, 'because if a generation falls out, after us, then the opera tradition won't be kept. This cannot happen. You must do it.'[60] Solti, unable a resist an appeal to his conscience, cabled his acceptance to Webster and proposed September 1961 as a starting date. Six months later, he discovered that the Los Angeles Philharmonic board had appointed a junior conductor, Zubin Mehta, without his approval. Solti tore up his Los Angeles contract and committed himself fully to Covent Garden. This was the last thing Webster wanted: an experienced, omniscient music director.

'Although I became a very great friend with David Webster later,' said Solti, 'originally he didn't want me. When Kubelik departed he felt, I'm good enough, I can do it alone. He had great sympathy towards me as a conductor, but he didn't need a music director. Cost too much money, whatever. It was basically a power complex: he didn't want to yield the power. Drogheda and the board forced David Webster to engage me, really forced him.'[61]

Sharing a car to Aldeburgh for the première of *A Midsummer Night's Dream* in June 1960, Webster did not speak a word to Solti throughout the three-hour journey. Solti volunteered to conduct the London première of Britten's new opera in a production by Webster's friend, John Gielgud. He knew how to make himself agreeable, and Webster was impressed by his musicianship. But the General Administrator was in torment. Although he had been knighted in the New Year's honours list, he felt unappreciated. Drogheda had curtailed his powers to hire and fire. De Valois was being more than usually difficult. And even on the American front which he had pioneered, Rudolf Bing at the Met bypassed him by dealing with his assistant, Tooley. Webster was fifty-seven and facing a critical career decision.

He called Arnold Goodman and asked if he could get him another job. Moments later, Goodman received a call from John Davis, chairman of Southern Television, where Webster was already on the board. Davis was looking for a new managing director. Would Webster do? said the lawyer. Delighted, said Davis. So was Webster, when Goodman passed on the offer.

Days later, Davis reported an obstacle. Was Goodman aware, he demanded, that Webster was homosexual? Not that it mattered to Davis personally, but his board would never accept a homosexual at the head of a television channel watched by women and children. The offer was summarily withdrawn. Webster lied about it to his lover, telling Jimmy that he had been unable to tear himself away from Covent Garden.[62] Whichever version was believed, he was now a life prisoner of the institution he had created.

CHAPTER 7

Act Two: Enter the Jew
(1961–70)

IT WAS CLEAR to many who were young at the time, clearer even than it would seem in retrospect, that the 60s ushered in an immense and irrevocable change in most fields of human relations. Sex, with the advent of the birth-control pill, was detached from marriage, forethought and the expectation of lasting romance. Love acquired new connotations with the decriminalization of homosexuality and the lowering of the age of consent. The price of error was reduced by legalized abortion; infants born to single mothers were relieved of the stigma of bastardy. Moral censorship eased after Penguin Books in 1960 successfully defended publishing a paperback edition of *Lady Chatterley's Lover*, overcoming the bewigged indignation of prosecuting counsel who asked the jury if they would wish their 'wives and servants' to read D. H. Lawrence's novel of cross-class couplings and Anglo-Saxon words. It went on to sell two million copies. According to the poet Philip Larkin, 'Sexual intercourse began/ in 1963,/between the "Chatterley" trial/ and the Beatles' first LP.'[1]

Yet, while the 60s are usually surveyed through smug shades of sex, soft drugs and pop songs, the loosening of stays was not the sole force of social transformation, nor the greatest. The tectonic plates of accepted conduct were shifting and relations between generations would never be the same again. Young people, scornful of elders who had acquiesced in two world wars and now contemplated a nuclear third, opted to live for today and forget about 'saving up to get married'. They left home to live alone, or informally with others. Where, in 1961, one in eight British homes was single-occupancy, by 1997 a quarter of all households consisted of one person living alone.[2] The nuclear family was consigned to the scrapheap.

Grandparents and invalid aunts were packed off to institutions, cast upon the mercies of an ever-expanding Welfare State.

Street-long communities were torn apart by high-rise architects, acting on behalf of manipulative local authorities who favoured the depersonalized tower blocks developed in Stalin's police state. The face of English urban life was being surgically restructured in fast-begrimed cement and concrete. The idea of 'community' was abolished and the word itself hijacked to imply a collectivity of interest, rather than a care for neighbours. In the momentum of demolition, a caste of property developers and asset strippers made themselves conspicuously rich. Also on the rise were new-age fashion and music entrepreneurs who pursued the spare cash in young people's pockets with an alternate vision of Arcadia. London, famed for its sober tailoring, became a Mecca of flowing peacock fabrics. Liverpool, noisiest of ports, gave birth to the Mersey Beat. Manchester, bristling with Victorian severity, nourished an ulterior media culture. The idea of England was being altered day by day.

Other western countries would be shaken by similar fissures, but the shock struck deepest in London because it was here that the 60s started to swing. Ever since the curtain rose on *Look Back in Anger*, Jimmy Porter's rage had served as rocket fuel for a resurgent English theatre, cinema and fiction. The kitchen-sink novels of John Braine, David Storey and Alan Sillitoe, swiftly filmed, vented a strikingly similar tone of pent-up frustrations. Within months of its première, the Osborne play was transmitted nationwide by Granada Television, the independent Manchester-based franchise. It scored a sixty-two per cent rating. Late in 1960, Granada brought forth two new strands of programming – a soap opera, *Coronation Street*, set in the kind of back-to-back terraces that were fast being torn down; and a current affairs weekly, *World in Action*, that tore into politics like a polecat with prey. The independent television trail-blazers – Granada, ATV, Thames – were owned by movie and music-hall impresarios of Russian-Jewish stock and manned by classless Oxbridge graduates who believed in the power of television to inform and democratize. *World in Action*'s first producer was a 28-year-old Glaswegian, Jeremy Isaacs. 'I joined Granada Television,' said Isaacs, 'because Sidney Bernstein wanted to use television cameras to reveal the democratic process to the people of this country. He televised the 1958 by-election at Rochdale when the

BBC were shit-scared of touching any electoral issue in case anything they said or did upset the parties.'[3]

At the BBC, in the autumn of 1960, a new director-general, the establishmentarian Hugh Carleton-Greene, began the process of converting a dowdy maiden aunt into a medium that reflected, and stimulated, swirling currents of public uncertainty. Social documentaries, sharper comedy and, in November 1962, the satirical lash of *That Was The Week That Was* informed the nation of its own state of flux. In November 1966, the critic Kenneth Tynan deliberately uttered the word 'fuck' on live BBC television and civilization was deemed to have come to an end. After the show, the American writer Mary McCarthy said, 'I suppose it's an historic moment.' She missed the point entirely. History was made matter-of-factly in the 60s, as one taboo tumbled after another.

In an Age of Ego, when gratification was instant and self-awareness the be-all and end-all, national ideals and enterprises were bound to take a back seat. The trick in any revolution is to stay in touch with public sentiment without succumbing to demotic pressure. The worst mistake is to turn one's back on the tide – which is what Covent Garden proceeded to do. The company was in the ascendant, but each triumph confirmed its fixity of purpose and ignored the fast-changing culture. The men who ran Covent Garden were middle-aged at a time when the world around them was young again.

Just how oblivious the company was to the risks of cultural drift is illustrated by its response to overtures from pace-setting Granada. Aware that the BBC were not screening much opera or ballet because of a never-ending fees dispute, an opera-loving Granada man, Denis Forman, suggested that the ROH and Granada should get round the problem by jointly engaging top artists to perform both on stage and in studio – thus bypassing the unions and ensuring the ROH a priceless stream of prime-time exposure. Summoned with his chairman, Sidney Bernstein, to explain the idea over lunch, Forman found himself in the Royal Box facing a formidable line-up of Drogheda, Webster, de Valois, Ashton and Professor Lionel Robbins. Their attitude could hardly have been more condescending:

They chattered endlessly about the scandals and credulities of the opera and ballet world, throwing in countless names and nicknames which meant nothing to Sidney or me. 'Have you heard who's going with Dukey for a snug week in Cannes?' one would say, and the rest would cry, 'No. Who? Who?' When the tease had run its time and the answer was given, 'Bim', they were all convulsed with laughter for several minutes. Sidney and I ate our food in isolation until coffee, when Garrett Drogheda said, 'Now, Sidney, tell us about your film idea.'

'Not film, said Sidney, 'television.' And he put me in to bat. It was clear that Webster had not read the paper and that no one else was even faintly interested . . . I was glad when Drogheda cut me short by saying, 'How interesting, but if it is about television we must of course ask the BBC first.'[4]

There were two whole seasons to run before Solti took over, and Webster made the most of his last chance to wield artistic authority. In 1959-60 he splashed out on a Zeffirelli double-bill of *Cavalleria Rusticana* and *I Pagliacci*, on Giulini conducting *The Barber of Seville*, and on a production of Verdi's *Macbeth* in which the role intended for Sutherland was taken by the cockney sparrow, Amy Shuard. Popular in the upper galleries, Shuard once swanned in to the refectory on a blistering hot day dressed in a fur coat. 'Ere, Amy,' shouted a stagehand, 'ain't yer hot in that fur?' Shuard quipped back in broadest Clerkenwell: 'Em as az furs, wears 'em.' The following year saw more of the same – a Giulini/Zeffirelli *Falstaff* with Geraint Evans in a heaven-sent role, Gielgud directing Britten's new opera, *A Midsummer Night's Dream*, and Serafin conducting *La Sonnambula* with Sutherland sleep-walking in place of the elusive Callas.

Webster was under continuous pressure from Drogheda and the Board to secure a seasonal commitment from the temperamental Greek, but Callas, torn between heart and art, was drifting in the slipstream of her shipowner lover, Onassis. London was not uppermost in her mind, and she was further troubled by clear signs of vocal decline. Walter Legge, her record producer, was powerless to make her return – but, before quitting the Board in mutual distrust, he did Covent Garden one good turn. It was Legge who urged Otto Klemperer, in his mid-seventies, to make a belated and momentous début at the Royal Opera House. Klemperer, a legend of pre-Hitler Berlin, had been retrieved from destitution by Legge and now towered over London's concert life as chief conductor of the Philharmonia Orchestra. Although maimed by brain surgery, manic-depressive episodes and such bizarre accidents as setting fire to himself in bed, he possessed so secure a sense of musical structure that players swore they could anticipate the ending of a symphony in the tempo he set for the opening bars. In Beethoven and Mahler he possessed unchallengeable authority. Even Herbert von Karajan, no respecter of colleagues, came to his Royal Festival Hall dressing room after an *Eroica* to say, 'I hope I shall live to conduct the Funeral March as well as you have done.'[5] In earlier classics he could seem exasperatingly slow, but musicians revered his fearless integrity, and feared his inflexible rigour, allied to a scathing wit.

Webster had first approached him in 1956 to conduct *Fidelio*, Beethoven's liberation opera, but Klemperer was unimpressed by the ROH production. Webster promised new sets, and Legge urged him to extend his concert-hall success to the higher-income opera house audience. Klemperer duly consented, on condition he could hand-pick the cast and direct them himself. In February 1960, Legge informed Webster that 'Dr Klemperer and I have just been discussing the necessary cast for the performances of *Fidelio*, which he will conduct at Covent Garden. What we (*sic*) have in mind is: Leonore = Jurinac; Florestan = Vickers; Rocco = (Gottlob) Frick; Marzelline = Lipp; Pizarro = Hotter; ... Minister (Eberhard) Waechter'[6] The only change to this stellar cast was the substitution of Elsie Morison for the unavailable Wilma Lipp. Webster sent Christopher West to act as assistant producer and allocated the infirm conductor a cupboard-sized changing room a few feet from the stage.

Klemperer found the conditions antiquated and dangerous -'I almost had to crawl on all fours to get into the orchestra pit,' he told his daughter, Lotte[7] – but he insisted on smoking his pipe and was, according to orchestral players, the only conductor ever allowed to puff in the pit.[8] They had trouble fathoming his downbeat and had to restart the overture several times before he was satisfied. He made an early gaffe by addressing the first horn, Tony Tunstall, as 'Mr Tuckwell', mistaking him for the famous principal of the London Symphony Orchestra, but the players were awestruck by his certitude and he rewarded the ones he liked best with interval cigarettes. They were, he said, 'no Philharmonia' but they tried hard.[9] Webster regularly came down to make sure he was content, and the singers proved accommodating, with the exception of Vickers who contested some of his tempi, though respectfully enough to avoid disruption.

Fidelio, seldom a crowd-puller, sold out within twenty-four hours. Klemperer was visibly nervous on the première night, 24 February 1961, and his spirits were not raised by an interval visit from Walter Legge who told him, '*Das Publikum ist noch ganz kalt* (the public is stone-cold).' But the woodwind chord that opens the second act emanated an irresistible tension, and the audience were gripped as if by a John Buchan thriller. At the final curtain, Webster presented Klemperer with a huge bouquet and a hand-written card that he treasured ever after. It read: 'You have conquered Covent Garden.'

Webster lost no time in booking Klemperer for *Magic Flute* the following winter with an all-British cast: Joan Carlyle as Pamina, Sutherland as Queen of the Night, Richard Lewis as Tamino, Geraint Evans as Papageno. Klemperer and West were to direct again, and Drogheda proposed Oskar Kokoschka as designer. Klemperer agreed to see the Austrian *émigré* artist in his Zurich apartment, greeting him with the cordial remark that he would have preferred sets by Picasso. Kokoschka, no less sweetly, said that he had only wanted to design the *Flute* for Furtwängler – 'and he, alas, died.' Lotte Klemperer hovered within earshot, fearing violence, but the two men had a hearty chuckle and parted firm friends and non-partners.[10] The ROH *Magic Flute* was ultimately designed by Georg Eisler, son of the socialist composer.

Rehearsals were marred by Sutherland's late arrival and grudging attitude. When the dress rehearsal overran, she returned for the finale in street clothes. Klemperer stopped her in mid-aria and asked her to follow his tempo. Bonynge, in the stalls, yelled out: 'Don't take any notice of him, Joanie. He's mad!'[11] Klemperer, whose hearing was starting to fail, apparently missed the remark. On opening night he held his beat and left Sutherland to flounder. In her memoirs, almost forty years later, she complained that his rhythm was irregular and she was advised by the orchestra leader, Charles Taylor: 'Don't watch him, Joan dear. You just go, and we'll be with you.'[12] Geraint Evans, of the same production, recalled: 'Klemperer had a fantastic sense of tempo. Sometimes it might seem to be slow, but it would always be all of a piece with the performance as he phrased it. Nor did he vary from one performance to another as some conductors do. I once asked a repetiteur to time my arias with a stopwatch at three successive Klemperer performances, and all three were exactly the same, an incredible consistency.'[13]

Sutherland left after three nights, but not before the *Flute* had been so slammed in the press that Legge, a stranger to loyalty, pondered transferring his *Fidelio* recording, which was due directly afterwards, to Karajan in Berlin. He need not have feared. In the subterranean studio at Kingsway Hall, Klemperer was unassailable and the recording was one of the greatest opera sets ever made.

His third legacy to Covent Garden was *Lohengrin* in 1963, with a German producer, Josef Gielen, recommended by Solti ('never listen to a colleague,' he told his daughter) and Régine Crespin awkwardly cast as Elsa. Despite ugly sets and variable singing, one critic hailed it as the greatest Wagner experience since the war[14] and Martin Cooper extolled 'a quite extraordinary splendour of tone and fineness of detail'.[15] Klemperer returned once more to Covent Garden, in March 1969 at the age of eighty-three, to preside over a *Fidelio* revival, six performances that sealed his mighty career in the opera house. Although his involvement was limited and late, he bestowed on Covent Garden a sense of confidence and continuity, linking it by his physical presence and moral authority to a chain of tradition that stretched back to his mentor, Gustav Mahler.

He grumbled mildly of a certain 'dilettantism'[16] which meant that everything had to stop for tea and everyone disappeared to the country for weekends, no matter what state the production was in. But he admired the company's spirit and he left behind a lasting imprint. He was, said Reggie Goodall, his repetiteur, 'a supreme musician – I had nothing but respect and devotion for him.'[17] Those who played and sang for Klemperer could never get his organic beat out of their system.

The Royal Ballet were dancing in Russia in June 1961, another of Madam's dreams come true, when news broke that would change its destiny. Appearing at the Kirov and the Bolshoi was an affirmation of Ninette de Valois's place in the Diaghilev line; she rejoiced in restoring to Russia a chunk of forsaken heritage. She was also keen for her dancers to absorb authentic Russian traditions of the kind they had gaped at when the Bolshoi danced in London.

Three days after opening in Leningrad, one of the ballerinas, Georgina Parkinson, managed to get through by phone to her husband in London. He told her that a young soloist had broken free from the Kirov Ballet at Le Bourget airport in Paris and requested political asylum. At the height of the Cold War, weeks before the Berlin Wall went up, the defection made the world's front-pages.

Nothing was reported in Russia for days until the Central Committee of the Communist Party had discussed the affair and issued a statement averring that Rudolf Hametovich Nureyev, aged twenty-three, had betrayed his motherland and run off with a Frenchwoman. The Kremlin sent a sharp note to the Elysée Palace warning that cultural exchanges between the two countries would be terminated if Nureyev was ever allowed to appear with a French state ensemble. The rest of the Kirov company flew on to London to make an acclaimed début at Covent Garden. Of the male lead, Yuri Soloviev, Andrew Porter reported that 'we have seen no one quite like him'.[18] Nureyev was not the best, nor the best known, dancer in the Kirov. Soviet ballet would survive without him.

Whether Nureyev would survive in the West was less certain. Trailed by photographers and KGB spies, he took work with the eccentric Marquis de Cuevas's travelling troupe, partnering the American ballerina, Rosella Hightower. That summer, he had a brief affair with her compatriot Maria Tallchief, before falling for the austere Danish dancer, Erik Bruhn, who became his lifelong lover. In Copenhagen he also found a teacher he could trust, the Russian emigrée Vera Volkova, who once taught Margot Fonteyn. But Nureyev was acutely homesick for his family and desperately needed to strike roots. Back in the USSR, he was put on trial *in absentia* for treason and his family were placed under surveillance. The sentence was seven years imprisonment and the secret services would be ordered to bring him back, by kidnap if necessary. Nureyev was frightened, insecure and forlorn.

Then, in October, there was a call for him one night at Volkova's flat. Would he dance with Margot Fonteyn in a charity gala at the Theatre Royal, Drury Lane? Galina Ulanova had dropped out under Kremlin pressure and Colette Clark, Kenneth's daughter, had persuaded Fonteyn that their best bet was the recent Kirov defector.

'He says he wants to dance with you,' Clark told Fonteyn.

'I've never set eyes on him,' said Fonteyn. 'Ask Vera if he's a good dancer.'

'Vera says he's adamant about dancing with you,' reported Clark, phoning back and forth to Copenhagen, 'and he's marvellous.'

'He sounds rather tiresome to me,' sighed Margot.[19]

Nureyev demanded to dance *Spectre of the Rose* with Fonteyn, but she had already assigned the duet to John Gilpin, and the Russian had to settle for a *Swan Lake pas de deux* with Rosella Hightower.

He insisted, however, that Ashton must choreograph a solo for him. Flying in to finalize arrangements, he took a taxi from Heathrow and turned up at the Panamanian Embassy, where Fonteyn and Arias had been reinstated after the comic coup. She ordered tea, five sugars for Rudolf, and took his measure between sips. 'I like him nine-tenths,' she told Colette Clark, 'but once or twice I saw a steely look in his eye.'[20] Before returning to Denmark, Nureyev attended class with Fonteyn under a false Polish name. 'You're that Russian fellow, aren't you?' demanded David Blair, who had just succeeded Michael Somes as Fonteyn's company partner. Nureyev stared him down, maintaining his fake identity. Blair never stood a chance.

The afternoon gala, a fundraiser for the Royal Academy of Dancing, was a sensational success. 'He's better than Nijinsky,' gasped the dowager Lady Diana Cooper, to her neighbour, Cecil Beaton. 'This boy,' noted Beaton, 'a peasant til he was seventeen when he won a scholarship to be trained as a dancer – looks like all the young Beatniks of today. Genius is not too strong a word to describe his quality and talent.'[21] The next morning, Ninette de Valois called Fonteyn to tell her she had engaged Nureyev for *Giselle*. 'Do you want to do it with him?' she demanded.

'Oh my goodness,' said Fonteyn, 'I think it would be like mutton dancing with lamb. Don't you think I'm too old?'[22] She was nineteen years his senior, and looked it. But after consulting her husband, Fonteyn decided that Nureyev was going to be the hottest thing in ballet and she had no choice: either dance with him, or get out. She called Madam and accepted the role. Nureyev's fee was £500 for three performances; Fonteyn was paid £400 a night. They were in no sense equals, not yet and perhaps never.

Nureyev had one reservation. Fearing a kidnap bid, he dared not stay in a hotel. Could he lodge with Fonteyn at the Embassy? She was unsure, more for reasons of state security than sexual risk. In the event, he proved the perfect house-guest, enduring a diet of English cold meats in polite silence. From their first rehearsal, though, Nureyev asserted his natural authority. 'Most of the men say "I will do it your way, how does it go?"' wrote Fonteyn. 'Rudolf, however, said, "Don't you think this way better?"'[23] No Englishman had ever handled her with such arrogant aplomb. Giselle, a role she had never fully possessed, suddenly became hers.

At Nureyev's ROH début, on 21 February 1962, there were twenty-three curtain calls. As the ovations swelled, Fonteyn plucked a rose from her bouquet and handed it to Nureyev, who dropped on one knee and lavished her hand with kisses. At that precise moment, the legend was born, stopping ballet history in its tracks and changing the course of English culture. 'If one person can come in and spoil the Royal Ballet style,' said Ninette de Valois, 'we deserve for it to be spoiled.'[24] The dream that British ballet, like British opera, could be nurtured entirely from kith-and-kin resources died that night. For the Royal Ballet to hold its own on the world stage, it would have to shed national pride and engage with the best. Nureyev was a revelation; he was also the start of a policy reversal. Soon to follow on the Covent Garden stage were his lover, Erik Bruhn, and Bruhn's Bulgarian-born ex-fiancée, Sonia Arova.

'I'm afraid I will ruin your *Swan Lake*,' Nureyev warned Fonteyn after seeing her dance with Blair. 'Just you try,' she replied.[25] There was give and take, grit and grace, in their relationship. She could defuse his tantrums with a shaft of wit, shattering the surge of violence on a surface of toughened glass. The impermeable Fonteyn became his cornerstone, and London his second home. As the French Government caved in to Soviet threats, cancelling his dates at the Paris Opéra, Nureyev accepted the title of Permanent Guest Artist at Covent Garden.

Through Nadia Nerina's husband, the businessman Charles Gordon, he found himself an agent in Sandor Gorlinsky, who managed Maria Callas and fixed him up with a tax shelter in Luxembourg. Nureyev gave little further thought to money. It was 1969 before he achieved fee parity with Fonteyn, at two thousand dollars a night. The impresario Victor Hochhauser, who managed his later tours, said: 'Rudolf was a gentleman. He was not cheap, but once we shook hands on a fee that was it – he never mentioned money again.'[26] Nureyev seldom bothered to collect his pay at Covent Garden. He sent tradesmen to John Tooley, who paid what they were owed and deducted it from Nureyev's fees. At one stage, Tooley was paying off a doctor, an anaesthetist, a firm of dry-cleaners, an irate landlord (for 'dilapidation') and a clutch of parking tickets.[27]

Nureyev was a free spirit, a roaming Tatar of Muslim and Mongol blood. He did not want to be tied down by worldly cares. 'I am twenty-four,' he declared in a precocious 1962 autobiography. 'I don't want to be told where my proper future lies, what is the "right" way to develop. I shall try to find this out for myself. That is what I mean by freedom.'[28]

For Madam, he brought a deeper form of liberation, releasing her from constant frets. Anxious about the effortless superiority of Russian ballet and the high-octane energy of American upstarts, she knew that her male dancers lacked training, technique and hunger for success. With Nureyev's arrival, her troubles were over. 'Until Rudi came along,' said one young company male, 'all a man had to do to get into the Royal Ballet was, more or less, turn up and show willing. Nureyev completely changed the pace. Where our chaps did little more than daintily hold a ballerina in the air, Rudi was macho man. He engaged with female dancers, manhandled them, threw them around. It was exciting, virile. He had worked with Russia's best and possessed a phenomenal memory. He could show you anything they did, and you could then try it yourself.'[29] Christopher Gable, Anthony Dowell, Nicholas Johnson, David Wall and others emerging from the Royal Ballet school were quick to pick up tips. 'The standard of virtuosity rose, literally, by leaps and bounds,'[30] said Fonteyn.

Nureyev, the least monogamous of men, danced with other leading ladies, notably Sibley, Beriosova, Anya Linden and Seymour, who called him 'a completely honest dancer – he won't cheat or take a cheap way out.'[31] The tension that preceded each performance, changing his shoes obsessively amid a torrent of curses until the moment came to go on stage, generated a magnetism that outshone his female, politely-English partners. 'The age of the ballerina is over,'[32] sighed Fonteyn, who alone could hold her own.

For Madam, he could do no wrong. At rehearsal he would sit on the floor, his head resting on her knee. No one could remember such *lèse-majesté*. 'If Rudolf asked for the lights to be changed, the lights would be changed,' said Sibley. 'It didn't matter that we'd all been asking, or that Michael (Somes) or the top people had all been asking for years. The moment Rudolf said it, it was done – he had that effect on Madam.'[33]

She urged him to contribute choreography, starting with a ten-minute *Corsaire* that was applauded for fully twice as long as its duration, and followed by a glittering *Bayadère*. Ashton, initially wary of competition, grew fascinated by the rippling eroticism of Nureyev and Fonteyn. In March 1963 he showcased them as *Marguerite and Armand* to the same Alexandre Dumas plot as Verdi's *La traviata*, with Somes, Fonteyn's former partner, cast incestuously as the heroine's brooding father. It was, wrote Richard

Buckle, 'romanticism to the nth degree, a Puccini opera in miniature, with music by Liszt . . . and it was only ever danced by the artists for whom it was created'.[34] Some critics condemned the ballet as 'a specimen of the personality cult', and according to Nerina 'it couldn't have been more kitsch'.[35] But it was exactly what the golden couple needed, and at just the right time.

Five weeks later they took the ballet to America, where saturation coverage and screaming crowds ushered them into a howl of fame. John Martin, ex-critic of the New York *Times*, warned that Nureyev's 'gigolo' antics would destroy Fonteyn and the Royal Ballet, but among those begging for tickets were Greta Garbo, Princess Grace of Monaco and Mrs Jacqueline Kennedy, who invited the pair (with Ashton) back to tea at the White House, where Rudolf sat in the President's chair. Madam beamed, knowing that her company had outshone the whole of American ballet and would be a fixture at the Met for so long as Fonteyn and Nureyev drew breath. Nureyev, increasingly mercurial, managed to get arrested for loitering in the streets of Toronto at three o'clock in the morning and made headlines once again. Balanchine warned Cecil Beaton that 'he is too selfish, and a dancer cannot afford to be selfish. Nureyev will end up badly, you'll see. He'll be like Pavlova.'[36] A stench of sour grapes trailed in his wake, along with a whiff of danger.

Fonteyn, said the lonely Nureyev, was the only person who truly understood him. She owed him her second life, as he owed her his second home. What the public witnessed on stage was a menopausal woman turning back the clock in lubricious encounters with a dark stranger half her age. He was her elixir of youth, and she his giver of purpose.

Their sexuality could hardly have been more explicit. Whether or not they were lovers in real life was hotly speculated in gossip columns and around fashionable dinner-tables without a shred of concrete evidence. The issue would be of no pressing interest to cultural historians had not their ardent physicality completely changed the course of the Royal Ballet's policy and identity. Fonteyn was coyly ambiguous when writing about the affair in her memoirs. 'As I was obviously very fond of Rudolf and spent so much time with him,' she wrote, 'it was food for scandal for those who liked it that way. I decided there was little I could do but wait for it to pass. The truth will out eventually, I thought.'[37]

'She must have had an affair with him,' said Nerina, 'because it showed on stage.'[38] Others, including Nureyev's secretary Joan Thring, were equally convinced that sex was 'out of the question . . . there was never any sign of anything like that.'[39] Nureyev preferred boys and had a prodigious appetite for casual sex. He was also headily in love with Bruhn. Fonteyn was fastidious, private and puritanical. On paper, they seem ill-matched, but the heart and loins are seldom ruled by logic.

'She was very sexy,' recalled Nicholas Johnson. 'I was the same age as Rudi, and I could have fancied her. In class and rehearsal, you can usually tell if two dancers have had sex from the way they treat each other. Rudi was very brutal to Margot, abused her terribly and called her all sorts of names. We all assumed they were lovers, or had been.'[40]

'In America,' said Laura Connor who toured with them in the late 1960s, 'they were never apart. He clung to her. She was his protection – he was very scared the KGB would come and get him. Margot was every inch a lady. Rudolf was a peasant. He did everything with his hands, ate with his hands, even wiped his bottom without paper. There are no physical secrets among dancers, and most of us believed that they slept together.'[41]

Nureyev himself told friends they had been lovers, but his accounts were contradictory and unreliable. The full facts of the affair, if ever there was one, may never come to light. They are, in any event, less interesting than the illusion they created on stage and the almost symbiotic intimacy they enjoyed in private. Fonteyn and Nureyev were probably as close as two human beings can get. They drew closer still after June 1964 when Fonteyn's husband, Tito Arias, was shot five times in his car while waiting at traffic lights in Panama City. Fonteyn and Nureyev had been dancing that night in Bath, where the violinist Yehudin Menuhin ran a music festival, and were returning from dinner when Diana Menuhin, a former dancer, broke the news as gently as she could. Fonteyn screamed, and ran through the hotel to an empty ballroom, where Nureyev found her and took her in his arms. Tito had been rushed to hospital but was expected to live. The would-be assassin was a political ally, Alfredo Jimenez, and press reports assumed that the attack had been politically motivated. It emerged years later that Tito, a wanton marriage-breaker, had seduced the wife of Jimenez, who shot him in a fit of sexual jealousy. Fonteyn, keeping up appearances as ever, told British diplomats that the attack was 'a put-up job' by 'three or four' conspirators whom she refused to name.[42] It is a mark of her national importance that these comments were promptly encoded and wired home to the Foreign Secretary.

Having ascertained that her husband was out of danger, Fonteyn decided to stay and dance, with Nureyev, a new *pas de deux* by Kenneth MacMillan that they were due to tour in Australia. The première of *Divertimento* was so intensely acclaimed that they danced the whole piece twice. The following day, Fonteyn flew to Panama to extricate her paralysed husband from a primitive hospital and transport him to the spinal injuries unit at Stoke Mandeville, back home. That summer Tito suffered a further collapse and almost died, losing his power of speech. His medical bills were crippling, and his children looked to Fonteyn to pay for their weddings. She had no alternative but to carry on dancing. Whenever possible, she took Tito along, feeding him solicitously, spoon by spoon. She lost none of her good humour or manners, but a steely look entered her eye and there was no more talk of retirement. She could not afford to give up, and would end up dancing longer than any ballerina in history, a career span of almost fifty years.

Her relentless, almost superhuman determination proved a mixed blessing for Covent Garden. Delighted as friends were that Margot had coped so well with tragedy, fears were voiced for the next line of soloists whose chances she was unwittingly blighting. Nerina, whom Buckle thought 'had three times Fonteyn's strength and technique'[43] saw the writing on the wall and retired in 1966, aged thirty-eight. Anya Linden, who married the supermarket heir John Sainsbury, quit a year earlier at thirty-two. Beriosova danced on langorously without ever claiming the fame she deserved. Sibley, Merle Park and Seymour would suffer collateral damage. 'I think all those three girls – Merle and Lynn and Antoinette – one day hoped to take over the company,' said Kenneth MacMillan. 'But the charisma of Fonteyn by then was so huge that it wasn't possible at that moment. And it was a shame, because it was the right moment when those girls could have zoomed up. A whole stream of dancers was eclipsed, and I don't only feel it about those three. I feel it about Svetlana Beriosova, also Nadia Nerina. But I don't know if that was anybody's fault, or if it just happened.'[44]

It was not Fonteyn's fault, said James Monahan, Park's husband, 'because it was up to the management, not to her, to see that opportunities were given to the young; and managements are – must be – inclined to favour the sure box-office success over the doubtful returns on a probationer. Yet the fact is that very fine dancers – Beriosova and Nerina among others – languished in the Fonteyn shadow and that . . . progress to the top of the Royal Ballet became discouragingly slow.'[45]

The blame for this sclerosis must be apportioned between Nureyev, for keeping Fonteyn ageless, and Ninette de Valois for cherishing Nureyev as her heaven-sent salvation and solution to all woes. Her admiring biographer explains this as 'the policy of an inspired general taking a calculated risk to improve a position'.[46] In fact, Madam was ready to give up the moment she saw her company was safe with Ashton at the helm and Fonteyn and Nureyev on stage for the forseeable future. She was almost sixty-five and longed to spend more time with her long-suffering husband of whom, by all accounts, she was touchingly fond. There were also physical causes. Her arthritis was getting worse and she was prone to migraine attacks that did nothing to soften her severe demeanour. On her last trip to America she told Drogheda that she was coming home by boat, since 'that jet migraine lasted thirty hours and I can't face another'.[47] Sibley recalls being invited with Somes for drinks at her riverside house in Barnes, only to be told they had come on the wrong day.

'What are you doing ringing my bell?' shouted Madam in her dressing-gown from an upstairs window. 'Well, since you're here, I suppose you had better come up.' They followed her to the bedroom and sat on the counterpane. Before she could even pour them a drink she had blown up at Somes, who cowered mutely beneath the storm. Suddenly, she stopped shrieking and said, 'thank you, dears, I feel much better now, the migraine has completely gone'.[48]

Three days after the première of *Marguerite and Armand*, Ninette de Valois announced her retirement, effective that summer. Her departure had been negotiated for nearly a year while Ashton, her designated successor, begged her to stay on a few extra months to allow him to remount *Romeo and Juliet* before having to shoulder the burdens of office.[49] The *Romeo* revival was the first casualty of his regime. Hearing that MacMillan had advanced on a staging of the same story, Ashton gave way with apparent good grace before starting to grumble about the chores of leadership. Madam, knowing his frailties, had installed three of her most trusted lieutenants in supporting roles. John Field, who had joined the Sadler's Wells

Ballet in 1939, was to run the touring company; John Hart, who had preceded him by a year, was put in charge of the rehearsal roster; Michael Somes became chief repetiteur. Madam insisted there should be no public farewell from the stage of the Royal Opera House and slipped away silently to look after her school, convinced that her legacy to the nation was in safe hands.

What could not be forseen was that Ninette de Valois would live past the end of the century, watching over her creation and charging into its affairs whenever things went wrong – as soon they would.

Georg Solti entered the Royal Opera House like a cyclone, a whirr of cosmic energy that brooked no resistance. 'In the German theatre where he had been working, the Generalmusikdirektor was emperor, his word unquestioningly obeyed,' said Bernard Keefe, a young conductor who had taken over Harewood's role as opera co-ordinator. 'Solti didn't find the efficiency he expected. It took him a long time to get used to the English way of doing things, where instead of giving orders you say, "don't you think it might be an idea. . . ?"'[50]

He raged against cramped rehearsal space, crowded rehearsal schedules, a phlegmatic chorus master and the absence of what he regarded as basic professional standards. 'You tell Sir Webster that this is what I want,' he would instruct the go-between Keefe.

'Hmm, I'd better think about that,' was Webster's murmured reply.

'I wanted discipline, precision; I was not used to people telling me, No,' recalled Solti. 'An opera house is like a military operation. You don't tell the general it can't be done.'[51]

He told the Board in his very first presentation that they would have to restructure the opera company, turning it from a repertory group that revived popular operas fifteen times a year with random cast changes to something resembling the Italian *stagione* system, where operas were produced with the same well-rehearsed cast and conductor for a run of six or seven performances. Webster demurred, saying Covent Garden could not afford a lot of new productions and complete restagings of old ones. Four new shows a year was the most the budget could manage. Nonsense, said Solti, and opened with ten.

There was not enough Mozart and Strauss being done, he complained. Many of the conductors were inadequate and he was not going to waste his time performing operas in English when there were not enough first-class native singers to cover all the roles. 'My God, it looks like Nibelheim!' he exclaimed on seeing the backstage offices. He told his first press conference that he intended to make Covent Garden the best opera house in the world, a dangerous boast. 'I thought there was no one there who knew anything at all about how to run an opera house,' he later said.

His high-handedness gave instant offence. William Bundy, the self-important technical director, rushed into Webster's office in high dudgeon after being ordered about his business by the hard-driving music director. 'Bill,' said Webster, 'if you're going to offer me your resignation, I have to tell you I'll accept it.' Morris Smith, the orchestral director and Webster's confidant, was outraged by Solti's demand that he should admit a few women to the orchestra. John Lanigan, the Australian tenor, christened him 'the Screaming Skull', an epithet that found its way into the satirical magazine *Private Eye*. 'He came along and made out as if we were some hick outfit,' said the conductor Edward Downes, who profited under Solti's leadership. 'But he inherited a company that was on a high, after all the hard work of Rankl, Kleiber and Kubelik. Solti just got lucky.'[52]

Internal dissension trickled out to the press room, where critics were prepared to hold Solti to his promise of world dominance. Almost inevitably, the first two seasons were an overwhelming let-down. Solti opened in September 1961 with Gluck's *Iphigénie en Tauride*, never much of a sensation, followed by a sepulchral *Don Giovanni* that was undermined by Solti's clashes with the languid director, Zeffirelli. A visionary triple-bill of Puccini's *Gianni Schicchi*, Ravel's *L'heure espagnole* and Arnold Schoenberg's scarily modernist *Erwartung* closed the season. The choice of director was inspired, but the brilliantly witty Peter Ustinov seemed to run out of ideas before the evening was over. There was polite criticism of Solti's hard-driven tempi, especially in Mozart.

A resplendent *Siegfried* launched his second season, directed by the estimable Hans Hotter and featuring Wolfgang Windgassen and Birgit Nilsson in the central roles. Solti's *Ring* recording was appearing to much acclaim, and few found fault with his Wagner nights, which continued with a *Walküre* revival. Three weeks into the season, however, Solti suffered a fiasco with Verdi's *Forza del Destino* in which the Hollywood producer Sam Wanamaker projected Goya paintings dimly and irrelevantly on to a screen above the stage and Solti's hand-picked soprano proved wholly inaudible. Outbursts of booing broke out in the main auditorium, untypically for an English audience. Solti's car was defaced and rotten vegetables were thrown as he drove away. The assaults were boisterous rather than life-threatening, but the music director did not see them that way.

A victim of institutionalized anti-Semitism in his native Hungary and then a Hitler refugee in gelid Switzerland, Solti was hyper-naturally sensitive to any hint of hostility from crowds or the organs of power. Accustomed to supportive reviews from a non-combative German press, he misconstrued the more robust notices of English critics as being personally or racially motivated. In Solti's mind there formed the spectre of an anti-Solti campaign driven by demagogic editors, disgruntled opera-goers and mutinous staff which was capable of inflicting, if not physical damage to his person, then lasting damage to his hard-earned career. Solti, to the end of his long and happy life, wore the fragility of a refugee touchingly on his sleeve.

He told his record producer, John Culshaw, that he did not know how long he would last at Covent Garden. Drogheda began urging Webster to renew his contract, which had to be negotiated two years in advance. Both sides were under pressure. Covent Garden could not afford to lose Solti after a single term without getting blighted as a company that could not keep a music director. Solti, for his part, saw London as his springboard to the English-speaking world. He did not want to leave defeated, but the noises in his inner ear could not be ignored.

England in the early 60s was gripped by racial tensions. With demand for cheap labour rising in the nationalized industries, particularly the National Health Service and transport systems, large numbers of immigrants had been arriving from Caribbean, African and Asian dominions. Averaging fifty thousand a year for a decade, the tide swelled to 136,400 in 1961 and 95,000 in the first half of 1962.[53] At the start of the decade, the Prime Minister's principal private secretary had written in his diary: 'The country is in a bad way. It is difficult to see how our economic ills can be cured and at the moment nothing that is done seems to be more than a short-term palliative. The remedy for fifty million people living in an island which can maintain thirty million and no longer leads the world in industrial exports or capital assets invested abroad is hard to find.'[54]

Racial violence erupted on the streets of Notting Hill. Oswald Mosley's pre-war Fascists reconvened as the British National Party and staged menacing rallies in Trafalgar Square. Jews, too, were made to feel uneasy. There was much adverse coverage of property barons and 'asset-strippers' like Charles Clore and Jack Cotton, who bought up small businesses and sold them off after exploiting their untapped value. The financier Freddy Greenwood achieved national notoriety when he borrowed funds from his own building society, fled to Israel and was brought back to face a jail sentence. Jews were in the news, and not in a favourable light.

Solti, looking around the Royal Opera House, saw one Jewish face – Isaiah Berlin – on the Board and none in senior management. Other races were conspicuously absent; the attitude was antediluvian. When the Royal Ballet toured South Africa in 1959, it deliberately omitted a South African-born company member, Johaan Mosaval. Angry fellow-dancers visited Mosaval's mother and invited her to a show they gave for a non-white audience in Cape Town City Hall. The company's policy, however, was to play along with apartheid, ignoring the riots that blew up in Sharpeville during the tour and the seminal 'winds of change' speech by their own Prime Minister which effectively ended South Africa's Commonwealth membership. So keen were the Royal Ballet to appease the apartheid regime that they asked Svetlana Beriosova to leave behind her husband, the Harley Street psychiatrist Mohammed Masud Khan on the grounds that he 'might be an unwelcome guest'.[55] Questions were asked in the House of Commons. The Opposition Leader, Hugh Gaitskell, declared that 'the introduction of racial discrimination into art and sport is repugnant to all of us' and demanded to know why it should be tolerated in a company subsidized by the Arts Council. Butler replied that this was an internal matter for the Royal Ballet; neither Government nor Arts Council had been consulted.[56] The ROH, for its part, made no apology.

Solti had no reason to be aware of this backdrop, but he felt the prejudice intuitively and experienced discomfort from both chorus and orchestra members. 'They called me a Prussian – me, a Hungarian Jew,' he exclaimed.[57] He was angry at the Home Office for putting him down as 'Georg', Germanizing his Hungarian forename, György. In contact with the press, he felt like a hound at bay. 'Solti believed the British press were against him,' said Sheila Porter. 'He was very upset by one William Mann review (in *The*

Times) and felt there was an anti-Semitic tinge to much of what was written. I heard this from his personal assistant, Enid Blech, who was also Jewish. The way Solti put it was, "They don't like me because I'm Jewish." I tried to tell him they didn't like him not because he was Jewish but because he was foreign.'[58]

When Webster and Drogheda sat him down to contract talks in December 1962 Solti 'opened by saying that after careful thought and consideration with his wife he had decided that he did not wish to continue after the (initial) three-year term.'[59] He had a lengthy list of grievances. The orchestra was beyond improvement so long as it had to play trash for ballets like *La fille mal gardée*. He needed a bigger ensemble and better players. The chorus master had to go: Robinson was 'indolent' and knew neither German nor Italian. He could not understand why both a stage director and a technical director were needed when neither Bundy nor Sullivan possessed a spark of imagination. As for himself,

> his presence as Musical Director at Covent Garden was adding little to his stature. He felt unhappy about the attitude of the press . . . and felt that far too little was being done to counter this attitude and to build up his personal position . . . He had nothing to live by but his name . . . He had a duty to himself as well as to Covent Garden . . . G.S. then spoke of Andrew Porter's *Walküre* notice which had, in one respect, compared Solti adversely with Goodall. He could not understand how I, as Chairman of Covent Garden, could tolerate such a thing in the paper with which I was identified. I said that I had complained of what was written, but that I was in a particularly difficult position.

Extraordinarily, after such frank exchanges, Drogheda won him over and the conversation ended with Solti agreeing to a three-year renewal. In a codicil to his new contract, it was agreed that the orchestra would be expanded to one hundred and forty-five players. Solti, in his own hand, inserted that the chorus master must be replaced, and that the chief press officer, Bill Beresford, would either be sacked or removed from handling the opera company. Neither of these conditions was fulfilled and Solti seems to have forgotten about them once his sense of well-being began to improve.

It was not, however, the end of the state of siege that persisted with the national press. Drogheda rang the press office insistently to demand that pressure be brought to bear on adversarial critics, particularly upon Andrew Porter. 'You're a friend of his,' he told Beresford. 'You must lean on him not to write so harshly about us.'

'If I did that,' said Beresford, 'the press would lose confidence in me. You'd better speak to Sheila.'

'Why does your brother write such wretched things about us?' stormed Drogheda at the assistant press officer.

'Why does your music critic write such wretched things?' she coolly replied.

Drogheda flailed about, reluctant to confront his cherished critic. He ordered Webster to look into the efficiency of the press office, and got more than he bargained for. 'I think we should replace the woman,' said Webster.[60] Drogheda panicked: 'Please don't dispense with Miss Porter without ref'ce to me. Andrew's reaction will be very bad.'[61] A more considered note followed the next day:

> It is not simply a question of Andrew's reaction, which will surely be very violent because he and his sister are twins, but I am sure hostility and a sense of victimization will be stirred up amongst all the critics.
>
> It was probably a mistake in the first instance to take the sister of one of the leading critics on to the staff, but having done so I really think one must be more careful about laying her off.[62]

Webster, for his part, grew less concerned about press reaction the more frantic Drogheda and Solti became. When Solti approached him with a sniffy newspaper report of one of his press conferences, Webster told Tooley to send it to the lawyers, Rubinstein Nash, with a view to issuing libel proceedings.[63] Solti, delighted that someone was taking his pain seriously, let the matter drop. He warmed to Webster, who plied him with well-chosen compliments. Solti, turning fifty while guest-conducting at the Met, received a cable from his General Administrator: 'I have heard with a shock that you are daring to celebrate your extreme youth today stop nevertheless I send you affectionate greetings David.'

Solti replied:'I your youthful Music Director wish to thank you for your greetings on the occasion. They were very much appreciated.'[64]

The fondness between them grew to the point that when word arrived of his sister's death in Hungary, it was to Webster of all people that Solti turned for words of consolation.[65] Their intimacy was the more remarkable for the fact that Solti was unsympathetic to homosexuals and Webster had little time for Jews. Both knew that it was in their interest to get along, but each sensed the other's outsiderness and responded intuitively to a fellow-outcast.

The only person to leave Covent Garden at Solti's direct insistence was Bernard Keefe who, after 'a very awkward year',[66] slipped away to pursue a conducting career. 'Personal assistant: Ingpen oder andere *not* Keefe,' wrote Solti in a bilingual memo to himself.[67] He asked his own agent to become Head of Opera Planning. 'Solti got hold of me and said, you've got to come, you cannot say No,' remembered Joan Ingpen. 'So I went to see David Webster and said, I can think of all sorts of reasons why you would not want me. First, I'm an agent. Second, I'm a woman.

'David said: "Think it over, my dear, before you sell your business. Then I'll put it to the Directors. I should tell you, though, that when Solti goes, I'll defend you as best I can, but you appreciate that this job is linked to the music director's." '[68]

A self-made woman in her mid-forties, Ingpen had co-founded the Philharmonia with Walter Legge and managed the London Mozart Players before founding her own agency. She breezed into Covent Garden to find 'everything was so behindhand, they hadn't even completed the casting for the following season'. She introduced five-year planning, a Stalinist device that she later transported to the Paris Opéra and the Met, making it the industry norm.

Rival agents bridled at her elevation and two of them, Lise Askonas and John Coast, protested furiously to Webster. They had good reason, for Ingpen endorsed Solti's standards of international quality and was prone to overlook middling British singers with whom both agents were overstocked. Their protests were in vain, for Ingpen had the full confidence of Solti and Webster; their fears were also groundless for she and her singers were fastidious in an old-fashioned English way about avoiding favouritism.

'After I had been there about nine months,' Ingpen related, 'Geraint Evans sidled up to me in the canteen and said, would you like a tea? Then he said, I don't know if you've noticed but some of us, your former artists, have kept away from you for a while . . .'

Her most delicate task was to secure appearances from her former star, Joan Sutherland, who now insisted on singing only with her husband in the pit. Webster said, 'Bonynge wants to be a conductor?

Over my dead body.'[69] Solti, too, was adamant. He said, 'what am I supposed to do, engage a bad conductor?'[70] Under Ingpen's persuasion, he finally agreed to let Bonynge into Covent Garden, 'provided I am not here'.

These developments suited Webster to perfection, for he knew that Ingpen was no threat to his position and a useful ally in the taming of Solti. By charm, diplomacy and a bit of luck, he had not only regained influence in the opera company but had extended his sway to the Royal Ballet, where he overrode his old friend Ashton and took control of booking Nureyev. 'Now that he has been lifted into the rare atmosphere shared only with Callas, where he discusses his performances with you,' griped Drogheda, 'one feels somewhat in the dark: but I should like to know whether and, if so, to what extent, he will be with us through 1964.'[71] Weeks later the chairman complained: 'I have been told that Nureyev himself is very perplexed as to where he really stands with us. It seems to me that since you took over the direct negotiation with him, matters are not progressing as they should.'[72] Webster was serenely unperturbed by these blasts from on high. 'When I asked if the Board had been informed about one or other of our plans,' recalled Ingpen, 'David would smile and say, "I don't think we'll tell them about that, do you?"'[73]

The ship of state was starting to list. In July 1962, Harold Macmillan sacked seven Cabinet ministers in an attempt to shore up an unpopular Government. From then on, nothing went right for the man they once called 'Supermac'. In November, an Admiralty clerk, William Vassall, was jailed for eighteen years for passing secrets to Moscow. The KGB had subjected Vassall to homosexual blackmail and Fleet Street quivered with rumours of further treacheries.

A thick fog descended on London, the worst since the abolition of coal burning fires in 1952. It was followed by the coldest spell since 1947. Hugh Gaitskell, the Labour leader, came down with pneumonia, was admitted to the Middlesex Hospital and sent home for Christmas. In the opening days of the New Year, Macmillan's one big idea was brought down in flames by a resounding 'Non!' from President Charles de Gaulle, avenging France's wartime humiliations by denying Britain entry to the European Economic Community.

That same week, Gaitskell died of a mysterious viral infection. In a leadership poll of Labour MPs, the Gaitskellite vote split between the drunken George Brown and the dull James Callaghan, leaving the Bevanite Harold Wilson triumphant. Roy Jenkins, on the right of the party, felt 'revulsion'[74] and many centrists could not overcome their distrust of a man they blamed for Labour's fall from power in 1951. But the shrewd and self-confident Wilson overrode their reservations to ignite public opinion with promises of a new Britain 'forged in the white heat' of technological revolution. Beside his synthetic optimism, the Tories stumbled from one disgrace to the next.

In March 1963, the Secretary of State for War, John Profumo, told Parliament that there had been 'no impropriety whatever' in his friendship with a call-girl, Christine Keeler. He was lying, and two weeks later resigned. Keeler, it transpired, had also been sleeping with a Soviet naval attaché, Evgeny Ivanov. The sex-and-spies hysteria whipped up in Parliament and the press by Wilson's grubby aide, George Wigg, damaged the Government beyond repair. 'Are We Going Sex Crazy?' demanded the *Daily Herald*.

In July 1963, the highbrow magazine *Encounter* published a 'Suicide of the Nation?' issue. The following month, thieves hijacked a mail train and made off with a million pounds in used notes, entering legend as the Great Train Robbers and shattering confidence in those twin Victorian legacies, the railways and Royal Mail. A property crash brought down one of the biggest dealers, Jack Cotton. With Ian Fleming's thrillers topping the bestseller lists, the Government was obliged to admit that a former Foreign Office official, Kim Philby, had escaped to Moscow to join his brother-spies, Burgess and Maclean. A security investigation led by Lord Denning blamed the Prime Minister for his credulity in handling the Profumo affair. Macmillan, sixty-nine, collapsed under the strain and in October, from his hospital bed, resigned. Crushing Rab Butler's ambitions, he advised the Queen to appoint the 14th Earl of Hume, a Scottish landowner who had served on Neville Chamberlain's staff at the Munich Agreement. A more retrograde appointment could hardly have been imagined.

Yet when Wilson was finally elected Prime Minister in October 1964 it was with a wafer-thin majority of seven, a qualified endorsement in dangerous times. Both of the Big Powers had lost leaders in the previous twelve months – Kennedy assassinated, and Khrushchev deposed by Leonid Brezhnev and Alexei Kosygin. Britain's footprint on the world map was shrinking as its last African colonies rushed to independence. Its economy was fragile, its exports unwanted and worryingly unreliable as industrial strife took its toll on their reputation for quality and dependability. The country was like an anchorless ship, drifting between armoured continental blocs.

Culturally, however, its vitality had never been greater. Like Vienna at the turn of the century, capital of a disintegrating empire, London in the mid-60s hummed, buzzed and swung with the sounds, sights and frights of a new civilization. Sex was, as in Vienna, the fulcrum of social change and, for outsiders, the main attraction. The revolution produced a miniskirt that conquered the Paris catwalks, a mini-car that mocked American gas-guzzlers and a mini-boom in visual arts. A 'School of London' gathered around the artists David Hockney and R. B. Kitaj. Everyone wanted to have their hair cut by Vidal Sassoon and their clothes bought on Carnaby Street. British cinema flickered back to life. A National Theatre was finally formed at the Old Vic, with Laurence Olivier in charge and *Hamlet* as its curtain-raiser. For Shakespeare's four hundredth birthday, in 1964, Olivier acted his first *Othello*.

But the most powerful of magnets was the new music, which stemmed not from London but from decaying Liverpool with its idle docks, ugly housing, morbid churches and laconic resilience. In under-street, city-centre dens and cavernous clubs, teenaged frustrations found expression in a counter-culture that mimicked American hard-rock but drew its strengths from Celtic balladry and English eloquence. A group called 'The Beatles' entered the lower reaches of the top twenty in November 1962 with a single, 'Love Me Do.' Five months later they topped the charts with their second release, 'Please, Please Me'. For the remainder of the decade until their disbandment in 1970, the Beatles set the pace in a global process that turned popular culture into a generational weapon, the voice of youthful rejection and the antithesis of traditional, establishmentarian music.

The force behind the Beatles was a portly Liverpool shopkeeper with a passion for symphonic concerts and a taste for rough trade that led to him getting beaten up on several occasions and arrested in public lavatories. Brian Epstein had something in common with David Webster. In his mid-twenties, he ran a sheet-music and musical instrument offshoot of his family's furniture business, building up record sales so rapidly that, by the time he met the Beatles, he had a chain of nine shops across the city and was the biggest record retailer in the north-west. Neatly dressed and well-spoken, Epstein spent much of his time on the shop floor talking to customers. When teenagers kept telling him of 'this fab group' at the Cavern, he went down one lunchtime to hear for himself and signed the four musicians to a management contract, taking twenty-five per cent of gross receipts. Epstein cleaned up the Beatles' act, put them in suits, sacked their drummer Pete Best and signed them to EMI. Until his death of a drugs overdose in 1967, Epstein was the guiding influence of a genre of Mersey Beat that embraced, beyond the Beatles, the varied talents of Gerry and the Pacemakers, Billy J. Kramer and the Cavern's hat-check girl, little Cilla Black who, nearly forty years later, was still a popular entertainer.

A man of refined tastes, Epstein held subscriptions to the Tuesday night and Musica Viva concerts of the Liverpool Philharmonic Orchestra and became friendly with its promiscuous conductor, John Pritchard. As the Beatles took off, Epstein hired a record-counter manager from Lewis's, Peter Brown, with whom he was 'best friends'.[75] Brown moved in with Pritchard. The divergent realms of popular and serious music were joined by many such strands; the Beatles' producer, George Martin, was classically trained and the harmonic sophistication of their early LPs was supplied by soloists from the London orchestras.

William Mann, *The Times'* music critic, named John Lennon and Paul McCartney 'the outstanding English composers of 1963', extolling their 'chains of pandiatonic clusters' and Mahlerian 'flat-submediant key switches'.[76] Richard Buckle in the *Sunday Times* called them simply 'the greatest composers since Beethoven'.[77] There were dissenting voices as well, not all of them reactionary. Glenn Gould, the thoughtful Canadian pianist, dismissed the Beatles as a 'happy, cocky, belligerently resourceless brand of harmonic primitivism'.[78] Aaron Copland, on the other hand, recognized their work in 1967 as 'music of quality'.[79] Whichever view prevailed, there is no denying the grip that Beatlemania exerted on the artistic climate of their times, particularly on their home territory, without the slightest concession to cultural relativism. It was Covent Garden's great misfortune that the years of its highest attainments coincided with a pop revolution that suborned cultural values, stole press headlines and monopolized the attention of the rising generation, and generations to come.

*

The Wilson Government was not expected to be culture-friendly. Its priorities were the economy, industrial relations, education, housing and any other blight that could be lumped under its vote-catch slogan, 'thirteen years of Tory misrule'. Wilson – dynamic, quick-witted and still under 50 – wanted to be seen as another J. F. Kennedy and much play was made of his 'first hundred days'. Mistrusting his own party, he introduced to British governance the dubious feature of a kitchen cabinet, formed around his secretary Marcia Williams, the economist 'Tommy' Balogh, the party's press liaison officer Gerald Kaufman and the tale-bearer George Wigg. A taint of cronyism clung to Wilson throughout his premiership. Nevertheless, his freedom from party and Whitehall allowed this deceptive little man to move in unorthodox and sometimes imaginative directions.

Harold Wilson smoked a pipe, poured Worcester sauce on his supper and dressed like a bank clerk, but he enjoyed an occasional night out and and was mildly appreciative of culture. Taken to the Royal Ballet one night by Jack Donaldson, he recited to Ashton all the ballets he had witnessed on official visits to Moscow, reeling off a roll of dancers whom the director knew only by name. 'I liked the leader very much,' said Ashton. 'He is the first politician who has seen a ballet and remembered anything about it after.'[80]

Two days after entering Downing Street, Wilson telephoned Jennie Lee, Bevan's widow. 'I've got a job for you to do,' he said. 'Find a desk and pack your handbag.'[81] The job he had in mind was something junior in Health, but Lee opted instead for a vacancy in the Ministry of Public Building and Works (MPBW), where she set about tackling arts policy. If the Cabinet liked her proposals, Wilson promised, she would be given ministerial status.

After Nye's death, Lee had become involved with a community theatre, Centre 42, formed by the left-wing writers Arnold Wesker, Doris Lessing, Shelagh Delaney and Bernard Kops. She believed in taking arts to the people and bettering their lives. Her first year in the lower echelons of government was spent visiting arts companies and forming a dislike for the Arts Council. In the White Paper she wrote for Cabinet, she proposed a revision of the arm's length principle, breaking up the annual tango between Treasury providers and Arts Council distributors. The arts, she argued, were being absurdly funded through four departments of state. The Treasury looked after museums, galleries and the ACGB grant; the Department of Education and Science (DES) funded, for some reason, the Victoria and Albert and National Science museums; the Ministry for Housing and Local Government pumped money into municipal arts; and her own MPBW was responsible for historic buildings. Bring them all under one roof, urged Lee, away from the Treasury which was stifling artistic growth. The arts needed a large increase in subsidy, especially outside London.

Her paper was published in February 1965 under the Prime Minister's name and debated in the House of Commons. After winning a secure majority in the General Election of April 1965, Wilson, true to his word, appointed Jennie Lee as Britain's first Minister for the Arts. She was installed at the DES, out of Treasury reach, and took added responsibility for Wilson's pet project, an Open University that could provide tutorship and grant degrees to working people who had missed out on tertiary education.

Lee's arrival provoked consternation at the Arts Council, but not at Covent Garden, where the canny Drogheda had been courting the still-comely minister. A class warrior to her fingertips, Lee's every instinct rebelled at the sight of an ermined eleventh earl, but Drogheda was a strikingly handsome man with a perpetual ocular twinkle and he courted her with the chaste and yearning courtesy of a medieval troubadour. Across social barriers, they found much to like in one another. In one of her first letters from the DES, Jennie Lee thanked Drogheda for some public compliments and asked him for a breakdown of Covent Garden costs. She added, winningly: 'You have my sympathy in trying to do the impossible.'[82] Drogheda, thus encouraged, updated her on the crippling expense of closing the ROH for essential rewiring and warned that the ROH deficit was approaching £300,000. He also offered help in extending opera and ballet to the deprived regions. Whatever befell the arts under Wilson, Covent Garden had secured itself a safety-net.

Lee could not move ahead without shaking up the Arts Council. She called her solicitor, who was also her downstairs neighbour in a mansion block near Victoria, and asked if he would like to become a member of the Council. Arnold Goodman was delighted. Two weeks later she called again. Would he like to be chairman? 'It was flattering to be asked, and a job that I was very willing to do,'[83] said Goodman, eager to reap the rewards of well-cultivated connections. Cottesloe, confidently expecting a second term, was waiting to open an Arts Council meeting when a senior Treasury official arrived with a letter, telling him his time was up.[84]

Goodman would become the most influential fixer England had ever seen, chairing a multiplicity of public bodies and quangos (Quasi-Autonomous Non-Governmental Organizations) that sprang up whenever Wilson and his successors feared to grasp a nettle. He was, at one time or other, chairman of the Housing Corporation; the National Building Agency; the Theatres Trust; English National Opera; Motability; the National Book League; the Observer Trust; British Lion Films; and others too numerous to list. 'Tell them I'm on my way,' was his catchphrase. Goodman was the man for all crises, a purveyor of panaceas for people in power. The arts, in his hands, were but a means to a more exalted end.

The pudgy son of East End traders, Abraham Goodman – he became Arnold after the war – served as a deskbound Major at Southern Command before making his name as a legal firm-buster. He sweet-talked his first practice into merging with Rubinstein Nash, then stomped out to found Goodman Derrick, taking along many of Rubinstein's eminent clients. Such bustling enterprise was uncommon in the placid waters of English law, but Goodman was no common lawyer. A restless man with a nagging conscience, his corpulence belied a mental agility that could strip any issue to its particulars and rattle off a dazzling response at twice the Pitman's dictation speed. He was wasted on the law, and aspired to superior planes of intellectual and ethical activity. 'No one believes that serving the legal system is a sacred cause,' he averred.[85]

Through George Wigg, whom he had met as a colonel at Southern Command, he got to mingle with the Bevanites. In March 1957 he received a phone call from an irate Jennie Lee. The *Spectator*, a political weekly then owned by the Tory MP Ian Gilmour, had reported that three Labour luminaries had been conspicuously the worse for drink at a conference of the Italian Socialist Party in Venice. The article, written by Jenny Nicholson, wife of a Reuters bureau chief and daughter of the poet Robert Graves, was flimsy grounds for a libel action, but Bevan had suffered grievously at the hands of the Tory press and sought urgent redress. The words that incensed him were these:

And there was the occasional appearance of Messrs [Nye] Bevan, Morgan Phillips [General Secretary of the Labour Party] and Richard Crossman [MP] who puzzled the Italians by their capacity to fill themselves like tanks with whisky and coffee, while they (because of their livers and also because they are abstemious by nature) were keeping going on mineral water and an occasional coffee. Although the Italians were never sure if the British delegation were sober, they always attributed to them an immense political acumen.[86]

Bevan, who drank wine and generally in moderation, hated to be typecast as a boozy tourist on a fraternal freebie. He demanded an apology, but Goodman went one further. When Phillips and Crossman swore affidavits that all three men had been sober as judges, he issued writs for libel. Gilmour offered several forms of apology, all of them toyed with by Goodman and then rebuffed. 'I had the distinct feeling that he was whipping it up,' said Gilmour. 'I was also convinced that he knew his clients were lying. He saw it as a case that would put him on the map.'[87] After a short trial attended by intense publicity, an inept defence and a one-sided judge, Lord Goddard, the jury awarded each plaintiff £2,500 in damages, plus costs. Gilmour was shaken and Jenny Nicholson distraught; she fell sick with stress and died not long after from cancer. Goodman, on the other hand, was made.

In his diary, Crossman confessed that both Bevan and Phillips had indeed been drunk and that all three had lied under oath. Whether Goodman was aware of their perjury or not,[88] it did him no harm to be seen supporting men of power through thick and thin, truth and lies, acting for might against right. To the suspicious Harold Wilson, he possessed exactly the right qualities to be his private lawyer and personal adviser on matters.

Fearing the 'lottery of the law', Goodman liked to get his way by means of threat and bluster. In July 1964, shortly before the election, the pro-Labour *Sunday Mirror*, chasing Tory sex scandals, ran a headline: 'Peer and a Gangster: Yard Inquiry.'[89] No names were mentioned, but ten days later the German magazine *Stern* noted that Lord Boothby was 'in trouble'. The Tory peer, a long-term lover of Harold Macmillan's wife, was passing his dotage among rough boys supplied for his pleasure by the East End thugs, Ronnie and Reggie Kray. Taking Goodman's advice, Boothby wrote to *The Times* denying homosexuality and any link with criminals. Goodman then bore down upon the *Mirror* and exacted a grovelling apology, the dismissal of the editor responsible and a punitive forty thousand pounds in damages for Boothby.

The public settlement, however, was less than half the sordid story. Wilson had been informed that the *Mirror* possessed a compromising photograph not only of Boothby but also of his own ally, Tom Driberg. Fearing the electoral impact of a cross-party sex scandal, he sent Driberg to see Goodman, who used Wilson's name to bludgeon the *Mirror* into submission. Goodman, in his memoirs, omits this shameful episode, indicative as it was of his evolving *modus operandi*. It was not the majesty of the law that Goodman brandished at miscreants but (like the Kray gang) the awe of his fearsome friends. The Boothby business opened the door of his chambers to Tory as well as Labour politicians. 'It became a habit, in sticky times, for people to reach for their Goodman,' said Gilmour.[90] Edward Heath, the next Tory leader, came to confide in the lumbering solicitor, whom he had first met as a schoolboy. Another client was the Liberal Party leader, Jeremy Thorpe. The Newspaper Publishers' Association, alarmed at Goodman's assaults on press freedom, appointed him their chairman – from which position he exerted an ever tighter stranglehold on what was printed, or at his insistence not printed, about his august clientele. For the next twenty years a hand-delivered letter on Goodman Derrick notepaper carried more clout in Fleet Street than a full-blown libel writ from any other law firm.

No sooner was Wilson elected than he consulted Goodman on issues great and small, from the survival of the Royal Philharmonic Orchestra to the secession of a white minority regime in Rhodesia, where the Prime Minister's personal solicitor conducted a secret state mission without much success. The RPO's difficulties marked Goodman's first encounter with the arts in crisis. Three years after Beecham's death, the last of his ensembles was going broke and in danger of losing its title, bestowed by the crusty Royal Philharmonic Society. Wilson had been nobbled by the general secretary of the Musicians' Union, an old-school Marxist called Hardie Ratcliffe, who raised fears of string players and their infants begging for bread on the streets of London. There were also appeals from the RPO chairman, none other than the almost-disgraced Lord Boothby. Wilson got the Home Secretary, Frank Soskice, to ask the Palace for a Royal Warrant that would let the orchestra keep its name. Then he called Goodman, tracking him down in a restaurant, and asked him to apply his mighty mind to the matter.

Goodman, unfamiliar with the ways of orchestras, formed a

committee on which Ratcliffe and Sir David Webster, representing the Orchestral Employers Association, were the key members. The Arts Council's music director, John Denison, volunteered to act as secretary but was brushed aside. Goodman brought in a music-loving, newly-landed South African barrister, Leonard Hoffmann, 'to learn the ropes', as he put it. He called the first meeting at five o'clock on Christmas Eve and made it clear that his aim was to save the orchestra.[91] After that, as Hoffmann recalled, the process was little more than a financial haggle between Ratcliffe and Jennie Lee. 'Having ascertained how much money was available,' said Hoffmann, 'we simply wrote a report saying that was the amount of money that ought to be spent.'[92] The Goodman report concluded that although the RPO was under-employed, there was enough work in the capital for 'three and a half' orchestras, and the Arts Council should provide for them all.

Goodman's much-hailed solution actually resolved nothing at all. The RPO staggered along, competing for film sessions and Strauss nights with three superior rivals, themselves often short of work. Meanwhile, large parts of east and south-west England never got to hear a proper symphony concert. It would have made more sense to have recommended a national redistribution of orchestras, relocating the RPO to Nottingham or Bristol, but Goodman was not in the habit of looking beyond his brief. He was a quick-fixer, not a strategic thinker, and he left London's orchestral wounds suppurating beneath a piece of sticking-plaster, storing up venom for future emergencies. Thirty years later, the London orchestral crisis brought the Arts Council to the very brink of collapse.

The only useful outcome was a London Orchestral Concerts Board (LOCB) to keep peace between the hostile bands. Its chairman was David Webster who, behind a façade of neutrality, was secretly negotiating to employ the London Symphony Orchestra at Covent Garden. The idea was to remodel the LSO along the lines of the Vienna Philharmonic, whose members worked for the opera house but were also organized as an independent concert orchestra. A deal was struck with the LSO manager, Ernest Fleischmann, only for the players to reject the terms. Webster was disappointed but not daunted. He recognized that the orchestra he had created with such cavalier optimism in 1946 now hung like a lead weight on the ROH finances. He had no sentimental attachment to his orchestra and no fear of the Musicians Union. He wanted to leave Covent Garden on a sound financial footing and was looking further into the difficult future than Goodman dared to gaze.

As chairman of the Arts Council, Goodman posed as a lavish public benefactor. Around his council table, Goodman saw the noble head of Henry Moore, the country's foremost sculptor. Beside him sat the next Poet Laureate, Cecil Day-Lewis. Further down he recognized the great actress Dame Peggy Ashcroft, the opera administrator Lord Harewood, the historian Alan Bullock and the photographer Lord Snowdon, husband of Princess Margaret. It was an élite phalanx of the great and the good, the trendy and the ascendant. And lording it over them all was a Jewish solicitor of modest birth, an apotheosis of the English melting-pot.

In contrast to his predecessors, Goodman decided to be an executive chairman, replacing the secretary general, Nigel Abercrombie with a fellow-solicitor, Hugh Willatt. The chairmanship demanded large chunks of unpaid time, but Goodman's practice was massively prosperous, and most client problems could be resolved with one of his effortlessly threatening letters. His regular clients included the leading publishers and television bosses whom he had taken away from Rubinstein Nash, as well as some of the sharper operators in the London property market, notably Max Rayne and the swash-buckling Harry Hyams. It did not trouble Goodman that their interests clashed with his chairmanship of the Housing Corporation.

He also kept his door open to the up-and-coming. The young Rupert Murdoch was a valued client, as was Brian Epstein who employed Goodman to steer the Beatles' company, Northern Songs Limited, on to the London Stock Exchange. The result of this venture was that John Lennon and Paul McCartney lost control of the songs they were writing, which landed in due course in the lap of the American pop singer, Michael Jackson.

Goodman's attitude to money was cavalier. A collector of celebrities, he often 'forgot' to invoice influential clients. Lord Gibson, a director of the *Financial Times*, went to see him on National Trust business. After several meetings, Gibson said: 'Arnold, I really can't continue coming here unless you send me a bill.' 'Tell me,' said Goodman, hands clasped across his expansive girth, 'do I look hungry to you?'[93] It was on the arms of Gibson and his FT associate Lord Drogheda that the ascendant power-broker was introduced to the House of Lords on 20 July 1965, as Baron Goodman of the City of Westminster.

Under his leadership, the delicate fabric of Keynes's arm's-length provision was mangled and wrenched into a shapeless muddle. Instead of the Arts Council negotiating its grant with the Treasury and disbursing it after judicious discussion, the Arts Council chairman now obtained his grant from the Minister for the Arts and handed it out according to a policy they jointly devised. Goodman and Lee met for supper every Sunday night in his flat. 'They would sit on the floor examining (Government papers), and Goodman would suggest suitable memos that she might care to write to him, and suitable replies that she might care to receive from him,' reported Lee's biographer.[94] It was said that Lee knew little about the arts and relied on Goodman for guidance. The process was possibly more synergetic. Something resembling love blossomed between them. It was not sexual – 'how can I love that body?' said Jennie Lee[95] – and each had other objects of desire: hers a younger man and his unchecked power. What bound them together was an affinity of outlook and his constant attentiveness with flowers and other flatteries. What caused disquiet was the covert way in which they manipulated the arts and erased the lines that should have separated Government aims from Arts Council action. 'It wasn't Lee at all who determined policy,' said Hugh Willatt. 'It was Arnold all along.'[96]

In Lee's first two years as minister, she achieved a near-doubling of the Arts Council's grant, from £3.9 million to £7.2 million. By the time Labour were ousted in 1970, the grant had almost trebled. Goodman spread the extra money liberally, endowing rundown theatres with improvement grants and lavishing awards on little magazines and local groups. The rush of cash altered the artistic climate in Britain, encouraging fringe performers – and many charlatans – to believe that any goal was within their grasp and that the arts were now central to the national purpose. In an inevitable side-effect, much rubbish flourished and many weak companies came to believe that the arts owed them a living.

There was a paradox at the heart of the chairman's outlook. Goodman believed in excellence and argued that it should be disseminated outwards from London where the top companies were to be found. But when it came to dealing with centres of excellence, his attitude was highly equivocal. It was Goodman who proposed a forced merger between the newborn National Theatre and the Royal Shakespeare Company, a move thwarted by fierce resistance from Willatt. Towards Covent Garden, Goodman exhibited a distinct ambivalence. There were trendy voices on his Council who resented its existence. 'Foolish decisions were made like keeping Covent Garden Opera alive,' said Dr Jonathan Miller, the Cambridge satirist and physician. 'It should have been throttled, along with the world of old-boy networks, the tattered representatives of the Establishment.'[97] Goodman sympathized with such iconoclasms, but yearned with every fibre of his being to be accepted into the Establishment. Torn between heart and mind, he loudly praised the Royal Opera House while reducing its share of the Arts Council cake. Against the triple rations that he sprayed around the rest of the arts, Covent Garden received no more than a forty per cent increase in the Lee-Goodman years (£1,026,000 to £1,420,000) much of it consumed by twenty-five per cent inflation and Wilson's fourteen per cent devaluation of the national currency.

'I warned Arnold that he could not carry on throwing money at the grass-roots and depriving the mainstream,' said John Tooley. 'He replied that if we ever got in trouble he would bale us out.'[98] Drogheda became so agitated at Goodman's silky meanness that he threatened to go over his head to the Treasury and seek the restoration of a direct grant. 'If he went to the Treasury,' said Goodman, 'they'd give him a cup of tea, and that's all he'd get.'[99]

'Arnold liked to say he was a Robin Hood, taking from the rich and giving to the poor, but not too much,' recalled Lord Gibson.[100] In this golden era of British arts, Keynes's flagship suffered an insidious erosion in its finances and centrality. Goodman was no friend of Covent Garden, nor was he easily circumvented. He had the ear of the Prime Minister any evening of the week, and restricted press criticism by means of threat and bluster. At no time, as chairman of the Arts Council, did he openly express a negative opinion of the ROH. But in retirement, as Master of an Oxford college, he let slip his parvenu sense of exclusion. The Royal Opera House, said Goodman, was

> a centre of snobbery, where people go to look at and despise those who are poorer than themselves, and to admire others for being richer. *It makes no serious contribution to the arts.*[101]

Asked why he went there so often, Goodman replied: 'It is true that I maintain an outrageously expensive box at Covent Garden, which I share with five other people . . . It provides personal satisfaction to the relatively few individuals who can derive continuous pleasure from attending a succession of great operas.'[102] The Blessed Arnold might go down in cultural myth as the greatest benefactor of British arts, eclipsing even the mighty Keynes. Yet, on closer examination, his attitude was duplicitous, unprincipled and, in the long term, profoundly damaging for both of Keynes's prime creations. Despite inherent tensions in their relationship, the Arts Council and Covent Garden had shared until now a common purpose. From Goodman onwards, they sang in different keys.

A cloud lifted from the Royal Ballet the day that Madam retired. The age of austerity was over, now the fun could begin. Fred Ashton was one of the few men in the kingdom who could make the Queen Mother laugh. Where Madam ruled by fear and fanatical ambition, Fred radiated a languid charm that concealed a ferocious dedication to detail. He was flippant, lazy and frequently naughty. Dancers longed to please him, and some boys at the Royal Ballet School knew what he liked. There was no need for chaperoning because Fred was the director, and it says much for his gentle, slightly diffident nature that there were no complaints of abuse. Beside him, Michael Somes, John Hart and John Field attended to the rigours of planning and administration but with Fred at the helm a lilt of lightness entered the Royal Ballet and dancers never knew what to expect next.

'I had just danced my first *Fille mal gardée*,' related Nicholas Johnson, 'and was sitting in my dressing-room in full make-up when Sir Fred walked in. "Well done!" he said, and then he walked right past me and pee'd into the sink. Can you imagine? The great Ashton urinating in the sink where I was about to wash my face. "Couldn't hold it in for another two flights of stairs," he explained.'[103]

There was never any distance between Ashton and his dancers, but familiarity did not lessen their respect for the man and his art. 'I have never been so frightened of anyone as I was of Sir Fred,'[104] said Antoinette Sibley, who plucked up courage and went to his house in Marlborough Street to ask why he had not entrusted her with a major role. When Ashton tried her out soon after in *Les Patineurs*, Sibley froze on the night and left the stage unapplauded, but the choreographer was not unimpressed. He decided she needed a partner, and had a young candidate in mind.

The board and Webster were pressuring him to write a new ballet for Fonteyn and Nureyev, but Ashton was bored with Margot and wary of the wild man of the steppes. Despite a South American childhood, Ashton was culturally English and the best of his ballets were steeped in subtle half-tones which, he felt, no foreigner could grasp. He longed to nurture an English male dancer of undisputed world class, the like of which had yet to be seen. The boy he picked for Sibley was a vulnerable-looking lad of twenty who had barely survived the ruthless cull of the Royal Ballet School. 'To me it was a reign of terror,' said Anthony Dowell. 'There was a headmistress that really smelt fear. She knew the victims and played on me quite a bit. But I never thought of giving up. I knew it was leading to getting me on to the magic world of the stage. And I knew I was talented. I sensed that people recognized a facility.

'Madam was pretty formidable. At a school performance, *Swan Lake*, I was one of three boys and I had a certain problem with a step turning in the air. I was a left turner and I had to go to the right. She just called me down after this rehearsal and said, "look, dear, if you can't do this step I'll have to take you out of it." My world fell apart. I broke down and collapsed in a terrible dressing room in the bowels of the Royal Opera House. Suddenly I looked up and there was this person talking to me. And it was Michael Somes. I thought, crikey.

'He said, "come on, we're going to sort this out." And he took me into a practice room about the size of a cupboard, off the side of the canteen, and he tried to analyse why this step was going wrong. Sorted it out, got me doing it, put me back together, then each day he might see me round the building and say, "how's it going? let's try again." The next rehearsal, I did it in front of de Valois. She didn't say anything. I just knew I wasn't taken out.'[105] BBC cameras caught Madam putting young dancers through their paces with Nureyev in attendance. She is looking the other way when Nureyev points to Dowell and says, 'look, there's your next principal dancer.' 'Madam wasn't that keen on me,' lamented Dowell.

Dowell entered the Royal Ballet at seventeen and danced his first solo two years later. When Ashton paired him with Sibley, she was a rising star and he was prancing in the corps. 'It was Ashton who put us together,' he said. 'It wasn't accidental. With his amazing eye he knew that those were the two people to come. Maybe not – maybe he just saw that she was right for Titania and I was right for Oberon.'[106]

For the Shakespeare tetracentenary, Ashton ordered a triple-bill of two new ballets by himself and MacMillan to go with Helpmann's time-worn *Hamlet*. Ashton's contribution was *The Dream*, set by John Lanchbery to sections of Mendelssohn's music for *A Midsummer Night's Dream* and a libretto by Somes. It was a brilliant condensation, airily suggesting the familiar plot without having to follow it literally, and the starry new pair were warmly, if perplexedly, received. For what they represented was an ironic commentary to the heroic-erotic coupling of Fonteyn and Nureyev. Sibley was cocky and assertive, Dowell wistful and submissive. Their physical dialogue was knowing, sensual yet coolly in control of the sexual possibilities. Ashton had rewired Shakespeare along 60s lines of changing gender roles. *The Dream* was written off by Clive Barnes in the trade press as 'a disappointment . . . one of his second best ballets',[107] but Porter in the FT acclaimed it as 'purest lyric poetry'[108] and future scholars would recognize *The Dream* as the acme of Ashton's style. In the story of Covent Garden, it established the company's first partnership of equals, itself a sign of the times.

Sibley and Dowell, Anthony and Antoinette, would became inseparable and mutually dependent, in life as on stage. When Sibley's marriage to Somes fell apart in 1968, Dowell dispatched his maiden aunt, Joan, to look after the heartbroken ballerina. When Dowell suffered career-threatening injuries, Sibley took him to her childhood teacher, Winifred Edwards, who readjusted his horizons. When Sibley remarried, Dowell was godfather to her son. They were the model of symbiosis, the pattern for post-Margot regeneration.

Another couple was forming concurrently under more searching eyes. Kenneth MacMillan, the anguished-looking choreographer, had first paired Lynn Seymour, the lushest of ballerinas, with Christopher Gable, a nice-looking but technically limited East End lad, in a shattering 1960 ballet of rape, *The Invitation*. Liking what he saw, MacMillan drew the dancers into a clique, 'always giggling away in corners together, sharing private jokes'.[109] 'Kenneth MacMillan was always with us,' wrote Seymour. 'He looked upon (our circle) as his special little brood and we looked upon him as our precocious little boy. I saw him daily and talked with him on the phone every night, even after we just had drinks or dinner together.'[110]

Like Antony Tudor, whom Madam had evicted, MacMillan founded his choreography on the intricacies of human psychology. 'He liked to find out who in the company was having romances and would often choose to work together with two people who had just split up.'[111] Himself predominantly gay and painfully involved with one of his set designers, MacMillan was seeking variations on conventional romance. For the Shakespeare triple-bill, he cast Seymour and Gable with Nureyev in a troilistic ballet, *Images of Love,* that pitted his perfect couple violently against one another for the love of an elusive outsider. The music was ill-adjusted to the dance, since MacMillan hardly bothered to communicate with his composer, Peter Tranchell, and the press were flummoxed by Seymour's 'profane' and Gable's 'sacred' passion for Nureyev. MacMillan, meanwhile, was moving on to the highest of Shakespearean ballet summits.

Ever since the Bolshoi danced Leonid Lavrovsky's *Romeo and Juliet* in 1956, Covent Garden had craved its own setting of Prokofiev's honeyed score. The yearning increased when the Bolshoi repeated its showpiece in the summer of 1963. A plan to send Ashton to Moscow with *Fille* in exchange for Lavrovsky and *Romeo* fell foul of the diplomatic fog that descended with Khrushchev's dismissal. Ashton had already tried his hand at *Romeo* in Copenhagen; John Cranko had done another at Stuttgart.

In May 1964, directly after *Images of Love*, Seymour danced Cranko's Juliet in Stuttgart, her first overseas engagement. On her return, MacMillan told her that Ashton had given him the go-ahead to create a full-length ROH *Romeo and Juliet* for herself and Gable. 'Our three-way collaboration would be electric,' felt Seymour.[112] They rushed off to see Zeffirelli's acclaimed Old Vic production with Judi Dench and John Stride, notable for its quasi-adolescent ambience. MacMillan declared that his intended pair were even more emphatically 'the very anatomy of young love'.

There was only one snag: Seymour discovered she was pregnant. 'My life was dedicated to the ballet,' she later confessed, with self-unsparing candour. 'We could have other children, I reasoned. Juliet was mine. Juliet was the bonding of my partnership with Christopher Gable. Juliet was a priceless gift from Kenneth, glazed especially for me.' When her husband, the press photographer Colin Jones, went on assignment to Russia, Seymour took herself to a backstreet abortionist and, for the equivalent of three months' ROH pay, had the pregnancy terminated. The decision would wreck her first marriage, but worse was in store.

Ashton announced the Royal Ballet's new season with *Romeo and*

Juliet as its main attraction. To Seymour's incredulity, Fonteyn and Nureyev were billed as the lovers. Distraught, she tried to reach MacMillan, but he was not answering his phone.

> When we finally cornered Kenneth at our next rehearsal, he looked positively sickly. His sad brown eyes were embedded in deep dark hollows. The Garden had already hurt him by refusing to let him mount a ballet to Mahler's *Song of the Earth*, which he [later] staged for Cranko's company in Stuttgart. Now, with *Romeo*, he was once again up against the Establishment.[113]

Or so the choreographer felt. The reality was more enmeshed in MacMillan's inability to stand up for his convictions. He had proposed the Mahler piece in 1962 to Madam who loathed the idea, remembering that the detested Tudor had started out with Mahler's *Songs of the Death of Children*. Despite her distaste, she took his project to the board, where it met with fierce opposition from Mahler lovers, who felt that the work was perfect in itself, and that the expense of a tenor and soprano soloist was unjustified. After a heated debate, the matter was put to expert arbitration. Sir Adrian Boult, no ballet lover, ruled against MacMillan. Cranko, ever eager to pique his former bosses and please a friend, called MacMillan to Stuttgart to stage his Mahler creation. The German press raved and offers of work came flooding his way. To their credit, Drogheda and the board instantly overturned their verdict and, within a year, welcomed *Song of the Earth* to Covent Garden, with Nureyev, Dowell, Seymour and the Brazilian Marcia Haydée alternating in the principal roles. No lasting harm had been done.

With Romeo, however, the damage was deep and irreparable. Sol Hurok, the American impresario, had been griping for some time about how much more it cost him to import the Royal Ballet rather than the Kirov or Bolshoi. Moving the Royal Ballet sets alone cost twice as much, and the fees were beyond comparison.[114] Hurok carried clout at Covent Garden. On hearing that MacMillan was planning *Romeo and Juliet*, he told Ashton that while British audiences might welcome a new pairing, Americans wanted to see Fonteyn and Nureyev. Ashton and Webster apparently failed to inform the board of his veto, for neither the ROH archives nor Drogheda's papers contain any mention of it. MacMillan was simply told to replace Seymour-Gable with Fonteyn-Nureyev, and he gave in without much of a fight. His friend, the designer Nicholas Georgiadis, told Seymour that MacMillan had gone 'straight to the top, above Ashton' in his efforts to overturn the decision, but there is no evidence of any such intervention. On the contrary, Seymour now learned that MacMillan wanted to split her up from Gable, who was down to dance second cast while she danced fifth and last. This, she felt, was 'the ultimate betrayal'.[115] It took a snarl from Ninette de Valois to restore the Seymour-Gable partnership.

MacMillan's *Romeo and Juliet* opened on 2 February 1965 to a rapturous ovation and forty-three curtain calls. Fonteyn had required MacMillan to revise his young-lovers concept, which would have looked absurd on a matron of forty-five, and Nureyev gave a strangely indeterminate account of Romeo. Fonteyn confided that she could never manage one critical moment, where Juliet decides to go to Friar Laurence, which Seymour handled magically.[116] In New York, she and Nureyev were applauded for forty minutes. At Covent Garden, praise for the secondary casts outshone the première pair. Seymour and Gable were described as 'near perfect', the choreography fitting Lynn's plump form 'like a glove'. Sibley gave 'the performance of her life' alongside Dowell, who danced 'better than ever before'. As third change, Merle Park and Donald MacLeary were 'rare and memorable'.[117] MacMillan, whether out of despair or weakness, had allowed each couple to develop the role individualistically.

Seymour performed the balcony scene with Gable on television in her native Canada, and scored a notable success in several US cities. In the autumn, she and Gable danced the ballet in Rome and Milan, while her ex-husband Colin was clearing his belongings from their flat. She was seeing a thyroid specialist for her weight, a psychiatrist for depression and Winifred Edwards for moral support. The perils of *Romeo and Juliet* had brought this passionate dancer to the brink of breakdown and destroyed any prospect of a lasting duet with Gable, who gave up soon after for an acting career, appearing with the RSC in Peter Brook's production of *A Midsummer Night's Dream* and on screen in Ken Russell's *Women in Love*. The official version that 'everyone survived'[118] the Romeo fiasco did not apply to the two dancers on whose bodies the key roles had been moulded. Gable lost his patience and Lynn Seymour her innocence on the rack of Covent Garden politics.

Nor did the repercussions end with the ballet's triumph. Fonteyn and Nureyev saw *Romeo* as their ticket to freedom and loosened their links with the Royal Ballet. Ashton's directorship was also destabilized. Drogheda told Webster that the casting confusion had led him to wonder whether all was well with the company. Nadia Nerina had been to see him, terribly upset that she and Beriosova had been left out of *Romeo*. 'MacMillan had told her that he would like her to do it, *but that he had nothing to do with the casting.*' Nerina complained that 'the general state of the company's morale was low . . . that Lynn Seymour was as discontented as she was . . . (and) that everything was being done to promote Sibley in a very unfair way.' She felt the best hope for the Royal Ballet was for Fonteyn to replace Ashton as director.[119] Insuperably frustrated, Nerina quit the company and hung up her pumps.

The knives were out for Sir Fred, as they had never been for Madam. Relations with Field had soured and the administrator slipped away to run the touring Sadler's Wells Ballet. Ashton's tolerance for MacMillan was also running out. 'Fred loathed Kenneth,' said Bill Beresford. 'One night after a well-received MacMillan première, at the far end of the Crush Bar where the man who ran Moët et Chandon dispensed free champagne to senior staff, Fred moaned, "I might as well be in the gutter. The public don't respect me any more. Just listen to the way they applauded Kenneth in there."'[120]

While staging *Song of the Earth* in Stuttgart, the Scotsman was approached by a man from West Berlin and offered the ballet directorship of the Deutsche Oper. He reported the offer to Ashton, in the hope that he would be implored to remain at Covent Garden. Ashton advised him to leave, saying the experience would do him good. So, in the summer of 1966, Britain's ascendant choreographer packed his bags and left for Germany, accompanied by Lynn Seymour as his principal ballerina. 'I'll be the management in Berlin,' he told her, 'this is our chance.'[121]

The departures marked a major breach in Madam's edifice, a disruption of the seamless continuity she had sought to assure. Behind the scenes, she raged at Ashton's weakness. The director sought redemption in a new ballet, *Monotones*, after Erik Satie's *Trois Gymnopédies*. It was exquisite, as ever, and the following season he extended it with a stretch of Satie's *Trois Gnossiennes*. Dowell and Sibley stood out in a cast of six, and comparisons were drawn with his epic *Symphonic Variations*. However, with MacMillan gone, Ashton was looking old and isolated and anxious souls on the board began contemplating his removal. The publisher Mark Bonham-Carter, chairman of the ballet committee, urged in May 1966 that John Field should be groomed as the next director. By November that year, he sounded a warning to the main board. Ashton, he said, was 'not by temperament or inclination suited to running a company'. Nor was he spending enough time creating ballets: 'in fact, we are getting the worst of both worlds'.[122] The nettle had to be grasped, he said, and the sooner the better. Webster, reluctant to move in haste, gave gentle advice to his old friend. 'Our troubles come in two ways,' he said. 'Mainly through the fact that the company feel they have no real care taken of them as individuals. Some of them refuse to go to Jack [Hart] saying "what is the use for I won't get anything even if I go". Some of them feel that his response to them is in almost all cases detached to a degree which has no personal appreciation of them as human beings ... This lack of interest and excitement is expressed in all the little things of day to day activities. I used the phrase to you yesterday that the main company has the feeling that nobody loves them! ... I think it is absolutely essential to the well-being of the company that we bring in to London John Field.'[123] Ashton, however, refused either to share power or to wield it and the Royal Ballet continued to grizzle as the 60s swung on.

Maria Callas telephoned Webster towards the end of 1963 and told him she was ready, after five years' absence, to return. She wanted to sing *Tosca*, and without delay. Webster had Zeffirelli, whom she trusted, about to produce *Rigoletto* for Solti in February 1964. He inserted three *Tosca*s in January and had the two casts rehearsing side by side, one in the morning, the other in the afternoon. They had six weeks in which to mount an opera and Callas, now forty, would not give an inch. Her fee was astronomical – fifteen hundred pounds a night, net of taxes, plus her suite at the Savoy and first-class return fares to Paris. She needed constant reassurance and seemed neurotically insecure about her voice, forever on the cusp of cancellation. Yet behind these anxieties lived an artist who was guided solely by her faith in art. 'I am a very simple woman,' she said, 'and I am a very moral woman. I do not mean that I claim to be a "good" woman, as the word is: that is for others to judge; but I am a moral woman in that I see clearly what is right and wrong for me, and I do not confuse them or evade them.'[124]

In rehearsal one day, Tito Gobbi, playing the cruel governor Scarpia, pinned her backwards, arms outstretched, as if to rape her. 'You want him,' Zeffirelli whispered to Callas. 'You know you want him to violate you, and that's what you can't deal with.'[125] Callas knew what she had to do. She poured herself a glass of water, drank it, stopping in mid-motion as she spied a knife on the table. As Scarpia approached again, she seized the knife, turned and stabbed him to death. No one present had ever witnessed an act of such concentrated ferocity.

On the morning of her opening night, she was running a temperature with bronchitis but for once repressed thoughts of cancellation and turned up at the stage door in good time. As she rushed into the church at the end of the first act to warn her lover of impending danger, she tore the hem of her silk dress on a protruding nail. Callas did not look down, because her character, Tosca, would never have been distracted by a torn hem. A grainy, monochrome off-air recording of the second act reveals Callas at her most luminous, ringed in waves of nervous energy, her charisma at its most compelling. A mushrooming roar of pent-up emotion greeted the final curtain, a moment when opera split the atom of physical matter. The carpers continued to carp – 'you should have heard what singing teachers were saying in the intervals,' sniffed Hope-Wallace[126] – but Callas possessed *Tosca* as no diva before or since. The stabbing, wrote Hope-Wallace, 'happened almost on the spur of the moment and took Scarpia completely by surprise! Think what that means to anyone who has seen fifty or more *Tosca*s.' Zeffirelli's production would still be in service at Covent Garden more than thirty years later.

Next morning, Webster heard from Peter Diamand, a Callas fan who was director of the Holland Festival:

> After having telephoned this morning with Maria and having heard from her – and from others too – what a triumphant event last night's *Tosca* must have been, I feel the urge to congratulate and to thank you for having made this possible.
>
> I believe I can somehow realize the great risk which you took when planning this performance: nobody could fore-tell, when you invited Maria, in what form she would be – in fact, whether she would appear at all. Many, very many, who admire Maria had become careful, even doubtful. That you felt that an artist as

Maria is worth *any* risk, – that to bring her back to the stage would not only provide her audiences with a unique experience but will also undoubtedly help her to resume her task which she, temporarily, seemed to have neglected: this deserves the greatest admiration and sincere gratitude from all who believe in opera and feel that there is no operatic artist comparable to Maria.[127]

An even richer compliment was paid by Rudolf Bing, who offered Callas six thousand dollars, more than twice her ROH fee, to repeat *Tosca* at the Met. She returned home in good spirits to sing *Norma* for Zeffirelli in Paris and resume her life in waiting for the fickle Onassis. Callas did not need British critics and French cat-callers to tell her that her top C had gone and her middle range was ravaged. She managed to record *Tosca* that autumn and sang two runs in Paris and New York, but the prospect of four more *Tosca*s at Covent Garden the following summer was suddenly too much to bear. Two days before opening night, she had not arrived at the Savoy. That evening, she rang Webster at home saying she was suffering from dangerously low blood pressure. Webster begged her to come and sing at least the last performance, a charity gala before the Queen on 5 July 1965. Out of fondness for him, she consented.

The first three *Tosca*s were sung by Marie Collier. The fourth was the last time Maria Callas ever set foot on an opera stage. With unerring artistry, and heeding no voice but her own, she ended her international opera career on the very spot where it had begun just twelve years before. There would be comeback rumours aplenty in the next few years and gossip enough to fill ten books, but the rest of her short life formed a tragic coda to the foregoing glory. Onassis soon forsook her for the widowed Jacqueline Kennedy. A recital tour with the tenor Giuseppe di Stefano verged on travesty. She declined to appear at Webster's farewell gala. 'It was always my hope that she might still return,' lamented John Tooley,[128] on hearing of her death of a heart attack, at home in Paris in September 1977, aged fifty-three.

The ROH fallout was considerable. Zeffirelli never worked again at Covent Garden, apparently unable to contemplate a reprise of his finest two hours. 'They won't come near me',[129] he complained, but over the years he rejected repeated overtures.

Marie Collier, who stood in so bravely for Callas, reaped a

whirlwind of world attention and was swamped with offers that she could neither handle nor resist. Her first loyalty, she declared, was to Covent Garden,[130] but a turbulent private life and too much travelling played havoc with her consistency. After three years of ups and downs Solti decided that her German was too poor for Covent Garden. 'You know that I admire your work in other roles,' he said, 'and I am very willing to talk to you personally if you want to see me, but I have given this matter a lot of thought, and Sir David knows and understands my attitude.'[131] In April 1971, her agent was informed that Covent Garden were replacing her in a long-planned role. Eight months later, Marie Collier fell to her death during a drunken party from a high window in Leicester Square, a few blocks away from the Royal Opera House. She was forty-four years old, and left four children.

Solti himself became embroiled in a tempestuous row with Webster. Hearing that Callas was to sing one *Tosca* for the Queen but none for the public who had queued for days to hear her, Solti demanded that she sing all four nights or none. Webster demurred. Solti went to Drogheda and said Callas was being allowed to set a dangerous precedent. 'This is not a serious opera house,' he raged, 'no serious house would allow such nonsense.' He produced a letter of resignation. Drogheda begged him to withdraw it. Solti went to the opera house with the letter in his pocket. He stayed to greet the Queen, but left before Callas began to sing.

Drogheda implored him to calm down. 'I must tell you how distressed I have been by the knowledge that you yourself have been so upset,' said the chairman, insisting that there had been no choice but to let Callas have her way. 'One must remember that extremely high prices have been paid for tickets, and as the money is to go to the Benevolent Fund we cannot possibly make refunds. One must remember, too, that the Queen agreed to come on the understanding that she would hear Callas.'[132] Webster added his apologies and Solti was appeased, though not unconditionally. 'I am very happy with your assurances that in future you will do everything to avoid this situation occurring again,' he told Webster, 'and I hope that you will understand that I feel this to be a very fundamental question in my partnership with you. If for any reason a similar situation re-occurred, the consequences must be very serious.'[133] His insistence on professionalism was absolute and he would not waste time on capricious singers, urging that even the effulgent Birgit Nilsson should be sent packing if she persisted in her unreasonable financial demands. But he was not a man to bear grudges and he seldom referred to a row once he had put it behind him.

For all the demonic energy that led John Lanigan to christen him 'the Screaming Skull', there was an almost child-like trustfulness and lovability about Solti that many found irresistible. Once he liked someone, he permitted limitless liberties. During a rehearsal in the Crush Bar, the huge Scottish bass David Ward lifted him on to the table and said, 'Georg, shut up.' Solti simply laughed. In a tricky passage of Ravel's *L'heure espagnole*, he told Lanigan, 'John, dear, I beat it twelve here.' 'Don't worry, Maestro,' said the cocky Aussie, 'I never look.'[134] Solti roared with laughter. Michael Langdon and the tenor Kenneth Macdonald were forever playing practical jokes on him. On a trip to Israel, Macdonald convinced Solti that the captain of a Royal Navy frigate wanted to give him a lift by sea from Haifa to Tel Aviv. Solti reciprocated by getting a rabbi to phone the tenor and thank him effusively for agreeing to sing in Hebrew. After Macdonald died of a heart attack during a London Opera Centre rehearsal in October 1970, Solti sent his family a cheque every Christmas.

When the young conductor Mark Elder had his wallet stolen, Solti said 'how much was in it?' and replaced the loss. If a singer that he liked got into vocal difficulties, he would ring up his fellow-Hungarian Vera Rozsa to arrange remedial coaching. John Tooley, remarried in 1968 to his former ROH secretary, Patsy Bagshawe, was invited to honeymoon at Solti's Italian villa at Roccamare.

The familial atmosphere that Solti fostered was kept warm by his trusted secretary, Enid Blech, who once ran the London Mozart Players for her husband, Harry. 'Enid held court in Solti's outer office,' recalled a regular visitor. 'She smoked cheroots, made very good black coffee and spoke fluent Italian so the continental artists were always hanging around her.'[135] Contrary to popular myth, the Solti environment at Covent Garden was unusually light and happy. It was also wide open to newcomers. Solti was always on the look-out for talent, even within his own profession, and future conductors like Elder and Jeffrey Tate owed their first steps to his patronage. 'Whatever one may think of Solti as an interpreter,' said Richard Armstrong, who went on to head Welsh and Scottish National Operas, 'one thing is unarguable: he was a fantastic opera-house musical director. He knew all the tricks, what the priorities were. All

I tried to do when I had the responsibility was to model WNO in a similar way.'[136]

At an altogether more exalted level, Solti socialized easily with the Droghedas and their friends, Isaiah Berlin and Burnet Pavitt. He was naturally convivial, curious about other people, a wry anecdotalist and compelling dinner guest. The patrician chairman was completely enchanted, almost in love.

'My dear Georg,' lamented Drogheda in the summer of 1964, 'It seems a very long time since I heard from you. I fear that I am no longer in your thoughts. This saddens me, but there is nothing I can do about it. I realize that you prefer to take other people into your confidence. It is always slightly depressing, but I must just be philosophical, I suppose.'[137]

'My dear Garrett,' replied Solti from an Israeli hotel. 'I am very sorry that you feel neglected by me, but you know very well that the contrary is true, and that you are continuously in my thoughts.'[138] 'I suspect that this is a slight over-statement,' responded Drogheda, 'but it is nice nevertheless to be told it'.[139]

The following season fulfilled all of the chairman's fondest hopes. Solti opened in September 1964 with his first full *Ring*, in a production directed by the august Hans Hotter, who also sang Wotan, alternating with David Ward. The sets were by Günther Schneider-Siemssen, and Wilhelm Pitz of Bayreuth was imported to impart fresh discipline to Douglas Robinson's chorus. Herbert von Karajan slipped incognito into several performances and emerged with Schneider-Siemssen as his Salzburg designer. Covent Garden had spotted him first.

Many of the *Ring* singers were British, several of them new-comers. Josephine Veasey, a Solti discovery, sang Fricka in *Rheingold*. In *Götterdämmerung*, ten out of thirteen roles were internally cast, including Rita Hunter as Third Norn, Collier and Veasey as Gutrune and Waltraute, Maureen Guy as Flosshilde and a Welsh newcomer, Gwynneth Jones, as Wellgunde.

The Covent Garden *Ring* was the first time Solti had conducted the tetralogy sequentially. The press reception was initially muted, but warmed up as the cycle came round again five times in the next six seasons. 'I have seen twenty-five productions of the *Ring*,' said one veteran, 'and that was the best.'[140] By the time Decca issued the first-ever recorded *Ring* in October 1966, Solti was on the point of establishing himself as the most famous living Wagner conductor.

He followed the Ring with *Arabella*, a light-hearted, often under-played romp by Richard Strauss whom the conductor had got to know and love in post-war Munich. Lisa Della Casa and Dietrich Fischer-Dieskau led a note-perfect cast. Visconti, meanwhile, presented a scintillating *Trovatore*, Gwyneth Jones dropped an 'n' from her name as it went up in lights and the Belfast soprano Heather Harper shone for Solti in a revival of Offenbach's *Tales of Hoffmann*. Both Jones and Harper were snapped up by Bayreuth and Solti took credit for developing yet another fresh strand of British singers. He also acquiesced to Joan Sutherland's return as *Lucia*, conducted by her husband.

A season which seemed to fire on all cylinders ended in June 1965 with the boldest work ever ventured at Covent Garden, the British première of Arnold Schoenberg's *Moses and Aron*. Schoenberg was box-office frostbite and the board had debated his demerits for years before Isaiah Berlin convinced Drogheda of the moral imperative. Schoenberg had conceived his opera in response to the rise of Nazism; its inarticulate hero, Moses, needs his brother Aron to convey a divine message that can neither be transmitted nor received with anything resembling total accuracy.

Solti first shied away from the challenge, then agreed to conduct on hearing that Pritchard and Colin Davis were being approached. He persuaded the composer's fierce widow, Gertrud, to agree to a new English translation, but fifteen months before the première he listened to a *Moses* recording and told Drogheda that Covent Garden could not possibly afford the rehearsal time for so complex a work. On the opera sub-committee, Sir Thomas Armstrong mounted a rear-guard resistance, protesting against noisy atonalities. It took a letter from Isaiah Berlin to stiffen Solti's resolve. *Moses and Aron*, argued the Oxford don, was 'noble, austere and uncompromising . . . a new chapter in the history of opera.' Stagings in Zurich and Berlin had given no impression of its magnitude. The first conductor and opera house to do so would reap eternal glory.[141] In a parallel memo to Webster, Berlin tipped Nino Sanzogno of Milan, and the young composers Pierre Boulez and Bruno Maderna as standby conductors if Solti proved immovable.[142] The music director, however, was back on side and ordered Edward Downes to start orchestral rehearsals fully ten months before the première.

Solti, who admitted that without an undercoat of tonal harmony he had no idea how to conduct *Moses*, demanded the aid of a

visionary director. He proposed Visconti, who was busy, then Peter
Brook. His third choice was Peter Hall, a storm force in British
theatre who had formed the Royal Shakespeare Company in
Stratford and rebased it in London. Not quite thirty-five years old,
Hall commanded the respect of senior actors and the favour of
Arnold Goodman. He had always wanted to direct opera and had
written to Webster in 1954 describing it as 'my chief ambition in
life'.[143] But apart from a 1957 dabble at Sadler's Wells with *The
Moon and Sixpence*, by an ROH repetiteur John Gardner, he had yet
to direct an opera. Webster offered him Verdi's *Macbeth* (1959), *A
Midsummer Night's Dream* (1960), *Forza del Destino* (1961) and
the sanitized *Katerina Izmailova* by Dmitri Shostakovich (1963), all
of which he declined. He was on the point of rejecting *Moses and
Aron* when the conductor came on the phone. 'Solti yelled at me
with his engaging mixture of charm and hysteria,' recalled Hall. 'He
said it was my responsibility, no, *my duty*, to work at Covent
Garden.'[144]

With his regular designer John Bury, Hall overtaxed the ROH
stage crew and had the obstructionist production manager John
Sullivan removed. He imported live animals, including an inconti-
nent camel from Chessington Zoo and, taking one look at the prim
and proper women's chorus, engaged Soho strippers for the orgy
scene around the Golden Calf. When the chorus men were ordered
to strap on phalluses, the *News of the World* ran a front-page shock-
horror and the Lord Chamberlain, who was responsible for
theatrical censorship, was only narrowly persuaded to permit the
production. The box-office was besieged by curiosity seekers and all
six performances sold out.

The much-feared Mrs Schoenberg, arriving in a two-piece tweed
suit in the middle of summer, pronounced the orgy too tame. Enid
Blech, sensing trouble, took her shopping and returned with a
Yorkshire terrier that kept the widow occupied for the rest of her
visit. Solti told a press conference: 'You'll find it difficult at first, but
for me, now, it is just like Mozart.' He had acquired a personal
affinity with the work, both for its biblical rectitude and for the
character of Moses who, like the music director, could not always
make himself understood.

Moses and Aron was an unqualified triumph for the whole
company, especially for Forbes Robinson and Richard Lewis, two
underrated British singers who took the title roles. There were three

hundred people on stage – 'more Israelites,' remarked Goodman with inverted anti-Semitism, 'than in the stalls' – and all the leading names in British arts rushed to catch the show. Among them was Karl Rankl, attending Covent Garden for the first time since his dismissal.

Webster, during the orgy scene, retreated prudishly to the Crush Bar. Solti, a connoisseur of feminine pulchritude, complained that his own head was buried too intently in the score to see anything of interest. Richard Lewis tried to punch a journalist for peeking at the strippers – whom Stella Chitty, the stage manager, covered up as they pranced into the wings. All told, this most austere of operas occasioned more fun and legends than a hatful of Italian fripperies and established Covent Garden as an international contender, equal to Vienna or the Met, just as Isaiah Berlin had predicted.

Solti glowed with delight. His octogenarian teacher, Zoltán Kodály, had come from Hungary to attend his session at the East End Roxy cinema that Webster had converted into a rehearsal hall and grandly renamed the London Opera Centre. Kodály, no lover of Schoenberg and sparing with compliments, praised his pupil's progress and Solti was 'as pleased as can be'.[145] He still found the working conditions inadequate but he enjoyed the atmosphere at Covent Garden, and his personal life had taken a decisive turn that would attach him to England for good and all.

His marriage to Hedi was coming apart. 'I never read a book before I met her, and in London she showed me which forks to use,' he confided.[146] But they had been together twenty years and his pursuit of other women placed an intolerable stress on their relationship. In her eyes, he remained the wild-eyed, half-grown Hungarian refugee who had stolen her away from her professorial first husband, a member of the Swiss parliament.

He left Hedi in their Kensington house and moved into a suite at the Savoy, where amorous whispers abounded. 'How any woman could resist him when he smiled, I don't know,'[147] said an orchestral player. It was rumoured that Solti gave white mink coats to the singers he bedded, but with modest fees and Hedi's maintenance to pay he could barely have afforded a fake stole. Promiscuity was fun, but Solti was a man who needed security. Then, one Saturday morning, a mishap at the Covent Garden press office transformed his troubled existence.

Bill Beresford and Sheila Porter had been planning coverage of the forthcoming *Ring* when Porter mentioned a young BBC television reporter, Valerie Pitts, who worked for regional news and presented the daily children's programme, *Play School.* 'Why don't I ring Val and get her to do something?' said Porter.

Pitts had an assignment that had fallen through, and a spare camera crew. She turned up at the Savoy for 11 a.m., as agreed, and hung around waiting for Beresford. He rushed in panting apologies and, leaving the crew in the lobby, took the willowy blonde presenter up in the lift to Solti's room on the eighth floor. They were not the only ones running late. 'The door opened,' said Beresford, 'and Solti stood there, his face lathered in shaving cream, naked except for a towel round his waist. I had never seen such a hairy man. His body was covered in black hair, like a bear. Very embarrassed, he asked us to wait downstairs. As we took the lift down, Val said: "Did you see all that hair on him?"'

When the television interview was over, Solti invited them both for a drink at the bar. 'Do you like opera?' he asked Valerie Pitts.

'Oh yes,' she said.

'Have you been to many?'

'No, but we just came back from holiday and stopped in Frankfurt, where we saw a dreadful thing, all about lesbians. It was by Johann Strauss.'

Solti said: 'I think you might mean a different Strauss, and was it called *Elektra*?'[148]

At this point, Beresford 'pleaded pressure of work and tactfully withdrew'. 'If Bill hadn't arrived late,' reminisced Valerie, 'I'd never have met Solti personally. He would have sat down in front of the camera and I'd have said, "tell me about the *Ring*." '[149]

Their romance was strewn with obstacles. Valerie was married, to a man called James Sargant, and Solti was not yet divorced. She was only twenty-four, less than half his age, and her upright parents in Leeds were aghast. Solti pursued her with relentless ardour, bombarding her with roses and phone calls from around the world. 'I was a laid-back English girl and he took me by storm,' she said. 'He used to say: you only have one life, you must make every minute count.' 'I had to urge Valerie to marry him,' said Joan Ingpen. 'She was sent to me by Georg to tell her why she should agree.' The couple married in November 1967 and, when two daughters were born, Solti bought a house in Elsworthy Road, Hampstead, and elected to raise his family in England. The letter from the Home

Office conferring citizenship on this eternal wanderer was framed in gold and kept in pride of place at the doorway of his studio.

When Drogheda approached him for a third contract renewal, Solti replied: 'I am only too happy.'[150] There was some dickering over how many nights he would conduct and his scale of pay over the next five years (£10,000 p.a. rising to £14,500), but Solti felt himself at home and among friends. The only reservations came from Webster, who wanted to start grooming Colin Davis of Sadler's Wells as the next music director – 'very much a change for the worse,' sniffed Drogheda[151] – and from a new board member, Professor Claus Moser of the London School of Economics who considered Solti's remuneration excessive. Drogheda, in a clinching memorandum, noted that 'it is generally agreed that Solti's presence at Covent Garden has been of enormous benefit for the standing of the House.'[152] The *Sun* newspaper captioned him: 'Solti, the Beatle of Covent Garden'.[153]

There remained, however, pockets of resistance. A small knot of opera-goers could not abide Solti's hard-driven interpretations. Some orchestral players fulminated against him for making records with the Vienna Philharmonic, arguing that much of his repertoire, 'including that wonderful Ring, was learned at Covent Garden'.[154] 'Dear Sir David,' began one anonymous letter to Webster, written in block capitals with a Willesden postmark, 'In heaven's name why don't you fire Solti? Soon no international artist will want to work with him (Vickers, Del Monaco, Birgit Nilson (*sic*) etc). Besides who wants to hear the Ring or Otello under Solti's selfish baton. Can't you fire him before it's too late? Your faithful gallerites (some of them).'[155]

The hatred peaked in July 1966, when Solti emerged from the stage door to find his white Mercedes-Benz daubed with the words: 'Solti go home'. To a Hungarian Jew who had lost relatives in the Holocaust, the assault was horrifying. Interviewed by the *Daily Express*, he exercised maximum restraint. 'It's very hurtful,' said Solti, 'not the sort of thing I'd expect British people to do.'

Drogheda reacted with sympathetic outrage. 'David told me that, after you left us last Monday and went back to your car, you found that some idiot had scrawled offensive things on it,' he wrote. 'How absolutely damnable for you. I can imagine nothing more unpleasant ... Everything possible will be done to discern the identity of the particular idiot who is plaguing you.'[156]

A private detective, one Robert F. Forde, was engaged. He was told to keep watch on Solti's car during three *Magic Flute* nights and to mingle with the Crush Bar crowd in the intervals. Forde, with his associate, Mr K. R. Lodge, reported back that they 'did not overhear any conversations of interest to us. . . . The only jeering heard during Mr Solti's curtain calls came from a young man sitting to the left of row B, who booed once. He appeared to be alone and there was definitely no sign of an organized demonstration.' The two private eyes then searched the building for clues, but only found a rash of stickers in the gentlemen's lavatory proclaiming 'Solti must stay'.[157]

The second half of Solti's decade was more relaxed. New productions were cut to three or four a year and Solti often left the plums to his prospective successors. Contrary to the jibes, he was not a greedy conductor and he aimed for continuity. The only group he failed to impress was the critics. In Frankfurt a reviewer, once won over, tended to remain broadly supportive. In the competitive British press, critics judged each show on merit, regardless of form. The best of them could never be counted as 'supporters' in the way that sports writers supported a particular team or manager. Solti found their unpredictability perplexing, and Drogheda was driven to distraction by his own man. On reading Andrew Porter's FT account of Solti's *Ring*, he sent a memo to Gordon Newton, the editor, saying: 'It is now impossible for me to remain as chairman of the Covent Garden Opera Company and as managing director of the *Financial Times*. Would you please inform me which position you wish me to relinquish?'[158] Porter had attacked the casting of the *Ring* as 'unforgivable',[159] an imputation that drove Drogheda wild. Advised by Newton that his impulsive resignation would inflict damage on both institutions, he sat down and fired off a volley at Porter in the nastiest terms he could muster:

> I would have thought that if anyone should write helpfully it is Andrew Porter. Instead of which, it seems that the presence of your sister on the staff makes you seize opportunities to be unhelpful. Apart from this, I do long for the day when you will develop a little bit of humility, and begin to question the accuracy of some of your more offensive positive statements.[160]

Porter's reply to his employer was a model of critical detachment.

'My dear Garrett,' he wrote,

I will ignore your muddled letter – the greater part of which is based on a careless misreading of my *Götterdämmerung* notice – except where it raises certain issues of principle affecting my work for this paper. You seem unable to grasp these, so, once again, I will set them out for you:

1) So long as I am music critic of the *Financial Times* its reviews will be independent and stand in no special relationship to Covent Garden . . .

2) I will not, despite your wishes, apply to you, or to my sister, for 'inside information' that has not been made generally available to all critics. I refuse to discuss Covent Garden affairs privately with my sister. She is in a position of confidence, and it is monstrous of you to propose that I should use a family relationship to take professional advantage of this.

. . . It must be plain to you what is wrong with this *Ring*, as well as the many things that are right. I hope you can distinguish between inevitable, and so forgivable, weaknesses and the wrong things, the 'bétises', that could have been right given the initial careful thought, good sense and strong direction which, on all but the musical side, Covent Garden so sadly lacks.

My tone here may sound severe (even 'offensive'). But believe me, we are working for the same end, and it is never 'helpful' for a critic to lower his sights below the Attainable.[161]

Drogheda noted in the margin that Porter had rung him 'to apologize for his letter in advance of my seeing it', but the vigour of his riposte resounds ringingly against the latterday acquiescence of many critics to the editorial priorities and media interests of their multinational proprietors.

Neither man flinched from administering further blows. 'Your arrogance and conceit are almost insupportable,' sputtered Drogheda after Porter had begun a review of Handel's *Saul* with the words, 'If Covent Garden Opera had a proper sense of its national responsibilities . . .'[162] 'What a beastly, unappreciative letter to receive,' exclaimed Porter of another memo. 'Sometimes I wonder why I go on working so hard for this paper.'[163] Drogheda signed off one vituperation: 'I am devoted to you, even though you madden me.'[164]

That sentiment was mutual. Maddening as Drogheda could be with his chivvying notes and winter-dawn phone calls, he made people sit up and take notice. There was an impresarial energy about Drogheda that raised Covent Garden from its dowdy English origins to a venue of international chic. The performers played their part in adding glamour, but it was the chairman who put fizz and pride into the company and won it a place in the sun. Isaiah Berlin, returning to the board after a three-year absence in New York, put his clever finger on the essence of Drogheda's input. 'The real point,' he told the chairman, 'is that Covent Garden has become an absolutely central part of London and, indeed, British culture. ... It is as intrinsic and traditional and national as the BBC, and that would not have happened without – as you very well know and do not need me to tell you, although I do so with the greatest pleasure – your administration.'[165] On reading this encomium Drogheda was, momentarily, becalmed with contentment.

Sir David Webster, surveying the world from the vastness of his office, had equal cause for satisfaction. The company had become the Royal Opera and he basked in reflected glory. Many of his daily dreads had vanished. Madam was off in Turkey forming a national ballet, Legge was banished, Drogheda left him mostly in peace and even the immigration officials at Heathrow airport had given up impeding his foreign singers. All a tenor had to say was 'Royal Opera House' and the gates of the kingdom swung open.

The running of the business was supervised by Tooley, his heir apparent, who made a habit of walking down the orchestral passage in rehearsal breaks and greeting everyone by name. 'You've got to be around all the time,' he said, 'talking to the players, stage crew and artists.'[166] The more Tooley was around, the less people saw of Webster, making his interventions the more momentous. Once, in the heat of a new production, the stage crew theatened to call a strike against the director. 'Someone turned to me,' recalled Ken Davison, director of the Friends, 'and hissed, "Get Webster".

'So I rushed up to his office, was let in by Muriel Kerr, and found him sitting quietly at an absolutely bare desk. He made a sign to Miss Kerr, who produced a file full of cheques which he proceeded laboriously to sign, about twenty of them.

'Then he said to me: "Now what seems to be the matter?"

'By this time I had calmed down, and told him quietly that there was a problem with the producer and the stage staff were about to walk out, and perhaps he should take a look.

'He got up, put on his coat and hat, very dapper, took his stick, and came down with me on to the stage, as if he had just come in from the street.

"Everybody all right?" he said mildly. "Anything I can help with?"

'And that was the end of the trouble. Everyone at Covent Garden trusted him to put things right.'[167]

The paternalist approach seldom failed, but Webster's was not a stable family. There were favourites and black sheep, insiders and outsiders. Those who crossed the line were ousted. Bill Beresford was called in by Webster after ten years in the press office and told 'it is time you moved on'. He was given no reason. In the mail one morning, he found a large personal cheque signed by Burnet Pavitt, a member of the board. Beresford sent it back, appalled by the patronizing gesture. His eviction, he discovered, had been wangled by Bill Bundy, the obstreperous stage boss who had Webster's ear and was also close to Sheila Porter, the deputy press officer. 'Horrendously ugly'[168] and 'a complete bastard,[169] Bundy made enemies recklessly. 'He was incredibly insecure, poor fellow,' said Tooley. One moonless night, on his way home from the theatre, Bundy was set upon and savagely beaten. His assailants were never caught; the prime suspects were members of his own crew.

Much of the early informality still prevailed. A North London schoolgirl who wrote to Webster asking if she could sketch dancers was allowed to sit in the wings any night she liked.[170] An Oxford student who came asking for a job was told, 'come and see me again next year'.[171] Hearing that Martinelli, the non-pareil pre-war Otello, was in town for the fiftieth anniversary of his début, Webster went out before the curtain and made an impromptu speech in honour of the mighty tenor. The death of Bruno Walter was similarly commemorated. It was his house, and he could do in it as he liked.

His bonhomie was disturbed only when an external foe loomed from the vanquished past, challenging Covent Garden's hegemony. The Sadler's Wells Opera had been doing well under the baton of Colin Davis and the leadership of Norman Tucker and his artistic administrator, Stephen Arlen. The company had made a successful European tour with Charles Mackerras and was nurturing new singers under the guidance of Leonard Hancock, once of Covent

Garden. Its subsidiary troupe, the old Carl Rosa, toured opera around the land.

The problem for Sadler's Wells was, as ever, its inability to make ends meet in a theatre which seated fewer than fifteen hundred. The company had to move to survive, and the obvious venue was the South Bank beside the emergent National Theatre. Tucker had put in for a South Bank plot as early as 1954. Both the Arts Council and the Tory-ruled Greater London Council were offering large grants to create a prestigious arts park, a concretization of the Festival of Britain idea. All it needed was Government approval.

Seen from Covent Garden, a transpontine, multi-disciplinary arts centre with an inbuilt opera house posed a direct threat. The matter was never formally raised and Drogheda denied employing dirty tricks, but strings were pulled to bar Sadler's Wells from the South Bank. Jennie Lee was gently persuaded that the costs would be extortionate. Arnold Goodman changed his mind. Despite GLC support and a heartfelt appeal from Laurence Olivier, Lee vetoed the South Bank opera house in order, she said, to save the National Theatre.

The decision was a recipe for planning blight. The South Bank complex arose as an unsightly, uncoordinated mess, a permanent blot on the riverscape. Sadler's Wells was almost sunk by the setback. Norman Tucker, blaming Covent Garden's 'antagonism',[172] suffered a nervous breakdown and retired. His capable successor, Stephen Arlen, was compensated by Goodman with a lease on a West End 2,900-seater, the Coliseum, five minutes' walk from the ROH. This time, Webster objected vociferously. Too close for comfort, he argued, and too large for the tender English voices that Sadler's Wells was supposed to be developing. But this was token resistance, not to be taken seriously. The underdog company moved into St Martin's Lane and Lilian Baylis's building became a venue for travelling players.

Quietly triumphant, Webster began to face the future. The death of his orchestral manager Morris Smith in October 1967, unmourned in the orchestra, was a sharp reminder that the founding fathers were fading out. Webster's term had been extended beyond the statutory retirement age, to 1970, when he would be sixty-seven. He also needed to replace Ashton, who was as old as himself, and Solti, who had accepted the conductorship of the Chicago Symphony Orchestra. Although Drogheda begged him to stay on for a further eighteen months, saying it was 'mad' to instal new opera, ballet and management teams simultaneously,[173] Webster was in a rush to settle the succession. He was not feeling at all well, and may have suffered a mild stroke. He mislaid his glasses at meetings and his speech was sometimes slurred. 'He had lost interest,' said one observer.[174] A proud man, Webster did not wish to be seen at less than his best.

His first duty was to dispose of Fred Ashton, his oldest friend in the arts. Madam had come banging around again complaining that the Royal Ballet was in disarray. Field was threatening to quit, Hart was not working out, Somes had the unpleasant habit of hitting people who disagreed with him and Ashton was his usual languid self. Ninette de Valois had never got over Kenneth MacMillan's defection to Berlin and wanted him back. MacMillan, too, was keen to return. Berlin had been, for him, a blur of drunken misery. He never managed to learn German or win public acclaim. Lynn Seymour found new friends and lovers, leaving him bitterly isolated. Egon Seefehlner, the Berlin intendant, begged Webster to take him back. 'He's drunk all the time and turns up to rehearsals in dressing-gown and pyjamas. Quite unacceptable in Berlin,' said Seefehlner.

Webster had often mentioned to Tooley, his right-hand man, that Ashton was due to retire at the same time as himself. 'Have you discussed this with Fred?' asked Tooley.

'No, I don't need to,' was Webster's reply.

'He was rather dismissive when questioned,' recalled Tooley. 'All he said was, "well of course there's going to be a change in '70, Ashton's going. You know that John, so why do you ask?"'

Tooley was given to understand that 'it had to do with something that happened in the 1930s homosexual arts scene, in which both were prominent. Ashton represented some sort of icon for David and he did not want to leave him behind. Also, de Valois was constantly saying, Fred must go. He must make room for younger people.'[175]

One morning in April 1968, Ashton was called to Webster's office and told that they would be retiring together in July 1970. 'Aren't you going to consult me about a successor?' quavered the great choreographer. Webster shook his head. 'That's all been settled,' he said.

'That was a very unhappy day,' recalled Tooley. 'I couldn't be present at the start of the disastrous meeting. When I went into the room, there was a crestfallen Ashton. He looked at me and said,

"John, I've been sacked." "Not sacked," said David, "Fred is just going with me." '[176]

The repercussions were colossal. Ashton told Somes and Hart that they were all being dismissed, and if they wanted to leave immediately he would willingly join them. He then phoned John Lanchbery, his chief conductor. 'Fred lived around the corner and would often call to say, put on the kettle, John, I'm coming over for a chat. On this occasion, I'll never forget it, he said: Put on the kettle, John, I've been sacked.'[177]

The Royal Ballet were dancing in New York when word arrived of Ashton's enforced retirement. 'We were completely shattered,' said Sibley, 'much more so than when we knew Madam was going. We were doing *Cinderella*, and everyone on stage was crying. Anthony and I had to carry that performance.'[178]

As Webster flew out to reassure the stricken dancers. Tooley pursued him with a panicky telegram:

DROGHEDA ROBBINS NINETTE BELIEVE IMMEDIATE PRESS ANNOUNCEMENT ESSENTIAL OTHERWISE SIGN WEAKNESS AND POSSIBILITY LEAKING DISTORTED VERSION STOP PHONING JOHN[179]

Nothing was announced, and the unpleasantness persisted. The Queen Mother, Ashton's friend, was notably displeased. Nureyev, who had given up pestering Ashton for choreography after going five years with only one new role, was distraught when Ashton dissolved in tears in his dressing-room. Mark Bonham-Carter, chairman of the ballet committee, feared that Ashton might take his work elsewhere, 'and while I believe we can straighten all this out eventually, the MacMillan/Ashton relationship does not help too much.'[180]

'We all blamed Webster,' said Sibley. Even de Valois let it be known that 'Webster should have changed his mind',[181] although the anti-Ashton pressure had come mostly from her. Ashton went to his grave believing Madam and MacMillan had acted in cahoots to unseat him. He never forgave MacMillan, or dared to confront the terrifying Madam. 'Fred was very suspicious of de Valois and her motives,' said Tooley. 'He was very much of the view that if it's going to be my fate to go, because that's what she wants, then maybe I have to go along with it.'[182]

Ever the artist, Ashton responded to adversity with a masterpiece. He was struck by the tragic figure of the elderly Edward Elgar, adored as England's great composer yet creatively washed up and superseded by younger men. Ashton built a flashback ballet upon Elgar's breakthrough work, the *Enigma Variations*, celebrating an idyll of youthful friendship. In Ashton's ballet, lost English values of leisure, companionship and honour shone to the fore, along with a wrenching compassion for the ageing genius who danced at its centre. Derek Rencher played Elgar, Beriosova his wife, Sibley the flirtatious Dorabella and Dowell a rumbustious architect. Staged six months after Ashton's demission, the ballet pulsated with personal resonances. 'We all knew what Fred was choreographing about,' said Beriosova, in her greatest role, 'but when he was thinking about Elgar, he forgot himself.'[183] Kenneth Clark wept at the première, telling Ashton he was 'an incomparable maestro'. Both of his remaining seasons contained significant new works, *Lament of the Waves* and *The Creatures of Prometheus*. 'I would have liked Fred to stay on for another three-four years,' confessed Tooley with the benefit of hindsight.

Solti was urged by his new wife to conduct *Enigma*. 'I kept on saying to him, go on, do it,'[184] she said. Solti explained that he hated making the music hover while the dancers did their stuff and had sworn never to conduct ballet again after working with Colonel de Basil's company at Covent Garden in 1938 and having to leave the pit at speed on the last night after forcing the dancers to follow authentic tempi. 'He loved looking at ballet,' said Valerie Solti, but in his entire decade at Covent Garden Solti never once conducted a ballet evening. Sibley, meeting him in Drogheda's box, berated him for the state of the orchestra which played beautifully for him and 'appallingly' when she danced *Swan Lake*. He smiled apologetically. As far as Solti was concerned, the union of opera and ballet at Covent Garden was an administrative convenience. He looked after the opera, and to hell with the rest.

Replacing so forthright a conductor was never going to be easy and Webster was not prepared to look far. He had earmarked Colin Davis back in 1965 and was unusually resolute in persuading the board that Covent Garden Opera needed the artistic leadership of a native son if it was not to lose sight of its founding mission. 'We all felt that we must appoint a British conductor,' said Drogheda.[185] John Pritchard, Webster's original favourite, had pitched his tent at

Glyndebourne; Charles Mackerras was deemed unready; and Reginald Goodall was too eccentric.

That left a straight choice between Davis and the house conductor, Edward Downes, who had performed wonders in revivals and brought off a tremendous staging of *Katerina Izmailova*. Downes was hard-working, plain-spoken and painfully myopic after eye surgery. Davis was regarded as the finest English prospect since the war after substituting for Klemperer in a *Don Giovanni*. Solti, who was kept fully consulted, suggested the job should be split, Downes looking after Italian and Slavonic operas and Davis presiding over Mozart, French music and moderns ('He doesn't do Wagner,' giggled Webster, 'that means we can get Kempe back').[186] Covent Garden, he warned, could ill afford to lose Downes.

The board, however, decided it had to be one or the other. The two professional musicians around the table, Sir Thomas Armstrong and Sir Keith Falkner, voted for Downes as the better trainer and all-rounder. The majority chose Davis as the better known figure. They were under time pressure to make a decision, as Davis was being courted by the Boston Symphony Orchestra. His fame was spreading fast while Downes was a well-kept local secret.

In a masterly summary by Denis Rickett, on his second stint as secretary to the board, Webster was instructed to negotiate 'an arrangement which would enable Davis and Downes to work together fruitfully and harmoniously at Covent Garden', with Davis as music director and Downes as principal conductor. That was unacceptable to the loser, who resigned from the staff and went off to establish Australian Opera in its resplendent Sydney harbour house. But Downes was too loyal and sentimental a man to turn his back on Covent Garden and returned to conduct there every year, a record he maintained to the end of the century. Goodall, meanwhile, cycled off to Sadler's Wells where he so illuminated a home-cast *Meistersinger* that he was garlanded as England's first Wagnerian, much to Solti's annoyance (the Hungarian Jew had never forgiven the former Hitler admirer his unrenounced Fascist opinions). The *Ring* that Goodall went on to conduct at the Coliseum in Andrew Porter's translation was broad and deep where Solti's was brisk and fiery, a genuinely alternative interpretation. A *New York Times* critic found it superior to anything on show at Bayreuth,[187] and London became an unexpected Mecca for Wagner worshippers. However, Goodall's Indian summer, allied to the loss of Edward Downes, left the ROH severely under-strength in the conducting department.

Davis asserted his credentials in the seasons before his accession with *The Midsummer Marriage* and *The Trojans*, removing some of the opprobrium from Tippett's opera but failing to match Kubelik's revelations in Berlioz. *The Trojans* was notable for a last-minute débutante, Janet Baker, who stepped in for Josephine Veasey as Dido and revealed a momentous talent. Baker had come up through the Glyndebourne chorus and Scottish Opera. There was now more than one way for an English singer to make a name and the new music director would need to attract and inspire the next national crop. Davis seemed to have all the right credentials. He worked easily with singers and had great respect for orchestral musicians. One morning he came into rehearsal to find the pit floor unswept. A call to Bram Gay, Smith's successor as orchestral manager, elicited the information that the cleaner was sick. Davis asked Gay to descend:

> At the pit door he offered me the choice of two brooms. He'd sent the orchestra to the canteen and the pit staff were aready moving chairs. He and I swept the floor. The message was clear. This was typical of the man.[188]

When push came to shove, Davis would always side with the working musician against the suits and allsorts of company management. He despised dilettantes and abhorred the press, even at its most fawning. When Harold Rosenthal, who had felt shut out of Covent Garden by Solti's massive competence, offered himself as dramaturg, or literary adviser, to the inexperienced music director, Davis refused to give him the time of day. As a conductor, he had few pretensions beyond solid technique and intensive preparation. 'I'm not a supremely gifted musician like Karajan, nor like Toscanini,' he said. 'I have been very, very lucky to have a balance between my brains and my feelings and my capacity as a musician. The man who is incredibly gifted from a very early age and is admired and adored from a very early age has a much more difficult time than I do . . . I know my limitations pretty well.'[189] Beyond the charming modesty was an unfathomable capacity to ignite a performance from within, until it glowed and shimmered with dramatic tension.

The only doubt about Davis concerned his solidity. At Sadler's

Wells, he had asked to be released from his contract before three years were up. There were cogent personal reasons. His fifteen-year marriage to a Sadler's Wells soprano, April Cantelo, was breaking up, and his love for their Iranian au pair Ashra Naini (known as 'Shamsi') was being thwarted by her inability or unwillingness to return to England. He moved into a dank basement, where mushrooms grew in his shoes. On leaving Sadler's Wells, he expected to become chief conductor of the London Symphony Orchestra but displayed such emotional turmoil on an Asian tour that only six players gave him their vote. He found a job with the BBC Symphony Orchestra and happiness in his remarriage in 1964. 'I set out to tame myself and to put all this energy into a more positive form,' he told the psychiatrist Anthony Clare, 'to overcome these seedy bouts of temper and rage.'[190] Devoted to Shamsi and their young family, he gave up work during school holidays to spend the time with his children. His box at Covent Garden was often given to parents he had met at the school gates. He loved to read esoteric works of psychology and spirituality and preached personal growth, seemingly at peace with himself.

Yet there was always about Davis a touch of insecurity, especially where stagecraft was concerned. Unlike Solti, who had spent his teens scurrying around the backstage, Davis was not '*un homme de théâtre*' and had no feel for thespian rituals and rhythms. At Sadler's Wells he had relied heavily upon a director of productions, Glen Byam Shaw, who 'was deeply hurt and felt badly let down'[191] when the music director upped and left. At Covent Garden, the Droghedas invited Davis to dinner with Peter Hall. 'I felt sure they would be attracted to one another,' said the wily chairman. '. . . Within days Colin was more or less saying to me that unless he had Peter to work alongside of him he did not think he could undertake the position of musical director at all. This meant creating a new post of artistic director.'[192] Davis, in a letter to Drogheda, stipulated that they should be 'on completely equal terms',[193] surrendering half of his directorial authority without a qualm. Hall, who was the most sought-after stage director and administrator in the country, had several irons in the fire, including an approach from Glyndebourne; but in March 1969 he agreed to join Davis at Covent Garden, 'with Peter on the artistic side very much the dominant voice'.[194]

All that remained was to anoint Webster's successor. John Tooley had served a patient apprenticeship since 1955. Webster was fond of

John Maynard Keynes (1944), inventor of the cultural economy and first chairman of the ROH

Ninette de Valois, dancing *Coppelia* at Sadler's Wells

Constant Lambert, musical firebird of English ballet, before he was ejected from Covent Garden

David Webster, ROH general administrator, scouting for singers in Munich with his music director, Karl Rankl (Photo: Sabine Toepffer)

Erich Kleiber, transformatory conductor (sketch by Eugen Spiro, c. 1949)

Operatic tea break in Gaumont Cinema, Cardiff, March 1954: (l to r) Constance Shacklock, Geraint Evans, James Johnston, Mr Brooks (cinema manager), Sylvia Fisher

Off to Africa, 1953: (l to r) Eric Mitchell, Elizabeth Latham (stage manager), Fred Dalberg, Joan Sutherland, Norman Walker, Constance Shacklock, Jess Walters (photo: PA/Reuter)

Fonteyn dances with Rudolf Nureyev to Yehudi Menuhin's violin on the
night her husband was shot, June 1964 (photo: David Farrell)

Georg Solti with protégée Kiri te Kanawa (photo: Mike Evans)

Colin Davis offers his baton to the heir to the throne (photo: Friends of ROH, photographer unknown)

Solti cues in Bernard Haitink, 1987

Ashton, after being sacked as Royal Ballet director

Kenneth MacMillan, his morose successor

Anthony Dowell, future RB director (sketches by Zsuszi Roboz)

Madam, still formidably in command

Antoinette Sibley, home-grown star and Dowell's dancing partner (sketches by Zsuzsi Roboz)

ROH Chairman Sir Claus Moser (left) receives a million-pound first-instalment from arts minister Norman St John Stevas, general director John Tooley watching intently (photo: Friends of the ROH)

Last-gasp populism: Paul Findlay presents opera in the Covent Garden piazza (photo: Richard Smith)

Mary Allen, in recovery, cultivates her Sussex garden

him and Drogheda found him presentable. Neither wanted to advertise the post because Tooley, they felt, 'might regard the decision to advertise as an indication of a lack of confidence in him.'[195] Two board members, Annan and Moser, warned that this was politically unwise. When Arnold Goodman got wind of the handover, he demanded an open selection procedure. Drogheda refused. Goodman was adamant: 'To us it remains a simple mystery that you can contemplate filling one of the most important musical appointments in the world by the sitting deputy without inviting anyone else to air his claims. To you it remains a total bewilderment that we can think this odd.'[196]

'I saw a serious issue of principle,' noted Drogheda. 'We had taken Arts Council finance "without strings", yet now on a matter where the right course of action seemed so clear, they were putting pressure on us. I knew that Tooley might be lost to us if the humiliating process of advertising was forced upon us, and that would be a serious matter for CG. But almost more important I felt that if as a board we settled on a given line for the good of the House, we could not bow to outside pressure to take another, or rather I could not be Chairman under such circumstances . . . In the whole of my Chairmanship, this was potentially the most dangerous area of conflict with the State . . . A Labour government, determined to shatter "establishment" methods in the pursuit of "democracy" picked on CG as a test case. I thought this was illogical, impractical and unfair.'[197]

In the event, an English compromise was reached. The Arts Council held a meeting with the ROH board, which agreed to send a notice of the vacancy to a select handful of qualified individuals. In Goodman's account, 'prospective candidates were telephoned with discouraging intimations that if they wanted to apply they could but their prospects were minimal.'[198] In fact, six men were notified by letter – John Denison of the Royal Festival Hall; Moran Caplan, the Glyndebourne administrator; Stephen Arlen; the Decca *Ring* producer, John Culshaw; Peter Diamand of the Holland Festival; and the Rt. Hon. The Earl of Harewood, who had the strongest credentials and appetite for the job.

Harewood had been Webster's right-hand man before he went off to run the Edinburgh Festival. His private life had undergone a public upheaval when he left his first wife, Marion, for Patricia Tuckwell, sister of the LSO hornist. While Harewood awaited Royal assent to his divorce under a siege of pressmen, Drogheda gave him refuge in his house the night before the couple flew abroad to get married. This was a personal kindness, not a professional courtesy. He would not allow Harewood, under any circumstances, to succeed Webster.

Harewood wanted the job and began lobbying for it. Alarmed, Drogheda took Harewood to lunch and made him an offer: withhold your application, and I will appoint you to the board with a view to succeeding me as chairman. Harewood was torn. He was still on the right side of fifty and keen to run an opera house, but as chairman he could reshape Covent Garden and as a wealthy landowner he did not need the salary or the duties of nightly attendance. Upon reflection, he accepted Drogheda's offer and joined the board.[199] Those who pressed his claims to Webster's post were fobbed off by Drogheda, each with a different excuse. Goodman, who knew Harewood as chairman of the Arts Council's music panel, was told that the ROH staff wanted Tooley, and that the Royal Family were so shocked by Harewood's divorce that they might boycott Covent Garden if he was in charge. Ken Davison was told that Drogheda could not forgive Harewood for some business at the London Opera Centre that cost Joan Cross her job. Drogheda told his mistress that Harewood was unsuitable because he was bound to spend too much time on his estates, near Leeds.[200] The truth of the matter is that Drogheda never trusted Harewood and was determined to neutralize him.

Diamand, the only foreign candidate, credulously submitted his credentials to the search committee which immediately found them 'not comparable to the claims of John Tooley'.[201] He was invited to a pro forma interview at the Treasury, a matter of days before the unstoppable announcement of Tooley's succession. Honour had been satisfied, but the job was plainly fixed and a House of Commons Committee was sufficiently disturbed to call a special hearing and denounce the Royal Opera House for underhandedness – its first formal public condemnation.

As for Harewood, Drogheda had him where he wanted. When Harewood asked to be named vice-chairman, Drogheda refused but strung him along. 'So far as the chairmanship itself is concerned,' he said, 'I don't know when you would like me to disappear from the scene. My idea was that I should see Solti out, so to speak . . .'[202]

At board meetings Harewood was full of ideas and Drogheda wanted none of them. Harewood held that more operas should be sung in English and backed a proposal from Davis and Hall for a vernacular *Marriage of Figaro*. Drogheda was incensed, fearing damage to the Royal Opera's international prestige. The suspicion dawned that he might not let Harewood succeed him after all. Goodman called the Palace and asked the Queen's Private Secretary, Sir Michael Adeane, if H.M. would object to having her cousin as ROH chairman. The reply was that she would not mind, albeit 'expressed in a fashion that indicated no great enthusiasm for the appointment'.[203]

Then, before blue blood flowed, Sadler's Wells was devastated by the death of Stephen Arlen from a five-week oesophageal cancer in January 1972. Harewood was approached by the company's chairman, David McKenna, and accepted the managing directorship without delay. He resigned from the ROH board and was thanked by Drogheda for his contribution in a letter expressing hope that the two theatres would 'work closely together in what is essentially a common cause'.[204] Before the year was out, Drogheda wrote to the Arts Council chairman, 'quietly boiling over the fearful disloyalty of George Harewood in attacking Covent Garden as he did in that interview with *Time Out*'.[205] There would be further irritations.

Harewood renamed his company English National Opera and challenged Covent Garden wherever he sensed a vulnerability. He demanded ever-larger slices of the Arts Council cake, founded a sister company in Leeds as English Opera North and missed no opportunity to depict ENO as the People's Opera and Covent Garden as the crusty toffs. Drogheda, for his part, was glad to see him go. Socially, the two earls remained on cordial terms. Theirs had been a very English conflict, with no apparent rancour. In years to come, though, loyalists would wonder aloud whether Harewood might not have saved the soul and spirit of the original Covent Garden. 'This would have become a very different company,' ruminated Edward Downes, 'if George Harewood had taken over.'[206]

Exciting as these events might have looked through opera glasses, the world outside was in the final throes of 60s revolution and would never be the same again. The American war in Vietnam bred a culture of protest and narcotics. The Soviet-led invasion of Czechoslovakia crushed hopes of a nuclear thaw and spread geopolitical despair. Martin Luther King and Robert Kennedy were assassinated. Students took to the streets, their cause varying from one western capital to the next. De Gaulle was driven from office in Paris, Lyndon B. Johnson in Washington. Harold Wilson, briefly boosted by England's 1966 World Cup soccer victory, was brought low by devaluation and his inability to tackle industrial chaos. Ireland, long dormant, awoke to sectarian violence.

As authority was mocked by its own ineptitude, the counter-culture thrived. Rock music was the language of revolution. London swung as never before. The Beatles disbanded, outshouted by the next wave. Brian Epstein and Brian Jones of the Rolling Stones died of drug overdoses. The cast of an imported musical, *Hair*, stood up and faced a West End audience stark naked. Dramatists grappled with *The National Health* (Peter Nichols), *The Ruling Class* (Peter Barnes) and *Time Present* (John Osborne). Fringe theatre was the medium for even freer forms of expression, liberated from state subsidy and self-censorship. 'The formative stage in my career,' wrote a future ROH general director, 'coincided with the explosive growth of the fringe in the late 1960s and early 70s.'[207]

Amid such ferment, the Royal Opera House risked looking irrelevant and out of touch. William Glock, newly added to the board, brought in the radical figure of Pierre Boulez, who had proclaimed 'burn down the opera houses!' Boulez conducted an impressive *Pelléas et Mélisande* on an abstract backdrop by Josef Svoboda and made a fine Philips recording, but never undertook another ROH production. In an effort to appear with-it, two new operas were commissioned, the first for a dozen years. *Hamlet*, by the deadly serialist Humphrey Searle, was abandoned half-way through its second performance when the Canadian baritone Victor Braun declared himself unable to sing another note. *Victory*, by Richard Rodney Bennett, who had written the delightful *Jazz Calendar* for a Frederick Ashton ballet, was an insipid dramatization of a Joseph Conrad story, inoffensively tonal and dedicated to Hans Werner Henze. Neither opera filled many seats, but *Victory* at least served some purpose as indigenous gloss on a crowning achievement.

Solti had long talked of taking Covent Garden into Europe and the Foreign Office were keen to establish a cultural presence in wall-torn Berlin. In April 1970, Solti led the Royal Opera to Germany with two Verdi productions, *Don Carlos* and *Falstaff*, which were acclaimed, and the Bennett opera, which escaped unbooed. Solti himself was lionized, Gwyneth Jones adored and Geraint Evans hugely roared by a public which had known no other Falstaff except Dietrich Fischer-Dieskau. The public, said the *Frankfurter Allgemeine Zeitung*, were 'beside themselves with enthusiasm'.[208] Apart from Regina Resnik (Mistress Quickly) and Carlo Cossuta (Don Carlos), the entire cast was British. Jennie Lee cabled her congratulations – 'We are all so proud of you!' – and the company came home on a high, having scaled the twin peaks of Munich and Berlin. It had taken less than twenty-five years to go from nullity to dominance. The only regret was that Webster could not witness the triumph: he was away in New York with the Royal Ballet, trying to rebuild bridges.

'The Royal Ballet had a fantastic success,' reported Lincoln Kirstein to Drogheda, 'due I am sad to say almost entirely to Nureyev. To me he is a vulgar acrobat. Margot should really not dance, but the company and in particular Dowell, were magnificent. I saw quite a bit of Fred, who is bitter and uncomfortable.'[209] The wounds were too deep to heal.

Webster had slipped and fallen in the market the previous winter and spent a few days in hospital. He remained unwell and unwilling to face the inevitable. On 30 June 1970, Covent Garden gave him a Farewell Gala. Seven conductors and some forty soloists took part, among them Sutherland, Vickers, Veasey, Gobbi, Shuard, Jones and Evans – all his favourites bar one, the irretrievable Callas. Benjamin Britten wrote an opening fanfare, the Queen Mother and Prince Charles were in attendance and Drogheda and Ashton paid warm tribute. There was no contribution from the Royal Ballet, which was rehearsing Ashton's Farewell and nursing his grievance.

When Webster tried to address the house, he choked on his speech and left the stage whispering, 'thank you.' At a Savoy lunch given by the Friends of Covent Garden, he got up to reply to Ashton's witty speech but, after a few words, broke down and began to cry. The artists and staff clubbed together to buy him a David Hockney portrait, to be hung in the Royal Opera House, and a pair of claret decanters for his Weymouth Street sideboard. Ten months later, on 10 May 1971, on a weekend in Brighton, he suffered a second stroke and died. Many felt his life had ended the day he left the opera house.

Geraint Evans overheard Webster's name mentioned one day in a buzz of chorus room conversation.

'You were very fond of him, weren't you?' he asked the chorus.

'Fond of him?' said one man. 'We loved him.'[210]

Webster, wrote the *Daily Telegraph* obituarist, had been 'the anchorman on whom all else depended'.[211] At his Thanksgiving Service in the Church of the Holy Sepulchre, High Holborn, the choir contained a clutch of international soloists. Ninette de Valois recited a poem by Yeats, John Tooley read the Lesson, Geraint Evans delivered a moving eulogy, Davis conducted Jon Vickers in 'Total Eclipse' from *Samson*, and Solti conducted Heather Harper in the 'Liebestod' from *Tristan und Isolde*.

Muriel Kerr stayed on a while to deal with his correspondence and supervise the erection of a memorial plaque at St Paul's Church, Covent Garden. She, too, did not enjoy a long retirement. In the spring of 1975, it was said, 'Muriel Kerr went home one night, put her affairs in order, took herself to hospital in a taxi and died. That was typical of Muriel. Never making any trouble for anybody.'[212] Davis and the orchestra performed at her obsequies.

At the time of Webster's death there were fifty-one of his founding team still on the payroll, including the repetiteur Norman Feasey and a bartender, Winnie Pradier, who had served since before the war.[213] Many had stayed out of loyalty to Webster, others owed their survival to his latterday laxity. Their time was now up, and the old guard were unsentimentally dispersed.

The curtain had fallen on the opening acts at Covent Garden, and the public streamed out in search of refreshment.

CHAPTER 8

The Long Interval: Propping up the Crush Bar
(1971–87)

THE PREDOMINANT COLOUR was brown. Suits, skirts, sweaters, leather and leisurewear came in all shades from auburn to rust, with large checks and loopy patterns on an unfailingly tan background. Even theatrical sets went brown, the actors vanishing into a modish murk as directors and a looming energy crisis kept the lighting low. Just why fashion should have dictated the colour of fecal waste to be the epochal hue is a matter for psychologists to investigate. It may have mirrored economic and political pessimism as much as cultural confusion, for the 70s were a decade in which assumptions of established authority were continually under threat. Palestinian hijackers and Gulf oil producers held industrialized nations to ransom. The West Indies whipped the white Commonwealth at cricket. China detonated nuclear devices. The president of the United States, Richard M. Nixon, was brought down by two newspaper men investigating a break-in. German and Italian industrialists were kidnapped and sometimes murdered by their children's friends. The holders of power were revealed to be powerless and the organs of state cracked under pressure. It was an era of glum uncertainty.

Harold Wilson called a general election in June 1970, persuaded by the opinion polls that victory was assured. To his bewilderment, the resurgent Tories under Edward Heath turfed him out of Downing Street. Wilson's failure to curb the unions had precipitated his downfall. The number of strikes in 1970 approached four thousand. Ten million working days were lost. The Tories, in a strategy meeting at Selsdon Park Hotel, near Croydon, resolved to legislate against union power, relax controls of prices and incomes, slash public expenditure and stimulate private enterprise through a series of tax cuts. The apparatus of state health and welfare benefits, divided and often duplicated between central and local government, was to be streamlined. Hospitals and housing estates would be built on a larger, more efficient scale. Those applying for benefits would be means-tested to reduce fraud. The featherbedding of failing industries with state subsidies to stem unemployment would be phased out. It was a bold programme, misguided in parts and some years ahead of its time. It might have worked had Heath held his nerve and fulfilled his Selsdon manifesto. But within a month after taking office, the Government suffered a crippling blow. Iain Macleod, architect of New Toryism and Chancellor of the Exchequer, died of a heart attack aged 56. No other senior figure had his zeal and charisma, and the Heath regime sagged into a soggy mode of climbdown and make-do.

It would be trite, though true, to describe Edward Heath as the worst Prime Minister of the century. He came into power with the best intentions and was brought down by extreme circumstances and the prevailing wisdom of a fatalistic Civil Service whose post-imperial aim was 'the management of decline'. Heath was a self-made man of the lower middle classes. Home Counties born and bred, he had applied for an organ scholarship at Oxford, where the examiner, Dr Thomas Armstrong, steered him gently towards Modern Greats. Heath continued to enjoy music, and sailing, as his favoured recreations. On becoming Prime Minister, he was congratulated by the likes of William Walton – 'Thank God you're in!' – and Carlo Maria Giulini, who 'thanked providence with all (my) heart for having placed the reins of government of this great country in the hands of a man whose concerns and political decisions will always be illuminated and enriched by the strength of his own rich spiritual and artistic experiences.'[1] There was also a supportive cable from Sir Thomas Armstrong, retired principal of the Royal Academy of Music and Covent Garden board member.

The London Symphony Orchestra came begging the new Prime Minister to conduct an Elgar overture at its November 1971 gala, which he did to his own evident satisfaction. The Royal Opera House was more circumspect. Drogheda had lunched Heath at the *Financial Times* and found him sulky and self-centred. A lifelong bachelor with few intimate attachments, Heath preferred the anonymities of orchestral mass to the human tangles of opera and ballet. Nor was he much impressed by ermined earls and scantily clad ballet dancers. However, an appointment that he made two weeks after election drew Edward Heath inextricably into Covent Garden.

Every incoming Prime Minister reshuffles the Private Office at 10 Downing Street, 'the single most important section'[2] of the power apparatus. The Private Office is headed by two civil servants, a Principal Private Secretary and a Foreign Affairs Secretary. The relationship between PPS and Prime Minister is among the closest in government, reaching a point where 'neither should need to finish a sentence to be completely understood by the other'.[3] No person in the country has easier access to power than the PM's PPS.

The man Heath picked as his Principal Private Secretary was Robert Armstrong, a stripe-shirted Treasury high-flier – Eton, Oxford, and, by nice coincidence, the only son of his Oxford examiner, Thomas Armstrong. Charming where Heath was truculent, unflappable in times of crisis, Robert Armstrong possessed an effortless authority and the capacity to inspire affection as much as respect, both from colleagues and from Prime Ministers of both parties.

For two years, Armstrong had served as Secretary to the Board of the Royal Opera House. He warned Drogheda that he might have to miss some board meetings, but there were two junior officials, Elizabeth Beavan and Andrew Edwards, who could take minutes and he very much hoped the Board would accommodate his changed situation. 'I am delighted that you can carry on helping Covent Garden,'[4] was Drogheda's silky reply.

From now on, the ROH would be but a heartbeat away from the centre of power. Where Attlee, Churchill, Eden, Macmillan and Douglas-Home hardly noticed the opera house, and Wilson had left cultural affairs to Jennie Lee, Armstrong's Prime Ministers became dutiful attenders. Drogheda was quickly keen to ascertain what advantage the ROH could reap from its Secretary's unexpected promotion.

He asked Armstrong to procure a knighthood for Solti. Armstrong suggested that he route the request through the Foreign Office since the conductor was not a British citizen. When it came to making the award, however, he arranged for the Prime Minister to present the insignia to the conductor at a post-curtain party in the Crush Bar.

Drogheda was growing concerned about Margot Fonteyn, who had been made a Dame but had no pension arrangements.

Armstrong mentioned that there was a discreet fund at the Prime Minister's disposal with which he could purchase an annuity for especially deserving citizens, giving them an unofficial state pension. The beneficiary was not allowed to know where the money came from, and all involved were sworn to secrecy. This tidy little Downing Street kitty was not accountable to Parliament, contravening a core principle of the British constitution. Its existence, never previously disclosed, is one of the funny little ways by which public good could be done with a nod and a wink from the person at the Prime Minister's right hand.

Both Armstrong and the ROH board were acutely sensitive to the delicacy of his position. 'Robert wouldn't be addressed,' said an official who attended board meetings for fifteen years. 'Even at times of financial crisis, I can only recall one occasion when someone asked for the matter to be brought to the PM's attention. "Perhaps the Prime Minister might be persuaded to look into this," was what was said, and nothing ever came of it. That was not the way to go about things.'[5]

The influence Armstrong wielded was contained in the raising of an eyebrow and a faint change of vocal inflexion. 'Yes, Prime Minister,' could signify anything from wholehearted assent to severe disapproval. Only an insider could tell the difference, and Armstrong was the ultimate insider. 'Never negotiate in public,' was one of his watchwords. Being 'economical with the truth' was a famous circumlocution that he employed in Australia some years later, on being sent abroad to lie for his country. Armstrong, with the classical propriety of an Old Etonian, wrote to *The Times*[6] on the day of his retirement pointing out that the evasion was not original: it had been coined by the eighteenth-century political writer, Edmund Burke.

So subtle a mandarin would never betray a confidence or curry favour, nor would the ROH board wish to discomfit him by suggesting it. It was enough to have Robert Armstrong sitting in the Prime Minister's anteroom for Covent Garden to feel secure and looked after. 'One had the feeling that we were extremely well protected,' said a senior staffer. 'People in power, whether they were left or right, knew about Covent Garden.'[7]

The incoming ROH team had much in common with the new Government. Tooley, Hall and Davis were all southerners of modest background, self-motivated and temperate. Hall and Davis were in their early forties, Tooley was 46. They spoke the same language, shared the same style. MacMillan, a Scot, grew up in Great Yarmouth on the Norfolk coast and never quite got to grips with middle-class style. Even more out of step was the bluff John Field, a northerner in his early fifties.

MacMillan came home a man reborn. On his way back from Berlin, he had stopped in Munich to see some Cranko ballets and go mountain climbing with his fellow-choreographer. On the morning of their first excursion, he collapsed in his hotel room. Doctors diagnosed a severe vascular spasm, brought on by overwork and heavy drinking. He was warned to give up alcohol and never touched another drop. In London, he stayed for a while with Georgina Parkinson and her husband. Lynn Seymour, his closest friend, had given birth to twins and was still enjoying her life in Germany. A loner through life, MacMillan had never seemed more isolated.

His first act at Covent Garden was to merge the touring troupe with the main company, dismissing two dozen soloists and replacing Field's 'Number Two Company' with an experimental New Group. His stated aims were to raise standards, cut costs, and give the provinces a chance to see more stars and new work. The cull was crudely carried out and deeply destabilizing in a ballet world that had known nothing but growth. MacMillan had his known favourites and Field protected a small knot of travellers. 'There were some of us who did not fit into either camp,' lamented Wayne Sleep, a brilliant young virtuoso dancer. 'Although we were not sacked, we did find ourselves marginalized, out on a limb, working but redundant.'[8] Several dancers resigned. Those who survived were roughly treated by Somes.

Field insisted on the title 'co-director', but MacMillan refused to treat him as an equal. He was reduced to Administrative Director. Then MacMillan saw a playbill on which Field's name figured above his own and exploded with rage. Field, friendless, was forced to resign before the season was three months old. He went on to become ballet director at La Scala, Milan, and later to run the Royal Academy of Dancing. Having danced for Madam since 1939, he was banished to the fringes of memory.

In place of Field, Tooley brought back Peter Wright, a former Sadler's Wells stalwart who had worked with Cranko since 1961 and developed steadily as a choreographer under Ashton's aegis. Wright took over the burdens of administration and touring. On the main stage, MacMillan opened with a hit, importing Jerome Robbins to stage *Dances at a Gathering* with a madcap mazurka for Nureyev and Dowell that seemed to proclaim 'anything you can do I can do better'. For the New Group he engaged Glen Tetley, an ex-Robbins American whose Nederlands Dans Theater flashed full-frontal nudity on the Sadler's Wells stage and whose first contribution to Covent Garden was the ironically titled *Field Figures*, with wavy music by Karlheinz Stockhausen. MacMillan made ballets for the New Group with modern music. But the mainspring of his opening season was *Anastasia*, a three-act expansion of a Seymour showcase he had created in Berlin, the story of a woman in a madhouse who claimed she was the sole survivor of the Russian royal family.

Seymour had returned with her twins, bought a house in Chiswick and danced for Robbins. 'In Lynn Seymour we had at last a ballerina whose whole body was as expressive as a Russian's,' wrote Richard Buckle. 'She was an even more wonderful actress than Fonteyn and far more a child of the period, with an appeal which went straight to the hearts of young people.'[9] Her success was integral to MacMillan's, glossing his profundity with high charisma, and in *Anastasia* – with Beriosova, Derek Rencher, Sibley, Dowell and the cream of the Royal Ballet in support – she gave proof of her virtuosic maturity. Yet the ballet bombed. It was too long and too adhesive to the three full-length symphonies by Tchaikovsky and Martinů chosen by the choreographer. MacMillan was booed at the curtain and the press was rough. 'Little short of disastrous,' said the *Guardian*, 'dull and repetitious' was the *Telegraph* verdict. Roughest of all was *The Times*, whose critic John Percival called the choreography an 'insipid copy' of Ashton's *Enigma Variations* and Grigorievich's *Spartacus* for the Bolshoi.

Drogheda, more than usually agitated, berated *The Times* arts editor, John Higgins, a former FT man, who agreed to curb his Crankophile critic. 'If I had a bet,' Drogheda told MacMillan, 'I would put a small sum on the unlikelihood of *The Times* ballet notices continuing in the same strain; and I do not say this to you in a frivolous manner.'[10] MacMillan appreciated his concern, but was badly damaged. 'One feels so helpless in times like this,' he replied, 'and of course you can imagine how deeply depressed I am.'[11] He went to see a psychiatrist and entered three years of analysis, not a happy augury for the new era – the more so when, that selfsame month, the Royal Opera team came unstuck.

*

The handover season from Solti to Davis was dominated by the surgent energies of Peter Hall, who directed all of the new productions, one for Davis and two for Solti. Davis chimed in with a Tippett commission, *The Knot Garden*, dedicated to Sir David Webster and signifying an attempt to grapple with contemporary confusions. Tippett had discovered America and come back with a taste for jazz, gay liberation, esoteric cults and unconventional relationships. 'The new set-up at Covent Garden believes that (this) is the kind of work to coax a new and "wider" audience,' noted the sceptical Philip Hope-Wallace.[12] Tippett's plot was typically shambolic, involving a black and white male gay couple, a female freedom fighter and a black-bearded psychoanalyst singing such hip lines as 'play it cool' and 'sure, baby'.

The audience, said Hall, 'will have to participate, we must make them participate. They may scream resentfully because opera is being dragged into the 1970s. But then something will have happened. That's why Colin Davis and I feel that there could be no better work for us with which to start our adventure together.'[13]

Davis and Hall gave it their all. The director ripped out the prompt box and extended the stage over the orchestra pit to bring the young singers – Yvonne Minton, Josephine Barstow, Robert Tear – closer to the audience. Jill Gomez, as the teenaged Flora, volunteered to wear a bikini and have the top ripped off to enliven a rape fantasy. 'That's absolutely brilliant,' said Hall, but the rapist balked at his duties and only detopped her on the opening night, when a clatter of coins signified that gentlemen in the stalls were reaching for their opera glasses. Davis conducted with passion and conviction and the cast were irreproachable, but the hope of *The Times* critic[14] that the opera would receive 'umpteen' revivals was quixotic. Although foreign intendants came to view the novelty, none took it back and Tippett remained a defiantly English delicacy, his swingers' opera outdated before it was sung.

Of Solti's departing glories, *Eugene Onegin* was sung in English because the conductor and cast knew no Russian, and *Tristan und Isolde* was almost capsized by a stupendous row between director and diva. 'I threatened to leave,' said Birgit Nilsson, 'because I didn't like the terrible way the *Liebestod* was staged by Peter Hall. First it was so dark I was tripping over Tristan's body. Then Hall wanted Tristan – Jess Thomas – to stand up behind me during the last part of the scene. He had tomato juice all over him, and I got smeared with it. I looked ridiculous. Solti said I should do whatever I wanted. He would take the blame . . . Of course Solti blamed me when Hall said he didn't want to have his work ruined by stars who changed everything.'[15]

She was not alone in her reservations. Andrew Porter began his FT review: 'Poor Mr Solti! Once again a performance prepared by him with love and care, with delicate attention to detail and passionate concern for musical effect, has been spoiled by insensitive, unimaginative inscenation.'[16] Hall had cut right across the grain of Wagnerian interpretation, neither embracing tradition nor convincingly overturning it. Solti would partner him again in a 1983 Bayreuth *Ring*, at the end of which the distressed maestro said he never wanted to conduct opera again. Hall's Covent Garden *Tristan* was panned by Harold Schonberg in the *New York Times* as 'the pipsqueak posturings of a director determined to show his cleverness'. Porter called it 'cheap'.

A week into the *Tristan* run, Hall told Tooley that he was unhappy. A week later, on 4 July 1971, two months before he formally became Director of Productions, Hall asked to be released from his contract: 'I have to admit to a great mistake,' he told Drogheda. 'The only course open to me is to recognize it and to apologize to you personally and publicly.'[17] He had underestimated the amount of work involved – 'to do the job properly I would have to devote all my time to it' – and discovered that he was temperamentally better suited to festival productions than to repertoire opera. He begged forgiveness from the board, from Tooley and particularly from Colin Davis: 'He gave me half his new kingdom gladly, and it is a poor way to answer his generosity. Working with him was one of the best experiences of my life.' But nothing in the world would persuade him to stay at Covent Garden.

Drogheda was thunderstruck. It was, he would say, the bitterest blow of his chairmanship. 'It is hardly necessary for me to tell you that I was most distressed to receive your letter,' he replied to Hall. 'I played a great part in bringing you together with Colin eighteen months ago, and therefore I have a very considerable sense of personal responsibility.'[18] Privately, he could not quite bring himself to believe the reasons that Hall had given.

That weekend, the *Sunday Times* accused the board of obstructing Hall's bold plans and precipitating his resignation. Hall denied having talked to the press and reiterated his regrets: 'I can only repeat that I am very very sorry.'[19] Drogheda was unconvinced, however, and a consolatory letter from Arnold Goodman only intensified his suspicions. 'In the end,' said the Arts Council chairman, 'it may be for the best that the release of Hall's remarkable talents for full theatrical employment is of no small advantage.'[20]

On reading the words 'full theatrical employment' Drogheda smelt a rat. He phoned Max Rayne, the property developer and Goodman crony who was chairman-elect of the National Theatre. Rayne was abroad on holiday. On his return, he planned to depose Laurence Olivier from the NT helm and it did not take a genius to guess whom he had earmarked as successor. Rayne eventually returned Drogheda's call, insisting (without being asked) that his 'knowledge of what has transpired between Covent Garden and Peter Hall is limited to what has been published in the press'.[21] Over-anxiously, he also reported the exchange to Goodman who, four days later, wrote to Drogheda in identical terms assuring him that neither he nor Rayne knew 'anything' about the reasons for Peter Hall leaving Covent Garden. They protested too much.

The truth, revealed in Hall's memoirs and Drogheda's papers, confirms that Hall met Goodman at Glyndebourne earlier that summer and told him that he was unhappy at Covent Garden. The arch-fixer 'greeted the news with delight'[22] and set up a lunch with Rayne in his flat, where they offered Hall the National Theatre. Hands were shaken and nothing was announced for eight months, until Olivier was eased out. Tooley reckoned that Hall was aware of the plot to drop Olivier before he jacked in his ROH job.[23] Hall, in his memoirs, admitted that he 'behaved badly'.[24] He was, without doubt, the best man for the National Theatre, but the intrigue that took him there was more questionable than any of the Covent Garden appointments. Thanks to Goodman, Hall's transfer escaped uncensured. Thanks also to Goodman, Hall's National Theatre was awarded a giant slice of the Arts Council budget, second only to Covent Garden's.

Hall, said the theatre's historian, 'needed the National'[25] to restabilize a brilliant career that was in danger of going off the rails. Famously uxorious (he would marry five times), he craved a home he could call his own. He also coveted fame, money and fun. Before he even warmed his seat at the NT, Hall arranged to direct operas at Glyndebourne, present a weekly arts show on television and make commercials for a brand of wallpaper ('Very Peter Hall. Very Sanderson'). In an era of fiscal stringency, his consumption was conspicuous and politically criticized, fomenting unrest within his own company. He would not have lasted long at Covent Garden and both Tooley and Drogheda came round to the view that 'it is better that it should have happened now rather than later'.[26]

The abruptness of his exit, however, threw plans for the next two seasons into chaos. Hall had put himself down to direct many of the new productions. Substitutes had to be scrambled. Happily, a new staff producer, John Copley, successor to Christopher West and Ande Anderson, came quietly into his own and established an unfussy house style. By the time *Figaro* came on stage in December, Hall was barely missed. The main legacy of his brief ROH encounter was a cloud of mistrust that fell between the worlds of English theatre and opera, ending the Keynesian dream of cross-pollination. From now on Covent Garden would look mostly abroad for its directors, severing its ties with Shakespearian stagecraft.

The personal consequences were messier and more protracted. On leaving, Hall snapped a limb off the three-legged directors' table, leaving Tooley and Davis to wobble precariously. 'Colin took it very badly,' said Tooley. 'He was feeling desperately insecure, really needed every prop he could find.'[27] Never high on confidence, Davis had relied on Hall to push plans past a board whom he mistrusted and openly attacked. He possessed neither the charm nor the force of a Solti to get what he wanted. When denied, he turned tetchy and reticent. Even in repose he needed constant reassurance, supplied at first by his close friend, the ardent Berlioz scholar, critic and conductor, David Cairns. Davis, many felt, never fully recovered from the shock of Hall's abandonment and would search for years for a second Hall.

Tooley, on the other hand, showed neither pain nor discomfiture. His talent was to keep a steady hand on the tiller. In the eye of any storm, he was impervious and courteous, insisting that all was well and the show would go on. Like the captain of the *Titanic*, he confided in no one and steadfastly performed his duty. He told his wife not to get too close to anyone at Covent Garden, 'in case he had to sack them'. There was something unflappably English about Tooley's phlegm, suppressing the possibility of adversity. 'He was quite reticent about telling me if anybody was ill,' said his wife, 'he didn't want me to know.'

He trotted out an inventive lexicon of bureacratic euphemisms – 'indisposed, unavailable, unforeseen circumstances,' to cover up for errant artists. A ballet conductor whom he sacked as a 'baleful influence'[28] would be lauded in his memoirs as 'devoted'. There was a rapid dismantlement of Solti aides. 'Colin and I didn't want Joan Ingpen to go,'[29] said John Tooley. Ingpen's version differed slightly. 'I went to Colin with a list of casts,' she recalled. 'He said: "I'd like you to leave. You're dangerous to me."'[30] Ingpen went on to become Head of Casting at the Met, the best they ever had; Davis found the help he needed from a German casting director, Helga Schmidt. In Tooley's mind, the facts were rearranged to fit the image he aimed to project of a happy family enterprise, untroubled by strife. If he could never be the father that Webster was, Tooley cast himself as the elder brother, the shoulder to cry on. He greeted every staff member by name and inquired solicitously after little Johnny's eleven-plus results or the old man's operation.

Like the politicians of his day, Tooley was not so much a leader as a conciliator. Heath, in government, lost his resolve to confront the unions and focused his energies on entering the European Community. He metricated shillings and pence into pounds and pee and replaced an unpopular purchase tax with an unwelcome Value Added Tax, fuelling inflation and stalling industrial growth. Prices shot up by ninety per cent in the first half of the decade.[31] The miners won a 'spectacular'[32] wage rise of twenty-five per cent after a seven-week strike that caused electricity blackouts at Covent Garden and across the land. Heath's attempts to enforce a prices and wages freeze failed to appease either side of a raging industrial war. His blustery, unapproachable personality inspired neither trust nor warmth.

Tooley, more transparently, made himself available to all people at all times, without giving of himself. After a bout of hepatitis, he moved into a company flat that was ten minutes' walk from the theatre. He could be at his desk each morning before breakfast and seldom left the premises before the curtain went up for the second act. 'I used to get it in the neck sometimes,' he divulged, 'when, for perfectly legitimate reasons, I was in Zurich or at the Festival Hall, and people in the company would say, where were you last night, John? Pity you weren't here, rattling good performance, you missed something.

'I was there most nights. I used to drive down to our house in

Wiltshire after the show on Friday night and I'd quite often get the train back Saturday afternoon to see the curtain up and maybe stay for one act before catching the train back. Very often I came back Sunday afternoon for a concert. It was a seven-day week. The fact is that institutions function well if there is somebody around who will give the time to drive them.'[33] 'He would occasionally have a Saturday off,' his wife confirmed.

Like Webster, he spoke no languages, but Patsy had spent three years with a United Nations agency in Rome and she made the Italian singers feel at home. Tooley displayed neither passion nor colour. He seldom raised his voice. He inherited from Webster a certain emollience, which allowed old lags and abuses to flourish. Ingpen, arriving at the Met, found tighter financial control and greater efficiency than she had left behind. Stars were paid much the same in both houses – Joan Sutherland was on five thousand dollars a night – but staff earned less at the Met and the backstage was better run. 'At Covent Garden, there was always trouble with stagehands,' she reported.

Tooley promoted William Bundy to Technical Director, in charge of all backstage operations. Bundy did not improve with age, nor did the backstage ambience. When he was finally obliged to retire at 65 in 1976, Tooley brought him back for the next six years as a freelance lighting director, regardless of his choleric disposition. 'This was a family,' said Tooley. 'If Bill Bundy blew his top, someone would rally round. The tempo was extreme. I took the view that we would get people out of their problems, and we did.' His doctrine of mutually assured assistance added a new dimension to the Websterian family myth. An organism that was always inward looking now grew dangerously inbred. People invested their entire lives in the house. Many looked no further for emotional fulfilment. Bundy's first wife, the stage manager Stella Chitty, found her second husband in the orchestra: a percussionist called Jack Wakely who, on stressful first nights, would knock on Tooley's door an hour before curtain up, spread a towel on his desk and administer a vigorous back massage to the retitled General Director. The family, in Tooley's view, was the essence of the house, a cause to be championed in its own right. Assured of its importance, it became, in parts, a breeding ground for slackness and indiscipline. In any clash between a family member and an outsider, Tooley would support his staff against all but the most exalted artists.

He missed little that went wrong, but his eye for an artist was never the equal of Webster's. His was not a quicksilver mind, and he turned for advice to the senior European intendants – Rolf Liebermann in Hamburg and Paris and Günther Rennert in Munich. Not that they could have helped him much, for his job was tougher than theirs. Where German houses would shut for a week before a new production, Covent Garden had to open every night or go bust. Where the French government always bailed out the Opéra, the ROH lived from one Arts Council grant to the next, in hope and in fear.

Tooley's was the loneliest post in operadom and he held his cards close to his chest. He gave up strong drink after his hepatitis and was to be found most intervals at the mirror end of the Crush Bar, sipping a small glass of wine and conversing with staff and patrons. He mingled with the upper classes and affected a cut-glass accent but never passed for one of the privileged. Unlike Webster, he was not a man to advertise his desires and frustrations.

'I don't think anybody ever got to know John,' said Paul Findlay, who spent twelve years as his assistant. 'What he adopted was a position where he listened. Few of his ideas were original. It was always a question of whom he had talked to last.'[34]

'He had, it was often said, a cushion-quality: the tendency to display the impression of the last chap who had sat on him,' said his orchestra manager, Bram Gay. 'It was an impression only; no one sat on John Tooley . . . He steered his own course in the end.'[35]

The inhibited, dedicated general director deserved some luck in the deadly months that followed Peter Hall's departure. He was rewarded that winter by a gift from heaven. A New Zealand soprano who had been knocking around London for three years was taken on to the staff by Colin Davis. Tested as a Flower Maiden in *Parsifal* and Xenia in *Boris Godunov*, she swanned off for the summer to sing the Countess in *Marriage of Figaro* at Santa Fe, New Mexico. She returned home to hear that Colin Davis wanted her as the centrepiece of John Copley's hurriedly recast *Figaro*. 'John absolutely didn't want me to do the part,' said Kiri te Kanawa. 'He'd seen me at the Opera Centre and knew I was a lazy, useless woman, and he didn't think I was old enough.'[36] Davis, however, was enchanted by the tonal purity of this half-Maori beauty (with whom he was once caught by his secretary wrestling on the floor),[37] and Copley agreed to start rehearsing her six weeks before the rest of the cast, led by the experienced Geraint Evans, Reri Grist, Victor Braun and Patricia Kern. So home-made a production, designed by Stefanos Lazaridis, would need a touch of magic to achieve ignition and that was where Kiri came in.

'At the first orchestral rehearsal,' recalled Lilian Watson who was making her début as Barbarina, 'when I heard her sing "Dove Sono", it was obvious she was destined for big things. There was a rustle in the pit as the sound hit them, an intake of breath.'[38] Victor Braun, who bought her a drink at the Nag's Head, warned Kiri that she was going to have a terrific success. 'Don't talk stupid,' she retorted, 'I'm only a student – I'll do my best.'[39] She was a plain-spoken girl who lived with her Australian husband in the stockbroker belt and commuted daily to Covent Garden by train. There were no starry pretensions to Kiri te Kanawa.

On the night of 1 December 1971, Davis struck up a scintillating *Figaro* overture, asserting his own credentials as the finest English Mozartian since Beecham. With 'Porgi amor' Kiri 'knocked the place flat'.[40] Ovations mounted with each successive aria. Serene, beautiful and tonally secure, she was framed by Davis's limpid, unforced rhythms, so different from Solti's adrenalized interpretations. By the time she reached 'Dove sono' in Act Three the applause was overwhelming and Davis paused to allow her a curtain call, but Kiri had promised Copley not to break the action. Her husband, Des, spent most of the evening in the Crush Bar, settling his nerves with gin-and-tonics.

Next morning, the press united in proclaiming the birth of a star – 'a teenage goddess' – in *Times* hyperbole. Philip Hope-Wallace struck a note of caution, averring that Kiri 'is too fresh an artist' for the Countess role and Desmond Shawe-Taylor suggested that she was not a full-grown Sutherland sensation but a promising talent 'on the threshold of international fame'. A day or two later Kiri was congratulated in the corridors by one of her contemporaries, Teresa Cahill. 'I bet Karajan will be ringing you soon,' giggled Cahill. 'He already has,' said Kiri.[41]

For Colin Davis and Covent Garden the rewards were immense. The new music director had staked his shirt on an ingénue and given her perfect musical support. He could not, said Andrew Porter, 'have made a better start' and there was much else to suggest spring in the air. Davis launched a clearout of what he regarded as deadwood in the chorus, orchestra and company of singers. 'Those of us who were over fifty were gradually being phased out,'[42] noted Michael

Langdon. 'You can stay here and do nothing,' Davis told the valuable John Lanigan, 'but I have nothing for you.'[43] David Ward, the English Wotan, was pensioned off. Amy Shuard, the cockney Turandot, was cut to once a season; she died soon of a heart attack, aged fifty.

For those singers who remained on the payroll, 'working at Covent Garden had become just a job'.[44] Kiri te Kanawa, as soon as her contract was up in 1973, cut loose and joined the jet-set. Typically for her time, she showed little social or emotional attachment to the company and its members. 'I don't ever remember partying,' she said. 'It was always straight home and settle down. I had an hour and a half to travel home to Esher.'[45]

Nor did she deepen her affinity with the music director. 'Colin had a family and children,' she said, 'he didn't really have time to expand. He had a bigger life outside. For him, it was like coming into work. Tooley was a good friend to me, if you can say there are friends in this business.'

Slow and late in learning roles, she required intensive tuition, especially in German operas where she (like Davis) felt least secure. It was with Solti that she formed her warmest association, studying the Strauss heroines. 'I turned myself inside out for Solti,' she recalled. 'I knew I could learn so much from him. I used to ring up and say, can I come round for a cup of tea? His door was always open.'

Unlike Davis, who was a specialist conductor and introspective man, Solti was an all-rounder and all-too-human maestro, who chased the nubile Kiri around his studio and pinned her to the couch.

'What about Valerie?' quavered Kiri.

'She will never know,' panted Solti.

'Yes she will,' said the spunky singer, 'because I'll bloody tell her.'[46] Her finest recordings, including *Figaro*, were conducted by Solti.

Covent Garden was no longer a magnet for Anglophone singers, or even the destination of choice. Lilian Watson, who spent four years with Welsh National Opera before her ROH début, never contemplated joining the staff. 'John Tooley did his best to make you feel welcome,' she said. 'He would always be there at the start of a rehearsal period, greeting everybody by name, how are you, nice to see you. The doormen would also recognize you, which is more than can be said for Vienna. It was a good place for a British singer to come home to, but it was not home.'[47] In the modern world, there was no reason to regard Covent Garden as more than a mainline station on the singing circuit, neither a sacred cause nor a special case.

Janet Baker, another glowing attraction with deep English roots, felt much the same. She maintained a stubborn independence and, though many of her finest hours and her final nights were seen at Covent Garden, she felt no sentimental attachment to the place. 'I think the House itself is a complete coquette,' she wrote. 'She was quite prepared to give herself to the production team today, she lets the stage staff believe they own the stage: we have the dressing-rooms and that part of the stage in between the dropped curtain and the pit, and the audience is allowed the foyers and the seats. But really, she belongs to herself.'[48]

The arts under Edward Heath were pushed off the Cabinet table and into the red box of a second-rank minister, the Paymaster General. Viscount Eccles was a collector of artefacts and watercolours and a patron of the English potters Bernard Leach and Lucie Rie. A bluff, well-heeled amateur known to back-benchers as 'Smarty-boots' for his immaculate turnout, David Eccles believed the arts should help pay their own way. He introduced entry charges at museums and refused to oppose the imposition of VAT on theatre and concert tickets, pushing up prices by a tenth and more. In his second year, however, Eccles achieved a twenty-five per cent increase in the Arts Council's grant and while much of the money was consumed by stagflation it nonetheless signified an extension of Tory support for the Keynesian principle.

Having landed extra money, Eccles was not going to leave it in the lap of Arnold Goodman, whom he disliked and mistrusted. Goodman had been too close to his Labour predecessor Jennie Lee and maintained a direct line to his own Prime Minister. Eccles saw him as a threat and a snob, squandering public money on a handful of London causes. He called for the largesse to be spread among the shires, with special emphasis on amateur groups and English craftsmanship. 'We had to get rid of Arnold Goodman,' explained Eccles. 'He didn't want to do anything outside London.'[49]

'Arnold didn't want to go,' recalled his successor, 'but Eccles would not give him another term.'[50] One morning, Patrick Gibson received a call from the Paymaster General at his office in the

Financial Times. 'Your name came to me while I was in the bath,' said Eccles winningly. 'Don't touch it,' said the FT chairman Oliver Poole, on being told that Gibson had been dangled the Arts Council. Gibson, imbued with a sense of public duty and a passion for the arts, could not refuse.

No one was made happier by his acceptance than Garrett Drogheda, who counted Gibson among his most trusted associates and looked forward to a restoration of Covent Garden's preferential status. Once again, he imagined, the opera house and Arts Council would walk hand in glove to the Treasury. Gibson, however, was as even-handed as he was amiable. Over his five years as chairman, he established a doctrine for distributing subsidy more evenly around the country. As the Arts Council grant trebled – from £11.9 million (1971–2) to £37.15 million (1976-77) – the ROH share fell from twenty to fifteen per cent (£1.6 to £4.3 million). In real terms, with inflation raging and the pound unsteady, the value of its state grant declined by almost one-fifth.

'Pat Gibson was a wonderful chairman, absolutely fair at all times,' said an ROH board member, somewhat ruefully.[51] Drogheda suppressed his regrets and remained on friendly terms. 'I had no trouble from Garrett,' said Gibson. 'It was Max Rayne at the National Theatre who used to send me robust letters, ending: "However, very best regards".'[52]

There was one large trump left in Drogheda's hand. No sooner had Arnold Goodman left the Arts Council than Drogheda lured him on to the board of Covent Garden, where he served for ten years. The fact that Goodman was also a director of English National Opera and, from 1977, its chairman, did not appear conflictual to this most impartial of lawyers who, at one and the same time, represented the Conservative, Labour and Liberal party leaders. What Drogheda sought from Goodman was influence and access; what Goodman expected in return was pride, pomp and a feeling that he was central to every institution and individual that mattered.

With his usual skill, Goodman left no fingerprints. His file in the ROH archives is completely empty, cleared as if by order. His notes to Drogheda were sparing and his attendances infrequent. 'I frankly regarded the activities of the board as almost entirely irrelevant to the conduct of the opera house,' wrote Goodman in his memoirs. 'I found the discussions long-winded and rarely reaching any conclusion that was reflected in action. They bore a resemblance to an expensive engine that had no transmission to the wheels. It chugged on pointlessly at tea-time meetings where the only compensation originally was the excellent smoked salmon sandwiches. I can trace my increasing irregularity of attendance to the disappearance of the expensive sandwiches and their replacement by an inferior paste.'[53]

Goodman was being, as ever, over-modest and casual with the truth. 'Arnold's qualities were not political,' said Claus Moser. 'He occasionally brought crucial wisdom to difficult issues, such as: was this a moment when we should write to the minister? Later, when we had a threatened strike in the orchestra, Arnold was chairman of ENO. I attended his negotiations and he attended ours, and there I saw his sheer brilliance as a negotiator. He always referred to Covent Garden as "The Opera House" even when he was at ENO. But Arnold was a natural chairman – he was not made by God to sit on somebody else's board. And by the way, we never had smoked salmon sandwiches.'[54]

Goodman's chief attraction to Covent Garden was his unrivalled range of contacts. The ROH was seriously short of money. Large sums were needed to sustain the international standards that had been so painfully attained. In addition, an opportunity that loomed just around the corner would require more capital than the company had ever seen. The Government and Greater London Council were planning to remove the fruit and vegetable market from Covent Garden to the other side of the river. The market was unsightly and noisome, they said, a traffic hazard and a blight on London's tourist potential.

These were the official reasons for vacating the site. There were other, less trumpeted grounds. Britain was in the grip of a property boom as investors, fearful of industrial disorder, put their money into bricks and mortar. Contracts and kickbacks were flying like confetti, and politicians of both ruling parties became tainted. Labour's fiefdom in north-east England was comprehensively corrupted by a crooked architect, John Poulson. The Tories lost their Home Secretary, Reginald Maudling, over business deals with a property developer. The need to clear Covent Garden was dictated as much by investment potential as by any urge for modernization.

Committees had been discussing the removal of the market since 1961 and Drogheda spoke up in the House of Lords to demand a share of the free space for the Royal Opera House. He took a

Commons committee around the building, demonstrating its dangerous squalor, and he impressed on ministers the inefficiency of having operas rehearsed in an East End cinema and the ballet in a West London gym. Finally, he wrote directly to Robert Armstrong 'asking him whether he could possibly help us over the acquisition of the Royal Opera freehold,' and recognizing that 'he will probably be furious'.[55] In January 1974, just as the property boom burst, Drogheda was told that the ROH would be allowed to acquire the great Floral Hall and some extra land – but there would be no extra money for development.

This was cork-popping news, intoxicating and hazardous in equal measure. With enough room to accommodate both companies and the chance to turn a Victorian opera house into a modern marvel, Covent Garden could outshine the new National Theatre which had been built and furnished to the last teaspoon from public money. Covent Garden, however, would have to find private money, and where it might come from was unclear. The ROH board was dominated by airy intellectuals of another era, great minds and grey beards. Drogheda had recruited the groceries baron John Sainsbury, who had given sterling support to Madam's ballet school since marrying the dancer Anya Linden, but he was now the only businessman on board. Sainsbury, in his early forties, was also chairman of the Friends of Covent Garden, the 11,000-strong educational and social group whose president was Marion Thorpe, Lord Harewood's ex-wife now remarried to the Liberal Party leader. The Friends could be counted on for small change and gentle suasion, but ten million pounds would be needed for renewing the house and the need was pressing. So Drogheda did what noblemen have done since the dawn of time. He turned to his Jews.

His first lunch with Goodman as a director dealt with tapping rich Jews to support Covent Garden. Goodman himself was persuaded to donate a set of chairs to the orchestra. His friend Max Rayne sent a thousand-pound cheque.[56] Another Goodman crony, Harry Kissin, set up and chaired a Redevelopment Trust. A Danzig-born lawyer who made his fortune trading commodities, Kissin was a member of Harold Wilson's inner circle, along with the banker Siegmund Warburg and the raincoat maker, Joe Kagan. Kissin in 1973 made himself unpopular in the City by taking over the blueblood merchant bank Guinness Mahon. He earned further notoriety at the Royal Opera House by having legal papers served on him in his box one night. Drogheda gave Kissin a seat on the board but held him at arm's length, sending Ken Davison to deal with him on Trust matters.

Drogheda was not conventionally anti-Semitic in the manner of his City contemporaries. Warburg, who introduced short lunches and Eurobonds to the Square Mile, had been snubbed by the banking set and saw his firm dubbed 'the nightclub' for carrying on working past five o'clock. Jews were excluded from old firms and golf clubs. 'We can't have the likes of Paul Hamlyn in British publishing,' sniffed the patrician Harold Macmillan of a bumptious refugee.

Drogheda eschewed such prejudices. He was proud to call Solti his friend and to embrace such civilized, establishmentarian Jews as Goodman, Berlin and Claus Moser. But he was wary of self-made Jews and could not fathom their motives. 'Never forget, George,' he lectured the thrusting young chairman of Maples fusty furniture store, 'what is an Englishman's by privilege, the Jew has to acquire by merit.'[57]

George Whyte was one of a new breed of quick-thinking entrepreneurs who were shaking up the retail sector. Hungarian by birth, he grew up in the Blitz and got hooked on Covent Garden as a fourteen-year-old schoolboy on seeing the City Ballet of New York in 1946. 'Covent Garden was my alma mater,' said Whyte.[58] A well-rounded man, who studied piano and science in London and Paris, he founded his own design business, was taken over by Maples and so energized the firm that in seven years its shares shot up elevenfold. Still in his thirties, he asked if he could help the opera house.

Drogheda invited Whyte to dinner at Lord North Street with Bernard Delfont, the television magnate. Over coffee and cigars, Drogheda said, 'I wonder if you could help me with something? I've got the Queen Mother coming to this Gala and we're about six thousand pounds short. Can you think of a couple of chaps who might like to sit next to Her Majesty in the Royal Box?' Whyte, looking at Delfont, said, 'I will if you will,' and they split the bill. But when the Gala evening came around, Whyte was away skiing. He had no particular desire to meet the Queen Mum, whose views on Jews were known to be reactionary. Whyte told Drogheda he would organize a fundraising drive for the redevelopment, but would need a seat on the board to run it efficiently. Drogheda was aghast at his presumption. A seat on the board, he replied, was an honour bestowed by the Minister in the name of Her Majesty. He could not nominate for such an honour a man he hardly knew. If, after a few years of attending the finance committee and raising lots of money, Whyte would prove himself worthy as an Englishman he might, just might, be co-opted on to the board, but he could not promise anything.[59] Drogheda told Tooley: 'You must get the idea of George Whyte as a Board Member out of your system. I am not willing to consider making him a Member of the Board.'[60] Whyte, mystified and hurt, melted away. Over the next decade, he applied himself to artistic and charitable causes in Switzerland, Israel and the Far East, before making a further, equally futile, effort to save the opera house.

Salesman that he was, Drogheda was confused by altruism. A Cincinnati businessman called Corbett offered to finance a new production of Gounod's *Faust*, provided its Mephisto could be sung by the American bass-baritone, Norman Treigle. The board was torn between gracious acceptance and total disgust. Goodman threatened to resign if dollars dictated artistic policy. Drogheda asked him to draft a reply, outlining the *amour propre* of the situation. Goodman's letter to the American was a masterpiece of English hypocrisy. Having thanked Corbett for an offer which 'would make it possible for the House to have a new production', he added:

> So far as Mr Norman Treigle is concerned, he is, of course, known to us, and his claims would naturally be taken into consideration for any suitable role for which he was qualified and available. We could not, of course, give any further assurance in relation to his employment; nevertheless the Board of Covent Garden will accept with great enthusiasm the proposal on your part to finance the special production referred to and we are indeed most grateful for so generous an offer.[61]

Faust was duly staged in November 1973 with Treigle as Mephisto and the Corbett Foundation paying the bills. Treigle turned out to be a heavy drinker who could not be bothered to rehearse a role he claimed to know. Threatened with the sack if he did not at least attend the general rehearsal, he turned up on crutches. Kiri te Kanawa, who sang Marguerite, was blighted by the tension and the production was roundly condemned. This did not stop the ROH board agreeing to a further gift from Corbett for Donizetti's *L'elisir d'amore* two years later. Sadly, Treigle took an overdose of sleeping pills on top of his whisky diet in February 1975, ending Corbett's involvement in Covent Garden without any point of principle having been established.

It was now painfully clear that the opera house needed new streams of funding. The state would pay the wage bill but not the costs of production. Big business was the obvious target, but there was no strategy involved. Whenever a new season was planned, members of the board and trust would ring around their friends and colleagues, soliciting funds for one show or another. A list of 'corporate members' began to appear at the front of opera and ballet brochures, and fulsome pages of thanks were offered to those 'who made this production possible'. Imperial Tobacco, hemmed with government health warnings, paid for *Un Ballo in Maschera*. Barings, the private bank, and Commercial Union Assurance underwrote a new *Ring*. Among the steadiest donors were J. Sainsbury Limited, the supermarket chain, and the Linbury Trust of Anya Linden and John Sainsbury, which funded four new ballets in as many years. Without such gifts, the ROH would have been reduced to dull revivals. Yet, essential as fundraising had become, nothing was done to recruit the know-how and purposefulness that American opera houses brought to the serious business of raising money.

To the board's surprise, and admittedly his own, it was John Tooley who came up with the most innovative form of external sponsorship. He and Colin Davis were anxious to attract a younger audience and in the summer of 1971 succeeded in packing the stalls with young faces for a Proms week by ripping out 400 seats and charging cinema prices for *Boris Godunov*. The BBC, on this occasion, covered the deficit. The following year, Tooley persuaded the Midland Bank to fund the summer Proms, which they continued to do for quarter of a century, eager as all banks are to reach a new generation. 'John, it's good for you; it's good for us; let's stay together,'[62] said the Midland chairman, Sir Archibald Forbes.

Students would queue all night for fifty-pence tickets and Sergeant Martin, the commissionaire, crammed seven hundred bodies into the steaming arena. Dress code was suspended. 'I would wear shoes if I were you, madam,' Martin advised one flaky, long-haired blonde, 'you never know what debris there is on our floors.' The Crush Bar sold beer, coffee and rolls at street prices instead of champagne and smoked salmon. Neophytes were lured into the opera house and smitten for life, more perhaps than at any time since the opening euphoria. Tooley, in retrospect, accounted it as one of his two greatest initiatives. In 1975, he extended the scheme to ballet nights in a tent, the 'Big Top', in Battersea Park. There was a heady air of renewal about these improvisations, which persisted throughout the decade. The only objections came from Drogheda, worried about 'upsetting Covent Garden's regular clientele'.[63]

Marshalling the upper crust to support the redevelopment, Drogheda was picky about whose pockets he picked. For the launch banquet, still some years ahead, he would refuse to invite the 'wrong sort of person', ruling out many a new-money millionaire. Sir Charles Clore was one of the wealthiest men in London and a regular at Covent Garden, where he noisily appreciated good singing before departing, blonde on arm, to his table at Annabel's, the place to be seen. Clore was the country's take-over king, the first to agglomerate asset-rich businesses for no reason other than the urge to expand. 'It was a natural part of his make-up to adopt the brutal approach,' said an admirer. 'He was a zealot for money, his grasping for it was a form of gluttony, an appetite which was voracious, never satistfied.'[64] Abandoned by his beautiful wife, Clore vented his frustrations on commercial and sexual conquests. He once told Nureyev how much he admired his single-minded pursuit of wealth: was it possible that a dancer could earn a million a month, tax-free? Clore was not a subtle man, not Drogheda's type, though word was out that, in failing health, he was trying to give away much of his money.

Hearing about the appeal, Clore called his married daughter, Vivien Duffield. 'Have you been invited to this dinner at the Guildhall?' he demanded.

'No,' said Vivien, 'have you?'

'No,' said Clore. 'Pity, because I was looking to do one big thing and we could have done the whole of the development.'

'Rubbish,' said Vivien, 'we've never done anything that big.'

'Well, I'm looking to do something big,' said Clore.[65]

The price of a new building was small beer for the Clores, but Drogheda could not bring himself to ask. To let in a man like Clore would lower the tone, undoing his efforts to bury Covent Garden's plebeian beginnings. He intended to leave the opera house at the summit of society and the centre of national affairs.

Three days into 1973, the ROH mounted the opening and closing nights of a ten-day 'Fanfare for Europe', marking Britain's entry to the Common Market. Acclaimed by Edward Heath as 'our country's greatest achievement',[66] the treaty was welcomed by the business sector and intelligentsia and resented by industrial workers and empire loyalists. It was an act of disunion that inaugurated a year of insurrection as Heath's Government lost its grip on the economy and the unions rose in rebellion. But for the Royal Opera House, representing the establishmentarian view and discarding its little-England antecedents, Europe was the great leap forward. With the Queen in her Box and Heath beaming like a beacon, John Copley and Patrick Garland assembled a night full of stars in a panoply of music and drama. Laurence Olivier, Sybil Thorndike and Judi Dench gave readings; Schwarzkopf, Gobbi, Régine Crespin, Peter Pears, Janet Baker, Geraint Evans and the fresh-voiced Kiri te Kanawa did the singing. 'It was a marvellous evening,' said Heath, in a thank-you note to Kiri, 'and it was a special pleasure to see how naturally the British contribution (in which I include the Common-wealth contribution) dovetailed into the European contribution.'[67] The closing gala was built around ballet and Drogheda impressed upon Kenneth MacMillan the 'great honour that Covent Garden should have been chosen both to open and close the ten day's festivities.'[68] Little did he know that this was the last time that century the ROH would figure at the centre of a national celebration.

A quirk of fate had raised MacMillan from the sloughs of despond. Taken by an art-dealer friend, Jeffrey Solomons, to see a Clint Eastwood film, *Play Misty for Me*, he clicked with another member of the party, an Australian artist called Deborah Williams. He took her to see his ballet, *Triad*, and asked her to sail with him to America on the *QEII*, as he hated flying and was still (as he told Drogheda) 'under my Doctor's supervision'.[69] He also asked to marry her, only to discover that Williams was not yet divorced. She had come to London, working as a waitress and nanny, in order to get over a failed marriage. MacMillan's need for her was so profound that she moved in with him and he, in response, grew in strength and confidence. 'When Deborah came on the scene,' said Tooley, 'he did open up quite a lot. He found in her a very close ally and someone who was feeding him huge emotional support and was also valuable for bouncing off ideas in the way he had done with Lynn Seymour.'

The American trip was unhappy. *Anastasia* was booed and

MacMillan was hounded by Ashton fanatics. 'They followed him down the street as he left the stage door, they screamed and spat at him,' recalled Monica Mason.[70] The arrival of another Soviet defector, Natalia Makarova, added zest to the coming season. Deborah fell pregnant, Makarova danced Juliet to Nureyev's Romeo and a setting of Kurt Weill's *Seven Deadly Sins*, with the Canadian Jennifer Penney in the central role and Lynn Seymour uproariously self-parodying as Greed in one of her obese phases, kept the much-feared critics at bay. Even the death of John Cranko, who choked on his vomit after taking an in-flight sleeping pill, could not cloud MacMillan's golden summer. In August 1973, as Deborah awaited the birth of their daughter, he choreographed a three-act *Manon*. His sights were set ever higher.

Manon was overlong and undercharacterized, maimed by a mid-rehearsal injury to Antoinette Sibley. 'I never knew what her ailment was,' said MacMillan, 'I never knew and I never found out . . . I had to finish it and Antoinette wasn't around, but the whole stimulus for doing it was her.'[71] Determined to deliver on time, he created the rest of the title role on Jenny Penney and reviewers zoomed in on that central weakness. *Manon* was deemed a flop by many critics, none more influential than Clive Barnes, who descended from the *New York Times* to preview the Royal Ballet's next US tour. Barnes, a Londoner and Ashton fan, revelled in his newfound notoriety as 'Butcher of Broadway'. He attacked MacMillan both in print and on the dinner circuit and his views blighted box-office sales. Soon after *Manon* opened in New York, MacMillan learned of a plot to replace it, mid-run, with Nureyev's *Nutcracker*. 'If you take *Manon* off,' he said quietly, 'I'll put the company on a plane and we'll fly home.'[72]

As if to relieve the pressure, MacMillan conjured up *Elite Syncopations*, to ragtime music by Scott Joplin. It was one of the few ballets ever to rock the belly of the Royal Opera House with irrepressible mirth, an instant hit. When the director married Deborah, in the spring of 1974, Peter Wright was best man – a symbol of the peace that seemed to be settling on the company. Even the rumblings of Lynn Seymour, who resented Deborah and was newly pregnant herself, did not greatly ruffle the waters. Seymour went to see MacMillan's psychoanalyst and was dismayed to learn that he never mentioned her. Their detachment grew, and an altogether calmer atmosphere settled at the head of the Royal Ballet.

*

At the Royal Opera, Colin Davis was having a rocky time. After the dream start came a string of disappointments. *Nabucco*, limply cast, demonstrated that he was not much of an early Verdian. *Don Giovanni* was loudly booed. A hangover from Hall's time, it was linked to a planned Davis recording for Philips. Over lunch one Saturday, Tooley and Davis persuaded Peter Brook to direct, but by Monday morning the wily genius had pulled out. The house team of Copley and Lazarides stepped in, investing the production with trivial ideas and a squeaking metal-rod set with huge slats in the floor where singers caught their feet. The cast was weak and local: Peter Glossop, Gwyneth Jones, Geraint Evans, Wendy Fine, Stuart Burrows.

Davis, on opening night, poked his tongue at the booing audience. In a newspaper interview, he showed signs of stress. 'Are they out to destroy me?' he railed.[73] John Pope-Hennessy, queenly director of the Victoria & Albert Museum and an increasingly outspoken board member, described the performance as 'one of the coarsest . . . I had ever heard. It was badly designed, in feeble, derivative, messy sets and was produced with a hideous literalness which would have made the meaning of every syllable evident to an audience of Eskimos . . . Colin Davis' behaviour before the curtain seemed to me undignified and reprehensible .. [Davis] appears (in the few conversations I have had with him) to have the brain of a sparrow, little operatic experience and a minus quantity of taste.'[74]

Davis assured Drogheda that he was 'not in the least despondent'[75] and had found a new helpmeet in the German director, Götz Friedrich, who would produce Peter Hall's intended *Ring* and then stay on as director of productions. His arrival would necessitate a renewal of the music director's contract for a minimum eight years,[76] a prospect that left board members feeling 'very unenthusiastic'.[77] Their spirits were not raised when the experienced Czech producer, Vaclav Kaslik, stormed out before the première of *Tannhäuser* in September 1973. In a letter to Tooley, copied to every arts editor on Fleet Street, Kaslik accused Davis of being a theatrical dilettant: 'Perhaps it will be remembered that in Covent Garden my production of *Pelléas et Mélisande* ran in harmonious collaboration between Boulez and all the cast, until Colin Davis with his production ideas and demands completely broke the production of *Nabucco* and *Tannhäuser*. While Covent Garden has at the head of the artistic management such an untheatrically thinking Colin Davis there will be no place for me here.' Hours later, under invisible pressures, Kaslik withdrew his letter, having 'no desire to harm anyone's personality or integrity'. In a parting note to Drogheda he added: 'The form of communication chosen by Mr Colin Davis was extremely outrageous indeed.'[78] *Tannhäuser* was doomed. Jon Vickers had pulled out of the title role, citing blasphemy. His substitute Richard Cassilly fell sick and was replaced at the last moment by the German understudy Wolfgang Kassel, singing opposite the large American soprano, Jessye Norman. 'Do you happen to know why it was that Kassel was engaged?' demanded Drogheda. 'His voice is far from pleasing, his appearance is totally unconvincing and he is stiff and wooden in his acting.'[79] The performance did little to enhance the conductor's credentials as a Wagnerian and Drogheda decided to leave the next chairman to settle Davis' future. 'He is a strange chap!' said Drogheda to his successor, 'and all I can say to you is jolly good luck.'[80]

Drogheda found Davis opaque and ungracious. 'Colin has so often made the Board feel they had no useful part to play and were simply an impediment in his way,' he complained.[81] He also found MacMillan aloof and Tooley overburdened with detail. He was sixty-three years old and in fine health, but the fun had gone out of being chairman. The country was going to the dogs and his friends were getting out. Andrew Porter, his treasured critic, had gone to write for the *New Yorker* and his twin sister, Sheila, had quit to work for Hurok in New York after incurring MacMillan's displeasure. Drogheda's last mistress had gone off with a flashy conductor and the flunkey who guarded his box was killed in a car accident in the Cromwell Road. Covent Garden was not the same without them.

Having made his decision, he was upset to learn that the succession would not be in his gift, as it had been in Waverley's. Watched by Goodman, the board would have to follow due process. A committee was appointed, headed by Lord Robbins and comprising Goodman, Bonham-Carter and the newly-knighted Sir Claus Moser. Drogheda had a candidate in mind but said nothing for fear of prejudicing his chances. 'Garrett was one of my heroes,' said John Sainsbury. 'I was aware that he thought me helpful and reliable, but I wasn't aware that he thought of me as chairman material – only that the chairmanship wasn't falling out exactly as he would have liked.'[82]

The wheels of selection began to turn. Moser nominated Lord Annan, a Keynes protégé who was one of the best connected men in the country. Goodman and Bonham-Carter favoured the more colourful John Pope-Hennessy, who bestrode the museum world. Robbins donned a worried look and wondered whether it would be fitting for the chief executive of a publicly-funded museum to be chairman of a state-funded opera house. He wrote to the head of the civil service, William Armstrong, seeking clarification. Armstrong, the ultimate authority on mandarin law, wrote back that this would be technically improper since the money for the V&A and the ROH came from the same source. As a matter of principle, however, he added that this had nothing to do with Pope-Hennessy being a civil servant. If, for example, the committee were to pick Claus Moser, who was director of the Central Office of Statistics, there would be no grounds for objection. 'At this point,' said Moser, 'I was removed from the committee.'[83]

For six months, he heard nothing more. Then, one night at a party in June 1973, someone whispered to him that he was to be the next chairman. 'I went straight to see the Prime Minister, Mr Heath,' recalled Moser, 'and he kindly agreed – on condition that my work at the COS came first, which I assured him it would. There is no doubt that his passion for music contributed to his decision.'

Moser was 'surprised and thrilled' beyond words. Having entered the country in 1936 as a 13-year-old Jewish refugee from Berlin, he had grown used to the snubs of outsiderhood and never expected to reach the heart of the English establishment. A wartime officer in the RAF, he was mocked in the mess for being unable to play the piano without a score before him – though he could deliver a Beethoven sonata or Mozart concerto to near-concert standard. His seriousness was the antithesis of English amateurism. There was also a fun-loving side to his character, but it did not dilute the deadly earnest of his middle-European devotion to music and duty.

As an academic, said Moser, 'I never had a new idea in my life. I was a good teacher but I wasn't a great scholar. If I hadn't met Lionel Robbins, who became my greatest friend and put me on the Robbins Committee (for education reform), I would have gone on being a backroom academic.' On the committee, he met Harold Wilson who gave him the keys to the national safe. In 1957, Moser had asked to spend his sabbatical year at the Central Office of Statistics but was turned down 'because I was of German birth and this was a high-security office'. Seven years later, Wilson named him head of the COS. 'I said, "but I was turned down to work there over security clearance". He said, "well I'm asking you to run it as permanent secretary."' That, said Moser, was the moment when he felt he had been accepted. When someone described him as 'the first foreigner to head the opera house', he took it as a compliment.

'I don't know why they appointed me,' said Moser. 'There was no question that music and opera had been at the centre of my life since I was a little boy in Berlin. So if they wanted commitment, they knew they would get it. Secondly, since my profession had been statistics, economics and finance, I think they saw in me somebody who might take an interest in the financial problems. I couldn't have wanted anything more, and I worked very hard at it.'

When the board debated his appointment, the only objection came from John Sainsbury, who argued that Moser was a music buff with no concern for ballet. 'I was a dissenting voice,' Sainsbury admitted, 'in the sense that we wanted the ballet to be looked after. And maybe that did some good, actually. It made Claus try very hard to consider the ballet, even though he was an opera man. It was a fair point to make. When I was on the board I don't remember ever feeling that Claus was not doing enough for the ballet. I remember saying John Tooley's impossible, he's not giving the ballet enough stage time, but no such feelings about Claus.'

Sainsbury had not coveted the chairmanship. He was in the throes of taking his company public in 1974 and, with a young family at home, 'couldn't have entertained it at all'.[84] Moser came to value Sainsbury as 'a superlative board member, probably the most influential'. To boost the ballet, he co-opted Colette Clark, daughter of the art historian and friend of Fonteyn, as the first woman to sit on the ROH board.

Drogheda sounded content with the outcome. 'Claus seems to me an admirable choice,' he assured Pope-Hennessy, 'and I think that his very close links with Whitehall as head of the COS must be immensely valuable, with finance an eternal problem and re-development of such paramount importance.'[85] He went off on a long holiday, leaving Moser to deal with Colin Davis, which he did briskly. Davis was granted a two-year extension with no further talk of renewal until after the *Ring*. Moser also agreed to consider Götz Friedrich, the *Ring* producer, as director of productions, provided he could work within tight budgets. The general financial situation, he told Drogheda, 'terrifies me'.[86]

Securing a real-terms increase in state subsidy was no longer an option, no matter how well Moser wined and dined his political contacts. 'I used to argue that it was an honour for a government to support the arts,' he said, 'I grew up to believe that this was integral to being a decent country.' But the economy was now in freefall. Property prices crashed, taking down a small bank and undermining fiscal confidence. Fuel prices soared after the 1973 Yom Kippur War and the Government began printing petrol ration books. Some £1.2 billion was cut from public spending. The miners worked to rule, aggravating the fuel crisis. When they called an all-out strike, Heath imposed a three-day working week, then called an election under the slogan, 'Who Governs Britain?' The question itself exposed his impotence. Ministers went on the BBC's 'Today' programme, telling the nation to brush its teeth in the dark and share bathwater with family and friends. Oxford Street lit its windows with candles and storm lamps. Theatres went dark half the week.

Heath lost the February 1974 election by 297 seats to Wilson's 301. Having failed to entice Jeremy Thorpe's Liberals into a coalition, he went to Buckingham Palace to submit his resignation. 'Come along, Robert,' he barked at Armstrong after leaving the royal presence. 'I'm sorry, Mr Heath,' said the perfect civil servant, 'I must wait here for the Prime Minister.'

Wilson formed a minority Government and, in an October poll, won an overall majority of three. Having bought off the miners, he saw inflation rise by twenty per cent in a year. Unemployment topped one million for the first time since the war and the International Monetary Fund threatened to call in a loan unless savage curbs were imposed on state spending. Wilson gave up in April 1976, making way for his avuncular Chancellor, James Callaghan, but the Liberal-backed Labour Government was never stable and dying MPs had to be trundled in on stretchers to save it from defeat. Amid perpetual crisis, Covent Garden kept its contacts alive. 'Harold Wilson we only asked to ballet,' reflected Moser, 'because he only liked one ballet, so he came each year to *Swan Lake*. Jim Callaghan did his duty; Roy Jenkins and Denis Healey came more often.' Thorpe, the Liberal leader, had to retire when charged with attempted murder. He was acquitted, but ruined; his defence solicitor was, needless to say, Arnold Goodman.

The new minister for the arts was, promisingly for Covent

Garden, none other than Jack Donaldson, Drogheda's best friend. Donaldson had many friends, among them Lord Gibson, chairman of the Arts Council, who gave him land to build a house on his Sussex farm. He was not much of a minister, however, and was putty in the hands of departmental officials. 'Lord Donaldson is being paid by the tax-payer,' thundered the Heritage conservator Hugh Leggatt, 'and if he does not understand what he is talking about he should resign.' The only mark left by 'weak, tired, sweet and affectionate'[87] Jack Donaldson in three years was a Heritage Fund that he set up primarily for the purpose of giving Covent Garden a million pounds towards redevelopment. In retirement, Donaldson returned to Covent Garden to help his wife, Frankie, write a glowing account of the opera house that was published by another of his good friends, George Weidenfeld.

Gibson also returned to Covent Garden, rejoining the board after giving up the Arts Council in 1977, weary of the fruitless struggle and the gravelly zeal of his Yorkshire-accented secretary-general, Roy Shaw. Gibson preferred his deputy secretary-general, Angus Stirling, whom he hired to run the National Trust and co-opted on to the Covent Garden board. The connections between giver and receiver were still cosy, but neither man had much success in squeezing extra cash from the Arts Council. With the best will in Whitehall, there was no money to be had, and no notion of how to raise the country from its doldrums. The only sector to thrive was British pop music which, for the first time since the Beatles, captured the moment with the punk phenomenon, along with approximately one-quarter of the global music market.

The nightly news in those dark years was usually led by a live report from ACAS, the Arbitration, Conciliation and Advisory Service, which stepped into industrial disputes and came up with compromises that carefully avoided long-term solutions. The more ACAS intervened, the more disputes there were. Kenneth MacMillan, in hospital for an operation on his foot, survived a catering strike and lived on lettuce and salad cream. The National Theatre was under union siege from the night it opened in October 1976. Dissension spread to Covent Garden, where Tooley shrank from confrontation and adopted an ACAS outlook, giving ground to increasingly aggressive stage and musicians unions. The arch procrastinator had given way to the generic mediator. 'The first strike I ever saw was in Australia,' said Antoinette Sibley. 'We never had that sort of thing at the Garden. But in the final rehearsal that Anthony (Dowell) and I did of Rudolf's *Nutcracker*, the orchestra just put down their instruments in the middle and walked out.'[88]

The epoch of post-war positivism was buried on 17 July 1974, the night of Drogheda's farewell gala. Fonteyn, Nureyev, Ashton, Gobbi, Solti, Kiri, Sibley, Dowell, Makarova and Davis studded the bill. Goodman packed the brochure with adverts from his best clients, including Rupert Murdoch and his soaraway *Sun*, the proceeds going to the ROH Benevolent Fund. Jennie Lee read an interminable eulogy. 'Then Garrett spoke. He was not the least sentimental. He was the perfect paradigm of patrician ease. He was willowy, smiling, devil-may-care, casual; yet all the time absolutely controlled in what he said and his manner of delivery. Every word was audible and to the point. He was his usual mischievous self; quite cheeky to the Queen, telling her that now she had found the way he hoped she might make a habit of patronizing the opera, yet respectful at the same time. He even hiccuped into the loud speaker slung around his neck, apologizing for the surprisingly amplified sound. Now no non-gent would ever ride supremely over that sort of incident.'[89]

Prince Philip lodged a private protest over the *lèse-majesté* but Drogheda was unrepentant. He bowed to no one in his own realm, and no one would ever rule Covent Garden as he had done. He awoke next morning with 'a strange sense of emptiness'.[90] Weeks later he suffered a second shock when Gibson replaced him as chairman of the *Financial Times*. Drogheda was disconsolate. A life that had been full day and night now loomed empty. He vacated his house in Lord North Street, which belonged to the FT, and moved to the country, commuting to Covent Garden to assist with fundraising and join Moser in deputations to senior ministers. Moser counted on him to raise ten million pounds and help contest a raucous campaign by Covent Garden residents to block the project. The original scheme incorporated an underground car-port and an arched shopping arcade, not unlike Vienna's. Drogheda staunchly supported his successor. He remained an imposing figure, and when he strode through the door flunkeys scurried to obey his commands.

Asked in a valedictory radio interview if he was optimistic about the company's future, he sounded hesitant. 'It's like saying, are you optimistic about the future of Britain,' mused Drogheda. 'I . . . don't know. To say unequivocally Yes I was would be perhaps a little bit foolhardy at the present time, because there are so many divisive forces at work and we are faced with such grave economic problems here. I am quite certain that talent exists at Covent Garden, and I think it would be a major tragedy, for all the effort and work which has been put into building up the place over these years since the war . . . to say that all this is to be set to naught would be terribly sad, and I myself do not think that opera and ballet as art forms are going to die.'[91]

Moser's enthusiasm for the arts appeared insatiable. In twenty years on the board, he attended two thousand performances. His happiest moment, he said, was a compliment from Karl Böhm, the octogenarian Straussian and unregenerate ex-Nazi. Delighted to discover an English opera house whose chairman spoke German and played music, he patted his host on both cheeks and said, 'Herr Moser, sei wie Sie sind – stay the same as you are.'

With the change of chairman, Tooley had an opportunity to assert greater executive authority. He failed to do so, inhibited as much by his years in Webster's shadow as by Moser's unsuspected vigour. The erudite, short-fused academic did not tolerate fools or trust much to chance. He decided to be 'very hands-on, perhaps too much so',[92] talking to Tooley daily and meeting him at least four times a week. A gregarious man, he invited the Tooleys – along with the Gibsons, the Armstrongs and others of the Covent Garden in-crowd – to share his summer holidays at a chalet his Swiss wife, Mary, had inherited in Arosa. 'I liked John enormously from very early on and thought we got on terribly well,' said Moser. 'I said any number of times to Mary when we had difficulties, the great thing is I always enjoy going in to see John, or ringing him up and being with him.'

Tooley was more circumspect about his second chairman. Early in Moser's tenure, he reported to his assistant, Paul Findlay, that they had enjoyed a frank exchange of views. 'We agreed that we are not the same sort of person,' said Tooley, 'but we respect each other and can make a go of it.'[93]

The tide turned for Colin Davis in June 1974, not with the *Ring* but with a classic never previously seen at Covent Garden. *La clemenza di Tito* was Mozart's last stage work, shelved for a century and a half after initial success. With Janet Baker as the dominatrix Vitellia and

Davis teasing out subtleties in one of Mozart's thinner scores, the production was cheered to the echo and exported to La Scala, Milan, where Davis was hailed as a master-restorer. (Tooley was terrified that he would get booed by the notorious claques.)

Six months later came *Das Rheingold* and *Die Walküre*. The third *Ring* segment, *Siegfried*, was delayed by a year for economic reasons and the apotheotic *Götterdämmerung* was put back until September 1976. The delay worked in favour of Davis, whose authority grew through the slow unfurling. 'My God, this is going to be an appalling *Ring*,' was the initial orchestral reaction; but by the first repetition of the full cycle players found 'we believed in him; he had developed a feeling for it, and paced it well.'[94] Andrew Porter, returning from New York to review the climax, had nothing but admiration for the conductor. 'Not since Kempe in the 'fifties have I heard a *Götterdämmerung* in Covent Garden conducted with so apt a blend of naturalness and passion; with power and eloquence in the orchestral playing but no training of spotlights, as it were, on individual instrumental marvels or the conductor's artfulness; with buoyant "breathing" support for the singers, alert, not dictatorial.'[95]

The production was another matter. Porter called it 'a disaster, scenically, dramatically, and therefore – since the elements cannot be separated – musically.' Getting personal, he added: 'I think indignation is called for – indignation first of all with the Covent Garden Board of directors. Did they really sit down, talk to Friedrich, look at (Josef) Svoboda's preliminary sketches and say: Yes, that's just the kind of *Ring* the Royal Opera House needs?'[96] The notice appeared, unusually, on page three of the *Financial Times*. Moser found it 'deeply upsetting' and complained to Drogheda,[97] who shrugged wearily.

It appears that no plan for the *Ring* was ever shown to Tooley or to the Board. Friedrich was not a man who liked to be second-guessed. An apostle of the doctrinaire Walter Felsenstein, whose collectivist ideals conformed with East German Marxism, Friedrich skipped West from Berlin's Komische Oper in 1972 without appreciably altering his operatic orientation. He became chief regisseur at the Hamburg State Opera and chief proponent of the 'progressive' approach to opera production, a *Weltanschauung* that employed dark backgrounds, industrial technology, obscure dialectics and occasional political inferences. At Bayreuth, he had the chorus give a clenched-fist Marxist salute in *Tannhäuser*. 'The opera of the bourgeoisie,' he said, 'too often did, and still does, ignore true social relationships both in the works and, so far as such relationships are necessary, between stage and audience.'[98]

At Covent Garden he harangued the chorus for an hour with philosophical abstractions, but did not seem overly concerned by a loss of visual coherence from one scene to the next. Don't bother your heads with where the story takes place, he told the singers: the stage is the world and that's all one needs to know. 'To open up the drama of the *Ring*, not to encapsulate it,' was his aim. 'Not to encircle its ideas, but rather to offer them up as questions; not to iron out the variety of Wagner's thought process but to present it in all its contradictions – these are among the objects of our production.'[99] His inconclusiveness appealed powerfully to the contemplative Davis, who defended Friedrich with great vigour. 'It's all very well to say, go back and do what Wagner wanted,' Davis declared, 'but what he wanted wasn't really practical; it couldn't be done. Wagner himself wasn't successful in staging it the way he imagined it . . . So you're forced to do something else. And as the Ring is essentially an opera of ideas, it doesn't really depend on the physical facts of dragons or people riding horses through clouds. This is all poetic nonsense, and can be done only in one's own imagination.'[100]

Not everyone disliked Friedrich's *Ring*. The modernist critic Peter Heyworth found it 'the most illuminating production of the *Ring* I have seen' and Philip Hope-Wallace, who had endured more *Ring*s than any man in England, was prepared to believe that 'it may yet become clearer'. Among the cast, the New Zealander Donald McIntyre stood out as Wotan, but Helge Brilioth's Siegfried and Berit Lindholm's Brünnhilde were fast forgotten.

Those who visited Bayreuth in the summer of 1976 for the centennial *Ring*, produced by Patrice Chéreau and conducted by Boulez, brought home reports of an austere beauty and intellectual unity beside which the Friedrich effort appeared muddled and provincial. The Chéreau *Ring* would be filmed in thirteen parts and serialized on television the world over, the first known instance of an opera being made into soap. Covent Garden, meanwhile, made do with the Friedrich version for years to come, unable to afford anything better. Both Tooley and Moser counted it, somewhat ruefully, as a highlight of their epoch. Friedrich, said Paul Findlay, 'brought a level of staging we hadn't seen at Covent Garden. He unified the four works and did a lot of damage to the theatre in terms of technical time. His style of working was not what this country wanted but it was stimulating.'[101] Davis maintained that 'the Ring we did with Götz Friedrich was really revolutionary, nothing like that had been seen at Covent Garden ever before and it resulted in boos and cheers, and more boos and more cheers. But it released Covent Garden from the conventional setting, and in that sense I think we did something useful.'[102]

'Colin always needed a partner and thought he had found one in Götz,' said Findlay. Moser asked Friedrich to become director of productions. The German declined, citing pressures of work in Hamburg. They settled on a reduced role as Principal Producer for the next four years. 'Unfortunately,' noted Tooley, 'this became little more than a title, and he made no input to our deliberations on planning and casting.'[103] In 1981, Friedrich became head of the Deutsche Oper in West Berlin, a taxing position that he held for the rest of the century. He remained, nonetheless, the producer of choice at Covent Garden, even after a violent falling-out with Davis over *Idomeneo*, where the conductor bridled at his thoughts on Mozart and Isaiah Berlin in the boardroom demolished them in a devastating display of wit and erudition. The satirists at *Private Eye* kept up the attack on the interventionist director. Why did the Germans lose the war? asked the *Eye*. Because it was over-produced.

Davis, growing in confidence, turned to *Peter Grimes*, the crucible of British opera, and deconstructed it. There was too much pity, he felt, in the version enshrined by Peter Pears, and not enough anger. Davis, with a young Australian director Elijah Moshinsky, and Jon Vickers in the pivotal role, outraged the dying composer by stripping *Grimes* of his constraints. 'The violence that is overt and latent in *Peter Grimes*,' said Davis, 'the whole way that Peter defies the world – there is a famous line of his, "this is whatever day I say it is" – is the arrogance of a frantic mind which is on the edge of the abyss. Vickers was an amazing theatrical animal. He was physically frightening. He embodied for me Peter Grimes, and I have never done it since because I can't see what I can do without him. I'm sure Ben Britten didn't very much approve of what we did but it only shows that a composer doesn't always know the resilience of the pieces he has created.'[104]

'To be on stage with Vickers was fantastic,' said Teresa Cahill, who played one of the nieces. 'He gave off so much electricity you didn't want to get closer than eight feet of him.'[105]

Vickers played *Grimes* as pure monster. 'I believe Benjamin Britten saw an opportunity here,' he said. 'In his anxiety to win sympathy and compassion for the homosexual world, he plunged into the whole psychology of human rejection . . . In doing so, he created a work of art so great that to continue to portray it in this cameo, almost chamber-like way, limiting it to the experience of one man in a situation, was not doing the work justice . . . This is the story of mankind's anguish, not a human being, nor a petty little group of feminists or homosexuals or Hasidic Jews – nothing like that! It's majestic, and I don't think that it was all recognized.'[106]

The motivating force of Davis's directorship was modernization, freshening up familiar works and expanding the repertoire with novelties. He commissioned four world premières, two by rising talents and the others by established composers. *Taverner* by Peter Maxwell Davies and *Thérèse* by John Tavener were half-baked. *We Come to the River* by Hans Werner Henze aroused higher hopes, but the composer was in an ultra-Marxist phase and the outcome was pure agit-prop. Originally titled 'The General' and then 'The Privates', it was rudely referred to internally as 'The General's privates come to the river'. There were fifty-eight artists on stage, and sometimes fewer heads in the house. To cheer up his colleagues, the tenor Robert Tear announced one night that he had good news – 'they're letting them in free'. Then he added: 'but they'll have to pay to get out.'

Tippett's fourth opera, *The Ice Break*, replete with laser beams and inconsequential plot, went down no better. Tippett, whom Davis had unsuccessfully nominated for the Board, complained that Covent Garden had become a 'gala house' and was no place for a composer. Davis tried to talk Vickers and Kiri te Kanawa into reviving *The Midsummer Marriage* and Tooley was personally upset when Tippett's final opera, *New Year*, opened in Houston and Glyndebourne. If Tippett failed to match Britten's fame, it was not for want of friends at the Royal Opera House. He was, however, right to point out that the house now catered to a richer crowd and would never again entertain new work by an unproven British composer. It was in the mid-1970s that seat prices rose beyond the means of school-kids, newlyweds and pensioners. Buying a ticket to the opera was a fifteen-pound investment, as much as many people earned in a week, and a hundred times more than the starting prices. A large part of the audience became socially self-selecting, and the first accusations of 'élitism' were heard. The Board ignored the omens and pushed prices up, season by season, in order to stay solvent.

Tooley kept his door open to composers but could offer little more than tea and sympathy. He displayed no strong tastes in new music, or much else for that matter. When pressed for a preference, he named John Eaton, an American of extreme obscurity. 'I particularly regret that the commissioning programme collapsed,' said Tooley on the eve of retirement, 'and that we were unable to get the new works that were done more firmly into the repertoire; instead, far too often we had to put in pot-boilers to obtain revenue.'[107] He was not alone in this predicament. Peter Hall at the National Theatre told John Osborne, author of *Look Back in Anger*, that he would take off any new play that did not sell ninety per cent of the house. With shrinking subsidy, there was no margin for error. But Hall was able to make room for manoeuvre and it was he, not Tooley, who devised a role for the most original of English composers, taking on Harrison Birtwistle as his music director and getting him to write original music for Tony Harrison's version of *The Oresteia* and arrangements of Mozart and Salieri for the National's greatest hit, Peter Shaffer's *Amadeus*. In the realms of imagination, daring and novelty, the National Theatre outstripped Covent Garden as the Vietnamese out-thought the Americans.

Colin Davis concentrated on pushing out the walls of standard repertoire with early Verdi operas and Meyerbeer's long-unseen and unwisely resuscitated *L'Africaine*. He conducted *The Rake's Progress*, which Webster had coveted back in 1951, as well as a *Lulu* in which Friedrich's American wife, Karan Armstrong, shrieked mercilessly for three interminable acts, confirming many prejudices about the music of Alban Berg. She did herself no favours by telling an evening paper that Lulu was a girl 'who liked her orgasms', and the production was loudly deplored by the Berg scholar, George Perle. It took a further decade for Glyndebourne and the regional companies to demonstrate that *Lulu* could be sung sweetly, affectingly, and to a national television audience.

For all Davis's efforts, Covent Garden was losing creative edge. Glyndebourne, with Pritchard and Bernard Haitink in the pit and

Peter Hall as productions director, mingled sparkling Strauss and Mozart with modernist severities. Glyndebourne's *Rake* had sets by David Hockney which lodged in the memory long after Covent Garden's was forgotten. English National Opera, with Harewood in command, undertook a complete Janáček cycle, as well as much Britten, some French frivolities and one UK première that claimed world attention: the madcap creation of *Le Grand Macabre* by the Hungarian exile, György Ligeti. Mackerras was music director through much of the 1970s, followed briefly by Charles Groves, and then by a duopoly of Mark Elder as music director and David Pountney as director of productions. It was ENO that would pioneer movie-style sex-and-violence with David Alden's chainsaw *Mazeppa* and Jonathan Miller's resetting of *Rigoletto* among New York mafiosi. Harewood gave young directors a licence to thrill. ENO got talked about while Covent Garden got bogged down.

ENO's regional wing seceded in 1978 as Opera North, another hotbed of invention. Singers now had a choice between playing it straight at Covent Garden, or playing it interesting elsewhere. After five 'pretty awful'[108] years, Davis had won the confidence of the audience, only to get blocked by a conservative board. 'It's possible Colin would have liked to be more involved in the daily running of the house,' said Moser. 'He was quite good at meetings. Possibly he felt underused. Colin could take a very intelligent interest in financial problems and was more willing to discuss criticism of performances than some other people in the house.'[109]

But it would have taken a leader of spectacular energy and tyrannical disposition to turn the company around, and Davis was not that kind of man. The single most significant quality that Colin Davis brought to Covent Garden was an almost saintly degree of selflessness. Unlike most music directors, Davis was a stranger to egotism. Where James Levine at the Met excluded any maestro who might show him up, Davis set about engaging the best in his field. Claudio Abbado, music director of La Scala, led the cavalcade with *Un ballo in maschera*, disliking the orchestra but agreeing to return once it had improved. Riccardo Muti, his Milan successor, led Verdi's *Macbeth* and Bellini's *I Capuleti e i Montecchi*. Both had been offered revivals by Solti, but Davis gave them new productions. Solti himself was welcomed back seasonally. Zubin Mehta, Lorin Maazel, Haitink, Edo de Waart and Gennady Rozhdestvensky joined the roster. No opera house on earth could boast such a line-up. Under Davis, Covent Garden became the conductors' house par excellence, the place where top batons proved their mettle. 'Colin had no hang-ups about other conductors,' said Tooley, 'He was so open. When I said we ought to have Carlos Kleiber he said, yes, go get him, it'll be terrific.'[110]

Kleiber was the topping on the cake. Son of the fondly-remembered Erich and every bit as combustible, he pursued a capricious career, cancelling almost as often as he conducted and limiting himself to those few operas in which his father excelled, as if to prove some peculiar oedipal point. He had just walked out on a Hamburg *Falstaff* when Covent Garden, hit by a Levine cancellation at three weeks' notice (he never got to work at the ROH), wondered if he might like to conduct *Der Rosenkavalier*, his father's trademark opera. Kleiber hesitated, issued a catalogue of extraneous demands (including a hotel with a swimming pool, a rarity in central London), and finally turned up in the pit with a scowl on his face, as if daring anyone to compare him to Erich. When Norman Feasey, the elderly repetiteur, greeted him with 'I remember your father', Kleiber's face clouded over and he made no reply.

He devoted the first three-hour rehearsal to the Prelude, a piece of music lasting one minute and a half. Taking their seats for the next rehearsal, several players found slips of paper on their stands – Kleibergrams they called them. 'This bit I think could be more forceful and audible,' read one note. 'Many thanks and kind regards, Yours, C. Kleiber.' His rehearsals were so intense that players took hours to unwind. 'Working with him must always be an electric experience,' said the orchestral manager, Bram Gay. 'The orchestra is never relaxed. The better the work goes the greater the tension because the more fragile the creation . . . An evening with him is one of the great lifetime opportunities for self-realization; not exhaust-ing but liberating. It is something for which we have been waiting and working all our lives.'[111] 'I have to go to the pub with some of the lads and steam off by going over the performance again verbally, over a pint,' said the orchestral leader, John Brown.[112]

After the June 1974 *Rosenkavalier*, an explosive success, Kleiber returned in 1977 for *Elektra*, with Birgit Nilsson, and in 1979 for *Bohème*. He gave no press interviews and could never be guaranteed to turn up, but the posting of his name on a playbill would cause box-office phone-lines to be jammed for hours and some buffs would cross the Atlantic on the off-chance of getting a ticket, so scarce and intense were his appearances. Kleiber never demanded a new production and stepped in twice at short notice for an *Otello* that he refashioned in unforgettable unity. On his nights off, he went to watch other conductors. 'Did you see Lorin Maazel last night?' he teased Tooley, who disliked Maazel. 'Best display of conducting you'll ever see in your life.'[113]

'Shall we do it differently tonight?' he would say on entering the pit, keeping every player on the edge of a seat. 'You dared not look anywhere but at him,' said Teresa Cahill who sang in *Rosenkavalier* and *Elektra*. 'He made tiny variations, so mercurial, always different.'[114] That Covent Garden could attract so rare a performer was a feather in its cap, much envied by the much-richer Met, where Kleiber did not appear until 1988. But Kleiber was never a part of the ROH furniture. Players were warned that he could walk out at the slightest excuse. In 1980 he declared a boycott of London orchestras after receiving poor reviews with the LSO. During his second ROH *Otello*, in 1986, with Placido Domingo and Katia Ricciarelli, he grew visibly bored. Appeals for his return were politely declined. Kleiber never conducted again at Covent Garden. He had left his mark on his father's spot, and that seemed to suffice.

Stability at the ballet was proving chimerical. MacMillan, neurotic and thin-skinned, was irresistibly attractive to the vultures who cluster around every creative being. Fearful of exposing a hint of his genuine vitality in press interviews, his public persona was that of a withdrawn, irritable, vulnerable artist. MacMillan was a thoughtful man trapped in a job that called for action. When the pressures mounted, no one in authority lifted a finger to save him.

Enmity skulked in the wings of his stage. Ashton, adored by dancers and the board, avoided contributing any new work for the first six years of MacMillan's directorship. When he finally produced *A Month in the Country*, on Turgenev's tale of a young tutor who subverts the family he serves, the press panted and fawned as they never did for MacMillan. The board, too, were thrilled that Ashton had chosen a story translated by Isaiah Berlin and music by Chopin that Berlin had suggested. Lynn Seymour danced the central role of Natalya Petrovna, with Dowell as the tutor. The ballet was ravishingly beautiful but neither physically as challenging nor emotionally as draining as *Enigma*. The response, however, was ecstatic. In New York, Clive Barnes acclaimed Ashton as 'our greatest choreographer' and Seymour received the kind of star treatment hitherto accorded only to Fonteyn. Many of the accolades were a thinly coded reproach to MacMillan, whose cable of thanks to Ashton was clipped and cold: 'Your ballet is exquisite. Thank you for doing it.'[115]

Ashton had little more to give. Frustrated by his decline, the anti-MacMillanites led by John Percival of *The Times* – 'poisonous Perce' in ROH parlance – cast around for a gladiator. They began agitating for the directorship to be given to Nureyev, whom MacMillan had neglected in his desire to advance the young pair of Waynes, Eagling and Sleep.

Nureyev let it be known that he was 'very unhappy' with MacMillan. When de Valois and Ashton were in charge, his agent complained, 'there were a considerable number of performances offered to him, and also discussions about new productions, and new works for him, whilst now it becomes an ordinary routine type of engagement.'[116] He remained the most captivating dancer in the west, an enigmatic object of universal curiosity. A reporter from *Women's Wear Daily* asked him, 'Mr Nureyev, I am sure my readers would like a word about your sex life.' Nureyev rose, put on his coat and, turning to leave, said: 'sporadic'.[117]

Fonteyn still shared his limelight. For a Friends of Covent Garden Christmas show, Ken Davison asked Ashton to dance the *Merry Widow* waltz with his ageless muse. 'You mean ballroom dancing?' said Ashton, aghast. 'But that would be impossible – you see, Margot is such a terrible dancer.' In 1976, at the age of fifty-six, she appeared on the ROH stage as MacMillan's teenaged Juliet.

Her shadow fell heavy on the company. Beriosova took to the bottle. Sibley found happiness in a second marriage and spent much of her time in consulting rooms, dogged by a knee injury. MacMillan was unable to cheer them up. He could not give dancers the sense of family and fun that de Valois and Ashton had so freely bestowed.

Against rumblings of dinosaurs and rumours of conspiracy, it seems remarkable that so sensitive a man managed to produce any new work at all. Yet in each season of MacMillan's directorship there was at least one work that stretched the limbs and the imagination in unforeseen directions. 'He felt he had to prove himself with every ballet,' explained his wife. 'There was an atmosphere of terror, a fear of failure. He was severely undermined and depressed, on medication. It shortened his life.'[118]

MacMillan's *Four Seasons*, to music from Verdi's *Sicilian Vespers* suggested by Andrew Porter, was almost too difficult for its dancers, some of whom felt it was as if they were being taught to fly. *Rituals*, set to Béla Bartók's sonata for two pianos and percussion, was derived from the kabuki and kung-fu he had witnessed in Japan. It soared way above the comprehension of *Nutcracker* critics and audiences. Percival in *The Times*, damning with faint praise, warned that MacMillan had returned to the 'confident experimentalism' of his early works. The ballet ended with Seymour, in childbirth, attended by Monica Mason as midwife, exploring uncharted areas of female intimacy.

Under pressure, often under siege, MacMillan found scant sympathy from the company hierarchy. Tooley, though he understood ballet, had little confidence in MacMillan's judgement and was not prepared to fight his cause. 'What he lacked as a creative artist,' said Tooley, 'was the true means of putting a ballet together that was consistently of a high standard from beginning to end.'[119]

MacMillan was keen to revive *The Prince of the Pagodas*, one of the company's nagging failures. Britten had fallen out with John Cranko, its choreographer, and could hardly bring himself to look at the score. MacMillan admired Britten's music and had built one of his early ballets, *Winter's Eve*, upon *Variations on a Theme of Frank Bridge*. To rescue *Pagodas*, though, he would need to make cuts and required the composer's approval. He set off with Tooley for Aldeburgh on what Tooley recalled as 'one of the most uncomfortable days of my life'.

Britten greeted them with: 'I understand you want to make cuts, which passages do you have in mind?'

Whichever page MacMillan pointed to, he exclaimed 'oh, that's one of my favourite stretches in the whole ballet.' When MacMillan asked to remove the *pas de deux* and variations from the finale, Britten snapped, 'why?'

'Because it's too much for the boy,' said the choreographer.

'Really?' said Britten acidly, 'I modelled it exactly on what Petipa did in *Swan Lake*.'

Unable to sway the dying composer, MacMillan turned to one who was dead and safely out of copyright. He decided to set Gabriel Fauré's haunting *Requiem* as a graphic protest against the horrors of war, and included it in the seasonal plans that he set before the board. To his dismay, the proposal was shot down after John Pope-Hennessy sanctimoniously suggested that misrepresentation of a requiem might offend religious feelings among the audience. The museum director seemed unaware that Fauré himself had not been in the least bit religious, and that the board was not constituted to act as a guardian of faith. MacMillan, who had been slapped down once before over *Song of the Earth*, looked to his fellow-directors for support and found none. Neither Tooley nor Davis was prepared to protest, let alone resign.

So MacMillan did what he had done before, staging *Requiem* in Stuttgart to tumultuous acclaim in November 1976, before bringing it home to a pusillanimous Covent Garden, where even sworn enemies were swayed to applaud.

'Given such criticism and administrative burdens,' wrote Tooley, 'everything was pointing to MacMillan's resignation and, in June 1977, it was announced.' Reading this typical Tooleyism, it would appear that nobody, neither Tooley nor the board, bore any degree of responsibility for his departure. MacMillan's resignation was kept under wraps until a successor had been lined up, at which point the press were told that he feared that running the company was ruining his creative flow. There was no mention of the Fauré scandal, which fuelled his decision to quit, nor of two key triggers, never previously disclosed, that directly precipitated his departure.

Early in 1977, MacMillan had to be reminded to look at his contract which was due to expire a year later. He was no good with money and not earning nearly as much in wages and royalties as Ashton who, in his time, had been Covent Garden's top earner. MacMillan's salary was £16,000, one-third less than Colin Davis's; his fee for a full-length ballet was a paltry £850. With a wife and child to support, he needed a pay rise but was told this would be untenable under the Government's income and wages freeze.

Taking professional advice, he formed a company with his wife and became its employee, asking Tooley to hire his services from 'The Partnership'. Tooley consulted the ROH lawyers, Rubinsteins, who dismissed the notion as a 'tax convenience' which breached the pay code and could get the company penalized by the Government.[120] Tooley offered MacMillan a salary of £22,500, but he was hurt by the imputation that he had been trying to cheat the system. He remembered how, as a rising choreographer, he had been forced to take a pay cut while creating *Romeo and Juliet* because it took time off from his duties as a dancer. He felt exploited by Covent Garden and unrewarded.

He was not the only one to feel that way. Nureyev, in May 1977, withdrew *Bayadère* from the Royal Ballet after finding he was being paid a nightly royalty of eight and a half dollars. Tooley, in a panic, offered him a hundred dollars, but Nureyev was hurt at being ripped off and took his work away. MacMillan did not respond to Tooley's pay offer. Added to the insult of being undervalued, the injury of being underpaid was almost the final straw.

The *coup de grâce* came from the supreme controller of British ballet. 'Kenneth came home one day,' said Deborah MacMillan, 'and said to me: "I have just been told that we're doing a new *Sleeping Beauty* and Madam will be directing it. I am no longer Director of the Royal Ballet."'[121]

Madam giveth and Madam taketh away, blessed be her name. Having sacked Sir Fred to make way for youth, Ninette de Valois now tired of MacMillan. She was almost eighty years old and racked with arthritic pain, but her vigour was undimmed and she remained the ultimate arbiter at both company and school, exercising absolute power without the burdens of responsibility. There was always, in Madam, a redeeming quality of caprice. Even at her most awesome, she could laugh at and contradict herself. An admirer characterized her around this time as 'changeable as a day in March; inflexible as a rock; irascible, benign; fiery, mild; intuitive, unaware; self-effacing, domineering; belligerent, shy; reticent (not often), voluble; arrogant, modest; giggly, dignified ... the contradictions proliferate.'[122] The danger with any such outsized personality lies with their acolytes, who seize upon each passing whim as if it were scriptural law. There was no decree from Madam that MacMillan must go; but the hangers-on, citing her desire to renew the famous *Beauty*, made common cause with the Ashton clique to undermine MacMillan's authority and enforce his resignation.

Madam's whim prevailed again when it came to a successor. Nureyev was sounded out by Tooley and seemed interested, but he needed to dance every night to stay in peak condition and would have left slim pickings for company principals. Peter Wright was also given brief consideration – too brief, some felt. The ultimate heir was an amiable outsider who had never danced with de Valois, having hitched the whole of his career to her sworn rival, Marie

Rambert. Norman Morrice had joined Rambert's school as a boy and her troupe as a dancer in 1952, spending a year in America with Martha Graham to study the advances in modern ballet. In the mid-60s, Rambert appointed him assistant director with orders to rescue her company by turning it into a contemporary ensemble. Morrice duly reinvented Rambert, leading a so-called 'dance explosion' that drew young audiences to watch works by Martha Graham, Glen Tetley, Christopher Bruce and Twyla Tharp. Graham herself helped found the London Contemporary Dance Theatre, led by Robin Howard and Robert Cohan. There was now more than one invitation to the dance, and the Royal crest looked stuffy and jaded beside the bristling upstarts.

Morrice led Rambert until 1974, when he went off to develop his own choreography. He was an appealing candidate, mop-topped in a roll-neck sweater, and any fears that he might teach the Royal radical steps were scotched at his inaugural press conference when Morrice declared that MacMillan would remain the principal choreographer. For all his modernizing zeal, Morrice was a traditionalist at heart. In a centennial radio greeting to Madam, he reminded her of the afternoon, 'just after I became director of the Royal Ballet, when you both, you and Marie Rambert, invited yourselves to tea at my flat, which happened to be in the basement of Rambert's house. I thought I was going to be grilled about what I was doing with the Royal Ballet. But when both of you arrived, you started chatting to each other and for the next two hours I was practically ignored so long as I kept the tea and biscuits coming. . . . I had you tick me off from time to time but you never held any kind of grudge.'[123]

What appealed to Madam was Morrice's determination to return her company to its roots, nurturing a new line of English dancers to the exclusion of all foreigners. 'Anyone who heard Norman speak at that time would have been swayed by him,' said a key supporter. 'The company lacked purpose and he was giving it direction for the first time since Madam retired.'[124]

Initially, it shone quite brightly. Madam's *Beauty* awoke memories of the 1946 epic with brilliant contributions from Seymour and Monica Mason, alternating as Carabosse. De Valois hopped through the rehearsals in a high orthopaedic collar and, after tripping on the studio steps, a foot in plaster. After the première, she was ordered into hospital for a week, to rest the broken foot.

'With Madam, you either survived or you didn't,' reflected

Mason, who had been terrified by Madam as a girl, 'because I saw her terrifying others.' Mason was now in her thirties and Seymour past forty. They stood up to Madam as strongminded women and she fitted the role to their distinctive personalities. 'She worked in great haste,' said Mason, 'with an ability to put in six words what I couldn't say in a hundred. There were never any doubts.' Mason, who lived in Kew, took to giving the old lady a lift home to Barnes after performances. Although her marriage broke up and she moved to the other side of the river, she continued chauffeuring Madam for the pleasure and privilege of her ceaseless conversation. One night as she pulled up outside her flat, Madam said, 'You are naughty, you know. You haven't told me you no longer live in Kew, and you're not married any more.' Mason replied, 'No, Madam, I'm not, but – this may sound like me being a total creep – I treasure every moment with you.' Madam said, 'Well I enjoy talking to you but it's out of your way and you're not to do it any more.'[125]

MacMillan, freed of the directorship, turned in his most compelling drama for years, an account of the notorious Austrian royal murder and suicide at the hunting lodge of *Mayerling*. Intensely erotic, it featured Seymour in her last MacMillan creation, with David Wall as Crown Prince Rudolf in place of the injured Dowell. The ballet was filmed for television and universally praised, but it marked an end rather than a new beginning. Morrice was keen to advance youngsters like Lesley Collier and Stephen Jeffries. Seymour found herself being passed over for her favourite roles. When her protests fell on deaf ears, she waltzed out of the company and went to Munich as director of the Bavarian State Ballet. Dowell, recovering from injury, joined American Ballet Theatre as a star replacement for Misha Baryshnikov who had defected to City Ballet.

Midway through his exile year, someone sent Dowell a clipping from the *Daily Telegraph* announcing Sibley's retirement. MacMillan, too, felt more appreciated at ABT than at Covent Garden. Jerome Robbins, who added a touch of Broadway pizzazz to the MacMillan era, never returned under Morrice. On 18 May 1979, Margot Fonteyn danced a new Ashton piece on her sixtieth birthday; five weeks later, she danced for the last time on pointe. In one short season, the Royal Ballet lost all its stars. Technically, its standards were slipping. After a US tour the ballet chairman Mark Bonham-Carter warned that they had been 'fortunate just to get away with it'.[126] Morrice, aiming to restore the company's core values, succeeded only in turning the clock back to bare rudiments.

The redevelopment appeal was not going well. At a Guildhall banquet in February 1979, Moser announced that £2,495,388 had been raised from private sources, of which the Linbury Trust had given 'by far the largest single donation'. The Government and Greater London Council had each pledged a million, but the total was barely half the initial target of £7.8 million which would pay for converting a rear extension of the opera house into rehearsal studios and dressing-rooms.

Royal help was summoned. Prince Charles, Patron of the ROH, spent three days filming what he called 'the appalling and outdated' backstage conditions. His documentary was distributed to cinemas by EMI, whose chairman, Sir Joseph Lockwood, was executive vice-chairman of the appeal. In May, BBC-1 screened an hour-long documentary about the dangerous and antiquated working conditions. Three weeks later, the newscaster Richard Baker made a televised appeal to the nation, which brought in all of thirteen thousand pounds. Prince Charles played his cello at a charity auction. Princess Margaret, always a good friend to the Ballet, went on a five-city US fundraiser and returned with half a million pounds. The kitty was still short, but there was enough in hand to start work on the rear extension. The saga of redevelopment had begun. It was expected to be completed in ten years. No one imagined it would take twice as long and cost twenty times as much.

Even at this early stage, there were fears that the company's attention was directed more towards raising money than towards raising standards. Harold Rosenthal, who loyally exhorted his readers to support the redevelopment appeal, complained of a two-tier opera house – starry international casts to impress 'potential business sponsors' and *vin ordinaire* for the rest of the time. Revivals were poorly cast and stand-ins, when needed, were flown in from Europe rather than whistled up locally. If Teresa Berganza dropped out of Massenet's *Werther*, the first-choice replacement should have been Sarah Walker or Josephine Veasey rather than an unknown and unimpressive Viorica Cortez from Paris.[127]

Tooley, in an evasive reply, admitted that financial constraints had forced him to leave many roles without a cover. 'Our aims and purposes are clear,' he protested, without specifying these noble objectives. The only justification he offered for according Covent Garden its special status was the 'quality' of its product, superior and more consistent than any other opera house. As for the redevelopment, it was being run by professional fundraisers and project managers, and did not impinge on artistic planning.[128] Everything, stressed Tooley, was under control. Even as he wrote, the country was undergoing one of its greatest political upheavals.

In May 1979, the Conservatives under Margaret Thatcher were swept to power by an electorate weary of a 'winter of discontent' in which municipal services had been paralysed by strikes, leaving refuse uncollected, schools shut and corpses unburied. 'Leicester Square is one large dump,' noted a prominent theatregoer, 'and every restaurant is approached through rubbish.'[129] In the coldest winter since 1947, domestic pipes froze and shop shelves were bare. Thatcher promised to tame the unions, reward enterprise and reduce the tax burden. She was returned with a majority of forty-three but, with the Heathite half of her party terrified of change, she proceeded cautiously at first. By abolishing subsidies for ailing industries, she laid whole towns to waste. A poignant press photo showed the Prime Minister surveying the twisted girders of a 'development site' where, until lately, a steel industry had blazed.

As unemployment reached Depression levels of three million and riots erupted in Brixton and Liverpool, Thatcher wooed working-class voters with the right to buy the homes they rented from local authorities. On the wings of a victory over Argentina in the Falklands War, she won re-election in 1983, crushing a fissipated opposition by a hundred and forty-four seats. Margaret Thatcher then proceeded to do what she wanted, routing the unions in an ugly standoff with desperate miners and reversing the public ownership of British industry by selling off the steel, coal and transport resources that Labour had nationalized. The Keynesian prescription for economic and social intervention was ripped up and ridiculed. Monetarism and market forces were the new orthodoxies.

Deploring consensus, Margaret Thatcher never seemed content unless she had a crusade to wage. One by one, she dismantled the institutions of the Welfare State, preserving only the sacred cow of the National Health Service which, she declared, 'is safe in our hands'. For her own eye operation, the Prime Minister went to Switzerland. For musical pleasures, she summered at Salzburg. For all her exhortations of national pride, she was easily convinced that other countries managed the important things much better than her own.

One of the first to recognize her exceptional determination was Sir Robert Armstrong who, sidelined to the Home Office under James Callaghan, sought out the opposition leader and invited her to the opera. Despite his early allegiance to the detested Ted Heath, Thatcher promoted Armstrong to Cabinet Secretary, head of the civil service. He remained also, with her full consent, Secretary to the Board of Covent Garden. To the access he had enjoyed under Heath, Armstrong now added real power. He was responsible, for example, for interrogating new ministers for possible security risks. Alan Clark, son of Kenneth, was summoned to his office and confronted with two files. The red file contained intelligence about the racist National Front, which viewed Clark as a potential sympathizer. Reaching for the orange file, Armstrong said, 'There are also certain matters of personal conduct . . . which could quite possibly leave you open to blackmail.' Clark, a compulsive philanderer, assured him that the girls in question were now respectably married. Armstrong gave a knowing smile and, after inquiring after Clark's sister whom he knew from the Covent Garden boardroom, sent the junior minister on his way.[130]

Authoritative as he was, Armstrong never forgot where his first loyalties lay. 'Civil servants are servants of the Crown,' he ruled. 'For all practical purposes the Crown in this context means and is represented by the Government of the day.'[131] He stood for continuity – 'I'm not sure that the underlying requirements of civil servants have changed really in four hundred years,' he told a BBC interviewer[132] – and was viewed by Lord Annan of the ROH board as one of the 'consensus men'[133] who had brought the country to its knees by yielding to union demands in the interests of peace and quiet. He was never a Thatcherite or, as the leader would have put it, 'one of us', and he was forced to submit to a ferocious review of his beloved civil service by a task force led by Derek Rayner of the Marks & Spencer department store. This dreaded unit, known as Rayner's Raiders, was out to eradicate waste, overmanning and the kind of bureaucratic circumlocution of which Armstrong was a grand master. Its chief of staff was a renegade civil servant, Clive Priestley, who quoted 'good management' manuals and employed a revolutionary rhetoric that appealed to the Prime Minister. 'If you think of the great reform movements of the past, they have all been attended by long periods of pain and agony,' Priestley proclaimed. 'The movement which triumphed is that which held power for long enough and was bloody-minded for long enough.'[134]

Throwing open his drawers to the raiders and deferring always to representatives of the Crown, Armstrong defended the traditional order with all the connections and craft at his command. He was caricatured in a popular BBC comedy series as 'Sir Humphrey', the pin-striped official who frustrates the activism of politicians. The programme was one of Mrs Thatcher's favourites; she even wrote a spoof episode herself. But Armstrong's ability to protect old establishments was strained to snapping point when the Prime Minister launched a direct assault on his favourite bastion.

The advance of Thatcherism had been greeted with dismay at the Royal Opera House. Its chairman, a Labour Party member since 1945, had clashed with Margaret Thatcher when she was minister for education in Heath's Government and he was in charge of statistics. 'I was never a friend of hers,' said Moser. 'She knew I was Labour and I don't think she liked me particularly.' Apart from John Sainsbury, a hard-line Tory, there was not a Thatcherite on the board and the need was now so desperate that Moser had to go begging, cap in hand, for an audience with the Prime Minister.

The appeal had fallen far short of its target and another million pounds was needed before work could begin on the rear extension. Moser convinced Norman St John Stevas, a royalist grandee who was Minister for the Arts, that the situation was critical and together they were granted an audience at Number 10. 'When we arrived,' Moser recalled, 'she said, "I suppose you want more money and you, Norman, can't find it somewhere else." We desperately needed money for building at the back, and we got another million pounds. There was another occasion when I went to see her with Drogheda. Mrs Thatcher, although she was very tough, was very committed to the opera house.'

More than any premier except Heath, Margaret Thatcher enjoyed going to the opera and, as Prime Minister, went twice a year. 'I remember her coming to *Trovatore*,' said Moser. 'We had a party in the Royal Box of people she knew – the Armstrongs and others. She came in looking as if she hadn't worked all day. She had read the story of *Trovatore* and asked me some detailed question about something in Act Two which I couldn't answer. We had a good evening. It ended around quarter to eleven and I said, Prime Minister

I expect you'll have to go. She said, can't we have coffee? So we all sat down and chatted away til midnight. Next morning I picked up the paper and saw that she had left at six for the Falklands.'[135]

Supportive though she was, there was nothing that irked Thatcher more than what she called 'whingeing'. Persistent financial demands from the ROH for money provoked sudden and drastic retribution. In 1982, she ordered her second arts minister, Paul Channon (Stevas had been sacked for alleged extravagance), to investigate whether the ROH was spending its public grant prudently and efficiently. To avoid suspicions of victimization, the Royal Shakespeare Company was selected for similar treatment. A sense of dread descended when it was learned that the inquisitors were to be headed by the zealous and unyielding Clive Priestley.

This was a dangerous precedent, a declaration of no-confidence in the Arts Council, whose officials attended every ROH board meeting and scrutinized the accounts. The Council, even under a true-blue Tory chairman, William Rees-Mogg, had become an object for scorn in Downing Street, a talking shop that never got anything done. Rees-Mogg, a former *Times* editor, was famed for the irrefutable logic and airy impracticality of many of his leading articles. His major policy initiative at the Arts Council was called 'The Glory of the Garden'; it advocated removing national companies from London and scattering them around the regions. Rees-Mogg and his secretary-general Luke Rittner – a shrewd Thatcherite who was mocked by arts mandarins for having no degree and only two 'O' levels – were no friends of Covent Garden. In the slipstream of the Priestley team, the Arts Council summoned Tooley, Moser and the deputy chairman, Sir Denis Forman, in May 1983 to give account of themselves. 'Claus looked defeated from the outset,' noted the V&A's Roy Strong, husband of Julia Trevelyan Oman, a regular ROH production designer.

He was never in control of the debate, virtually at one point asking the Council to formulate policy for him . . . There was not really a voice raised in their defence, apart from the fact that we all recognized the need for a prestigious opera house and appreciated the success of the Ballet.

After they left we were asked what we thought. I was beckoned to lead off and said that the rot was at the top and reflected the composition of the Board, which was by no means a consumer's microcosm, and that it, together with the management, lacked any sense of direction. Earlier, I had drawn attention to the appallingly low morale in Covent Garden which was rotting the *esprit* of the workforce. The delegation struck one as rather helpless, arrogant and obsessed with money. Everything was put down to lack of it, not lack of ideas.[136]

Priestley, meanwhile, was going through the opera house with a fine toothcomb, with interludes for arduous trips to La Scala, the Met, Vienna, Berlin, the Kirov and the Bolshoi to compare Covent Garden with its competitors. Returning to the ROH boardroom, Priestley was greeted by the lion's last roar. Lord Goodman was aroused when Priestley handed out questionnaires for the directors to fill in.

No one present raised the slightest objection until I announced that he had no business to do what he was doing, that this was the most outrageous breach of the time-honoured principle that artistic subsidy was not related to government control. We had a rather heated scene. At one stage I informed him that after reading his questionnaire – he had come flanked by two assistants – there were in my view only six people in the world competent to answer it, and I was unhappy to say that those six did not include his party of three. Mr Priestley – an inoffensive and no doubt efficient gentleman – was clearly nonplussed by my onslaught and departed rather flushed.[137]

For the better part of a year, Tooley and Moser walked on egg-shells, encouraged only by the knowledge that Priestley was himself a theatregoer and was taking guidance from such wily professionals as Peter Diamand and Hugues Gall, head of the Geneva Opera. When the report was finally delivered in September 1983 to Thatcher's third arts minister in four years, the sybaritic and Wagner-loving Earl of Gowrie, it singled out Tooley's 'friendly, intrigue-free, supportive' management for special commendation – to the disgust of Rees-Mogg's Arts Council which wanted him sacked.

Priestley's main proposal was that the Royal Opera and Royal Ballet should be run as separate cost-centres and placed on three-year funding cycles, which would enable them to improve budget

planning and avoid crises. Priestley found a creeping deficit at
Covent Garden that he expected to reach three million pounds
within a year. He urged the Government to write off the shortfall and
raise the next grant by ten per cent, to £12.35 million. Thereafter, the
funding should be pegged to inflation, not a penny more or less.

There were alternatives to increased funding, he suggested. The
company could reduce the corps de ballet and opera chorus, disband
the Sadler's Wells Royal Ballet, or cut back the opera to a pre-war
festival season. Such measures, however, 'would write off the
substantial investment of public funds that have been made over the
past thirty-seven years; would reduce the value for money to be had
from the very substantial grant that would still remain to be paid to
the truncated ROH; and, in the case of the SWRB option, would
deprive the provinces of the benefits of ROH companies.'[138]

Tooley and Moser were jubilant. 'It's very nice to be told that we
are grossly underfunded,' said their spokesman. 'It's what we have
been saying all along.'[139] But the Priestley Report was not a clean
bill of health. The raiders found the ROH to be inefficient in many
areas and urged it to cut staff and reform work practices. Some guest
artists were grossly overpaid, overtime pay was out of control and
there was no point in touring the Royal Opera around the country; it
cost too much.

And this was where Priestley came unstuck. For Covent Garden to
survive it needed to be seen as a national asset. Only one of its three
companies, the SWRB, could now afford to set foot outside London
and in the house itself, opera had become 'relatively inaccessible'
due to high seat prices. The company could not reach more people
without slashing prices, which would only increase its losses. There
was little chance of reaching out through television, since one union
or artist was forever in dispute over extra fees. Priestley quoted
Isaiah Berlin's belief that 'opera is today, no less than yesterday,
intrinsic to the culture of a developed society,' but he failed to show
how opera might enrich society when it was available only to the
moneyed classes in the capital area.

Like Priestley, no one at Covent Garden could see beyond the end
of Bow Street. Tooley, incensed by the Treasury's refusal to scrap
VAT on ROH tickets, declared that the tax would mean 'spiritual
death' for the nation. His assertion sounded all the more insensitive
at a time when the weekly state benefit to an unemployed couple was
£47.85; the nightly cost to the state of two seats at Covent Garden

was £42.00.[140] The misery was no longer shared equally, as it had been after the war. Under Thatcherism, the gulf between haves and have-nots was widening. Those who lived on state handouts could never hope to share in the nation's 'spiritual life'.

The outcome of the Priestley Report was unsatisfactory to all concerned. The Government increased Covent Garden's subsidy to the recommended £12.35 million in 1984-85, but stalled again the following year. Lord Harewood at ENO protested that his grant had now fallen to less than half of Covent Garden's. A Manchester businessman, Raymond Slater, who had spent two million pounds renovating the Palace Theatre after being promised a Royal Opera tour, cancelled a £100,000 grant to Covent Garden, along with all other arts sponsorships. Priestley became chairman of the Greater London Arts Board. Tooley brandished his report at every politician who came his way, until eyes glazed over.

Among the Priestley findings that were swept back under the carpet was his concern about a certain boardroom irregularity:

> I have also recommended that the Secretariat which the Civil Service has provided to the Board since 1947 should be replaced by one formed by the ROH's permanent staff. This implies no adverse criticism of the existing Secretariat or their predecessors, but simply that an institution with an annual turnover of close on twenty million pounds should be capable of finding itself a competent Secretariat.[141]

Capable, perhaps, but unwilling to give up its agent in Downing Street, any more than the Prime Minister was prepared to tell her Cabinet Secretary, Sir Robert Armstrong, to relinquish his free nights at the opera. No further mention was made of this impertinent proposal, and for the rest of Armstrong's career and beyond Covent Garden continued to be served, free of charge, by some of the most superior officials in Whitehall.

Hardly a season went by now without the opera house having to cancel new productions for want of funds. The absence of novelty left the box office reliant on a flow of stars to entice operagoers to see an old show for a second or third time. The top-noters were never numerous, and female glamour in particular was scarce. From the very outset, Covent Garden had relied on a Flagstad, a Schwarzkopf, a Callas or a Nilsson to quicken the pulse and shorten the breath. These titans had retired and their successors were less bankable. Joan Sutherland had her fans, but the vehicles chosen by her omniscient husband were outlandish and expensive. Richard Bonynge was carving a niche for himself as a hunter of historic truffles. He retrieved Donizetti's *Lucrezia Borgia* from archival dust, followed by Massenet's *Esclarmonde*, a production that was shipped over from San Francisco at a cost of sixty thousand pounds. The diva herself was paid six thousand a night. By the second performance, she was unwell. Since there was no understudy, the rest of the cast bravely turned out in a make-do *Madam Butterfly*. There were five airings of *Esclarmonde*, which the *Daily Telegraph* called 'grotesque' and *The Times* 'meretricious'. The singers referred to it as *Excrement*, but this was the nature of diva-bait and the diva did as she pleased. In the next three seasons, she returned only once to Covent Garden.

Janet Baker retired from opera in 1981. Gwyneth Jones, another home-reared dame turned inconsistent, her screech and scoop nights saved from booing only by her regal bearing. Casting operas became all the trickier once Helga Schmidt resigned in poor health in 1979. It took five years to instal a replacement – Peter Mario Katona of the Hamburg Opera – and in that time the consistency of singing wobbled as badly as Dame Gwyneth as Desdemona.

The one stroke of fortune that befell the Royal Opera was the royal apotheosis of its prize soprano. Kiri te Kanawa had progressed through Mozart and Strauss into the Verdian roles of Amelia (*Simon Boccanegra*) and Desdemona (*Otello*), which she sang with serene beauty but no dramatic force. She was earning half a million pounds a year and, managed by her husband, Desmond, sometimes sounded less than fresh. Nevertheless, whenever she appeared in London, *The Times*' op-ed columnist Bernard Levin would clear his page of human rights abuses and bureaucratic muddle and deliver a paean of overpraise. When music critics were underwhelmed by a Covent Garden charity recital, Levin charged to her defence. 'Did you ever read such a pack of miserable, spiritless wretches as the critics who reviewed the performance in yesterday's papers?' he demanded. 'What thin and vinegary liquor has been substituted for blood in the veins of Mr Hope-Wallace, that he could say her performance of the Jewel Song failed to excite? What ailed our own Mr Higgins, a most learned and sharp-eared canary-fancier that he found the evening "a shade unsatisfying"? Failed to excite? A shade unsatisfying? I tell you, if this pair had been present at the miracle of the loaves and the fishes, one of them would have complained that there was no lemon to go with the fish, and the other would have demanded more butter for the bread.'[142]

A superior Kiri fan proved more influential. On 1 April 1981, she received a call asking her to sing at Charles's wedding. 'Charles who?' she said. The Prince of Wales, at thirty-two the world's most eligible bachelor, had chosen to marry a nineteen-year-old nursery teacher of noble birth, Lady Diana Spencer. He wanted Kiri to sing them out after the service.

The date fitted neatly in her diary. She had seven Elviras (*Don Giovanni*) and four Fiordiligis (*Cosi fan tutte*) to sing in an ROH Mozart Festival in July. Charles came to see *Don Giovanni* and found her 'wonderfully sexy and seductive'.[143] He invited her and Des back to the Palace, where she barely spoke to Diana.

On 29 July, decked out in a canary-coloured gown and cheeky, quiche-shaped hat, Kiri te Kanawa trilled Handel's 'Let the Bright Seraphim' while the ill-fated newlyweds signed the register and swanned down the aisle of St Paul's Cathedral. Seven hundred million people all over the world watched her on live television – the equivalent, said the US newscaster Tom Brokaw, of 'two hundred and fifty thousand Covent Garden audiences at the same time'.[144] The point was not lost on the ambitious soprano who, in her haste to make the wedding, had omitted to wear knickers, or so she later revealed.

Learning new roles had never been her forte and she was losing what little appetite she once felt for character growth. Rehearsing Puccini's *Manon Lescaut* at Covent Garden in May 1983, Dame Kiri (she was ennobled a year after the wedding) seemed so sullen and unprepared that the conductor Giuseppe Sinopoli threatened to walk out a week before opening night. 'He tried to get me fired,' raged Kiri.[145] The impulsive Italian was taken aside and warned that the Queen Mother was coming to the Gala performance and, unless he wagged his stick like a good boy, he would never work on these shores again. Kiri also balked at working with Götz Friedrich, whose production had been shipped in from Hamburg after Piero Faggioni's sets proved too big for the ROH stage. The second-hand *Lescaut*, was about ten boos short of a total disaster. Dame Kiri, said one critic,[146] 'had a less than comprehensive grasp' of her role.

That summer she met the sports impresario Mark McCormack on a golf course and began a new career. McCormack reckoned she would be better off singing concert arias in large arenas rather than fixed-fee operas in a two thousand-seat house. Kiri, the adopted child of poor parents, was keen. McCormack set up outdoor gigs in Australian vineyards and tennis courts. 'We made Kiri more money than she'd ever made before,'[147] he bragged. Kiri said it was 'inappropriate' to discuss her art in pecuniary terms, but from now on opera ceased to be the mainspring of her existence and she gave up learning new roles.

For want of a top soprano, Covent Garden was thrown upon the mercy of tenors. There were five lyric tenors of Mediterranean origin and comparable merit, two of whom soared above the rest. Luciano Pavarotti was a Covent Garden discovery. In 1963 Joan Ingpen, needing an understudy for the wayward Giuseppe di Stefano, checked out an all-Italian *Rigoletto* in Dublin and came home with Pavarotti and the baritone Piero Cappuccilli. The unknown Pavarotti, just twenty-seven, took over all but one of di Stefano's *Bohème*s, as well as a television spot on *Sunday Night at the London Palladium*. Most nights he watched TV in his hotel room, understanding barely a word. Weekends he spent with Enid Blech in Sussex, where she taught him to ride a horse. He was booked by Glyndebourne for *Idomeneo* and enjoyed the company's iron discipline. Then Richard Bonynge spotted him as the only tenor tall and loud enough to look Joan Sutherland in the eye. They took him on an Australian tour, won him a Decca contract and set up his US début. From the night he hit nine top Cs in succession in Donizetti's *Daughter of the Regiment* at the Metropolitan Opera in February 1972, Pavarotti was the biggest tenor in America since Caruso. He had sung the role before at Covent Garden, but on this night the press had been hyped up to fever pitch by his personal publicist, Herbert Breslin, and Pavarotti was crowned 'King of the High Cs'. He soon had five albums simultaneously in Billboard's classical top ten.

Pavarotti was a softie at heart. He talked wistfully of his time at Glyndebourne and his early struggles as a competition singer in Wales. He cherished the memory of Enid Blech and remained friendly with the Bonynges and Joan Ingpen. But towards Covent Garden, he blanked out. In a 1995 autobiography, he gave the company one glancing mention, as if it were alien territory.

The impediment, for 'Big Lucy', was John Tooley. Pavarotti was a dispenser of bear-hugs. Tooley, emotionally inhibited, resisted his embrace. 'I had a love-hate relationship with Luciano,' said Tooley. 'He used to accuse me of engaging the "Spanish Mafia" at his expense. And of course we went for them because they were more reliable.' In Tooley's book, reliability scored higher than magic.

In preference to Pavarotti, Tooley favoured the elegant Alfredo Kraus, the thin-toned José Carreras and the glorious Giacomo Aragall, whose talents were stunted by incurable stage fright. Above all, Tooley hitched his schedules to the one tenor that Pavarotti feared as a rival.

Placido Domingo had reached Covent Garden by the scenic route. Spanish born, he was singing with the Mexico National Opera at eighteen, followed by three years in Tel Aviv and a stint at New York City Opera. He made his début in Vienna in 1967, at the Met in 1968 and at La Scala the following season. By the time he opened his throat as Cavaradossi at Covent Garden on 8 December 1971, Domingo had sung two Verdi *Requiem*s in London under Carlo Maria Giulini and Leonard Bernstein and was a fully-fledged world star.

Arriving at the start of Tooley's regime, in the very week of Kiri's triumph, Domingo chimed in perfectly with the general director's wishes. Businesslike where Pavarotti was bumptious, urbane to the Italian's abrupt, Domingo liked to say 'yes'. He was intelligent, hard-working and unfailingly punctual, a management's dream. He also knew three times as many roles as Pavarotti and could sing, apart from Italian and Spanish, in French, English, Hebrew (for Tel Aviv), German and Russian. As if this were not enough, he played the piano, conducted and longed to direct. In Tooley he found a management tutor, a confidant and friend. Seeing them together, one sensed a cautious symbiosis of two tidy men who always looked twice before putting a foot forward. Tooley would do his utmost to keep Domingo happy. When the tenor's eldest son, by a short-lived teenage marriage, was lodging in Northampton, Tooley drove up regularly to visit and report on his progress.

Domingo invested his fees in several properties, including a house in Chelsea and a flat in Covent Garden, where he or his son would stay. When vacant, he rented rooms to visiting singers. In Vienna he rented out a whole apartment block near the Staatsoper, saving the penthouse for himself.

This most organized of tenors took care to create a good working atmosphere. 'Most stars nowadays don't even speak to the chorus,' observed Constance Shacklock, whose adopted daughter sang at the ROH. 'Domingo is the exception. He knows every chorister by name.'

Tooley raved about his 'really extraordinary musicality, and his ability to use his voice to dramatic ends in a way not matched by any other.'[148] Domingo reciprocated with florid praise for the unprepossessing manager. For the rest of his career, he never missed a season at Covent Garden. Pavarotti, no fool, saw which way the scales were tipped. From the early 80s he turned capricious, cancelling as often as he sang. At the Lyric Opera in Chicago, another Domingo stronghold, he missed twenty-six out of forty-one contracted appearances between 1981 and 1989. At Covent Garden, he furnished a plethora of excuses. His father was sick; Calaf in *Turandot* was too taxing for his voice; finally, in February 1983, he telexed from Australia that he was too poorly to sing in *Tosca* – only to be snapped by press photographers on a South Sea island with a new girlfriend. He turned up for *Aida* the following season and virtually wrecked Jean-Pierre Ponnelle's new production, refusing to obey the simplest of directions. His next cancellation was *Tosca*, complaining that backstage dust at the ROH might trigger an allergy. 'I spoke to him on the phone,' said Tooley, 'and I said I want evidence of the allergy. He said, I'll get it to you. Some time later he sent me a paper from a New York laboratory which had done very serious analysis.' The final straw was a demand by Pavarotti, the morning after singing before the Prince and Princess of Wales, for a twenty thousand pound reward.

It dawned on Tooley that Pavarotti, who had a profitable sideline in open-air arena concerts, could not care less if he never sang again at Covent Garden. His booming fan club might wail, but Domingo was an acceptable substitute, ever ready to help out. Tooley would fly to the ends of the earth to squeeze extra dates out of him, and Domingo seldom refused. He owned the role of Otello at Covent Garden; also of Samson in Saint-Saëns's opera and of Hoffmann in Offenbach's. In July 1984, he led the Royal Opera to the United States with four *Turandot*s in Los Angeles, coinciding with the Olympic Games. Never had the Royal Opera known a more loyal or obliging servant. He was Covent Garden's *chanteur noble* as Anthony Dowell was its *danseur noble*.

Then, catastrophe. In September 1985, while Domingo was warming up for *Otello* in Chicago, an earthquake struck Mexico City, killing hundreds, including Domingo's aunt, uncle and two cousins in the district where he grew up. He took a private plane to the disaster zone and, in a dust-choked voice, issued a statement that wrecked the world's opera schedules. 'I am asking every theatre in the world to give me one year's leave of absence, starting immediately,' he told me down a crackly telephone. 'I expect they will make difficulties. That is why I am now asking them publicly through you: Let me go!' He aimed to spend the year giving concerts to raise enough money to rehouse two hundred families.

A week later he flew to Barletta on Italy's Adriatic coast, to shoot *Otello* in a medieval castle with Franco Zeffirelli. 'I could not abandon the film,' he said. 'A film like this costs ten million dollars to make and involves many jobs. I know live opera also costs money but . . . they can find another tenor to fill my sixty performances for a year. After that I will see where I go.'[149] On set in Barletta, he was almost unapproachable with gloom. On camera all day, he spent the evenings and half the night on the phone to opera managers, clearing his diary. The first of his relief concerts took place in nearby Bari. It raised a hundred thousand dollars but left a residue of bitterness when two sopranos pulled out of the supporting cast and Domingo's voice cracked after two arias. A party of schoolchildren gave him two hundred dollars from their pocket money.

He had not been filming for more than a week when John Tooley flew in, desperate for a word. Incongruous in a three-piece suit in the Adriatic heat, Tooley begged Domingo to reinstate his *Otello* at Covent Garden. The entire season hinged on his appearance, and the house hoped to make a profit of £150,000 by increasing seat prices for the show. 'Outrageous,' said Domingo. 'These operas are for the public. How can they afford £75 a ticket?' For two days, Tooley and Margherita Stafford, Domingo's London agent, fluttered around the fringes of the set before the tenor gave way. He would sing *Otello*, he agreed, but not in a new production. 'Right now I am not at my best,' he protested. Before Tooley left, he yielded completely.

Domingo never let him down.

But the Domingo who returned to Covent Garden in January 1987 was a changed man. His Otello was grey-toned and dispiriting. His aid efforts for Mexico sold poorly. When he announced on the Des O'Connor chat show that he was cancelling a Wembley concert at twenty-four hours notice 'because the tickets were too high,' one promoter told a newspaper: 'I want the head of Placido Domingo.' Legal action ensued, and Domingo parted company acrimoniously from his long-suffering agent. Soon after, he cancelled *Lohengrin*. The music press reported that 'the Royal Opera is at the end of its tether with Domingo'.[150] This was overstated, but an irritation had set in with the enforced Otello and Domingo found it hard to recapture his élan. 'I had a sour time adjusting myself to singing in England,' he told me. 'I was shocked, electrified, by some of the reactions. We are not machines, and we have an instrument that is very much affected by the emotions. If you are not completely happy, you cannot sing. You need your happiness to sing.' What Tooley needed was a top-note tenor, happy or not. The departure of Pavarotti and disgruntlement of Domingo were dangerously weakening the company's prospects, and his own.

The disappearance of guest artists at the Royal Ballet took a heavy toll at the box-office. After two years of purified Englishness, Norman Morrice gave in and asked Tooley to re-engage Nureyev. The wounded Tatar brooded on the invitation, telexing his assent five minutes before the annual press conference, and too late to change the printed casts. 'I am mortified by what happened,' Tooley told him. 'I could not reach Ninette de Valois, who is organizing the cast of *Sleeping Beauty* and when we eventually did, later in the day, she said that much as she would have liked you to appear she simply could not cope with explanations to the dancers and the large re-arrangement of casting which your presence at this late hour would have meant.

'I understand all of this, and I hope you will. Since things have got to this point, the last thing that any of us want is a further deterioration of your relationship with the Royal Ballet. That is not in any of our interests. Rudolf, please understand the situation, please accept my apologies for our failure to implement your decision for the reasons which I have explained.'[151] The hint of desperation in Tooley's note was unmistakable. Without a bankable star, the ballet would lose not only its overseas tours but its home audience to the sparkier Rambert and LCDT, where Seymour and Sleep were trying their hands at choreography. Nureyev, for his part, longed to return. He had been a company member of the Royal Ballet in all but name and missed its home comforts. Angry and frustrated, he told a television interviewer that 'the moment Margot ceased to dance . . . there was an incredible urge to demote me, to turn me from identity to nonentity.'[152] He went on to describe the ROH management as 'a sack of shit'.

He finally returned in March 1982 after a five-year absence, 'galumphing' (as one insider put it) comically yet charismatically through his youthful roles. He was forty-four years old and pushing himself as hard as ever. His fee was fourteen hundred pounds, a pittance compared to the four thousand paid to the baritone Geraint Evans, another fading stalwart. Nureyev was about to become artistic director of the Paris Opéra Ballet and danced only a few times more at the ROH – in 1984, 1988 and at a 1990 fundraiser for Margot Fonteyn, who was dying of cancer in Panama. Nureyev himself was by then stricken with Aids and did not have long to live. He never ceased to regret his rift with the Royal Ballet which, had decisions fallen differently, he might have led as director and galvanized in the way that he revitalized the Paris Opéra.

Other foreigners now slipped back into the schedules. Makarova danced *Giselle* and Mikhail Baryshnikov, the USSR's greatest dancing loss since Nureyev, appeared in a new Ashton piece, *Rhapsody*, to mark the Queen Mother's eightieth birthday. His American lover, the volatile Gelsey Kirkland, danced Juliet opposite the newly repatriated Anthony Dowell in a fixed-smile season marking the jubilee of English ballet. Half a century after Madam founded the Vic-Wells Ballet there was no English ballerina of world rank and only Dowell to fly the ensign among the men.

The onus of continuity lay heavily on the shoulders of Kenneth MacMillan, far more so than when he had been director. MacMillan did not disappoint. His 1980s ballets extended his skills as a social critic and story-teller. *Gloria*, using Francis Poulenc's soprano-sung setting of the Roman Catholic Mass – this time without board veto – evoked the futility of the First World War, just as Mrs Thatcher and the US President Ronald Reagan upped the ante in Cold War rhetoric. *Isadora* recreated the life and loves of the legendary American dancer, Isadora Duncan, to a new score by Richard Rodney Bennett. Innovatively, he split the title role between a dancer, Merle Park, and an actress, Mary Miller, who spoke words from Duncan's memoirs. 'Isadora', said MacMillan, 'was a more serious as well as a more tragic person than most people appreciate.'[153] He might well have been speaking about himself. 'It would be unfair to blame MacMillan for trivializing Isadora Duncan's life,' snarled Percival on *The Times*. 'She began that process when she wrote a lurid, often fictional, autobiography.'[154]

Knighted in 1983, MacMillan pressed ahead with *Valley of Shadows* – a realization of the Italian Holocaust memoir, *The Garden of the Finzi-Continis* – and *Different Drummer*, which used the atonalities of Webern and Schoenberg to rework Georg Büchner's original 1835 story of Berg's opera *Wozzeck*. He then picked up his long-delayed ambition to recreate Britten's *Prince of Pagodas*, the composer's executors having sensibly authorized his proposed cuts. None of his ballets met with instant acclaim, even within the company. It was in the nature of his art that it revealed its merits steadily over a period of time.

Morrice gave MacMillan all the support he needed, intervening to retrieve *Manon* from the scrapheap and restoring it to the staple repertoire. Lynn Seymour was still keen to bring him to Munich, but their contact ended when MacMillan slapped her face in the foyer on a Covent Garden first night after hearing her criticize the costumes his wife had designed for a new production of *Solitaire*. Morrice sought to encourage new choreography within the company, setting David Bintley and Ashley Page on the road to distinguished careers. But MacMillan was the Royal Ballet's guiding light, as Ashton had been before him, and his work was gaining favour abroad. In September 1984, Baryshnikov enticed him to become Associate Director of American Ballet Theater, with the prospect of establishing his work on a larger stage.

MacMillan was reluctant to spend time in New York without knowing how his work was being treated back home. In the rehearsal warren at Baron's Court, he struck up a conversation with Monica Mason, who was retiring early with persistent injury. 'I was friendly with Kenneth but I never had a meal with him, never went to his house, never knew him socially outside the company,' recalled Mason. 'One day, when he said to me in a corridor, "would you like to be my assistant?" I said, "yes". He said, "you're not meant to answer, you're meant to go away and think about it."

'I said, "there's nothing to think about."

'He said, "I'll see you in two days."'

Mason became MacMillan's eyes and ears, taking rehearsals and telephoning him daily reports – 'he hated not knowing what was going on.' Every MacMillan ballet was based on trial and error and consumed by a pervasive self-doubt. 'When he was making *Gloria*,' recalled Mason, 'he had done the *pas de deux* and we came to the first big movement for corps de ballet. He was very tense. We went into rehearsal and the miracles started happening. At the end of an hour and a half he let everybody go. He turned to me, "what do you think of that?" I'm taking notes and thinking, boys come in on the right . . . do a semi-circle .. so he said, "would you say it was all right?" I said, "yes . . ." He said, "that was the worst rubbish, there is not a single thing I can keep out of today's rehearsal, tomorrow we'll start all over again." It was only on the third go that he got it.'

Upright, discreet and self-contained, Mason turned into more than a choreographer's amanuensis. Dancers came to her with their fears and niggles and she became the first port of call for anyone with an injury. Raised in South Africa, she had seen English dancers on tour as a child and all she ever wanted to do was work with the Royal Ballet. She represented its conscience and continuity.

Morrice lost credibility. He quickly set about grooming a successor. Anthony Dowell had returned from America a changed man. He had relished the limelight at ABT but recognized the grim realities of balletic business in an open market. 'The real eye-opener,' he said, 'was that they had a lay-off period and some of those dancers were serving tables in restaurants. It was tough. People were very hungry, the energy level was terrific. America opened me up as a person.' He did not have much longer to dance and wanted to recommit to the Royal Ballet.

He was given two seasons to understudy Morrice. Much of the time he spent in the rehearsal room, attacking slackened techniques. Dowell was not quite sure whether he had what it took to run a company and cast around for oracles to support his next move. He harked back to the lowest moment of his career, losing Prince Rudolf's role in *Mayerling* because he could not recover fast enough from injury. 'I was being trained back to fitness,' he recalled, 'by a wonderful lady called Winifred Edwards, who came back in her eighties to retrain me (Monica carries on Miss Edwards' traditions). Kenneth when he created a ballet had to do the central *pas de deux* and work the rest around it. I think I created one small section. I knew it wasn't ready. Miss Edwards was telling me I wasn't ready, and Kenneth couldn't wait. So I waved it goodbye, the biggest career blow I ever suffered.

'Funnily enough, after one of these training sessions we walked out and I remember crossing the road with her when out of the blue Miss Edwards said: "Anthony I think one day you should think of being director of the Royal Ballet." I didn't think it was mad, because I respected her so much. But it really shocked me and made me think.'

The crucial push came from Ninette de Valois who, in her mid-eighties, had just deposed the head of the Royal Ballet School – the accomplished James Monahan, former head of the BBC World Service and (as James Kennedy) dance critic of the *Guardian* – and replaced him with his embittered ex-wife, Merle Park. That kind of casting always made Madam cackle. Dowell had never been one of her favourites – 'she liked the naughty ones, and Anthony was so good,' said Sibley – but he was loyal, hard-working and above all respectful. 'I knew that she was for it – she let it be known,' said Dowell. 'Afterwards, she sent wonderful little letters of encouragement. That kept me going.'

Morrice had been due to hand over in mid-1985 but returned from a Far East tour with an attack of toxoplasmosis that caused him to take several months of sick leave. 'I was thrown in at the deep end,' said Dowell, who had just turned forty. 'It is staggering how he has matured,' said one insider.[155] Tooley relieved him of many administrative chores and Monica Mason agreed to assist him, in addition to MacMillan. 'It's quite hard serving two masters,' she reflected, 'but I was serving the company, and that's what everybody has always done.'

Some doubted whether Dowell was strong enough to impose his will. 'Anthony,' said Wayne Sleep, 'hated any kind of scene.'[156] But Ashton and MacMillan, who had twisted his body one way and another as a dancer, submitted meekly to his programming decisions. Madam was generally compliant. 'It's much harder for you, dear,' she said, 'than it was for me. I didn't have to waste time with unions and working practices and all that.' She was still 'very visible'[157] in the day-to-day workings of the company.

When Dowell put on his first *Swan Lake* at Christmas 1986, she objected loudly to the décor and lighting. 'As you get older, the eyesight goes and nothing in the show was ever light enough for her,' said Dowell. 'It obviously hit a nerve and she let fly. I just rallied and shouted right back at her.' Years later, there was a note of astonishment in his voice as he relived his resistance. It was the moment he came of age as director of the Royal Ballet, a post he would hold longer than anyone, except Madam herself.

The annual curtain-raiser for the Royal Opera was turning into a coconut shy. Bored by a lack of new productions and exacerbated by second-rate casts, several members of the press stored up their venom for the traditional coffee morning in the Crush Bar and, once the next season's programme had been distributed, let fly with all the adjectives in their quiver at the hapless trio of Tooley, Moser and Davis, sitting upon the dais. The panellists' body language invited attack. Moser would sit, arms folded and legs crossed, looking morose and away from Tooley. Davis stared down at the floor.

In fairness, there were isolated bouquets of praise. Verdi's *Macbeth*, conducted by Riccardo Muti, was considered the most exciting show in years, and the production of *Boris Godunov* by the Russian exile, Andrei Tarkovsky, conducted by Claudio Abbado, bore the unmistakable imprint of living history. Many were encouraged by the showing of a lone episode of Karlheinz Stockhausen's seven-day opera, *Licht* (Isaiah Berlin found it 'most melodious'; a friend replied: 'pure Palm Court'). A pair of rare Zemlinsky one-acters imported from Hamburg via the Edinburgh Festival showed a further spark of enterprise. On the whole, however, these glints of light were lost in the gloom and the press colloquies were dominated by cancellations, monetary losses and general moans. In November 1982, Alan Blyth of the *Daily Telegraph* and Brian Magee, a Cambridge don and future chairman of the Arts Council's music panel, demanded the head of Colin Davis. Both called for Mackerras to succeed, while others set up a clamour for Muti. Tom Sutcliffe of the *Guardian* said few tears would be shed if the opera house were shut down until its entire board and management could be replaced.

'Something old, something new, something borrowed, something blue,' quipped Sutcliffe of another meagre seasonal offering. 'Are you accusing us of disseminating pornography?' snapped Davis.

Comparisons with ENO were invariably unfavourable. Harewood had made way for a hotshot trio of Peter Jonas, David Pountney and Mark Elder who called themselves 'The Power House'. They continually renewed the stock. The spring of 1986 saw two world premières – Ferruccio Busoni's half-forgotten *Doctor Faust* in an authentic completion, and a semi-electronic *Mask of Orpheus* by Harrison Birtwistle which, many in the first-night audience felt, was the biggest breakthrough for British opera since *Peter Grimes*. The Austrian pianist Alfred Brendel went one further. He was overheard telling Sir Isaiah Berlin, as they left the Coliseum, that this was the finest English opera since Purcell's. Much of what ENO did was fresh, challenging, infuriating. Much of Covent Garden's output was stuffy, predictable and stale.

Dissent was not confined to the press. The Arts Council, itself squeezed by Thatcherite constraints, froze the Covent Garden grant with the aim, never openly admitted, of shaking out the board and management. There were also elements on the Covent Garden board who demanded change, causing Tooley no end of discomfiture. The main agitator was Sir Denis Forman who, with the Bernsteins, had made Granada the country's most watchable television station. Forman was personally responsible for one of the great serial dramas, Paul Scott's post-imperial cycle, *The Jewel in the Crown*. One-footed from a war wound and sporting red braces, Forman was a practising musician who had rescued the venerable music publishers, Novello, and published *The Musical Times*. He took a look at the ROH books and demanded radical measures. 'Forman would say, your chorus is too big, get rid of it,' recalled an eye-witness. 'This was heresy. All there was left of the opera company, after all, was a chorus and orchestra.'[158]

'Denis Forman was a great shooter from the hip,' said Tooley. 'Intelligent, well informed, passionate about opera and ballet. Often sent people off on wild goose chases.' Resentful of being bossed about, Tooley demanded a seat on the board and was refused. To his further dismay, Forman was made deputy chairman and joined Moser in dealing with the Arts Council, where Tooley was disliked.

Forman apart, most of the board were consumed by a sense of divine right. 'What one wants on a board is not a bunch of people who think the same thing,' recollected Moser. 'We had some crises and tough times, but there was a wonderful feeling of unity on the board in wanting the opera house to survive. John Sainsbury and Isaiah Berlin and Pat Gibson and Colette Clark all brought different attributes but whatever our politics we were always united, that's why we were quite powerful.'

Powerful, perhaps, but not uniformly effective. Moser had fattened the board with finance men to handle the redevelopment, which was not going well. The phase-one appeal for ten million pounds was reached only in 1985. 'The first phase ran out of money before they could double-glaze the windows,' reported a board member. 'So the loudest noise in the rehearsal room was a ghetto-blaster playing in James Street.'[159]

The next stage would cost five times as much, fifty-six million pounds, half of which would be raised by erecting an adjacent office block for sale or rent. John Sainsbury took charge of choosing architects. From an open contest, he picked a young partnership of Jeremy Dixon and Edward Jones, whose main project to date had been restoring a tree-lined Victorian street in North Kensington. Where most architects were prisoners of glassy modernism, Dixon and Jones had reconverted to early classicism. Their fervour for Inigo Jones and his designs infected Sainsbury and his conservative committee with a vision to restore the gutted market area to an imaginary splendour. Sainsbury then left the board, after fifteen years' service, to focus on the National Gallery, where he endowed an extension wing under the chairmanship of his former ROH colleague, Lord Annan. Sainsbury continued to keep a watchful eye on the Royal Ballet and was committed to be the lead donor in Covent Garden's reconstruction. When the Royal Opera and Royal Ballet were split (on Priestley's recommendation) into separate cost centres, he returned as chairman of the ballet board. In due course, he acquired a significant extraneous role as chairman of the Governors of the Royal Ballet, a group that existed and met independently of the ROH.

The board was reinforced with the likes of Lord Richardson, recently retired Governor of the Bank of England; the chief executive of Lloyd's, Ian Hay Davison; the chairman of Commercial Union Assurance, Sir Francis Sandilands; the IBM chairman Sir Edwin Nixon; and a property developer, Christopher Benson. All appointments needed Downing Street approval but, with the Cabinet Secretarys in attendance, this proved no more than a formality. The ROH board, once composed of scholars and gentlemen, was now packed with City suits. Forman, to inject a discordant note, co-opted a protégé of his, the television producer Jeremy Isaacs who had invented Channel Four (on the strength of a report by the ubiquitous Lord Annan) as an outlet for alternative and minority broadcasting. He and Tooley took against one another on sight, which is hardly surprising given the undeclared sub-text. 'I set my heart on appointing Jeremy (in John's place),' said Moser. 'When Denis and

I appointed him to the board, we shared this hypothetical thought that he could become the successor.'

Into this ferment returned George Whyte, the self-made furniture magnate whose earlier ideas had been rejected by Drogheda. Whyte, ten years on, volunteered to spend three months at Covent Garden and produce a business plan. Moser accepted his offer, but fretted that he should take care not 'to upset the staff'. Tooley sat in at the meeting, looking worried. 'I am a man who wants to provide solutions,' Whyte noted, 'but I don't believe this can work if they are processed by people who may be the source of the problems.'[160]

Whyte set about gathering information. Moser told him he thought Tooley was good with artists but weak on finance. Goodman said Moser had been a poor chairman and blamed himself for the appointment. Whyte found little communication between Tooley and Moser. He discussed artist fees with Peter Katona and was shocked to discover that conductors were being paid twenty thousand Swiss francs a night, well above the going rate in Europe. Other items of waste and inefficiency sprang to view backstage, but Whyte quickly decided that Covent Garden could not be saved by nit-picking and cost-cutting. What was needed was a new vision to raise the company's profile and finances, a strategy that combined modern marketing and merchandising methods. An independent Enterprise Board was needed to refocus the company's image and outlook. Among Whyte's ideas was a package for Concorde-class tourists, combining the Savoy and QEII with nights at the opera and dinners with the artists. The house could be utilized in summer for prestige ROH study courses in opera and ballet, a profitable and proselytizing sideline. No single scheme, and he proposed fifty of them, would raise less than quarter of a million pounds.

Whyte looked at the redevelopment and found it wanting. Half the projected cost of fifty-seven million pounds was supposed to come from the sale of new offices and shops around the opera house, to the disgust of local residents. London was basking in another of its property booms, but if prices fell before the building was finished the ROH would be left with a crippling shortfall. Whyte, in a dazzling, holistic report, urged the ROH to scrap its property deals and create an international cultural centre in the available space, funded by wealthy Far Eastern and European nations. The idea was, perhaps, quixotic – and no part of the plan could be made to work independently of the whole, but the Report deserved serious consideration. What it got from the ROH board was dead silence.

Ten months later, Whyte gave an interview to the *Sunday Times*. 'No one wants a third-rate office block that is going to be a disaster for the area, when they could have a resplendent international development,' he argued.[161] Whyte had spent £25,000 of his own money by this time. He offered to spend twice as much again on a feasibility study for the international cultural centre. He went before the Board and declared that 'at no time did I have anything but the interests of the House at heart'. They all but threw him out. He told Moser: 'You have mentioned on a number of occasions that you find my proposals attractive, on the other hand you do not wish to impede the implementation of your own scheme, which has no doubt incurred internal costs.'[162]

The Times, in a leading article, urged Covent Garden 'to market itself actively by one means or another'.[163] In a letter to the editor, Drogheda proclaimed that the main problem at Covent Garden was underfunding, and 'for this the fault rests clearly with the Government, who have so far failed to honour the recommendations of the Priestley Report.' He added: 'I do not believe sums of the order required could ever be raised through the ideas being put forward by Mr George Whyte, with whom Covent Garden first had talks fifteen years ago.'[164] Moser was never man enough to contradict his charismatic predecessor. 'One of the reasons we can't go along with your plan,' he told Whyte, 'is that Drogheda is against you.'

'These people on the Board believed they were there by God's will,' Whyte concluded. 'Apart from Forman, they were interested only in self-perpetuation and not in taking responsibility.'[165]

On 30 June 1987, Westminster City Council overruled local protests and granted outline planning permission for the next phase of ROH development, offices and all. The seeds of future disaster were being set in cement and concrete.

Internally, tectonic plates started to shift. To head the newly devolved opera company, Tooley hired Eva Wagner, dispossessed daughter of Bayreuth, who rolled up in a Porsche with her own office furniture, all glass and chrome. She lasted two years and left little impression – except on Moser, who doted on her. The reshaping of the Royal Opera would take place over and above the head of its nominal director.

Paul Findlay, Tooley's assistant, emerged as a driving force, while

Peter Katona made himself indispensable as casting director. It was Findlay who suggested live relays of opera on to a big screen in the Covent Garden piazza, the most populist venture since the Proms. And it was Findlay again who pushed for the introduction of surtitles – a running translation projected above the stage – over the objections of boardroom traditionalists and opera critics. 'I don't think one goes to the opera to *read*,' sniffed Rodney Milnes, Rosenthal's heir at *Opera*. 'What should be an act of great concentration between performers and audience is broken when the eyes flicker elsewhere. If people go unprepared to the opera, that's their lookout. Why should they spoil the enjoyment of those who do prepare?'[166] Tooley agreed to poll the audience, ninety-four per cent of whom endorsed the surtitles. 'I'm sure they are going to be very popular,' muttered Milnes, 'just like public executions.'

Findlay, a gangling man of deceptively boyish manner, was coming up as a contender. He had the support of the staff and more hands-on experience than Tooley had when he succeeded Webster, having organized and led tours of both companies to the Far East and the United States. 'I was Tooley's Tooley,' said Findlay. 'I had done everything except cook, sing and dance.' What counted now was how well he could play the board game.

The first casualty was Colin Davis. The music director had become moody and withdrawn, showing little interest in any productions but his own. One night when the singing was scrappy and the applause tepid, he told Findlay: 'I've never been music director of this place, not in the sense that Solti was. Solti did what he wanted. Whenever I wanted to do something and John didn't, he would find a million reasons why it couldn't happen.'

His relations with Tooley had cooled. 'They used to be thick as thieves,' said Patsy Tooley, 'but there weren't as many dinners with Colin and Shamsi as before.' Despite his alienation, Davis refused to give up. 'He wanted to work in London, to be with his wife and children,' said Tooley. 'Ideally he would have liked to conduct one of the London orchestras, but that was not forthcoming.' When Tooley broke the news that his contract would not be renewed beyond 1986, Davis was 'desperate'.[167] 'Colin did feel that he was asked to leave too early,' agreed Moser. 'I would have been happier to renew him than some others on the board.'

'It seemed to me a perfectly rational decision by the board,' said Tooley. 'But Colin saw it as something other than that. He felt there were knives out for him, which was absolutely untrue.'

He had been music director for fifteen years, too long by half. Had he left, like Solti, at the end of a decade, he would have departed in glory. As it was, he slunk away with a *Fidelio* in a patchwork production that was booed louder than anything since the 1973 *Don Giovanni*. Only Rosenthal found a kind word to say for the music director, postulating that the Solti and Davis eras at Covent Garden would be seen, in time, 'to be as important as were the Mahler, Toscanini and Krauss regimes in Vienna, Milan and Munich'.[168]

Tooley approached the obvious successors and was turned down flat by the first three. Muti was waiting to inherit La Scala when Abbado moved on, Abbado had his eye on Vienna and Daniel Barenboim would not work for London wages. Zubin Mehta, then head of the New York Philharmonic, was interested and thought Tooley had promised him the job, but the board cast a veto. Mehta's flying visits to Covent Garden had been marred by haste and make-do.

Tooley then suggested that they should abolish the post altogether. 'One of John's lines was, we don't need a music director,' said Findlay. 'I have been here thirty years, he said, I can handle most of that.'

When the board balked, he went looking for the conductor who would need him most. It was Moser who first approached Bernard Haitink, music director of Amsterdam's Concertgebouw Orchestra for quarter of a century and of Glyndebourne for the past decade. He had also been chief conductor of the London Philharmonic. Despite his titular authority, Haitink had always leaned heavily on artistic and administrative partners. At Glyndebourne, Peter Hall supplied the ideas. In Amsterdam they came from artistic directors. Haitink was an excellent conductor but neither an innovator nor a decision maker. When Tooley approached him, he weighed the offer, slept on it, and declined. Twice more Tooley thrust the crown upon him, and twice more Haitink refused. 'I did not think I was the man for it,' he told me at the time. 'It would drive me mad; it was a tremendous risk. But I was fifty-five and it could be my last challenge.'

When he resigned from Glyndebourne, George Christie exploded with anger, outraged that Covent Garden could poach his music director with the divine right of a medieval warlord. The press responded with joyous anticipation and relief at the ending of tedium. Haitink earned extra points by promising to ban fly-by-night stars and renew the bond between Covent Garden and the world beyond. 'There's such a gap between the *Royal* Opera House and the public and musicians outside,' he declared. 'Too much accent on this establishment thing. We must get rid of it.'[169] His inaugural production, a bleak and gripping *Jenůfa* directed by the Russian exile Yuri Lyubimov, saw the experimental introduction of surtitles on alternate nights. 'I noticed the difference,' Haitink exulted. 'The hairs stood up on the back of my neck when I felt the audience understanding every word that was being sung.' In the second act, when the foster-mother drowns Jenůfa's illegitimate baby, the sobbing in the left-hand stalls almost drowned out the cellos. Later in the season, he conducted the ballet thrillingly in a Stravinsky triple bill, the first time since Lambert that a top-notch conductor had led the dancers.

To cover for Haitink's lack of operatic confidence, Jeffrey Tate was brought in as principal conductor; he soon made way for the veteran Edward Downes, who had never been away for long. Downes had the privilege of taking over a run of *Salome* from Christoph von Dohnanyi in which Maria Ewing stripped down to the very buff for a full half-minute, against the feeble protestations of her director husband, Peter Hall. Downes, whose vision was impaired, claimed he saw sequins in her pubic hair. Suddenly, the music was looking up.

'John believed that bringing Bernard in would ensure him another period,' said Findlay. 'His biggest shock was that Bernard did not go to the wall to insist on John staying. Bernard made his point at a board meeting but would not stand up for it.' Tooley was told soon after that his term would end in the summer of 1988, a month after his sixty-fourth birthday.

'I had not expected a renewal,' he said in retrospect. 'I talked about it with Haitink, who wanted it a lot. But I said it's time for appointing somebody who would see the company through the renovation of the house.' Internally, Tooley complained he was being cut off without means of support, although the board agreed to pay him two years' severance, taking him past retirement age, and his salary was raised to a respectable £100,000.

He implored the board to replace him with an opera professional like the Anglophile Hugues Gall, or Brian McMaster who was doing well at Welsh National Opera. John Sainsbury nominated an American called Henry Wrong who was running the City of

London's new Barbican Centre, having previously worked at Rudolf Bing's right hand at the Met.

A selection panel was formed, comprising Moser, Forman, Gibson, Colette Clark and Brian Nicholson. They overrode Tooley's advice, snubbed Sainsbury's man and overlooked Findlay who was backed by most of the staff. Forman and Moser had determined two years earlier that Isaacs should succeed, and the rest of the board were in accord. 'Angus Stirling had got it into his head after the big-screen relay in the piazza that what Covent Garden needed was a television person,' said an eye-witness. 'Tooley lost his temper. "What you need," he said, " is someone who can put on a show in the house night after night."'[170]

A last-minute impediment arose. The BBC had riled Mrs Thatcher with a run of hostile programmes. She demanded the head of its director-general, Alisdair Milne. The biggest job in broadcasting was up for grabs and Isaacs was a prime candidate. He apologized to the ROH board and put in his c.v. There were two contenders of equal merit – David Dimbleby, who was backed by the BBC chairman, 'Duke' Hussey; and Isaacs, favoured by the deputy chairman and former Labour MP, Joel Barnett. When the panel hit stalemate, they reached an English compromise and chose a BBC apparatchik, Michael Checkland. He picked a deputy, John Birt, from independent television, and was deposed before long in his favour. Isaacs or Dimbleby might have spared the BBC the ravages that followed, but the Governors were too timid to choose a strong personality.

Deprived of the job he really wanted, Isaacs became available to Covent Garden on the rebound. Tooley vainly argued that he had disqualified himself by looking elsewhere, but this cut no ice with the board. Isaacs gave in his notice at Channel 4, and told his populist successor, Michael Grade: 'I am handing on to you a sacred trust. If you screw it up, if you betray it, I'll come back and throttle you.'[171] He was as different from Tooley as opera from ballet. For six uneasy months, he shadowed the outgoing general director, under the sharp eye of a new chairman.

Moser, too, had given up. He was out of tune with the times and getting nowhere with the politicians. 'The Labour years always seemed rather easier from our point of view,' he reflected. 'My last two or three years were very tough. I ended on a low.' At his parting press conference, he made a 'final and urgent' plea for more money to an unheeding Government.

Moser had intended to hand over the chair to Forman but the Granada chief was nursing a dying wife. He next thought of nominating Armstrong, who was due to retire from Whitehall the following year, but thought better of it. The next chairman had to be someone Mrs Thatcher trusted, but who could also stand up to her. The man who sprang to mind was John Sainsbury, a notable contributor to Conservative Party funds and powerful business figure. 'I had left the board and had no idea whether they would want me back,' said the supermarket chief. 'When I was approached I found it a very difficult decision, because of the pressure of my other responsibilities. I thought for some time about it and decided that I couldn't commit myself for a full term. I would only accept if they agreed that I could only commit myself to serving for two years while they found someone else.'

'John Sainsbury believed he had to get an undertaking from Thatcher that she would help,' said an ROH insider. 'He went to Downing Street and came back saying that if we doubled the box-office and sponsorship they would help.'

Corks popped in the Royal Ballet. 'We were thrilled,' said Dowell, delighted that a ballet fan would lead the board, the first since Keynes. In his opening set of accounts, Sainsbury reversed the natural order and introduced the ballet season ahead of the opera. 'Retail is detail,' he proclaimed several times daily, and he pursued minutiae with the zeal of a man who was proud to know, to the nearest hundred, how many bags of frozen peas the English bought each day. Short of temper, he brooked no contradiction and subjected staff and directors to shouting fits if they persisted in defying his will. Tooley, unaccustomed to rough treatment, was almost glad to be going. Few were aware that Sainsbury's chairmanship was short-term and stopgap.

On his last day as general director, Tooley was asked on television what had been his greatest disaster. He was stumped for an answer. There had been no failures. Everything at the Garden had been simply perfect.

Called upon to make a farewell address to the staff, Tooley turned to a close colleague and confided: 'I have been here eighteen years and it is very difficult to say what my achievements were. The only thing I can say is: I have kept this place afloat. This may sound dreadful to the outside, but anyone on the inside will know what it means.'

CHAPTER 9

Act Three, On a Spree
(1987–96)

THE SMELLS HAD gone and, with them, the character of the *quartier*.
Covent Garden was no longer a market but a burgeoning tourist trap
of boutiques, restaurants and faked shop fronts that concealed the
superior sort of offices: publishers, property lawyers and the like.
The craftsmen and artisans who occupied the less salubrious lofts
were driven out by spiralling rents. Armourers, saddlers, silver-
makers and many humbler guilds vanished from the district, to be
replaced by chocolatiers, pizza parlours and sweater shops. The last
remnants of local skills were located inside the opera house, where
milliners and scene-painters rubbed shoulders with stagehands who
were themselves the sons and cousins of departed costermongers. In
due course, they too would be evicted, along with the police from
their famous station on Bow Street – all, in some way or other,
driven out by the ever-expanding opera house.

A raggle-taggle resistance movement formed. Six thousand
people lived in Covent Garden and not all of them welcomed the
prospect of two years' upheaval and a twenty-three million pound
office block to show for it. In August 1987, two months after the
ROH obtained planning permission from Westminster Council, the
Covent Garden Community Association applied to the High Court
for a judicial review. They argued that tenanted land which had
been given to the opera house for art's sake should not be used for
commercial development, and that Westminster had broken its
own rules by allowing more offices in a heritage conservation
area. Among the cited outrages against local history was the ROH
plan to demolish the imposing Floral Hall, a Victorian crystal
palace of bygone blooms, half-destroyed by fire in 1956.

As the dispute rippled outwards, new players leaped into the pond. A property company, Tottingham's, based in Columbus, Ohio, received encouragement from the ROH board to submit a neighbour-friendly scheme involving retail and residential elements. A conductor called Denis Vaughan – a former Beecham pupil who lived in a Floral Street flat opposite the opera house and waited for a ten-minute call that never came – floated an idea of linking the ROH to the Coliseum, the Lyceum and the Theatre Royal Drury Lane in an integrated performing arts village, akin to George Whyte's grounded vision. Vaughan was a dreamer whose inch-thick missives were binned unread by ROH directors, but he was tenacious, energetic and sometimes far-sighted. The only way to fund a sensible rebuilding of the ROH, he maintained, was to create a National Lottery for the purpose. Don't be absurd, he was told. Just you wait, said Vaughan.

Moser had been dismissive of protestors and dreamers. Sainsbury, alert to their disruptive potential, detailed Covent Garden's new head of public affairs, Ewen Balfour, to bend an ear to their plaints. Balfour, an engaging man from the Central Office of Information with a mystifying range of contacts in every tier of public life, drew the sting from the dissentients as the legal action took its course. Once learned counsel shuffled their briefs, matters got local and personal. The Board accused several of its tenants, restaurateurs on short-term leases, of funding the costly CGCA court action for personal gain. Attempts were made to discredit the Association's most voluble activist, Jim Monahan, an architect and son of the ex-director of the Royal Ballet School. He was alleged to have private axes to grind. Monahan said: 'My main reason for belonging to the CGCA is to continue the battle to maintain central London as a place where those on low incomes can live, and where the quality of life is not completely consumed by commercial, short-term interests.'[1]

It took six months for the review to come to court. Before Isaacs took office, he was warned that closure would have to be postponed from 1992 to 1995 at the earliest. In February 1988 the High Court ruled that Westminster had acted lawfully in granting planning consent. The CGCA appealed. In September, the Court of Appeal upheld the ruling. Leave to appeal to the House of Lords was denied. There was nothing now to stop the redevelopment from going ahead, except an attack of second thoughts within the ROH.

A new Technical Director, John Harrison, joined the company in

November 1988. He warned that the plans did not provide nearly enough space. The architects were sent back to the drawing board. A new plan was submitted to Westminster, this time without an office block or underground parking. Fifteen years of preparation and a great deal of money had gone to waste. The Royal Opera House was fifteen million pounds in the red at Coutts. The estimated cost of redevelopment rocketed from £56 million to £150 million in a year. The grim comedy was about to begin.

England in the latter half of 1987 descended from serenity to confusion. A sequence of preternatural events fell from a clear blue sky. In July, Margaret Thatcher became the first Prime Minister of her century to be re-elected for a third term. With a vast majority and little opposition, she rammed through an unfettered programme of privatizations, along with contentious reforms of the health, education and local taxation systems. Satisfaction among the propertied classes was unconfined.

In August, a gunman walked around the quiet, middle-England town of Hungerford, killing fourteen people and wounding fifteen in an unprecedented imitation of American-style massacres. On 16 October the worst hurricane on record sowed terror and havoc across the south of the country, ripping roofs off houses and paralysing rail and roadways. Three days later, the London Stock Exchange saw ten per cent of its share values wiped out on Black Monday. In November, the IRA bombed a Remembrance Day parade in Enniskillen. Two weeks later, a fire at King's Cross Underground Station killed thirty passengers and injured hundreds. Each disaster was horrific in itself; together they suggested a turning of tides, a blight on the new prosperity. In a fractious atmosphere of deepening gloom, people no longer trusted essential services or the established powers to cope with the unforeseen. The strongest leader since Churchill was also the most reviled.

Margaret Thatcher's third victory had unleashed triumphalist yelps from the newly rich. This was the age of Loadsamoney, a character minted by the comedian Harry Enfield from the yuppies and yahoos who thronged City bars and lit their cigars with ten pound notes. The yuppies were young upwardly-mobile professionals; the yahoos were brightly-coated traders who stoked a fever of speculation and walked away with six-digit bonuses. Unaccustomed to wealth, they looked for conspicuous ways to spend it. Opera, extravagant and loud, appealed. The first mobile phones went off in the Covent Garden foyer. Opera was *nouveau chic*. Record attendances were reported at ENO and Welsh National Opera, eighty-five and eighty-seven per cent respectively. Entrepreneurs got in on the act, putting on an *Aida* spectacular at Earl's Court and selling a hundred thousand tickets at twenty and twenty-five pounds apiece. The opera cost £1.5 million to produce and made a big enough profit for two of its co-promoters, Harvey Goldsmith and Mark McCormack, to attempt further ventures. At Covent Garden, Lyubimov's much-lauded *Jenůfa* had cost £529,300. It recouped £199,900 from a ninety-two per cent box-office and £150,000 more in sponsorship. The net loss was £179,400. The bulk of the costs were inbuilt: chorus and orchestra together amounted to £114,000, almost a quarter of the budget.

John Sainsbury, who knew the price of everything, gave orders to up the ante. Tickets were increased by up to forty per cent. Isaacs, a socialist and populist, recorded no objection. Paul Findlay said: 'That's the end of the opera house.' He was proved wrong, at first, as money rushed in through every door. Then, as recession gripped, top seats went unsold and the deficit grew. Worse, an impression had been given that opera and ballet could be self-financing. One Tory think-tanker went so far as to urge minority arts like opera, reaching two per cent of the populace, to shake off the shackles of subsidy and follow market forces: 'to create the kind of partnership with the British public that forty years of state subsidy have totally failed to achieve.'[2]

Such contentions were music to the ears of a new breed of Tory MPs who refused lunch at the Arts Council and privately advocated its abolition. Margaret Thatcher was herself intent on rolling back state involvement. She had ears for the likes of the conductor Lorin Maazel, a Downing Street dinner guest, who told her that London's musicians were a load of wastrels.

The portents for Covent Garden grew poorer. The new Arts Council chairman was a millionaire property developer, Peter Palumbo, who promised an increased grant but failed to deliver. Sainsbury, needing money for running costs and redevelopment, did as Drogheda had done before him: he turned to the Jews. At Glyndebourne one summer's night, he wooed Alex Alexander, chairman of Allied Lyons, to become chairman of the ROH Trust. George Christie was incensed. 'Hast thou killed and also taken possession?'[3] he raged (or words to that effect), as his chief fundraiser went the red-carpet way of his music director. For a while, the two opera companies were barely on speaking terms. Christie, as chairman of the Arts Council's music panel, was in a position to exact fiscal retribution on the ROH grant.

Alexander, a Czech-born Hitler refugee, reorganized the ROH Trust, squeezing his suppliers for donations whether they liked arts or not. He brought on board as deputy chairman the redoubtable Vivien Duffield, heir to the Clore millions, along with her friend Gail Ronson, wife of the Heron Group chairman who would go to jail for his part in the Guinness share-dealing scandal. Duffield had built a wing on to the Tate Gallery and saved a Constable for the nation, receiving no more than a cursory thank-you note from a junior minister three weeks later. 'I'd rather give the money to my East End Jews,' she told a dinner partner. 'At least they're grateful.'[4]

At Covent Garden, she demanded a say in how her money was spent. 'I was under no illusions,' she reported. 'I said I would need a place on the board if they wanted me (on the Trust). John (Sainsbury) was more pro-female than Moser. It was a seriously establishment board, nobody too brazen. They all thought I was slightly mad to undertake a job like this.'[5]

It was not in Vivien Duffield's nature to be inconspicuous. There was much muttering behind cupped hands about the '*haute juiverie*' who were taking over the opera house. It was all right for a Jew to be chairman or general director, but for rich Jews to think they owned the place was simply *de trop*, my dear. The more money Mrs Duffield and John Sainsbury pledged to the opera house, the more antagonism they aroused. 'Great credit to the generosity of these millionaires who are donating portions of their wealth to the public,' sneered Jim Monahan. 'But this is done for the public good on *their* terms . . . It is the power that such benefactors have to twist and contort public projects that is my main concern.'[6]

Two weeks before Jeremy Isaacs took over, Sir Frederick Ashton died in his sleep, a month short of his eighty-fourth birthday. The country-churchyard funeral, in late August, was ill-attended. The great goodbyes were said at Westminster Abbey in November, in the presence of the Queen Mother, Princess Margaret, peers of the realm and four generations of Royal Ballet dancers, great and small. Ninette de Valois led the mourning. Margot Fonteyn, herself near death, sent a fond eulogy from her Panamanian *hacienda*, likening

Ashton to Shakespeare 'for his extraordinary understanding of the human heart and mind and his ability to illuminate them through his own art form.' To many, it marked the end of an age. To Isaacs, entering unfamiliar realms, it posed an immediate conundrum.

Ashton had named his late sister's son, Anthony Russell-Roberts, as his executor and heir. Russell-Roberts was Administrative Director of the Royal Ballet. A former Tooley aide, he had gone to work at the Paris Opéra before returning as chief executive of the RB. No one had foreseen the difficulty this could cause when Ashton died. The Royal Ballet, which danced more of Ashton's work than any other company, would be run by a man who earned a royalty every time his ballets were performed. Anthony Dowell, as artistic director, had the first and final say on what the RB would dance and who was to appear in it, but the administrative director had an input into the programming process and influence over the dancers whose contracts he negotiated. In Whitehall, his position would have required one of those moral clarifications from the Cabinet Secretary. At Covent Garden, it became part of an uncritically cosy set-up.

Isaacs disliked Russell-Roberts and wanted to replace him with someone he trusted. He was warned this might be unwise. If Ashton's heir were to withdraw his uncle's works, the Royal Ballet would not have much to dance. The general director swallowed hard and accepted the unacceptable.

He next tried to dismiss Paul Findlay, who had been appointed at Haitink's insistence as Director of the Royal Opera. 'Jeremy phoned me about a week after he had arrived and said he wanted to get rid of Paul,' recalled Tooley. 'I told him he would lose Haitink if he did, so he backed down.'

Isaacs and Findlay were physically and temperamentally ill-suited. Isaacs was squat, abrasive and modernist in outlook, Findlay was tall, courteous and traditionalist. The son of a philosophy professor, his whirlygig outflow of ideas and activity could be disconcerting. Isaacs decided to second-guess Findlay with two backstop appointments – John Cox as director of productions and Patrick Carnegy as dramaturg. Together with Haitink and the casting director Peter Katona, they made up the artistic directorate of the Royal Opera, in which Findlay's voice was paramount.

Haitink was in one of his morose periods, between wives and perpetually on the verge of resignation. Findlay calmed him down and kept him working. 'Bernard wanted to cancel everything,' he recalled. 'He wanted to get back to Holland. Didn't get on with Isaacs. His time span for a meeting was forty minutes. One of the greatest disappointments for me as Opera Director was that he had so few suggestions to make.' His reticence was well founded. 'Lacking any distinctive taste of his own,' said Carnegy, 'Haitink became the victim of those who had to decide things for him.'[7]

Haitink encouraged Findlay to engage the best guest conductors. He also welcomed the return of Edward Downes, who would contribute the biggest repertory idea of the Isaacs decade: a cycle of all Verdi's operas, from the immature *Oberto* to a climactic *Falstaff* on the centenary (in 2001) of his death.

Findlay brought back Solti, a close personal friend, after a three-year absence. He nurtured the young Italians Daniele Gatti and Carlo Rizzi, and encouraged Sian Edwards, the first woman to conduct at Covent Garden (she joined the staff in 1988). One day, Findlay had a call from the stage door saying there was a Russian to see him. The name was unfamiliar, but Findlay came down to greet the visitor, who introduced himself as the new Director of the Kirov Opera. Valery Gergiev, thirty-five, was on his first trip abroad with a basic phrasebook, having inherited the famous theatre as the Soviet Union under Mikhail Gorbachev entered its dying phase. At the Royal Opera House, he saw a revival of Tarkovsky's *Boris Godunov*. 'I want to show that in Russia,' he declared. He could not pay a kopek, but Findlay had an idea. The BBC wanted to screen *Boris* but could not afford stage-union fees. If he shipped it to Russia, they could film it for free.

Gergiev was ecstatic. He talked Findlay into co-producing two Prokofiev operas, *Fiery Angel* and *War and Peace*, at the Kirov with British directors. During Findlay's tenure, he conducted often and brilliantly at Covent Garden – 'I have heard nothing like it since Furtwängler,' said one vocal authority.[8] Haitink told Tooley he had never heard the strings play so well.[9]

'All credit to Jeremy,' said Findlay, 'he gave me my head. I was allowed to put on ten new productions a year, after years of nothing.' Isaacs was less ecstatic. At Channel Four he had built his own staff from scratch and commanded personal loyalty. Here, he inherited inbred structures and uncongenial executives whose wages were kept on a separate payroll to prevent the lower orders from knowing what they earned. Labour relations were antediluvian. The rest of the country had ended its industrial warfare while Covent Garden was still tuning up. The orchestra came out on strike, only to be bribed back by a gift from a mysterious donor. The chorus walked out next, bitter at seeing their wages fall below ENO parity. 'We had been pushed into a corner,' said one non-activist. 'You had to be a soloist to get into this chorus, go into the Crush Bar and sing an aria to the music director before you were accepted, and do it again every two years. We sang in five languages, ENO in one. We earned less than train drivers, £176 maximum a week. They never treated us as artists. They just said, "there's no extra money". But if the orchestra came out, a week later they'd give them a rise.'[10] Backstage members of the Broadcasting and Entertainment Alliance (BETA, later Bectu), staged wildcat stoppages.

Trouble also simmered at the Ballet, where MacMillan's long-awaited revision of Cranko's *Prince of the Pagodas* was disrupted in mid-rehearsal. 'I remember being on stage,' said Anthony Dowell, 'and I was playing the emperor. Suddenly I was the only person on stage and they were having a meeting, threatening to black the first night. Monica and I had to go up and talk to the company. Wayne (Eagling) was the leader, and I just couldn't agree with all of that.'

Isaacs settled the chorus dispute to get his first season opened on time, and walked around the house radiating good will. A gregarious man with a capacious range of interests, he would stop and chat with all and sundry but, unlike Tooley, was never accepted as part of the 'family', never a 'Gardener'. It was held against him that he lunched in restaurants and only once joined the toilers in the steamy staff canteen. During intervals, he avoided the Crush Bar, disappearing with favoured guests to his redecorated office. 'This was a paternalistically run family concern,' he reflected, 'in the sense that everybody who was there had a feeling for what the House wanted to achieve. People worked in the accounts department for very inadequate pay because on the tannoy in their office they could hear the sound of a rehearsal and could, perhaps, get cheap tickets for the night. They felt that they belonged to the House and had a job there for life.

'There was no fixed retirement age. You could not get anyone out of the orchestra or chorus unless you engaged in ludicrous, protracted, undignified procedures to show them that they could not perform as well as they used to. I said, if you're not good enough, you're out. We lost that sense of family where nobody could do you any harm because you belonged. The family was broken, though, under the pressure of decades of underfunding of which the Thatcher years were the most evident. The family home, which I entered as a stranger, ended for good in the years that I was there.'

His inaugural press conference was a rumbustious affair, introducing a Five Year Plan to increase new productions, visiting companies and outside broadcasts. He specifically promised to reinstate *La Juive*, a mid-Victorian blockbuster with three strong tenors and a Jewish heroine. 'If a general director with the name of Jeremiah Israel Isaacs cannot put on *La Juive* at Covent Garden,' he laughed, 'then the job's not worth having.' He would be forced to eat those words, ungarnished.

Extrovert, extravagant and expansive, Isaacs was a refreshing antidote to the thin-blooded Tooley. His love for music blazed through every utterance, a legacy of his Glasgow childhood. 'I owe it all to my parents,' he avowed. His father, a bookish man, had a jeweller's shop. His mother was a busy family doctor who took her three sons to symphony concerts after cooking Sunday lunch and taught them to appreciate fine art by acquiring a Josef Herman oil painting, the cornerstone of Isaacs' collector's instinct for modern Scottish art. 'My great wish is that everybody should grow up in an environment where they can be exposed to what the arts can do for their lives,' he prayed. Though he forsook religious faith, he displayed a fiery adherence to his family, his Jewish heritage and certain restless ideals of education and self-betterment.

At Oxford, he was President of the Union. In television he caught an echo of ancestral values from Sidney Bernstein who 'absolutely forbade anyone to say on his channel, "I'm sorry that's all we've got time for."' The new medium existed to spread information, and hence opportunity, democracy and equality. In *The World at War*, Isaacs reinvented the historical documentary on a massive scale, employing first-hand sources to relate the course of the conflict. At Channel Four, he had a licence to be quirky and diverse, appealing to ethnic, sexual and special-interest minorities; as the BBC abandoned highbrow viewing in a ratings war, Isaacs put out whole operas on Sunday afternoons. For relaxation, he read Greek poetry.

Sentimental to a fault, Isaacs could be brutally insensitive. He was deeply wounded by the death of a brother by a Palestinian bomb in Jerusalem and by the tragic demise of his first wife, Tamara, from breast cancer. He would burst into tears on recounting these losses.

'I was a bad husband,' he confessed to an opera house colleague. A few days later, he sacked the man without a trace of emotion.

Two years after his first wife's death, Isaacs married Gillian Widdicombe, a former *Financial Times* critic who had advised Channel Four on its opera broadcasts. A stunning beauty when young, Widdicombe snared many artistic admirers, first among them the Earl of Drogheda. She introduced the old man to her new husband, who bestowed a paternal blessing. 'Garrett became very fond of Jeremy,' said Widdicombe. 'When I asked him what advice he would give a general director's wife he said: Don't appear to know too much, they'll dislike you for it.' Widdicombe's position was doubly delicate; she was about to become Arts Editor of the *Observer* newspaper and was expected to report even-handedly on the country's costliest arts institution while married to its chief. As a token of her detachment, she engaged as music critic the repatriated Andrew Porter, who recalled a more glorious past.

Drogheda now cut a sad figure around the opera house. His wife, Joan, had succumbed to Alzheimer's Disease and he nursed her at home, refusing to subject her to the indignities of institutional care. 'Towards the end she could not remember her own name,' said a visiting friend, 'but she could sit at the piano and play a Mozart sonata, note perfect.' A few days before Christmas 1989, Joan Drogheda died. Solti, hearing the news, telephoned the ex-chairman to offer condolences. There was no answer. The earl had taken to his bed and died on Christmas Eve. 'It was like Tristan and Isolde,' said Solti, fighting back tears, 'they could not live without each other.'

A new *Ring* was needed to set the regime on its way. Haitink had demanded it as 'a crucial part of my work as music director', never having conducted the cycle before. He nominated Lyubimov as director after their *Jenůfa* triumph, overlooking his lack of Wagner experience. Isaacs, visiting the septuagenarian Russian exile in Jerusalem, was alarmed to hear that he found much of it 'terrible nonsense'. Back in the house, Paul Hernon designed a foldaway set that could be taken on the road when Covent Garden closed, to be set up before five thousand viewers in the Royal Albert Hall, or fifty thousand in a football stadium. 'We can really widen our audience appeal,' enthused Findlay.

It was not to be. Lyubimov turned up with few ideas, no German and halting English. He was mocked by James Morris, singing

Wotan, and the production attracted critical obloquy – 'lacking in motivation, unnecessarily fussy, sometimes astonishingly inept,' wrote Paul Griffiths in *The Times*.[11] *Rheingold* was saved from ignominy only by Haitink's assured conducting. It was clear after the opening segment that the cycle could not be allowed to proceed under Lyubimov, nor could it be abandoned without paying off huge casts and throwing the schedules into chaos. Helge Schmidt, Tooley's erstwhile casting director, pointed out to Findlay that Götz Friedrich was running a *Ring* in Berlin in which most of the ROH cast had already sung. It differed from his last London *Ring* in its 'concept' of an underground tunnel through which all human life flowed. 'The space is different,' said Friedrich. 'I hope it can be interesting because there are many things I want to review. It is not an emergency *Ring*.'[12]

It was more of a hand-me-down *Ring* – cobbled together, banged about and displaying little vitality. Friedrich, in middle-age, wore executive suits and delivered to budget. Haitink burnished the orchestra to high sheen, sometimes at the expense of his singers. 'I wish he'd remember we are here sometimes,' grumbled the tenor René Kollo,[13] who declined a return invitation.

The next let-down was Piero Faggioni, commissioned to produce and design a *Trovatore* on sets so flexible they could serve two other operas. The sets proved dismal and the costumes so heavy that Domingo threatened to tear his tunic off. The Spanish director Nuria Espert was brought in for *Madam Butterfly*, *Rigoletto* and a humdrum *Carmen*, featuring the stressed-out Maria Ewing, whose marriage to Peter Hall had ruptured.

Against these and other embarrassments, there were scintillating delights in each of Isaacs' first three seasons. *Un re in ascolto (A King Listens)* by Luciano Berio, premièred at the Salzburg Festival, sparkled with circus acrobatics and drew a ninety-two per cent attendance. *The Cunning Little Vixen* marked the ROH début of Simon Rattle, the rising British conductor who had fallen out with Tooley in 1979 over the apparent mistreatment of his wife, Elise Ross, cast as *Thérèse* in John Tavener's opera and then dropped. Rattle, no linguist, performed the Janáček opera in English, despite the availability of surtitles. He was loudly acclaimed, and never returned. 'He wasn't comfortable at Covent Garden,' said Lilian Watson, who sang the Vixen. 'Some of the music staff dug their heels in and did it their way. His style of working didn't appeal to them.' In addition to house recalcitrance, Rattle bridled against the snobbishness he perceived in London, ever an active deterrent for a Liverpudlian who devoted the first chunk of his career to the City of Birmingham Symphony Orchestra and the next to the Berlin Philharmonic.

Isaacs' third season produced a world première. Harrison Birtwistle's *Gawain* wove a circular spell around Arthurian legend of green knights and chaste damsels. Rough-toned at times, but also tartly tender, the opera was intended for Haitink but the Dutchman ducked out in favour of Elgar Howarth, who had premièred *Mask of Orpheus*. Peter Sellars, the Californian director, withdrew because he found the work 'anti-feminist'.

Repeated in 1994, the opera attracted organized heckling from a gang of frustrated neo-romantic composers who made more headlines by cat-calling than they ever would by writing music. Birtwistle's was a shy, stubborn, English art that drew its strengths from a rural upbringing and a fixation with Greek drama. 'I haven't invented a language,' he once told me. 'What I do is somehow joined up to something that came before it. Tradition is not aping the past but making the future. That's why I like to think that what I do is tradition.' *Gawain* was, in its way, a *Parsifal* for modern times. It did not conquer the world despite three Covent Garden revivals, but the composer's fame spread from Chicago to Berlin as a result of his ROH success. Isaacs had stuck his neck out for Birtwistle, more than Tooley had done for Tippett, or Webster for Britten, after *Billy Budd*.

He invited readers of a new daily, the *Independent*, to support young composers and librettists who were struggling to write their first opera. Close to a thousand individuals chipped in a hundred pounds each to the 'Garden Venture' and six short operas were duly produced at the Donmar Theatre. They ranged from the inept to the egregious, but the scheme drew widespread attention to the fresh water that Isaacs was trying to pump into a stagnant pond.

Downes's ambitious Verdi project got under way with *Attila*, unstaged in living memory. The production budget was just £205,000. But when staff costs and overheads were taken into account, the run of eight performances cost £1.27 million, of which £928,000 was recovered in tickets, sponsorship and catering, leaving a deficit of £344,000. It was not possible for Covent Garden to put on any kind of opera, no matter how modest, without losing large sums of money against a static public grant. Two operas scheduled for Isaacs' third season, Massenet's *Don Quichotte* and Gluck's *Iphigénie en Tauride*, had to be sacrificed on the altar of cost.

There was no margin for error, and physical safety was daily at risk in a Victorian manufactory that worked stagehands round the clock, bare-handedly hauling hunks of scenery. 'This was manual labour that was clumsy, inefficient, repetitive and dangerous,' said Isaacs. One Friday evening, working at his desk, his eye strayed to a silent television monitor on his wall. Men seemed to be running diagonally across the stage, where they were setting up that night's *Don Carlos*, the venerable Visconti production. Isaacs rushed downstairs. 'On the floor is a bloodied body,' he reported a week later. 'Over it, a nurse, a fireman and a couple of his mates are giving artificial respiration, trying to keep him alive. "Come on, Greg,"' they call to him, "keep going."'[14] It was no use. Greg Bellamy, a member of B crew, had been crushed beneath a slippage of plywood flooring. He was pronounced dead on arrival at hospital. The news paralysed the backstage. Isaacs watched as

> bells are rung to bring the audience from the bars into the theatre. I go out front to tell them what has happened, and that the performance is cancelled. Silently, they accept and leave the theatre, some donating their ticket refunds to the widow.[15]

On Sunday, before a packed house, a Verdi *Requiem* was sung for Greg Bellamy, with dancers and crewmen holding candles on stage. Agnes Baltsa, Katia Ricciarelli, Arthur Davies and Samuel Ramey were the soloists and Colin Davis came in to conduct. The takings were given to the victim's family. The ROH was fined a thousand pounds by a Health and Safety tribunal some months later, and measures were taken to minimize further risks. But in a crumbling theatre and on knife-edge deadlines it was only a matter of time before someone else got hurt. 'Greg Bellamy's death called attention, as nothing else could, to the urgent need for the redeveloped opera house,' said Isaacs.

A pall of anxiety hung over the Royal Ballet. Directly after the Ashton commemoration, the company set off in high spirits for Australia. The tour was happy and cloud-free. Only Brisbane, the last stop, posed a problem. A triple bill with MacMillan's *Rite of Spring* was not selling well. The Queensland promoter called Anthony Dowell two weeks beforehand and asked if he could substitute *Swan Lake*. MacMillan reluctantly agreed.

On the afternoon of the performance, around five o'clock, MacMillan felt unwell and went to visit a Brisbane friend, who happened to be a doctor. 'The doctor walked him straight into the hospital next door, and that's where he had the heart attack and the stroke,' recalled Monica Mason. 'It was very serious and we were terrified he wouldn't pull through. I stayed on in Australia for a three-week holiday, always phoning Deborah to see how he was. By the end of the holiday it looked brighter. I remember Deborah saying to me, "this was very serious. we just don't know how long he can survive. It can happen at any time. It could be in rehearsal with you and something terrible could happen."' The company's creative pulse was unsteady, but MacMillan was a resilient man and, without Ashton at his shoulder, was keen to get back to work.

Dowell meanwhile buckled down to strengthening the ensemble. There were some good ballerinas coming through – Alessandra Ferri, Bryony Brind, Fiona Chadwick – all home-grown products, but the icy sheen of stardom was absent. Then, two windfalls transformed the picture. Nureyev, on his penultimate visit, brought along a sleek Parisienne who had partnered him since 1984, when she was just nineteen. Sylvie Guillem had it all: glamour, beauty, *hauteur* and a gymnastic agility that defied the laws of anatomy and gravity. At twenty-three she had the strut of a champion and the nerves of an iceberg. Nureyev hoped to draw from her the elixir of youth that he had bestowed on Fonteyn, but any dreams of rejuvenation were dashed by the advance of his disease. Beside Guillem, he looked wasted and not long for this world. She, beside him, refused to be treated as an ingénue and demanded independence.

On her second trip to London, dancing *Giselle*, she was chatting to Anthony Dowell after rehearsal when he said, as a pleasantry, 'Sylvie, it would be lovely if you could give us a little more time.' Before the week was out, she was talking terms with Anthony Russell-Roberts and preparing to move in as Principal Guest Artist. News of her defection in February 1989 devastated French ballet. 'A national catastrophe,' *Le Monde* called it. Nureyev was wounded, and told her so. 'Rudolf was angry at me when I left,' she said.

'Doesn't she know I would have married her?' he told a friend.[16]

When Nureyev had got over his resentment, he gave Dowell some advice on handling his last creation. 'We were talking on the phone, and he suddenly came up with one of his brilliant phrases,' Dowell remembered. 'He said to me, talking about Sylvie: "treat with iron glove."' Guillem would be a law unto herself.

Fifteen months later, the leading man of the Bolshoi signed up with the Royal Ballet. Irek Mukhamedov was thirty years old, at the peak of his powers, and fed up with the powers that be. Communism was crumbling, but dancers were still subjected to the iron rule of Yuri Grigorovich and the company commissars. 'I was tired of being a Soviet hero, of supporting Grigorovich, the state, communism,' he explained. '. . . It was time I took responsibility for myself and Masha and the baby.'[17] Russell-Roberts met him in Vienna in an attempt to head him off from following Baryshnikov to America. A weekend in the country – at Ashton's former home, Chandos Lodge, now inhabited by the Russell-Roberts family – sealed the deal. On the Monday he met Dowell who 'liked him immediately'. Isaacs was summoned to the Soviet Embassy and rebuked for having encouraged the dancer to break his contract with the Bolshoi; defection was no longer regarded as political betrayal but as commercial malpractice.

Mukhamedov, like Nureyev, was a Tatar. Unlike Nureyev, he was house-trained. Elegant, well-mannered and generous, Mukhamedov was the ultimate dream-teamer, an artist who raised others on the wings of his own attainments. Half-clad, he was the hottest thing London had seen in tights for many a long year. All of his allure and exuberance was saved for the stage. In class, he was focused, studious and infinitely considerate. Seeing a visitor sitting with one leg extended, he quietly asked me to tuck it under the chair 'to make sure you don't get injured'. No fuss, no reproach, just the meticulous attentiveness that is the mark of all high-fliers.

'There can be resentment if the (artistic) visitors are not obviously better than our own people,' said Darcey Bussell, a rising ballerina. 'But Irek is part of the company now. He has class with the rest of the boys and they all learn from watching him.' He came, said Ninette de Valois, 'not as a distinguished visitor; he came to learn. His presence is a marvellous tonic for the company, his different style and schooling an example to everyone.'[18]

The only sour note was struck by Wayne Eagling. 'The people

who lose out from the star policy are the English dancers,' he snapped, echoing a moan that had rumbled through Covent Garden since the first foreign singers docked in 1947. 'The public should not get the idea that only big names are worth watching.'[19] Eagling left the company the following year to run the Dutch National Ballet.

With two world-beaters in harness, the extra costs approved by a balletomane chairman, the Royal Ballet recovered its twinkle. Excitement and attendances rose sharply. So did standards. Attention was finally directed to the orchestral accompaniment, which was generally appalling. The self-effacing Ashley Lawrence had been eased out as conductor in 1987; he was felled three years later by a heart attack in a Tokyo street. His successor, Isaiah Jackson from the American Deep South, made no impression on hard-bitten musicians of the ROH pit. Only when Haitink conducted – *Romeo and Juliet* was his second ballet – did the orchestra play as if they meant it. Jackson was replaced in 1990 by Barry Wordsworth, a solid English professional.

Isaacs now pitched into strategic restructuring. The Sadler's Wells Royal Ballet was going all over the country and going nowhere in terms of aims and identity. He proposed to rebase the company in Birmingham, where Simon Rattle's orchestra and a sympathetic city council were reinvigorating cultural life. The move was designed to appeal to the Arts Council's devolutionary demands.

Madam, who still had power of veto, was persuaded of the worthiness of the cause through a good deal of shouting into her ear-trumpet. Peter Wright, the company's quietly effective director, was warily in favour. David Bintley, his principal choreographer and intended successor, was thrilled. Reins were grabbed and roots planted. The amorphous second company finally gained a life of its own as the Birmingham Royal Ballet.

MacMillan, back at work, was delighted with Mukhamedov. 'He must remember all his mistakes,' he said at their first rehearsal, 'I will use them.'[20] He gave him a one-act ballet, *Winter Dreams*, and coached him steadily in the great heroic roles. He picked out Darcey Bussell for *Prince of the Pagodas*, spotting her potential 'far more presciently than anybody else'.[21] The ballet was riding high and MacMillan, perhaps for the first time in his professional life, seemed happy. 'We got lulled,' said Monica Mason, his assistant, 'into a false sense of security.'

*

The world was turning at alarming speed. The fortified wall that had divided Europe since the war was breached. Communism crumbled in one state after another until even the Soviet Union, crucible of working-class revolution, was abolished. The West had won the war, but dared not claim victory, military or moral. Most western economies, mired in recession and fearful of being overrun by cheap labour and products from the liberated east, erected a new wall of protectionism and xenophobia.

The arts, having sat out the Cold War, had no message for the messy peace. After the initial celebratory Beethoven Ninths in Berlin, bureaucrats set about reducing the surfeit of orchestras and theatres that resulted from German reunification. At the centre of events and the heart of European music, few tears were shed for the atrophying of culture. State-subsidized opera houses began staging commercial musicals to turn a profit. The arts establishment was too intent on survival to reflect and direct public concerns. At a time when rock stars rallied to relieve famine in Africa and film stars made political careers, the stylized, regimented, timeworn antics of opera singers and ballet dancers bore scant relevance to the burning issues of the day. The old justifications rang hollow. To the proverbial man on the Clapham omnibus, the survival of the Royal Opera House mattered less than the threatened bankruptcy of a third-division football club.

Jeremy Isaacs, faced with a funding freeze, resolved to spend his way out of trouble. He increased the thousand-strong payroll – already twice the size of Webster's family firm – by an extra hundred staff, including, and necessitating for the first time, a personnel manager. In a considerable personal coup, he persuaded Luciano Pavarotti to return after a seven-year absence, parading him at the Savoy Hotel before a ravenous mob of press snappers. The 1990 Three Tenors Concert during the soccer World Cup had led Pavarotti and Domingo to bury their rivalries above the reedy tones of José Carreras, who was miraculously recovered from leukaemia. All three now enjoyed pop-star status, earning a million dollars nightly in open-air arena concerts.

Pavarotti did not come cheap. Isaacs maintained that his fee was held in line with the prevalent top nightly rate of ten thousand pounds, but any deal with Pavarotti involved a ream of incidentals that cost several times more than his singing wage. Three or four

Concorde seats, Savoy suites, expensive gifts and sundry attentions made Big Lucy an expensive luxury that could be justified only by inflating seat prices – and thereby excluding the popular audience he had been booked to attract. Pavarotti sang fifteen performances in three productions during Isaacs' nine years. He enjoyed, to all appearances, a happy rapport with the General Director, which is more than could be said of Domingo, who complained to Tooley that he felt unappreciated. 'Jeremy didn't have much time for him,' said Tooley, 'he wasn't that interested in performers.'

Domingo had his fervent supporters, among them Vivien Duffield. 'He is the least affected of them all,' she said, 'no entourages and limos. Somebody who will give up two hours after a gruelling performance so that every single one of those little ladies who stood outside in the rain got a word and a kiss – *il faut le faire*, as they say. There aren't many in the business like that.'

Domingo sang thirty-six performances in the Isaacs period and conducted twice; he had a London property portfolio to look after and a genuine attachment to the house. When his dresser, Julio, suffered severe burns in a domestic accident, Domingo paid his medical bills.

Carreras sang eighteen times, never as impressively as before, though his female fans were legion. The cost was extortionate, and only the rich could afford to watch. 'It is against my nature to charge people *anything* to listen to music,' grumbled Haitink.[22]

As resources tightened, half a million pounds was lost each year on industrial disputes. The orchestra, perpetually murmurous, found ever more ingenious causes for dissent. Rejecting a five and a half per cent pay rise, they halted rehearsals for Meyerbeer's long-unseen *Les Huguenots* by demanding the four interval breaks specified by the composer. 'There was not one person in the management of the ROH who had a qualification in music,' said shop steward Robert Trory. The players turned up in the pit in casual clothes, distributing leaflets among the audience to explain their grievance. Isaacs took stock of the worsening situation and shut the house. It took a week of dark nights and ACAS mediation to get it reopened. *The Times*, in an editorial, advised Covent Garden to sack its turbulent musicians and replace them with one of London's underworked symphony orchestras. 'Isaacs was impossible to deal with,' said Trory. 'He only liked the sound of his own voice.'

Isaacs, hemmed in on all sides, went to the Arts Council and told them that he was prepared to run up a deficit. Unless funding was increased, he told the press, the result would be 'Armageddon'. His chairman implored Mrs Thatcher to cough up, but the Prime Minister was otherwise preoccupied. Her new arts minister, David Mellor, was keen on music but nurtured ill-feeling for Covent Garden where, he alleged, his visually-impaired wife, Judith, had been snubbed by the General Director and reception staff.

The Arts Council ordered Isaacs to balance the books or risk the consequences. Coutts made anxious noises about the overdraft. Isaacs flew to Berlin with Findlay to tell Friedrich that his *Ring* would have to be given without *Götterdämmerung*, because the rehearsals meant too many black nights. Friedrich agreed to fewer rehearsals and Findlay, rejigging the schedules, inserted twelve *Rigoletto*s and *Bohème*s to boost box-office takings.

'You bloody fool!' exclaimed Isaacs.

'What do you mean?' said his Opera Director.

'That kills Sainsbury's position with the PM,' fumed Isaacs. 'He was going to go to her and say, this theatre can't even put on a *Ring* cycle any more. That would have impressed her.'

Margaret Thatcher was on her last legs. In November 1990, six weeks before a United Nations victory in the Gulf War might have repaired her popularity, she failed to see off a leadership challenge from the disgruntled Michael Heseltine. Having ruled longer than any Prime Minister since Pitt, she was brought down by her strident opposition to European integration and her hectoring way with Cabinet colleagues. Her successor, John Major, was an unimposing man from humble beginnings who liked to go to the opera; his wife, Norma, had written a semi-official biography of Joan Sutherland. On New Year's Eve, they watched Sutherland's farewell gala, sitting with Sainsbury in the Royal Box. Major had sympathy for the Royal Opera House, and promised support.

Things were looking up, but not for the chairman. Bereft of the leader he loved, and concerned about the future of his family firm, John Sainsbury announced his resignation on 9 April 1991. Sainsbury had been an authoritarian chairman, short-fused and shouting red-faced at members of board and staff alike. His relations with Isaacs had grown tense when he found the general director cropping up as late-night television interviewer with his own BBC slot, *Face to Face*. 'Do the job we're paying you to do,' he yelled at Isaacs in full public view. 'The shouting at board meetings was unbelievable,' recalled Findlay. 'It was counter-productive.'

Where Moser liked to be liked, Sainsbury had no such need. He would turn up with his briefcase at the end of a day's work, march into Isaacs' office and demand full account of current business. For closer briefings, he summoned Ewen Balfour to report to him at Sainsbury headquarters, costing Balfour the confidence of his General Director.

'John resigned because he realized that to be a proper chairman of the opera house during the redevelopment was a full-time job,' said Vivien Duffield. 'And he wanted to apply himself to J Sainsbury Ltd. I genuinely believe that to do the job properly he felt it needed more time than he could give.'

Sainsbury reminded the board that he had agreed to serve for two years and remained twice as long. 'I stayed four years but I didn't stay for the fifth,' he reflected, 'because I had one year left at Sainsbury's and there were a lot of things that I wanted to do there.' He had created the most profitable retailer in the land and feared for its future under his techno-minded cousin, David, who was a reluctant grocer, harbouring woolly leftish views. Employees who saw the cousins pass one another in the corridor noted that their eyes never met. 'It was my life,' said John Sainsbury of the company.[23] By the time his cousin stepped down, accepting a junior minister's post in the Labour Government in September 1998, the firm had fallen far behind Tesco and there were no family members left in senior management. The provenders of the British middle classes had lost their way.

Saving the business was one pressing reason for John Sainsbury's early resignation. 'But the underlying reason,' he told me, 'was that the Government were getting more and more difficult and the squeeze on the opera house finances was terrible. I was so appalled by a Government that I supported being so mistaken about the arts in general and the opera house particularly. Palumbo had given me all sorts of reassurances but was unable to give us what we needed. The more difficult the issue, the more time one has to give to it, and I knew I could not do it. Little did I know that they would choose someone as chairman who was almost as busy as I was. I had no say in the matter. . . .'

Looking around the boardroom, the eyes fell on Angus Stirling, director general of the National Trust under Lord Gibson's chairmanship. Stirling was preparing for the Trust's centenary as a conserver of English houses and landscapes. His hands were full, but offers like the ROH chairmanship do not come more than twice in a life and he was unable to refuse. 'I should never have let Angus do it,' said his mentor, Lord Gibson.

'Angus is one of the nicest men in the world,' said Vivien Duffield. 'We never had an argument about anything. I had terrible rows with Jeremy. You'd say good morning to him, and he'd say, what's good about this morning? bloody awful morning!'

Stirling belonged to the class of Englishmen who rise without trace. After Eton and Cambridge, he had done spells in fine arts and banking before his discreet competence at the Arts Council brought him under Gibson's wing. His main attraction to the ROH board was his experience in handling public subsidy. He had connections at every level of the Council, and it was hoped that his quiet diplomacy would succeed where Sainsbury's bluster had so demonstrably failed.

These hopes were soon dashed. Palumbo told Stirling that Covent Garden deserved 'double or treble' its present grant, but he said that two or three times without delivering extra cash. The Arts Council was itself under investigation from the National Audit Office. Seeing the Covent Garden deficit reach £3.1 million, the Council ordered an inquiry by the educationalist Mary Warnock, the second such investigation in a decade. The ROH invited a parallel inquiry from the accountants Price Waterhouse. Both gave the company a generally clean bill of health and recommended a higher level of public funding. Warnock called for clearer management objectives, a break-even budget and an end to Royal Ballet touring. She warned that the redevelopment scheme would be ruinous unless the Government paid the bills and recommended that it should be shelved. The house should modernize internally and await a better day. Price Waterhouse found internal savings of one million pounds a year, adding that the company's 'sense of economy is poor'.

Nothing came of either report, nor of the new Prime Minister's avowed sympathies for Covent Garden. Major appointed his close ally David Mellor to the Cabinet as chief secretary to the Treasury, one of the most powerful positions in Government with virtual right of veto over departmental budgets. Shortly before the 1992 election, the grinning, gap-toothed Mellor arranged for ENO to be given ten million pounds to buy the freehold of its building, the Coliseum. The gift was smeared in some quarters as an electoral bribe to the arts; at Covent Garden it provoked tears of consternation.

ENO's powerhouse had run out of steam and Peter Jonas was on his way to run the Bavarian State Opera in Munich, leaving a large deficit and leaking roof to Dennis Marks, a BBC producer with no previous experience of running a theatre. His music director, equally innocent, was to be Sian Edwards. ENO, in disarray, was being richly rewarded while Covent Garden, at peak performance, was penalized on every side. 'They felt completely unloved and quite helpless,' was the view of a senior Arts Council official.[24] Suspicions of double standards were not unfounded. After the election, which Major won to general surprise, Mellor was rewarded with a job fitted to his own tastes. The Department of National Heritage brought together his love of arts, sport, travel and broadcasting. Its permanent secretary was to be Hayden Phillips, a Whitehall high-flier who was aiming for the Cabinet Office and somehow wound up on playground duty. Related by marriage to the former ballet chairman Mark Bonham-Carter, Phillips took a sceptical interest in Covent Garden and, notch by notch, tightened the Government's grip over all the public arts.

Had the new Department acted as decisively as it talked, a shaft of clarity might have pierced the muddled process of public funding and restored a sense of purpose. Instead, the Department acted as another layer of buck-passing so that nothing of importance ever got decided except under dire emergency. Whether the country needed a new opera house and how it was to be paid for and rebuilt was never debated as a matter of principle, though its exigencies crossed departmental desks on a monthly, sometimes weekly, basis. The Prime Minister, for his part, offered occasional poultices. When a Hong Kong businessman, Stanley Ho, while weekending at Chequers, expressed his desire to contribute to a British good cause, Major directed him to Covent Garden which relieved him of two and a half million pounds – saving the companies from mid-1990s insolvency.

Isaacs grew increasingly frustrated. 'I have never been in a position where I couldn't raise the money I wanted,' he told Findlay. Running a television channel, he recalled, 'we used to spend at most four weeks of the year working out a budget. Here, someone comes in to discuss budgets with me three times a week.'[25] The satisfactions of a showman were buried beneath a pile of insolubles.

He got little support from below. 'He is terribly unpopular with singers, conductors, administrators and in particular with the dancers,' noted a veteran Gardener. 'It seems that he was in New York when the Royal Ballet opened and he did not go to the first night. Having read the good notices he [told the company]: "Perhaps we can look forward to the same standard of dancing in London." I understand he was booed by the dancers.'[26]

Company members, accustomed to seeing Tooley at the Crush Bar six nights a week, complained that Isaacs was seldom in attendance. Isaacs maintained that he spent 'three or four' evenings a week in the theatre. Tooley, whose wife divorced him shortly after his retirement on grounds of 'unreasonable behaviour', served as a focus for discontent. Bewildered and embittered, he hung around the backstage and orchestral corridor, talking to 'the family', until Sainsbury pointedly told him to stay away. When Peter Wright gave way to David Bintley at the Birmingham Royal Ballet, Isaacs told the outgoing director, 'whatever you do, don't do to David what John Tooley did to me.'

Isaacs, with little to lose, decided to sweep the decks of relics of the Tooley era. He fired Ewen Balfour, ignoring a mass petition for his reinstatement, which Bernard Haitink prominently signed. Balfour was well liked. He was also well connected. Questions were asked in the House of Commons. In a political crisis, Balfour was a man to have on your side. When he left, Jim Monahan of the CGCA said: 'This is the best thing that has ever happened to us.' Balfour, like Bill Beresford before him, found a large cheque in his post, an anonymous gift from a sympathetic board member.

Also chopped were Patrick Carnegy, John Cox and Paul Findlay, the nucleus of the opera team. 'Jeremy was perfectly within his rights,' said Findlay equably. 'My contract was coming up, and he wanted to have his own man.' Findlay went on to run the Royal Philharmonic Orchestra, with Balfour as his righthand man, and later the Kirov Theatre for Gergiev.

To head the Royal Opera Isaacs brought in Nicholas Payne, a deceptively jolly Old Etonian who had put Opera North firmly on the map with modernist stagings that looked radical in London, let alone Leeds. Balfour was replaced by Keith Cooper who, at ENO, had caught the eye by blazoning a half-naked stagehand with a snake round his neck as an advertisement for *The Magic Flute*. Isaacs craved style and profile. He would get more than he bargained for.

His own contract was up for renewal, as were Dowell's and Haitink's. The two artistic directors were nodded through. Isaacs was asked to leave the room while his case was discussed. David Mellor had made no secret that he wanted Isaacs' head. The Arts Council, unable to interfere, made disapproving noises. Forman, who was leaving the board, passionately extolled Isaacs' achievements. It was a close call. By a single vote, according to an eye-witness, Jeremy Isaacs was granted a mandate to take the company through the closure period and into its rebuilt home. To balance the books, the chorus was cut from seventy-two to sixty, and seat prices were raised yet again. The top ticket for a Domingo night now exceeded two hundred pounds.

At the Westminster Abbey memorial service for Margot Fonteyn, on 2 July 1991, Ninette de Valois gave the first dull speech of her long life. The age of oratory was over. Madam now lived in a sheltered flat beside the river at Barnes, where Anthony Dowell visited her weekly to report on the ballet's progress. Her presence was no longer seen, but sensed. Many an innovative proposal would be shot down by Dowell with the words, 'Madam wouldn't like it.' To her own frustration, Ninette de Valois had become a reactionary impediment to the balletic progress she had always espoused.

For the present, the auguries were good. Mukhamedov and Guillem worked strictly apart, but the Tatar found a shining foil in the twenty-year-old Darcey Bussell when creating MacMillan's *Winter Dreams*. They came unstuck in *Manon*, where Bussell on pointe proved half a head taller than the hero, but Viviana Durante, another home-grown dancer, fitted perfectly. Her eleventh-hour insertion provoked rumours of a diva war in the popular press, always good for business. Mukhamedov danced *Romeo and Juliet* with Durante, as well as MacMillan's next ballet, *The Judas Tree*, a grim tale of gang-rape set against a backdrop of Canary Wharf, London's newest commercial development. Bussell, growing in stature, developed a stage rivalry with Guillem. William Forsythe, the American choreographer, gave them a jazzy joint showcase, *In the Middle Somewhat Elevated*. Ashley Page and William Tuckett, company members both, showed a gift for choreography.

MacMillan, at sixty-three, was full of ideas and contentment, eager to rework his life's repertoire upon the infinitely pliant Mukhamedov. 'In those last years after Fred, Kenneth felt a sense of relief,' said Monica Mason. 'He did say, you mustn't think I'm always going to be here. I'm going to retire, it'll be just wonderful.

I said, will I come round and go through cast lists? He said, maybe, maybe not.'

He intended to rework *Anastasia*, he told Dowell, 'redoing the role of Rasputin for Irek, and he was really quite fired up about how he would do it in a totally different concept.' First, however, he would restage *Mayerling*, with Mukhemadov as the homicidal Prince Rudolf. The house was packed for the opening night, 29 October 1992, and just before the curtain went up Isaacs, whose seat was directly across the aisle, moved across 'to touch his arm and wish him luck'. Many in the house that night were conscious of an extra surge of pre-performance tension. During the first interval it was clear that the company had a hit on its hands. In the second break, MacMillan went backstage and was late returning to his seat.

'I don't know why I was the one who went on the search,' said Dowell, 'but I must have picked up on Deborah's anxiety and started to look for him, went to the stage door and there heard a fireman talking of someone who had collapsed. I asked where, and I ended up in a part of the opera house where I had never been before (it was one of the phases of development where the opera got new dressing rooms, but not the ballet – surprise, surprise) and there he was, on the floor, lifeless, with a St John's Ambulance nursing person.

'I rushed back, and couldn't find my way. Finally found Deborah, took her by the hand and told her to come with me. I had never seen a dead person before and I was witnessing a terribly private moment, holding on to her while she was over the body, saying all these private things.'

A press officer, Janine Limberg, stumbled upon them and was sent to fetch Monica. The ballet was nearly over and arrangements had to be made. Rumours filtered down to the dancers as they flitted on and off stage. 'Deborah's first concern was Charlotte (her daughter) so we just got in a taxi and rushed back to fetch her,' said Mason.

Isaacs was informed. He responded warmly and impetuously. He could not allow the public to jubilate while a man lay dead, nor could he withhold information from a confused and anxious cast, Mukhemadov visibly on the brink of tears. He walked on stage, raised a hand for silence and announced: 'It is with deep sadness, and in shock, that I have to tell you that the great master whose work we have seen performed here tonight, Kenneth MacMillan, has, during the performance, suffered a heart attack and died. I ask you to stand, and to leave the theatre quietly.'[27]

This was unwise, inappropriate and, as Isaacs subsequently acknowledged, technically illegal. A death may not be announced in England until a doctor has certified it; nor, as a matter of form, should anyone be notified ahead of the next of kin. On the night MacMillan died, Isaacs gave the news to a thronged house before it was broken to the dead man's child. He argued in retrospect that the public was 'entitled to know then that in their presence a great spirit had departed, rather than reading the news of his death the next day.'[28] The public had no such right, legal or moral. What Isaacs should have announced was that MacMillan had been taken seriously ill and conveyed to hospital. Weeks later, after the first wave of bereavement, Deborah MacMillan called on Isaacs in his office and told him, in no uncertain Antipodean terms, what she thought of his conduct that night. He had made a drama out of a personal tragedy and that, in her view, was unconscionable. In the hospital, the only ones to sit with her beside the body late into the night were Monica Mason and an old friend, Peter Brownlee.

MacMillan's death gutted the Royal Ballet of its creative engine. 'Now he's dead, they call him a genius,' said Deborah MacMillan, bitterly. There was talk of appointing Bintley or Page as resident choreographer, but neither was of comparable stature. A fateful decision was taken to leave the creative post vacant. Dowell brought in Tetley, William Forsythe, Twyla Tharp and other grand names to stage one-off shows, but their fleeting visits left no residue in an organization whose glorious past dwarfed its diminished present and stunted its unseen future.

Six weeks later, the Royal Ballet suffered a second hammerblow to its morale. All summer long, the Murdoch press had been trailing the stench of royal scandal. An apparently authorized biography of Diana, Princess of Wales, serialized in the *Sunday Times*, exposed the misery of her marriage to Prince Charles, her bulimia and attempted suicide. Charles was Patron of the Royal Opera House, Diana its biggest fan. She was never that keen on opera and used to summon someone from the ROH, usually the obliging Ken Davison, to explain the plot to her at Kensington Palace two or three days beforehand. When surtitles were introduced, she dispensed with this courtesy but seldom seemed to enjoy the show unless Pavarotti was on song. The ballet, however, she adored. As a girl, she had learned to dance. As an adult she relished the physical freedom of dancers, so remote from the stiffness of royalty. She came to the ballet early and often, seldom with Charles. Her companion was more likely to be a girlfriend, dressed like herself in a mannish suit. House manager Trevor Jones, who had known her before she married as his son's nursery teacher, would admit her via a side entrance on Floral Street, incognito and unnoticed.

In happier times, Diana had conspired with the dancer Wayne Sleep to give Charles a surprise birthday gift. Each winter, Ken Davison put on a Friends Gala at Covent Garden in which ballerinas sang and sopranos danced and everyone sent themselves up something rotten. Prince Charles, as Patron, was persuaded to participate in one sketch, which he greatly relished. The following year, 1985, Diana slipped out of the Royal Box in mid-gala, changed out of her red velvet gown into a slinky silvery dress, and showed up on stage with Sleep in a funny, well-rehearsed routine to a Billy Joel song, 'Uptown Girl'.

'I said, look, it's not going to be good for you to look bad,' recalled Sleep. 'Comedy is very difficult to do in ballet terms, not to look completely cod. And she said, oh dear. But then I found out she was game to try a few things, and with honesty and fun it could work, tongue-in-cheek, very chic.'[29] Sleep was five foot two, six inches shorter than the princess. Midway through the routine he hoisted her high above his head and carried her across the stage. 'She kept looking up at Charles,' reported a press photographer.[30]

There were eight curtain calls and the audience were enraptured, all except Charles who tried to look pleased. He told Sleep that Diana was a 'terrific' dancer, but friends were given to understand that he found the dress too slinky and the act undignified. Back at the Palace he vented his displeasure. Diana was downcast.

As the marriage foundered, she increased her attendances at the ballet. She would show up spontaneously for morning rehearsals, with the young princes in tow, favouring senior ROH officials with outrageous indiscretions. Not a word leaked out, such was their affection for her. The press were on the rampage. In November 1992, the *Daily Mirror* and Murdoch's *Sun* published extracts from tapped telephone chats between Prince Charles and his lover, Camilla Parker-Bowles. On 9 December John Major told a hushed House of Commons that the royal pair were to separate. After three more years of media wars and salacious revelations, they divorced in July 1996. Diana won custody of the princes and a fifteen million pound settlement, but lost the title of HRH, Her Royal Highness. The following day she severed her patronage of almost one hundred charities and public causes. Among the six she retained was English National Ballet, testifying to the depth of her love of dance.

Having left Charles, Diana avoided the ROH. The ballet felt orphaned, bereft of its cheerleader in the Royal Box, its champion on the board and its choreographer in residence. As closure loomed, the Royal Ballet was fatally weakened.

David Mellor did not last long. The breezy, high-living Heritage Secretary had offended Rupert Murdoch by defending the BBC against the predations of his satellite broadcasting business. Mellor was easy prey. A nightclub hostess, introduced to a Sunday newspaper by a dubious publicist, confessed to having sex with the minister, who allegedly wore a Chelsea shirt and liked to have his toes sucked. When these revelations failed to procure his dismissal, tabloid hounds 'discovered' that the pro-Palestinian Mellor had accepted a paid family holiday from the daughter of a PLO paymaster. Hours after his sacking on 1 October 1992, the *Sun*'s front page crowed: 'From Toe Job to No Job'.

It was a seminal moment in public affairs. The gutter press had won a gruesome victory and politicians of both main parties cowered in fear. Murdoch's men were not finished with Mellor. Young reporters taken on by the *Sunday Times*, were ordered to 'dig dirt on Mellor',[31] *pour encourager les autres*. Media owners were flexing their pecs. The humiliation of the Heritage Secretary was the prelude to a tide of 'sleaze' that would engulf and bring down the Major Government. The downgrading of public ethics accelerated. Murdoch led the prurient pack into the royal bedchambers. His red-top *Sun* masqueraded as the *vox populi*. It mixed tittle-tattle about television soap operas with reams of sport and a generalized sneer at 'toffs'. The arts, if mentioned, were crudely derided. Subsidy was a euphemism for rich people getting seats paid for by the poor. The Royal Opera House was ripe for plucking, though not quite yet.

John Major, in his election manifesto, had promised to create a National Lottery to relieve recessional gloom. The project was entrusted to the next National Heritage Secretary, Peter Brooke, an end-of-line career politician who showed no particular enthusiasm for anything, but a dogged loyalty to his Prime Minister. It fell to Hayden Phillips, the department's permanent secretary, to make the rules by which Lottery profits would be kept out of Treasury hands and distributed to five good causes, including the arts. Phillips coined a ghastly word 'additionality', to signify that Lottery money could not be used for running costs or extant projects. It was new money, destined for new initiatives.

Denis Vaughan, prophet of the Lottery, was appalled. The operational method, he argued, was too costly; the yield to the arts would be no more than 5.6 per cent of the pot; and most of the money would be invested in buildings instead of new audiences.

'I believe,' declared Jeremy Isaacs, 'that the National Lottery was invented to find a responsible route for a Government that knew it ought to put its own hand in its pocket and pay for a national lyric theatre, but couldn't find the courage to do it.' As far as Covent Garden was concerned, it was the intended beneficiary, a view it impressed upon the Arts Council, which was designated to distribute the cash. Brooke and Phillips wanted the problem off their doorstep. The Department was under fire for a hundred million pound overspend on the prison-like new British Library, an epic bureaucratic disaster.

At this stage, no one knew how much cash the Lottery would produce. The Arts Council guessed fifty million pounds, and formed a new department under Jeremy Newton to administer it. Peter Gummer, public relations adviser to the Prime Minister and brother of the Environment Secretary, was the supervising Council member. Endless procedural meetings were held. Entire forests were pulped into policy papers. When the balls first rolled on Saturday 19 November 1994, the Lottery overtook the football pools as the Englishman's weekly flutter. The first year's yield to the arts was £271.6 million, almost half as much again as the Council's existing budget of £190 million. The Council was left dangerously lop-sided, with more cash in Gummer's lap than in the chairman's. It was also in no position to command public confidence, having barely recovered from a crippling cock-up.

One sunny morning in July 1993, the Council's secretary general, Anthony Everitt, had summoned the press to discuss the future of the London orchestras. Funding had not flowed easier since the Goodman report thirty years earlier, and all four self-governing orchestras were in varying degrees of difficulty. The LSO, conducted by Colin Davis and resident at the Barbican, were in relative clover, having won a million pounds from the City of London to match their

Arts Council grant. The RPO, managed by Paul Findlay, were, as ever, near the breadline. The Philharmonia and London Philharmonic were, as ever, at each other's throats.

Everitt, and his music director Ken Baird, announced that the Arts Council had decided to fund only two orchestras, but could not decide which. A panel under Sir Leonard Hoffmann, Goodman's former rapporteur, would make recommendations. The officials smiled at television cameras as they delivered the death sentence on two renowned ensembles. Baird's face fell moments later when he heard the present writer denounce the deed on television as unnecessary, unworkable and an abdication of statutory responsibilities. The Council had not anticipated opposition.

Over the next five months, fur flew. Findlay pulled Valery Gergiev out of a Russian hat as the RPO's key attraction. The Philharmonia hooked Judy Grahame, the LPO's former marketing chief, to publicize its involvement with the venerable composer György Ligeti. The LPO huffed and puffed. Goodman emerged from retirement to say the Arts Council should resign. 'Orchestral music is the last thing they should be cutting,' he growled, 'it's one of the few arts we are famous for.'[32]

Hoffmann's panel split down the middle. Two members felt the contest was too close to call; three others backed the Philharmonia. Palumbo, the Council chairman, was dead set on cutting his client base. He ruled that the Philharmonia should be saved alongside the LSO, the other two could die. The LPO chairman, Elliott Bernerd, a tough property developer, refused to accept the Solomonian verdict. He called Palumbo on a Saturday night and threatened him and the Council with legal action. Palumbo crumbled and a statement was issued on the Monday that all four orchestras would continue to receive funding. Baird and the music panel chairman Brian Magee resigned, followed by Everitt. Palumbo's term ended soon after.

The next chairman was Lord Gowrie, the former arts minister. He called in Everitt's deputy, Mary Allen. 'When did you first hear of this orchestra plan?' he demanded. 'The day before it was announced,' said Allen. 'That's all right, then,' sighed Gowrie, appointing her secretary general.

Allen, daughter of a poet and actress of Irish extraction, assembled a brisk new cadre of women executives. In budget week, Allen would come in each morning at six and lock the building when she left at night. In dealing with arts clients, she played bad cop to Gowrie's good cop.

Gowrie had won the chairmanship over the Prime Minister's chum, Peter Gummer, and the piano-playing north-eastern industrialist Ernest Hall. He was a passionate Wagnerian who summered in Bayreuth and believed in the right of every citizen to see a new *Ring* twice a decade. He persuaded Sainsbury of his commitment to Covent Garden and was given to understand by Downing Street that it looked favourably on the ROH redevelopment.

Mary Allen, before her promotion, had been the Council's observer at ROH board meetings. She was alarmed at Isaacs' deficits and Stirling's indecisiveness. In two years of board minutes, hardly a single issue had been satisfactorily resolved. No theatres had been rented for the closure period. Costs were vague and programmes unplanned. Three board members – Duffield, the Labour academic Tessa Blackstone and the printing magnate Robert Gavron – pressed for action, which Stirling airily deferred.

Questions of principle had scarcely been considered. Was it in Covent Garden's best interest to rebuild a two thousand seat house when it could sell the site and build a four thousand seater, with an eye to Met-like financial independence? Why would it cost the ROH £214 million to rebuild, when Glyndebourne could knock down its old hall and build a brand new one for thirty-five million, all of it privately raised?

Allen demanded facts, not waffle. Peter Gummer, who chaired a joint AC-ROH committee to implement the Warnock proposals, warned that he could not sign a blank Lottery cheque. 'The opera house would come to these meetings, in the person of Jeremy, unable to talk in matters of detail,' said an observer. 'It was all rhetoric. It was like wrestling with jelly.'[33]

Gummer and Allen went to the Heritage Department to canvass support. 'Hayden, we need to get tough with the opera house,' said Allen, 'but we can't unless the Government are on our side.' Phillips, in classic Whitehall fashion, said: 'why don't we take it a little more gently, be a little less confrontational?'[34]

The cost had hit £214 million pounds and Stirling was demanding first dip into the Lottery hat. Isaacs, by his own admission, 'fondly imagined that I, or the Chairman, would write a simple, eloquent letter stating our need' and the Lottery cheque would arrive by return of post. When he saw the application form, with hundreds of questions and demands for professional validation, he erupted in rage and frustration.

Keith Cooper was charged with preparing the paperwork, which he did by aggrandizing his own department and distributing research tasks around the house. Cooper was a tall, engaging character who made Vivien Duffield laugh aloud and kept her abreast of internal plots, as Balfour had done for Sainsbury. He completed the application in the week that Lottery tickets went on sale. On 4 January 1995, the first working morning of a new year, Isaacs staged a glitzy photo-opportunity on the Arts Council's doorstep with two dancers, Darcey Bussell and Bruce Sansom, and two singers, Thomas Allen and Simon Keenlyside, handing in the application.

It took six months to get an answer while the Arts Council pursued due diligence, a process that Isaacs deemed wasteful. Six weeks after receiving the ROH submission, the Arts Council published the findings of a 'geological survey' into the 'provision of Lyric Theatre (Dance and Opera) in London' – in plain English, a study of how many stages the capital needed. Covent Garden, ENO, Sadler's Wells and the South Bank Centre were all putting in simultaneously for huge Lottery grants. Dennis Stevenson, head of the Pearson publishing group and a former member of the Warnock panel, was asked to report whether the theatres should rebuild, and when: it would be calamitous if they all shut at the same time. His report identified the need for a medium-sized dance house – ideally, Sadler's Wells – but indicated that there was not enough operatic demand to justify ROH and ENO running at full steam. Despite the hype of an opera boom, audiences had remained static over quarter of a century. The average age of Coliseum goers was forty-four years old, of Covent Garden audiences fifty-five. London's ballet public had shrunk from half a million attenders to fewer than 200,000 people annually. Stevenson recommended that ENO should cut back its opera output, produce large-scale dance and get out more into the regions.

As regards closure, Covent Garden deserved priority, but Sadler's Wells should rebuild first, thereby providing a temporary home and potentially younger audience for the Royal Ballet during the ROH shutdown. Stevenson was assisted in his work by three expert arts administrators: Graham Devlin, Stephen Phillips and Genista McIntosh of the National Theatre. Their approach was cool, dis-passionate and non-partisan. It made a significant contribution to the planning process and was warmly received by the Arts Council. 'All options are open,' said Mary Allen, 'The only ones we will not endorse are simultaneous closure for Covent Garden and ENO, or the dismantling of either company.'[35]

The Stevenson report was ignored at Covent Garden (and in Isaacs' memoirs) and denounced by ENO's intemperate boss for its 'breathless urgency'. Marks, and ENO, were in trouble. The deficit was rising, Sian Edwards would soon resign and the Arts Council femocracy had demanded as a condition of approving Marks' contract renewal that he should seek counselling to enable him to work better with powerful women. Over the next two years, until Marks departed, ENO entered its darkest night since the schism of 1945. Audiences fell and programming stultified. Yet Government officials noted drily that, no matter how dire ENO's plight, the crisis was kept within a constitutional remit, whereas at Covent Garden, the faintest whiff of anxiety would send Stirling, Sainsbury or some shadowy official scuttling into Downing Street for succour.

Successive Heritage Secretaries were so irked by this intimacy that Hayden Phillips was ordered to investigate secret links between the Royal Opera House and the Cabinet Office. He found that Robert Armstrong, long retired, had attempted to hand over his ROH Secretaryship to his Downing Street successor, Sir Robin Butler, only to be vetoed by Margaret Thatcher. His seat went to a top Treasury man, Andrew Edwards, and nothing that Phillips could do would dislodge him. Powerful interests were protecting the *status quo* and making sure that Covent Garden was well served.

On 20 July 1995, Gowrie announced the Arts Council's largest Lottery grant – a total of £78.5 million to be given to Covent Garden, £55 million for the development itself, and £23.5 million to cover extra costs entailed during the two-year closure from July 1997. Eighteen conditions were attached to the award, at Allen's and Gummer's insistence, and Gowrie was careful to stipulate that even larger amounts were likely to be given to future regional applicants. It was an oddly defensive performance from a normally upbeat man.

Isaacs invited the press back to Covent Garden, uncorked a few bottles of wine, and was pictured on the next morning's front pages holding Stirling's arm aloft in sunlit triumph outside the Floral Hall. Gowrie was asked to justify the award in an op-ed article for the *Daily Telegraph*. The case he made was so incoherent that I, just off a flight from Australia, was obliged to produce an eleven-hundred word comment piece in ninety minutes flat. There was no question in my jet-lagged mind of opposing the grant – it was a matter of simple national interest. The ROH was the acme of British arts. Ascendant, it nurtured the broader arts economy with values and ideas. Deprived, it depressed the creative aspiration.

> In a country that does not like to give the impression of being good at anything (I wrote), Covent Garden achieves high standards almost by stealth. It is a barometer for the national culture . . . It gives London the chimera of civility and luxury that many of its hoteliers and cabbies have worked so valiantly to destroy . . . [Its] underlying objective is to entertain, to represent and, at times, to elevate the national mood.[36]

Other broadsheets generally concurred. The *Sun*, that good Friday, raised a cackle of controversy. Ever since the Lottery started, tabloid newspapers had fostered a delusion that its revenue somehow belonged to those who bought tickets – as if beer-drinkers were empowered to tell brewers how to spend their profits. Any spending on culture was élitist and snobbish. Thus did the *Sun* set upon Covent Garden:

FURY AS MORE LOTTERY CASH GOES DOWN THE DRAIN
IT'S THE GREEDY BEGGAR'S OPERA
Exclusive by Lenny Lottery

A storm erupted last night over the extra £100 million (sic) Lottery handout for opera lovers – instead of the ordinary Lottery punters. Furious Labour MP Tony Banks blasted the Arts Council for dishing out cash to 'people who never bought a Lottery ticket in their lives.' He stormed, 'Most of the millions raised by the Lottery come from working class punters. But they are getting nothing back.'

Arts Council chairman Lord Gowrie defended the payouts, insisting opera was 'not just for toffs' despite £120 ticket prices. He said, 'Opera audiences I have seen around the country are very often struggling professionals. *They are middle class people – not very rich toffs.*' He added he would have liked to have given the Royal Opera an EXTRA £10 million to help lower ticket prices.[37]

The *Sun* set up a hotline for readers to vote on whether the opera house should get a hundred million pounds, untroubled by factual precision. That day, fifteen thousand people were said to have rung the 'No' line. The next morning, the Sun resumed its attack in a telly-punned editorial: 'This Opera Windfall's* Appalling'

> Not one penny more must go to the bunch of Toscas at the Royal Opera House.
>
> The people's verdict in our You The Jury vote could not be clearer.
>
> They don't want their lottery money squandered on the minority pastimes of the well-heeled when genuine causes like medical research charities are losing out. Those who hand out lottery cash lack two things: common sense and the common touch.

No politician dared challenge the self-appointed voice of the people. The *Sun* was not read by arts lovers, but it was tamely obeyed by ministers who knew the price of its disfavour. In political circles, Covent Garden became from that day on a dirty word, never to be uttered with approbation or, if possible, at all. The new Heritage Secretary, Virginia Bottomley, just two weeks in office, said nothing. 'The lottery has been absurdly mishandled from the point of view of the public relations of government,' raged Isaacs. 'We were sitting ducks for whatever the *Sun* wanted to do to us.'[38]

The following week, the *Sun* kitted out half a dozen readers in top hats and tails and sent them for a fun night at the opera. 'The Prime Minister,' said Isaacs, 'and the secretary of state for National Heritage should have been standing on their feet saying to people, "we've brought this lottery in, it's succeeding beyond our wildest expectations . . . and hats off to the ROH which has got there first." But of course they didn't do that. They just stood back and said, "oh dear, why is Jeremy being photographed with his thumbs up?" '[39]

There was no point in apportioning blame. Lasting damage had been done to the ROH, and some of it, *pace* Isaacs, was self-inflicted.

If Nicholas Payne suffered the torments of managing opera, he hid

---

* viz. Oprah Winfrey

them well behind a fixed jollity and a hobbyist's passion for tiny details of past casting. There was much else that he kept concealed. Getting information out of Payne was as easy as getting decisions from his chairman. At Opera North, as chief executive, Payne was personally in charge of repertoire and budgets. At the ROH, he had to seek budget clearance from Isaacs, repertoire approval from the board, and date co-ordination from the Royal Ballet. His tactic was to keep all plans close to his chest until absolutely forced to disclose. This drove some colleagues to despair, and the ballet directors to spitting fury. Payne could rely on boardroom support from Isaacs and Duffield, while Dowell and Russell-Roberts went naked into the negotiating chamber and emerged skinned. Dowell muttered of a 'Capulets and Montagues' situation as relations between the Royal Opera and Royal Ballet hissed and spluttered.

'We would be asked once a programme had been planned, and sometimes printed, to make changes,' complained Dowell. 'One season we had our usual Christmas fare of *Nutcracker* and *Cinderella*, and the board said, could you put *Swan Lake* and *Beauty* in? It put enormous strains on the company. The rehearsal time got very tight, and we only just got things together. Anthony (Russell-Roberts) would come out of a financial meeting and we'd be asked to make savings, or help revenue by adding a populist work.'[40] In their last four seasons in the opera house, the ballet were allowed fewer than half as many new productions as the opera. Audiences grew weary of repetition and critics condemned Dowell for lack of imagination. His music director, Barry Wordsworth, urged him to get tough with the board. 'There would have been no point in me standing and screaming,' sighed Dowell, 'anyway, it's not my style.' He took the criticism to heart and, visibly stressed, retreated from public view. 'When you're a dancer and you read reviews, the knife goes in but you find ways of working round it,' he explained. 'When you are director, it reflects on the company and I feel incredibly responsible. I know what is good and bad, and I think we have brought standards up. If the rep has been changed it's because of financial problems, that's why.'

Payne, by contrast, radiated success. He inherited many of Findlay's best schemes, and found the music director a man reborn. Bernard Haitink, twice divorced and past sixty, had found love in the orchestra. He married the viola player Patricia Bloomfield and moved into a terraced house near Harrods, giving up all threats of resignation. 'I have changed,' Haitink told me. 'My roots are now in London. I work well here. I love the English mentality, living as an artist in a community where you can read so many press opinions, not like New York where there is only the *Times*. I admire the English for, with so little money, organizing opera groups. I admire the English singers, they are very well brought up, and the English orchestral musicians. Even if I did not work here, I would still live here.'[41]

'Nicholas doesn't know how lucky he was that Bernard found Patricia,' said Findlay ruefully. Haitink opened Payne's era with a triumphant *Meistersinger*, deftly directed by Graham Vick on a traditionalist setting by Graham Hudson, and with two English masters, John Tomlinson and Thomas Allen, in central roles. The Wagners of Bayreuth attended; British and American singers had come to dominate their festival. Haitink exuded authority and joy. This was one of those rare opera nights where everything worked.

Haitink continued with Janáček's *Katya Kabanova*, directed by Trevor Nunn of the RSC, and effulgently sung by Elena Prokina, one of Gergiev's fresh crop. Payne indulged his sense of whimsy with Massenet's *Chérubin*, never previously seen at Covent Garden. Its English director, Tim Albery, demanded slower tempi than the Russian conductor, Gennady Rozhdestvensky, was prepared to beat. Rozhdestvensky walked out. *Prima la musica*? Not under Payne's regime, which prized deconstruction above textual fidelity. The show was predictably trivial, as was Giordano's *Fedora*, revived at the instigation of José Carreras, who sang opposite Mirella Freni, pushing sixty but vocally immaculate. Carreras looked worried. He was under police investigation in Rome for allegedly receiving secret fee boosters from the opera house. Pavarotti was appearing in the Philippines at twenty-five thousand pesos (or six hundred pounds) a ticket. Domingo pulled out of Covent Garden's *Fanciulla* in order to join the other two in Los Angeles for a World Cup concert in which they shared sixteen million dollars for record and media rights. Covent Garden, meanwhile, announced a million-pound budget cut and Isaacs vacated Webster's spacious office to make way for shops and offices at the rear of the building.

The next season was starstruck. Roberto Alagna arrived in September 1994 to rehearse Gounod's *Roméo et Juliette*, straight from his wife's funeral. Alagna, just thirty, had been discovered singing in a Paris pizza house and had lately made his mark at La Scala. Word of his bereavement trickled out, rendering his Romeo –

sung to the Juliette of the Rumanian Leontina Vaduva and watched from the stalls by his orphaned daughter – all the more poignant. 'It has the credibility of cinema,'[42] said Alagna, on seeing the video.

Backstage, he met another Romanian soprano who was rehearsing *La traviata*. Angela Gheorghiu, a rail worker's daughter, had auditioned at Covent Garden a few weeks after graduating from the Bucharest Academy. Peter Katona liked her style and booked her for *Bohème*. Solti, eighty-two and full of vigour, saw her sing Mimi and engaged her for *Traviata*, a work he had never conducted before. The director, Richard Eyre, head of the National Theatre, had never produced an opera before. 'Everybody was fresh, open to ideas,' said Gheorghiu. 'We began reading the text, each word without music.'[43]

'I never tired of watching Solti at work with the orchestra and singers,' wrote Eyre, 'punching the air, moulding, sculpting, caressing, on his toes in a half-crouch like a boxing trainer, singing and shouting like a muezzin. "Play this *forte*," he crowed to the cellos. "Break your wrists, and break my heart." '[44] Eyre, an opera sceptic, was overwhelmed.

The resultant drama was so spare and moving that BBC-2, for the first time in years, cleared its schedules and carried the opera live. Gheorghiu was an overnight star, in the same month as Alagna conquered all hearts as Romeo. They were smitten with one another. 'From Angela Gheorghiu,' glowed Alagna, 'I learned to sing with happiness.' 'It's true,' purred Gheorghiu, 'always.'[45]

Celebrity ensued, followed by notoriety. The golden pair fell out, in quick succession, with the Met, La Scala and Solti. As doors slammed, their fame grew. Not since Mario and Grisi in the middle of the nineteenth century had opera experienced a singing couple of equal calibre. Together, they were too much for the faint-hearted. Rumours suppurated around them like lava down Etna's slopes and colleagues walked on hot coals. At Covent Garden, they were proof that the old stage had lost none of its capacity to sow stardust. The spot where Callas found her voice and Sutherland her *métier*, where Fonteyn came of age and Nureyev restored her youth, possessed an alchemist's magic that was matched by no other. It was to Covent Garden that the Alagnas owed their romance and fortune.

But while stars were born beneath the royal crest, English singers for whom the theatre had been founded felt generally disaffected. A month after the lovebirds left, the Lancastrian soprano Amanda

Roocroft turned up to sing Fiordiligi in an almost home-grown cast of *Così fan tutte*, directed by Jonathan Miller. Roocroft, at twenty-eight, was growing out of Mozart and into big Italian roles. Nurtured at the Royal Northern College of Music, she was spotted by the critic Michael Kennedy and tipped as 'the soprano the world's leading opera houses would soon be fighting over'. Many did, but not Covent Garden which expected English singers to make a name abroad to prove that they were of appropriate 'international' calibre. Roocroft was well liked by Findlay and Payne, but was not prepared to wait for them to call. She made Munich her base and was effectively lost to London audiences.

Jane Eaglen, an English Wagnerian who also sang the fiercest Norma since Callas, bedded down in the United States. Bryn Terfel, the boisterous Welsh baritone, appeared twice that spring at Covent Garden – as Jokanaan in *Salome* and Balstrode in *Peter Grimes* – and then put the venue on his back-burner. He reckoned that as many Welshmen came to hear him at the Met as at Covent Garden.[46] The world was shrinking and loyalties were no longer local, but more than one singer complained that, at the ROH, patriotic pride had been displaced by the inverted snobbery of Gucci-shod cosmopolites.

The last relic of national self-assertion was to be found in the preference that Isaacs professed for British directors of post-modern tendencies. Hall was passé, Eyre and Nunn hard to fault. But what really excited Isaacs was a clever-dick director who could decon-struct a classic and make it look contemporary. It was precisely for this reason that he had hired Payne, who obliged by assigning Wagner's *Ring* not to some clapped-out German spouting Marxist dialectics but to a British director who was making real waves. Richard Jones was a respected professional who believed in the director's right to take the fifth amendment. His work was invariably dramatic but often obtuse. It included innovative open-air operas for the Bregenz Festival in Austria, Sondheim in the West End, Molière at the National Theatre, modern plays on and off Broadway and a side-splitting *Love for Three Oranges* at Opera North and ENO. Jones throughout never explained his methods or meanings.

At Covent Garden he missed meetings and was so late in delivering Nigel Lowery's designs that Haitink turned fractious. Introduced to the Jones concept by Nicholas Payne, Haitink slumped into his seat as one outrage after another was paraded before his unbelieving eyes: grotesque Rhinemaidens in rubbery breasts, a stretch limousine, an aeroplane. 'What can I say?' he moaned.

'What the director was anxious to establish was the image of time passing,' explained Payne.

'Do you think the audience will understand that?' Haitink demanded, 'even for me it's difficult to understand what he means . . . You can't just ignore everything that Wagner asked for.'[47]

Payne reported his dismay to Isaacs, who replied: 'In the last resort, if you and I are persuaded that the thing is right . . . Bernard will go along with it.' As, indeed, he did, keeping his eyes well down. Haitink was deemed the saving grace of the Jones-Lowery *Ring* by critics who split generationally over its merits. Michael Kennedy, in the *Sunday Telegraph*, wrote a protest note to Wagner in Valhalla. Rupert Christiansen, in the *Daily Telegraph*, found the production refreshingly anti-intellectual.

'There was no intention to outrage for its own sake,' said Payne, 'but there has been an intention to disturb, because we think that Wagner's work is disturbing. Beneath that, you have in Richard Jones a deeply serious director who has gone back to the text and back to what the music means. His direction is about ideas. It's not, in that sense, decorative. It's about getting to the meaning of Wagner's deeply pessimistic view of human failings.'[48]

In the teacup of British arts, a minor tempest raged. It would have quickly blown over were it not for the fact that every doubt and blunder was captured by television cameras and relayed to living rooms across the nation and, soon after, across America.

Jeremy Isaacs believed, at the very core of his being, in the power of television to uplift minds and improve the world. He had no hesitation in allowing a BBC team the run of the opera house, from board meetings to backstage dangers, with the aim of showing the extraordinary dedication practised and excellence achieved in the national lyric theatre. There was no other way of getting on television; the unions ruled out live relays and the BBC had all but given up covering the arts. To win the hearts of the nation, he aimed to appeal over the heads of broadsheet critics and tabloid saboteurs. 'Get the readers of the *Sun* on your side,'[49] urged Peter Gummer, the public relations magnate. In his eagerness to set the cameras rolling, Isaacs waived editorial approval of the project and, according to a senior member of the production team, accepted in writing that a proportion of the material filmed might turn out to be derogatory of the ROH.[50]

The series' director, Michael Waldman, had worked as a researcher on Isaacs' 1980 televisual history of Ireland. He was a trusted colleague from whom Isaacs expected the usual courtesies of contact and consultation. His confidence was misplaced. Waldman 'never came'[51] to share his thoughts with the industry veteran.

Television had changed in the 90s, its values contorted by satellite competition, confrontational chat shows and wall-to-wall sports. The story that Waldman was seeking was not the one Isaacs hoped to tell. He was competing for primetime audiences with laddish comedy, live football and topless starlets. His commitment could not be faulted: he gave up a year of his life to filming daily routines that had his cameramen aching with tedium. Out of the humdrum stuff of meetings, memos and arts politics, Waldman constructed six compellingly watchable episodes about an institution in distress.

The House commanded audiences of four million, high for BBC-2. It aroused gasps of sympathy for stagehands who risked life and limb in the cause of an art they barely glimpsed, and of admiration for the low-paid and unsung auxiliaries who laboured around the clock to put a show on stage. Given television's predilection for the exotic and unnatural, it was a fair and balanced portrait. But the television eye invariably distorts, and what lodged in the public memory was not the company's halo but its horrors.

Keith Cooper, sacking a box office manager and hurling a phone at the wall, was the unquestioned star of the series; he would be swamped by offers of marriage and other, less reputable proposals. Two barmen in the Crush Bar who had not exchanged a word for years provided an entertaining sub-plot. A stage door concierge with singing ambitions hammed it up for all he was worth, harmlessly.

The gruesome bits were the informalities. Nicholas Payne was heard complaining to Isaacs about 'the fucking rah-rahs' he had to smile at on opening nights. Isaacs was seen, naked from the waist up, dressing in black tie and yellow socks for a gala. 'Undignified,' exclaimed Joseph Volpe, tough-minded manager of New York's Met. 'What was he doing, auditioning for a Tarzan movie?'[52]

A French mezzo, Magali Damonte, hauled from cooking family dinner in Marseilles to stand in as Carmen at Covent Garden, was thrown on stage without rehearsal and left to find her own way around. The Carmen she replaced, Denyce Graves, was refused a dining table for her family because they had all been grabbed by the rah-rahs. Fiona Chadwick, a popular Royal Ballet principal, was seen dancing her last Juliet, moments after being told that, after sixteen years with the company, she was surplus to requirements.

Against the backdrop of sacrifice, high-jinks and mishaps, the board were seen languidly discussing financial crisis. 'Unless this board actually pulls its fingers out,' warned Vivien Duffield, 'we're going to lose the children's matinées.' 'The fact is,' sighed Angus Stirling, 'that we have a £2.2 million accumulated deficit and if we do not earn the money we are going to go down the chute.' Nobody seemed unduly panicked.

At the Arts Council, Isaacs, Cooper and the deputy chairman Sir James Spooner reviewed the closure plans with Peter Gummer, Mary Allen, the dance chairman Prue Skene and finance director Lew Hodges.

'The least-cost option,' said Hodges, 'would be to stop performing for two years, saving forty million pounds.'

'Ridiculous,' snorted Spooner. 'Patrons do not give money for bricks and mortar but to support their world-class opera and ballet companies. If there are no performances for two years, three years, whatever, then sponsorship will simply dry up.'

'That's like saying, fuck it, we don't want you any more,' exploded Isaacs.

No one seemed to recall that the original Lottery application made no mention of the companies continuing to perform during closure.

The House showed up many of the cracks that were surfacing in the company as it approached the dreaded date of closure with little planned beyond. Although many scenes were more than two years old by the time they reached the screen, a fatal impression was conveyed of an enterprise adrift, holed below the water line but still dancing in the ballroom and dickering on deck. The perceptual damage was irreparable. 'Fly on the wall that nearly brought the House down,' was one newspaper's verdict.[53]

From the first night of transmission, 16 January 1996, Isaacs' position was undermined. He had announced the previous spring that he would retire in September 1997, when he turned sixty-five, but *The House* and its attendant events put paid to any hopes of glory.

A month before the series was screened, relations with the Arts Council reached an all-time low. Isaacs demanded the right to 'draw down' some of the Lottery money earmarked for redevelopment. The Council replied that they could not release the funds until the ROH fulfilled the eighteen conditions of the grant, including a balanced budget and a confirmed programme for the closure period.

Mary Allen, alarmed at the lack of an integrated monthly cash flow report, put a mole into the house in the form of Richard Pulford, a former Arts Council deputy secretary-general. Pulford's brief was to report to her weekly, daily if necessary, on the company's solvency and on its progress in meeting the eighteen conditions. A man of dry wit and infinite patience, Pulford had earned his spurs in many an arts crisis. He had singlehandedly rescued local funding when Margaret Thatcher abolished the metropolitan authorities and had been joint chief of London's perpetually troubled South Bank Centre. What he found at Covent Garden was a drift into debt and a lack of clear decisions. 'A failure of senior management,' he called it. 'How the various departments have been allowed to plan on this basis is an interesting question, the answer to which must lie at the top of the organization,'[54] said Pulford.

Isaacs, facing close budgetary scrutiny, slashed the payroll. He cut a hundred jobs one week, two hundred the next. Four days before Christmas 1995 he had a meeting with the Arts Council which was 'so horrible that I have suppressed the memory, having only a dim recollection of abuse and recrimination, of men and women behaving badly'.[55]

Eye-witnesses recall that Lord Gowrie opened with a statement so airy and obtuse that, after quarter of an hour, Angus Stirling leaned across the table and said, in his gentlest voice, 'Grey, it's obvious that something is terribly wrong. Please tell us what it is.' Gowrie abandoned his peroration and handed over to Mary Allen. She reported that the Council had decided that no Lottery handout could be given to Covent Garden until its budgets balanced and its closure was acceptably planned. Sir James Spooner rose, so violently that his chair crashed to the ground. 'I have to go,' he said, 'but I can tell you this: if you want the whole thing back in your laps, we'll give it to you. We'll put it into liquidation.'

For the next two hours, one side 'hammered at the table saying "give us the cash" and the other side said, "no, we will not".' The meeting ended with an agreement to send in a team of independent accountants from KPMG. Isaacs was seen kicking the corridor wall, but progress had been made.[56] Once the audit had been conducted the only outstanding obstacle would be where the companies should perform during the exile years. Isaacs had set his face against the Arts Council's favoured option.

Sadler's Wells had been given a £27 million Lottery grant to rebuild and its chief executive Ian Albery had offered to co-ordinate his timetable to give the ROH first use of the renovated theatre from November 1997. Isaacs snubbed the offer gracelessly. 'Surely a bird in the hand is worth two in the bush?' said Albery. Isaacs muttered something about there being no restaurants in the neighbourhood. Sadler's Wells was a community theatre, drawing, as in Lilian Baylis's time, on a local audience of pensioners, school parties and council tenants. Under Albery's direction it was starting to buzz as a place for new dance. An experimental, all-male *Swan Lake*, choreographed by Matthew Bourne and starring the Royal Ballet's undervalued Adam Cooper, proved so exciting that it earned two West End runs and a Christmas show on television. Small as it was, with only fifteen hundred seats, Sadler's Wells was able to take risks. Its lottery win was resented at Covent Garden, where malicious tongues accused the Arts Council of pandering to a Sadler's Wells board member by name of Cherie Booth, Q.C., wife of a fast-rising Labour MP, Tony Blair.

The theatres Isaacs wanted to book were both in the West End: the Lyceum and Drury Lane. The latter was occupied by the long-running *Miss Saigon*, whose producer, Cameron Macintosh, refused to budge. The Lyceum's owners demanded a crippling rental and, while waiting interminably for an ROH decision, did a deal with Andrew Lloyd Webber for a revival of *Jesus Christ Superstar*.

Isaacs, while driving to work, was struck by a vacant site beside Tower Bridge. He suggested building a temporary theatre which another organization, perhaps Disney, could inherit when the Royal companies moved back home. Plans were drawn up and months slipped by. Planning permission was granted by the local authority on 18 December 1996. Two weeks later, just before *The House* aired, the scheme was abandoned for want of a willing partner. Disney were not answering the phone and the architects told Isaacs that it was now too late to erect the tent in time for the company's exile.

Visiting Isaacs in his office that week, I asked him for the fall-back plan. There was none. He seemed unfocused, his eyes straying to television monitors on the wall and his sentences drifting into thin air. He was still hoping that the temporary theatre could be built. He told the board on 22 January 'there was just a chance that the Tower Bridge theatre project might again become a realistic option'. That faint hope was extinguished when the Environment Secretary John Gummer, Peter's brother, called in the proposal for a public inquiry. Eighteen months before closure, the ROH had nowhere to go. 'The right decision would have been to delay closure, and therefore the redevelopment, until clear plans had been crystallized,' said the ROH finance director, Clive Timms. Postponement was unthinkable, said Isaacs.[57]

Anxieties flared. Vivien Duffield demanded that Peter Gummer should be brought on to the board to push things along and mend bridges with the Arts Council. Some wanted him to succeed Stirling without delay, but the rules stated that the chairman had to be a serving board member for at least three months. Gummer was co-opted in March 1996, arousing adverse press comment. It seemed improper that the Lottery gamekeeper should join the opera house poachers without breaking stride. It seemed also unwise to appoint one of John Major's closest advisers as chairman-designate when the Tory Government was on its last legs. The warnings went unheeded. Gummer's arrival coincided with the release of Lottery funds. At his first meeting, Clive Timms told the board that the costs of exile could well exceed the projected twenty million pounds. Twenty-seven and thirty-four were the figures he mentioned. An enraged Robert Gavron demanded, and received, the finance director's immediate resignation. Matters were no longer being discussed with the augustan calm of a Waverley or the detailed attentiveness of a Drogheda, a Moser or a Sainsbury.

For want of a homeless shelter, Sadler's Wells was pressed into service. 'The last time I had seen Jeremy,' said Albery, 'he told me, "Ian, don't bother, we're not coming to Sadler's Wells. We – do – not – want – to go to Sadler's Wells."'[58] Albery booked the Pina Bausch dance ensemble as his opening attraction and the Rambert company as his mainstay. Suddenly there was a call from Isaacs. 'Ian, you have to do something to help us.' Next came a call from Clive Priestley, chairman of the London Arts Board: 'You've got to help Covent Garden.' Finally, at a meeting with Mary Allen, funding pressure was exerted. Albery refused to cancel his scheduled dates and told Covent Garden they would have to fit in as best they could. Like many arts professionals, he was unwilling to grant favours to the haughty and bullying Royal Opera House.

The Royal Opera booked blocks of time at the Barbican Centre, the Royal Festival Hall and the rundown Shaftesbury Theatre on the edge of the West End. The Royal Ballet rented Labatt's Apollo in Hammersmith, six miles from its natural habitat and beside a thundering flyover. For the rest, the companies would tour Japan, America, Germany, Finland and anywhere else that would have them at short notice. In July, Pulford reported to Mary Allen that the ROH had done just enough to satisfy the eighteen conditions, though problems persisted.

Allen attended the interviews for Isaacs' successor as the Arts Council's observer. The selection process had been botched. An approach to Hugues Gall, director of the Paris Opéra, was sent to his former post in Geneva. The invitation to Peter Jonas was mailed not to the Intendant's office at the Bavarian State Opera but to the Ministry of Culture, arousing unfounded doubts about his loyalty. The only foreign applicant of appropriate calibre was Gerard Mortier, the Salzburg Festival's engagingly modernist opera boss. Mortier was asked: 'What would you do if the Government cuts the Arts Council grant and you are obliged to cut your repertoire at three months' notice?' Mortier replied, 'but this doesn't happen . . .' Someone sourly replied, 'it just has.' Mortier was asked back for a second interview. He left saying, 'all they wanted to do was steal my ideas.'

The remaining candidates were Brian Dickie of Glyndebourne and three internal contenders: Nicholas Payne, Anthony Russell-Roberts and the personnel director, Mike Morris. None inspired confidence. Payne, who had been nominated by Isaacs, seemed unwilling to answer any question that was put to him. 'If he could have said nothing, he would have,' said one interviewer.

Allen received a call from Genista McIntosh, executive director of the lately ennobled Royal National Theatre, saying she had heard the job was still open. Should she apply? With all speed, said Allen, putting her in touch with the head-hunters. The two women saw themselves as allies in a male-dominated field. McIntosh was the National's backroom girl, sorting out the nuts and bolts while Richard Eyre ruled the glamorous repertoire. A child of the Welfare

State, just short of fifty years old, she had only ever worked in subsidized theatre, first at the RSC and then at the National beside Eyre who was about to step down. She believed passionately in the citizen's right to enjoy the summits of cultural attainment but, although a Labour diehard, she took a practical view of the benefits of private sponsorship. 'Unlike some,' she told theatre students, 'I don't think the introduction of private sector funding was a pollutant.'[59]

Before McIntosh could send in her c.v., one of the head-hunters took Mary Allen aside and said: 'You could do this job. Why don't you apply?' Allen cocked her head and said she might consider it if Peter Gummer wanted her. She and Gummer had clashed fiercely at the Arts Council. In the rarified world of public relations, he did not expect a woman to overrule him and was taken aback when Allen did. Over time, they achieved a productive, if combustible, relationship.

Gummer responded enthusiastically to Allen's nomination and tried to talk her into the job. He also sounded out Stirling, who added his blessing. But Allen was concerned about leaving the Arts Council, where the Lottery Director was out of action with a broken skull and Lord Gowrie would be lost without her. She threw her support behind McIntosh who, in a sparkling interview, won over the panel, with one exception. Gummer said: 'I don't think she's good at handling stress.' It took several meetings before he was persuaded.

The announcement of Genista McIntosh's appointment on 4 July 1996 was widely acclaimed. She was a woman of proven theatrical know-how and dedication – calm, assiduous and self-effacing where Isaacs was blustery, mercurial and vain. Isaacs had been awarded a knighthood the previous weekend. Peter Gummer, ennobled by John Major, would succeed Stirling under his new title, Lord Chadlington. He was chuffed with the job, remarking that he had been going to the opera weekly for thirty-two years. He could not wait to get started.

Isaacs, however, was not the type go quietly. He had left Channel Four with a threat to throttle his successor and he did not like being cast as the villain in Covent Garden's downslide. He smarted at having to cut four operas – *Norma*, *Il Corsaro* (Verdi), *The Golden Cockerel* (Rimsky-Korsakov) and *Hérodiade* (Massenet) from his final season, leaving only two new shows: Verdi's *Macbeth* and

Palestrina by Hans Pfitzner, an eighty-year fixture in the German repertoire that had never been staged in Britain. The Royal Opera was celebrating its jubilee. Isaacs wanted to go out with a bang. In the event, he was lucky to escape with a whimper.

In the midst of his travails – with the Arts Council withholding its Lottery cheque, the Tower Bridge tent collapsing and *The House* oozing weekly into the nation's living rooms – Isaacs was snapped at seven one morning leaving the house of a senior colleague's estranged wife. A *Daily Mail* reporter asked on the doorstep if he was having an affair with Anne Dunhill, whose marriage to Anthony Russell-Roberts had broken up over his liaison with a Danish dancer. Isaacs said nothing. Dunhill, a tobacco heiress, told the *Mail* that he had been helping 'with my Latin translation'. She would later provide the paper with an amplified account and adapt her experiences as romantic fiction. 'Jeremy knew I was going to write a novel about us,' she told the *Mail*. 'It was my first time as an adultress and it was all quite exciting, rather like being a spy. I thought he had an open marriage. When he told me he didn't, I was conscience-stricken. But I persuaded myself that if it wasn't me, it would be someone else.'[60]

Isaacs held his tongue. Then, interviewed four years later about his memoir of the opera house which made no mention of the affair, he issued a snarl of defiance at the press. It was, he said 'a straight case of kiss and tell, which is a nastiness that obtrudes into British life to a degree which was unheard of thirty years ago and which is now commonplace. We all make mistakes, and that was a serious mistake on my part. I was stupid. I thought I was trying to help this woman over a bad patch. She obviously brought herself to believe it would last. But it was comparatively brief. ... It is completely behind me. Gillian has – whom I love very much – has put up with me. So it's over. Over. Finished. Gone. And yet a newspaper will leap and pay money to print it. It is – dreadful.'[61]

What Isaacs had failed to appreciate was that *Sun* and television exposure had made him a minor public figure, and hence a target for tabloid intrusion. Winning the Lottery and pulling on yellow socks for the camera had backfired in an ugly and predictable fashion, making public knowledge of a private lapse. Someone, perhaps Keith Cooper, should have warned him to watch his back. But Cooper had his hands full with a broadsheet press that were baying for human sacrifice as the price for the company's ineptitude.

Wounded and besieged, Isaacs was not alone in his plight. The tabloids, in a feeding frenzy, had staked out a dozen allegedly errant Tory MPs in their eagerness to exploit 'sleaze' and bring down an outworn Government. England at the close of the century was a snoopers' paradise, where no home was safe from long lenses and the Princess of Wales was hounded by paparazzi every hour of the day and night. She would be driven to her death. Jeremy Isaacs escaped slightly wounded to his natural habitat.

He had a television job to return to, in a production company set up by Gillian Widdicombe and producer Martin Smith five minutes' walk away from the ROH. Since the end of 1994, Isaacs had been involved in the making of *Cold War*, a twenty-four part sequel to *World at War*, and *Millennium*, a ten-part retrospect. 'I was general director of the Royal Opera House where it was agreed I could be involved in one major outside project,'[62] Isaacs explained. He credited Smith with driving the project. 'I have been there to back him up and,' wrote Isaacs, '. . . occasionally pointed the way.'[63] Widdicombe maintained that Isaacs 'hardly ever came in to the office'.[64] Nevertheless, people in authority wondered why the ROH board had allowed Isaacs to accept an absorbing extra-curricular role in the very years when all of his attention was required to steer the complex redevelopment and plan the unresolved closure period. No matter how tough conditions grew at the opera house, Isaacs kept one foot firmly in the television camp.

Genista McIntosh worked out six months' notice at the Royal National Theatre. She would take up her post in January 1997, and Isaacs was asked to leave as soon as she arrived, without so much as a day's handover. He would be paid a full salary for not working the following nine months. Stirling and Chadlington felt he was 'dying to go'. Isaacs was ambivalent. He did not like being evicted and would remain a board member until the house closed. His final half-year passed almost without incident, in a state of suspended animation. As the year ended, Chadlington noted that staff costs were half a million over budget. A further quarter of a million pounds had been lost in South America. Isaacs' last financial statement showed a deficit of three million pounds, of which two million pounds could be clawed back in identified savings. 'I feel I gee'd the place up a bit and handed it over in reasonable nick to my successors,' he said in parting.[65] 'He could have worked wonders if he had kept his mind on the job,' observed a senior Government official.[66]

Isaacs did not go gently. 'I was pushed,' he rasped in a television interview,[67] angering the rest of the board who felt he had been treated more fairly than perhaps he deserved. Months later he popped up as chairman of the London wing of the Salzburg Festival Trust, competing for donations and upmarket ticket sales with his former employer.

There were to be no ROH farewells for Isaacs, at his own insistence. He would return for the ceremonial closure in July 1997, announcing then from the stage that 'opera has a future here so long as two forces unite to defend it: the dedication of those on stage and behind who give it, and the passion of the audience – your passion – to enjoy it.'

In an open letter to his successor, Isaacs urged her to attend rehearsals, make a fuss of singers and get to bed before three in the morning. Above all, he exhorted her to innovate. 'Whatever the financial pressures that argue otherwise,' he wrote, 'it is crucial that we do not let a great lyric theatre slide, as it all too easily can, into the unthinking habit of safe repertory and safe production style. Adventure, I know, will be one of your watchwords, too.'[68]

Of the many qualities that Jeremy Isaacs had brought to Covent Garden, his dynamism had transformed the internal atmosphere and his modernist aspirations the production style. But the television know-how for which he was hired had rebounded against the institution in the most malevolent way. Television, under Jeremy Isaacs, turned the Royal Opera House into soap opera.

There was worse to come. The comic-opera era was about to unfold.

CHAPTER 10

Act Four: Where's the Door?
(January to August 1997)

ENGLAND, AT THE start of 1997, trembled on the brink of seismic upheaval. After eighteen years of Conservative rule, Tony Blair's renovated Labour Party had reclaimed the centre ground and was positioning itself to take power. Although its appeal was pitched at Middle England and its fiscal policies were prudent, Labour's agenda was radical. It aimed to set up independent governments for Scotland, Wales and Northern Ireland, to abolish the hereditary powers of the House of Lords and to rush a reluctant island into closer co-operation with Europe.

Aided by some of the best brains in the advertising and media industries, Blair employed the soap-powder trick and rebranded his party 'New' Labour. It was not so much a slogan as a statement of intent. All that was new would be hailed as healthy, useful and progressive. The old was soiled, tacky and corrupt. In the gleaming world of New Labour, the Royal Opera House and the traditional arts belonged decidedly to the old.

Genista McIntosh, known as Jenny, had one foot on either side of the old-new divide. An opera lover who bought her own tickets, she adored the excess and immediacy of live performance. Opera, she wrote, 'like all forms of theatre, is dependent for its power on performers and audience being present together in the same space at the same time to share an experience that will never be repeated again in exactly the same way. Mechanical reproductions, no matter how remarkable, cannot compare with the excitement and energy of being there, with all senses fully engaged . . . We must not breed a generation of opera lovers "spoilt" by the perfection of recorded sound . . . This is one of many reasons for ensuring that there are seats in opera houses available at prices people can afford.'[1]

As a card-carrying populist, however, she deplored the exclusivism of the house she had chosen to lead. Along with many in the arts, she had watched aghast as the company's antics brought the entire sector into disrepute. 'The allocation of £78 million to the ROH in 1995 (and their reaction to it) was probably the single most damaging event in the recent history of the arts in the UK,' she wrote. 'It gave licence to the latent hostility to art and artists that has been evident in this country for a long time.'[2]

To McIntosh and the theatrical profession, Covent Garden was no longer a flagship for British arts but a pirate vessel, afloat on the high seas and a danger to shipping. Her mission, as she saw it, was to bring the ROH back under the union flag, to tone down its élitism, renew its pact with the public and make its existence acceptable to her friends in New Labour. It was a Herculean task, but one that she approached with every semblance of confidence. A ballet board member who sat beside her at an early meeting felt she was 'thrilled about the job when she first arrived'.[3]

Equine featured and smartly dressed, McIntosh entered the opera house on 6 January and set about touring its far-flung departments. She radiated warmth and raised morale wherever she trod. 'She's lovely,' gushed one long-serving Gardener whose job would soon be abolished. Among McIntosh's first tasks would be to halve the payroll for closure, reducing the number of employees to five hundred and forty.

As Chief Executive, she entered the boardroom two rungs lower than Isaacs, who had been General Director and a member of the board. She was greeted courteously but condescendingly. Chadlington let it be known that he was in charge, while Vivien Duffield's voice was heard on all matters pertaining to money. The abrasive Mrs Duffield needed to raise one hundred million pounds in the next three years to pay for the redevelopment. 'I think people are probably scared of me,' she said, as McIntosh arrived, 'they are scared of anyone who points out what is wrong.'[4]

Tensions flared between the ROH Trust, which Mrs Duffield chaired, and the main board. She had hired Millbank Public Relations, at five thousand pounds a month 'to position the House and management team as sensitive, responsible, considerate, realistic' and 'good custodians of Lottery money'. She was not prepared to rely on Chadlington, whose company, Shandwick, flagged itself as 'the international leader in global reputation management'.

At a performing level, there was aggravated friction between the opera and ballet companies with Nicholas Payne riding roughshod over the two Anthonies, Dowell and Russell-Roberts. In talks with Sadler's Wells, Payne was team-leader with the Anthonies 'clinging on to his tails'.[5] The Arts Council had stipulated as a condition of the Lottery that ballet should have parity with opera. 'It was my impression that the interest of the Covent Garden board lay heavily with the opera company,' observed Prue Skene, who chaired the Arts Council's dance panel. Neither Chadlington nor McIntosh had a primary passion for ballet, which was squeezed at every turn. Dowell had prepared a fairly ambitious dance programme for the closure period. He emerged from the boardroom with the schedule in shreds, garnished with *Nutcracker*s and *Swan Lake*s. If he refused to accept the changes, Dowell was told, the Royal Ballet could be disbanded. 'Our priority had to be finding a way to keep the company going at full strength through the closure,' was the reason that McIntosh gave.[6]

'Anthony was absolutely suicidal,' said his friend, Dame Antoinette Sibley. 'He is fantastically loyal and would give his life for the company, but there came a point where they got to him.'

'I remember thinking, I just can't,' confessed Dowell. 'I took a walk over the Waterloo bridge because I had booked an appointment with Jenny and didn't know what to say. The responsibility was eating away at me, every day there was a new situation. The anxiety was wearing me thin. It was awful to wake up every morning nervous and dreading what you're going in for.

'Jenny was not long here, she had come in as a wonderful breath of air. I felt doubly bad at saying this to someone like her. But she was a wonderful listener, very sensible and very practical. She said to me, "this is awful, but your health must come first".'

Dowell went away to consider his position. By the time he returned, Genista McIntosh was gone.

Managing an opera house in the modern era was a high wire act with an alarming casualty toll. In the mid-90s, the Sovrintendente of La Scala, Carlo Fontana, was sacked for political reasons and reinstated after boycott threats by Pavarotti. Two music directors of the Bastille Opéra, Daniel Barenboim and Myung Whun Chung, were fired on grounds of cost and repertoire, each winning huge damages in court. Finland built itself an opera house after seventy-five years of statehood and lost both the music director and the finance director within the first season; the artistic director followed two years later. Israel created an opera house for its jubilee, performing a triple public sacrifice in the opening season of the managing director, the music director and the Mayor of Tel Aviv, who had reportedly fiddled the street-paving budgets to fund the palace of art. The Teatro Real in Madrid reopened six years late, having lost both music director and artistic director amid charges of 'rampant provincialism and xenophobia'; the Liceo in Barcelona burned down and was con-stitutionally restructured.

Resignations were the roughage that kept the opera machine in working order, the spice that titivated tongues between acts of art. Ruptures were routine and rarely evoked much interest beyond a claque of cognoscenti. What happened to Genista McIntosh, how-ever, became a national issue, presenting as it did a mirror image of the spirit of the times. Shrouded in mystery and misinformation, it became the focus for two public inquiries and a political backlash that brought the ROH to the verge of abolition.

There was nothing out of the ordinary about her first two months. At the end of January, Deborah MacMillan (who succeeded Skene in the chair of the Arts Council's dance panel) complained that the dress rehearsal of *Prince of the Pagodas*, in front of a paying audience, was also the first time the orchestra had played the music in the presence of dancers.[7] *Plus ça change*. Weeks later, a crucial film section was omitted from *Anastasia*. McIntosh maintained that its absence 'did not detract from the performance'.[8]

The deficit figure fluctuated. In the absence of a finance director it was hard to know exactly how much cash was in hand. Uncertainty can breed anxiety, but McIntosh's dilemma was no worse than Isaacs' had been in his last six months without a finance director. The new chief executive appeared in February before Skene's Lottery panel, with Chadlington, to outline their plans for the closure period. Chadlington made the opening remarks, but McIntosh carried the rest of the meeting. 'The tensions between them had not yet surfaced,' said Skene. If McIntosh resented Chadlington planting himself and a secretary in an office next to hers, she said nothing. Once, when she came to the Arts Council looking wan, Mary Allen sought her out and said, 'you do know, don't you, that we'll give you any and every support that we can. Any time you need us, we're here for you.'[9] On 20 March, Allen informed

McIntosh that the Council had agreed to hand over the £23.5 million second tranche of Lottery money – on condition that it received in future 'integrated monthly cashflow' statements.[10] Members of the Council were getting edgy over the lack of clear financial information from the ROH.

At the end of March, McIntosh announced plans for the first season of exile. The best news was that Haitink had agreed to stay on as music director. 'It seems almost beyond comprehension,' noted the *Daily Telegraph*, 'that Covent Garden should have left its closure plans so late and so incomplete.'[11] Ismene Brown, the *Telegraph*'s robust dance critic, described the season as a 'betrayal' of the Royal Ballet. 'There will be six new opera productions in the first six months. And for the ballet? None.' She reported that 'wholly unacceptable pressures' had been exerted on Dowell 'to abandon by far the best option – to take the Royal Ballet to the nation's cities (agreement had even been reached with other ballet companies).'[12] Brown urged the ballet to declare its independence of the ROH management.

Internal rifts were widening. In one of two interviews that she gave as chief executive, McIntosh described the ROH as a company that had been 'put together in bits, rather than springing into coherent life like the National Theatre'.[13] She formed an executive board to pull the strands together, but her executives were disunited. Three of them – Payne, Russell-Roberts and Morris – had contested her job. 'I wish we had been more supportive as a management team when she began to feel the strain,' said Keith Cooper in retrospect. 'I don't think we supported her enough.'[14]

There was not much she could do to harmonize relations between the Board, the Friends and the fundraising Trust. Vivien Duffield, not the most reticent of activists, articulated her requirements in a stentorian tone that could chill the faint-hearted. 'Just for the record,' said Duffield, 'I never had a row with Jenny. I don't think I was ever in the same room alone with Jenny.'

In April, the country went into abeyance for a General Election. Chadlington spent much of his time at Downing Street. He urged John Major to run a television campaign depicting Tony Blair as the Devil. Major, knowing that Blair was a religious man, fastidiously refused. With his mind on impending political disaster, Chadlington eased his grip on the ROH controls.

McIntosh and Allen met in Hayden Phillips' office to survey the political outlook. An official noted that McIntosh looked thin and spent the whole meeting with her legs wound around the chair, talking slightly off the agenda.[15]

A letter written by Lord Gowrie to the *Sunday Times* kept the stew simmering. Irked by criticism of the Arts Council's handling of ROH grants, Gowrie described the original closure plans as 'quite frankly, a shambles'.[16] His criticism was directed at Stirling and Isaacs but was misconstrued as a coded attack on the new regime. Allen and Chadlington had a working breakfast on 25 April to calm the waters.

Chadlington confided that he was worried about McIntosh. As early as the second week of February, he had been warned by the head-hunter, Michael Knight, who was searching for a new finance director, that McIntosh was in 'a state of increasing personal crisis'.[17] At the end of February, she went to Chadlington and told him she wanted to leave; he gently dissuaded her. On the 27th, the board commended her 'excellent and unstinting' work. By mid-April, McIntosh felt she could take it no longer. On the 16th, she asked to resign. Chadlington urged her to give it one last try. Neither showed any sign of stress outside their private offices.

McIntosh plied an upbeat line to the press. 'Until now, everyone has been preoccupied with endings,' she said. 'I think we've reached the point when people can talk about beginnings.'[18] At a board meeting on 28 April she appeared cool and in control.

Two days later, Chadlington took Mary Allen to breakfast and confirmed that McIntosh was wobbling. Allen reacted coolly. The Arts Council had, at any given time, two or three orchestral and theatre managers who were desperate to quit and were being held in place by strong tea and sympathy. Some survived, others not. Knowing McIntosh, Allen expected her to pull through. She suggested that he should consult the Heritage Department, meaning Hayden Phillips.

In the small hours of 2 May, Labour romped to power. Key supporters, McIntosh included, were summoned by Blair's campaign manager and Herbert Morrison's grandson, Peter Mandelson, to dance the night away at the Royal Festival Hall, artistic totem of Labour power, old and new. McIntosh was unable to share the jubilation. Four days later, on 6 May, she told Chadlington that she could not carry on. He asked her to sleep on it. She said she could neither eat nor sleep; he advised her not to risk her health. The next morning she wrote a two-page resignation letter by hand from her home in Tufnell Park and had it delivered to the Connaught Hotel, where the chairman was having a lunchtime meeting. Her tone was regretful but firm; she asked to leave as quickly as possible.

Pandemonium ensued. Chadlington called Mary Allen after lunch and offered her the chief executive's job. He demanded an immediate answer. Allen was used to making quick decisions. Friends said that she weighed, on the one hand, her loyalty to Lord Gowrie and the Arts Council and, on the other, her ambition and career plan. The pay at Covent Garden was fifty per cent higher than she was earning as secretary general of the ACE, just over ninety thousand a year. She knew the parameters of the job, having scrutinized it for five years, and felt she could do better than previous incumbents. She had experience of running an arts centre at Brentford, on the western outskirts of London, and an early career as an actress. She was forty-five years old and knew that the best jobs do not often come begging.

Personal security is usually paramount in decisions of this sort. Gowrie's ACE chairmanship, under Labour, was bound to be brief; his successor might want a different secretary general. In Allen's mind, there was an additional concern. Her husband, Nigel Pantling, head of corporate finance at Hambros Bank, had been involved that spring in an ill-timed takeover bid for the Co-operative Wholesale Society, one of the Labour Party's historic adjuncts. The bid aborted and Pantling now faced an inquiry from the Securities and Futures Authority which could rule him out of City work for years. There was no imputation of dishonesty, but his earning power was likely to be drastically curtailed whatever the findings of the inquiry. The inquiry continues. A better job was an offer his wife could not lightly refuse. Taking all these factors quickly into consideration, Mary Allen accepted the job – on condition that each and every member of the ROH board separately endorsed her appointment. Chadlington began phoning them for approval.

One board member, Robert Gavron, had given half a million pounds to New Labour's election fund and was friendly with the newly installed Heritage Secretary, Chris Smith. Chadlington asked Gavron to set up an emergency meeting with Smith, that very day if possible. Smith had been a minister for half a week. A bookish man with a doctorate in the Lakeland poets, he was the first member of a British Cabinet to live an openly gay lifestyle. Before the election, he had been intensively coached by Labour veterans and former civil servants not to let himself be dominated by the Whitehall mandarinate. With these strictures possibly in mind, Smith apparently omitted to tell his permanent secretary, Hayden Phillips, that he was seeing the Covent Garden chairman on a matter of great urgency. Had Phillips known of the meeting, he would have been duty-bound to attend and might well have influenced the outcome. Instead, a junior official took minutes.

Chadlington, battered by his electoral débâcle, informed the neophyte minister that his chief executive had resigned and that he wanted to poach Mary Allen from the Arts Council, subject to Gowrie's permission. It was essential to make a rapid appointment without a proper selection process, he stressed, because of the company's difficult financial situation. Chadlington made it clear, he later maintained, that Allen might not be able to take up the job instantaneously; her availability would depend on Gowrie's willingness to let her go without serving notice. He emerged from the meeting under the impression that Smith was 'happy'.[19]

The official minute, submitted to a subsequent inquiry, gave a slightly different account. Smith declared himself 'extremely unhappy about many of the circumstances that had arisen', but agreed, after a long discussion, not to 'raise any further objections' so long as Chadlington conveyed his reservations to the Arts Council and the ROH Board. Smith would later tell a public inquiry that he had no idea Allen would not start work until September. Had he been told this salient fact he 'would have questioned even more strongly the circumstances of urgency which they were pressing upon me.'[20] Given that he and Chadlington were political enemies, they were unlikely to sing the same tune. The departmental record suggests that Chadlington was being frugal with the facts. However, Chadlington did not have all the facts to hand; he had no way of knowing whether Gowrie would release Allen, or make her work out three months' notice.

He reported back to Allen, who tried to catch Gowrie before he left the Arts Council that evening. She found him in his hat and coat, and booked an appointment for eleven o'clock next morning. On being told of her proposed transfer, Gowrie was shocked, bitter and bewildered – 'gob-smacked', as he later put it. He trusted Allen and, though their relationship was entirely proper, liked to refer to her as 'my working wife'. He viewed her departure as a marital betrayal. All he could say by way of blessing was, 'well, at least you're going off with a friend of mine'.

For the next five days, the entire cast kept up appearances and not a word leaked to the press. On Monday 12 May, the ROH board met at Chadlington's company, Shandwick, to ratify Allen's appointment. One member who was in America was reached by phone and told that McIntosh was leaving for the sake of her health, to be replaced by Mary Allen. 'I was presented,' said Jeremy Isaacs, 'with a *fait accompli*.'[21] He would have recommended that Payne and Morris form an interim management until a strong candidate was selected by due process. 'I was rung up in Israel,' said Vivien Duffield, 'and by that time it was a *fait accompli*.'

After the board dispersed, Chadlington spoke to Gowrie, who phoned around his Council members to tell them that Mary Allen was going to Covent Garden. The following day, Gowrie announced her departure to the press, insisting that he had 'been consulted throughout' and that the ROH 'could not have made a more appropriate appointment given the special circumstances'. Chadlington simultaneously welcomed Mary Allen's appointment, along with a new finance director, Richard Hall. He worded the announcements himself, overriding a last-minute demurral from Genista McIntosh on the reasons given for her resignation.

McIntosh, he said, was leaving 'due to ill health . . . I and all my colleagues wish her a speedy return to full health and much success and happiness in the future'. Chadlington added that he rushed the appointment through because, as he had told Chris Smith, 'we would go bust if we didn't choose a chief executive straight away . . . those who say I acted too speedily simply do not understand the financial situation of the house.'[22]

The B-word – bust, bankrupt, broke – had been uttered for the first time. It would become a refrain of Chadlington's, a thin red line of defence. Under press questioning, he admitted that the deficit had shot up to four and a half million pounds, but there was no immediate cause for concern. Mary Allen would take up her duties in September once she had wound up her former job and taken a well-earned holiday. The Arts Council met the next morning, Wednesday. Allen promptly realized that she could not give advice on anything pertaining to its largest client which she was about to join. She asked to be released immediately, but resolved, with Chadlington, to take a break in the hope of avoiding the opprobrium that had attended his own direct transfer from the giver to the receiver.

She had, in any event, been advised to take some rest after a stubborn chest infection and a debilitating course of antibiotics. Clearing her desk, Mary Allen retreated to her Suffolk cottage, where she received a warm note of congratulation and encouragement from Genista McIntosh, who was in another rural refuge, hiding from the press. Both women asked for nothing more than to lie low until the storm blew over.

But this was not to be a teacup squall. So much about the transfer was couched in the euphemisms and ambiguities of spin doctors that the public interest was piqued. Staff at the ROH, distressed at McIntosh's departure, hissed Chadlington when he gave them the news. Chris Smith, smarting from being wrongfooted in his first public act, called a departmental inquiry into the 'probity' of the Royal Opera House. Parliament was stirring and the press were up in arms. Rodney Milnes in *The Times* accused Chadlington and Allen of colluding in the removal of McIntosh and 'mounting what looks very much like a coup'.[23] The present writer, in the *Daily Telegraph*, argued that what Covent Garden needed from a new Heritage Secretary was 'a public inquiry and a new constitution to protect the house in future from the pressures that put paid to Genista McIntosh's best intentions.'[24]

Inquiries flowed hot and fast. Lord Gowrie appointed a respected lawyer, Edward Walker-Arnott, to investigate allegations of collusion. Walker-Arnott would discover 'a long history of uneasiness' between the the Arts Council and Covent Garden, but no active wrongdoing. Barely had his inquest opened than Parliament got into the act. Gerald Kaufman, sometime press secretary to Harold Wilson and now chairman of the National Heritage Select Committee, announced that his inquiry would be held in public, with the protagonists called to account in front of television cameras. Chadlington's speed strategy had spectacularly backfired.

Doubt was instantly cast on the official reasons for McIntosh's departure. Friends and family let it be known that she was neither physically nor mentally ill, aware that any such imputation could damage her future prospects. McIntosh herself wrote to *The Times*,[25] denying reports that she had been pushed out by conspiracies or pressures. 'The decision to leave was mine alone,' she said.

In her eventual evidence before the Kaufman committee, McIntosh was gently questioned about the reasons for her decision.

'I left because I was extremely unhappy in the job,' she said. 'There is no doubt that being extremely unhappy causes one to be very distressed.'

'What was causing you distress?' asked one MP.

'It was caused partly by what I regard now, looking back, as a mismatch between me and the organization.'

Pressed again on the issue of ill health, she conceded: 'Had I continued in my job, I might well have become ill.'

In a further memorandum to Kaufman, unpublished in his report, McIntosh attempted to clarify differences of interpretation over the reason given for her departure. She had never been ill, she said, and she doubted the need to say that she was. But by the time she voiced her doubts matters were too far advanced and any delay would have caused embarrassment. Lord Chadlington was entitled to believe that, had she continued in the job, she might well have become ill; and he acted on his judgement in the best interests of the opera house. For her part, she wished it to be known that she dissented from his decision to ascribe her departure to health reasons, though not strongly enough to stop him from doing so, or in any way questioning his good intentions.[26]

No further light was shed on the matter and Genista McIntosh was allowed to leave the public arena with her integrity intact. She never said another word about her time at Covent Garden. She told colleagues, as she told Kaufman, that she found the company's structures 'diffuse' and 'fragmented'. She felt uncomfortable with internal conflicts and was unused to being shouted at by members of the board. None of this amounted to credible grounds for resignation. The mystery persists, and only a private confessor or psychoanalyst may be in possession of the full story.

The theatre closes ranks to protect its own as rigorously as the legal and medical professions. A recent Data Protection Act blocks public access to key documents in the public domain. McIntosh's associates, including ROH board members who were shown a copy of her resignation letter, sealed their lips. Nevertheless, a close scrutiny of ambient events and internal documents reveals a great deal about the motives that made McIntosh's resignation inevitable.

Word of her unhappiness percolated the upper echelons of English theatre from mid-February, when a sabotaged meeting appeared to affect her previously positive attitude. McIntosh had gone to Sadler's Wells to finalize rental contracts with its manager

Ian Albery, an ex-West End man with a strong public ethos. Albery knew McIntosh from the National and considered her 'totally honest, totally skilled'. She arrived in Islington to find two board members awaiting her. One was Chadlington, the other James Butler, a director of the accountants KPMG and a close associate of Vivien Duffield. Asked afterwards if she had not thought of attending this crucial meeting, Duffield said, 'no, I sent a strong man'.

Overcoming her surprise at being shadowed, McIntosh went into the meeting with two directors in tow. Barely had she begun to speak than Chadlington jumped in, telling Albery: 'You're negotiating with me now.' McIntosh dropped her head and said nothing for the rest of the meeting. Albery, incensed at her humiliation, exacted tough terms, some three hundred thousand pounds more than he expected to charge. 'There are many ways of skinning somebody in the theatre,' he laughed.[27] When McIntosh returned days later to sign the contracts she told him, 'Ian, you know I would never have agreed to this deal.'

It was a turning point in her relations with the board, a moment when McIntosh recognized that they could treat her like a vassal, damaging her standing in the wider theatrical world. Chadlington would later tell Mary Allen: 'I wasn't undermining Jenny, and it's terribly important they should not think I am undermining you.'[28] One of his close allies, expressing high regard for McIntosh, said: 'Peter is not a man who sits silently at meetings – he likes to get things done.'[29] To Albery, it did not look quite so amicable. 'To be treated like that,' he said, 'amounted to constructive dismissal.' Even if all the participants had taken Trappist vows – and several versions of the meeting soon raged like bushfire on the theatrical grapevine – the incident would have triggered a survival instinct in a less sensitive mind than McIntosh's. All she had to offer was proven competence. When that was overidden, her future was at stake.

Her resignation letter to Chadlington touched delicately but pointedly on such fears. She was finding the job increasingly difficult, she said, despite the board's support. Her best option, she felt, was to escape before the job overwhelmed her and affected her standard of performance. The concern she expressed was not for her physical well-being but for her professional reputation. An unhappy spell at a problem-ridden opera house would blight her prospects of ever returning to a senior position in the theatre world. When Chadlington showed her his press release, she asked him to omit any mention of health or anything else that might provoke damaging speculation. She wanted to walk out of the Royal Opera House untouched, for better or worse, and ready to resume her career. In a private communication to a close colleague, she confessed that she lacked the courage to tackle the ROH and felt that Mary Allen was being extremely brave – always a double-edged compliment.

The fuzzy reasons for her departure were nothing more sinister than an over-developed sense of self-preservation, allied to her known virtues of prudence and caution. She received a £23,000 pay-off and in August returned to her old job in the Royal National Theatre, alongside Trevor Nunn. She also joined the Trust Board of Sadler's Wells Theatre, cementing her friendship with Ian Albery. Two years later, Tony Blair elevated her to the peerage. A friend who tried over lunch, on her way to the House of Lords, to get her to discuss Covent Garden elicited nothing more than a pained and distant look.

The first three administrators of the Royal Opera House ruled for forty-two years, the fourth for just four months and a week. For the next four months, there was to be a vacuum. Lord Chadlington alternated with Sir Kit McMahon, former Governor of the Bank of England (and chairman of the ROH development board), in manning the office.

A redundancy deal was struck with the stage union, Bectu, allowing for the dismissal of virtually the entire stage and front-of-house staff in exchange for Bectu being authorized to represent clerical employees, an unprecedented concession to internal activists. Chris Smith kept well clear of the enterprise after his initial blunder, but New Labour was serving notice of future intent. Mark Fisher, the second-rank arts minister, told Chadlington publicly that he must convert the ROH into the 'people's opera house', an ominously vague term. 'My objective,' said Fisher, 'was to underline the importance that the Government attaches to improving access to the ROH, notably through more low-cost seats, more touring and use of broadcast facilities.'[30] A retroactive price tag was being pinned to the Lottery cheque, in an untested currency called 'access'.

At the end of June, as Britain handed Hong Kong back to China in an end-of-empire ceremony, the ROH deficit crept over five million pounds and members of the board were asked, for the first time, 'to consider whether the House is a going concern' – as the minutes put it[31] – or whether it should be put into liquidation. A loan of a million pounds each from two unnamed supporters (apparently Sainsbury and Duffield) staved off the need for instant action, but this was a crisis deferred, not a problem solved. Early bookings for the exile season looked gloomy, with the ballet at Labatt's Apollo running at barely ten per cent of budget.

On stage, events were building up to a dramatic conclusion. The production of *Macbeth* was cancelled a week before opening night because, amid mass redundancies and backstage wind-down, there had not been enough rehearsal time. Nicholas Payne took responsibility for a projected £200,000 loss and offered his resignation to the board, which refused to accept it. Another executive resignation could have undermined confidence and brought the house down.

On Saturday 12 July, Haitink gave a repetition of his masterly *Meistersinger* and on Monday 14th the Prince of Wales came to a closing gala, sealed with a *Sleeping Beauty*'s kiss from Darcey Bussell. The opening twirl of 1946 was a fitting farewell to the venerable old building. The Prime Minister conspicuously failed to attend. He was planning a party at Number Ten for the New Britain – a motley of fashion designers, Formula One racers, media types and rock singers, notably the Gallaghers of Oasis, who represented his vision of the nation reborn.

The next morning, the wreckers moved in. Patrons, passers-by and anyone with an eye for memorabilia were invited to take objects from the skips. Two former singers walked off with red velvet seats, which they transplanted to their television lounges.

Ten days later, the Kaufman committee held its first hearings, a fairly low-key examination of Gowrie, McIntosh and Isaacs, followed by Chadlington and the editor of *Opera*, Rodney Milnes. The sessions attracted little attention as the media unwound for the summer. A brief exchange between Kaufman and McIntosh gave some foreboding of the horrors in store. Had she, asked Kaufman solicitously, been shocked by the ROH's 'clubbiness'? McIntosh dodged the question; this was not a word she would have used. He rephrased the question. Had the clubbable atmosphere made her feel 'like an intruder?' Genista McIntosh gave an unseasonally wintry smile. 'Let's say that's not entirely unfair, chairman,' she replied.

One Friday afternoon, I went to see Solti to discuss his forthcoming memoirs. Sitting in his studio in a heavy cardigan and rollneck sweater, shivering despite the summer heat, he looked happier and more relaxed than I had ever seen him. His elder daughter, Gabrielle, was getting engaged that evening and the whole family were about to go on holiday, to his summer house in Italy. We talked about his struggles and successes, his future plans and his abiding love of women. 'Vat you want,' he upbraided me, 'I should be homosexual?'

The only worries on his mind were the general decline in musical attendances and the future of Covent Garden. He intended to do something about both issues when he got back. He was going to talk to Paul McCartney, who lived up the road, to see how they could enliven symphony concerts and he would get hold of Tony Blair to tell him he had to help the opera house. 'This can not go on,' said Solti, separating each syllable. The next morning, he left his adoptive country, never to return alive.

CHAPTER 11

Coming up for Eyre
(September 1997 to November 1998)

ON THE MORNING of 31 August 1997, the country awoke to the hushed tones of newscasters struggling to cope with the dignities of grief. Diana, Princess of Wales – 'the People's Princess' as Tony Blair renamed her that day – had been killed in a Paris car-smash with her lover, Dodi Fayed, after being pursued all month by swarms of photographers. She was thirty-six years old.

During the day crowds began to gather at the royal palaces. Many laid flowers, some wept. Diana's death had opened a floodgate of emotions. Alive, she had sought out the doomed and the deprived, visiting hospitals unannounced at the dead of night, holding hands with men who were dying of Aids. Her rejection by Prince Charles struck chords in the lives of many lone women. In her long-running media war with the Royal Family, she spoke for a new post-familial social order, while the Queen seemed locked into a rigid, failing nuclear capsule. Rejecting the dreary remoteness of other royals, Diana did workouts, took her sons to the movies and chose exotic lovers of Asian and Middle Eastern extraction. In the months before her death she had exposed herself to the war in Bosnia and waged a campaign against landmines that blew the legs off little children.

She was a wish-symbol of New Britain: liberal, multicultural and touchingly vulnerable. The stiff upper lip had given way to the brimming eye. England was acknowledging emotion. The spirit of the Blitz had dissolved in a wash of genuine mourning and sentimental indulgence, some of it resembling self-pity. The writer Julian Barnes called it 'look-at-me-grief'. Diana herself had been wealthy, white and a scion of one of England's oldest dynasties.

All week long, the crowds grew and the media were baffled. Reaction was rising from the ground up, and no one knew where it began, or might end. 'London is in a pre-revolutionary situation,' said a visiting historian. The Royal parks were flung open at night and thousands milled by floodlight at the gates of Kensington Palace, their flowers and messages piled above head height. Half a million letters were received at Buckingham Palace. The Queen was forced to break all precedent and bow to the coffin, as anti-monarchism surged and swelled. On the morning of the funeral, a Saturday, London was as still as Yukon City after the gold ran out. Elton John sobbed a song at Westminster Abbey and Earl Spencer, Diana's brother, delivered a barbed eulogy. The cortège was waved through the streets by citizens standing fifteen thick. 'Bye, Di,' they cried. Half the population watched on television. Twenty-one million copies of Elton John's song were sold in aid of Diana's charities. Cabinet ministers talked of renaming the August bank holiday Diana Day, and Heathrow, Diana Airport.

Many pontificated about changes in the national character, as Virginia Woolf had done in 1910.[1] The country, they said, would never be the same again. That assumption was partly true, but for other, political reasons. In Scotland and Wales, a devolution referendum that month dispelled the aftermath of Diana's death with a heady foretaste of independence. In Northern Ireland, the IRA had agreed an 'unequivocal' ceasefire. In London, the Prime Minister called for a new 'age of compassion'. Strangely, at a time of death, there was an intimation of new beginnings.

Coming home from Diana's funeral, I was informed of the death of Georg Solti. He had suffered a heart attack while on holiday and, chatting in bed in a hospital in Antibes, was felled by a relapse. Many in the world of music found his death at eighty-four as hard to accept as Diana's. He seemed indestructible, a force of destiny. With Solti gone, the podium lost the last of its titans.

At the next meeting of the ROH board, Vivien Duffield suggested that something should be done to commemorate Princess Diana, whose association with the ROH, 'though less than with ENB, had been considerable'. She recalled that the late princess had 'attended many performances at the House and had even danced on the stage with Wayne Sleep'.[2] The board might consider naming a ballet studio after her. They liked that idea, urging Mrs Duffield to raise funds for the purpose from the American Friends of Covent Garden.

The meeting was otherwise preoccupied with financial shortfalls and the Arts Council's preposterous refusal to show them an advance copy of the Walker-Arnott report which, it was stressed, 'had been prepared with public money'. Judging by the minutes, no board member saw fit to mention the death of Georg Solti, let alone to stand in tribute to an artist who, more than anyone, had raised Covent Garden's sights from the insular to the international.

Mary Allen turned up for work on the morning after Diana's death, refreshed and invigorated after an 'insulation' period in which she had no contact with either the Arts Council or Covent Garden. She spent the day finding her way around the warren of temporary Floral Street offices and meeting senior staff. She found the situation confusing and decided to keep a diary. Other senior staff were also keeping a private log of internal conversations, some at their lawyers' advice. The element of trust was fast evaporating. Allen eventually published her diaries; other records fell into my hands. Together, they reveal a portrait of the way capable people behave under the lash of events beyond their control and in hourly anticipation of disaster. There were few smiles, or lifeboats, to spare. At least on the *Titanic*, there had been time to dance before the men on the bridge realized that they were going down.

Allen's first priority was to redress the company's negative image. She told the flamboyant Keith Cooper that his job would be restructured to cover sales and broadcasting; a new executive would handle external relations with the public, press and politicians. Cooper was wounded but compliant. Allen's next task was to persuade Nicholas Payne of the Royal Opera and Anthony Russell-Roberts of the Royal Ballet to accept that there would have to be a unified artistic strategy, a mission foredoomed to failure. 'One of the first things Mary said to me,' Payne recalled, 'was, "you know I'm keeping a diary." I thought to myself, better be careful what you say in front of her.'

On the Friday of her first week, Allen had a two hour meeting with the finance director, Richard Hall. Expecting to see a planned deficit of £800,000 for the twenty-seven months of closure, she was shown a ten million pound black hole – on top of the existing £4.7 million accumulated deficit. The entire ROH annual turnover was only forty million pounds. 'Some mistake, surely,' she muttered, asking Hall to run another set of calculations. There was always a possibility that heads of department had slipped in extra costs between one chief executive and the next. Hall came back with the same bottom line.

There had been no mistake and, from that moment on, there would be no turning back.

The mystery of the unforeseen millions has yet to be satisfactorily resolved. John Tooley maintained that, in his time, Covent Garden had 'the most sophisticated management reporting information system in the operatic world', a cashflow control so admirable that the Met sent a man over to copy it. Jeremy Isaacs argued that he knew at all times how much money was coming in and going out, and that he left the company with 'adequate contingencies'.[3] Two teams of independent accountants had clawed over the books since his departure. The Arts Council had inserted its own monitor, Richard Pulford, to survey the balancing of budgets. Genista McIntosh had been financially competent and the acting finance director, in the year between Timms and Hall, had been by all accounts outstanding.

Yet, during the repeated crunching of numbers, a gap of ten million pounds had eluded some of the finest accountants and administrators in the kingdom – not to mention two top bankers and an accountancy firm director on the ROH board. As she wrestled with the balance sheets, Allen would uncover 'an almost total absence of proper financial information or controls'.[4] She concluded that the systems had broken down during the upheavals of closure, but this did not explain the forecasting lacunae over two previous years when Mary Allen, at the Arts Council, kept demanding firm financial targets and failed to receive them.

It would be presumptuous and pointless to attach blame to any individual for these prolonged shortcomings. In the 'diffuse and fragmented' structure of the ROH, the fault lay with the failures over half a century to weld the company into a coherent unity where ballet and opera companies talked to one another and the sundry trusts and supporters' groups worked together to a common purpose. Allen, in her first board meeting, gave a grim presentation which showed how individual departments made their own budgets and then refused to meet them. If they ran out of cash, they were used to being bailed out. In purely organizational terms, the ROH had become virtually unmanageable.

Administratively, it was years behind the times. When Judy Grahame joined as director of external relations, she found that no computer in the building could communicate with any other, because every department had purchased a different brand of software. Managers guarded their secrets and defended fiefdoms. Gardeners conspired and protected each other's jobs. Grahame, who had brilliantly repositioned the Philharmonia Orchestra during the Hoffmann process, was hard pressed to conceive an overall image strategy for an antiquated edifice that appeared so cracked and torn.

Where the money would be found to bridge the ten million pound gap was unknown. Any hopes of extra Lottery help could be ruled out. Late in August, it became clear that New Labour aimed to halve Lottery spending on the arts and divert the surplus to a sixth good cause – itself, specifically to new health and education projects. The Government was also refusing to let the ROH use money from the sale of surplus buildings for its running costs. The Arts Council was in a huff and the usual sources of spare cash – such as the benevolent patrons of the Drogheda Circle – were being stretched to their limits by Vivien Duffield's £100 million development appeal.

The board, faced with the facts, were, as Allen put it, 'terrified – like rabbits in headlights'.[5] The chairman refused to sign off the previous year's accounts since he could not confirm that the company was a going concern. It is illegal under English law for a firm to continue trading if it goes into debt and has no prospect of sufficient incoming funds. Members of the board could be held personally liable in such circumstances; they could even face criminal charges. It was suddenly no longer an honour to be on the ROH board but distinctly a danger. Faces went white around the board table as Chadlington asked for time to work on a rescue plan.

In her third week at Covent Garden, I ran into Mary Allen at a champagne breakfast in the National Gallery, after a private viewing of the Seurat exhibition. She sounded cheerily upbeat and told me how much she was enjoying the job. Her laughter rang a tone too bright, but I was dashing off to catch a flight to Washington D.C. and made a mental note to pay closer attention to Covent Garden when I got back at the end of the month.

Attention then got deflected by upheavals at ENO where Dennis Marks had resigned; with suspicious alacrity, the Arts Council gave ENO a five million pound 'stabilization' grant to pay off debts and put its house in order. The man favoured to succeed Marks was Nicholas Payne, who was fed up with Covent Garden in-fighting and preferred to run a theatre his own way, without worrying about ballets and building work. Paul Daniel, his former partner at Opera North, was to become ENO's music director and there was an opportunity to renew their dream team. Payne received a mollifying call from Mary Allen, who could not afford to lose him.

The Royal Opera season had opened quietly at the Barbican with Handel's *Giulio Cesare* and Rameau's *Platée*. Spirits rose with *The Turn of the Screw* in Deborah Warner's production, vindicating Payne's decision to branch into more intimate operas than would normally be seen at Covent Garden. Regular patrons had no trouble finding the Barbican or coping with Britten. Where they bridled was at the windswept Labatt's Apollo and the dilapidated Shaftesbury Theatre, home to a *Merry Widow* that failed to raise much of a laugh.

The pigeons were racing home to splatter ROH heads. The Royal Ballet lost £750,000 in a month and the *Widow* wept for want of stardust. Felicity Lott did her best, but the part had been cast for Kiri te Kanawa, and she had lost faith in Covent Garden, or vice versa. 'Singers are the last people that matter (there),' she told a BBC talk show. 'It has not had good management for quite a long time. The last time they called me was three years ago.'

This was a large exaggeration from an artist undergoing a painful divorce, but other strictures that she uttered rang painfully true. At Covent Garden, said Kiri, 'they have no people on the ground to help the singers. When you are giving your body (to the audience, which is what you do when you sing) you need somebody there. At the Met they still truly look after you. They have one person babysitting. We need babysitting. We need our bottoms wiped a lot and we need a lot of pampering, because we're special. We do think of ourselves as being more special than other people.'[6] During the closure, she announced her retirement from opera. She would never sing again with the company that made her. 'Covent Garden?' she said to me. 'I don't think they even know my telephone number.'

She was not the only star to stay away. Bryn Terfel made it clear that he would not appear with the Royal Opera during its wandering years.[7] The Italian mezzo Cecilia Bartoli, whose records outsold every other diva apart from Callas, was happy to sing opera at the Barbican, but not with the troupe from the Royal.[8] Pavarotti and Carreras were not interested, and only Domingo showed concern and support. The exile era lacked glamour and the public voted with its feet.

On the penultimate day of October, the Kaufman committee resumed its hearings. It could hardly have picked a tougher day for the ROH. All month long, Mary Allen had been battling with insolvency. The company had paid out £600,000 in cheques when there was only £400,000 in its account, a mishap attributed to antiquated ledger keeping. Chadlington was arranging emergency cover from a blind trust, but Allen had called in lawyers and liquidation practitioners and knew what had to be done if the creditors came pressing. At this moment there was no prospect of paying the next month's wages.

At an extraordinary board meeting on the 20th, Richard Hall and the KPMG auditor had outlined the gravity of the position and Vivien Duffield called for immediate liquidation to stop the financial haemorrhaging. A second meeting was scheduled for the afternoon of Thursday the 30th at which the company's fate would be decided.

That morning, the *Guardian* ran a front-page report saying that ROH cheques were bouncing and salaries were in arrears. Keith Cooper had categorically denied this when approached by the reporter and Robert Gavron, who was chairman of the *Guardian* and an ROH board member, hit the roof and promised to read the riot act.[9] Damage, however, had been done, and arts correspondents hovered like carrion crows as Mary Allen took her seat in committee room 15, in front of the renamed Culture, Media and Sport Committee – 'National Heritage' having been banned by New Labour as oldspeak.

Both Allen and Chadlington had rehearsed their lines at a mock tribunal earlier in the week, standard procedure when appearing before a hostile panel. Allen had been advised by Cooper to wear a black polo neck sweater, to cover up her neck which reddened when she grew agitated. She was asked by Kaufman if she wanted to make a short statement.

While Allen was speaking, Gerald Kaufman had shuffled his papers and put on a show of looking uninterested. An embittered man of caustic wit, with the clammy eye and handshake of a captive dolphin, he had been dropped without obvious cause from Labour's front bench in 1992 and at sixty-seven saw no further hope of high office. This was the nearest he would ever get to wielding power. Kaufman was an avid consumer of culture and a ticket-buying opera buff who, like David Mellor, suffered from feelings of alienation at the Royal Opera House. In plain words, he could not bear the neighbours:

There were all those people air-kissing each other (he would write in the *Spectator*); all those people rearranging their seating after the interval according to some recondite social ritual; all those people who could somehow get served when I never could in the Crush Bar – providing, of course, that they were standing at the Crush Bar at all rather than sitting at little reserved tables and ingesting cold chicken or smoked salmon.

Most aggravating of all, there were all those people who did not give a damn about the opera; who chatted to each other during the performances (and rounded on me in fury when I remonstrated) or fanned themselves distractingly with their bulkily expensive programmes; who stared at the programme before the start of a production of *The Marriage of Figaro* and exclaimed in genuine surprise, 'It's by Mozart!' What is more, the lot of them were being subsidized not only by my taxes but by the taxes of people less well-off than themselves who would never get the chance to go to Covent Garden, even if they were so inclined.[10]

For Kaufman, as he confirmed with his own vitriolic pen, this was a grudge match, a chance for the aggrieved anorak to strike back at the black-tied snobs. He was not particularly fussy where the blows landed, so long as they dented the pride of an institution he had come to need and despise. If ever a politician played to the public gallery, it was Gerald Kaufman that autumn morning.

When Mary Allen finished her statement, he ignored everything she said and launched into a languid Mancunian diatribe, his dry tone and laid-back demeanour masking the acrid words. 'It's a shambles, isn't it?' he began.

'I think that the Arts Council would be nuts to give you an extra penny until you have sorted yourselves out,' he continued. Of the present management, he added, 'You are running things incompetently and not doing your jobs.'

Allen replied as best she could, but got the worse of the exchange. Kaufman interrogated her about Genista McIntosh's departure and waved a letter, which he threatened to publish, from which he alleged that McIntosh had 'been asked to leave the opera house immediately', seemingly against her will. In the letter (which I have seen) McIntosh confirms that it was her own wish to leave immediately. Kaufman had been bluffing; he never placed this document on the open record. His aim, it seemed, was to nail a culprit for the chief executive's departure, the event that had triggered his investigation.

Allen was followed in the hot seat by Vivien Duffield, who gave as good as she got, declaring 'I don't see how any great public institution can survive on passing round the begging bowl.' Kaufman was cowed by her maternal ferocity, and any mirth rebounded against him. Jim Monahan then gave evidence for the Covent Garden Community Association, alleging without much evidence that Lottery money was being used to pay for a smart new boardroom for Lord Chadlington and his friends. The committee adjourned for a week and the press rushed off to its deadlines. The comedy in Committee Room 15 was proving a hotter ticket than *The Merry Widow*.

Downcast, the ROH team went back to Floral Street for a board meeting so surreal it could have been designed by Dali. Four members announced that they wanted to liquidate the company; the other four had no solution in mind. The meeting opened with a trawl around the table in which each and every director offered to resign, either out of regret for past negligence or out of sympathy for the embattled chairman. None of their misgivings were recorded in the minutes by Andrew Edwards, the retired Treasury official, but Chadlington asked to receive their resignations in writing so that he could, if necessary, dump them in the Government's lap.

The legal advisers then trooped in and advised that neither resignation nor liquidation would save the directors from personal consequences. If the ROH collapsed, they could be held responsible for its debts. Some, like Chadlington and Mrs Duffield, might be left after settlement with a few off-shore millions for their old age, but the composer Michael Berkeley, a recent recruit, was seen fingering his collar, fearing perhaps that his family could lose the roof over its head. Anyone involved with Covent Garden in any position of responsibility was now trapped, unable to get on with managing the crisis or to get out. As in the fall of Rome, events were mightier than the men and women in command.

There were only two options left. Either the Government could be induced to step in, which seemed unlikely, or money would have to be begged from a source whose existence came as a surprise to several board members. The Floral Trust had been set up in 1994 as a vehicle for donations from an overseas supporter. It had raised twenty million pounds, twenty-five with interest, apparently from the Sultan of Brunei's brother. England, in distress, was pumping the reservoirs of imperial goodwill. Both Prince Charles and John Major had solicited help from Asian well-wishers. The Floral Trust was created over dinner at Highgrove, the Prince's country estate.

Much of the money in the trust had already gone to the builders, but ten or twelve million pounds were thought to remain. The tricky bit was that there were five trustees, including the ROH chairman, who might refuse to surrender the money for an unforeseen emergency, aware of their fiduciary responsibility and of the interest the Charity Commissioners might take in their decisions. Chadlington would argue for the release of the remaining funds, supported by George Magan, a friend of Mrs Duffield's. But there was no telling what screws Sir Angus Stirling and Sir Jeremy Isaacs would turn on their stumbling successors in exchange for signing their reprieve. It might come down to a casting vote by the fifth trustee, Lord Carrington, the distinguished former Foreign Secretary and NATO Secretary General.

The board meeting broke up with an appeal to the chairman to raid the Floral Trust and an authorization to Mary Allen to renew the loan facility at Coutts, ensuring that the wages got paid. It would take around twelve million, the advisers said, to save the ROH from going bankrupt and the money had to be raised within a month.

Gravity turned to forced jollity as the condemned men and women rolled up two nights later at the Sainsbury Wing of the National Gallery to celebrate its donor's seventieth birthday. Lord Sainsbury, the former ROH chairman, looked as florid as the incumbent looked ashen. Mary Allen sidled up to Hayden Phillips and warned that they might need to have a word in the next few days.

Early on Monday morning, 3 November, Chadlington went to see Chris Smith. It was their first encounter since the panic session over Mary Allen's appointment and they might have been expected to compare notes before appearing the next day in Kaufman's dock. Smith appeared acutely uncomfortable. His position was under threat and he was about to take another hasty decision. Two opera houses were on fire and all the headlines were being usurped by a back-bench MP while H. M.'s Secretary of State for Culture, Media and Sport fiddled. His political advisers urged him to do something, anything; Hayden Phillips advised caution. Smith's job was not yet at risk. He enjoyed a personal friendship with the Prime Minister and could be relied upon to raise his hand in Cabinet against the ambitious Chancellor, Gordon Brown. But Kaufman was running away with his show and a weak performance before his committee could cost Smith his career.

He had to act quickly. He could not splash cash on opera without incurring the populist wrath of his party. Nor could he let the ROH founder without being implicated in the crash. His inclination was to let the company go under, proceed with the development and reconstitute a new performing ensemble in time for the opening. Hayden Phillips was of much the same opinion. They were on the point of ordering the Arts Council to stop all further Lottery payments when a fax arrived from Richard Hall, the ROH finance director, clarifying what would happen if the ROH was allowed to go bust. Not only would the main company cease trading, said Hall, but the associated Royal Opera House Developments Limited would be dragged down with it. The development would stop and the land on which it stood would fall into the hands of liquidators, to be sold to the highest bidder in order to pay off ROH debts. The Government would then be held responsible for causing one of London's prime cultural sites to be sold for a song to alien commercial interests. 'Oh, my God,' said Phillips on reading the fax. He told Smith that the Government, too, was paralysed in this situation, unable to do anything but sit tight and await developments.

So Smith did what ministers do in moments of irresoluble crisis – he asked his permanent secretary for advice, and was told to pass the buck.

Hours before entering Kaufman's chamber, Smith announced a review of 'The Future of Lyric Theatre in London'. The Government, he said, could not afford to subsidize both Covent Garden and ENO in separate homes. They should both move in to the new ROH, sell the Coliseum, and use the proceeds to pay off debts. ENO should spend more time taking its work around the country. A 'radical solution' was needed. 'I am not interested in buildings,' said Smith. 'Taking money out of bricks and mortar and putting it into artistic activity may be the best way forward.'[11]

He had asked Sir Richard Eyre, outgoing chief of the Royal National Theatre, to examine his proposal and report to him by May 1998. 'I encourage you to think freely and creatively,' said Smith in a letter to Eyre, making no secret where his preference lay. Any blame for the outcome, however, would rest with Eyre. When Mark Fisher, the arts minister, announced on BBC's *Newsnight* that Eyre 'supports our plan and will make it work', Smith slapped him down without delay. 'He said what he said, and he has been told off for it,' said the Culture Secretary;[12] Fisher was to be sacked in the next reshuffle. The whole purpose of appointing Eyre was to wash the blood off ministerial hands.

Eyre had refused three times before succumbing to the call of conscience. 'Chris did turn it on very strongly,' he explained, 'it was like being a subaltern in the First World War and being told that England Expects . . . Also, having spent years banging a drum, privately and publicly, for a Labour government, it would be churlish when asked to do something for them that could provide stability for the performing arts to say, "no".'[13] Smith apart, Hayden Phillips was a close personal friend and his persuasion proved decisive.

The prospect of yet another review was greeted with despair at Covent Garden, where Eyre was remembered as an operaphobe and close colleague of Genista McIntosh. ENO's music director Paul Daniel declared himself 'greatly concerned' that the company would lose its identity and audience if it was forced to share with the ROH. He stepped up on the Coliseum stage after conducting Janáček's *From the House of the Dead* to share his concerns with the audience, who responded with roars of solidarity. Daniel cancelled all his concert dates to campaign for ENO's independence. The Musicians Union demanded an urgent meeting with Smith and Eyre. Lord Sainsbury declared that it would be 'a cause of national humilation if London should have only one opera house when every other major European capital has two or more.'[14]

Smith had won the round. Next morning, the press whistled his Eyre loud and clear, and Kaufman was outshone. Their confrontation promised rich entertainment and when Smith arrived at Committee Room 15, the overcrowding was dangerous. 'If Covent Garden could get this attendance,' carped Kaufman, 'its financial problems would be over.' The nation waited to see how hard Kaufman would press a party comrade whose elevation he must have envied.

Smith in a blue suit, Kaufman in grey, eyed one another like bantams at a weigh-in. 'I look forward to constructive and fruitful relations with the committee in the years ahead,' jabbed Smith.

'How do we get there from here?' retorted Kaufman, taking him through the process of Mary Allen's recruitment. Smith denied he had done anything to influence staff appointments at the ROH.

Kaufman read out apparent differences in Chadlington's account of their meeting.

'You, sir, are as Secretary of State, a custodian of the English language,' said Kaufman. 'Would you be good enough to reconcile these two statements?'

'I was actually very unhappy,' said Smith. 'I did indicate my high regard for Mary Allen and was extremely sorry to see her leave the Arts Council.'

Kaufman turned the questioning over to his committee. Why was the permanent secretary not present at that meeting? demanded Damian Green, MP. Smith shifted nervously in his seat and replied that an official of the department had been present throughout. Michael Fabricant MP asked why, when setting up the Eyre review, he had also announced its intended conclusion. 'This is a proposal which, I believe, could help to solve a number of long-term problems affecting the theatre in London,' said Smith. 'If Richard Eyre comes up with an alternative plan, I will listen very carefully.'

'Do I also take it,' said Kaufman, 'that, whatever Lord Gowrie may answer about funding, you are not prepared to put more taxpayers' money into Covent Garden?'

'I have no more taxpayers' money to spend,' replied Smith.

The bout ended quietly with Smith promising to 'listen carefully and seriously to your views', and vacating his seat for Gowrie, whose retirement had been announced. After desultory questioning, the ACE chairman gave way to Chadlington and Allen; the show was dying on its feet when Chadlington asked to make a statement clarifying the issue of Genista McIntosh's resignation. He was stopped by Kaufman. He then stopped Kaufman in his tracks by declaring that the ROH could go broke within days. 'Unless we can find a solution on our own, then the House will become insolvent,' intoned the ROH chairman. It was Kaufman's turn to be gob-smacked, upstaged for the second time in a day. 'I believe there is a way through,' Chadlington added. 'It is going to be difficult, but I think we have a small opportunity to get through it.'

Kaufman, conscious that any superfluous word could close the opera house, said gently: 'Are you able to expand on that? If not, I shall not press you.' Chadlington replied: 'Chairman, I would be grateful if you did not press me at this time.'

Next morning, the *Guardian* front-paged: 'Going Broke – the Opera'. Allen, expecting to find creditors at her door, slipped out of the office and made her way to a critical meeting of the Floral Trust, where tempers flared. Isaacs, according to Allen's account, was furious at being blamed before Kaufman for the financial crisis and told Chadlington that he would publicly challenge his version. George Magan had unexpectedly withdrawn his support from the rescue grant. Half-way through the meeting, Allen reckoned that they were going down. She had reckoned without Angus Stirling, one of nature's born chairmen, who allowed everyone to let off steam before steering the debate elegantly to a pre-ordained conclusion. The Floral Trust would give the ROH ten and half million pounds for running costs over the next two years, on condition that other donors continued to fund the development, and that the company remained solvent. There were to be more conditions, but the Trust was not yet ready to reveal them.

Waving the Floral Trust's piece of paper, endorsed by Stirling 'as a true record of the meeting', Chadlington rushed back to the ROH and into an extraordinary board meeting, like Chamberlain after Munich. A decision had to be made there and then, he said: either accept the rescue package or go into liquidation. In addition to the Floral money, he had a pledge of an extra two million pounds from donors who wished to remain anonymous. One identity can now be revealed. Shaun Woodward, married to a Sainsbury heiress and a close friend of the late Princess Diana, had worked on John Major's election team with Lord Chadlington and was an opera devotee – a named supporter of ENO. One million from the Woodward Trust over the next two years would tide the company over until reopening.

Chadlington went around the table seeking endorsement for his package. Most members quickly raised their hands. Michael Berkeley, who was absent, assented in writing but worried 'about throwing good money after bad'. Vivien Duffield had a shouting match with Mary Allen, after which both felt much better. Under the circumstances, everyone behaved rather well. The rescue was approved and the press were informed that the opera house had been saved at the eleventh hour by anonymous well-wishers. *Plus ça change*, said the cynics. For the rich, there would always be an opera house.

The rest of November passed in a state of suspended reality as the political and performing worlds awaited Gerald Kaufman's report.

On the 7th, Isaiah Berlin died, providentially spared from witnessing the finale of the farce. That morning, I dropped in on Mary Allen to see how she was getting on. She found me, she told her diary, 'hypnotically sympathetic, and I find myself telling him all kinds of things that I probably shouldn't.'[15] I remember thinking how pale she looked on her black leather sofa, and how brittle – a changed woman from the confident oligarch I had known at the Arts Council. We had friends in common and gossiped awhile. I caught myself choking back a question, anxious not to be told any personal confidences that I could neither report nor ignore.

Mary told me that, five weeks into the job, she had sought to resign. 'I went through a long dark night of the soul and thought, I've got to get out – anything, anything to get out of this place,' she said. Her husband and chairman talked her round over the course of a turbulent weekend. In one telephone exchange with Chadlington, she told him that she 'fully understood why Genista McIntosh had quit – I warned him we had a structural problem that no one could live with.' The chairman appealed to her sense of responsibility. 'I told her that there were five hundred people whose jobs depended on us,' he said, 'as well as donors who had given seventy million pounds to the House, and we had to do our best for them.' Had Allen quit, he told me, 'we could not have got through the past month.'

Nothing had been solved by the rescue announcement, Allen warned. 'The box office went into reverse last Wednesday,' she said. 'We gave more money back than we took in.' The details of the rescue needed fine-tuning and the Floral trustees appeared to be back-tracking. By the end of the following week, her former deputy at the Arts Council, Graham Devlin, said he could not sign the next cheque of Lottery money until he had received confirmation of the Floral Trust donation. Once again there would be no cash in hand at the end of the month to pay the wages.

The Floral conditions were stringent. In addition to cast-iron assurances of continued ACE support, they demanded written guarantees of the viability of the development and of the company after the house reopened. They intended to use the company's real estate as security for the return of their money if the enterprise collapsed. The killer clause amounted to outright interference with the company's autonomy. Stirling and his fellow-trustees demanded that a 'professional adviser' be appointed immediately 'to assist the executive team over the next four to six months'.[16] This was an affront to Mary Allen, who said she would have to resign if her authority was being undermined.

Chadlington called another emergency board at two p.m. on 19 November, announcing that the company would go bankrupt in five hours' time, when the payroll button was pressed at Coutts, unless they agreed to the Floral Trust conditions – the last of which would have to be negotiated carefully to ensure that Mary Allen did not quit. He had warned Hayden Phillips that they were on the brink of going under, and the Government had not blinked. There was no chance of an official rescue, nor would Whitehall allow money from the sale of properties to be used to run the company.

Across town, the Arts Council and the Floral Trust were eyeballing one another, each refusing, like infants behind the shed, 'to show mine before you show me yours'. Unless one fund or the other opened up by seven that evening, the ROH was finished. Richard Hall asked for, and received, permission from the board to pass essential papers to an administrator at the accountancy firm Arthur Andersen, who would take over that night if the company declared itself insolvent.

As afternoon darkened into wintry evening, accusations, bluffs and documents flew back and forth. Mary Allen phoned Coutts and asked them to delay the payroll run by half an hour, to seven-thirty. The request was highly irregular, she was told; they would do their best. She tried, and failed, to reach the Coutts chairman by phone. As the lights went out in neighbouring offices, the Arts Council and Floral Trust were still refusing to budge until each was sure that the other would move. If British generals had behaved like this at Waterloo, this cultural history would be written in French.

Five minutes before seven-thirty, Graham Devlin rang Mary Allen to say that he had released Lottery funds and she could tell the bank to pay the wages. The Floral Trust would shell out in the morning. Late that night, Allen caught a train in the wrong direction as she stumbled her way back home.

The Royal Opera House was no longer running, but reeling about, like a mugging victim, the lifeblood gushing from its head. Its direction was staggered and inconclusive. No passers-by would rush to help, and one more blow could finish it off.

On 24 November, the board accepted the Floral Trust ultimata without much protest. The trustees explained, reasonably enough, that their donor had given them plenipotentiary powers and they were obliged *to have been seen* to act properly as trustees in the event 'that things later went wrong'.[17] Everybody dealing with the opera house was now cladding themselves in legal chainmail. Mary Allen asked the board to engage a lawyer to negotiate the terms under which the 'professional adviser' would work beside her. She could not discuss the matter directly with Chadlington, as he was also a director of the Floral Trust. The ROH Trust, under Vivien Duffield, had instructed a QC to protect their position.

What the press would make of the Floral Trust gift was preying on their minds, the more so since the Trust and its donor were insisting on total anonymity. Judy Grahame accepted the external relations job that week. She told Mary Allen that, in the absence of real information, several journalists were speculating that she was having an affair with Chadlington. In fact, their working relationship had been strained to snapping point.

Copies of the Kaufman report arrived on the afternoon of Tuesday, 2 December, embargoed until ten-thirty the next morning. This was an astute publicity device, designed to procure double coverage. It allowed the press, having read the report, to conjecture its contents accurately overnight before reporting them in detail with official reactions the following day.

Kaufman's solution was comprehensive: sack the chairman, the board and the chief executive and start again. 'We would prefer to see the Royal Opera House run by a philistine with the requisite financial acumen than by the succession of opera and ballet lovers who have brought a great and valuable institution to its knees,' was one of the more eye-catching phrases. Vivien Duffield and Robert Gavron were specifically exonerated. Chris Smith was half-forgiven for failing to tell his permanent secretary that he was meeting the opera house chairman. Lord Gowrie was sent on his way with a friendly wave. Angus Stirling and Jeremy Isaacs were accused of 'disastrous misjudgements'. Chadlington was spared blame for the financial crisis but excoriated for his role in Genista McIntosh's departure and his inability to staunch the losses, 'a failure which ensured that a fragile financial position became acute'.

The most blistering criticism was directed at Mary Allen whose account of her appointment was disbelieved. 'We found Ms Allen's convoluted explanation of her actions entirely unconvincing,' said Kaufman in bold type. 'Given her experience of public office, Ms

Allen's conduct fell seriously below the standards to be expected of the principal officer of a public body whose loyalty should first and foremost be to the organization[18] which employs her.'

This was savage stuff, the kind of comment that puts people on the street and ensures they never work again. Allen stood condemned before the bar of public service, potentially debarred from public office. She had no right of appeal. Her press statement said: 'I absolutely reject and refute the criticisms about my appointment. I am angry that I have been singled out for criticism of an intemperate kind. I have been there for only three months. I have done what I could in that time.'[19]

She offered her resignation next morning at eight-thirty to a board meeting hastily convened at Shandwick. The board implored her to stay on, unanimously reaffirming 'their complete confidence' in her. She had received dozens of messages of support, including a fax from Bernard Haitink. Unwisely, she agreed to remain.

Lord Chadlington then offered to resign. To his evident surprise, the board accepted his resignation. 'He was very bitter,' observed Keith Cooper.[20] He had planned to devote his leisure years to working for a place that had given him lifelong pleasure, but he was thrown overboard in order to save the ship. Chadlington went quietly. Six months later he sold Shandwick to an American giant, denying that its weak performance in the past year had been affected by his involvements at the opera house. John Major wrote to *The Times*, decrying the need for his resignation as 'bizarre' and dismissing Kaufman's report as a 'parody' of good parliamentary procedure, 'unjust' in its tone and conclusions.[21] When Chadlington went, the million pound offer from the Woodward Trust also evaporated. 'I thought Peter was terribly good,' said Vivien Duffield. 'He loved the place, had an absolute passion for it. It was politically the wrong time. The whole thing was a disaster.'[22]

The rest of the board submitted their resignations but agreed to continue in a caretaker role under Sir James Spooner, the deputy chairman, until Chris Smith replaced them. They trooped off to the Department to see Smith, who promised to come up with an 'action plan'. He asked Mary Allen to stay on. When someone wondered why any person in their right mind would join the board of a company that could go bankrupt at any moment, and for which they might become personally liable, the Secretary of State looked confused. The game was up. He would have to give the next chairman and directors a Government guarantee that Covent Garden would not be allowed to go under.

Kaufman was jubilant, crowing his triumph in the *Spectator*. 'Had it not been for me,' he bragged, 'all [the wicked old ways] might have resumed when the House reopened . . . I do believe that the disclosures about the state of the ROH's finances emerging from our Committee proceedings did help to open Smith's eyes somewhat wider and to spur him to take action by setting up a working party on lyric theatre under Sir Richard Eyre.'[23] Kaufman's rhetoric was denounced by Chadlington as 'hysterical hyperbole'.[24] George Christie of Glyndebourne, no friend of Covent Garden's, called it 'a piece of grotesque irresponsibility'.[25] Kaufman himself protested his high intentions a mite too much. There was, however, one line in his report that rang true to all who knew the way the arts in Britain were run. 'There is no future for the Royal Opera House,' declared Kaufman, 'unless someone accepts responsibility for the sorry train of events we have described.'[26]

The Secretary of State was now back-pedalling as hard as he could to put an ocean between himself and the preposterous proposal he had made to Eyre. Paul Daniel's agitation had paid off. ENO supporters had been talking to the Blairs and Smith now said that his idea of cramming ENO into forced accommodation with the Covent Garden companies had been merely intended to stimulate discussion. 'I know that ENO has a devoted audience and many committed friends,' he wrote. 'I count myself one of them.'[27]

In mid-December the Royal Opera went to Suffolk, where Mary Allen lived, to put on Francesca Zambello's production of *Paul Bunyan* at Britten's festival stage near Aldeburgh. This little-known piece was the young Britten's first attempt at an opera, more a *Singspiel* or American musical, and it worked like a dream, transferring to the Shaftesbury Theatre as a hot Christmas ticket. Nicholas Payne's chamber opera schedule had scored another hit; he was proving invaluable to the headless ROH.

Mary Allen was being pressed by the Floral Trust to let their 'professional adviser' get started. The first investigator from accountants Coopers & Lybrand she dismissed as 'a complete Rottweiler'. She was offered a second choice, Pelham Allen, and found him sensitive and astute. She was wrestling with defining an acceptable form to their relationship when her knee gave way. It was strapped by a woman from the Occupational Health Unit but she had to hobble on a crutch to the next board meeting, which Vivien Duffield attended with her personal lawyer. The atmosphere was tense. Board members decided that they would not stay on beyond 10 January, after which Chris Smith could do his worst. Mary Allen reported that the Kaufman hearings had cost the box-office somewhere between £250,000 and £400,000. There were more lawyers and accountants in the room that day than directors and executives.

The holiday break was protracted that year, Christmas falling on a Thursday and precipitating two weeks of idleness. Mary Allen returned to the office on Monday, 5 January, to find a screed of faxes from Pelham Allen, who was settling down with the figures. He introduced himself to the board as a 'turn-around specialist' or 'company doctor', a man who spent his life bringing ailing firms back from the brink.

Allen hared off with Harvey Goldsmith, the rock impresario, to renegotiate with Sadler's Wells. 'I would never have signed such a deal,' growled Goldsmith at Ian Albery. 'I was told by my board to exact commercial terms,' said the Sadler's Wells boss sweetly.[28]

Allen was still limping heavily. 'Let me tell you about a knee operation I once had,' said Anthony Dowell at an executive meeting, describing the procedure in such gory detail that Allen's natural pallor turned ghostly white. 'That's what will happen to you if you don't get it treated now,' warned the ballet director. He recommended a surgeon who, after a scan, booked her in for a cartilage operation.

Over Christmas, she felt that something had given way inside her. 'I'd had enough,' she decided. 'There is only so much one can do.'[29] She phoned Hayden Phillips, who begged, 'Not now, please not now.' She then rang Graham Devlin at the Arts Council who said, 'Mary, I'm about to go to Florida, can it wait until I'm gone?' She laughed, and carried on working, awaiting her call from the Eyre Review. She pronounced herself confident of its outcome because Eyre's panel was being advised by Melanie Leech, a senior official in Smith's department, who, said Allen, 'is a good friend of mine'. What she failed to appreciate was that, in the maelstrom of English arts, friendship counted for naught when survival was at stake. Leech told colleagues that she avoided taking Allen's calls. Battered by Kaufman, shadowed by the Floral Trust, overshadowed by Eyre and damaged below the knee, Mary Allen clung on literally as a lame duck leader.

The two most prestigious jobs in British arts were going begging and few were tempted by the honour, or the headache. Downing Street presented Chris Smith with a list of businessmen who deserved to be rewarded for switching support to New Labour at the last election. Near the top was Gerry Robinson, chairman of Granada plc, a man widely reviled for reducing the jewel of British television to a channel of soaps and gameshows. 'It was shedding £100 million cash the year I arrived,' he explained.[30] Robinson was an expansionist. He bought London Weekend Television and Yorkshire Tyne-Tees TV and extended Granada's catering interests through a fiercely contested takeover of Trust House Forte. He also served for a while as chairman of Murdoch's BSkyB, in which Granada held an interest.

Robinson was planning further takeovers to establish Granada as the unrivalled leader in British commercial broadcasting. He was eyeing Scottish TV and Carlton, the London weekday franchise. Any such takeover would need the consent of the Department of Culture, Media and Sport, which could feel reasonably confident that he would not kick up too much of a fuss at the Arts Council.

Robinson exuded Irish charm and shrewd analysis. Privately, he loved the theatre, painted landscapes and played his children a piece of classical music before they went to bed, believing the arts to be morally improving. In commercial life, however, Robinson rode roughshod over his own predilections in his drive for growth and profitability. The ninth son of a Donegal carpenter, his personal fortune exceeded ten million pounds and he intended to retire young to enjoy it. He took eight weeks holiday a year. Robinson's plans for the ACE were to strip it down to ten members, devolve powers to regional boards and disenfranchise the turbulent chairmen of art-form panels. He would bring the Arts Council to heel and give the Government no cause for discomfort.

With the ACE under control, Hayden Phillips invited Vivien Duffield and Robert Gavron to the Department's new offices on Trafalgar Square to apprise them of the next ROH chairman. They were shown a list of three – David Davies, a businessman; John Eatwell, an economist and sometime escort of Tessa Blackstone's, the former ballet board chair; and Sir Colin Southgate, chairman of the £3.4 billion music conglomerate, EMI.

None was self-recommending. Davies was virtually unknown. Eatwell was master of Queen's College Cambridge and a Labour peer whose passion was contemporary dance. He had once left a performance of Ashton's *Enigma Variations* saying, 'we don't want more of that'. Duffield and Gavron noted that he had no experience of running a business and would be overwhelmed by Covent Garden's difficulties.

That left Southgate. A gangling man, reassuringly deep voiced, he ran a global company whose roster ran from Caruso to the Spice Girls. He had made his pile by exercising share options and attended Covent Garden frequently on EMI's £180 corporate tickets. He was acceptable, but only just. Duffield wondered if the field could not be extended. The best chairman, she felt, would be Sir Dennis Stevenson, head of Pearsons plc (Drogheda's old firm) and a long-standing Labour supporter who played the violin at night and bought more concert tickets than he ever managed to attend. Stevenson knew the opera house inside out from conducting the last review of lyric theatre, only two years before. He had also transformed the Tate Gallery in ten years as chairman. Phillips frowned. Stevenson would not do. Too independent minded, likely to make waves.

Duffield and Gavron agreed to meet Southgate and took the short-list back to the board, where it was received without enthusiasm. Someone asked to make a last-ditch nomination. What about Sir Robin Butler, Armstrong's successor as Cabinet Secretary and now Master of University College, Oxford? Surely Hayden Phillips would appreciate having an arch-mandarin at the opera. Gavron promised to convey the suggestion, which Phillips dismissed. He should have made the position clearer, perhaps. The outgoing board were not being offered a choice but an ultimatum. Southgate, who was fifty-nine, had told Downing Street that he was retiring from EMI and would make himself available full time to sort out the opera. His was an offer the board were not allowed to refuse.

Southgate's appointment was announced on the day Nicholas Payne resigned to become general director of ENO, a fresh blow to the Royal Opera. Southgate was trotted out to meet the press. He promised to make the ROH accessible to all sectors of the public. Asked whether this meant universal access, he said: 'We mustn't downgrade the opera house. I don't want to sit next to somebody in a singlet, a pair of shorts and a smelly pair of trainers. I'm a relaxed individual, but I'm passionate about standards of behaviour.'

The next morning, his comments were plastered across the top of the *Guardian*'s front page, above a photograph of a black-tied ROH gala audience.[31] A reader in Newport wrote in: 'Sir Colin Southgate has a nerve. The amount of subsidy on his ticket is more than an ordinary person's weekly wage packet.'[32] Southgate learned his lesson. From that day on, he refused to give press interviews, a peculiar reticence for the head of a public-funded institution.

Chris Smith was next up for a grilling. Gerald Kaufman called him back to tell his Committee how its recommendations were being implemented. Smith reported that 'Sir Colin Southgate has made a vigorous start,' appointing Vivien Duffield as vice-chairman, Lord Eatwell as chairman of the ballet board and Michael Berkeley as chairman of the opera board.

Kaufman opened with his customary civilities. 'Be so kind as to speak more loudly than you usually do,' he told the Secretary of State, 'you being a person of modest and retiring disposition.' Being sweet-talked in public by Gerald Kaufman was a bit like being nuzzled by a pet jellyfish.

The committee's deputy chairman, Michael Fabricant, accused Smith of 'taking the same hands-off approach that [ACE] were taking while the [ROH] was going through its problems.' Smith replied: 'I do not believe it is right or sensible for the Secretary of State or the Department to become involved in detailed managerial decisions.' 'Every time we make a criticism,' snapped Fabricant, 'you come back with *mea non culpa*.'

Two women MPs on the committee led the cries for Mary Allen's head. 'The chief executive is still there,' protested Clare Wood, 'but (she) has not made the necessary changes. We were not impressed by Mary Allen's explanation of events. The circumstances of her appointment were, to say the least, unsatisfactory.'

'Everyone agrees on that,' said Smith, 'but I had no power to appoint Mary Allen or to dismiss her.'

The chairman weighed in. He brandished a letter from Keith Cooper, revealing that the *Barber of Seville* and *Marriage of Figaro* were playing to fifty and sixty per cent houses, against a budget forecast of eighty per cent. 'That shambles,' said Kaufman, 'has continued utterly unabated and without the tiniest effort to control it.' Smith replied: 'I am not in charge of the [ROH]. I am sometimes very glad of that particular fact.'

'Much as I love this Government,' sighed Kaufman theatrically, 'we are entitled to some answers.' Smith replied that Southgate's first priority would be to satisfy himself whether the ROH was viable. 'Will he cancel the rest of the season?' Kaufman pressed. 'That is precisely a matter he wishes to look at urgently,' said Smith.

Southgate appeared to have made up his mind about Mary Allen. The music business had been a male preserve, with few women in senior positions. Allen returned two days after her operation, too soon for her own good. She had words with the finance director, Richard Hall, and decided at the same time to get rid of Keith Cooper and the technical director, John Harrison, in a night of the long knives, known as 'management restructuring'. Pelham Allen, the professional adviser, would take over finance while Judy Grahame reorganized marketing (Harrison was later reinstated). Grahame lengthened the list, dismissing the marketing director Andrew Stokes and opera press officer, Helen Anderson. Both were popular Gardeners. Keith Cooper went off to serve tables at his lover's restaurant in Shepherd's Bush, and made a documentary for the BBC. Vivien Duffield, who enjoyed having him around, turned furiously against the chief executive.

Time was running out for Mary Allen. Bernard Haitink wrote a letter in her defence to *Opera* magazine, which was clamouring for her head. 'What is desperately needed at the moment is a modicum of stability,' said Haitink. 'A third change of leadership within a year is not the answer.'[33] On 18 March, Haitink went into hospital for a heart bypass operation, putting him out of action for the rest of the season. Hours earlier, Colin Southgate had called in Judy Grahame and told her to start preparing the company's submission to the Eyre Review. He intended to propose a different structure, with an artistic director on top, followed by a chief executive. Allen's post was to be downgraded. Grahame asked him to tell the chief executive; when he failed to do so, she did. Mary Allen knew that this was the end.

For three torrid months the board and the Government had been begging her to stay; now she was cast off without the courtesy of an explanation. On 25 March she appeared before the board and resigned. The official reason was 'a growing difference of views over future plans for the organization'. Pouring herself a stiff Scotch, she cleared her desk and left.

'And then there were none,' crowed Kaufman in a paid article for the *Evening Standard*. 'With the resignation of Mary Allen as chief executive, the entire top team that ran the ROH has gone. That was what the House of Commons Culture, Media and Sports Committee insisted should happen when we issued our celebrated (notorious?) report four months ago. We were accused of going over the top. We have been vindicated.'[34]

Mary Allen responded with an open letter to Eyre, attacking the Government's 'apathy' to Covent Garden and 'the way in which such a highly trained human resource is being wasted'.[35] A few days after her departure, I took her to tea at the Langham Hotel. She had been shopping for household furnishings on Oxford Street and was preparing to get on with her life. 'I believe everything is sortable,' she said. 'There is no organization so dysfunctional that it cannot be sorted out. Two things scuppered me. The huge debt and the Kaufman Report.' She was heading for Suffolk to cultivate her garden for a while, but two years would pass before she could resume her career. Cancer, the sister of stress, struck at her breast and she underwent surgery and chemotherapy. Like Genista McIntosh, Mary Allen had entered the opera house with a buoyant reputation. Unlike her, she lingered too long and departed damaged in body and spirit.

The opera house was now in the hands of Pelham Allen until, as he put it, the board selected 'a general director of the highest artistic reputation and distinction'.[36] Richard Jarman, once of Scottish Opera, stepped in temporarily to fill Payne's shoes.

'It is symptomatic,' said Genista McIntosh in a muted side-blast, 'that the ROH was briefly run by a chief executive seconded from the accountancy partnership Coopers & Lybrand. In my view, you cannot separate managing such institutions from their artistic philosophy.'[37] The artistic credibility of the opera house was being called into question.

As if to nullify such doubts, that month the Royal Opera swept the board at the *Evening Standard*'s annual theatre awards. Sir Edward Downes, picking up the trophies, said the company had been 'run down – dumbed down – to a level that is dangerous in the extreme . . . What we are celebrating in these awards is the way the company has fought against attack. These are people who, in a damn-you-all way, have produced performances that are outstanding, despite all this. These are people who don't work from nine to five. They do it as a vocation, because this is what they have been born for, for the nation.'[38]

*

Eyre was running late and the spin doctors were getting busy. A report was planted in the *Sunday Times*, suggesting that this most public-spirited of men was about to recommend privatization. Bectu members called a protest rally and Eyre was obliged to send a private letter to Pelham Allen and ENO's Russell Willis Taylor, affirming that no one had yet been apprised of the contents of his report, 'because only I know what I intend to recommend'.[39]

While the nation waited, Chris Smith published a slim volume of essays under the title *Creative Britain*. Wrapped in blotches by the fashionable post-modernist Damien Hirst, it affirmed New Labour's faith in a 'Cool Britannia' in which shlock art, advertising and pop music were valued as progressive and profitable while traditional arts were scorned as 'unmodernized' and parasitical.

Colin Southgate flew to Los Angeles to fulfil his promise to get shot of EMI. Half his plan had already foundered. His designated successor, the diminutive American Jim Fifield, had walked away from the company with an eight-digit pay-off. Southgate headed to California to clinch a sale. He had been negotiating a takeover for months with the Canadian distillers, Seagrams, who owned Universal Pictures. When Southgate got off the plane, they told him not to bother. PolyGram, owned by Philips in Holland, had nipped in at a lower price and sold their labels to Universal. Southgate was left at the altar like a jilted bride and had to stay on as EMI chairman until he found a new successor or buyer. The unplanned distraction compounded his ROH woes and shortened his temper.

Eyre was due to report on 1 May but that week he was rehearsing the Royal Opera revival of *La Traviata* at the Royal Albert Hall. 'The reason the report has taken such an inordinately long time,' he told a *Guardian* diarist, 'is simply that never having directed an Andrew Lloyd Webber musical, I have to earn a living, which does rather interfere with voluntary work. At least you lot (journalists) get paid to write about the Royal Opera House.' Between the lines of that remark lurked a green-eyed envy for his *Cats*-rich successor, Trevor Nunn, along with a puritanical resentment of all who fed off the fruits of public-funded arts. Other asides from Eyre referred to the anomaly of Placido Domingo earning one hundred times as much for singing *Otello* at Covent Garden as the £200 paid to England's finest actors who played the role at the Royal National Theatre.

Prudish in his dislike of excess, Eyre was neither a visionary nor a stirrer, but a quiet operator who got things done and, from time to time, scored a hit. Under Eyre, the National conquered the West End with *Guys and Dolls* and staged a fistful of well-crafted new plays. It was a model company with balanced budgets. Eyre rarely rose to the bait of self-publicity. A family man, married for twenty-five years to a television producer who made *Pride and Prejudice* for the BBC, he was untouched by gossip. A book of memoirs hinted that his life was a rebellion against his Rabelaisian father, a naval officer turned farmer who voted Tory and advised his son to 'fuck his way around the world'.[40] Richard, who read English at Cambridge under Kingsley Amis, became a moral socialist. As a servant of the arts and a supporter of New Labour, he felt his report could benefit both causes.

As publication drifted into June, rumours abounded. A tip that Eyre was angling for Allen's job at Covent Garden was reported by the *Independent* ('he'd rather walk barefoot to Scunthorpe,' said his sister). Mary Allen began writing a column for *The Times*.

On 6 June, a housebound Ninette de Valois marked her hundredth birthday. 'Tell me,' she demanded, 'is there any excitement in the world?'[41] Tony Blair was collared one night at his table in a smart London restaurant, The Ivy, by the composer Harrison Birtwistle, who ticked him off loudly about Labour's neglect of the arts. 'We're getting it wrong, aren't we?' murmured Blair to the Barbican Centre manager, John Tusa, as they entered a conference hall. 'Is it a question of money?'

A day before Eyre's report came off the presses, Blair invited a small group of arts chiefs to brief him on the crisis. Over tea and cupcakes at Downing Street, one leader after another told the Prime Minister of the need for extra funding and a degree of respect for heritage arts. Eyre himself delivered a synoptic overview of the funding shortage and demanded an extra sixty million pounds. The conductor Sir Simon Rattle described the collapse of instrumental teaching in schools, a drop of 150,000 pupils in five years. Tusa spoke of the support the arts could deliver in return – and Blair seemed impressed, apologizing for his negligence and promising 'to write the arts into the core script' of Government activity. 'I think I saw a Prime Minister who does believe in the role arts can play in a civilized society,' said Sir Dennis Stevenson.[42] To muddy the waters, Downing Street spin doctors assured a *Times* columnist that Blair had merely been 'in listening mode' and had no intention of favouring middle-class habits. 'Politically speaking,' *The Times* was told, 'Covent Garden is on Planet Zog.'[43]

Southgate, taking Blair at his word, leaked a letter he had written to Chris Smith, demanding a doubling of subsidy – without which the house could not reopen. Even if every performance in the new house sold out, he warned, there would be an annual shortfall of fifteen million pounds.[44] In tone, timing, and temerity, his note could hardly have been less judicious. 'I am particularly surprised,' said Smith, 'that such a request should be made now, in advance of consideration of Sir Richard Eyre's recommendations on financial stability and planning, efficient management and value for public money. These must be the priority, before any meaningful discussion of future funding requirements can take place.'

Smith's letter was published as an adjunct to the Eyre Report, in an operation orchestrated to attract minimum attention. The report was released on a day when England's football team were playing a do-or-die World Cup tie against Argentina. The television news would run late that night, and the next morning's papers would be full of England's fate (they lost, of course). Smith's officials restricted entry to Eyre's press conference to two specialist correspondents from each national newspaper and broadcast medium.

At three o'clock in the afternoon of 30 June, the select few were shepherded into a windowless cellar-room in the Department of Culture, Media and Sport and given half an hour to read the 150-page report before questioning Eyre and Smith. Eyre appeared dour, subdued and defensive. Smith sounded petulant. 'I am glad to see we've got a full house here,' he began and, echoing Kaufmann's jibe, 'it is more than Covent Garden can manage.'

That cheap shot set the tone. 'It is our intention that the ROH should continue to receive public subsidy, and that ENO should remain at the Coliseum as its own home base,' declared Smith, nullifying his original proposal. There was little more to add. Eyre had examined all other options and found them wanting. Privatization he ruled out because it would mean writing off all the public money that had been invested over the years in Covent Garden – a weak argument, since such write-offs are inherent to every privatization. He was tempted by an idea of mine to separate the management of theatres from the running of the performing companies; he had also toyed with abolishing the Arts Council. In the end, he said, the Government had three choices – either to decide that the arts did not merit state support; or to carry on as before; or, as he would recommend, to make a real commitment on the basis of 'excellence, artistic integrity, accessibility, accountability and cost effectiveness' by greatly increasing its subsidy for the arts.

'My belief,' wrote Eyre, 'is that, at the end of this process, additional funds will be needed, if the companies are fully to deliver the objectives of the Review.' He went on to argue that 'a huge increase in funding is unrealistic', but 'a substantial increase is essential'.[45] Yet, as if to spare Smith's blushes, he portrayed Covent Garden as undeserving of the largesse he was recommending. 'I think it would be disastrous,' said Eyre, 'if the Royal Opera House were to be given special, remedial treatment.'

Eyre spoke bitterly about Covent Garden. 'It's a tragedy,' he said, 'that the ROH has been perceived as a barometer of the arts. What alarms me is that the whole world of the subsidized arts has been tainted by the opprobrium that is attached to the Royal Opera House.'

Richard Morrison, in *The Times*,[46] called the report 'a great waste: I have never read an official arts report that is so elegantly written, so full of sane suggestions and well-argued observations about the running of theatres and yet so illogical when approaching the central issues.' In the *Daily Telegraph* I lamented 'a painfully missed opportunity for which opera will pay a mortal price in the years to come'.[47] The entire sector had been hungry for challenge and prepared to respond to a new agenda; Eyre had let them down, and let the Government off the hook.

To cover their nakedness, Eyre and Smith launched into tirades against Covent Garden which they depicted as a citadel of vanity and waste. Eyre complained primly that the ROH kept two-thirds as many executives on salaries over £30,000 as any other arts company. In fact, the Royal Opera and Royal Ballet each had ten employees, including music directors, earning over £30,000. The Royal National Theatre had eight. Eyre's information was three years out of date.

Smith condemned Covent Garden for failing to submit a business plan. The ROH replied that it had a letter from Smith's office agreeing that there was no point in writing a business plan without knowing what levels of funding it could expect.

By the weekend the report was shelved. By the summer's end, it was forgotten. The newspapers were preoccupied with a soccer player, David Beckham, who was blamed for the Argentine defeat, and with the impending anniversary of Princess Diana's death. The Archbishop of Canterbury warned against a renewed outpouring of public grief. The Archbishop of York attacked those who were 'clinging to the icon . . . wallowing in her death'.[48] England was in the grip of a millennial marian cult, while older beliefs foundered for want of glamour and immediacy.

The opening pages of Eyre's report had envisaged a Utopian England in which

> our corrosive class divisions would dissolve, crime among young men would be curbed, and unemployment would be eased. Our political immaturity would be cured, our insular attitudes towards Europe and our paranoia about our national identity would be dispelled. We would put an end to our ignorance and suspicion of science, our diffidence about learning, and abolish the cultural apartheid which divides the country between those who go to galleries, theatres and opera houses, and those who feel themselves excluded from them.[49]

The way to achieve this utopia, said Eyre, repeating a Blairite mantra, was 'education, education, education'. Three days after he uttered these words, the Guardian topped its front page with the headline: 'ROH sacks head of education on first day'.[50]

Covent Garden's propensity for self-damage was not exhausted. Janet Robertson, turning up for work as head of opera education, was greeted by the personnel director, Mike Morris. He handed her a letter reading: 'I regret to inform you that the ROH has decided not to confirm your appointment.' She was then escorted off the premises. Robertson told the *Guardian* that in a previous meeting with Pelham Allen she had been told that the company's commitment to education was 'nothing more than lip service'.

Richard Eyre, approached for a reaction, purpled his phraseology. 'It makes me blind with anger,' said Eyre. 'This confirms my worst fears of bad faith and it's in a tragically time-honoured tradition of opera house own-goals. It confirms my view, which I spell out in the report, that unless there is a total change of mindset they can't survive. It appears that they have not taken on board the report. Unless they get the message soon, they will just sink into the sea.'

The facts of the matter were more prosaic than they appeared, although the handling of the affair could not have been clumsier. Covent Garden was a pioneer in arts education. The Royal Ballet toured sink estates with its 'chance to dance' programme, inspiring children of deprived backgrounds with respect for their bodies and awareness of their talent. The brightest were offered free coaching and occasionally scholarships to the Royal Ballet School. The Royal Opera tapped into London schools for child actors and choruses. It was spreading opera awareness still wider through a range of teaching aids. Its Write an Opera project had been adopted by a hundred and fifty schools in several countries. Stuffy as it was at the top, the company's roots were grassy and the singers and dancers seldom refused to give freely of their time to preach their art to bright-eyed school assemblies.

Janet Robertson had been hired by Nicholas Payne to run a vibrant department. She got off on the wrong foot with Pelham Allen, complaining about her £25,000 salary and demanding a raise. Allen felt that she lacked the right attitude and asked Judy Grahame to administer a formal warning. Resentments simmered and a decision was taken not to allow Robertson to start work.

Grahame was herself at loggerheads with murmurous staff over her sacking of two Gardeners. The Bectu representative Sofie Mason, a graduate who worked in the publications department selling advertising space in opera and ballet programmes, called a union meeting where she uttered a number of wild and unfounded allegations about Grahame. A motion of no-confidence in the external affairs director was passed. Copies of Mason's allegations were circulated to eighteen journalists. She was immediately suspended, pending disciplinary action. E-mails proclaiming 'Sofie Mason is a martyr' flew around the company and beyond. Grahame reached for libel lawyers.

The dispute was brought to Southgate, who decided that Mason had committed a dismissable offence and should be sacked. He was advised that the company could not afford more bad publicity, a probable clerical strike and £50,000 in dispute proceedings. The chairman backed down and called for conciliation. On 7 July, Mason and Bectu withdrew all allegations against Grahame, without an apology. Both sides agreed 'not to comment any further on this'.[51]

Behind the scenes, tempers seethed. Bectu claimed victory and the executive team felt betrayed. Southgate was overheard calling the opera house 'a nest of vipers'. It was an eye-opening moment that pushed the chairman towards a radical decision.

At the Kaufman committee a week later, Richard Eyre said: 'Unless the ROH regards itself as an organization that exists for the public good, and if they won't change . . . there is no justification for them to continue to receive public support.'

On 22 July, Darryl Jaffray, the ballet's education officer, was named ROH Director of Education. That afternoon, Southgate called a board meeting to deal with the financial insolubles. The time for soft shoe shuffles was over. He was ready to go for broke.

And, all the while, the opera sang and the ballet danced, in unfamiliar places and on borrowed time. I caught up with the Royal Ballet in Frankfurt, staying in one of the world's most exclusive hotels. The owner of the Frankfurter Hof, a devotee of classical dance, was putting up the dancers for the price of a Scunthorpe bed-and-breakfast. Thanks to the American choreographers John Neumeier, William Forsythe and Mark Morris, Germany was a world leader in contemporary dance, but its ballet fans hungered for the sight of a traditional ensemble dancing to a live orchestra, in place of pre-recorded tapes.

The musicians of Frankfurt had never played for dancers before and stumbled through the first act of Ashton's *Cinderella* with some alarming judders. The performance came together in the second act under the cool baton of the Royal Ballet's latest music director, a young woman of thirty-three with two small daughters at home. Andrea Quinn had inherited the baton from Barry Wordsworth, who blew out after failing to get his repertoire ideas past the two Anthonies and the ever-depressing board. 'Anthony Dowell doesn't like confrontation,' said Wordsworth, 'he can't stand up to anyone.'

'I think Andrea is on a hiding to nothing,' he added. 'She is as good a conductor as they are ever likely to get, but she'll only be good if they let her get on with the job. They have thrown out a lot of good conductors, and some[52] have died in a ditch.' John Lanchbery, another predecessor, intoned a solemn warning. 'The main thing,' he advised, 'is to fight every inch of the way against the Opera. They'll steal all your rehearsal time.'

Quinn certainly had the composure, as well as the confidence of Dowell, who warmed to her 'exciting ideas' for new ballets to music by Birtwistle and the minimalist Kevin Volans. How she would cope with the hard hats of the ROH orchestra remained to be seen. What was evident in Frankfurt, though, was that the Royal Ballet danced just as well with a strange band in the pit as they did with their home orchestra. Later in the year, they would make their first Irish appearance, at the Grand Opera House in Belfast, accompanied by the sensitive and enthusiastic Ulster Orchestra. Extraordinarily, it was the ballet's only UK residency outside London during the closure years.

The Royal Opera were also breaking new ground, ending their first exile year at Savonlinna, in the month of the midnight sun. When the sun shines, the semi-covered castle courtyard beside a Finnish lake is a splendid place to watch opera. That summer, it rained continuously and temperatures were ten degrees below normal. The dress rehearsal of Verdi's *I Masnadieri* was abandoned in blinding gales. During the performances, singers, players and audience alike were soaked to the skin. 'There was an extraordinary intimacy,' growled Sir Edward Downes, who conducted.

The following night, they gave *Peter Grimes*, unseen in Finland since 1947. The audience were gripped by the Moshinsky production, with Anthony Rolfe-Johnson in the Jon Vickers role. They leaped to their feet, roaring and stamping – 'behaving like Spaniards,' as the festival director put it. The orchestra played in shirts soaked to transparency, several men surrendering their jackets to female colleagues. 'It was sheer, bloody-minded pride,' said the conductor, Elgar Howarth. Afterwards, they cycled ten kilometres to a spartan student hostel, where no hot meal awaited them. The fortitude was admirable – but it was British grit more than company spirit. Several players, including the leader, David Nolan, were well-known London freelancers filling in for the opera tour. The myth of the essential ROH orchestra was ripe for lancing.

Offstage, Royal Opera education officers were helping twenty-eight Finnish eleven year olds to create their own *Grimes*, the first such schools project in a country noted for the excellence of its music education. On the final night, the cast gave a party for John Dobson, the veteran comprimario, who was calling it a day after playing character roles at Covent Garden since Solti's era. He was the last surviving member of the company of singers and many an eye was moist as high times were recalled. There was no one from the management team to bid him farewell, nor had any member of board came out to brave the nordic elements. The Royal Opera flew home, and on to the Edinburgh Festival, feeling chilled and undervalued.

Pelham Allen, three months into the job, was looking wan and drawn.

Having spent his working life nursing companies back to health, he told colleagues that he had never seen anything quite like Covent Garden. Normally, he found debt, fraud and neglect of duty; here, apart from some of the usual problems, there was incompetence, intrigue and external interference of every kind from politicians, the press, high society and trade unions. The staff fell into two groups – dedicated and deeply conservative, or dedicated and deeply malicious. He found the company 'virtually unmanageable'.[53]

Allen's skills did not come cheap. For its 'professional advisers', Coopers & Lybrand billed the ROH for £50,248.33 (including VAT) for the first fortnight, around five thousand pounds per working day. The charges for Pelham Allen himself were two hundred and fifty pounds an hour.[54] Things could not carry on like this for long.

On 27 July, the executive team were summoned on their mobile phones to an unscheduled meeting at EMI. They found Southgate and Allen in a fifth-floor conference room, with a war plan written out by Allen on a wall-screen. Southgate said, 'this has got to stop' and handed over to Allen, who ran through an eight-point strategy. They were about to shut down the ROH company and make everyone redundant. Orchestra and chorus were to be disbanded.

The ballet company would be kept going, if necessary by reverting ownership to the Royal Ballet Governors, whose chairman was Lord Sainsbury. However, the two Anthonies were to be dismissed and the dancers would have to agree new contracts within three months.

The building work would continue and finish in time; the Trust and Friends would be kept going as separate bodies.

An artistic director would be quickly appointed – Southgate had someone in mind – and the company would reopen in 1999, slimmed down, but with much the same structure.

All the executives enthusiastically endorsed the plan, but each and every one of them argued that the structure had to be changed. Southgate dismissed their views and charged off with Allen to see Chris Smith.

They reported back the next day, saying Smith was in agreement and would allow the subsidy for 1999 to be spent on redundancy costs. This was not enough, in Southgate's opinion, to allow the ROH to reopen in the black. He decided to resign, booking a 5.00 p.m. appointment that Thursday with Chris Smith to tell him so. At five-thirty, he showed up at the Floral Hall for a topping-out ceremony looking decidedly more cheerful. Smith had offered no more money, but had praised him to the skies. Southgate made an impromptu speech. 'And when we reopen,' he said grandly, 'all the people buying seats up there can look down on us nobs in the Floral Hall.' His executives groaned, thanking heaven that no press were within earshot.

Allen went off for a week's family holiday. He returned to find the war-plan watered down and Southgate avoiding bellicose talk. He had been advised by a close business associate to tone it down. The new strategy was called 'managed transition'. It involved calling off the 1999 performance schedule, and telling staff they would be dismissed if by January they had not signed improved contracts, surrendering extra payments for broadcasts and similar perks. The point on which Southgate now stood firm was that he would definitely resign if Smith did not offer more money in exchange for the efficiencies he was about to achieve.

At eight forty-five on Monday 7 September, Southgate and Allen went to see Smith. The figures they presented spoke for themselves. The ROH was now thirteen million pounds in debt; that sum would reach twenty million by March 2000 if performances continued. The solution was to stop and rethink. 'We have been asked to make the ROH less élitist and to bring ticket prices down,' said Southgate. 'We want to do this, but we can't without money. It's a circle we cannot square.'[55] Smith replied that he was prepared to give more money if the opera house showed willingness to change. He asked for time to reflect and promised an answer by the end of the day.

Southgate returned to EMI deeply dejected. Late in the afternoon, he was rung by Eatwell who had picked up hopeful political signals. At six in the evening, Smith sent round a letter, praising Southgate for his 'visionary approach towards securing the ROH's long-term future'. He promised more money but did not say how much.

The board gathered on Tuesday for a meeting attended by the new junior arts minister Alan Howarth. His preliminary bromides were interrupted by a raging Vivien Duffield, who said 'I've heard all this smooth talk before.' She demanded to know whether the

Government would support the company or not. Howarth said it was up to the Arts Council to decide how much money the ROH would receive. Graham Devlin said the ACE could not make that decision until the Government announced how much extra it was providing. The familiar old dodgem routine was broken up by Lord Eatwell, who said that unless an extra £5.5 million was received in December – 'not five million or five point two' – it was curtains for the opera house. Both Howarth and Devlin agreed that something of that order could be arranged, with an extra ten million the following year. Southgate smiled and proclaimed salvation.

Tough letters were sent to the Musicians Union, Equity and Bectu. The secret fallback plan was that, if agreement was not quickly obtained, the company would shut down and there would be no reopening before September 2000 at the earliest. A fallback announcement was drafted: 'The Board of the ROH today agreed to solvently wind-down its existing operation and to build a new organization from scratch.'

Staff meetings and a press conference were called around noon on Wednesday to deliver the news. The chorus took it worst, convinced they were all to be sacked; their director, Terry Edwards, had advised Eyre that there was no need to employ a full-time chorus. The orchestra were informed during *Ring* rehearsals with Haitink, whose face darkened. Bectu members gathered at Conway Hall, a relic of Victorian public-spiritedness, to hear Southgate say, 'It's hard for all of you who have given your heart and soul to this place, but it has gone from decade to decade, from crisis to crisis, and this has got to stop.' The ballet received the news during rehearsals at Sadler's Wells.

It was not so much the revised agreements that caused dismay as the realization that, once the house opened, there would be no more than two hundred and twenty performances a year, which was the most that could be afforded at present levels of subsidy. Most of the salaried artists would be on part-time contracts. 'We're being offered seventy-nine per cent of our existing salary,' said a chorus singer. 'We would become part-time but they require us to be available all the year, so we couldn't take on other work.'

The unions called it 'cultural vandalism'. Sofie Mason set about organizing a celebrity rally in defence of ROH staff. Edward Downes got up a petition that he would present at Downing Street. Nine conductors wrote to *The Times* in support of the orchestra and chorus. The letter was signed by Colin Davis, Daniel Barenboim, Pierre Boulez, Valery Gergiev, Carlos Kleiber, James Levine, Zubin Mehta, Simon Rattle and Mstislav Rostropovich;[56] three of the signatories had never conducted at Covent Garden.

This was predictable ferment, nothing to furrow Pelham Allen's brow. The two factors he was watching were the music director and the donors. Haitink's choler was rising. He demanded a meeting with Allen and the acting Royal Opera director Richard Jarman. Nothing they could say sufficed to reassure him. Haitink declared that artistic standards could not be maintained if the company stopped performing and that any gap in the performing year would cause the best players in his orchestra to seek work elsewhere. After a week of growing concern, he sent a resignation letter to Southgate.

The chairman went to see him a week later and, with the help of an EMI recording executive, persuaded Haitink to suspend his decision while he tried to salvage part of the 1999 programme. But in the week between his letter and their meeting, Haitink had spoken in Edinburgh to Hugh Canning of the *Sunday Times*. News of his resignation appeared in the Sunday paper and panic set in at the prospect of another bout of bad publicity. At the end of the month, Haitink wrote to Chris Smith offering to remain in his post in exchange for his support for reinstating a skeleton opera season in 1999. He argued that the company would lose artists, audiences and himself if it stopped performing. Smith, not wanting to be embroiled in a high-profile row, told Covent Garden to relax the total shutdown. This was the first crack in the salvation plan.

The dancers, meanwhile, had written to Lord Sainsbury, imploring him to help them in their plight. Sainsbury addressed the Royal Ballet at the end of the month and told them 'it's going to be all right'. The company wanted them to accept 36-week contracts. He backed full employment. 'As chairman of the Governors of the Royal Ballet, there was clearly a need to be very concerned at what was going on,' said Sainsbury. 'We had to get involved and say that the company needed to be looked after rather more than they were going to be, in terms of how many weeks they were going to be employed. The Governors would never accept that they should only be employed for six months of the year.'

Sainsbury let it be known that the Royal Ballet would go it alone if the ROH failed to deliver acceptable terms. Given that he was a leading donor to the ROH, his threat was twin-edged. 'In order to keep the (ballet) at the opera house,' said Sainsbury, 'we had to do some tough talking. I was wearing several hats, also as chairman of the appeal, and I was saying (to Southgate) that in no way could you expect people to give money to an opera house that was only going to function for part of the year. If that was going to be the case, I, for one, could not accept that this was the organization we were pledging money to.'

Southgate backtracked again, promising to keep the dancers on full employment and work towards a year-round programme in the new house. 'The compromise,' said Sainsbury, 'was that it was to be built up to a point where it could operate fully. It was terrible that it came to that.' A second strand snapped in the rescue plan.

Then Vivien Duffield weighed in with a letter to Southgate from her lawyers, restating the commitment of her trustees to the ROH but stipulating that the plans to perform for just thirty-five weeks a year were incompatible with the aims of their five million pound donation. Unless Southgate agreed to achieve a full forty-five week schedule for the Royal Opera and Royal Ballet within three years of reopening, there would be no further money from her trusts. There was no point in giving money to a building; it was the performing companies that she intended to support. Southgate, faced with the loss of his chief fundraiser and lead donor, caved in. Pelham Allen's rescue plan lay in ruins.

Allen had done his best. He was a good man, with good intentions, but nothing in his commercial experience had confronted him with so many conflictual forces, all shouting at the top of their voices. In the midst of a crisis meeting, with executives telling him that everything hung in the balance, he took his coat at five o'clock and said he had to go. Ninety minutes later, he walked back into the meeting. To a sympathetic colleague, he confided that he had been to a memorial service for a close relative. In the hysteria of the opera house, Pelham Allen kept his human priorities intact.

Mercifully for Allen, his time was almost up. At the board meeting of 8 September, the Board had appointed the next boss of the ROH. It had reached the decision by a circuitous route and for most of the wrong reasons. But, like a shaft of sunlight that falls upon a storm-tossed sea, it was a harbinger of calmer times, a settler of nerves.

All summer long, Southgate had been telling his board that he was going to appoint an artistic director and he had an excellent person in mind. She was Sarah Billinghurst, casting director at the Metropolitan Opera in New York, and a human barrier between its aggressive general manager, Joseph Volpe, and its music director, James Levine. Billinghurst was in her early fifties, a New Zealander who had spent her whole career in opera houses.

There were immediate objections from the usual quarters, namely Vivien Duffield. Had Billinghurst ever run an opera house? Er, no. Had she any experience of a mixed economy of state and private subvention? Also not. Did she control the Met's $163 million budget, two-and-a-half times larger than Covent Garden's? Negative.

Nevertheless, Southgate was set on having her and flew to New York to finalize details. Before he left, someone suggested to him that there was an American he should meet who could work under Billinghurst as her administrator. His name was Michael Kaiser and few in England, apart from Deborah MacMillan, had heard of him.

Lady MacMillan, who chaired the ACE's dance panel, had been catching up with old contacts at American Ballet Theater, where her husband had spent some of his happiest months. She knew Kaiser as the director who turned ABT around financially in the mid-90s after years of famine. 'They need someone like you at Covent Garden,' she told him over dinner. 'You think so?' said Kaiser.

Some days later, he called back and said, 'I want to do it.'

MacMillan said, 'You must be off your head.'

Back home, she told John Tooley, who passed his name on to a board member. Southgate agreed to meet Kaiser while he was in New York.

Neither man will exactly say what passed at that meeting, but Kaiser made it clear to Southgate that he wanted the top job and, no disrespect, would not work under Sarah Billinghurst. Southgate was smitten by a man who knew his mind. He asked Billinghurst if she would be Kaiser's number two, and she likewise refused. She had virtually cleared her desk at the Met when Southgate told her he was giving the job to Michael Kaiser.

It was at the shutdown meeting of 8 September that Michael Kaiser, under Any Other Business, walked in to meet the board. All the executives except Pelham Allen were asked to leave the room.

Kaiser turned on a beam of reassurance and within moments had the board at his feet. 'My career,' he said, 'is about finding new resources for the arts and saving money.' He was not interested in problems, only in solutions. Such positivism had not been heard in the boardroom since Isaiah Berlin was at his philosophical peak.

There was only one objection. Chris Smith, Richard Eyre, Colin Southgate and the Floral Trust had all agreed that the next boss at Covent Garden was to be an artistic director, not an administrator. Pelham Allen was present as the Floral Trust's guardian of good conduct. He had to leave the room momentarily to go to the toilet. By the time he returned, Michael Kaiser had been appointed Executive Director, reporting directly to the board.

CHAPTER 12

And so to Bed

(December 1998 to December 1999)

THE WORLD WAS in the grip of an unprecedented fit of prurience. Bill Clinton, president of the United States, had, like many who attained that office, lied and screwed his way to power. Once there, his enemies made valiant efforts to expose the lies. Failing that, they turned the spotlight on screwing.

For the whole of 1998, newspapers described the president's sexual habits in anatomical detail. He admitted, finally, to oral sex with a White House intern. Clinton survived the attempt to impeach him, but his presidency was tarnished.

A backlash was inevitable. America, in its next election, would choose between two dullards. The rest of the world was torn between its right to know and its instinct to ignore. In Russia, a drunken, incapable president with links to organized crime was allowed to hand over to a chosen protégé, rather than face investigation and trial. Germany's unifying ex-president, Helmut Kohl, was caught laundering party donations. His successor was cashiered, but Kohl escaped with a caution. The Clinton carnival had revealed limits to the embarrassment of power. It aroused a universal longing to restore purity and a presumption of honesty in elected leaders.

In Britain, Tony Blair enjoyed a higher opinion poll rating than any Prime Minister since polling began. His ministers might err, but Blair was put on a pedestal and the public willed him to be above reproach – 'you know me, I'm a decent kind of guy,' was the basis of his appeal. When his wife, Cherie, fell pregnant in her mid-forties, the event was regarded as a triumph of fidelity, decency and faith, the antithesis of Tory 'sleaze'.

Michael Kaiser stepped directly from the Clinton impeachment to the canonization of Blair. He arrived in a climate that had turned kind to leaders. Kaiser was good at making organizations work and projecting a positive outlook. He cannot, however, have anticipated the halo that would come his way as, prudently and methodically, he set about putting together again the Humpty Dumpty of English arts.

In fairness to all concerned, most of the repairs had been carried out before Michael Kaiser took up his post. In the two months before his arrival, Southgate and the personnel director, Mike Morris, hammered out union agreements and limited work-force reductions. Morris wrote off his own job.

The *Ring* resounded at the Royal Albert Hall and hundreds queued outside but many seats gaped empty because Friends and donors had not returned their allocations. Haitink grumbled that the chairman had not bothered to attend. Relations between Southgate and his deputy, Vivien Duffield, remained tense and Lord Sainsbury was keeping his powder dry. The Clore and Duffield Foundations announced a seven million pound bequest in October for educational and interactive devices to help children get more out of visits to museums and art galleries. A Jewish school in poverty-line Hackney received £400,000 for a language and technology wing. The Weizman Institute in Israel was given three million dollars for a Clore Garden of Science. Mrs Duffield refused to answer questions about the Royal Opera House.[1]

'I am not at all surprised to read that Mrs Vivien Duffield is reconsidering her donation to the ROH redevelopment,' wrote the former deputy chairman, Sir James Spooner, in a letter to *Opera* and *The Times*. 'I am sure that she and the other major six, seven and eight-figure donors (and even some minor five-figure donors like my wife and myself) feel dreadfully let down. It must seem to many that Perfidious Albion is alive and well in certain corridors in Westminster. I would hope that those concerned are, in their hearts, thoroughly ashamed of the hideous damage they are causing to two of this country's star assets and to all who work in or for them.'[2] Chris Smith said nothing, but Tony Blair told the opera director Nicholas Hytner that the money needed to regenerate the arts was 'a drop in the ocean'; the problem was, how to sell it to readers of the *Sun*?[3]

Within the ravaged company, the head of marketing, Gillian Brierley, quit after five months, complaining of lack of staff co-operation. Judy Grahame resigned, her contract paid out in full. The *Daily Telegraph*, in an editorial, wrote:

> To lose one highly respected executive in unexplained circumstances is unfortunate, to lose two sounds like negligence. Three seems reckless and four in eighteen months suggests that the organization is careering out of control. The ROH put out business-as-usual signs yesterday after the abrupt resignation of its public affairs director, Judy Grahame. Like the two chief executives and marketing director – all women – who preceded her in a rush to the door, Ms Grahame was unable immediately to give her version of events without breaching the terms of her severance agreement.
>
>   However, anyone with an eye for institutional psychology must be aware that the neurosis inherent in every opera house has slipped at Covent Garden into the darker realms of psychosis. Privately, senior executives past and present describe the place as unmanageable.[4]

Nevertheless, by the end of October Southgate was able to announce that 'substantial progress had been made with artists and staff on new arrangements'. The unions claimed they had saved jobs, the management that they had cut some. Little had been resolved beyond the saving of face on both sides.

A bigger capitulation was taking place to the north. No sooner had the ROH announced cuts in its 1999 season than Ian Albery warned that without the revenue from the Opera House residency, Sadler's Wells would go bust. 'This has blown out twenty-five weeks of programming and unless something happens very soon we will be closed,' he said.[5] The rebuilt Sadler's Wells, due to open on 12 October, was also four million pounds short of its £48 million building costs.

Albery threatened to sue Covent Garden for a million pounds in lost revenue and penalty clauses. The ROH retorted that it was being made a 'scapegoat' by Sadler's Wells to divert attention from its own financial crisis.[6] The Blairs were alerted. Nobody in authority wanted to be held responsible for closing their local theatre.

On the day the Wells reopened, the Arts Council announced that it had 'secured compensation' of £1.35 million pounds for Sadler's Wells. The deal, it was reported, 'amounts to a full settlement of

Covent Garden's contract, give or take £50,000'.[7] Michael Berkeley, a member of the ROH board, gave a yelp of anguish. He admitted that Covent Garden were liable for a million but 'expressed dismay that (ACE) was insisting that Covent Garden pay a further £350,000'.[8] This seemed like punitive retribution from a Council which had its thumbprints all over the Sadler's Wells-ROH contract and bore equal responsibility for its fulfilment.* There was no escaping the conclusion that Covent Garden, far from being the flagship of British arts, was now the favourite whipping boy. Six months later, the Arts Council coughed up, without a squeak of protest, an additional six million pound Lottery grant to Sadler's Wells to cover the construction shortfall. Had Covent Garden been able to rely on such generosity, it would never have landed in the present mess.

On Armistice Day, 11 November, Chris Smith met Bernard Haitink and bowed to his terms. He also assured Lord Sainsbury and Mrs Duffield that the Royal companies would eventually return to year-round performance. The donors unstopped their cheques and Haitink withdrew his resignation, once he was convinced that the orchestra would continue to play through the following year. The consequences of this climbdown were generally uncalculated.

The orchestra was costing the company four million pounds a year. In the judgement of most conductors, it was not the equal of London's four self-employed concert orchestras, and on ballet nights it played appallingly. Approaches had been made to the RPO and one other ensemble to take over at Covent Garden if the ROH orchestra were to be disbanded. Engaging independent orchestras, free of holiday, sickness and pension costs, would have saved the ROH well over a million pounds a year.

Opera festivals like Glyndebourne and Salzburg were all the more exciting for having top-flight international orchestras playing in the pit. Newer opera companies like Los Angeles were formed without an orchestra, relying on the local philharmonic. There was no compelling reason for Covent Garden to keep its own band except for union resistance, sentimental attachments and Haitink's solidarity with an orchestra in which his wife had once played. Unwilling to grasp the nettle, Chris Smith caved in and the rescue plan was aborted. Every critical issue was fudged into a formula that allowed

---

* in fact, the ACE ultimately paid the £350,000 itself

Smith to release extra funds and Michael Kaiser to start work with a clean sheet.

A few days after Kaiser's arrival, we had breakfast at the Waldorf Hotel. A pale, roly-poly man in his mid-forties, Kaiser was sounding out opinion formers without taking much interest in the causes of past discomfort. His eyes were fixed on a future in which the opera house would offer access to all and the highest standard of performance. It would be a light unto the nations, developing a training programme for managers from other companies and unifying British arts behind their greatest asset. The two smaller theatres within the building would enable them to engage, for the first time, with solo and chamber performances and develop educational outreach to untold heights. 'This is a group of people that has gone through a war,' he said, 'and I want to give them hope.'

There was something admirable about his optimism, in view of the company's rampant unpopularity. Kaiser was brisk and business-like, courteous and attentive, yet he appeared self-effacing to the point that I could hardly identify a single personality trait. My mystification was widely shared. Casting around the American opera and orchestral sectors and their attendant media, I found hardly anyone who had heard of Kaiser, and the few who had met him knew nothing about him. Even in the ballet world, where he had performed most of his wonders, people described him as efficient and valuable but could not bring themselves to say what he was like. Michael Kaiser was a man without a shadow – a consultant who came to the aid of ailing organizations and left them feeling much better. Covent Garden represented the biggest challenge of his life. When his mother read the *Telegraph* headline that greeted his arrival – 'Chaos Reigns as Kaiser enters Opera House'[9] – she phoned him and said, 'have you gone off your head?'

A New Yorker by birth, he would sing in a synagogue choir on Saturday mornings and spend the afternoon watching rehearsals of the Philharmonic, where his grandfather had played. He thought of having his voice trained professionally, and thought better of it. He went to Brandeis University and MIT, and in his mid-twenties formed a business consultancy that attracted such blue-chip clients as General Motors and IBM. He sold up in 1985 and went to work in the arts, for the State Ballet of Missouri, the Pierpont Morgan Library and the Alvin Ailey Dance Theater Foundation. In 1994 he founded his second consultancy, this time devoted to arts management. His clients included the Detroit Symphony Orchestra and the South African government, his only overseas involvement. In 1995, he took command of American Ballet Theater as its executive director.

Four years was the longest he had spent in any post, and he seemed to make neither enemies nor close friends. Deborah MacMillan, invited to dinner at his apartment, found herself among a group of his MIT contemporaries who were running huge companies and making millions. 'You should know,' said one of these high-fliers, 'that Michael was the brightest of us all.'

Kaiser himself admitted to no attachments. He had a dog, which he left with a friend in New York. His greatest joy in life, he said, was to make things work.

The parallels with Webster were startling: both were single men and single-minded with no life to speak of outside the theatre. Like Webster, he never appeared flustered. Covent Garden was about to pass from the hurly-burly of four chief executives in less than two years to the deep, deep calm of Michael Kaiser.

But there was more to Kaiser than a good bedside manner and a willingness to tell people what they wanted to hear. He represented a change of style that caught English colleagues unprepared. One of Kaiser's first acts was to dispense with the three-person secretariat that had served the chief executive since Isaacs' time. He required one secretary, and when she was out to lunch Michael Kaiser answered the phone himself. There were to be no barriers or formalities at the top.

Anthony Dowell was the first to be struck – dumbstruck – by the new chief's style. A few days before Kaiser's arrival, the Royal Ballet's leading male dancer, Tetsuya 'Teddy' Kumakawa decided to break away and form his own troupe, the K Ballet. 'I'm very disappointed,' said Dowell. Two weeks later five more dancers defected to join him, leaving the company with just three principal full-time men. Dowell was devastated. 'What are we going to do?' he sighed. 'This is a terrific opportunity,' said Kaiser. 'Go out and hire the five best male dancers in the world.' There was a deathly hush. No one had ever suggested anything so bold at the Royal Ballet since Nureyev shook the company's foundations. What is more, Kaiser was the first person to run the company with real ballet know-how.

Kaiser's approach to problems was not to cover up or deny but to

admit the difficulty and promise, 'we'll fix it'. His transparency was
rare in the arts, and in the tight-lipped ROH it amounted to a cultural
revolution. At one stage, when I challenged the budgets, he invited
me in to go over the books, itemizing profit and loss with no
apparent concern for commercial confidentiality. His candour was
not so much refreshing as disarming. Within weeks, the press had
turned from sour to supportive. Suddenly, everyone was willing
Michael Kaiser to succeed. The *Guardian* headlined him 'The
Turnaround King of Opera',[10] and the catchphrase caught on. Soon
after, the *New York Times* reported that 'Mr Turnaround' had become
his nickname. Kaiser made no objection. 'It does help to come from
the outside,' he said, 'because my experience of troubled organizations is that when you are in the midst of all the problems, everyone
is focused on the past. Who caused the problem? How did we get
into this mess? They point fingers at each other, the staff blames the
board, the board blames the staff. And no one is saying, "where do
we go from here?"'[11]

It was not all smooth sailing from here on in. The first choice for
artistic director of the Royal Opera turned them down. Francesca
Zambello, the American director of *Paul Bunyan*, said she could not
take the job, because no one would tell her who was in charge –
herself as artistic director, or Kaiser as ROH executive director. In a
letter to Southgate, she said, 'at present the managerial structure,
and my own commitments, make this an enticing possibility best
contemplated in the future.' To a press inquiry she added, 'I don't
think they really know what they want. The company needs to
rethink its whole role.'[12]

There was better luck on the conductor front. While Gergiev,
Gatti, Rattle and Riccardo Chailly had declared themselves
unavailable, and a campaign for Mark Elder, the former ENO music
director, ran out of steam, a little-known London-born Italian
entered the frame.

Antonio Pappano was music director of the Monnaie Theatre in
Brussels and a regular at Bayreuth. He had the reputation of being
able to work with anyone – indeed, he was the only conductor who
could propitiate the volatile lovebirds, Angela Gheorghiu and
Roberto Alagna.

Pappano had been working with voices since he was ten years old,
coming home from school to a Marylebone studio to play piano for

the singers his father was coaching. A family tragedy, the death of a sibling, took the Pappanos to a fresh start in America, but for Tony, just short of forty, the chance to lead Covent Garden was a wheel turned full circle. 'I have been told that I am on the list,' he remarked in Brussels that winter. 'I have not been formally courted but I'm being told what's going on.'[13] A fortnight later he was formally appointed.

Pappano had experienced Covent Garden at its worst, in 1989. 'It was a nightmare,' he said. 'I had, in the first seven nights of *Bohème*, seven different tenors. Jerry Hadley cancelled the première and Dennis O'Neill dropped out twice. Then *William Tell* was pulled one night and they asked me for an extra *Bohème* – and in the pit I found a *William Tell* orchestra. I thought I had a lot to say about *Bohème*, but the situation just got me in knots and it didn't go as it should. I got blasted in the press. People warned me, don't read the reviews.'

In another opera house, someone would have thrown an arm round his shoulder and taken him out to get drunk. At Covent Garden he was treated like a leper. 'I don't remember anyone in the house who was on my side. You walk around, and people know you've been blasted.' He had never returned. What swayed him was Southgate's insistence – Pappano was an EMI recording artist – and an instant rapport with Kaiser. In accepting the job, he insisted that Kaiser extend his own contract to 2005, so that they would have at least three years together in harness.

His appointment solved a nagging structural dilemma. Eyre had decreed that the Royal Opera needed an artistic director at the helm. Pappano said: 'It has to be clear that the music director is the artistic head of the house. He should be there at least seven months of the year. In addition to planning and conducting operas, he should be playing chamber music with the orchestra musicians, doing recitals with young artists.'

This was just what the doctor ordered. Pappano would be the first music director since Solti to know the nuts and bolts of an opera house, the intricacies of programming and the rewards of foresight. He would also be the company's youngest ever music director. The future was starting to look brighter.

At a topping-out ceremony, Chris Smith promised that Covent Garden would become 'a model of good practice in education and access'. Southgate declared that the building 'belonged to the nation', paid for by ordinary people out of their Lottery bets. A gaggle of local residents heckled the proceedings. Eerily, a hydraulic yellow van drew up to clean the street-lamps. On its side was the legend: David Webster Limited.

In the summer of 1999, Kaiser declared Covent Garden's financial crisis to be over. 'We will not be going back for more money to the Arts Council saying we need an extra bit otherwise we can't finish the building – that won't happen,' he said. 'Nor will we say we need an extra bit, otherwise we can't have the season we planned. While we want as much as we can get, I am realistic about the difficulties that all governments have in exceeding inflation when it comes to arts grants.'[14]

This was music to Chris Smith's ears. Not only was Kaiser planning to run a full season on twenty million pounds subsidy, but he was planning to raise an endowment to underpin new work. When the house reopened, said Kaiser, 'we are going to be in the best financial shape we have known in our history'.

For two dedicated years, Vivien Duffield had been going around tapping people and companies for money. 'We've got Vivien coming Monday morning,' one would hear. 'She thinks she's going to get fifty. She'll be lucky to get ten.' Duffield was a shrewd judge of donor character. 'I used to write on a piece of paper what I thought I was going to get, and I was usually right,' she said.

'It was quite businesslike with the corporates. We gave them something that they wanted. It was based on the Glyndebourne scale. They had sort of priced themselves into leagues beforehand. But I'm much better at individuals.'

She had perfected a technique of making a request that could not be refused. 'The only reason I can do it is that people do it to me, and I'm quite impervious about it,' she laughed. 'I go to Israel three times a year, where the word chutzpah was invented.

'There's a Jewish form of fundraising which my Uncle David was expert at. He'd get up at a dinner for Nightingale House (an old age home) and say, "Come on Shmulley, look what your wife's got round her neck, and look at that new car outside – what's the number plate? A new Bentley. What's this you're giving me? £10,000? Come on now, you can make it twenty." And he'd tear up the pledge. At least I haven't resorted to that.'

Duffield was tantalizingly close to her hundred-million target and focusing on small donations. She started a seat-naming campaign, in which anyone could put a plaque on a seat from £500 upwards. A number of ballerinas clubbed together and named a seat in memory of a man who used to send them flowers every night. One woman gave £5,000 for a seat in the stalls on which the anonymous plaque read: 'the seat in which I met the love of my life'.

On a rather grander scale, a pair of Darcey Bussell fans named her dressing-room and a woman whose mother had been in the chorus put her name on their rehearsal room. At the top of the range, three donors had given over ten million – herself, Sainsbury and the Floral Trust. Thirteen more had given over one million. With time running out, the total was in the upper eighties and stalling. During the Eyre review she had lost a million-pound pledge and she was busy trying to woo it back.

The final windfall came by a circuitous route. Alberto Vilar was a Cuban-American who made his fortune tracking new-tech stocks in the dawn of mass computing. He had been among the earliest investors in Microsoft and now he was giving large sums away to the places that gave him most pleasure.

He gave twenty-five million dollars to the Metropolitan Opera and four million more to the Salzburg Festival. He liked to be known as the biggest donor wherever he gave and loved seeing his name in lights. His favourite director was Franco Zeffirelli. When the Italian arrayed his forces on the Met stage, Vilar liked to say that he could see where every dollar was spent; he had no time for minimal stagings.

As co-ordinator of his munificence, he employed Charles Kay, Solti's former secretary, but Vilar liked to make his own decisions and was touchy about how he was received. At a post-concert dinner in London, he sat next to the banker Jacob Rothschild and his wife, Serena, who was involved with the Covent Garden appeal. They put him in touch with Sir Colin Southgate, but Vilar did not like what he was told. Southgate said he could not be the lead donor, since that honour had been claimed by Duffield and Sainsbury. He was about to walk away when Michael Kaiser suggested that, for ten million pounds, they could rename the Floral Hall after him. Others would claim credit for the donation, but Vilar made no secret of the clinching factor. 'If it hadn't been for Michael Kaiser,' he told a business friend, 'I would never have given money to Covent Garden.' Kaiser had given the donor all he wanted without yielding an inch on principle or precedence. Vilar was keen on education. The Vilar Floral Hall would help spread opera to new enthusiasts.[15]

*

One morning in the middle of the year, Sir Anthony Dowell was feeling weighed down by company reshuffles and continuing press attacks when he looked out of the window at the building site across Floral Street. 'Come on,' he said to his secretary, Jeanetta, and to Anthony Russell-Roberts, 'let's have a look.' After a hard-hat tour, Dowell said to himself 'it's going to be something wonderful'. He decided at that moment to see the Royal Ballet into its quarters, and then leave as quickly as possible. 'I have been through the mill in the last few years,' he exhaled.[16]

The building was breathtaking. The ballet rehearsal and dressing-rooms were bathed in sunlight, a far cry from dingy Baron's Court. The fourth-floor staff canteen had one of the best views in London and people ascending the escalator opposite the main entrance could catch a glimpse of Nelson's column if they inclined their heads to the right. There was a sun terrace running around half the roof, giving views of Whitehall and the River Thames. For the first time, the Royal Opera House was looking outward, behaving like a part of the great city.

The entrance halls were airy and marbled. Gone were the red baize curtains and the flunkey at the door, the choking of dust and the claustrophobic sensation, 'abandon hope all ye who enter'.

Jeremy Dixon, the architect, confessed himself 'amazed that the board didn't lose heart and give up two or three times during this process'. He had designed a huge backstage, with room for six sets to be stored intact and thirty more broken up (the rest were stored in Wales).

Everything had been constructed according to instructions given almost thirty years earlier. The potential of new technology hardly entered the picture. Barcelona, which was rebuilding the Liceo after fire in less than two years, had included planning for virtual-reality stage sets and live-relay screens around the lobby. The Met had introduced seat-back surtitles, so much easier on the eye than a screen hung above the proscenium. None of these innovations were considered at Covent Garden or mentioned to the architect. As technology hurtled ahead into a new millennium, this was definedly a twentieth-century building for two nineteenth-century art forms – a museum, to all intents and purposes, rather than a magnet for the lively arts.

*

Early in November, New Labour banned most hereditary peers from the House of Lords. Among those disenfranchised was the twelfth Earl of Drogheda, Derry Moore, photographer son of the former Covent Garden chairman. He lamented the passing of tradition in a *Guardian* diary and found greater distress among the lords who remained than among those who departed into history.

The ballet moved into their new quarters that week, thrilling to unaccustomed luxury. The orchestra checked in soon after, finding showers, lockers and proper shelves for their instruments. Some rehearsal rooms were unheated, others freshly painted, giving grief to the singers. On the 22nd, Cherie Blair bowled up to open the Linbury Studio Theatre, donated by John Sainsbury and Anya Linden. Her pregnancy was hot news and press photographers were out in force. A multi-ethnic audience of kids from local schools had been herded in to see their first ballet. 'For too long,' said Mrs Blair, 'the message that went out from this house was that arts are for the privileged few. All that has changed now.' The children sat mutely through a routine of classical ballet, livening up when the music turned minimalist and the dancing modern in *'Still Life' at the Penguin Café*. As the kids went off to consume boxed lunches in the Floral Hall, I saw the diminutive American director, Peter Sellars, leaving the stage door looking worried. Trouble? We would soon hear about it.

The next morning it transpired that Covent Garden was cancelling one of its three opening operas, and by far the most exciting – György Ligeti's *Le grand macabre*, imported from Salzburg where it had been a huge hit. The reason given was software failures, affecting the movement of scene-shifting wagons. The truth was slightly more complex. One stagehand admitted that they were inadequately trained – three weeks in a classroom before having to stage a full rehearsal. Half the stage crew were new, and the machinery was complex. 'One night it was the wagons, the next the hydraulics. No one knew why,' he said.[17] Kaiser had shed his jacket and put his shoulder to the wheel, to no obvious purpose except raising morale.

Cancelling the Ligeti opera relieved last-minute rehearsal pressure, but infuriated the composer and the conductor, Esa-Pekka Salonen, who were among the last to be told. Without Salzburg topping, the opening programme looked weakly repetitive – a new *Falstaff* with Bryn Terfel and a repeat of Birtwistle's *Gawain*. The ballet was no livelier than the usual Christmas fare.

A squalid row had broken out between the opera and the ballet as to who should go first on opening night. Haitink, on seeing Dowell's ballet programme, said it was far too long. He offered to boycott the opening night unless cuts were made. Dowell had designed a synoptic portrait of the Royal Ballet's work from 1946 to the present. He slashed his programme to an hour and seventeen minutes, shedding contributions by John Cranko and Jerome Robbins. Haitink was still not pacified, grumbling that it was too much for his poor orchestra, who would be overtired by the time they reached Wagner in the second half.

Although the evening was meant to open with Darcey Bussell dancing a spell from *Sleeping Beauty* with which she had put the house to rest thirty months before, Dowell decided to yield precedence in order to save the show. 'Would you like to go first?' he offered Haitink, who gracelessly accepted. The legend of two arts in one company had never seemed more ridiculous.

Tension mounted as the opening approached. Tradition, decorum and board preference dictated that it should be a black-tie occasion. A message arrived from Downing Street: did it have to be black tie? The Prime Minister hated dressing up. When the form was confirmed, Downing Street spin-doctors went tale-bearing to the tabloids about the toffs at Covent Garden. Some people in power never tired of playing class war.

On 1 December, Tony and Cherie Blair arrived in black tie, long gown and matching fixed grins. The Queen, with Prince Philip two scowls behind, glided through the portals in an ankle-length cream and gold dress designed to match the refurbished interiors. Sir Colin Southgate seemed to be forcibly restraining himself from taking Her Majesty by the arm. Vivien Duffield bobbed and curtsied, Michael Kaiser gave a trim little bow. In a breach with tradition, the royal party forsook the Royal Box and sat with the political classes, among them two ex-premiers, Thatcher and Heath. Of all the élite guests, Queen Elizabeth the Queen Mother, now ninety-nine years old, was the only one who seemed to be enjoying herself, perhaps remembering the night almost fifty-four years earlier when she had challenged the lack of refreshments. Tonight, it was free champagne for all and, as in 1946, nothing at all to eat.

Past chief executives jostled chairmen past and present, assuring one another that there were no hard feelings. The great and the good turned out in force. Only the gifted were absent. Joan Sutherland and

Kiri te Kanawa had not been invited. 'We weren't asked,' said Dame Joan tersely. Art took second place on the invitation list to social and political rank.

Colin Southgate was the first on stage, acclaiming the new opera house as 'the most technically advanced theatre in the world'. Then the microphone failed. BBC screens were twice blacked out during the evening by loss of power. There were no stage sets and the house felt unready. Chris Smith called it 'a miracle' and confessed there were times he never believed it would come into being. That afternoon he had been called to the floor of the Commons to admit that the hundred and twenty million pound Lottery grant he had approved for an Olympic stadium in Wembley had been a mistake since the space could not in his estimation accommodate both track and team-sport events. At least half the money was irrecoverable. With one stroke of the pen he had blown three-quarters of the amount of Lottery money invested in Covent Garden. Yet there was no howl from the tabloids, because the money was wasted with good sporting intentions, and no grilling from Kaufman because there was not as much fun to be had in exposing sporting negligence as there was in mocking the arts.

When the music finally struck up, spirits sank. Haitink had decided to open with the *Oberon* overture that Weber wrote for Covent Garden in 1826. Next came Domingo and Deborah Polaski in the love duet from *Walküre*. An assorted septet delivered the finale of *Fidelio*. It was a woefully becalmed festivity, lumpen with German dumplings and not a twinkle of light or an echo of the company's national identity. Two of the female singers were American, the third came from Lapland. Had England run out of sopranos who could sing a Beethoven set piece?

The ballet, by contrast, glittered and soared. Bussell reopened all eyes with *Beauty*'s Rose Adagio in the 1946 choreography, kicking off a chronological survey compiled with wit and fine taste. Ashton was remembered in clips from *Symphonic Variations*, *Cinderella* and later glories. Nureyev's role in *Bayadère* was revived by Irek Mukhamedov. Guillem swooped and swooned in MacMillan's *Manon* and Bussell and Jonathan Cope ran away with *Prince of the Pagodas*. The minimalist scores and modern choreography for '*Still Life' at the Penguin Café* and *Fearful Symmetries* showed that there was still some life remaining in dance, which is more than could have been said for the opera. When the curtain fell, first priorities had been restored. The ballet had triumphed at Covent Garden, while the opera seemed confused, stolid and uncertain. The wheel had turned full circle.

CHAPTER 13

Lie Back and Think of England
(2000–2100 European time)

EVER SINCE THE Festival of Britain in 1951, Labour had looked upon itself as the party of parties. The bash it put on for the opening of the third Christian millennium was designed to wow the world, no expense spared. A chain of fireworks along the Thames, an orange cloud of parachutists descending on Tower Bridge, the 'biggest ever' street parade and, to cap it all, a countdown entertainment at the Millennium Dome in the presence of the Queen and everyone who counted in New Labour's vision of New Britain. Paul Daniel and the orchestra of English National Opera performed a spiritual new meditation by Sir John Tavener, who protested at the absence of God's name in the text he had been given to set. Willard White, the West Indian-born bass, sang 'Amazing Grace'.

At the stroke of midnight, Tony Blair and Her Majesty clinked champagne glasses. He then *lèse-majesté*'d his arm into hers for a rendition of 'Auld Lang Syne'. After that, it was party all the way with a riot of Brazilian dancing and an 'erotic aerial ballet' beneath the brave new cupola. There was some muttering at an absence of indigenous relevance, but the show was intended to reflect a nation that had emerged from primordial insularity to embrace all the world had to offer in randomly equal opportunity.

The Dome, designed by the New Labour peer and former Arts Council deputy chairman Richard Rogers, emblemified the dawning century, its pylons stretching hopefully into the sky. Blair called it 'the envy of the world'. It had cost £758 million to build, of which a generous £449 million had come from the Millennium Commission, using National Lottery funds. This was almost six times the amount invested in the new ROH, and the Dome was not expected to survive longer than twenty-five years. Is it a visionary leap, wondered the novelist J. G. Ballard, 'or a gigantic folly, the equivalent of the South Sea Bubble, a vast balloon inflated by the promises of PR men?'[1]

The answer came with the speed of e-commerce. By the end of its opening week, the Dome was in trouble, running well below visitor targets and drawing glum reactions for the length of its queues and the mediocrity of its exhibits. By the end of the month, the Dome's operators had to go back to Millennium Commission for a sixty-million-pound 'loan' to enable them to continue trading. The money would be repaid from profits, they promised, but early projections indicated an annual loss of as much as twenty-three million pounds. 'This is a misuse of donated funds,' said the Institute of Charity Fund Managers.[2] Every pound that was poured into the Dome was a pound taken away from good causes and the arts.

The subsidy per Dome visitor amounted to thirty pounds, on top of the twenty pound admission price. This compared with £27.50 seat subsidy at the Royal Opera House, and eight pounds at Sadler's Wells.[3] The Dome was draining the nation of funds for education and enlightenment. A week into its second month, the Dome's chief executive, Jennie Page, was replaced by a Frenchman, a marketing executive from Euro Disney. The putative second Festival of Britain had made a mockery of national pride, bypassing the creative gene and substituting a rush of Gallic fast-sell gimmickry.

It was not the only post-war shibboleth to crack. 'Labour admits NHS in crisis,'[4] blared a front-page splash that winter as the crucible of the Welfare State proved unable to cope with a mild flu epidemic. Patients in Kent were shuttled across to French hospitals and German television viewers were warned to leave Britain fast if they felt sick. Britain had the lowest survival rate for heart disease and cancer in western Europe.

A fifty-five-year-old woman in Middlesborough was told that she would have to pay ten thousand pounds if she wanted a routine course of aggressive chemotherapy for ovarian cancer, as her local health authority could not afford it. 'I just didn't believe it,' said Jackie O'Donnell, 'because in this country we were brought up to believe that we would get the best treatment available.'[5] In Leeds, seventy-three-year-old Mavis Skeet was sentenced to death when her operation for oesophageal cancer was postponed four times until it became inoperable.

Tony Blair was shocked at this 'dreadful' latter case and accepted 'the responsibility to put this situation right'.[6] But it would take more than money to repair the nation's health. The NHS was now the largest employer in Europe, a behemoth in which cost control was all but impossible except in the most generalized forms. But no politician dared break it up. Of all the post-war values, the NHS remained a sacred shrine. Like a five-headed deity, no one believed it brought good health, but it could not be touched – just in case.

At the heart of its problems was a shortage of funds that derived partly from past economic crises and partly from expensive new drugs and treatments coming on to the market. When Viagra was released, promising renewed potency and mental equilibrium to men with erectile dysfunction, Blair's Health Secretary Frank Dobson announced at first that the pills, costing eight pounds each, would not be available on the NHS. He later modified his position, urging doctors to prescribe Viagra only in 'exceptional circumstances', such as paralysis victims. This advice was ruled illegal by a High Court judge,[7] but few health authorities could, in any case, afford to dispense the drug.

Spending on health in Britain was running at £55.7 billion a year, or 6.8 per cent of gross domestic product. This compared with 9.6 per cent in France, 10.7 per cent in Germany and 14 per cent in the United States. New Labour in its election campaign had promised an extra billion pounds for the NHS. Frank Dobson, when he entered office, was told that this would amount to roughly one week's spending, and would make no appreciable difference.[8]

Blair now pledged to raise health spending within six years to European levels, but much of the money was bound to be whittled away in wage rises for the gargantuan payroll, without appreciable improvements in patient care. Blair ordered the appointment of a national supervisor of critical care – a cancer 'czar', a heart 'supremo', swelling the bureaucracy still further.

There were two alternatives: either raise taxes, or encourage a higher uptake of private health insurance, as prevailed in the United States and most of Europe. Neither option was electorally accept-able, and no mainstream politician was prepared to propose more than a tinkering at the edges with this ailing relic of national consensus. England, on the threshold of a new millennium, was literally the sick man of Europe, its leaders unable to venture a cure.

The opening of the Royal Opera House was not much happier than the Dome. After the gala came Verdi's *Falstaff*, which Haitink conducted heavily, as if it were Wagner. Bryn Terfel played the comic hero with an apt blend of pomposity and self-pity, but the rest of the cast was undistinguished and Paul Brown's set resembled the BBC's cultish pre-school programme, *Teletubbies*. Backstage, crews wrestled with untested machinery and stubborn software.

By mid-January, twelve opera performances had been cancelled, including a schools matinée of *Gawain*, which left teachers and pupils bewailing their waste of curricular preparation. A ballet triple bill was abandoned mid-way through the performance when the sets would not budge. In *Nutcracker*, the Christmas tree failed to materialize and in *Gawain* the audience were kept waiting forty minutes for a trap-door to open. Many left during the delays to catch the last train home. There was not much by way of apology or compensation.

Patrons complained of a strident public address system and a lack of customer care at the front of the house, where the attendants were new and half-trained. 'I have been coming here for fifty-three years, and nobody knows me any more,' wailed a retired gentleman's outfitter.

The Crush Bar had been demolished and the space turned over to corporate entertainment. The fashionable round bars in the Floral Hall were crowded and lacked conviviality. The Hall itself looked like a cross between an airport concourse and a shopping arcade. It was soon to be hired out for barmitzvahs and weddings.

There were voluminous complaints about ticketing. Kaiser had promised to bring down prices. In fact, many seats were more expensive than before. A former ROH singer, Joan Carlyle, paid £150 for a seat with partial sightlines. Sir Peter Hall complained that not many people could, like himself, afford a pair of £150 seats for a *Rosenkavalier*. Chris Smith had let it be known that he did not want to see the 'same old faces' in the stalls and expected further price cuts to attract 'a better social mix'. There were, at last, facilities for the disabled, but MPs complained that twenty-four seats were far too few.

By mid-January, Bectu were demanding that the house should be shut until backstage problems were resolved. The Musicians Union said, 'our patience is running out'. The *Sunday Times* reported that the orchestra was in revolt and that a million pounds had been lost in the opening month. Kaiser kept his cool. 'All along we have evaluated whether we can get shows on safely and efficiently,' he said. 'So long as we can do that, we stay open.' The losses incurred had been about one-third of press guesstimates. He was negotiating with Bectu to allow all-night working on wagon tests.

In most other countries, the curtain would have fallen there and then. France, when it opened the Bastille Opéra for the glorious bicentenary of the 1789 Revolution, shut it again for the rest of the year until officials were satisfied that it worked. But this was England, where the state kept its hands off the arts until they lost money or offended ministers. Covent Garden could not afford to shut down for fear it would not be allowed to reopen. The Prime Minister hated the place, the culture secretary was looking to score points and the rest of the arts regarded it still as the whore of Babylon, a place of immoral and wasteful excess. Kaiser had no alternative but to put a brave face on the setbacks and carry on sweet-talking until the software came right. He was unable to propose radical measures without upsetting a fragile status quo. Like the NHS, the ROH was trapped in the misery of its own myth.

By March, matters had settled down sufficiently for people to attend the opera house in reasonable expectation that a show would start and finish on time, and they might retrieve their coats afterwards with less than half an hour's wait. A smile was seen on Anthony Dowell's drawn face, though that might have been an indication of demob-happiness. As Dowell put together tribute evenings to Ashton and MacMillan and the first revival for forty years of Ninette de Valois' *Coppélia*, televised live, his successor was about to be announced.

There were no fewer than fifty applicants, ten of them serious contenders. Kevin McKenzie of American Ballet Theater was Kaiser's favourite, along with Ross MacGibbon, a former RB dancer and busy filmmaker. Derek Deane, head of English National Ballet, was in the reckoning, as was Nureyev's Paris deputy, Patricia Ruanne, who had the support of the Sainsburys. Lynn Seymour put in a late bid, partnered by the choreographer Mark Baldwin. Parties formed behind Irek Mukhamedov, approaching the end of his dancing career, and Sylvie Guillem, who had just revived *Marguerite and Armand* with the Parisian Nicolas Le Riche, the first pair to dance the roles since Fonteyn and Nureyev.

The victor was an Australian, unknown in Britain. Ross Stretton, head of Australian Ballet, had not seen the Royal Ballet dance for three years but had strong views on its problems. 'I think it needs somebody to take a look from the outside, somebody with no axe to grind,' he said.[9] The company had to be 'remotivated' and would benefit from working with the European choreographers Jiri Kylian and Maurice Béjart, and their disciples. Kaiser, who had admired Stretton as a dancer at ABT, was impressed by his energy. Deborah MacMillan, who remembered him as one of her husband's New York principals, said: 'Kenneth thought Ross was a beautifully trained dancer, a perfect partner and a good company man.'[10] Not everyone was convinced that this was what the company needed. Since the death of MacMillan, whose works were danced in a dozen companies the world over, the Royal Ballet had not made a single contribution to dance repertoire. What it needed, more than Mr Motivator, was creative force at its helm, a choreographer who would remind the world of the uniqueness of English ballet, if such uniqueness still existed – and, if not, what was the company's purpose?

Another Australian, Gailene Stock, took over that month as head of the Royal Ballet School. She bemoaned the lack of good British male dancers. 'I am wondering why it is harder to find the raw talent here than it was in Australia,' she told Ismene Brown. 'Maybe it's the sedentary lives they lead in front of the television and the computer.'[11] Had English ballet fallen so low that it could be mocked and run by ex-colonials who, when Madam ruled the roost, had barely a tutu between them from Sydney to Perth? Certainly, its fortunes seemed to be on the slide. The men Dowell had imported to replace his defectors were Cuban, Russian and Swedish. Viviana Durante, the company's complete all-rounder, followed Adam Cooper into freelance exile. Stars of English National Ballet posed in their underwear for *Loaded*, a lads' mag, which billed them on its cover as 'Bra-less'. There was not much left to shed, it seemed, before ballet in Britain hit rock-bottom. Andrea Quinn, music director of the Royal Ballet, resigned after clashes with the Covent Garden orchestra and joined New York City Ballet.

Yet, early that year, the men of Matthew Bourne's unsubsidized *Swan Lake* returned for a second run in the West End, demonstrating that there was a viable audience for classical dance and an appetite for fresh ideas that seemed to have deserted the public sector. Bourne was staging *My Fair Lady* for the Royal National Theatre, but could not find the time or inclination to work with the Royal Ballet. He was about to make a bold move. In March, his company,

Adventures in Motion Pictures, took a lease on the vacant Old Vic, where Lilian Baylis had founded the public-spirited tradition, the stage where Ninette de Valois created English ballet. Bourne was sensitive to the symbolism. 'Anybody who knows me,' he said, 'knows that I love the history of theatre and dance, and the Old Vic is where British music and dance were born.'[12] It was a homecoming of sorts, perhaps a new beginning.

Elsewhere in the arts, resentments rumbled and heaved. Sir Richard Eyre, in a public lecture,[13] implored the Government to appoint a 'theatre czar' to rescue the drama sector from intensive care. Three symphony orchestras teetered on the brink of insolvency, awaiting a rescue package from the Arts Council that came with strings attached. The Council had squandered whatever trust it once owned among the arts to deal kindly and fairly with clients. Gerry Robinson, its chairman, announced that he would not serve a second term. Chris Smith formed a ministerial unit called Quest whose task was to monitor the Arts Council and, potentially, to take over arts funding in the event of its abolition, which many deemed desirable.

The saddest of spectres was Sir Peter Hall, obliged at seventy to work abroad because his own country would not sustain his brimming ambitions. Hall had asked the Arts Council for a half-million pound guarantee against loss – not a subsidy, he insisted – to continue running a repertory company that he had founded at the Old Vic and taken to the West End. They refused. New Labour was no friend to old age. Hall threatened to form an alternative Arts Council, made up of real artists, who would expose the ACE as a pen-pushing sham.

He went to America to direct Shakespeare in Los Angeles, and again to stage a cycle of ten new plays set in ancient Greece. 'I wanted to do it here with the Royal Shakespeare Company,' he lamented. 'They would have done it, but they haven't got any money. In Denver, population 3.5 million they found me eight million dollars. Here, population fifty-five million, nothing. It drives me mad, this country. Chris Smith is nice enough but he has no clout. The arts are starved of cash. Blair doesn't care. He isn't remotely interested. And I voted for him . . .'[14]

His was a common wail – that Governments of both parties refused to sustain the arts with amounts so tiny, 'they wouldn't even show up in the national accounts'.[15] Jeremy Isaacs, back in his television habitat, never tired of telling people how much easier it was to run an international opera house in Europe, with twice as much subsidy as in Britain. On the Continent, however, opera and ballet were state-run operations. Peter Jonas, the intendant in Munich, had a senior Treasury official sitting in an adjacent room to tell him what he could, and could not, put on. There was great respect for tradition in Bavaria, but limited room for adventure. The vitality of English opera and dance was rooted in a mixed economy of state and private subsidy, and Jonas would sometimes look back wistfully at the hair-raising risks he had taken at ENO.

In Europe, too, governments were cutting back on art subsidies in an age of mounting social costs. The German capital, Berlin, with three opera houses and seven orchestras, was facing severe rationalization. Italy was looking to reduce its thirteen opera houses, and La Scala was being encouraged to go private if it could find sufficient corporate sponsorship. France had stopped building cultural monuments, amid a rash of recriminations. The opera house in Lyon, lavishly rebuilt in 1993, was closed down after inspectors declared the stage and its machinery too dangerous for use. Similar problems afflicted the Bastille, the Bibliothèque Nationale and the Paris musical Conservatoire.

In England, the funding emphasis shifted away from live performance to capital conservation. The biggest expansion in British arts over the last decade of the twentieth century was the Tate Gallery, which built offshoots in Liverpool and Cornwall and a massive annexe opposite St Paul's Cathedral, designed to represent 'modern' – more precisely, post-modern – British art. Museum culture was redefining itself in an age of computers and virtual reality, while performing culture was mired in unchanged conditions of fixed labour costs, fickle audiences, and an ever-shrinking base of educated audiences who would spend their last penny to see a show. 'There must be vibrant audiences longing to come, fighting to come, pushing their way into spaces to live an experience that they feel is life-enhancing,' said Peter Brook, the theatrical doyen-in-exile. 'That is what theatre is about,' he told an awards audience, 'and yet – the opposite is true. The impossible-to-define theatre of next year, and the next hundred years, and the next millennium, will never happen unless that audience-cash-success criterion ... is also questioned, and with equal confidence one acclaims the bold work that empties the theatre and asserts the right to fail.'[16]

That right had been progressively withdrawn from the Royal Opera House in particular, and English performing arts in general, over a quarter of a century. The need for success produced safety-first programming which, in turn, foisted a fusty image upon lyric theatre. Opera, after its Big Bang mini-boom in the late 1980s, reverted overwhelmingly to its middle-class, middle-aged core audiences and ceased to be 'cool'.

In a culture of instant e-mails, two-minute pop-songs and whittled down attention spans, a full evening at the opera was more than most twenty-somethings could contemplate, let alone afford. The cross-section of teachers, clerical workers, college students, other ranks and curiosity seekers who thronged the Royal Opera House in its formative period were now banned – both by price and by self-perception. This was not the sort of place where young people would feel comfortable or find like-minded contemporaries. Unless some educational and economic miracle were to make opera irresistible and accessible once again to audiences of all ages and backgrounds, its claim to represent the nation would continue to be ridiculed as a privileged sham.

So where had it all gone wrong? How had a country which once put funding for the Royal Opera House before its daily bread ration reverted in prosperity to John Bull's cultural indifference? Had nothing improved in the national character after half a century of state-supported art?

As far as the ROH was concerned, executives and artists, past and present, overwhelmingly blamed its decline and fall on persistent and progressive underfunding. The bare statistics support their case. Between 1970 and 1997, Arts Council grants to Covent Garden rose from £1.4 million to £20 million. Over that period inflation octupled. In 1997, the grant was worth therefore half as much in purchasing value as it had been in 1970.[17] That is a severe and unsustainable decline, unforgivable in the view of arts supporters.

Seen from the Treasury side, however, the grant can be shown to have remained relatively constant in terms of general Government spending. It represented in 1997 exactly the same proportion of state expenditure as it had in 1970. Any shortfall had been happily compensated by private donations and sponsorships. The state, in this light, had done its bit.

Other factors entered the equation. The fees for stars and senior staff exploded in the last quarter of the twentieth century,[18] making the running of an international opera house the exclusive preserve of the world's wealthiest cities. These sums were themselves dwarfed by the soaring rewards for success in sports and light entertainment. If Domingo commanded £20,000 for singing a role at Covent Garden or the Met, it was a fraction of the million dollars he could have earned from singing in the park, or of the ten million dollars that a baby-faced Spice Girl could collect from a single record track. Managerial salaries were comparably disproportionate. Webster, who depressed his own wage packet to maintain a tight salary structure, earned in 1948 roughly the same as Matt Busby, manager of the Cup-winning Manchester United,[19] who was paid £1,750, plus bonus. Michael Kaiser, equally frugal, received £125,000 in the year 2000, one-eighth of the published salary of Alex Ferguson, manager of European Cup-winning Manchester United, who took home a cool million.

The rewards in art and entertainment had become disproportionate to the creativity and effort involved, and distortionate to general economic trends. To accuse the arts of extravagance, as politicians habitually did, was to ignore the heartless exploitation of working-class fans by club owners, record companies and the stars themselves. The reasons for Covent Garden's decline were partly self-inflicted, but they did not include wild indulgence, or, *pace* Kaufman and Smith, persistent wastage of public funds. Nor could underfunding be cited as the precipitant and principal cause. Money, for once, was not the root of all evil.

The underlying cause was loss of purpose and relevance. When Ninette de Valois founded Sadler's Wells Ballet, its aim was to cultivate an English form of dance for a popular audience. Over time and triumph, the company became international in reputation and ability. What it stood for got lost in transition.

Ask its outgoing artistic director Anthony Dowell what the Royal Ballet represents today, and he struggles for a definition:

> I know the value of this company, what had been achieved. When asked about my vision, I said that a classical company should remain a classical company because that creates the best dancers, and that's what I tried to move on. And a certain quality in the package. I think I have kept alive certain things in the company that do not exist in others.

Monica Mason, his deputy, speaks in terms of heritage preservation:

> For me, this is the best company in the world, because we have the best repertoire, the best working situation and the most extraordinary heritage from de Valois to the end of Anthony Dowell's reign. Since the 1930s there has been one continuous line running through. Most companies haven't had a history like that. It represents the most wonderful opportunity for young dancers to discover their talents in classical ballet.

Lynn Seymour, ever a dissident voice, challenged some of those assumptions:

> The Royal Ballet isn't doing anything to distinguish it from any other company, and in fact is quite a lot below the standard of other companies we see these days . . . I think the nation needs to feel a sense of ownership about English ballet – the same sense of ownership about Ashton as it feels about Shakespeare.[20]

But how to get to the point where the nation resumes its rightful ownership of English ballet is something no one can envision. De Valois' clarity of purpose and the need she identified for having a national ballet have faded in her successors and cannot perhaps be redefined so long as the founder casts her living shadow over the troubled proceedings.

The point of having an opera company at Covent Garden was that it should awaken and cultivate undeveloped realms of English culture and language. But the Royal Opera stopped singing in English. Then it disbanded its company of English singers. What survives is an orchestra, not of the best; a chorus at subsistence level; and an administration. The company cannot afford to tour the UK. Its national purpose has become invisible.

A former chairman, Claus Moser, defines its uniqueness through the continuity of its last three music directors:

> Why the opera house has been reborn is because we had three outstanding music directors in Solti, Davis and Haitink – it's like Karajan and the Berlin Philharmonic: the standards never slipped.

That traditional argument is meaningful, though only to a

diminishing caste of aesthetes. It is not a basis on which an artistic enterprise can attract broad public support.

The splendid bass singer John Tomlinson, a favourite Wotan at Covent Garden and Bayreuth, attacked domestic criticism of Covent Garden as 'parochial':

> Covent Garden is one of the three or four Eiffel Towers of the opera world, with Vienna, the Met, La Scala as the others. The tradition of opera as real music theatre is second to none in Britain, if only people would realize it.[21]

But how could they be expected to realize it, when only a minority within an arts-loving minority could afford to experience it. The cost of reducing tickets at Covent Garden to the levels of the Bastille or the Metropolitan Opera would amount to ten or fifteen million pounds a year, more than the entire subsidy for ENO. The Met and the Bastille kept tickets affordable by building new houses with four thousand seats. Covent Garden kept them exclusive by rebuilding with just 2,141 seats. This cardinal misjudgement alone will prevent the ROH from ever again becoming a popular venue.

'How much importance we attach to making opera and ballet accessible to all depends on what society we believe ourselves to be,'[22] intoned Jeremy Isaacs. His perception was typically accurate, but the face of society had changed in his lifetime and no longer shared his ideals. A country which was prepared to spend less than half on its health than the United States was also a country that would eke one-third as much to the arts as the German state. A mean, puritanical, pig-ignorant streak dominated the media agenda, and it precluded, as Tony Blair rightly perceived, any renewal of artistic altruism on the part of central Government.

What the arts had lost, apart from a reasonable level of funding, were their roots in a society that was changing both aspirationally and demographically. The ability to sing, dance, play the piano, write a poem or paint a picture to the best of one's ability was no longer prized in an Internet world where entertainment was obtainable at the press of a button and refinement was a suspect quality, tainted with politically-incorrect 'élitism'. The arts were scarcely taught in school, except with marks or careers in mind, and those who missed these skills at an early age would never learn to seek and appreciate the summits of art. The audience of the future was being eroded in the nation's schoolrooms. The J. B. Priestley characters who sought to 'better themselves' by attending concerts and operas were now more likely to pleasure themselves at a football match or disco.

As the improving dimension of the performing arts declined, so did their roots in English society. The second half of the twentieth century was a period of mass immigration, the diasporas arriving so thick and fast that they did not need to shed indigenous cultures and immerse themselves, as earlier waves had done, in a dominant host culture. Instead, there flourished a Joseph's coat of mini-cultures in which the western heritage of song and dance was but one contender among many. Its centrality could not be taken for granted in a multi-cultural society whose younger members sought a borderless breadth of experiences. Covent Garden could not claim to stand for England, when England was busily redefining itself.

Around one quarter of the populace of central London boroughs, those within an hour's journey of Covent Garden, were estimated to belong to ethnic minorities for whom the Royal Opera House meant little or nothing in terms of tradition, pleasure and aspiration.

The company's roots in its own city were thinning. Critically, the roots in its immediate locality were destroyed when the market was uprooted, the porters no longer whistling at passing ballerinas or lending a hand backstage, and many of the inhabitants affronted by the opera house's assaults on their environment. It was this loss of relevance and roots, more than any personal or financial failure, that brought successive ROH boards to their knees and prevented them from seeing beyond the end of their aquiline noses.

And then there were the residues of unresolved structural faults, going back to the company's formation. Maynard Keynes, when he created the ROH, intended to run it as an executive chairman, with a general administrator attending to daily business. Keynes died before the house was fully operational and the relative powers of chairman, board members and chief executive were never clarified. Conflicts could usually be settled over a cup of tea, but when it came down to a clash of personalities there was no constitutional framework on which to fall back. Many of the 1990s crises could be ascribed less to individual error than to institutional weakness. By the end of the first season in the reopened opera house, those frailties were fatally exposed.

Sir Colin Southgate had never got on well with his deputy, Vivien

Duffield. He allowed her to be removed from the board as soon as the money she had collected and donated was safely banked. Dame Vivien, honoured in the June 2000 birthday list, could do nothing but go gracefully. However, the board's ingratitude was duly noted by many who had given, or were thinking of giving, private donations. No American opera house would have treated a benefactor so shabbily.

That summer, relations between the board and executive director reached breaking point. Southgate is said to have resented the credit given to Kaiser for restoring the company, while Kaiser resisted having his decisions questioned and second-guessed by the chairman. The final straw was the appointment to the board of Peter Hemmings, retired manager of Scottish Opera and Los Angeles Opera and a man whose professional skills ran parallel to Kaiser's. Hemmings was there, potentially, to shadow the boss. 'This is not a board I can work with,' Kaiser told an American colleague. In the first week of June he crossed the Atlantic to pitch for top jobs at the Kennedy Center in Washington and the Lincoln Center in New York. On 19 June, he announced his resignation from the Royal Opera House. 'For personal reasons,' said Kaiser, 'it is time for me to return to my home.'

He had not settled well in London, missing his Manhattan friends and his dog, which had sadly died. But the principal reason for announcing his departure after only 19 months was neither social nor personal, but primarily structural. The imbalanced relationship between the board and its executive director had rendered the company effectively unmanageable.

Fingers were pointed at the board and a cry went up for Southgate's head, but the loss of a fifth chief in three years signalled that it was not so much the chairman as the system that was at fault. The board was appointed by a government which now contributed less than one-third of the budget. It no longer represented charitable supporters, disenfranchised with Vivien Duffield's departure, and took no heed of consumer views. Alberto Vilar, who had endowed the Floral Hall with ten million pounds and was planning to give more, sounded the alarm on the day that Kaiser quit. 'Michael was someone I could relate to and respect,' he said. 'I will need to know that his successor is someone I can work with.'[23]

Although Kaiser had never been expected to stay for life, his swift exit provoked a plummeting of morale and a sense of foreboding among the incoming opera and ballet chiefs, Antonio Pappano and Ross Stretton. The ROH remained conspicuously on the sick-list and in need of urgent reconstruction.

So what is to be done? The need for redefinition is urgent, for without it Covent Garden cannot survive. Four reviews in two decades – Priestley, Warnock, Stevenson, Eyre – failed to produce decisive change as politicians of both main parties fudged and fiddled. Given the near-certainty that no opera house will ever be funded to sustainable levels in a twenty-first century England, there are only two solutions on offer: the radical and the prudent.

The radical route separates performing companies from buildings. The ROH, Coliseum and Sadler's Wells would be put under a unified public administration. The Royal Ballet, Royal Opera, ENO, ENB, Ballet Rambert – and regional companies if they so wished – would each have a fixed residency period in its preferred house and a chance to bid for extra periods against foreign and commercial promoters, such as the Kirov and Raymond Gubbay. The performing companies would be relieved of the overheads of building maintenance and freed to concentrate on making art. The Royal Ballet and Royal Opera would shed their historic enmity and go their separate ways, fruitfully and sometimes collaboratively.

The building administration would shed the daily intrusion of artistic foibles and begin to formulate a performing-arts policy for the capital city, a policy in which repertorial risk could be safely balanced against box-office bankrollers. Both the ROH and Coliseum would have a resident orchestra, booked competitively by the season, playing with all comers. This would free the performing companies to take productions to the regions and abroad, working with local orchestras instead of expensively touring their own.

The plan is more likely to appeal to believers in a controlled economy – Eyre was 'enticed'[24] by it – but it has the virtues of saving money and, above all, liberating artists from internecine strife and unnecessary baggage. Radical plans, however, require political courage – a quality that is seldom to be found in bottom-of-the-table Cabinet ministers – along with a great deal of goodwill which has been conspicuously wanting in the performing arts industry. Without a fairly high level of mutual respect and tolerance between the performing companies, the plan cannot work.

There is a simpler option. It is called privatization and it is supported by strategists on all sides of the political spectrum, for reasons both negative and positive. Melvyn Bragg, the Labour peer, has urged that the ROH should be privatized because 'it is an albatross around the neck of arts subsidy'.[25] Graham Serjeant, the *Times* business columnist, has called for arts subsidy to be abolished altogether because most arts companies can be funded privately and the sums involved are so minute that they distort political judgement. Arts subsidy, wrote Serjeant, 'fuels disproportionate controversy' and thereby damages the arts.[26]

Critically, Governments no longer give money to the arts out of the goodness of their hearts. It is eked out with a show of reluctance and a degree of malice for the tabloids to chew. Sooner or later it will be cut off altogether. The Royal Opera House would be better off without it, sooner rather than later.

To sustain a privately-funded Royal Opera House requires two preconditions – a high and regular flow of donations and a substantial endowment to cover against loss. The first condition has always been deemed inapplicable to British circumstances, since the Treasury, in exchange for funding the Arts Council, has refused to allow donations to the arts to be set against personal tax.

No longer. In his Budget of March 2000, the Labour Chancellor Gordon Brown, persuaded by charities and the ACE chairman Gerry Robinson, made two important concessions. He allowed donations through the Gift Aid scheme to qualify for full tax relief, and absolved gifts of shares from Capital Gains Tax. The regime was not quite as liberal as the American way of giving, where a thousand dollars given to the Met would cost the donor five hundred dollars after tax relief, but it opened the way to large-scale benefaction. The shares concession was designed to attract dozens of newly-rich Internet entrepreneurs to leave their mark on the arts. Tax experts viewed the measures as revolutionary and attractive.

Raising money for the arts was becoming relatively easy. Vivien Duffield collected a hundred million pounds in two and a half years. Claus Moser who, as chairman of the ROH struggled to raise a million, now raised a hundred million for the British Museum Development Trust. The country was awash with cash and the desire to do good. Funding a private Royal Opera House would require twenty-five million a year, which was not beyond the end of a rainbow.

Raising the endowment might prove trickier. There was twenty-five million to start with, left over from Vivien Duffield's appeal; another hundred million should suffice. If the Government could be persuaded to donate its next five years' grant in a single cheque, that would set the ROH free in a single bound and shut the book on half a century of underhand conniving and mutual irritation.

The new ROH would have its own building, £125 million in the bank and no pretension to represent anything but itself. Its chairman would not be appointed or approved by Downing Street. He or she would be the biggest donor, the vice-chairman the second biggest. That is how it works, mostly, at Carnegie Hall and the Kennedy Center. The rest of the board would be chosen for what they can give, in cash and expertise. The moment public money stops flowing in, Covent Garden would cease to be a public issue – any more than Glyndebourne or Goodwood is a public issue. It would also become cheaper and simpler to run without having constantly to consult the Arts Council and conform to its labyrinthine twists of policy. Giving up state subsidy, the ROH would have nothing to lose but its chains.

Michael Kaiser has given the matter considerable thought. 'We are heading towards a no-subsidy situation,' he admitted, 'but it can't be done cold-turkey. I think about it a lot. I believe passionately in taking the arts to the widest possible public – not as a public right, but as a public responsibility.'[27]

Whatever the final outcome, those who care for English culture must demand that Covent Garden be put on a stable footing and spared the tortures of uncertainty as it resumes the quest for excellence. It has lost its flagship status and embodies few values beyond its own survival. It is an opera house, no more, no less. Its future should have no bearing on the state of the nation.

Notes

Chapter 1
Come Into the Garden, Awed
1. L. P. Hartley, *The Go-Between*.
2. Earl of Harewood in Rosenthal, *Two Centuries*, xii.
3. Author's interview.
4. Lady Tooley, author's interview.
5. Interview with Alexander Chancellor, January 1998.
6. Brougham, 18–19.
7. Dr Andrew Renton, author's interview.
8. Derek Wyatt, at House of Commons select committee on culture, 21.i.98.
9. Bracewell, 5.

Chapter 2
Drinks at the Bar. 6.45
1. Ziegler, 324.
2. Memorandum of 13.viii.1945, cf. Bryant, 363.
3. Orwell, *The English People*. Collins, 1947. Written between September 1943 and May 1944 (cf. Orwell, Collected Essays).
4. Orwell, loc. cit.
5. Taylor, 600.
6. Announcement by Sir John Anderson, incorporated in Arts Council Charter, 9.viii.1946.
7. Reported in *The Times*, 13.vi.1945.
8. BBC Broadcast, printed in *The Listener*, 12.vii.1945.
9. Bryant, 363.
10. Oscar A. H. Schmitz, *Das Land ohne Musik: Englische Gesellschaftsprobleme*. Munich (Müller), 1914.

11. Carey, 140.
12. Guthrie, 97.
13. De Valois, 77.
14. Atkins, Newman, 29.
15. Procter-Gregg, 153.
16. Related by Richard Bebb.
17. Clark, *The Other Half*, 25.
18. Ellis, 338.
19. Thomas Jones, 'The origins of CEMA', CEMA Bulletin, May 1942.
20. Macmillan, 305.
21. Mary Glasgow, in Milo Keynes, Essays (1975), 261–2.
22. Clark, *The Other Half*, 28.
23. Ellis, 434.
24. Sinclair, 34–5.
25. Clark, loc.cit, 26.
26. Russell, 71.
27. Keynes (ed.), Lopokova, 13.
28. Article in the *Observer*, 1947, cited in Ellis, 500.
29. Milo Keynes, Essays (1975), 4.
30. Landstone, 67.
31. Glasgow, in W. M. Keynes, Essays, loc. cit.
32. General Theory, 235.
33. loc. cit., 29.
34. Harrod, 462.
35. Skidelsky, vol 2, 537.
36. *Daily Telegraph*, Arts & Books, v.1998.
37. William Rees-Mogg, article in *The Times*, 10.xi.1983.
38. Including a 1994 biography 'for young people', by Jeffrey Escoffier, in a series of Lives of Notable Gay Men and Lesbians.
39. Skidelsky, vol 2, 537–8.
40. Skidelsky, vol 1, 67.
41. Skidelsky, vol 1, 248.
42. Quoted by Annan, 56.
43. Bell, 145.
44. Milo Keynes, Essays, 142.
45. *The Economic Consequences of the Peace*.
46. Skidelsky, vol 1, 287–8.
47. Grant diary entry, in Spalding, 204.
48. Skidelsky, vol 1, 349.

49. Spalding, 75.
50. Spalding, 210.
51. Skidelsky, vol 2, 93.
52. Spalding, 334.
53. In Milo Keynes, Essays, 49.
54. Milo Keynes, Essays, 3.
55. Hill and Keynes, 333.
56. Kavanagh, 116.
57. Milo Keynes, Lopokova, 81.
58. Kavanagh, 115.
59. Frederick Ashton in Milo Keynes, Lopokova, 117.
60. De Valois, 98.
61. Kirstein, 241.
62. Walker, 317.
63. loc. cit.
64. Lopokova, 170.
65. Hennessy, 102.
66. W. M. Keynes, Essays, 264.
67. Landstone, 67.
68. Walker, 316.
69. Kavanagh, 256.
70. Blunt, 231.
71. Clark, 131.
72. Blunt, 233.
73. Keynes, Essays, 269.
74. Recollection of John Denison, q.v., author's interview.
75. Clark, 131.
76. Blunt, 237.
77. Reid, 234–6 and Jefferson 190–3.
78. Foreword to Stephen Williams, *Come to the Opera!*, Hutchinson, 1947.
79. CGA, letter from Washington dated 6.xi.1944.
80. De Valois, 154.
81. Kavanagh, 308.
82. Guthrie, 195.
83. Webster, in CGB1, 63.
84. CGB1, 63.
85. CGB1, 63.
86. *Irish Times*, 28.ii.1946.
87. J. M. Keynes, Lopokova, 121.

88. Harrod, 623.
89. Beaton, 231.
90. W. M. Keynes, Essays, 270.
91. Drogheda, 226.
92. CGA, letter dated 23.ii.1945.
93. CGA, letter of 6.xi.1944.
94. CGA, trustees tribute to Keynes, 7.v.1946.
95. Guthrie, 197.

Chapter 3
Enter the Leader (1946–47)

1. Quoted in Sked and Cook, 28.
2. Alan Jefferson, conversation with the author.
3. Healey, 69.
4. Burton, 149.
5. Interview with Delia Barnaby.
6. Barnaby.
7. See Drogheda, 232.
8. John Denison, author's interview.
9. CGA, 14.ix.1945.
10. CGA, 1.iv.1946.
11. Montague Haltrecht, interview with the author.
12. Shead, 10.
13. De Valois, 112.
14. Sir Edward Downes's comment to the author, July 1998.
15. Savage, 95.
16. See Lebrecht, *When the Music Stops*, 112–13.
17. Rosen, 248–9.
18. CGA, and Rosen, 250.
19. CGA, letter of 25.ii.1946. The chronology in Donaldson is inaccurate and misleading.
20. Rosen, 251.
21. Rosen, 253.
22. 'Delighted with Keynes letter(,) the view which is Clark's and mine.' (CGA, 16.iii.1946).
23. CGA.
24. CGA, 29.i.1958.
25. *The Other Half*, 132.
26. *The Times*, 17.vi.1946.
27. Source withheld by request.

28. Schoenberg, 75–6.
29. Brook (D.), 143.
30. Constance Shacklock, author's interview.
31. Author's interview.
32. Savage, 114.
33. CGA, 7.xii.1946.
34. Author's interview.
35. CGA memo, 12.xi.1946.
36. CGA: DW to Keynes, 1.i.1946.
37. Foreman, 270.
38. Mandinian, 19.
39. CGA: Ashton to DW, 14.x.1946.
40. Shead, 148.
41. Shead, 148–9.
42. Shead, 118.
43. Thomas, 45.
44. Private communication, 2.ii.1947.
45. Franklin, 124-5; the incident is corroborated by Irene Thomas, p.48.
46. Witnessed by Alan Jefferson, 1.x.1950, and related to the author.
47. Interview with the author.
48. CG25, p.26.
49. CGA, n.d., March 1946.
50. Langdon, 26.
51. Author's interview.
52. Interview with the author.
53. Thomas, 47.
54. Thomas, 66.
55. Drogheda, 232.
56. DNB, article by John Tooley.
57. Haltrecht, 22.
58. Clark, 129.
59. Glasgow memoirs, quoted in Witts, 460.
60. Witts, loc. cit.
61. Clark, 133.
62. Wheeler-Bennett, 362.
63. Drogheda, 230.
64. Wheeler-Bennett, 316.
65. Tucker, 47.

66. Wheeler-Bennett, 368.

67. CGA various memos, notably 22.vii.1946.

68. Wheeler-Bennett, 366.

69. Drogheda, 227.

70. Wheeler-Bennett, 367.

71. Drogheda, 227.

72. Wheeler-Bennett, 367.

73. CGA, memo of 25.iv.1947.

74. Drogheda, 230.

75. John Denison, author's interview.

Chapter 4
Overture and Beginners (1947–51)

1. Orwell, Essays, 'Writers Against Leviathan', 466.

2. Hollis, 131.

3. Tony Benn, at NHS 50th anniversary service.

4. In *The Listener*, 29.v.1941.

5. Carpenter, 156.

6. Lucas, 92.

7. Note written in 1993 to accompany EMI's release of a 1947 recording of *Grimes* excerpts. EMI CMS 7 64727 2.

8. Eric Blom in the *Birmingham Post*.

9. Scott Goddard in the *News Chronicle*.

10. Edmund Wilson, *Europe Without Baedeker*, NY, 1947, pp. 186-91.

11. Letter to Basil Wright's mother, dated 18.vi.1945, reproduced by permission of © the Trustees of the Britten-Pears Foundation and may not be further reproduced without permission.

12. Chronologically: Stockholm, Basle, Zurich, Tanglewood (US première, cond. Leonard Bernstein), Antwerp (1946); Brno, Milan, Copenhagen, Budapest, Hamburg, Mannheim, Berlin, Graz, Brussels, Paris (1947); New York, Los Angeles, Philadelphia, Boston, Oldenburg, Stanford University, Cal., San Francisco (1948); Helsinki, Strasbourg, Colmar (1949).

13. Evans recollections in 1993, notes to EMI recording CMS 7 64727 2.

14. *Evening Standard*, 14.vii.1946.

15. *Time and Tide*, October 1946.

16. Hinrichsen's Musical Year Book, 1947–8.

17. Blunt, 257.

18. Ashton and Piper quotes in Kavanagh, 338.
19. Kennedy, Britten, 49.
20. Apart from *The Partisans* by Inglis Gundry, which had an airing in St Pancras Town Hall in May 1946, and never since.
21. CGA, DW to Britten, 15.xi.1946.
22. CGA, 24.vii.1946 and other files.
23. CGA, Britten to DW, 15.v.1948.
24. CGA, DW to Britten, 14.vi.1948 © the Trustees of the Britten-Pears Foundation.
25. Haltrecht, 68.
26. Carey, 182.
27. CGA, minute of meeting on 24.vii.1946.
28. Carey, 184.
29. Covent Garden press statement, October 1946
30. Donaldson, 71.
31. Carpenter, *Envy*, 60.
32. Carpenter, loc. cit.
33. McArthur, 223.
34. Biancolli, vi.
35. Kells.
36. Desmond Shawe-Taylor, quoted Rosenthal, 576.
37. Interview with Susannah Herbert, *Daily Telegraph*, 2.v.1998.
38. Brook, 47.
39. Franklin, 121.
40. Franklin, 123.
41. Brook, 51.
42. Haltrecht, 126.
43. 12.xi.1949.
44. Author's interview.
45. *Sunday Times*, 13.xi.1949.
46. Brook, 59.
47. Coward, 172.
48. CGA, DW to JA, 25.vii.1947.
49. CGA: Weekly expenses of joint opera and ballet seasons.
50. CGA: E. Hale to Mary Glasgow, 27.i.1948.
51. Press reports, 5.i.1949.
52. *The Times*.
53. *News Chronicle*, 7.i.1949; information supplied by Webster: CGA.
54. *Daily Telegraph*, 17.i.1949.

55. CGA.
56. *Sunday Times*, 10.vi.1951.
57. John Denison, author's interview.
58. CGA: DW to Rankl, 2.iii.1950.
59. CGA: Wilson to Webster, 23.ix.1947.
60. CGA.
61. CGA: Wilson to Kenneth Stevenson, 15.i.1951.
62. Recollection by Constance Shacklock.
63. CGA: DW to JA, 16.xii.1949.
64. Author's interview, March 1998.
65. *Musical America*, 1.xi.1949.
66. De Valois, 187.
67. Robinson, 313.
68. Fonteyn, 113.
69. De Valois, 187.
70. Robinson, 315.
71. Clarke, 244.
72. Robinson, 309.
73. Kavanagh, 372.
74. Author's interview.
75. Channel 4 TV, 'Secret Lives', 4.ii.1999.
76. CGA: Jane Clark to DW, 3.v.1948.
77. Channel 4 TV, 'Secret Lives', 4.ii.1999.
78. Edwin Denby, *Ballet* magazine, viii.1952.
79. Shearer, author's interview.
80. *Musical America*, 1.xi.1950.
81. Author's interview.
82. Author's interview; source withheld by request.
83. Shearer, Menuhin, Sibley: author's interviews.
84. Christine Beckley, in Newman, 38.
85. Peter Gellhorn, author's interview.
86. Kennedy, 219.
87. Recollection by Joan Ingpen, author's interview.
88. Author's interview.
89. Eliot, 19.
90. Christine Rankl, interview with the author.
91. CGA: 2.iii.1950.
92. CGA: 2.iii.1950.
93. CGA: 3.iii.1950.
94. Recalled by Christine Rankl.

95. Elizabeth Latham, author's interview.
96. Desmond Shawe-Taylor in the *New Statesman*, 16.xii.1950.
97. Steven Rose, author's interview.
98. Savage, 128.
99. Savage, 128.
100. CGA: Clark to DW, 16.xii.1950.
101. Author's interview.
102. CGA, 10.ii.1951.
103. CGA, 9.ii.1951.
104. Information from Christine Rankl.
105. CGA: 20.iv.1951.
106. CGA: DW to Anderson, 7.v.1951.
107. Gellhorn, author's interview.
108. Langdon, 37,
109. CGA: Kerr to Rankl, 6.vi.1952.
110. CGA: DW to Rankl, 22.vi.1953.
111. CGA: DW to Wilfred Stiff, 31.vii.1962.

Chapter 5
First Act, Forbidden Acts (1951–59)

1. FOB, 9.
2. Samuel Johnson, 7.iv.1775.
3. FOB, 8–9.
4. FOB, 69.
5. op. cit.
6. Donoughue and Jones, 493.
7. Banham and Hillier, 176–89.
8. Castle, 192.
9. Tiratsoo, 103.
10. See Roberts, 243–85.
11. Goldschmidt, 72.
12. Recalled by Christine Rankl.
13. Letter from Mary Glasgow to Berthold Goldschmidt, 23.v.1950.
14. Berthold Goldschmidt, author's interview.
15. CGA: JB to DW, 9.v.1951.
16. CGA: Webster to Anderson, 19.v.1951.
17. Kennedy, Barbirolli, 225.
18. Neville Cardus (ed.), *Kathleen Ferrier, a memoir*. Hamish Hamilton, 1954, p. 52.

19. Savage, 139.
20. Hope-Wallace, 91.
21. CGA: EJD to DW, 29.xi.1952.
22. loc. cit.
23. Savage, 138.
24. Carpenter, Britten, 298.
25. Public Record Office document, cited *Guardian*, 17.viii.1998.
26. Eric Crozier, 'Writers Remembered: E. M. Forster', *The Author*, Winter 1990, p. 123.
27. Hope-Wallace, 98.
28. Channel 4: J'Accuse – Benjamin Britten.
29. *Sunday Telegraph*, 22.ii.1998.
30. *Observer*, 22.ii.1998.
31. Carpenter, Britten, 300.
32. cf Coward, 181.
33. CGA, letter of 9.xii.1951.
34. CGA, undated DW memo.
35. See Carpenter, Britten, 312.
36. Harewood.
37. CGA: BB to DW, 20.xi.1952: © the Trustees of the Britten-Pears Foundation and may not further be reproduced without written permission.
38. See Conway, 119–20.
39. Donald Mitchell and Hans Keller (eds.), *Benjamin Britten; A Commentary on his Works from a Group of Specialists*. Rockliff, 1952.
40. CGA: BB to DW, 28.v.1953.
41. Beaton diary entry for 4.xi.1952; Beaton, 243.
42. Savage, 142.
43. Colville, 715–6.
44. Letter to a friend quoted by Donald Mitchell in booklet for EMI recording of *Gloriana*, 1993.
45. Harewood, 138.
46. Drogheda, 239.
47. Rosenthal, *Mad*, 109.
48. CGA, DW file n.d. (assuredly 1958 from internal references).
49. Opera Annual 1954–5 (ed. Harold Rosenthal), p. 31.
50. Author's interview.
51. Haltrecht, 157.
52. Gay, 109.

53. See Drogheda, 285.
54. CGA: C. West to DW, 11.v.1950.
55. Recalled by Alan Jefferson.
56. CGA: DW to Clifford, 18.viii.1951.
57. *Opera*, Jan. 1954, p. 8.
58. Author's interview.
59. Major, 22.
60. Interview with *Classical Singer*, vol X, no. xii, October 1999, p. 7.
61. Braddon, 46.
62. Recalled by Miss Ingpen.
63. CGA: DW to Callas, 12.vii.1952.
64. *Manchester Guardian*, 9.xi.1952.
65. Braddon, 51.
66. Stassinopoulos, 131.
67. CGA, n.d.
68. Schwarzkopf, 202.
69. Personal communication.
70. John Tolansky: 'The Royal Opera, 50 glorious years'. Classic FM, 1.i.1997
71. Drogheda, 266.
72. Langdon, 49.
73. CGA: DW to BBC, 25.vii.1958.
74. Drogheda, 265.
75. Conrad, 318.
76. *Observer*, 18.ix.1977, from 1970 interview with Kenneth Harris.
77. Conrad, 325.
78. Harewood, 231.
79. Braddon, 97.
80. John Tooley, in John Drummond, 'A Price Worth Paying', Radio 3, tx 3.iv.1999.
81. Author's interview.
82. CGA: Pooley (AC) to JA, 14.ii.1952.
83. CGA: JA to Pooley, 20.ii.1952.
84. Norman Tucker, in Opera Annual 1954–5, p. 33.
85. Clark, *The Other Half*, 134.
86. Clark, op. cit.
87. Source withheld on request.
88. Information from John Denison.

89. CGA: K. Clark to Waverley, 18.xi.1953.
90. CGA: Waverley to KC, 10.xii.1953.
91. GDA, 1.i.1955.
92. CGA: Drogheda to Tooley, 22.vi.1972, adding: 'I don't think he will get in anybody's way. . .' Lund died 18.xi.1974.
93. *Opera*, Jan. 1956, William Mann.
94. *Dance and Dancers*, Aug. 1955, Peter Williams on *The Lady and the Fool.*
95. Interview with the author.
96. CGA, HDR file, 30.x.1950; not five pounds as reported by Rosenthal in his memoirs, p. 88.
97. Comments by Alan Jefferson and Ken Davison.
98. CGA: SW to DW, 29.vii.1953.
99. CGA: DW to HDR, 31.x.1958.
100. CGA: HDR to DW, 15.xii.1959.
101. CGA, 12.vi.1960.
102. *The Times*, 28.viii.1951.
103. Savage, 152.
104. Related to the author by Schuyler Chapin, Heifetz's agent; corroborated in Susannah Walton, 148.
105. Bayan Northcott, *Sunday Telegraph*, 21.xi.1976, quoted Kennedy, 188.
106. Tippett, 218.
107. CGA: SW to DW, 8.iii.1954.
108. 'This Opera Baffles Us Too, Say Singers'; article by James Thomas in *News Chronicle*, 26.i.1955.
109. Ross-Russell, 69.
110. 'This Opera Baffles . . .' loc. cit.
111. Tippett, 216.
112. *Daily Express*, 28.i.1955.
113. Verbatim first-hand account of the conversation reported to the author by Arts Council observer, John Denison.
114. Author's interview.
115. Gay, 157.
116. Comments to the author by Elsie Morison, Iris Kells, Elizabeth Latham and others.
117. *The Times*, 18.vi.1955.
118. *People*, 24.vii.1955.
119. Higgins, 268.
120. Carpenter, 335.

121. *Sunday Express*, 25.x.1953.
122. *Daily Express*, 9.iv.1959.
123. As Webster confided to John Denison.
124. Source withheld.
125. Kavanagh, 358.
126. CGA: Jane Clark to DW, 5.i.1953.
127. Drogheda, 237.
128. Author's interview.
129. BB to DW, 4.i.1957 (after 1st night of *Prince of Pagodas*) © the Trustees of the Britten Pears Foundation.
130. Stewart, 215.
131. *Daily Telegraph*, 9.vii.1956.
132. Stewart, 214.
133. CGA.
134. *Dance and Dancers*, Aug. 55, p. 5.
135. Buckle, 276.
136. Macaulay, 61.
137. See David Vaughan, 'London Revisited', *Dance and Dancers*, October 1956, p. 13.
138. Franks, 76.
139. Interview with the author, April 1998.
140. *Dance and Dancers*, October 1956, p. 5.
141. *Daily Express*, 4.x.1956.
142. *Dancing Times*, Nov. 1956, p. 73.
143. *Undine, Tagesbuch eines Ballets*. Munich (Piper), 1959; transl. Mary Whittall for DG recording 453-467-2.
144. John Lanchbery, interview with *Dance and Dancers*, March 1962.
145. Lecture at the Royal Society of Arts, 29.v.1957; *Dance and Dancers*, July 1957.
146. Downes, author's interview.
147. Author's interview.
148. Harewood, 159.
149. Author's interview.
150. Rosenthal, 660.
151. Author's interview.
152. Reported to the author by Miss Leigh.
153. CGA: DW to RK, n.d.
154. Gielgud, 185–6.
155. GDA: IB to GD, 1.vi.1956.

156. GDA, Waverley file, 28.ix.1956.

157. CGA: EJD to DW, 7.vi.1957.

158. CGA: EG to DW, 14.vi.1957.

159. See Ales Brezina, 'The first version of *The Greek Passion* by Bohuslav Martinů', Bregenz Festival brochure, 1999.

160. CGA: 9.xii.1957, RK to Opera Subcommittee chairman.

161. *The Times*, 27.vi.1956.

162. Drogheda, 247.

163. GDA, 14.v.1957.

164. Author's interview, 1982.

165. Author's interview.

166. Interviewed by John Drummond, 'A Price Worth Paying', Radio 3 3.iv.1999.

167. CG 25, p52.

168. Author's interview.

169. Sorley Walker, 318.

170. Wheeler-Bennett, 403.

Chapter 6
Short Interval: Champagne, Canapés and Nature Calls (1959–60)

1. Newton, 93.

2. Author's interview.

3. Strong, 48.

4. Information from Bill Beresford.

5. Walker, 320.

6. Donaldson, *A Twentieth Century Life*, 167.

7. Goodman, 303.

8. Author's interview.

9. Fane, 222.

10. Colin Clark, 48.

11. Lees-Milne, *Fourteen Friends*, 221.

12. Source withheld.

13. John Denison, author's interview.

14. GDA, Waverley file, 8.xi.1956.

15. Donaldson, *Twentieth Century Life*, 165.

16. Newton, 93.

17. Conversation with the author.

18. GDA: Drogheda to DW, 31.x.1960.

19. Private information.

20. Paul Findlay, author's interview.

21. Source withheld.
22. GDA: undated memo in Drogheda's hand.
23. Drogheda, 234.
24. Hansard, 23.i.1959
25. *Opera*, April 1958.
26. Tucker, 127.
27. John Denison, 'Subsidies for Opera in Great Britain', in Opera Annual 8, p. 23.
28. Author's interview.
29. Evans, 103.
30. Langdon, 52.
31. Zeffirelli, 148.
32. Langdon, 52.
33. Author's interview.
34. Schwarzkopf, 197.
35. Langdon, 52.
36. *Guardian* and *Financial Times*, 18.ii.1959.
37. Joan Ingpen, author's interview.
38. GDA: GD to DW, 10.i.1960.
39. Braddon, 122.
40. Related to the author by Joan Ingpen.
41. Culshaw, 293–4.
42. Culshaw, 295.
43. Author's interview.
44. John Tolansky: 'The Royal Opera, 50 glorious years'. Classic FM, 1.i.1997.
45. Haltrecht, 246.
46. Tolansky, loc. cit.
47. *Musical America*, September 1964, p. 12.
48. Advertisement, *Daily Express*, xii.1963.
49. Interview with the author.
50. Fonteyn, 175.
51. Channel 4, 'Secret Lives', 4.ii.1999.
52. Roboz/Monahan, 79.
53. Author's interview.
54. Newman, 93.
55. Sheila Bloom, in Newman, 95.
56. GDA: de Valois to DW, 15.ix.1960.
57. Author's interview.
58. Notes to meeting of 23.ii.1960.

59. Drogheda, 280.
60. Related by Solti to the author, February 1990.
61. Interview, Feb. 1990.
62. cf. Goodman 300, Haltrecht 260; and personal information.

Chapter 7
Act Two: Enter the Jew (1961–70)
  1. Larkin, 'Annus Mirabilis'.
  2. *Guardian*, 2.x.1999.
  3. Interviewed on BBC Radio 4, 'Front Row', 28.x.1999.
  4. Forman, 129.
  5. Heyworth, 264.
  6. CGA: Legge to DW, 9.ii.1960.
  7. Heyworth, 288.
  8. Information received from Andrew McGee.
  9. Information from Lotte Klemperer, Andrew McGee and others.
10. Letter from Lotte Klemperer to Webster, 19.v.1961, quoted by permission of the Otto Klemperer Archive, Zurich.
11. Observed by Bill Beresford.
12. Sutherland, 132.
13. Evans, 194.
14. *Times Educational Supplement*, anon.
15. *Daily Telegraph*, 9.iv.1963.
16. Lotte Klemperer, comment to the author.
17. Lucas, 148.
18. FT, 24.vi.1961.
19. Fonteyn, 204–5.
20. Fonteyn, 206.
21. Beaton, 345.
22. Fonteyn, 208.
23. Fonteyn, 209.
24. Maude Gosling, 'Nureyev in the West'. *Ballet Review*, Spring 1994.
25. Fonteyn, 209.
26. Comments to the author.
27. CGA, Nureyev file.
28. Nureyev, 122.
29. Nicky Johnson, author's interview.
30. Fonteyn, *Magic of Dance*, 67.
31. Seymour, 307.

32. Fonteyn, *Magic of Dance*, 67.
33. Newman, 120.
34. Buckle, 277.
35. Kavanagh, 472.
36. Beaton, 380.
37. Fonteyn, 221.
38. Channel 4, 'Secret Lives', 4.ii.1999.
39. Solway, 300.
40. Author's interview.
41. Author's interview.
42. Public Records Office, FO 371 184933, dispatch by British Ambassador, Madrid.
43. Buckle, 276.
44. Newman, 149.
45. Roboz, 79.
46. Sorley Walker, 291.
47. GDA: De Valois to Drogheda, 16.ix.1960.
48. Recounted by Sibley to the author.
49. GDA: Mark Bonham-Carter to Drogheda, 10.x.1962.
50. Author's interview.
51. Author's interview, February 1990.
52. Comments to the author.
53. cf. Roberts, 218.
54. Colville 649, entry for 30.v.1952.
55. GDA, file memo, 26.vi.1959.
56. Hansard, 10.xii.1959.
57. To the author.
58. Author's interview.
59. GDA, memo of the meeting, kept by Drogheda.
60. GDA, 27.xi.1962.
61. loc. cit.
62. GDA: GD to DW, 28.xi.1962.
63. CGA, Solti file, 21.vi.1963.
64. CGA: DW to GS, 21.x.1963.
65. Information from Valerie Solti.
66. BK comment to the author.
67. Solti archives.
68. Interview with the author.
69. Bernard Keefe, to the author.
70. Recalled by Ingpen.

71. GDA: GD to DW, 10.xi.1963.
72. GDA: GD to DW, 18.xii.1963.
73. Author's interview.
74. Ziegler, 134.
75. Conway, 139.
76. *The Times*, 27.xii.1963.
77. *Sunday Times*, 29.xii.1963.
78. *High Fidelity*, November 1967.
79. Kozinn, 12.
80. Donaldson, *Twentieth Century Life*, 185–6.
81. Hollis, 254.
82. GDA: JL to GD, 16.vi.1965.
83. Goodman, 265.
84. Recalled by John Denison.
85. Selbourne, 192.
86. *Spectator*, 1.iii.1957.
87. Comments to the author.
88. See Brivati, 50.
89. *Sunday Mirror*, 12.vii.1964.
90. Author's interview.
91. Recounted by John Denison.
92. Brivati, 117.
93. Author's interview.
94. Hollis, 260.
95. Hollis, 364.
96. Witts, 471.
97. Sinclair, 162.
98. Author's interview.
99. Recalled by Lord Gibson.
100. Author's interview.
101. Selbourne, 198.
102. Selbourne, loc. cit.
103. Author's interview.
104. Author's interview.
105. Author's interview.
106. Newman, 128.
107. *Dance and Dancers*, May 1964.
108. FT, 3.iv.1964.
109. Bill Beresford, author's interview.
110. Seymour, 222–3.

111. Author's interview.
112. Seymour, 230.
113. Seymour, 247.
114. GDA ballet file, Edward Perper to Sol Hurok, 3.vii.1963 et alii.
115. Seymour, 251.
116. Information from Ken Davison.
117. Fernau Hall and James Kelsey, *Ballet Today*, March/April 1965, pp. 16–18.
118. Tooley, 150.
119. GDA: GD to DW, 20.iv.1966.
120. Author's interview.
121. Seymour, 264.
122. GDA: MBC to GD, 22.xi.1966.
123. CGA: DW to FA 9.iii.1967.
124. *Observer*, 18.ix.1977 (from 1970 interview with Kenneth Harris).
125. Zeffirelli, 188.
126. *Guardian*, 22.i.1964.
127. CGA: Diamand to DW, 22.i.1964.
128. ROH press statement, 16.ix.1977.
129. Interview with the author, Barletta, 1987.
130. CGA: Gorlinsky to DW, 10.ii.1967.
131. CGA: Solti to Collier, 4.iii.1968.
132. GDA: GD to GS, 1.vii.1965.
133. GDA: GS to DW, 2.vii.1965.
134. Savage, 121.
135. Valerie Solti, author's interview.
136. Interview in *The Times*, 9.ix.1988.
137. GDA: GD to GS, 18.vi.1964.
138. GDA: GS to GD, 22.vi.1964.
139. GDA: GD to GS, 29.vi.1964.
140. Ken Davison, author's interview.
141. GDA: IB to GD, 10.ii.1964.
142. GDA: IB to DW, 25.ii.1964.
143. Fay, 71.
144. Hall, 222.
145. Solti, 19.
146. Interview with the author, vii.1997.
147. Alan Taylor, in Tolansky (CFMROH, 1.i.19.97).

148. Recounted to the author by Beresford.
149. Author's interview.
150. GDA: GD to DW, 2.viii.1965.
151. GDA: GD to BP, 7.ii.1965.
152. GDA: GD to Board, 28.x.1965.
153. *Sun*, 13.vii.1967.
154. Gay, 110.
155. CGA, Solti file, 31.iii.1964.
156. GDA: GD to GS, i.vii.1966.
157. CGA, 6.vii.1966.
158. Newton, 96.
159. FT, 21.ix.1964.
160. GDA.
161. GDA: AP to GD, 26.ix.1964.
162. GDA: GD to AP, 24.vi.1965.
163. GDA: AP to GD, 24.iii.1965.
164. GDA: GD to AP, 8.vii.1968.
165. GDA: IB to GD, 13.i.1970.
166. Author's interview.
167. Author's interview.
168. Ken Davison.
169. Bill Beresford.
170. Information from Lady Lightman.
171. Paul Findlay, author's interview.
172. Tucker, 127.
173. GDA: GD to DW, 21.xii.1967.
174. Observations by Bill Beresford, Alan Jefferson and others.
175. Author's interview.
176. Author's interview.
177. Author's interview.
178. Author's interview.
179. CGA, 29.iv.1968.
180. GDA: MBC to GD, 11.x.1971.
181. Kavanagh, 502.
182. Author's interviews.
183. Kavanagh, 508.
184. Author's interview.
185. Drogheda, 325
186. Recounted by Joan Ingpen.
187. John Rockwell, 29.viii.1973.

188. Gay, 153.
189. Clare, 67.
190. Clare, 52.
191. Tucker, 82.
192. Drogheda, 326.
193. GDA: CD to GD, 22.ii.no year.
194. Drogheda, loc. cit.
195. Private annexe to board minutes, 28.i.1969.
196. Goodman to GD, 15.iv.1969.
197. GDA, n.d.
198. Goodman, 305.
199. GDA: Harewood to GD, 9.iv.1969.
200. Private information.
201. GDA, undated report by Lord Robbins.
202. GDA: GD to Harewood, 7.i.1970.
203. Goodman, 306.
204. GDA: GH to GD, 18.iv.1972; GD to GH, 19.iv.1972.
205. GDA: GD to Lord Gibson, 4.xii.1972.
206. Conversation with the author.
207. Genista McIntosh, in Gottlieb and Chambers, 121.
208. FAZ, 25.iv.1970.
209. GDA: Kirstein to GD, 2.iv.1970.
210. Evans, 243.
211. *Daily Telegraph*, 13.v.1971.
212. Recounted by Valerie Solti.
213. Source: *About the House*, Spring 1971.

Chapter 8
The Long Interval: Propping up the Crush Bar (1971–87)

1. Heath, 309.
2. Hennessy, 383.
3. Hennessy, 384.
4. GDA: GD to Armstrong, 6.vii.1970.
5. Source withheld.
6. *The Times*, 5.i.1988.
7. Paul Findlay, author's interview.
8. Sleep, 84.
9. Buckle, 280.
10. GDA: GD to KM, 28.vii.1971.
11. GDA: KM to GD, 29.vii.1971.

12. *Guardian*, 3.xii.1970.
13. Interview with Harold Rosenthal, *Opera*, xii.1970.
14. William Mann, *The Times*.
15. *Opera Monthly*, July 1988, interview with Sam H. Shirakawa.
16. FT, 16.vi.1971.
17. GDA: PH to GD, 4.vii.1971.
18. GDA: GD to PH, 7.vii.1971.
19. GDA: PH to GD, 12.vii.1971.
20. CGA, quoted in Fay, 206.
21. GDA: Rayne to GD, 30.vii.1971.
22. Hall, 261.
23. Fay, 206, and personal information.
24. Hall, 230.
25. Lewis, 99.
26. GDA: JT to GD and Colin Anderson, 6.vii.1971.
27. Author's interview.
28. GDA: JT to GD, 28.ii.1972.
29. Interview with the author.
30. Author's interview.
31. The RPI Index stood at 513.9 in 1970, and 950.0 in 1975.
32. Castle, 441.
33. Author's interview.
34. Author's interview.
35. Gay, 158.
36. Fingleton, 94.
37. See Jenkins and d'Antal, 196.
38. Author's interview.
39. Fingleton, 95.
40. Donald McIntyre, in Jenkins and D'Antal, 183.
41. Cahill, author's interview.
42. Langdon, 166.
43. Reported to Joan Ingpen.
44. loc. cit.
45. Author's interview.
46. Reported by Kiri to the author.
47. Author's interview.
48. Baker, 27.
49. Sinclair, 188.
50. Lord Gibson, author's interview.
51. Claus Moser, author's interview.

52. Author's interview.
53. Goodman, 306.
54. Author's interview.
55. GDA: GD to Claus Moser, 31.xii.1973.
56. GDA: Goodman to GD, 10.vii.1972.
57. George Whyte, author's interview.
58. Author's interview.
59. GWA.
60. GDA: GD to JT, 28.vi.1972.
61. GDA: Goodman to GD, 6.xii.1972.
62. Tooley, 278.
63. Drogheda, 323.
64. Gordon, 43.
65. Recounted to the author by Vivien Duffield.
66. Heath, 394.
67. Fingleton, 111.
68. GDA: GD to KM, 17.i.1973.
69. GDA: MacMillan to GD, 1972, n.d.
70. Author's interview.
71. Newman, 175.
72. Deborah MacMillan, author's interview.
73. *Evening Standard*, 13.vii.1973.
74. GDA: JP-H to GD, 19.iv.1973.
75. GDA, 15.iv.1973.
76. GDA: CD to GD, 26.viii.1973.
77. GDA: Robbins to GD, 16.v.1973.
78. GDA: Kaslik to GD, 22.ix.1973.
79. GDA: GD to Pavitt, 10.x.1973.
80. GDA: GD to CM, 9.vii.1974.
81. GDA: GD to JT, 16.v.1973.
82. Author's interview.
83. Author's interview.
84. Author's interview.
85. GDA: GD to JP-H, 20.vi.1973.
86. GDA: CM to GD, 8.xii.1973.
87. Strong, 183.
88. Author's interview.
89. James Lees-Milne, *A Mingled Measure*, 177.
90. Drogheda, 348.
91. Interview with Harold Rosenthal, 'Music Weekly', BBC Radio,

4.vi.1974.
92. Author's interview.
93. Author's interviews.
94. Mattheopoulos, 161.
95. *Financial Times*, 19.ix.1976.
96. loc. cit.
97. GDA: Moser to GD, 18.x.1976.
98. Interview with Tom Sutcliffe, *About the House*, Summer 1974, p. 59.
99. *About the House*, Christmas 1974, p. 10.
100. Mattheopoulos, 160.
101. Author's interview.
102. CFM-50.
103. Tooley, 44.
104. CFM-50, loc. cit.
105. Author's interview.
106. Interview with Max Loppert, *Opera*, August 1984, pp. 836–42.
107. *Classical Music* magazine, 9.vii.1988.
108. *Opera*, viii.1986, p. 876.
109. Author's interview.
110. Author's interview.
111. Gay, 143.
112. Mattheopoulos, 442.
113. Tooley, author's interview.
114. Author's interview.
115. Kavanagh, 555.
116. CGA: Gorlinsky to JT, 26.v.1977.
117. Ken Davison, to author.
118. Author's interview.
119. Author's interview.
120. CGA, 29.iii.1977.
121. Deborah MacMillan, author's interview.
122. Monahan, 34.
123. Radio 3, De Valois centennial tribute, v.1998.
124. Anonymity requested.
125. Author's interview.
126. Donaldson, 175.
127. *Opera*, August 1979, pp. 738–9.
128. *Opera*, October 1979, pp. 937–40.

129. Strong, 234.
130. cf. Clark Diaries, 17–18.
131. Hennessy, 346.
132. cf. Ranelagh, 80.
133. Annan, 347.
134. Hennessy, 589
135. Author's interview.
136. Strong, 335.
137. Goodman, 307.
138. Priestley, 4–5.
139. Author's interview with Ken Davison, *Classical Music* magazine, n.d.
140. Pick, 153.
141. Priestley, 52.
142. Quoted in Fingleton, 159–60.
143. Fingleton, 180.
144. Jenkins, 247.
145. Jenkins, 270.
146. *Time Out*'s Martin Hoyle, in Jenkins, 270.
147. Author's interview.
148. Mattheopoulos, *Bravo*, 57.
149. Author's interview, see *Sunday Times*, 13.x.1985 and 9.iii.1986.
150. *Classical Music*, 14.v.1988, p. 1.
151. CGA: JT to RN 11.ii.1981.
152. Solway, 427.
153. *Sunday Times* magazine, 26.iv.1981, p. 23.
154. *The Times*, 2.v.1981.
155. Ken Davison, private correspondence.
156. Sleep, 95.
157. Dowell to the author.
158. Findlay, author's interview.
159. Jeremy Isaacs, author's interview.
160. All quotes: GWA.
161. *Sunday Times*, 18.i.1987, interview with Robert Hewison.
162. GWA: GW to Moser, 10.iii.1987.
163. *The Times*, 2.iii.1987.
164. *The Times*, 3.iii.1987.
165. Author's interview.
166. Author's interview, *Sunday Times*, 22.vi.1986

167. Tooley to the author.
168. *Opera*, August 1986, p. 875.
169. Author's interview, *Sunday Times*, 5.x.1986.
170. Source withheld.
171. Isaacs, *Storm Over 4*, 197.

Chapter 9
Act Three, On a Spree (1987–96)
 1. CGCA website, 10.x.1999.
 2. Douglas Mason, 'Let's scrap the art of the state', *Evening Standard*, 13.v.1987.
 3. Kings I, xxi, 19.
 4. Wyatt, 346.
 5. Author's interview.
 6. *Classical Music*, 23.ix.1995, p. 11.
 7. 'How Long Before Ofop Steps In?', *London Review of Books*, 16.iii.2000, p.226.
 8. Richard Bebb, to the author.
 9. Tooley, 202.
10. Source withheld.
11. *The Times*, n.d.
12. *Guardian*, 13.xii.1988, p. 35
13. Source withheld.
14. In *The Listener*, 20.iv.1989.
15. Loc. cit.
16. Solway, 496–7.
17. Taylor, 194–5.
18. Taylor, ix.
19. *Sunday Times* magazine, loc. cit. both Bussell and Eagling.
20. *Sunday Times* magazine, 18.xi.1990.
21. Isaacs, author's interview.
22. *The Times*, 31.i.1990, interview with Richard Morrison.
23. *Daily Telegraph* magazine, xii.2000.
24. Source withheld.
25. Findlay, author's interview.
26. Private communication.
27. Isaacs, 136.
28. loc. cit.
29. Interview with Ismene Brown, *Daily Telegraph*, 3.viii.1998.
30. Reg Wilson, in Bedell Smith, 160.

31. Confided to the author.
32. Author's interview, *Daily Telegraph*, 28.x.1993.
33. Source withheld.
34. Source withheld.
35. See Norman Lebrecht, 'Blight at the Opera', *Daily Telegraph*, 27.ii.1995.
36. *Daily Telegraph*, 21.vii.1995.
37. *Sun*, 21.vii.1995.
38. Interview in *Opera*, iv.1997, p. 396
39. *Opera*, loc. cit.
40. Author's interview.
41. *Daily Telegraph*, 1.v.1995.
42. Author's interview.
43. Author's interview.
44. *BBC Music* magazine, xi.1996, p. 59.
45. Author's interviews, June 1995.
46. Author's interview, April 1995.
47. *The House:* Settling Scores.
48. Tolansky, CFM-50, 1.i.1997.
49. Isaacs, 242.
50. Source withheld.
51. Isaacs, 244.
52. *Daily Telegraph*, 8.xii.1997.
53. *Independent*, n.d.
54. Pulford to Mary Allen, 4.ii.1996, copy in private possession.
55. Isaacs, 300.
56. Sources withheld.
57. 'Trouble at the House', a programme by Keith Cooper.
58. Author's interview.
59. Gottlieb, Chambers, 124.
60. *Daily Mail*, 23.x.1999, p. 24: 'Adultery, Deceit and the Secret Passion that Rocked the Royal Opera House'.
61. *Guardian*, 5.xi.1999, interview with Sabine Durrant.
62. *Guardian*, 9.ix.1998.
63. loc. cit.
64. Comments to the author.
65. Interview with BBC Radio 4 'Front Row', ix.1999.
66. Source withheld.
67. 'Trouble at the House' by Keith Cooper.
68. *BBC Music* magazine, xi.1996, p. 44.

Chapter 10
Act Four: Where's the Door? (January to August 1997)
1. *BBC Music* magazine, xi.1996, p. 45.
2. Gottlieb, Chambers, 126.
3. Antoinette Sibley, author's interview.
4. *Daily Telegraph*, 14.i.1997, interview with Jan Moir.
5. Source withheld.
6. *Daily Telegraph*, 10.v.1997.
7. Minutes of ROH/AC monitoring committee, 30.i.1997.
8. *Daily Telegraph*, 12.iv.1997.
9. Eye-witness account.
10. MA to JM, 20.iii.1997, doc. in Walker-Arnott report.
11. Article by NL, 5.iv.1997.
12. *Daily Telegraph*, 12.iv.1997.
13. *Daily Telegraph*, 10.v.1997, interview with Rupert Christiansen.
14. *Sunday Telegraph*, 29.iii.1998.
15. Source withheld.
16. Original letter in author's possession, published 20.iv.1997.
17. Submission by Chadlington to CMSC, 4.xi.1997.
18. *Daily Telegraph*, 10.v.1997.
19. Evidence to CMSC, p. xxiv.
20. loc. cit.
21. Isaacs, 315.
22. *Daily Telegraph*, 15.v.1997.
23. *The Times*, 14.v.1997.
24. *Daily Telegraph*, 15.v.1997.
25. *The Times*, 15.v.1997.
26. GM to Kaufman, 8.ix.1997, copy seen by author.
27. Author's interview.
28. Conveyed by Mary Allen to the author.
29. Source withheld.
30. *Daily Telegraph*, 26.iv.1997.
31. Board minutes, 30.vi.1997.

Chapter 11
Coming up for Eyre (September 1997 to November 1998)
1. Q.v. chapter two, p. 31.
2. Minutes to board meeting of 29.ix.1997, p. 9.
3. Author's interviews.

4. Allen, 9.
5. Allen, 57.
6. Parkinson, BBC1, 27.ii.1998.
7. Confided to the author.
8. Interview with the author.
9. Board minutes, 30.x.1997.
10. *Spectator*, 6.xii.1997, p. 15.
11. *Daily Telegraph*, 4.xi.1997.
12. *Guardian*, 7.xi.1997.
13. Interview with Michael Billington, *Guardian*, 2.v.1998.
14. *Daily Telegraph*, 5.xi.1997.
15. Allen, 120.
16. ROH board minutes, 19.xi.1997.
17. ROH board minutes, 24.xi.1997.
18. i.e. the Arts Council.
19. *Daily Telegraph*, 4.xii.1997.
20. 'Trouble at the House'.
21. *The Times*, 8.xii.1997.
22. Author's interview.
23. *Spectator*, 6.xii.1997, pp. 15–16.
24. *Spectator*, 13.xii.1997, pp. 20–21.
25. *Sunday Telegraph*, n.d.
26. CMSC, xviii.
27. Open letter to the National Campaign for the Arts, n.d.
28. Recounted by Albery.
29. Author's interview.
30. William Kay, 'Looking for a Fight', *Independent*, 2.ii.2000.
31. *Guardian*, 16.i.1998.
32. *Guardian*, 17.i.1998.
33. *Opera*, ii.1998, p. 144.
34. *Evening Standard*, 26.iii.1998.
35. *The Times*, 2.iv.1998.
36. Allen, letter to *The Times*, 3.iv.1998.
37. Gottlieb, Chambers, 15.
38. *Evening Standard* awards Savoy Hotel, 19.iii.1997.
39. Eyre to Russell Willis Taylor and Pelham Allen, 7.iv.1998.
40. Richard Eyre, *Utopia and Other Places*.
41. Author's interview.
42. All comments: interviews with the author.
43. Simon Jenkins, in the same column (1.vii.1998), curiously

asserted that 'Smith had deputed one of his own officials to write the Eyre Report.'
44. *The Times*, 19.vi.1998.
45. Eyre, pp. 31, 118.
46. *The Times*, 3.vii.1998, p. 35.
47. *Daily Telegraph*, 1.vii.1998, p. 20.
48. *Sunday Times*, 5.vii.1998, p. 1.
49. Eyre, 6.
50. *Guardian*, 3.vii.1998.
51. ROH press release, 7.vii.1998.
52. Two, actually.
53. Source withheld.
54. Memo leaked to *Evening Standard*, quoted in *Opera*, vii.1998, p. 766.
55. *Guardian*, 10.x.1998.
56. *The Times*, 27.x.1998.

Chapter 12
And so to Bed (December 1998 to December 1999)

1. *Guardian* and *Daily Telegraph*, 23.x.1998, *Jewish Chronicle*, 9.x.1998.
2. *Opera*, xii.1998, pp. 1405–6.
3. *Opera*, xii.1998, p. 140.
4. *Daily Telegraph*, 10.x.1998.
5. *Classical Music*, 10.x.1998.
6. *The Times*, 1.x.1998.
7. *Daily Telegraph*, 15.x.1998.
8. *The Times*, 19.x.1998.
9. *Daily Telegraph*, 13.ix.1998.
10. *Guardian*, 4.i.1999.
11. *NY Times*, 15.ii.1999.
12. Author's interview.
13. Author's interview.
14. *Daily Telegraph*, 23.vi.1999.
15. Source withheld.
16. *The Times*, 2.vi.1999.
17. Source withheld.

Chapter 13

Lie Back and Think of England (2000–2100 European time)

1. *Sunday Telegraph*, 8.i.2000.
2. *Daily Telegraph*, 28.i.2000.
3. cf. Rowan Moore, 'True Cost of a Great Day Out', *Evening Standard*, 18.i.2000.
4. *Guardian*, 9.i.2000.
5. *NY Times*, 10.ii.2000.
6. Interview with David Frost, BBC-1, 16.i.2000.
7. cf. *Daily Telegraph*, 17.v.1999.
8. Source withheld.
9. Interview with Ismene Brown, *Daily Telegraph*, 17.iii.2000.
10. *The Times*, 16.iii.2000.
11. *Daily Telegraph*, 18.iii.2000.
12. *Evening Standard*, 23.iii.2000.
13. At LAMDA, 23.iii.2000.
14. *Sunday Telegraph*, 26.iii.2000, interview with Gyles Brandreth.
15. Hall, interview with *The Times*, 13.iii.2000.
16. Peter Brook Awards, Theatre Museum, 9.xi.1999.
17. cf. CMCS, Appendix 3.
18. cf. Lebrecht, *When the Music Stops*.
19. Michael Crick and David Smith, *Manchester United, the Betrayal of a Legend*. Pelham Books, 1989, p. 21.
20. Interview with Ismene Brown, *Daily Telegraph*, 7.iv.2000.
21. Interview with Fiona Maddocks, *Observer*, 22.ii.1998.
22. Isaacs, 334–5.
23. Author's interview.
24. Eyre, 4.
25. *Daily Telegraph*, x.1998.
26. *The Times*, 23.xii.1999.
27. Comments to the author, March 2000.

Bibliography

A. Archives, newspapers, periodicals, reports, databases:

CFM-50   Classic FM documentary for fiftieth anniversary of ROH
CGA   Archive of the Royal Opera House, Covent Garden
CGB   Covent Garden Books (a series issued intermittently, 1947–60)
CG25   Covent Garden, 25 years of opera and ballet (exhibition catalogue), Victoria and Albert Museum, 1971
CMSC   Culture Media and Sport Committee, First report, The Royal Opera House, vol. 1. London, 25 November, 1997
DNB   Dictionary of National Biography, Oxford University Press, 1995
EYRE   The Eyre Review: The future of lyric theatre in London. The Stationery Office, 30. vi. 1998.
FOB   Festival of Britain catalogue, 1951.
GDA   Lord Drogheda's correspondence files (private collection)
GSA   Georg Solti archive (private)
GWA   George Whyte archive (private)

DTel   Daily Telegraph
FT   Financial Times
Gdn   The Guardian
MusAm   Musical America
NYT   New York Times
Op   Opera magazine
Obs   Observer
STel   Sunday Telegraph
STim   Sunday Times

B. BOOKS (major works consulted)
(place of publication is London, unless stated)

Mary Allen, *A House Divided*. Simon & Schuster, 1998.

Noel Annan, *Our Age*. Weidenfeld & Nicolson, 1990.

Dennis Arundel, *The Story of Sadler's Wells, 1683–1964*. Hamish Hamilton, 1965.

Harold Atkins and Archie Newman, *Beecham Stories*. Robson, 1978.

Janet Baker, *Full Circle*. Julia MacRae, 1982.

Mary Banham and Bevis Hiller (eds), *A Tonic to the Nation; the Festival of Britain, 1951*. Thames and Hudson, 1976.

Paul Banks (ed.), *Britten's Gloriana; essays and sources*. Woodbridge, The Boydell Press, 1993.

Cecil Beaton (ed. Richard Buckle), *Selected Diaries*. Weidenfeld & Nicolson, 1979.

Sally Bedell Smith, *Diana; the life of a troubled princess*. Aurum, 1999.

Quentin Bell, *Virginia Woolf*. 2 vols. The Hogarth Press, 1972.

Patrick Belshaw, *A Kind of Private Magic*. Andre Deutsch, 1994.

Louis Biancolli, *The Flagstad Manuscript*. William Heinemann, 1953.

Wilfrid Blunt, *John Christie of Glyndebourne*. Theatre Art Books (NY), 1968.

Alan Blyth, *Colin Davis*. Ian Allan (Shepperton), 1972.

Michael Bracewell, *England is Mine; pop life in Albion from Wilde to Goldie*. HarperCollins, 1997.

Russell Braddon, *Joan Sutherland*. William Collins, 1962.

Peter Brinson and Clement Crisp, *A Guide to the Repertory, Ballet and Dance*. David and Charles (Newton Abbot), 1980.

Brian Brivati, *Lord Goodman*. Richard Cohen Books, 1999.

Donald Brook, *International Gallery of Conductors*. Rockliff, 1951.

Peter Brook, *Threads of Time; a memoir*. Methuen, 1998.

Henrietta Brougham, Christopher Fox, Ian Pace, *Uncommon Grounds; the music of Michael Finnissy*. Ashgate, 1998.

Chris Bryant, *Stafford Cripps; the first modern Chancellor*. Hodder & Stoughton, 1997.

Richard Buckle, *Diaghilev*. Weidenfeld & Nicolson, 1979.

Humphrey Burton, *Leonard Bernstein*. Faber & Faber, 1994.

Angus Calder, *The People's War*. Panther Books, 1971.

Humphrey Carpenter, *Benjamin Britten; a biography*. Faber & Faber, 1992.

Humphrey Carpenter, *The Envy of the World; fifty years of the BBC Third Programme and Radio 3*. Weidenfeld & Nicolson, 1996.

Barbara Castle, *Fighting All the Way*. Macmillan, 1993.

Anthony Clare, *In the Psychiatrist's Chair*. Heinemann, 1992.

Anthony Clare, *In the Psychiatrist's Chair II*. Heinemann, 1995.

Kenneth Clark, *Another Part of the Wood*, John Murray, 1974.

Kenneth Clark, *The Other Half*, John Murray, 1977.

Mary Clarke, *The Sadler's Wells Ballet; a history and appreciation*. A. & C. Black, 1955.

Helen Conway, *Sir John Pritchard; his life in music*. Andre Deutsch, 1993.

Nöel Coward, *Diaries* (ed. Payne and Morley). Weidenfeld & Nicolson, 1982.

John Culshaw, *Putting the Record Straight*. Secker & Warburg, 1981.

Hugh David, *On Queer Street*. HarperCollins, 1997.

Norman Davies, *Europe*. Oxford University Press, 1996.

Michael De-La-Noy, *Eddy; the life of Edward Sackville-West*. Arcadia Books (2nd edition), 1999.

Frances Donaldson, *The Royal Opera House in the Twentieth Century*. Weidenfeld & Nicolson, 1988.

Frances Donaldson, *A Twentieth Century Life*. Weidenfeld & Nicolson, 1992.

Ninette de Valois, *Come Dance with Me; a memoir, 1898–1956*. Hamish Hamilton, 1959.

Bernard Donoughue and G. W. Jones, *Herbert Morrison; portrait of a politician*. Weidenfeld & Nicolson, 1973.

T. S. Eliot, *Notes Towards a Definition of Culture*. Faber & Faber, 1948.

E. L. Ellis, *T. J., A Life of Dr Thomas Jones, CH*. University of Wales Press (Cardiff), 1992.

Geraint Evans (with Noel Goodwin), *A Knight at the Opera*. Michael Joseph, 1984.

Ifor Evans and Mary Glasgow, *The Arts in England*. The Falcon Press, 1949.

Richard Eyre, *Utopia and Other Places*. Bloomsbury, 1993.

Julian Fane, *Eleanor*. Constable, 1993.

Stephen Fay, *Power Play; the life and times of Peter Hall*. Hodder & Stoughton, 1995.

David Fingleton, *Kiri*. Collins, 1982.

Margot Fonteyn, *Autobiography*. Hamish Hamilton, (rev. edn) 1989

Margot Fonteyn, *The Magic of Dance*. BBC Publications, 1980.

Denis Forman, *Persona Granada*. Andre Deutsch, 1997.

James Fox, *White Mischief*. Penguin, 1987.

David Franklin, *Basso Cantante*. George Duckworth & Co, 1970.

Bram Gay, *Trumpet Involuntary; an orchestral life*. Thames Publishing, 1995.

John Gielgud (with John Miller and John Powell), *An Actor and his Time*. Sidgwick & Jackson, 1979.

Tito Gobbi, *My Life*. Futura Books, 1980.

Arnold Goodman, *Tell Them I'm On My Way*. Chapmans, 1993.

Arnold Goodman, *Not for the Record* (selected writings and speeches). Andre Deutsch, 1973.

Charles Gordon, *The Two Tycoons*. Hamish Hamilton, 1984.

Vera Gottlieb and Colin Chambers (ed.), *Theatre in a Cool Climate*. Amber Lane Press (Oxford), 1999.

Tyrone Guthrie, *A Life in the Theatre*. Hamish Hamilton, 1960.

Tyrone Guthrie (ed.), *Opera in English*. Bodley Head, 1945.

F. E. Halliday, *An Illustrated Cultural History of England*. Thames and Hudson, 1967.

Montague Haltrecht, *The Quiet Showman; Sir David Webster and the Royal Opera House*. Collins, 1975.

Joan Hammond, *A Voice, a Life*. Victor Gollancz, 1970.

R. F. Harrod, *The Life of John Maynard Keynes*. Macmillan, 1951.

Roy Hattersley, *Fifty Years On; a prejudiced history of Britain since the War*. Little, Brown, 1997.

Peter Hennessy, *Whitehall*. Secker & Warburg, 1989.

Robert Hewison, *Culture & Consensus; England, art and politics since 1940*. Methuen (revised edition), 1997.

Christopher Hibbert, *Wellington; a personal history*. HarperCollins, 1997.

Patrick Higgins, *Heterosexual Dictatorship*. Fourth Estate, 1996.

Polly Hill and Richard Keynes (eds), *Lydia & Maynard; the letters of Lydia Lopokova and John Maynard Keynes*. Andre Deutsch, 1989.

Patricia Hollis, *Jennie Lee; a life*. Oxford University Press, 1997.

Philip Hope-Wallace, *Words and Music*. William Collins, 1981.

Editors of *Opera News*, *The Golden Horseshoe; the life and times of the Metropolitan Opera House*. Viking (NY), 1965.

Robert Hutchinson, *The Politics of the Arts Council*. Sinclair Browne, 1982.

Jeremy Isaacs, *Never Mind the Moon*. Bantam Press, 1999.

Jeremy Isaacs, *Storm Over 4*. Weidenfeld & Nicolson, 1986.

Alan Jefferson, *Sir Thomas Beecham; a centenary tribute*. Macdonald & Jane's, 1979.

Alan Jefferson, *Elisabeth Schwarzkopf*. Victor Gollancz, 1996.

George Jellinek, *Callas; portrait of a prima donna*. Anthony Gibbs and Phillips, 1960.

Garry Jenkins & Stephen d'Antal, *Kiri; her unsung story*. HarperCollins, 1998.

John Joel, *I Paid the Piper*. Howard Baker, 1970.

Thomas Jones, CH, LD, *A Diary with Letters, 1931–1950*. Oxford University Press, 1954.

Ludovic Kennedy, *On My Way to the Club*. Collins, 1989.

Michael Kennedy, *Britten*. J. M. Dent & Sons, 1981.

Michael Kennedy, *Portrait of Walton*. Oxford University Press, 1989.

Jürgen Kesting, *Maria Callas*. transl. John Hunt. Quartet, 1992.

John Maynard Keynes, *The General Theory of Employment, Interest and Money*. Macmillan, 1936.

John Maynard Keynes (ed. Donald Moggridge), *Collected Writings, volume XXVIII; social, political and literary writings*. Macmillan (for the Royal Economic Society), 1982.

Milo Keynes (ed.), *Essays on John Maynard Keynes*. Cambridge University Press, 1975.

Milo Keynes (ed.) *Lydia Lopokova*. Weidenfeld & Nicolson, 1993.

Lincoln Kirstein, *Mosaic; memoirs*. FSG (NY), 1994.

Allan Kozinn, *The Beatles*. Phaidon Press, 1995.

Heinrich Kralik, *The Vienna Opera*. Vienna, 1955.

C. P. Landstone, *Off-Stage; a personal record of the first twelve years of state-sponsored drama in Great Britain*. Elek, 1953.

James Lees-Milne, *Ancestral Voices*. Chatto & Windus, 1975.

James Lees-Milne, *Fourteen Friends*. John Murray, 1996.

James Lees-Milne, *Through Wood and Dale*. John Murray, 1998.

Roger Lewis, *The Real Life of Lawrence Olivier*. Century, 1996.

John Lucas, *England and Englishness*. The Hogarth Press, 1990.

John Lucas, *Reggie; the life of Reginald Goodall*. Julia MacRae Books, 1993.

Edwin McArthur, *Flagstad; a personal memoir*. Alfred A. Knopf (NY), 1965.

Lord Macmillan, *A Man of Law's Tale*. Macmillan, 1953.

Norma Major, *Joan Sutherland; the authorised biography*. Macdonald, 1987.

Edward Mandinian (photographer), *Purcell's The Fairy Queen; as presented by the Sadler's Wells Ballet and The Covent Garden Opera*. John Lehmann, 1948.

Arthur Marwick, *British Society Since 1945*. Penguin (3rd edition), 1996.

Lawrence D. Mass, *Confessions of a Jewish Wagnerite*. Cassell, 1994.

Martin Mayer, *The Met*. Thames & Hudson, 1983.

Richard Mayne, *Postwar; the dawn of today's Europe*. Thames & Hudson, 1983.

Barry Miles, *Paul McCartney; many years from now*. Secker & Warburg, 1997.

Andrew Motion, *The Lamberts*. Chatto & Windus, 1986.

Barbara Newman, *Antoinette Sibley; reflections of a ballerina*. Hutchinson, 1986.

Sir Gordon Newton (ed. Malcolm Rutherford), *A Peer Without Equal*. Privately published, 1997.

Nigel Nicolson, (ed.), *The Letters of Virginia Woolf* (vol. III). Hogarth Press, 1977.

Rudolf Nureyev (edited by Alexander Bland), *The Autobiography of Rudolf Nureyev*. Hodder & Stoughton, 1962.

Charles Osborne, *Giving it Away*. Secker & Warburg, 1986.

George Orwell, *The English People*. Collins, 1947.

Sonia Orwell and Ian Angus (eds), *The Collected Essays, Journalism and Lectures of George Orwell* (vols I–IV). Penguin Books, 1970.

John Percival, *Theatre in my Blood; a biography of John Cranko*. The Herbert Press. 1983.

Donna Perlmutter, *Shadowplay; the life of Antony Tudor*. Limelight Editions (NY), 1995.

John Pick, *Managing the Arts? the British experience*. Rhinegold, 1986.

V. S. Pritchett, *London Perceived*. Chatto & Windus, 1962.

Humphrey Procter-Gregg, *Beecham Remembered*. Duckworth, 1976.

Pierre-Jean Rémy, *Maria Callas; a tribute*. Macdonald and Jane's, 1978.

Andrew Roberts, *Eminent Churchillians*. Weidenfeld & Nicolson, 1994.

Philip Roberts, *The Royal Court Theatre and the Modern Stage*. Cambridge University Press, 1999.

Harlow Robinson, *The Last Impresario; the life, times and legacy of Sol Hurok*. Viking (NY), 1994.

Zsuzsi Roboz (with text by James Monahan), *British Ballet Today*. Davis-Poynter, 1980.

Carol Rosen, *The Goossens; a musical century*. Andre Deutsch, 1993.

Noel Ross-Russell, *There Will I Sing; a biography of Richard Lewis, CBE*. Open Gate Press, 1996.

Peter Rowland, *Lloyd George*. Barrie & Jenkins, 1975.

Bertrand Russell, *The Autobiography of Bertrand Russell, 1872–1914*. George Allen & Unwin, 1967.

Richard Temple Savage, *A Voice from the Pit; reminiscences of an orchestral musician*. David & Charles (Newton Abbot), 1988.

Erwin Stein (ed.), Arnold Schoenberg, *Letters*. Faber & Faber, 1964.

Elisabeth Schwarzkopf, *On and Off the Record; a memoir of Walter Legge*. Faber & Faber, 1982.

Meryle Secrest, *Kenneth Clark*. Weidenfeld & Nicolson, 1984.

Richard Shead, *Constant Lambert*. Simon Publications, 1973.

Andrew Sinclair, *Arts and Cultures; the history of the 50 years of the Arts Council of Great Britain*. Sinclair-Stevenson, 1995.

Alan Sked and Chris Cook, *Post-War Britain; a political history*. Penguin (4th edition), 1993.

Robert Skidelsky, *John Maynard Keynes; hopes betrayed, 1883–1920*. Macmillan, 1983.

Robert Skidelsky, *John Maynard Keynes; the economist as saviour, 1920–1937*. Macmillan, 1992.

Terry Slasberg, *The pleasure was mine . . . 40 years as a concert agent*. Thames Publishing, 1993.

Wayne Sleep, *Precious Little Sleep*. Boxtree, 1996.

Diane Solway, *Nureyev*. Weidenfeld & Nicolson, 1998.

Frances Spalding, *Duncan Grant*. Chatto & Windus, 1997.

Margaret Stewart, *English Singer; the life of Steuart Wilson*. George Duckworth & Co., 1970.

Joan Sutherland, *A Prima Donna's Progress*. Weidenfeld & Nicolson, 1997.

A. J. P. Taylor, *English History, 1914–1945*. Oxford University Press, 1966.

Irene Thomas, *The Bandsman's Daughter*. Macmillan, 1979.

Edward Thorpe, *Kenneth MacMillan; the man and the ballets*. Hamish Hamilton, 1985.

Michael Tippett, *Those Twentieth Century Blues*. Hutchinson, 1991.

Nick Tiratsoo (ed.), *From Blitz to Blair*. Weidenfeld & Nicolson, 1997.

John Tooley, *In House; Covent Garden, 50 years of opera and ballet*. Faber & Faber, 1999.

J. C. Trewin, *Peter Brook; a biography*. Macdonald, 1971.

Penelope Turing, *Hans Hotter; man and artist*. John Calder, 1983.

Katherine Sorley Walker, *Ninette de Valois; idealist without illusions*. Dance Books, 1998.

Ian Wallace, *Promise me you'll sing MUD*. John Calder, 1975.

Geoffrey Wansell, *Terence Rattigan; a biography*. Fourth Estate, 1995.

John W. Wheeler-Bennett, *John Anderson, Viscount Waverley*. Macmillan, 1962.

Eric Walter White, *The Arts Council of Great Britain*. Davis Poynter, 1975.

Richard Witts, *Artist Unknown; an alternative history of the Arts Council*. Little, Brown, 1988.

Hugo Young, *One of Us*. Macmillan, 1989.

Franco Zeffirelli, *Zeffirelli*. Weidenfeld & Nicolson, 1986.

Philip Ziegler, *London at War*, 1939–1945. Sinclair-Stevenson, 1995.

Philip Ziegler, *Harold Wilson*. HarperCollins, 1993.

Index